RMENIA | **AUSTRALIA** | **AUSTRIA** | **AZERBAIJAN** | **BAHAMAS** | **BAHRAIN** | **BANGLADESH**

HERZEGOVINA | **BOTSWANA** | **BRAZIL** | **BRUNEI** | **BULGARIA** | **BURKINA FASO** | **BURMA**

CHILE | **CHINA** | **COLOMBIA** | **COMOROS** | **CONGO** | **COSTA RICA** | **CROATIA**

CUADOR | **EGYPT** | **EL SALVADOR** | **EQUATORIAL GUINEA** | **ERITREA** | **ESTONIA** | **ETHIOPIA**

ERMANY | **GHANA** | **GREECE** | **GREENLAND** | **GRENADA** | **GUATEMALA** | **GUINEA**

INDIA | **INDONESIA** | **IRAN** | **IRAQ** | **IRELAND** | **ISRAEL** | **ITALY**

EA, NORTH |  **KOREA, SOUTH** | **KUWAIT** | **KYRGYZSTAN** | **LAOS** | **LATVIA** | **LEBANON**

CEDONIA | **MADAGASCAR** | **MALAWI** | **MALAYSIA** | **MALDIVES** | **MALI** | **MALTA**

OROCCO | **MOZAMBIQUE** | **NAMIBIA** | **NAURU** | **NEPAL** | **NETHERLANDS** | **NEW ZEALAND**

ANAMA | **PAPUA NEW GUINEA** | 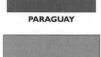 **PARAGUAY** | **PERU** | **PHILIPPINES** | **POLAND** | **PORTUGAL**

DI ARABIA |  **SENEGAL** | **SEYCHELLES** | **SIERRA LEONE** | **SINGAPORE** | **SLOVAK REPUBLIC** | **SLOVENIA**

VINCENT |  **SUDAN** | **SURINAM** |  **SWAZILAND** | **SWEDEN** | **SWITZERLAND** |  **SYRIA**

TUNISIA | **TURKEY** | **TURKMENISTAN** |  **TUVALU** | **UGANDA** | **UKRAINE** |  **UNITED ARAB EMIRATES**

ETNAM |  **WESTERN SAMOA** | **YEMEN** |  **YUGOSLAVIA** |  **ZAÏRE** | **ZAMBIA** | **ZIMBABWE**

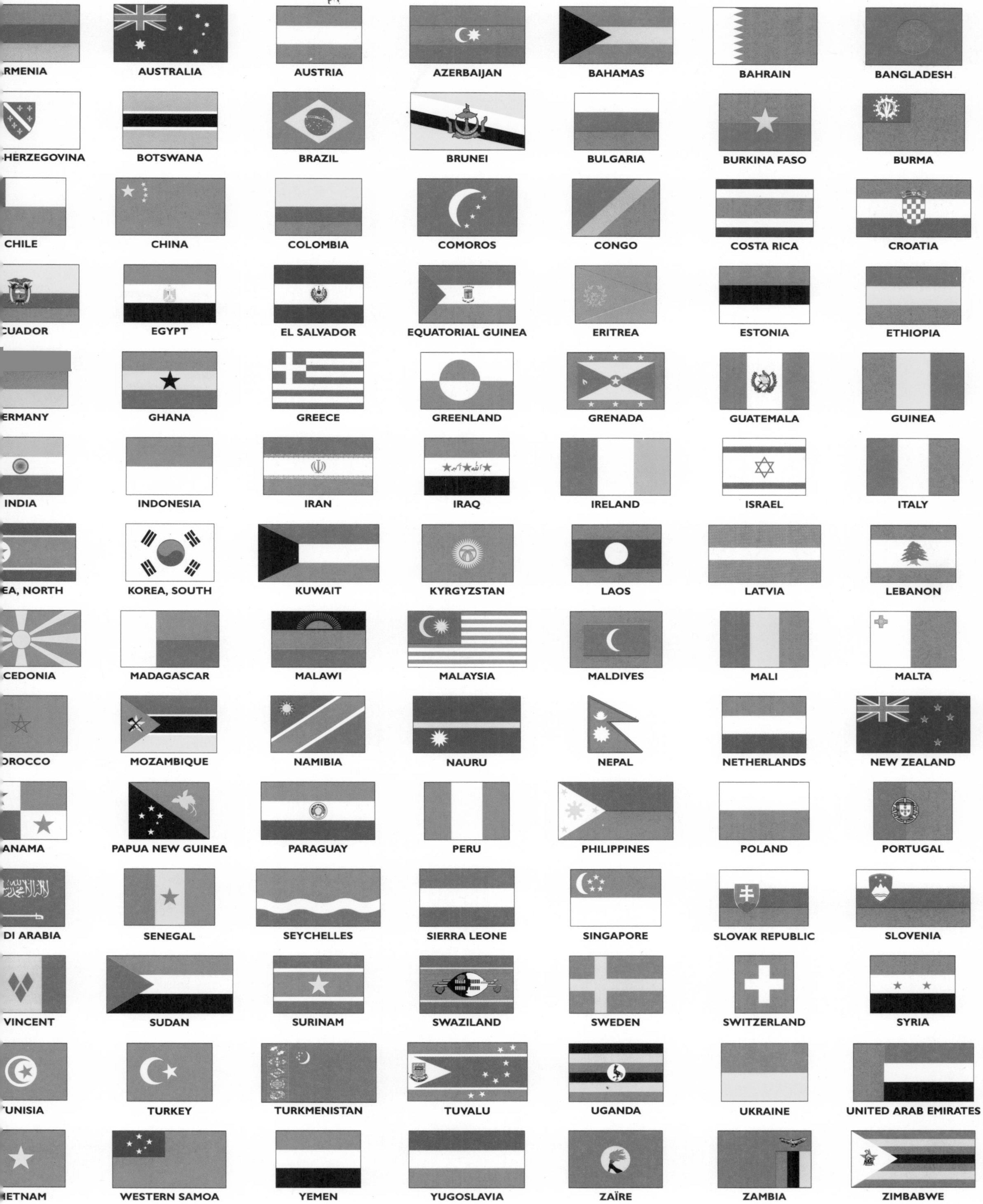

OXFORD

CONCISE
ATLAS
OF THE
WORLD

THIRD EDITION

CONTENTS

Acknowledgements
Introduction to World Geography
Cartography by Philip's

Geography Consultants:
Professor M. Monmonier, Syracuse University, N.Y., USA
Professor M.J. Tooley, University of St Andrews, UK
Dr C. Clarke, Oxford University, UK

Illustrations:
Stefan Chabluk

George Philip Limited,
an imprint of Reed Books,
Michelin House, 81 Fulham Road, London SW3 6RB,
and Auckland, Melbourne, Singapore and Toronto

Cartography by Philip's

Published in North America by
Oxford University Press, Inc.,
198 Madison Avenue,
New York, N.Y. 10016, U.S.A.

Oxford is a registered trademark of Oxford University Press

Library of Congress Cataloging-in-Publication Data

George Philip Limited.
  Concise atlas of the world / [cartography by Philip's].—3rd ed.
  p. cm.
  Includes index.
  Rev. ed. of: Concise atlas of the world.
  ISBN 0–19–521265–7
  1. Children's atlases. I. Concise atlas of the world. II. Oxford
  University Press. III. Title.
  G1021.C74   1996 <G&M>
  912—dc20   96-17385
                   CIP
              MAP AC

ISBN 0–19–521265–7

Printing (last digit):
9 8 7 6 5 4 3

Printed in Hong Kong

World Statistics: Countries

This alphabetical list includes all the countries and territories of the world. If a territory is not completely independent, then the country it is associated with is named. The area figures give the total area of land, inland water and ice. The population figures are 1995 estimates. The annual income is the Gross National Product per capita in US dollars. The figures are the latest available, usually 1994.

Country/Territory	Area km² Thousands	Area miles² Thousands	Population Thousands	Capital	Annual Income US $
Adélie Land (Fr.)	432	167	0.03	–	–
Afghanistan	652	252	19,509	Kabul	220
Albania	28.8	11.1	3,458	Tirana	340
Algeria	2,382	920	25,012	Algiers	1,650
American Samoa (US)	0.20	0.08	58	Pago Pago	2,600
Andorra	0.45	0.17	65	Andorra La Vella	14,000
Angola	1,247	481	10,020	Luanda	600
Anguilla (UK)	0.1	0.04	8	The Valley	6,800
Antigua & Barbuda	0.44	0.17	67	St John's	6,390
Argentina	2,767	1,068	34,663	Buenos Aires	7,290
Armenia	29.8	11.5	3,603	Yerevan	660
Aruba (Neths)	0.19	0.07	71	Oranjestad	17,500
Ascension Is. (UK)	0.09	0.03	1.5	Georgetown	–
Australia	7,687	2,968	18,107	Canberra	17,510
Austria	83.9	32.4	8,004	Vienna	23,120
Azerbaijan	86.6	33.4	7,559	Baku	730
Azores (Port.)	2.2	0.87	238	Ponta Delgada	–
Bahamas	13.9	5.4	277	Nassau	11,500
Bahrain	0.68	0.26	558	Manama	7,870
Bangladesh	144	56	118,342	Dhaka	220
Barbados	0.43	0.17	263	Bridgetown	6,240
Belarus	207.6	80.1	10,500	Minsk	2,930
Belgium	30.5	11.8	10,140	Brussels	21,210
Belize	23	8.9	216	Belmopan	2,440
Benin	113	43	5,381	Porto-Novo	420
Bermuda (UK)	0.05	0.02	64	Hamilton	27,000
Bhutan	47	18.1	1,639	Thimphu	170
Bolivia	1,099	424	7,900	La Paz/Sucre	770
Bosnia-Herzegovina	51	20	3,800	Sarajevo	2,500
Botswana	582	225	1,481	Gaborone	2,590
Brazil	8,512	3,286	161,416	Brasília	3,020
British Indian Ocean Terr. (UK)	0.08	0.03	0	–	–
Brunei	5.8	2.2	284	Bandar Seri Begawan	9,000
Bulgaria	111	43	8,771	Sofia	1,160
Burkina Faso	274	106	10,326	Ouagadougou	300
Burma (Myanmar)	677	261	46,580	Rangoon	950
Burundi	27.8	10.7	6,412	Bujumbura	180
Cambodia	181	70	10,452	Phnom Penh	600
Cameroon	475	184	13,232	Yaoundé	770
Canada	9,976	3,852	29,972	Ottawa	20,670
Canary Is. (Spain)	7.3	2.8	1,494	Las Palmas/Santa Cruz	–
Cape Verde Is.	4	1.6	386	Praia	870
Cayman Is. (UK)	0.26	0.10	31	George Town	20,000
Central African Republic	623	241	3,294	Bangui	390
Chad	1,284	496	6,314	Ndjaména	200
Chatham Is. (NZ)	0.96	0.37	0.05	Waitangi	–
Chile	757	292	14,271	Santiago	3,070
China	9,597	3,705	1,226,944	Beijing	490
Christmas Is. (Aus.)	0.14	0.05	2	The Settlement	–
Cocos (Keeling) Is. (Aus.)	0.01	0.005	0.6	West Island	–
Colombia	1,139	440	34,948	Bogotá	1,400
Comoros	2.2	0.86	654	Moroni	520
Congo	342	132	2,593	Brazzaville	920
Cook Is. (NZ)	0.24	0.09	19	Avarua	900
Costa Rica	51.1	19.7	3,436	San José	2,160
Croatia	56.5	21.8	4,900	Zagreb	4,500
Cuba	111	43	11,050	Havana	1,250
Cyprus	9.3	3.6	742	Nicosia	10,380
Czech Republic	78.9	30.4	10,500	Prague	2,730
Denmark	43.1	16.6	5,229	Copenhagen	26,510
Djibouti	23.2	9	603	Djibouti	780
Dominica	0.75	0.29	89	Roseau	2,680
Dominican Republic	48.7	18.8	7,818	Santo Domingo	1,080
Ecuador	284	109	11,384	Quito	1,170
Egypt	1,001	387	64,100	Cairo	660
El Salvador	21	8.1	5,743	San Salvador	1,320
Equatorial Guinea	28.1	10.8	400	Malabo	360
Eritrea	94	36	3,850	Asmara	500
Estonia	44.7	17.3	1,531	Tallinn	3,040
Ethiopia	1,128	436	51,600	Addis Ababa	100
Falkland Is. (UK)	12.2	4.7	2	Stanley	–
Faroe Is. (Den.)	1.4	0.54	47	Tórshavn	23,660
Fiji	18.3	7.1	773	Suva	2,140
Finland	338	131	5,125	Helsinki	18,970
France	552	213	58,286	Paris	22,360
French Guiana (Fr.)	90	34.7	154	Cayenne	5,000
French Polynesia (Fr.)	4	1.5	217	Papeete	7,000
Gabon	268	103	1,316	Libreville	4,050
Gambia, The	11.3	4.4	1,144	Banjul	360
Georgia	69.7	26.9	5,448	Tbilisi	560
Germany	357	138	82,000	Berlin/Bonn	23,560
Ghana	239	92	17,462	Accra	430
Gibraltar (UK)	0.007	0.003	28	Gibraltar Town	5,000
Greece	132	51	10,510	Athens	7,390
Greenland (Den.)	2,176	840	59	Godthåb (Nuuk)	9,000
Grenada	0.34	0.13	94	St George's	2,410
Guadeloupe (Fr.)	1.7	0.66	443	Basse-Terre	9,000
Guam (US)	0.55	0.21	155	Agana	6,000
Guatemala	109	42	10,624	Guatemala City	1,110
Guinea	246	95	6,702	Conakry	510
Guinea-Bissau	36.1	13.9	1,073	Bissau	220
Guyana	215	83	832	Georgetown	350
Haiti	27.8	10.7	7,180	Port-au-Prince	800
Honduras	112	43	5,940	Tegucigalpa	580
Hong Kong (UK)	1.1	0.40	6,000	–	17,860
Hungary	93	35.9	10,500	Budapest	3,330
Iceland	103	40	269	Reykjavik	23,620
India	3,288	1,269	942,989	New Delhi	290
Indonesia	1,905	735	198,644	Jakarta	730
Iran	1,648	636	68,885	Tehran	4,750
Iraq	438	169	20,184	Baghdad	2,000
Ireland	70.3	27.1	3,589	Dublin	12,580
Israel	27	10.3	5,696	Jerusalem	13,760
Italy	301	116	57,181	Rome	19,620
Ivory Coast	322	125	14,271	Yamoussoukro	630
Jamaica	11	4.2	2,700	Kingston	1,390
Jan Mayen Is. (Nor.)	0.38	0.15	0.06	–	–
Japan	378	146	125,156	Tokyo	31,450
Johnston Is. (US)	0.002	0.0009	1	–	–
Jordan	89.2	34.4	5,547	Amman	1,190
Kazakstan	2,717	1,049	17,099	Alma-Ata	1,540
Kenya	580	224	28,240	Nairobi	270
Kerguelen Is. (Fr.)	7.2	2.8	0.7	–	–
Kermadec Is. (NZ)	0.03	0.01	0.1	–	–
Kiribati	0.72	0.28	80	Tarawa	710
Korea, North	121	47	23,931	Pyŏngyang	1,100
Korea, South	99	38.2	45,088	Seoul	7,670
Kuwait	17.8	6.9	1,668	Kuwait City	23,350
Kyrgyzstan	198.5	76.6	4,738	Bishkek	830
Laos	237	91	4,906	Vientiane	290
Latvia	65	25	2,558	Riga	2,030
Lebanon	10.4	4	2,971	Beirut	1,750
Lesotho	30.4	11.7	2,064	Maseru	660
Liberia	111	43	3,092	Monrovia	800
Libya	1,760	679	5,410	Tripoli	6,500
Liechtenstein	0.16	0.06	31	Vaduz	33,510
Lithuania	65.2	25.2	3,735	Vilnius	1,310
Luxembourg	2.6	1	408	Luxembourg	35,850
Macau (Port.)	0.02	0.006	490	Macau	7,500
Macedonia	25.7	9.9	2,173	Skopje	730
Madagascar	587	227	15,206	Antananarivo	240
Madeira (Port.)	0.81	0.31	253	Funchal	–
Malawi	118	46	9,800	Lilongwe	220
Malaysia	330	127	20,174	Kuala Lumpur	3,160
Maldives	0.30	0.12	254	Malé	820
Mali	1,240	479	10,700	Bamako	300
Malta	0.32	0.12	367	Valletta	6,800
Marshall Is.	0.18	0.07	55	Dalap-Uliga-Darrit	1,500
Martinique (Fr.)	1.1	0.42	384	Fort-de-France	3,500
Mauritania	1,025	396	2,268	Nouakchott	510
Mauritius	2.0	0.72	1,112	Port Louis	2,980
Mayotte (Fr.)	0.37	0.14	101	Mamoundzou	1,430
Mexico	1,958	756	93,342	Mexico City	3,750
Micronesia, Fed. States of	0.70	0.27	125	Palikir	1,560
Midway Is. (US)	0.005	0.002	2	–	–
Moldova	33.7	13	4,434	Chişinău	1,180
Monaco	0.002	0.0001	32	Monaco	16,000
Mongolia	1,567	605	2,408	Ulan Bator	400
Montserrat (UK)	0.10	0.04	11	Plymouth	4,500
Morocco	447	172	26,857	Rabat	1,030
Mozambique	802	309	17,800	Maputo	80
Namibia	825	318	1,610	Windhoek	1,660
Nauru	0.02	0.008	12	Yaren District	10,000
Nepal	141	54	21,953	Katmandu	160
Netherlands	41.5	16	15,495	Amsterdam/The Hague	20,710
Neths Antilles (Neths)	0.99	0.38	199	Willemstad	9,700
New Caledonia (Fr.)	19	7.3	181	Nouméa	6,000
New Zealand	269	104	3,567	Wellington	12,900
Nicaragua	130	50	4,544	Managua	360
Niger	1,267	489	9,149	Niamey	270
Nigeria	924	357	88,515	Abuja	310
Niue (NZ)	0.26	0.10	2	Alofi	–
Norfolk Is. (Aus.)	0.03	0.01	2	Kingston	–
Northern Mariana Is. (US)	0.48	0.18	47	Saipan	11,500
Norway	324	125	4,361	Oslo	26,340
Oman	212	82	2,252	Muscat	5,600
Pakistan	796	307	143,595	Islamabad	430
Palau	0.46	0.18	17	Koror	2,260
Panama	77.1	29.8	2,629	Panama City	2,580
Papua New Guinea	463	179	4,292	Port Moresby	1,120
Paraguay	407	157	4,979	Asunción	1,500
Peru	1,285	496	23,588	Lima	1,490
Philippines	300	116	67,167	Manila	830
Pitcairn Is. (UK)	0.03	0.01	0.06	Adamstown	–
Poland	313	121	38,587	Warsaw	2,270
Portugal	92.4	35.7	10,600	Lisbon	7,890
Puerto Rico (US)	9	3.5	3,689	San Juan	7,020
Qatar	11	4.2	594	Doha	15,140
Queen Maud Land (Nor.)	2,800	1,081	0	–	–
Réunion (Fr.)	2.5	0.97	655	Saint-Denis	3,900
Romania	238	92	22,863	Bucharest	1,120
Russia	17,075	6,592	148,385	Moscow	2,350
Rwanda	26.3	10.2	7,899	Kigali	200
St Helena (UK)	0.12	0.05	6	Jamestown	–
St Kitts & Nevis	0.36	0.14	45	Basseterre	4,470
St Lucia	0.62	0.24	147	Castries	3,040
St Pierre & Miquelon (Fr.)	0.24	0.09	6	Saint Pierre	–
St Vincent & Grenadines	0.39	0.15	111	Kingstown	1,730
San Marino	0.06	0.02	26	San Marino	20,000
São Tomé & Príncipe	0.96	0.37	133	São Tomé	330
Saudi Arabia	2,150	830	18,395	Riyadh	8,000
Senegal	197	76	8,308	Dakar	730
Seychelles	0.46	0.18	75	Victoria	6,370
Sierra Leone	71.7	27.7	4,467	Freetown	140
Singapore	0.62	0.24	2,990	Singapore	19,310
Slovak Republic	49	18.9	5,400	Bratislava	1,900
Slovenia	20.3	7.8	2,000	Ljubljana	6,310
Solomon Is.	28.9	11.2	378	Honiara	750
Somalia	638	246	9,180	Mogadishu	500
South Africa	1,220	471	44,000	C. Town/Pretoria/Bloem.	2,900
South Georgia (UK)	3.8	1.4	0.05	–	–
Spain	505	195	39,664	Madrid	13,650
Sri Lanka	65.6	25.3	18,359	Colombo	600
Sudan	2,506	967	29,980	Khartoum	750
Surinam	163	63	421	Paramaribo	1,210
Svalbard (Nor.)	62.9	24.3	4	Longyearbyen	–
Swaziland	17.4	6.7	849	Mbabane	1,050
Sweden	450	174	8,893	Stockholm	24,830
Switzerland	41.3	15.9	7,268	Bern	36,410
Syria	185	71	14,614	Damascus	5,700
Taiwan	36	13.9	21,100	Taipei	11,000
Tajikistan	143.1	55.2	6,102	Dushanbe	470
Tanzania	945	365	29,710	Dodoma	100
Thailand	513	198	58,432	Bangkok	2,040
Togo	56.8	21.9	4,140	Lomé	330
Tokelau (NZ)	0.01	0.005	2	Nukunonu	–
Tonga	0.75	0.29	107	Nuku'alofa	1,610
Trinidad & Tobago	5.1	2	1,295	Port of Spain	3,730
Tristan da Cunha (UK)	0.11	0.04	0.33	Edinburgh	–
Tunisia	164	63	8,906	Tunis	1,780
Turkey	779	301	61,303	Ankara	2,120
Turkmenistan	488.1	188.5	4,100	Ashkhabad	1,400
Turks & Caicos Is. (UK)	0.43	0.17	15	Cockburn Town	5,000
Tuvalu	0.03	0.01	10	Fongafale	600
Uganda	236	91	21,466	Kampala	190
Ukraine	603.7	233.1	52,027	Kiev	1,910
United Arab Emirates	83.6	32.3	2,800	Abu Dhabi	22,470
United Kingdom	243.3	94	58,306	London	17,970
United States of America	9,373	3,619	263,563	Washington, DC	24,750
Uruguay	177	68	3,186	Montevideo	3,910
Uzbekistan	447.4	172.7	22,833	Tashkent	960
Vanuatu	12.2	4.7	167	Port-Vila	1,230
Vatican City	0.0004	0.0002	1	–	–
Venezuela	912	352	21,800	Caracas	2,840
Vietnam	332	127	74,580	Hanoi	170
Virgin Is. (UK)	0.15	0.06	20	Road Town	–
Virgin Is. (US)	0.34	0.13	105	Charlotte Amalie	12,000
Wake Is.	0.008	0.003	0.30	–	–
Wallis & Futuna Is. (Fr.)	0.20	0.08	13	Mata-Utu	–
Western Sahara	266	103	220	El Aaiún	300
Western Samoa	2.8	1.1	169	Apia	980
Yemen	528	204	14,609	Sana	800
Yugoslavia	102.3	39.5	10,881	Belgrade	1,000
Zaïre	2,345	905	44,504	Kinshasa	500
Zambia	753	291	9,500	Lusaka	370
Zimbabwe	391	151	11,453	Harare	540

WORLD STATISTICS: PHYSICAL DIMENSIONS

Each topic list is divided into continents and within a continent the items are listed in order of size. The order of the continents is as in the atlas. The bottom part of many of the lists is selective in order to give examples from as many different countries as possible. The figures are rounded as appropriate, and both metric and imperial measurements are given.

WORLD, CONTINENTS, OCEANS

	km²	miles²	%
The World	509,450,000	196,672,000	–
Land	149,450,000	57,688,000	29.3
Water	360,000,000	138,984,000	70.7
Asia	44,500,000	17,177,000	29.8
Africa	30,302,000	11,697,000	20.3
North America	24,241,000	9,357,000	16.2
South America	17,793,000	6,868,000	11.9
Antarctica	14,100,000	5,443,000	9.4
Europe	9,957,000	3,843,000	6.7
Australia & Oceania	8,557,000	3,303,000	5.7
Pacific Ocean	179,679,000	69,356,000	49.9
Atlantic Ocean	92,373,000	35,657,000	25.7
Indian Ocean	73,917,000	28,532,000	20.5
Arctic Ocean	14,090,000	5,439,000	3.9

OCEAN DEPTHS

Atlantic Ocean	m	ft
Puerto Rico (Milwaukee) Deep	9,220	30,249
Cayman Trench	7,680	25,197
Gulf of Mexico	5,203	17,070
Mediterranean Sea	5,121	16,801
Black Sea	2,211	7,254
North Sea	660	2,165

Indian Ocean	m	ft
Java Trench	7,450	24,442
Red Sea	2,635	8,454

Pacific Ocean	m	ft
Mariana Trench	11,022	36,161
Tonga Trench	10,882	35,702
Japan Trench	10,554	34,626
Kuril Trench	10,542	34,587

Arctic Ocean	m	ft
Molloy Deep	5,608	18,399

MOUNTAINS

Europe		m	ft
Mont Blanc	*France/Italy*	4,807	15,771
Monte Rosa	*Italy/Switzerland*	4,634	15,203
Dom	*Switzerland*	4,545	14,911
Liskamm	*Switzerland*	4,527	14,852
Weisshorn	*Switzerland*	4,505	14,780
Taschorn	*Switzerland*	4,490	14,730
Matterhorn/Cervino	*Italy/Switzerland*	4,478	14,691
Mont Maudit	*France/Italy*	4,465	14,649
Dent Blanche	*Switzerland*	4,356	14,291
Nadelhorn	*Switzerland*	4,327	14,196
Grandes Jorasses	*France/Italy*	4,208	13,806
Jungfrau	*Switzerland*	4,158	13,642
Grossglockner	*Austria*	3,797	12,457
Mulhacén	*Spain*	3,478	11,411
Zugspitze	*Germany*	2,962	9,718
Olympus	*Greece*	2,917	9,570
Triglav	*Slovenia*	2,863	9,393
Gerlachovka	*Slovak Republic*	2,655	8,711
Galdhöpiggen	*Norway*	2,468	8,100
Kebnekaise	*Sweden*	2,117	6,946
Ben Nevis	*UK*	1,343	4,406

Asia		m	ft
Everest	*China/Nepal*	8,848	29,029
K2 (Godwin Austen)	*China/Kashmir*	8,611	28,251
Kanchenjunga	*India/Nepal*	8,598	28,208
Lhotse	*China/Nepal*	8,516	27,939
Makalu	*China/Nepal*	8,481	27,824
Cho Oyu	*China/Nepal*	8,201	26,906
Dhaulagiri	*Nepal*	8,172	26,811
Manaslu	*Nepal*	8,156	26,758
Nanga Parbat	*Kashmir*	8,126	26,660
Annapurna	*Nepal*	8,078	26,502
Gasherbrum	*China/Kashmir*	8,068	26,469
Broad Peak	*China/Kashmir*	8,051	26,414
Xixabangma	*China*	8,012	26,286
Kangbachen	*India/Nepal*	7,902	25,925
Trivor	*Pakistan*	7,720	25,328
Pik Kommunizma	*Tajikistan*	7,495	24,590
Elbrus	*Russia*	5,642	18,510
Demavend	*Iran*	5,604	18,386
Ararat	*Turkey*	5,165	16,945
Gunong Kinabalu	*Malaysia (Borneo)*	4,101	13,455
Fuji-San	*Japan*	3,776	12,388

Africa		m	ft
Kilimanjaro	*Tanzania*	5,895	19,340
Mt Kenya	*Kenya*	5,199	17,057
Ruwenzori (Margherita)	*Uganda/Zaïre*	5,109	16,762
Ras Dashan	*Ethiopia*	4,620	15,157
Meru	*Tanzania*	4,565	14,977
Karisimbi	*Rwanda/Zaïre*	4,507	14,787
Mt Elgon	*Kenya/Uganda*	4,321	14,176
Batu	*Ethiopia*	4,307	14,130
Toubkal	*Morocco*	4,165	13,665
Mt Cameroon	*Cameroon*	4,070	13,353

Oceania		m	ft
Puncak Jaya	*Indonesia*	5,029	16,499
Puncak Trikora	*Indonesia*	4,750	15,584
Puncak Mandala	*Indonesia*	4,702	15,427
Mt Wilhelm	*Papua New Guinea*	4,508	14,790
Mauna Kea	*USA (Hawaii)*	4,205	13,796
Mauna Loa	*USA (Hawaii)*	4,170	13,681
Mt Cook	*New Zealand*	3,753	12,313
Mt Kosciusko	*Australia*	2,237	7,339

North America		m	ft
Mt McKinley (Denali)	*USA (Alaska)*	6,194	20,321
Mt Logan	*Canada*	5,959	19,551
Citlaltepetl	*Mexico*	5,700	18,701
Mt St Elias	*USA/Canada*	5,489	18,008
Popocatepetl	*Mexico*	5,452	17,887
Mt Foraker	*USA (Alaska)*	5,304	17,401
Ixtaccihuatl	*Mexico*	5,286	17,342
Lucania	*Canada*	5,227	17,149
Mt Steele	*Canada*	5,073	16,644
Mt Bona	*USA (Alaska)*	5,005	16,420
Mt Whitney	*USA*	4,418	14,495
Tajumulco	*Guatemala*	4,220	13,845
Chirripó Grande	*Costa Rica*	3,837	12,589
Pico Duarte	*Dominican Rep.*	3,175	10,417

South America		m	ft
Aconcagua	*Argentina*	6,960	22,834
Bonete	*Argentina*	6,872	22,546
Ojos del Salado	*Argentina/Chile*	6,863	22,516
Pissis	*Argentina*	6,779	22,241
Mercedario	*Argentina/Chile*	6,770	22,211
Huascaran	*Peru*	6,768	22,204
Llullaillaco	*Argentina/Chile*	6,723	22,057
Nudo de Cachi	*Argentina*	6,720	22,047
Yerupaja	*Peru*	6,632	21,758
Sajama	*Bolivia*	6,542	21,463
Chimborazo	*Ecuador*	6,267	20,561
Pico Colon	*Colombia*	5,800	19,029
Pico Bolivar	*Venezuela*	5,007	16,427

Antarctica		m	ft
Vinson Massif		4,897	16,066
Mt Kirkpatrick		4,528	14,855

RIVERS

Europe		km	miles
Volga	*Caspian Sea*	3,700	2,300
Danube	*Black Sea*	2,850	1,770
Ural	*Caspian Sea*	2,535	1,575
Dnepr (Dnipro)	*Volga*	2,285	1,420
Kama	*Volga*	2,030	1,260
Don	*Volga*	1,990	1,240
Petchora	*Arctic Ocean*	1,790	1,110
Oka	*Volga*	1,480	920
Dnister (Dniester)	*Black Sea*	1,400	870
Vyatka	*Kama*	1,370	850
Rhine	*North Sea*	1,320	820
N. Dvina	*Arctic Ocean*	1,290	800
Elbe	*North Sea*	1,145	710

Asia		km	miles
Yangtze	*Pacific Ocean*	6,380	3,960
Yenisey–Angara	*Arctic Ocean*	5,550	3,445
Huang He	*Pacific Ocean*	5,464	3,395
Ob–Irtysh	*Arctic Ocean*	5,410	3,360
Mekong	*Pacific Ocean*	4,500	2,795
Amur	*Pacific Ocean*	4,400	2,730
Lena	*Arctic Ocean*	4,400	2,730
Irtysh	*Ob*	4,250	2,640
Yenisey	*Arctic Ocean*	4,090	2,540
Ob	*Arctic Ocean*	3,680	2,285
Indus	*Indian Ocean*	3,100	1,925
Brahmaputra	*Indian Ocean*	2,900	1,800
Syrdarya	*Aral Sea*	2,860	1,775
Salween	*Indian Ocean*	2,800	1,740
Euphrates	*Indian Ocean*	2,700	1,675
Amudarya	*Aral Sea*	2,540	1,575

Africa		km	miles
Nile	*Mediterranean*	6,670	4,140
Zaïre/Congo	*Atlantic Ocean*	4,670	2,900
Niger	*Atlantic Ocean*	4,180	2,595
Zambezi	*Indian Ocean*	3,540	2,200
Oubangi/Uele	*Zaïre*	2,250	1,400
Kasai	*Zaïre*	1,950	1,210
Shaballe	*Indian Ocean*	1,930	1,200
Orange	*Atlantic Ocean*	1,860	1,155
Cubango	*Okavango Swamps*	1,800	1,120
Limpopo	*Indian Ocean*	1,600	995
Senegal	*Atlantic Ocean*	1,600	995

Australia		km	miles
Murray–Darling	*Indian Ocean*	3,750	2,330
Darling	*Murray*	3,070	1,905
Murray	*Indian Ocean*	2,575	1,600
Murrumbidgee	*Murray*	1,690	1,050

North America		km	miles
Mississippi–Missouri	*Gulf of Mexico*	6,020	3,740
Mackenzie	*Arctic Ocean*	4,240	2,630
Mississippi	*Gulf of Mexico*	3,780	2,350
Missouri	*Mississippi*	3,780	2,350
Yukon	*Pacific Ocean*	3,185	1,980
Rio Grande	*Gulf of Mexico*	3,030	1,880
Arkansas	*Mississippi*	2,340	1,450
Colorado	*Pacific Ocean*	2,330	1,445
Red	*Mississippi*	2,040	1,270
Columbia	*Pacific Ocean*	1,950	1,210
Saskatchewan	*Lake Winnipeg*	1,940	1,205

South America		km	miles
Amazon	*Atlantic Ocean*	6,450	4,010
Paraná–Plate	*Atlantic Ocean*	4,500	2,800
Purus	*Amazon*	3,350	2,080
Madeira	*Amazon*	3,200	1,990
São Francisco	*Atlantic Ocean*	2,900	1,800
Paraná	*Plate*	2,800	1,740
Tocantins	*Atlantic Ocean*	2,750	1,710
Paraguay	*Paraná*	2,550	1,580
Orinoco	*Atlantic Ocean*	2,500	1,550
Pilcomayo	*Paraná*	2,500	1,550
Araguaia	*Tocantins*	2,250	1,400

LAKES

Europe		km²	miles²
Lake Ladoga	*Russia*	17,700	6,800
Lake Onega	*Russia*	9,700	3,700
Saimaa system	*Finland*	8,000	3,100
Vänern	*Sweden*	5,500	2,100

Asia		km²	miles²
Caspian Sea	*Asia*	371,800	143,550
Aral Sea	*Kazakstan/Uzbekistan*	33,640	13,000
Lake Baykal	*Russia*	30,500	11,780
Tonlé Sap	*Cambodia*	20,000	7,700
Lake Balqash	*Kazakstan*	18,500	7,100

Africa		km²	miles²
Lake Victoria	*East Africa*	68,000	26,000
Lake Tanganyika	*Central Africa*	33,000	13,000
Lake Malawi/Nyasa	*East Africa*	29,600	11,430
Lake Chad	*Central Africa*	25,000	9,700
Lake Turkana	*Ethiopia/Kenya*	8,500	3,300
Lake Volta	*Ghana*	8,500	3,300

Australia		km²	miles²
Lake Eyre	*Australia*	8,900	3,400
Lake Torrens	*Australia*	5,800	2,200
Lake Gairdner	*Australia*	4,800	1,900

North America		km²	miles²
Lake Superior	*Canada/USA*	82,350	31,800
Lake Huron	*Canada/USA*	59,600	23,010
Lake Michigan	*USA*	58,000	22,400
Great Bear Lake	*Canada*	31,800	12,280
Great Slave Lake	*Canada*	28,500	11,000
Lake Erie	*Canada/USA*	25,700	9,900
Lake Winnipeg	*Canada*	24,400	9,400
Lake Ontario	*Canada/USA*	19,500	7,500
Lake Nicaragua	*Nicaragua*	8,200	3,200

South America		km²	miles²
Lake Titicaca	*Bolivia/Peru*	8,300	3,200
Lake Poopo	*Peru*	2,800	1,100

ISLANDS

Europe		km²	miles²
Great Britain	*UK*	229,880	88,700
Iceland	*Atlantic Ocean*	103,000	39,800
Ireland	*Ireland/UK*	84,400	32,600
Novaya Zemlya (N.)	*Russia*	48,200	18,600
Sicily	*Italy*	25,500	9,800
Corsica	*France*	8,700	3,400

Asia		km²	miles²
Borneo	*South-east Asia*	744,360	287,400
Sumatra	*Indonesia*	473,600	182,860
Honshu	*Japan*	230,500	88,980
Celebes	*Indonesia*	189,000	73,000
Java	*Indonesia*	126,700	48,900
Luzon	*Philippines*	104,700	40,400
Hokkaido	*Japan*	78,400	30,300

Africa		km²	miles²
Madagascar	*Indian Ocean*	587,040	226,660
Socotra	*Indian Ocean*	3,600	1,400
Réunion	*Indian Ocean*	2,500	965

Oceania		km²	miles²
New Guinea	*Indonesia/Papua NG*	821,030	317,000
New Zealand (S.)	*Pacific Ocean*	150,500	58,100
New Zealand (N.)	*Pacific Ocean*	114,700	44,300
Tasmania	*Australia*	67,800	26,200
Hawaii	*Pacific Ocean*	10,450	4,000

North America		km²	miles²
Greenland	*Atlantic Ocean*	2,175,600	839,800
Baffin Is.	*Canada*	508,000	196,100
Victoria Is.	*Canada*	212,200	81,900
Ellesmere Is.	*Canada*	212,000	81,800
Cuba	*Caribbean Sea*	110,860	42,800
Hispaniola	*Dominican Rep./Haiti*	76,200	29,400
Jamaica	*Caribbean Sea*	11,400	4,400
Puerto Rico	*Atlantic Ocean*	8,900	3,400

South America		km²	miles²
Tierra del Fuego	*Argentina/Chile*	47,000	18,100
Falkland Is. (E.)	*Atlantic Ocean*	6,800	2,600

MAP PROJECTIONS

MAP PROJECTIONS

A map projection is the systematic depiction on a plane surface of the imaginary lines of latitude or longitude from a globe of the earth. This network of lines is called the graticule and forms the framework upon which an accurate depiction of the earth is made. The map graticule, which is the basis of any map, is constructed sometimes by graphical means, but often by using mathematical formulae to give the intersections of the graticule plotted as x and y co-ordinates. The choice between projections is based upon which properties the cartographer wishes the map to possess, the map scale and also the extent of the area to be mapped. Since the globe is three dimensional, it is not possible to depict its surface on a two dimensional plane without distortion. Preservation of one of the basic properties listed below can only be secured at the expense of the others and the choice of projection is often a compromise solution.

Correct Area

In these projections the areas from the globe are to scale on the map. For example, if you look at the diagram at the top right, areas of 10° x 10° are shown from the equator to the poles. The proportion of this area at the extremities are approximately 11:1. An equal area projection will retain that proportion in its portrayal of those areas. This is particularly useful in the mapping of densities and distributions. Projections with this property are termed **Equal Area, Equivalent or Homolographic.**

Correct Distance

In these projections the scale is correct along the meridians, or in the case of the Azimuthal Equidistant scale is true along any line drawn from the centre of the projection. They are called **Equidistant.**

Correct Shape

This property can only be true within small areas as it is achieved only by having a uniform scale distortion along both x and y axes of the projection. The projections are called **Conformal** or **Orthomorphic.**

In order to minimise the distortions at the edges of some projections, central portions of them are often selected for atlas maps. Below are listed some of the major types of projection.

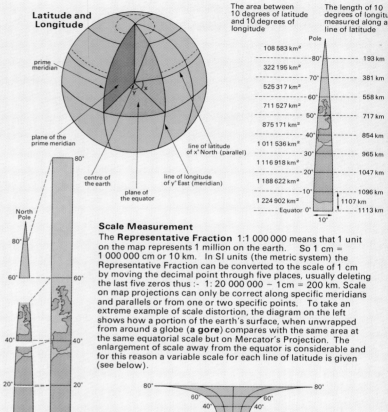

Latitude and Longitude

prime meridian

plane of the prime meridian

centre of the earth

plane of the equator

line of latitude of x° North (parallel)

line of longitude of y° East (meridian)

North Pole

The area between 10 degrees of latitude and 10 degrees of longitude

108 583 km²	
322 195 km²	
525 317 km²	
711 527 km²	
875 171 km²	
1 011 536 km²	
1 116 918 km²	
1 188 622 km²	
1 224 902 km²	

The length of 10 degrees of longitude measured along a line of latitude

Pole
80° — 193 km
70° — 381 km
60° — 558 km
50° — 717 km
40° — 854 km
30° — 965 km
20° — 1047 km
10° — 1096 km
1107 km
Equator 0° — 1113 km
10°

Scale Measurement

The **Representative Fraction** 1:1 000 000 means that 1 unit on the map represents 1 million on the earth. So 1 cm = 1 000 000 cm or 10 km. In SI units (the metric system) the Representative Fraction can be converted to the scale of 1 cm by moving the decimal point through five places, usually deleting the last five zeros thus :- 1 : 20 000 000 − 1cm = 200 km. Scale on map projections can only be correct along specific meridians and parallels or from one or two specific points. To take an extreme example of scale distortion, the diagram on the left shows how a portion of the earth's surface, when unwrapped from around a globe (**a gore**) compares with the same area at the same equatorial scale but on Mercator's Projection. The enlargement of scale away from the equator is considerable and for this reason a variable scale for each line of latitude is given (see below).

0 800 1600 km

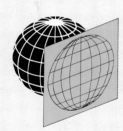

AZIMUTHAL OR ZENITHAL PROJECTIONS

These are constructed by the projection of part of the graticule from the globe onto a plane tangential to any single point on it. This plane may be tangential to the equator (**equatorial case**), the poles (**polar case**) or any other point (**oblique case**). Any straight line drawn from the point at which the plane touches the globe is the shortest distance from that point and is known as a **great circle**. In its **Gnomonic** construction *any* straight line on the map is a great circle, but there is great exaggeration towards the edges and this reduces its general uses. There are five different ways of transferring the graticule onto the plane and these are shown on the right. The central diagram below shows how the graticules vary, using the polar case as the example.

Equidistant | **Equal-Area** | **Orthographic** | **Gnomonic** | **Stereographic (conformal)**

Oblique Case

The plane touches the globe at any point between the equator and poles. The oblique orthographic uses the distortion in azimuthal projections away from the centre to give a graphic depiction of the earth as seen from any desired point in space. It can also be used in both Polar and Equatorial cases. It is used not only for the earth but also for the moon and planets.

Polar Case

The polar case is the simplest to construct and the diagram below shows the differing effects of all five methods of construction comparing their coverage, distortion etc., using North America as the example.

Equatorial Case

The example shown here is Lambert's Equivalent Azimuthal. It is the only projection which is both equal area and where bearing is true from the centre.

Stereographic

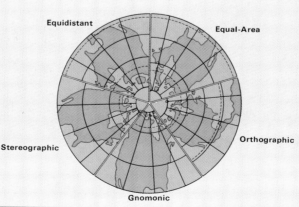

Equidistant

Equal-Area

Orthographic

Gnomonic

CONICAL PROJECTIONS

These use the projection of the graticule from the globe onto a cone which is tangential to a line of latitude (termed the **standard parallel**). This line is always an arc and scale is always true along it. Because of its method of construction it is used mainly for depicting the temperate latitudes around the standard parallel i.e. where there is least distortion. To reduce the distortion and include a larger range of latitudes, the projection may be constructed with the cone bisecting the surface of the globe so that there are two standard parallels each of which is true to scale. The distortion is thus spread more evenly between the two chosen parallels.

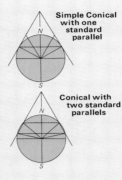

Simple Conical
with one
standard
parallel

Conical with
two standard
parallels

Bonne

This is a modification of the simple conic whereby the true scale along the meridians is sacrificed to enable the accurate representation of areas. However scale is true along each parallel but shapes are distorted at the edges.

Simple Conic

Scale is correct not only along the standard parallel but also along all meridians. The selection of the standard parallel used is crucial because of the distortion away from it. The projection is usually used to portray regions or continents at small scales.

Lambert's Conformal Conic

This projection uses two standard parallels but instead of being equal area as Albers, it is Conformal. Because it has comparatively small distortion, direction and distances can be readily measured and it is therefore used for some navigational charts.

Albers Conical Equal Area

This projection uses two standard parallels and once again the selection of the two specific ones relative to the land area to be mapped is very important. It is equal area and is especially useful for large land masses oriented East-West, for example the U.S.A.

CYLINDRICAL AND OTHER WORLD PROJECTIONS

Cylindrical with
two standard parallels

This group of projections are those which permit the whole of the Earth's surface to be depicted on one map. They are a very large group of projections and the following are only a few of them. Cylindrical projections are constructed by the projection of the graticule from the globe onto a cylinder tangential to the globe. In the examples shown here the cylinder touches the equator, but it can be moved through 90° so it touches the poles - this is called the **Transverse Aspect**. If the cylinder is twisted so that it touches anywhere between the equator and poles it is called the **Oblique Aspect**. Although cylindrical projections can depict all the main land masses, there is considerable distortion of shape and area towards the poles. One cylindrical projection, **Mercator** overcomes this shortcoming by possessing the unique navigational property that any straight drawn on it is a line of constant bearing (**loxodrome**), i.e. a straight line route on the globe crosses the parallels and meridians on the map at the same angles as on the globe. It is used for maps and charts between 15° either side of the equator. Beyond this enlargement of area is a serious drawback, although it is used for navigational charts at all latitudes.

Simple Cylindrical

Mercator

Mollweide

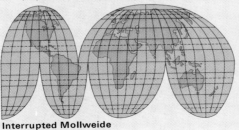

Sanson-Flamsteed

Mollweide and Sanson-Flamsteed

Both of these projections are termed **pseudo-cylindrical**. They are basically cylindrical projections where parallels have been progressively shortened and drawn to scale towards the poles. This allows them to overcome the gross distortions exhibited by the ordinary cylindrical projections and they are in fact Equal Area, Mollweide's giving a slightly better shape. To improve the shape of the continents still further they, like some other projections can be **Interrupted** as can be seen below, but this is at the expense of contiguous sea areas. These projections can have any central meridian and so can be 'centred' on the Atlantic, Pacific, Asia, America etc. In this form both projections are suitable for any form of mapping statistical distributions.

Hammer

This is not a cylindrical projection, but is developed from the Lambert Azimuthal Equal Area by doubling all the East-West distances along the parallels from the central meridian. Like both Sanson–Flamsteed and Mollweide it is distorted towards its edges but has curved parallels to lessen the distortion.

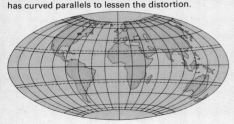

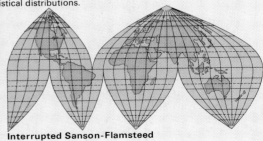

Interrupted Mollweide

Interrupted Sanson-Flamsteed

USER GUIDE

Organization of the atlas

Prepared in accordance with the highest standards of international cartography to provide accurate and detailed representation of the earth, the atlas is made up of four separate sections and is organized with ease of use in mind.

The first section of the atlas consists of up-to-date world geographical and demographical statistics, graphics on map projections intended to help the reader understand how cartographers create and use map projections, and this user guide.

The second section of the atlas, the 32-page United States Maps section, has blue page borders and offers comprehensive coverage of the United States and its outlying areas, with climate and agricultural maps, politically colored maps with some topographical detail, maps of major urban areas, and a 16-page index with longitude and latitude coordinates.

The third section of the atlas, the 32-page Introduction to World Geography section, consists of thematic maps, graphs, and charts on a range of geographical and demographical topics, and a subject index.

The fourth and final section of the atlas, the 96-page World Maps section, has gray page borders and covers the earth continent by continent in the classic sequence adopted by cartographers since the 16th century. This section begins with Europe, then Asia, Africa, Australia and Oceania, North America, and South America. For each continent, there are maps at a variety of scales: first, physical relief maps and political maps of the whole continent, then large scale maps of the most important or densely populated areas.

The governing principle is that by turning the pages of the World Maps section, the reader moves steadily from north to south through each continent, with each map overlapping its neighbors. Immediately following the maps in the World Maps section is the comprehensive index to the maps, which contains 44,000 entries of both place names and geographical features. The index provides the latitude and longitude coordinates as well as letters and numbers, so that locating any site can be accomplished with speed and accuracy.

Map presentation

All of the maps in the atlas are drawn with north at the top (except for the map of the Arctic Ocean and the map of Antarctica). The maps in the United States Maps section and the World Maps section contain the following information in their borders: the map title; the scale; the projection used; the degrees of latitude and longitude; and on the physical relief maps, a height and depth reference panel identifying the colors used for each layer of contouring. In addition to this information, the maps in the World Maps section also contain locator diagrams which show the area covered, the page numbers for adjacent maps, and the letters and numbers used in the index for locating place names and geographical features.

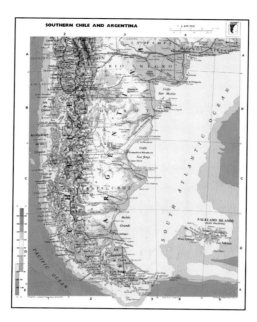

Map symbols

Each map contains a vast amount of detail which is conveyed clearly and accurately by the use of symbols. Points and circles of varying sizes locate and identify the relative importance of towns and cities; different styles of type are employed for administrative, geographical and regional place names. A variety of pictorial symbols denote landscape features such as glaciers, marshes and reefs, and man-made structures including roads, railroads, airports, canals and dams. International borders are shown by red lines. Where neighboring countries are in dispute, the maps show the *de facto* boundary between nations, regardless of the legal or historical situation. The symbols are explained on the first page of each of the map sections.

Map scales

The scale of each map is given in the numerical form known as the representative fraction. The first figure is always one, signifying one unit of distance on the map; the second figure, usually in millions, is the number by which the map unit must be multiplied to give the equivalent distance on

LARGE SCALE		
1: 1 000 000	1 cm = 10 km	1 inch = 16 miles
1: 2 500 000	1 cm = 25 km	1 inch = 39.5 miles
1: 5 000 000	1 cm = 50 km	1 inch = 79 miles
1: 6 000 000	1 cm = 60 km	1 inch = 95 miles
1: 8 000 000	1 cm = 80 km	1 inch = 126 miles
1: 10 000 000	1 cm = 100 km	1 inch = 158 miles
1: 15 000 000	1 cm = 150 km	1 inch = 237 miles
1: 20 000 000	1 cm = 200 km	1 inch = 316 miles
1: 50 000 000	1 cm = 500 km	1 inch = 790 miles
SMALL SCALE		

the earth's surface. Calculations can easily be made in centimeters and kilometers, by dividing the earth units figure by 100 000 (i.e. deleting the last five 0s). Thus 1:1 000 000 means l cm = 10 km. The calculation for inches and miles is more laborious, but 1 000 000

divided by 63 360 (the number of inches in a mile) shows that 1:1 000 000 means approximately 1 inch = 16 miles. The table shown provides distance equivalents for scales down to 1:50 000 000.

Measuring distances

Although each map is accompanied by a scale bar, distances cannot always be measured with confidence because of the distortions involved in portraying the curved surface of the earth on a flat page. As a general rule, the larger the map scale (i.e. the lower the number of earth units in the representative fraction), the more accurate and reliable will be the distance measured. On small scale maps such as those of the world and of entire continents, measurement may only be accurate along the standard parallels, or central axes, and should not be attempted without considering the map projection.

Latitude and longitude

Accurate positioning of individual points on the earth's surface is made possible by reference to the geometrical system of latitude and longitude. Latitude parallels are drawn west–east around the earth and numbered by degrees north and south of the Equator, which is designated 0° of latitude. Longitude meridians are drawn north–south and numbered by degrees east and west of the prime meridian, 0° of longitude, which passes through Greenwich in England. By referring to these coordinates and their subdivisions of minutes (1/60th of a degree) and seconds (1/60th of a minute), any place on earth can be located to within a few hundred yards. Latitude and longitude are indicated by blue lines on the maps; they are straight or curved according to the projection employed. Reference to these lines is the easiest way of determining the relative positions of places on different large scale maps, and for plotting compass directions.

Name forms

For ease of reference, both English and local name forms appear in the atlas. Oceans, seas and countries are shown in English throughout the atlas; country names may be abbreviated to their commonly accepted form (e.g. Germany, not The Federal Republic of Germany). Conventional English forms are also used for place names on the smaller scale maps of the continents. However, local name forms are used on all large scale and regional maps, with the English form given in brackets only for important cities – the large scale map of Eastern Europe and Turkey thus shows Moskva (Moscow). For countries which do not use a Roman script, place names have been transcribed according to the systems adopted by the British and US Geographic Names Authorities. For China, the Pin Yin system has been used, with some more widely known forms appearing in brackets, as with Beijing (Peking). Both English and local names appear in the index to the world maps.

UNITED STATES MAPS

SETTLEMENTS

◻ WASHINGTON D.C. ▪ Tampa ◉ Fresno ● Waterloo ◎ Ventura ○ Barstow ○ Blythe ○ Hope

Settlement symbols and type styles vary according to the scale of each map and indicate the importance of towns on the map rather than specific population figures

ADMINISTRATION

───── International Boundaries

·········· Internal Boundaries

National Parks, Recreation Areas and Monuments

Country Names
CANADA

Administrative Area Names
MICHIGAN

COMMUNICATIONS

───── Major Highways

⌒ Other Principal Roads

≍ Passes

✈ ＋ ○ Airports and Airfields

⌒ Principal Railroads

·--·- Railroads Under Construction

⌒ Other Railroads

╕---╘ Railroad Tunnels

⊔⊔⊔⊔⊔ Principal Canals

PHYSICAL FEATURES

⌒ Perennial Streams

·-·-· Intermittent Streams

⬭ Perennial Lakes and Reservoirs

◌ Intermittent Lakes and Salt Flats

Swamps and Marshes

▱ Permanent Ice and Glaciers

▲ 8848 Elevations in meters

▼ 8050 Sea Depths in meters

1134 Height of Lake Surface Above Sea Level in meters

I meter is approx. 3.3 feet

CITY MAPS

In addition to, or instead of, the symbols explained above, the following symbols are used on the city maps between pages 20-29

▨ Urban Areas

⌒ Limited Access Roads

⌒ Aqueducts

▨ Woodland and Parks

⌒ Secondary Roads

·---· Ferry Routes

⌒ State Boundaries

✕ Airports

⌒ Canals

⌒ County Boundaries

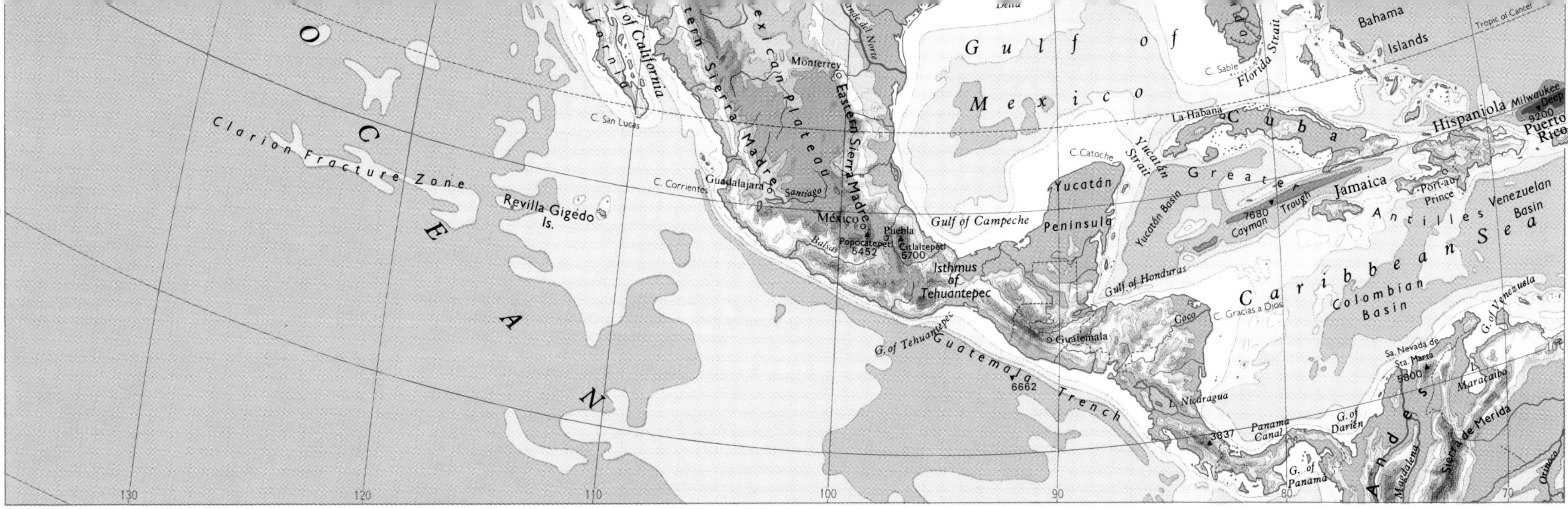

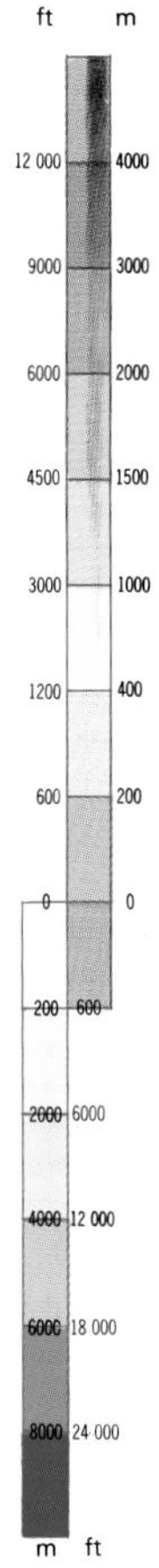

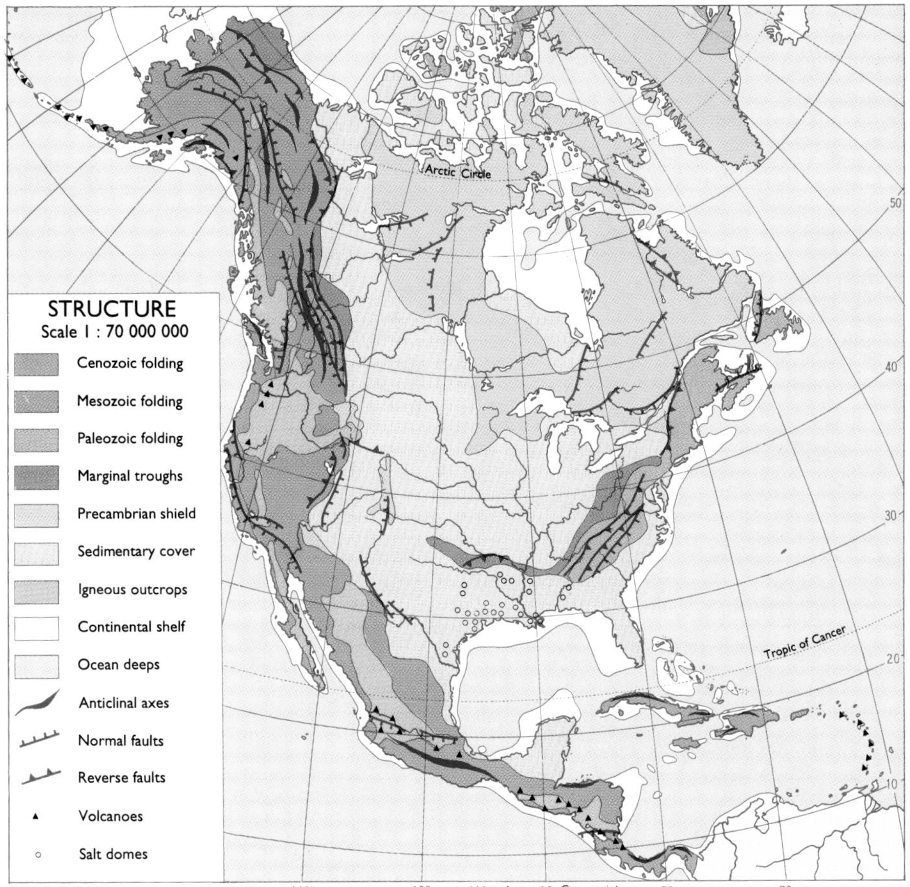

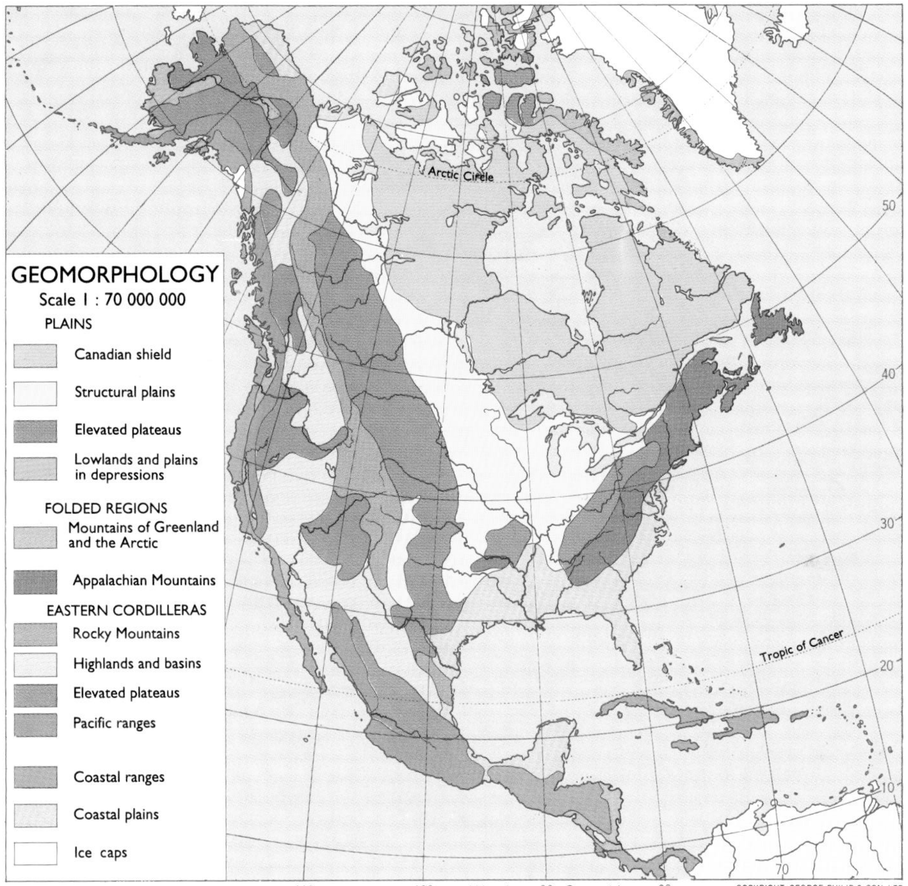

1:30 000 000

100 0 100 200 300 400 500 600 700 miles
100 0 200 400 600 800 1000 km

GEOMORPHOLOGY
Scale 1:70 000 000

PLAINS
Canadian shield
Structural plains
Elevated plateaus
Lowlands and plains in depressions

FOLDED REGIONS
Mountains of Greenland and the Arctic
Appalachian Mountains

EASTERN CORDILLERAS
Rocky Mountains
Highlands and basins
Elevated plateaus
Pacific ranges
Coastal ranges
Coastal plains
Ice caps

STRUCTURE
Scale 1:70 000 000

Cenozoic folding
Mesozoic folding
Paleozoic folding
Marginal troughs
Precambrian shield
Sedimentary cover
Igneous outcrops
Continental shelf
Ocean deeps
Anticlinal axes
Normal faults
Reverse faults
Volcanoes
Salt domes

Projection: Bonne

m / ft
4000 12 000
3000 9000
2000 6000
1500 4500
1000 3000
400 1200
200 600
0 0
200 600
2000 6000
4000 12 000
6666 18 000
8000 24 000

Map labels (left panel)
Bahama Islands, Gulf of Mexico, Cuba, La Habana, Jamaica, Greater Antilles, Hispaniola, Puerto Rico, Milwaukee, Caribbean Sea, Lesser Antilles, Colombian Basin, Venezuelan Basin, Sierra Maestra, Cayman Trough, Yucatán Peninsula, Yucatán Basin, Yucatán Strait, Gulf of Honduras, Gulf of Campeche, C. Catoche, Guatemala, Isthmus of Tehuantepec, Gulf of Tehuantepec, Guatemala Trench, Mexican Plateau, Eastern Sierra Madre, Western Sierra Madre, México, Guadalajara, C. Corrientes, Gulf of California, C. San Lucas, California, Revilla-Gigedo Is., Clarion Fracture Zone, PACIFIC OCEAN, Tropic of Cancer, Arctic Circle, West from Greenwich

1:70 000 000

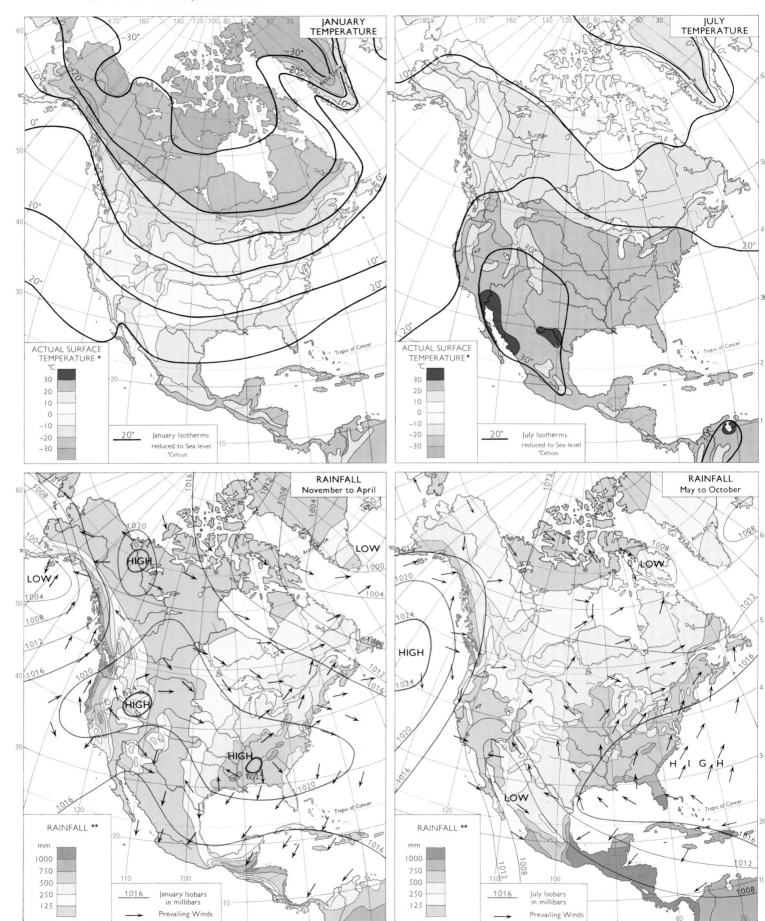

JANUARY TEMPERATURE

ACTUAL SURFACE TEMPERATURE *
°C
30
20
10
0
-10
-20
-30

20° — January Isotherms reduced to Sea-level *Celsius*

JULY TEMPERATURE

ACTUAL SURFACE TEMPERATURE *
°C
30
20
10
0
-10
-20
-30

20° — July Isotherms reduced to Sea-level *Celsius*

RAINFALL
November to April

RAINFALL **
mm
1000
750
500
250
125

1016 — January Isobars in millibars
→ Prevailing Winds

RAINFALL
May to October

RAINFALL **
mm
1000
750
500
250
125

1016 — July Isobars in millibars
→ Prevailing Winds

Projection: *Lambert's Equivalent Azimuthal*

West from 70 Greenwich

*To convert °C to °F, multiply by 1.8, then add 32   **1 in equals 25.4mm

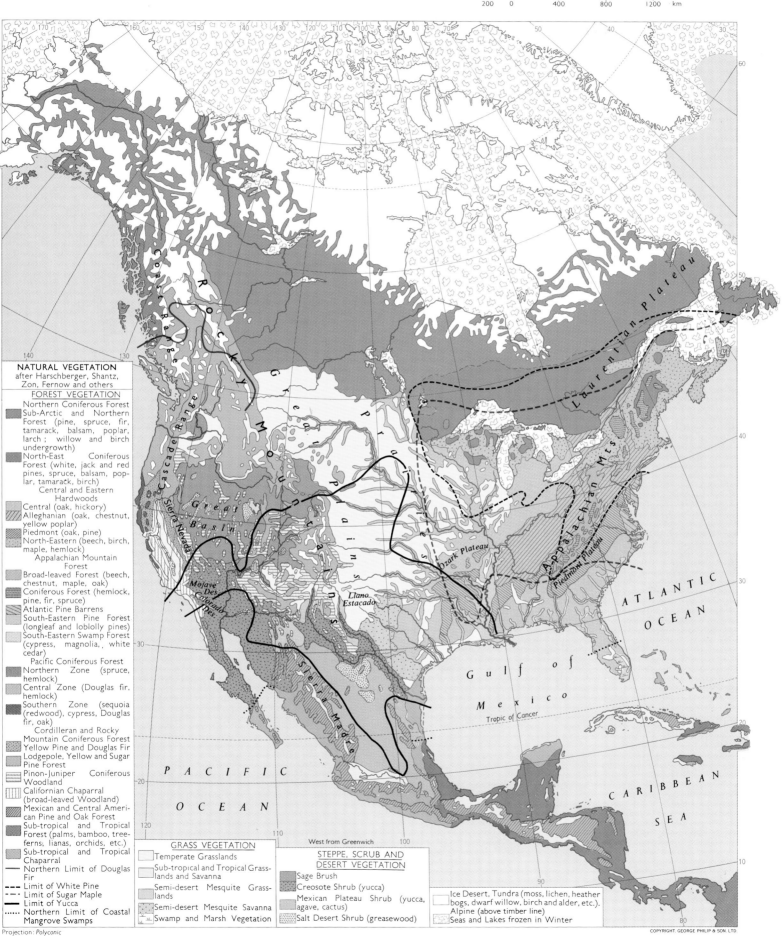

1:32 000 000

NATURAL VEGETATION
after Harschberger, Shantz, Zon, Fernow and others

FOREST VEGETATION

Northern Coniferous Forest
Sub-Arctic and Northern Forest (pine, spruce, fir, tamarack, balsam, poplar, larch; willow and birch undergrowth)
North-East Coniferous Forest (white, jack and red pines, spruce, balsam, poplar, tamarack, birch)

Central and Eastern Hardwoods
Central (oak, hickory)
Alleghanian (oak, chestnut, yellow poplar)
Piedmont (oak, pine)
North-Eastern (beech, birch, maple, hemlock)

Appalachian Mountain Forest
Broad-leaved Forest (beech, chestnut, maple, oak)
Coniferous Forest (hemlock, pine, fir, spruce)
Atlantic Pine Barrens
South-Eastern Pine Forest (longleaf and loblolly pines)
South-Eastern Swamp Forest (cypress, magnolia, white cedar)

Pacific Coniferous Forest
Northern Zone (spruce, hemlock)
Central Zone (Douglas fir, hemlock)
Southern Zone (sequoia (redwood), cypress, Douglas fir, oak)

Cordilleran and Rocky Mountain Coniferous Forest
Yellow Pine and Douglas Fir
Lodgepole, Yellow and Sugar Pine Forest
Pinon-Juniper Coniferous Woodland
Californian Chaparral (broad-leaved Woodland)
Mexican and Central American Pine and Oak Forest
Sub-tropical and Tropical Forest (palms, bamboo, tree-ferns, lianas, orchids, etc.)
Sub-tropical and Tropical Chaparral

— Northern Limit of Douglas Fir
--- Limit of White Pine
-·-·- Limit of Sugar Maple
━━ Limit of Yucca
····· Northern Limit of Coastal Mangrove Swamps

GRASS VEGETATION
Temperate Grasslands
Sub-tropical and Tropical Grasslands and Savanna
Semi-desert Mesquite Grasslands
Semi-desert Mesquite Savanna
Swamp and Marsh Vegetation

STEPPE, SCRUB AND DESERT VEGETATION
Sage Brush
Creosote Shrub (yucca)
Mexican Plateau Shrub (yucca, agave, cactus)
Salt Desert Shrub (greasewood)

Ice Desert, Tundra (moss, lichen, heather bogs, dwarf willow, birch and alder, etc.).
Alpine (above timber line)
Seas and Lakes frozen in Winter

West from Greenwich

PACIFIC OCEAN

ATLANTIC OCEAN

Gulf of Mexico

Tropic of Cancer

CARIBBEAN SEA

Projection: *Polyconic*

HAWAII
1:10 000 000

Projection : Albers' Equal Area with two standard parallels .

West from Greenwich

National Capital ★
State Capital ■ ● ● ● ●

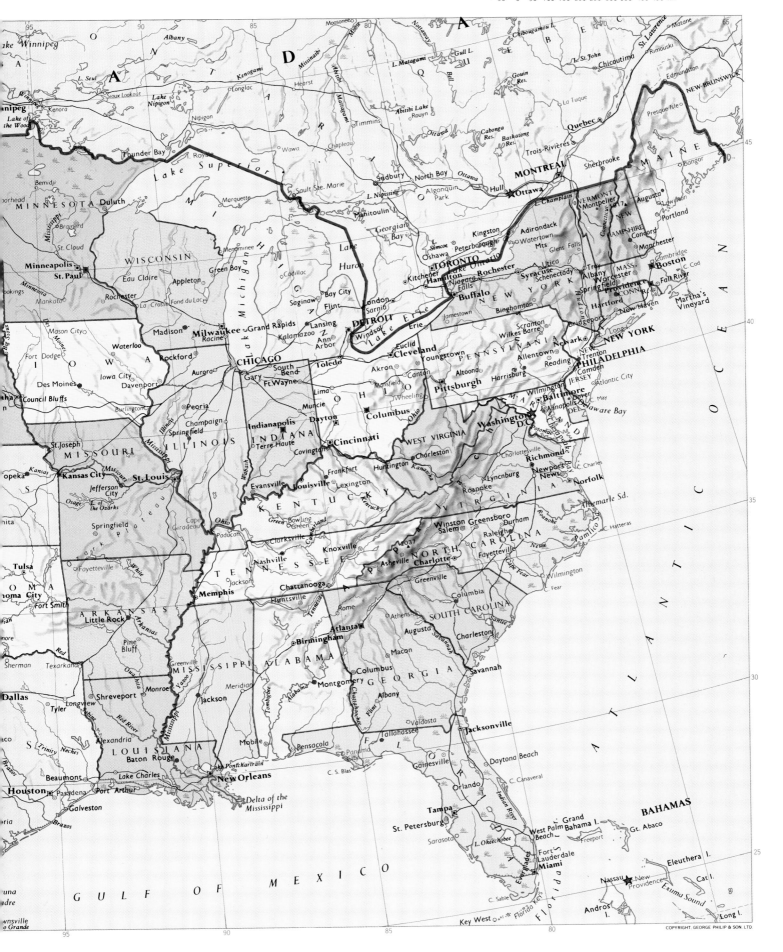

1:12 000 000

50   0   50   100   150   200   250   300 miles
50   0   50 100 150 200 250 300 350 400 450 km

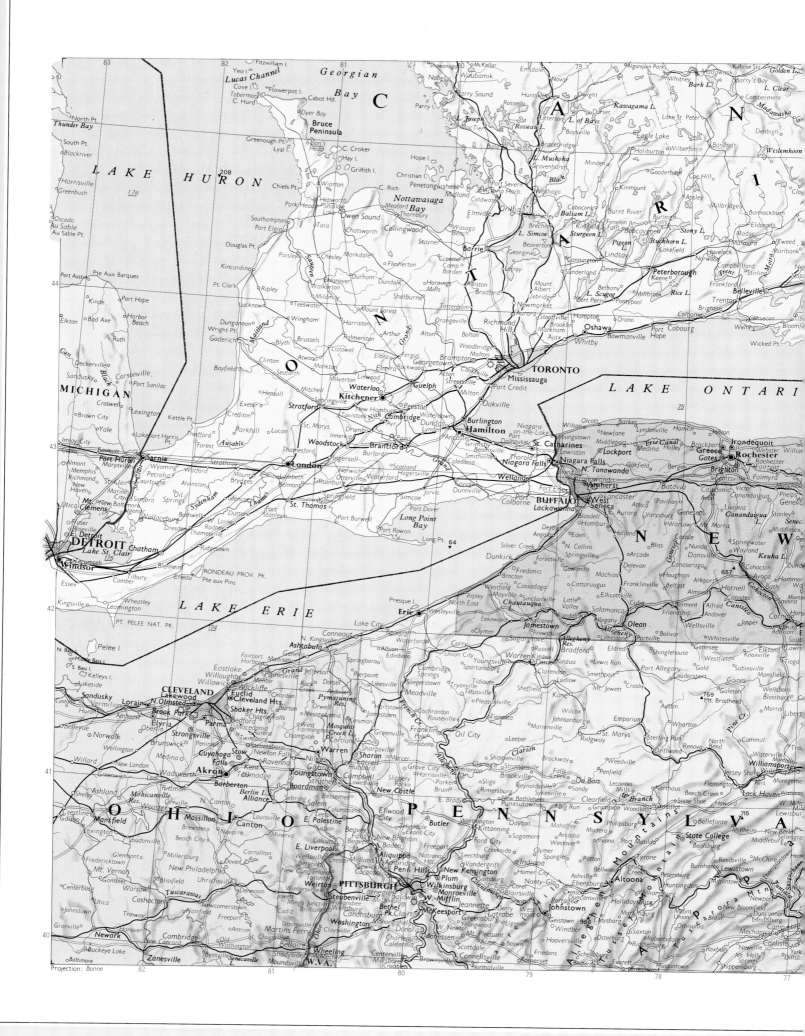

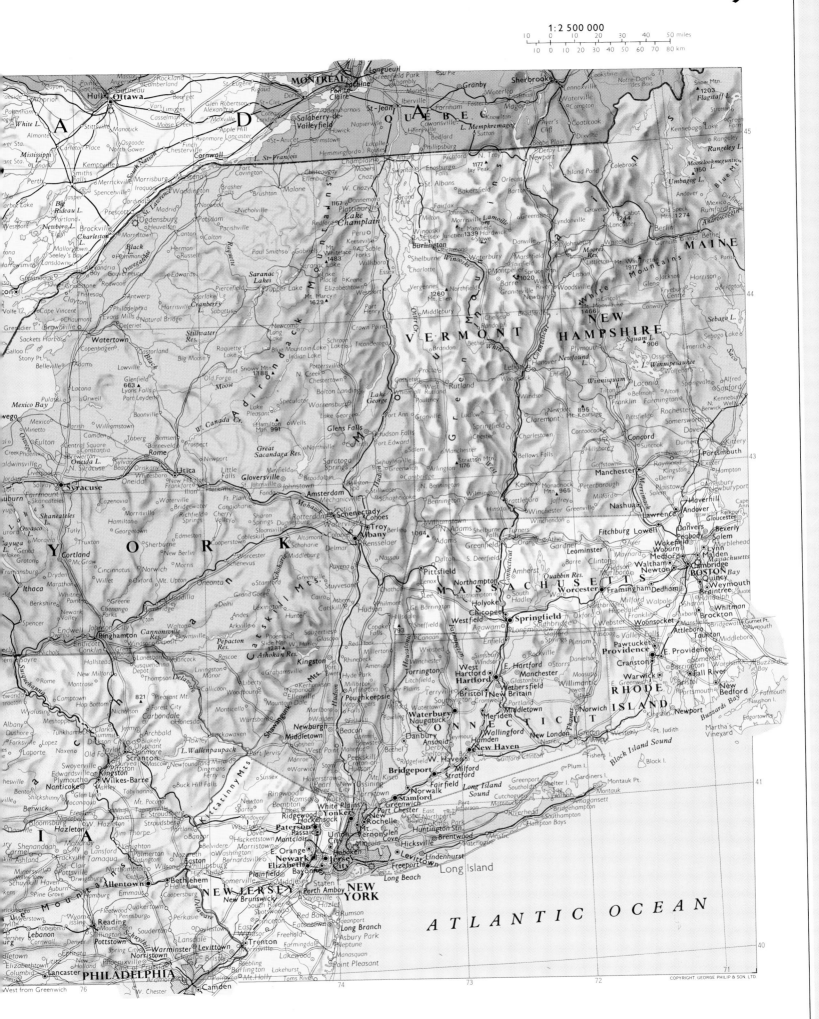

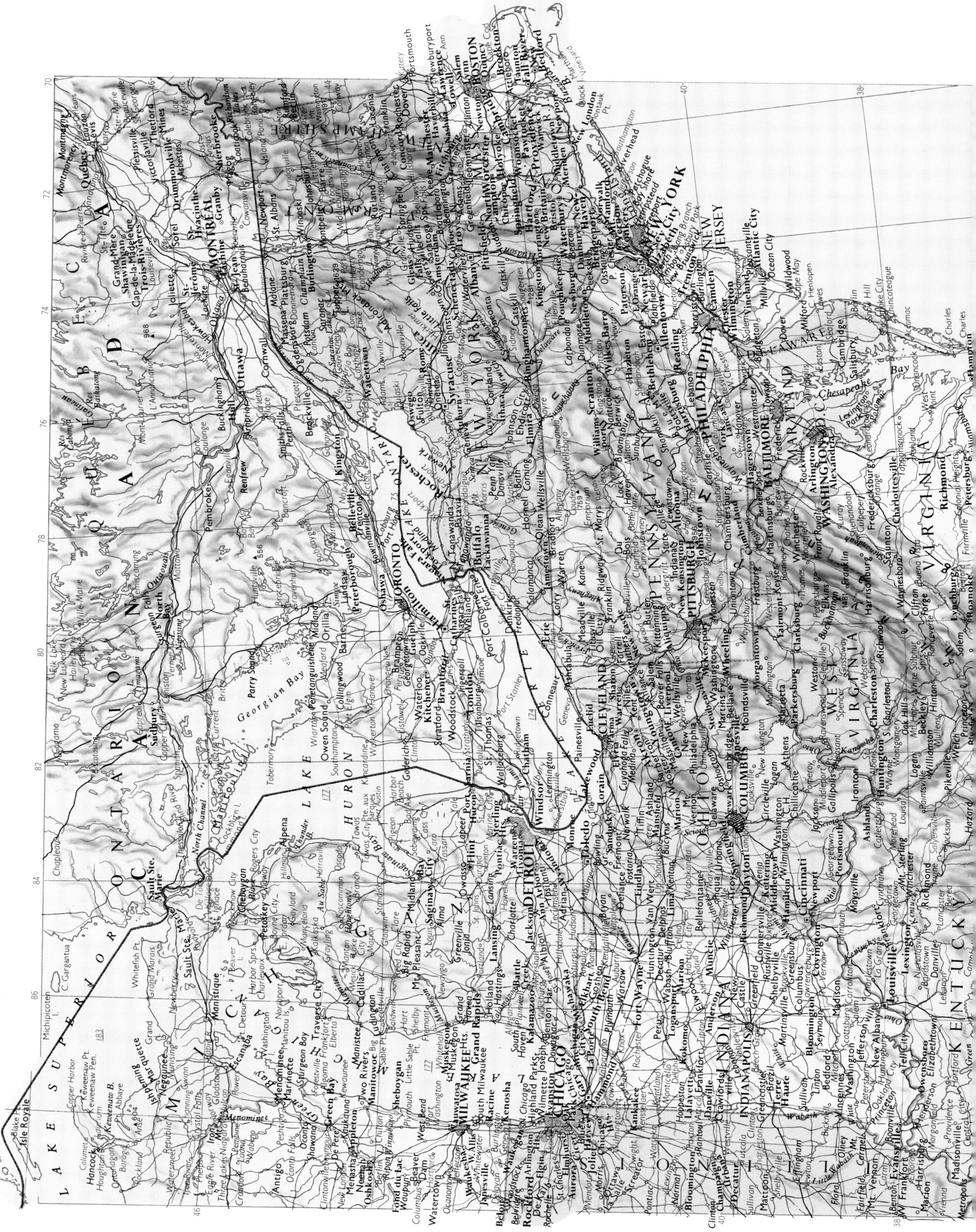
LAKE SUPERIOR
LAKE HURON
LAKE ONTARIO
LAKE ERIE
ONTARIO
QUEBEC
MICHIGAN
NEW YORK
PENNSYLVANIA
OHIO
INDIANA
KENTUCKY
VIRGINIA
WEST VIRGINIA
MARYLAND
NEW JERSEY
CHICAGO
MILWAUKEE
DETROIT
CLEVELAND
PITTSBURGH
TORONTO
MONTREAL
OTTAWA
BUFFALO
PHILADELPHIA
BALTIMORE
WASHINGTON
BOSTON
NEW YORK
INDIANAPOLIS
COLUMBUS

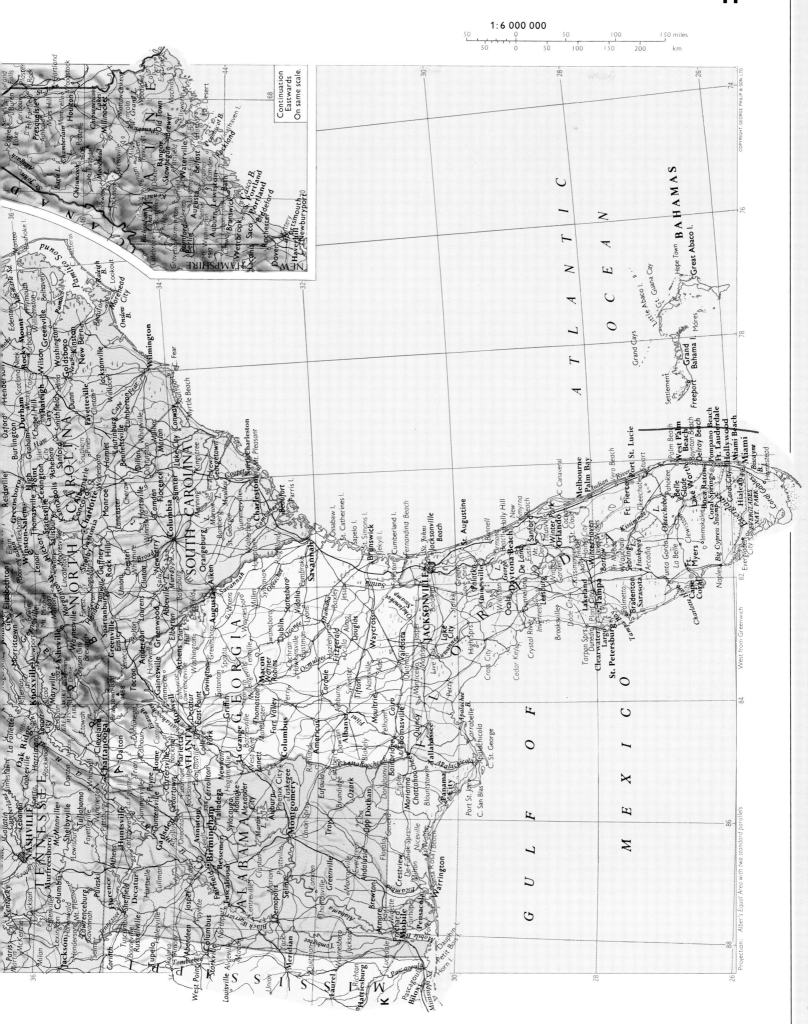

1 : 6 000 000

50   1:6 000 000   50   100   150 miles
50   0   50   100   150   200   km

Continuation
Eastwards
On same scale.

COPYRIGHT GEORGE PHILIP & SON LTD

MAINE

NEW HAMPSHIRE

ATLANTIC

OCEAN

BAHAMAS

Great Abaco I.

Grand Bahama I.

NORTH CAROLINA

SOUTH CAROLINA

GEORGIA

ALABAMA

MISSISSIPPI

TENNESSEE

F L O R I D A

G U L F   O F

M E X I C O

ATLANTA

NASHVILLE

JACKSONVILLE

Montgomery

Tallahassee

Miami

West from Greenwich

Projection: Alber's Equal Area with two standard parallels

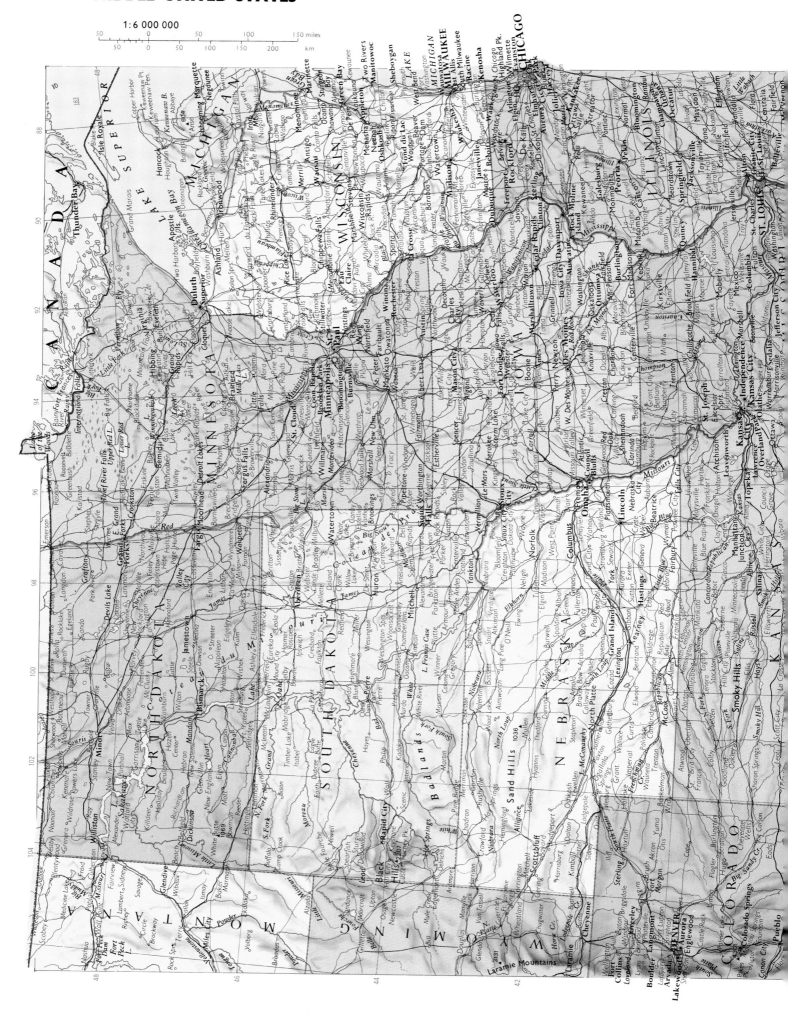

1 : 6 000 000

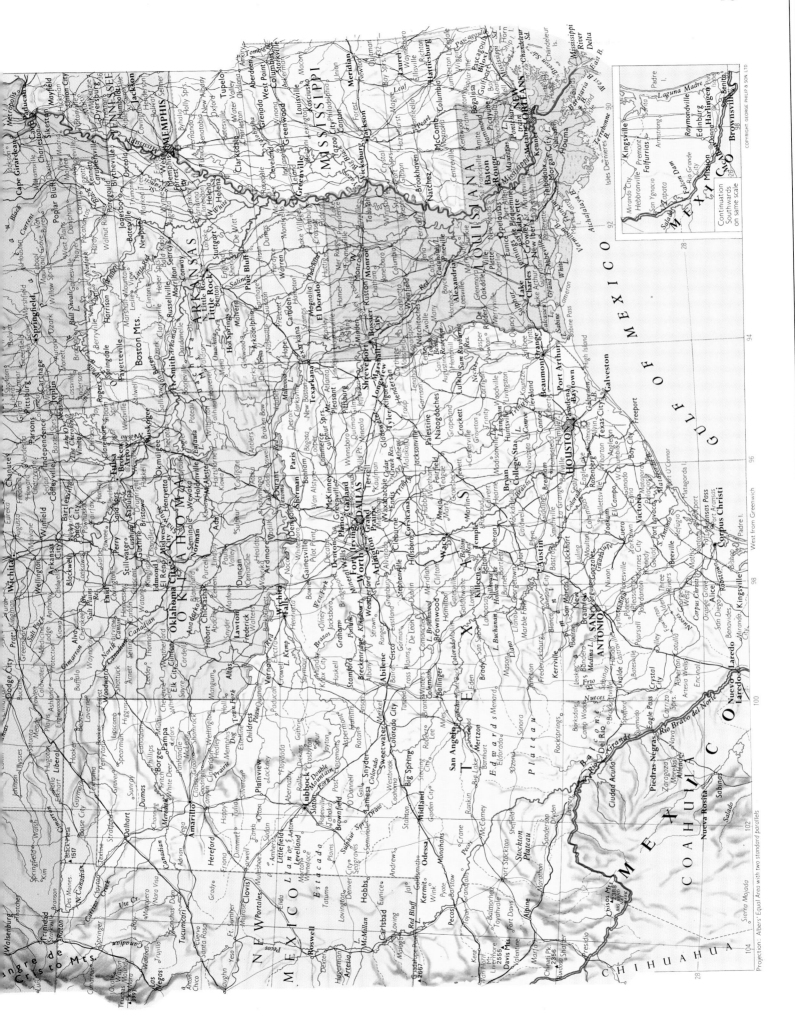

Projection: Albers' Equal Area with two standard parallels

West from Greenwich

COPYRIGHT GEORGE PHILIP & SON LTD

Continuation
Southwards
on same scale

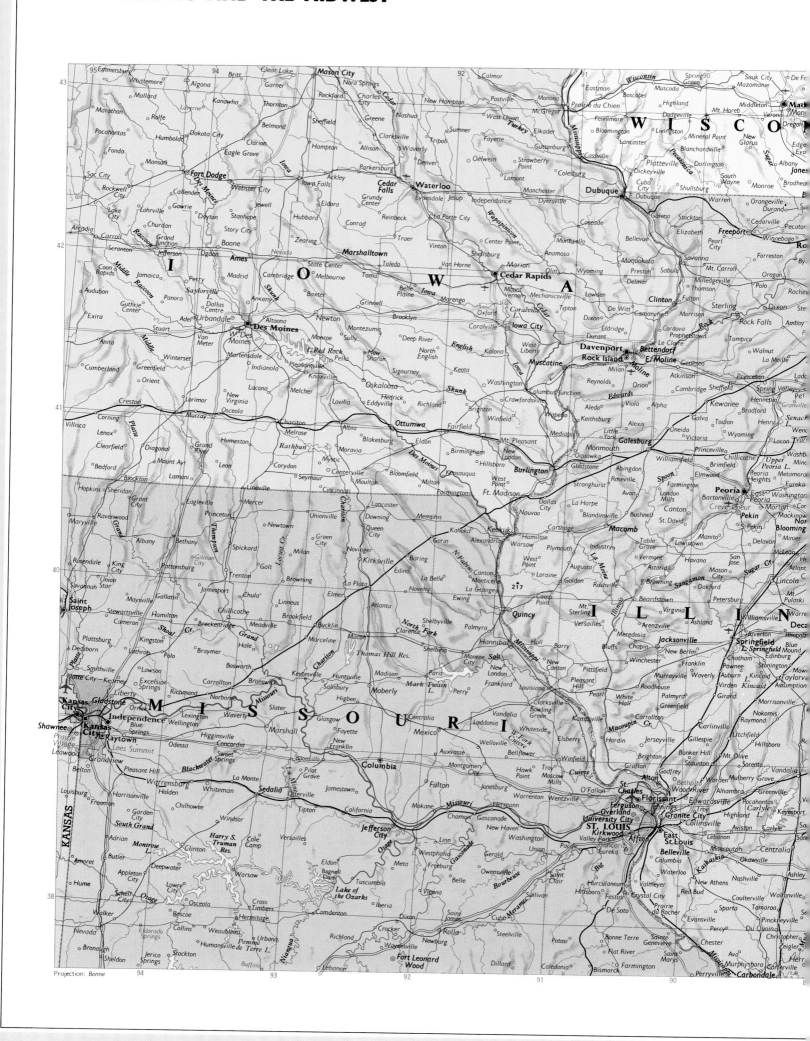

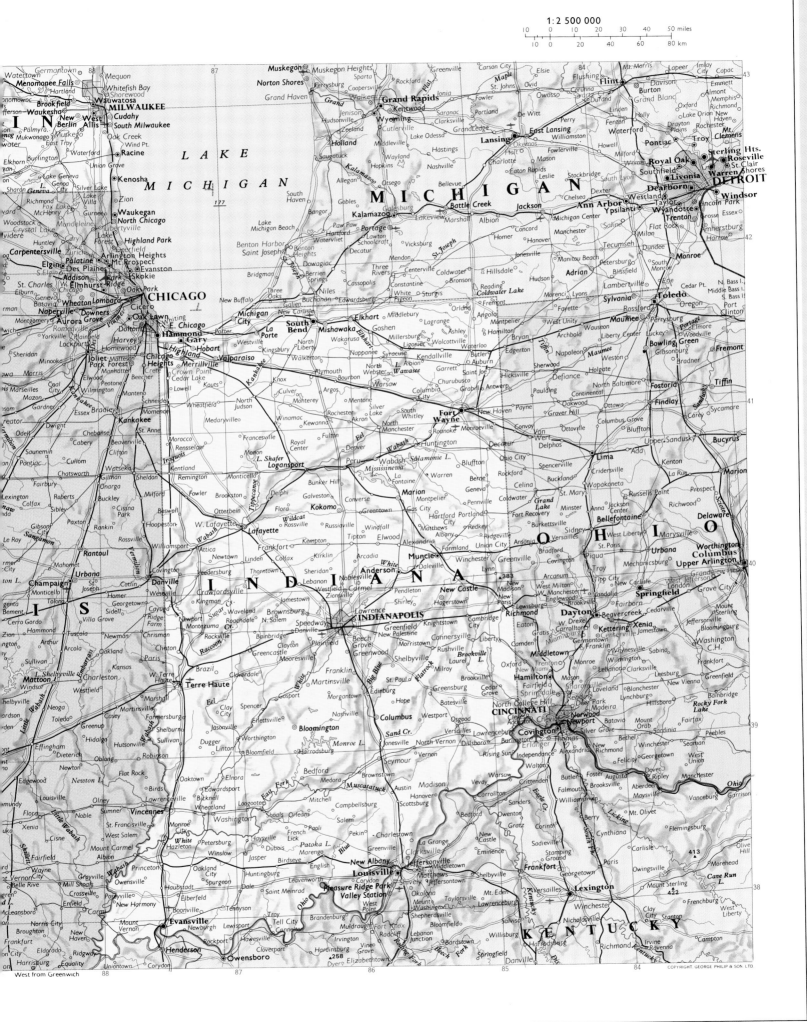

1:2 500 000

10   0   10   20   30   40   50 miles

10   0   20   40   60   80 km

LAKE

MICHIGAN

MICHIGAN

WIN

MILWAUKEE

CHICAGO

INDIANA

OHIO

ILLINOIS

INDIANAPOLIS

CINCINNATI

Louisville

Lexington

KENTUCKY

Evansville

Owensboro

West from Greenwich   88   87   86   85   84   COPYRIGHT GEORGE PHILIP & SON LTD

1:6 000 000

50   0   50   100 miles

50   0   50   100   150 km

Projection: Albers Equal Area with two standard parallels   West from Greenwich

SEATTLE-PORTLAND
REGION
On same scale

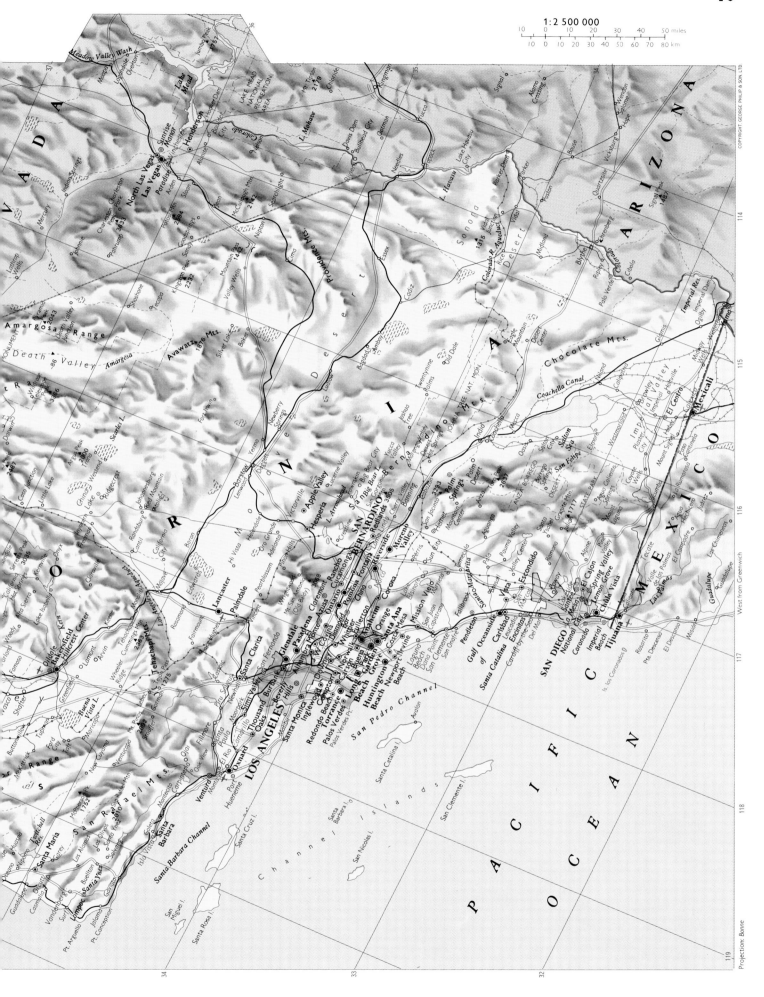

1 : 2 500 000

10 0 10 20 30 40 50 miles

10 0 10 20 30 40 50 60 70 80 km

NEVADA

ARIZONA

CALIFORNIA

MEXICO

PACIFIC OCEAN

Death Valley

Amargosa Range

Las Vegas

North Las Vegas

Henderson

L. Mead

Lake Havasu

Colorado R.

Mojave Desert

Sonora Desert

Chocolate Mts.

Salton Sea

El Centro

Mexicali

Yuma

Tijuana

SAN DIEGO

Chula Vista

Oceanside

Carlsbad

Escondido

San Clemente

Santa Ana

Anaheim

LOS ANGELES

Long Beach

Pasadena

Glendale

Burbank

Santa Monica

Inglewood

Torrance

Huntington Beach

Newport Beach

Irvine

Costa Mesa

Orange

Fullerton

Buena Park

Garden Grove

Pomona

Ontario

SAN BERNARDINO

Riverside

Moreno Valley

Redlands

Fontana

Rancho Cucamonga

Chino

Corona

Palm Springs

Indio

Coachella

Bakersfield

Oildale

Lancaster

Palmdale

Santa Clarita

Thousand Oaks

Simi Valley

Oxnard

Ventura

Santa Barbara

Santa Maria

Lompoc

Channel Islands

Santa Catalina I.

San Clemente I.

Santa Cruz I.

Santa Rosa I.

San Miguel I.

San Nicolas I.

Santa Barbara Channel

San Pedro Channel

Gulf of Santa Catalina

Mt. San Gorgonio

Imperial Dam

Joshua Tree Nat. Mon.

West from Greenwich

Projection: Bonne

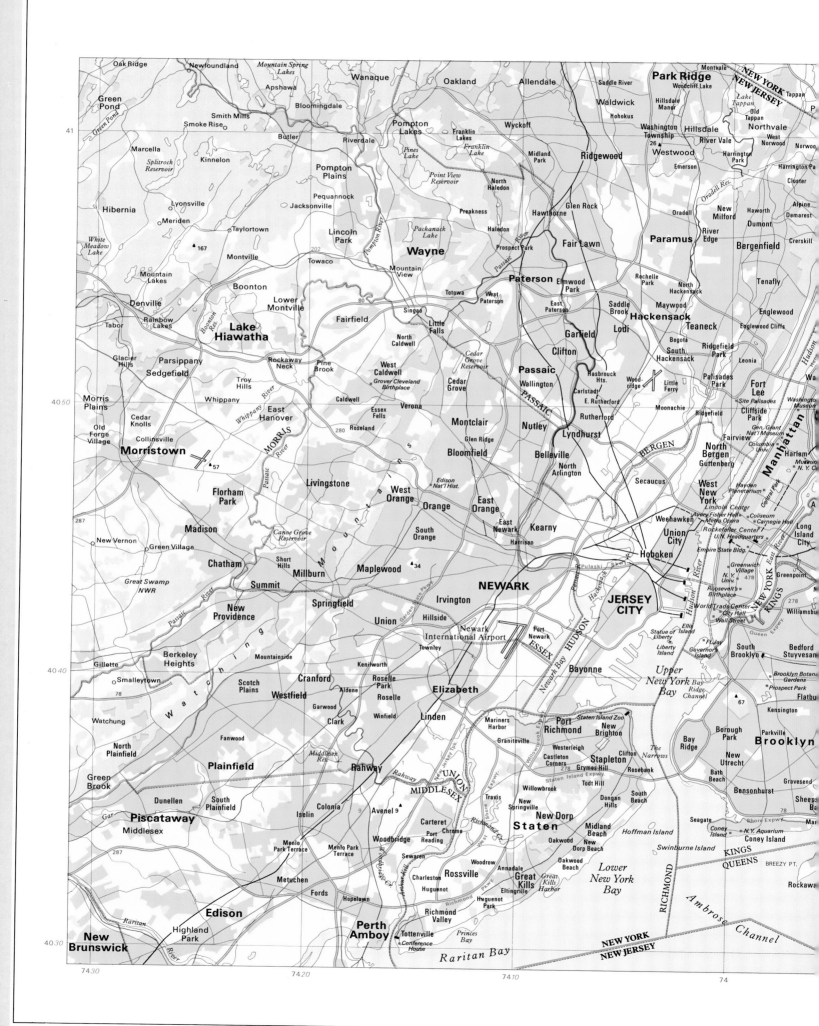

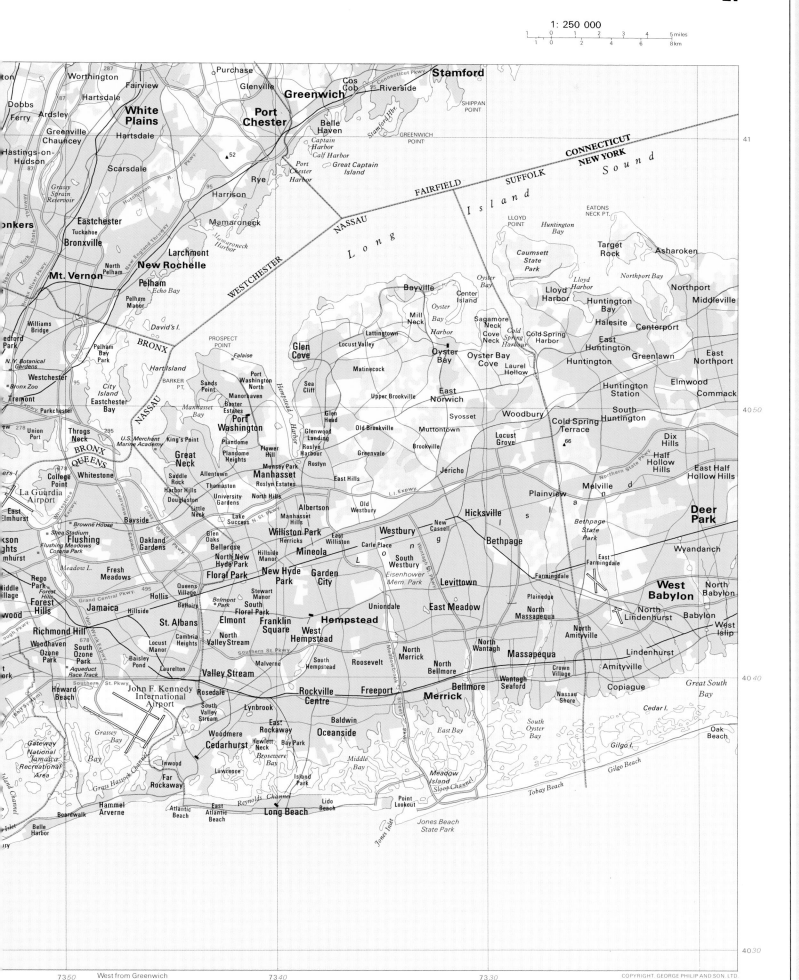

1 : 250 000

1   0   1   2   3   4   5 miles
1   0   2   4   6   8 km

COPYRIGHT. GEORGE PHILIP AND SON. LTD.

1 : 250 000

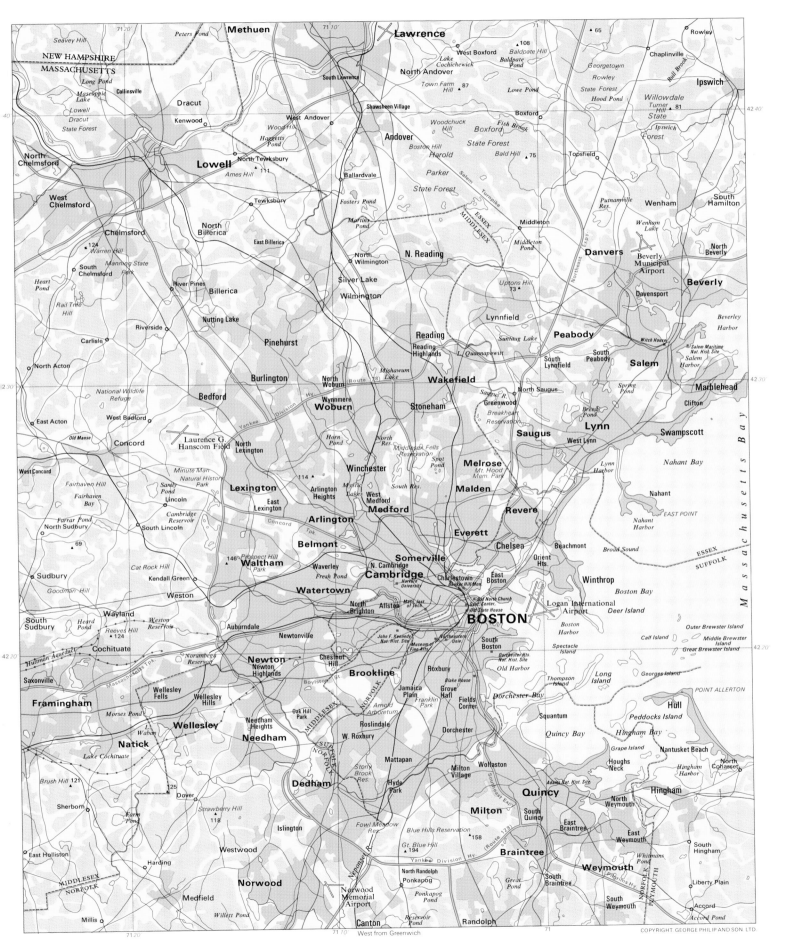

1: 250 000

COPYRIGHT GEORGE PHILIP AND SON LTD.

West from Greenwich

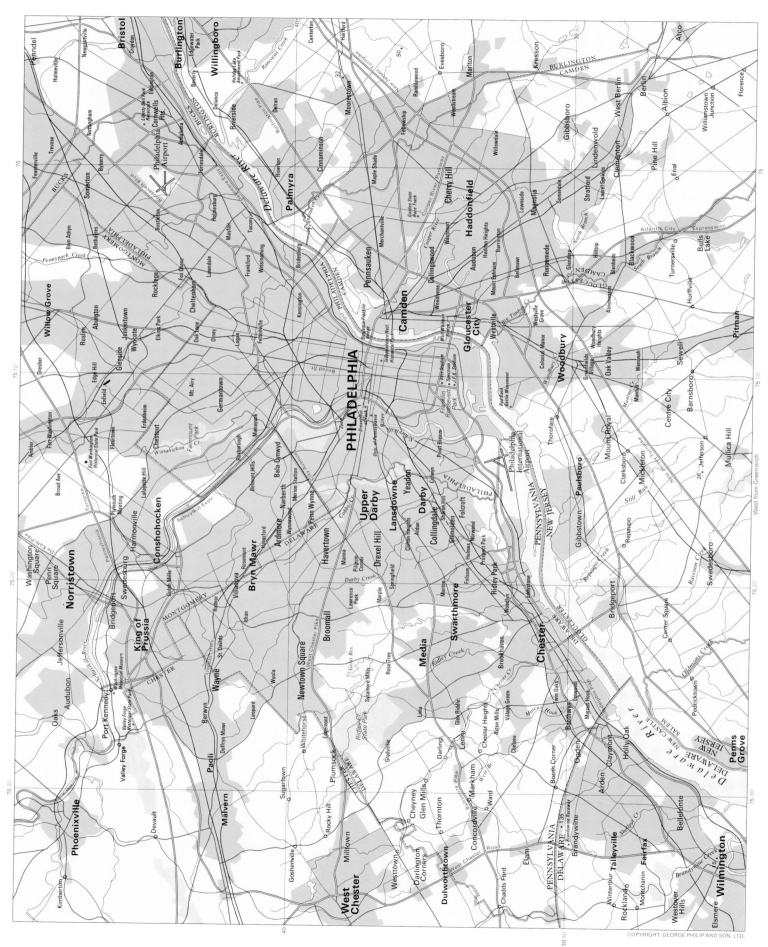

1: 250 000

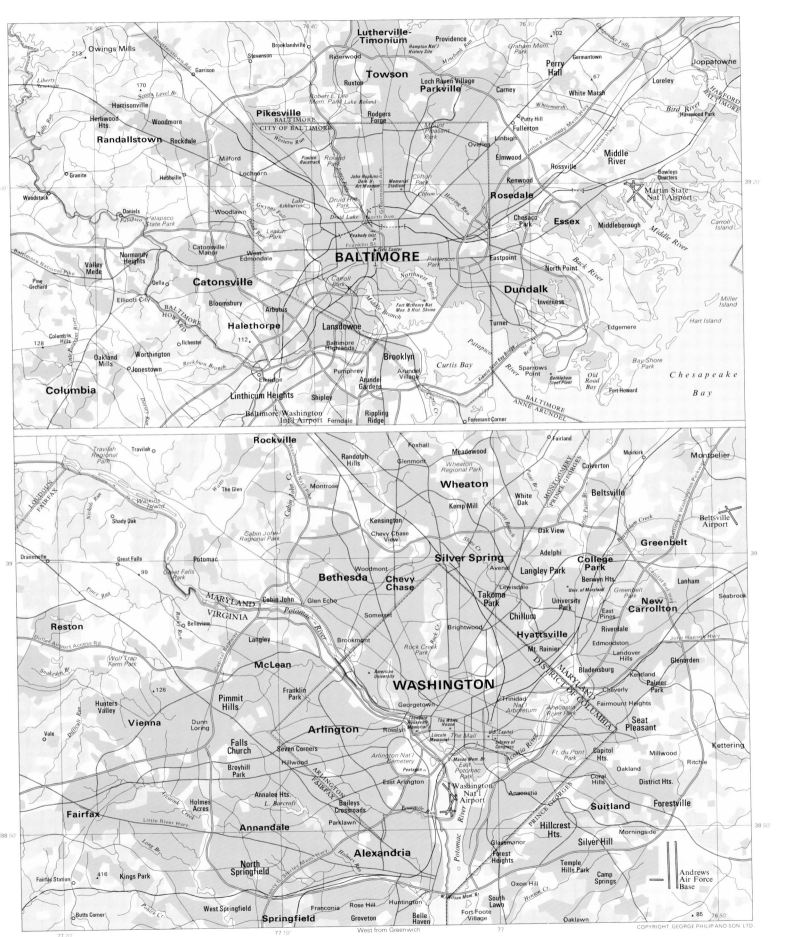

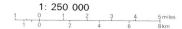

1 : 250 000

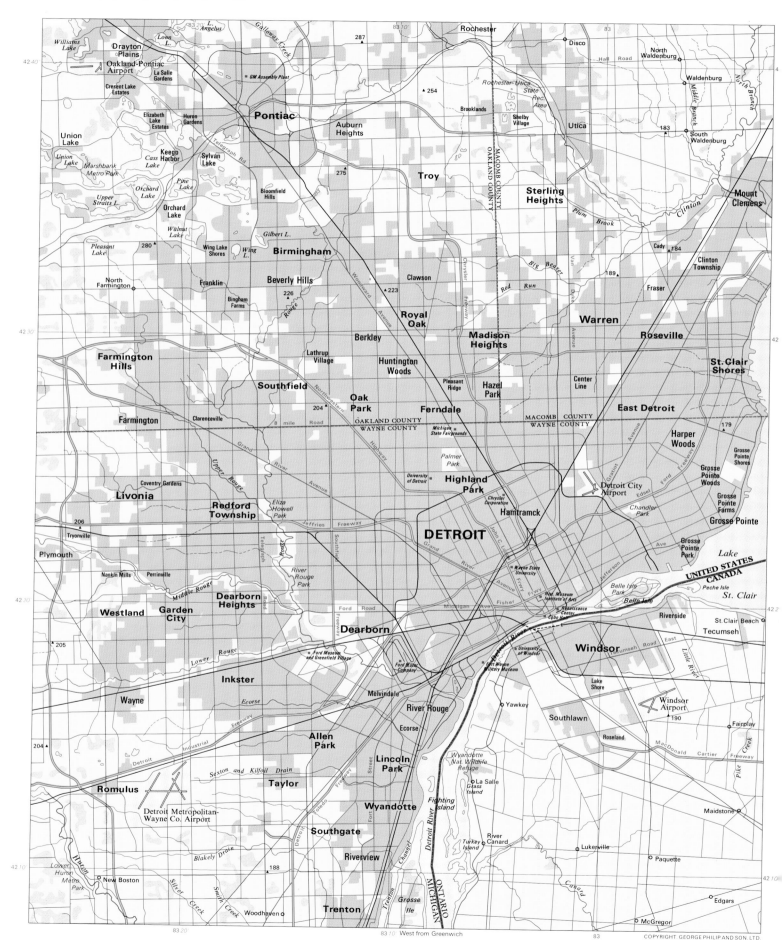

Williams Lake

Drayton Plains

Oakland-Pontiac Airport

La Salle Gardens

Cresent Lake Estates

Elizabeth Lake Estates

Huron Gardens

Pontiac

Union Lake

Union Lake

Keego Harbor

Cass Lake

Sylvan Lake

Marshbank Metro Park

Orchard Lake

Pine Lake

Upper Straits L.

Orchard Lake

Walnut Lake

Pleasant Lake

North Farmington

Wing Lake Shores

Wing L.

Birmingham

Franklin

Beverly Hills

Bingham Farms

Farmington Hills

Farmington

Clarenceville

Lathrup Village

Southfield

Oak Park

Coventry Gardens

Livonia

Redford Township

Eliza Howell Park

Plymouth

Tryonville

Nankin Mills

Perrinville

Westland

Garden City

Dearborn Heights

Wayne

Inkster

Romulus

Detroit Metropolitan-Wayne Co. Airport

Allen Park

Taylor

New Boston

Woodhaven

Trenton

Southgate

Riverview

Wyandotte

Lincoln Park

River Rouge

Melvindale

Ecorse

Ecorse

Ford Museum and Greenfield Village

Ford Motor Company

Dearborn

River Rouge Park

Rochester

Disco

North Waldenburg

Hall Road

Waldenburg

GM Assembly Plant

Rochester Utica State Rec. Area

Brooklands

Shelby Village

Utica

South Waldenburg

Troy

Sterling Heights

Mount Clemens

Auburn Heights

Bloomfield Hills

Clawson

Clinton Township

Royal Oak

Berkley

Madison Heights

Fraser

Warren

Roseville

Huntington Woods

Pleasant Ridge

Hazel Park

Center Line

St. Clair Shores

Ferndale

OAKLAND COUNTY
WAYNE COUNTY

Michigan State Fairgrounds

MACOMB COUNTY
WAYNE COUNTY

East Detroit

Harper Woods

Palmer Park

University of Detroit

Highland Park

Chrysler Corporation

Hamtramck

Detroit City Airport

Chandler Park

Grosse Pointe Woods

Grosse Pointe Shores

Grosse Pointe Farms

Grosse Pointe

DETROIT

Wayne State University

Hist. Museum of Arts

Renaissance Center
Cobo Hall

Belle Isle Park

Belle Isle

Grosse Pointe Park

UNITED STATES
CANADA

Peche Isle

St. Clair

Lake St. Clair

Riverside

St. Clair Beach

Tecumseh

Windsor

University of Windsor

Fort Wayne Military Museum

Yawkey

Lake Shore

Windsor Airport

Fairplay

Southlawn

Roseland

Wyandotte Nat. Wildlife Refuge

La Salle Glass Island

Maidstone

Fighting Island

Turkey Island

River Canard

Lukerville

Paquette

Grosse Ile

ONTARIO
MICHIGAN

Edgars

McGregor

1: 250 000

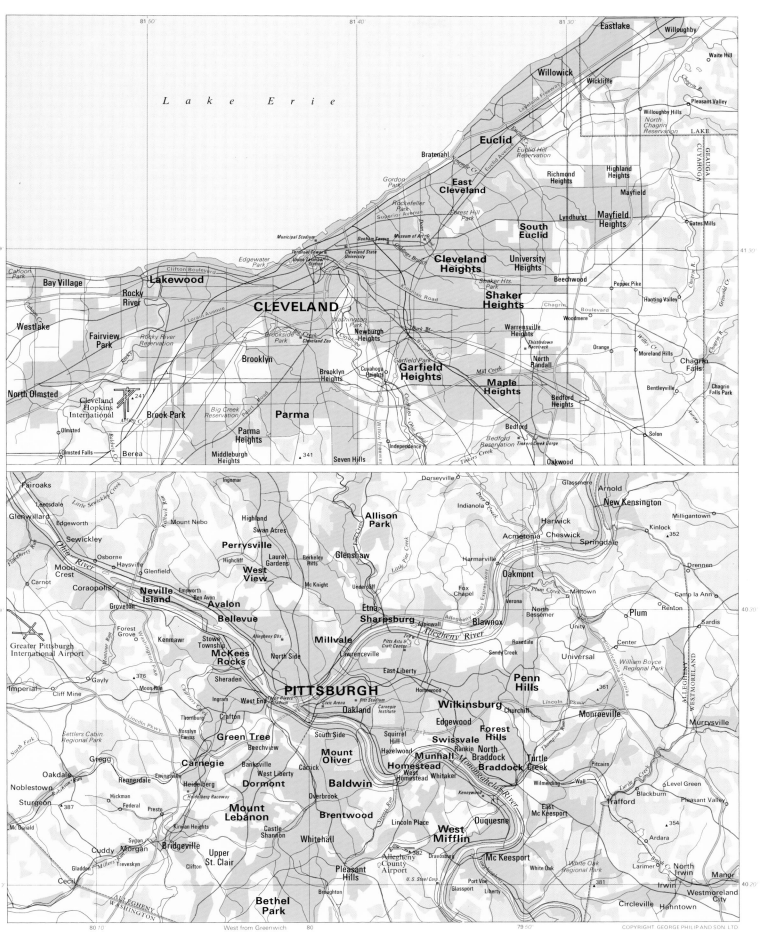

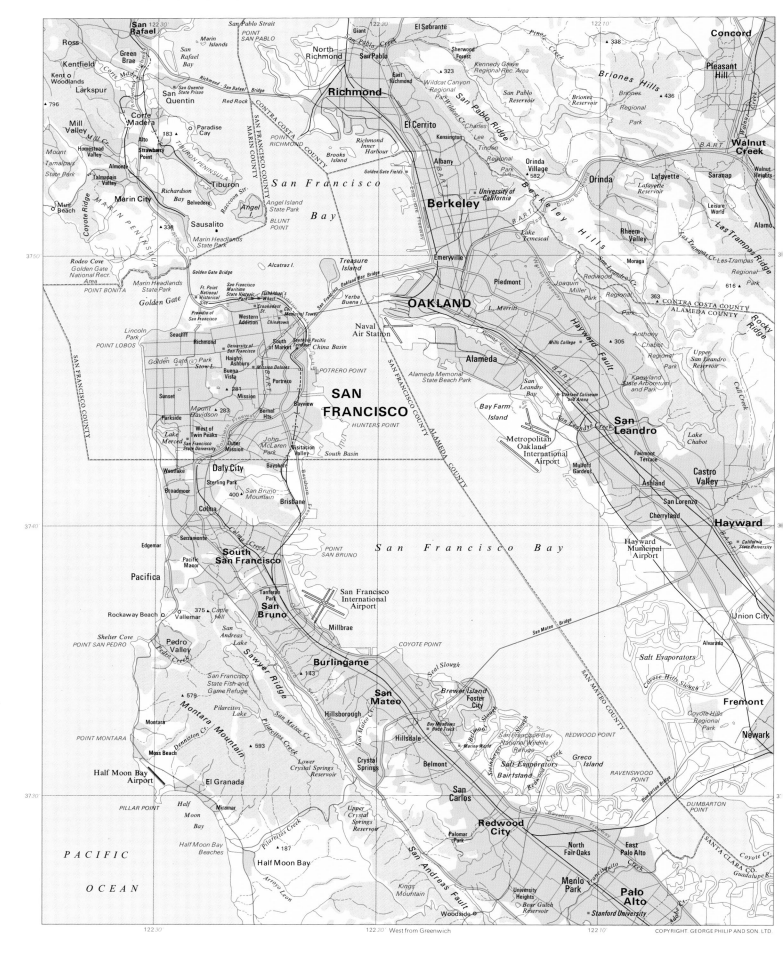

1: 250 000

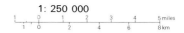

1 : 250 000

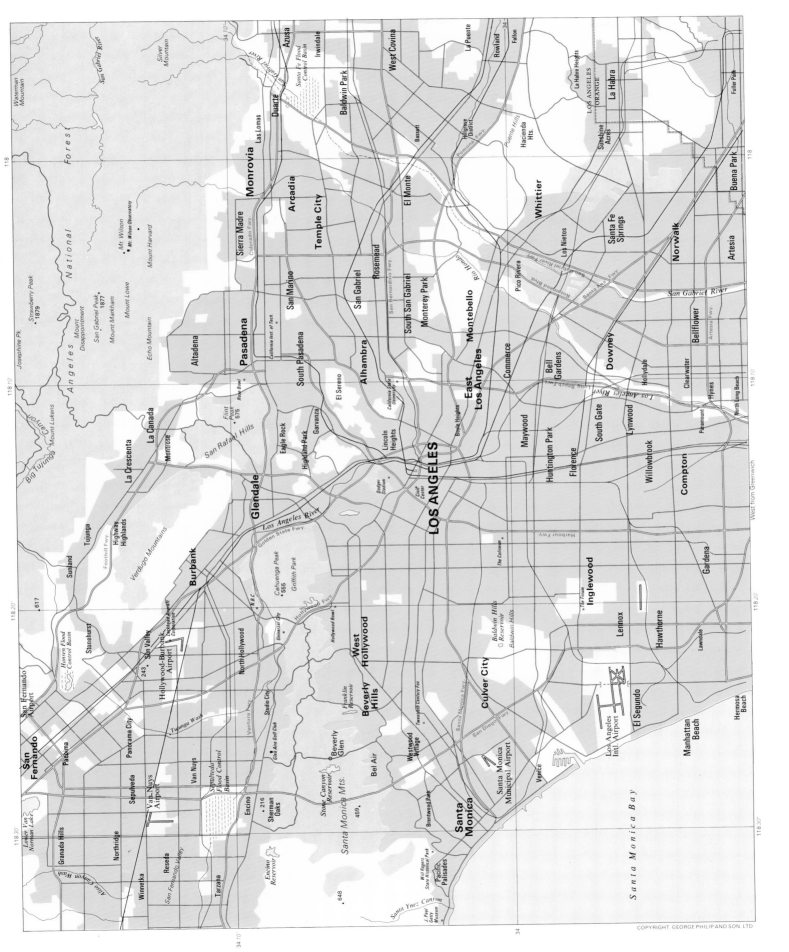

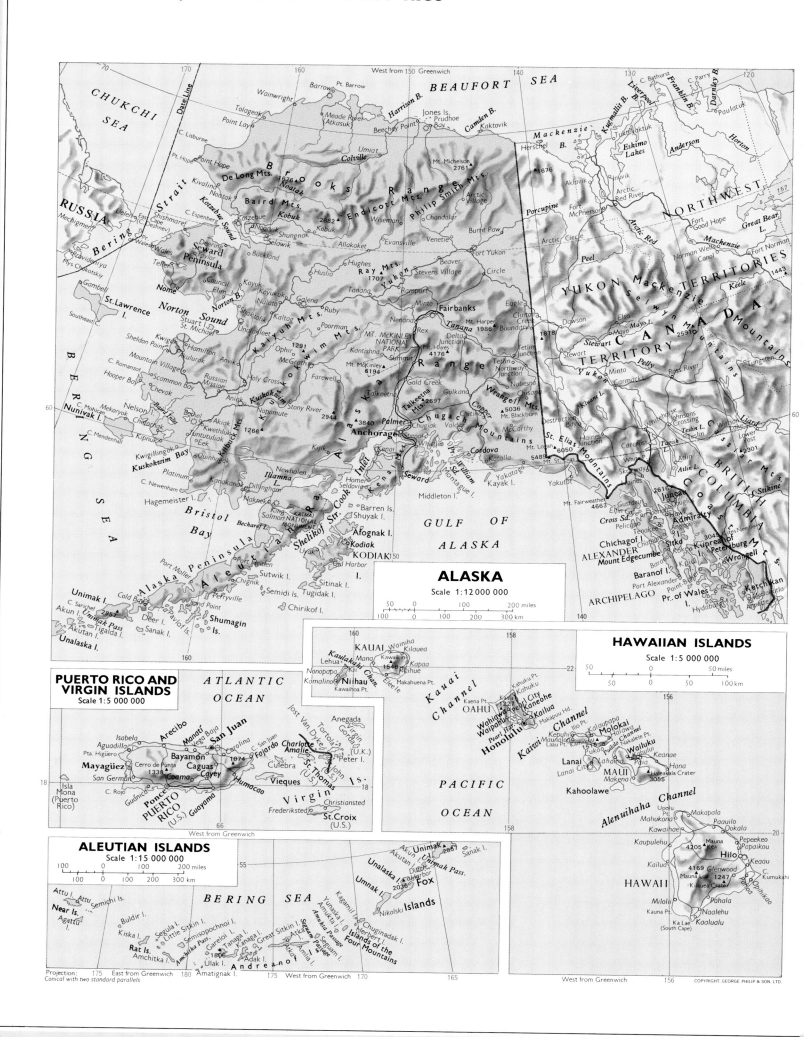

ALASKA

Scale 1:12 000 000

HAWAIIAN ISLANDS

Scale 1:5 000 000

PUERTO RICO AND VIRGIN ISLANDS

Scale 1:5 000 000

ALEUTIAN ISLANDS

Scale 1:15 000 000

Projection:
Conical with two standard parallels

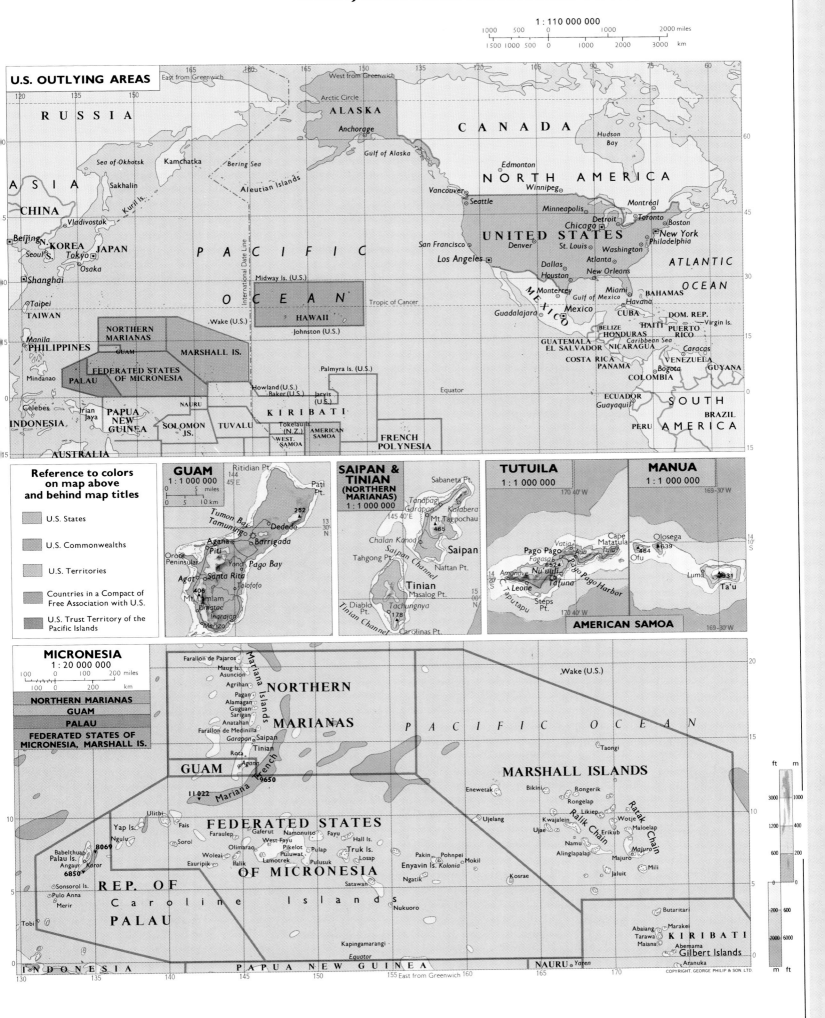

INDEX

UNITED STATES & OUTLYING AREAS

This index lists all the place names which appear on the large scale maps of the United States and outlying areas (pages which precede this index). Place names for the rest of the world can be found in the World Maps Index at the end of the atlas.

The number in dark type which follows each name in the index refers to the page number on which the place or feature is located. The geographical coordinates which follow the page number give the latitude and longitude of each place. The first coordinate indicates the latitude – the distance north or south of the Equator. The second coordinate indicates the longitude – the distance east or west of the Greenwich Meridian. Both latitude and longitude are measured in degrees and minutes (there are 60 minutes in a degree). Rivers are indexed to their mouths or confluences. A solid square ■ follows the name of a country, while an open square □ signifies that the name is a state. An arrow → follows the name of a river.

The alphabetic order of names composed of two or more words is governed by the first word and then by the second. Names composed of a proper name (Alaska) and a description (Gulf of) are positioned alphabetically by the proper name. All names beginning St. are alphabetized under Saint and those beginning Mc under Mac.

Abbreviations used in the index

Ala. — Alabama
Amer. — America, American
Ariz. — Arizona
Ark. — Arkansas
B. — Bay
C. — Cape
Calif. — California
Chan. — Channel
Colo. — Colorado
Conn. — Connecticut
Cr. — Creek
D.C. — District of Columbia
Del. — Delaware
Dist. — District
E. — East, Eastern
Fla. — Florida
G. — Gulf
Ga. — Georgia
Gt. — Great
I.(s) — Island(s)
Ill. — Illinois
Ind. — Indiana
Kans. — Kansas
Ky. — Kentucky
L. — Lake
La. — Louisiana
Ld. — Land
Mass. — Massachusetts
Md. — Maryland
Mich. — Michigan
Minn. — Minnesota
Miss. — Mississippi
Mo. — Missouri
Mont. — Montana
Mt.(s) — Mountain(s)
N. — North, Northern
N.B. — New Brunswick
N.C. — North Carolina
N. Dak. — North Dakota
N.H. — New Hampshire
N.J. — New Jersey
N. Mex. — New Mexico
N.Y. — New York
Nat. Mon. — National Monument
Nat. Park — National Park
Nat. Rec. Area. — National Recreation Area
Nebr. — Nebraska
Nev. — Nevada
Okla. — Oklahoma
Oreg. — Oregon
Pa. — Pennsylvania
Pac. Oc. — Pacific Ocean
Pass. — Passage
Pen. — Peninsula
Pk. — Peak
Pt. — Point
R. — Rio, River
R.I. — Rhode Island
Ra.(s) — Range(s)
Res. — Reserve, Reservoir, Reservation
S.C. — South Carolina
S. Dak. — South Dakota
Sa. — Serra, Sierra
Sd. — Sound
St. — Saint
Ste. — Sainte
Str. — Strait
Tenn. — Tennessee
Tex. — Texas
U.S.A. — United States of America
Va. — Virginia
Vt. — Vermont
Wash. — Washington
W. — West, Western
W. Va. — West Virginia
Wis. — Wisconsin
Wyo. — Wyoming

A

Abbaye, Pt., *Mich.* **10** 46 58N 88 8W
Abbeville, *La.* **13** 29 58N 92 8W
Abbeville, *S.C.* **11** 34 11N 82 23W
Abbotsford, *Wis.* **12** 44 57N 90 19W
Aberdeen, *Ala.* **11** 33 49N 88 33W
Aberdeen, *Idaho* **16** 42 57N 112 50W
Aberdeen, *S. Dak.* **12** 45 28N 98 29W
Aberdeen, *Wash.* **18** 46 59N 123 50W
Abernathy, *Tex.* **13** 33 50N 101 51W
Abert, L., *Oreg.* **16** 42 38N 120 14W
Abilene, *Kans.* **12** 38 55N 97 13W
Abilene, *Tex.* **13** 32 28N 99 43W
Abingdon, *Ill.* **14** 40 48N 90 24W
Abingdon, *Va.* **11** 36 43N 81 59W
Absaroka Range, *Wyo.* . **16** 44 45N 109 50W
Accomac, *Va.* **10** 37 43N 75 40W
Ackerman, *Miss.* **13** 33 19N 89 11W
Ada, *Minn.* **12** 47 18N 96 31W
Ada, *Okla.* **13** 34 46N 96 41W
Adams, *Mass.* **9** 42 38N 73 7W
Adams, *N.Y.* **9** 43 49N 76 1W
Adams, *Wis.* **12** 43 57N 89 49W
Adams Mt., *Wash.* **18** 46 12N 121 30W
Adel, *Ga.* **11** 31 8N 83 25W
Adelanto, *Calif.* **19** 34 35N 117 22W
Adin, *Calif.* **16** 41 12N 120 57W
Adirondack Mts., *N.Y.* .. **9** 44 0N 74 0W
Admiralty I., *Alaska* **30** 57 30N 134 30W
Admiralty Inlet, *Wash.* . **16** 48 8N 122 58W
Adrian, *Mich.* **15** 41 54N 84 2W
Adrian, *Tex.* **13** 35 16N 102 40W
Affton, *Miss.* **14** 38 33N 90 20W
Afognak I., *Alaska* **30** 58 15N 152 30W
Afton, *N.Y.* **9** 42 14N 75 32W
Agana, *Guam* .... **31** 13 28N 144 45 E
Agattu I., *Alaska* ...... **30** 52 25N 172 30 E
Agua Caliente Springs, *Calif.* **19** 32 56N 116 19W
Aguadilla, *Puerto Rico* . **30** 18 26N 67 10W
Aguanga, *Calif.* **19** 33 27N 116 51W
Aiken, *S.C.* **11** 33 34N 81 43W
Ainsworth, *Nebr.* **12** 42 33N 99 52W
Aitkin, *Minn.* **12** 46 32N 93 42W
Ajo, *Ariz.* **17** 32 22N 112 52W
Akiak, *Alaska* **30** 60 55N 161 13W
Akron, *Colo.* **12** 40 10N 103 13W
Akron, *Ohio* **8** 41 5N 81 31W
Akulurak, *Alaska* **30** 62 40N 164 35W
Akun I., *Alaska* **30** 54 11N 165 32W
Akutan I., *Alaska* **30** 54 7N 165 55W
Alabama □ **11** 33 0N 87 0W
Alabama →, *Ala.* **11** 31 8N 87 57W
Alameda, *Calif.* **28** 37 46N 122 15W
Alameda, *N. Mex.* **17** 35 11N 106 37W
Alameda County, *Calif.* . **28** 37 40N 122 10W
Alamo, *Nev.* **19** 36 21N 115 10W
Alamogordo, *N. Mex.* .. **17** 32 54N 105 57W
Alamosa, *Colo.* **17** 37 28N 105 52W
Alaska □ **30** 64 0N 154 0W
Alaska, G. of, *Pac. Oc.* . **30** 58 0N 145 0W
Alaska Peninsula, *Alaska* **30** 56 0N 159 0W
Alaska Range, *Alaska* .. **30** 62 50N 151 0W
Alava, C., *Wash.* **16** 48 10N 124 44W
Albany, *Ga.* **11** 31 35N 84 10W
Albany, *Minn.* **12** 45 38N 94 34W
Albany, *N.Y.* **9** 42 39N 73 45W
Albany, *Oreg.* **16** 44 38N 123 6W
Albany, *Tex.* **13** 32 44N 99 18W
Albemarle, *N.C.* **11** 35 21N 80 11W
Albemarle Sd., *N.C.* **11** 36 5N 76 0W
Albert Lea, *Minn.* **12** 43 39N 93 22W
Albia, *Iowa* **14** 41 2N 92 48W
Albion, *Idaho* **16** 42 25N 113 35W
Albion, *Mich.* **15** 42 15N 84 45W
Albion, *Nebr.* **12** 41 42N 98 0W
Albuquerque, *N. Mex.* . **17** 35 5N 106 39W
Alcatraz I., *Calif.* **28** 37 49N 122 25W
Alcoa, *Tenn.* **11** 35 48N 83 59W
Alcova, *Wyo.* **16** 42 34N 106 43W
Alder, *Mont.* **16** 45 19N 112 6W
Alder Pk., *Calif.* **18** 35 53N 121 22W
Aledo, *Ill.* **14** 41 12N 90 45W
Alenuihaha Channel, *Hawaii* **30** 20 30N 156 0W
Aleutian Is., *Pac. Oc.* ... **30** 52 0N 175 0W
Aleutian Ra., *Alaska* ... **30** 55 0N 155 0W
Alexander, *N. Dak.* **12** 47 51N 103 39W
Alexander Arch., *Alaska* **30** 56 0N 136 0W
Alexander City, *Ala.* ... **11** 32 56N 85 58W
Alexandria, *Ind.* **15** 40 16N 85 41W
Alexandria, *La.* **13** 31 18N 92 27W
Alexandria, *Minn.* **12** 45 53N 95 22W
Alexandria, *S. Dak.* **12** 43 39N 97 47W
Alexandria, *Va.* **25** 38 49N 77 6W
Alexandria Bay, *N.Y.* ... **9** 44 20N 75 55W
Alfred, *Maine* **9** 43 29N 70 43W
Algoma, *Wis.* **10** 44 36N 87 26W
Algona, *Iowa* **14** 43 4N 94 14W
Alhambra, *Calif.* **29** 34 5N 118 9W
Alice, *Tex.* **13** 27 45N 98 5W
Aliceville, *Ala.* **11** 33 8N 88 9W
Aliquippa, *Pa.* **8** 40 37N 80 15W
All American Canal, *Calif.* **17** 32 45N 115 15W
Allakaket, *Alaska* **30** 66 34N 152 39W
Allegan, *Mich.* **15** 42 32N 85 51W
Allegheny →, *Pa.* **8** 40 27N 80 1W
Allegheny Plateau, *Va.* . **10** 38 0N 80 0W
Allen Park, *Mich.* **26** 42 14N 83 12W
Allentown, *Pa.* **9** 40 37N 75 29W
Alliance, *Nebr.* **12** 42 6N 102 52W
Alliance, *Ohio* **8** 40 55N 81 6W
Allison Park, *Pa.* **27** 40 33N 79 56W
Alma, *Ga.* **11** 31 33N 82 28W
Alma, *Kans.* **12** 39 1N 96 17W
Alma, *Mich.* **10** 43 23N 84 39W
Alma, *Nebr.* **12** 40 6N 99 22W
Alma, *Wis.* **12** 44 20N 91 55W
Almanor, L., *Calif.* **16** 40 14N 121 9W
Alpaugh, *Calif.* **18** 35 53N 119 29W
Alpena, *Mich.* **10** 45 4N 83 27W
Alpine, *Ariz.* **17** 33 51N 109 9W
Alpine, *Calif.* **19** 32 50N 116 46W
Alpine, *Tex.* **13** 30 22N 103 40W
Alta Sierra, *Calif.* **19** 35 42N 118 33W
Altadena, *Calif.* **29** 34 11N 118 8W
Altamaha →, *Ga.* **11** 31 20N 81 20W
Altamont, *N.Y.* **9** 42 43N 74 3W
Altavista, *Va.* **10** 37 6N 79 17W
Alton, *Ill.* **14** 38 53N 90 11W
Altoona, *Pa.* **8** 40 31N 78 24W
Alturas, *Calif.* **16** 41 29N 120 32W
Altus, *Okla.* **13** 34 38N 99 20W
Alva, *Okla.* **13** 36 48N 98 40W
Alvarado, *Tex.* **13** 32 24N 97 13W
Alvin, *Tex.* **13** 29 26N 95 15W
Alzada, *Mont.* **12** 45 2N 104 25W
Amargosa →, *Calif.* ... **19** 36 14N 116 51W
Amargosa Range, *Calif.* **19** 36 20N 116 45W
Amarillo, *Tex.* **13** 35 13N 101 50W
Amatignak I., *Alaska* ... **30** 51 16N 179 6W
Amboy, *Calif.* **19** 34 33N 115 45W
Amchitka I., *Alaska* .... **30** 51 32N 179 0 E
Amchitka Pass., *Alaska* . **30** 51 30N 179 0W
American Falls, *Idaho* .. **16** 42 47N 112 51W
American Falls Reservoir, *Idaho* **16** 42 47N 112 52W
American Samoa ■, *Pac. Oc.* **31** 14 20S 170 40W
Americus, *Ga.* **11** 32 4N 84 14W
Ames, *Iowa* **14** 42 2N 93 37W
Amesbury, *Mass.* **9** 42 51N 70 56W
Amherst, *Mass.* **9** 42 23N 72 31W
Amherst, *Tex.* **13** 34 1N 102 25W
Amite, *La.* **13** 30 44N 90 30W
Amlia I., *Alaska* **30** 52 4N 173 30W
Amory, *Miss.* **11** 33 59N 88 29W
Amsterdam, *N.Y.* **9** 42 56N 74 11W
Amukta I., *Alaska* **30** 52 30N 171 16W
Anaconda, *Mont.* **16** 46 8N 112 57W
Anacortes, *Wash.* **18** 48 30N 122 37W
Anadarko, *Okla.* **13** 35 4N 98 15W
Anaheim, *Calif.* **19** 33 50N 117 55W
Anamoose, *N. Dak.* **12** 47 53N 100 15W
Anamosa, *Iowa* **14** 42 7N 91 17W
Anatone, *Wash.* **16** 46 8N 117 8W
Anchorage, *Alaska* **30** 61 13N 149 54W
Andalusia, *Ala.* **11** 31 18N 86 29W
Anderson, *Calif.* **16** 40 27N 122 18W
Anderson, *Ind.* **15** 40 10N 85 41W
Anderson, *Mo.* **13** 36 39N 94 27W
Anderson, *S.C.* **11** 34 31N 82 39W
Andover, *Mass.* **23** 42 39N 71 7W
Andreanof Is., *Alaska* .. **30** 52 0N 178 0W
Andrews, *S.C.* **11** 33 27N 79 34W
Andrews, *Tex.* **13** 32 19N 102 33W
Andrews Air Force Base, *Md.* **25** 38 48N 76 52W
Anegada I., *Virgin Is.* .. **30** 18 45N 64 20W
Angeles National Forest, *Calif.* **29** 34 15N 118 5W
Angels Camp, *Calif.* ... **18** 38 4N 120 32W
Angleton, *Tex.* **13** 29 10N 95 26W
Angola, *Ind.* **15** 41 38N 85 0W
Angoon, *Alaska* **30** 57 30N 134 35W
Aniak, *Alaska* **30** 61 35N 159 32W
Animas, *N. Mex.* **17** 31 57N 108 48W
Ann, C., *Mass.* **9** 42 38N 70 35W
Ann Arbor, *Mich.* **15** 42 17N 83 45W
Anna, *Ill.* **13** 37 28N 89 15W
Annandale, *Va.* **25** 38 50N 77 12W
Annapolis, *Md.* **10** 38 59N 76 30W
Annette, *Alaska* **30** 55 2N 131 35W
Anniston, *Ala.* **11** 33 39N 85 50W
Annville, *Pa.* **9** 40 20N 76 31W
Anoka, *Minn.* **12** 45 12N 93 23W
Ansley, *Nebr.* **12** 41 18N 99 23W
Anson, *Tex.* **13** 32 45N 99 54W
Ansonia, *Conn.* **9** 41 21N 73 5W
Antero, Mt., *Colo.* **17** 38 41N 106 15W
Anthony, *Kans.* **13** 37 9N 98 2W
Anthony, *N. Mex.* **17** 32 0N 106 36W
Antigo, *Wis.* **12** 45 9N 89 9W
Antimony, *Utah* **17** 38 7N 112 0W
Antioch, *Calif.* **18** 38 1N 121 48W

Blackfoot

ntler, N. Dak. 12 48 59N 101 17W
ntlers, Okla. 13 34 14N 95 37W
nton, Tex. 13 33 49N 102 10W
nton Chico, N. Mex. 17 35 12N 105 9W
ntonito, Colo. 17 37 5N 106 0W
nvik, Alaska 30 62 39N 160 13W
nza, Calif. 19 33 35N 116 39W
pache, Okla. 13 34 54N 98 22W
palachee B., Fla. 11 30 0N 84 0W
palachicola, Fla. 11 29 43N 84 59W
palachicola —►, Fla. 11 29 43N 84 58W
postle Is., Wis. 12 47 0N 90 40W
ppalachian Mts., Va. 10 38 0N 80 0W
pple Valley, Calif. 19 34 32N 117 14W
ppleton, Wis. 10 44 16N 88 25W
ransas Pass, Tex. 13 27 55N 97 9W
rapahoe, Nebr. 12 40 18N 99 54W
rbuckle, Calif. 18 39 1N 122 3W
rcadia, Calif. 29 34 7N 118 1W
rcadia, Fla. 11 27 13N 81 52W
rcadia, La. 13 32 33N 92 55W
rcadia, Nebr. 12 41 25N 99 8W
rcadia, Wis. 12 44 15N 91 30W
rcata, Calif. 16 40 52N 124 5W
rchbald, Pa. 9 41 30N 75 32W
rco, Idaho 16 43 38N 113 18W
rctic Village, Alaska 30 68 8N 145 32W
rdmore, Okla. 13 34 10N 97 8W
rdmore, Pa. 24 40 0N 75 19W
rdmore, S. Dak. 12 43 1N 103 40W
recibo, Puerto Rico 30 18 29N 66 43W
rgonne Forest, Ill. 22 41 42N 87 53W
rguello, Pt., Calif. 19 34 35N 120 39W
rgus Pk., Calif. 19 35 52N 117 26W
rgyle, Minn. 12 48 20N 96 49W
rivaca, Ariz. 17 31 37N 111 25W
rizona □ 17 34 0N 112 0W
rkadelphia, Ark. 13 34 7N 93 4W
rkansas □ 13 35 0N 92 30W
rkansas —►, Ark. 13 33 47N 91 4W
rkansas City, Kans. 13 37 4N 97 2W
rlee, Mont. 16 47 10N 114 5W
rlington, Mass. 23 42 24N 71 9W
rlington, Oreg. 16 45 43N 120 12W
rlington, S. Dak. 12 44 22N 97 8W
rlington, Va. 25 38 53N 77 7W
rlington, Wash. 18 48 12N 122 8W
rlington Heights, Ill. 22 42 5N 87 54W
rlington National
Cemetery, D.C. 25 38 52N 77 4W
rmour, S. Dak. 12 43 19N 98 21W
rmstrong, Tex. 13 26 56N 97 47W
rnett, Okla. 13 36 8N 99 46W
rnold, Calif. 18 38 15N 120 20W
rnold, Nebr. 12 41 26N 100 12W
rrow Rock Res., Idaho 16 43 45N 115 50W
rrowhead, L., Calif. 19 34 16N 117 10W
rroyo Grande, Calif. 19 35 7N 120 35W
rtesia, Calif. 29 33 51N 118 5W
rtesia, N. Mex. 13 32 51N 104 24W
rtesia Wells, Tex. 13 28 17N 99 17W
rtesian, S. Dak. 12 44 1N 97 55W
rundel Gardens, Md. 25 39 12N 76 37W
rvada, Wyo. 16 44 39N 106 8W
rvin, Calif. 19 35 12N 118 50W
sbury Park, N.J. 9 40 13N 74 1W
sh Fork, Ariz. 17 35 13N 112 29W
sh Grove, Mo. 13 37 19N 93 35W
shburn, Ga. 11 31 43N 83 39W
sheboro, N.C. 11 35 43N 79 49W
sherton, Tex. 13 28 27N 99 46W
sheville, N.C. 11 35 36N 82 33W
shford, Wash. 16 46 46N 122 2W
shland, Kans. 13 37 11N 99 46W
shland, Ky. 10 38 28N 82 38W
shland, Maine 11 46 38N 68 24W
shland, Mont. 16 45 36N 106 16W
shland, Nebr. 12 41 3N 96 23W
shland, Ohio 8 40 52N 82 19W
shland, Oreg. 16 42 12N 122 43W
shland, Pa. 9 40 45N 76 22W
shland, Va. 10 37 46N 77 29W
shland, Wis. 12 46 35N 90 53W
shley, N. Dak. 12 46 2N 99 22W
shtabula, Ohio 8 41 52N 80 47W
shton, Idaho 16 44 4N 111 27W
sotin, Wash. 16 46 20N 117 3W
spen, Colo. 17 39 11N 106 49W
spermont, Tex. 13 33 8N 100 14W
storia, Oreg. 18 46 11N 123 50W
tascadero, Calif. 17 35 32N 120 44W
tchafalaya B., La. 13 29 25N 91 25W
tchison, Kans. 12 39 34N 95 7W
thens, Ala. 11 34 48N 86 58W
thens, Ga. 11 33 57N 83 23W
thens, N.Y. 9 42 16N 73 49W
thens, Ohio 10 39 20N 82 6W
thens, Pa. 9 41 57N 76 31W
thens, Tenn. 11 35 27N 84 36W
thens, Tex. 13 32 12N 95 51W
tka, Alaska 30 52 5N 174 40W
tkasuk, Alaska 30 70 30N 157 20W
tkinson, Nebr. 12 42 32N 98 59W
tlanta, Ga. 11 33 45N 84 23W
tlanta, Tex. 13 33 7N 94 10W
tlantic, Iowa 12 41 24N 95 1W
tlantic City, N.J. 10 39 21N 74 27W
tmore, Ala. 11 31 2N 87 29W
Atoka, Okla. 13 34 23N 96 8W
Atolia, Calif. 19 35 19N 117 37W
Attalla, Ala. 11 34 1N 86 6W
Attica, Ind. 15 40 18N 87 15W
Attleboro, Mass. 9 41 57N 71 17W
Attu, Alaska 30 52 56N 173 15 E
Atwater, Calif. 18 37 21N 120 37W
Atwood, Kans. 12 39 48N 101 3W
Au Sable —►, Mich. 10 44 25N 83 20W
Auberry, Calif. 18 37 7N 119 29W
Auburn, Ala. 11 32 36N 85 29W
Auburn, Calif. 18 38 54N 121 4W
Auburn, Ind. 15 41 22N 85 4W
Auburn, N.Y. 9 42 56N 76 34W
Auburn, Nebr. 12 40 23N 95 51W
Auburndale, Fla. 11 28 4N 81 48W
Audubon, Iowa 14 41 43N 94 56W
Augusta, Ark. 13 35 17N 91 22W
Augusta, Ga. 11 33 28N 81 58W
Augusta, Kans. 13 37 41N 96 59W
Augusta, Maine 11 44 19N 69 47W
Augusta, Mont. 16 47 30N 112 24W
Augusta, Wis. 12 44 41N 91 7W
Aukum, Calif. 18 38 34N 120 43W
Ault, Colo. 12 40 35N 104 44W
Aurora, Colo. 12 39 44N 104 52W
Aurora, Ill. 15 41 45N 88 19W
Aurora, Mo. 13 36 58N 93 43W
Aurora, Nebr. 12 40 52N 98 0W
Austin, Minn. 12 43 40N 92 58W
Austin, Nev. 16 39 30N 117 4W
Austin, Tex. 13 30 17N 97 45W
Avalon, Calif. 19 33 21N 118 20W
Avalon, Pa. 27 40 30N 80 4W
Avawatz Mts., Calif. 19 35 40N 116 30W
Avenal, Calif. 18 36 0N 120 8W
Avery, Idaho 16 47 15N 115 49W
Avila Beach, Calif. 19 35 11N 120 44W
Avon, S. Dak. 12 43 0N 98 4W
Aztec, N. Mex. 17 36 49N 107 59W
Azusa, Calif. 29 34 7N 117 54W

B

Babb, Mont. 16 48 51N 113 27W
Bad —►, S. Dak. 12 44 21N 100 22W
Bad Axe, Mich. 8 43 48N 83 0W
Bad Lands, S. Dak. 12 43 40N 102 10W
Badger, Calif. 18 36 38N 119 1W
Bagdad, Calif. 19 34 35N 115 53W
Baggs, Wyo. 16 41 2N 107 39W
Bagley, Minn. 12 47 32N 95 24W
Bainbridge, Ga. 11 30 55N 84 35W
Bainbridge, N.Y. 9 42 18N 75 29W
Bainville, Mont. 12 48 8N 104 13W
Baird, Tex. 13 32 24N 99 24W
Baird Inlet, Alaska 30 60 50N 164 18W
Baird Mts., Alaska 30 67 0N 160 0W
Baker, Calif. 19 35 16N 116 4W
Baker, Mont. 12 46 22N 104 17W
Baker, Oreg. 16 44 47N 117 50W
Baker Mt., Wash. 16 48 50N 121 49W
Bakersfield, Calif. 19 35 23N 119 1W
Bald Knob, Ark. 13 35 19N 91 34W
Baldwin, Fla. 11 30 18N 81 59W
Baldwin, Mich. 10 43 54N 85 51W
Baldwin, Pa. 27 40 23N 79 58W
Baldwin Park, Calif. 29 34 5N 117 57W
Baldwinsville, N.Y. 9 43 10N 76 20W
Baldy Peak, Ariz. 17 33 54N 109 34W
Ballinger, Tex. 13 31 45N 99 57W
Balmorhea, Tex. 13 30 59N 103 45W
Balta, N. Dak. 12 48 10N 100 2W
Baltimore, Md. 25 39 17N 76 37W
Baltimore Washington
International Airport,
Md. 25 39 11N 76 41W
Bamberg, S.C. 11 33 18N 81 2W
Bandera, Tex. 13 29 44N 99 5W
Bangor, Maine 11 44 48N 68 46W
Bangor, Pa. 9 40 52N 75 13W
Banning, Calif. 19 33 56N 116 53W
Bar Harbor, Maine 11 44 23N 68 13W
Baraboo, Wis. 12 43 28N 89 45W
Baraga, Mich. 12 46 47N 88 30W
Baranof I., Alaska 30 57 0N 135 0W
Barataria B., La. 13 29 20N 89 55W
Barberton, Ohio 8 41 0N 81 39W
Barbourville, Ky. 11 36 52N 83 53W
Bardstown, Ky. 15 37 49N 85 28W
Barksdale, Tex. 13 29 44N 100 2W
Barnesville, Ga. 11 33 3N 84 9W
Barneveld, N.Y. 9 43 16N 75 14W
Barnhart, Tex. 13 31 8N 101 10W
Barnsville, Minn. 12 46 43N 96 28W
Barques, Pt. Aux, Mich. 10 44 4N 82 58W
Barre, Mass. 9 42 25N 72 6W
Barre, Vt. 9 44 12N 72 30W
Barren Is., Alaska 30 58 45N 152 0W
Barrington, R.I. 9 41 44N 71 18W
Barrow, Alaska 30 71 18N 156 47W
Barrow Pt., Alaska 30 71 24N 156 29W
Barstow, Calif. 19 34 54N 117 1W
Barstow, Tex. 13 31 28N 103 24W
Bartlesville, Okla. 13 36 45N 95 59W
Bartlett, Calif. 18 36 29N 118 2W
Bartlett, Tex. 13 30 48N 97 26W
Bartow, Fla. 11 27 54N 81 50W
Basin, Wyo. 16 44 23N 108 2W
Bassett, Nebr. 12 42 35N 99 32W
Bassett, Va. 11 36 46N 79 59W
Bastrop, Tex. 13 30 7N 97 19W
Batavia, N.Y. 8 43 0N 78 11W
Batesburg, S.C. 11 33 54N 81 33W
Batesville, Ark. 13 35 46N 91 39W
Batesville, Miss. 13 34 19N 89 57W
Batesville, Tex. 13 28 58N 99 37W
Bath, Maine 11 43 55N 69 49W
Bath, N.Y. 8 42 20N 77 19W
Baton Rouge, La. 13 30 27N 91 11W
Battle Creek, Mich. 15 42 19N 85 11W
Battle Lake, Minn. 12 46 17N 95 43W
Battle Mountain, Nev. 16 40 38N 116 56W
Baudette, Minn. 12 48 43N 94 36W
Baxley, Ga. 11 31 47N 82 21W
Baxter Springs, Kans. 13 37 2N 94 44W
Bay City, Mich. 10 43 36N 83 54W
Bay City, Oreg. 16 45 31N 123 53W
Bay City, Tex. 13 28 59N 95 58W
Bay Minette, Ala. 11 30 53N 87 46W
Bay St. Louis, Miss. 13 30 19N 89 20W
Bay Springs, Miss. 13 31 59N 89 17W
Bay Village, Ohio 27 41 29N 81 53W
Bayamón, Puerto Rico 30 18 24N 66 10W
Bayard, Nebr. 12 41 45N 103 20W
Bayfield, Wis. 12 46 49N 90 49W
Bayonne, N.J. 20 40 40N 74 6W
Baytown, Tex. 13 29 43N 94 59W
Beach, N. Dak. 12 46 58N 104 0W
Beacon, N.Y. 9 41 30N 73 58W
Bear L., Utah 16 41 59N 111 21W
Bearcreek, Mont. 16 45 11N 109 6W
Beardstown, Ill. 14 40 1N 90 26W
Bearpaw Mts., Mont. 16 48 12N 109 30W
Beatrice, Nebr. 12 40 16N 96 45W
Beatty, Nev. 18 36 54N 116 46W
Beaufort, N.C. 11 34 43N 76 40W
Beaufort, S.C. 11 32 26N 80 40W
Beaumont, Calif. 19 33 56N 116 58W
Beaumont, Tex. 13 30 5N 94 6W
Beaver, Alaska 30 66 22N 147 24W
Beaver, Okla. 13 36 49N 100 31W
Beaver, Utah 17 38 17N 112 38W
Beaver City, Nebr. 12 40 8N 99 50W
Beaver Dam, Wis. 12 43 28N 88 50W
Beaver Falls, Pa. 8 40 46N 80 20W
Beaver I., Mich. 10 45 40N 85 33W
Becharof L., Alaska 30 57 56N 156 23W
Beckley, W. Va. 10 37 47N 81 11W
Bedford, Ind. 15 38 52N 86 29W
Bedford, Iowa 14 40 40N 94 44W
Bedford, Mass. 23 42 29N 71 15W
Bedford, Ohio 8 41 23N 81 32W
Bedford, Va. 10 37 20N 79 31W
Beech Grove, Ind. 15 39 44N 86 3W
Beechey Point, Alaska 30 70 27N 149 18W
Beeville, Tex. 13 28 24N 97 45W
Belen, N. Mex. 17 34 40N 106 46W
Belfast, Maine 11 44 26N 69 1W
Belfield, N. Dak. 12 46 53N 103 12W
Belfry, Mont. 16 45 9N 109 1W
Belgrade, Mont. 16 45 47N 111 11W
Belhaven, N.C. 11 35 33N 76 37W
Bell Gardens, Calif. 29 33 58N 118 9W
Bellaire, Ohio 8 40 1N 80 45W
Belle Fourche, S. Dak. 12 44 40N 103 51W
Belle Fourche —►,
S. Dak. 12 44 26N 102 18W
Belle Glade, Fla. 11 26 41N 80 40W
Belle Plaine, Iowa 14 41 54N 92 17W
Belle Plaine, Minn. 12 44 37N 93 46W
Bellefontaine, Ohio 15 40 22N 83 46W
Bellefonte, Pa. 8 40 55N 77 47W
Belleville, Ill. 14 38 31N 89 59W
Belleville, Kans. 12 39 50N 97 38W
Belleville, N.J. 20 40 48N 74 9W
Belleville, N.Y. 9 43 46N 76 10W
Bellevue, Idaho 16 43 28N 114 16W
Bellevue, Pa. 27 40 29N 80 3W
Bellflower, Calif. 29 33 53N 118 8W
Bellingham, Wash. 18 48 46N 122 29W
Bellmore, N.Y. 21 40 39N 73 31W
Bellows Falls, Vt. 9 43 8N 72 27W
Bellville, Tex. 13 29 57N 96 15W
Bellwood, Ill. 22 41 53N 87 53W
Belmont, Mass. 23 42 24N 71 10W
Beloit, Kans. 12 39 28N 98 6W
Beloit, Wis. 14 42 31N 89 2W
Belton, S.C. 11 34 31N 82 30W
Belton, Tex. 13 31 3N 97 28W
Belton Res., Tex. 13 31 8N 97 32W
Beltsville, Md. 25 39 2N 76 55W
Belvidere, Ill. 15 42 15N 88 50W
Belvidere, N.J. 9 40 50N 75 5W
Belzoni, Miss. 13 33 11N 90 29W
Bemidji, Minn. 12 47 28N 94 53W
Benavides, Tex. 13 27 36N 98 25W
Bend, Oreg. 16 44 4N 121 19W
Benicia, Calif. 18 38 3N 122 9W
Benkelman, Nebr. 12 40 3N 101 32W
Bennettsville, S.C. 11 34 37N 79 41W
Bennington, N.H. 9 43 0N 71 55W
Benson, Ariz. 17 31 58N 110 18W
Benton, Ark. 13 34 34N 92 35W
Benton, Calif. 18 37 48N 118 32W
Benton, Ill. 14 38 0N 88 55W
Benton Harbor, Mich. 15 42 6N 86 27W
Beowawe, Nev. 16 40 35N 116 29W
Berea, Ky. 10 37 34N 84 17W
Bergenfield, N.J. 20 40 55N 73 58W
Bering Sea, Pac. Oc. 30 58 0N 171 0 E
Bering Strait, Alaska 30 65 30N 169 0W
Berkeley, Calif. 28 37 52N 122 17W
Berkeley Springs, W. Va. 10 39 38N 78 14W
Berkley, Mich. 26 42 29N 83 11W
Berlin, Md. 10 38 20N 75 13W
Berlin, N.H. 9 44 28N 71 11W
Berlin, Wis. 10 43 58N 88 57W
Bernado, N. Mex. 17 34 30N 106 53W
Bernalillo, N. Mex. 17 35 18N 106 33W
Berryville, Ark. 13 36 22N 93 34W
Berthold, N. Dak. 12 48 19N 101 44W
Berthoud, Colo. 12 40 19N 105 5W
Bertrand, Nebr. 12 40 32N 99 38W
Berwick, Pa. 9 41 3N 76 14W
Berwyn, Ill. 22 41 50N 87 47W
Bessemer, Ala. 11 33 24N 86 58W
Bessemer, Mich. 12 46 29N 90 3W
Bethany, Mo. 14 40 16N 94 2W
Bethel, Alaska 30 60 48N 161 45W
Bethel Park, Pa. 27 40 19N 80 1W
Bethesda, Md. 25 38 59N 77 6W
Bethlehem, Pa. 9 40 37N 75 23W
Bethpage, N.Y. 21 40 45N 73 29W
Beulah, N. Dak. 12 47 16N 101 47W
Beverly, Mass. 23 42 33N 70 52W
Beverly, Wash. 16 46 50N 119 56W
Beverly Hills, Calif. 29 34 5N 118 24W
Beverly Hills, Mich. 26 42 31N 83 15W
Bicknell, Ind. 15 38 47N 87 19W
Bicknell, Utah 17 38 20N 111 33W
Biddeford, Maine 11 43 30N 70 28W
Bieber, Calif. 16 41 7N 121 8W
Big Bear City, Calif. 19 34 16N 116 51W
Big Bear Lake, Calif. 19 34 15N 116 56W
Big Belt Mts., Mont. 16 46 30N 111 25W
Big Bend National Park,
Tex. 13 29 20N 103 5W
Big Black —►, Miss. 13 32 3N 91 4W
Big Blue —►, Kans. 12 39 35N 96 34W
Big Creek, Calif. 18 37 11N 119 14W
Big Cypress Swamp, Fla. 11 26 12N 81 10W
Big Falls, Minn. 12 48 12N 93 48W
Big Fork —►, Minn. 12 48 31N 93 43W
Big Horn Mts. = Bighorn
Mts., Wyo. 16 44 30N 107 30W
Big Lake, Tex. 13 31 12N 101 28W
Big Moose, N.Y. 9 43 49N 74 58W
Big Muddy Cr. —►, Mont. 12 48 8N 104 36W
Big Pine, Calif. 18 37 10N 118 17W
Big Piney, Wyo. 16 42 32N 110 7W
Big Rapids, Mich. 10 43 42N 85 29W
Big Sable Pt., Mich. 10 44 3N 86 1W
Big Sandy, Mont. 16 48 11N 110 7W
Big Sandy Cr. —►, Colo. 12 38 7N 102 29W
Big Sioux —►, S. Dak. 12 42 29N 96 27W
Big Spring, Tex. 13 32 15N 101 28W
Big Springs, Nebr. 12 41 4N 102 5W
Big Stone City, S. Dak. 12 45 18N 96 28W
Big Stone Gap, Va. 11 36 52N 82 47W
Big Stone L., Minn. 12 45 30N 96 35W
Big Sur, Calif. 18 36 15N 121 48W
Big Timber, Mont. 16 45 50N 109 57W
Bigfork, Mont. 16 48 4N 114 4W
Bighorn, Mont. 16 46 10N 107 27W
Bighorn —►, Mont. 16 46 10N 107 28W
Bighorn Mts., Wyo. 16 44 30N 107 30W
Bikini Atoll, Pac. Oc. 31 12 0N 167 30 E
Bill, Wyo. 12 43 14N 105 16W
Billerica, Mass. 23 42 33N 71 15W
Billings, Mont. 16 45 47N 108 30W
Biloxi, Miss. 13 30 24N 88 53W
Bingham, Maine 11 45 3N 69 53W
Bingham Canyon, Utah 16 40 32N 112 9W
Binghamton, N.Y. 9 42 6N 75 55W
Bird City, Kans. 12 39 45N 101 32W
Birmingham, Ala. 11 33 31N 86 48W
Birmingham, Mich. 26 42 33N 83 13W
Bisbee, Ariz. 17 31 27N 109 55W
Biscayne B., Fla. 11 25 40N 80 12W
Bishop, Calif. 18 37 22N 118 24W
Bishop, Tex. 13 27 35N 97 48W
Bismarck, N. Dak. 12 46 48N 100 47W
Bison, S. Dak. 12 45 31N 102 28W
Bitter Creek, Wyo. 16 41 33N 108 33W
Bitterroot —►, Mont. 16 46 52N 114 7W
Bitterroot Range, Idaho 16 46 0N 114 20W
Bitterwater, Calif. 18 36 23N 121 0W
Biwabik, Minn. 12 47 32N 92 21W
Black —►, Ark. 13 35 38N 91 20W
Black —►, Wis. 12 43 57N 91 22W
Black Hills, S. Dak. 12 44 0N 103 45W
Black L., Mich. 10 45 28N 84 16W
Black Mesa, Okla. 13 36 58N 102 58W
Black Range, N. Mex. 17 33 15N 107 50W
Black River Falls, Wis. 12 44 18N 90 51W
Black Warrior —►, Ala. 11 32 32N 87 51W
Blackburn, Mt., Alaska 30 61 44N 143 26W
Blackduck, Minn. 12 47 44N 94 33W
Blackfoot, Idaho 16 43 11N 112 21W
Blackfoot —►, Mont. 16 46 52N 113 53W

Blackfoot River Reservoir

Blackfoot River Reservoir, Idaho 16 43 0N 111 43W
Blacksburg, Va. 10 37 14N 80 25W
Blackstone, Va. 10 37 4N 78 0W
Blackwell, Okla. 13 36 48N 97 17W
Blackwells Corner, Calif. 19 35 37N 119 47W
Blackwood, N.J. 24 39 48N 75 4W
Blaine, Wash. 18 48 59N 122 45W
Blair, Nebr. 12 41 33N 96 8W
Blake Pt., Mich. 12 48 11N 88 25W
Blakely, Ga. 11 31 23N 84 56W
Blanca Peak, Colo. 17 37 35N 105 29W
Blanchard, Okla. 13 35 8N 97 39W
Blanco, Tex. 13 30 6N 98 25W
Blanco, C., Oreg. 16 42 51N 124 34W
Blanding, Utah 17 37 37N 109 29W
Block I., R.I. 9 41 11N 71 35W
Bloomer, Wis. 12 45 6N 91 29W
Bloomfield, Iowa 14 40 45N 92 25W
Bloomfield, N.J. 20 40 48N 74 12W
Bloomfield, N. Mex. 17 36 43N 107 59W
Bloomfield, Nebr. 12 42 36N 97 39W
Bloomingdale, N.J. 20 41 0N 74 15W
Bloomington, Ill. 14 40 28N 89 0W
Bloomington, Ind. 15 39 10N 86 32W
Bloomsburg, Pa. 9 41 0N 76 27W
Blossburg, Pa. 8 41 41N 77 4W
Blountstown, Fla. 11 30 27N 85 3W
Blue Island, Ill. 10 41 40N 87 40W
Blue Island, Ill. 22 41 40N 87 40W
Blue Lake, Calif. 16 40 53N 123 59W
Blue Mesa Reservoir, Colo. 17 38 28N 107 20W
Blue Mts., Oreg. 16 45 15N 119 0W
Blue Mts., Pa. 9 40 30N 76 30W
Blue Rapids, Kans. 12 39 41N 96 39W
Blue Ridge Mts., N.C. 11 36 30N 80 15W
Bluefield, Va. 10 37 15N 81 17W
Bluff, Utah 17 37 17N 109 33W
Bluffton, Ind. 15 40 44N 85 11W
Blunt, S. Dak. 12 44 31N 99 59W
Bly, Oreg. 16 42 24N 121 3W
Blythe, Calif. 19 33 37N 114 36W
Boca Raton, Fla. 11 26 21N 80 5W
Boerne, Tex. 13 29 47N 98 44W
Bogalusa, La. 13 30 47N 89 52W
Bogata, Tex. 13 33 28N 95 13W
Boise, Idaho 16 43 37N 116 13W
Boise City, Okla. 13 36 44N 102 31W
Bolivar, Mo. 13 37 37N 93 25W
Bolivar, Tenn. 13 35 12N 89 0W
Bonham, Tex. 13 33 35N 96 11W
Bonne Terre, Mo. 14 37 55N 90 33W
Bonners Ferry, Idaho 16 48 42N 116 19W
Bonsall, Calif. 19 33 16N 117 14W
Booker, Tex. 13 36 27N 100 32W
Boone, Iowa 14 42 4N 93 53W
Boone, N.C. 11 36 13N 81 41W
Booneville, Ark. 13 35 8N 93 55W
Booneville, Miss. 11 34 39N 88 34W
Boonville, Ind. 15 38 3N 87 16W
Boonville, Mo. 14 38 58N 92 44W
Boonville, N.Y. 9 43 29N 75 20W
Borah Peak, Idaho 16 44 8N 113 47W
Borger, Tex. 13 35 39N 101 24W
Boron, Calif. 19 35 0N 117 39W
Borrego Springs, Calif. 19 33 15N 116 23W
Bossier City, La. 13 32 31N 93 44W
Boston, Mass. 23 42 21N 71 3W
Boswell, Okla. 13 34 2N 95 52W
Bottineau, N. Dak. 12 48 50N 100 27W
Boulder, Colo. 12 40 1N 105 17W
Boulder, Mont. 16 46 14N 112 7W
Boulder City, Nev. 19 35 59N 114 50W
Boulder Creek, Calif. 18 37 7N 122 7W
Boulder Dam = Hoover Dam, Ariz. 19 36 1N 114 44W
Boundary, Alaska 30 64 4N 141 6W
Boundary Peak, Nev. 18 37 51N 118 21W
Bountiful, Utah 16 40 53N 111 53W
Bovill, Idaho 16 46 51N 116 24W
Bowbells, N. Dak. 12 48 48N 102 15W
Bowdle, S. Dak. 12 45 27N 99 39W
Bowie, Ariz. 17 32 19N 109 29W
Bowie, Tex. 13 33 34N 97 51W
Bowling Green, Ky. 10 36 59N 86 27W
Bowling Green, Ohio 15 41 23N 83 39W
Bowman, N. Dak. 12 46 11N 103 24W
Boyce, La. 13 31 23N 92 40W
Boyne City, Mich. 10 45 13N 85 1W
Boynton Beach, Fla. 11 26 32N 80 4W
Bozeman, Mont. 16 45 41N 111 2W
Brackettville, Tex. 13 29 19N 100 25W
Braddock, Pa. 27 40 24N 79 51W
Bradenton, Fla. 11 27 30N 82 34W
Bradford, Pa. 8 41 58N 78 38W
Bradley, Ark. 13 33 6N 93 39W
Bradley, Calif. 18 35 52N 120 48W
Bradley, S. Dak. 12 45 5N 97 39W
Brady, Tex. 13 31 9N 99 20W
Brainerd, Minn. 12 46 22N 94 12W
Braintree, Mass. 23 42 12N 71 0W
Brandywine, Del. 24 39 49N 75 32W
Branford, Conn. 9 41 17N 72 49W
Branson, Colo. 13 37 1N 103 53W
Branson, Mo. 13 36 39N 93 13W
Brasstown Bald, Ga. 11 34 53N 83 49W
Brattleboro, Vt. 9 42 51N 72 34W
Brawley, Calif. 19 32 59N 115 31W
Brazil, Ind. 15 39 32N 87 8W
Brazos →, Tex. 13 28 53N 95 23W
Breckenridge, Colo. 16 39 29N 106 3W
Breckenridge, Minn. 12 46 16N 96 35W
Breckenridge, Tex. 13 32 45N 98 54W
Bremerton, Wash. 18 47 34N 122 38W
Brenham, Tex. 13 30 10N 96 24W
Brentwood, Pa. 27 40 22N 79 59W
Breton Sd., La. 13 29 35N 89 15W
Brevard, N.C. 11 35 14N 82 44W
Brewer, Maine 11 44 48N 68 46W
Brewer, Mt., Calif. 18 36 44N 118 28W
Brewster, N.Y. 9 41 23N 73 37W
Brewster, Wash. 16 48 6N 119 47W
Brewton, Ala. 11 31 7N 87 4W
Bridgehampton, N.Y. 9 40 56N 72 19W
Bridgeport, Calif. 18 38 15N 119 14W
Bridgeport, Conn. 9 41 11N 73 12W
Bridgeport, Nebr. 12 41 40N 103 6W
Bridgeport, Pa. 24 39 48N 75 21W
Bridgeport, Tex. 13 33 13N 97 45W
Bridger, Mont. 16 45 18N 108 55W
Bridgeton, N.J. 10 39 26N 75 14W
Bridgeville, Pa. 27 21 0N 80 6W
Bridgewater, Mass. 9 41 59N 70 58W
Bridgewater, S. Dak. 12 43 33N 97 30W
Briggsdale, Colo. 12 40 38N 104 20W
Brigham City, Utah 16 41 31N 112 1W
Brighton, Colo. 12 39 59N 104 49W
Brinkley, Ark. 13 34 53N 91 12W
Bristol, Conn. 9 41 40N 72 57W
Bristol, Pa. 24 40 6N 74 53W
Bristol, R.I. 9 41 40N 71 16W
Bristol, S. Dak. 12 45 21N 97 45W
Bristol, Tenn. 11 36 36N 82 11W
Bristol B., Alaska 30 58 0N 160 0W
Bristol L., Calif. 17 34 23N 116 50W
Bristow, Okla. 13 35 50N 96 23W
Britton, S. Dak. 12 45 48N 97 45W
Broad →, S.C. 11 34 1N 81 4W
Broadus, Mont. 12 45 27N 105 25W
Broadview, Ill. 22 41 51N 87 52W
Brockport, N.Y. 8 43 13N 77 56W
Brockton, Mass. 9 42 5N 71 1W
Brockway, Mont. 12 47 18N 105 45W
Brogan, Oreg. 16 44 15N 117 31W
Broken Bow, Nebr. 12 41 24N 99 38W
Broken Bow, Okla. 13 34 2N 94 44W
Bronte, Tex. 13 31 53N 100 18W
Bronx, N.Y. 21 40 50N 73 52W
Bronxville, N.Y. 21 40 56N 73 49W
Brook Park, Ohio 27 41 24N 81 48W
Brookfield, Ill. 22 41 48N 87 50W
Brookfield, Mo. 14 39 47N 93 4W
Brookhaven, Miss. 13 31 35N 90 26W
Brookings, Oreg. 16 42 3N 124 17W
Brookings, S. Dak. 12 44 19N 96 48W
Brookline, Mass. 23 42 19N 71 7W
Brooklyn, Md. 25 39 13N 76 35W
Brooklyn, N.Y. 20 40 37N 73 57W
Brooklyn, Ohio 27 41 26N 81 44W
Brooks Ra., Alaska 30 68 40N 147 0W
Brooksville, Fla. 11 28 33N 82 23W
Brookville, Ind. 15 39 25N 85 1W
Broomall, Pa. 24 39 58N 75 22W
Brothers, Oreg. 16 43 49N 120 36W
Browerville, Minn. 12 46 5N 94 52W
Brownfield, Tex. 13 33 11N 102 17W
Browning, Mont. 16 48 34N 113 1W
Brownsville, Oreg. 16 44 24N 122 59W
Brownsville, Tenn. 13 35 36N 89 16W
Brownsville, Tex. 13 25 54N 97 30W
Brownwood, Tex. 13 31 43N 98 59W
Brownwood, L., Tex. 13 31 51N 98 35W
Brundidge, Ala. 11 31 43N 85 49W
Bruneau, Idaho 16 42 53N 115 48W
Bruneau →, Idaho 16 42 56N 115 57W
Brunswick, Ga. 11 31 10N 81 30W
Brunswick, Maine 11 43 55N 69 58W
Brunswick, Md. 10 39 19N 77 38W
Brunswick, Mo. 14 39 26N 93 8W
Brush, Colo. 12 40 15N 103 37W
Bryan, Ohio 15 41 28N 84 33W
Bryan, Tex. 13 30 40N 96 22W
Bryant, S. Dak. 12 44 35N 97 28W
Bryn Mawr, Pa. 24 40 1N 75 19W
Bryson City, N.C. 11 35 26N 83 27W
Buchanan, L., Tex. 13 30 45N 98 25W
Buchon, Pt., Calif. 18 35 15N 120 54W
Buckeye, Ariz. 17 33 22N 112 35W
Buckhannon, W. Va. 10 39 0N 80 8W
Buckland, Alaska 30 65 59N 161 8W
Buckley, Wash. 16 47 10N 122 2W
Bucklin, Kans. 13 37 33N 99 38W
Bucyrus, Ohio 15 40 48N 82 59W
Buellton, Calif. 19 34 37N 120 12W
Buena Park, Calif. 29 33 51N 118 1W
Buena Vista, Colo. 17 38 51N 106 8W
Buena Vista, Va. 10 37 44N 79 21W
Buena Vista L., Calif. 19 35 12N 119 18W
Buffalo, Mo. 14 37 39N 93 6W
Buffalo, N.Y. 8 42 53N 78 53W
Buffalo, Okla. 13 36 50N 99 38W
Buffalo, S. Dak. 12 45 35N 103 33W
Buffalo, Wyo. 16 44 21N 106 42W
Buford, Ga. 11 34 10N 84 0W
Buhl, Idaho 16 42 36N 114 46W
Buhl, Minn. 12 47 30N 92 46W
Buldir I., Alaska 30 52 21N 175 56 E
Bull Shoals L., Ark. 13 36 22N 92 35W
Bunker Hill Monument, Mass. 23 42 21N 71 3W
Bunkie, La. 13 30 57N 92 11W
Bunnell, Fla. 11 29 28N 81 16W
Buras, La. 13 29 22N 89 32W
Burbank, Calif. 29 34 11N 118 18W
Burbank, Ill. 22 41 44N 87 47W
Burkburnett, Tex. 13 34 6N 98 34W
Burke, Idaho 16 47 31N 115 49W
Burley, Idaho 16 42 32N 113 48W
Burlingame, Calif. 28 37 35N 122 22W
Burlington, Colo. 12 39 18N 102 16W
Burlington, Iowa 14 40 49N 91 14W
Burlington, Kans. 12 38 12N 95 45W
Burlington, Mass. 23 42 30N 71 13W
Burlington, N.C. 11 36 6N 79 26W
Burlington, N.J. 24 40 4N 74 54W
Burlington, Vt. 9 44 29N 73 12W
Burlington, Wash. 18 48 28N 122 20W
Burlington, Wis. 10 42 41N 88 17W
Burnet, Tex. 13 30 45N 98 14W
Burney, Calif. 16 40 53N 121 40W
Burns, Oreg. 16 43 35N 119 3W
Burns, Wyo. 12 41 12N 104 21W
Burnt Paw, Alaska 30 67 2N 142 43W
Burwell, Nebr. 12 41 47N 99 8W
Bushnell, Ill. 12 40 33N 90 31W
Bushnell, Nebr. 12 41 14N 103 54W
Butler, Mo. 14 38 16N 94 20W
Butler, Pa. 8 40 52N 79 54W
Butte, Mont. 16 46 0N 112 32W
Butte, Nebr. 12 42 58N 98 51W
Buttonwillow, Calif. 19 35 24N 119 28W
Buzzards Bay, Mass. 9 41 45N 70 37W
Byers, Colo. 12 39 43N 104 14W
Byhalia, Miss. 13 34 52N 89 41W
Bylas, Ariz. 17 33 8N 110 7W

C

Cabazon, Calif. 19 33 55N 116 47W
Cabinet Mts., Mont. 16 48 0N 115 30W
Cabool, Mo. 13 37 7N 92 6W
Caddo, Okla. 13 34 7N 96 16W
Cadillac, Mich. 10 44 15N 85 24W
Caguas, Puerto Rico 30 18 14N 66 2W
Cairo, Ga. 11 30 52N 84 13W
Cairo, Ill. 13 37 0N 89 11W
Calais, Maine 11 45 11N 67 17W
Calcasieu L., La. 13 29 55N 93 18W
Caldwell, Idaho 16 43 40N 116 41W
Caldwell, Kans. 13 37 2N 97 37W
Caldwell, Tex. 13 30 32N 96 42W
Calexico, Calif. 19 32 40N 115 30W
Calhoun, Ga. 11 34 30N 84 57W
Caliente, Nev. 17 37 37N 114 31W
California, Mo. 14 38 38N 92 34W
California □ 17 37 30N 119 30W
California, University of, Calif. 28 37 52N 122 15W
California City, Calif. 19 35 10N 117 55W
California Hot Springs, Calif. 19 35 51N 118 41W
Calipatria, Calif. 19 33 8N 115 31W
Calistoga, Calif. 18 38 35N 122 35W
Callaway, Nebr. 12 41 18N 99 56W
Calumet, Mich. 10 47 14N 88 27W
Calumet City, Ill. 22 41 37N 87 32W
Calvert, Tex. 13 30 59N 96 40W
Calwa, Calif. 18 36 42N 119 46W
Camanche Reservoir, Calif. 18 38 14N 121 1W
Camarillo, Calif. 19 34 13N 119 2W
Camas, Wash. 18 45 35N 122 24W
Camas Valley, Oreg. 16 43 2N 123 40W
Cambria, Calif. 18 35 34N 121 5W
Cambridge, Idaho 16 44 34N 116 41W
Cambridge, Mass. 23 42 22N 71 6W
Cambridge, Md. 10 38 34N 76 5W
Cambridge, Minn. 12 45 34N 93 13W
Cambridge, N.Y. 9 43 2N 73 22W
Cambridge, Nebr. 12 40 17N 100 10W
Cambridge, Ohio 8 40 2N 81 35W
Camden, Ala. 11 31 59N 87 17W
Camden, Ark. 13 33 35N 92 50W
Camden, Maine 11 44 13N 69 4W
Camden, N.J. 24 39 56N 75 7W
Camden, S.C. 11 34 16N 80 36W
Camden, B., Alaska 30 70 30N 145 0W
Camdenton, Mo. 14 38 1N 92 45W
Cameron, Ariz. 17 35 53N 111 25W
Cameron, La. 13 29 48N 93 20W
Cameron, Mo. 14 39 44N 94 14W
Cameron, Tex. 13 30 51N 96 59W
Camino, Calif. 18 38 44N 120 41W
Camp Crook, S. Dak. 12 45 33N 103 59W
Camp Nelson, Calif. 19 36 8N 118 39W
Camp Wood, Tex. 13 29 40N 100 1W
Campbell, Calif. 18 37 17N 121 57W
Campbellsville, Ky. 10 37 21N 85 20W
Canadian, Tex. 13 35 55N 100 23W
Canadian →, Okla. 13 35 28N 95 3W
Canandaigua, N.Y. 8 42 54N 77 17W
Canarsie, N.Y. 21 40 38N 73 53W
Canaveral, C., Fla. 11 28 27N 80 32W
Canby, Calif. 16 41 27N 120 52W
Canby, Minn. 12 44 43N 96 16W
Canby, Oreg. 18 45 16N 122 42W
Cando, N. Dak. 12 48 32N 99 12W
Cannon Ball →, N. Dak. 12 46 20N 100 38W
Canon City, Colo. 12 38 27N 105 14W
Cantil, Calif. 19 35 18N 117 58W
Canton, Ga. 11 34 14N 84 29W
Canton, Ill. 14 40 33N 90 2W
Canton, Miss. 13 32 37N 90 2W
Canton, Mo. 14 40 8N 91 32W
Canton, N.Y. 9 44 36N 75 10W
Canton, Ohio 8 40 48N 81 23W
Canton, Okla. 13 36 3N 98 35W
Canton, S. Dak. 12 43 18N 96 35W
Canton L., Okla. 13 36 6N 98 35W
Canutillo, Tex. 17 31 55N 106 36W
Canyon, Tex. 13 34 59N 101 55W
Canyon, Wyo. 16 44 43N 110 36W
Canyonlands National Park, Utah 17 38 15N 110 0W
Canyonville, Oreg. 16 42 56N 123 17W
Cape Charles, Va. 10 37 16N 76 1W
Cape Fear →, N.C. 11 33 53N 78 1W
Cape Girardeau, Mo. 13 37 19N 89 32W
Cape May, N.J. 10 38 56N 74 56W
Capitan, N. Mex. 17 33 35N 105 35W
Capitola, Calif. 18 36 59N 121 57W
Carbondale, Colo. 16 39 24N 107 13W
Carbondale, Ill. 14 37 44N 89 13W
Carbondale, Pa. 9 41 35N 75 30W
Cardiff-by-the-Sea, Calif. 19 33 1N 117 17W
Carey, Idaho 16 43 19N 113 57W
Carey, Ohio 15 40 57N 83 23W
Caribou, Maine 11 46 52N 68 1W
Carlin, Nev. 16 40 43N 116 7W
Carlinville, Ill. 14 39 17N 89 53W
Carlisle, Pa. 8 40 12N 77 12W
Carlsbad, Calif. 19 33 10N 117 21W
Carlsbad, N. Mex. 13 32 25N 104 14W
Carlyle, Ill. 12 38 37N 89 22W
Carmel, N.Y. 9 41 26N 73 41W
Carmel-by-the-Sea, Calif. 18 36 33N 121 55W
Carmel Valley, Calif. 18 36 29N 121 43W
Carmi, Ill. 15 38 5N 88 10W
Carmichael, Calif. 18 38 38N 121 19W
Carnegie, Pa. 27 40 24N 80 5W
Caro, Mich. 10 43 29N 83 24W
Carol City, Fla. 11 25 56N 80 16W
Caroline Is., Pac. Oc. 31 8 0N 150 0 E
Carpinteria, Calif. 19 34 24N 119 31W
Carrabelle, Fla. 11 29 51N 84 40W
Carrington, N. Dak. 12 47 27N 99 8W
Carrizo Cr. →, N. Mex. 13 36 55N 103 55W
Carrizo Springs, Tex. 13 28 31N 99 52W
Carrizozo, N. Mex. 17 33 38N 105 53W
Carroll, Iowa 14 42 4N 94 52W
Carrollton, Ga. 11 33 35N 85 5W
Carrollton, Ill. 12 39 18N 90 24W
Carrollton, Ky. 15 38 41N 85 11W
Carrollton, Mo. 14 39 22N 93 30W
Carson, N. Dak. 12 46 25N 101 34W
Carson City, Nev. 18 39 10N 119 46W
Carson Sink, Nev. 16 39 50N 118 25W
Cartersville, Ga. 11 34 10N 84 48W
Carthage, Ark. 13 34 4N 92 33W
Carthage, Ill. 14 40 25N 91 8W
Carthage, Mo. 13 37 11N 94 19W
Carthage, S. Dak. 12 44 10N 97 43W
Carthage, Tex. 13 32 9N 94 20W
Caruthersville, Mo. 13 36 11N 89 39W
Casa Grande, Ariz. 17 32 53N 111 45W
Cascade, Idaho 16 44 31N 116 2W
Cascade, Mont. 16 47 16N 111 42W
Cascade Locks, Oreg. 18 45 40N 121 54W
Cascade Ra., Wash. 18 47 0N 121 30W
Cashmere, Wash. 16 47 31N 120 28W
Casmalia, Calif. 19 34 50N 120 32W
Casper, Wyo. 16 42 51N 106 19W
Cass City, Mich. 10 43 36N 83 11W
Cass Lake, Minn. 12 47 23N 94 37W
Casselton, N. Dak. 12 46 54N 97 13W
Cassville, Mo. 13 36 41N 93 52W
Castaic, Calif. 19 34 30N 118 38W
Castle Dale, Utah 16 39 13N 111 1W
Castle Rock, Colo. 12 39 22N 104 51W
Castle Rock, Wash. 18 46 17N 122 54W
Castro Valley, Calif. 28 37 42N 122 4W
Castroville, Calif. 18 36 46N 121 45W
Castroville, Tex. 13 29 21N 98 53W
Cat I., Miss. 13 30 14N 89 6W
Catahoula L., La. 13 31 31N 92 7W
Cathlamet, Wash. 18 46 12N 123 23W
Catlettsburg, Ky. 10 38 25N 82 36W
Catonsville, Md. 25 39 16N 76 43W
Catskill, N.Y. 9 42 14N 73 52W
Catskill Mts., N.Y. 9 42 10N 74 25W
Cavalier, N. Dak. 12 48 48N 97 37W
Cave City, Ky. 10 37 8N 85 58W
Cayey, Puerto Rico 30 18 7N 66 10W
Cayuga L., N.Y. 9 42 41N 76 41W
Cedar →, Iowa 14 41 17N 91 21W
Cedar City, Utah 17 37 41N 113 4W
Cedar Creek Reservoir, Tex. 13 32 11N 96 4W

Creston

Creston, Calif. 18 35 32N 120 33W
Creston, Iowa 14 41 4N 94 22W
Creston, Wash. 16 47 46N 118 31W
Crestview, Calif. 18 37 46N 118 58W
Crestview, Fla. 11 30 46N 86 34W
Crete, Nebr. 12 40 38N 96 58W
Crockett, Tex. 13 31 19N 95 27W
Crooked →, Oreg. 16 44 32N 121 16W
Crookston, Minn. 12 47 47N 96 37W
Crookston, Nebr. 12 42 56N 100 45W
Crooksville, Ohio 10 39 46N 82 6W
Crosby, Minn. 12 46 29N 93 58W
Crosbyton, Tex. 13 33 40N 101 14W
Cross City, Fla. 11 29 38N 83 7W
Cross Plains, Tex. 13 32 8N 99 11W
Cross Sound, Alaska 30 58 0N 135 0W
Crossett, Ark. 13 33 8N 91 58W
Croton-on-Hudson, N.Y. 9 41 12N 73 55W
Crow Agency, Mont. 16 45 36N 107 28W
Crowell, Tex. 13 33 59N 99 43W
Crowley, La. 13 30 13N 92 22W
Crowley, L., Calif. 18 37 35N 118 42W
Crown Point, Ind. 15 41 25N 87 22W
Crows Landing, Calif. 18 37 23N 121 6W
Crystal City, Mo. 14 38 13N 90 23W
Crystal City, Tex. 13 28 41N 99 50W
Crystal Falls, Mich. 10 46 5N 88 20W
Crystal River, Fla. 11 28 54N 82 35W
Crystal Springs, Miss. 13 31 59N 90 21W
Cuba, N. Mex. 17 36 1N 107 4W
Cudahy, Wis. 15 42 58N 87 52W
Cuero, Tex. 13 29 6N 97 17W
Cuervo, N. Mex. 13 35 2N 104 25W
Culbertson, Mont. 12 48 9N 104 31W
Culebra, Isla de, Puerto Rico 30 18 19N 65 18W
Cullman, Ala. 11 34 11N 86 51W
Culpeper, Va. 10 38 30N 78 0W
Culver City, Calif. 29 34 1N 118 23W
Cumberland, Md. 10 39 39N 78 46W
Cumberland, Wis. 12 45 32N 92 1W
Cumberland →, Tenn. 11 36 15N 87 0W
Cumberland I., Ga. 11 30 50N 81 25W
Cumberland Plateau, Tenn. 11 36 0N 85 0W
Cummings Mt., Calif. 19 35 2N 118 34W
Currant, Nev. 16 38 51N 115 32W
Current →, Ark. 13 36 15N 90 55W
Currie, Nev. 16 40 16N 114 45W
Currituck Sd., N.C. 11 36 20N 75 52W
Curtis, Nebr. 12 40 38N 100 31W
Cushing, Okla. 13 35 59N 96 46W
Custer, S. Dak. 12 43 46N 103 36W
Cut Bank, Mont. 16 48 38N 112 20W
Cuthbert, Ga. 11 31 46N 84 48W
Cutler, Calif. 18 36 31N 119 17W
Cuyahoga Falls, Ohio 8 41 8N 81 29W
Cynthiana, Ky. 15 38 23N 84 18W

D

Dade City, Fla. 11 28 22N 82 11W
Daggett, Calif. 19 34 52N 116 52W
Dahlonega, Ga. 11 34 32N 83 59W
Dakota City, Nebr. 12 42 25N 96 25W
Dalhart, Tex. 13 36 4N 102 31W
Dallas, Oreg. 16 44 55N 123 19W
Dallas, Tex. 13 32 47N 96 49W
Dalton, Ga. 11 34 46N 84 58W
Dalton, Mass. 9 42 28N 73 11W
Dalton, Nebr. 12 41 25N 102 58W
Daly City, Calif. 28 37 42N 122 26W
Dana, Mt., Calif. 18 37 54N 119 12W
Danbury, Conn. 9 41 24N 73 28W
Danby L., Calif. 17 34 13N 115 5W
Danforth, Maine 11 45 40N 67 52W
Daniel, Wyo. 16 42 52N 110 4W
Danielson, Conn. 9 41 48N 71 53W
Dannemora, N.Y. 9 44 43N 73 44W
Dansville, N.Y. 8 42 34N 77 42W
Danvers, Mass. 23 42 34N 70 56W
Danville, Ill. 15 40 8N 87 37W
Danville, Ky. 15 37 39N 84 46W
Danville, Va. 11 36 36N 79 23W
Darby, Mont. 16 46 1N 114 11W
Darby, Pa. 24 39 55N 75 16W
Dardanelle, Ark. 13 35 13N 93 9W
Dardanelle, Calif. 18 38 20N 119 50W
Darlington, S.C. 11 34 18N 79 52W
Darlington, Wis. 14 42 41N 90 7W
Darrington, Wash. 16 48 15N 121 36W
Darwin, Calif. 19 36 15N 117 35W
Dauphin I., Ala. 11 30 15N 88 11W
Davenport, Calif. 18 37 1N 122 12W
Davenport, Iowa 14 41 32N 90 35W
Davenport, Wash. 16 47 39N 118 9W
David City, Nebr. 12 41 15N 97 8W
Davis, Calif. 18 38 33N 121 44W
Davis Dam, Ariz. 19 35 11N 114 34W
Davis Mts., Tex. 13 30 50N 103 55W
Dawson, Ga. 11 31 46N 84 27W
Dawson, N. Dak. 12 46 52N 99 45W
Dayton, Ohio 10 39 45N 84 12W
Dayton, Tenn. 11 35 30N 85 1W
Dayton, Wash. 16 46 19N 117 59W
Daytona Beach, Fla. 11 29 13N 81 1W
Dayville, Oreg. 16 44 28N 119 32W
De Funiak Springs, Fla. 11 30 43N 86 7W
De Kalb, Ill. 15 41 56N 88 46W
De Land, Fla. 11 29 2N 81 18W
De Leon, Tex. 13 32 7N 98 32W
De Long Mts., Alaska 30 68 30N 163 0W
De Pere, Wis. 10 44 27N 88 4W
De Queen, Ark. 13 34 2N 94 21W
De Quincy, La. 13 30 27N 93 26W
De Ridder, La. 13 30 51N 93 17W
De Smet, S. Dak. 12 44 23N 97 33W
De Soto, Mo. 14 38 8N 90 34W
De Tour Village, Mich. 10 46 0N 83 56W
De Witt, Ark. 13 34 18N 91 20W
Deadwood, S. Dak. 12 44 23N 103 44W
Dearborn, Mich. 26 42 19N 83 10W
Dearborn Heights, Mich. 26 42 20N 83 17W
Death Valley, Calif. 19 36 15N 116 50W
Death Valley Junction, Calif. 19 36 20N 116 25W
Death Valley National Monument, Calif. 19 36 45N 117 15W
Decatur, Ala. 11 34 36N 86 59W
Decatur, Ga. 11 33 47N 84 18W
Decatur, Ill. 14 39 51N 88 57W
Decatur, Ind. 15 40 50N 84 56W
Decatur, Tex. 13 33 14N 97 35W
Decorah, Iowa 12 43 18N 91 48W
Dedham, Mass. 23 42 15N 71 10W
Deer I., Alaska 30 54 55N 162 18W
Deer Lodge, Mont. 16 46 24N 112 44W
Deer Park, N.Y. 21 40 46N 73 19W
Deer Park, Wash. 16 47 57N 117 28W
Deer River, Minn. 12 47 20N 93 48W
Deering, Alaska 30 66 4N 162 42W
Defiance, Ohio 15 41 17N 84 22W
Del Mar, Calif. 19 32 58N 117 16W
Del Norte, Colo. 17 37 41N 106 21W
Del Rio, Tex. 13 29 22N 100 54W
Delano, Calif. 19 35 46N 119 15W
Delavan, Wis. 15 42 38N 88 39W
Delaware, Ohio 15 40 18N 83 4W
Delaware □ 10 39 0N 75 20W
Delaware →, Del. 10 39 15N 75 20W
Delhi, N.Y. 9 42 17N 74 55W
Dell City, Tex. 17 31 56N 105 12W
Dell Rapids, S. Dak. 12 43 50N 96 43W
Delphi, Ind. 15 40 36N 86 41W
Delphos, Ohio 15 40 51N 84 21W
Delray Beach, Fla. 11 26 28N 80 4W
Delta, Colo. 17 38 44N 108 4W
Delta, Utah 16 39 21N 112 35W
Deming, N. Mex. 17 32 16N 107 46W
Demopolis, Ala. 11 32 31N 87 50W
Denair, Calif. 18 37 32N 120 48W
Denison, Iowa 12 42 1N 95 21W
Denison, Tex. 13 33 45N 96 33W
Denton, Mont. 16 47 19N 109 57W
Denton, Tex. 13 33 13N 97 8W
Denver, Colo. 12 39 44N 104 59W
Denver City, Tex. 13 32 58N 102 50W
Deposit, N.Y. 9 42 4N 75 25W
Derby, Conn. 9 41 19N 73 5W
Dernieres, Isles, La. 13 29 2N 90 50W
Des Moines, Iowa 14 41 35N 93 37W
Des Moines, N. Mex. 13 36 46N 103 50W
Des Moines →, Iowa 12 40 23N 91 25W
Des Plaines, Ill. 22 42 2N 87 54W
Deschutes →, Oreg. 16 45 38N 120 55W
Desert Center, Calif. 19 33 43N 115 24W
Desert Hot Springs, Calif. 19 33 58N 116 30W
Detour, Pt., Mich. 10 45 40N 86 40W
Detroit, Mich. 26 42 20N 83 2W
Detroit, Tex. 13 33 40N 95 16W
Detroit City Airport, Mich. 26 42 24N 83 0W
Detroit Lakes, Minn. 12 46 49N 95 51W
Detroit-Wayne Airport, Mich. 26 42 13N 83 20W
Devils Den, Calif. 18 35 46N 119 58W
Devils Lake, N. Dak. 12 48 7N 98 52W
Dexter, Mo. 13 36 48N 89 57W
Dexter, N. Mex. 13 33 12N 104 22W
Diablo, Mt., Calif. 18 37 53N 121 56W
Diablo Range, Calif. 18 37 20N 121 25W
Diamond Mts., Nev. 16 39 50N 115 30W
Diamond Springs, Calif. 18 38 42N 120 49W
Diamondville, Wyo. 16 41 47N 110 32W
Dickinson, N. Dak. 12 46 53N 102 47W
Dickson, Tenn. 11 36 5N 87 23W
Dickson City, Pa. 9 41 29N 75 40W
Dierks, Ark. 13 34 7N 94 1W
Dighton, Kans. 12 38 29N 100 28W
Dilley, Tex. 13 28 40N 99 10W
Dillingham, Alaska 30 59 3N 158 28W
Dillon, Mont. 16 45 13N 112 38W
Dillon, S.C. 11 34 25N 79 22W
Dimmitt, Tex. 13 34 33N 102 19W
Dingmans Ferry, Pa. 9 41 13N 74 55W
Dinosaur National Monument, Colo. 16 40 30N 108 45W
Dinuba, Calif. 18 36 32N 119 23W
Disappointment, C., Wash. 16 46 18N 124 5W
Divide, Mont. 16 45 45N 112 45W
Dixon, Calif. 18 38 27N 121 49W
Dixon, Ill. 14 41 50N 89 29W
Dixon, Mont. 16 47 19N 114 19W
Dixon, N. Mex. 17 36 12N 105 53W
Dodge Center, Minn. 12 44 2N 92 52W
Dodge City, Kans. 13 37 45N 100 1W
Dodgeville, Wis. 14 42 58N 90 8W
Dodson, Mont. 16 48 24N 108 15W
Doland, S. Dak. 12 44 54N 98 6W
Dolores, Colo. 17 37 28N 108 30W
Dolores →, Utah 17 38 49N 109 17W
Dolton, Ill. 22 41 37N 87 35W
Donaldsonville, La. 13 30 6N 90 59W
Donalsonville, Ga. 11 31 3N 84 53W
Doniphan, Mo. 13 36 37N 90 50W
Donna, Tex. 13 26 9N 98 4W
Dormont, Pa. 27 40 23N 80 2W
Dorris, Calif. 16 41 58N 121 55W
Dos Palos, Calif. 18 36 59N 120 37W
Dothan, Ala. 11 31 13N 85 24W
Douglas, Alaska 30 58 17N 134 24W
Douglas, Ariz. 17 31 21N 109 33W
Douglas, Ga. 11 31 31N 82 51W
Douglas, Wyo. 12 42 45N 105 24W
Douglasville, Ga. 11 33 45N 84 45W
Dove Creek, Colo. 17 37 46N 108 54W
Dover, Del. 10 39 10N 75 32W
Dover, N.H. 9 43 12N 70 56W
Dover, N.J. 9 40 53N 74 34W
Dover, Ohio 8 40 32N 81 29W
Dover-Foxcroft, Maine 11 45 11N 69 13W
Dover Plains, N.Y. 9 41 43N 73 35W
Dowagiac, Mich. 15 41 59N 86 6W
Downey, Calif. 29 33 56N 118 8W
Downey, Idaho 16 42 26N 112 7W
Downieville, Calif. 18 39 34N 120 50W
Doylestown, Pa. 9 40 21N 75 10W
Drain, Oreg. 16 43 40N 123 19W
Drake, N. Dak. 12 47 55N 100 23W
Drexel Hill, Pa. 24 39 56N 75 18W
Driggs, Idaho 16 43 44N 111 6W
Drummond, Mont. 16 46 40N 113 9W
Drumright, Okla. 13 35 59N 96 36W
Dryden, Tex. 13 30 3N 102 7W
Du Bois, Pa. 8 41 8N 78 46W
Du Quoin, Ill. 14 38 1N 89 14W
Duanesburg, N.Y. 9 42 45N 74 11W
Duarte, Calif. 29 34 8N 117 57W
Dublin, Ga. 11 32 32N 82 54W
Dublin, Tex. 13 32 5N 98 21W
Dubois, Idaho 16 44 10N 112 14W
Dubuque, Iowa 14 42 30N 90 41W
Duchesne, Utah 16 40 10N 110 24W
Duckwall, Mt., Calif. 18 37 58N 120 7W
Duluth, Minn. 12 46 47N 92 6W
Dulworthtown, Pa. 24 39 54N 75 33W
Dumas, Ark. 13 33 53N 91 29W
Dumas, Tex. 13 35 52N 101 58W
Duncan, Ariz. 17 32 43N 109 6W
Duncan, Okla. 13 34 30N 97 57W
Dundalk, Md. 25 39 16N 76 30W
Dunedin, Fla. 11 28 1N 82 47W
Dunkirk, N.Y. 8 42 29N 79 20W
Dunlap, Iowa 12 41 51N 95 36W
Dunmore, Pa. 9 41 25N 75 38W
Dunn, N.C. 11 35 19N 78 37W
Dunnellon, Fla. 11 29 3N 82 28W
Dunning, Nebr. 12 41 50N 100 6W
Dunseith, N. Dak. 12 48 50N 100 3W
Dunsmuir, Calif. 16 41 13N 122 16W
Dupree, S. Dak. 12 45 4N 101 35W
Dupuyer, Mont. 16 48 13N 112 30W
Duquesne, Pa. 27 40 22N 79 52W
Durand, Mich. 15 42 55N 83 59W
Durango, Colo. 17 37 16N 107 53W
Durant, Okla. 13 33 59N 96 25W
Durham, N.C. 11 35 59N 78 54W
Duryea, Pa. 9 41 20N 75 45W
Dutch Harbor, Alaska 30 53 53N 166 32W
Dwight, Ill. 15 41 5N 88 26W
Dyersburg, Tenn. 13 36 3N 89 23W

E

Eads, Colo. 12 38 29N 102 47W
Eagle, Alaska 30 64 47N 141 12W
Eagle, Colo. 16 39 39N 106 50W
Eagle Butte, S. Dak. 12 45 0N 101 10W
Eagle Grove, Iowa 14 42 40N 93 54W
Eagle L., Calif. 16 40 39N 120 45W
Eagle L., Maine 11 46 20N 69 22W
Eagle Lake, Tex. 13 29 35N 96 20W
Eagle Nest, N. Mex. 17 36 33N 105 16W
Eagle Pass, Tex. 13 28 43N 100 30W
Eagle Pk., Calif. 18 38 10N 119 25W
Eagle River, Wis. 12 45 55N 89 15W
Earle, Ark. 13 35 16N 90 28W
Earlimart, Calif. 19 35 53N 119 16W
Earth, Tex. 13 34 14N 102 24W
Easley, S.C. 11 34 50N 82 36W
East B., La. 13 29 0N 89 15W
East Chicago, Ind. 22 41 38N 87 26W
East Cleveland, Ohio 27 41 32N 81 35W
East Detroit, Mich. 26 42 27N 82 58W
East Grand Forks, Minn. 12 47 56N 97 1W
East Greenwich, R.I. 9 41 40N 71 27W
East Hartford, Conn. 9 41 46N 72 39W
East Helena, Mont. 16 46 35N 111 56W
East Jordan, Mich. 10 45 10N 85 7W
East Lansing, Mich. 15 42 44N 84 29W
East Liverpool, Ohio 8 40 37N 80 35W
East Los Angeles, Calif. 29 34 1N 118 10W
East Meadow, N.Y. 21 40 42N 73 31W
East Orange, N.J. 20 40 46N 74 11W
East Point, Ga. 11 33 41N 84 27W
East Providence, R.I. 9 41 49N 71 23W
East St. Louis, Ill. 14 38 37N 90 9W
East Stroudsburg, Pa. 9 41 1N 75 11W
East Tawas, Mich. 10 44 17N 83 29W
East Walker →, Nev. 18 38 52N 119 10W
Eastchester, N.Y. 21 40 57N 73 49W
Eastlake, Ohio 27 41 38N 81 28W
Eastland, Tex. 13 32 24N 98 49W
Eastman, Ga. 11 32 12N 83 11W
Easton, Md. 10 38 47N 76 5W
Easton, Pa. 9 40 41N 75 13W
Easton, Wash. 18 47 14N 121 11W
Eastport, Maine 11 44 56N 67 0W
Eaton, Colo. 12 40 32N 104 42W
Eatonton, Ga. 11 33 20N 83 23W
Eatontown, N.J. 9 40 19N 74 4W
Eau Claire, Wis. 12 44 49N 91 30W
Eden, N.C. 11 36 29N 79 53W
Eden, Tex. 13 31 13N 99 51W
Eden, Wyo. 16 42 3N 109 26W
Edenton, N.C. 11 36 4N 76 39W
Edgar, Nebr. 12 40 22N 97 58W
Edgartown, Mass. 9 41 23N 70 31W
Edgefield, S.C. 11 33 47N 81 56W
Edgeley, N. Dak. 12 46 22N 98 43W
Edgemont, S. Dak. 12 43 18N 103 50W
Edina, Mo. 14 40 10N 92 11W
Edinburg, Tex. 13 26 18N 98 10W
Edison, N.J. 20 40 31N 74 22W
Edmeston, N.Y. 9 42 42N 75 15W
Edmond, Okla. 13 35 39N 97 29W
Edmonds, Wash. 18 47 49N 122 23W
Edna, Tex. 13 28 59N 96 39W
Edwards, Calif. 19 34 55N 117 51W
Edwards Plateau, Tex. 13 30 45N 101 20W
Edwardsville, Pa. 9 41 15N 75 56W
Eek, Alaska 30 60 14N 162 2W
Effingham, Ill. 15 39 7N 88 33W
Egeland, N. Dak. 12 48 38N 99 6W
Ekalaka, Mont. 12 45 53N 104 33W
El Cajon, Calif. 19 32 48N 116 58W
El Campo, Tex. 13 29 12N 96 16W
El Centro, Calif. 19 32 48N 115 34W
El Cerrito, Calif. 28 37 54N 122 18W
El Dorado, Ark. 13 33 12N 92 40W
El Dorado, Kans. 13 37 49N 96 52W
El Granada, Calif. 28 37 30N 122 28W
El Monte, Calif. 29 34 3N 118 1W
El Paso, Tex. 17 31 45N 106 29W
El Paso Robles, Calif. 18 35 38N 120 41W
El Portal, Calif. 18 37 41N 119 47W
El Reno, Okla. 13 35 32N 97 57W
El Rio, Calif. 19 34 14N 119 10W
El Segundo, Calif. 29 33 55N 118 24W
Elba, Ala. 11 31 25N 86 4W
Elbert, Mt., Colo. 17 39 7N 106 27W
Elberta, Mich. 10 44 37N 86 14W
Elberton, Ga. 11 34 7N 82 52W
Eldon, Mo. 14 38 21N 92 35W
Eldora, Iowa 14 42 22N 93 5W
Eldorado, Ill. 15 37 49N 88 26W
Eldorado, Tex. 13 30 52N 100 36W
Eldorado Springs, Mo. 14 37 52N 94 1W
Electra, Tex. 13 34 2N 98 55W
Eleele, Hawaii 30 21 54N 159 35W
Elephant Butte Reservoir, N. Mex. 17 33 9N 107 11W
Elfin Cove, Alaska 30 58 12N 136 22W
Elgin, Ill. 15 42 2N 88 17W
Elgin, N. Dak. 12 46 24N 101 51W
Elgin, Nebr. 12 41 59N 98 5W
Elgin, Nev. 17 37 21N 114 32W
Elgin, Oreg. 16 45 34N 117 55W
Elgin, Tex. 13 30 21N 97 22W
Elida, N. Mex. 13 33 57N 103 39W
Elim, Alaska 30 64 37N 162 15W
Elizabeth, N.J. 20 40 39N 74 12W
Elizabeth City, N.C. 11 36 18N 76 14W
Elizabethton, Tenn. 11 36 21N 82 13W
Elizabethtown, Ky. 10 37 42N 85 52W
Elizabethtown, Pa. 9 40 9N 76 36W
Elk City, Okla. 13 35 25N 99 25W
Elk Grove, Calif. 18 38 25N 121 22W
Elk River, Idaho 16 46 47N 116 11W
Elk River, Minn. 12 45 18N 93 35W
Elkhart, Ind. 15 41 41N 85 58W
Elkhart, Kans. 13 37 0N 101 54W
Elkhorn →, Nebr. 12 41 8N 96 19W
Elkin, N.C. 11 36 15N 80 51W
Elkins, W. Va. 10 38 55N 79 51W
Elko, Nev. 16 40 50N 115 46W
Ellendale, N. Dak. 12 46 0N 98 32W
Ellensburg, Wash. 16 46 59N 120 34W
Ellenville, N.Y. 9 41 43N 74 24W
Ellinwood, Kans. 12 38 21N 98 35W
Ellis, Kans. 12 38 56N 99 34W
Ellisville, Miss. 13 31 36N 89 12W
Ellsworth, Kans. 12 38 44N 98 14W
Ellwood City, Pa. 8 40 52N 80 17W
Elma, Wash. 18 47 0N 123 25W

Georgetown

lmhurst, *Ill.* **22** 41 53N 87 55W
lmira, *N.Y.* **8** 42 6N 76 48W
lmont, *N.Y.* **21** 40 42N 73 42W
lmwood Park, *Ill.* **22** 41 55N 87 48W
loy, *Ariz.* **17** 32 45N 111 33W
lsinore, *Utah* **17** 38 41N 112 9W
lwood, *Ind.* **15** 40 17N 85 50W
lwood, *Nebr.* **12** 40 36N 99 52W
ly, *Minn.* **12** 47 55N 91 51W
ly, *Nev.* **16** 39 15N 114 54W
lyria, *Ohio* **8** 41 22N 82 7W
mery, *Utah* **17** 38 55N 111 15W
mmetsburg, *Iowa* **14** 43 7N 94 41W
mmett, *Idaho* **16** 43 52N 116 30W
mpire State Building,
N.Y. **20** 40 44N 73 59W
mporia, *Kans.* **12** 38 25N 96 11W
mporia, *Va.* **11** 36 42N 77 32W
mporium, *Pa.* **8** 41 31N 78 14W
ncinal, *Tex.* **13** 28 2N 99 21W
ncinitas, *Calif.* **19** 33 3N 117 17W
ncino, *N. Mex.* **17** 34 39N 105 28W
nderlin, *N. Dak.* **12** 46 38N 97 36W
ndicott, *N.Y.* **9** 42 6N 76 4W
ndicott, *Wash.* **16** 46 56N 117 41W
ndicott Mts., *Alaska* **30** 68 0N 152 0W
ngland, *Ark.* **13** 34 33N 91 58W
nglewood, *Colo.* **12** 39 39N 104 59W
nglewood, *Kans.* **13** 37 2N 99 59W
nid, *Okla.* **13** 36 24N 97 53W
nnis, *Mont.* **16** 45 21N 111 44W
nnis, *Tex.* **13** 32 20N 96 38W
nterprise, *Oreg.* **16** 45 25N 117 17W
nterprise, *Utah* **17** 37 34N 113 43W
numclaw, *Wash.* **18** 47 12N 121 59W
phraim, *Utah* **16** 39 22N 111 35W
phrata, *Wash.* **16** 47 19N 119 33W
rie, *Pa.* **8** 42 8N 80 5W
rie, L., *N. Amer.* **8** 42 15N 81 0W
rskine, *Minn.* **12** 47 40N 96 0W
rwin, *Tenn.* **11** 36 9N 82 25W
scalante, *Utah* **17** 37 47N 111 36W
scalante →, *Utah* **17** 37 24N 110 57W
scambia →, *Fla.* **11** 30 32N 87 11W
scanaba, *Mich.* **10** 45 45N 87 4W
scondido, *Calif.* **19** 33 7N 117 5W
spenberg, C., *Alaska* **30** 66 33N 163 36W
ssex, *Md.* **25** 39 18N 76 28W
stancia, *N. Mex.* **17** 34 46N 106 4W
stelline, *S. Dak.* **12** 44 35N 96 54W
stelline, *Tex.* **13** 34 33N 100 26W
stherville, *Iowa* **12** 43 24N 94 50W
tawah →, *Ga.* **11** 34 20N 84 15W
towah, *Tenn.* **11** 35 20N 84 32W
uclid, *Ohio* **27** 41 34N 81 33W
udora, *Ark.* **13** 33 7N 91 16W
ufaula, *Ala.* **11** 31 54N 85 9W
ufaula, *Okla.* **13** 35 17N 95 35W
ufaula L., *Okla.* **13** 35 18N 95 21W
ugene, *Oreg.* **16** 44 5N 123 4W
unice, *La.* **13** 30 30N 92 25W
unice, *N. Mex.* **13** 32 26N 103 10W
ureka, *Calif.* **16** 40 47N 124 9W
ureka, *Kans.* **13** 37 49N 96 17W
ureka, *Mont.* **16** 48 53N 115 3W
ureka, *Nev.* **16** 39 31N 115 58W
ureka, *S. Dak.* **12** 45 46N 99 38W
ureka, *Utah* **16** 39 58N 112 7W
ustis, *Fla.* **11** 28 51N 81 41W
vans, *Colo.* **12** 40 23N 104 41W
vanston, *Ill.* **22** 42 3N 87 41W
vanston, *Wyo.* **16** 41 16N 110 58W
vansville, *Ind.* **15** 37 58N 87 35W
vansville, *Wis.* **14** 42 47N 89 18W
veleth, *Minn.* **12** 47 28N 92 32W
verett, *Mass.* **23** 42 24N 71 3W
verett, *Wash.* **18** 47 59N 122 12W
verglades, The, *Fla.* **11** 25 50N 81 0W
verglades City, *Fla.* **11** 25 52N 81 23W
verglades National
Park, *Fla.* **11** 25 30N 81 0W
vergreen, *Ala.* **11** 31 26N 86 57W
vergreen Park, *Ill.* **22** 41 43N 87 42W
verson, *Wash.* **16** 48 57N 122 22W
vesboro, *N.J.* **24** 39 54N 74 56W
wing, *Nebr.* **12** 42 16N 98 21W
xcelsior Springs, *Mo.* **14** 39 20N 94 13W
xeter, *Calif.* **18** 36 18N 119 9W
xeter, *N.H.* **9** 42 59N 70 57W
xeter, *Nebr.* **12** 40 39N 97 27W

F

abens, *Tex.* **17** 31 30N 106 10W
agatogo, *Amer. Samoa* **31** 14 17S 170 41W
air Lawn, *N.J.* **20** 40 56N 74 7W
air Oaks, *Calif.* **18** 38 39N 121 16W
airbank, *Ariz.* **17** 31 43N 110 11W
airbanks, *Alaska* **30** 64 51N 147 43W
airbury, *Nebr.* **12** 40 8N 97 11W
airfax, *Del.* **24** 39 47N 75 32W
airfax, *Okla.* **13** 36 34N 96 42W
airfax, *Va.* **25** 38 50N 77 19W
airfield, *Ala.* **11** 33 29N 86 55W
airfield, *Calif.* **18** 38 15N 122 3W
Fairfield, *Conn.* **9** 41 9N 73 16W
Fairfield, *Idaho* **16** 43 21N 114 44W
Fairfield, *Ill.* **15** 38 23N 88 22W
Fairfield, *Iowa* **14** 40 56N 91 57W
Fairfield, *Mont.* **16** 47 37N 111 59W
Fairfield, *Tex.* **13** 31 44N 96 10W
Fairhope, *Ala.* **11** 30 31N 87 54W
Fairmead, *Calif.* **18** 37 5N 120 10W
Fairmont, *Minn.* **12** 43 39N 94 28W
Fairmont, *W. Va.* **10** 39 29N 80 9W
Fairmount, *Calif.* **19** 34 45N 118 26W
Fairplay, *Colo.* **17** 39 15N 106 2W
Fairport, *N.Y.* **8** 43 6N 77 27W
Fairview, *Mont.* **12** 47 51N 104 3W
Fairview, *Okla.* **13** 36 16N 98 29W
Fairview, *Utah* **16** 39 50N 111 0W
Fairview Park, *Ohio* **27** 41 26N 81 52W
Fairweather, Mt., *Alaska* **30** 58 55N 137 32W
Faith, *S. Dak.* **12** 45 2N 102 2W
Fajardo, *Puerto Rico* **30** 18 20N 65 39W
Falcon Dam, *Tex.* **13** 26 50N 99 20W
Falfurrias, *Tex.* **13** 27 14N 98 9W
Fall River, *Mass.* **9** 41 43N 71 10W
Fall River Mills, *Calif.* **16** 41 3N 121 26W
Fallbrook, *Calif.* **17** 33 25N 117 12W
Fallon, *Mont.* **12** 46 50N 105 8W
Fallon, *Nev.* **16** 39 28N 118 47W
Falls Church, *Va.* **25** 38 53N 77 11W
Falls City, *Nebr.* **12** 40 3N 95 36W
Falls City, *Oreg.* **16** 44 52N 123 26W
Falmouth, *Ky.* **15** 38 41N 84 20W
Famoso, *Calif.* **19** 35 37N 119 12W
Farewell, *Alaska* **30** 62 31N 153 54W
Fargo, *N. Dak.* **12** 46 53N 96 48W
Faribault, *Minn.* **12** 44 18N 93 16W
Farmerville, *La.* **13** 32 47N 92 24W
Farmington, *Calif.* **18** 37 55N 120 59W
Farmington, *Mich.* **26** 42 26N 83 22W
Farmington, *N. Mex.* **17** 36 44N 108 12W
Farmington, *Utah* **16** 41 0N 111 12W
Farmington →, *Conn.* **9** 41 51N 72 38W
Farmington Hills, *Mich.* **26** 42 29N 83 23W
Farmville, *Va.* **10** 37 18N 78 24W
Farrell, *Pa.* **8** 41 13N 80 30W
Farwell, *Tex.* **13** 34 23N 103 2W
Faulkton, *S. Dak.* **12** 45 2N 99 8W
Fawnskin, *Calif.* **19** 34 16N 116 56W
Fayette, *Ala.* **11** 33 41N 87 50W
Fayette, *Mo.* **14** 39 9N 92 41W
Fayetteville, *Ark.* **13** 36 4N 94 10W
Fayetteville, *N.C.* **11** 35 3N 78 53W
Fayetteville, *Tenn.* **11** 35 9N 86 34W
Fear, C., *N.C.* **11** 33 50N 77 58W
Feather →, *Calif.* **16** 38 47N 121 36W
Felton, *Calif.* **18** 37 3N 122 4W
Fennimore, *Wis.* **14** 42 59N 90 39W
Fenton, *Mich.* **15** 42 48N 83 42W
Fergus Falls, *Minn.* **12** 46 17N 96 4W
Fernandina Beach, *Fla.* **11** 30 40N 81 27W
Ferndale, *Calif.* **16** 40 35N 124 16W
Ferndale, *Mich.* **26** 42 27N 83 7W
Ferndale, *Wash.* **18** 48 51N 122 36W
Fernley, *Nev.* **16** 39 36N 119 15W
Ferriday, *La.* **13** 31 38N 91 33W
Ferron, *Utah* **17** 39 5N 111 8W
Fertile, *Minn.* **12** 47 32N 96 17W
Fessenden, *N. Dak.* **12** 47 39N 99 38W
Filer, *Idaho* **16** 42 34N 114 37W
Fillmore, *Calif.* **19** 34 24N 118 55W
Fillmore, *Utah* **17** 38 58N 112 20W
Findlay, *Ohio* **15** 41 2N 83 39W
Finley, *N. Dak.* **12** 47 31N 97 50W
Firebaugh, *Calif.* **18** 36 52N 120 27W
Fitchburg, *Mass.* **9** 42 35N 71 48W
Fitzgerald, *Ga.* **11** 31 43N 83 15W
Five Points, *Calif.* **18** 36 26N 120 6W
Flagler, *Colo.* **12** 39 18N 103 4W
Flagstaff, *Ariz.* **17** 35 12N 111 39W
Flambeau →, *Wis.* **12** 45 18N 91 14W
Flaming Gorge Dam,
Utah **16** 40 55N 109 25W
Flaming Gorge
Reservoir, *Wyo.* **16** 41 10N 109 25W
Flandreau, *S. Dak.* **12** 44 3N 96 36W
Flat River, *Mo.* **13** 37 51N 90 31W
Flathead L., *Mont.* **16** 47 51N 114 8W
Flattery, C., *Wash.* **18** 48 23N 124 29W
Flaxton, *N. Dak.* **12** 48 54N 102 24W
Flint, *Mich.* **15** 43 1N 83 41W
Flint →, *Ga.* **11** 30 57N 84 34W
Floodwood, *Minn.* **12** 46 55N 92 55W
Flora, *Ill.* **10** 38 40N 88 29W
Floral Park, *N.Y.* **21** 40 43N 73 42W
Florala, *Ala.* **11** 31 0N 86 20W
Florence, *Ala.* **11** 34 48N 87 41W
Florence, *Ariz.* **17** 33 2N 111 23W
Florence, *Calif.* **29** 33 57N 118 13W
Florence, *Colo.* **12** 38 23N 105 8W
Florence, *Oreg.* **16** 43 58N 124 7W
Florence, *S.C.* **11** 34 12N 79 46W
Floresville, *Tex.* **13** 29 8N 98 10W
Florham Park, *N.J.* **20** 40 46N 74 23W
Florida □ **11** 28 0N 82 0W
Floydada, *Tex.* **13** 33 59N 101 20W
Flushing, *N.Y.* **21** 40 45N 73 49W
Folkston, *Ga.* **11** 30 50N 82 0W
Follett, *Tex.* **13** 36 26N 100 8W
Fond du Lac, *Wis.* **12** 43 47N 88 27W
Ford City, *Calif.* **19** 35 9N 119 27W
Fordyce, *Ark.* **13** 33 49N 92 25W
Forest, *Miss.* **13** 32 22N 89 29W
Forest City, *Iowa* **12** 43 16N 93 39W
Forest City, *N.C.* **11** 35 20N 81 52W
Forest Grove, *Oreg.* **18** 45 31N 123 7W
Forest Hills, *N.Y.* **21** 40 42N 73 51W
Forest Hills, *Pa.* **27** 40 25N 79 51W
Forestville, *Md.* **25** 38 50N 76 52W
Forestville, *Wis.* **10** 44 41N 87 29W
Forks, *Wash.* **18** 47 57N 124 23W
Forman, *N. Dak.* **12** 46 7N 97 38W
Forrest City, *Ark.* **13** 35 1N 90 47W
Forsyth, *Ga.* **11** 33 2N 83 56W
Forsyth, *Mont.* **16** 46 16N 106 41W
Fort Apache, *Ariz.* **17** 33 50N 110 0W
Fort Benton, *Mont.* **16** 47 49N 110 40W
Fort Bragg, *Calif.* **16** 39 26N 123 48W
Fort Bridger, *Wyo.* **16** 41 19N 110 23W
Fort Collins, *Colo.* **12** 40 35N 105 5W
Fort Davis, *Tex.* **13** 30 35N 103 54W
Fort Defiance, *Ariz.* **17** 35 45N 109 5W
Fort Dodge, *Iowa* **12** 42 30N 94 11W
Fort Garland, *Colo.* **17** 37 26N 105 26W
Fort Hancock, *Tex.* **17** 31 18N 105 51W
Fort Irwin, *Calif.* **19** 35 16N 116 34W
Fort Kent, *Maine* **11** 47 15N 68 36W
Fort Klamath, *Oreg.* **16** 42 42N 122 0W
Fort Laramie, *Wyo.* **12** 42 13N 104 31W
Fort Lauderdale, *Fla.* **11** 26 7N 80 8W
Fort Lee, *N.J.* **20** 40 50N 73 58W
Fort Lupton, *Colo.* **12** 40 5N 104 49W
Fort Madison, *Iowa* **14** 40 38N 91 27W
Fort Meade, *Fla.* **11** 27 45N 81 48W
Fort Morgan, *Colo.* **12** 40 15N 103 48W
Fort Myers, *Fla.* **11** 26 39N 81 52W
Fort Payne, *Ala.* **11** 34 26N 85 43W
Fort Peck, *Mont.* **16** 48 1N 106 27W
Fort Peck Dam, *Mont.* **16** 48 0N 106 26W
Fort Peck L., *Mont.* **16** 48 0N 106 26W
Fort Pierce, *Fla.* **11** 27 27N 80 20W
Fort Pierre, *S. Dak.* **12** 44 21N 100 22W
Fort Scott, *Kans.* **13** 37 50N 94 42W
Fort Smith, *Ark.* **13** 35 23N 94 25W
Fort Stanton, *N. Mex.* **17** 33 30N 105 31W
Fort Stockton, *Tex.* **13** 30 53N 102 53W
Fort Sumner, *N. Mex.* **13** 34 28N 104 15W
Fort Valley, *Ga.* **11** 32 33N 83 53W
Fort Walton Beach, *Fla.* **11** 30 25N 86 36W
Fort Wayne, *Ind.* **15** 41 4N 85 9W
Fort Worth, *Tex.* **13** 32 45N 97 18W
Fort Yates, *N. Dak.* **12** 46 5N 100 38W
Fort Yukon, *Alaska* **30** 66 34N 145 16W
Fortuna, *Calif.* **16** 40 36N 124 9W
Fortuna, *N. Dak.* **12** 48 55N 103 47W
Fossil, *Oreg.* **16** 45 0N 120 9W
Fosston, *Minn.* **12** 47 35N 95 45W
Fostoria, *Ohio* **15** 41 10N 83 25W
Fountain, *Colo.* **12** 38 41N 104 42W
Fountain, *Utah* **16** 39 41N 111 37W
Fountain Springs, *Calif.* **19** 35 54N 118 51W
Four Mountains, Is. of,
Alaska **30** 53 0N 170 0W
Fowler, *Calif.* **18** 36 38N 119 41W
Fowler, *Colo.* **12** 38 8N 104 2W
Fowler, *Kans.* **13** 37 23N 100 12W
Fowlerton, *Tex.* **13** 28 28N 98 48W
Fox Is., *Alaska* **30** 52 30N 166 0W
Foxpark, *Wyo.* **16** 41 5N 106 9W
Frackville, *Pa.* **9** 40 47N 76 14W
Framingham, *Mass.* **23** 42 18N 71 23W
Frankfort, *Ind.* **15** 40 17N 86 31W
Frankfort, *Kans.* **12** 39 42N 96 25W
Frankfort, *Ky.* **15** 38 12N 84 52W
Frankfort, *Mich.* **10** 44 38N 86 14W
Franklin, *Ky.* **11** 36 43N 86 35W
Franklin, *La.* **13** 29 48N 91 30W
Franklin, *Mass.* **9** 42 5N 71 24W
Franklin, *N.H.* **9** 43 27N 71 39W
Franklin, *Nebr.* **12** 40 6N 98 57W
Franklin, *Pa.* **8** 41 24N 79 50W
Franklin, *Tenn.* **11** 35 55N 86 52W
Franklin, *Va.* **11** 36 41N 76 56W
Franklin, *W. Va.* **10** 38 39N 79 20W
Franklin D. Roosevelt L.,
Wash. **16** 48 18N 118 9W
Franklin L., *Nev.* **16** 40 25N 115 22W
Franklin Park, *Ill.* **22** 41 55N 87 52W
Franklin Square, *N.Y.* **21** 40 41N 73 40W
Franklinton, *La.* **13** 30 51N 90 9W
Franks Pk., *Wyo.* **16** 43 58N 109 18W
Frederick, *Md.* **10** 39 25N 77 25W
Frederick, *Okla.* **13** 34 23N 99 1W
Frederick, *S. Dak.* **12** 45 50N 98 31W
Fredericksburg, *Tex.* **13** 30 16N 98 52W
Fredericksburg, *Va.* **10** 38 18N 77 28W
Fredericktown, *Mo.* **13** 37 34N 90 18W
Fredonia, *Ariz.* **17** 36 57N 112 32W
Fredonia, *Kans.* **13** 37 32N 95 49W
Fredonia, *N.Y.* **8** 42 26N 79 20W
Freehold, *N.J.* **9** 40 16N 74 17W
Freel Peak, *Nev.* **18** 38 52N 119 54W
Freeland, *Pa.* **9** 41 1N 75 54W
Freeman, *Calif.* **19** 35 35N 117 53W
Freeman, *S. Dak.* **12** 43 21N 97 26W
Freeport, *Ill.* **14** 42 17N 89 36W
Freeport, *N.Y.* **21** 40 39N 73 35W
Freeport, *Tex.* **13** 28 57N 95 21W
Fremont, *Calif.* **28** 37 33N 122 2W
Fremont, *Mich.* **10** 43 28N 85 57W
Fremont, *Nebr.* **12** 41 26N 96 30W
Fremont, *Ohio* **15** 41 21N 83 7W
Fremont →, *Utah* **17** 38 24N 110 42W
Fremont L., *Wyo.* **16** 42 57N 109 48W
French Camp, *Calif.* **18** 37 53N 121 16W
French Creek →, *Pa.* **8** 41 24N 79 50W
Frenchglen, *Oreg.* **16** 42 50N 118 55W
Frenchman Cr. →,
Mont. **16** 48 31N 107 10W
Frenchman Cr. →, *Nebr.* **12** 40 14N 100 50W
Fresno, *Calif.* **18** 36 44N 119 47W
Fresno Reservoir, *Mont.* **16** 48 36N 109 57W
Friant, *Calif.* **18** 36 59N 119 43W
Frio →, *Tex.* **13** 28 26N 98 11W
Friona, *Tex.* **13** 34 38N 102 43W
Fritch, *Tex.* **13** 35 38N 101 36W
Froid, *Mont.* **12** 48 20N 104 30W
Fromberg, *Mont.* **16** 45 24N 108 54W
Front Range, *Colo.* **16** 40 25N 105 45W
Front Royal, *Va.* **10** 38 55N 78 12W
Frostburg, *Md.* **10** 39 39N 78 56W
Fullerton, *Calif.* **19** 33 53N 117 56W
Fullerton, *Nebr.* **12** 41 22N 97 58W
Fulton, *Mo.* **14** 38 52N 91 57W
Fulton, *N.Y.* **9** 43 19N 76 25W
Fulton, *Tenn.* **11** 36 31N 88 53W

G

Gadsden, *Ala.* **11** 34 1N 86 1W
Gadsden, *Ariz.* **17** 32 33N 114 47W
Gaffney, *S.C.* **11** 35 5N 81 39W
Gail, *Tex.* **13** 32 46N 101 27W
Gainesville, *Fla.* **11** 29 40N 82 20W
Gainesville, *Ga.* **11** 34 18N 83 50W
Gainesville, *Mo.* **13** 36 36N 92 26W
Gainesville, *Tex.* **13** 33 38N 97 8W
Galax, *Va.* **11** 36 40N 80 56W
Galena, *Alaska* **30** 64 44N 156 56W
Galesburg, *Ill.* **14** 40 57N 90 22W
Galiuro Mts., *Ariz.* **17** 32 30N 110 20W
Gallatin, *Tenn.* **11** 36 24N 86 27W
Gallipolis, *Ohio* **10** 38 49N 82 12W
Gallup, *N. Mex.* **17** 35 32N 108 45W
Galt, *Calif.* **18** 38 15N 121 18W
Galva, *Ill.* **14** 41 10N 90 3W
Galveston, *Tex.* **13** 29 18N 94 48W
Galveston B., *Tex.* **13** 29 36N 94 50W
Gambell, *Alaska* **30** 63 47N 171 45W
Gamerco, *N. Mex.* **17** 35 34N 108 46W
Ganado, *Ariz.* **17** 35 43N 109 33W
Ganado, *Tex.* **13** 29 2N 96 31W
Gannett Peak, *Wyo.* **16** 43 11N 109 39W
Gannvalley, *S. Dak.* **12** 44 2N 98 59W
Garapan, *Pac. Oc.* **31** 15 12N 145 53 E
Garber, *Okla.* **13** 36 26N 97 35W
Garberville, *Calif.* **16** 40 6N 123 48W
Garden City, *Kans.* **13** 37 58N 100 53W
Garden City, *Mich.* **26** 42 20N 83 20W
Garden City, *N.Y.* **21** 40 43N 73 38W
Garden City, *Tex.* **13** 31 52N 101 29W
Garden Grove, *Calif.* **19** 33 47N 117 55W
Gardena, *Calif.* **29** 33 53N 118 17W
Gardiner, *Mont.* **16** 45 2N 110 22W
Gardiners I., *N.Y.* **9** 41 6N 72 6W
Gardner, *Mass.* **9** 42 34N 71 59W
Gardnerville, *Nev.* **18** 38 56N 119 45W
Gareloi I., *Alaska* **30** 51 48N 178 48W
Garey, *Calif.* **19** 34 53N 120 19W
Garfield, *N.J.* **20** 40 52N 74 6W
Garfield, *Wash.* **16** 47 1N 117 9W
Garfield Heights, *Ohio* **27** 41 25N 81 37W
Garland, *Utah* **16** 41 47N 112 10W
Garner, *Iowa* **14** 43 6N 93 36W
Garnett, *Kans.* **12** 38 17N 95 14W
Garrison, *Mont.* **16** 46 31N 112 49W
Garrison, *N. Dak.* **12** 47 40N 101 25W
Garrison, *Tex.* **13** 31 49N 94 30W
Garrison Res. =
Sakakawea, L., *N. Dak.* **12** 47 30N 101 25W
Gary, *Ind.* **22** 41 35N 87 23W
Gassaway, *W. Va.* **10** 38 41N 80 47W
Gastonia, *N.C.* **11** 35 16N 81 11W
Gatesville, *Tex.* **13** 31 26N 97 45W
Gaviota, *Calif.* **19** 34 29N 120 13W
Gaylord, *Mich.* **10** 45 2N 84 41W
Genesee, *Idaho* **16** 46 33N 116 56W
Genesee →, *N.Y.* **8** 43 16N 77 36W
Geneseo, *Ill.* **14** 41 27N 90 9W
Geneseo, *Kans.* **12** 38 31N 98 10W
Geneva, *Ala.* **11** 31 2N 85 52W
Geneva, *N.Y.* **8** 42 52N 76 59W
Geneva, *Nebr.* **12** 40 32N 97 36W
Geneva, *Ohio* **8** 41 48N 80 57W
Geneva, L., *Wis.* **15** 42 38N 88 30W
Genoa, *N.Y.* **9** 42 40N 76 32W
Genoa, *Nebr.* **12** 41 27N 97 44W
George, L., *Fla.* **11** 29 17N 81 36W
George, L., *N.Y.* **9** 43 37N 73 33W
George West, *Tex.* **13** 28 20N 98 7W
Georgetown, *Colo.* **16** 39 42N 105 42W
Georgetown, *D.C.* **25** 38 54N 77 3W
Georgetown, *Ky.* **10** 38 13N 84 33W

Georgetown

Georgetown, *S.C.* **11** 33 23N 79 17W
Georgetown, *Tex.* **13** 30 38N 97 41W
Georgia □ **11** 32 50N 83 15W
Geraldine, *Mont.* **16** 47 36N 110 16W
Gering, *Nebr.* **12** 41 50N 103 40W
Gerlach, *Nev.* **16** 40 39N 119 21W
Gettysburg, *Pa.* **10** 39 50N 77 14W
Gettysburg, *S. Dak.* **12** 45 1N 99 57W
Geyser, *Mont.* **16** 47 16N 110 30W
Giant Forest, *Calif.* **18** 36 36N 118 43W
Gibbon, *Nebr.* **12** 40 45N 98 51W
Giddings, *Tex.* **13** 30 11N 96 56W
Gila →, *Ariz.* **17** 32 43N 114 33W
Gila Bend, *Ariz.* **17** 32 57N 112 43W
Gila Bend Mts., *Ariz.* **17** 33 10N 113 0W
Gillette, *Wyo.* **12** 44 18N 105 30W
Gilmer, *Tex.* **13** 32 44N 94 57W
Gilroy, *Calif.* **18** 37 1N 121 34W
Girard, *Kans.* **13** 37 31N 94 51W
Glacier Park, *Mont.* **16** 48 30N 113 18W
Glacier Peak, *Wash.* **16** 48 7N 121 7W
Gladewater, *Tex.* **13** 32 33N 94 56W
Gladstone, *Mich.* **10** 45 51N 87 1W
Gladwin, *Mich.* **10** 43 59N 84 29W
Glasco, *Kans.* **12** 39 22N 97 50W
Glasco, *N.Y.* **9** 42 3N 73 57W
Glasgow, *Ky.* **10** 37 0N 85 55W
Glasgow, *Mont.* **16** 48 12N 106 38W
Glastonbury, *Conn.* **9** 41 43N 72 37W
Glen Canyon Dam, *Ariz.* **17** 36 57N 111 29W
Glen Canyon National Recreation Area, *Utah* **17** 37 15N 111 0W
Glen Cove, *N.Y.* **21** 40 52N 73 38W
Glen Lyon, *Pa.* **9** 41 10N 76 5W
Glen Ullin, *N. Dak.* **12** 46 49N 101 50W
Glencoe, *Ill.* **22** 42 7N 87 44W
Glencoe, *Minn.* **12** 44 46N 94 9W
Glendale, *Ariz.* **17** 33 32N 112 11W
Glendale, *Calif.* **29** 34 9N 118 14W
Glendale, *Oreg.* **16** 42 44N 123 26W
Glendive, *Mont.* **12** 47 7N 104 43W
Glendo, *Wyo.* **12** 42 30N 105 2W
Glenmora, *La.* **13** 30 59N 92 35W
Glenns Ferry, *Idaho* **16** 42 57N 115 18W
Glenrock, *Wyo.* **16** 42 52N 105 52W
Glens Falls, *N.Y.* **9** 43 19N 73 39W
Glenshaw, *Pa.* **27** 40 32N 79 58W
Glenview, *Ill.* **22** 42 4N 87 48W
Glenville, *W. Va.* **10** 38 56N 80 50W
Glenwood, *Ark.* **13** 34 20N 93 33W
Glenwood, *Hawaii* **30** 19 29N 155 9W
Glenwood, *Iowa* **12** 41 3N 95 45W
Glenwood, *Minn.* **12** 45 39N 95 23W
Glenwood Springs, *Colo.* **16** 39 33N 107 19W
Globe, *Ariz.* **17** 33 24N 110 47W
Gloucester, *Mass.* **9** 42 37N 70 40W
Gloucester City, *N.J.* **24** 39 53N 75 7W
Gloversville, *N.Y.* **9** 43 3N 74 21W
Gogebic, L., *Mich.* **12** 46 30N 89 35W
Golconda, *Nev.* **16** 40 58N 117 30W
Gold Beach, *Oreg.* **16** 42 25N 124 25W
Gold Creek, *Alaska* **30** 62 46N 149 41W
Gold Hill, *Oreg.* **16** 42 26N 123 3W
Golden, *Colo.* **12** 39 42N 105 15W
Golden Gate, *Calif.* **16** 37 54N 122 30W
Golden Gate, *Calif.* **28** 37 48N 122 30W
Golden Gate Bridge, *Calif.* **28** 37 49N 122 28W
Goldendale, *Wash.* **16** 45 49N 120 50W
Goldfield, *Nev.* **17** 37 42N 117 14W
Goldsboro, *N.C.* **11** 35 23N 77 59W
Goldsmith, *Tex.* **13** 31 59N 102 37W
Goldthwaite, *Tex.* **13** 31 27N 98 34W
Goleta, *Calif.* **19** 34 27N 119 50W
Goliad, *Tex.* **13** 28 40N 97 23W
Gonzales, *Calif.* **18** 36 30N 121 26W
Gonzales, *Tex.* **13** 29 30N 97 27W
Gooding, *Idaho* **16** 42 56N 114 43W
Goodland, *Kans.* **12** 39 21N 101 43W
Goodnight, *Tex.* **13** 35 2N 101 11W
Goodsprings, *Nev.* **17** 35 50N 115 26W
Goose L., *Calif.* **16** 41 56N 120 26W
Gorda, *Calif.* **18** 35 53N 121 26W
Gordon, *Nebr.* **12** 42 48N 102 12W
Gorman, *Calif.* **19** 34 47N 118 51W
Gorman, *Tex.* **13** 32 12N 98 41W
Goshen, *Calif.* **18** 36 21N 119 25W
Goshen, *Ind.* **15** 41 35N 85 50W
Goshen, *N.Y.* **9** 41 24N 74 20W
Gothenburg, *Nebr.* **12** 40 56N 100 10W
Gowanda, *N.Y.* **8** 42 28N 78 56W
Grace, *Idaho* **16** 42 35N 111 44W
Graceville, *Minn.* **12** 45 34N 96 26W
Grady, *N. Mex.* **13** 34 49N 103 19W
Grafton, *N. Dak.* **12** 48 25N 97 25W
Graham, *N.C.* **11** 36 5N 79 25W
Graham, *Tex.* **13** 33 6N 98 35W
Graham, Mt., *Ariz.* **17** 32 42N 109 52W
Granada, *Colo.* **13** 38 4N 102 19W
Granbury, *Tex.* **13** 32 27N 97 47W
Grand →, *Mo.* **14** 39 23N 93 7W
Grand →, *S. Dak.* **12** 45 40N 100 45W
Grand Canyon, *Ariz.* **17** 36 3N 112 9W
Grand Canyon National Park, *Ariz.* **17** 36 15N 112 30W
Grand Coulee, *Wash.* **16** 47 57N 119 0W
Grand Coulee Dam, *Wash.* **16** 47 57N 118 59W
Grand Forks, *N. Dak.* **12** 47 55N 97 3W
Grand Haven, *Mich.* **15** 43 4N 86 13W
Grand I., *Mich.* **10** 46 31N 86 40W
Grand Island, *Nebr.* **12** 40 55N 98 21W
Grand Isle, *La.* **13** 29 14N 90 0W
Grand Junction, *Colo.* **17** 39 4N 108 33W
Grand L., *La.* **13** 29 55N 92 47W
Grand Lake, *Colo.* **16** 40 15N 105 49W
Grand Marais, *Mich.* **10** 46 40N 85 59W
Grand Rapids, *Mich.* **15** 42 58N 85 40W
Grand Rapids, *Minn.* **12** 47 14N 93 31W
Grand Teton, *Idaho* **16** 43 54N 111 50W
Grand Valley, *Colo.* **16** 39 27N 108 3W
Grande, Rio →, *Tex.* **13** 25 58N 97 9W
Grandfalls, *Tex.* **13** 31 20N 102 51W
Grandview, *Wash.* **16** 46 15N 119 54W
Granger, *Wash.* **16** 46 21N 120 11W
Granger, *Wyo.* **16** 41 35N 109 58W
Grangeville, *Idaho* **16** 45 56N 116 7W
Granite City, *Ill.* **14** 38 42N 90 9W
Granite Falls, *Minn.* **12** 44 49N 95 33W
Granite Mt., *Calif.* **19** 33 5N 116 28W
Granite Peak, *Mont.* **16** 45 10N 109 48W
Grant, *Nebr.* **12** 40 53N 101 42W
Grant, Mt., *Nev.* **16** 38 34N 118 48W
Grant City, *Mo.* **14** 40 29N 94 25W
Grant Range, *Nev.* **17** 38 30N 115 25W
Grants, *N. Mex.* **17** 35 9N 107 52W
Grants Pass, *Oreg.* **16** 42 26N 123 19W
Grantsburg, *Wis.* **12** 45 47N 92 41W
Grantsville, *Utah* **16** 40 36N 112 28W
Granville, *N. Dak.* **12** 48 16N 100 47W
Granville, *N.Y.* **10** 43 24N 73 16W
Grapeland, *Tex.* **13** 31 30N 95 29W
Grass Range, *Mont.* **16** 47 0N 109 0W
Grass Valley, *Calif.* **18** 39 13N 121 4W
Grass Valley, *Oreg.* **16** 45 22N 120 47W
Grayling, *Mich.* **10** 44 40N 84 43W
Grays Harbor, *Wash.* **16** 46 59N 124 1W
Grays L., *Idaho* **16** 43 4N 111 26W
Great Barrington, *Mass.* **9** 42 12N 73 22W
Great Basin, *Nev.* **16** 40 0N 117 0W
Great Bend, *Kans.* **12** 38 22N 98 46W
Great Bend, *Pa.* **9** 41 58N 75 45W
Great Falls, *Mont.* **16** 47 30N 111 17W
Great Kills, *N.Y.* **20** 40 32N 74 9W
Great Neck, *N.Y.* **21** 40 48N 73 44W
Great Plains, *N. Amer.* **2** 47 0N 105 0W
Great Salt L., *Utah* **16** 41 15N 112 40W
Great Salt Lake Desert, *Utah* **16** 40 50N 113 30W
Great Salt Plains L., *Okla.* **13** 36 45N 98 8W
Great Sitkin I., *Alaska* **30** 52 3N 176 6W
Great Smoky Mts. Nat. Pk., *Tenn.* **11** 35 40N 83 40W
Greater Pittsburgh International Airport, *Pa.* **27** 40 29N 80 13W
Greeley, *Colo.* **12** 40 25N 104 42W
Greeley, *Nebr.* **12** 41 33N 98 32W
Green →, *Ky.* **10** 37 54N 87 30W
Green →, *Utah* **17** 38 11N 109 53W
Green B., *Wis.* **10** 45 0N 87 30W
Green Bay, *Wis.* **10** 44 31N 88 0W
Green Cove Springs, *Fla.* **11** 29 59N 81 42W
Green River, *Utah* **17** 38 59N 110 10W
Green Tree, *Pa.* **27** 40 25N 80 4W
Greenbelt, *Md.* **25** 39 0N 76 52W
Greenbush, *Minn.* **12** 48 42N 96 11W
Greencastle, *Ind.* **15** 39 38N 86 52W
Greene, *N.Y.* **9** 42 20N 75 46W
Greenfield, *Calif.* **18** 36 19N 121 15W
Greenfield, *Calif.* **19** 35 15N 119 0W
Greenfield, *Ind.* **15** 39 47N 85 46W
Greenfield, *Iowa* **14** 41 18N 94 28W
Greenfield, *Mass.* **9** 42 35N 72 36W
Greenfield, *Mo.* **13** 37 25N 93 51W
Greenport, *N.Y.* **9** 41 6N 72 22W
Greensboro, *Ga.* **11** 33 35N 83 11W
Greensboro, *N.C.* **11** 36 4N 79 48W
Greensburg, *Ind.* **15** 39 20N 85 29W
Greensburg, *Kans.* **13** 37 36N 99 18W
Greensburg, *Pa.* **8** 40 18N 79 33W
Greenville, *Ala.* **11** 31 50N 86 38W
Greenville, *Calif.* **18** 40 8N 120 57W
Greenville, *Ill.* **14** 38 53N 89 25W
Greenville, *Maine* **11** 45 28N 69 35W
Greenville, *Mich.* **15** 43 11N 85 15W
Greenville, *Miss.* **13** 33 24N 91 4W
Greenville, *N.C.* **11** 35 37N 77 23W
Greenville, *Ohio* **15** 40 6N 84 38W
Greenville, *Pa.* **8** 41 24N 80 23W
Greenville, *S.C.* **11** 34 51N 82 24W
Greenville, *Tenn.* **11** 36 13N 82 51W
Greenville, *Tex.* **13** 33 8N 96 7W
Greenwich, *Conn.* **21** 41 1N 73 38W
Greenwich, *N.Y.* **9** 43 5N 73 30W
Greenwood, *Miss.* **13** 33 31N 90 11W
Greenwood, *S.C.* **11** 34 12N 82 10W
Gregory, *S. Dak.* **12** 43 14N 99 20W
Grenada, *Miss.* **13** 33 47N 89 49W
Grenora, *N. Dak.* **12** 48 37N 103 56W
Gresham, *Oreg.* **18** 45 30N 122 26W
Greybull, *Wyo.* **16** 44 30N 108 3W
Gridley, *Calif.* **18** 39 22N 121 42W
Griffin, *Ga.* **11** 33 15N 84 16W
Grinnell, *Iowa* **14** 41 45N 92 43W
Groesbeck, *Tex.* **13** 30 48N 96 31W
Groom, *Tex.* **13** 35 12N 101 6W
Grosse Pointe, *Mich.* **26** 42 23N 82 54W
Groton, *Conn.* **9** 41 21N 72 5W
Groton, *S. Dak.* **12** 45 27N 98 6W
Grouse Creek, *Utah* **16** 41 42N 113 53W
Groveland, *Calif.* **18** 37 50N 120 14W
Grover City, *Calif.* **19** 35 7N 120 37W
Groveton, *N.H.* **9** 44 36N 71 31W
Groveton, *Tex.* **13** 31 4N 95 8W
Grundy Center, *Iowa* **14** 42 22N 92 47W
Gruver, *Tex.* **13** 36 16N 101 24W
Guadalupe, *Calif.* **19** 34 59N 120 33W
Guadalupe →, *Tex.* **13** 28 27N 96 47W
Guadalupe Peak, *Tex.* **17** 31 50N 104 52W
Guam ■, *Pac. Oc.* **31** 13 27N 144 45 E
Guánica, *Puerto Rico* **30** 17 58N 66 55W
Guayama, *Puerto Rico* **30** 17 59N 66 7W
Guernsey, *Wyo.* **12** 42 19N 104 45W
Gueydan, *La.* **13** 30 2N 92 31W
Guilford, *Maine* **11** 45 10N 69 23W
Gulfport, *Miss.* **13** 30 22N 89 6W
Gulkana, *Alaska* **30** 62 16N 145 23W
Gunnison, *Colo.* **17** 38 33N 106 56W
Gunnison, *Utah* **16** 39 9N 111 49W
Gunnison →, *Colo.* **17** 39 4N 108 35W
Guntersville, *Ala.* **11** 34 21N 86 18W
Gurdon, *Ark.* **13** 33 55N 93 9W
Gustavus, *Alaska* **30** 58 25N 136 44W
Gustine, *Calif.* **18** 37 16N 121 0W
Guthrie, *Okla.* **13** 35 53N 97 25W
Guttenberg, *Iowa* **14** 42 47N 91 6W
Guymon, *Okla.* **13** 36 41N 101 29W
Gwinn, *Mich.* **10** 46 19N 87 27W

H

Hackensack, *N.J.* **20** 40 53N 74 3W
Haddonfield, *N.J.* **24** 39 53N 75 2W
Hagemeister I., *Alaska* **30** 58 39N 160 54W
Hagerman, *N. Mex.* **13** 33 7N 104 20W
Hagerstown, *Md.* **10** 39 39N 77 43W
Hailey, *Idaho* **16** 43 31N 114 19W
Haines, *Alaska* **30** 59 14N 135 26W
Haines, *Oreg.* **16** 44 55N 117 56W
Haines City, *Fla.* **11** 28 7N 81 38W
Halawa, *Hawaii* **30** 21 9N 156 47W
Haleakala Crater, *Hawaii* **30** 20 43N 156 16W
Halethorpe, *Md.* **25** 39 14N 76 41W
Haleyville, *Ala.* **11** 34 14N 87 37W
Half Moon B., *Calif.* **28** 37 29N 122 28W
Half Moon Bay, *Calif.* **28** 37 27N 122 25W
Hallettsville, *Tex.* **13** 29 27N 96 57W
Halliday, *N. Dak.* **12** 47 21N 102 20W
Hallstead, *Pa.* **9** 41 58N 75 45W
Halstad, *Minn.* **12** 47 21N 96 50W
Hamburg, *Ark.* **13** 33 14N 91 48W
Hamburg, *Iowa* **12** 40 36N 95 39W
Hamburg, *Pa.* **9** 40 33N 75 59W
Hamden, *Conn.* **9** 41 23N 72 54W
Hamilton, *Alaska* **30** 62 54N 163 53W
Hamilton, *Mo.* **12** 39 45N 93 59W
Hamilton, *Mont.* **16** 46 15N 114 10W
Hamilton, *N.Y.* **9** 42 50N 75 33W
Hamilton, *Ohio* **15** 39 24N 84 34W
Hamilton, *Tex.* **13** 31 42N 98 7W
Hamlet, *N.C.* **11** 34 53N 79 42W
Hamlin, *Tex.* **13** 32 53N 100 8W
Hammond, *Ind.* **22** 41 35N 87 29W
Hammond, *La.* **13** 30 30N 90 28W
Hammonton, *N.J.* **10** 39 39N 74 48W
Hampton, *Ark.* **13** 33 32N 92 28W
Hampton, *Iowa* **14** 42 45N 93 13W
Hampton, *N.H.* **9** 42 57N 70 50W
Hampton, *S.C.* **11** 32 52N 81 7W
Hampton, *Va.* **10** 37 2N 76 21W
Hamtramck, *Mich.* **26** 42 23N 83 4W
Hana, *Hawaii* **30** 20 45N 155 59W
Hancock, *Mich.* **12** 47 8N 88 35W
Hancock, *Minn.* **12** 45 30N 95 48W
Hancock, *N.Y.* **9** 41 57N 75 17W
Hanford, *Calif.* **18** 36 20N 119 39W
Hankinson, *N. Dak.* **12** 46 4N 96 54W
Hanksville, *Utah* **17** 38 22N 110 43W
Hannaford, *N. Dak.* **12** 47 19N 98 11W
Hannah, *N. Dak.* **12** 48 58N 98 42W
Hannibal, *Mo.* **14** 39 42N 91 22W
Hanover, *N.H.* **9** 43 42N 72 17W
Hanover, *Pa.* **10** 39 48N 76 59W
Happy, *Tex.* **13** 34 45N 101 52W
Happy Camp, *Calif.* **16** 41 48N 123 23W
Harbor Beach, *Mich.* **10** 43 51N 82 39W
Harbor Springs, *Mich.* **10** 45 26N 85 0W
Hardin, *Mont.* **16** 45 44N 107 37W
Hardman, *Oreg.* **16** 45 10N 119 41W
Hardy, *Ark.* **13** 36 19N 91 29W
Harlan, *Iowa* **12** 41 39N 95 19W
Harlan, *Ky.* **11** 36 51N 83 19W
Harlem, *Mont.* **16** 48 32N 108 47W
Harlem, *N.Y.* **20** 40 48N 73 56W
Harlingen, *Tex.* **13** 26 12N 97 42W
Harlowton, *Mont.* **16** 46 26N 109 50W
Harney Basin, *Oreg.* **16** 43 30N 119 0W
Harney L., *Oreg.* **16** 43 14N 119 8W
Harney Peak, *S. Dak.* **12** 43 52N 103 32W
Harper, Mt., *Alaska* **30** 64 14N 143 51W
Harper Woods, *Mich.* **26** 42 26N 82 56W
Harriman, *Tenn.* **11** 35 56N 84 33W
Harrisburg, *Ill.* **15** 37 44N 88 32W
Harrisburg, *Nebr.* **12** 41 33N 103 44W
Harrisburg, *Oreg.* **16** 44 16N 123 10W
Harrisburg, *Pa.* **8** 40 16N 76 53W
Harrison, *Ark.* **13** 36 14N 93 7W
Harrison, *Idaho* **16** 47 27N 116 47W
Harrison, *Nebr.* **12** 42 41N 103 53W
Harrison Bay, *Alaska* **30** 70 40N 151 0W
Harrisonburg, *Va.* **10** 38 27N 78 52W
Harrisonville, *Mo.* **14** 38 39N 94 21W
Harrisville, *Mich.* **8** 44 39N 83 17W
Hart, *Mich.* **10** 43 42N 86 22W
Hartford, *Conn.* **9** 41 46N 72 41W
Hartford, *Ky.* **10** 37 27N 86 55W
Hartford, *S. Dak.* **12** 43 38N 96 57W
Hartford, *Wis.* **12** 43 19N 88 22W
Hartford City, *Ind.* **15** 40 27N 85 22W
Hartselle, *Ala.* **11** 34 27N 86 56W
Hartshorne, *Okla.* **13** 34 51N 95 34W
Hartsville, *S.C.* **11** 34 23N 80 4W
Hartwell, *Ga.* **11** 34 21N 82 56W
Harvard University, *Mass.* **23** 42 22N 71 7W
Harvey, *Ill.* **22** 41 36N 87 39W
Harvey, *N. Dak.* **12** 47 47N 99 56W
Harwood Heights, *Ill.* **22** 41 57N 87 47W
Haskell, *Okla.* **13** 35 50N 95 40W
Haskell, *Tex.* **13** 33 10N 99 44W
Hastings, *Mich.* **15** 42 39N 85 17W
Hastings, *Minn.* **12** 44 44N 92 51W
Hastings, *Nebr.* **12** 40 35N 98 23W
Hatch, *N. Mex.* **17** 32 40N 107 9W
Hatteras, C., *N.C.* **11** 35 14N 75 32W
Hattiesburg, *Miss.* **13** 31 20N 89 17W
Havana, *Ill.* **14** 40 18N 90 4W
Havasu, L., *Ariz.* **19** 34 18N 114 28W
Haverhill, *Mass.* **9** 42 47N 71 5W
Haverstraw, *N.Y.* **9** 41 12N 73 58W
Havertown, *Pa.* **24** 39 58N 75 18W
Havre, *Mont.* **16** 48 33N 109 41W
Haw →, *N.C.* **11** 35 36N 79 3W
Hawaii □ **30** 19 30N 156 30W
Hawaii I., *Pac. Oc.* **30** 20 0N 155 0W
Hawaiian Is., *Pac. Oc.* **30** 20 30N 156 0W
Hawarden, *Iowa* **12** 43 0N 96 29W
Hawkinsville, *Ga.* **11** 32 17N 83 28W
Hawley, *Minn.* **12** 46 53N 96 19W
Hawthorne, *Calif.* **29** 33 54N 118 21W
Hawthorne, *Nev.* **16** 38 32N 118 38W
Haxtun, *Colo.* **12** 40 39N 102 38W
Hay Springs, *Nebr.* **12** 42 41N 102 41W
Hayden, *Ariz.* **17** 33 0N 110 47W
Hayden, *Colo.* **16** 40 30N 107 16W
Hayes, *S. Dak.* **12** 44 23N 101 1W
Haynesville, *La.* **13** 32 58N 93 8W
Hays, *Kans.* **12** 38 53N 99 20W
Hayward, *Calif.* **28** 37 40N 122 4W
Hayward, *Wis.* **12** 46 1N 91 29W
Hazard, *Ky.* **10** 37 15N 83 12W
Hazel Park, *Mich.* **26** 42 28N 83 5W
Hazelton, *N. Dak.* **12** 46 29N 100 17W
Hazen, *N. Dak.* **12** 47 18N 101 38W
Hazen, *Nev.* **16** 39 34N 119 3W
Hazlehurst, *Ga.* **11** 31 52N 82 36W
Hazlehurst, *Miss.* **13** 31 52N 90 24W
Hazleton, *Pa.* **9** 40 57N 75 59W
Healdsburg, *Calif.* **18** 38 37N 122 52W
Healdton, *Okla.* **13** 34 14N 97 29W
Hearne, *Tex.* **13** 30 53N 96 36W
Heart →, *N. Dak.* **12** 46 46N 100 50W
Heavener, *Okla.* **13** 34 53N 94 36W
Hebbronville, *Tex.* **13** 27 18N 98 41W
Heber Springs, *Ark.* **13** 35 30N 92 2W
Hebgen L., *Mont.* **16** 44 52N 111 20W
Hebron, *N. Dak.* **12** 46 54N 102 3W
Hebron, *Nebr.* **12** 40 10N 97 35W
Hecla, *S. Dak.* **12** 45 53N 98 9W
Hedley, *Tex.* **13** 34 52N 100 39W
Helena, *Ark.* **13** 34 32N 90 36W
Helena, *Mont.* **16** 46 36N 112 2W
Helendale, *Calif.* **19** 34 44N 117 19W
Helper, *Utah* **16** 39 41N 110 51W
Hemet, *Calif.* **19** 33 45N 116 58W
Hemingford, *Nebr.* **12** 42 19N 103 4W
Hemphill, *Tex.* **13** 31 20N 93 51W
Hempstead, *N.Y.* **21** 40 42N 73 37W
Hempstead, *Tex.* **13** 30 6N 96 5W
Henderson, *Ky.* **15** 37 50N 87 35W
Henderson, *N.C.* **11** 36 20N 78 25W
Henderson, *Nev.* **19** 36 2N 114 59W
Henderson, *Tenn.* **11** 35 26N 88 38W
Henderson, *Tex.* **13** 32 9N 94 48W
Hendersonville, *N.C.* **11** 35 19N 82 28W
Henlopen, C., *Del.* **10** 38 48N 75 6W
Hennessey, *Okla.* **13** 36 6N 97 54W
Henrietta, *Tex.* **13** 33 49N 98 12W
Henry, *Ill.* **14** 41 7N 89 22W
Henryetta, *Okla.* **13** 35 27N 95 59W
Heppner, *Oreg.* **16** 45 21N 119 33W
Herbert I., *Alaska* **30** 52 45N 170 7W
Hereford, *Tex.* **13** 34 49N 102 24W
Herington, *Kans.* **12** 38 40N 96 57W
Herkimer, *N.Y.* **9** 43 0N 74 59W
Herman, *Minn.* **12** 45 49N 96 9W
Hermann, *Mo.* **12** 38 42N 91 27W
Hermiston, *Oreg.* **16** 45 51N 119 17W

Keewatin

Hernandez, *Calif.* **18** 36 24N 120 46W
Hernando, *Miss.* **13** 34 50N 90 0W
Herreid, *S. Dak.* **12** 45 50N 100 4W
Herrin, *Ill.* **14** 37 48N 89 2W
Hesperia, *Calif.* **19** 34 25N 117 18W
Hetch Hetchy Aqueduct, *Calif.* **18** 37 29N 122 19W
Hettinger, *N. Dak.* **12** 46 0N 102 42W
Hi Vista, *Calif.* **19** 34 45N 117 46W
Hialeah, *Fla.* **11** 25 50N 80 17W
Hiawatha, *Kans.* **12** 39 51N 95 32W
Hiawatha, *Utah* **16** 39 29N 111 1W
Hibbing, *Minn.* **12** 47 25N 92 56W
Hickory, *N.C.* **11** 35 44N 81 21W
Hickory Hills, *Ill.* **22** 41 43N 87 50W
Hicksville, *N.Y.* **21** 40 46N 73 30W
Higgins, *Tex.* **13** 36 7N 100 2W
High Island, *Tex.* **13** 29 34N 94 24W
High Point, *N.C.* **11** 35 57N 80 0W
High Springs, *Fla.* **11** 29 50N 82 36W
Highland Park, *Ill.* **15** 42 11N 87 48W
Highland Park, *Mich.* **26** 42 24N 83 6W
Highmore, *S. Dak.* **12** 44 31N 99 27W
Hiko, *Nev.* **18** 37 32N 115 14W
Hill City, *Idaho* **16** 43 18N 115 3W
Hill City, *Kans.* **12** 39 22N 99 51W
Hill City, *Minn.* **12** 46 59N 93 36W
Hill City, *S. Dak.* **12** 43 56N 103 35W
Hillcrest Heights, *Md.* **25** 38 50N 76 57W
Hillman, *Mich.* **10** 45 4N 83 54W
Hillsboro, *Kans.* **12** 38 21N 97 12W
Hillsboro, *N. Dak.* **12** 47 26N 97 3W
Hillsboro, *N.H.* **9** 43 7N 71 54W
Hillsboro, *N. Mex.* **17** 32 55N 107 34W
Hillsboro, *Oreg.* **18** 45 31N 122 59W
Hillsboro, *Tex.* **13** 32 1N 97 8W
Hillsdale, *Mich.* **15** 41 56N 84 38W
Hillsdale, *N.J.* **20** 41 0N 74 2W
Hillsdale, *N.Y.* **9** 42 11N 73 30W
Hilo, *Hawaii* **30** 19 44N 155 5W
Hinckley, *Utah* **16** 39 20N 112 40W
Hingham, *Mass.* **23** 42 14N 70 54W
Hingham, *Mont.* **16** 48 33N 110 25W
Hinsdale, *Ill.* **22** 41 47N 87 56W
Hinsdale, *Mont.* **16** 48 24N 107 5W
Hinton, *W. Va.* **10** 37 40N 80 54W
Hobart, *Okla.* **13** 35 1N 99 6W
Hobbs, *N. Mex.* **13** 32 42N 103 8W
Hoboken, *N.J.* **20** 40 44N 74 3W
Hogansville, *Ga.* **11** 33 10N 84 55W
Hogeland, *Mont.* **16** 48 51N 108 40W
Hohenwald, *Tenn.* **11** 35 33N 87 33W
Hoisington, *Kans.* **12** 38 31N 98 47W
Holbrook, *Ariz.* **17** 34 54N 110 10W
Holden, *Utah* **16** 39 6N 112 16W
Holdenville, *Okla.* **13** 35 5N 96 24W
Holdrege, *Nebr.* **12** 40 26N 99 23W
Holland, *Mich.* **15** 42 47N 86 7W
Hollidaysburg, *Pa.* **8** 40 26N 78 24W
Hollis, *Okla.* **13** 34 41N 99 55W
Hollister, *Calif.* **18** 36 51N 121 24W
Hollister, *Idaho* **16** 42 21N 114 35W
Holly, *Colo.* **12** 38 3N 102 7W
Holly Hill, *Fla.* **11** 29 16N 81 3W
Holly Springs, *Miss.* **13** 34 46N 89 27W
Hollywood, *Calif.* **17** 34 7N 118 25W
Hollywood, *Fla.* **11** 26 1N 80 9W
Holton, *Kans.* **12** 39 28N 95 44W
Holtville, *Calif.* **19** 32 49N 115 23W
Holy Cross, *Alaska* **30** 62 12N 159 46W
Holyoke, *Colo.* **12** 40 35N 102 18W
Holyoke, *Mass.* **9** 42 12N 72 37W
Homedale, *Idaho* **16** 43 37N 116 56W
Homer, *Alaska* **30** 59 39N 151 33W
Homer, *La.* **13** 32 48N 93 4W
Homestead, *Fla.* **11** 25 28N 80 29W
Homestead, *Oreg.* **16** 45 2N 116 51W
Homestead, *Pa.* **27** 40 24N 79 55W
Hominy, *Okla.* **13** 36 25N 96 24W
Hondo, *Tex.* **13** 29 21N 99 9W
Honey L., *Calif.* **18** 40 15N 120 19W
Honolulu, *Hawaii* **30** 21 19N 157 52W
Hood, Mt., *Oreg.* **16** 45 23N 121 42W
Hood River, *Oreg.* **16** 45 43N 121 31W
Hoodsport, *Wash.* **18** 47 24N 123 9W
Hooker, *Okla.* **13** 36 52N 101 13W
Hoonah, *Alaska* **30** 58 7N 135 27W
Hooper Bay, *Alaska* **30** 61 32N 166 6W
Hoopeston, *Ill.* **15** 40 28N 87 40W
Hoover Dam, *Ariz.* **19** 36 1N 114 44W
Hop Bottom, *Pa.* **9** 41 42N 75 46W
Hope, *Ark.* **13** 33 40N 93 36W
Hope, *N. Dak.* **12** 47 19N 97 43W
Hope, Pt., *Alaska* **30** 68 20N 166 50W
Hopkins, *Mo.* **14** 40 33N 94 49W
Hopkinsville, *Ky.* **11** 36 52N 87 29W
Hopland, *Calif.* **18** 38 58N 123 7W
Hoquiam, *Wash.* **18** 46 59N 123 53W
Horn I., *Miss.* **11** 30 14N 88 39W
Hornbeck, *La.* **13** 31 20N 93 24W
Hornbrook, *Calif.* **16** 41 55N 122 33W
Hornell, *N.Y.* **8** 42 20N 77 40W
Hornitos, *Calif.* **18** 37 30N 120 14W
Horse Creek, *Wyo.* **12** 41 57N 105 10W
Horton, *Kans.* **12** 39 40N 95 32W
Hosmer, *S. Dak.* **12** 45 34N 99 28W
Hot Creek Range, *Nev.* **16** 38 40N 116 20W
Hot Springs, *Ark.* **13** 34 31N 93 3W
Hot Springs, *S. Dak.* **12** 43 26N 103 29W
Hotchkiss, *Colo.* **17** 38 48N 107 43W
Houck, *Ariz.* **17** 35 20N 109 10W
Houghton, *Mich.* **12** 47 7N 88 34W
Houghton L., *Mich.* **10** 44 21N 84 44W
Houlton, *Maine* **11** 46 8N 67 51W
Houma, *La.* **13** 29 36N 90 43W
Houston, *Mo.* **13** 37 22N 91 58W
Houston, *Tex.* **13** 29 46N 95 22W
Howard, *Kans.* **13** 37 28N 96 16W
Howard, *S. Dak.* **12** 44 1N 97 32W
Howe, *Idaho* **16** 43 48N 113 0W
Howell, *Mich.* **15** 42 36N 83 56W
Hualapai Peak, *Ariz.* **17** 35 5N 113 54W
Huasna, *Calif.* **19** 35 6N 120 24W
Hubbard, *Tex.* **13** 31 51N 96 48W
Hudson, *Mich.* **15** 41 51N 84 21W
Hudson, *N.Y.* **9** 42 15N 73 46W
Hudson, *Wis.* **12** 44 58N 92 45W
Hudson, *Wyo.* **16** 42 54N 108 35W
Hudson →, *N.Y.* **9** 40 42N 74 2W
Hudson Falls, *N.Y.* **9** 43 18N 73 35W
Hughes, *Alaska* **30** 66 3N 154 15W
Hugo, *Colo.* **12** 39 8N 103 28W
Hugoton, *Kans.* **13** 37 11N 101 21W
Hull, *Mass.* **23** 42 18N 70 54W
Humacao, *Puerto Rico* **30** 18 9N 65 50W
Humble, *Tex.* **13** 29 59N 93 18W
Humboldt, *Iowa* **14** 42 44N 94 13W
Humboldt, *Tenn.* **13** 35 50N 88 55W
Humboldt →, *Nev.* **16** 39 59N 118 36W
Hume, *Calif.* **18** 36 48N 118 54W
Humphreys, Mt., *Calif.* **18** 37 17N 118 40W
Humphreys Peak, *Ariz.* **17** 35 21N 111 41W
Hunter, *N. Dak.* **12** 47 12N 97 13W
Hunter, *N.Y.* **9** 42 13N 74 13W
Huntingburg, *Ind.* **15** 38 18N 86 57W
Huntingdon, *Pa.* **8** 40 30N 78 1W
Huntington, *Ind.* **15** 40 53N 85 30W
Huntington, *N.Y.* **21** 40 52N 73 25W
Huntington, *Oreg.* **16** 44 21N 117 16W
Huntington, *Utah* **16** 39 20N 110 58W
Huntington, *W. Va.* **10** 38 25N 82 27W
Huntington Beach, *Calif.* **19** 33 40N 118 5W
Huntington Park, *Calif.* **29** 33 58N 118 13W
Huntington Woods, *Mich.* **26** 42 28N 83 10W
Huntsville, *Ala.* **11** 34 44N 86 35W
Huntsville, *Tex.* **13** 30 43N 95 33W
Hurley, *N. Mex.* **17** 32 42N 108 8W
Hurley, *Wis.* **12** 46 27N 90 11W
Huron, *Calif.* **18** 36 12N 120 6W
Huron, *S. Dak.* **12** 44 22N 98 13W
Huron, L., *Mich.* **8** 44 30N 82 40W
Hurricane, *Utah* **17** 37 11N 113 17W
Huslia, *Alaska* **30** 65 41N 156 24W
Hutchinson, *Kans.* **13** 38 5N 97 56W
Hutchinson, *Minn.* **12** 44 54N 94 22W
Huttig, *Ark.* **13** 33 2N 92 11W
Hyannis, *Nebr.* **12** 42 0N 101 46W
Hyattsville, *Md.* **25** 38 57N 76 58W
Hydaburg, *Alaska* **30** 55 12N 132 50W
Hyndman Peak, *Idaho* **16** 43 45N 114 8W
Hyrum, *Utah* **16** 41 38N 111 51W
Hysham, *Mont.* **16** 46 18N 107 14W

I

Ida Grove, *Iowa* **12** 42 21N 95 28W
Idabel, *Okla.* **13** 33 54N 94 50W
Idaho □ **16** 45 0N 115 0W
Idaho City, *Idaho* **16** 43 50N 115 50W
Idaho Falls, *Idaho* **16** 43 30N 112 2W
Idaho Springs, *Colo.* **16** 39 45N 105 31W
Idria, *Calif.* **18** 36 25N 120 41W
Iliamna L., *Alaska* **30** 59 30N 155 0W
Iliff, *Colo.* **12** 40 45N 103 4W
Ilio Pt., *Hawaii* **30** 21 13N 157 16W
Ilion, *N.Y.* **9** 43 1N 75 2W
Illinois □ **14** 40 15N 89 30W
Illinois →, *Ill.* **14** 38 58N 90 28W
Imbler, *Oreg.* **16** 45 28N 117 58W
Imlay, *Nev.* **16** 40 40N 118 9W
Immokalee, *Fla.* **11** 26 25N 81 25W
Imperial, *Calif.* **19** 32 51N 115 34W
Imperial, *Nebr.* **12** 40 31N 101 39W
Imperial Beach, *Calif.* **19** 32 35N 117 8W
Imperial Dam, *Ariz.* **19** 32 55N 114 25W
Independence, *Calif.* **18** 36 48N 118 12W
Independence, *Iowa* **14** 42 28N 91 54W
Independence, *Kans.* **13** 37 14N 95 42W
Independence, *Mo.* **14** 39 6N 94 25W
Independence, *Oreg.* **16** 44 51N 123 11W
Independence Mts., *Nev.* **16** 41 20N 116 0W
Indian →, *Fla.* **11** 27 59N 80 34W
Indiana, *Pa.* **8** 40 37N 79 9W
Indiana □ **15** 40 0N 86 0W
Indianapolis, *Ind.* **15** 39 46N 86 9W
Indianola, *Iowa* **14** 41 22N 93 34W
Indianola, *Miss.* **13** 33 27N 90 39W
Indio, *Calif.* **19** 33 43N 116 13W
Inglewood, *Calif.* **29** 33 57N 118 19W
Ingomar, *Mont.* **16** 46 35N 107 23W
Inkom, *Idaho* **16** 42 48N 112 15W
Inkster, *Mich.* **26** 42 17N 83 16W
Interior, *S. Dak.* **12** 43 44N 101 59W
International Falls, *Minn.* **12** 48 36N 93 25W
Inverness, *Fla.* **11** 28 50N 82 20W
Inyo Mts., *Calif.* **17** 36 40N 118 0W
Inyokern, *Calif.* **19** 35 39N 117 49W
Iola, *Kans.* **13** 37 55N 95 24W
Ione, *Calif.* **18** 38 21N 120 56W
Ione, *Wash.* **16** 48 45N 117 25W
Ionia, *Mich.* **15** 42 59N 85 4W
Iowa □ **12** 42 18N 93 30W
Iowa City, *Iowa* **14** 41 40N 91 32W
Iowa Falls, *Iowa* **14** 42 31N 93 16W
Ipswich, *Mass.* **23** 42 41N 70 50W
Ipswich, *S. Dak.* **12** 45 27N 99 2W
Iron Mountain, *Mich.* **10** 45 49N 88 4W
Iron River, *Mich.* **12** 46 6N 88 39W
Ironton, *Mo.* **13** 37 36N 90 38W
Ironton, *Ohio* **10** 38 32N 82 41W
Ironwood, *Mich.* **12** 46 27N 90 9W
Irvine, *Ky.* **15** 37 42N 83 58W
Irvington, *N.Y.* **20** 40 42N 74 13W
Isabel, *S. Dak.* **12** 45 24N 101 26W
Isabela, *Puerto Rico* **30** 18 30N 67 2W
Ishpeming, *Mich.* **10** 46 29N 87 40W
Isla Vista, *Calif.* **19** 34 25N 119 53W
Island Falls, *Maine* **11** 46 1N 68 16W
Island Pond, *Vt.* **9** 44 49N 71 53W
Isle Royale, *Mich.* **12** 48 0N 88 54W
Isleta, *N. Mex.* **17** 34 55N 106 42W
Isleton, *Calif.* **18** 38 10N 121 37W
Ismay, *Mont.* **12** 46 30N 104 48W
Istokpoga, L., *Fla.* **11** 27 23N 81 17W
Ithaca, *N.Y.* **9** 42 27N 76 30W
Ivanhoe, *Calif.* **18** 36 23N 119 13W

J

Jackman, *Maine* **11** 45 35N 70 17W
Jacksboro, *Tex.* **13** 33 14N 98 15W
Jackson, *Ala.* **11** 31 31N 87 53W
Jackson, *Calif.* **18** 38 21N 120 46W
Jackson, *Ky.* **10** 37 33N 83 23W
Jackson, *Mich.* **15** 42 15N 84 24W
Jackson, *Minn.* **12** 43 37N 95 1W
Jackson, *Miss.* **13** 32 18N 90 12W
Jackson, *Mo.* **13** 37 23N 89 40W
Jackson, *Ohio* **10** 39 3N 82 39W
Jackson, *Tenn.* **11** 35 37N 88 49W
Jackson, *Wyo.* **16** 43 29N 110 46W
Jackson Heights, *N.Y.* **21** 40 44N 73 53W
Jackson L., *Wyo.* **16** 43 52N 110 36W
Jacksonville, *Ala.* **11** 33 49N 85 46W
Jacksonville, *Calif.* **18** 37 52N 120 24W
Jacksonville, *Fla.* **11** 30 20N 81 39W
Jacksonville, *Ill.* **14** 39 44N 90 14W
Jacksonville, *N.C.* **11** 34 45N 77 26W
Jacksonville, *Oreg.* **16** 42 19N 122 57W
Jacksonville, *Tex.* **13** 31 58N 95 17W
Jacksonville Beach, *Fla.* **11** 30 17N 81 24W
Jacob Lake, *Ariz.* **17** 36 43N 112 13W
Jal, *N. Mex.* **13** 32 7N 103 12W
Jalama, *Calif.* **19** 34 29N 120 29W
Jaluit I., *Pac. Oc.* **31** 6 0N 169 30 E
Jamaica, *N.Y.* **21** 40 42N 73 48W
James →, *S. Dak.* **12** 42 52N 97 18W
Jamestown, *Ky.* **10** 36 59N 85 4W
Jamestown, *N. Dak.* **12** 46 54N 98 42W
Jamestown, *N.Y.* **8** 42 6N 79 14W
Jamestown, *Tenn.* **11** 36 26N 84 56W
Janesville, *Wis.* **14** 42 41N 89 1W
Jasper, *Ala.* **11** 33 50N 87 17W
Jasper, *Fla.* **11** 30 31N 82 57W
Jasper, *Minn.* **12** 43 51N 96 24W
Jasper, *Tex.* **13** 30 56N 94 1W
Jay, *Okla.* **13** 36 25N 94 48W
Jayton, *Tex.* **13** 33 15N 100 34W
Jean, *Nev.* **19** 35 47N 115 20W
Jeanerette, *La.* **13** 29 55N 91 40W
Jefferson, *Iowa* **14** 42 1N 94 23W
Jefferson, *Tex.* **13** 32 46N 94 21W
Jefferson, *Wis.* **15** 43 0N 88 48W
Jefferson, Mt., *Nev.* **16** 38 51N 117 0W
Jefferson, Mt., *Oreg.* **16** 44 41N 121 48W
Jefferson City, *Mo.* **14** 38 34N 92 10W
Jefferson City, *Tenn.* **11** 36 7N 83 30W
Jeffersonville, *Ind.* **15** 38 17N 85 44W
Jena, *La.* **13** 31 41N 92 8W
Jenkins, *Ky.* **10** 37 10N 82 38W
Jennings, *La.* **13** 30 13N 92 40W
Jermyn, *Pa.* **9** 41 31N 75 31W
Jerome, *Ariz.* **17** 34 45N 112 7W
Jersey City, *N.J.* **20** 40 42N 74 4W
Jersey Shore, *Pa.* **8** 41 12N 77 15W
Jerseyville, *Ill.* **14** 39 7N 90 20W
Jesup, *Ga.* **11** 31 36N 81 53W
Jetmore, *Kans.* **13** 38 4N 99 54W
Jewett, *Tex.* **13** 31 22N 96 9W
Jewett City, *Conn.* **9** 41 36N 72 0W
Johannesburg, *Calif.* **19** 35 22N 117 38W
John Day, *Oreg.* **16** 44 25N 118 57W
John Day →, *Oreg.* **16** 45 44N 120 39W
John F.Kennedy International Airport, *N.Y.* **21** 40 38N 73 46W
John H. Kerr Reservoir, *N.C.* **11** 36 36N 78 18W
Johnson, *Kans.* **13** 37 34N 101 45W
Johnson City, *N.Y.* **9** 42 7N 75 58W
Johnson City, *Tenn.* **11** 36 19N 82 21W
Johnson City, *Tex.* **13** 30 17N 98 25W
Johnsondale, *Calif.* **19** 35 58N 118 32W
Johnstown, *N.Y.* **9** 43 0N 74 22W
Johnstown, *Pa.* **8** 40 20N 78 55W
Joliet, *Ill.* **15** 41 32N 88 5W
Jolon, *Calif.* **18** 35 58N 121 9W
Jonesboro, *Ark.* **13** 35 50N 90 42W
Jonesboro, *Ill.* **13** 37 27N 89 16W
Jonesboro, *La.* **13** 32 15N 92 43W
Jonesport, *Maine* **11** 44 32N 67 37W
Joplin, *Mo.* **13** 37 6N 94 31W
Joppatowne, *Md.* **25** 39 24N 76 21W
Jordan, *Mont.* **16** 47 19N 106 55W
Jordan Valley, *Oreg.* **16** 42 59N 117 3W
Joseph, *Oreg.* **16** 45 21N 117 14W
Joseph City, *Ariz.* **17** 34 57N 110 20W
Joshua Tree, *Calif.* **19** 34 8N 116 19W
Joshua Tree National Monument, *Calif.* **19** 33 55N 116 0W
Jourdanton, *Tex.* **13** 28 55N 98 33W
Judith →, *Mont.* **16** 47 44N 109 39W
Judith, Pt., *R.I.* **9** 41 22N 71 29W
Judith Gap, *Mont.* **16** 46 41N 109 45W
Julesburg, *Colo.* **12** 40 59N 102 16W
Julian, *Calif.* **19** 33 4N 116 38W
Junction, *Tex.* **13** 30 29N 99 46W
Junction, *Utah* **17** 38 14N 112 13W
Junction City, *Kans.* **12** 39 2N 96 50W
Junction City, *Oreg.* **16** 44 13N 123 12W
Juneau, *Alaska* **30** 58 18N 134 25W
Juniata →, *Pa.* **8** 40 30N 77 40W
Juntura, *Oreg.* **16** 43 45N 118 5W
Justice, *Ill.* **22** 41 44N 87 49W

K

Ka Lae, *Hawaii* **30** 18 55N 155 41W
Kaala, *Hawaii* **30** 21 31N 158 9W
Kadoka, *S. Dak.* **12** 43 50N 101 31W
Kaena Pt., *Hawaii* **30** 21 35N 158 17W
Kagamil I., *Alaska* **30** 53 0N 169 43W
Kahoka, *Mo.* **14** 40 25N 91 44W
Kahoolawe, *Hawaii* **30** 20 33N 156 37W
Kahuku Pt., *Hawaii* **30** 21 43N 157 59W
Kahului, *Hawaii* **30** 20 54N 156 28W
Kailua Kona, *Hawaii* **30** 19 39N 155 59W
Kaiwi Channel, *Hawaii* **30** 21 15N 157 30W
Kaiyuh Mts., *Alaska* **30** 64 30N 158 0W
Kake, *Alaska* **30** 56 59N 133 57W
Kaktovik, *Alaska* **30** 70 8N 143 38W
Kalama, *Wash.* **18** 46 1N 122 51W
Kalamazoo, *Mich.* **15** 42 17N 85 35W
Kalamazoo →, *Mich.* **15** 42 40N 86 10W
Kalaupapa, *Hawaii* **30** 21 12N 156 59W
Kalispell, *Mont.* **16** 48 12N 114 19W
Kalkaska, *Mich.* **10** 44 44N 85 11W
Kamalino, *Hawaii* **30** 21 50N 160 14W
Kamiah, *Idaho* **16** 46 14N 116 2W
Kanab, *Utah* **17** 37 3N 112 32W
Kanab →, *Ariz.* **17** 36 24N 112 38W
Kanaga I., *Alaska* **30** 51 45N 177 22W
Kanakanak, *Alaska* **30** 59 0N 158 58W
Kanarraville, *Utah* **17** 37 32N 113 11W
Kanawha →, *W. Va.* **10** 38 50N 82 9W
Kane, *Pa.* **8** 41 40N 78 49W
Kaneohe, *Hawaii* **30** 21 25N 157 48W
Kankakee, *Ill.* **15** 41 7N 87 52W
Kankakee →, *Ill.* **15** 41 23N 88 15W
Kannapolis, *N.C.* **11** 35 30N 80 37W
Kansas □ **12** 38 30N 99 0W
Kansas →, *Kans.* **12** 39 7N 94 37W
Kansas City, *Kans.* **14** 39 7N 94 38W
Kansas City, *Mo.* **14** 39 6N 94 35W
Kantishna, *Alaska* **30** 63 31N 151 5W
Kapaa, *Hawaii* **30** 22 5N 159 19W
Karlstad, *Minn.* **12** 48 35N 96 31W
Karnes City, *Tex.* **13** 28 53N 97 54W
Kaskaskia →, *Ill.* **14** 37 58N 89 57W
Katalla, *Alaska* **30** 60 12N 144 31W
Katmai National Park, *Alaska* **30** 58 20N 155 0W
Kauai, *Hawaii* **30** 22 3N 159 30W
Kauai Channel, *Hawaii* **30** 21 45N 158 50W
Kaufman, *Tex.* **13** 32 35N 96 19W
Kaukauna, *Wis.* **10** 44 17N 88 17W
Kaupulehu, *Hawaii* **30** 19 43N 155 53W
Kawaihae, *Hawaii* **30** 20 3N 155 50W
Kawaihoa Pt., *Hawaii* **30** 21 47N 160 12W
Kawaikimi, *Hawaii* **30** 22 5N 159 29W
Kayak I., *Alaska* **30** 59 56N 144 23W
Kaycee, *Wyo.* **16** 43 43N 106 38W
Kayenta, *Ariz.* **17** 36 44N 110 15W
Kaysville, *Utah* **16** 41 2N 111 56W
Keaau, *Hawaii* **30** 19 37N 155 2W
Keams Canyon, *Ariz.* **17** 35 49N 110 12W
Keanae, *Hawaii* **30** 20 52N 156 9W
Kearney, *Nebr.* **12** 40 42N 99 5W
Kearny, *N.J.* **20** 40 45N 74 9W
Keeler, *Calif.* **18** 36 29N 117 52W
Keene, *Calif.* **19** 35 13N 118 33W
Keene, *N.H.* **9** 42 56N 72 17W
Keewatin, *Minn.* **12** 47 24N 93 5W

Keller

Keller, Wash. 16 48 5N 118 41W
Kellogg, Idaho 16 47 32N 116 7W
Kelso, Wash. 18 46 9N 122 54W
Kemmerer, Wyo. 16 41 48N 110 32W
Kemp, L., Tex. 13 33 46N 99 9W
Kenai, Alaska 30 60 33N 151 16W
Kenai Mts., Alaska 30 60 0N 150 0W
Kendallville, Ind. 15 41 27N 85 16W
Kendrick, Idaho 16 46 37N 116 39W
Kenedy, Tex. 13 28 49N 97 51W
Kenmare, N. Dak. 12 48 41N 102 5W
Kennebec, S. Dak. 12 43 54N 99 52W
Kennett, Mo. 13 36 14N 90 3W
Kennewick, Wash. 16 46 12N 119 7W
Kenosha, Wis. 15 42 35N 87 49W
Kensington, Kans. 12 39 46N 99 2W
Kent, Ohio 8 41 9N 81 22W
Kent, Oreg. 16 45 12N 120 42W
Kent, Tex. 13 31 4N 104 13W
Kentfield, Calif. 28 37 57N 122 33W
Kentland, Ind. 15 40 46N 87 27W
Kenton, Ohio 15 40 39N 83 37W
Kentucky □ 10 37 0N 84 0W
Kentucky →, Ky. 15 38 41N 85 11W
Kentucky L., Ky. 11 37 1N 88 16W
Kentwood, La. 13 31 0N 90 30W
Kentwood, La. 13 30 56N 90 31W
Keokuk, Iowa 14 40 24N 91 24W
Kepuhi, Hawaii 30 21 10N 157 10W
Kerman, Calif. 18 36 43N 120 4W
Kermit, Tex. 13 31 52N 103 6W
Kern →, Calif. 19 35 16N 119 18W
Kernville, Calif. 19 35 45N 118 26W
Kerrville, Tex. 13 30 3N 99 8W
Ketchikan, Alaska 30 55 21N 131 39W
Ketchum, Idaho 16 43 41N 114 22W
Kettle Falls, Wash. 16 48 37N 118 3W
Kettleman City, Calif. 18 36 1N 119 58W
Kevin, Mont. 16 48 45N 111 58W
Kewanee, Ill. 14 41 14N 89 56W
Kewaunee, Wis. 10 44 27N 87 31W
Keweenaw B., Mich. 10 47 0N 88 15W
Keweenaw Pen., Mich. 10 47 30N 88 0W
Keweenaw Pt., Mich. 10 47 25N 87 43W
Keyser, W. Va. 10 39 26N 78 59W
Keystone, S. Dak. 12 43 54N 103 25W
Kijik, Alaska 30 60 20N 154 20W
Kilauea, Hawaii 30 22 13N 159 25W
Kilauea Crater, Hawaii 30 19 25N 155 17W
Kilbuck Mts., Alaska 30 60 30N 160 0W
Kilgore, Tex. 13 32 23N 94 53W
Killdeer, N. Dak. 12 47 26N 102 48W
Killeen, Tex. 13 31 7N 97 44W
Kim, Colo. 13 37 15N 103 21W
Kimball, Nebr. 12 41 14N 103 40W
Kimball, S. Dak. 12 43 45N 98 57W
Kimberly, Idaho 16 42 32N 114 22W
King City, Calif. 18 36 13N 121 8W
King of Prussia, Pa. 24 40 5N 75 22W
Kingfisher, Okla. 13 35 52N 97 56W
Kingman, Ariz. 19 35 12N 114 4W
Kingman, Kans. 13 37 39N 98 7W
Kings →, Calif. 18 36 3N 119 50W
Kings Canyon National Park, Calif. 18 36 50N 118 40W
Kings Mountain, N.C. 11 35 15N 81 20W
King's Peak, Utah 16 40 46N 110 27W
Kingsburg, Calif. 18 36 31N 119 33W
Kingsley, Iowa 12 42 35N 95 58W
Kingsport, Tenn. 11 36 33N 82 33W
Kingston, N.Y. 9 41 56N 73 59W
Kingston, Pa. 9 41 16N 75 54W
Kingston, R.I. 9 41 29N 71 30W
Kingstree, S.C. 11 33 40N 79 50W
Kingsville, Tex. 13 27 31N 97 52W
Kinsley, Kans. 13 37 55N 99 25W
Kinston, N.C. 11 35 16N 77 35W
Kiowa, Kans. 13 37 1N 98 29W
Kiowa, Okla. 13 34 43N 95 54W
Kipnuk, Alaska 30 59 56N 164 3W
Kirkland, Ariz. 17 34 25N 112 43W
Kirksville, Mo. 14 40 12N 92 35W
Kiska I., Alaska 30 51 59N 177 30 E
Kissimmee, Fla. 11 28 18N 81 24W
Kissimmee →, Fla. 11 27 9N 80 52W
Kit Carson, Colo. 12 38 46N 102 48W
Kittanning, Pa. 8 40 49N 79 31W
Kittatinny Mts., N.J. 9 41 0N 75 0W
Kittery, Maine 11 43 5N 70 45W
Kivalina, Alaska 30 67 44N 164 33W
Klamath →, Calif. 16 41 33N 124 5W
Klamath Falls, Oreg. 16 42 13N 121 46W
Klamath Mts., Calif. 16 41 20N 123 0W
Klein, Mont. 16 46 24N 108 33W
Klickitat, Wash. 16 45 49N 121 9W
Knights Ferry, Calif. 18 37 50N 120 40W
Knights Landing, Calif. 18 38 48N 121 43W
Knox, Ind. 15 41 18N 86 37W
Knox City, Tex. 13 33 25N 99 49W
Knoxville, Iowa 14 41 19N 93 6W
Knoxville, Tenn. 11 35 58N 83 55W
Kobuk, Alaska 30 66 55N 156 52W
Kobuk →, Alaska 30 66 55N 157 0W
Kodiak, Alaska 30 57 47N 152 24W
Kodiak I., Alaska 30 57 30N 152 45W
Kokomo, Ind. 15 40 29N 86 8W
Konawa, Okla. 13 34 58N 96 45W
Kooskia, Idaho 16 46 9N 115 59W
Koror, Pac. Oc. 31 7 20N 134 28 E
Kosciusko, Miss. 13 33 4N 89 35W
Kotzebue, Alaska 30 66 53N 162 39W
Kotzebue Sound, Alaska 30 66 20N 163 0W
Kountze, Tex. 13 30 22N 94 19W
Koyuk, Alaska 30 64 56N 161 9W
Koyukuk →, Alaska 30 64 55N 157 32W
Kremmling, Colo. 16 40 4N 106 24W
Kualakahi Chan, Hawaii 30 22 2N 159 53W
Kuiu I., Alaska 30 57 45N 134 10W
Kulm, N. Dak. 12 46 18N 98 57W
Kumukahi, C., Hawaii 30 19 31N 154 49W
Kupreanof I., Alaska 30 56 50N 133 30W
Kuskokwim →, Alaska 30 60 5N 162 25W
Kuskokwim B., Alaska 30 59 45N 162 25W
Kuskokwim Mts., Alaska 30 62 30N 156 0W
Kwethluk, Alaska 30 60 49N 161 26W
Kwigillingok, Alaska 30 59 51N 163 8W
Kwiguk, Alaska 30 62 46N 164 30W
Kyburz, Calif. 18 38 47N 120 18W

L

La Barge, Wyo. 16 42 16N 110 12W
La Belle, Fla. 11 26 46N 81 26W
La Canada, Calif. 29 34 12N 118 12W
La Conner, Wash. 16 48 23N 122 30W
La Crescenta, Calif. 29 34 13N 118 14W
La Crosse, Kans. 12 38 32N 99 18W
La Crosse, Wis. 12 43 48N 91 15W
La Fayette, Ga. 11 34 42N 85 17W
La Follette, Tenn. 11 36 23N 84 7W
La Grande, Oreg. 16 45 20N 118 5W
La Grange, Calif. 18 37 42N 120 27W
La Grange, Ga. 11 33 2N 85 2W
La Grange, Ill. 22 41 48N 87 53W
La Grange, Ky. 10 38 25N 85 23W
La Grange, Tex. 13 29 54N 96 52W
La Guardia Airport, N.Y. 21 40 46N 73 52W
La Habra, Calif. 29 33 56N 117 57W
La Harpe, Ill. 14 40 35N 90 58W
La Jara, Colo. 17 37 16N 105 58W
La Junta, Colo. 13 37 59N 103 33W
La Mesa, Calif. 19 32 46N 117 3W
La Mesa, N. Mex. 17 32 7N 106 42W
La Moure, N. Dak. 12 46 21N 98 18W
La Pine, Oreg. 16 43 40N 121 30W
La Plant, S. Dak. 12 45 9N 100 39W
La Porte, Ind. 15 41 36N 86 43W
La Push, Wash. 18 47 55N 124 38W
La Salle, Ill. 14 41 20N 89 6W
La Selva Beach, Calif. 18 36 56N 121 51W
Laau Pt., Hawaii 30 21 6N 157 19W
Lac du Flambeau, Wis. 12 45 58N 89 53W
Lackawanna, N.Y. 8 42 50N 78 50W
Lacona, N.Y. 9 43 39N 76 10W
Laconia, N.H. 9 43 32N 71 28W
Lacrosse, Wash. 16 46 51N 117 58W
Ladysmith, Wis. 12 45 28N 91 12W
Lafayette, Colo. 12 39 58N 105 12W
Lafayette, Ind. 15 40 25N 86 54W
Lafayette, La. 13 30 14N 92 1W
Lafayette, Tenn. 11 36 31N 86 2W
Laguna, N. Mex. 17 35 2N 107 25W
Laguna Beach, Calif. 19 33 33N 117 47W
Lahaina, Hawaii 30 20 53N 156 41W
Lahontan Reservoir, Nev. 16 39 28N 119 4W
Lake Alpine, Calif. 18 38 29N 120 0W
Lake Andes, S. Dak. 12 43 9N 98 32W
Lake Anse, Mich. 10 46 42N 88 25W
Lake Arthur, La. 13 30 5N 92 41W
Lake Charles, La. 13 30 14N 93 13W
Lake City, Colo. 17 38 2N 107 19W
Lake City, Fla. 11 30 11N 82 38W
Lake City, Iowa 14 42 16N 94 44W
Lake City, Mich. 10 44 20N 85 13W
Lake City, Minn. 12 44 27N 92 16W
Lake City, S.C. 11 33 52N 79 45W
Lake George, N.Y. 9 43 26N 73 43W
Lake Havasu City, Ariz. 19 34 27N 114 22W
Lake Hiawatha, N.J. 20 40 52N 74 22W
Lake Hughes, Calif. 19 34 41N 118 26W
Lake Isabella, Calif. 19 35 38N 118 28W
Lake Mead National Recreation Area, Ariz. 19 36 15N 114 30W
Lake Mills, Iowa 12 43 25N 93 32W
Lake Providence, La. 13 32 48N 91 10W
Lake Village, Ark. 13 33 20N 91 17W
Lake Wales, Fla. 11 27 54N 81 35W
Lake Worth, Fla. 11 26 37N 80 3W
Lakeland, Fla. 11 28 3N 81 57W
Lakeside, Ariz. 17 34 9N 109 58W
Lakeside, Calif. 19 32 52N 116 55W
Lakeside, Nebr. 12 42 3N 102 26W
Lakeview, Oreg. 16 42 11N 120 21W
Lakewood, Colo. 12 39 44N 105 5W
Lakewood, N.J. 9 40 6N 74 13W
Lakewood, Ohio 27 41 29N 81 49W
Lakin, Kans. 13 37 57N 101 15W
Lakota, N. Dak. 12 48 2N 98 21W
Lamar, Colo. 12 38 5N 102 37W
Lamar, Mo. 13 37 30N 94 16W
Lambert, Mont. 12 47 41N 104 37W
Lame Deer, Mont. 16 45 37N 106 40W
Lamesa, Tex. 13 32 44N 101 58W
Lamont, Calif. 19 35 15N 118 55W
Lampasas, Tex. 13 31 4N 98 11W
Lamy, N. Mex. 17 35 29N 105 53W
Lanai City, Hawaii 30 20 50N 156 55W
Lanai I., Hawaii 30 20 50N 156 55W
Lancaster, Calif. 19 34 42N 118 8W
Lancaster, Ky. 10 37 37N 84 35W
Lancaster, N.H. 9 44 29N 71 34W
Lancaster, Pa. 9 40 2N 76 19W
Lancaster, S.C. 11 34 43N 80 46W
Lancaster, Wis. 14 42 51N 90 43W
Lander, Wyo. 16 42 50N 108 44W
Lanesboro, Pa. 9 41 57N 75 34W
Lanett, Ala. 11 32 52N 85 12W
Langdon, N. Dak. 12 48 45N 98 22W
Langley Park, Md. 25 38 59N 76 58W
Langlois, Oreg. 16 42 56N 124 27W
Langtry, Tex. 13 29 49N 101 34W
Lansdale, Pa. 9 40 14N 75 17W
Lansdowne, Md. 25 39 14N 76 39W
Lansdowne, Pa. 24 39 56N 75 15W
Lansford, Pa. 9 40 50N 75 53W
Lansing, Mich. 15 42 44N 84 33W
Laona, Wis. 10 45 34N 88 40W
Lapeer, Mich. 15 43 3N 83 19W
Laporte, Pa. 9 41 25N 76 30W
Laramie, Wyo. 12 41 19N 105 35W
Laramie Mts., Wyo. 12 42 0N 105 30W
Larchmont, N.Y. 21 40 55N 73 44W
Laredo, Tex. 13 27 30N 99 30W
Larimore, N. Dak. 12 47 54N 97 38W
Larkspur, Calif. 28 37 56N 122 32W
Larned, Kans. 12 38 11N 99 6W
Las Animas, Colo. 12 38 4N 103 13W
Las Cruces, N. Mex. 17 32 19N 106 47W
Las Vegas, N. Mex. 17 35 36N 105 13W
Las Vegas, Nev. 19 36 10N 115 9W
Lassen Pk., Wash. 16 40 29N 121 31W
Lathrop Wells, Nev. 19 36 39N 116 24W
Laton, Calif. 18 36 26N 119 41W
Laurel, Miss. 13 31 41N 89 8W
Laurel, Mont. 16 45 40N 108 46W
Laurens, S.C. 11 34 30N 82 1W
Laurinburg, N.C. 11 34 47N 79 28W
Laurium, Mich. 10 47 14N 88 27W
Lava Hot Springs, Idaho 16 42 37N 112 1W
Laverne, Okla. 13 36 43N 99 54W
Lawrence, Kans. 12 38 58N 95 14W
Lawrence, Mass. 23 42 43N 71 7W
Lawrenceburg, Ind. 15 39 6N 84 52W
Lawrenceburg, Tenn. 11 35 14N 87 20W
Lawrenceville, Ga. 11 33 57N 83 59W
Laws, Calif. 18 37 24N 118 20W
Lawton, Okla. 13 34 37N 98 25W
Laytonville, Calif. 16 39 41N 123 29W
Le Mars, Iowa 12 42 47N 96 10W
Le Roy, Kans. 13 38 5N 95 38W
Le Sueur, Minn. 12 44 28N 93 55W
Lead, S. Dak. 12 44 21N 103 46W
Leadville, Colo. 17 39 15N 106 18W
Leaf →, Miss. 13 30 59N 88 44W
Leakey, Tex. 13 29 44N 99 46W
Leamington, Utah 16 39 32N 112 17W
Leavenworth, Kans. 12 39 19N 94 55W
Leavenworth, Wash. 16 47 36N 120 40W
Lebanon, Ind. 15 40 3N 86 28W
Lebanon, Kans. 12 39 49N 98 33W
Lebanon, Ky. 10 37 34N 85 15W
Lebanon, Mo. 14 37 41N 92 40W
Lebanon, Oreg. 16 44 32N 122 55W
Lebanon, Pa. 9 40 20N 76 26W
Lebanon, Tenn. 11 36 12N 86 18W
Lebec, Calif. 19 34 50N 118 52W
Lee Vining, Calif. 18 37 58N 119 7W
Leech L., Minn. 12 47 10N 94 24W
Leedey, Okla. 13 35 52N 99 21W
Leeds, Ala. 11 33 33N 86 33W
Leesburg, Fla. 11 28 49N 81 53W
Leesville, La. 13 31 9N 93 16W
Lefors, Tex. 13 35 26N 100 48W
Lehi, Utah 16 40 24N 111 51W
Lehighton, Pa. 9 40 50N 75 43W
Lehua I., Hawaii 30 22 1N 160 6W
Leland, Miss. 13 33 24N 90 54W
Lemhi Ra., Idaho 16 44 30N 113 30W
Lemmon, S. Dak. 12 45 57N 102 10W
Lemon Grove, Calif. 19 32 45N 117 2W
Lemoore, Calif. 18 36 18N 119 46W
Lennox, Calif. 29 33 56N 118 21W
Lenoir, N.C. 11 35 55N 81 32W
Lenoir City, Tenn. 11 35 48N 84 16W
Lenora, Kans. 12 39 37N 100 0W
Lenox, Mass. 9 42 22N 73 17W
Lenwood, Calif. 19 34 53N 117 7W
Leola, S. Dak. 12 45 43N 98 56W
Leominster, Mass. 9 42 32N 71 46W
Leon, Iowa 14 40 44N 93 45W
Leonardtown, Md. 10 38 17N 76 38W
Leoti, Kans. 12 38 29N 101 21W
Leslie, Ark. 13 35 50N 92 34W
Leucadia, Calif. 19 33 4N 117 18W
Levan, Utah 16 39 33N 111 52W
Levelland, Tex. 13 33 35N 102 23W
Levittown, N.Y. 21 40 43N 73 31W
Levittown, Pa. 9 40 9N 74 51W
Lewellen, Nebr. 12 41 20N 102 9W
Lewes, Del. 10 38 46N 75 9W
Lewis Range, Mont. 16 48 5N 113 5W
Lewisburg, Pa. 8 40 58N 76 54W
Lewisburg, Tenn. 11 35 27N 86 48W
Lewiston, Idaho 16 46 25N 117 1W
Lewiston, Maine 11 44 6N 70 13W
Lewistown, Mont. 16 47 4N 109 26W
Lewistown, Pa. 8 40 36N 77 34W
Lexington, Ill. 15 40 39N 88 47W
Lexington, Ky. 15 38 3N 84 30W
Lexington, Mass. 23 42 26N 71 13W
Lexington, Miss. 13 33 7N 90 3W
Lexington, Mo. 14 39 11N 93 52W
Lexington, N.C. 11 35 49N 80 15W
Lexington, Nebr. 12 40 47N 99 45W
Lexington, Oreg. 16 45 27N 119 42W
Lexington, Tenn. 11 35 39N 88 24W
Lexington Park, Md. 10 38 16N 76 27W
Libby, Mont. 16 48 23N 115 33W
Liberal, Kans. 13 37 3N 100 55W
Liberal, Mo. 13 37 34N 94 31W
Liberty, Mo. 14 39 15N 94 25W
Liberty, Tex. 13 30 3N 94 48W
Lida, Nev. 17 37 28N 117 30W
Lihue, Hawaii 30 21 59N 159 23W
Lima, Mont. 16 44 38N 112 36W
Lima, Ohio 15 40 44N 84 6W
Limon, Colo. 12 39 16N 103 41W
Lincoln, Ill. 14 40 9N 89 22W
Lincoln, Kans. 12 39 3N 98 9W
Lincoln, Maine 11 45 22N 68 30W
Lincoln, N. Mex. 17 33 30N 105 23W
Lincoln, Nebr. 12 40 49N 96 41W
Lincoln Park, Mich. 26 42 14N 83 9W
Lincolnton, N.C. 11 35 29N 81 16W
Lincolnwood, Ill. 22 42 1N 87 45W
Lind, Wash. 16 46 58N 118 37W
Linden, Calif. 18 38 1N 121 5W
Linden, N.J. 20 40 38N 74 14W
Linden, Tex. 13 33 1N 94 22W
Lindsay, Calif. 18 36 12N 119 5W
Lindsay, Okla. 13 34 50N 97 38W
Lindsborg, Kans. 12 38 35N 97 40W
Lingle, Wyo. 12 42 8N 104 21W
Linthicum Heights, Md. 25 39 12N 76 41W
Linton, Ind. 15 39 2N 87 10W
Linton, N. Dak. 12 46 16N 100 14W
Lipscomb, Tex. 13 36 14N 100 16W
Lisbon, N. Dak. 12 46 27N 97 41W
Lisburne, C., Alaska 30 68 53N 166 13W
Litchfield, Conn. 9 41 45N 73 11W
Litchfield, Ill. 14 39 11N 89 39W
Litchfield, Minn. 12 45 8N 94 32W
Little Belt Mts., Mont. 16 46 40N 110 45W
Little Blue →, Kans. 12 39 42N 96 41W
Little Colorado →, Ariz. 17 36 12N 111 48W
Little Falls, Minn. 12 45 59N 94 22W
Little Falls, N.Y. 9 43 3N 74 51W
Little Fork →, Minn. 12 48 31N 93 35W
Little Humboldt →, Nev. 16 41 1N 117 43W
Little Lake, Calif. 19 35 56N 117 55W
Little Missouri →, N. Dak. 12 47 36N 102 25W
Little Red →, Ark. 13 35 11N 91 27W
Little Rock, Ark. 13 34 45N 92 17W
Little Sable Pt., Mich. 10 43 38N 86 33W
Little Sioux →, Iowa 12 41 48N 96 4W
Little Snake →, Colo. 16 40 27N 108 26W
Little Wabash →, Ill. 15 37 55N 88 5W
Littlefield, Tex. 13 33 55N 102 20W
Littlefork, Minn. 12 48 24N 93 34W
Littleton, N.H. 9 44 18N 71 46W
Live Oak, Fla. 11 30 18N 82 59W
Livermore, Calif. 18 37 41N 121 47W
Livermore, Mt., Tex. 13 30 38N 104 11W
Livingston, Calif. 18 37 23N 120 43W
Livingston, Mont. 16 45 40N 110 34W
Livingston, N.J. 20 40 47N 74 18W
Livingston, Tex. 13 30 43N 94 56W
Livonia, Mich. 26 42 24N 83 22W
Llano, Tex. 13 30 45N 98 41W
Llano →, Tex. 13 30 39N 98 26W
Llano Estacado, Tex. 13 33 30N 103 0W
Loa, Utah 17 38 24N 111 39W
Lock Haven, Pa. 8 41 8N 77 28W
Lockeford, Calif. 18 38 10N 121 9W
Lockhart, Tex. 13 29 53N 97 40W
Lockney, Tex. 13 34 7N 101 27W
Lockport, N.Y. 8 43 10N 78 42W
Lodge Grass, Mont. 16 45 19N 107 22W
Lodgepole, Nebr. 12 41 9N 102 38W
Lodgepole Cr. →, Wyo. 12 41 20N 104 30W
Lodi, Calif. 18 38 8N 121 16W
Lodi, N.J. 20 40 52N 74 5W
Logan, Kans. 12 39 40N 99 34W
Logan, Ohio 10 39 32N 82 25W
Logan, Utah 16 41 44N 111 50W
Logan, W. Va. 10 37 51N 81 59W
Logan International Airport, Mass. 23 42 21N 71 0W
Logansport, Ind. 15 40 45N 86 22W
Logansport, La. 13 31 58N 94 0W
Lolo, Mont. 16 46 45N 114 5W
Loma, Mont. 16 47 56N 110 30W
Loma Linda, Calif. 19 34 3N 117 16W
Lometa, Tex. 13 31 13N 98 24W
Lompoc, Calif. 19 34 38N 120 28W
London, Ky. 10 37 8N 84 5W
London, Ohio 15 39 53N 83 27W
Lone Pine, Calif. 18 36 36N 118 4W
Long Beach, Calif. 19 33 47N 118 11W
Long Beach, N.Y. 21 40 35N 73 40W
Long Beach, Wash. 18 46 21N 124 3W

Millerton

ong Branch, N.J. **9** 40 18N 74 0W
ong Creek, Oreg. **16** 44 43N 119 6W
ong I., N.Y. **9** 40 45N 73 30W
ong Island Sd., N.Y. **9** 41 10N 73 0W
ong Pine, Nebr. **12** 42 32N 99 42W
ongmont, Colo. **12** 40 10N 105 6W
ongview, Tex. **13** 32 30N 94 44W
ongview, Wash. **18** 46 8N 122 57W
onoke, Ark. **13** 34 47N 91 54W
ookout, C., N.C. **11** 34 35N 76 32W
orain, Ohio **8** 41 28N 82 11W
ordsburg, N. Mex. **17** 32 21N 108 43W
os Alamos, Calif. **19** 34 44N 120 17W
os Alamos, N. Mex. **17** 35 53N 106 19W
os Altos, Calif. **18** 37 23N 122 7W
os Angeles, Calif. **29** 34 3N 118 13W
os Angeles Aqueduct, Calif. **19** 35 22N 118 5W
os Angeles International Airport, Calif. **29** 33 56N 118 23W
os Banos, Calif. **18** 37 4N 120 51W
os Lunas, N. Mex. **17** 34 48N 106 44W
os Olivos, Calif. **19** 34 40N 120 7W
oudon, Tenn. **11** 35 45N 84 20W
ouisa, Ky. **10** 38 7N 82 36W
ouisiana, Mo. **14** 39 27N 91 3W
ouisiana □ **13** 30 50N 92 0W
ouisville, Ky. **15** 38 15N 85 46W
ouisville, Miss. **13** 33 7N 89 3W
oup City, Nebr. **12** 41 17N 98 58W
oveland, Colo. **12** 40 24N 105 5W
ovell, Wyo. **16** 44 50N 108 24W
ovelock, Nev. **16** 40 11N 118 28W
oving, N. Mex. **13** 32 17N 104 6W
ovington, N. Mex. **13** 32 57N 103 21W
owell, Mass. **23** 42 38N 71 16W
ower L., Calif. **16** 41 16N 120 2W
ower Lake, Calif. **18** 38 55N 122 37W
ower Red L., Minn. **12** 47 58N 95 0W
owville, N.Y. **9** 43 47N 75 29W
ubbock, Tex. **13** 33 35N 101 51W
ucedale, Miss. **11** 30 56N 88 35W
ucerne Valley, Calif. **19** 34 27N 116 57W
udington, Mich. **10** 43 57N 86 27W
udlow, Calif. **19** 34 43N 116 10W
udlow, Vt. **9** 43 24N 72 42W
ufkin, Tex. **13** 31 21N 94 44W
uling, Tex. **13** 29 41N 97 39W
uma, Amer. Samoa **31** 14 15S 169 32W
umberton, Miss. **13** 31 0N 89 27W
umberton, N.C. **11** 34 37N 79 0W
umberton, N. Mex. **17** 36 56N 106 56W
und, Nev. **16** 38 52N 115 0W
uning, Nev. **16** 38 30N 118 11W
uray, Va. **10** 38 40N 78 28W
usk, Wyo. **12** 42 46N 104 27W
utherville-Timonium, Md. **25** 39 25N 76 36W
uverne, Minn. **12** 43 39N 96 13W
yman, Wyo. **16** 41 20N 110 18W
ynchburg, Va. **10** 37 25N 79 9W
ynden, Wash. **18** 48 57N 122 27W
yndhurst, N.J. **20** 40 49N 74 8W
ynn, Mass. **23** 42 28N 70 57W
ynwood, Calif. **29** 33 55N 118 12W
yons, Colo. **12** 40 14N 105 16W
yons, Ga. **11** 32 12N 82 19W
yons, Ill. **22** 41 48N 87 49W
yons, Kans. **12** 38 21N 98 12W
yons, N.Y. **8** 43 5N 77 0W
ytle, Tex. **13** 29 14N 98 48W

M

Mabton, Wash. **16** 46 13N 120 0W
McAlester, Okla. **13** 34 56N 95 46W
McAllen, Tex. **13** 26 12N 98 14W
McCall, Idaho **16** 44 55N 116 6W
McCamey, Tex. **13** 31 8N 102 14W
McCammon, Idaho **16** 42 39N 112 12W
McCarthy, Alaska **30** 61 26N 142 56W
McCloud, Calif. **16** 41 15N 122 8W
McClure, L., Calif. **18** 37 35N 120 16W
McClusky, N. Dak. **12** 47 29N 100 27W
McComb, Miss. **13** 31 15N 90 27W
McConaughy, L., Nebr. **12** 41 14N 101 40W
McCook, Nebr. **12** 40 12N 100 38W
McDermitt, Nev. **16** 41 59N 117 43W
McFarland, Calif. **19** 35 41N 119 14W
McGehee, Ark. **13** 33 38N 91 24W
McGill, Nev. **16** 39 23N 114 47W
McGregor, Iowa **14** 43 1N 91 11W
Machias, Maine **11** 44 43N 67 28W
McIntosh, S. Dak. **12** 45 55N 101 21W
Mackay, Idaho **16** 43 55N 113 37W
McKees Rocks, Pa. **27** 40 28N 80 3W
McKeesport, Pa. **27** 40 21N 79 51W
McKenzie, Tenn. **11** 36 8N 88 31W
McKenzie →, Oreg. **16** 44 7N 123 6W
Mackinaw City, Mich. **10** 45 47N 84 44W
McKinley, Mt., Alaska **30** 63 4N 151 0W
McKinney, Tex. **13** 33 12N 96 37W
McLaughlin, S. Dak. **12** 45 49N 100 49W
McLean, Tex. **13** 35 14N 100 36W
McLean, Va. **25** 38 56N 77 10W
McLeansboro, Ill. **15** 38 6N 88 32W
McLoughlin, Mt., Oreg. **16** 42 27N 122 19W
McMillan, L., N. Mex. **13** 32 36N 104 21W
McMinnville, Oreg. **16** 45 13N 123 12W
McMinnville, Tenn. **11** 35 41N 85 46W
McNary, Ariz. **17** 34 4N 109 51W
Macomb, Ill. **14** 40 27N 90 40W
Macon, Ga. **11** 32 51N 83 38W
Macon, Miss. **11** 33 7N 88 34W
Macon, Mo. **14** 39 44N 92 28W
McPherson, Kans. **13** 38 22N 97 40W
McPherson Pk., Calif. **19** 34 53N 119 53W
McVille, N. Dak. **12** 47 46N 98 11W
Madera, Calif. **18** 36 57N 120 3W
Madill, Okla. **13** 34 6N 96 46W
Madison, Fla. **11** 30 28N 83 25W
Madison, Ind. **15** 38 44N 85 23W
Madison, N.J. **20** 40 45N 74 25W
Madison, Nebr. **12** 41 50N 97 27W
Madison, S. Dak. **12** 44 0N 97 7W
Madison, Wis. **14** 43 4N 89 24W
Madison →, Mont. **16** 45 56N 111 31W
Madison Heights, Mich. **26** 42 29N 83 6W
Madisonville, Ky. **10** 37 20N 87 30W
Madisonville, Tex. **13** 30 57N 95 55W
Madras, Oreg. **16** 44 38N 121 8W
Madre, Laguna, Tex. **13** 27 0N 97 30W
Magdalena, N. Mex. **17** 34 7N 107 15W
Magee, Miss. **13** 31 52N 89 44W
Magnolia, Ark. **13** 33 16N 93 14W
Magnolia, Miss. **13** 31 9N 90 28W
Mahanoy City, Pa. **9** 40 49N 76 9W
Mahnomen, Minn. **12** 47 19N 95 58W
Mahukona, Hawaii **30** 20 11N 155 52W
Maine □ **11** 45 20N 69 0W
Makapuu Hd., Hawaii **30** 21 19N 157 39W
Makena, Hawaii **30** 20 39N 156 27W
Malad City, Idaho **16** 42 12N 112 15W
Malaga, N. Mex. **13** 32 14N 104 4W
Malakoff, Tex. **13** 32 10N 96 1W
Malden, Mass. **23** 42 26N 71 3W
Malden, Mo. **13** 36 34N 89 57W
Malheur →, Oreg. **16** 44 4N 116 59W
Malheur L., Oreg. **16** 43 20N 118 48W
Malibu, Calif. **19** 34 2N 118 41W
Malone, N.Y. **9** 44 51N 74 18W
Malta, Idaho **16** 42 18N 113 22W
Malta, Mont. **16** 48 21N 107 52W
Malvern, Ark. **13** 34 22N 92 49W
Malvern, Pa. **24** 40 2N 75 31W
Mammoth, Ariz. **17** 32 43N 110 39W
Mana, Hawaii **30** 22 2N 159 47W
Manasquan, N.J. **9** 40 8N 74 3W
Manassa, Colo. **17** 37 11N 105 56W
Manatí, Puerto Rico **30** 18 26N 66 29W
Mancelona, Mich. **10** 44 54N 85 4W
Manchester, Conn. **9** 41 47N 72 31W
Manchester, Ga. **11** 32 51N 84 37W
Manchester, Iowa **14** 42 29N 91 27W
Manchester, Ky. **10** 37 9N 83 46W
Manchester, N.H. **9** 42 59N 71 28W
Mandan, N. Dak. **12** 46 50N 100 54W
Mangum, Okla. **13** 34 53N 99 30W
Manhasset, N.Y. **21** 40 47N 73 39W
Manhattan, Kans. **12** 39 11N 96 35W
Manhattan, N.Y. **20** 40 48N 73 57W
Manhattan Beach, Calif. **29** 33 53N 118 25W
Manila, Utah **16** 40 59N 109 43W
Manistee, Mich. **10** 44 15N 86 19W
Manistee →, Mich. **10** 44 15N 86 21W
Manistique, Mich. **10** 45 57N 86 15W
Manitou Is., Mich. **10** 45 8N 86 0W
Manitou Springs, Colo. **12** 38 52N 104 55W
Manitowoc, Wis. **10** 44 5N 87 40W
Mankato, Kans. **12** 39 47N 98 13W
Mankato, Minn. **12** 44 10N 94 0W
Manning, S.C. **11** 33 42N 80 13W
Mannington, W. Va. **10** 39 32N 80 21W
Mansfield, La. **13** 32 2N 93 43W
Mansfield, Mass. **9** 42 2N 71 13W
Mansfield, Ohio **8** 40 45N 82 31W
Mansfield, Pa. **8** 41 48N 77 5W
Mansfield, Wash. **16** 47 49N 119 38W
Manteca, Calif. **18** 37 48N 121 13W
Manteo, N.C. **11** 35 55N 75 40W
Manti, Utah **16** 39 16N 111 38W
Manton, Mich. **10** 44 25N 85 24W
Manua Is., Amer. Samoa **31** 14 13S 169 35W
Manville, Wyo. **12** 42 47N 104 37W
Many, La. **13** 31 34N 93 29W
Manzano Mts., N. Mex. **17** 34 40N 106 20W
Maple Heights, Ohio **27** 41 25N 81 33W
Mapleton, Oreg. **16** 44 2N 123 52W
Maplewood, N.J. **20** 40 43N 74 16W
Maquoketa, Iowa **14** 42 4N 90 40W
Marana, Ariz. **17** 32 27N 111 13W
Marathon, N.Y. **9** 42 27N 76 2W
Marathon, Tex. **13** 30 12N 103 15W
Marble Falls, Tex. **13** 30 35N 98 16W
Marblehead, Mass. **23** 42 29N 70 51W
Marengo, Iowa **14** 41 48N 92 4W
Marfa, Tex. **13** 30 19N 104 1W
Mariana Trench, Pac. Oc. **31** 13 0N 145 0 E
Marianna, Ark. **13** 34 46N 90 46W
Marianna, Fla. **11** 30 46N 85 14W
Marias →, Mont. **16** 47 56N 110 30W
Maricopa, Ariz. **17** 33 4N 112 3W
Maricopa, Calif. **19** 35 4N 119 24W
Marietta, Ga. **11** 33 57N 84 33W
Marietta, Ohio **10** 39 25N 81 27W
Marin City, Calif. **28** 37 52N 122 30W
Marina, Calif. **18** 36 41N 121 48W
Marine City, Mich. **10** 42 43N 82 30W
Marinette, Wis. **10** 45 6N 87 38W
Marion, Ala. **11** 32 38N 87 19W
Marion, Ill. **14** 37 44N 88 56W
Marion, Ind. **15** 40 32N 85 40W
Marion, Iowa **14** 42 2N 91 36W
Marion, Kans. **12** 38 21N 97 1W
Marion, Mich. **10** 44 6N 85 9W
Marion, N.C. **11** 35 41N 82 1W
Marion, Ohio **15** 40 35N 83 8W
Marion, S.C. **11** 34 11N 79 24W
Marion, Va. **11** 36 50N 81 31W
Marion, L., S.C. **11** 33 28N 80 10W
Mariposa, Calif. **18** 37 29N 119 58W
Marked Tree, Ark. **13** 35 32N 90 25W
Markham, Ill. **22** 41 35N 87 41W
Markleeville, Calif. **18** 38 42N 119 47W
Marksville, La. **13** 31 8N 92 4W
Marlboro, Mass. **9** 42 19N 71 33W
Marlin, Tex. **13** 31 18N 96 54W
Marlow, Okla. **13** 34 39N 97 58W
Marmarth, N. Dak. **12** 46 18N 103 54W
Marple, Pa. **24** 39 56N 75 21W
Marquette, Mich. **10** 46 33N 87 24W
Marsh I., La. **13** 29 34N 91 53W
Marsh L., Minn. **12** 45 5N 96 0W
Marshall, Ark. **13** 35 55N 92 38W
Marshall, Mich. **15** 42 16N 84 58W
Marshall, Minn. **12** 44 25N 95 45W
Marshall, Mo. **14** 39 7N 93 12W
Marshall, Tex. **13** 32 33N 94 23W
Marshall Is. ■, Pac. Oc. **31** 9 0N 171 0 E
Marshalltown, Iowa **14** 42 3N 92 55W
Marshfield, Mo. **13** 37 15N 92 54W
Marshfield, Wis. **12** 44 40N 90 10W
Mart, Tex. **13** 31 33N 96 50W
Martha's Vineyard, Mass. **9** 41 25N 70 38W
Martin, S. Dak. **12** 43 11N 101 44W
Martin, Tenn. **13** 36 21N 88 51W
Martin L., Ala. **11** 32 41N 85 55W
Martin State National Airport, Md. **25** 39 19N 76 25W
Martinez, Calif. **18** 38 1N 122 8W
Martinsburg, W. Va. **10** 39 27N 77 58W
Martinsville, Ind. **15** 39 26N 86 25W
Martinsville, Va. **11** 36 41N 79 52W
Maryland □ **10** 39 0N 76 30W
Marysvale, Utah **17** 38 27N 112 14W
Marysville, Calif. **18** 39 9N 121 35W
Marysville, Kans. **12** 39 51N 96 39W
Marysville, Ohio **15** 40 14N 83 22W
Maryville, Tenn. **11** 35 46N 83 58W
Mason, Nev. **18** 38 56N 119 8W
Mason, Tex. **13** 30 45N 99 14W
Mason City, Iowa **14** 43 9N 93 12W
Massachusetts □ **9** 42 30N 72 0W
Massachusetts B., Mass. **9** 42 20N 70 50W
Massapequa, N.Y. **21** 40 41N 73 28W
Massena, N.Y. **9** 44 56N 74 54W
Massillon, Ohio **8** 40 48N 81 32W
Matagorda, Tex. **13** 28 42N 95 58W
Matagorda B., Tex. **13** 28 40N 96 0W
Matagorda I., Tex. **13** 28 15N 96 30W
Mathis, Tex. **13** 28 6N 97 50W
Mattawamkeag, Maine **11** 45 32N 68 21W
Mattituck, N.Y. **9** 40 59N 72 32W
Maui, Hawaii **30** 20 48N 156 20W
Maumee, Ohio **15** 41 34N 83 39W
Maumee →, Ohio **15** 41 42N 83 28W
Mauna Kea, Hawaii **30** 19 50N 155 28W
Mauna Loa, Hawaii **30** 19 30N 155 35W
Maupin, Oreg. **16** 45 11N 121 5W
Maurepas, L., La. **13** 30 15N 90 30W
Mauston, Wis. **12** 43 48N 90 5W
Max, N. Dak. **12** 47 49N 101 18W
Mayagüez, Puerto Rico **30** 18 12N 67 9W
Maybell, Colo. **16** 40 31N 108 5W
Mayer, Ariz. **17** 34 24N 112 14W
Mayfield, Ky. **11** 36 44N 88 38W
Mayfield Heights, Ohio **27** 41 31N 81 28W
Mayhill, N. Mex. **17** 32 53N 105 29W
Maysville, Ky. **15** 38 39N 83 46W
Mayville, N. Dak. **12** 47 30N 97 20W
Maywood, Calif. **29** 33 59N 118 12W
Maywood, Ill. **22** 41 52N 87 52W
McGrath, Alaska **30** 62 58N 155 40W
Mead, L., Ariz. **19** 36 1N 114 44W
Meade, Kans. **13** 37 17N 100 20W
Meade River = Atkasuk, Alaska **30** 70 30N 157 20W
Meadow Valley Wash →, Nev. **19** 36 40N 114 34W
Meadville, Pa. **8** 41 39N 80 9W
Meares, C., Oreg. **16** 45 37N 124 0W
Mecca, Calif. **19** 33 34N 116 5W
Mechanicsburg, Pa. **8** 40 13N 77 1W
Mechanicville, N.Y. **9** 42 54N 73 41W
Medford, Mass. **23** 42 25N 71 7W
Medford, Oreg. **16** 42 19N 122 52W
Medford, Wis. **12** 45 9N 90 20W
Media, Pa. **24** 39 55N 75 23W
Medical Lake, Wash. **16** 47 34N 117 41W
Medicine Bow, Wyo. **16** 41 54N 106 12W
Medicine Bow Pk., Wyo. **16** 41 21N 106 19W
Medicine Bow Ra., Wyo. **16** 41 10N 106 25W
Medicine Lake, Mont. **12** 48 30N 104 30W
Medicine Lodge, Kans. **13** 37 17N 98 35W
Medina, N. Dak. **12** 46 54N 99 18W
Medina, N.Y. **8** 43 13N 78 23W
Medina, Ohio **8** 41 8N 81 52W
Medina →, Tex. **13** 29 16N 98 29W
Medina L., Tex. **13** 29 32N 98 56W
Meeker, Colo. **16** 40 2N 107 55W
Meeteetse, Wyo. **16** 44 9N 108 52W
Mekoryok, Alaska **30** 60 20N 166 20W
Melbourne, Fla. **11** 28 5N 80 37W
Mellen, Wis. **12** 46 20N 90 40W
Mellette, S. Dak. **12** 45 9N 98 30W
Melrose, Mass. **23** 42 27N 71 2W
Melrose, N. Mex. **13** 34 26N 103 38W
Melrose Park, Ill. **22** 41 53N 87 53W
Melstone, Mont. **16** 46 36N 107 52W
Memphis, Tenn. **13** 35 8N 90 3W
Memphis, Tex. **13** 34 44N 100 33W
Mena, Ark. **13** 34 35N 94 15W
Menard, Tex. **13** 30 55N 99 47W
Menasha, Wis. **10** 44 13N 88 26W
Mendenhall, C., Alaska **30** 59 45N 166 10W
Mendocino, Calif. **16** 39 19N 123 48W
Mendocino, C., Calif. **16** 40 26N 124 25W
Mendota, Calif. **18** 36 45N 120 23W
Mendota, Ill. **14** 41 33N 89 7W
Menlo Park, Calif. **28** 37 26N 122 11W
Menominee, Mich. **10** 45 6N 87 37W
Menominee →, Wis. **10** 45 6N 87 36W
Menomonie, Wis. **12** 44 53N 91 55W
Mer Rouge, La. **13** 32 47N 91 48W
Merced, Calif. **18** 37 18N 120 29W
Merced Pk., Calif. **18** 37 36N 119 24W
Meredith, L., Tex. **13** 35 43N 101 33W
Meriden, Conn. **9** 41 32N 72 48W
Meridian, Idaho **16** 43 37N 116 24W
Meridian, Miss. **11** 32 22N 88 42W
Meridian, Tex. **13** 31 56N 97 39W
Merkel, Tex. **13** 32 28N 100 1W
Merrick, N.Y. **21** 40 39N 73 32W
Merrill, Oreg. **16** 42 1N 121 36W
Merrill, Wis. **12** 45 11N 89 41W
Merriman, Nebr. **12** 42 55N 101 42W
Merryville, La. **13** 30 45N 93 33W
Mertzon, Tex. **13** 31 16N 100 49W
Mesa, Ariz. **17** 33 25N 111 50W
Meshoppen, Pa. **9** 41 36N 76 3W
Mesick, Mich. **10** 44 24N 85 43W
Mesilla, N. Mex. **17** 32 16N 106 48W
Mesquite, Nev. **17** 36 47N 114 6W
Metairie, La. **13** 29 58N 90 10W
Metaline Falls, Wash. **16** 48 52N 117 22W
Methuen, Mass. **23** 42 43N 71 12W
Metlakatla, Alaska **30** 55 8N 131 35W
Metropolis, Ill. **13** 37 9N 88 44W
Metropolitan Oakland International Airport, Calif. **28** 37 43N 122 13W
Mexia, Tex. **13** 31 41N 96 29W
Mexico, Mo. **14** 39 10N 91 53W
Miami, Ariz. **17** 33 24N 110 52W
Miami, Fla. **11** 25 47N 80 11W
Miami, Tex. **13** 35 42N 100 38W
Miami →, Ohio **10** 39 20N 84 40W
Miami Beach, Fla. **11** 25 47N 80 8W
Miamisburg, Ohio **15** 39 38N 84 17W
Michelson, Mt., Alaska **30** 69 20N 144 20W
Michigan □ **10** 44 0N 85 0W
Michigan, L., Mich. **10** 44 0N 87 0W
Michigan City, Ind. **15** 41 43N 86 54W
Micronesia, Federated States of ■, Pac. Oc. **31** 11 0N 160 0 E
Middle Alkali L., Calif. **16** 41 27N 120 5W
Middle Loup →, Nebr. **12** 41 17N 98 24W
Middle River, Md. **25** 39 21N 76 26W
Middleburg, N.Y. **9** 42 36N 74 20W
Middleport, Ohio **10** 39 0N 82 3W
Middlesboro, Ky. **11** 36 36N 83 43W
Middlesex, N.J. **9** 40 36N 74 30W
Middleton I., Alaska **30** 59 26N 146 20W
Middletown, Conn. **9** 41 34N 72 39W
Middletown, N.Y. **9** 41 27N 74 25W
Middletown, Ohio **15** 39 31N 84 24W
Middletown, Pa. **9** 40 12N 76 44W
Midland, Mich. **10** 43 37N 84 14W
Midland, Tex. **13** 32 0N 102 3W
Midlothian, Tex. **13** 32 30N 97 0W
Midwest, Wyo. **16** 43 25N 106 16W
Milaca, Minn. **12** 45 45N 93 39W
Milan, Mo. **14** 40 12N 93 7W
Milan, Tenn. **11** 35 55N 88 46W
Milbank, S. Dak. **12** 45 13N 96 38W
Miles, Tex. **13** 31 36N 100 11W
Miles City, Mont. **12** 46 25N 105 51W
Milford, Conn. **9** 41 14N 73 3W
Milford, Del. **10** 38 55N 75 26W
Milford, Mass. **9** 42 8N 71 31W
Milford, Pa. **9** 41 19N 74 48W
Milford, Utah **17** 38 24N 113 1W
Milk →, Mont. **16** 48 4N 106 19W
Mill City, Oreg. **16** 44 45N 122 29W
Mill Valley, Calif. **28** 37 54N 122 32W
Millburn, N.J. **20** 40 43N 74 19W
Mille Lacs L., Minn. **12** 46 15N 93 39W
Milledgeville, Ga. **11** 33 5N 83 14W
Millen, Ga. **11** 32 48N 81 57W
Miller, S. Dak. **12** 44 31N 98 59W
Millersburg, Pa. **8** 40 32N 76 58W
Millerton, N.Y. **9** 41 57N 73 31W

Millerton L.

Millerton L., *Calif.* **18** 37 1N 119 41W
Millinocket, *Maine* **11** 45 39N 68 43W
Milltown, *Pa.* **24** 39 57N 75 32W
Millvale, *Pa.* **27** 40 28N 79 59W
Millville, *N.J.* **10** 39 24N 75 2W
Millwood L., *Ark.* **13** 33 42N 93 58W
Milnor, *N. Dak.* **12** 46 16N 97 27W
Milolii, *Hawaii* **30** 19 11N 155 55W
Milton, *Calif.* **18** 38 3N 120 51W
Milton, *Fla.* **11** 30 38N 87 3W
Milton, *Mass.* **23** 42 14N 71 2W
Milton, *Pa.* **8** 41 1N 76 51W
Milton-Freewater, *Oreg.* **16** 45 56N 118 23W
Milwaukee, *Wis.* **15** 43 2N 87 55W
Milwaukie, *Oreg.* **18** 45 27N 122 38W
Mina, *Nev.* **17** 38 24N 118 7W
Minden, *La.* **13** 32 37N 93 17W
Mineola, *N.Y.* **21** 40 44N 73 38W
Mineola, *Tex.* **13** 32 40N 95 29W
Mineral King, *Calif.* **18** 36 27N 118 36W
Mineral Wells, *Tex.* **13** 32 48N 98 7W
Minersville, *Pa.* **9** 40 41N 76 16W
Minersville, *Utah* **17** 38 13N 112 56W
Minetto, *N.Y.* **9** 43 24N 76 28W
Minidoka, *Idaho* **16** 42 45N 113 29W
Minneapolis, *Kans.* **12** 39 8N 97 42W
Minneapolis, *Minn.* **12** 44 59N 93 16W
Minnesota □ **12** 46 0N 94 15W
Minot, *N. Dak.* **12** 48 14N 101 18W
Minto, *Alaska* **30** 64 53N 149 11W
Minturn, *Colo.* **16** 39 35N 106 26W
Mirando City, *Tex.* **13** 27 26N 99 0W
Mishawaka, *Ind.* **15** 41 40N 86 11W
Mission, *S. Dak.* **12** 43 18N 100 39W
Mission, *Tex.* **13** 26 13N 98 20W
Mississippi □ **13** 33 0N 90 0W
Mississippi →, *La.* **13** 29 9N 89 15W
Mississippi River Delta, *La.* **13** 29 10N 89 15W
Mississippi Sd., *Miss.* .. **13** 30 20N 89 0W
Missoula, *Mont.* **16** 46 52N 114 1W
Missouri □ **12** 38 25N 92 30W
Missouri →, *Mo.* **12** 38 49N 90 7W
Missouri Valley, *Iowa* .. **12** 41 34N 95 53W
Mitchell, *Ind.* **15** 38 44N 86 28W
Mitchell, *Nebr.* **12** 41 57N 103 49W
Mitchell, *Oreg.* **16** 44 34N 120 9W
Mitchell, *S. Dak.* **12** 43 43N 98 2W
Mitchell, Mt., *N.C.* **11** 35 46N 82 16W
Moab, *Utah* **17** 38 35N 109 33W
Moberly, *Mo.* **14** 39 25N 92 26W
Mobile, *Ala.* **11** 30 41N 88 3W
Mobile B., *Ala.* **11** 30 30N 88 0W
Mobridge, *S. Dak.* **12** 45 32N 100 26W
Moclips, *Wash.* **18** 47 14N 124 13W
Modena, *Utah* **17** 37 48N 113 56W
Modesto, *Calif.* **18** 37 39N 121 0W
Mohall, *N. Dak.* **12** 48 46N 101 31W
Mohawk →, *N.Y.* **9** 42 47N 73 41W
Mohican, C., *Alaska* **30** 60 12N 167 25W
Mojave, *Calif.* **19** 35 3N 118 10W
Mojave Desert, *Calif.* ... **19** 35 0N 116 30W
Mokelumne →, *Calif.* **18** 38 13N 121 28W
Mokelumne Hill, *Calif.* . **18** 38 18N 120 43W
Moline, *Ill.* **14** 41 30N 90 31W
Molokai, *Hawaii* **30** 21 8N 157 0W
Monahans, *Tex.* **13** 31 36N 102 54W
Mondovi, *Wis.* **12** 44 34N 91 40W
Monessen, *Pa.* **8** 40 9N 79 54W
Monett, *Mo.* **13** 36 55N 93 55W
Monmouth, *Ill.* **14** 40 55N 90 39W
Mono L., *Calif.* **18** 38 1N 119 1W
Monolith, *Calif.* **19** 35 7N 118 22W
Monroe, *Ga.* **11** 33 47N 83 43W
Monroe, *La.* **13** 32 30N 92 7W
Monroe, *Mich.* **15** 41 55N 83 24W
Monroe, *N.C.* **11** 34 59N 80 33W
Monroe, *Utah* **17** 38 38N 112 7W
Monroe, *Wis.* **14** 42 36N 89 38W
Monroe City, *Mo.* **14** 39 39N 91 44W
Monroeville, *Ala.* **11** 31 31N 87 20W
Monroeville, *Pa.* **27** 40 26N 79 46W
Monrovia, *Calif.* **29** 34 9N 118 1W
Montague, *Calif.* **16** 41 44N 122 32W
Montague I., *Alaska* **30** 60 0N 147 30W
Montalvo, *Calif.* **19** 34 15N 119 12W
Montana □ **16** 47 0N 110 0W
Montauk, *N.Y.* **9** 41 3N 71 57W
Montauk Pt., *N.Y.* **9** 41 4N 71 52W
Montclair, *N.J.* **20** 40 49N 74 12W
Monte Vista, *Colo.* **17** 37 35N 106 9W
Montebello, *Calif.* **29** 34 1N 118 8W
Montecito, *Calif.* **19** 34 26N 119 40W
Montello, *Wis.* **12** 43 48N 89 20W
Monterey, *Calif.* **18** 36 37N 121 55W
Monterey B., *Calif.* **18** 36 45N 122 0W
Monterey Park, *Calif.* ... **29** 34 3N 118 7W
Montesano, *Wash.* **18** 46 59N 123 36W
Montevideo, *Minn.* **12** 44 57N 95 43W
Montezuma, *Iowa* **14** 41 35N 92 32W
Montgomery, *Ala.* **11** 32 23N 86 19W
Montgomery, *W. Va.* **10** 38 11N 81 19W
Monticello, *Ark.* **13** 33 38N 91 47W
Monticello, *Fla.* **11** 30 33N 83 52W
Monticello, *Ind.* **15** 40 45N 86 46W
Monticello, *Iowa* **14** 42 15N 91 12W
Monticello, *Ky.* **11** 36 50N 84 51W
Monticello, *Minn.* **12** 45 18N 93 48W
Monticello, *Miss.* **13** 31 33N 90 7W
Monticello, *N.Y.* **9** 41 39N 74 42W
Monticello, *Utah* **17** 37 52N 109 21W
Montour Falls, *N.Y.* **8** 42 21N 76 51W
Montpelier, *Idaho* **16** 42 19N 111 18W
Montpelier, *Md.* **25** 39 3N 76 50W
Montpelier, *Ohio* **15** 41 35N 84 37W
Montpelier, *Vt.* **9** 44 16N 72 35W
Montrose, *Colo.* **17** 38 29N 107 53W
Montrose, *Pa.* **9** 41 50N 75 53W
Moorcroft, *Wyo.* **12** 44 16N 104 57W
Moorefield, *W. Va.* **10** 39 5N 78 59W
Mooresville, *N.C.* **11** 35 35N 80 48W
Moorhead, *Minn.* **12** 46 53N 96 45W
Moorpark, *Calif.* **19** 34 17N 118 53W
Moose Lake, *Minn.* **12** 46 27N 92 46W
Moosehead L., *Maine* **11** 45 38N 69 40W
Moosup, *Conn.* **9** 41 43N 71 53W
Mora, *Minn.* **12** 45 53N 93 18W
Mora, *N. Mex.* **17** 35 58N 105 20W
Moran, *Kans.* **13** 37 55N 95 10W
Moran, *Wyo.* **16** 43 53N 110 37W
Moravia, *Iowa* **14** 40 53N 92 49W
Moreau →, *S. Dak.* **12** 45 18N 100 43W
Morehead, *Ky.* **15** 38 11N 83 26W
Morehead City, *N.C.* **11** 34 43N 76 43W
Morenci, *Ariz.* **17** 33 5N 109 22W
Morgan, *Utah* **16** 41 2N 111 41W
Morgan City, *La.* **13** 29 42N 91 12W
Morgan Hill, *Calif.* **18** 37 8N 121 39W
Morganfield, *Ky.* **10** 37 41N 87 55W
Morganton, *N.C.* **11** 35 45N 81 41W
Morgantown, *W. Va.* **10** 39 38N 79 57W
Morongo Valley, *Calif.* . **19** 34 3N 116 37W
Morrilton, *Ark.* **13** 35 9N 92 44W
Morris, *Ill.* **15** 41 22N 88 26W
Morris, *Minn.* **12** 45 35N 95 55W
Morrison, *Ill.* **14** 41 49N 89 58W
Morristown, *Ariz.* **17** 33 51N 112 37W
Morristown, *N.J.* **20** 40 48N 74 26W
Morristown, *S. Dak.* **12** 45 56N 101 43W
Morristown, *Tenn.* **11** 36 13N 83 18W
Morro Bay, *Calif.* **18** 35 22N 120 51W
Morton, *Tex.* **13** 33 44N 102 46W
Morton, *Wash.* **18** 46 34N 122 17W
Morton Grove, *Ill.* **22** 42 2N 87 45W
Moscow, *Idaho* **16** 46 44N 117 0W
Moses Lake, *Wash.* **16** 47 8N 119 17W
Mosquero, *N. Mex.* **13** 35 47N 103 58W
Mott, *N. Dak.* **12** 46 23N 102 20W
Moulton, *Tex.* **13** 29 35N 97 9W
Moultrie, *Ga.* **11** 31 11N 83 47W
Moultrie, L., *S.C.* **11** 33 20N 80 5W
Mound City, *Mo.* **12** 40 7N 95 14W
Mound City, *S. Dak.* **12** 45 44N 100 4W
Moundsville, *W. Va.* **8** 39 55N 80 44W
Mount Airy, *N.C.* **11** 36 31N 80 37W
Mount Angel, *Oreg.* **16** 45 4N 122 48W
Mount Carmel, *Ill.* **15** 38 25N 87 46W
Mount Clemens, *Mich.* ... **8** 42 35N 82 53W
Mount Clemens, *Mich.* ... **26** 42 35N 82 53W
Mount Desert I., *Maine* . **11** 44 21N 68 20W
Mount Dora, *Fla.* **11** 28 48N 81 38W
Mount Edgecumbe, *Alaska* **30** 57 3N 135 21W
Mount Hope, *W. Va.* **10** 37 54N 81 10W
Mount Horeb, *Wis.* **14** 43 1N 89 44W
Mount Laguna, *Calif.* ... **19** 32 52N 116 25W
Mount Lebanon, *Pa.* **27** 40 22N 80 2W
Mount McKinley National Park, *Alaska* **30** 63 30N 150 0W
Mount Morris, *N.Y.* **8** 42 44N 77 52W
Mount Oliver, *Pa.* **27** 40 24N 79 59W
Mount Pleasant, *Iowa* .. **14** 40 58N 91 33W
Mount Pleasant, *Mich.* .. **10** 43 36N 84 46W
Mount Pleasant, *S.C.* ... **11** 32 47N 79 52W
Mount Pleasant, *Tenn.* .. **11** 35 32N 87 12W
Mount Pleasant, *Tex.* ... **13** 33 9N 94 58W
Mount Pleasant, *Utah* ... **16** 39 33N 111 27W
Mount Pocono, *Pa.* **9** 41 7N 75 22W
Mount Prospect, *Ill.* ... **22** 42 3N 87 55W
Mount Rainier National Park, *Wash.* **18** 46 55N 121 50W
Mount Royal, *N.J.* **24** 39 48N 75 13W
Mount Shasta, *Calif.* ... **16** 41 19N 122 19W
Mount Sterling, *Ill.* ... **14** 39 59N 90 45W
Mount Sterling, *Ky.* **15** 38 4N 83 56W
Mount Vernon, *Ind.* **15** 38 17N 88 57W
Mount Vernon, *N.Y.* **21** 40 54N 73 49W
Mount Vernon, *Ohio* **8** 40 23N 82 29W
Mount Vernon, *Wash.* **18** 48 25N 122 20W
Mount Wilson Observatory, *Calif.* ... **29** 34 13N 118 4W
Mountain Center, *Calif.* . **19** 33 42N 116 44W
Mountain City, *Nev.* **16** 41 50N 115 58W
Mountain City, *Tenn.* ... **11** 36 29N 81 48W
Mountain Grove, *Mo.* **13** 37 8N 92 16W
Mountain Home, *Ark.* **13** 36 20N 92 23W
Mountain Home, *Idaho* .. **16** 43 8N 115 41W
Mountain Iron, *Minn.* ... **12** 47 32N 92 37W
Mountain View, *Ark.* **13** 35 52N 92 7W
Mountain View, *Calif.* .. **18** 37 23N 122 5W
Mountain Village, *Alaska* **30** 62 5N 163 43W
Mountainair, *N. Mex.* ... **17** 34 31N 106 15W
Muddy Cr. →, *Utah* **17** 38 24N 110 42W
Mule Creek, *Wyo.* **12** 43 19N 104 8W
Muleshoe, *Tex.* **13** 34 13N 102 43W
Mullen, *Nebr.* **12** 42 3N 101 1W
Mullens, *W. Va.* **10** 37 35N 81 23W
Mullin, *Tex.* **13** 31 33N 98 40W
Mullins, *S.C.* **11** 34 12N 79 15W
Mulvane, *Kans.* **13** 37 29N 97 15W
Muncie, *Ind.* **15** 40 12N 85 23W
Munday, *Tex.* **13** 33 27N 99 38W
Munhall, *Pa.* **27** 40 24N 79 54W
Munising, *Mich.* **10** 46 25N 86 40W
Murdo, *S. Dak.* **12** 43 53N 100 43W
Murfreesboro, *Tenn.* **11** 35 51N 86 24W
Murphy, *Idaho* **16** 43 13N 116 33W
Murphys, *Calif.* **18** 38 8N 120 28W
Murphysboro, *Ill.* **14** 37 46N 89 20W
Murray, *Ky.* **11** 36 37N 88 19W
Murray, *Utah* **16** 40 40N 111 53W
Murray, L., *S.C.* **11** 34 3N 81 13W
Murrieta, *Calif.* **19** 33 33N 117 13W
Murrysville, *Pa.* **27** 40 25N 79 41W
Muscatine, *Iowa* **14** 41 25N 91 3W
Muskegon, *Mich.* **15** 43 14N 86 16W
Muskegon →, *Mich.* **10** 43 14N 86 21W
Muskegon Heights, *Mich.* **15** 43 12N 86 16W
Muskogee, *Okla.* **13** 35 45N 95 22W
Musselshell →, *Mont.* .. **16** 47 21N 107 57W
Myerstown, *Pa.* **9** 40 22N 76 19W
Myrtle Beach, *S.C.* **11** 33 42N 78 53W
Myrtle Creek, *Oreg.* **16** 43 1N 123 17W
Myrtle Point, *Oreg.* **16** 43 4N 124 8W
Mystic, *Conn.* **9** 41 21N 71 58W
Myton, *Utah* **16** 40 12N 110 4W

N

Naalehu, *Hawaii* **30** 19 4N 155 35W
Nabesna, *Alaska* **30** 62 22N 143 0W
Naches, *Wash.* **16** 46 44N 120 42W
Nacimiento Reservoir, *Calif.* **18** 35 46N 120 53W
Naco, *Ariz.* **17** 31 20N 109 57W
Nacogdoches, *Tex.* **13** 31 36N 94 39W
Nakalele Pt., *Hawaii* .. **30** 21 2N 156 35W
Naknek, *Alaska* **30** 58 44N 157 1W
Nampa, *Idaho* **16** 43 34N 116 34W
Nanticoke, *Pa.* **9** 41 12N 76 0W
Napa, *Calif.* **18** 38 18N 122 17W
Napa →, *Calif.* **18** 38 10N 122 19W
Napamute, *Alaska* **30** 61 30N 158 45W
Napanoch, *N.Y.* **9** 41 44N 74 22W
Naples, *Fla.* **11** 26 8N 81 48W
Napoleon, *N. Dak.* **12** 46 30N 99 46W
Napoleon, *Ohio* **15** 41 23N 84 8W
Nara Visa, *N. Mex.* **13** 35 37N 103 6W
Narrows, The, *N.Y.* **20** 40 37N 74 3W
Nashua, *Iowa* **14** 42 57N 92 32W
Nashua, *Mont.* **16** 48 8N 106 22W
Nashua, *N.H.* **9** 42 45N 71 28W
Nashville, *Ark.* **13** 33 57N 93 51W
Nashville, *Ga.* **11** 31 12N 83 15W
Nashville, *Tenn.* **11** 36 10N 86 47W
Nassau, *N.Y.* **9** 42 31N 73 37W
Natchez, *Miss.* **13** 31 34N 91 24W
Natchitoches, *La.* **13** 31 46N 93 5W
Natick, *Mass.* **23** 42 16N 71 21W
National City, *Calif.* . **19** 32 41N 117 6W
Natoma, *Kans.* **12** 39 11N 99 2W
Navajo Reservoir, *N. Mex.* **17** 36 48N 107 36W
Navasota, *Tex.* **13** 30 23N 96 5W
Neah Bay, *Wash.* **18** 48 22N 124 37W
Near Is., *Alaska* ...... **30** 53 0N 172 0 E
Nebraska □ **12** 41 30N 99 30W
Nebraska City, *Nebr.* .. **12** 40 41N 95 52W
Necedah, *Wis.* **12** 44 2N 90 4W
Neches →, *Tex.* **13** 29 58N 93 51W
Needham, *Mass.* **23** 42 16N 71 13W
Needles, *Calif.* **19** 34 51N 114 37W
Neenah, *Wis.* **10** 44 11N 88 28W
Negaunee, *Mich.* **10** 46 30N 87 36W
Neihart, *Mont.* **16** 47 0N 110 44W
Neilton, *Wash.* **16** 47 25N 123 53W
Neligh, *Nebr.* **12** 42 8N 98 2W
Nelson, *Ariz.* **17** 35 31N 113 19W
Nelson I., *Alaska* **30** 60 40N 164 40W
Nenana, *Alaska* **30** 64 34N 149 5W
Neodesha, *Kans.* **13** 37 25N 95 41W
Neosho, *Mo.* **13** 36 52N 94 22W
Neosho →, *Okla.* **13** 36 48N 95 18W
Nephi, *Utah* **16** 39 43N 111 50W
Neptune, *N.J.* **9** 40 13N 74 2W
Neuse →, *N.C.* **11** 35 6N 76 29W
Nevada, *Mo.* **14** 37 51N 94 22W
Nevada □ **16** 39 0N 117 0W
Nevada, Sierra, *Calif.* . **16** 39 0N 120 30W
Nevada City, *Calif.* ... **18** 39 16N 121 1W
Neville Island, *Pa.* ... **27** 40 30N 80 6W
New Albany, *Ind.* **15** 38 18N 85 49W
New Albany, *Miss.* **13** 34 29N 89 0W
New Albany, *Pa.* **9** 41 36N 76 27W
New Bedford, *Mass.* **9** 41 38N 70 56W
New Bern, *N.C.* **11** 35 7N 77 3W
New Boston, *Tex.* **13** 33 28N 94 25W
New Braunfels, *Tex.* ... **13** 29 42N 98 8W
New Britain, *Conn.* **9** 41 40N 72 47W
New Brunswick, *N.J.* ... **9** 40 30N 74 27W
New Carrollton, *Md.* ... **25** 38 58N 76 53W
New Castle, *Ind.* **15** 39 55N 85 22W
New Castle, *Pa.* **8** 41 0N 80 21W
New City, *N.Y.* **9** 41 9N 73 59W
New Cuyama, *Calif.* ... **19** 34 57N 119 38W
New Don Pedro Reservoir, *Calif.* **18** 37 43N 120 24W
New Dorp, *N.Y.* **20** 40 34N 74 8W
New England, *N. Dak.* .. **12** 46 32N 102 52W
New Hampshire □ **9** 44 0N 71 30W
New Hampton, *Iowa* ... **14** 43 3N 92 19W
New Haven, *Conn.* **9** 41 18N 72 55W
New Hyde Park, *N.Y.* .. **21** 40 43N 73 39W
New Iberia, *La.* **13** 30 1N 91 49W
New Jersey □ **9** 40 0N 74 30W
New Kensington, *Pa.* .. **8** 40 34N 79 46W
New Kensington, *Pa.* .. **27** 40 34N 79 46W
New Lexington, *Ohio* .. **10** 39 43N 82 13W
New London, *Conn.* ... **9** 41 22N 72 6W
New London, *Minn.* ... **12** 45 18N 94 56W
New London, *Wis.* **12** 44 23N 88 45W
New Madrid, *Mo.* **13** 36 36N 89 32W
New Meadows, *Idaho* .. **16** 44 58N 116 18W
New Melones L., *Calif.* . **18** 37 57N 120 31W
New Mexico □ **17** 34 30N 106 0W
New Milford, *Conn.* **9** 41 35N 73 25W
New Milford, *Pa.* **9** 41 52N 75 44W
New Orleans, *La.* **13** 29 58N 90 4W
New Philadelphia, *Ohio* **8** 40 30N 81 27W
New Plymouth, *Idaho* .. **16** 43 58N 116 49W
New Providence, *N.J.* .. **20** 40 42N 74 23W
New Richmond, *Wis.* .. **12** 45 7N 92 32W
New Roads, *La.* **13** 30 42N 91 26W
New Rochelle, *N.Y.* **21** 40 55N 73 45W
New Rockford, *N. Dak.* . **12** 47 41N 99 8W
New Salem, *N. Dak.* ... **12** 46 51N 101 25W
New Smyrna Beach, *Fla.* **11** 29 1N 80 56W
New Town, *N. Dak.* **12** 47 59N 102 30W
New Ulm, *Minn.* **12** 44 19N 94 28W
New York, *N.Y.* **20** 40 42N 74 0W
New York □ **9** 43 0N 75 0W
Newark, *Del.* **10** 39 41N 75 46W
Newark, *N.J.* **20** 40 43N 74 10W
Newark, *N.Y.* **8** 43 3N 77 6W
Newark, *Ohio* **8** 40 3N 82 24W
Newark International Airport, *N.J.* **20** 40 41N 74 10W
Newaygo, *Mich.* **10** 43 25N 85 48W
Newberg, *Oreg.* **16** 45 18N 122 58W
Newberry, *Mich.* **10** 46 21N 85 30W
Newberry, *S.C.* **11** 34 17N 81 37W
Newberry Springs, *Calif.* **19** 34 50N 116 41W
Newburgh, *N.Y.* **9** 41 30N 74 1W
Newburyport, *Mass.* ... **9** 42 49N 70 53W
Newcastle, *Wyo.* **12** 43 50N 104 11W
Newell, *S. Dak.* **12** 44 43N 103 25W
Newenham, C., *Alaska* . **30** 58 39N 162 11W
Newhalen, *Alaska* **30** 59 43N 154 54W
Newhall, *Calif.* **19** 34 23N 118 32W
Newkirk, *Okla.* **13** 36 53N 97 3W
Newman, *Calif.* **18** 37 19N 121 1W
Newmarket, *N.H.* **9** 43 5N 70 56W
Newnan, *Ga.* **11** 33 23N 84 48W
Newport, *Ark.* **13** 35 37N 91 16W
Newport, *Ky.* **15** 39 5N 84 30W
Newport, *N.H.* **9** 43 22N 72 10W
Newport, *Oreg.* **16** 44 39N 124 3W
Newport, *R.I.* **9** 41 29N 71 19W
Newport, *Tenn.* **11** 35 58N 83 11W
Newport, *Vt.* **9** 44 56N 72 13W
Newport, *Wash.* **16** 48 11N 117 3W
Newport Beach, *Calif.* .. **19** 33 37N 117 56W
Newport News, *Va.* **10** 36 59N 76 25W
Newton, *Iowa* **14** 41 42N 93 3W
Newton, *Mass.* **23** 42 19N 71 13W
Newton, *Miss.* **13** 32 19N 89 10W
Newton, *N.C.* **11** 35 40N 81 13W
Newton, *N.J.* **9** 41 3N 74 45W
Newton, *Tex.* **13** 30 51N 93 46W
Newtown Square, *Pa.* .. **24** 39 59N 75 24W
Nezperce, *Idaho* **16** 46 14N 116 14W
Niagara, *Mich.* **10** 45 45N 88 0W
Niagara Falls, *N.Y.* ... **8** 43 5N 79 4W
Niceville, *Fla.* **11** 30 31N 86 30W
Nicholasville, *Ky.* ... **15** 37 53N 84 34W
Nichols, *N.Y.* **9** 42 1N 76 22W
Nicholson, *Pa.* **9** 41 37N 75 47W
Niihau, *Hawaii* **30** 21 54N 160 9W
Nikolski, *Alaska* **30** 52 56N 168 52W
Niland, *Calif.* **19** 33 14N 115 31W
Niles, *Ill.* **22** 42 1N 87 48W
Niles, *Ohio* **8** 41 11N 80 46W
Niobrara, *Nebr.* **12** 42 45N 98 2W
Niobrara →, *Nebr.* ... **12** 42 46N 98 3W
Nipomo, *Calif.* **19** 35 3N 120 29W
Nixon, *Tex.* **13** 29 16N 97 46W
Noatak, *Alaska* **30** 67 34N 162 58W
Noatak →, *Alaska* **30** 68 0N 161 0W
Noblesville, *Ind.* **15** 40 3N 86 1W
Nocona, *Tex.* **13** 33 47N 97 44W
Noel, *Mo.* **13** 36 33N 94 29W
Nogales, *Ariz.* **17** 31 20N 110 56W
Nome, *Alaska* **30** 64 30N 165 25W
Nonopapa, *Hawaii* **30** 21 50N 160 15W
Noonan, *N. Dak.* **12** 48 54N 103 1W
Noorvik, *Alaska* **30** 66 50N 161 3W
Norco, *Calif.* **19** 33 56N 117 33W
Norfolk, *Nebr.* **12** 42 2N 97 25W
Norfolk, *Va.* **10** 36 51N 76 17W
Norfork Res., *Ark.* ... **13** 36 13N 92 15W
Normal, *Ill.* **14** 40 31N 88 59W
Norman, *Okla.* **13** 35 13N 97 26W
Norridge, *Ill.* **22** 41 57N 87 49W

Perry

Norris, *Mont.* **16** 45 34N 111 41W
Norristown, *Pa.* **24** 40 7N 75 20W
North Adams, *Mass.* **9** 42 42N 73 7W
North Bend, *Oreg.* **16** 43 24N 124 14W
North Bergen, *N.J.* **20** 40 48N 74 0W
North Berwick, *Maine* **9** 43 18N 70 44W
North Billerica, *Mass.* **23** 42 35N 71 16W
North Braddock, *Pa.* **27** 40 25N 79 51W
North Canadian →, *Okla.* **13** 35 16N 95 31W
North Carolina □ **11** 35 30N 80 0W
North Chelmsford, *Mass.* **23** 42 38N 71 23W
North Chicago, *Ill.* **15** 42 19N 87 51W
North Dakota □ **12** 47 30N 100 15W
North Fork, *Calif.* **18** 37 14N 119 21W
North Las Vegas, *Nev.* **19** 36 12N 115 7W
North Loup →, *Nebr.* **12** 41 17N 98 24W
North Olmsted, *Ohio* **27** 41 24N 81 55W
North Palisade, *Calif.* **18** 37 6N 118 31W
North Platte, *Nebr.* **12** 41 8N 100 46W
North Platte →, *Nebr.* **12** 41 7N 100 42W
North Powder, *Oreg.* **16** 45 2N 117 55W
North Reading, *Mass.* **23** 42 34N 71 5W
North Richmond, *Calif.* **28** 37 57N 122 22W
North Springfield, *Va.* **25** 38 48N 77 12W
North Tonawanda, *N.Y.* **8** 43 2N 78 53W
North Truchas Pk., *N. Mex.* **17** 36 0N 105 30W
North Vernon, *Ind.* **15** 39 0N 85 38W
Northampton, *Mass.* **9** 42 19N 72 38W
Northampton, *Pa.* **9** 40 41N 75 30W
Northbridge, *Mass.* **9** 42 9N 71 39W
Northbrook, *Ill.* **22** 42 7N 87 53W
Northern Marianas ■, *Pac. Oc.* **31** 17 0N 145 0 E
Northfield, *Ill.* **22** 42 5N 87 44W
Northfield, *Minn.* **12** 44 27N 93 9W
Northlake, *Ill.* **22** 41 54N 87 53W
Northome, *Minn.* **12** 47 52N 94 17W
Northport, *Ala.* **11** 33 14N 87 35W
Northport, *Mich.* **10** 45 8N 85 37W
Northport, *Wash.* **16** 48 55N 117 48W
Northway, *Alaska* **30** 62 58N 141 56W
Northwood, *Iowa* **12** 43 27N 93 13W
Northwood, *N. Dak.* **12** 47 44N 97 34W
Norton, *Kans.* **12** 39 50N 99 53W
Norton B., *Alaska* **30** 64 45N 161 15W
Norton Sd., *Alaska* **30** 63 50N 164 0W
Norwalk, *Calif.* **29** 33 54N 118 4W
Norwalk, *Conn.* **9** 41 7N 73 22W
Norwalk, *Ohio* **8** 41 15N 82 37W
Norway, *Mich.* **10** 45 47N 87 55W
Norwich, *Conn.* **9** 41 31N 72 5W
Norwich, *N.Y.* **9** 42 32N 75 32W
Norwood, *Mass.* **23** 42 11N 71 13W
Nottoway →, *Va.* **10** 36 33N 76 55W
Novato, *Calif.* **18** 38 6N 122 35W
Noxen, *Pa.* **9** 41 25N 76 4W
Noxon, *Mont.* **16** 48 0N 115 43W
Nueces →, *Tex.* **13** 27 51N 97 30W
Nulato, *Alaska* **30** 64 43N 158 6W
Nunivak I., *Alaska* **30** 60 10N 166 30W
Nutley, *N.J.* **20** 40 49N 74 9W
Nyack, *N.Y.* **9** 41 5N 73 55W
Nyssa, *Oreg.* **16** 43 53N 117 0W

O

Oacoma, *S. Dak.* **12** 43 48N 99 24W
Oahe, L., *S. Dak.* **12** 44 27N 100 24W
Oahe Dam, *S. Dak.* **12** 44 27N 100 24W
Oahu, *Hawaii* **30** 21 28N 157 58W
Oak Creek, *Colo.* **16** 40 16N 106 57W
Oak Forest, *Ill.* **22** 41 36N 87 44W
Oak Harbor, *Wash.* **18** 48 18N 122 39W
Oak Hill, *W. Va.* **10** 37 59N 81 9W
Oak Lawn, *Ill.* **22** 41 42N 87 44W
Oak Park, *Ill.* **22** 41 52N 87 46W
Oak Park, *Mich.* **26** 42 27N 83 11W
Oak Ridge, *Tenn.* **11** 36 1N 84 16W
Oak View, *Calif.* **19** 34 24N 119 18W
Oakdale, *Calif.* **18** 37 46N 120 51W
Oakdale, *La.* **13** 30 49N 92 40W
Oakes, *N. Dak.* **12** 46 8N 98 6W
Oakesdale, *Wash.* **16** 47 8N 117 15W
Oakhurst, *Calif.* **18** 37 19N 119 40W
Oakland, *Calif.* **28** 37 48N 122 17W
Oakland, *N.J.* **20** 41 2N 74 13W
Oakland, *Oreg.* **16** 43 25N 123 18W
Oakland City, *Ind.* **15** 38 20N 87 21W
Oakland Pontiac Airport, *Mich.* **26** 42 40N 83 24W
Oakley, *Idaho* **16** 42 15N 113 53W
Oakley, *Kans.* **12** 39 8N 100 51W
Oakmont, *Pa.* **27** 40 31N 79 50W
Oakridge, *Oreg.* **16** 43 45N 122 28W
Oasis, *Calif.* **19** 33 28N 116 6W
Oasis, *Nev.* **18** 37 29N 117 55W
Oatman, *Ariz.* **19** 35 1N 114 19W
Oberlin, *Kans.* **12** 39 49N 100 32W
Oberlin, *La.* **13** 30 37N 92 46W
Ocala, *Fla.* **11** 29 11N 82 8W
Oconomowoc, *Wis.* **12** 43 7N 88 30W
Ocate, *N. Mex.* **13** 36 11N 105 3W
Ocean City, *N.J.* **10** 39 17N 74 35W
Ocean Park, *Wash.* **18** 46 30N 124 3W
Oceano, *Calif.* **19** 35 6N 120 37W
Oceanside, *Calif.* **19** 33 12N 117 23W
Oceanside, *N.Y.* **21** 40 38N 73 37W
Ocilla, *Ga.* **11** 31 36N 83 15W
Ocmulgee →, *Ga.* **11** 31 58N 82 33W
Oconee →, *Ga.* **11** 31 58N 82 33W
Oconto, *Wis.* **10** 44 53N 87 52W
Oconto Falls, *Wis.* **10** 44 52N 88 9W
Octave, *Ariz.* **17** 34 10N 112 43W
Odessa, *Tex.* **13** 31 52N 102 23W
Odessa, *Wash.* **16** 47 20N 118 41W
O'Donnell, *Tex.* **13** 32 58N 101 50W
Oelrichs, *S. Dak.* **12** 43 11N 103 14W
Oelwein, *Iowa* **12** 42 41N 91 55W
Ofu, *Amer. Samoa* **31** 14 11 S 169 41W
Ogallala, *Nebr.* **12** 41 8N 101 43W
Ogden, *Iowa* **14** 42 2N 94 2W
Ogden, *Utah* **16** 41 13N 111 58W
Ogdensburg, *N.Y.* **9** 44 42N 75 30W
Ogeechee →, *Ga.* **11** 31 50N 81 3W
Ohio □ **10** 40 15N 82 45W
Ohio →, *Ohio* **10** 36 59N 89 8W
Oil City, *Pa.* **8** 41 26N 79 42W
Oildale, *Calif.* **19** 35 25N 119 1W
Ojai, *Calif.* **19** 34 27N 119 15W
Okanogan, *Wash.* **16** 48 22N 119 35W
Okanogan →, *Wash.* **16** 48 6N 119 44W
Okeechobee, *Fla.* **11** 27 15N 80 50W
Okeechobee, L., *Fla.* **11** 27 0N 80 50W
Okefenokee Swamp, *Ga.* **11** 30 40N 82 20W
Oklahoma □ **13** 35 20N 97 30W
Oklahoma City, *Okla.* **13** 35 30N 97 30W
Okmulgee, *Okla.* **13** 35 37N 95 58W
Okolona, *Miss.* **13** 34 0N 88 45W
Ola, *Ark.* **13** 35 2N 93 13W
Olancha, *Calif.* **19** 36 17N 118 1W
Olancha Pk., *Calif.* **19** 36 15N 118 7W
Olathe, *Kans.* **12** 38 53N 94 49W
Old Baldy Pk. = San Antonio, Mt., *Calif.* **19** 34 17N 117 38W
Old Dale, *Calif.* **19** 34 8N 115 47W
Old Forge, *N.Y.* **9** 43 43N 74 58W
Old Forge, *Pa.* **9** 41 22N 75 45W
Old Harbor, *Alaska* **30** 57 12N 153 18W
Old Town, *Maine* **11** 44 56N 68 39W
Olean, *N.Y.* **8** 42 5N 78 26W
Olema, *Calif.* **18** 38 3N 122 47W
Olney, *Ill.* **15** 38 44N 88 5W
Olney, *Tex.* **13** 33 22N 98 45W
Olosega, *Amer. Samoa* **31** 14 11 S 169 38W
Olton, *Tex.* **13** 34 11N 102 8W
Olympia, *Wash.* **18** 47 3N 122 53W
Olympic Mts., *Wash.* **18** 47 55N 123 45W
Olympic Nat. Park, *Wash.* **18** 47 48N 123 30W
Olympus, Mt., *Wash.* **18** 47 48N 123 43W
Omaha, *Nebr.* **12** 41 17N 95 58W
Omak, *Wash.* **16** 48 25N 119 31W
Onaga, *Kans.* **12** 39 29N 96 10W
Onalaska, *Wis.* **12** 43 53N 91 14W
Onamia, *Minn.* **12** 46 4N 93 40W
Onancock, *Va.* **10** 37 43N 75 45W
Onawa, *Iowa* **12** 42 2N 96 6W
Onaway, *Mich.* **10** 45 21N 84 14W
Oneida, *N.Y.* **9** 43 6N 75 39W
Oneida L., *N.Y.* **9** 43 12N 75 54W
O'Neill, *Nebr.* **12** 42 27N 98 39W
Oneonta, *Ala.* **11** 33 57N 86 28W
Oneonta, *N.Y.* **9** 42 27N 75 4W
Onida, *S. Dak.* **12** 44 42N 100 4W
Onslow B., *N.C.* **11** 34 20N 77 15W
Ontario, *Calif.* **19** 34 4N 117 39W
Ontario, *Oreg.* **16** 44 2N 116 58W
Ontario, L., *N. Amer.* **8** 43 20N 78 0W
Ontonagon, *Mich.* **12** 46 52N 89 19W
Onyx, *Calif.* **19** 35 41N 118 14W
Ookala, *Hawaii* **30** 20 1N 155 17W
Opelousas, *La.* **13** 30 32N 92 5W
Opheim, *Mont.* **16** 48 51N 106 24W
Ophir, *Alaska* **30** 63 10N 156 31W
Opp, *Ala.* **11** 31 17N 86 16W
Oracle, *Ariz.* **17** 32 37N 110 46W
Orange, *Calif.* **19** 33 47N 117 51W
Orange, *Mass.* **9** 42 35N 72 19W
Orange, *N.J.* **20** 40 46N 74 13W
Orange, *Tex.* **13** 30 6N 93 44W
Orange, *Va.* **10** 38 15N 78 7W
Orange Cove, *Calif.* **18** 36 38N 119 19W
Orange Grove, *Tex.* **13** 27 58N 97 56W
Orangeburg, *S.C.* **11** 33 30N 80 52W
Orcutt, *Calif.* **19** 34 52N 120 27W
Orderville, *Utah* **17** 37 17N 112 38W
Ordway, *Colo.* **12** 38 13N 103 46W
Oregon, *Ill.* **14** 42 1N 89 20W
Oregon □ **16** 44 0N 121 0W
Oregon City, *Oreg.* **18** 45 21N 122 36W
Orem, *Utah* **16** 40 19N 111 42W
Orinda, *Calif.* **28** 37 52N 122 10W
Orland, *Calif.* **18** 39 45N 122 12W
Orland Park, *Ill.* **22** 41 37N 87 52W
Orlando, *Fla.* **11** 28 33N 81 23W
Ormond Beach, *Fla.* **11** 29 17N 81 3W
Oro Grande, *Calif.* **19** 34 36N 117 20W
Orogrande, *N. Mex.* **17** 32 24N 106 5W
Oroville, *Calif.* **18** 39 31N 121 33W
Oroville, *Wash.* **16** 48 56N 119 26W
Osage, *Iowa* **12** 43 17N 92 49W
Osage, *Wyo.* **12** 43 59N 104 25W
Osage →, *Mo.* **14** 38 35N 91 57W
Osage City, *Kans.* **12** 38 38N 95 50W
Osawatomie, *Kans.* **12** 38 31N 94 57W
Osborne, *Kans.* **12** 39 26N 98 42W
Osceola, *Ark.* **13** 35 42N 89 58W
Osceola, *Iowa* **14** 41 2N 93 46W
Oscoda, *Mich.* **8** 44 26N 83 20W
Oshkosh, *Nebr.* **12** 41 24N 102 21W
Oshkosh, *Wis.* **12** 44 1N 88 33W
Oskaloosa, *Iowa* **14** 41 18N 92 39W
Ossabaw I., *Ga.* **11** 31 50N 81 5W
Ossining, *N.Y.* **9** 41 10N 73 55W
Oswego, *N.Y.* **9** 43 27N 76 31W
Othello, *Wash.* **16** 46 50N 119 10W
Otis, *Colo.* **12** 40 9N 102 58W
Ottawa, *Ill.* **15** 41 21N 88 51W
Ottawa, *Kans.* **12** 38 37N 95 16W
Ottumwa, *Iowa* **14** 41 1N 92 25W
Ouachita →, *La.* **13** 31 38N 91 49W
Ouachita, L., *Ark.* **13** 34 34N 93 12W
Ouachita Mts., *Ark.* **13** 34 40N 94 25W
Ouray, *Colo.* **17** 38 1N 107 40W
Outlook, *Mont.* **12** 48 53N 104 47W
Overlea, *Md.* **25** 39 21N 76 33W
Overton, *Nev.* **19** 36 33N 114 27W
Ovid, *Colo.* **12** 40 58N 102 23W
Owatonna, *Minn.* **12** 44 5N 93 14W
Owego, *N.Y.* **9** 42 6N 76 16W
Owens →, *Calif.* **18** 36 32N 117 59W
Owens L., *Calif.* **19** 36 26N 117 57W
Owensboro, *Ky.* **15** 37 46N 87 7W
Owensville, *Mo.* **14** 38 21N 91 30W
Owings Mills, *Md.* **25** 39 25N 76 48W
Owosso, *Mich.* **15** 43 0N 84 10W
Owyhee, *Nev.* **16** 41 57N 116 6W
Owyhee →, *Oreg.* **16** 43 49N 117 2W
Owyhee, L., *Oreg.* **16** 43 38N 117 14W
Oxford, *Miss.* **13** 34 22N 89 31W
Oxford, *N.C.* **11** 36 19N 78 35W
Oxford, *Ohio* **15** 39 31N 84 45W
Oxnard, *Calif.* **19** 34 12N 119 11W
Oyster Bay, *N.Y.* **21** 40 52N 73 31W
Ozark, *Ala.* **11** 31 28N 85 39W
Ozark, *Ark.* **13** 35 29N 93 50W
Ozark, *Mo.* **13** 37 1N 93 12W
Ozark Plateau, *Mo.* **13** 37 20N 91 40W
Ozarks, L. of the, *Mo.* **14** 38 12N 92 38W
Ozona, *Tex.* **13** 30 43N 101 12W

P

Paauilo, *Hawaii* **30** 20 2N 155 22W
Pacific Grove, *Calif.* **18** 36 38N 121 56W
Pacifica, *Calif.* **28** 37 38N 122 29W
Padre I., *Tex.* **13** 27 10N 97 25W
Paducah, *Ky.* **10** 37 5N 88 37W
Paducah, *Tex.* **13** 34 1N 100 18W
Page, *Ariz.* **17** 36 57N 111 27W
Page, *N. Dak.* **12** 47 10N 97 34W
Pago Pago, *Amer. Samoa* **31** 14 16 S 170 43W
Pagosa Springs, *Colo.* **17** 37 16N 107 1W
Pahala, *Hawaii* **30** 19 12N 155 29W
Pahoa, *Hawaii* **30** 19 30N 154 57W
Pahokee, *Fla.* **11** 26 50N 80 40W
Pahrump, *Nev.* **19** 36 12N 115 59W
Pahute Mesa, *Nev.* **18** 37 20N 116 45W
Paia, *Hawaii* **30** 20 54N 156 22W
Paicines, *Calif.* **18** 36 44N 121 17W
Pailolo Channel, *Hawaii* **30** 21 0N 156 40W
Painesville, *Ohio* **8** 41 43N 81 15W
Paint Rock, *Tex.* **13** 31 31N 99 55W
Painted Desert, *Ariz.* **17** 36 0N 111 0W
Paintsville, *Ky.* **10** 37 49N 82 48W
Paisley, *Oreg.* **16** 42 42N 120 32W
Pala, *Calif.* **19** 33 22N 117 5W
Palacios, *Tex.* **13** 28 42N 96 13W
Palatka, *Fla.* **11** 29 39N 81 38W
Palau ■, *Pac. Oc.* **31** 7 30N 134 30 E
Palermo, *Calif.* **16** 39 26N 121 33W
Palestine, *Tex.* **13** 31 46N 95 38W
Palisade, *Nebr.* **12** 40 21N 101 7W
Palisades, *N.Y.* **20** 41 1N 73 55W
Palm Beach, *Fla.* **11** 26 43N 80 2W
Palm Desert, *Calif.* **19** 33 43N 116 22W
Palm Springs, *Calif.* **19** 33 50N 116 33W
Palmdale, *Calif.* **19** 34 35N 118 7W
Palmer, *Alaska* **30** 61 36N 149 7W
Palmer Lake, *Colo.* **12** 39 7N 104 55W
Palmerton, *Pa.* **9** 40 48N 75 37W
Palmetto, *Fla.* **11** 27 31N 82 34W
Palmyra, *Mo.* **14** 39 48N 91 32W
Palmyra, *N.J.* **24** 40 0N 75 1W
Palo Alto, *Calif.* **28** 37 26N 122 8W
Palos Heights, *Ill.* **22** 41 40N 87 47W
Palos Hills Forest, *Ill.* **22** 41 40N 87 52W
Palos Verdes, *Calif.* **19** 33 48N 118 23W
Palos Verdes, Pt., *Calif.* **19** 33 43N 118 26W
Palouse, *Wash.* **16** 46 55N 117 4W
Pamlico →, *N.C.* **11** 35 20N 76 28W
Pamlico Sd., *N.C.* **11** 35 20N 76 0W
Pampa, *Tex.* **13** 35 32N 100 58W
Pana, *Ill.* **14** 39 23N 89 5W
Panaca, *Nev.* **17** 37 47N 114 23W
Panama City, *Fla.* **11** 30 10N 85 40W
Panamint Range, *Calif.* **19** 36 20N 117 20W
Panamint Springs, *Calif.* **19** 36 20N 117 28W
Pancake Range, *Nev.* **17** 38 30N 115 50W
Panguitch, *Utah* **17** 37 50N 112 26W
Panhandle, *Tex.* **13** 35 21N 101 23W
Paola, *Kans.* **12** 38 35N 94 53W
Paoli, *Pa.* **24** 40 2N 75 28W
Paonia, *Colo.* **17** 38 52N 107 36W
Papaikou, *Hawaii* **30** 19 47N 155 6W
Paradise, *Mont.* **16** 47 23N 114 48W
Paradise Valley, *Nev.* **16** 41 30N 117 32W
Paragould, *Ark.* **13** 36 3N 90 29W
Paramus, *N.J.* **20** 40 56N 74 2W
Paris, *Idaho* **16** 42 14N 111 24W
Paris, *Ky.* **15** 38 13N 84 15W
Paris, *Tenn.* **11** 36 18N 88 19W
Paris, *Tex.* **13** 33 40N 95 33W
Parish, *N.Y.* **9** 43 25N 76 8W
Park City, *Utah* **16** 40 39N 111 30W
Park Falls, *Wis.* **12** 45 56N 90 27W
Park Range, *Colo.* **16** 40 0N 106 30W
Park Rapids, *Minn.* **12** 46 55N 95 4W
Park Ridge, *Ill.* **22** 42 0N 87 50W
Park Ridge, *N.J.* **20** 41 2N 74 2W
Park River, *N. Dak.* **12** 48 24N 97 45W
Parker, *Ariz.* **19** 34 9N 114 17W
Parker, *S. Dak.* **12** 43 24N 97 8W
Parker Dam, *Ariz.* **19** 34 18N 114 8W
Parkersburg, *W. Va.* **10** 39 16N 81 34W
Parkfield, *Calif.* **18** 35 54N 120 26W
Parkston, *S. Dak.* **12** 43 24N 97 59W
Parkville, *Md.* **25** 39 23N 76 34W
Parma, *Idaho* **16** 43 47N 116 57W
Parma, *Ohio* **27** 41 24N 81 43W
Parma Heights, *Ohio* **27** 41 23N 81 45W
Parowan, *Utah* **17** 37 51N 112 50W
Parris I., *S.C.* **11** 32 20N 80 41W
Parshall, *N. Dak.* **12** 47 57N 102 8W
Parsons, *Kans.* **13** 37 20N 95 16W
Pasadena, *Calif.* **29** 34 9N 118 8W
Pasadena, *Tex.* **13** 29 43N 95 13W
Pascagoula, *Miss.* **13** 30 21N 88 33W
Pascagoula →, *Miss.* **13** 30 23N 88 37W
Pasco, *Wash.* **16** 46 14N 119 6W
Paso Robles, *Calif.* **17** 35 38N 120 41W
Passaic, *N.J.* **20** 40 51N 74 9W
Patagonia, *Ariz.* **17** 31 33N 110 45W
Patchogue, *N.Y.* **9** 40 46N 73 1W
Pateros, *Wash.* **16** 48 3N 119 54W
Paterson, *N.J.* **20** 40 54N 74 10W
Pathfinder Reservoir, *Wyo.* **16** 42 28N 106 51W
Patten, *Maine* **11** 46 0N 68 38W
Patterson, *Calif.* **18** 37 28N 121 8W
Patterson, *La.* **13** 29 42N 91 18W
Patterson, Mt., *Calif.* **18** 38 29N 119 20W
Paullina, *Iowa* **12** 42 59N 95 41W
Pauls Valley, *Okla.* **13** 34 44N 97 13W
Paulsboro, *N.J.* **24** 39 49N 75 14W
Pauma Valley, *Calif.* **19** 33 16N 116 58W
Pavlof Is., *Alaska* **30** 55 30N 161 30W
Pawhuska, *Okla.* **13** 36 40N 96 20W
Pawling, *N.Y.* **9** 41 34N 73 36W
Pawnee, *Okla.* **13** 36 20N 96 48W
Pawnee City, *Nebr.* **12** 40 7N 96 9W
Pawtucket, *R.I.* **9** 41 53N 71 23W
Paxton, *Ill.* **15** 40 27N 88 6W
Paxton, *Nebr.* **12** 41 7N 101 21W
Payette, *Idaho* **16** 44 5N 116 56W
Paynesville, *Minn.* **12** 45 23N 94 43W
Payson, *Ariz.* **17** 34 14N 111 20W
Payson, *Utah* **16** 40 3N 111 44W
Pe Ell, *Wash.* **18** 46 34N 123 18W
Peabody, *Mass.* **23** 42 32N 70 57W
Peach Springs, *Ariz.* **17** 35 32N 113 25W
Peale, Mt., *Utah* **17** 38 26N 109 14W
Pearblossom, *Calif.* **19** 34 30N 117 55W
Pearl →, *Miss.* **13** 30 11N 89 32W
Pearl City, *Hawaii* **30** 21 24N 157 59W
Pearl Harbor, *Hawaii* **30** 21 21N 157 57W
Pearsall, *Tex.* **13** 28 54N 99 6W
Pease →, *Tex.* **13** 34 12N 99 2W
Pebble Beach, *Calif.* **18** 36 34N 121 57W
Pecos, *Tex.* **13** 31 26N 103 30W
Pecos →, *Tex.* **13** 29 42N 101 22W
Pedro Valley, *Calif.* **28** 37 35N 122 28W
Peekskill, *N.Y.* **9** 41 17N 73 55W
Pekin, *Ill.* **14** 40 35N 89 40W
Pelham, *Ga.* **11** 31 8N 84 9W
Pelham, *N.Y.* **21** 40 54N 73 46W
Pelican, *Alaska* **30** 57 58N 136 14W
Pella, *Iowa* **14** 41 25N 92 55W
Pembina, *N. Dak.* **12** 48 58N 97 15W
Pembine, *Wis.* **10** 45 38N 87 59W
Pembroke, *Ga.* **11** 32 8N 81 37W
Pend Oreille →, *Wash.* **16** 49 4N 117 37W
Pend Oreille L., *Idaho* **16** 48 10N 116 21W
Pendleton, *Calif.* **19** 33 16N 117 23W
Pendleton, *Oreg.* **16** 45 40N 118 47W
Penn Hills, *Pa.* **27** 40 27N 79 50W
Penn Yan, *N.Y.* **8** 42 40N 77 3W
Pennsauken, *N.J.* **24** 39 57N 75 5W
Pennsylvania □ **10** 40 45N 77 30W
Pensacola, *Fla.* **11** 30 25N 87 13W
Peoria, *Ariz.* **17** 33 35N 112 14W
Peoria, *Ill.* **14** 40 42N 89 36W
Perham, *Minn.* **12** 46 36N 95 34W
Perris, *Calif.* **19** 33 47N 117 14W
Perry, *Fla.* **11** 30 7N 83 35W
Perry, *Ga.* **11** 32 28N 83 44W
Perry, *Iowa* **14** 41 51N 94 6W

Perry

Perry, *Maine* **11** 44 58N 67 5W
Perry, *Okla.* **13** 36 17N 97 14W
Perry Hall, *Md.* **25** 39 24N 76 28W
Perrysville, *Pa.* **27** 40 32N 80 1W
Perryton, *Tex.* **13** 36 24N 100 48W
Perryville, *Alaska* **30** 55 55N 159 9W
Perryville, *Mo.* **14** 37 43N 89 52W
Perth Amboy, *N.J.* **20** 40 30N 74 16W
Peru, *Ill.* **14** 41 20N 89 8W
Peru, *Ind.* **15** 40 45N 86 4W
Peshtigo, *Mich.* **10** 45 4N 87 46W
Petaluma, *Calif.* **18** 38 14N 122 39W
Peterborough, *N.H.* **9** 42 53N 71 57W
Petersburg, *Alaska* **30** 56 48N 132 58W
Petersburg, *Ind.* **15** 38 30N 87 17W
Petersburg, *Va.* **10** 37 14N 77 24W
Petersburg, *W. Va.* **10** 39 1N 79 5W
Petit Bois I., *Miss.* **11** 30 12N 88 26W
Petoskey, *Mich.* **10** 45 22N 84 57W
Phelps, *N.Y.* **8** 42 58N 77 3W
Phelps, *Wis.* **12** 46 4N 89 5W
Phenix City, *Ala.* **11** 32 28N 85 0W
Philadelphia, *Miss.* **13** 32 46N 89 7W
Philadelphia, *Pa.* **24** 39 58N 75 10W
Philadelphia Airport, *Pa.* **24** 40 4N 75 1W
Philadelphia International Airport, *Pa.* **24** 39 52N 75 14W
Philip, *S. Dak.* **12** 44 2N 101 40W
Philip Smith Mts., *Alaska* **30** 68 0N 146 0W
Philipsburg, *Mont.* **16** 46 20N 113 18W
Phillips, *Tex.* **13** 35 42N 101 22W
Phillips, *Wis.* **12** 45 42N 90 24W
Phillipsburg, *Kans.* **12** 39 45N 99 19W
Phillipsburg, *N.J.* **9** 40 42N 75 12W
Philmont, *N.Y.* **9** 42 15N 73 39W
Philomath, *Oreg.* **16** 44 32N 123 22W
Phoenix, *Ariz.* **17** 33 27N 112 4W
Phoenix, *N.Y.* **9** 43 14N 76 18W
Phoenixville, *Pa.* **24** 40 7N 75 31W
Picayune, *Miss.* **13** 30 32N 89 41W
Pico Rivera, *Calif.* **29** 33 59N 118 5W
Piedmont, *Ala.* **11** 33 55N 85 37W
Piedmont Plateau, *S.C.* **11** 34 0N 81 30W
Pierce, *Idaho* **16** 46 30N 115 48W
Pierre, *S. Dak.* **12** 44 22N 100 21W
Pigeon, *Mich.* **10** 43 50N 83 16W
Piggott, *Ark.* **13** 36 23N 90 11W
Pikes Peak, *Colo.* **12** 38 50N 105 3W
Pikesville, *Md.* **25** 39 22N 76 41W
Pikeville, *Ky.* **10** 37 29N 82 31W
Pilot Point, *Tex.* **13** 33 24N 96 58W
Pilot Rock, *Oreg.* **16** 45 29N 118 50W
Pima, *Ariz.* **17** 32 54N 109 50W
Pimmit Hills, *Va.* **25** 38 54N 77 12W
Pinckneyville, *Ill.* **14** 38 5N 89 23W
Pine, *Ariz.* **17** 34 23N 111 27W
Pine Bluff, *Ark.* **13** 34 13N 92 1W
Pine City, *Minn.* **12** 45 50N 92 59W
Pine Flat L., *Calif.* **18** 36 50N 119 20W
Pine Ridge, *S. Dak.* **12** 43 2N 102 33W
Pine River, *Minn.* **12** 46 43N 94 24W
Pine Valley, *Calif.* **19** 32 50N 116 32W
Pinecrest, *Calif.* **18** 38 12N 120 1W
Pinedale, *Calif.* **18** 36 50N 119 48W
Pinehurst, *Mass.* **23** 42 31N 71 12W
Pinetop, *Ariz.* **17** 34 8N 109 56W
Pinetree, *Wyo.* **16** 43 42N 105 52W
Pineville, *Ky.* **11** 36 46N 83 42W
Pineville, *La.* **13** 31 19N 92 26W
Pinnacles, *Calif.* **18** 36 33N 121 19W
Pinon Hills, *Calif.* **19** 34 26N 117 39W
Pinos, Mt., *Calif.* **19** 34 49N 119 8W
Pinos Pt., *Calif.* **17** 36 38N 121 57W
Pioche, *Nev.* **17** 37 56N 114 27W
Pipestone, *Minn.* **12** 44 0N 96 19W
Piqua, *Ohio* **15** 40 9N 84 15W
Piru, *Calif.* **19** 34 25N 118 48W
Piscataway, *N.J.* **20** 40 34N 74 27W
Pismo Beach, *Calif.* **19** 35 9N 120 38W
Pittsburg, *Kans.* **13** 37 25N 94 42W
Pittsburg, *Tex.* **13** 33 0N 94 59W
Pittsburgh, *Pa.* **27** 40 26N 79 59W
Pittsfield, *Ill.* **14** 39 36N 90 49W
Pittsfield, *Mass.* **9** 42 27N 73 15W
Pittsfield, *N.H.* **9** 43 18N 71 20W
Pittston, *Pa.* **9** 41 19N 75 47W
Pixley, *Calif.* **18** 35 58N 119 18W
Placerville, *Calif.* **18** 38 44N 120 48W
Plain Dealing, *La.* **13** 32 54N 93 42W
Plainfield, *N.J.* **20** 40 36N 74 24W
Plainfield, *N.J.* **9** 40 37N 74 25W
Plains, *Kans.* **13** 37 16N 100 35W
Plains, *Mont.* **16** 47 28N 114 53W
Plains, *Tex.* **13** 33 11N 102 50W
Plainview, *Nebr.* **12** 42 21N 97 47W
Plainview, *Tex.* **13** 34 11N 101 43W
Plainville, *Kans.* **12** 39 14N 99 18W
Plainwell, *Mich.* **10** 42 27N 85 38W
Planada, *Calif.* **18** 37 16N 120 19W
Plankinton, *S. Dak.* **12** 43 43N 98 29W
Plano, *Tex.* **13** 33 1N 96 42W
Plant City, *Fla.* **11** 28 1N 82 7W
Plaquemine, *La.* **13** 30 17N 91 14W
Plateau du Coteau du Missouri, *N. Dak.* **12** 47 9N 101 5W
Platinum, *Alaska* **30** 59 1N 161 49W
Platte, *S. Dak.* **12** 43 23N 98 51W
Platte →, *Mo.* **14** 39 16N 94 50W
Platteville, *Colo.* **12** 40 13N 104 49W
Plattsburgh, *N.Y.* **9** 44 42N 73 28W
Plattsmouth, *Nebr.* **12** 41 1N 95 53W
Pleasant Hill, *Calif.* **28** 37 56N 122 4W
Pleasant Hill, *Mo.* **14** 38 47N 94 16W
Pleasant Hills, *Pa.* **27** 40 20N 79 58W
Pleasanton, *Tex.* **13** 28 58N 98 29W
Pleasantville, *N.J.* **10** 39 24N 74 32W
Plentywood, *Mont.* **12** 48 47N 104 34W
Plum I., *N.Y.* **9** 41 11N 72 12W
Plummer, *Idaho* **16** 47 20N 116 53W
Plymouth, *Calif.* **18** 38 29N 120 51W
Plymouth, *Ind.* **15** 41 21N 86 19W
Plymouth, *Mass.* **9** 41 57N 70 40W
Plymouth, *N.C.* **11** 35 52N 76 43W
Plymouth, *Pa.* **9** 41 14N 75 57W
Plymouth, *Wis.* **10** 43 45N 87 59W
Plymouth Meeting, *Pa.* **24** 40 6N 75 17W
Pocahontas, *Ark.* **13** 36 16N 90 58W
Pocahontas, *Iowa* **14** 42 44N 94 40W
Pocatello, *Idaho* **16** 42 52N 112 27W
Pocomoke City, *Md.* **10** 38 5N 75 34W
Pohnpei, *Pac. Oc.* **31** 6 55N 158 10 E
Point Baker, *Alaska* **30** 56 21N 133 37W
Point Hope, *Alaska* **30** 68 21N 166 47W
Point Lay, *Alaska* **30** 69 46N 163 3W
Point Pleasant, *W. Va.* **10** 38 51N 82 8W
Pointe-à-la Hache, *La.* **13** 29 35N 89 55W
Pojoaque Valley, *N. Mex.* **17** 35 54N 106 1W
Polacca, *Ariz.* **17** 35 50N 110 23W
Pollock, *S. Dak.* **12** 45 55N 100 17W
Polo, *Ill.* **14** 41 59N 89 35W
Polson, *Mont.* **16** 47 41N 114 9W
Pomeroy, *Ohio* **10** 39 2N 82 2W
Pomeroy, *Wash.* **16** 46 28N 117 36W
Pomona, *Calif.* **19** 34 4N 117 45W
Pompano Beach, *Fla.* **11** 26 14N 80 8W
Pompeys Pillar, *Mont.* **16** 45 59N 107 57W
Pompton Plains, *N.J.* **20** 40 58N 74 18W
Ponca, *Nebr.* **12** 42 34N 96 43W
Ponca City, *Okla.* **13** 36 42N 97 5W
Ponce, *Puerto Rico* **30** 18 1N 66 37W
Ponchatoula, *La.* **13** 30 26N 90 26W
Pond, *Calif.* **19** 35 43N 119 20W
Pontchartrain L., *La.* **13** 30 5N 90 5W
Pontiac, *Ill.* **15** 40 53N 88 38W
Pontiac, *Mich.* **26** 42 38N 83 17W
Poorman, *Alaska* **30** 64 5N 155 48W
Poplar, *Mont.* **12** 48 7N 105 12W
Poplar Bluff, *Mo.* **13** 36 46N 90 24W
Poplarville, *Miss.* **13** 30 51N 89 32W
Porcupine →, *Alaska* **30** 66 34N 145 19W
Port Alexander, *Alaska* **30** 56 15N 134 38W
Port Allegany, *Pa.* **8** 41 48N 78 17W
Port Allen, *La.* **13** 30 27N 91 12W
Port Angeles, *Wash.* **18** 48 7N 123 27W
Port Aransas, *Tex.* **13** 27 50N 97 4W
Port Arthur, *Tex.* **13** 29 54N 93 56W
Port Austin, *Mich.* **8** 44 3N 83 1W
Port Chester, *N.Y.* **21** 41 0N 73 40W
Port Clinton, *Ohio* **15** 41 31N 82 56W
Port Gibson, *Miss.* **13** 31 58N 90 59W
Port Heiden, *Alaska* **30** 56 55N 158 41W
Port Henry, *N.Y.* **9** 44 3N 73 28W
Port Hueneme, *Calif.* **19** 34 7N 119 12W
Port Huron, *Mich.* **10** 42 58N 82 26W
Port Isabel, *Tex.* **13** 26 5N 97 12W
Port Jefferson, *N.Y.* **9** 40 57N 73 3W
Port Jervis, *N.Y.* **9** 41 22N 74 41W
Port Lavaca, *Tex.* **13** 28 37N 96 38W
Port O'Connor, *Tex.* **13** 28 26N 96 24W
Port Orchard, *Wash.* **18** 47 32N 122 38W
Port Orford, *Oreg.* **16** 42 45N 124 30W
Port Richmond, *N.Y.* **20** 40 38N 74 7W
Port St. Joe, *Fla.* **11** 29 49N 85 18W
Port Sanilac, *Mich.* **8** 43 26N 82 33W
Port Townsend, *Wash.* **18** 48 7N 122 45W
Port Washington, *N.Y.* **21** 40 49N 73 41W
Port Washington, *Wis.* **10** 43 23N 87 53W
Portage, *Wis.* **12** 43 33N 89 28W
Portageville, *Mo.* **13** 36 26N 89 42W
Portales, *N. Mex.* **13** 34 11N 103 20W
Porterville, *Calif.* **18** 36 4N 119 1W
Porthill, *Idaho* **16** 48 59N 116 30W
Portland, *Conn.* **9** 41 34N 72 38W
Portland, *Maine* **11** 43 39N 70 16W
Portland, *Mich.* **15** 42 52N 84 54W
Portland, *Oreg.* **18** 45 32N 122 37W
Portola, *Calif.* **18** 39 49N 120 28W
Portsmouth, *N.H.* **9** 43 5N 70 45W
Portsmouth, *Ohio* **10** 38 44N 82 57W
Portsmouth, *R.I.* **9** 41 36N 71 15W
Portsmouth, *Va.* **10** 36 50N 76 18W
Post, *Tex.* **13** 33 12N 101 23W
Post Falls, *Idaho* **16** 47 43N 116 57W
Poteau, *Okla.* **13** 35 3N 94 37W
Poteet, *Tex.* **13** 29 2N 98 35W
Potomac →, *Md.* **10** 38 0N 76 23W
Potsdam, *N.Y.* **9** 44 40N 74 59W
Potter, *Nebr.* **12** 41 13N 103 19W
Pottstown, *Pa.* **9** 40 15N 75 39W
Pottsville, *Pa.* **9** 40 41N 76 12W
Poughkeepsie, *N.Y.* **9** 41 42N 73 56W
Poulsbo, *Wash.* **18** 47 44N 122 39W
Poway, *Calif.* **19** 32 58N 117 2W
Powder →, *Mont.* **12** 46 45N 105 26W
Powder River, *Wyo.* **16** 43 2N 106 59W
Powell, *Wyo.* **16** 44 45N 108 46W
Powell L., *Utah* **17** 36 57N 111 29W
Powers, *Mich.* **10** 45 41N 87 32W
Powers, *Oreg.* **16** 42 53N 124 4W
Powers Lake, *N. Dak.* **12** 48 34N 102 39W
Pozo, *Calif.* **19** 35 20N 120 24W
Prairie →, *Tex.* **13** 34 30N 99 23W
Prairie City, *Oreg.* **16** 44 28N 118 43W
Prairie du Chien, *Wis.* **14** 43 3N 91 9W
Pratt, *Kans.* **13** 37 39N 98 44W
Prattville, *Ala.* **11** 32 28N 86 29W
Premont, *Tex.* **13** 27 22N 98 7W
Prentice, *Wis.* **12** 45 33N 90 17W
Prescott, *Ariz.* **17** 34 33N 112 28W
Prescott, *Ark.* **13** 33 48N 93 23W
Presho, *S. Dak.* **12** 43 54N 100 3W
Presidio, *Tex.* **13** 29 34N 104 22W
Presque Isle, *Maine* **11** 46 41N 68 1W
Preston, *Idaho* **16** 42 6N 111 53W
Preston, *Minn.* **12** 43 40N 92 5W
Preston, *Nev.* **16** 38 55N 115 4W
Price, *Utah* **16** 39 36N 110 49W
Prichard, *Ala.* **11** 30 44N 88 5W
Priest →, *Idaho* **16** 48 12N 116 54W
Priest L., *Idaho* **16** 48 35N 116 52W
Priest Valley, *Calif.* **18** 36 10N 120 39W
Prince of Wales, C., *Alaska* **30** 65 36N 168 5W
Prince of Wales I., *Alaska* **30** 55 47N 132 50W
Prince William Sd., *Alaska* **30** 60 40N 147 0W
Princeton, *Ill.* **14** 41 23N 89 28W
Princeton, *Ind.* **15** 38 21N 87 34W
Princeton, *Ky.* **10** 37 7N 87 53W
Princeton, *Mo.* **14** 40 24N 93 35W
Princeton, *N.J.* **9** 40 21N 74 39W
Princeton, *W. Va.* **10** 37 22N 81 6W
Prineville, *Oreg.* **16** 44 18N 120 51W
Prospect Heights, *Ill.* **22** 42 6N 87 54W
Prosser, *Wash.* **16** 46 12N 119 46W
Protection, *Kans.* **13** 37 12N 99 29W
Providence, *Ky.* **10** 37 24N 87 46W
Providence, *R.I.* **9** 41 49N 71 24W
Providence Mts., *Calif.* **17** 35 10N 115 15W
Provo, *Utah* **16** 40 14N 111 39W
Prudhoe Bay, *Alaska* **30** 70 18N 148 22W
Pryor, *Okla.* **13** 36 19N 95 19W
Pueblo, *Colo.* **12** 38 16N 104 37W
Puerco →, *N. Mex.* **17** 34 22N 107 50W
Puerto Rico ■, *W. Indies* **30** 18 15N 66 45W
Puget Sound, *Wash.* **16** 47 50N 122 30W
Pukoo, *Hawaii* **30** 21 4N 156 48W
Pulaski, *N.Y.* **9** 43 34N 76 8W
Pulaski, *Tenn.* **11** 35 12N 87 2W
Pulaski, *Va.* **10** 37 3N 80 47W
Pullman, *Wash.* **16** 46 44N 117 10W
Punta Gorda, *Fla.* **11** 26 56N 82 3W
Punxsatawney, *Pa.* **8** 40 57N 78 59W
Purcell, *Okla.* **13** 35 1N 97 22W
Putnam, *Conn.* **9** 41 55N 71 55W
Puyallup, *Wash.* **18** 47 12N 122 18W
Pyote, *Tex.* **13** 31 32N 103 8W
Pyramid L., *Nev.* **16** 40 1N 119 35W
Pyramid Pk., *Calif.* **19** 36 25N 116 37W

Q

Quakertown, *Pa.* **9** 40 26N 75 21W
Quanah, *Tex.* **13** 34 18N 99 44W
Quartzsite, *Ariz.* **19** 33 40N 114 13W
Queens, *N.Y.* **21** 40 42N 73 50W
Quemado, *N. Mex.* **17** 34 20N 108 30W
Quemado, *Tex.* **13** 28 58N 100 35W
Questa, *N. Mex.* **17** 36 42N 105 36W
Quincy, *Calif.* **18** 39 56N 120 57W
Quincy, *Fla.* **11** 30 35N 84 34W
Quincy, *Ill.* **12** 39 56N 91 23W
Quincy, *Mass.* **23** 42 14N 71 0W
Quincy, *Wash.* **16** 47 22N 119 56W
Quinhagak, *Alaska* **30** 59 45N 161 54W
Quitman, *Ga.* **11** 30 47N 83 34W
Quitman, *Miss.* **11** 32 2N 88 44W
Quitman, *Tex.* **13** 32 48N 95 27W

R

Racine, *Wis.* **15** 42 41N 87 51W
Radford, *Va.* **10** 37 8N 80 34W
Rahway, *N.J.* **20** 40 36N 74 17W
Rainier, *Wash.* **18** 46 53N 122 41W
Rainier, Mt., *Wash.* **18** 46 52N 121 46W
Raleigh, *N.C.* **11** 35 47N 78 39W
Raleigh B., *N.C.* **11** 34 50N 76 15W
Ralls, *Tex.* **13** 33 41N 101 24W
Ramona, *Calif.* **19** 33 2N 116 52W
Rampart, *Alaska* **30** 65 30N 150 10W
Ranchester, *Wyo.* **16** 44 54N 107 10W
Randallstown, *Md.* **25** 39 21N 76 46W
Randolph, *Mass.* **9** 42 10N 71 2W
Randolph, *Utah* **16** 41 40N 111 11W
Rangeley, *Maine* **9** 44 58N 70 39W
Rangely, *Colo.* **16** 40 5N 108 48W
Ranger, *Tex.* **13** 32 28N 98 41W
Rankin, *Tex.* **13** 31 13N 101 56W
Rantoul, *Ill.* **15** 40 19N 88 9W
Rapid City, *S. Dak.* **12** 44 5N 103 14W
Rapid River, *Mich.* **10** 45 55N 86 58W
Rat Islands, *Alaska* **30** 52 0N 178 0 E
Raton, *N. Mex.* **13** 36 54N 104 24W
Ravena, *N.Y.* **9** 42 28N 73 49W
Ravenna, *Nebr.* **12** 41 1N 98 55W
Ravenswood, *W. Va.* **10** 38 57N 81 46W
Rawlins, *Wyo.* **16** 41 47N 107 14W
Ray, *N. Dak.* **12** 48 21N 103 10W
Ray Mts., *Alaska* **30** 66 0N 152 0W
Raymond, *Calif.* **18** 37 13N 119 54W
Raymond, *Wash.* **18** 46 41N 123 44W
Raymondville, *Tex.* **13** 26 29N 97 47W
Rayne, *La.* **13** 30 14N 92 16W
Rayville, *La.* **13** 32 29N 91 46W
Reading, *Mass.* **23** 42 31N 71 5W
Reading, *Pa.* **9** 40 20N 75 56W
Red →, *La.* **13** 31 1N 91 45W
Red →, *N. Dak.* **12** 49 0N 97 15W
Red Bank, *N.J.* **9** 40 21N 74 5W
Red Bluff, *Calif.* **16** 40 11N 122 15W
Red Bluff L., *N. Mex.* **13** 31 54N 103 55W
Red Cloud, *Nebr.* **12** 40 5N 98 32W
Red Lake Falls, *Minn.* **12** 47 53N 96 16W
Red Lodge, *Mont.* **16** 45 11N 109 15W
Red Mountain, *Calif.* **19** 35 37N 117 38W
Red Oak, *Iowa* **12** 41 1N 95 14W
Red Rock, L., *Iowa* **14** 41 22N 92 59W
Red Slate Mt., *Calif.* **18** 37 31N 118 52W
Red Wing, *Minn.* **12** 44 34N 92 31W
Redding, *Calif.* **16** 40 35N 122 24W
Redfield, *S. Dak.* **12** 44 53N 98 31W
Redford Township, *Mich.* **26** 42 23N 83 17W
Redlands, *Calif.* **19** 34 4N 117 11W
Redmond, *Oreg.* **16** 44 17N 121 11W
Redwood City, *Calif.* **28** 37 29N 122 13W
Redwood Falls, *Minn.* **12** 44 32N 95 7W
Reed City, *Mich.* **10** 43 53N 85 31W
Reeder, *N. Dak.* **12** 46 7N 102 57W
Reedley, *Calif.* **18** 36 36N 119 27W
Reedsburg, *Wis.* **12** 43 32N 90 0W
Reedsport, *Oreg.* **16** 43 42N 124 6W
Refugio, *Tex.* **13** 28 18N 97 17W
Reidsville, *N.C.* **11** 36 21N 79 40W
Reinbeck, *Iowa* **14** 42 19N 92 36W
Reno, *Nev.* **18** 39 31N 119 48W
Renovo, *Pa.* **8** 41 20N 77 45W
Rensselaer, *Ind.* **15** 40 57N 87 9W
Rensselaer, *N.Y.* **9** 42 38N 73 45W
Renton, *Wash.* **18** 47 29N 122 12W
Republic, *Mich.* **10** 46 25N 87 59W
Republic, *Wash.* **16** 48 39N 118 44W
Republican →, *Kans.* **12** 39 4N 96 48W
Republican City, *Nebr.* **12** 40 6N 99 13W
Reserve, *N. Mex.* **17** 33 43N 108 45W
Reston, *Va.* **25** 38 57N 77 20W
Revere, *Mass.* **23** 42 25N 71 1W
Rex, *Alaska* **30** 64 10N 149 20W
Rexburg, *Idaho* **16** 43 49N 111 47W
Reyes, Pt., *Calif.* **18** 38 0N 123 0W
Rhinelander, *Wis.* **12** 45 38N 89 25W
Rhode Island □ **9** 41 40N 71 30W
Rice Lake, *Wis.* **12** 45 30N 91 44W
Rich Hill, *Mo.* **13** 38 6N 94 22W
Richardton, *N. Dak.* **12** 46 53N 102 19W
Richey, *Mont.* **12** 47 39N 105 4W
Richfield, *Idaho* **16** 43 3N 114 9W
Richfield, *Utah* **17** 38 46N 112 5W
Richland, *Ga.* **11** 32 5N 84 40W
Richland, *Oreg.* **16** 44 46N 117 10W
Richland, *Wash.* **16** 46 17N 119 18W
Richland Center, *Wis.* **12** 43 21N 90 23W
Richlands, *Va.* **10** 37 6N 81 48W
Richmond, *Calif.* **28** 37 56N 122 22W
Richmond, *Ind.* **15** 39 50N 84 53W
Richmond, *Ky.* **15** 37 45N 84 18W
Richmond, *Mo.* **12** 39 17N 93 58W
Richmond, *Tex.* **13** 29 35N 95 46W
Richmond, *Utah* **16** 41 56N 111 48W
Richmond, *Va.* **10** 37 33N 77 27W
Richmond Hill, *N.Y.* **21** 40 41N 73 50W
Richton, *Miss.* **11** 31 16N 88 56W
Richwood, *W. Va.* **10** 38 14N 80 32W
Ridgecrest, *Calif.* **19** 35 38N 117 40W
Ridgeland, *S.C.* **11** 32 29N 80 59W
Ridgewood, *N.J.* **20** 40 59N 74 6W
Ridgewood, *N.Y.* **21** 40 42N 73 52W
Ridgway, *Pa.* **8** 41 25N 78 44W
Rifle, *Colo.* **16** 39 32N 107 47W
Rigby, *Idaho* **16** 43 40N 111 55W
Riggins, *Idaho* **16** 45 25N 116 19W
Riley, *Oreg.* **16** 43 32N 119 28W
Rimrock, *Wash.* **18** 46 38N 121 10W
Ringling, *Mont.* **16** 46 16N 110 49W
Rio Grande →, *Tex.* **13** 25 57N 97 9W
Rio Grande City, *Tex.* **13** 26 23N 98 49W
Rio Vista, *Calif.* **18** 38 10N 121 42W
Ripley, *Tenn.* **13** 35 45N 89 32W
Ripon, *Calif.* **18** 37 44N 121 7W
Ripon, *Wis.* **10** 43 51N 88 50W
Rison, *Ark.* **13** 33 58N 92 11W
Ritzville, *Wash.* **16** 47 8N 118 23W
River Rouge, *Mich.* **26** 42 16N 83 8W
Riverdale, *Calif.* **18** 36 26N 119 52W
Riverdale, *N.Y.* **21** 40 54N 73 54W
Riverhead, *N.Y.* **9** 40 55N 72 40W
Riverside, *Calif.* **19** 33 59N 117 22W

Selmer

Selmer, Tenn. 11 35 10N 88 36W
Seminoe Reservoir, Wyo. 16 42 9N 106 55W
Seminole, Okla. 13 35 14N 96 41W
Seminole, Tex. 13 32 43N 102 39W
Semisopochnoi I., Alaska 30 51 55N 179 36 E
Senatobia, Miss. 13 34 37N 89 58W
Seneca, Oreg. 16 44 8N 118 58W
Seneca, S.C. 11 34 41N 82 57W
Seneca Falls, N.Y. 9 42 55N 76 48W
Seneca L., N.Y. 8 42 40N 76 54W
Sentinel, Ariz. 17 32 52N 113 13W
Sequim, Wash. 18 48 5N 123 6W
Sequoia National Park, Calif. 18 36 30N 118 30W
Settlement Pt., Bahamas 11 26 40N 79 0W
Sevier, Utah 17 38 39N 112 11W
Sevier →, Utah 17 39 4N 113 6W
Sevier L., Utah 16 38 54N 113 9W
Seward, Alaska 30 60 7N 149 27W
Seward, Nebr. 12 40 55N 97 6W
Seward Pen., Alaska 30 65 0N 164 0W
Seymour, Conn. 9 41 24N 73 4W
Seymour, Ind. 15 38 58N 85 53W
Seymour, Tex. 13 33 35N 99 16W
Seymour, Wis. 10 44 31N 88 20W
Shafter, Calif. 19 35 30N 119 16W
Shafter, Tex. 13 29 49N 104 18W
Shaker Heights, Ohio 27 41 28N 81 33W
Shakopee, Minn. 12 44 48N 93 32W
Shaktolik, Alaska 30 64 20N 161 15W
Shamokin, Pa. 9 40 47N 76 34W
Shamrock, Tex. 13 35 13N 100 15W
Shandon, Calif. 18 35 39N 120 23W
Shaniko, Oreg. 16 45 0N 120 45W
Sharon, Mass. 9 42 7N 71 11W
Sharon, Pa. 8 41 14N 80 31W
Sharon Springs, Kans. 12 38 54N 101 45W
Sharpsburg, Pa. 27 40 29N 79 56W
Shasta, Mt., Calif. 16 41 25N 122 12W
Shasta L., Calif. 16 40 43N 122 25W
Shattuck, Okla. 13 36 16N 99 53W
Shaver L., Calif. 18 37 9N 119 18W
Shawano, Wis. 10 44 47N 88 36W
Shawnee, Okla. 13 35 20N 96 55W
Sheboygan, Wis. 10 43 46N 87 45W
Sheffield, Ala. 11 34 46N 87 41W
Sheffield, Mass. 9 42 5N 73 21W
Sheffield, Tex. 13 30 41N 101 49W
Shelburne Falls, Mass. 9 42 36N 72 45W
Shelby, Mich. 10 43 37N 86 22W
Shelby, Mont. 16 48 30N 111 51W
Shelby, N.C. 11 35 17N 81 32W
Shelbyville, Ill. 15 39 24N 88 48W
Shelbyville, Ind. 15 39 31N 85 47W
Shelbyville, Tenn. 11 35 29N 86 28W
Sheldon, Iowa 12 43 11N 95 51W
Sheldon Point, Alaska 30 62 32N 164 52W
Shelikof Strait, Alaska 30 57 30N 155 0W
Shelton, Conn. 9 41 19N 73 5W
Shelton, Wash. 18 47 13N 123 6W
Shenandoah, Iowa 12 40 46N 95 22W
Shenandoah, Pa. 9 40 49N 76 12W
Shenandoah, Va. 10 38 29N 78 37W
Shenandoah →, Va. 10 39 19N 77 44W
Sheridan, Ark. 13 34 19N 92 24W
Sheridan, Wyo. 16 44 48N 106 58W
Sherman, Tex. 13 33 40N 96 35W
Sherwood, N. Dak. 12 48 57N 101 38W
Sherwood, Tex. 13 31 18N 100 45W
Sheyenne, N. Dak. 12 47 50N 99 7W
Sheyenne →, N. Dak. 12 47 2N 96 50W
Ship I., Miss. 13 30 13N 88 55W
Shippensburg, Pa. 8 40 3N 77 31W
Shiprock, N. Mex. 17 36 47N 108 41W
Shishmaref, Alaska 30 66 15N 166 4W
Shoshone, Calif. 19 35 58N 116 16W
Shoshone, Idaho 16 42 56N 114 25W
Shoshone L., Wyo. 16 44 22N 110 43W
Shoshone Mts., Nev. 16 39 20N 117 25W
Shoshoni, Wyo. 16 43 14N 108 7W
Show Low, Ariz. 17 34 15N 110 2W
Shreveport, La. 13 32 31N 93 45W
Shumagin Is., Alaska 30 55 7N 159 45W
Shungnak, Alaska 30 66 52N 157 9W
Shuyak I., Alaska 30 58 31N 152 30W
Sibley, Iowa 12 43 24N 95 45W
Sibley, La. 13 32 33N 93 18W
Sidney, Mont. 12 47 43N 104 9W
Sidney, N.Y. 9 42 19N 75 24W
Sidney, Nebr. 12 41 8N 102 59W
Sidney, Ohio 15 40 17N 84 9W
Sierra Blanca, Tex. 17 31 11N 105 22W
Sierra Blanca Peak, N. Mex. 17 33 23N 105 49W
Sierra City, Calif. 18 39 34N 120 38W
Sierra Madre, Calif. 29 34 9N 118 3W
Sigurd, Utah 17 38 50N 111 58W
Sikeston, Mo. 13 36 53N 89 35W
Siler City, N.C. 11 35 44N 79 28W
Siloam Springs, Ark. 13 36 11N 94 32W
Silsbee, Tex. 13 30 21N 94 11W
Silver City, N. Mex. 17 32 46N 108 17W
Silver City, Nev. 16 39 15N 119 48W
Silver Cr. →, Oreg. 16 43 16N 119 13W
Silver Creek, N.Y. 8 42 33N 79 10W
Silver Hill, Md. 25 38 49N 76 55W
Silver L., Calif. 18 38 39N 120 6W
Silver L., Calif. 19 35 21N 116 7W
Silver Lake, Oreg. 16 43 8N 121 3W
Silver Spring, Md. 25 39 0N 77 1W
Silverton, Colo. 17 37 49N 107 40W
Silverton, Tex. 13 34 28N 101 19W
Silvies →, Oreg. 16 43 34N 119 2W
Simi Valley, Calif. 19 34 16N 118 47W
Simmler, Calif. 19 35 21N 119 59W
Sinclair, Wyo. 16 41 47N 107 7W
Sinton, Tex. 13 28 2N 97 31W
Sioux City, Iowa 12 42 30N 96 24W
Sioux Falls, S. Dak. 12 43 33N 96 44W
Sirretta Pk., Calif. 19 35 56N 118 19W
Sisseton, S. Dak. 12 45 40N 97 3W
Sisters, Oreg. 16 44 18N 121 33W
Sitka, Alaska 30 57 3N 135 20W
Skagway, Alaska 30 59 28N 135 19W
Skokie, Ill. 22 42 2N 87 42W
Skowhegan, Maine 11 44 46N 69 43W
Skunk →, Iowa 14 40 42N 91 7W
Skykomish, Wash. 16 47 42N 121 22W
Slaton, Tex. 13 33 26N 101 39W
Sleepy Eye, Minn. 12 44 18N 94 43W
Slidell, La. 13 30 17N 89 47W
Sloansville, N.Y. 9 42 45N 74 22W
Sloughhouse, Calif. 18 38 26N 121 12W
Smith Center, Kans. 12 39 47N 98 47W
Smithfield, N.C. 11 35 31N 78 21W
Smithfield, Utah 16 41 50N 111 50W
Smithville, Tex. 13 30 1N 97 10W
Smoky Hill →, Kans. 12 39 4N 96 48W
Snake →, Wash. 16 46 12N 119 2W
Snake Range, Nev. 16 39 0N 114 20W
Snake River Plain, Idaho 16 42 50N 114 0W
Snelling, Calif. 18 37 31N 120 26W
Snohomish, Wash. 18 47 55N 122 6W
Snow Hill, Md. 10 38 11N 75 24W
Snowflake, Ariz. 17 34 30N 110 5W
Snowshoe Pk., Mont. 16 48 13N 115 41W
Snowville, Utah 16 41 58N 112 43W
Snyder, Okla. 13 34 40N 98 57W
Snyder, Tex. 13 32 44N 100 55W
Soap Lake, Wash. 16 47 23N 119 29W
Socorro, N. Mex. 17 34 4N 106 54W
Soda L., Calif. 17 35 10N 116 4W
Soda Springs, Idaho 16 42 39N 111 36W
Sodus, N.Y. 8 43 14N 77 4W
Soledad, Calif. 18 36 26N 121 20W
Solomon, N. Fork →, Kans. 12 39 29N 98 26W
Solomon, S. Fork →, Kans. 12 39 25N 99 12W
Solon Springs, Wis. 12 46 22N 91 49W
Solvang, Calif. 19 34 36N 120 8W
Solvay, N.Y. 9 43 3N 76 13W
Somers, Mont. 16 48 5N 114 13W
Somerset, Colo. 17 38 56N 107 28W
Somerset, Ky. 10 37 5N 84 36W
Somerset, Mass. 9 41 47N 71 8W
Somerton, Ariz. 17 32 36N 114 43W
Somerville, Mass. 23 42 23N 71 5W
Somerville, N.J. 9 40 35N 74 38W
Sonora, Calif. 18 37 59N 120 23W
Sonora, Tex. 13 30 34N 100 39W
South Baldy, N. Mex. 17 33 59N 107 11W
South Bend, Ind. 15 41 41N 86 15W
South Bend, Wash. 18 46 40N 123 48W
South Boston, Va. 11 36 42N 78 54W
South C. = Ka Lae, Hawaii 30 18 55N 155 41W
South Cape, Hawaii 30 18 58N 155 24 E
South Carolina □ 11 34 0N 81 0W
South Charleston, W. Va. 10 38 22N 81 44W
South Dakota □ 12 44 15N 100 0W
South Euclid, Ohio 27 41 31N 81 32W
South Fork →, Mont. 16 47 54N 113 15W
South Fork, American →, Calif. 18 38 45N 121 5W
South Gate, Calif. 29 33 56N 118 12W
South Haven, Mich. 15 42 24N 86 16W
South Holland, Ill. 22 41 36N 87 36W
South Loup →, Nebr. 12 41 4N 98 39W
South Milwaukee, Wis. 15 42 55N 87 52W
South Pasadena, Calif. 29 34 7N 118 8W
South Pass, Wyo. 16 42 20N 108 58W
South Pittsburg, Tenn. 11 35 1N 85 42W
South Platte →, Nebr. 12 41 7N 100 42W
South River, N.J. 9 40 27N 74 23W
South San Francisco, Calif. 28 37 39N 122 24W
South Sioux City, Nebr. 12 42 28N 96 24W
Southampton, N.Y. 9 40 53N 72 23W
Southbridge, Mass. 9 42 5N 72 2W
Southeast C., Alaska 30 62 56N 169 39W
Southern Pines, N.C. 11 35 11N 79 24W
Southfield, Mich. 26 42 28N 83 15W
Southgate, Mich. 26 42 11N 83 12W
Southington, Conn. 9 41 36N 72 53W
Southold, N.Y. 9 41 4N 72 26W
Southport, N.C. 11 33 55N 78 1W
Spalding, Nebr. 12 41 42N 98 22W
Spanish Fork, Utah 16 40 7N 111 39W
Sparks, Nev. 18 39 32N 119 45W
Sparta, Ga. 11 33 17N 82 58W
Sparta, Wis. 12 43 56N 90 49W
Spartanburg, S.C. 11 34 56N 81 57W
Spearfish, S. Dak. 12 44 30N 103 52W
Spearman, Tex. 13 36 12N 101 12W
Spenard, Alaska 30 61 11N 149 55W
Spencer, Idaho 16 44 22N 112 11W
Spencer, Iowa 12 43 9N 95 9W
Spencer, N.Y. 9 42 13N 76 30W
Spencer, Nebr. 12 42 53N 98 42W
Spencer, W. Va. 10 38 48N 81 21W
Spirit Lake, Idaho 16 47 58N 116 52W
Spofford, Tex. 13 29 10N 100 25W
Spokane, Wash. 16 47 40N 117 24W
Spooner, Wis. 12 45 50N 91 53W
Sprague, Wash. 16 47 18N 117 59W
Sprague River, Oreg. 16 42 27N 121 30W
Spray, Oreg. 16 44 50N 119 48W
Spring City, Utah 16 39 29N 111 30W
Spring Mts., Nev. 17 36 0N 115 45W
Spring Valley, Minn. 12 43 41N 92 23W
Springdale, Ark. 13 36 11N 94 8W
Springdale, Wash. 16 48 4N 117 45W
Springer, N. Mex. 13 36 22N 104 36W
Springerville, Ariz. 17 34 8N 109 17W
Springfield, Colo. 13 37 24N 102 37W
Springfield, Ill. 14 39 48N 89 39W
Springfield, Mass. 9 42 6N 72 35W
Springfield, Mo. 13 37 13N 93 17W
Springfield, N.J. 20 40 42N 74 18W
Springfield, Ohio 15 39 55N 83 49W
Springfield, Oreg. 16 44 3N 123 1W
Springfield, Tenn. 11 36 31N 86 53W
Springfield, Va. 25 38 46N 77 10W
Springfield, Vt. 9 43 18N 72 29W
Springvale, Maine 9 43 28N 70 48W
Springville, Calif. 18 36 8N 118 49W
Springville, N.Y. 8 42 31N 78 40W
Springville, Utah 16 40 10N 111 37W
Spur, Tex. 13 33 28N 100 52W
Stafford, Kans. 13 37 58N 98 36W
Stafford Springs, Conn. 9 41 57N 72 18W
Stamford, Conn. 9 41 3N 73 32W
Stamford, Tex. 13 32 57N 99 48W
Stamps, Ark. 13 33 22N 93 30W
Stanberry, Mo. 12 40 13N 94 35W
Standish, Mich. 10 43 59N 83 57W
Stanford, Mont. 16 47 9N 110 13W
Stanislaus →, Calif. 18 37 40N 121 14W
Stanley, Idaho 16 44 13N 114 56W
Stanley, N. Dak. 12 48 19N 102 23W
Stanley, Wis. 12 44 58N 90 56W
Stanton, Tex. 13 32 8N 101 48W
Staples, Minn. 12 46 21N 94 48W
Stapleton, N.Y. 20 40 36N 74 5W
Stapleton, Nebr. 12 41 29N 100 31W
Starke, Fla. 11 29 57N 82 7W
Starkville, Colo. 13 37 8N 104 30W
Starkville, Miss. 11 33 28N 88 49W
State College, Pa. 8 40 48N 77 52W
Staten Island, N.Y. 20 40 34N 74 9W
Statesboro, Ga. 11 32 27N 81 47W
Statesville, N.C. 11 35 47N 80 53W
Statue of Liberty, N.J. 20 40 41N 74 2W
Stauffer, Calif. 19 34 45N 119 3W
Staunton, Ill. 14 39 1N 89 47W
Staunton, Va. 10 38 9N 79 4W
Steamboat Springs, Colo. 16 40 29N 106 50W
Steele, N. Dak. 12 46 51N 99 55W
Steelton, Pa. 8 40 14N 76 50W
Steelville, Mo. 14 37 58N 91 22W
Stephen, Minn. 12 48 27N 96 53W
Stephenville, Tex. 13 32 13N 98 12W
Sterling, Colo. 12 40 37N 103 13W
Sterling, Ill. 14 41 48N 89 42W
Sterling, Kans. 12 38 13N 98 12W
Sterling City, Tex. 13 31 51N 101 0W
Sterling Heights, Mich. 26 42 35N 83 3W
Steubenville, Ohio 8 40 22N 80 37W
Stevens Point, Wis. 12 44 31N 89 34W
Stevens Village, Alaska 30 66 1N 149 6W
Stigler, Okla. 13 35 15N 95 8W
Stillwater, Minn. 12 45 3N 92 49W
Stillwater, N.Y. 9 42 55N 73 41W
Stillwater, Okla. 13 36 7N 97 4W
Stillwater Range, Nev. 16 39 50N 118 5W
Stilwell, Okla. 13 35 49N 94 38W
Stockett, Mont. 16 47 21N 111 10W
Stockton, Calif. 18 37 58N 121 17W
Stockton, Kans. 12 39 26N 99 16W
Stockton, Mo. 14 37 42N 93 48W
Stoneham, Mass. 23 42 29N 71 5W
Stony River, Alaska 30 61 47N 156 35W
Storm Lake, Iowa 12 42 39N 95 13W
Stove Pipe Wells Village, Calif. 19 36 35N 117 11W
Strasburg, N. Dak. 12 46 8N 100 10W
Stratford, Calif. 18 36 11N 119 49W
Stratford, Conn. 9 41 12N 73 8W
Stratford, Tex. 13 36 20N 102 4W
Strathmore, Calif. 18 36 9N 119 4W
Stratton, Colo. 12 39 19N 102 36W
Strawberry Reservoir, Utah 16 40 8N 111 9W
Strawn, Tex. 13 32 33N 98 30W
Streator, Ill. 15 41 8N 88 50W
Streeter, N. Dak. 12 46 39N 99 21W
Stromsburg, Iowa 12 41 7N 97 36W
Stroudsburg, Pa. 9 40 59N 75 12W
Struthers, Ohio 8 41 4N 80 39W
Stryker, Mont. 16 48 41N 114 46W
Stuart, Fla. 11 27 12N 80 15W
Stuart, Nebr. 12 42 36N 99 8W
Stuart I., Alaska 30 63 55N 164 50W
Sturgeon Bay, Wis. 10 44 50N 87 23W
Sturgis, Mich. 15 41 48N 85 25W
Sturgis, S. Dak. 12 44 25N 103 31W
Stuttgart, Ark. 13 34 30N 91 33W
Stuyvesant, N.Y. 9 42 23N 73 45W
Sudan, Tex. 13 34 4N 102 32W
Suffolk, Va. 10 36 44N 76 35W
Sugar City, Colo. 12 38 14N 103 40W
Suitland, Md. 25 38 50N 76 55W
Sullivan, Ill. 15 39 36N 88 37W
Sullivan, Ind. 15 39 6N 87 24W
Sullivan, Mo. 14 38 13N 91 10W
Sulphur, La. 13 30 14N 93 23W
Sulphur, Okla. 13 34 31N 96 58W
Sulphur Springs, Tex. 13 33 8N 95 36W
Sulphur Springs Draw →, Tex. 13 32 12N 101 36W
Sumatra, Mont. 16 46 37N 107 33W
Summer L., Oreg. 16 42 50N 120 45W
Summerville, Ga. 11 34 29N 85 21W
Summerville, S.C. 11 33 1N 80 11W
Summit, Alaska 30 63 20N 149 7W
Summit, Ill. 22 41 47N 87 47W
Summit, N.J. 20 40 43N 74 21W
Summit Peak, Colo. 17 37 21N 106 42W
Sumner, Iowa 14 42 51N 92 6W
Sumter, S.C. 11 33 55N 80 21W
Sun City, Ariz. 17 33 36N 112 17W
Sun City, Calif. 19 33 42N 117 11W
Sunburst, Mont. 16 48 53N 111 55W
Sunbury, Pa. 9 40 52N 76 48W
Suncook, N.H. 9 43 8N 71 27W
Sundance, Wyo. 12 44 24N 104 23W
Sunnyside, Utah 16 39 34N 110 23W
Sunnyside, Wash. 16 46 20N 120 0W
Sunnyvale, Calif. 18 37 23N 122 2W
Sunray, Tex. 13 36 1N 101 49W
Sunshine Acres, Calif. 29 33 56N 117 59W
Supai, Ariz. 17 36 15N 112 41W
Superior, Ariz. 17 33 18N 111 6W
Superior, Mont. 16 47 12N 114 53W
Superior, Nebr. 12 40 1N 98 4W
Superior, Wis. 12 46 44N 92 6W
Superior, L., N. Amer. 10 47 0N 87 0W
Sur, Pt., Calif. 18 36 18N 121 54W
Surf, Calif. 19 34 41N 120 36W
Susanville, Calif. 16 40 25N 120 39W
Susquehanna →, Pa. 9 39 33N 76 5W
Susquehanna Depot, Pa. 9 41 57N 75 36W
Sussex, N.J. 9 41 13N 74 37W
Sutherland, Nebr. 12 41 10N 101 8W
Sutherlin, Oreg. 16 43 23N 123 19W
Sutter Creek, Calif. 18 38 24N 120 48W
Sutton, Nebr. 12 40 36N 97 52W
Sutwik I., Alaska 30 56 34N 157 12W
Suwannee →, Fla. 11 29 17N 83 10W
Swainsboro, Ga. 11 32 36N 82 20W
Swampscott, Mass. 23 42 28N 70 53W
Swarthmore, Pa. 24 39 54N 75 20W
Sweet Home, Oreg. 16 44 24N 122 44W
Sweetwater, Nev. 18 38 27N 119 9W
Sweetwater, Tex. 13 32 28N 100 25W
Sweetwater →, Wyo. 16 42 31N 107 2W
Swissvale, Pa. 27 40 25N 79 52W
Sylacauga, Ala. 11 33 10N 86 15W
Sylvania, Ga. 11 32 45N 81 38W
Sylvester, Ga. 11 31 32N 83 50W
Syracuse, Kans. 13 37 59N 101 45W
Syracuse, N.Y. 9 43 3N 76 9W

T

Tacoma, Wash. 18 47 14N 122 26W
Taft, Calif. 19 35 8N 119 28W
Taft, Tex. 13 27 59N 97 24W
Tahoe, L., Nev. 18 39 6N 120 2W
Tahoe City, Calif. 18 39 10N 120 9W
Takoma Park, Md. 25 38 58N 77 0W
Talihina, Okla. 13 34 45N 95 3W
Talkeetna, Alaska 30 62 20N 150 6W
Talkeetna Mts., Alaska 30 62 20N 149 0W
Talladega, Ala. 11 33 26N 86 6W
Tallahassee, Fla. 11 30 27N 84 17W
Talleyville, Del. 24 39 48N 75 32W
Tallulah, La. 13 32 25N 91 11W
Tama, Iowa 14 41 58N 92 35W
Tamaqua, Pa. 9 40 48N 75 58W
Tampa, Fla. 11 27 57N 82 27W
Tampa B., Fla. 11 27 50N 82 30W
Tanana, Alaska 30 65 10N 152 4W
Tanana →, Alaska 30 65 10N 151 58W
Taos, N. Mex. 17 36 24N 105 35W
Tappahannock, Va. 10 37 56N 76 52W
Tarboro, N.C. 11 35 54N 77 32W
Tarpon Springs, Fla. 11 28 9N 82 45W
Tarrytown, N.Y. 9 41 4N 73 52W
Tatum, N. Mex. 13 33 16N 103 19W
Tau, W. Samoa 31 14 15S 169 30W
Taunton, Mass. 9 41 54N 71 6W
Tawas City, Mich. 10 44 16N 83 31W
Taylor, Alaska 30 65 40N 164 50W
Taylor, Mich. 26 42 13N 83 15W
Taylor, Nebr. 12 41 46N 99 23W
Taylor, Pa. 9 41 23N 75 43W
Taylor, Tex. 13 30 34N 97 25W
Taylor, Mt., N. Mex. 17 35 14N 107 37W
Taylortown, N.J. 20 40 56N 74 23W
Taylorville, Ill. 14 39 33N 89 18W
Teague, Tex. 13 31 38N 96 17W

Washington

Washington, *N.J.* **9** 40 46N 74 59W
Washington, *Pa.* **8** 40 10N 80 15W
Washington, *Utah* **17** 37 8N 113 31W
Washington □ **16** 47 30N 120 30W
Washington, Mt., *N.H.* **9** 44 16N 71 18W
Washington Heights, *N.Y.* **20** 40 50N 73 55W
Washington I., *Wis.* **10** 45 23N 86 54W
Washington National Airport, *D.C.* **25** 38 51N 77 2W
Watching Mountains, *N.J.* **20** 40 42N 74 20W
Water Valley, *Miss.* **13** 34 10N 89 38W
Waterbury, *Conn.* **9** 41 33N 73 3W
Waterford, *Calif.* **18** 37 38N 120 46W
Waterloo, *Ill.* **14** 38 20N 90 9W
Waterloo, *Iowa* **14** 42 30N 92 21W
Waterloo, *N.Y.* **8** 42 54N 76 52W
Watersmeet, *Mich.* **12** 46 16N 89 11W
Waterton-Glacier International Peace Park, *Mont.* **16** 48 45N 115 0W
Watertown, *Conn.* **9** 41 36N 73 7W
Watertown, *Mass.* **23** 42 22N 71 10W
Watertown, *N.Y.* **9** 43 59N 75 55W
Watertown, *S. Dak.* **12** 44 54N 97 7W
Watertown, *Wis.* **15** 43 12N 88 43W
Waterville, *Maine* **11** 44 33N 69 38W
Waterville, *N.Y.* **9** 42 56N 75 23W
Waterville, *Wash.* **16** 47 39N 120 4W
Watervliet, *N.Y.* **9** 42 44N 73 42W
Watford City, *N. Dak.* **12** 47 48N 103 17W
Watkins Glen, *N.Y.* **8** 42 23N 76 52W
Watonga, *Okla.* **13** 35 51N 98 25W
Watrous, *N. Mex.* **13** 35 48N 104 59W
Watseka, *Ill.* **15** 40 47N 87 44W
Watsonville, *Calif.* **18** 36 55N 121 45W
Waubay, *S. Dak.* **12** 45 20N 97 18W
Wauchula, *Fla.* **11** 27 33N 81 49W
Waukegan, *Ill.* **15** 42 22N 87 50W
Waukesha, *Wis.* **15** 43 1N 88 14W
Waukon, *Iowa* **12** 43 16N 91 29W
Wauneta, *Nebr.* **12** 40 25N 101 23W
Waupaca, *Wis.* **12** 44 21N 89 5W
Waupun, *Wis.* **12** 43 38N 88 44W
Waurika, *Okla.* **13** 34 10N 98 0W
Wausau, *Wis.* **12** 44 58N 89 38W
Wautoma, *Wis.* **12** 44 4N 89 18W
Wauwatosa, *Wis.* **15** 43 3N 88 0W
Waverly, *Iowa* **14** 42 44N 92 29W
Waverly, *N.Y.* **9** 42 1N 76 32W
Wawona, *Calif.* **18** 37 32N 119 39W
Waxahachie, *Tex.* **13** 32 24N 96 51W
Waycross, *Ga.* **11** 31 13N 82 21W
Wayland, *Mass.* **23** 42 21N 71 20W
Wayne, *Mich.* **26** 42 16N 83 22W
Wayne, *N.J.* **20** 40 55N 74 14W
Wayne, *Nebr.* **12** 42 14N 97 1W
Wayne, *Pa.* **24** 40 2N 75 24W
Wayne, *W. Va.* **10** 38 13N 82 27W
Waynesboro, *Ga.* **11** 33 6N 82 1W
Waynesboro, *Miss.* **11** 31 40N 88 39W
Waynesboro, *Pa.* **10** 39 45N 77 35W
Waynesboro, *Va.* **10** 38 4N 78 53W
Waynesburg, *Pa.* **10** 39 54N 80 11W
Waynesville, *N.C.* **11** 35 28N 82 58W
Waynoka, *Okla.* **13** 36 35N 98 53W
Weatherford, *Okla.* **13** 35 32N 98 43W
Weatherford, *Tex.* **13** 32 46N 97 48W
Weaverville, *Calif.* **16** 40 44N 122 56W
Webb City, *Mo.* **13** 37 9N 94 28W
Webster, *Mass.* **9** 42 3N 71 53W
Webster, *S. Dak.* **12** 45 20N 97 31W
Webster, *Wis.* **12** 45 53N 92 22W
Webster City, *Iowa* **14** 42 28N 93 49W
Webster Green, *Mo.* **12** 38 38N 90 20W
Webster Springs, *W. Va.* **10** 38 29N 80 25W
Weed, *Calif.* **16** 41 25N 122 23W
Weedsport, *N.Y.* **9** 43 3N 76 35W
Weiser, *Idaho* **16** 44 10N 117 0W
Welch, *W. Va.* **10** 37 26N 81 35W
Wellesley, *Mass.* **23** 42 17N 71 17W
Wellington, *Colo.* **12** 40 42N 105 0W
Wellington, *Kans.* **13** 37 16N 97 24W
Wellington, *Nev.* **18** 38 45N 119 23W
Wellington, *Tex.* **13** 34 51N 100 13W
Wells, *Maine* **9** 43 20N 70 35W
Wells, *Minn.* **12** 43 45N 93 44W
Wells, *Nev.* **16** 41 7N 114 58W
Wellsboro, *Pa.* **8** 41 45N 77 18W
Wellsville, *Mo.* **14** 39 4N 91 34W
Wellsville, *N.Y.* **8** 42 7N 77 57W
Wellsville, *Ohio* **8** 40 36N 80 39W
Wellsville, *Utah* **16** 41 38N 111 56W
Wellton, *Ariz.* **17** 32 40N 114 8W
Wenatchee, *Wash.* **16** 47 25N 120 19W
Wendell, *Idaho* **16** 42 47N 114 42W
Wendover, *Utah* **16** 40 44N 114 2W
Weott, *Calif.* **16** 40 20N 123 55W
Wesley Vale, *N. Mex.* **17** 35 3N 106 2W
Wessington, *S. Dak.* **12** 44 27N 98 42W
Wessington Springs, *S. Dak.* **12** 44 5N 98 34W
West, *Tex.* **13** 31 48N 97 6W
West B., *La.* **13** 29 3N 89 22W
West Babylon, *N.Y.* **21** 40 43N 73 21W
West Bend, *Wis.* **10** 43 25N 88 11W
West Branch, *Mich.* **10** 44 17N 84 14W
West Chelmsford, *Mass.* **23** 42 36N 71 22W
West Chester, *Pa.* **10** 39 58N 75 36W
West Chester, *Pa.* **24** 39 57N 75 35W
West Columbia, *Tex.* **13** 29 9N 95 39W
West Covina, *Calif.* **29** 34 4N 117 55W
West Des Moines, *Iowa* **14** 41 35N 93 43W
West Frankfort, *Ill.* **14** 37 54N 88 55W
West Hartford, *Conn.* **9** 41 45N 72 44W
West Haven, *Conn.* **9** 41 17N 72 57W
West Helena, *Ark.* **13** 34 33N 90 38W
West Hempstead, *N.Y.* **21** 40 41N 73 38W
West Hollywood, *Calif.* **29** 34 5N 118 21W
West Memphis, *Ark.* **13** 35 9N 90 11W
West Mifflin, *Pa.* **27** 40 21N 79 53W
West Monroe, *La.* **13** 32 31N 92 9W
West New York, *N.J.* **20** 40 46N 74 0W
West Orange, *N.J.* **20** 40 46N 74 15W
West Palm Beach, *Fla.* **11** 26 43N 80 3W
West Plains, *Mo.* **13** 36 44N 91 51W
West Point, *Ga.* **11** 32 53N 85 11W
West Point, *Miss.* **11** 33 36N 88 39W
West Point, *Nebr.* **12** 41 51N 96 43W
West Point, *Va.* **10** 37 32N 76 48W
West Rutland, *Vt.* **9** 43 38N 73 5W
West View, *Pa.* **27** 40 31N 80 2W
West Virginia □ **10** 38 45N 80 30W
West Walker →, *Nev.* **18** 38 54N 119 9W
West Yellowstone, *Mont.* **16** 44 40N 111 6W
Westbrook, *Maine* **11** 43 41N 70 22W
Westbrook, *Tex.* **13** 32 21N 101 1W
Westbury, *N.Y.* **21** 40 45N 73 35W
Westby, *Mont.* **12** 48 52N 104 3W
Westchester, *Ill.* **22** 41 51N 87 53W
Westend, *Calif.* **19** 35 42N 117 24W
Westernport, *Md.* **10** 39 29N 79 3W
Westfield, *Mass.* **9** 42 7N 72 45W
Westfield, *N.J.* **20** 40 39N 74 20W
Westhope, *N. Dak.* **12** 48 55N 101 1W
Westlake, *Ohio* **27** 41 27N 81 54W
Westland, *Mich.* **26** 42 19N 83 22W
Westminster, *Md.* **10** 39 34N 76 59W
Westmorland, *Calif.* **17** 33 2N 115 37W
Weston, *Mass.* **23** 42 22N 71 17W
Weston, *Oreg.* **16** 45 49N 118 26W
Weston, *W. Va.* **10** 39 2N 80 28W
Westport, *Wash.* **16** 46 53N 124 6W
Westville, *Ill.* **15** 40 2N 87 38W
Westville, *Okla.* **13** 35 58N 94 40W
Westwood, *Calif.* **16** 40 18N 121 0W
Westwood, *Mass.* **23** 42 12N 71 13W
Wethersfield, *Conn.* **9** 41 42N 72 40W
Wewoka, *Okla.* **13** 35 9N 96 30W
Weymouth, *Mass.* **23** 42 12N 70 57W
Wharton, *N.J.* **9** 40 54N 74 35W
Wharton, *Tex.* **13** 29 19N 96 6W
Wheatland, *Wyo.* **12** 42 3N 104 58W
Wheaton, *Md.* **25** 39 2N 77 1W
Wheaton, *Minn.* **12** 45 48N 96 30W
Wheeler, *Oreg.* **16** 45 41N 123 53W
Wheeler, *Tex.* **13** 35 27N 100 16W
Wheeler Pk., *N. Mex.* **17** 36 34N 105 25W
Wheeler Pk., *Nev.* **17** 38 57N 114 15W
Wheeler Ridge, *Calif.* **19** 35 0N 118 57W
Wheeling, *W. Va.* **8** 40 4N 80 43W
White →, *Ark.* **13** 33 57N 91 5W
White →, *Ind.* **15** 38 25N 87 45W
White →, *S. Dak.* **12** 43 42N 99 27W
White →, *Utah* **16** 40 4N 109 41W
White Bird, *Idaho* **16** 45 46N 116 18W
White Butte, *N. Dak.* **12** 46 23N 103 18W
White City, *Kans.* **12** 38 48N 96 44W
White Deer, *Tex.* **13** 35 26N 101 10W
White Hall, *Ill.* **14** 39 26N 90 24W
White Haven, *Pa.* **9** 41 4N 75 47W
White House, The, *D.C.* **25** 38 53N 77 2W
White L., *La.* **13** 29 44N 92 30W
White Mts., *Calif.* **18** 37 30N 118 15W
White Mts., *N.H.* **9** 44 15N 71 15W
White Plains, *N.Y.* **21** 41 0N 73 46W
White River, *S. Dak.* **12** 43 34N 100 45W
White Sulphur Springs, *Mont.* **16** 46 33N 110 54W
White Sulphur Springs, *W. Va.* **10** 37 48N 80 18W
Whiteface, *Tex.* **13** 33 36N 102 37W
Whitefish, *Mont.* **16** 48 25N 114 20W
Whitefish Point, *Mich.* **10** 46 45N 84 59W
Whitehall, *Mich.* **10** 43 24N 86 21W
Whitehall, *Mont.* **16** 45 52N 112 6W
Whitehall, *N.Y.* **9** 43 33N 73 24W
Whitehall, *Pa.* **27** 40 21N 80 0W
Whitehall, *Wis.* **12** 44 22N 91 19W
Whitesboro, *N.Y.* **9** 43 7N 75 18W
Whitesboro, *Tex.* **13** 33 39N 96 54W
Whitetail, *Mont.* **12** 48 54N 105 10W
Whiteville, *N.C.* **11** 34 20N 78 42W
Whitewater, *Wis.* **15** 42 50N 88 44W
Whitewater Baldy, *N. Mex.* **17** 33 20N 108 39W
Whiting, *Ind.* **22** 41 41N 87 30W
Whitman, *Mass.* **9** 42 5N 70 56W
Whitmire, *S.C.* **11** 34 30N 81 37W
Whitney, Mt., *Calif.* **18** 36 35N 118 18W
Whitney Point, *N.Y.* **9** 42 20N 75 58W
Whittier, *Alaska* **30** 60 47N 148 41W
Whittier, *Calif.* **29** 33 58N 118 2W
Whitwell, *Tenn.* **11** 35 12N 85 31W
Wibaux, *Mont.* **12** 46 59N 104 11W
Wichita, *Kans.* **13** 37 42N 97 20W
Wichita Falls, *Tex.* **13** 33 54N 98 30W
Wickenburg, *Ariz.* **17** 33 58N 112 44W
Wiggins, *Colo.* **12** 40 14N 104 4W
Wiggins, *Miss.* **13** 30 51N 89 8W
Wilber, *Nebr.* **12** 40 29N 96 58W
Wilburton, *Okla.* **13** 34 55N 95 19W
Wildrose, *Calif.* **19** 36 14N 117 11W
Wildrose, *N. Dak.* **12** 48 38N 103 11W
Wildwood, *N.J.* **10** 38 59N 74 50W
Wilkes-Barre, *Pa.* **9** 41 15N 75 53W
Wilkesboro, *N.C.* **11** 36 9N 81 10W
Wilkinsburg, *Pa.* **27** 40 26N 79 52W
Willamina, *Oreg.* **16** 45 5N 123 29W
Willapa B., *Wash.* **16** 46 40N 124 0W
Willard, *N. Mex.* **17** 34 36N 106 2W
Willard, *Utah* **16** 41 25N 112 2W
Willcox, *Ariz.* **17** 32 15N 109 50W
Williams, *Ariz.* **17** 35 15N 112 11W
Williamsburg, *Ky.* **11** 36 44N 84 10W
Williamsburg, *Va.* **10** 37 17N 76 44W
Williamson, *W. Va.* **10** 37 41N 82 17W
Williamsport, *Pa.* **8** 41 15N 77 0W
Williamston, *N.C.* **11** 35 51N 77 4W
Williamstown, *N.Y.* **9** 43 26N 75 53W
Williamsville, *Mo.* **13** 36 58N 90 33W
Willimantic, *Conn.* **9** 41 43N 72 13W
Willingboro, *N.J.* **24** 40 3N 74 54W
Williston, *Fla.* **11** 29 23N 82 27W
Williston, *N. Dak.* **12** 48 9N 103 37W
Williston Park, *N.Y.* **21** 40 45N 73 39W
Willits, *Calif.* **16** 39 25N 123 21W
Willmar, *Minn.* **12** 45 7N 95 3W
Willow Brook, *Calif.* **29** 33 55N 118 13W
Willow Grove, *Pa.* **24** 40 8N 75 7W
Willow Lake, *S. Dak.* **12** 44 38N 97 38W
Willow Springs, *Mo.* **13** 37 0N 91 58W
Willowick, *Ohio* **27** 41 36N 81 30W
Willows, *Calif.* **18** 39 31N 122 12W
Wills Point, *Tex.* **13** 32 43N 96 1W
Wilmette, *Ill.* **10** 42 5N 87 42W
Wilmette, *Ill.* **22** 42 4N 87 42W
Wilmington, *Del.* **10** 39 45N 75 33W
Wilmington, *Del.* **24** 39 44N 75 32W
Wilmington, *Ill.* **15** 41 18N 88 9W
Wilmington, *N.C.* **11** 34 14N 77 55W
Wilmington, *Ohio* **15** 39 27N 83 50W
Wilsall, *Mont.* **16** 45 59N 110 38W
Wilson, *N.C.* **11** 35 44N 77 55W
Wilton, *N. Dak.* **12** 47 10N 100 47W
Winchendon, *Mass.* **9** 42 41N 72 3W
Winchester, *Conn.* **9** 41 53N 73 9W
Winchester, *Idaho* **16** 46 14N 116 38W
Winchester, *Ind.* **15** 40 10N 84 59W
Winchester, *Ky.* **15** 38 0N 84 11W
Winchester, *Mass.* **23** 42 26N 71 8W
Winchester, *N.H.* **9** 42 46N 72 23W
Winchester, *Tenn.* **11** 35 11N 86 7W
Winchester, *Va.* **10** 39 11N 78 10W
Wind →, *Wyo.* **16** 43 12N 108 12W
Wind River Range, *Wyo.* **16** 43 0N 109 30W
Windber, *Pa.* **8** 40 14N 78 50W
Windom, *Minn.* **12** 43 52N 95 7W
Window Rock, *Ariz.* **17** 35 41N 109 3W
Windsor, *Colo.* **12** 40 29N 104 54W
Windsor, *Conn.* **9** 41 50N 72 39W
Windsor, *Mich.* **26** 42 18N 83 0W
Windsor, *Mo.* **14** 38 32N 93 31W
Windsor, *N.Y.* **9** 42 5N 75 37W
Windsor, *Vt.* **9** 43 29N 72 24W
Windsor Airport, *Mich.* **26** 42 16N 82 57W
Winfield, *Kans.* **13** 37 15N 96 59W
Winifred, *Mont.* **16** 47 34N 109 23W
Wink, *Tex.* **13** 31 45N 103 9W
Winlock, *Wash.* **18** 46 30N 122 56W
Winnebago, *Minn.* **12** 43 46N 94 10W
Winnebago, L., *Wis.* **10** 44 0N 88 26W
Winnemucca, *Nev.* **16** 40 58N 117 44W
Winnemucca L., *Nev.* **16** 40 7N 119 21W
Winner, *S. Dak.* **12** 43 22N 99 52W
Winnetka, *Ill.* **22** 42 6N 87 43W
Winnett, *Mont.* **16** 47 0N 108 21W
Winnfield, *La.* **13** 31 56N 92 38W
Winnibigoshish, L., *Minn.* **12** 47 27N 94 13W
Winnipesaukee, L., *N.H.* **9** 43 38N 71 21W
Winnsboro, *La.* **13** 32 10N 91 43W
Winnsboro, *S.C.* **11** 34 23N 81 5W
Winnsboro, *Tex.* **13** 32 58N 95 17W
Winona, *Minn.* **12** 44 3N 91 39W
Winona, *Miss.* **13** 33 29N 89 44W
Winooski, *Vt.* **9** 44 29N 73 11W
Winslow, *Ariz.* **17** 35 2N 110 42W
Winsted, *Conn.* **9** 41 55N 73 4W
Winston-Salem, *N.C.* **11** 36 6N 80 15W
Winter Garden, *Fla.* **11** 28 34N 81 35W
Winter Haven, *Fla.* **11** 28 1N 81 44W
Winter Park, *Fla.* **11** 28 36N 81 20W
Winters, *Tex.* **13** 31 58N 99 58W
Winterset, *Iowa* **14** 41 20N 94 1W
Winthrop, *Mass.* **23** 42 22N 70 58W
Winthrop, *Minn.* **12** 44 32N 94 22W
Winthrop, *Wash.* **16** 48 28N 120 10W
Winton, *N.C.* **11** 36 24N 76 56W
Wisconsin □ **12** 44 45N 89 30W
Wisconsin →, *Wis.* **12** 43 0N 91 15W
Wisconsin Dells, *Wis.* **12** 43 38N 89 46W
Wisconsin Rapids, *Wis.* **12** 44 23N 89 49W
Wisdom, *Mont.* **16** 45 37N 113 27W
Wiseman, *Alaska* **30** 67 25N 150 6W
Wishek, *N. Dak.* **12** 46 16N 99 33W
Wisner, *Nebr.* **12** 41 59N 96 55W
Woburn, *Mass.* **23** 42 29N 71 10W
Wolf Creek, *Mont.* **16** 47 0N 112 4W
Wolf Point, *Mont.* **12** 48 5N 105 39W
Wood Lake, *Nebr.* **12** 42 38N 100 14W
Woodbury, *N.J.* **24** 39 50N 75 9W
Woodbury, *N.Y.* **21** 40 49N 73 27W
Woodfords, *Calif.* **18** 38 47N 119 50W
Woodlake, *Calif.* **18** 36 25N 119 6W
Woodland, *Calif.* **18** 38 41N 121 46W
Woodlawn, *Md.* **25** 39 19N 76 44W
Woodruff, *Ariz.* **17** 34 51N 110 1W
Woodruff, *Utah* **16** 41 31N 111 10W
Woodstock, *Ill.* **15** 42 19N 88 27W
Woodstock, *Vt.* **9** 43 37N 72 31W
Woodsville, *N.H.* **9** 44 9N 72 2W
Woodville, *Tex.* **13** 30 47N 94 25W
Woodward, *Okla.* **13** 36 26N 99 24W
Woody, *Calif.* **19** 35 42N 118 50W
Woonsocket, *R.I.* **9** 42 0N 71 31W
Woonsocket, *S. Dak.* **12** 44 3N 98 17W
Wooster, *Ohio* **8** 40 48N 81 56W
Worcester, *Mass.* **9** 42 16N 71 48W
Worcester, *N.Y.* **9** 42 36N 74 45W
Worland, *Wyo.* **16** 44 1N 107 57W
Wortham, *Tex.* **13** 31 47N 96 28W
Worthington, *Minn.* **12** 43 37N 95 36W
Wrangell, *Alaska* **30** 56 28N 132 23W
Wrangell Mts., *Alaska* **30** 61 30N 142 0W
Wray, *Colo.* **12** 40 5N 102 13W
Wrens, *Ga.* **11** 33 12N 82 23W
Wrighton Mt., *Ariz.* **17** 31 42N 110 51W
Wrightwood, *Calif.* **19** 34 21N 117 38W
Wyalusing, *Pa.* **9** 41 40N 76 16W
Wyandotte, *Mich.* **26** 42 12N 83 9W
Wymore, *Nebr.* **12** 40 7N 96 40W
Wyndmere, *N. Dak.* **12** 46 16N 97 8W
Wynne, *Ark.* **13** 35 14N 90 47W
Wyoming □ **16** 43 0N 107 30W
Wytheville, *Va.* **10** 36 57N 81 5W

X

Xenia, *Ohio* **15** 39 41N 83 56W

Y

Yadkin →, *N.C.* **11** 35 29N 80 9W
Yakataga, *Alaska* **30** 60 5N 142 32W
Yakima, *Wash.* **16** 46 36N 120 31W
Yakima →, *Wash.* **16** 47 0N 120 30W
Yakutat, *Alaska* **30** 59 33N 139 44W
Yalobusha →, *Miss.* **13** 33 33N 90 10W
Yampa →, *Colo.* **16** 40 32N 108 59W
Yankton, *S. Dak.* **12** 42 53N 97 23W
Yap Is., *U.S. Pac. Is. Trust Terr.* **31** 9 30N 138 10 E
Yates Center, *Kans.* **13** 37 53N 95 44W
Yazoo →, *Miss.* **13** 32 22N 90 54W
Yazoo City, *Miss.* **13** 32 51N 90 25W
Yellowstone →, *Mont.* **12** 47 59N 103 59W
Yellowstone L., *Wyo.* **16** 44 27N 110 22W
Yellowstone National Park, *Wyo.* **16** 44 40N 110 30W
Yellowtail Res., *Wyo.* **16** 45 6N 108 8W
Yermo, *Calif.* **19** 34 54N 116 50W
Yeso, *N. Mex.* **13** 34 26N 104 37W
Yoakum, *Tex.* **13** 29 17N 97 9W
Yonkers, *N.Y.* **21** 40 57N 73 52W
York, *Ala.* **11** 32 29N 88 18W
York, *Nebr.* **12** 40 52N 97 36W
York, *Pa.* **10** 39 58N 76 44W
Yorktown, *Tex.* **13** 28 59N 97 30W
Yorkville, *Ill.* **15** 41 38N 88 27W
Yosemite National Park, *Calif.* **18** 37 45N 119 40W
Yosemite Village, *Calif.* **18** 37 45N 119 35W
Youngstown, *N.Y.* **8** 43 15N 79 3W
Youngstown, *Ohio* **8** 41 6N 80 39W
Ypsilanti, *Mich.* **15** 42 14N 83 37W
Yreka, *Calif.* **16** 41 44N 122 38W
Ysleta, *N. Mex.* **17** 31 45N 106 24W
Yuba City, *Calif.* **18** 39 8N 121 37W
Yucca, *Ariz.* **19** 34 52N 114 9W
Yucca Valley, *Calif.* **19** 34 8N 116 27W
Yukon →, *Alaska* **30** 62 32N 163 54W
Yuma, *Ariz.* **19** 32 43N 114 37W
Yuma, *Colo.* **12** 40 8N 102 43W
Yunaska I., *Alaska* **30** 52 38N 170 40W

Z

Zanesville, *Ohio* **8** 39 56N 82 1W
Zapata, *Tex.* **13** 26 55N 99 16W
Zion National Park, *Utah* **17** 37 15N 113 5W
Zrenton, *Mich.* **26** 42 8N 83 12W
Zuni, *N. Mex.* **17** 35 4N 108 51W
Zwolle, *La.* **13** 31 38N 93 39W

INTRODUCTION TO
WORLD GEOGRAPHY

PLANET EARTH

Sun
Mercury
Mars
Saturn
Neptune
Venus
Earth
Jupiter
Uranus
Pluto

THE SOLAR SYSTEM

A minute part of one of the billions of galaxies (collections of stars) that comprises the Universe, the Solar System lies some 27,000 light-years from the center of our own galaxy, the 'Milky Way'. Thought to be over 4,700 million years old, it consists of a central sun with nine planets and their moons revolving around it, attracted by its gravitational pull. The planets orbit the Sun in the same direction – counterclockwise when viewed from the Northern Heavens – and almost in the same plane. Their orbital paths, however, vary enormously.

The Sun's diameter is 109 times that of Earth, and the temperature at its core – caused by continuous thermonuclear fusions of hydrogen into helium – is estimated to be 27 million degrees Fahrenheit. It is the Solar System's only source of light and heat.

PROFILE OF THE PLANETS

	Mean distance from Sun (million miles)	Mass (Earth = 1)	Period of orbit (Earth days)	Period of rotation (Earth days)	Equatorial diameter (miles)	Number of known satellites
Mercury	36.4	0.06	88 days	58.67	3,049	0
Venus	67.3	0.8	224.7 days	243.00	7,565	0
Earth	93.5	1.0	365.24 days	0.99	7,973	1
Mars	142.1	0.1	1.88 years	1.02	4,242	2
Jupiter	486.2	317.8	11.86 years	0.41	89,250	16
Saturn	891.9	95.2	29.63 years	0.42	75,000	20
Uranus	1,795.2	14.5	83.97 years	0.45	31,949	15
Neptune	2,814.2	17.1	164.80 years	0.67	30,955	8
Pluto	3,683.9	0.002	248.63 years	6.38	1,438	1

All planetary orbits are elliptical in form, but only Pluto and Mercury follow paths that deviate noticeably from a circular one. Near perihelion – its closest approach to the Sun – Pluto actually passes inside the orbit of Neptune, an event that last occurred in 1983. Pluto will not regain its station as outermost planet until February 1999.

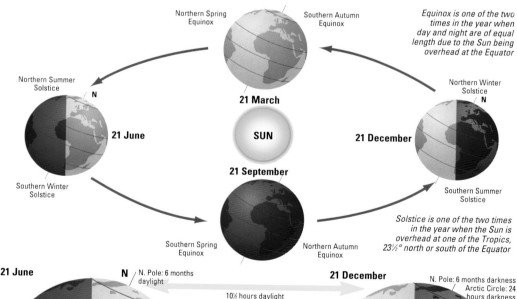

Northern Spring Equinox
Southern Autumn Equinox

Equinox is one of the two times in the year when day and night are of equal length due to the Sun being overhead at the Equator

Northern Summer Solstice
N

21 March

21 June

SUN

21 December

21 September

Northern Winter Solstice
N

Southern Winter Solstice

Southern Summer Solstice

Southern Spring Equinox

Northern Autumn Equinox

Solstice is one of the two times in the year when the Sun is overhead at one of the Tropics, 23½° north or south of the Equator

21 June

N / N. Pole: 6 months daylight

66½°

10½ hours daylight

12 hours daylight

LONG DAY 23½°

Sun's rays

13½ hours daylight

Equator

0°

12 hours daylight

SHORT DAY 23½°

10½ hours daylight

Antarctic Circle: 24 hours darkness
S. Pole: 6 months darkness

SHORT NIGHT
LONG NIGHT

21 December

N. Pole: 6 months darkness
Arctic Circle: 24 hours darkness

23½°

SHORT DAY

66½°

0°

23½°

Equator

LONG DAY

23½°

Antarctic Circle: 24 hours daylight
S. Pole: 6 months daylight

S

LONG NIGHT
SHORT NIGHT

THE SEASONS

The Earth revolves around the Sun once a year in a 'counterclockwise' direction, tilted at a constant angle of 23½°. In June, the northern hemisphere is tilted toward the Sun: as a result it receives more hours of sunshine in a day and therefore has its warmest season, summer. By December, the Earth has rotated halfway round the Sun so that the southern hemisphere is tilted toward the Sun and has its summer; the hemisphere that is tilted away from the Sun has winter. On 21 June the Sun is directly overhead at the Tropic of Cancer (23½° N), and this is midsummer in the northern hemisphere. Midsummer in the southern hemisphere occurs on 21 December, when the Sun is overhead at the Tropic of Capricorn (23½° S).

DAY AND NIGHT

The Sun appears to rise in the east, reach its highest point at noon, and then set in the west, to be followed by night. In reality it is not the Sun that is moving but the Earth revolving from west to east. Due to the tilting of the Earth the length of day and night varies from place to place and month to month.

At the summer solstice in the northern hemisphere (21 June), the Arctic has total daylight and the Antarctic total darkness. The opposite occurs at the winter solstice (21 December). At the Equator, the length of day and night are almost equal all year, at latitude 30° the length of day varies from about 14 hours to 10 hours, and at latitude 50° from about 16 hours to about 8 hours.

TIME

Year: The time taken by the Earth to revolve around the Sun, or 365.24 days.
Leap Year: A calendar year of 366 days, 29 February being the additional day. It offsets the difference between the calendar (365 days) and the solar year.
Month: The approximate time taken by the Moon to revolve around the Earth. The 12 months of the year in fact vary from 28 (29 in a Leap Year) to 31 days.
Week: An artificial period of 7 days, not based on astronomical time.
Day: The time taken by the Earth to complete one rotation on its axis.
Hour: 24 hours make one day. Usually the day is divided into hours AM (ante meridiem or before noon) and PM (post meridiem or after noon), although most timetables now use the 24-hour system, from midnight to midnight.

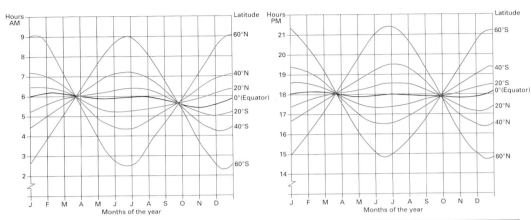

SUNRISE

SUNSET

THE MOON

Distance from Earth: 221,463 mi – 252,710 mi; Mean diameter: 2,160 mi; Mass: approx. 1/81 that of Earth; Surface gravity: one-sixth of Earth's; Daily range of temperature at lunar equator: 360°F; Average orbital speed: 2,300 mph

PHASES OF THE MOON

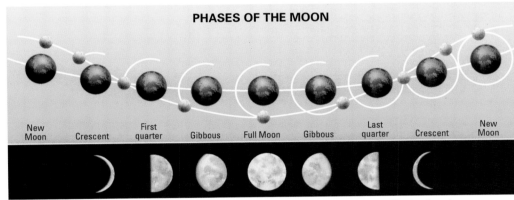

New Moon — Crescent — First quarter — Gibbous — Full Moon — Gibbous — Last quarter — Crescent — New Moon

The Moon rotates more slowly than the Earth, making one complete turn on its axis in just over 27 days. Since this corresponds to its period of revolution around the Earth, the Moon always presents the

same hemisphere or face to us, and we never see 'the dark side'. The interval between one full Moon and the next (and between new Moons) is about 29½ days – a lunar month. The apparent changes in the

shape of the Moon are caused by its changing position in relation to the Earth; like the planets, it produces no light of its own and shines only by reflecting the rays of the Sun.

ECLIPSES

When the Moon passes between the Sun and the Earth it causes a partial eclipse of the Sun (1) if the Earth passes through the Moon's outer shadow (P), or a total eclipse (2) if the inner cone shadow crosses the Earth's surface. In a lunar eclipse, the Earth's shadow crosses the Moon and, again, provides either a partial or total eclipse. Eclipses of the Sun and the Moon do not occur every month because of the 5° difference between the plane of the Moon's orbit and the plane in which the Earth moves. In the 1990s only 14 lunar eclipses are possible, for example, seven partial and seven total; each is visible only from certain, and variable, parts of the world. The same period witnesses 13 solar eclipses – six partial (or annular) and seven total.

Partial eclipse (1) — **Solar eclipse** — P P P

Total eclipse (2)

Lunar eclipse

TIDES

The daily rise and fall of the ocean's tides are the result of the gravitational pull of the Moon and that of the Sun, though the effect of the latter is only 46.6% as strong as that of the Moon. This effect is greatest on the hemisphere facing the Moon and causes a tidal 'bulge'. When the Sun, Earth and Moon are in line, tide-raising forces are at a maximum and Spring tides occur: high tide reaches the highest values, and low tide falls to low levels. When lunar and solar forces are least coincidental with the Sun and Moon at an angle (near the Moon's first and third quarters), Neap tides occur, which have a small tidal range.

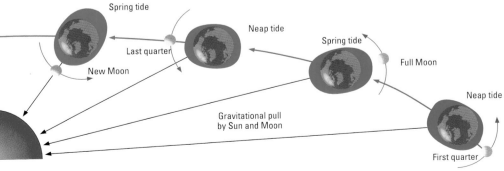

Spring tide — Neap tide — Spring tide — Last quarter — New Moon — Full Moon — Neap tide — Gravitational pull by Sun and Moon — First quarter

RESTLESS EARTH

THE EARTH'S STRUCTURE

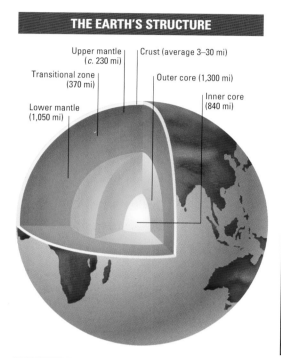

Upper mantle (c. 230 mi)
Crust (average 3–30 mi)
Transitional zone (370 mi)
Outer core (1,300 mi)
Inner core (840 mi)
Lower mantle (1,050 mi)

CONTINENTAL DRIFT

About 200 million years ago the original Pangaea land mass began to split into two continental groups, which further separated over time to produce the present-day configuration.

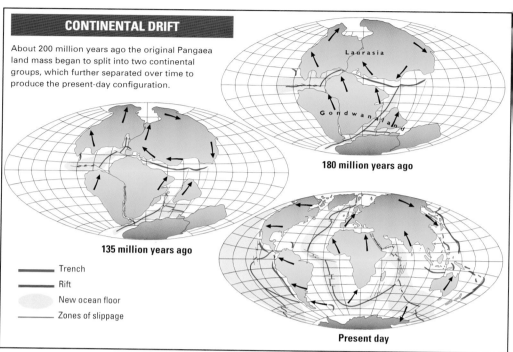

Laurasia

Gondwanaland

180 million years ago

135 million years ago

Trench
Rift
New ocean floor
Zones of slippage

Present day

EARTHQUAKES

Earthquake magnitude is usually rated according to either the Richter or the Modified Mercalli scale, both devised by seismologists in the 1930s. The Richter scale measures absolute earthquake power with mathematical precision: each step upward represents a tenfold increase in shockwave amplitude. Theoretically, there is no upper limit, but the largest earthquakes measured have been rated at between 8.8 and 8.9. The 12–point Mercalli scale, based on observed effects, is often more meaningful, ranging from I (earthquakes noticed only by seismographs) to XII (total destruction); intermediate points include V (people awakened at night; unstable objects overturned), VII (collapse of ordinary buildings; chimneys and monuments fall) and IX (conspicuous cracks in ground; serious damage to reservoirs).

Shockwaves reach surface
Epicenter
Ocean trench
Subduction zone
Origin or focus
Shockwaves travel away from focus

NOTABLE EARTHQUAKES SINCE 1900

Year	Location	Richter Scale	Deaths
1906	San Francisco, USA	8.3	503
1906	Valparaiso, Chile	8.6	22,000
1908	Messina, Italy	7.5	83,000
1915	Avezzano, Italy	7.5	30,000
1920	Gansu (Kansu), China	8.6	180,000
1923	Yokohama, Japan	8.3	143,000
1927	Nan Shan, China	8.3	200,000
1932	Gansu (Kansu), China	7.6	70,000
1934	Bihar, India/Nepal	8.4	10,700
1935	Quetta, India (now Pakistan)	7.5	60,000
1939	Chillan, Chile	8.3	28,000
1939	Erzincan, Turkey	7.9	30,000
1960	Agadir, Morocco	5.8	12,000
1962	Khorasan, Iran	7.1	12,230
1968	N.E. Iran	7.4	12,000
1970	N. Peru	7.7	66,794
1972	Managua, Nicaragua	6.2	5,000
1974	N. Pakistan	6.3	5,200
1976	Guatemala	7.5	22,778
1976	Tangshan, China	8.2	650,000
1978	Tabas, Iran	7.7	25,000
1980	El Asnam, Algeria	7.3	20,000
1980	S. Italy	7.2	4,800
1985	Mexico City, Mexico	8.1	4,200
1988	N.W. Armenia	6.8	55,000
1990	N. Iran	7.7	36,000
1993	Maharashtra, India	6.4	30,000
1994	Los Angeles, USA	6.6	57
1995	Kobe, Japan	7.2	5,000
1995	Sakhalin Is., Russia	7.5	2,000
1996	Yunnan, China	7.0	240

The highest magnitude recorded on the Richter scale is 8.9, in Japan on 2 March 1933 (2,990 deaths). The most devastating quake ever was at Shaanxi (Shenshi) province, central China, on 3 January 1556, when an estimated 830,000 people were killed.

STRUCTURE AND EARTHQUAKES

Mobile land areas
Submarine zones of mobile land areas
Stable land platforms
Mobile land areas
Submarine extensions of stable land platforms
Oceanic platforms

1976 ○ Principal earthquakes & dates

Earthquakes are a series of rapid vibrations originating from the slipping or faulting of parts of the Earth's crust when stresses within build up to breaking point. They usually happen at depths varying from 5 mi to 20 mi. Severe earthquakes cause extensive damage when they take place in populated areas, destroying structures and severing communications. Most initial loss of life occurs due to secondary causes such as falling masonry, fires and flooding.

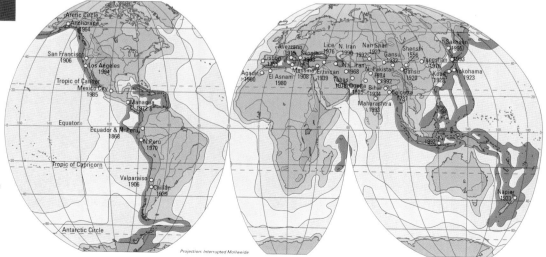

Projection: Interrupted Mollweide

PLATE TECTONICS

The drifting of the continents is a feature that is unique to Planet Earth. The complementary, almost jigsaw-puzzle fit of the coastlines on each side of the Atlantic Ocean inspired Alfred Wegener's theory of continental drift in 1915. The theory suggested that an ancient super-continent, which Wegener named Pangaea, incorporated all of the Earth's land masses and gradually split up to form today's continents.

The original debate about continental drift was a prelude to a more radical idea: plate tectonics. The basic theory is that the Earth's crust is made up of a series of rigid plates which float on a soft layer of the mantle and are moved about by continental convection currents within the Earth's interior. These plates diverge and converge along margins marked by earthquakes, volcanoes and other seismic activity. Plates diverge from mid-ocean ridges where molten lava pushes upward and forces the plates apart at a rate of up to 40 mm [1.6 in] a year; converging plates form either a trench (where the oceanic plate sinks below the lighter continental rock) or mountain ranges (where two continents collide).

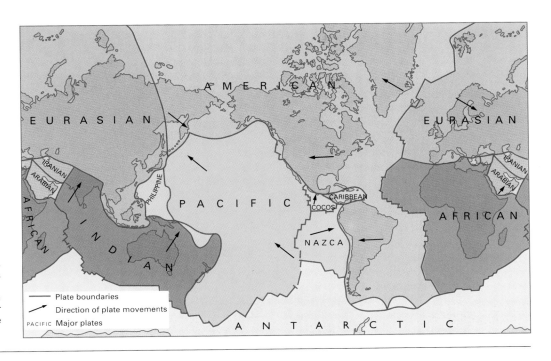

- —— Plate boundaries
- → Direction of plate movements
- PACIFIC Major plates

VOLCANOES

Ash and gas cloud

Volcanic bombs

Layers of cinders and lava from previous eruptions

Neck or pipe

Eruption at side vent

Lava flow

Main vent

Rock strata

Magma chamber

Volcanoes occur when hot liquefied rock beneath the Earth's crust is pushed up by pressure to the surface as molten lava. Some volcanoes erupt in an explosive way, throwing out rocks and ash (such as Anak Krakatoa in Indonesia); others are effusive, and lava flows out of the vent (Mauna Loa in Hawaii is a classic example); and there are volcanoes which are both (such as Mount Fuji, a composite volcano like the diagram opposite). Fast-flowing basaltic lava erupts at temperatures of between 1,800–2,200°F, close to the temperature of the upper mantle. An accumulation of lava and cinders around a vent creates cones of variable size and shape. As a result of many eruptions over centuries Mount Etna in Sicily has a circumference of over 120 km [75 miles].

Climatologists believe that volcanic ash, if ejected high enough into the atmosphere, can influence temperature and weather for several years afterward. The eruption of Mount Pinatubo in the Philippines ejected more than 20 million tons of dust and ash 32 km [20 miles] into the atmosphere and is believed to have accelerated ozone depletion over a large part of the globe.

DISTRIBUTION OF VOLCANOES

Today volcanoes might be the subject of considerable scientific study but they remain both dramatic and unpredictable, if not exactly supernatural: in 1991 Mount Pinatubo, 100 km [62 miles] north of the Philippines capital Manila, suddenly burst into life after lying dormant for more than six centuries.

Most of the world's active volcanoes occur in a belt around the Pacific Ocean, on the edge of the Pacific plate, called the 'ring of fire'. Indonesia has the greatest concentration with 90 volcanoes, 12 of which are active. The most famous, Krakatoa, erupted in 1883 with such force that the resulting tidal wave killed 36,000 people and tremors were felt as far away as Australia.

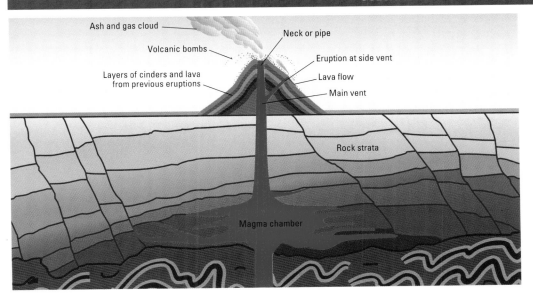

- ○ Submarine volcanoes
- ▲ Submarine volcanoes active since 1700
- —— Boundaries of tectonic plates

Projection: Interrupted Mollweide

LANDSCAPE

Above and below the surface of the oceans, the features of the Earth's crust are constantly changing. The phenomenal forces generated by convection currents in the molten core of our planet carry the vast segments or 'plates' of the crust across the globe in an endless cycle of creation and destruction. A continent may travel little more than 25 mm [1 in] per year, yet in the vast span of geological time this process throws up giant mountain ranges and creates new land.

Destruction of the landscape, however, begins as soon as it is formed. Wind, water, ice and sea, the main agents of erosion, mount a constant assault that even the hardest rocks can not withstand. Mountain peaks may dwindle by an inch or less each year, but if they are not uplifted by further movements of the crust they will eventually be reduced to rubble and transported away. Water is the most powerful agent of erosion – it has been estimated that 100 billion tons of rock are washed into the oceans every year.

Rivers and glaciers, like the sea itself, generate much of their effect through abrasion – pounding the landscape with the debris they carry with them. But as well as destroying they also create new landscapes, many of them spectacular: vast deltas like the Mississippi and the Nile, or the fjords cut by glaciers in British Columbia, Norway and New Zealand.

THE SPREADING EARTH

The vast ridges that divide the Earth's crust beneath each of the world's oceans mark the boundaries between tectonic plates that are gradually moving in opposite directions. As the plates shift apart, molten magma rises from the mantle to seal the rift and the sea floor slowly spreads toward the continental land masses. The rate of spreading has been calculated by magnetic analysis of the rock at around 40 mm [1.5 in] a year in the North Atlantic Ocean. Underwater volcanoes mark the line where the continental rise begins. As the plates meet, much of the denser ocean crust dips beneath the continental plate and melts back to the magma.

Sea-floor spreading in the Atlantic Ocean

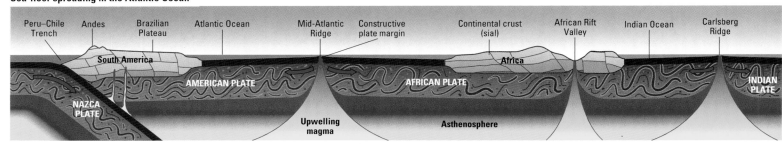

Sea-floor spreading in the Indian Ocean and continental plate collision

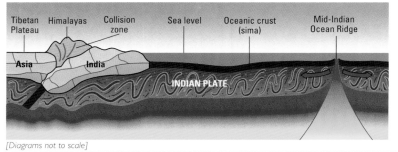

[Diagrams not to scale]

Oceanic and continental plate collision

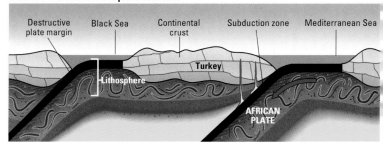

MOUNTAIN BUILDING

Mountains are formed when pressures on the Earth's crust caused by continental drift become so intense that the surface buckles or cracks. This happens where oceanic crust is subducted by continental crust or, more dramatically, where two tectonic plates collide: the Rockies, Andes, Alps, Urals and Himalayas resulted from such impacts. These are all known as fold mountains because they were formed by the compression of the rocks, forcing the surface to bend and fold like a crumpled rug. The Himalayas are formed from the folded former sediments of the Tethys Sea which was trapped in the collision zone between the Indian and Eurasian plates.

The other main mountain-building process occurs when the crust fractures to create faults, allowing rock to be forced upward in large blocks; or when the pressure of magma within the crust forces the surface to bulge into a dome, or erupts to form a volcano. Large mountain ranges may reveal a combination of those features; the Alps, for example, have been compressed so violently that the folds are fragmented by numerous faults and intrusions of molten igneous rock.

Over millions of years, even the greatest mountain ranges can be reduced by the agents of erosion (especially rivers) to a low rugged landscape known as a peneplain.

Types of faults: Faults occur where the crust is being stretched or compressed so violently that the rock strata break in a horizontal or vertical movement. They are classified by the direction in which the blocks of rock have moved. A normal fault results when a vertical movement causes the surface to break apart; compression causes a reverse fault. Horizontal movement causes shearing, known as a strike-slip fault. When the rock breaks in two places, the central block may be pushed up in a horst fault, or sink (creating a rift valley) in a graben fault.

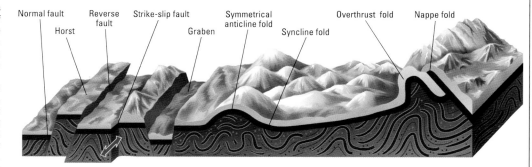

Types of fold: Folds occur when rock strata are squeezed and compressed. They are common therefore at destructive plate margins and where plates have collided, forcing the rocks to buckle into mountain ranges. Geographers give different names to the degrees of fold that result from continuing pressure on the rock. A simple fold may be symmetric, with even slopes on either side, but as the pressure builds up, one slope becomes steeper and the fold becomes asymmetric. Later, the ridge or 'anticline' at the top of the fold may slide over the lower ground or 'syncline' to form a recumbent fold. Eventually, the rock strata may break under the pressure to form an overthrust and finally a nappe fold.

Features of the natural landscape

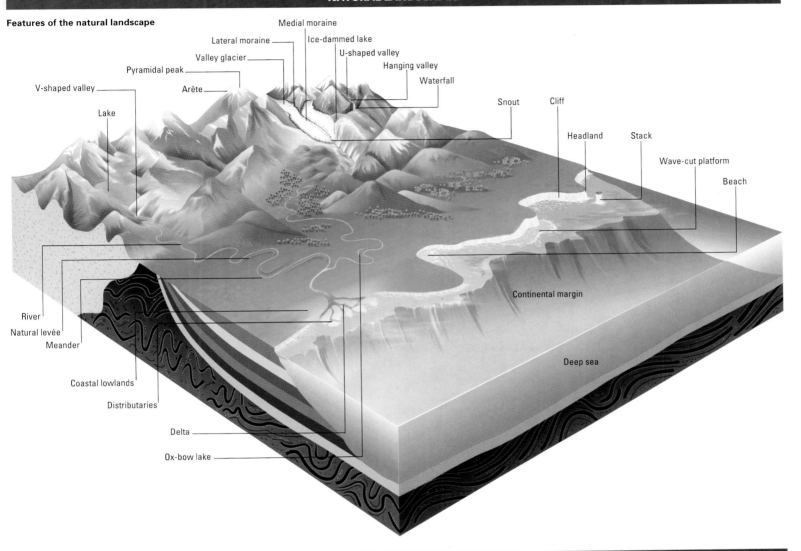

Medial moraine
Lateral moraine
Ice-dammed lake
Valley glacier
U-shaped valley
Pyramidal peak
Hanging valley
V-shaped valley
Waterfall
Arête
Snout
Cliff
Lake
Headland
Stack
Wave-cut platform
Beach
River
Natural levée
Meander
Continental margin
Coastal lowlands
Distributaries
Deep sea
Delta
Ox-bow lake

SHAPING FORCES: GLACIERS

Many of the world's most dramatic landscapes have been carved by ice sheets and glaciers. During the Ice Ages of the Pleistocene Epoch (over 10,000 years ago) up to a third of the land surface was glaciated; even today a tenth is covered in ice – the vast majority of this ice is locked up in vast ice sheets and ice caps. The world's largest ice sheet covers most of Antarctica and is up to 4,800 m [15,750 ft] thick. It is extremely slow moving, unlike valley glaciers which can move at rates of between a few inches and several feet a day.

Valley glaciers are found in mountainous regions throughout the world, except Australia. In the relatively short geological time scale of the recent ice ages, glaciers accomplished far more carving of the topography than did rivers and the wind. They are formed from compressed snow, called *névé*, accumulating in a valley head or cirque. Slowly the glacier moves downhill scraping away debris from the mountains and valleys through which it passes. The debris, or moraine, adds to the abrasive power of the ice. The amount of glacial debris is enormous – the sediments are transported by the ice to the edge of the glacier, where they are deposited or carried away by meltwater streams. The end of the glacier may not reach the bottom of the valley – the position of the snout depends on the rate at which the ice melts.

Glaciers create numerous distinctive landscape features from arête ridges and pyramidal peaks to ice-dammed lakes and truncated spurs, with the U-shape distinguishing a glacial valley from one cut by a river.

SHAPING FORCES: RIVERS

From their origins as small upland rills and streams channeling rainfall, or as springs releasing water that has seeped into the ground, all rivers are incessantly at work cutting and shaping the landscape on their way to the sea. The area of land drained by a river and all its tributaries is termed a drainage basin.

In highland regions stream flow may be rapid and turbulent, pounding rocks and boulders with enough violence to cut deep gorges and V-shaped valleys through softer rocks, or tumble as waterfalls over harder ones. Rocks and pebbles are moved along the stream bed either by saltation (bouncing) or traction (rolling), whilst lighter sediments are carried in suspension or dissolved in solution. This material transported by the river is termed its load.

As they reach more gentle slopes, rivers release some of the pebbles and heavier sediments they have carried downstream, flow more slowly and broaden out. Levées or ridges are raised along their banks by the deposition of mud and sand during floods. In lowland plains, where the gradient is minimal, the river drifts into meanders, depositing deep layers of sediment especially on the inside of each bend, where the flow is weakest. Here farmers may dig drainage ditches and artificial levées to keep the flood plain dry.

As the river finally reaches the sea, it deposits all its remaining sediments, and estuaries are formed where the tidal currents are strong enough to remove them; if not, the debris creates a delta, through which the river cuts outlet streams known as distributaries.

SHAPING FORCES: THE SEA

Under the constant assault from tides and currents, wind and waves, coastlines change faster than most landscape features, both by erosion and by the build-up of sand and pebbles carried by the sea. In severe storms, giant waves pound the shoreline with rocks and boulders; but even in much quieter conditions, the sea steadily erodes cliffs and headlands, creating new features in the form of sand dunes, spits and salt marshes. Beaches, where sand and shingle have been deposited, form a buffer zone between the erosive power of the waves and the coast. Because it is composed of loose material, a beach can rapidly adapt its shape to changes in wave energy.

Where the coastline is formed from soft rocks such as sandstones, debris may fall evenly and be carried away by currents from shelving beaches. In areas with harder rock, the waves may cut steep cliffs and wave-cut platforms; eroded debris is deposited as a terrace. Bays are formed when sections of soft rock are carved away between headlands of harder rock. These are then battered by waves from both sides, until the headlands are eventually reduced to rock arches and stacks.

A number of factors affect the rate of erosion in coastal environments. These vary from rock type and structure, beach width and supply of beach material, to the more complex fluid dynamics of the waves, namely the breaking point, steepness and length of fetch. Very steep destructive waves have more energy and erosive power than gentle constructive waves formed many miles away.

OCEANS

THE GREAT OCEANS

Relative sizes of the world's oceans

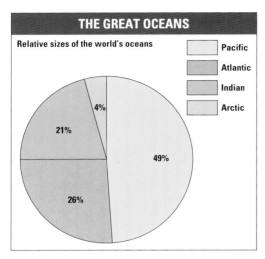

- Pacific
- Atlantic
- Indian
- Arctic

4%
21%
49%
26%

In a strict geographical sense there are only three true oceans – the Atlantic, Indian and Pacific. The legendary 'Seven Seas' would require these to be divided at the Equator and the addition of the Arctic Ocean – which accounts for less than 4% of the total sea area. The International Hydrographic Bureau does not recognize the Antarctic Ocean (even less the 'Southern Ocean') as a separate entity.

The Earth is a watery planet: more than 70% of its surface – almost 140,000,000 square miles – is covered by the oceans and seas. The mighty Pacific alone accounts for nearly 36% of the total, and 49% of the sea area. Gravity holds in around 320 million cubic miles of water, of which over 97% is saline.

The vast underwater world starts in the shallows of the seaside and plunges to depths of more than 36,000 feet. The continental shelf, part of the land mass, drops gently to around 600 feet; here the seabed falls away suddenly at an angle of 3° to 6° – the continental slope. The third stage, called the continental rise, is more gradual with gradients varying from 1 in 100 to 1 in 700. At an average depth of 16,000 feet there begins the aptly-named abyssal plain – massive submarine depths where sunlight fails to penetrate and few creatures can survive.

From these plains rise volcanoes which, taken from base to top, rival and even surpass the biggest continental mountains in height. Mount Kea, on Hawaii, reaches a total of 33,400 feet, almost 4,500 feet more than Mount Everest, though scarcely 40% is visible above sea level.

In addition there are underwater mountain chains up to 600 miles across, whose peaks sometimes appear above sea level as islands such as Iceland and Tristan da Cunha.

THE OCEAN DEPTHS

Average and maximum depths of the world's great oceans, in feet

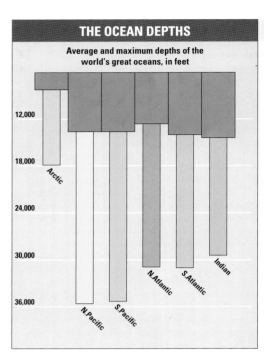

12,000
18,000
24,000
30,000
36,000

Arctic
N.Pacific
S.Pacific
N.Atlantic
S.Atlantic
Indian

OCEAN CURRENTS

January temperatures and ocean currents

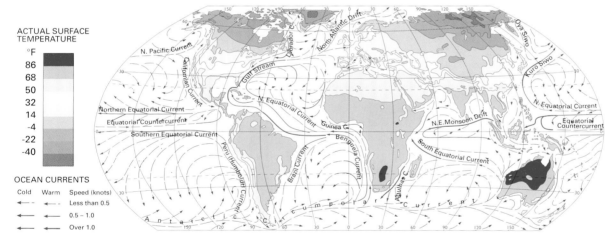

ACTUAL SURFACE TEMPERATURE

°F
86
68
50
32
14
-4
-22
-40

OCEAN CURRENTS
Cold Warm Speed (knots)
Less than 0.5
0.5 – 1.0
Over 1.0

July temperatures and ocean currents

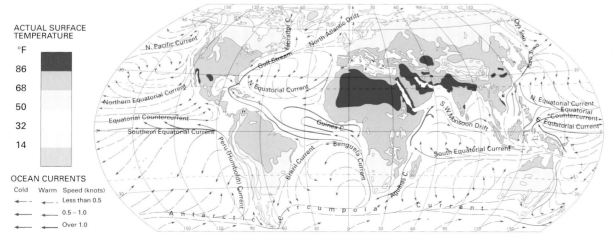

ACTUAL SURFACE TEMPERATURE

°F
86
68
50
32
14

OCEAN CURRENTS
Cold Warm Speed (knots)
Less than 0.5
0.5 – 1.0
Over 1.0

Moving immense quantities of energy as well as billions of tons of water every hour, the ocean currents are a vital part of the great heat engine that drives the Earth's climate. They themselves are produced by a twofold mechanism. At the surface, winds push huge masses of water before them; in the deep ocean, below an abrupt temperature gradient that separates the churning surface waters from the still depths, density variations cause slow vertical movements.

The pattern of circulation of the great surface currents is determined by the displacement known as the Coriolis effect. As the Earth turns beneath a moving object – whether it is a tennis ball or a vast mass of water – it appears to be deflected to one side. The deflection is most obvious near the Equator, where the Earth's surface is spinning eastward at 1,050 mph; currents moving poleward are curved clockwise in the northern hemisphere and counterclockwise in the southern.

The result is a system of spinning circles known as gyres. The Coriolis effect piles up water on the left of each gyre, creating a narrow, fast-moving stream that is matched by a slower, broader returning current on the right. North and south of the Equator, the fastest currents are located in the west and in the east respectively. In each case, warm water moves from the Equator and cold water returns to it. Cold currents often bring an upwelling of nutrients with them, supporting the world's most economically important fisheries.

Depending on the prevailing winds, some currents on or near the Equator may reverse their direction in the course of the year – a seasonal variation on which Asian monsoon rains depend, and whose occasional failure can bring disaster to millions.

WORLD FISHING AREAS

Main commercial fishing areas (numbered FAO regions)

Catch by top marine fishing areas, thousand tons (1992)

1.	Pacific, NW	[61]	26,667	29.3%
2.	Pacific, SE	[87]	15,317	16.8%
3.	Atlantic, NE	[27]	12,202	13.4%
4.	Pacific, WC	[71]	8,496	9.3%
5.	Indian, W	[51]	4,129	4.5%
6.	Indian, E	[57]	3,595	4.0%
7.	Atlantic, EC	[34]	3,591	3.9%
8.	Pacific, NE	[67]	3,470	3.8%

Principal fishing areas

Leading fishing nations

China 17.3% Peru 8.3% Japan 8.0% Chile 5.9% U.S.A. 5.9% Russia 4.4% India 4.3% Indonesia 3.6%

World total (1993): 111,762,080 tons
(Marine catch 83.1% Inland catch 16.9%)

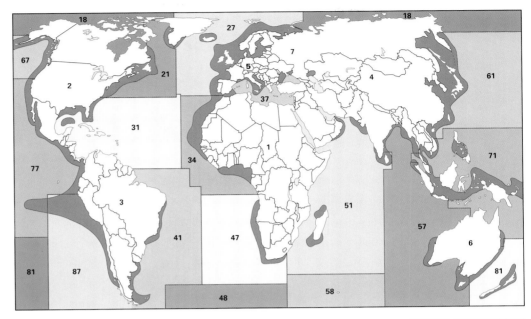

MARINE POLLUTION

Sources of marine oil pollution (latest available year)

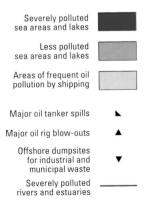

- Tanker operations
- Municipal wastes
- Tanker accidents
- Bilge and fuel oils
- Natural seeps
- Industrial waste
- Urban runoff
- Coastal oil refining
- Offshore oil rigs
- Other
- River runoffs

Pie: 22%, 22%, 12.5%, 9%, 7.5%, 6%, 3.5%, 3%, 1.5%, 1%, 12%

OIL SPILLS

Major oil spills from tankers and combined carriers

Year	Vessel	Location	Spill (barrels)**	Cause
1979	Atlantic Empress	West Indies	1,890,000	collision
1983	Castillo De Bellver	South Africa	1,760,000	fire
1978	Amoco Cadiz	France	1,628,000	grounding
1991	Haven	Italy	1,029,000	explosion
1988	Odyssey	Canada	1,000,000	fire
1967	Torrey Canyon	UK	909,000	grounding
1972	Sea Star	Gulf of Oman	902,250	collision
1977	Hawaiian Patriot	Hawaiian Is.	742,500	fire
1979	Independenta	Turkey	696,350	collision
1993	Braer	UK	625,000	grounding
1996	Sea Empress	UK	515,000	grounding

Other sources of major oil spills

1983	Nowruz oilfield	The Gulf	4,250,000†	war
1979	Ixtoc 1 oilwell	Gulf of Mexico	4,200,000	blow-out
1991	Kuwait	The Gulf	2,500,000†	war

** 1 barrel = 0.15 tons/159 lit./35 Imperial gal./42 US gal. † estimated

RIVER POLLUTION

Sources of river pollution, USA (latest available year)

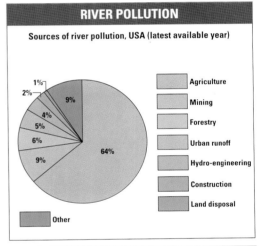

- Agriculture
- Mining
- Forestry
- Urban runoff
- Hydro-engineering
- Construction
- Land disposal
- Other

Pie: 64%, 9%, 9%, 6%, 5%, 4%, 2%, 1%

WATER POLLUTION

Severely polluted sea areas and lakes

Less polluted sea areas and lakes

Areas of frequent oil pollution by shipping

Major oil tanker spills ◤

Major oil rig blow-outs ▲

Offshore dumpsites for industrial and municipal waste ▼

Severely polluted rivers and estuaries ——

The most notorious tanker spillage of the 1980s occurred when the *Exxon Valdez* ran aground in Prince William Sound, Alaska, in 1989, spilling 267,000 barrels of crude oil close to shore in a sensitive ecological area. This rates as the world's 28th worst spill in terms of volume.

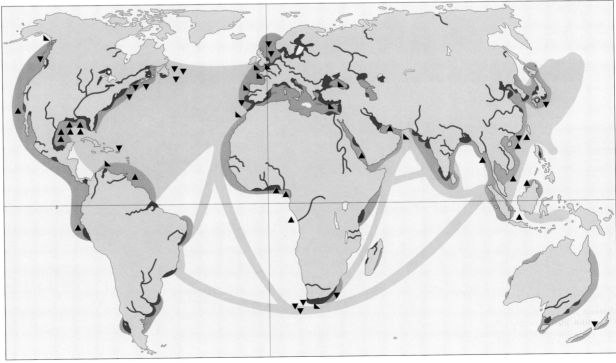

CLIMATE

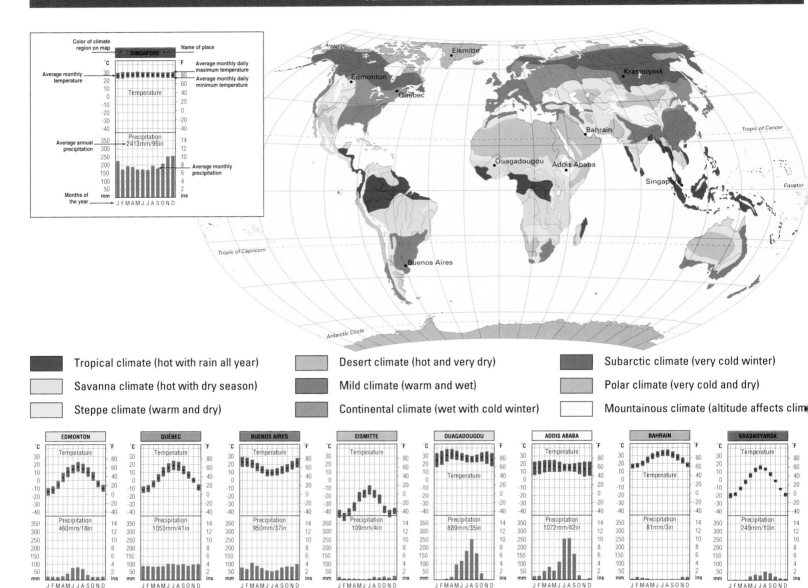

Tropical climate (hot with rain all year)

Savanna climate (hot with dry season)

Steppe climate (warm and dry)

Desert climate (hot and very dry)

Mild climate (warm and wet)

Continental climate (wet with cold winter)

Subarctic climate (very cold winter)

Polar climate (very cold and dry)

Mountainous climate (altitude affects clim

CLIMATE RECORDS

Temperature

Highest recorded shade temperature: Al Aziziyah, Libya, 58°C [136.4°F], 13 September 1922.

Highest mean annual temperature: Dallol, Ethiopia, 34.4°C [94°F], 1960–66.

Longest heatwave: Marble Bar, W. Australia, 162 days over 38°C [100°F], 23 October 1923 to 7 April 1924.

Lowest recorded temperature (outside poles): Verkhoyansk, Siberia, –68°C [–90°F], 6 February 1933.

Lowest mean annual temperature: Plateau Station, Antarctica, –56.6°C [–72.0°F]

Precipitation

Driest place: Arica, N. Chile, 0.8mm [0.03 in] per year (60-year average).

Longest drought: Calama, N. Chile, no recorded rainfall in 400 years to 1971.

Wettest place (12 months): Cherrapunji, Meghalaya, N.E. India, 26,470 mm [1,040 in], August 1860 to August 1861. Cherrapunji also holds the record for the most rainfall in one month: 930 mm [37 in], July 1861.

Wettest place (average): Mawsynram, India, mean annual rainfall 11,873 mm [467.4 in].

Wettest place (24 hours): Cilaos, Réunion, Indian Ocean, 1,870 mm [73.6 in], 15–16 March 1952.

Heaviest hailstones: Gopalganj, Bangladesh, up to 1.02 kg [2.25 lb], 14 April 1986 (killed 92 people).

Heaviest snowfall (continuous): Bessans, Savoie, France, 1,730 mm [68 in] in 19 hours, 5–6 April 1969.

Heaviest snowfall (season/year): Paradise Ranger Station, Mt Rainier, Washington, USA, 31,102 mm [1,224.5 in], 19 February 1971 to 18 February 1972.

Pressure and winds

Highest barometric pressure: Agata, Siberia (at 262 m [862 ft] altitude), 1,083.8 mb [32 in], 31 December 1968.

Lowest barometric pressure: Typhoon Tip, Guam, Pacific Ocean, 870 mb [25.69 in], 12 October 1979.

Highest recorded wind speed: Mt Washington, New Hampshire, USA, 371 km/h [231 mph], 12 April 1934. This is three times as strong as hurricane force on the Beaufort Scale.

CLIMATE

Climate is weather in the long term: the seasonal pattern of hot and cold, wet and dry, averaged over time (usually 30 years). At the simplest level, it is caused by the uneven heating of the Earth. Surplus heat at the Equator passes toward the poles, leveling out the energy differential. Its passage is marked by a ceaseless churning of the atmosphere and the oceans, further agitated by the Earth's diurnal spin and the motion it imparts to moving air and water. The heat's means of transport – by winds and ocean currents, by the continual evaporation and recondensation of water molecules – is the weather itself. There are four basic types of climate, each of which can be further subdivided: tropical, desert (dry), temperate and polar.

COMPOSITION OF DRY AIR

Nitrogen	78.09%	Sulfur dioxide	trace
Oxygen	20.95%	Nitrogen oxide	trace
Argon	0.93%	Methane	trace
Water vapor	0.2–4.0%	Dust	trace
Carbon dioxide	0.03%	Helium	trace
Ozone	0.00006%	Neon	trace

WINDCHILL FACTOR

In sub-zero weather, even moderate winds significantly reduce effective temperatures. The chart below shows the windchill effect across a range of speeds. Figures in the pink zone are not dangerous to well-clad people; in the blue zone, the risk of serious frostbite is acute.

	Wind speed (mph)				
	5	15	25	35	45
30°F	27	9	1	-4	-6
25°F	21	2	-7	-12	-14
20°F	16	-5	-15	-20	-22
15°F	12	-11	-22	-27	-30
10°F	7	-18	-29	-35	-38
5°F	0	-25	-36	-43	-46
0°F	-5	-31	-44	-52	-54
-5°F	-10	-38	-51	-58	-62
-10°F	-15	-45	-59	-67	-70
-15°F	-21	-51	-66	-74	-78
-20°F	-26	-56	-74	-82	-85

BEAUFORT WIND SCALE

Named after the 19th-century British naval officer who devised it, the Beaufort Scale assesses wind speed according to its effects. It was originally designed as an aid for sailors, but has since been adapted for use on the land.

Scale	Wind speed km/h	mph	Effect
0	0–1	0–1	**Calm** Smoke rises vertically
1	1–5	1–3	**Light air** Wind direction shown only by smoke drift
2	6–11	4–7	**Light breeze** Wind felt on face; leaves rustle; vanes moved by wind
3	12–19	8–12	**Gentle breeze** Leaves and small twigs in constant motion; wind extends small flag
4	20–28	13–18	**Moderate** Raises dust and loose paper; small branches move
5	29–38	19–24	**Fresh** Small trees in leaf sway; crested wavelets on inland waters
6	39–49	25–31	**Strong** Large branches move; difficult to use umbrellas; overhead wires whistle
7	50–61	32–38	**Near gale** Whole trees in motion; difficult to walk against wind
8	62–74	39–46	**Gale** Twigs break from trees; walking very difficult
9	75–88	47–54	**Strong gale** Slight structural damage
10	89–102	55–63	**Storm** Trees uprooted; serious structural damage
11	103–117	64–72	**Violent storm** Widespread damage
12	118+	73+	**Hurricane**

Conversions
°C = (°F − 32) x 5/9;   °F = (°C x 9/5) + 32;   0°C = 32°F
1 in = 25.4 mm;   1 mm = 0.0394 in;   100 mm = 3.94 in

TEMPERATURE

Average temperature in January

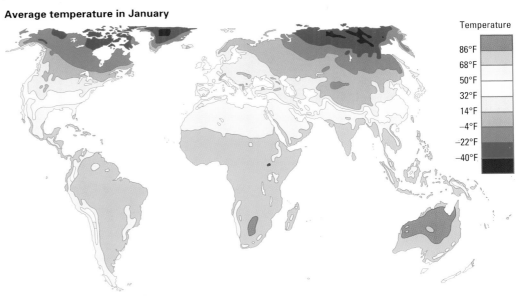

Temperature

	86°F
	68°F
	50°F
	32°F
	14°F
	−4°F
	−22°F
	−40°F

Average temperature in July

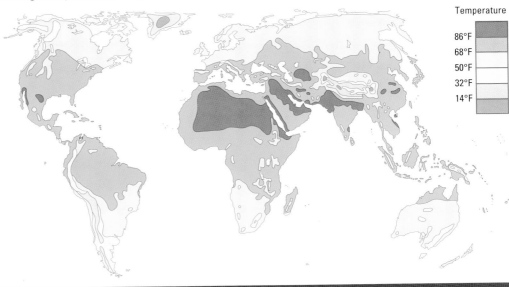

Temperature

	86°F
	68°F
	50°F
	32°F
	14°F

PRECIPITATION

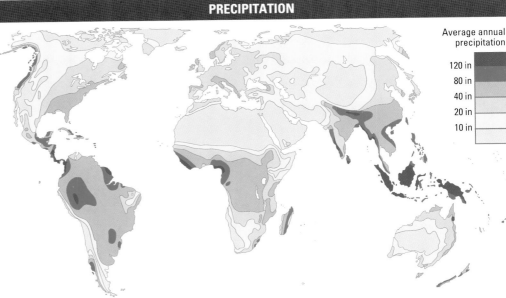

Average annual precipitation

	120 in
	80 in
	40 in
	20 in
	10 in

WATER AND VEGETATION

THE HYDROLOGICAL CYCLE

The world's water balance is regulated by the constant recycling of water between the oceans, atmosphere and land. The movement of water between these three reservoirs is known as the hydrological cycle. The oceans play a vital role in the hydrological cycle: 74% of the total precipitation falls over the oceans and 84% of the total evaporation comes from the oceans.

Transfer of water vapor

Evaporation from oceans

Precipitation

Evapotranspiration

Precipitation

Surface runoff

Runoff

Surface storage

Infiltration

Groundwater flow

WATER DISTRIBUTION

The distribution of planetary water, by percentage. Oceans and ice caps together account for more than 99% of the total; the breakdown of the remainder is estimated.

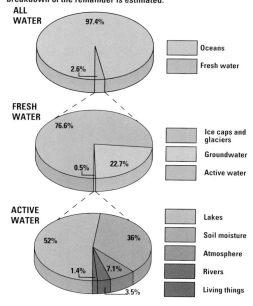

ALL WATER
97.4%
2.6%
- Oceans
- Fresh water

FRESH WATER
76.6%
0.5%
22.7%
- Ice caps and glaciers
- Groundwater
- Active water

ACTIVE WATER
52%
36%
1.4%
7.1%
3.5%
- Lakes
- Soil moisture
- Atmosphere
- Rivers
- Living things

WATER USAGE

Almost all the world's water is 3,000 million years old, and all of it cycles endlessly through the hydrosphere, though at different rates. Water vapor circulates over days, even hours, deep ocean water circulates over millennia, and ice-cap water remains solid for millions of years.

Fresh water is essential to all terrestrial life. Humans cannot survive more than a few days without it, and even the hardiest desert plants and animals could not exist without some water. Agriculture requires huge quantities of fresh water: without large-scale irrigation, most of the world's people would starve. Agriculture uses about 43% and industry 38% of all water withdrawals in the USA.

The United States is one of the heaviest users of water in the world. In the United States the per capita use for all purposes is about 6,000 liters per day. This is two to four times more than in Western Europe, where users pay up to 350% more for their water.

WATER UTILIZATION

The percentage breakdown of water usage by sector, selected countries (latest available year)

- Domestic
- Industrial
- Agriculture

	0	20	40	60	80	100
Mexico						
UK						
France						
Saudi Arabia						
Poland						
Algeria						
Egypt						
CIS						
USA						
Ghana						
India						
Australia						

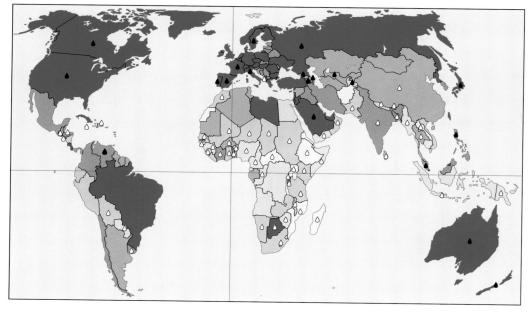

WATER SUPPLY

Percentage of total population with access to safe drinking water (1992)

- Over 90% with safe water
- 75 – 90% with safe water
- 60 – 75% with safe water
- 45 – 60% with safe water
- 30 – 45% with safe water
- Under 30% with safe water

⌀ Under 80 liters per person per day domestic water consumption

⬥ Over 320 liters per person per day

Least well-provided countries

Central African Rep...	12%	Madagascar	23%
Uganda	15%	Guinea-Bissau	25%
Ethiopia	18%	Laos	28%
Mozambique	22%	Swaziland	30%
Afghanistan	23%	Tajikistan	30%

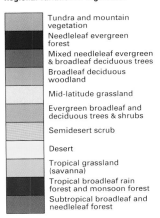

Regional variation in vegetation

- Tundra and mountain vegetation
- Needleleaf evergreen forest
- Mixed needleleaf evergreen & broadleaf deciduous trees
- Broadleaf deciduous woodland
- Mid-latitude grassland
- Evergreen broadleaf and deciduous trees & shrubs
- Semidesert scrub
- Desert
- Tropical grassland (savanna)
- Tropical broadleaf rain forest and monsoon forest
- Subtropical broadleaf and needleleaf forest

The map shows the natural 'climax vegetation' of regions, as dictated by climate and topography. In most cases, however, agricultural activity has drastically altered the vegetation pattern. Western Europe, for example, lost most of its broadleaf forest many centuries ago, while irrigation has turned some natural semidesert into productive land.

LAND USE BY CONTINENT

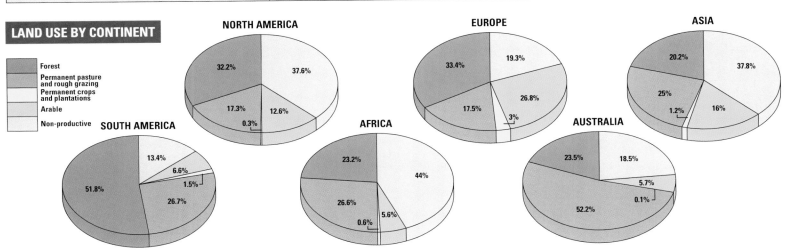

- Forest
- Permanent pasture and rough grazing
- Permanent crops and plantations
- Arable
- Non-productive

NORTH AMERICA
32.2%, 37.6%, 17.3%, 12.6%, 0.3%

EUROPE
33.4%, 19.3%, 17.5%, 26.8%, 3%

ASIA
20.2%, 37.8%, 25%, 16%, 1.2%

SOUTH AMERICA
51.8%, 13.4%, 6.6%, 1.5%, 26.7%

AFRICA
23.2%, 44%, 26.6%, 5.6%, 0.6%

AUSTRALIA
23.5%, 18.5%, 5.7%, 0.1%, 52.2%

FORESTRY: PRODUCTION

	Forest & woodland (million acres)	Annual production (1993, million cubic yards)	
		Fuelwood & charcoal	Industrial roundwood*
World	*9,854.1*	*2,453.5*	*1,999.3*
CIS	2,045.5	67.4	226.2
S. America	2,049.2	324.1	159.6
N. & C. America	1,753.9	205.0	767.4
Africa	1,691.6	645.6	77.8
Asia	1,211.3	1,133.3	363.8
Europe	388.7	66.6	356.0
Australasia	388.4	11.4	48.3

PAPER AND BOARD

Top producers (1993)**

USA	85,130
Japan	30,596
China	26,245
Canada	19,348
Germany	14,363

Top exporters (1993)**

Canada	14,211
Finland	9,396
USA	7,875
Sweden	7,723
Germany	5,249

* roundwood is timber as it is felled
** in thousand tons

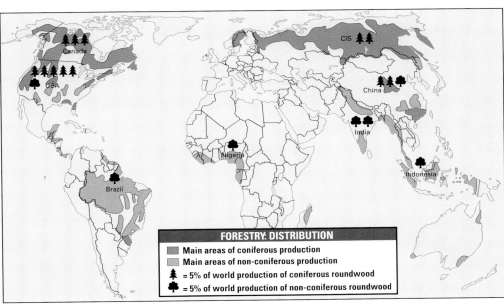

FORESTRY: DISTRIBUTION

- Main areas of coniferous production
- Main areas of non-coniferous production
- 🌲 = 5% of world production of coniferous roundwood
- 🌳 = 5% of world production of non-coniferous roundwood

ENVIRONMENT

Humans have always had a dramatic effect on their environment, at least since the invention of agriculture almost 10,000 years ago. Generally, the Earth has accepted human interference without obvious ill effects: the complex systems that regulate the global environment have been able to absorb substantial damage while maintaining a stable and comfortable home for the planet's trillions of lifeforms. But advancing human technology and the rapidly-expanding populations it supports are now threatening to overwhelm the Earth's ability to compensate.

Industrial wastes, acid rainfall, desertification and large-scale deforestation all combine to create environmental change at a rate far faster than the great slow cycles of planetary evolution can accommodate. As a result of overcultivation, overgrazing and overcutting of groundcover for firewood, desertification is affecting as much as 60% of the world's croplands. In addition, with fire and chainsaws, humans are destroying more forest in a day than their ancestors could have done in a century, upsetting the balance between plant and animal, carbon dioxide and oxygen, on which all life ultimately depends.

The fossil fuels that power industrial civilization have pumped enough carbon dioxide and other so-called greenhouse gases into the atmosphere to make climatic change a near-certainty. As a result of the combination of these factors, the Earth's average temperature has risen by almost 1°F since the beginning of the 20th century, and is still rising.

GLOBAL WARMING

Carbon dioxide emissions in tons per person per year (1991)

- Over 10 tons of CO_2
- 5 – 10 tons of CO_2
- 1 – 5 tons of CO_2
- Under 1 ton of CO_2

Changes in CO_2 emissions 1980–90

- ▲ Over 100% increase in emissions
- ▲ 50–100% increase in emissions
- ▽ Reduction in emissions
- — Coastal areas in danger of flooding from rising sea levels caused by global warming

High atmospheric concentrations of heat-absorbing gases, especially carbon dioxide, appear to be causing a steady rise in average temperatures worldwide – by as much as 3°F by the year 2020, according to some estimates. Global warming is likely to bring with it a rise in sea levels that may flood some of the Earth's most densely populated coastlines.

GREENHOUSE POWER

Relative contributions to the Greenhouse Effect by the major heat-absorbing gases in the atmosphere

The chart combines greenhouse potency and volume. Carbon dioxide has a greenhouse potential of only 1, but its concentration of 350 parts per million makes it predominate. CFC 12, with 25,000 times the absorption capacity of CO_2, is present only as 0.00044 ppm.

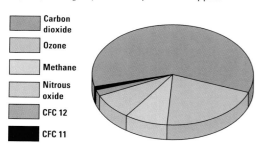

- Carbon dioxide
- Ozone
- Methane
- Nitrous oxide
- CFC 12
- CFC 11

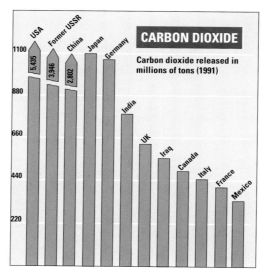

CARBON DIOXIDE

Carbon dioxide released in millions of tons (1991)

USA 5,435 · Former USSR 3,946 · China 2,802 · Japan · Germany · India · UK · Iraq · Canada · Italy · France · Mexico

TEMPERATURE RISE

The rise in average temperatures caused by carbon dioxide and other greenhouse gases (1960–2020)

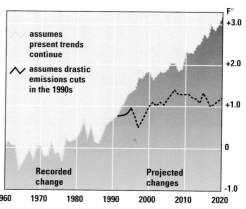

- assumes present trends continue
- assumes drastic emissions cuts in the 1990s

Recorded change — Projected changes

1960 1970 1980 1990 2000 2010 2020

THE GREENHOUSE EFFECT

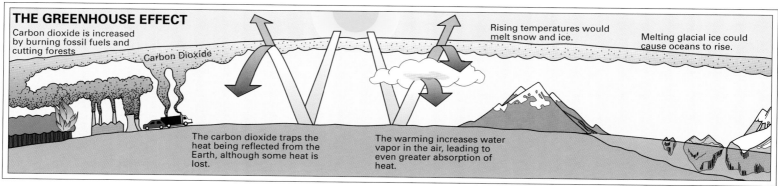

Carbon dioxide is increased by burning fossil fuels and cutting forests

Carbon Dioxide

Rising temperatures would melt snow and ice.

Melting glacial ice could cause oceans to rise.

The carbon dioxide traps the heat being reflected from the Earth, although some heat is lost.

The warming increases water vapor in the air, leading to even greater absorption of heat.

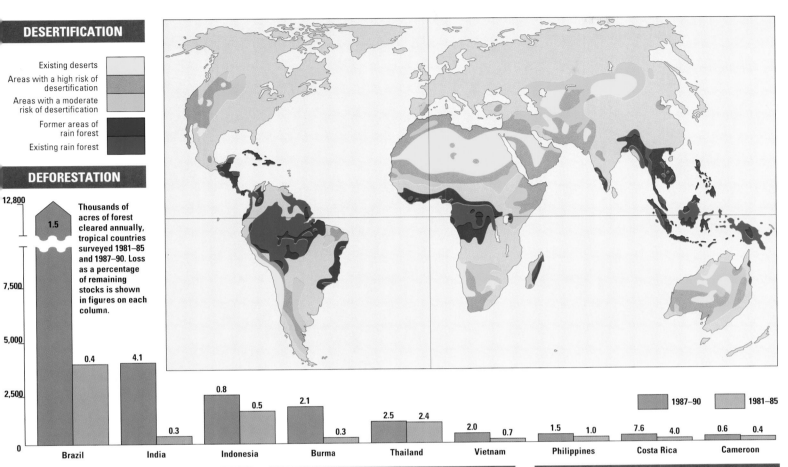

DESERTIFICATION

- Existing deserts
- Areas with a high risk of desertification
- Areas with a moderate risk of desertification
- Former areas of rain forest
- Existing rain forest

DEFORESTATION

Thousands of acres of forest cleared annually, tropical countries surveyed 1981–85 and 1987–90. Loss as a percentage of remaining stocks is shown in figures on each column.

12,800

	1987–90	1981–85

Brazil 1.5 / 0.4
India 4.1 / 0.3
Indonesia 0.8 / 0.5
Burma 2.1 / 0.3
Thailand 2.5 / 2.4
Vietnam 2.0 / 0.7
Philippines 1.5 / 1.0
Costa Rica 7.6 / 4.0
Cameroon 0.6 / 0.4

OZONE DEPLETION

The ozone layer (15–18 miles above sea level) acts as a barrier to most of the Sun's harmful ultraviolet radiation, protecting us from the ionizing radiation that can cause skin cancer and cataracts. In recent years, however, two holes in the ozone layer have been observed; one over the Arctic and the other, the size of the USA, over Antarctica. By 1993, ozone had been reduced to between a half and two-thirds of its 1970 amount. The ozone (O_3) is broken down by chlorine released into the atmosphere as CFCs (chlorofluorocarbons) – chemicals used in refrigerators, packaging and aerosols.

DEFORESTATION

The Earth's remaining forests are under attack from three directions: expanding agriculture, logging, and growing consumption of fuelwood, often in combination. Sometimes deforestation is the direct result of government policy, as in the efforts made to resettle the urban poor in some parts of Brazil; just as often, it comes about despite state attempts at conservation. Loggers, licensed or unlicensed, blaze a trail into virgin forest, often destroying twice as many trees as they harvest. Landless farmers follow, burning away most of what remains to plant their crops, completing the destruction.

ACID RAIN

Killing trees, poisoning lakes and rivers and eating away buildings, acid rain is mostly produced by sulfur dioxide emissions from industry and volcanic eruptions. By the late 1980s, acid rain had sterilized 4,000 or more of Sweden's lakes and left 45% of Switzerland's alpine conifers dead or dying, while the monuments of Greece were dissolving in Athens' smog. Prevailing wind patterns mean that the acids often fall many hundreds of miles from where the original pollutants were discharged. In parts of Europe acid deposition has slightly decreased, following reductions in emissions, but not by enough.

WORLD POLLUTION

Acid rain and sources of acidic emissions (latest available year)

Acid rain is caused by high levels of sulfur and nitrogen in the atmosphere. They combine with water vapor and oxygen to form acids (H_2SO_4 and HNO_3) which fall as precipitation.

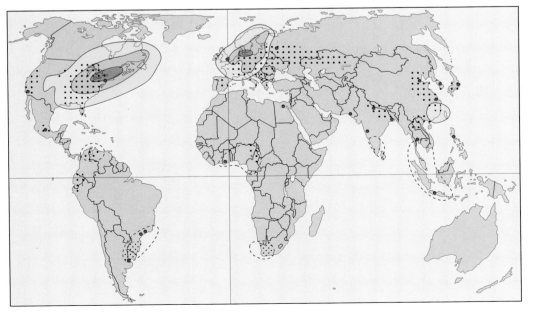

- Regions where sulfur and nitrogen oxides are released in high concentrations, mainly from fossil fuel combustion
- Major cities with high levels of air pollution (including nitrogen and sulfur emissions)

Areas of heavy acid deposition

pH numbers indicate acidity, decreasing from a neutral 7. Normal rain, slightly acid from dissolved carbon dioxide, never exceeds a pH of 5.6.

- pH less than 4.0 (most acidic)
- pH 4.0 to 4.5
- pH 4.5 to 5.0
- Areas where acid rain is a potential problem

15

CARTOGRAPHY BY PHILIP'S. COPYRIGHT REED INTERNATIONAL BOOKS LTD

POPULATION

Developed nations such as the USA have populations evenly spread across the age groups and, usually, a growing proportion of elderly people. The great majority of the people in developing nations, however, are in the younger age groups, about to enter their most fertile years. In time, these population profiles should resemble the world profile (even Kenya has made recent progress with reducing its birth rate), but the transition will come about only after a few more generations of rapid population growth.

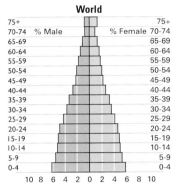

World

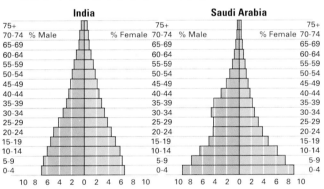

UK

Kenya

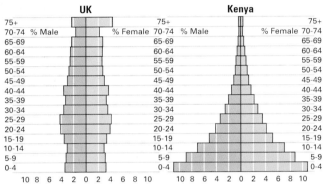

India

Saudi Arabia

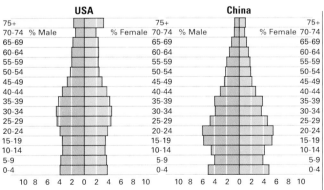

USA

China

MOST POPULOUS NATIONS [in millions (1995)]

1.	China	1,227	9.	Bangladesh	118	17.	Turkey	61
2.	India	943	10.	Mexico	93	18.	Thailand	58
3.	USA	264	11.	Nigeria	89	19.	UK	58
4.	Indonesia	199	12.	Germany	82	20.	France	58
5.	Brazil	161	13.	Vietnam	75	21.	Italy	57
6.	Russia	148	14.	Iran	69	22.	Ukraine	52
7.	Pakistan	144	15.	Philippines	67	23.	Ethiopia	52
8.	Japan	125	16.	Egypt	64	24.	Burma	47

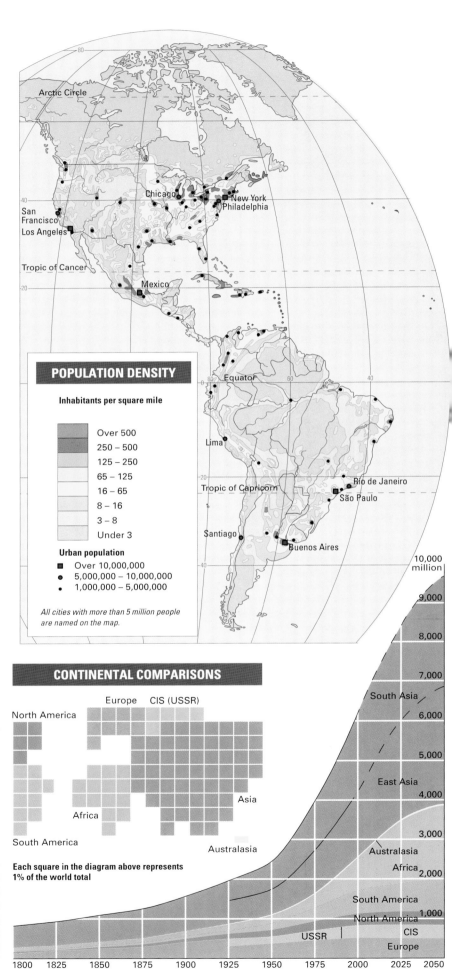

POPULATION DENSITY

Inhabitants per square mile

- Over 500
- 250 – 500
- 125 – 250
- 65 – 125
- 16 – 65
- 8 – 16
- 3 – 8
- Under 3

Urban population

- ■ Over 10,000,000
- ● 5,000,000 – 10,000,000
- • 1,000,000 – 5,000,000

All cities with more than 5 million people are named on the map.

CONTINENTAL COMPARISONS

North America
Europe   CIS (USSR)
Asia
Africa
South America
Australasia

Each square in the diagram above represents 1% of the world total

10,000 million
9,000
8,000
7,000
South Asia 6,000
5,000
East Asia 4,000
3,000
Australasia
Africa 2,000
South America
North America 1,000
USSR   CIS
Europe

1800 1825 1850 1875 1900 1925 1950 1975 2000 2025 2050

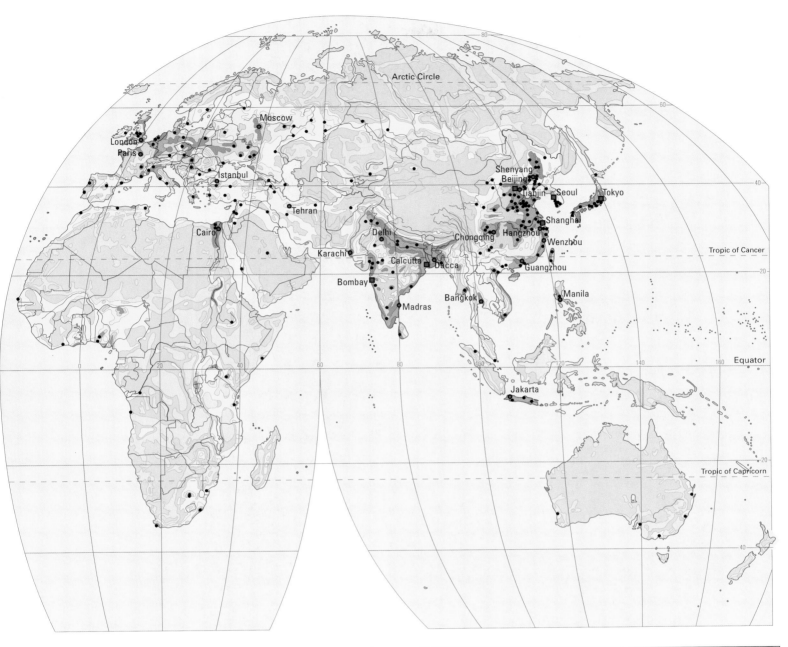

Arctic Circle

Moscow

London
Paris

Istanbul

Tehran

Cairo

Delhi

Karachi

Calcutta
Bombay

Madras

Shenyang
Beijing
Tianjin Seoul Tokyo

Shanghai
Chongqing Hangzhou
Wenzhou

Dacca

Guangzhou

Bangkok

Manila

Tropic of Cancer

Equator

Jakarta

Tropic of Capricorn

URBAN POPULATION

Percentage of total population living in towns and cities (1992)

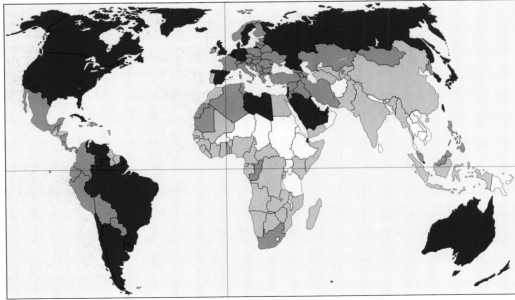

Over 75%

50 – 75%

25 – 50%

10 – 25%

Under 10%

Most urbanized

Singapore	100%
Belgium	97%
Kuwait	95%
Hong Kong	94%
Venezuela	91%

[USA 76%]

Least urbanized

Bhutan	6%
Rwanda	6%
Burundi	7%
Malawi	12%
Nepal	12%

THE HUMAN FAMILY

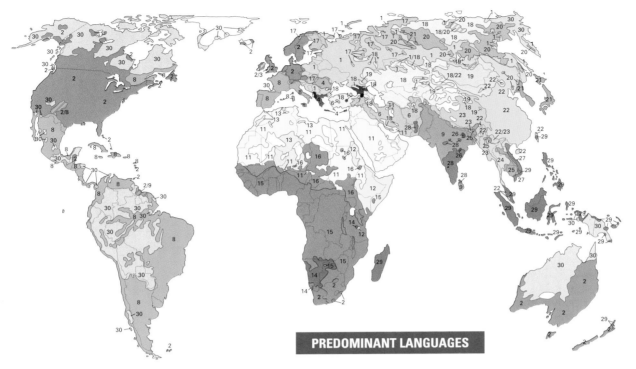

MOTHER TONGUES
Chinese 1,069 million (Mandarin 864), English 443, Hindi 352, Spanish 341, Russian 293, Arabic 197, Bengali 184, Portuguese 173, Malay-Indonesian 142, Japanese 125, French 121, German 118, Urdu 92, Punjabi 84, Korean 71.

OFFICIAL LANGUAGES
English 27% of the world population, Chinese 19%, Hindi 13.5%, Spanish 5.4%, Russian 5.2%, French 4.2%, Arabic 3.3%, Portuguese 3%, Malay 3%, Bengali 2.9%, Japanese 2.3%.

Language can be classified by ancestry and structure. For example, the Romance and Germanic groups are both derived from an Indo-European language believed to have been spoken 5,000 years ago.

PREDOMINANT LANGUAGES

INDO-EUROPEAN FAMILY
1	Balto-Slavic group (incl. Russian, Ukrainian)
2	Germanic group (incl. English, German)
3	Celtic group
4	Greek
5	Albanian
6	Iranian group
7	Armenian
8	Romance group (incl. Spanish, Portuguese, French, Italian)
9	Indo-Aryan group (incl. Hindi, Bengali, Urdu, Punjabi, Marathi)
10	CAUCASIAN FAMILY

AFRO-ASIATIC FAMILY
11	Semitic group (incl. Arabic)
12	Kushitic group
13	Berber group
14	KHOISAN FAMILY
15	NIGER-CONGO FAMILY
16	NILO-SAHARAN FAMILY
17	URALIC FAMILY

ALTAIC FAMILY
18	Turkic group
19	Mongolian group
20	Tungus-Manchu group
21	Japanese and Korean

SINO-TIBETAN FAMILY
22	Sinitic (Chinese) languages
23	Tibetic-Burmic languages
24	TAI FAMILY

AUSTRO-ASIATIC FAMILY
25	Mon-Khmer group
26	Munda group
27	Vietnamese
28	DRAVIDIAN FAMILY (incl. Telugu, Tamil)
29	AUSTRONESIAN FAMILY (incl. Malay-Indonesian)
30	OTHER LANGUAGES

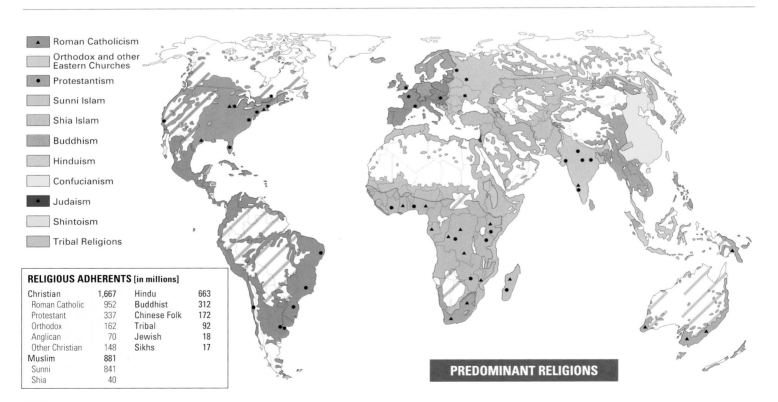

- ▲ Roman Catholicism
- Orthodox and other Eastern Churches
- • Protestantism
- Sunni Islam
- Shia Islam
- Buddhism
- Hinduism
- Confucianism
- ★ Judaism
- Shintoism
- Tribal Religions

RELIGIOUS ADHERENTS [in millions]
Christian	1,667	Hindu	663
Roman Catholic	952	Buddhist	312
Protestant	337	Chinese Folk	172
Orthodox	162	Tribal	92
Anglican	70	Jewish	18
Other Christian	148	Sikhs	17
Muslim	881		
Sunni	841		
Shia	40		

PREDOMINANT RELIGIONS

UNITED NATIONS

Created in 1945 to promote peace and cooperation and based in New York, the United Nations is the world's largest international organization, with 185 members and an annual budget of US $2.61 billion (1996–97). Each member of the General Assembly has one vote, while the permanent members of the 15-nation Security Council – USA, Russia, China, UK and France – hold a veto. The Secretariat is the UN's principal administrative arm. The 54 members of the Economic and Social Council are responsible for economic, social, cultural, educational, health and related matters. The UN has 16 specialized agencies – based in Canada, France, Switzerland and Italy, as well as the USA – which help members in fields such as education (UNESCO), agriculture (FAO), medicine (WHO) and finance (IFC). By the end of 1994, all the original 11 trust territories of The Trusteeship Council had become independent.

[The International Court of Justice is based in The Hague]

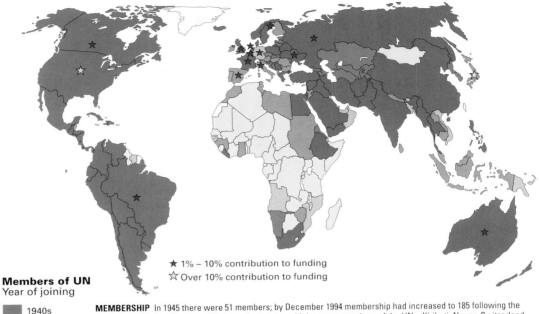

★ 1% – 10% contribution to funding
☆ Over 10% contribution to funding

Members of UN
Year of joining

- 1940s
- 1950s
- 1960s
- 1970s
- 1980s
- 1990s
- Non-members

MEMBERSHIP In 1945 there were 51 members; by December 1994 membership had increased to 185 following the admission of Palau. There are 7 independent states which are not members of the UN – Kiribati, Nauru, Switzerland, Taiwan, Tonga, Tuvalu and the Vatican City. All the successor states of the former USSR had joined by the end of 1992. The official languages of the UN are Chinese, English, French, Russian, Spanish and Arabic.
FUNDING The UN budget for 1996–97 is US $2.61 billion. Contributions are assessed by the members' ability to pay, with the maximum 25% of the total, the minimum 0.01%. Contributions for 1994–95 were: USA 25%, Japan 12.45%, Germany 8.93%, Russia 6.71%, France 6%, UK 5.02%, Italy 4.29%, Canada 3.11% (others 28.49%).
PEACEKEEPING Between 1988 and 1994, 21 new peacekeeping operations were mounted, compared with 13 such operations undertaken during the previous 40 years. There are currently 15 areas of UN patrol and 30,000 'blue berets'.

EU European Union (evolved from the European Community in 1993). The 15 members – Austria, Belgium, Denmark, Finland, France, Germany, Greece, Ireland, Italy, Luxembourg, Netherlands, Portugal, Spain, Sweden and the UK – aim to integrate economies, coordinate social developments and bring about political union. These members of what is now the world's biggest market share agricultural and industrial policies and tariffs on trade. The original body, the European Coal and Steel Community (ECSC), was created in 1951 following the signing of the Treaty of Paris.
EFTA European Free Trade Association (formed in 1960). Portugal left the original 'Seven' in 1989 to join what was then the EC, followed by Austria, Finland and Sweden in 1995. Only 4 members remain: Norway, Iceland, Switzerland and Liechtenstein.
ACP African-Caribbean-Pacific (formed in 1963). Members have economic ties with the EU.
NATO North Atlantic Treaty Organization (formed in 1949). It continues after 1991 despite the winding up of the Warsaw Pact. There are 16 member nations.
OAS Organization of American States (formed in 1948). It aims to promote social and economic cooperation between developed countries of North America and developing nations of Latin America.
ASEAN Association of Southeast Asian Nations (formed in 1967). Vietnam joined in July 1995.
OAU Organization of African Unity (formed in 1963). Its 53 members represent over 94% of Africa's population. Arabic, French, Portuguese and English are recognized as working languages.
LAIA Latin American Integration Association (1980). Its aim is to promote freer regional trade.
OECD Organization for Economic Cooperation and Development (formed in 1961). It comprises the 26 major Western free-market economies. The Czech Republic joined in December 1995. 'G7' is its 'inner group' of the USA, Canada, Japan, UK, Germany, Italy and France.
COMMONWEALTH The Commonwealth of Nations evolved from the British Empire; it comprises 16 Queen's realms, 32 republics and 5 indigenous monarchies, giving a total of 53.
OPEC Organization of Petroleum Exporting Countries (formed in 1960). It controls about three-quarters of the world's oil supply.

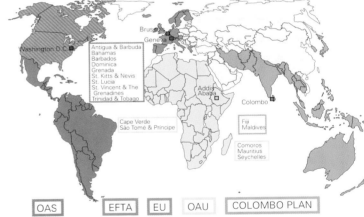

ARAB LEAGUE (formed in 1945). The League's aim is to promote economic, social, political and military cooperation. There are 21 member nations.
COLOMBO PLAN (formed in 1951). Its 26 members aim to promote economic and social development in Asia and the Pacific.

CARTOGRAPHY BY PHILIP'S. COPYRIGHT REED INTERNATIONAL BOOKS LTD

WEALTH

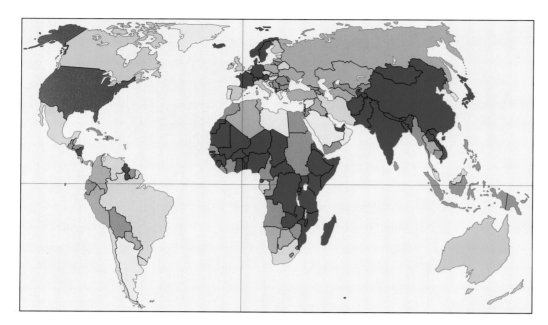

Gross National Product per capita: the value of total production divided by the population (1993)

- Over 400% of world average
- 200 – 400% of world average
- 100 – 200% of world average

[World average wealth per person US $5,359]

- 50 – 100% of world average
- 25 – 50% of world average
- 10 – 25% of world average
- Under 10% of world average

Richest countries		Poorest countries	
Switzerland	$36,410	Mozambique	$80
Luxembourg	$35,850	Ethiopia	$100
Liechtenstein	$33,510	Tanzania	$100
Japan	$31,450	Sierra Leone	$140

WEALTH CREATION

The Gross National Product (GNP) of the world's largest economies, US $ million (1993)

1.	USA	6,387,686	23.	Austria	183,530
2.	Japan	3,926,668	24.	Denmark	137,610
3.	Germany	1,902,995	25.	Indonesia	136,991
4.	France	1,289,235	26.	Saudi Arabia	131,000
5.	Italy	1,134,980	27.	Turkey	126,330
6.	UK	1,042,700	28.	Thailand	120,235
7.	China	581,109	29.	South Africa	118,057
8.	Canada	574,884	30.	Norway	113,527
9.	Spain	533,986	31.	Hong Kong	104,731
10.	Brazil	471,978	32.	Ukraine	99,677
11.	Russia	348,413	33.	Finland	96,220
12.	South Korea	338,062	34.	Poland	87,315
13.	Mexico	324,951	35.	Syria	81,700
14.	Netherlands	316,404	36.	Portugal	77,749
15.	Australia	309,967	37.	Greece	76,698
16.	Iran	300,000	38.	Israel	72,662
17.	India	262,810	39.	Malaysia	60,061
18.	Switzerland	254,066	40.	Venezuela	58,916
19.	Argentina	244,013	41.	Singapore	55,372
20.	Taiwan	225,000	42.	Philippines	54,609
21.	Sweden	216,294	43.	Pakistan	53,250
22.	Belgium	213,435	44.	Colombia	50,119

THE WEALTH GAP

The world's richest and poorest countries, by Gross National Product per capita in US $ (1993)

1.	Switzerland	36,410	1.	Mozambique	80
2.	Luxembourg	35,850	2.	Ethiopia	100
3.	Liechtenstein	33,510	3.	Tanzania	100
4.	Japan	31,450	4.	Sierra Leone	140
5.	Bermuda	27,000	5.	Nepal	160
6.	Denmark	26,510	6.	Bhutan	170
7.	Norway	26,340	7.	Vietnam	170
8.	Sweden	24,830	8.	Burundi	180
9.	USA	24,750	9.	Uganda	190
10.	Iceland	23,620	10.	Chad	200
11.	Germany	23,560	11.	Rwanda	200
12.	Kuwait	23,350	12.	Afghanistan	220
13.	Austria	23,120	13.	Bangladesh	220
14.	UAE	22,470	14.	Guinea-Bissau	220
15.	France	22,360	15.	Malawi	220
16.	Belgium	21,210	16.	Madagascar	240
17.	Netherlands	20,710	17.	Kenya	270
18.	Canada	20,670	18.	Niger	270
19.	Italy	19,620	19.	India	290
20.	Singapore	19,310	20.	Laos	290

GNP per capita is calculated by dividing a country's Gross National Product by its population.

CONTINENTAL SHARES

Shares of population and of wealth (GNP) by continent

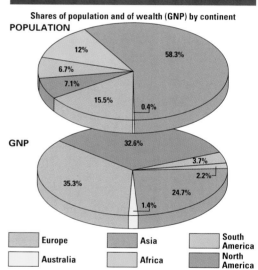

POPULATION
- 58.3%
- 12%
- 6.7%
- 7.1%
- 15.5%
- 0.4%

GNP
- 32.6%
- 3.7%
- 2.2%
- 24.7%
- 1.4%
- 35.3%

Europe	Asia		South America
Australia	Africa		North America

INFLATION

Average annual rate of inflation (1980–91)

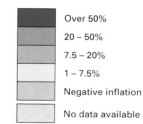

- Over 50%
- 20 – 50%
- 7.5 – 20%
- 1 – 7.5%
- Negative inflation
- No data available

Highest average inflation		Lowest average inflation	
Nicaragua	584%	Oman	–3.1%
Argentina	417%	Kuwait	–2.7%
Brazil	328%	Saudi Arabia	–2.4%
Peru	287%	Equatorial Guinea	–0.9%
Bolivia	263%	Albania	–0.4%
Israel	89%	Bahrain	–0.3%
Mexico	66%	Libya	0.2%

INTERNATIONAL AID

Aid provided or received, divided by the total population, in US $ (1993)

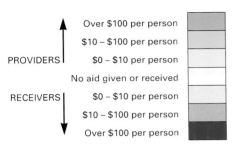

PROVIDERS
- Over $100 per person
- $10 – $100 per person
- $0 – $10 per person
- No aid given or received

RECEIVERS
- $0 – $10 per person
- $10 – $100 per person
- Over $100 per person

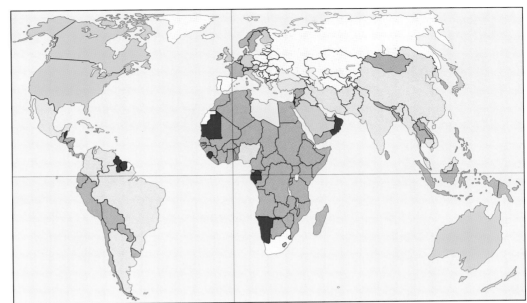

Top 5 providers		Top 5 receivers	
Kuwait	$261	Oman	$539
Denmark	$258	Sierra Leone	$269
Norway	$235	Israel	$243
Sweden	$202	Mauritania	$153
UAE	$197	Namibia	$106

DEBT AND AID

International debtors and the aid they receive (1993)

Although aid grants make a vital contribution to many of the world's poorer countries, they are usually dwarfed by the burden of debt that the developing economies are expected to repay. In 1992, they had to pay US $160,000 million in debt service charges alone – more than two and a half times the amount of Official Development Assistance (ODA) the developing countries were receiving, and US $60,000 million more than total private flows of aid in the same year. In 1990, the debts of Mozambique, one of the world's poorest countries, were estimated to be 75 times its entire earnings from exports.

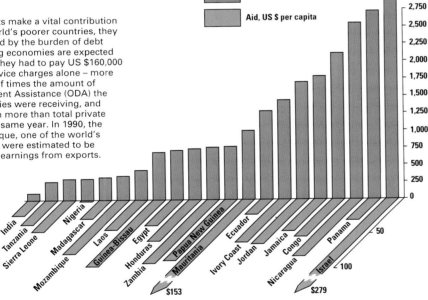

- Debt, US $ per capita
- Aid, US $ per capita

$4853

India, Tanzania, Sierra Leone, Nigeria, Madagascar, Mozambique, Laos, Guinea-Bissau, Egypt, Honduras, Zambia, Papua New Guinea, Mauritania, Ecuador, Ivory Coast, Jordan, Jamaica, Congo, Nicaragua, Panama, Israel

$153 $279

DISTRIBUTION OF SPENDING

Percentage share of household spending

- Food
- Medicine & Education
- Clothing
- Transport
- Energy & Housing
- Other

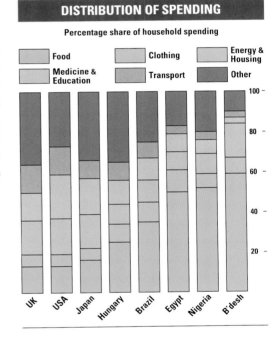

UK, USA, Japan, Hungary, Brazil, Egypt, Nigeria, B'desh

HIGH INCOME

Number of cars, televisions and telephones for each 10,000 people, selected high income countries (1993)

- Cars
- Televisions
- Telephones

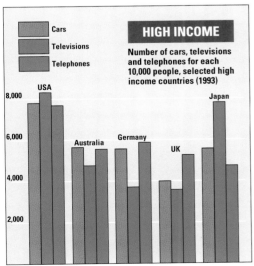

USA, Australia, Germany, UK, Japan

MIDDLE INCOME

Number of cars, televisions and telephones for each 10,000 people, selected middle income countries (1993)

- Cars
- Televisions
- Telephones

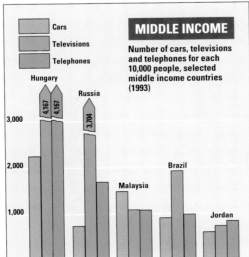

Hungary 4,167 4,167, Russia 3,704, Malaysia, Brazil, Jordan

LOW INCOME

Number of cars, televisions and telephones for each 10,000 people, selected low income countries (1993)

- Cars
- Televisions
- Telephones

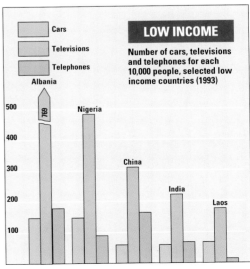

Albania 769, Nigeria, China, India, Laos

QUALITY OF LIFE

DAILY FOOD CONSUMPTION

Average daily food intake in calories per person (1992)

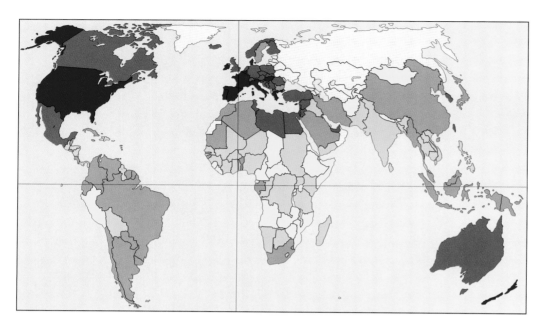

- Over 3,500 calories per person
- 3,000 – 3,500 calories per person
- 2,500 – 3,000 calories per person
- 2,000 – 2,500 calories per person
- Under 2,000 calories per person
- No available data

Top 5 countries		Bottom 5 countries	
Ireland	3,847 cal.	Mozambique	1,680 cal.
Greece	3,815 cal.	Liberia	1,640 cal.
Cyprus	3,779 cal.	Ethiopia	1,610 cal.
USA	3,732 cal.	Afghanistan	1,523 cal.
Spain	3,708 cal.	Somalia	1,499 cal.

HOSPITAL CAPACITY

Hospital beds available for each 1,000 people (1993)

Highest capacity		Lowest capacity	
Japan	13.6	Bangladesh	0.2
Kazakstan	13.5	Ethiopia	0.2
Ukraine	13.5	Nepal	0.3
Russia	13.5	Burkina Faso	0.4
Latvia	13.5	Afghanistan	0.5
North Korea	13.5	Pakistan	0.6
Moldova	12.8	Niger	0.6
Belarus	12.7	Mali	0.6
Finland	12.3	Indonesia	0.6
France	12.2	Guinea	0.6

[USA 4.6]

Although the ratio of people to hospital beds gives a good approximation of a country's health provision, it is not an absolute indicator. Raw numbers may mask inefficiency and other weaknesses: the high availability of beds in Kazakstan, for example, has not prevented infant mortality rates over three times as high as in the United Kingdom and the United States.

LIFE EXPECTANCY

Years of life expectancy at birth, selected countries (1990–95)

The chart shows combined data for both sexes. On average, women live longer than men worldwide, even in developing countries with high maternal mortality rates. Overall, life expectancy is steadily rising, though the difference between rich and poor nations remains dramatic.

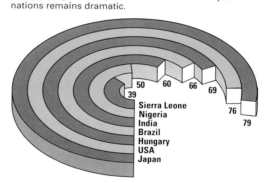

39 50 60 66 69 76 79

Sierra Leone
Nigeria
India
Brazil
Hungary
USA
Japan

CAUSES OF DEATH

Causes of death for selected countries by % (1988–92)

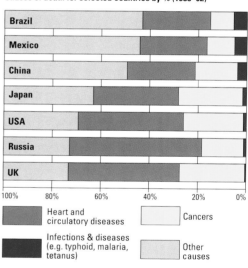

Brazil
Mexico
China
Japan
USA
Russia
UK

100% 80% 60% 40% 20% 0%

- Heart and circulatory diseases
- Cancers
- Infections & diseases (e.g. typhoid, malaria, tetanus)
- Other causes

CHILD MORTALITY

Number of babies who will die under the age of one, per 1,000 births (average 1990–95)

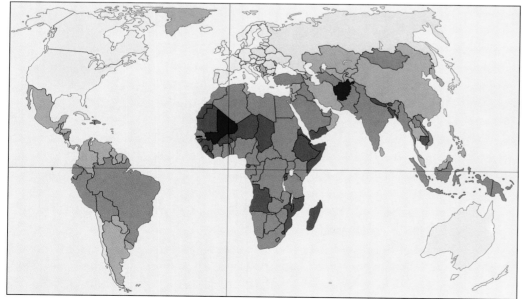

- Over 150 deaths per 1,000 births
- 100 – 150 deaths per 1,000 births
- 50 – 100 deaths per 1,000 births
- 20 – 50 deaths per 1,000 births
- 10 – 20 deaths per 1,000 births
- Under 10 deaths per 1,000 births

Highest child mortality		Lowest child mortality	
Afghanistan	162	Hong Kong	6
Mali	159	Denmark	6
Sierra Leone	143	Japan	5
Guinea-Bissau	140	Iceland	5
Malawi	138	Finland	5

[USA 8 deaths]

ILLITERACY

Percentage of the total population unable to read or write (1992)

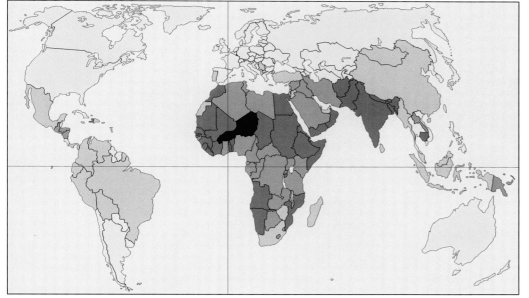

- Over 75% of population illiterate
- 50 – 75% of population illiterate
- 25 – 50% of population illiterate
- 10 – 15% of population illiterate
- Under 10% of population illiterate

Educational expenditure per person (latest available year)

Top 5 countries		Bottom 5 countries	
Sweden	$997	Chad	$2
Qatar	$989	Bangladesh	$3
Canada	$983	Ethiopia	$3
Norway	$971	Nepal	$4
Switzerland	$796	Somalia	$4

LIVING STANDARDS

At first sight, most international contrasts in living standards are swamped by differences in wealth. The rich not only have more money, they have more of everything, including years of life. Those with only a little money are obliged to spend most of it on food and clothing, the basic maintenance costs of their existence; air travel and tourism are unlikely to feature on their expenditure lists. However, poverty and wealth are both relative: slum dwellers living on social security payments in an affluent industrial country have far more resources at their disposal than an average African peasant, but feel their own poverty nonetheless. A middle-class Indian lawyer cannot command a fraction of the earnings of a counterpart living in New York, London or Rome; nevertheless, he rightly sees himself as prosperous.

The rich not only live longer, on average, than the poor, they also die from different causes. Infectious and parasitic diseases, all but eliminated in the developed world, remain a scourge in the developing nations. On the other hand, more than two-thirds of the populations of OECD nations eventually succumb to cancer or circulatory disease.

FERTILITY AND EDUCATION

Fertility rates compared with female education, selected countries (1990–92)

- Fertility rate: average number of children borne per woman
- Percentage of females aged 12–17 in secondary education

(Countries: Japan, Canada, Denmark, USA, Poland, Australia, UK, Brazil, Malaysia, Mexico, Egypt, Bolivia, China, India, Sudan, Ethiopia, Bangladesh, Mali)

WOMEN IN THE WORK FORCE

Women in paid employment as a percentage of the total work force (latest available year)

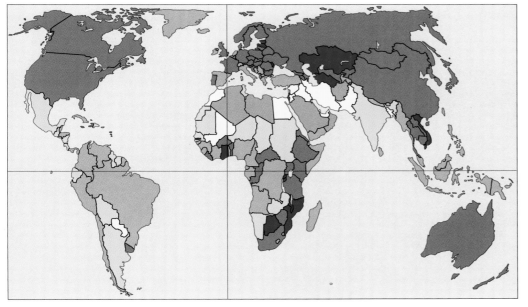

- Over 50% are women
- 40 – 50% are women
- 30 – 40% are women
- 20 – 30% are women
- 10 – 20% are women
- Under 10% are women

Most women in the work force		Fewest women in the work force	
Kazakstan	54%	Guinea-Bissau	3%
Rwanda	54%	Oman	6%
Botswana	53%	Afghanistan	8%
Burundi	53%	Libya	8%
Mozambique	52%	Algeria	9%

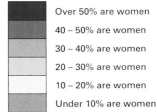

ENERGY

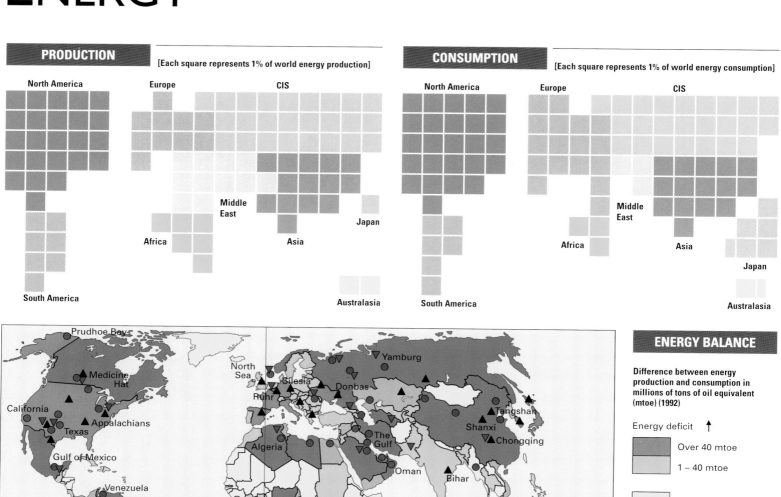

PRODUCTION

[Each square represents 1% of world energy production]

North America

Europe

CIS

Middle East

Africa

Asia

Japan

South America

Australasia

CONSUMPTION

[Each square represents 1% of world energy consumption]

North America

Europe

CIS

Middle East

Africa

Asia

Japan

South America

Australasia

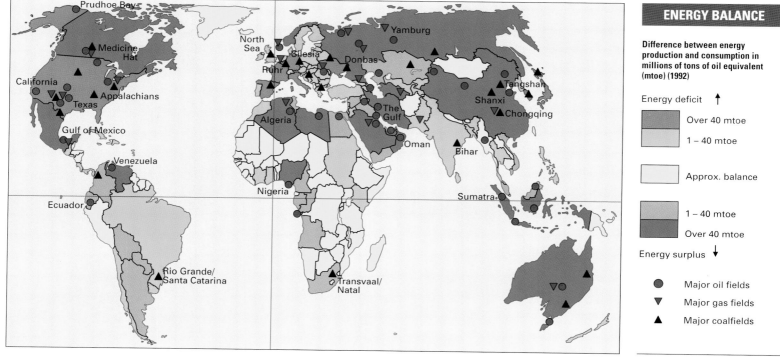

Prudhoe Bay

Yamburg

North Sea

Silesia

Ruhr

Donbas

Medicine Hat

California

Appalachians

Texas

Tangshan

Shanxi

Chongqing

The Gulf

Gulf of Mexico

Algeria

Oman

Bihar

Venezuela

Nigeria

Ecuador

Sumatra

Rio Grande/ Santa Catarina

Transvaal/ Natal

ENERGY BALANCE

Difference between energy production and consumption in millions of tons of oil equivalent (mtoe) (1992)

Energy deficit ↑

Over 40 mtoe

1 – 40 mtoe

Approx. balance

1 – 40 mtoe

Over 40 mtoe

Energy surplus ↓

● Major oil fields

▽ Major gas fields

▲ Major coalfields

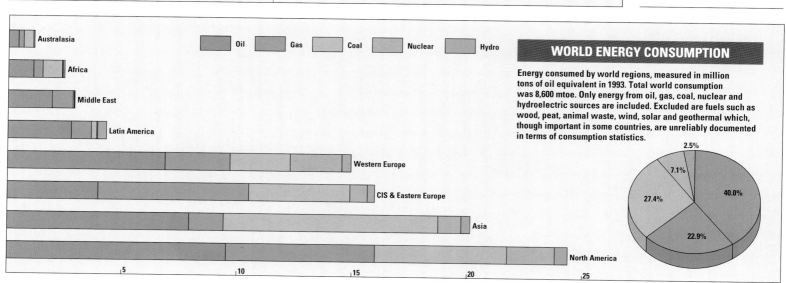

Australasia

Africa

Middle East

Latin America

Oil Gas Coal Nuclear Hydro

Western Europe

CIS & Eastern Europe

Asia

North America

WORLD ENERGY CONSUMPTION

Energy consumed by world regions, measured in million tons of oil equivalent in 1993. Total world consumption was 8,600 mtoe. Only energy from oil, gas, coal, nuclear and hydroelectric sources are included. Excluded are fuels such as wood, peat, animal waste, wind, solar and geothermal which, though important in some countries, are unreliably documented in terms of consumption statistics.

2.5%

7.1%

27.4%

40.0%

22.9%

5 10 15 20 25

24

ENERGY

Energy is used to keep us warm or cool, fuel our industries and our transport systems, and even feed us; high-intensity agriculture, with its use of fertilizers, pesticides and machinery, is heavily energy-dependent. Although we live in a high-energy society, there are vast discrepancies between rich and poor; for example, a North American consumes 13 times as much energy as a Chinese person. But even developing nations have more power at their disposal than was imaginable a century ago.

The distribution of energy supplies, most importantly fossil fuels (coal, oil and natural gas), is very uneven. In addition, the diagrams and map opposite show that the largest producers of energy are not necessarily the largest consumers. The movement of energy supplies around the world is therefore an important component of international trade. In 1993, total world movements in oil amounted to 1,515 million tons.

As the finite reserves of fossil fuels are depleted, renewable energy sources, such as solar, hydro-thermal, wind, tidal and biomass, will become increasingly important around the world.

NUCLEAR POWER

Percentage of electricity generated by nuclear power stations, leading nations (1994)

1. Lithuania	76%	11. Spain	35%
2. France	75%	12. Taiwan	32%
3. Belgium	56%	13. Finland	30%
4. Sweden	51%	14. Germany	29%
5. Slovak Rep.	49%	15. Ukraine	29%
6. Bulgaria	46%	16. Czech Rep.	28%
7. Hungary	44%	17. Japan	27%
8. Slovenia	38%	18. UK	26%
9. Switzerland	37%	19. USA	22%
10. South Korea	36%	20. Canada	19%

Although the 1980s were a bad time for the nuclear power industry (major projects ran over budget, and fears of long-term environmental damage were heavily reinforced by the 1986 disaster at Chernobyl), the industry picked up in the early 1990s. However, whilst the number of reactors is still increasing, orders for new plants have shrunk. This is partly due to the increasingly difficult task of disposing of nuclear waste.

HYDROELECTRICITY

Percentage of electricity generated by hydroelectric power stations, leading nations (1992)

1. Paraguay	99.9%	11. Zaïre	97.4%
2. Norway	99.6%	12. Cameroon	97.2%
3. Bhutan	99.6%	13. Albania	96.1%
4. Zambia	99.5%	14. Laos	95.3%
5. Ghana	99.3%	15. Iceland	94.8%
6. Congo	99.3%	16. Nepal	93.4%
7. Uganda	99.2%	17. Brazil	92.6%
8. Burundi	98.1%	18. Honduras	91.4%
9. Malawi	98.0%	19. Guatemala	89.7%
10. Rwanda	97.8%	20. Uruguay	89.0%

Countries heavily reliant on hydroelectricity are usually small and non-industrial: a high proportion of hydroelectric power more often reflects a modest energy budget than vast hydroelectric resources. The USA, for instance, produces only 9% of power requirements from hydroelectricity; yet that 9% amounts to more than three times the HEP generated by all of Africa.

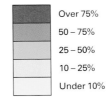

FUEL EXPORTS

Fuels as a percentage of total value of exports (latest available year)

- Over 75%
- 50 – 75%
- 25 – 50%
- 10 – 25%
- Under 10%

Direction of trade

- Coal
- Oil

Arrows show the major trade direction of selected fuels, and are proportional to export value.

MEASUREMENTS

For historical reasons, oil is still traded in 'barrels'. The weight and volume equivalents (shown right) are all based on average-density 'Arabian light' crude oil.

The energy equivalents given for a ton of oil are also somewhat imprecise: oil and coal of different qualities will have varying energy contents, a fact usually reflected in their price on world markets.

CONVERSION RATES
1 barrel = 0.15 tons or 159 liters or 35 Imperial gallons or 42 US gallons
1 ton = 6.67 barrels or 1,075 liters or 233 Imperial gallons or 280 US gallons
1 ton oil = 1.5 tons hard coal or 3.0 tons lignite or 10,900 kWh

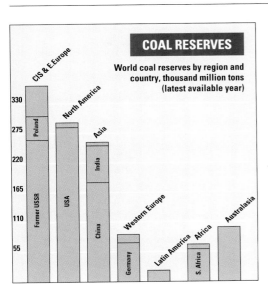

COAL RESERVES
World coal reserves by region and country, thousand million tons (latest available year)

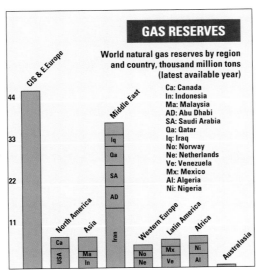

GAS RESERVES
World natural gas reserves by region and country, thousand million tons (latest available year)

Ca: Canada
In: Indonesia
Ma: Malaysia
AD: Abu Dhabi
SA: Saudi Arabia
Qa: Qatar
Iq: Iraq
No: Norway
Ne: Netherlands
Ve: Venezuela
Mx: Mexico
Al: Algeria
Ni: Nigeria

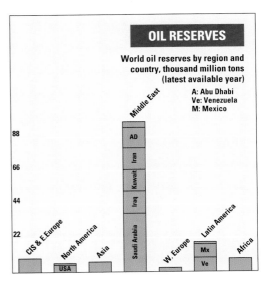

OIL RESERVES
World oil reserves by region and country, thousand million tons (latest available year)

A: Abu Dhabi
Ve: Venezuela
M: Mexico

PRODUCTION

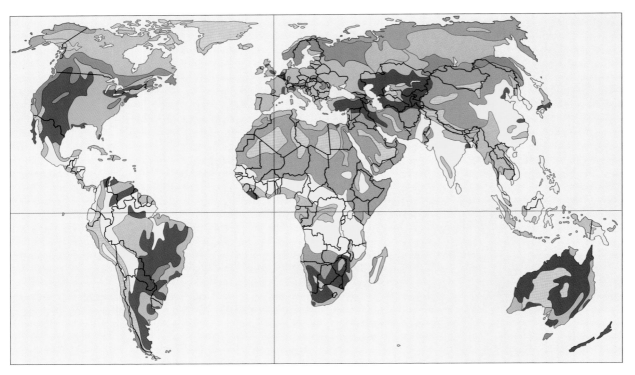

AGRICULTURE

Predominant type of farming or land use

Nomadic herding

Hunting, fishing and gathering

Subsistence agriculture

Commercial ranching

Commercial livestock and grain farming

Urban areas

Forestry

Unproductive land

The invention of agriculture transformed human existence more than any other. The whole business of farming is constantly developing: due mainly to new varieties of rice and wheat, world grain production has increased by over 70% since 1965. New machinery and modern techniques enable relatively few farmers to produce enough food for the world's 5,700 million people.

STAPLE CROPS

Wheat
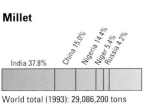
China 18.6% USA 11.6% India 10.1% Russia 7.5% France 5.2% Canada 4.9%

World total (1993): 620,902,700 tons

Rice
China 35.4% India 21.0% Indonesia 9.1% Bangladesh 5.3% Vietnam 4.2% Thailand 3.6%

World total (1993): 580,154,300 tons

Maize
USA 35.8% China 22.9% Brazil 6.7% Mexico 4.1% France 3.3%

World total (1993): 495,627,000 tons

Potatoes
Russia 13.2% Poland 12.6% China 12.2% Ukraine 7.3% USA 6.6% India 5.5%

World total (1993): 317,001,300 tons

Millet
India 37.8% China 15.0% Nigeria 14.4% Niger 5.4% Russia 4.2%

World total (1993): 29,086,200 tons

Rye
Russia 34.9% Poland 19.0% Germany 11.2% Belarus 10.7% Ukraine 4.5%

World total (1993): 28,820,000 tons

Soya
USA 44.3% Brazil 20.5% China 11.7% Argentina 9.6% India 4.1%

World total (1993): 122,112,100 tons

Cassava
Brazil 14.1% Nigeria 13.7% Zaïre 13.6% Thailand 12.8% Indonesia 10.6% Tanzania 4.4%

World total (1993): 168,990,800 tons

SUGARS

Sugarcane
Brazil 24.2% India 22.2% China 6.6% Cuba 4.2% Mexico 4.0% Pakistan 3.7%

World total (1993): 1,144,660,000 tons

Sugar beet
Ukraine 12.0% France 11.3% Germany 10.2% Russia 9.1% USA 8.5% Poland 5.5% Turkey 5.5%

World total (1993): 309,850,200 tons

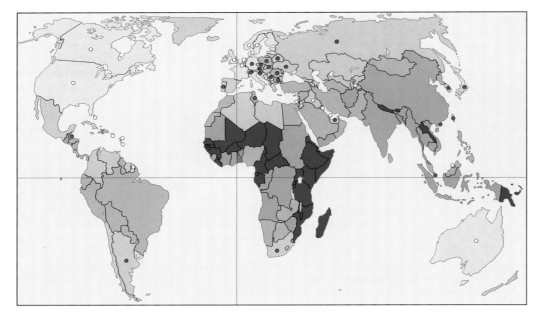

BALANCE OF EMPLOYMENT

Percentage of total work force employed in agriculture, including forestry and fishing (1990–92)

Over 75% in agriculture

50 – 75% in agriculture

25 – 50% in agriculture

10 – 25% in agriculture

Under 10% in agriculture

Employment in industry and services

• Over a third of total work force employed in manufacturing

○ Over two-thirds of total work force employed in service industries (work in offices, shops, tourism, transport, construction and government)

MINERAL PRODUCTION

*Figures for aluminum are for refined metal; all other figures refer to ore production

Copper
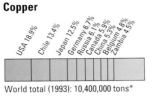
USA 18.9% | Chile 13.4% | Japan 12.5% | Germany 6.7% | Russia 6.1% | Canada 5.9% | Australia 5.3% | China 4.8% | Zambia 4.5%

World total (1993): 10,400,000 tons*

Iron
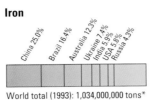
China 25.0% | Brazil 16.4% | Australia 12.3% | Ukraine 7.4% | India 5.9% | Russia 5.8% | 4.3%

World total (1993): 1,034,000,000 tons*

Chromium
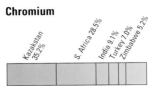
Kazakstan 35.2% | S. Africa 28.5% | India 9.1% | Turkey 7.0% | Zimbabwe 5.2%

World total (1993): 10,923,000 tons*

Gold

S. Africa 32.6% | USA 17.7% | Australia 13.0% | Canada 7.9% | Russia 6.8% | China 6.7%

World total (1993): 2,090 tons*

Uranium

Canada 27.8% | Kazakstan 8.2% | Uzbekistan 7.9% | Russia 7.3% | Australia 6.9% | S. Africa 5.2% | France 5.2% | Namibia 5.0%

World total (1993): 36,300 tons*

Lead
USA 22.7% | Russia 9.3% | UK 6.7% | Germany 6.2% | Japan 5.7% | China 5.6% | France 4.8%

World total (1993): 5,940,000 tons*

Tin

China 22.7% | Malaysia 20.7% | Indonesia 13.6% | Brazil 10.6% | Bolivia 7.6% | Peru 6.2% | Russia 4.5%

World total (1993): 242,000 tons*

Manganese
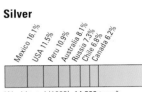
Ukraine 31.8% | China 19.1% | S. Africa 15.9% | Brazil 9.1% | Gabon 8.2% | Australia 6.6% | India 5.9%

World total (1993): 24,200,000 tons*

Silver
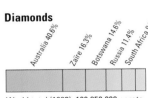
Mexico 16.1% | USA 11.5% | Peru 10.9% | Australia 8.1% | Russia 7.3% | Chile 6.9% | Canada 6.2%

World total (1993): 14,300 tons*

Aluminum
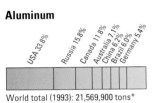
USA 33.8% | Russia 15.8% | Canada 11.8% | Australia 7.1% | China 6.2% | Brazil 6.0% | Germany 5.4%

World total (1993): 21,569,900 tons*

Mercury

China 25.0% | Mexico 20.7% | Russia 14.3% | Algeria 8.9% | Kyrgyzstan 6.0%

World total (1993): 4,620 tons*

Zinc
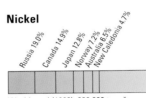
China 11.8% | Japan 10.3% | Canada 9.3% | Germany 7.7% | Belgium 5.6% | USA 5.6% | Russia 4.9%

World total (1993): 7,839,700 tons*

Nickel
Russia 19.0% | Canada 14.9% | Japan 12.8% | Norway 7.2% | Australia 6.5% | New Caledonia 4.7%

World total (1993): 869,000 tons*

Diamonds

Australia 40.6% | Zaire 16.3% | Botswana 14.6% | Russia 11.4% | South Africa 9.7%

World total (1993): 100,850,000 carats

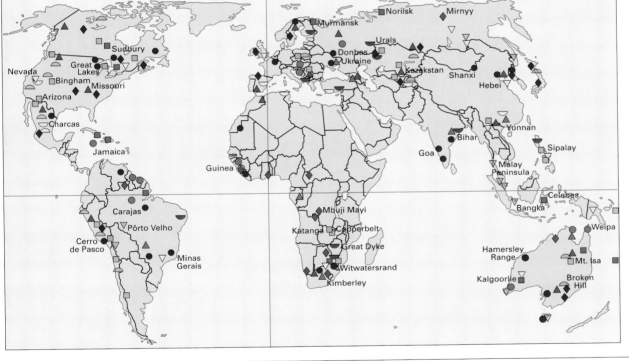

MINERAL DISTRIBUTION

The map shows the richest sources of the most important minerals.

Light metals
- ⬤ Bauxite

Base metals
- ▢ Copper
- ▲ Lead
- ▽ Mercury
- ▽ Tin
- ◆ Zinc

Iron and ferro-alloys
- ⬤ Iron
- ◖ Chrome
- ▲ Manganese
- ▪ Nickel

Precious metals
- ▽ Gold
- ◠ Silver

Precious stones
- ◆ Diamonds

The map does not show undersea deposits, most of which are considered inaccessible.

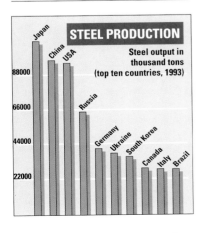

STEEL PRODUCTION
Steel output in thousand tons (top ten countries, 1993)

SHIPBUILDING
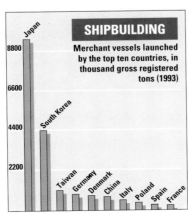
Merchant vessels launched by the top ten countries, in thousand gross registered tons (1993)

AUTOMOBILES
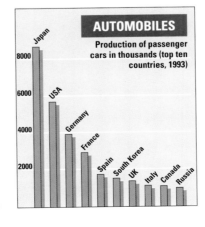
Production of passenger cars in thousands (top ten countries, 1993)

COMMERCIAL VEHICLES
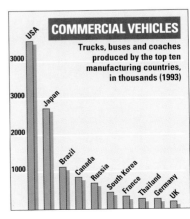
Trucks, buses and coaches produced by the top ten manufacturing countries, in thousands (1993)

CARTOGRAPHY BY PHILIP'S. COPYRIGHT REED INTERNATIONAL BOOKS LTD

27

TRADE

SHARE OF WORLD TRADE

Percentage share of total world exports by value (1993)

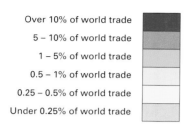

Over 10% of world trade
5 – 10% of world trade
1 – 5% of world trade
0.5 – 1% of world trade
0.25 – 0.5% of world trade
Under 0.25% of world trade

International trade is dominated by a handful of powerful maritime nations. The members of 'G7', the inner circle of OECD (see page 19), and the top seven countries listed in the diagram below, account for more than half the total. The majority of nations – including all but four in Africa – contribute less than one quarter of 1% to the worldwide total of exports; the EU countries account for 40%, the Pacific Rim nations over 35%.

THE GREAT TRADING NATIONS

The imports and exports of the top ten trading nations as a percentage of world trade (latest available year). Each country's trade in manufactured goods is shown in orange.

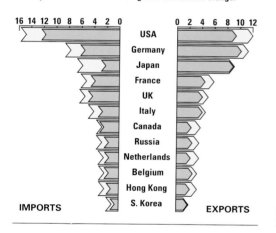

16 14 12 10 8 6 4 2 0   0 2 4 6 8 10 12

USA
Germany
Japan
France
UK
Italy
Canada
Russia
Netherlands
Belgium
Hong Kong
S. Korea

IMPORTS   EXPORTS

PATTERNS OF TRADE

Thriving international trade is the outward sign of a healthy world economy, the obvious indicator that some countries have goods to sell and others the wherewithal to buy them. Despite local fluctuations, trade throughout the 1980s grew consistently faster than output, increasing in value by almost 50% in the decade 1979–89. It remains dominated by the rich, industrialized countries of the Organization for Economic Development: between them, OECD members account for almost 75% of world imports and exports in most years. OECD dominance is just as marked in the trade in 'invisibles' – a column in the balance sheet that includes among other headings the export of services, interest payments on overseas investments, tourism and even remittances from migrant workers abroad. In the UK, invisibles account for more than half all trading income.

However, the size of these great trading economies means that imports and exports usually make up a small percentage of their total wealth: for example, in the case of export-conscious Japan, trade in goods and services amounts to less than 18% of GDP. In poorer countries, trade – often in a single commodity – may amount to 50% of GDP or more.

TRADED PRODUCTS

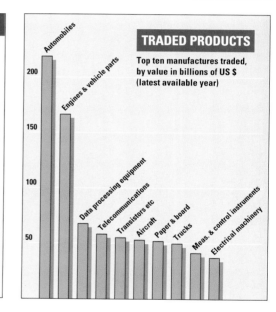

Top ten manufactures traded, by value in billions of US $ (latest available year)

Automobiles
Engines & vehicle parts
Data processing equipment
Telecommunications
Transistors etc
Aircraft
Paper & board
Trucks
Meas. & control instruments
Electrical machinery

BALANCE OF TRADE

Value of exports in proportion to the value of imports (1993)

Exports exceed imports by:
More than 40%
10 – 40%
10% either side
Imports exceed exports by:
10 – 40%
More than 40%

The total world trade balance should amount to zero, since exports must equal imports on a global scale. In practice, at least $100 billion in exports go unrecorded, leaving the world with an apparent deficit and many countries in a better position than public accounting reveals. However, a favorable trade balance is not necessarily a sign of prosperity: many poorer countries must maintain a high surplus in order to service debts, and do so by restricting imports below the levels needed to sustain successful economies.

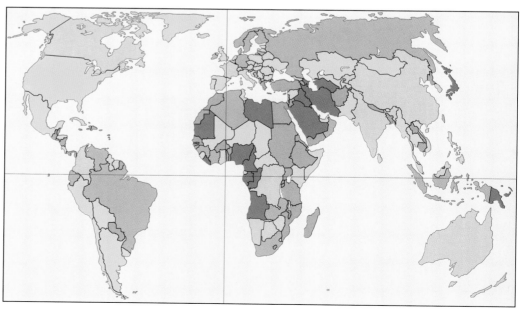

28

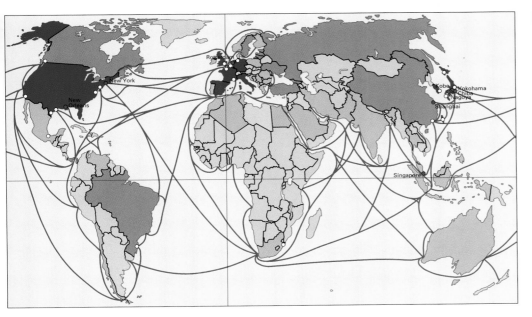

FREIGHT

Freight unloaded in millions of tons (latest available year)

- Over 100
- 50 – 100
- 10 – 50
- 5 – 10
- Under 5
- Landlocked countries

Major seaports

- ● Over 100 million tons per year
- ○ 50–100 million tons per year
- — Major shipping routes

CARGOES

Type of seaborne freight

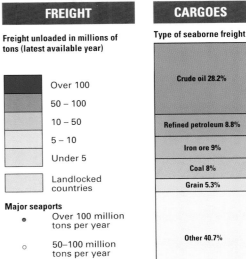

- Crude oil 28.2%
- Refined petroleum 8.8%
- Iron ore 9%
- Coal 8%
- Grain 5.3%
- Other 40.7%

MERCHANT FLEETS

Merchant fleets in thousand gross tonnage (1994). A large number of vessels are registered in Liberia and Panama but they are not part of the national fleet.

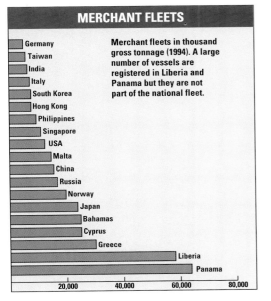

Germany, Taiwan, India, Italy, South Korea, Hong Kong, Philippines, Singapore, USA, Malta, China, Russia, Norway, Japan, Bahamas, Cyprus, Greece, Liberia, Panama

20,000 40,000 60,000 80,000

WORLD SHIPPING

World merchant fleet by type of vessel and deadweight tonnage (latest available year)

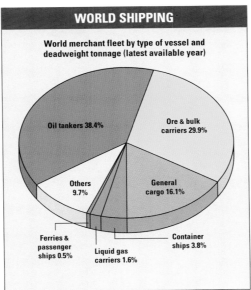

- Oil tankers 38.4%
- Ore & bulk carriers 29.9%
- General cargo 16.1%
- Others 9.7%
- Ferries & passenger ships 0.5%
- Liquid gas carriers 1.6%
- Container ships 3.8%

THE GREAT PORTS

The world's ten busiest ports by million tons of shipping arrivals (1992)

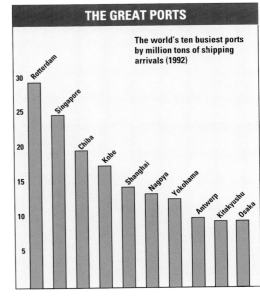

Rotterdam, Singapore, Chiba, Kobe, Shanghai, Nagoya, Yokohama, Antwerp, Kitakyushu, Osaka

DEPENDENCE ON TRADE

Value of exports as a percentage of Gross Domestic Product (1993)

- Over 50% GDP
- 40 – 50% GDP
- 30 – 40% GDP
- 20 – 30% GDP
- 10 – 20% GDP
- Under 10% GDP
- ● Most dependent on industrial exports (over 75% of total exports)
- ● Most dependent on fuel exports (over 75% of total exports)
- ○ Most dependent on mineral and metal exports (over 75% of total exports)

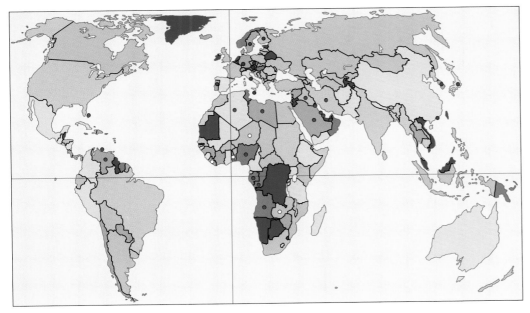

TRAVEL AND TOURISM

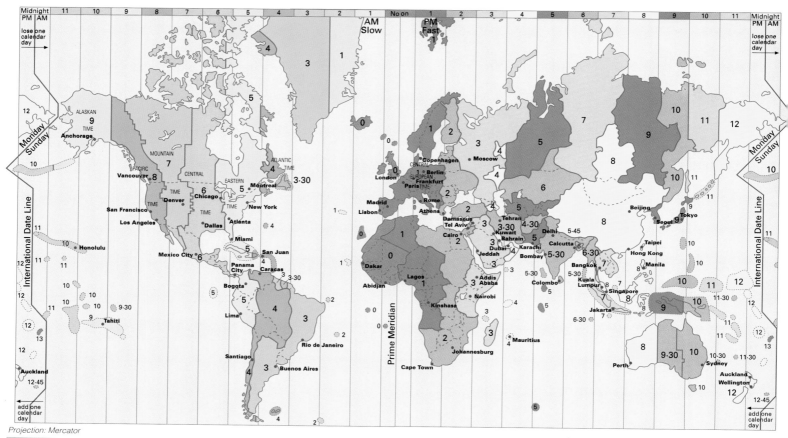

Projection: Mercator

TIME ZONES

Zones using GMT	Zones fast of GMT	Certain time zones are affected by the incidence of 'summer time' in countries where it is adopted.
Zones slow of GMT	Half-hour zones	
– – – International boundaries	Time zone boundaries	
10 Hours slow or fast of GMT	International Date Line	Actual Solar Time, when it is noon at Greenwich, is shown along the top of the map.

The world is divided into 24 time zones, each centered on meridians at 15° intervals, which is the longitudinal distance the sun travels every hour. The meridian running through Greenwich, London, passes through the middle of the first zone.

RAIL AND ROAD: THE LEADING NATIONS

Total rail network ('000 miles)	Passenger miles per head per year	Total road network ('000 miles)	Vehicle miles per head per year	Number of vehicles per mile of roads
1. USA 148.9	Japan 1,253	USA...........3,898.6	USA................7,766	Hong Kong ...176
2. Russia.............54.3	Belarus 1,167	India 1,839.7	Luxembourg.4,961	Taiwan 131
3. India..............38.8	Russia 1,134	Brazil 1,133.0	Kuwait...........4,503	Singapore.......94
4. China 33.5	Switzerland..1,099	Japan 702.3	France 4,435	Kuwait.............87
5. Germany 25.1	Ukraine 904	China............646.5	Sweden.........4,341	Brunei 60
6. Australia 22.2	Austria 725	Russia..........549.0	Germany 4,227	Italy 57
7. Argentina 21.2	France 628	Canada........527.5	Denmark 4,200	Israel 54
8. France............20.2	Netherlands 617	France 504.0	Austria 4,048	Thailand..........45
9. Mexico...........16.5	Latvia 570	Australia 503.2	Netherlands..3,716	Ukraine 45
10. Poland 15.5	Denmark 549	Germany 395.1	UK 3,563	UK 42
11. South Africa ...14.7	Slovak Rep. 535	Romania 286.8	Canada..........3,411	Netherlands....41
12. Ukraine 14.0	Romania..........528	Turkey 241.0	Italy 3,013	Germany........39

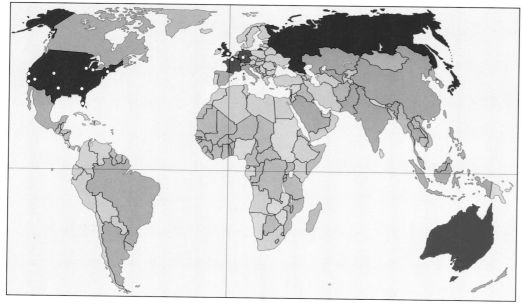

AIR TRAVEL

Passenger miles (the number of passengers – international and and domestic – multiplied by the distance flown by each passenger from the airport of origin) (1992)

	Over 60,000 million
	30,000 – 60,000 million
	6,000 – 30,000 million
	600 – 6,000 million
	300 – 600 million
	Under 300 million

o Major airports (handling over 25 million passengers in 1994)

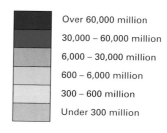

World's busiest airports (total passengers)

1. Chicago (O'Hare)
2. Atlanta (Hatsfield)
3. Dallas (Dallas/Ft Worth)
4. London (Heathrow)
5. Los Angeles (Intern'l)

World's busiest airports (international passengers)

1. London (Heathrow)
2. London (Gatwick)
3. Frankfurt (International)
4. New York (Kennedy)
5. Paris (De Gaulle)

DESTINATIONS

- ■ Cultural & historical centers
- ▫ Coastal resorts
- □ Ski resorts
- ▪ Centers of entertainment
- ■ Places of pilgrimage
- ■ Places of great natural beauty
- — Popular holiday cruise routes

VISITORS TO THE USA

International tourism receipts in US $ million (1993)

1. Japan 14,356
2. Canada 8,649
3. UK 8,151
4. Mexico 5,670
5. Germany 5,332
6. France 2,752
7. Australia 1,941
8. All others 27,320

In 1993 45.8 million foreigners visited the USA. Between them they spent $74 billion. The average length of stay was 17 nights.

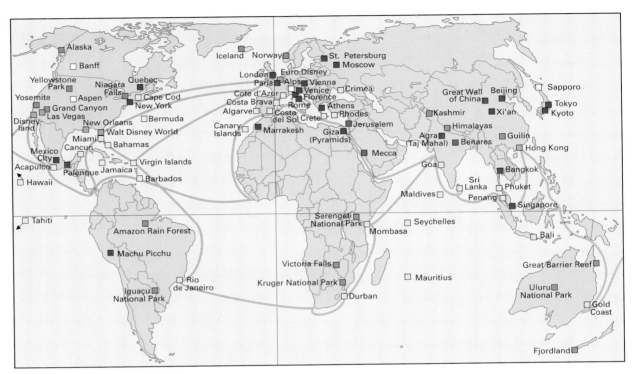

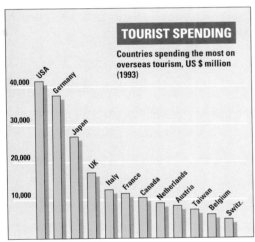

TOURIST SPENDING

Countries spending the most on overseas tourism, US $ million (1993)

IMPORTANCE OF TOURISM

	Arrivals from abroad (1992)	Receipts as % of GDP (1992)
1. France	59,590,000	1.9%
2. USA	44,647,000	0.9%
3. Spain	39,638,000	4.0%
4. Italy	26,113,000	1.8%
5. Hungary	20,188,000	3.3%
6. Austria	19,098,000	7.6%
7. UK	18,535,000	1.3%
8. Mexico	17,271,000	2.0%
9. China	16,512,000	0.9%
10. Germany	15,147,000	0.6%
11. Canada	14,741,000	1.0%
12. Switzerland	12,800,000	3.1%

Small economies in attractive areas are often completely dominated by tourism: in some West Indian islands tourist spending provides over 90% of total income. In cash terms the USA is the world leader: its 1992 earnings exceeded $53 billion, though that sum amounted to only 0.9% of GDP.

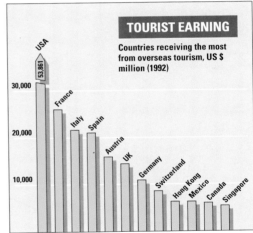

TOURIST EARNING

Countries receiving the most from overseas tourism, US $ million (1992)

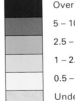

TOURISM

Tourism receipts as a percentage of Gross National Product (1992)

- Over 10% of GNP from tourism
- 5 – 10% of GNP from tourism
- 2.5 – 5% of GNP from tourism
- 1 – 2.5% of GNP from tourism
- 0.5 – 1% of GNP from tourism
- Under 0.5% of GNP from tourism

Largest percentage share of total world spending on tourism (1993)

USA 15%
Germany 14%
Japan 10%
UK 6%
Italy 5%

Largest percentage share of total world receipts from tourism (1993)

USA 19%
France 8%
Italy 7%
Spain 6%
Austria 4%

SUBJECT INDEX

WORLD MAPS

SETTLEMENTS

⬠ **PARIS**   ◼ **Berne**   ◉ **Livorno**   ⊙ **Brugge**   ◎ *Algeciras*   ○ *Fréjus*   ○ *Oberammergau*   ○ *Thira*

Settlement symbols and type styles vary according to the scale of each map and indicate the importance
of towns on the map rather than specific population figures

∴   Ruins or Archæological Sites   ˅   Wells in Desert

ADMINISTRATION

——— International Boundaries

– – – International Boundaries (Undefined or Disputed)

·········· Internal Boundaries

National Parks

Country Names

NICARAGUA

Administrative Area Names

KENT

CALABRIA

International boundaries show the *de facto* situation where there are rival claims to territory

---

COMMUNICATIONS

——— Principal Roads

‿ Other Roads

-·- Trails and Seasonal Roads

⋈ Passes

⊙ Airfields

‿ Principal Railroads

-·-·- Railroads Under Construction

‿ Other Railroads

⌐---⌐ Railroad Tunnels

⊔⊔⊔⊔ Principal Canals

PHYSICAL FEATURES

‿ Perennial Streams

·-·-· Intermittent Streams

⬭ Perennial Lakes

⬭ Intermittent Lakes

Swamps and Marshes

Permanent Ice and Glaciers

▲ 8848   Elevations (m)

▼ 8050   Sea Depths (m)

1134   Height of Lake Surface Above Sea Level (m)

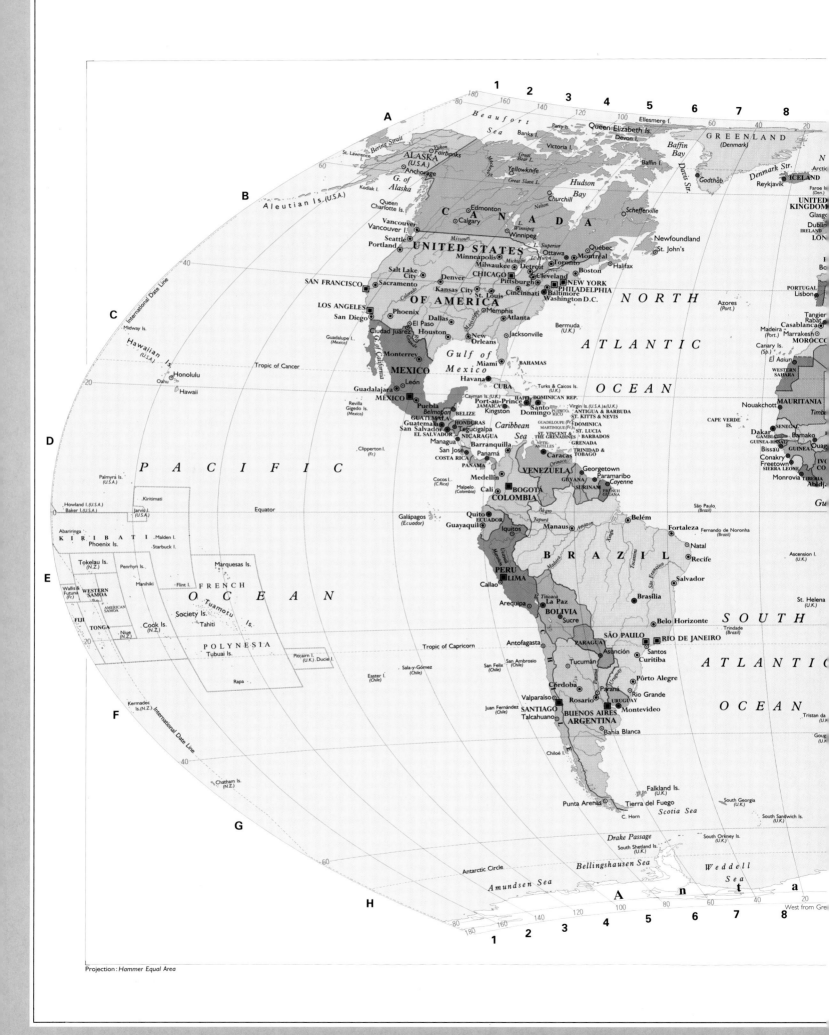

Projection: Hammer Equal Area

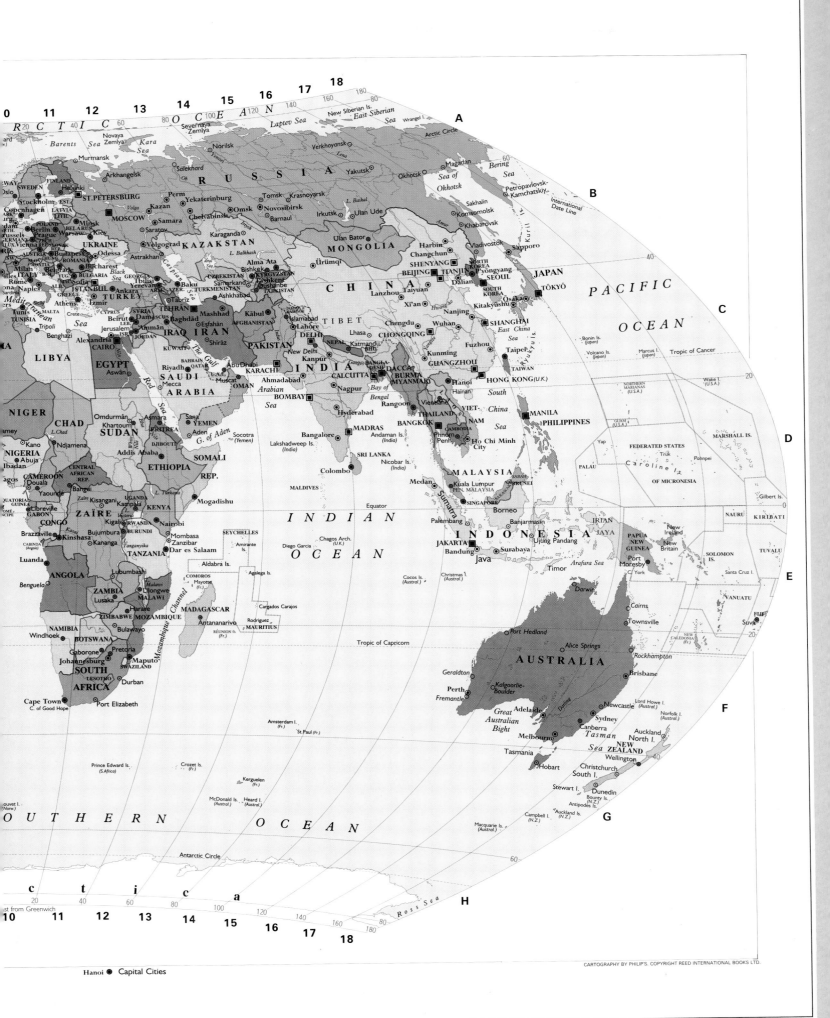

Hanoi ● Capital Cities

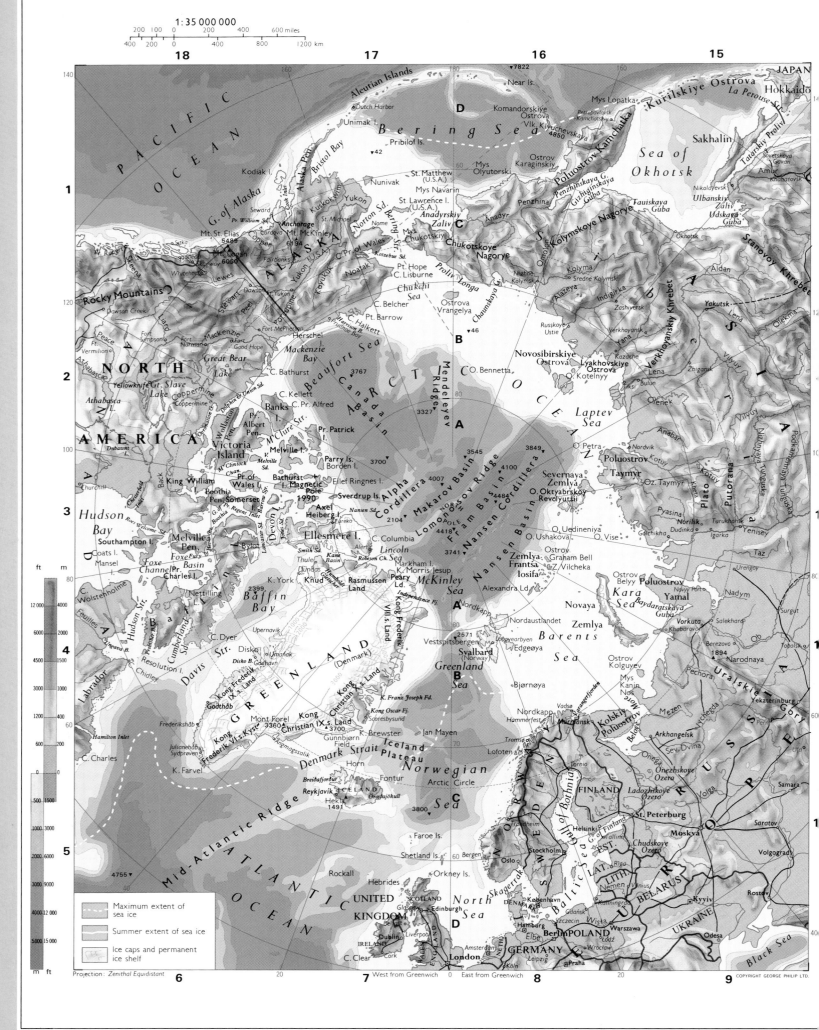

1 : 35 000 000

200 100 0   200   400   600 miles
400 200 0   400   800   1200 km

18   17   16   15

JAPAN

PACIFIC OCEAN

Bering Sea

Sea of Okhotsk

ARCTIC OCEAN

Beaufort Sea

Canada Basin

Laptev Sea

NORTH AMERICA

Hudson Bay

Baffin Bay

GREENLAND (Denmark)

Barents Sea

Kara Sea

Greenland Sea

Norwegian Sea

ICELAND

Denmark Strait

Mid-Atlantic Ridge

ATLANTIC OCEAN

North Sea

UNITED KINGDOM

IRELAND

GERMANY

POLAND

FINLAND

SWEDEN

NORWAY

RUSSIA

EUROPE

BELARUS

UKRAINE

Black Sea

Baltic Sea

Moskvá

St. Peterburg

London

Legend:
- Maximum extent of sea ice
- Summer extent of sea ice
- Ice caps and permanent ice shelf

ft   m
12 000 4000
6000   2000
4500   1500
3000   1000
1200   400
600   200
0   0
500   1500
1000   3000
2000   6000
3000   9000
4000 12 000
5000 15 000
m   ft

Projection: Zenithal Equidistant

6   7 West from Greenwich 0 East from Greenwich 8   9 COPYRIGHT GEORGE PHILIP LTD.

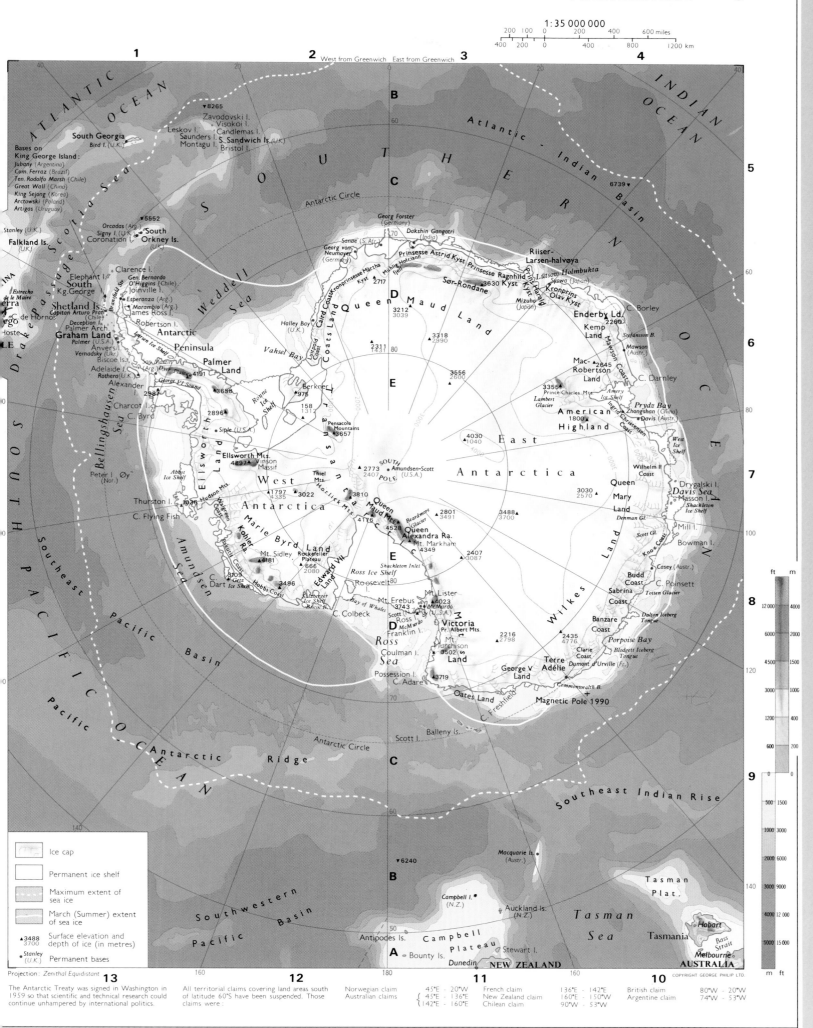

1:35 000 000

Scale markings:
200 100 0 200 400 600 miles
400 200 0 400 800 1200 km

West from Greenwich East from Greenwich

ATLANTIC OCEAN

INDIAN OCEAN

Atlantic - Indian Basin

South Georgia
Bird I. (U.K.)

Bases on
King George Island:
Jubany (Argentina)
Com. Ferraz (Brazil)
Ten. Rodolfo Marsh (Chile)
Great Wall (China)
King Sejong (Korea)
Arctowski (Poland)
Artigas (Uruguay)

▼8265
Zavodovski I.
Leskov I. ▼ Visokoi I. ▼ Candlemas I.
Saunders I. ▼ S. Sandwich Is. (U.K.)
Montagu I. ▼ Bristol I.

SOUTHERN

Antarctic Circle

SCOTIA SEA

Stanley (U.K.)
Falkland Is. (U.K.)

Orcadas (Arg.) ▼5552
Signy I. (U.K.) ● South
Coronation I. ● Orkney Is. (U.K.)

Georg Forster (Germany)
Dakshin Gangotri (India)
Sanae (S. Afr.)
Georg von Neumayer (Germany)
Prinsesse Astrid Kyst Prinsesse Ragnhild Kyst
Kronprinsesse Martha Mühlig Hofmann
Kyst Fjell 2717

Riiser-
Larsen-halvøya

Lützow-Holmbukta
Syowa (Japan)
Kronprins
Olav Kyst
Mizuho (Japan)

OCEAN

Elephant I.
South Gen. Bernardo O'Higgins (Chile)
Kg.George Esperanza (Arg.)
Shetland Is. (U.K.) Marambio (Arg.)
Capitan Arturo Prat (Chile) James Ross I.
Deception I. Robertson I.

Clarence I.

Sør-Rondane ▲3630

Enderby Ld. C. Borley
Kemp ▲2260
Land
Stefansson B.
Mawson (Austr.)

6739▼

Queen D Maud Land
Coats Land
Caird Coast
Luitpold Coast
Halley Bay (U.K.)
3212
3039

Graham Land
Palmer (U.S.A.)
Anvers I.
Vernadsky (Ukr.)
Adelaide I.
Rothera (U.K.)

Antarctic
Peninsula
Palmer
Land
Larsen Ice Shelf

3318
2990

Mac- ▲2645
Robertson
Land C. Darnley
3354▲ Prince Charles Mts.
Lambert Amery
Glacier Ice Shelf
American 1800▲ Zhongshan (China)
Highland Prydz Bay
Davis (Austr.)

Vahsel Bay
San Martin (Arg.)
Dyer Plateau 4191▲
Alexander I. ▲3658
2987▼
Charcot I.
C. Byrd

Berkner I.
Ronne 975▼
Ice Shelf
158 1312

2311
1431 80

3556
2600

4030
1040

East
Antarctica
1040

West
Ice Shelf

Siple (U.S.A.)
▲3657

Pensacola
Mountains

SOUTH Amundsen-Scott (U.S.A.)
2773 2407 POLE

Wilhelm II
Coast

Queen
Mary
Land

Drygalski I.
Davis Sea
Masson I.
Shackleton
Ice Shelf

Bellingshausen
Sea
Peter I Øy (Nor.)

Ellsworth Mts.
4897▲ Vinson
Massif

3030 ▲
2570

Thurston I.
1936▼
C. Flying Fish

West 1797
Antarctica 4335 3022
Horlick Mts.
3810

Thiel
Mts.

Queen
Maud Mts.
4116 Beardmore
4528 Glacier
2801 3491

3488 ▲
3700

Denman Gl.
Scott Gl.
Kno▲ Coast
Bowman I.

100

Mill I.

Hudson Mts.

Marie Byrd Land
Koller
Ra.

Mt. Sidley
▲4181 Rockefeller
Plateau
▲666
2080

Queen
Alexandra Ra.
Mt. Markham
4349

2407
3087

Budd
Coast
Casey (Austr.)
C. Poinsett
Sabrina
Coast Totten Glacier

Amundsen
Sea

3109▼ Getz
Dart Ice Shelf 2496 Ice Shelf

Shackleton Inlet

Banzare
Coast
Dalton Iceberg
Tongue

12000 4000

Sulzberger
Ice Shelf Ross Ice Shelf
Edward VII Roosevelt I.
Land 80

Bay of Whales
Mt. Erebus
C. Colbeck 4023 Mt. Lister
3743 4023
Scott (N.Z.)
Ross (U.S.A.) McMurdo (U.S.A.)

Porpoise Bay
Clarie Blodgett Iceberg
Coast Tongue

2435
4776

6000 2000

4500 1500

Pacific Basin

Ross
Sea
Coulman I.
Possession I.

Franklin I.
Victoria
Pr. Albert Mts.

Mt.
Murchison
3502
Land
2216
2798

George V
Land
Terre
Adélie

Dumont d'Urville (Fr.)
Commonwealth B.
Magnetic Pole 1990

3000 1000

1200 400

PACIFIC Antarctic Ridge

3719

Oates Land
C. Freshfield

600 200

Antarctic Circle

Scott I.

Balleny Is.

SOUTHEAST INDIAN RISE

0 0

OCEAN

▼6240

Macquarie Is. (Austr.)

500 1500

1000 3000

Campbell I. (N.Z.)

Auckland Is. (N.Z.)

Tasman
Plat.

2000 6000

Southwestern
Pacific

Tasman
Sea

3000 9000

4000 12000

Basin

Tasmania

Hobart

Bass
Strait

5000 15000

Antipodes Is. Campbell
Plateau Stewart I.
Bounty Is.
Dunedin **NEW ZEALAND**

Melbourne
AUSTRALIA

m ft

Legend

- Ice cap
- Permanent ice shelf
- Maximum extent of sea ice
- March (Summer) extent of sea ice
- ▲3488 / 3700 Surface elevation and depth of ice (in metres)
- ● Stanley (U.K.) Permanent bases

Projection: Zenithal Equidistant

COPYRIGHT GEORGE PHILIP LTD.

The Antarctic Treaty was signed in Washington in 1959 so that scientific and technical research could continue unhampered by international politics.

All territorial claims covering land areas south of latitude 60°S have been suspended. Those claims were:

Norwegian claim	45°E - 20°W	
Australian claims	45°E - 136°E	
	142°E - 160°E	
French claim	136°E - 142°E	
New Zealand claim	160°E - 150°W	
Chilean claim	90°W - 53°W	
British claim	80°W - 20°W	
Argentine claim	74°W - 53°W	

1 : 20 000 000

100   0   100   200   300   400 miles

100   0   100   200   300   400   500   600 km

Ob
Ural Mountains
Obshchi Syrt
Caspian Depression
Caspian Sea
Ural
Kama
Volga
Volga Hts.
Caucasus
Kura
Araxes
Kurdistan
Mesopotamia
Tigris
Euphrates
L. Urmia
L. Van
Elbrus 5633
Ararat 5165
Pontine Mts.
Anatolia (Asia Minor)

Pechora
N. Dvina
Mezen
Pechora
Onega
White Sea
Kola Pen.
Kanin Pen.
Nordkinn
North Cape
Lapland

Rybinsk Res.
Volga
Don
Oka
L. Onega
L. Ladoga
Neva
L. Chudskoye
Central Russian Uplands
Don
Donets
Dnieper
Dniester
Manych
Tsimlyansk Res.
Sea of Azov
Str. of Kerch
Crimea
Black Sea
Kerch

Ukraine
Bug
Prut
Pripet
Danube
Carpathians
Transylvanian Alps
Wallachia
Balkans
Rhodope
Bosphorus
Sea of Marmara
Aegean Sea
L. Tuz
Kizil Irmak
Taurus Mts.
Rhodes
Cyprus

Finland
Plain
Russian
G. of Finland
G. of Riga
Saaremaa
Aland
Gotland
Oland
Bornholm
Baltic Sea
North European Plain
Vistula
Oder
Niemen
W. Dvina
Dvina
Tatra 2663
Sudeten
Moravian Hts.
Plain of Hungary
Mur
Tisza
Bakony Forest
Drava
Sava
Danube
Dinaric Alps
Pindus
Morea
C. Matapan
Str. of Otranto
Ionian Is.
Ionian Sea
Olympus 2917
Str. of Messina

Norwegian Sea
Scandinavia
Vesterålen
Lofoten
Kebnekaise 2117
Torne
Ume
Indals
Mälaren
Scania
Trollhättan
Kattegat
Skagerrak
Jutland
Galdhöpiggen 2469
Glommen

Iceland
Arctic Circle
Oræfajökull 2119
Hvannadalshnúkur 2119
Rockall
Faroe Is.
Shetland Is.
Orkney Is.
Hebrides
Great Britain
Ben Nevis 1347
Snowdon 1085
British Isles
Ireland
Irish Sea
Celtic Sea
C. Clear
Land's End
English Channel
Channel Is.
Brittany
Ushant
Loire
Seine
Thames
North Sea
Helgoland
Elbe
Weser
Rhine
Harz
Erzgebirge
Bohemian Forest
Black Forest
Inn
Vosges
Ardennes
Taunus
Westerwald
Meuse
Hunsrück
Alps
Jura
Mont Blanc 4807
Po
Gran Sasso 2914
Apennines
Vesuvius 1277
Etna 3340
Corsica
Sardinia
Str. of Bonifacio
C. Bon
Pantelleria
Sicily
Malta
Ligurian Sea
Tyrrhenian Sea
Calabria

Massif Central
Cévennes
Rhône
Puy de Sancy
Garonne
G. of Lions
Pyrenees
Pico de Aneto 3404
Cantabrian Mts.
Old Castile
New Castile
Iberian Peninsula
Duero
Ebro
Guadiana
Sierra Morena
Andalusia
Sierra Nevada 3481
Mulhacén
Guadalquivir
Str. of Gibraltar
Africa
Plateau of the Shotts
Mediterranean Sea
Balearic Is.
Minorca
Majorca
Ibiza
Bay of Biscay
4897
Gironde
Garonne
C. Finisterre
Serra da Estrela
C. de São Vicente
C. da Roca
C. Trafalgar
ATLANTIC OCEAN
2861

Projection: Bonne
West from Greenwich   0   East from Greenwich

CARTOGRAPHY BY PHILIP'S. COPYRIGHT REED INTERNATIONAL BOOKS LTD.

m   ft
5000   15 000
4000   12 000
2000   6000
1000   3000
400   1200
200   600
0
200   600
3000   6000
2000   4000
4000   12 000
ft   m

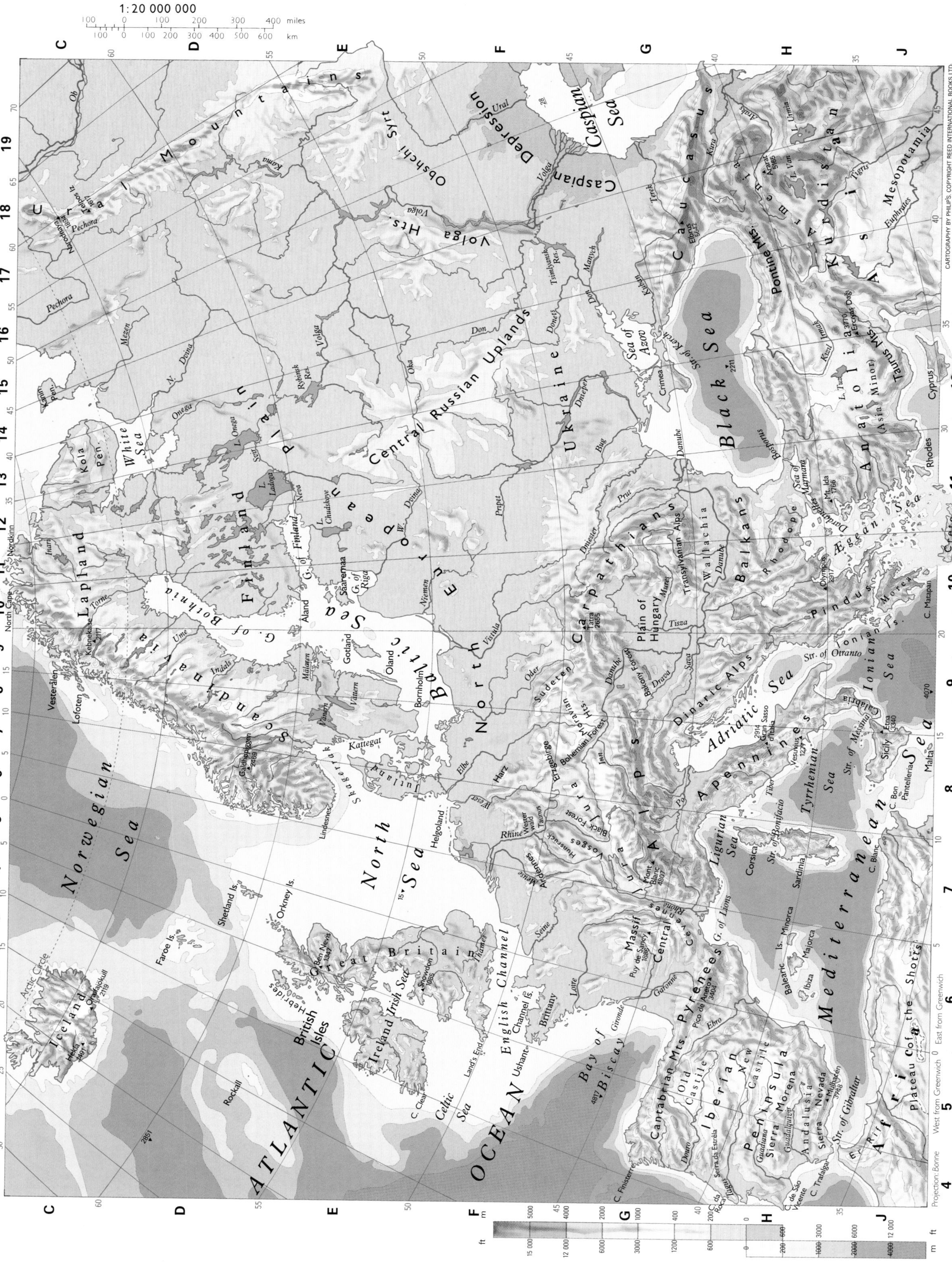

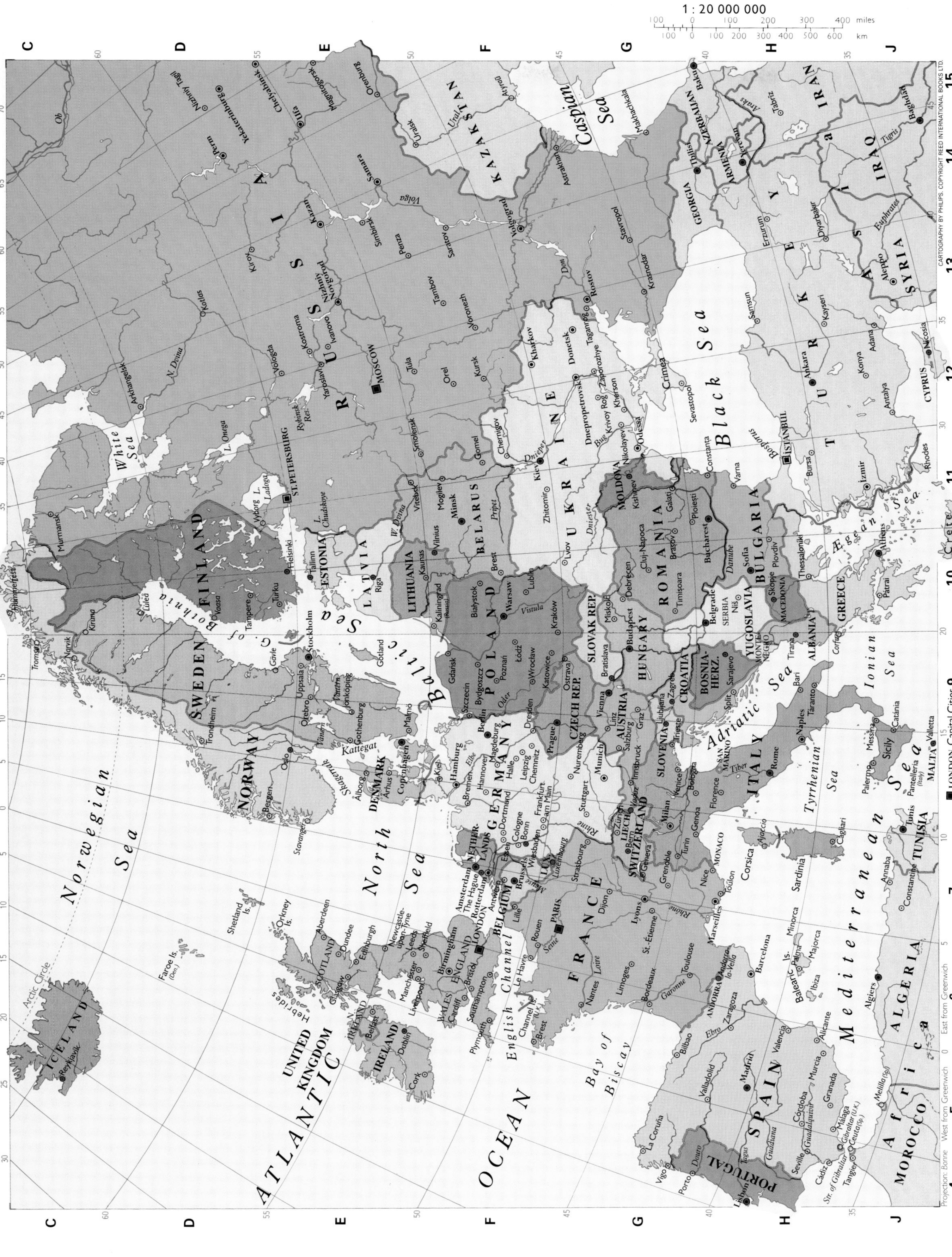

1 : 20 000 000

100   0   100   200   300   400   miles
100 0   100 200 300 400 500 600   km

ATLANTIC OCEAN

Norwegian Sea

North Sea

Baltic Sea

White Sea

Caspian Sea

Black Sea

Adriatic Sea

Mediterranean Sea

Aegean Sea

Ionian Sea

Tyrrhenian Sea

Bay of Biscay

English Channel

Gulf of Bothnia

Kattegat

RUSSIA
KAZAKSTAN
FINLAND
SWEDEN
NORWAY
ICELAND
UNITED KINGDOM
IRELAND
SCOTLAND
ENGLAND
WALES
DENMARK
NETHERLANDS
BELGIUM
GERMANY
FRANCE
SPAIN
PORTUGAL
ITALY
SWITZERLAND
AUSTRIA
CZECH REP.
SLOVAK REP.
POLAND
HUNGARY
SLOVENIA
CROATIA
BOSNIA HERZ.
YUGOSLAVIA
SERBIA
MONTENEGRO
MACEDONIA
ALBANIA
GREECE
ROMANIA
BULGARIA
MOLDOVA
UKRAINE
BELARUS
LITHUANIA
LATVIA
ESTONIA
TURKEY
GEORGIA
ARMENIA
AZERBAIJAN
IRAN
IRAQ
SYRIA
CYPRUS
MALTA
TUNISIA
ALGERIA
MOROCCO
Africa
SAN MARINO
MONACO
ANDORRA
LUX.
Crete
Sicily
Sardinia
Corsica
Crimea

Capital cities:
MOSCOW, ST. PETERSBURG, LONDON, PARIS, Rome, Madrid, Lisbon, Oslo, Stockholm, Helsinki, Copenhagen, Amsterdam, The Hague, Brussels, Berlin, Bonn, Vienna, Bratislava, Prague, Warsaw, Budapest, Ljubljana, Zagreb, Sarajevo, Belgrade, Skopje, Tiranë, Athens, Bucharest, Sofia, Kishinev, Kiev, Minsk, Vilnius, Riga, Tallinn, Ankara, Tbilisi, Yerevan, Baku, Baghdad, Nicosia, Valletta, Tunis, Algiers, Reykjavík, Dublin

■ LONDON Capital Cities 9

Projection: Bonne

West from Greenwich   0   East from Greenwich

Arctic Circle

CARTOGRAPHY BY PHILIP'S. COPYRIGHT REED INTERNATIONAL BOOKS LTD.

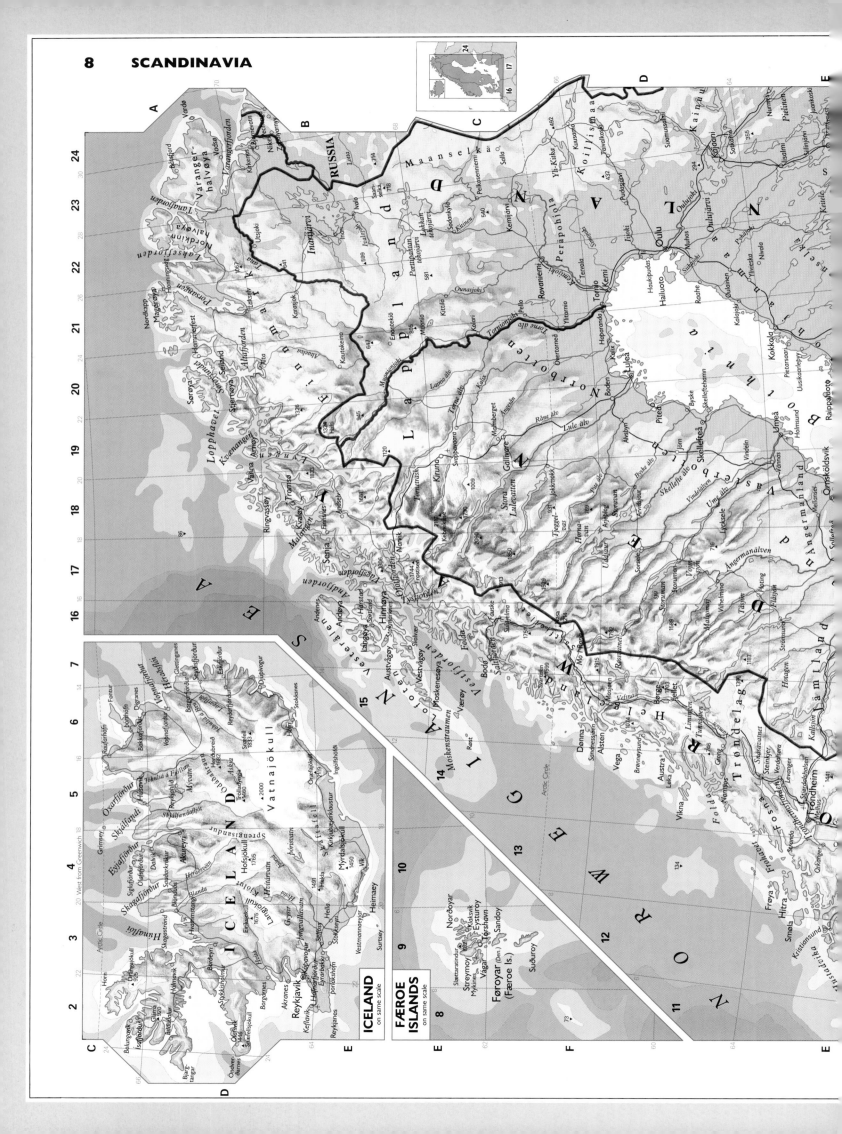

RUSSIA

F I N L A N D

L A P P L A N D

S W E D E N

N O R W A Y

I C E L A N D

ICELAND
on same scale

FÆROE ISLANDS
on same scale

Føroyar (Den.)
(Færoe Is.)

Reykjavik

Vatnajökull

Vestfjorden

Lofoten

Vesterålen

Trøndelag

Jämtland

Ångermanland

Norrbotten

Västerbotten

This map shows Scandinavia and the Baltic region, including Norway, Sweden, Finland, Denmark, Estonia, Latvia, Lithuania, and parts of Russia, Poland, and Germany.

1 : 5 000 000

50 · 0 · 50 · 100 miles
50 · 0 · 50 · 100 · 150 km

9

Projection: Conical with two standard parallels

East from Greenwich

F I N L A N D

E S T O N I A

L A T V I A

L I T H U A N I A

B A L T I C   S E A

Gulf of Finland

Gulf of Riga

Gulf of Bothnia

S W E D E N

N O R W A Y

D E N M A R K

G E R M A N Y

P O L A N D

Helsinki (Helsingfors)

Tallinn

Riga

Vilnius

Kaliningrad (Russia)

STOCKHOLM

KØBENHAVN (Copenhagen)

Oslo

Tampere

Skagerrak

Kattegat

Gotland

Öland

Bornholm

Åland (Ahvenanmaa)

Ålands hav

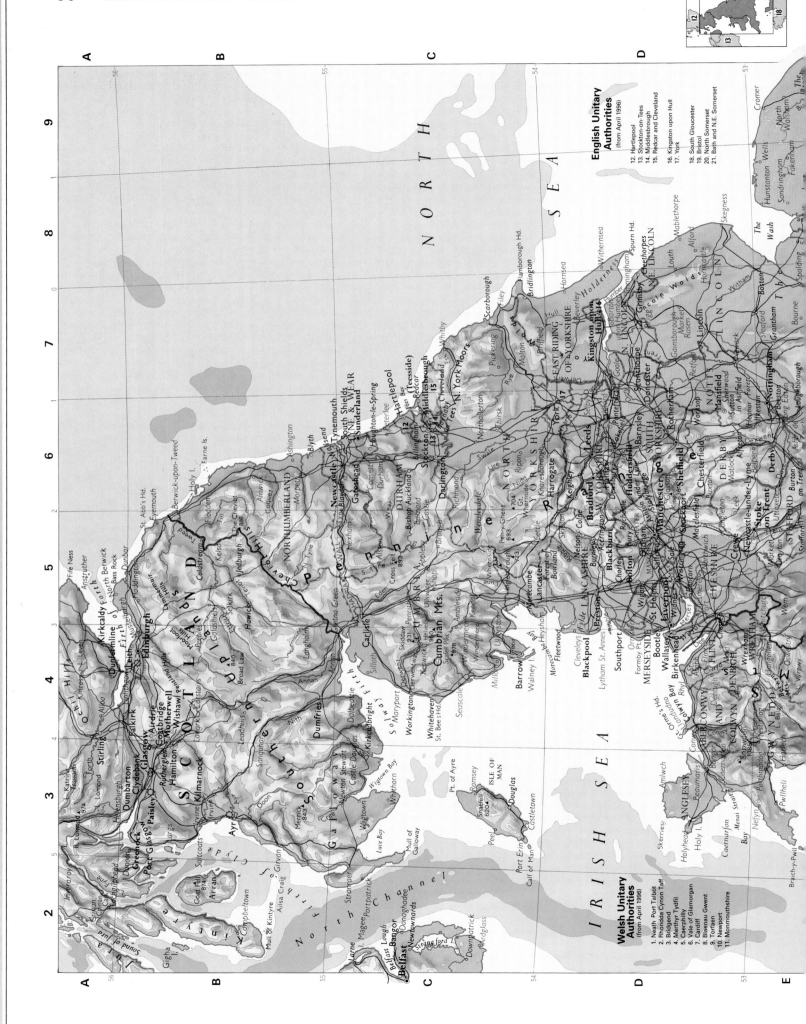

English Unitary Authorities
(from April 1996)

12. Hartlepool
13. Stockton-on-Tees
14. Middlesbrough
15. Redcar and Cleveland
16. Kingston upon Hull
17. York
18. South Gloucester
19. Bristol
20. North Somerset
21. Bath and N.E. Somerset

Welsh Unitary Authorities
(from April 1996)

1. Neath Port Talbot
2. Rhondda Cynon Taff
3. Merthyr Tydfil
4. Bridgend
5. Caerphilly
6. Vale of Glamorgan
7. Cardiff
8. Blaenau Gwent
9. Torfaen
10. Newport
11. Monmouthshire

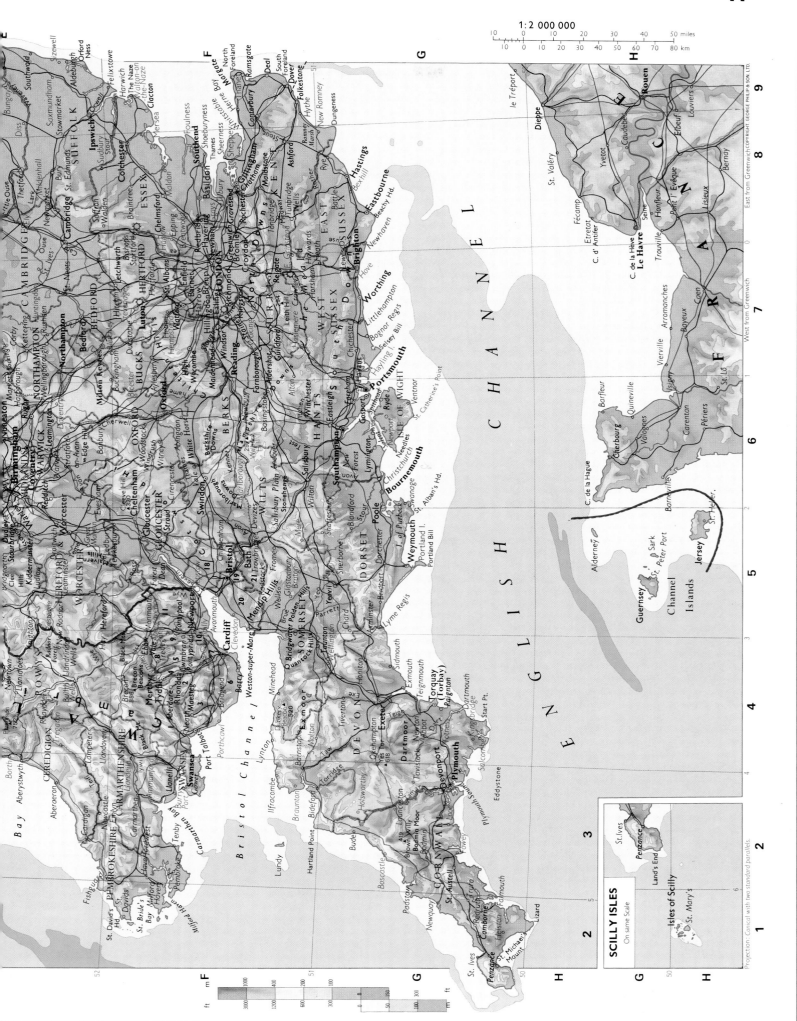

1:2 000 000

10   0   10   20   30   40   50 miles
10   0 10 20 30 40 50 60 70 80 km

Scottish Local Authorities
(From April 1996)

1. City of Aberdeen
2. Dundee City
3. West Dunbartonshire
4. East Dunbartonshire
5. City of Glasgow
6. Inverclyde
7. Renfrewshire
8. East Renfrewshire
9. North Lanarkshire
10. Falkirk
11. Clackmannan
12. West Lothian
13. City of Edinburgh
14. Midlothian

ORKNEY IS.
On same scale

Westray
Rousay
Eday
Sanday
Stronsay
Mainland
Stromness
Kirkwall
Shapinsay
ORKNEY
Hoy
Scapa Flow
South Ronaldsay
Pentland Firth
Dunnet Hd.
John o'Groats

SHETLAND IS.
On same scale

Unst
Fetlar
Yell
Yell Sound
Whalsay
SHETLAND
Mainland
Bressay
Scalloway
Lerwick
Foula
Sumburgh Hd.

Orkney Is.
Scapa Flow
South Ronaldsay
Hoy
Pentland Firth
Dunnet Hd.
Dounreay
Thurso
John o'Groats
Noss Hd.
Strathy Pt.
Halladale
Tongue
Wick
C. Wrath
Durness
Ben Hope 927
Lybster
Eddrachillis Bay
Reay Forest
L. Laxford
Naver
Butt of Lewis
Flannan Is.
Broad Bay
L. Roag
Stornoway
Eye Pen.
LEWIS
WESTERN ISLES
L. Seaforth
Tarbert
HARRIS
Lochinver
Enard Bay
B. More Assynt
L. Assynt
L. Shin
Lairg
Brora
Ord of Caithness
Helmsdale
Oykel
Golspie
Dornoch
Dornoch Firth
Tain
Tarbat Ness
Lossiemouth
Cullen
Portsoy
Banff
Macduff
Kinnaird's Head
Fraserburgh
Rattray Head
Peterhead
Buchan Ness
Ellon
Inverurie
Oldmeldrum
ABERDEENSHIRE
Aberdeen
Girdle Ness
Stonehaven
Inverbervie
Montrose
Brechin
Laurencekirk
Arbroath
Broughty Ferry
Dundee
North Sea
St. Andrews
Fife Ness
Anstruther
Buckhaven
Kirkcaldy
North Berwick
Bass Rock
Dunbar
St. Abb's Hd.
Eyemouth
Berwick-upon-Tweed
Holy I.
Flodden
The Cheviot 816
CHEVIOT HILLS
Coldstream
Kelso
Jedburgh
Hawick
Melrose
Galashiels
Selkirk
SOUTHERN UPLANDS
Broad Law
Moffat
Langholm
Lockerbie
Gretna Green
Annan
Carlisle
HADRIAN'S WALL
ENGLAND
Hexham
N. Tyne
Alston
Cross Fell 893
Penrith
Ullswater
Skiddaw 931
Workington
Solway Firth
DUMFRIES AND GALLOWAY
Dumfries
Castle Douglas
Dalbeattie
Kirkcudbright
Gatehouse of Fleet
Newton Stewart
Wigtown
Wigtown Bay
Whithorn
Luce Bay
Stranraer
Portpatrick
L. Ryan
Mull of Galloway
GALLOWAY
Merrick 843
SOUTH AYRSHIRE
Girvan
Ailsa Craig
Ballantrae
Dalmellington
Cumnock
Sanquhar
Leadhills
Biggar
Lanark
Carstairs
Peebles
Moorfoot Hills
Lammermuir Hills
Penicuik
Dalkeith
LOTHIAN
Musselburgh
Leith
EDINBURGH
Livingston
Bathgate
Linlithgow
Falkirk
Grangemouth
Alloa
Dunfermline
FIFE
Glenrothes
Cupar
Cowdenbeath
Kinross
L. Leven
KINROSS
Perth
Scone
Firth of Tay
Tayport
Crieff
Comrie
Callander
Dunblane
STIRLING
Stirling
Bannockburn
Denny
Cumbernauld
Kirkintilloch
Coatbridge
Airdrie
Motherwell
Wishaw
Hamilton
E. Kilbride
GLASGOW
Paisley
Johnstone
Rutherglen
Barrhead
Clydebank
Dumbarton
Port Glasgow
Greenock
Gourock
Helensburgh
NORTH AYRSHIRE
Irvine
Kilmarnock
SOUTH LANARKSHIRE
Troon
Prestwick
Ayr
EAST AYRSHIRE
Saltcoats
Ardrossan
Largs
Brodick
Arran
Goat Fell 874
Rothesay
Bute
Tarbert
Kintyre
Campbeltown
Mull of Kintyre
Gigha
Port Ellen
Bowmore
Islay
Jura
Sound of Jura
Rubh' a' Mhail
Colonsay
Crinan
Lochgilphead
Inveraray
L. Awe
L. Fyne
ARGYLL & BUTE
Oban
Firth of Lorn
Iona
Staffa
Mull
Ben More 966
Tobermory
Coll
Tiree
Pt. of Ardnamurchan
MORVERN
Ardgour
Ben Nevis 1343
Fort William
Glencoe
Ballachulish
Rannoch Moor
L. Rannoch
L. Tummel
Blair Atholl
Pitlochry
Pass of Killiecrankie
Forest of Atholl
Braemar
Lochnagar 1154
Ballater
Balmoral
Banchory
Aboyne
Alford
Tomintoul
Cairn Gorm
Cairn Toul 1291
Ben Macdhui 1311
Braes of Angus
Kirriemuir
Forfar
Blairgowrie
Alyth
Coupar Angus
Dunkeld
Aberfeldy
PERTH
Breadalbane
Ben Lawers 1214
L. Tay
Killin
Crianlarich
Ben More 1174
B. Vorlich 983
L. Earn
L. Katrine
Trossachs
Ben Lomond 974
L. Lomond
Dunoon
ATLANTIC OCEAN
NORTH CHANNEL
NORTHERN IRELAND
Belfast
Belfast Lough
Bangor
Newtownards
Larne
Ballymena
Ballycastle
Rathlin
Fair Hd.
Mull of Kintyre
Trostan 554
Rubha Hunish
Portree
Trotternish
Raasay
Rona
Scalpay
Kyle of Lochalsh
Cuillin Hills
Cuillin Sound
Canna
Rhum
Eigg
Muck
L. Moidart
Arisaig
Mallaig
Morar
L. Morar
L. Arkaig
L. Eil
Glenfinnan
LOCHABER
L. Garry
Glen Garry
Loch Ness
Fort Augustus
L. Oich
Newtonmore
Kingussie
Monadhliath Mts.
Aviemore
Grantown-on-Spey
BADENOCH
GRAMPIAN HIGHLANDS
Strathspey
Carrbridge
Nethy Bridge
Dufftown
Keith
Huntly
Turriff
BUCHAN
Deveron
MORAY
Rothes
Elgin
Forres
Nairn
Culloden Moor
Findhorn
Inverness
Beauly
Dingwall
Strathpeffer
Conon
Ben Wyvis 1045
Cromarty
Fortrose
Invergordon
Moray Firth
HIGHLAND
WEST HIGHLANDS
NORTH WEST HIGHLANDS
L. Maree
Gairloch
L. Gairloch
Poolewe
Ullapool
L. Broom
B. Dearg 1081
L. Fannich
Strome Ferry
L. Torridon
L. Carron
Glen Affric
Glen Moriston
Dornie
Hourn
L. Hourn
Glen Spean
Glen Roy
Sound of Sleat
Kyleakin
SKYE
L. Bracadale
Dunvegan
Sound of Harris
NORTH UIST
Lochmaddy
Benbecula
Monach Is.
SOUTH UIST
Lochboisdale
Ben More 620
Sound of Barra
Barra
Barra Hd.
OUTER HEBRIDES
INNER HEBRIDES
Little Minch
North Minch
Sound of Raasay
Inner Sound

Scale
ft   m
3000 1000
1200 400
600   200
300   100
0   0
50   150
100   300
m   ft

Projection: Conical with two standard parallels.

West from Greenwich

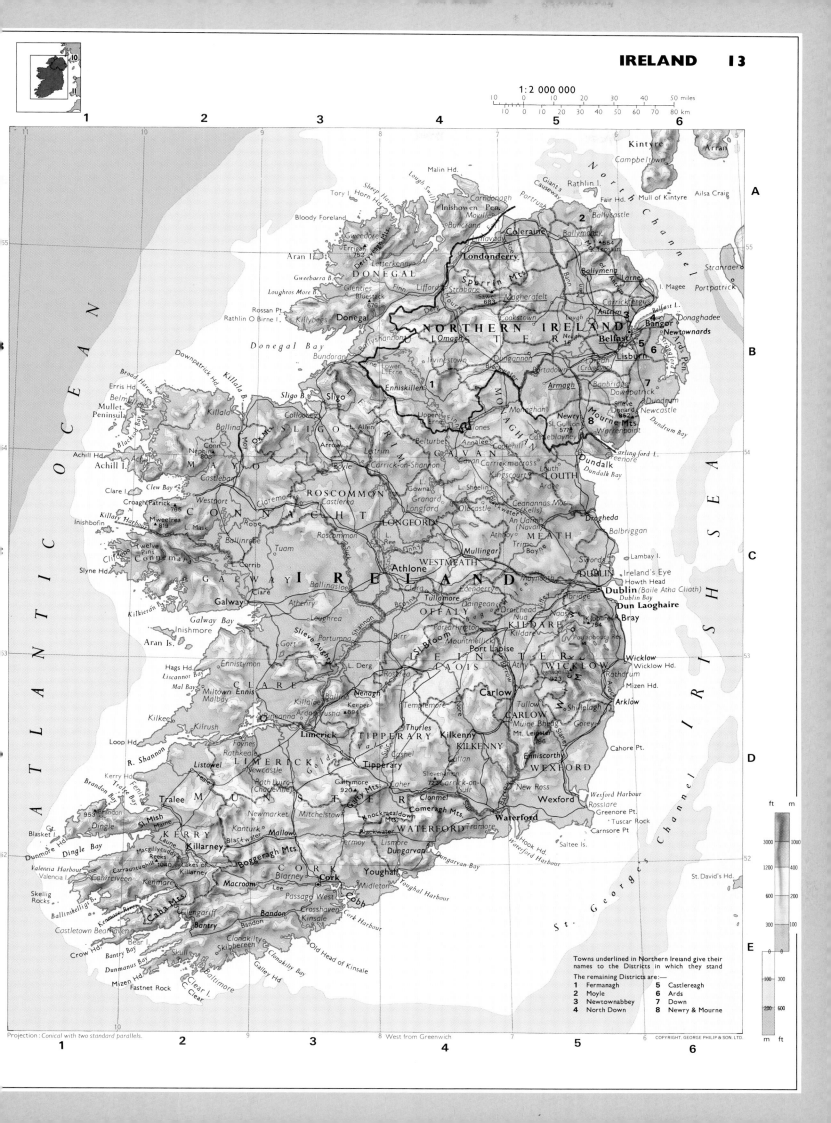

1:2 000 000

10   0   10   20   30   40   50 miles
10   0   10   20   30   40   50   60   70   80 km

Towns underlined in Northern Ireland give their
names to the Districts in which they stand

The remaining Districts are:—

1	Fermanagh	5	Castlereagh
2	Moyle	6	Ards
3	Newtownabbey	7	Down
4	North Down	8	Newry & Mourne

Projection : Conical with two standard parallels.

8 West from Greenwich   COPYRIGHT. GEORGE PHILIP & SON. LTD.

ft   m
3000 1000
1200 400
600   200
300   100
0   0
100   300
200   600
m ft

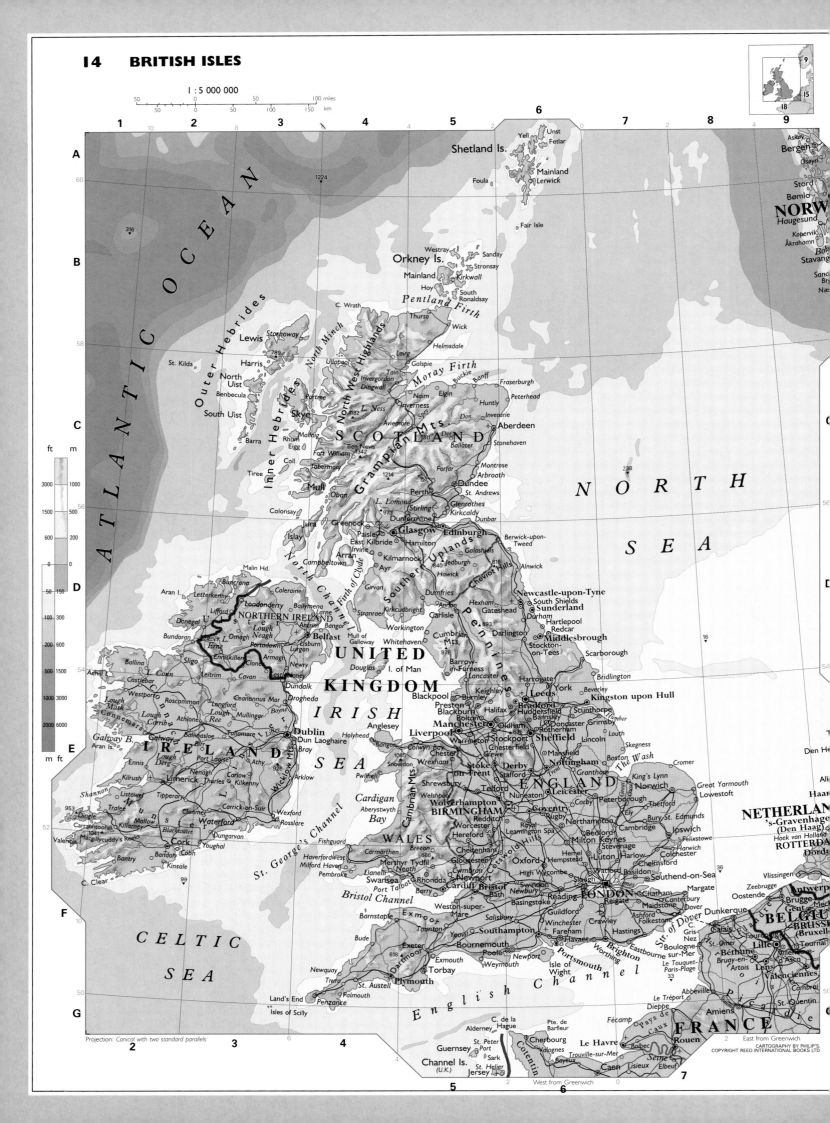

1 : 5 000 000

Projection: Conical with two standard parallels

CARTOGRAPHY BY PHILIP'S.
COPYRIGHT REED INTERNATIONAL BOOKS LTD

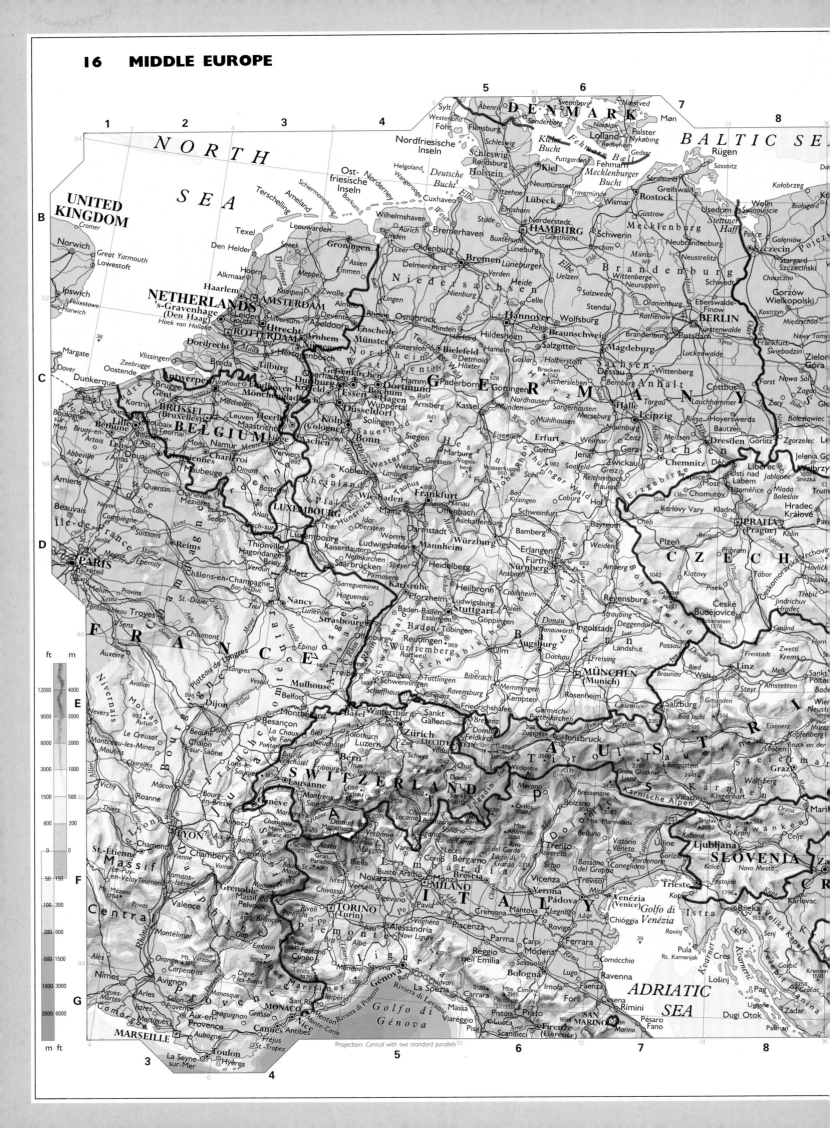

Map labels

NORTH SEA

BALTIC SEA

DENMARK

UNITED KINGDOM

NETHERLANDS

BELGIUM

LUXEMBOURG

GERMANY

FRANCE

SWITZERLAND

AUSTRIA

ITALY

SLOVENIA

CZECH

ADRIATIC SEA

Norwich · Cromer · Great Yarmouth · Lowestoft · Ipswich · Felixstowe · Harwich · Margate · Dover · Calais · Boulogne · Abbeville · Amiens · Beauvais · Paris · Créteil · Melun · Fontainebleau · Troyes · Sens · Auxerre · Avallon · Dijon · Nevers · Moulins · Vichy · Roanne · St-Étienne · Le-Puy-en-Velay · Lyon · Grenoble · Valence · Montélimar · Avignon · Nîmes · Arles · Marseille · Toulon · Hyères · La Seyne-sur-Mer · Nice · Cannes · Antibes · Monaco · Monte-Carlo

Den Helder · Amsterdam · Rotterdam · Utrecht · Haarlem · Leiden · Gouda · Hilversum · Apeldoorn · Arnhem · Nijmegen · Eindhoven · Breda · Tilburg · Antwerpen · Brugge · Gent · Brussel (Bruxelles) · Mechelen · Leuven · Liège · Namur · Charleroi · Mons · Maubeuge · Lille · Douai · Arras · Lens

Groningen · Leeuwarden · Assen · Emmen · Meppel · Zwolle · Enschede · Münster · Osnabrück · Bremen · Bremerhaven · Oldenburg · Wilhelmshaven · Emden · Hamburg · Lübeck · Kiel · Rostock · Schwerin · Hannover · Braunschweig · Wolfsburg · Magdeburg · Berlin · Potsdam · Frankfurt · Cottbus · Dresden · Leipzig · Halle · Chemnitz · Erfurt · Gera · Jena · Weimar · Gotha · Eisenach · Kassel · Göttingen · Paderborn · Bielefeld · Dortmund · Essen · Duisburg · Düsseldorf · Köln (Cologne) · Bonn · Aachen · Wuppertal · Bochum · Koblenz · Wiesbaden · Mainz · Frankfurt · Darmstadt · Mannheim · Heidelberg · Karlsruhe · Stuttgart · Pforzheim · Freiburg · München (Munich) · Augsburg · Ingolstadt · Regensburg · Nürnberg · Fürth · Würzburg · Bamberg · Bayreuth

Praha (Prague) · Plzeň · Liberec · Karlovy Vary · České Budějovice · Hradec Králové

Szczecin · Rügen · Kołobrzeg · Gorzów Wielkopolski · Zielona Góra

Basel · Zürich · Bern · Luzern · Genève · Lausanne · Neuchâtel · Interlaken · Chur · Innsbruck · Salzburg · Linz · Graz · Klagenfurt · Villach · Ljubljana

Milano · Torino (Turin) · Genova · Verona · Venézia (Venice) · Pádova · Bologna · Modena · Parma · Ferrara · Ravenna · Firenze (Florence) · Trieste · San Marino

Elevation scale

ft	m
12000	4000
9000	3000
6000	2000
3000	1000
1500	500
600	200
0	0
150	50
300	100
600	200
1500	500
3000	1000
6000	2000

m ft

Projection: Conical with two standard parallels

1:5 000 000

50   0   50   100 miles

50   0   50   100   150 km

LITHUANIA

BELARUS

POLAND

UKRAINE

SLOVAK REP.

HUNGARY

ROMANIA

MOLDOVA

YUGOSLAVIA

BULGARIA

BOSNIA-HERZEGOVINA

C. P.

Zatoka Gdańska

Kaliningrad (Russia)

Vilnius

MINSK

Warszawa (Warsaw)

KYYIV (Kiev)

BUDAPEST

BUCUREŞTI (Bucharest)

Beograd (Belgrade)

Bratislava

Sarajevo

Wejherowo, Rumia, Gdynia, Sopot, Gdańsk, Tczew, Elbląg, Braniewo, Gvardeysk, Chernyakhovsk, Gusev, Prienai, Marijampolė, Vileyka, Maladzyechna, Barysaw, Krupki, Shklow, Mstsislaw, Krychaw

Lębork, Bytów, Kościerzyna, Starogard Gdański, Malbork, Kwidzyn, Iława, Ostróda, Olsztyn, Kętrzyn, Gižycko, Suwałki, Augustów, Druskininkai, Varėna, Lida, Navahrudak, Valozhyn, Zhodzina, Cherven, Byhaw, Bykhaw, Cherykaw, Slawharad

Bydgoszcz, Toruń, Chełmno, Grudziądz, Brodnica, Rypin, Mława, Działdowo, Szczytno, Ełk, Łomza, Sokółka, Białystok, Hrodna, Masty, Vawkavysk, Slonim, Baranavichy, Klyetsk, Slutsk, Salihorsk, Babruysk, Zhlobin, Homyel, Dobrush

Inowrocław, Gniezno, Września, Włocławek, Płock, Ciechanów, Pułtusk, Ostrołęka, Ostrów Mazowiecka, Bielsk Podlaski, Pruzhany, Bereza, Yatselda, Luninyets, Pyetrykaw, Mazyr, Kalinkavichy, Loyew, Khoyniki, Rechytsa, Vasilevichy

Konin, Koło, Kutno, Łowicz, Legionowo, Mińsk Mazowiecki, Otwock, Siedlce, Łuków, Międzyrzec Podlaski, Biała Podlaska, Brest, Malaryta, Zhabinka, Kobryn, Dragichyn, Ivanava, Pinsk, Stolin, Davyd Haradok, Uborf, Yelsk, Ovruch, Chornobyl

Kalisz, Ostrów Wielkopolski, Sieradz, Zduńska Wola, Pabianice, Łódź, Tomaszów Mazowiecki, Radom, Puławy, Włodawa, Kamin-Kashyrskyy, Dubrovytsya, Olevsk, Belokorovichi, Novohrad-Volynskyy, Radomyshl, Malyn, Korosten, Oster

Wrocław, Oława, Kluczbork, Opole, Częstochowa, Piotrków Trybunalski, Radomsko, Skarżysko-Kamienna, Starachowice, Kielce, Ostrowiec Świętokrzyski, Lublin, Świdnik, Chełm, Novovolynsk, Lyuboml, Kovel, Staryy Chartoriysk, Rozhyshche, Kostopil, Sluch, Zhytomyr, Korostyshev, Kyyivske Vdskh., Dymer, Irpin, Vasylkiv

Oleśnica, Nysa, Brzeg, Tarnowskie Góry, Bytom, Zabrze, Gliwice, Chorzów, Katowice, Sosnowiec, Myszków, Zawiercie, Jędrzejów, Pińczów, Sandomierz, Stalowa Wola, Kraśnik, Zamość, Rava-Ruska, Volodymyr-Volynskyy, Oleksandriya, Kivertsi, Lutsk, Rivne, Zdolbuniv, Dubno, Ostroh, Slavuta, Shepetivka, Polonne, Berdychiv, Bila Tserkva

Racibórz, Opava, Ostrava, Havířov, Frýdek-Místek, Přerov, Zlín, Bielsko-Biała, Żywiec, Oświęcim, Kraków, Bochnia, Tarnów, Dębica, Mielec, Rzeszów, Jarosław, Przemyśl, Jasło, Krosno, Sanok, Yavoriv, Mostyska, Horodok, Lviv (Lvov), Zolochiv, Zbarazh, Ternopil, Skalat, Khmelnytskyy, Vinnytsya, Kozyatyn, Skvyra, Tarashcha

Trenčín, Považská Bystrica, Žilina, Martin, Ružomberok, Poprad, Prešov, Humenné, Nowy Sącz, Nowy Targ, Zakopane, Bardejov, Michalovce, Uzhhorod, Ivano-Frankivsk, Nadvirna, Kolomyya, Snyatyn, Chortkiv, Skala-Podilska, Kamyanets-Podilskyy, Mohyliv-Podilskyy, Bershad, Zhmerynka, Tulchyn, Vapnyarka, Balta, Uman, Haysyn

Bielé Karpaty, Nízke Tatry, Banská Bystrica, Zvolen, Prievidza, Topol'čany, Levice, Lučenec, Košice, Sátoraljaújhely, Chop, Mukacheve, Berehove, Khust, Vynohradiv, Rakhiv, Yasinya, Chernivtsi, Storozhynets, Hlyboka, Novoselytsya, Lipcani, Drochia, Soroca, Floreşti, Ananyiv, Kotovsk

Bratislava, Nové Zámky, Nitra, Komárno, Vác, Salgótarján, Ózd, Miskolc, Eger, Mezőkövesd, Hajdúböszörmény, Nyíregyháza, Satu Mare, Sighetu-Marmaţiei, Borşa, Vatra-Dornei, Rădăuţi, Suceava, Botoşani, Dorohoi, Edineţa, Bălţi, Făleşti, Orhei, Dubăsari, Rîbniţa, Camenca

Mosonmagyaróvár, Győr, Tatabánya, Esztergom, Dunakeszi, Érd, Székesfehérvár, Budapest, Cegléd, Szolnok, Mezőtúr, Karcag, Debrecen, Baia Mare, Carei, Zalău, Dej, Bistriţa, Piatra Neamţ, Roman, Iaşi, Ungheni, Chişinău, Tiraspol, Tighina, Rozdilna

Pápa, Veszprém, Ajka, Dunaújváros, Kecskemét, Kiskunfélegyháza, Nagykőrös, Békéscsaba, Oradea, Salonta, Cluj-Napoca, Turda, Reghin, Tîrgu Mureş, Bacău, Bîrlad, Vaslui, Huşi, Leova, Comrat, Cimişlia, Basarabeasca, Bilhorod-Dnistrovskyy

Nagykanizsa, Kaposvár, Pécs, Szekszárd, Baja, Kiskunhalas, Kiskőrös, Kalocsa, Szentes, Szeged, Makó, Gyula, Oroszháza, Hódmezővásárhely, Arad, Deva, Alba-Iulia, Sibiu, Sighişoara, Mediaş, Tîrnăveni, Odorheiu Secuiesc, Miercurea Ciuc, Sfîntu Gheorghe, Oneşti, Tecuci, Cahul, Vulcăneşti, Bolhrad, Tatarbunary, Artsyz

Subotica, Senta, Kikinda, Timişoara, Lugoj, Caransebeş, Reşiţa, Hunedoara, Simeria, Brad, Abrud, Petroşani, Cîmpulung, Braşov, Săcele, Făgăraş, Rîmnicu Vîlcea, Focşani, Rîmnicu Sărat, Galaţi, Brăila, Reni, Izmayil, Kiliya, Sulina

Sombor, Novi Sad, Petrovaradin, Zrenjanin, Vršac, Vojvodina, Bela Crkva, Vulcan, Porta Orientalis, Tîrgu-Jiu, Curtea de Argeş, Rîmnicu Vîlcea, Tîrgovişte, Ploieşti, Buzău, Slobozia, Feteşti, Călăraşi, Medgidia, Năvodari, Constanţa, Mangalia

Osijek, Vukovar, Vinkovci, Slavonski Brod, Bosanska Gradiška, Doboj, Tuzla, Bijeljina, Brčko, Šabac, Zemun, Pančevo, Smederevo, Požarevac, Dobreta-Turnu-Severin, Orşova, Craiova, Slatina, Caracal, Roşiori-de-Vede, Alexandria, Giurgiu, Ruse, Silistra, Tutrakan, Olteniţa, Dobrich, Balchik

Zenica, Travnik, Han Pijesak, Srebrnica, Titovo Užice, Valjevo, Kragujevac, Čačak, Kraljevo, Zaječar, Negotin, Bor, Vidin, Lom, Oryakhovo, Corabia, Turnu Măgurele, Zimnicea, Nikopol, Razgrad, Varna, Nos Kaliakra

Sarajevo, Visegrad, Svetozarevo, Kruševac, Bǎileşti

Lacul Razelm, Ozero Sasyk, Vylkove, Babadag, Tulcea

Mures, Criş, Olt, Dunărea (Danube), Sava, Drava, Tisza, Vistula, Dniester, Pripet, Buh, Nistru (Dniester), Prut, Siret

CARTOGRAPHY BY PHILIP'S. COPYRIGHT REED INTERNATIONAL BOOKS LTD

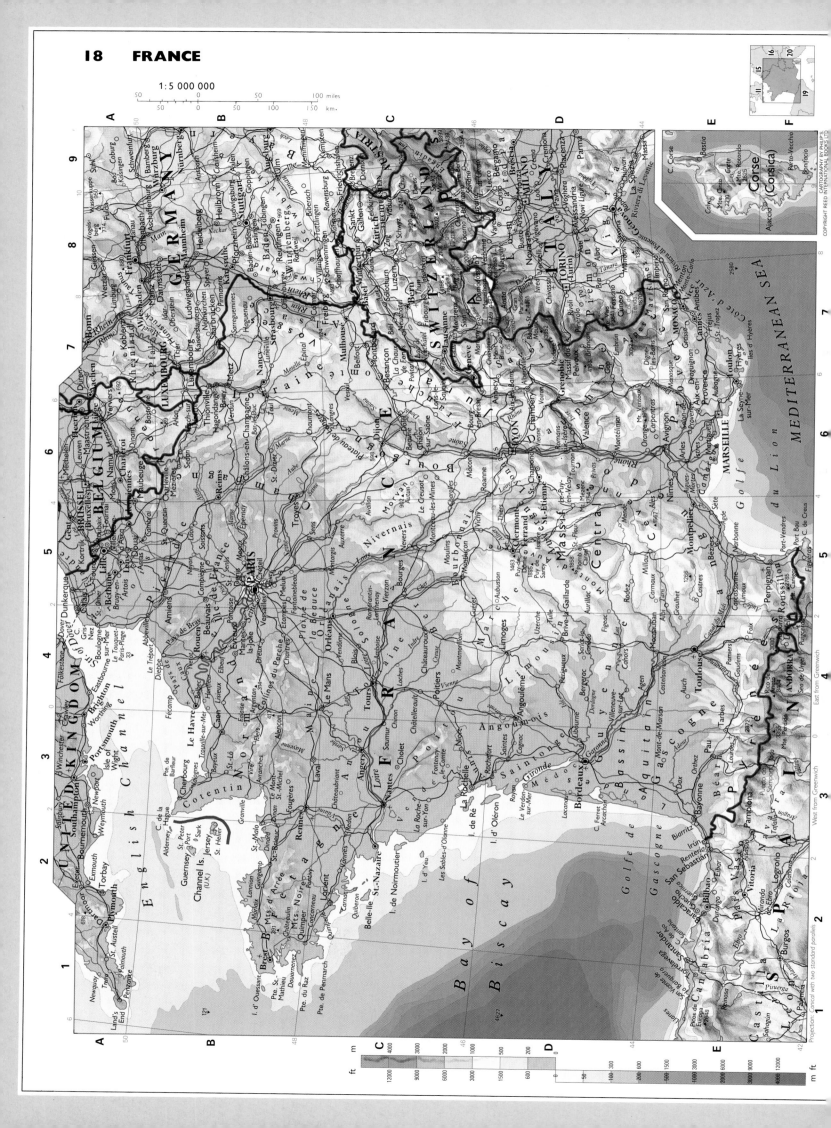

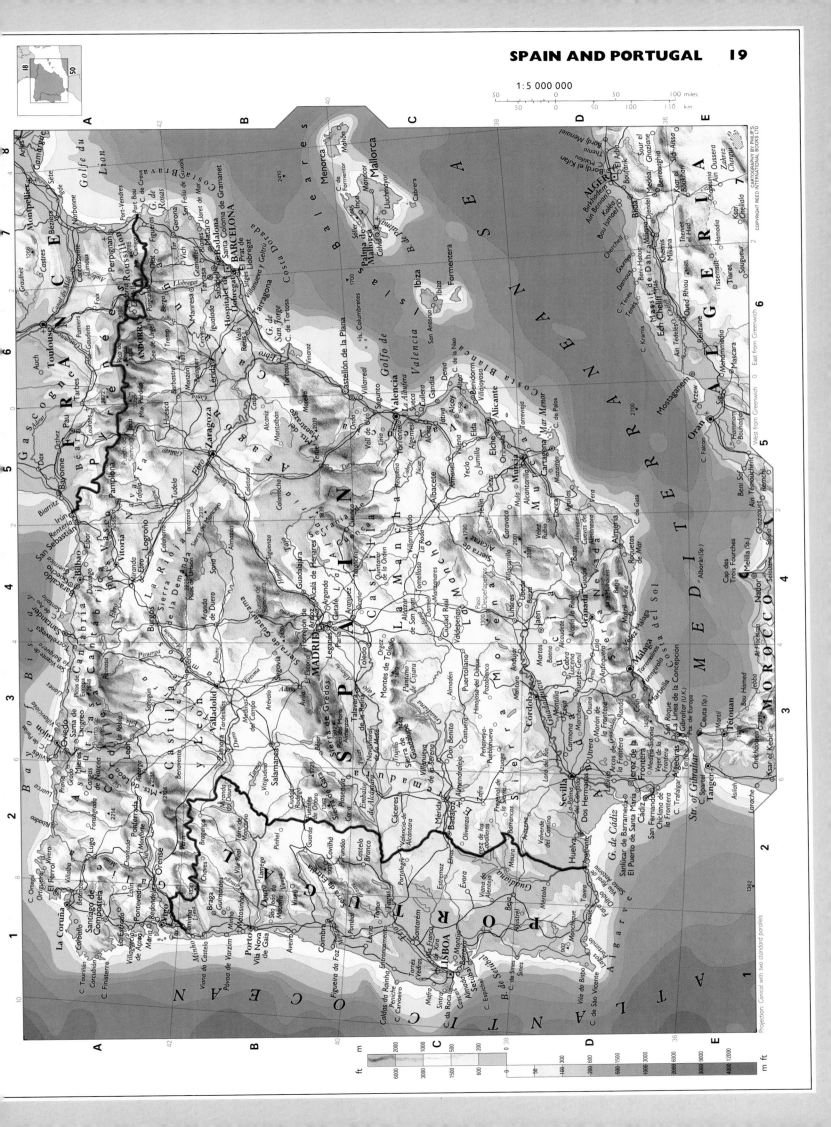

1 : 5 000 000

Projection: Conical with two standard parallels

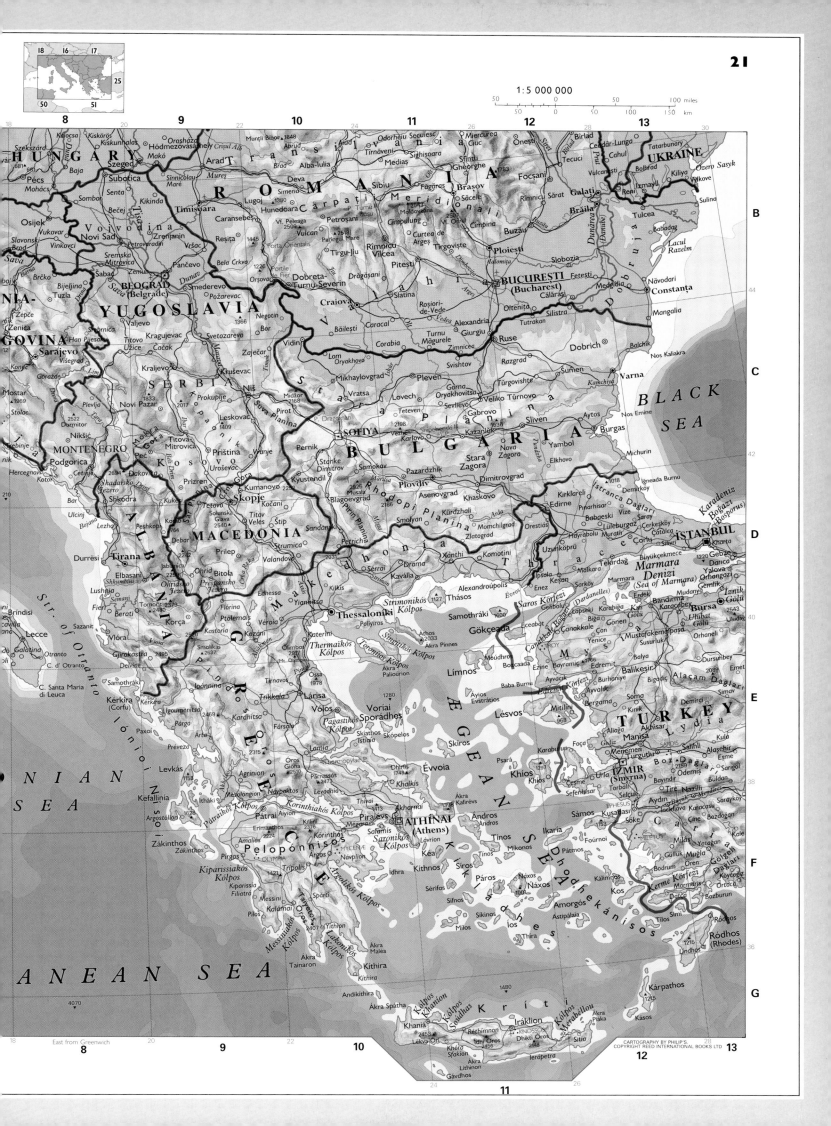

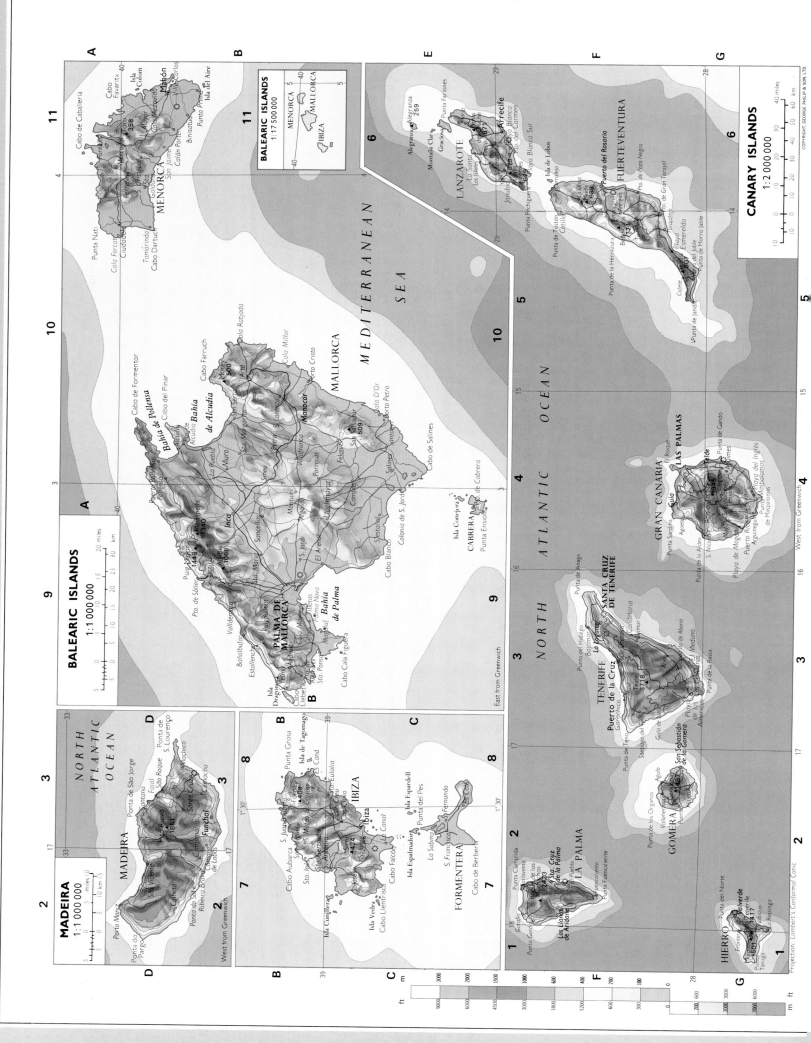

BALEARIC ISLANDS
1:17 500 000

MENORCA

MALLORCA

IBIZA

MEDITERRANEAN SEA

MENORCA

Cabo de Caballeria
Cabo Favaritx
Isla Colom
Mahón
Villa Carlos
Punta Prima
Isla del Aire
Fornells
Mercadal
Alayor
358
Cala Mezquida
Galdana
San Jaime
San Cristobal
Cala Portera
Binisafua
Punta Nati
Cala Forcat
Ciudadela
Tamaranda
Cabo Dartuct
Caldn Portens

MALLORCA

Cabo de Formentor
Cabo del Pinar
Cabo Farruch
Cala Ratjada
Artá
Cala Millor
Porto Cristo
Cabo D'Or
Cabo Petro
Cabo de Salines
Cabo Blanco
Monte 500
Pto. de Sóller
Puig Mayor 1445
1338
Inca
1068
La Puebla
Muro
Sta. Margarita
Pedro S. Llorenzo
Manacor
San Servera
Felanitx
Salvador 509
Porreras
Villafranca
Campos
Salinas
S. Jordi
El Arenal
Montuiri
Algaida
Sancellas
Sineu
La Puebla
Bahía de Alcudia
Bahía de Pollensa
Alcudia
Pto. Pollensa
PALMA DE MALLORCA
Bahía de Palma
Andraitx
Sta. Ponsa
Cabo Cala Figuera
Estellenchs
Bañalbufar
Valldemosa
Isla Dragonera
Lluchmayor

BALEARIC ISLANDS
1:1 000 000

CABRERA
Isla Conejera
Colonia de S. Jordi
Punta Ensiola
Isla de Cabrera

MADEIRA
1:1 000 000

NORTH ATLANTIC OCEAN

MADEIRA
Porto Mnz
Ponta do Sol
Ponta do Pargo
Ribeira Brava
Calheta
São Vicente
Santana
Faial
São Roque
Ponta de S. Lourenço
Ponta de São Jorge
Machico
Camacha
Funchal
Santa Cruz
Câmara de Lobos
Pco. Ruivo 1861
West from Greenwich

IBIZA

Punta Grosa
Isla de Tagomago
Punta de Tagomago
S. Carlos
Sta. Eulalia
IBIZA
S. Juan
Portinatx
S. Miguel
S. Antonio
409
S. Mateo
S. Rafael
452?
S. José
Cala Llonga
S. Agustin
Isla Cunillera
Cabo Aubarca
Isla Vedra
Cabo Llentrisca
Isla Espardell
Punta del Pes
Isla Espalmador
S. Francisco
S. Fernando
La Sabina
FORMENTERA
Cabo Berberia
Cabo Falcó

CANARY ISLANDS
1:2 000 000

COPYRIGHT GEORGE PHILIP & SON LTD

LANZAROTE
Alegranza 259
Montaña Clara
Graciosa
Punta Fariones
Arrecife
Pto. del Carmen
Playa Blanca
Isla de Lobos
Punta Pechiguera
Los Islotes

FUERTEVENTURA
Puerto del Rosario
La Oliva 688
Pto. de Gran Tarajal
Punta de Toston
Cotillo
Corralejo
Punta de la Herradura
Pto. de Pozo Negro
807
Punta de Morro Jable
Cofete
Playa de Jandia
Punta de Jandia

GRAN CANARIA
LAS PALMAS
El Roque
Teide
1950
Guía
Punta Sardina
Punta de Gando
Telde
S. Nicolas
Playa del Inglés
Agaete
Punta de Maspalomas
Maspalomas
Puerto Rico
Punta de la Aldea

TENERIFE
SANTA CRUZ DE TENERIFE
La Laguna
Puerto de la Cruz
Teide 3718
Punta de Anaga
Punta de Hidalgo
Bajamar
Candelaria
Güimar
Garachico
Punta de Teno
Guía de Isora
Isla de Abona
Punta de la Rasca
Playa de las Américas

GOMERA
SAN SEBASTIÁN DE LA GOMERA
1146
Agulo
Vallehermoso
Puerto de los Organos
Valle Gran Rey

LA PALMA
SANTA CRUZ DE LA PALMA
Roque de los Muchachos 2423
Punta Cumplida
Barlovento
Los Llanos de Aridane
Fuencaliente
Punta Gorda

HIERRO
VALVERDE
Frontera 1417
Punta del Norte
Restinga
Tanojo

NORTH ATLANTIC OCEAN

MEDITERRANEAN SEA

ft   m
9000 3000
6000 2000
4500 1500
3000 1000
1800   600
1200   400
600   200
300   100
0   0

ft   m
600   200
3000   1000
6000   2000

Projection: Lambert's Conformal Conic

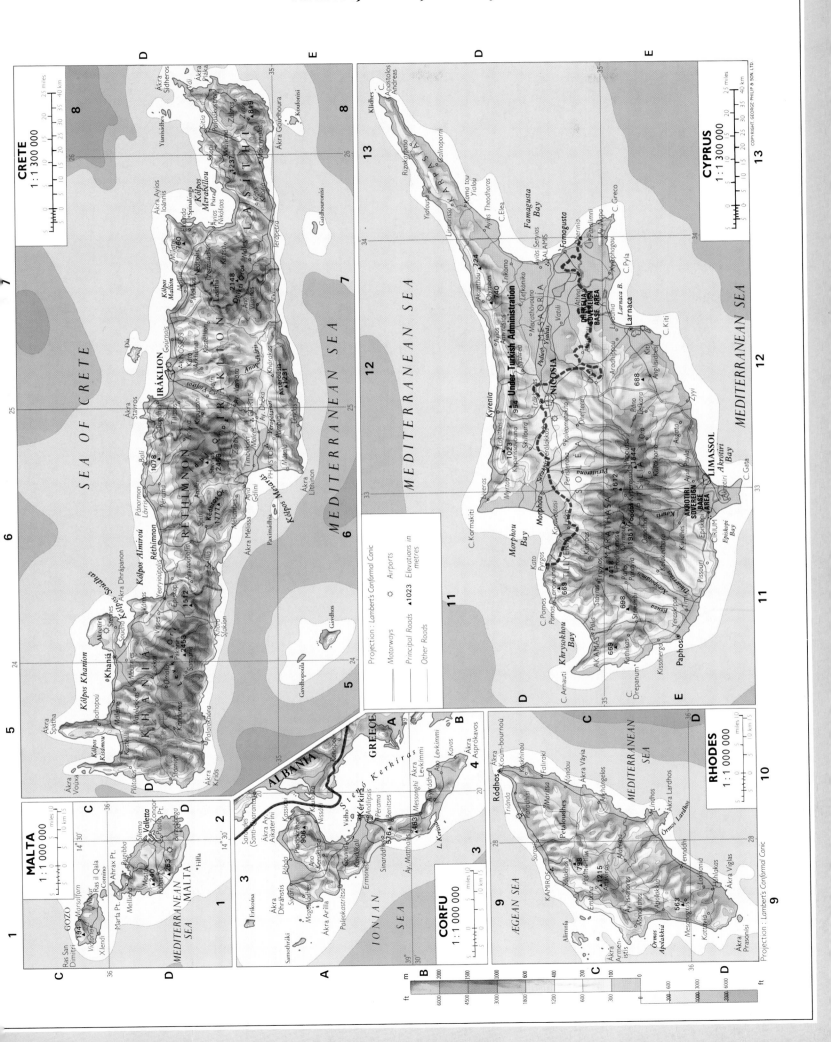

CRETE
1:1 300 000

MALTA
1:1 000 000

CORFU
1:1 000 000

CYPRUS
1:1 300 000

RHODES
1:1 000 000

SEA OF CRETE

MEDITERRANEAN SEA

IRÁKLION

KHANIÁ

Réthimnon

RÉTHIMNON

LASÍTHI

Díkti Óros

IONIAN SEA

ALBANIA

GREECE

Kérkira

AEGEAN SEA

Ródhos

NICOSIA

Famagusta

Larnaca

LIMASSOL

Paphos

Kyrenia

Morphou Bay

Famagusta Bay

Larnaca B.

Akrotiri Bay

Episkopi Bay

Under Turkish Administration

DHEKELIA SOVEREIGN BASE AREA

AKROTIRI SOVEREIGN BASE AREA

Projection: Lambert's Conformal Conic

Motorways

Airports

Principal Roads

▲1023 Elevations in metres

Other Roads

COPYRIGHT GEORGE PHILIP & SON LTD

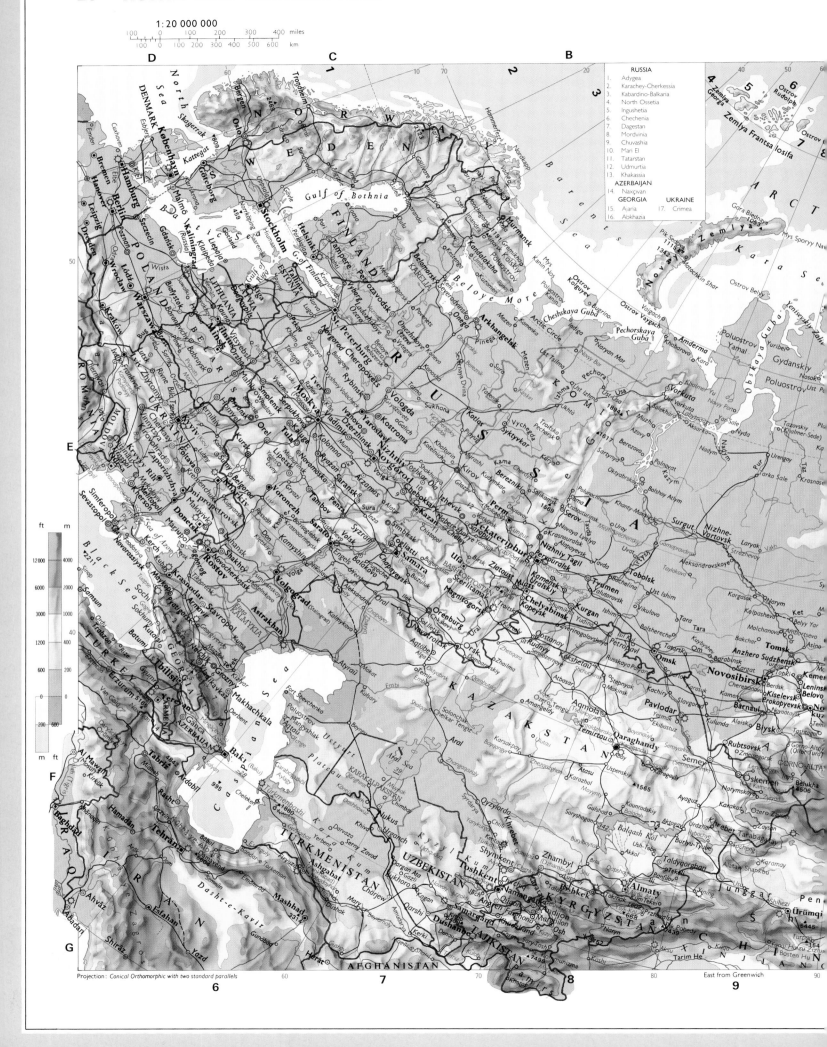

1:20 000 000

100 0 100 200 300 400 miles
100 0 100 200 300 400 500 600 km

| RUSSIA |
| 1. Adygea |
| 2. Karachey-Cherkessia |
| 3. Kabardino-Balkana |
| 4. North Ossetia |
| 5. Ingushetia |
| 6. Chechenia |
| 7. Dagestan |
| 8. Mordvinia |
| 9. Chuvashia |
| 10. Mari El |
| 11. Tatarstan |
| 12. Udmurtia |
| 13. Khakassia |
| AZERBAIJAN |
| 14. Naxçivan |
| GEORGIA   UKRAINE |
| 15. Ajaria   17. Crimea |
| 16. Abkhazia |

Projection: Conical Orthomorphic with two standard parallels

East from Greenwich

A   B   C

19

Mys Dezhneva
(East C.)

Chukchi
Sea

Ostrov Vrangelya
Ostrov Vrangelya

St. Lawrence I.
(U.S.A.)

D

Bering
Sea

OCEAN

Laptev Sea

East Siberian Sea

Novosibirskiye Ostrova

Severnaya
Zemlya

Ostrov Shmidta
Ostrov Pioner

Mys Arkticheskiy

Ostrov Komsomolets

Ostrov Oktyabrskoy
Revolyutsii

Ostrov Bolshevik

965

Poluostrov
Taymyr

Goryy
Byrranga

1146

Nordvik

Oz. Taymyr

Ostrov Bolshoy
Begichev

Tiksi

E

Zaliv
Shelikhova

Sea of
Okhotsk

Poluostrov
Kamchatka

Petropavlovsk-
Kamchatskiy

Sakhalin

Nikolayevsk
na-Am.

Komsomolsk

Khabarovsk

Sovetskaya
Gavan

Yuzhno-Sakhalinsk

Kurilskiye Ostrova

Hokkaido

Sapporo

Hakodate

R U S S I A

YAKUTSK

Verkhoyansk

Khrebet Cherskogo

Srednekolymsk

Kolyma

Magadan

Okhotsk

Arctic Circle

962

Vilyuysk

Yakutsk

Olekminsk

Vitim

Stanovoy Khrebet

Krasnoyarsk

Bratsk

Nizhneudinsk

Angarsk

Irkutsk

Ulan Ude

Chita

Blagoveshchensk

Birobidzhan

Hiamusi

Ussuriysk

Vladivostok

Nakhodka

Sea of
Japan

JAPAN

Honshū

Kanazawa

Toyama

Niigata

F

M O N G O L I A

Ulaanbaatar
(Ulan Bator)

Hangayn Nuruu

Hentiyn Nuruu

2800

Qiqihar

Harbin

Jilin

Changchun

Siping

Fushun

Shenyang

Anshan

NORTH
KOREA

Wŏnsan

P'yŏngyang

Dalian

SOUTH KOREA

Sŏul

Inch'ŏn

Taejŏn

Taegu

Pusan

Da Hinggan Ling

S E R E P U B L I C

G O B I

Hohhot

Baotou

Zhangjiakou

Beijing

Yingkou

Qingdao

Boundaries of
Republics

COPYRIGHT. GEORGE PHILIP & SON. LTD.

10   11   12   13   14

1:50 000 000

250   0   250   500   750   1000 miles
250   0   500   1000   1500 km

ARCTIC OCEAN

PACIFIC OCEAN

ATLANTIC OCEAN

INDIAN OCEAN

Greenland
Iceland
Norwegian Sea
Scandinavia
Svalbard
Novaya Zemlya
Severnaya Zemlya
Franz Josef Land
C. Chelyuskin
Taimyr Peninsula
Kara Sea
Barents Sea
White Sea
Kola Pen.
North Cape
Arctic Circle
British Isles
North Sea
Baltic Sea
Finland
Europe
North European Plain
Central Russian Uplands
Ural Mts.
West Siberian Plain
Central Siberian Plateau
Verkhoyansk Ra.
Cherski Ra.
Kolyma Ra.
New Siberian Is.
Wrangel I.
Chukot Pen.
Bering Strait
C. Dezhnev
Koryak Ra.
Kamchatka Pen.
Sredinny Ra.
Sea of Okhotsk
Sakhalin
Bering Sea
Aleutian Is.
Alaska
C. Alaska

Yenisei
Ob
Irtysh
Tobol
Ural
Don
Danube
Carpathians
Alps
Adriatic Sea
Mediterranean Sea
Cyprus
Anatolia
Taurus Mts.
Pontic Mts.
Black Sea
Caucasus
Elbruz
Bosporus
Caspian Sea
Elburz Mts.
Damavend
Zagros
Plateau of Iran
Hindu Kush
Karakoram Ra.
Pamirs
Tien Shan
Tarim Basin
Turfan Basin
Takla Makan
Lop Nor
Altai
Plateau of Mongolia
Sayan Mts.
Yablonovyy Ra.
Stanovoy Ra.
Amur
Manchurian Plain
Great Khingan Mts.
Sikhote Alin Ra.
Sea of Japan
Korea
Hokkaido
Honshu
Shikoku
Kyushu
Kuril Is.
Japan
Yellow Sea
East China Sea
Hwang
Great Plain of China
Si Kiang
Hainan
Taiwan
Ryukyu Is.
Luzon
Philippines
Mindanao
Mindanao Trench
Celebes Sea
Sulu Sea
Borneo
Palawan
South China Sea
Gulf of Tonkin
Mekong
Indo-China
Gulf of Thailand
Chao Phraya
Malay Pen.
Str. of Malacca
Isthmus of Kra
Sumatra
Java
Java Sea
Bali
Sunda Is.
Sumbawa
Sumba
Flores
Timor
Timor Sea
Arafura Sea
New Guinea
Australia
Molucca Sea
Halmahera
Ceram
Banda Sea
Celebes
Indonesia
Guam
Caroline Is.
Belau

Himalaya
Mt. Everest
Kunlun
Plateau of Tibet
Brahmaputra
Ganges
Yamuna
India
Thar Desert
Narmada
Western Ghats
Eastern Ghats
Bay of Bengal
Andaman Is.
Nicobar Is.
Ceylon
Palk Strait
Dondra Head
C. Comorin
Maldives
Lakshadweep Is.
Chagos Arch.
Indus
Sulaiman Ra.
Arabian Sea
The Gulf
Tigris
Euphrates
Mesopotamia
Syrian Desert
Arabia
Rub' al Khali (Empty Quarter)
An Nafud
Middle East
Dead Sea
Sinai
Red Sea
Nile
G. of Aden
Socotra
Ras Asir
Somali Pen.
Africa
Ethiopian Highlands
Libyan Desert
Equator
Tropic of Cancer
Amirante Is.
Seychelles
L. Victoria
L. Tanganyika
L. Malawi

East of Greenwich

Projection: Bonne 30

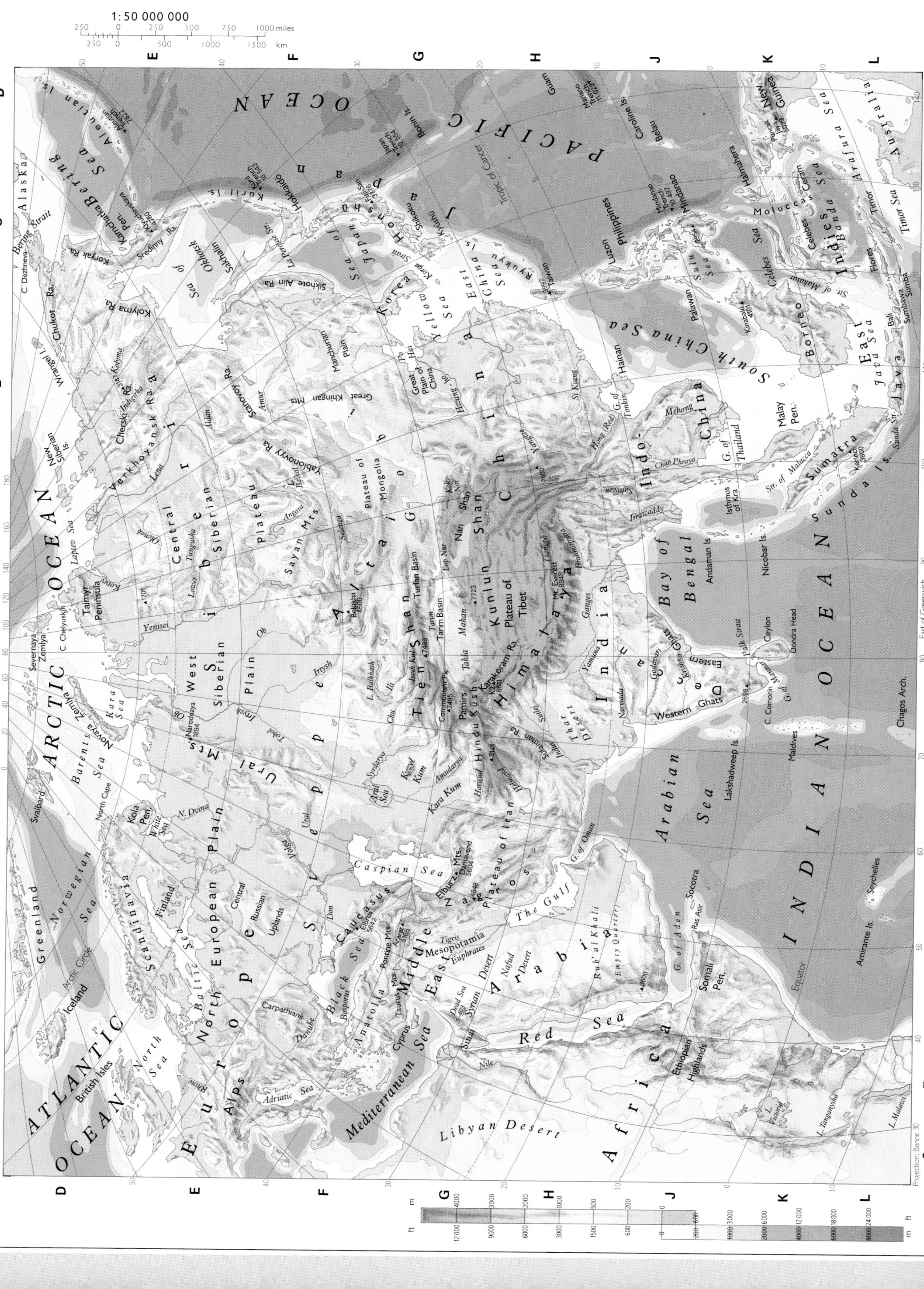

CARTOGRAPHY BY PHILIPS COPYRIGHT REED INTERNATIONAL BOOKS LTD.

ft   m
4000
3000
2000
1000
500
200
0
200–600
600–3000
3000–6000
6000–12 000
12 000–18 000
18 000–24 000

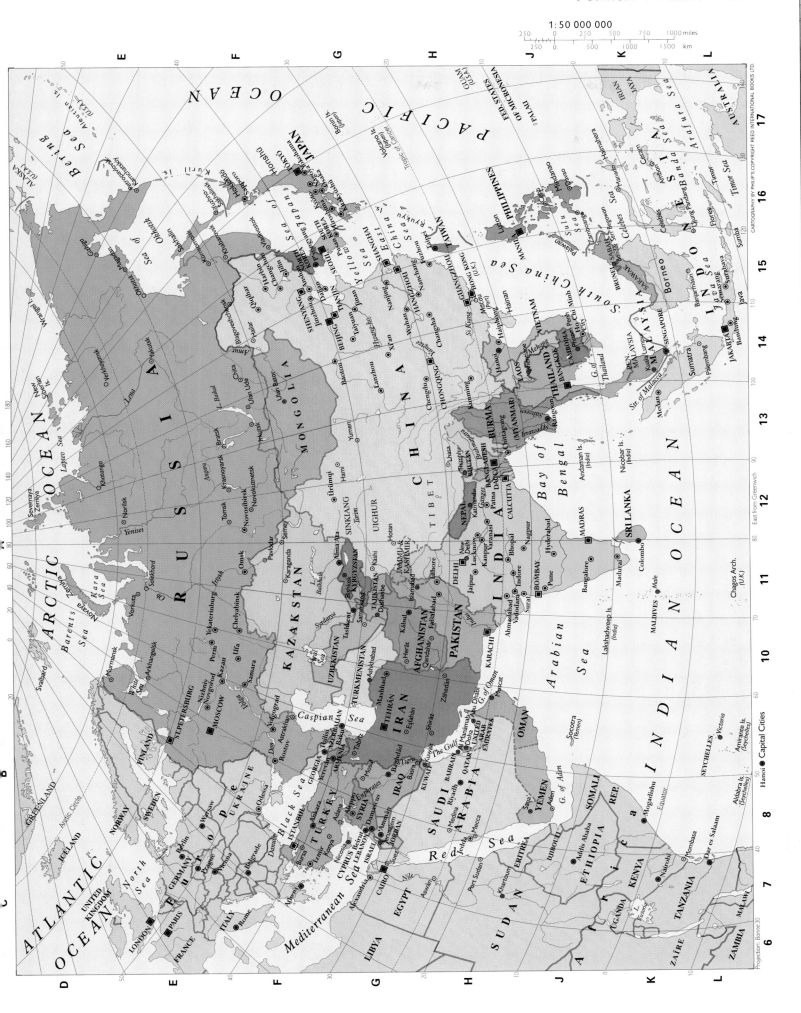

1 : 50 000 000

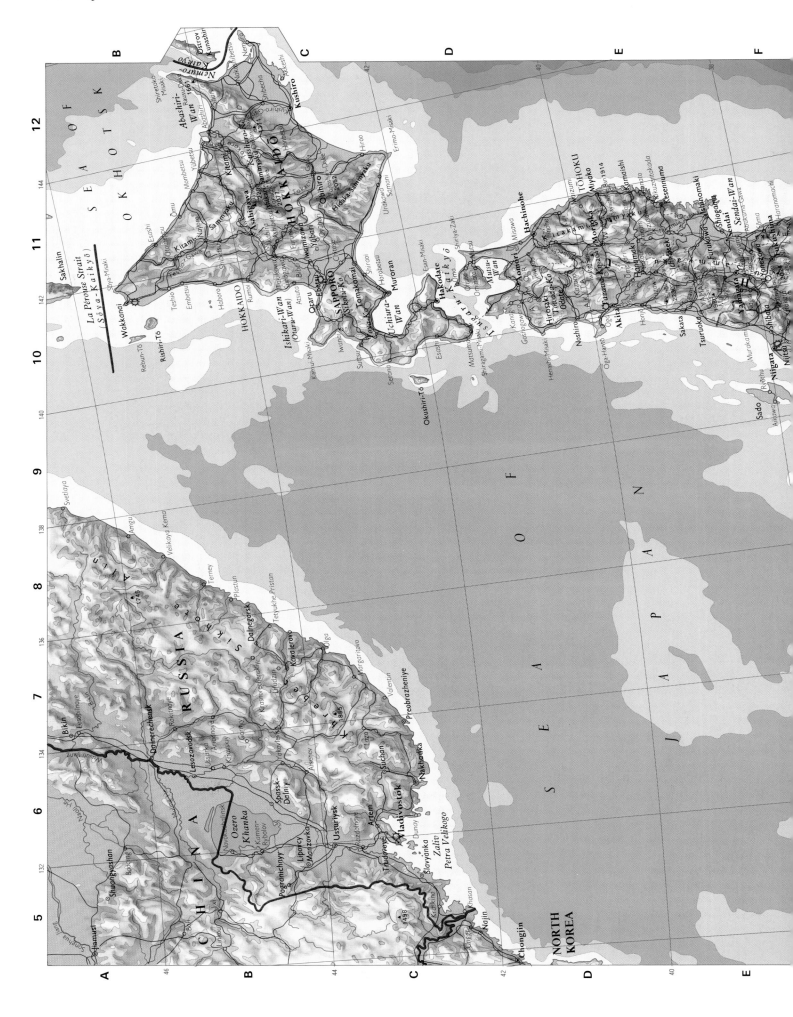

SEA OF OKHOTSK

Sakhalin

La Pérouse Strait
(Sōya-Kaikyō)

HOKKAIDO

SAPPORO

S E A   O F   J A P A N

SIKHOTE ALIN'

RUSSIA

CHINA

Ozero
Khanka

Vladivostok

Zaliv
Petra Velikogo

NORTH
KOREA

TOHOKU

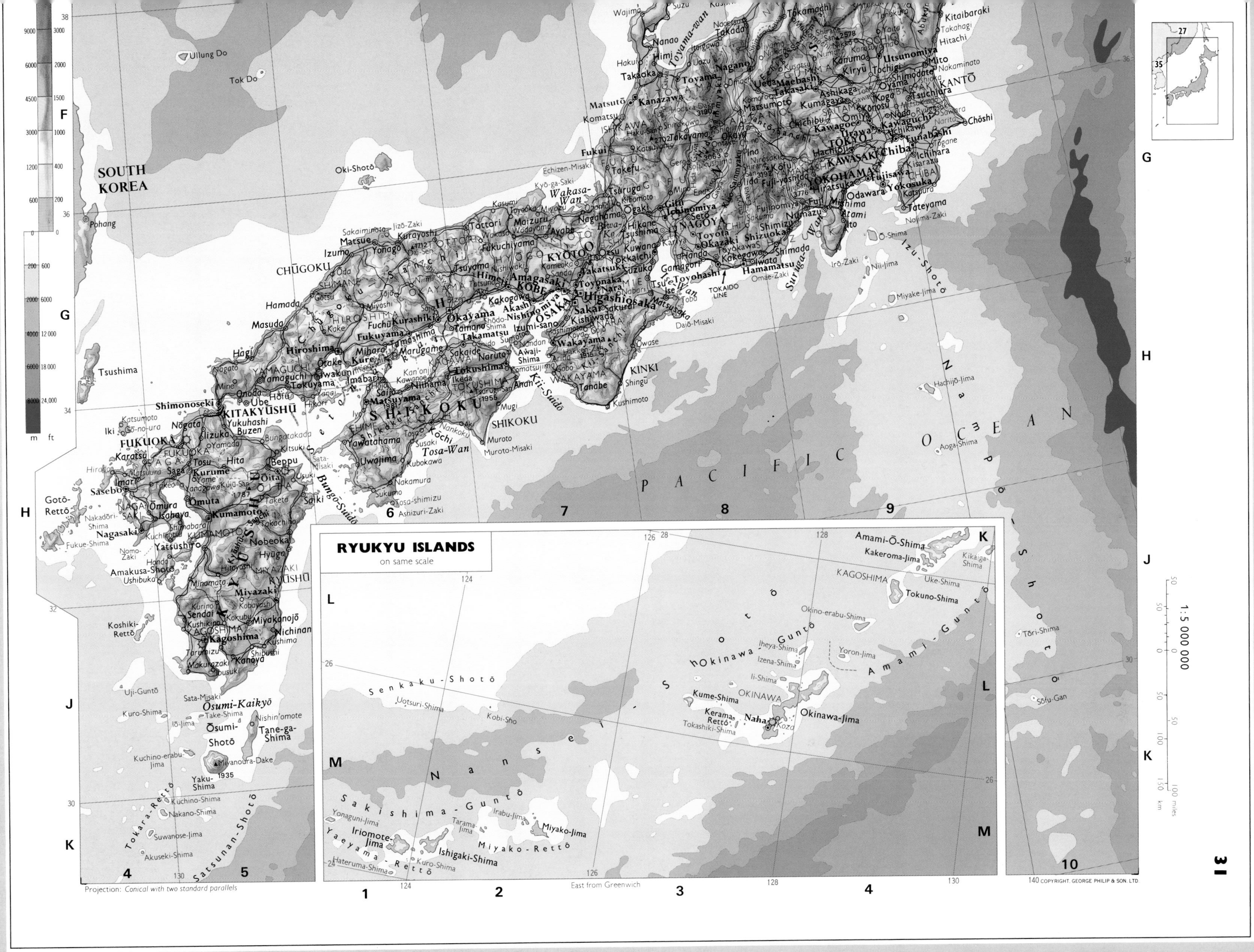

1:5 000 000

50 0 50 100 miles
50 0 50 100 150 km

RYUKYU ISLANDS
on same scale

SOUTH KOREA

PACIFIC OCEAN

KANTŌ
TOKYO
YOKOHAMA
KAWASAKI
CHIBA
NAGOYA
KYŌTO
KOBE
OSAKA
KINKI
SHIKOKU
KYŪSHŪ
KITAKYŪSHŪ
FUKUOKA
CHŪGOKU
HIROSHIMA
YAMAGUCHI
KAGOSHIMA
NAGASAKI
SASEBO
KUMAMOTO

Izu-Shotō
Hachijō-Jima
Miyake-Jima
Ō-Shima

Bungō-Suidō
Kii-Suidō
Tokaidō LINE

Tsushima
Oki-Shotō
Tok Do
Ullung Do
Pohang

Ōsumi-Kaikyō
Tane-ga-Shima
Yaku-Shima
Ōsumi-Shotō
Koshiki-Rettō
Amakusa-Shotō
Gotō-Rettō

Satsunan-Shotō
Tokara-Rettō
Kuchino-Shima
Nakano-Shima
Akuseki-Shima
Kuro-Shima
Suwanose-Jima
Uji-Guntō
Kuchino-erabu-Jima

Amami-Ō-Shima
Kakeroma-Jima
Tokuno-Shima
Uke-Shima
Kikaiga-Shima
KAGOSHIMA
Okino-erabu-Shima
Yoron-Jima
OKINAWA
Okinawa-Jima
Naha
Kume-Shima
Kerama Rettō
Iheya-Shima
Izena-Shima

Nansei-Shotō
Amami-Guntō
Okinawa-Guntō
Sakishima-Guntō
Miyako-Rettō
Miyako-Jima
Ishigaki-Shima
Iriomote-Jima
Yaeyama-Rettō
Yonaguni-Jima
Hateruma-Shima

Senkaku-Shotō
Uotsuri-Shima
Kobi-Sho

East from Greenwich

Projection: Conical with two standard parallels

140 COPYRIGHT GEORGE PHILIP & SON LTD

ft
3000
9000
6000
4500
3000
2000
1500
1000
600
400
200
0
m
200
600
1200
2000
4000
6000
12 000
18 000
24 000

Projection: Bonne

East from Greenwich

1:15 000 000

100   0   100   200   300   400 miles
100   0   100 200 300 400 500 600 km

27
40
38 37

6 7 8 9

Cities and places

Baykal
Chita
Sretensk
Nerchinsk
Olovyannaya
Borzya
Bukachacha
Svobodny
Shimanovsk
Chegdomyn
Aleksandrovsk
Poronaysk
C. Terpeniya

Sakhalin
Komsomolsk
Dolinsk
Yuzhno-Sakhalinsk
Kholmsk
La Perouse Str.

Ulan Ude
Olekski
Manzhouli
Oroqen Zizhiqi
Nenjiang
Obluchye
Birobidzhan
Khabarovsk
Troitskoye
Bikin

Hailar
Yilehuli Shan
Blagoveshchensk
Aihui
Bureya

Hulun Nur
Dutulun Shan
Buir Nur
Butha Qi
Bei'an
Yichun
Hegang
Hulin
Mishan
Wakkanai

Ozero Khanka
Asahigawa
Hokkaido
Sapporo
Otaru
Muroran
Kushiro
C. Erimo

Chaobaisang
Kerulen
Buynshan
Arxan
Solon
Qiqihar
Anda
Suihua
Hamusi
Shuangyashan

Tamsagbulag
Horqin Youyi Qianqi
Ulan Hot
Baicheng
Shuangcheng
HARBIN
Manchur
Jixi

Dzamin Uud
Abagnar Qi
Huolin Gol
Tao'an
Mudanjiang
Hakodate
Tsugaru-kaikyo
Aomori
Hachinohe
Morioka

Erenhot
Linxi
1949
Tongliao
CHANGCHUN
Shuangliao
Jilin
Duihua
Vladivostok
Nakhodka
Partizansk
Artem
Ussuriysk
Hunchun
Yanji

Duolun
Chifeng
Siping
Liaoyuan
Mashan
2744
Chongjin
Akita
Sakata
Ishinomaki

Hohhot
Jining
Zhangjiakou
Chengde
Fuxin
FUSHUN
SHENYANG
Liaoyang
Benxi
ANSHAN
Yingkou
Dandong
NORTH
Hungnam
Wonsan
Sado
Niigata
Koriyama
Utsunomiya

Datong
Xuanhua
Qinhuangdao
BEIJING (Peking)
Baoding
TIANJIN SHI
TIANJIN
Tangshan
Liaodong Wan
DALIAN
P'YONGYANG
Korea Bay
Kaesong
SOUL
Inch'on
Wajima
Toyama
Kanazawa
TOKYO
NAGOYA
YOKOHAMA
Yokosuka
Kawasaki

TAIYUAN
Yangquan
Shijiazhuang
HEBEI
Cangzhou
Bo Hai
Yantai
Weihai
SOUTH
Taejon
TAEGU
PUSAN
KOBE
OSAKA
Okayama
Hiroshima
Kure
Shizuoka
Hamamatsu
Wakayama
Sakai

Fenyang
Yuci
Taiyue Shan
Dezhou
Weifang
Ye Xian
JINAN
QINGDAO
YELLOW SEA
Kwangju
Masan
Shimonoseki
KITAKYUSHU
FUKUOKA
Matsuyama
Kochi
Shikoku

Changzhi
Linfen
Handan
Anyang
Zibo
Tai'an
Jining
SHANDONG
Cheju Do
1950
Saseb
Kumamoto
Nagasaki
Kyushu
Kagoshima
Tanega-shima

Sanmenxia
Luoyang
Xinxiang
Kaifeng
Zaozhuang
Lianyungang
Tongchuan
ZHENGZHOU
HENAN
Pingdingshan
Nanyang
Shangqiu
Shangshui
Xuzhou
Qingjiang
Yancheng
JIANGSU
Nantong

Xi'an
Xiangfan
Zhumadian
Bengbu
Huainan
Yangzhou
Taizhou
Changzhou
Wuxi
Suzhou
SHANGHAI SHI
SHANGHAI

Dabie Shan
NANJING
Ma'anshan
Wuhu
Wuxing
Jiaxing

Hefei
ANHUI
Tongling
WUHAN
Anqing
Hangzhou
Hangzhou Wan

Yichang
Shashi
Huangshi
Jiujiang
Tunxi
Shaoxing
Ningbo

Changde
Dongting Hu
Nanchang
Jingdezhen
Jinhua
Linhai
EAST CHINA SEA

Yiyang
Poyang Hu
Shangrao
Qu Jiang
Wenzhou
Amami-o-Shima

HUNAN
Changsha
Xiangtan
Pingxiang
JIANGXI
Jiujiang Shan
2120
Nanping

Shaoyang
Ji'an
Nanchang
Okinawa
Naha

Hengyang
Sanming
Fuzhou
RYUKYU-retto

Xing'an
Ganzhou
FUJIAN
Longyan
Quanzhou
Chilung
Sakishima Gunto

Shaoguan
Zhangzhou
Hsinchu
TAIPEI
Taichung
Changhua

Mei Xian
Chaozhou
Xiamen
Hengchun Shan
3997
TAIWAN (FORMOSA)

Wuzhou
GUANGDONG
GUANGZHOU
Huizhou
Shantou
T'ainan
T'aitung
Kaohsiung
Pingtung

Zhaoqing
Foshan
Jiangmen
HONG KONG (Br.)
Macau (Port.)

Maoming
Yangjiang
Zhanjiang
Haikou
Hainan Dao
HAINAN

SEA OF JAPAN
PACIFIC OCEAN
Tropic of Cancer
EAST CHINA SEA
SOUTH CHINA SEA
Pratas
Batan Is.
Babuyan Is.

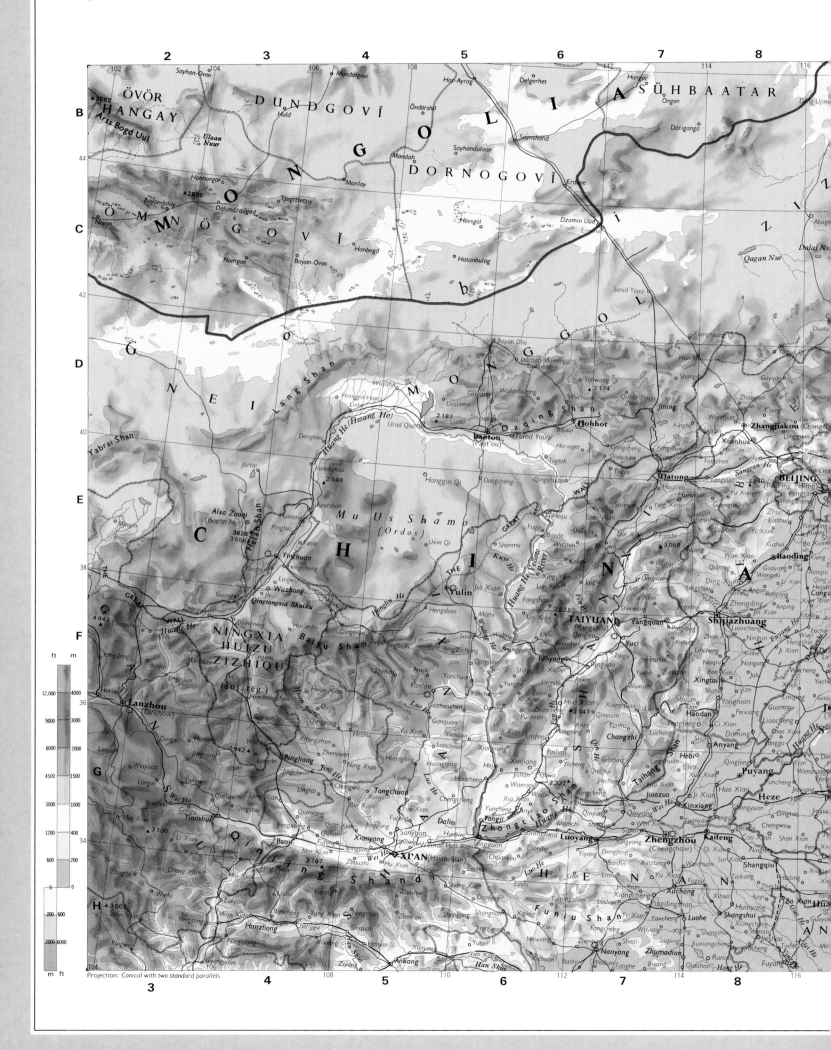

Projection: Conical with two standard parallels

27
31
32
33

9 10 11 12 13 14 15 16

1:6 000 000

50 0 50 100 150 miles

50 0 50 100 150 200 km

B

Horqin Youyi Qianqi

HARBIN (Ha'erpin)

HEILONGJIANG

Bin Xian

Ozero Khanka

R U S S I A

Turiy Rog

Jixi

Hulin He

Zhenlai

Nen Jiang

Maoxing Zhaoyuan Yanshou

Tao'an Anguang Songhua Jiang

Balicheng Acheng

Shangzhi

Yimianpo

Hulin He

Mudanjiang Muling Suifenhe Pogranichnyy

Maqiao

Ussuriysk (Voroshilov) Razdolnoye

C

Artem

Tongyu Fuyu Changchunling Wuchang Hailin Ning'an Dongning

Tavrichanka

Shenjingzi Jiutai Shulan Xinzhan Emu

Wangqing Hunchun

VLADIVOSTOK

Changchun **Jilin** Kirin

Jiaohe Dunhua Daxinggou Yanji

Shixian Slavyanka

Huaidezhen Fanjiatun Jiaohe Helong Kraskino

Posyet

D

Huaide Shuangyang Dongfeng Jingyu Antu

Shixian Unggi Sosura

Liaoyuan Panshi Huadian Fusong Musan

Najin

Siping Kaiyuan Hailong Shanchengzhen Linjiang Changbai Shan Puryong Ugodong

Tieling Qingyuan Tonghua Chongsong Chongjin

Fuxin Zhangwu Liao He Fushun Tonghua Linjiang 2541 Pyongdong Ondeajin

SHENYANG (Mukden) Huanren Inpundong Hyesan Simpungdong

Xinmin Benxi Huaijianzi 845 Manpojin Pungson Kimch'aek (Songjin)

L I A O N I N G Liaoyang Kapsan Kosong Tanch'on

Jinzhou **Anshan** 2522 Pujon chosuji Kwanggaeri

Jinxi Haicheng Kuandian Yalu Pyoktong Changjin chosuji Sinhung Sinpo Pukchong

Yingkou Gai Xian Dandong Supung Sk. Kanggye Oro Simpo Hamhung

NORTH Sinhung Hungnam

Xiongyuecheng Sinuiju Yongampo Taegwan Kujang

Wanfu Doriggan Chongju Kaech'on **KOREA** Tongjoson Man

E

Liaodong Wan Fu Xian Pakchon Hamhung Yonghung

Liaodong Jin Xian Sukchon Anju Tokch'on Wonsan

Lüshun Pikou Unsan Kangdong Munch'on **SEA OF**

DALIAN (Lüda) Chongju Tongyang Anbyon Kojo

Bo Hai **Korea** **P'YONGYANG** Songnim Pyonggang **JAPAN**

(Gulf of Chihli) **Bay** Chinnampo Suan Hoeyang 1638

TIANJIN (Tientsin) Cho-do Sariwon Nam-ch'on Kumhwa Hwach'on chosuji 1578 Yangyang

Tanggu Dagu Chaeryong Sinmak Kaesong Chunchon Kangnung

Oikou Changyon Haeju Panmunjom Uijongbu Hongchon

Paengnyong-do Ongjin Munsan Samchok Ullung-do

F

Huang He Cease Fire Line **SOUL** Wonju Yongwol

Penglai Longkou Yantai **INCH'ON** Suwon Ichon Chungju Chechon Ulchin

Laizhou Wan Weihai Osan Yoju Chongju

Ye Xian Mupingxian **SOUTH** Andong Yongdok

Shandong Bandao Shidao Hongsong **KOREA** Chongju Sangju Uisong Chongha

Weifang Chongan Chonan Kimch'on Pohang

Zibo Yidu Gaomi Laoshan Kunsan **Taejon** Sonsan

SHANDONG Jiao Xian Kanggyong Yongdong Waegwan Kyongju

Xintai Chonju **TAEGU** Chongdo Ulsan

QINGDAO (Ch'ingtao) Namwon 1915 Chinju Masan

G

HUANG HAI Sogo-ri Tamyang Chinhae **PUSAN**

(Yellow Sea) **Kwangju** Suwon Chungmu

Mokpo Posong Sunchon Korea Strait

Tsushima

JAPAN

Cheju Cheju-do

Hallim 1950 Onpyong-ni **Nagasaki**

Mosulp'o Sogwi-po Nakadori-jima

East from Greenwich

COPYRIGHT. GEORGE PHILIP & SON LTD.

9 10 11 12 13 14 15

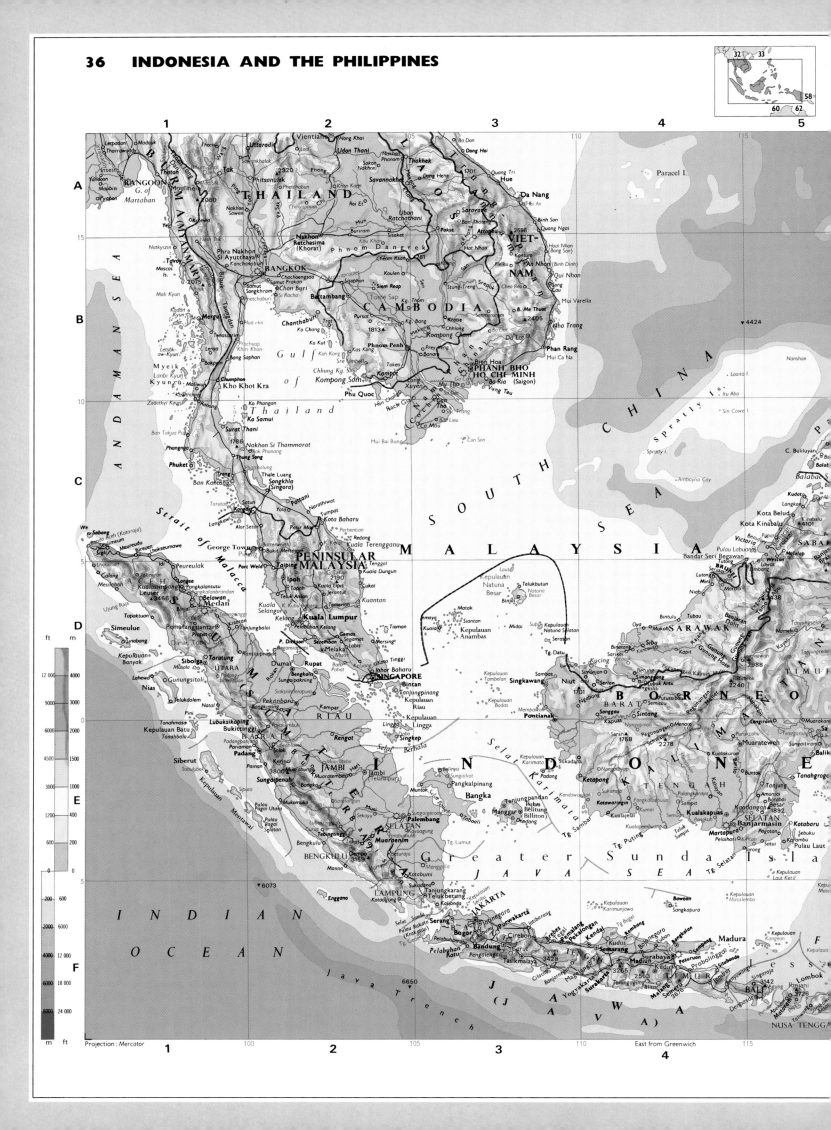

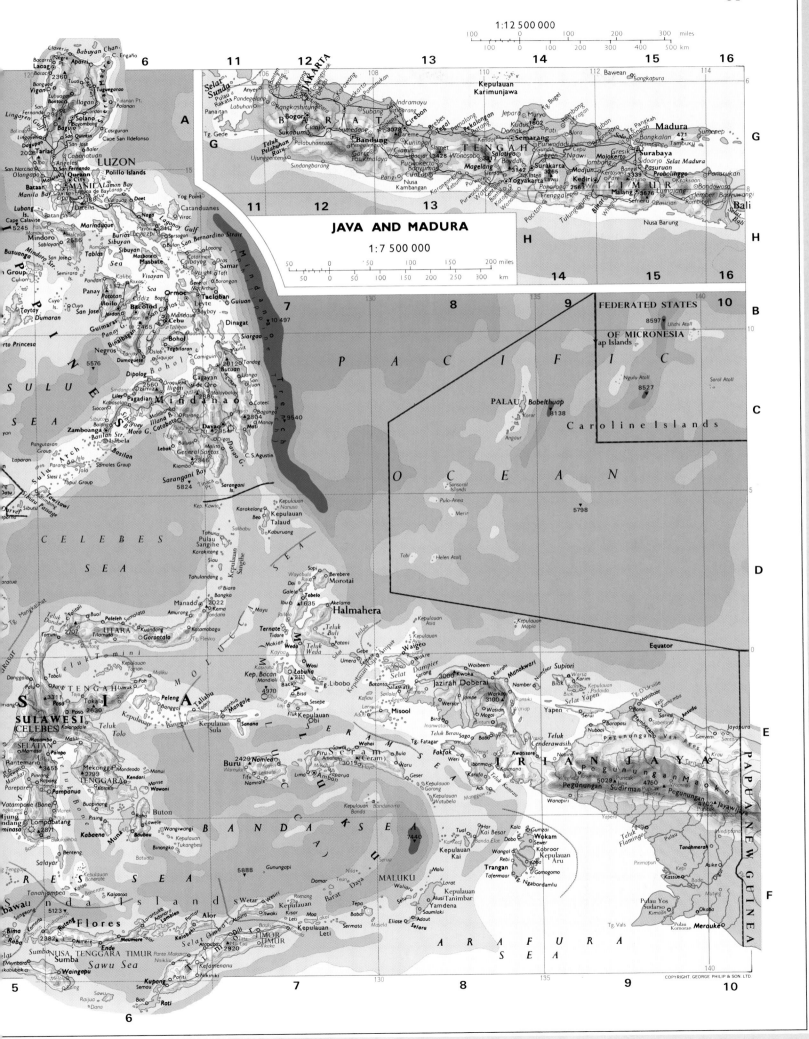

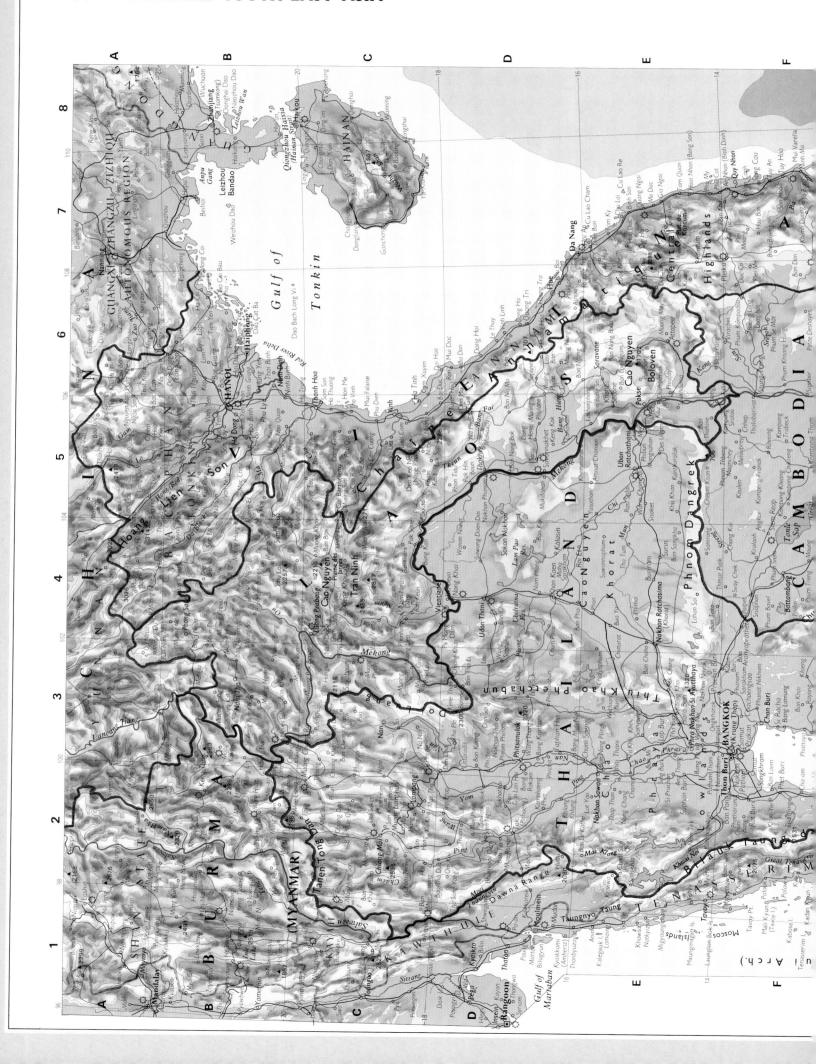

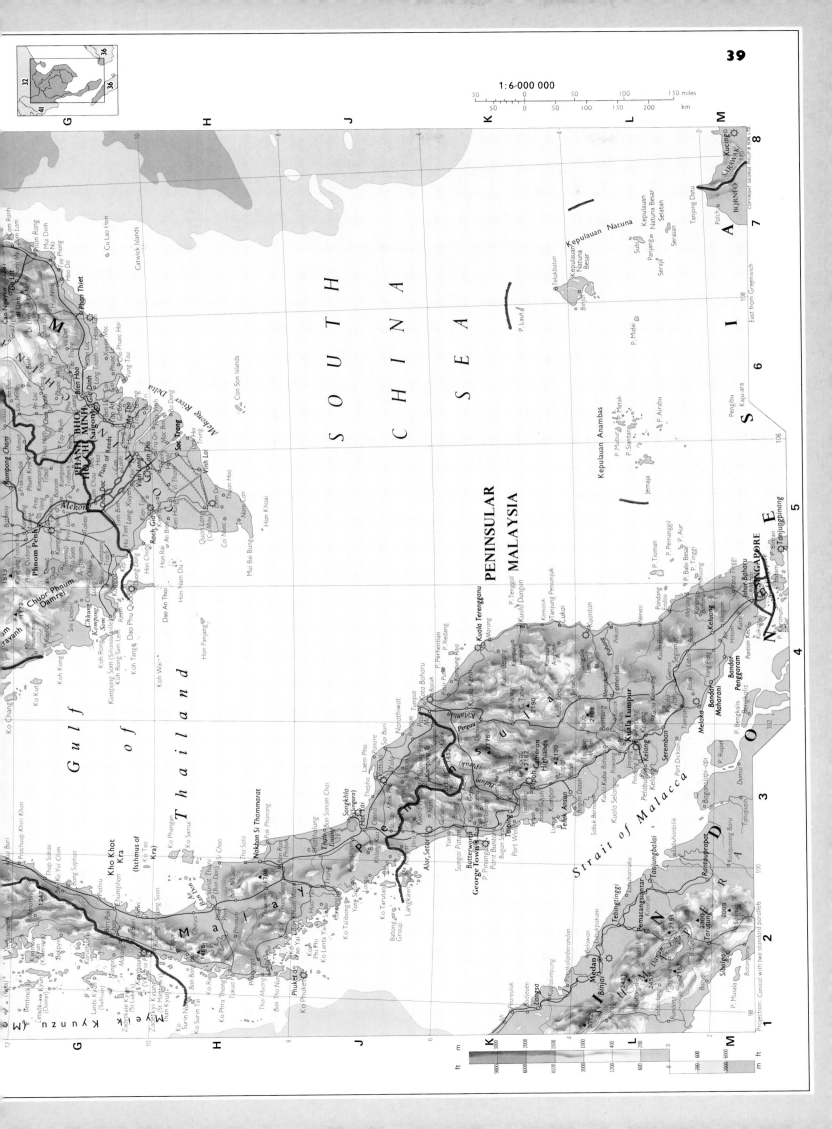

1 : 6 000 000

SOUTH

CHINA

SEA

Gulf

of

Thailand

PENINSULAR
MALAYSIA

Strait of Malacca

Kepulauan Natuna

Kepulauan Anambas

BORNEO

SINGAPORE

Projection: Conical with two standard parallels

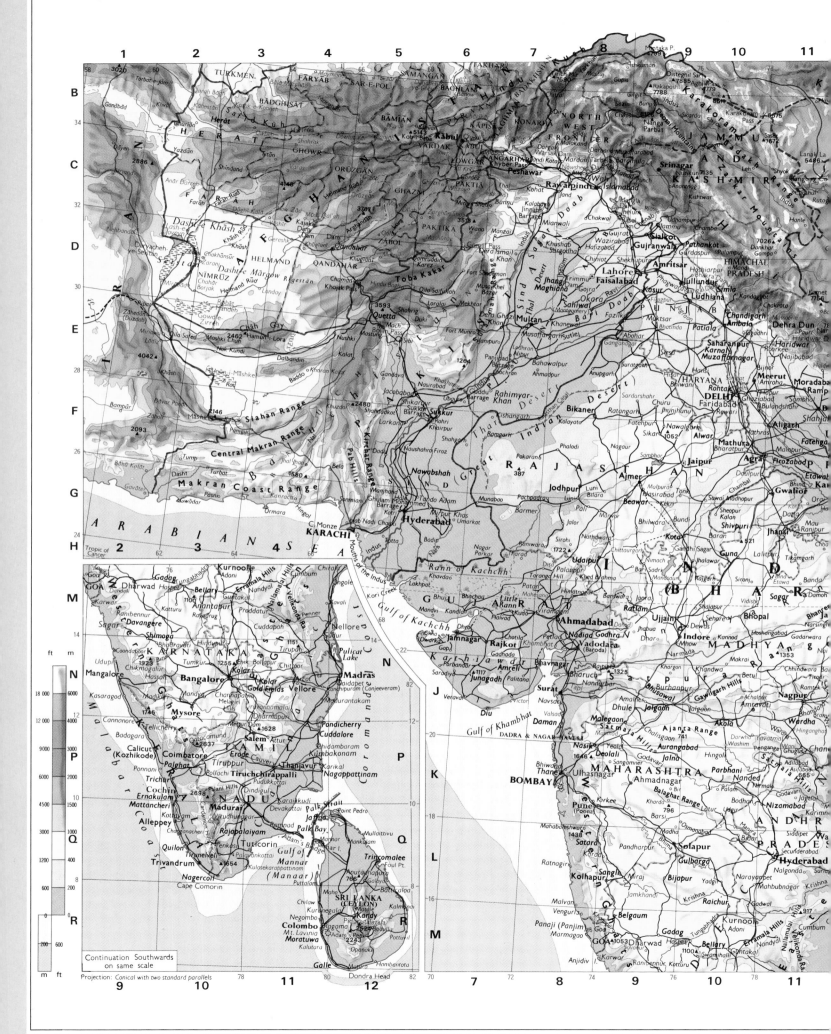

Continuation Southwards
on same scale

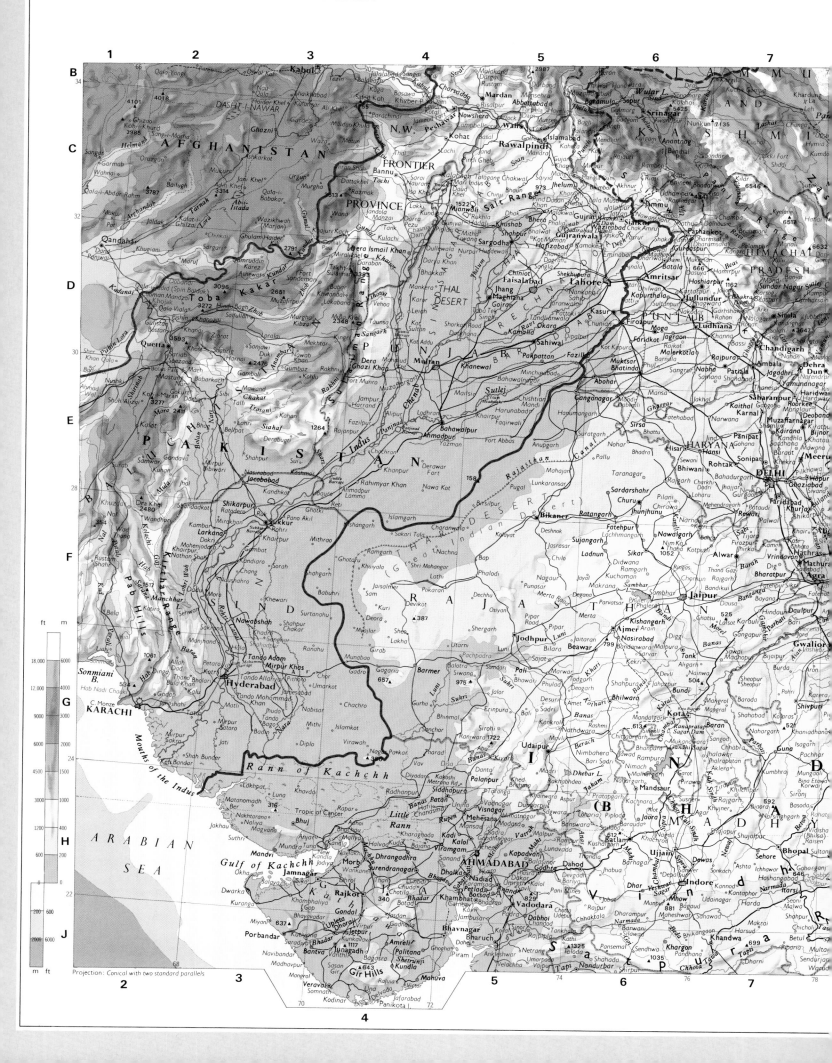

1 : 6 000 000

50   0   50   100 miles
50   0   50   100   150 km

JAMMU AND KASHMIR
On same scale as Main Map

CHINA

A

Kunlun Shan

Karakoram Range

SODA PLAINS

Aksai Chin

N.W. FRONTIER PROVINCE

PUNJAB

Gilgit

Indus

Deosai Mountains

Nanga Parbat

Skardu

Leh

Zaskar Mountains

Wular L.

Srinagar

Anantnag

KASHMIR

Rawalpindi

Islamabad

Jammu

HIMACHAL PRADESH

B

C

D

E

CHINA

Nganglong Kangri

Gangdise Shan

Nanda Devi

XIZANG

TIBET

Mt. Everest 8848

Kanchenjunga

SIKKIM

Gangtok

BHUTAN

ASSAM

Brahmaputra

Katmandu

Lalitpur Bhaktapur

Pokhara

Annapurna Manaslu

Dhaulagiri

N E P A L

Jumla

Moradabad

Rampur

Bareilly

Lucknow

KANPUR

Faizabad

Gorakhpur

Bahraich

Gonda

Allahabad

VARANASI

Mirzapur

U T T A R   P R A D E S H

Patna

BIHAR

Muzaffarpur

Darbhanga

Bhagalpur

Munger

Gaya

Hazaribag

Ranchi

Jamshedpur

Asansol

Durgapur

Bankura

CALCUTTA

Haora

Kharagpur

M A D H Y A   P R A D E S H

Jabalpur

Bilaspur

Raurkela

Raipur

Sambalpur

Maikala Range

BANGLADESH

DHAKA

Narayanganj

Faridpur

Jessore

Khulna

Barisal

Mymensingh

Rajshahi

Bogra

Sundarbans

Mouths of the Ganga

The Sandheads

F

G

H

J

East from Greenwich

COPYRIGHT GEORGE PHILIP & SON. LTD.

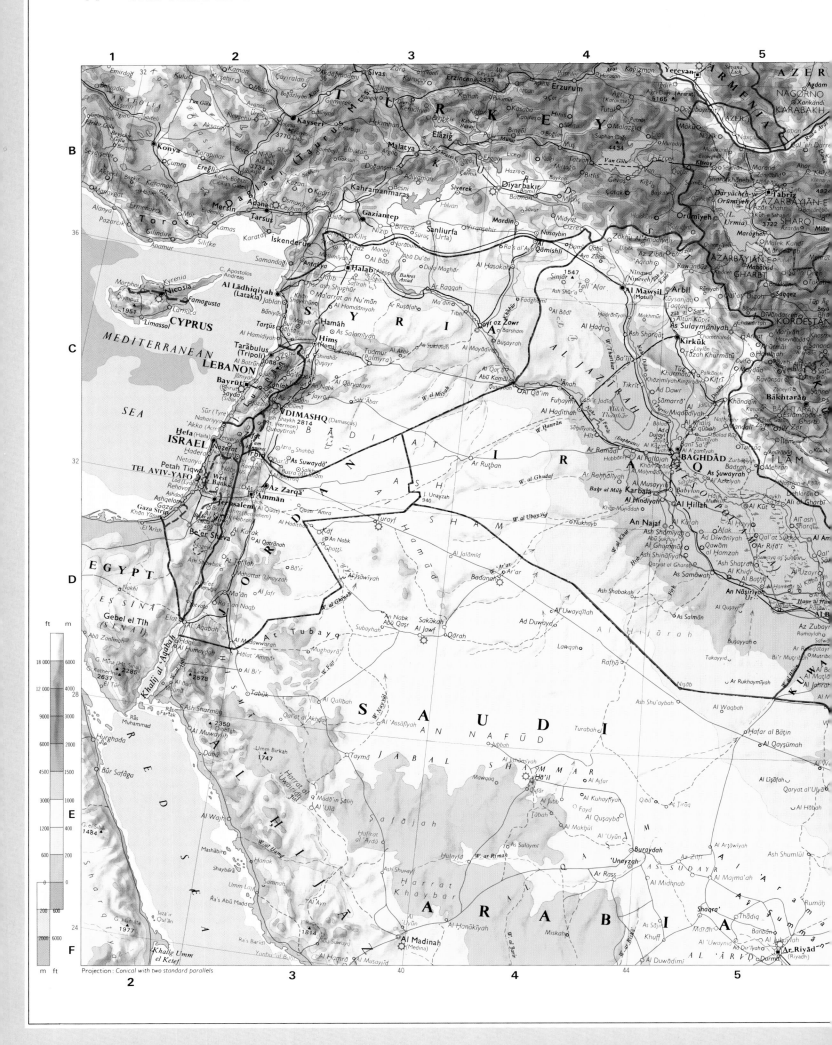

Projection: Conical with two standard parallels

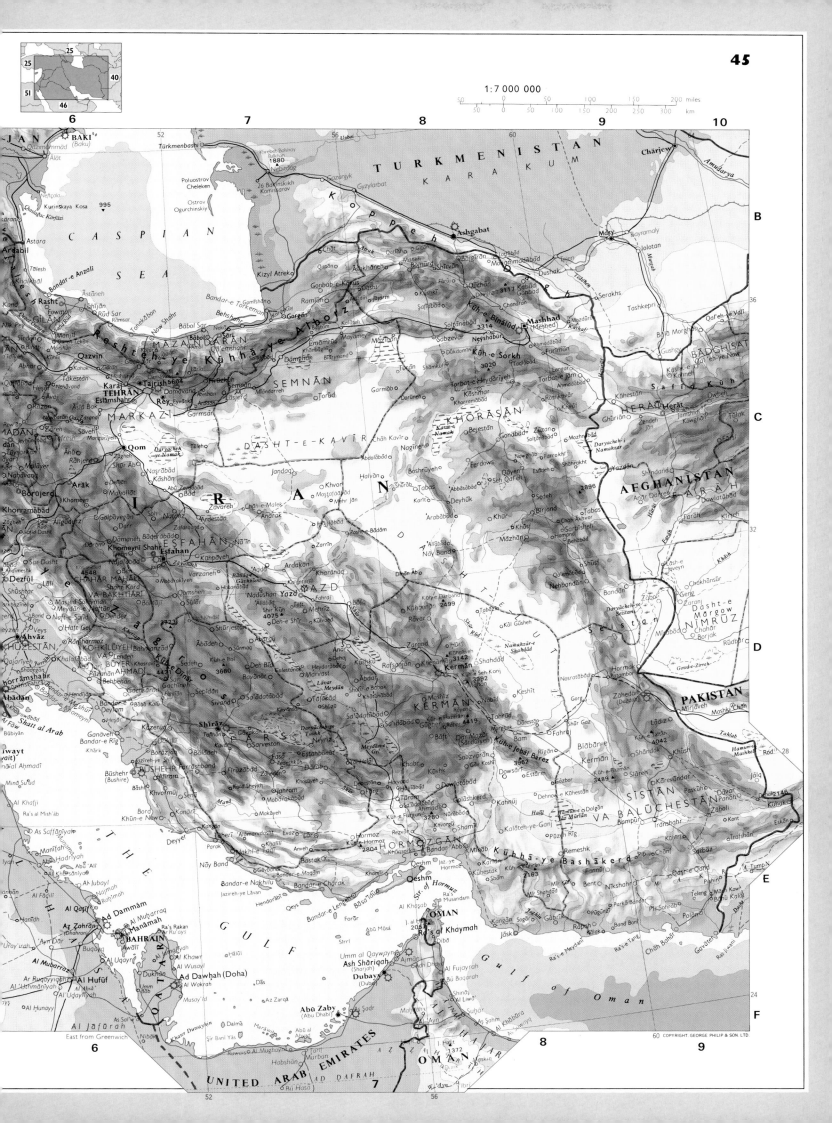

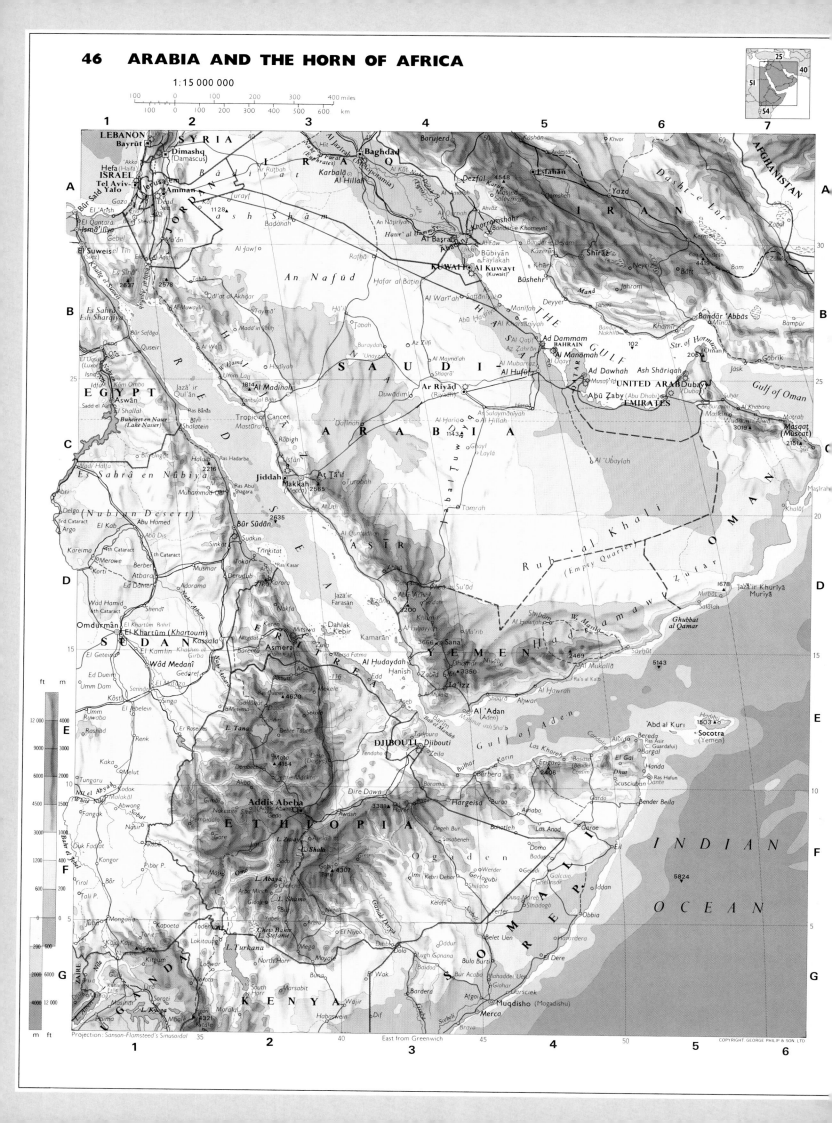

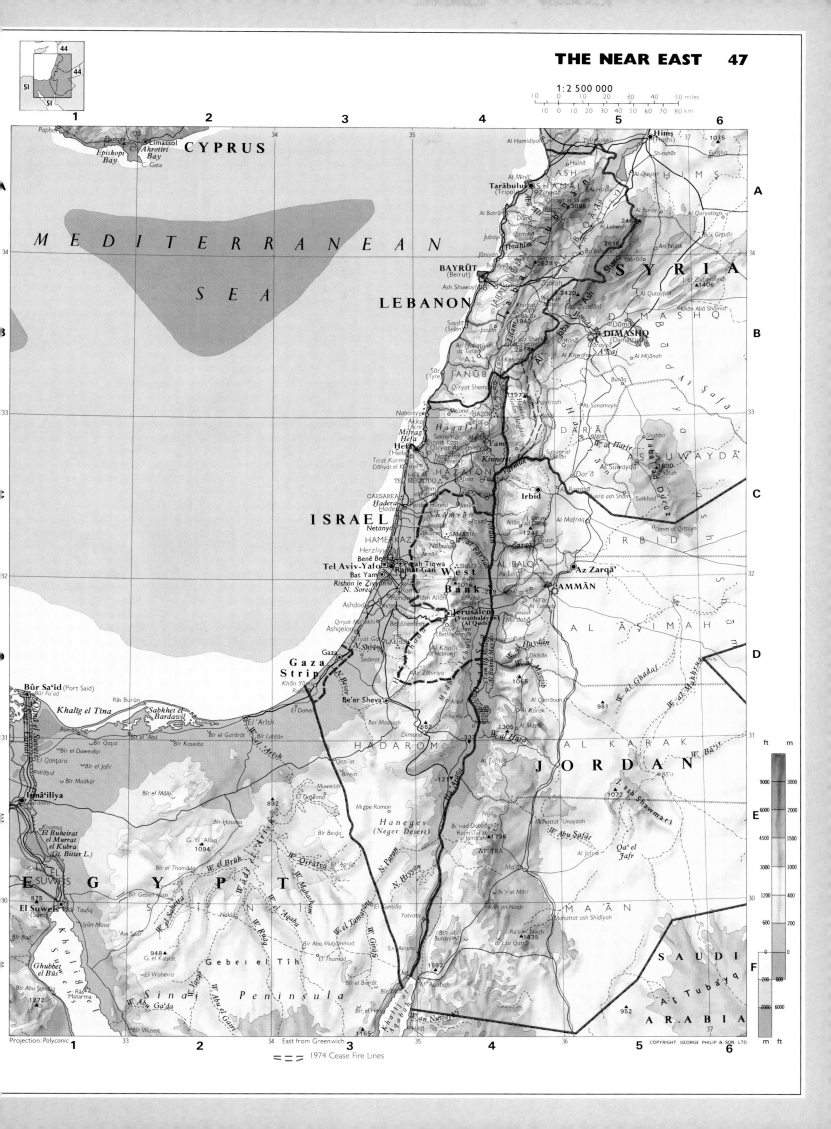

1:2 500 000

10   0   10   20   30   40   50 miles
10 0 10 20 30 40 50 60 70 80 km

CYPRUS

Paphos
Episkopı Bay
Akrotiri Bay
Limassol
C. Gata

M E D I T E R R A N E A N

S E A

LEBANON

BAYRŪT
(Beirut)

SYRIA

DIMASHQ
(Damascus)

ISRAEL

Tel Aviv-Yafo
Bat Yam
Rishon le Ziyyon

Gaza
Strip

West

Bank

Jerusalem
(Yerushalayim)
(Al Quds)

Bûr Sa'îd (Port Said)
Bûr Fu'âd

Khalîg el Tîna

Ismâ'îlîya

El Buheirat
el Murrat
el Kubra
(Gt. Bitter L.)

EL SUWEIS
El Suweis (Suez)

E G Y P T

S i n a i   P e n i n s u l a

Gebeı el Tîh

Hanegev
(Negev Desert)

HADAROM

Be'er Sheva

JORDAN

'AMMĀN
'Az Zarqā'

Irbid

AL KARAK

M A 'Ā N

PETRA

S A U D I

A R A B I A

Hims
(Homs)

Tarābulus
(Tripoli)

ft   m
9000   3000
6000   2000
4500   1500
3000   1000
1200   400
600   200
0   0
200   600
2000   6000
m   ft

Projection: Polyconic   East from Greenwich   COPYRIGHT. GEORGE PHILIP & SON LTD

=== 1974 Cease Fire Lines

1 : 42 000 000

200   0   200   400   600   800   1000   1200 miles
200   0   200 400 600 800 1000 1200 1400 1600 1800 km

1   **2**   **3**   **4**   **5**   **6**   **7**   **8**   **9**   **10**

NORTH

ATLANTIC

OCEAN

British Isles

Europe

Carpathians

B. of Biscay

Mont Blanc 4807

Alps

Apennines

Dinaric Alps

Adriatic Sea

Black Sea

Caucasus

Elbrus 5633

Caspian Sea

Aral Sea

Azores

6578

Iberian Peninsula

Pyrénées

Corsica

Sardinia

Sicily

Malta

Crete

Cyprus

Anatolia

Mediterranean Sea

Asia

Madeira

Str. of Gibraltar

High Plateaux

Saharan Atlas

C. Bon

5121

Levant

Mesopotamia

Tigris

Euphrates

Canary Is.

4165 Middle Atlas

High Atlas

Toubkal

Anti Atlas

Chott Djerid

G. of Gabès

Tripolitania

G. of Sidra

Cyrenaica

Syrian Desert

Arabia

The Gulf

Ras Nouâdhibou

Tasili Plateau

Hoggar

Libyan Desert

Egypt

Siwa Oasis

Al Kufrah

El Kharga

Mt Sinai 2285

Red Sea

Arabian Desert

Hejaz

Tropic of Cancer

Sahara

Adrar

Air

Tibesti

Nubian Desert

Nubia

Cape Verde Is.

Senegal

C. Vert

Senegambia

Gambia

Fouta Djalon

El Djouf

Bilma

L. Chad

Bahr el Ghazal

Wadai

Darfur

Kordofan

Sahel

Ras Dashen 4620

116

Albara

Barim

Bab el Mandeb

Ras Asir

G. of Aden

Soco

Niger

Volta

Niger

Benue

Chari

White Nile

Blue Nile

L. Tana

Ethiopian Highlands

Somali Peninsula

Guinea

Grain Coast

Gold Coast

Slave Coast

Ivory Coast

C. Palmas

Bight of Benin

Mt. Cameroon 4070

Bioko

Adamawa Highlands

Dar Banda

Bahr el Ghazâl

Bahr el Jebel

Uele

Shaballe

Juba

Bight of Bonny

I. de Principe

São Tomé

Gulf of Guinea

Ogooué

C. Lopez

Zaire

Oubangui

Congo

Uele

Zaire

L. Albert

Chutes Boyoma

Ruwenzori 5104

4321

Mt. Elgon

Turkana

5199

Mt. Kenya

Tana

Equator

Annobón

Ogooué

Basin

Kasai

Sankuru

Lualaba

L. Edward

L. Kivu

Victoria

5895 Kilimanjaro

INDIAN

OCEAN

Seychelles

ft   m

Ascension I.

Cuango

Cuanza

Kasai

Kwango

Tanganyika

Luvua

L. Mweru

Rungwe 296

Pemba I.

Aldabra Is.

SOUTH

St. Helena

Bié Plateau

Zambezi

Luapula

Bangweulu Swamp

Shaba

L. Nyasa (L. Malawi)

Shire

C. Delgado

Comoros

ATLANTIC

OCEAN

Cunene

C. Fria

Cubango

Cuando

Victoria Falls

Okavango Swamps

Zambezi

Limpopo

Mozambique Channel

Madagascar

2643

Mauriti

Réunion

Tropic of Capricorn

Walvis Bay

Namib Desert

Kalahari

Vaal

Orange

High Veld

Delagoa B.

Drakensberg

Algoa B.

3482

Compass Mt. 2505

Nieuweldberge

Great Karoo

Swartberge

C. of Good Hope

C. Agulhas

Projection: Azimuthal Equidistant

West from Greenwich

East from Greenwich

m ft

ft   m
12000 4000
9000   3000
6000   2000
3000   1000
1500   500
600   200
0   0
200   600
1000   3000
2000   6000
4000   12000

Tristan da Cunha

1   **2**   **3**   **4**   **5**   **6**   **7**   **8**   **9**

1 : 42 000 000

NORTH ATLANTIC OCEAN

UNITED KINGDOM
LONDON
NETH.
BELG.
GERMANY POLAND
Warsaw
Kiev
RUSSIA
Volgograd
KAZAKSTAN
PARIS
Prague
Vienna
CZECH REP.
SLOVAK REP.
HUNGARY
UKRAINE
Odessa
Aral Sea
FRANCE
SWITZ.
AUSTRIA
CROATIA
BOS.-HERZ.
YUG.
ROMANIA
Caspian Sea
B. of Biscay
ITALY
Adriatic Sea
ALB.
MAC.
BULGARIA
Black Sea
GEORGIA
ARM. AZER.
Baku
TURKMEN.

Azores (Port.)
Madrid
SPAIN
Corsica
Rome
Sardinia
Sicily
GREECE
Athens
Crete
TURKEY
Ankara
Mostul
ARM.
Tehrān

Lisbon
PORTUGAL
Madeira (Port.)
Algiers
Rabat
Tétouan
Fès
Casablanca
MOROCCO
Marrakesh
Constantine
Annaba
TUNISIA
Tunis
Sfax
MALTA
Mediterranean Sea
Tripoli
Misrātah
Benghazi
Alexandria
Port Said
CAIRO
El Faiyûm
CYPRUS
LEB.
SYRIA
Aleppo
Damascus
Tel Aviv-Jaffa
ISRAEL
Jerusalem
JORDAN
Suez
Baghdād
IRAQ
Basra
KUWAIT
Esfahān
IRAN
Tigris
Euphrates
Syrian Desert

Canary Is. (Sp.)
El Aaiún
WESTERN SAHARA
Fdérik
Dakhla
Ras Nouâdhibou
ALGERIA
In Salah
Tropic of Cancer
LIBYA
Marzūq
Al Jawf
EGYPT
Asyūt
Aswân
Wadi Halfa
Red Sea
Medina
Jedda
Mecca
SAUDI ARABIA
Riyadh
BAHRAIN
QATAR
The Gulf

VERDE IS.
C. Vert
Dakar
SENEGAL
GAMBIA
Banjul
GUINEA-BISSAU
Bissau
Conakry
Freetown
SIERRA LEONE
LIBERIA
Monrovia
St-Louis
Nouakchott
MAURITANIA
MALI
Bamako
GUINEA
Tombouctou
Niamey
BURKINA FASO
Ouagadougou
Bobo Dioulasso
IVORY COAST
Yamoussoukro
Bouaké
GHANA
Kumasi
Accra
Sekondi-Takoradi
Abidjan
TOGO
BENIN
Lomé
Porto Novo
Sahara
Agadès
NIGER
Kano
Maiduguri
Ndjamena
NIGERIA
Abuja
Ibadan
Lagos
Enugu
CHAD
Abéché
L. Chad
CAMEROON
Douala
Yaoundé
Malabo
EQUATORIAL GUINEA
SÃO TOMÉ & PRINCIPE
Port Harcourt
Bight of Benin
SUDAN
El Fâsher
El Obeid
Khartoum
Omdurmân
Atbara
Port Sudan
Wâd Medani
Malakâl
Wau
YEMEN
G. of Aden
Socotra (Yemen)
Ras Asir
DJIBOUTI
Djibouti
Asmera
ERITREA
Mesewa
ETHIOPIA
Addis Ababa
Harer
Berbera
SOMALI REP.
Mogadishu

Gulf of Guinea
Equator
GABON
Libreville
C. Lopez
Annobón
CONGO
Brazzaville
Pointe Noire
CABINDA (Angola)
Mbandaka
Kisangani
ZAÏRE
Zaïre
Ubangi
CENTRAL AFRICAN REP.
Bangui
UGANDA
Kampala
RWANDA
Kigali
BURUNDI
Bujumbura
L. Albert
L. Edward
L. Kivu
L. Victoria
KENYA
Kisumu
Nairobi
Kismayu
Mombasa
L. Turkana
Juba
INDIAN OCEAN
SEYCHELLES

SOUTH ATLANTIC OCEAN
Ascension I. (U.K.)
St. Helena (U.K.)
Matadi
Kinshasa
Kananga
Kasai
TANZANIA
Dodoma
Zanzibar
Dar es Salaam
L. Tanganyika
Luanda
Lobito
Namibe
ANGOLA
Huambo
Cunene
Likasi
Lubumbashi
Ndola
ZAMBIA
Lusaka
L. Mweru
L. Malawi
Lilongwe
Blantyre
MALAWI
Zambezi
MOZAMBIQUE
Moçambique
C. Delgado
COMOROS
Mayotte (Fr.)
Antsiranana
Mahajanga
Aldabra Is.

Tropic of Capricorn
NAMIBIA
Windhoek
C. Fria
Okavango
Livingstone
Harare
ZIMBABWE
Bulawayo
Beira
Limpopo
BOTSWANA
Gaborone
Johannesburg
Pretoria
Maputo
SWAZ.
Mbabane
Kimberley
Vaal
Orange
LESOTHO
Maseru
Durban
Toamasina
Antananarivo
Fianarantsoa
MADAGASCAR
Réunion (Fr.)
MAURITIUS

SOUTH AFRICA
Cape Town
C. of Good Hope
C. Agulhas
East London
Port Elizabeth

Tristan da Cunha (U.K.)

Projection: Azimuthal Equidistant
West from Greenwich
East from Greenwich
Dakar
Capital Cities
CARTOGRAPHY BY PHILIP'S. COPYRIGHT REED INTERNATIONAL BOOKS LTD.

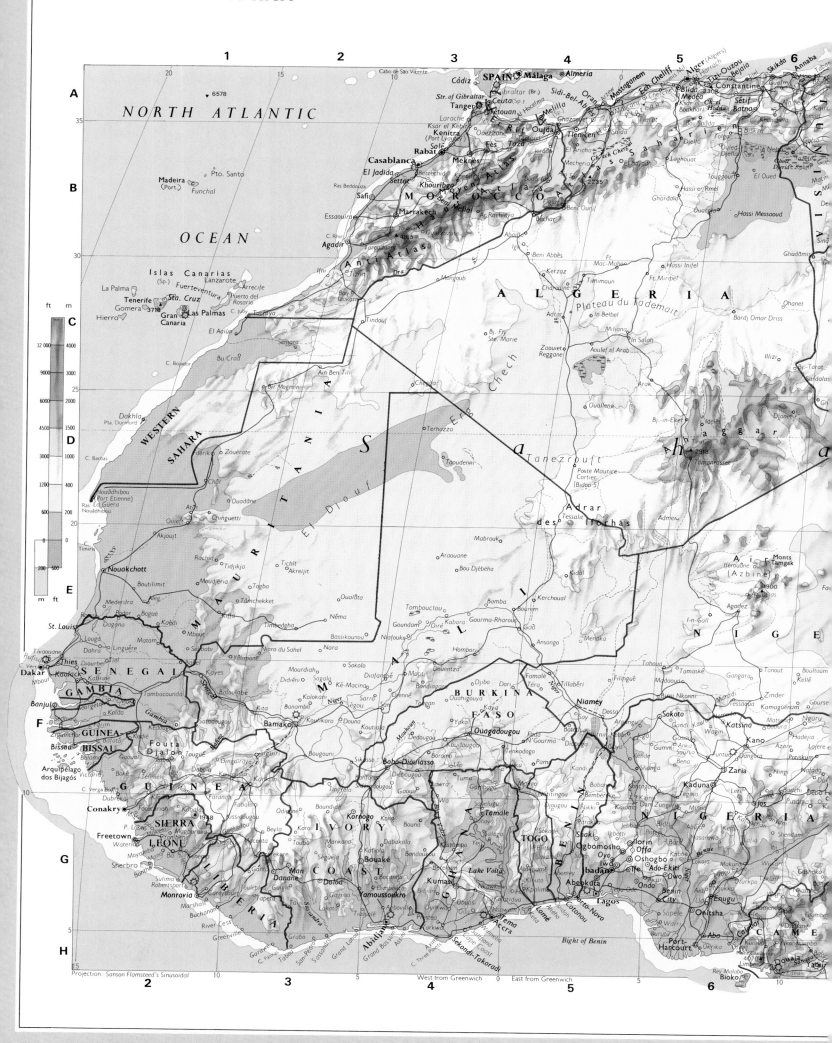

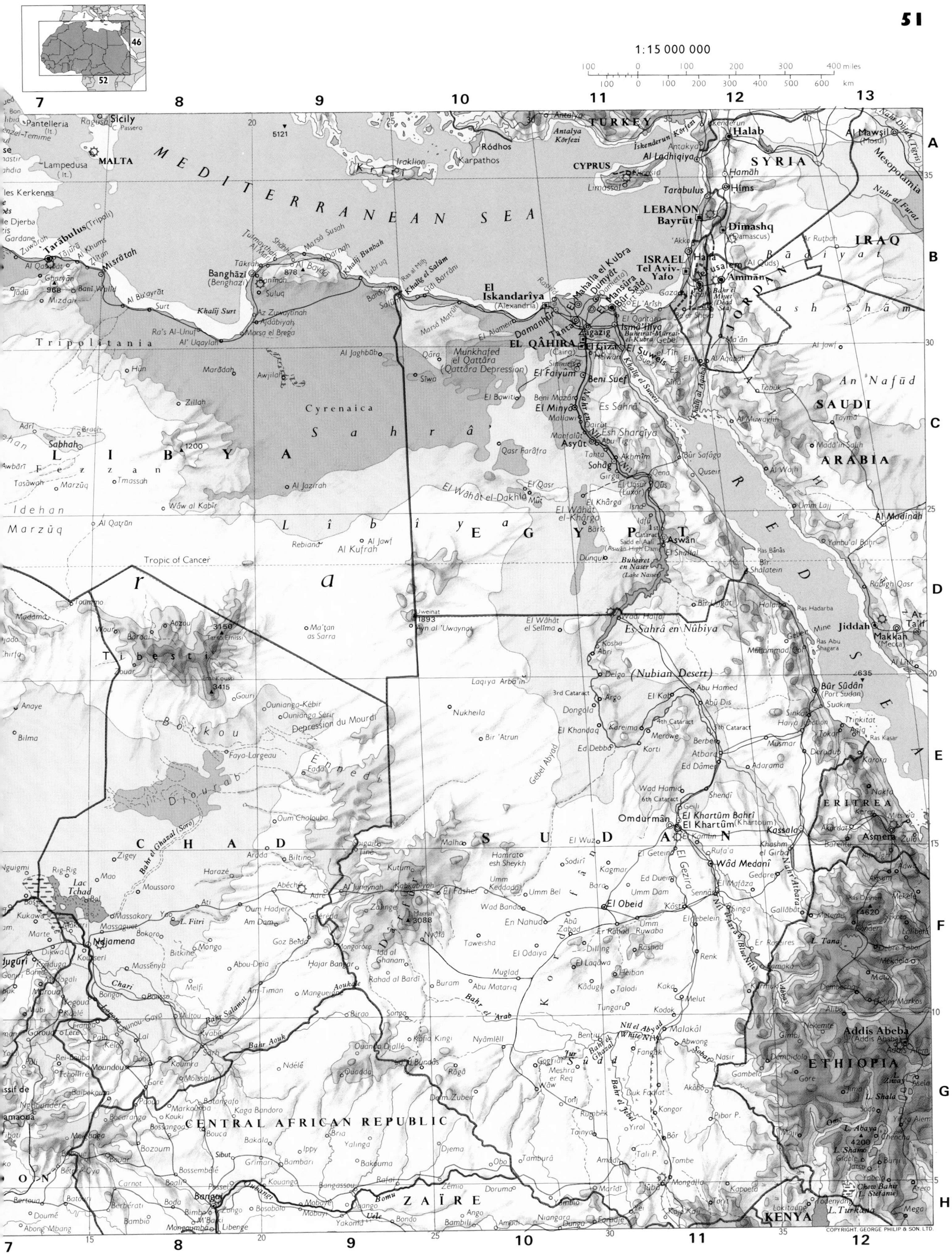

1:15 000 000

100   0   100   200   300   400 miles
100   0   100   200   300   400   500   600 km

7   8   9   10   11   12   13

MEDITERRANEAN SEA

TURKEY
Antalya
Antalya Körfezi
İskenderun Körfezi
İskenderun
Al Mawşil (Mosul)
Nahr Dijla (Tigris)
Halab
Ródhos
Karpathos
CYPRUS
Al Ladhiqiya
SYRIA
Limassol
Hamāh
Tarabulus
Hims
Mesopotamia
Ra's el Basit
LEBANON
Bayrūt
Dimashq (Damascus)
Ruṭban
IRAQ
Bādiyat
Krití
Iraklion
ISRAEL
Haifa
Tel Aviv-Yafo
Jerusalem (Al Quds)
Ammān
'Akko
Gaza
ash Shām
JORDAN
A

MALTA
Pantelleria (It.)
C. Passero
Sicily
Ragusa
C. Bon
Lampedusa (It.)
les Kerkenna
Île de Djerba
Gabès
Gardane
Tarabulus (Tripoli)
Az Zuwarah
Al Khums
Zlitan
Misrātah
Gharyān
968
Banī Walīd
Al Bu'ayrāt
Surt
Khalīj Surt
Az Zuwaytinah
Al' Uqaylah
Marsa el Brega
Ajdābiyah
Banghāzī (Benghazi)
Suluq
Barnīmah
Tūkrah
Al Bayda
878
Ra's el Milh
Darnah
Khalīj Bunbah
Tubruq
Sīdī Barrānī
Bardia
Marsa Matrûh
El 'Alamein
El Iskandarîya (Alexandria)
Damanhûr
El Mahalla el Kubra
Tanta
Zagazig
Damietta
Dumyât
Būr Sa'îd
El Qantara
Ismâ'îlîya
El Arîsh
Rafah
Bûr Fu'ad
El Qâhira (Cairo)
El Gîza
El Suweis (Suez)
B

Tripolitania
Hūn
Marādah
Awjilah
Al Jaghbūb
Qāra
Munkhafed el Qattâra (Qattâra Depression)
Siwa
El Faiyûm
Helwan
Beni Suef
El Minya
Beni Mazâr
Mallawi
Es Sahrâ
Esh Sharqîya
Dairût
Asyût
Abu Tig
Akhmîm
Sohâg
Tahta
Girga
Bûr Safâga
El Ghardaqa
Qena
Quseir
SAUDI
An Nafūd
Taymã
Tabūk
El Jwf
Al Muwayliḥ
Madā'in Salih
ARABIA
C

Sabhah
Zillah
1200
Marzūq
Tmassah
Wāw al Kabīr
Fezzan
Idehan
Marzūq
Al Qatrūn
Al Jawf
Rebiana
Al Kufrah
Tropic of Cancer
Sahrâ'
Libîya
EGYPT
El Wâhât el-Dakhla
Mût
El Qasr
El Khârga
El Wâhât el-Khârga
Baris
Qasr Farâfra
El Bawiti
Luxor
El Uqsur
Qûs
Isnâ
Idfû
Kôm Ombo
Aswân
Sadd el Aali (Aswan High Dam)
El Shallal
Al Wajh
Al Madinah
Al Qusair
D

Madama
Toummo
Zouar
Aozou
3150
Tarso Emissi
Tibesti
Bardaï
3415
Gouro
 Tropique
Uweinat
1893
'Ayn al 'Uwaynât
El Wâhât el Sellima
Es Sahrâ en Nûbiya
Buheiret en Naser (Lake Nasser)
Dunqula
Bîr Ungat
Halaib
Ras Hadarba
Jiddah
Makkah (Mecca)
At Tã'if
4200
Al Lith
Kosha
Abri
Delgo (Nubian Desert)
Laqiya Arbâ'in
Nukheila
Bîr 'Atrûn
Argo
3rd Cataract
Dongola
Kareima
Abu Hamed
El Kab
Abū Dis
El Khandaq
4th Cataract
Merowe
5th Cataract
Berber
Atbara
Sinkat
Haiya Junction
Trinkitat
Agig
Ras Kasar
Karora
E

Tibestı
Borkou
Faya-Largeau
Ennedi
Fada
Djourab
Bahr el Ghazal (Soro)
CHAD
Biltine
Abéché
Oum Hadjer
Ati
Am Dam
Goz Beïda
Mongororo
Adré
Tine
El Junayna
Kabkabiyah
El Fasher
3088
Nyālā
Zalingei
Kutum
Malha
Hamrat esh Sheykh
Sodiri
Umm Keddada
Umm Bel
Wad Banda
Taweisha
En Nahud
Er Rahad
Ed Dueim
Umm Dam
Ed Dâmer
Wad Hamid
6th Cataract
Shendi
Geili
Omdurmân
El Khartûm Bahrî
El Khartûm (Khartoum)
El Kamlin
Wad Medanî
Rufa'a
Geteina
El Gezira
Sennâr
Dinder
Khashm el Girba
Kassala
Er Rateiyes
L. Tana
Gedaref
El Mafâza
Gallâbât
Mekelé
4620
ERITREA
Keren
Asmera
Massawa
Zula
F

N'guigmi
Rig-Rig
Mao
Moussoro
Massakory
L. Fitri
Bitkine
Mongo
Massenya
Melfi
Aboû-Deïa
Hajar Banga
Birao
Rahad al Bardî
Buram
Abu Matariq
Muglad
Dilling
Kadugli
Talodi
Kaka
Tungaru
Renk
Kodok
Abwong
Malakâl
Nil el Abyad (White Nile)
Bentiu
Nasir
Sobat
Gambela
Addis Abeba (Addis Ababa)
ETHIOPIA
Dembidollo
Gore
Lac Tchad
Kukawa
Maïduguri
Dikwa
Marte
N'Djamena
Bokoro
Massaguet
Chari
Bongor
Kélo
Moundou
Doba
Lai
Koumra
Sarh
Moïssala
Ndélé
Ouadda
Bria
Yalinga
Djema
Bambari
Ippy
Bakala
CENTRAL AFRICAN REPUBLIC
G

Garoua
Ngaoundéré
Meiganga
Bozoum
Bossangoa
Bouca
Bossembélé
Bangui
Sibut
Grimari
Kouango
Bakouma
Rafai
Zémio
Mobaye
ZAÏRE
Bondo
Uele
Bomu
Bangassou
Ouango
Dorumo
Yakoma
Mongala
Juba
Torit
Kapoeta
L. Turkana
L. Stéfanie
Chew Bahir
Mega
KENYA
H

7   8   9   10   11   12

COPYRIGHT. GEORGE PHILIP & SON LTD.

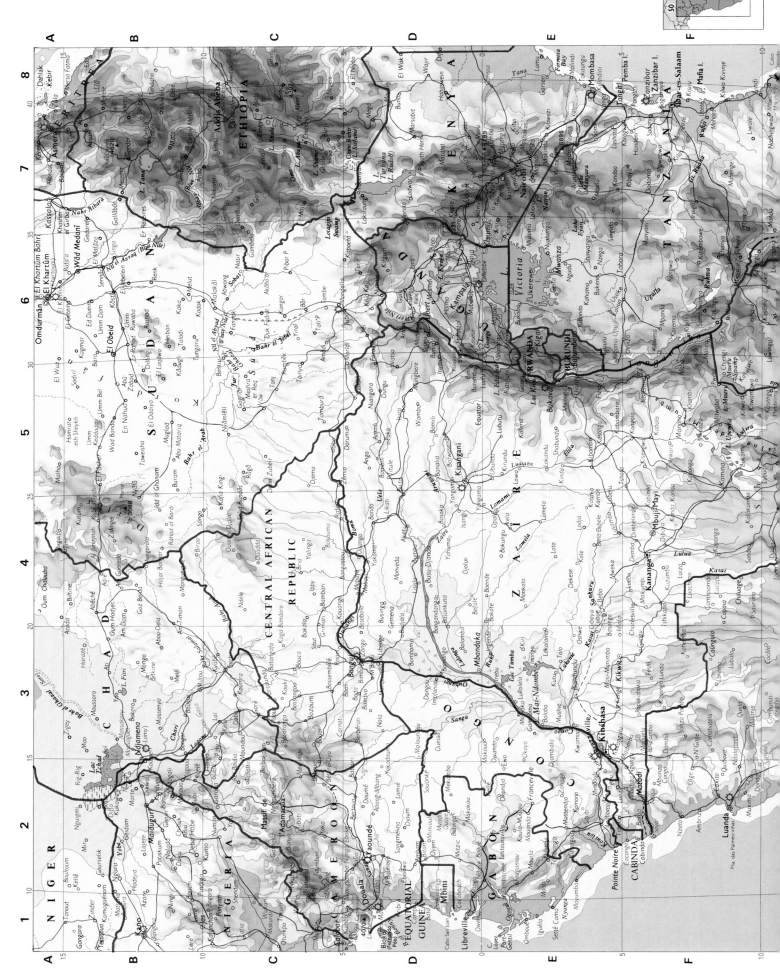

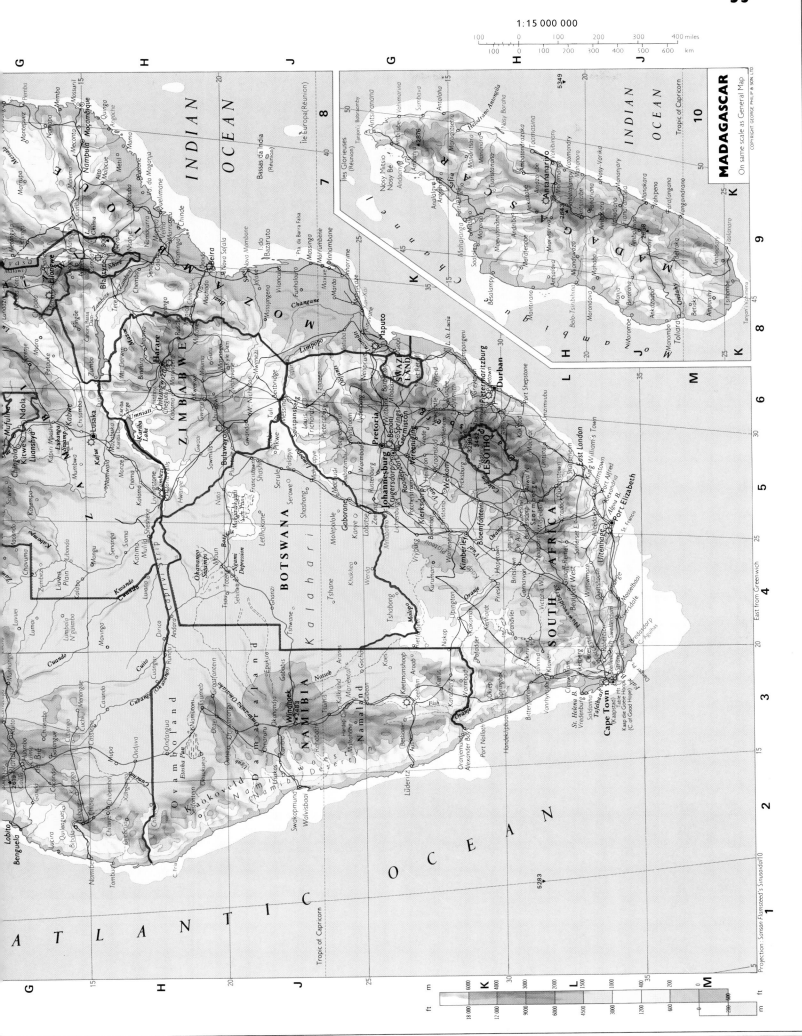

1:15 000 000

MADAGASCAR
On same scale as General Map

COPYRIGHT GEORGE PHILIP & SON, LTD.

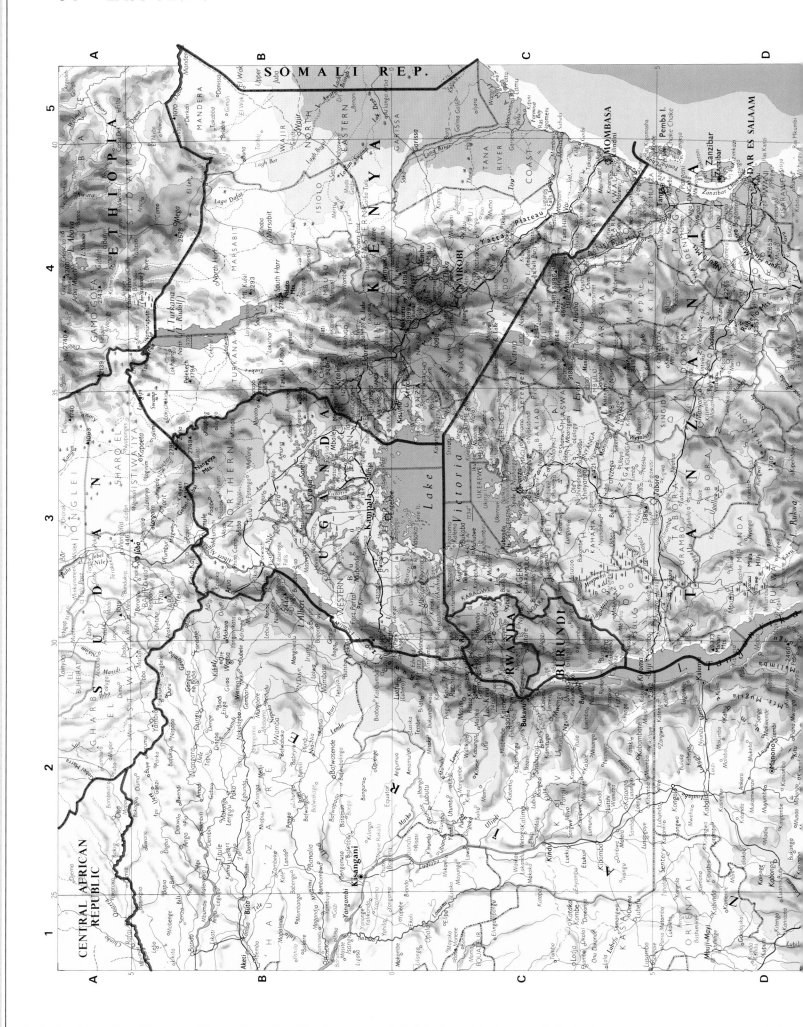

1 : 8 000 000

Projection : Lambert's Equivalent Azimuthal

COPYRIGHT GEORGE PHILIP & SON, LTD

East from Greenwich

53 55

1 **2** **3**

ANGOLA

CUANDO CUBANGO

WESTERN

SOUTH

ZAMBIA

Ponta Albina
Pta. da Marca
NAMIBE
Tombua
Cuanza
Chanhanga 15
Macope
Mupa N
Lagos
Catuala
Mulonga Plain Sioma
Senanga
Lubi
Zambezi
Kaloma
Tara

Ba. dos Tigres
Iona
Oncocua
Otchinjau
Chibemba
Cafu
Evale
Nehone
Chiquelequele
Cula
Capuça
Luiana
Katima Mulilo
Sesheke
Mwandi
Sindeo
Kabango

Foz do
Cunene
Chitado
Ruacana
Namacunde
Ondjiva
Naulila Cuamato
Chiede
Mienga
L. do Dungo
Marung
Mucusso
Dirico
Didimbo
Luana
Kongola
Livingstone

Baynes Mts. 2195
Hartmannberge
Steilrandberge
Ruacana Falls
Tshandi
Enana
Nkurenkuru
Cuangar
Calai
Rundu
Nyangana
Andara
Shakawe
Caprivi Strip
Victoria Falls

Etanga
Opuwo
Elim
Oshigambo
Ondangua
Tondoro
Lupala
Nyurpuru
Utukoto
Mucusse
Bagani
Mababe
Chobe Nat.
Park
Hwange
Nat. Park

Rocky Point
Hoarusib
Sesfontein
Natukanaoka Pan
Etosha Pan
Namutoni
Karakuwisa
Noma Omuramba
Tsodilo Hill 1300
Nxau-Nxau
Mababe Depression
Maseme
Dedo

Kaokoveld
Hoanib
Kamanjab
Okaukuejo
Tsumeb
Grootfontein
Okavango
Swamps
Nokaneng
Maun
Jovere ga
Motlamanyane
Gobokonkwane

Huab
Fransfontein
Outjo
Okaputa
Otavi 2148
Uchab
Omuramba Omatako
Aha Mts.
Kaukauveld
Tsau
Sehitwa
Makalamabedi
Moremaoto
Khumaga
Odiakwe
Tsigara

Khorixas
Otjiwarongo
Kalkfeld
Hochfeld
Eiseb
Rooiboklaagte
Ngami Depression
Maitengwe
Makgadikgadi
Salt Pan
Mopipi

NAMIBIA
Omaruru
Okombahe
Sandveld
Groothaagte
Great Tsau
L. Xau (L. Dow) 974
Kedia Hill
Khama
Country

Anichab
Brandberg 2606
Uis
Erongo 2350
Ounguati
Wilhelmstal
Epukiro
Epukiro
Rietfontein
Ghanzi
Dekar
Eerstrus
Rakops
Xhumo
Mmadisa
Letlhakane

Kaapkruis
Omaruru
Usakos
Karibib
Okahandja
Steinhausen
Mamuno
Kalkfontein
Kuke
Matapa
Shoshong
Serowe

Swakopmund
Walvisbaai
Khan
Trekkopje
Omitara
Witvlei
Gobabis
Tshwee
Okwa
Takachu
Khomodimo
Palapye

Walvisbaai (Walvis Bay)
Khomas Hochland
Windhoek
Aussberg
2483
Seeis
Witvleirivier
Sandfontein
Makunda
Chukudukraal
Mahalapye

Sandwich B.
Swakop
Hakos
Rehoboth
Dordabis
Nojane
Massering
Kang
Lephepe
Dinokwe

Tropic of Capricorn
Tubas
Garob
2351
Uhlenhorst
Ukwi
Lehututu
Dutlwe
Letlhakeng
Dibete

Conception B.
Tsirub
Leonardville
Aminuis
Hukuntsi
Lokgwabe
Tshane
Mochudi

Meob B.
Sossus Vlei
Hollams' Bird I.
Kam
Kalkrand
Aranos
Nossob
Molepolole
Gaborone
Ramotswa
Depredorp

Hardap Dam
Mariental
Stampriet
Werda
Ironstone Kopje
Kwedia
Kanye
Middleton

Maltahöhe
Namaland
Auob
Gochas
Kalahari
Kalahari Gemsbok National Park
Tshabong
Morokweng
Lobatse
Zeerust
Tlhabane

Gibeon
Nossob
Schwarzrand
Asab
Koes
Vytdraai
Kuruman
Tsineng
Vryburg
NORTH-WEST
Kruger
Rand

Spencer B.
Helmeringhausen
Bersebo
Tses
Askham
Kurumon
Reivilo
Schweizer-Reneke
Klerksdorp

Hottentotsbaai
Lüderitzbaai
Kolchab
Bethanien
Koes
Khuis
Ganyesa
Stella
Delareyville
Wolmaransstad
Bothaville

Halifax I.
Lüderitz
Kolmanskop
Aus
Konkiep
Seeheim
Gowachub
Groot Karasberge
Blaudhoek
Taung
Christiana
Bloemhof
Kroonstad

Hunsberge 1655
Klein-Karas
Kanus
Genab
Swartmodder
1855
Mabieskraal
Welkom
Virginia

Karasburg
Hamob
Longklip
Upington
Postmasburg
Griekwastad
Warrenton
Kimberley
Bloemfontein
FREE

Oranjemund
Ariamsvlei
Nakop
Augrabies
Keimoes
Groblershoop
Campbell
Boshof

Alexander Bay
Oranje
Goodhouse
Warmbad
Kakamas
Koegrabie
Douglas
FREE STATE

Port Nolloth
Steinkopf
Pella
Pofadder
Kenhardt
Putsonderwater
Jacobsdal
Petrusburg

ATLANTIC
Buffels
Okiep
Nababeep
Springbok
Aggeneys
Koegrabie
Niekerkshoop
Hopetown
Belmont
Edenburg

SOUTH AFRICA

OCEAN

Kamieskroon
Namaqualand
Pofadder
Prieska
Strydenburg
Philippolis
Trompsburg

NORTHERN CAPE
Grootvloer
Vanwyksvlei
Vosburg
Petrusville
Smithfield

Hondeklipbaai
Garies
Brandvlei
Sodium
Houtkraal
Philipstown
Springfontein

Biesiesfontein
Bitterfontein
Loeriesfontein
Sakrivier
Kareeberg
Carnarvon
De Aar
Colesberg
Noupoort
Burgersdorp

Koekenaap
Nuwerus
Kliprand
Williston
1667
Pampoenpoort
Hanover
Middelburg
Rosmead

Vredendal
Klawer
Calvinia
Vanrhynsdorp
Doring
1672
Victoria West
Hutchinson
Richmond
Kompasberg 2502
EASTERN

Lambert's Bay
Clanwilliam
Wuppertal
Great Karoo
Fraserburg
Nelspoort
Graaff-Reinet
Cradock
CAPE
Queenstown

St. Helena B.
Velddrif
Aurora
Citrusdal
Bo-Wadrif
Koedoesberge
Leeu-Gamka
Beaufort West
Murraysburg
Aberdeen
2369

Vredenburg
Saldanha
Hopefield
Piketberg
Porterville
Ladismith
Prince Albert
Klipplaat
Jansenville
Somerset East
Adelaide
Fort Beaufort

Moorreesburg
Malmesbury
Tulbagh
2249
Swartberge
Oudtshoorn
Willowmore
Kougaberg
Uitenhage

CAPE TOWN (Kaapstad)
Table Mt. 1086
Paarl
Worcester
Montagu
Little Karoo
George
Knysna
Port Elizabeth

Stellenbosch
Somerset West
Robertson
Swellendam
Langeberge
Mosselbaai
Algoa Bay
PORT ELIZABETH

Simonstown
Kaap die Goeie Hoop (Cape of Good Hope)
Strand
Caledon
Stormsrivier
Plettenbergbaai

Hermanus
Danger Pt.
Stanford
Elim
Bredasdorp
C. St. Francis

Quoin Pt.
C. Agulhas

ft m
9000 3000
6000 2000
4500 1500
3000 1000
1200 400
600 200
0 0
200 600
2000 6000
4000 12,000
m ft

Projection: Lambert's Equivalent Azimuthal

D
E

B
C
D

20
25
30

1 15 **2** 20 **3** 25 **4**

1 : 8 000 000

50   0   50   100   150   200 miles
50   0   100   200   300 km

5   **6**   **7**

MALAWI

B

MOZAMBIQUE

CHANNEL

Ile de Juan de Nova
(Réunion)

40   50

8

Iles Glorieuses
(Réunion)

Tanjon'i Bobraomby

Tanjon'i St. Sébastien
Toraka Leven
Ampombiantambo

Nosy Mitsio

Nosy Be
Betsaka

Antsiranana
Ambohitra
1475

A

Saikanosy Ampasindava
Anorotsangana
Helodranon' Ampasindava

Nosy Radama
Nosy Lava
Helodranon'i Narinda

Mahajanga
Katsepe
Mitsinjo

Soalala

15

Marovoay
Ankarafantsika

Mampikony

Besalampy

Maevatanana

Ankazobe

B

Tamboharano
Helodranon' Kotraika
Maintirano

Berevo
Bebao

Nosy Barren

Antsalova
Soahanina

Bekodoka
Sitampiky

Kandreho

Soaloka
Tsiroanomandidy

Betafo
Ankazobe

ANTANANARIVO

ANTANANARIVO

Toamasina

Masoarivo

Miandrivazo

Antsirabe
2643

20

Belo-
Tsiribihina

Morondava
Mahabo

Malaimbandy

D

Ambositra

Fandriana

Nosy-Varika

Belo

Befasy

Mandabe

Ambohimahasoa

Ifanadiana
Mananjary

Ankazoabo

Ranohira

FIANARANTSOA

C

Ankaramena

Manakara

Ihosy

Ivohibe
2658

Vohipeno

Manombo
Toliara

Tropic of Capricorn

Vangaindrano
Manara
Midongy Atsimo
Befotaka

Betioky

E

Ampanihy
Bekily
1956

Manantenana

D

Androka
Ampotaka
Tranoroa
Tsihombe
Bevoalavo
Beloha
Ankororoka

Taolanaro

Tanjon'i Vohimena

9

MADAGASCAR

On same scale as General Map

COPYRIGHT. GEORGE PHILIP & SON. LTD.

7   45   **8**

East from Greenwich

INDIAN

OCEAN

1 : 50 000 000

250   0   250   500   750   1000 miles
250   0   500   1000   1500 km

Physical map (top):

ft m
12000 4000
9000 3000
6000 2000
3000 1000
1500 500
600 200
0
0
200 600
1000 3000
2000 6000
4000 12000
6000 18000
8000 24000
m ft

Malay Peninsula
Str. of Malacca
Sumatra
Borneo
Celebes Sea
Str. of Makassar
Celebes
Halmahera
Sula Is.
Buru
Ceram
Ambon
Maoke Mts.
6029 Puncak Jaya
G. of Sarera
Admiralty Is.
New Ireland
Nauru
Gilbert Is.
Bismarck Arch.
New Guinea
Aru Is.
New Britain
9103
Bougainville
Solomon Is.
Owen Stanley Ra.
PACIFIC
Java Sea
Banda Sea
Tanimbar Is.
Flores Sea
Java
Flores
Timor
Arafura Sea
Melville I.
Thursday I.
C. York
Pt. of Papua
D'Entrecasteaux
Malaita
Ellice Is.
Sumbawa
Sumba
Torres Strait
C. Arnhem
Louisiade Arch.
San Cristobal
Santa Cruz Is.
Timor Sea
Arnhem Land
Gulf of Carpentaria
Cape York Pen.
Great Barrier Reef
Coral Sea
Guadalcanal
Espíritu Santo
Rotuma
Samoan
King Sd.
Victoria
Barkly Tableland
Flinders
Chesterfield Is.
Malakula
New Hebrides
Fiji Is.
Vanua Levu
Savai'i
Upol
Fitzroy
Tanami Desert
Australia
New Caledonia
Loyalty Is.
Viti Levu
Tonga Is.
INDIAN
North West C.
Mt. Bruce 1227
L. Disappointment
L. Mackay
Macdonnell Ras.
Hervey B.
Sandy C.
6658
Ashburton
L. Amadeus
Musgrave Ra.
Cooper
C. Byron
Tongatapu
10822
Tropic of Capricorn
Shark Bay
Gascoyne
L. Eyre
Warrego
Darling Downs
New England
Norfolk I.
OCEAN
L. Torrens
Frome
Darling
Kermadec Is.
OCEAN
Darling Ra.
L. Barlee
Nullarbor Plain
Gairdner
Eyre Pen.
Lachlan
Murray
Botany Bay
10047
Geographe Bay
C. Naturaliste
Great Australian Bight
Spencer Gulf
Kangaroo I.
Encounter B.
Australian Alps
C. Howe
Tasman
North C.
C. Leeuwin
P. Phillip B.
Bass Str.
Flinders I.
Sea
B. of Plenty
King I.
Ruapehu 2797
East C.
Hawke B.
Tasmania
South C.
North I.
South I.
Cook Strait
Mt. Cook 3753
Southern Alps
New Zealand
Stewart I.

Political map (bottom):

m ft

MALAYSIA
BRUNEI
PALAU
FEDERATED STATES OF MICRONESIA
MARSHALL IS.
Equator
Kuala Lumpur
SINGAPORE
Borneo
Celebes
Sula Is.
Ceram
IRIAN JAYA
PAPUA NEW GUINEA
New Ireland
NAURU
KIRIBATI
Sumatra
Buru
New Guinea
Madang
Rabaul
New Britain
Bougainville I.
PACIFIC
Java Sea
INDONESIA
Banda Sea
Aru Is.
Lae
Choiseul
SOLOMON IS.
Ujung Pandang
Tanimbar Is.
Santa Isabel
TUVALU
JAKARTA
Java
Flores
Timor
Arafura Sea
Torres Strait
Port Moresby
Honiara
Malaita
San Cristóbal
Funafuti
Sumbawa
Sumba
Kupang
Timor Sea
Santa Cruz Is.
Darwin
Katherine
Gulf of Carpentaria
Cooktown
CORAL SEA ISLANDS TERRITORY
Espíritu Santo
Rotuma
Is. Wallis & Futuna (Fr.)
WESTERN SAMOA
Wyndham
NORTHERN
Cairns
VANUATU
Broome
QUEENSLAND
Townsville
Vanua Levu
Apia
INDIAN
Mount Isa
Chesterfield Is.
Port Vila
Dampier
WESTERN
TERRITORY
Charters Towers
NEW CALEDONIA (Fr.)
Viti Levu
Onslow
AUSTRALIA
Alice Springs
Longreach
Rockhampton
Loyalty Is.
Suva
FIJI
AUSTRALIA
Quilpie
Charleville
Nouméa
TONGA
Wiluna
L. Eyre
Toowoomba
Brisbane
OCEAN
Nuku'alofa
Tropic of Capricorn
Oodnadatta
SOUTH
Cunnamulla
Warwick
Geraldton
Kalgoorlie-Boulder
AUSTRALIA
Bourke
NEW SOUTH
Norfolk I. (Aust.)
Perth
Port Pirie
Broken Hill
WALES
Newcastle
Lord Howe I. (Aust.)
Kermadec Is. (N.Z.)
Fremantle
Esperance
Mildura
A.C.T.
Sydney
Albany
Great Australian Bight
Adelaide
Canberra
Tasman
North I.
NEW ZEALAND
VICTORIA
Sea
Auckland
Ballarat
Geelong
Melbourne
New Plymouth
Hamilton
King I.
Bass Str.
Napier
TASMANIA
Launceston
South I.
Wellington
Hobart
Greymouth
Nelson
Invercargill
Dunedin
Christchurch
Chatham Is. (N.Z.)
International Date Line

Projection: Bonne
90 East from Greenwich 100

● Canberra Capital Cities

CARTOGRAPHY BY PHILIP'S.COPYRIGHT REED INTERNATIONAL BOOKS LTD

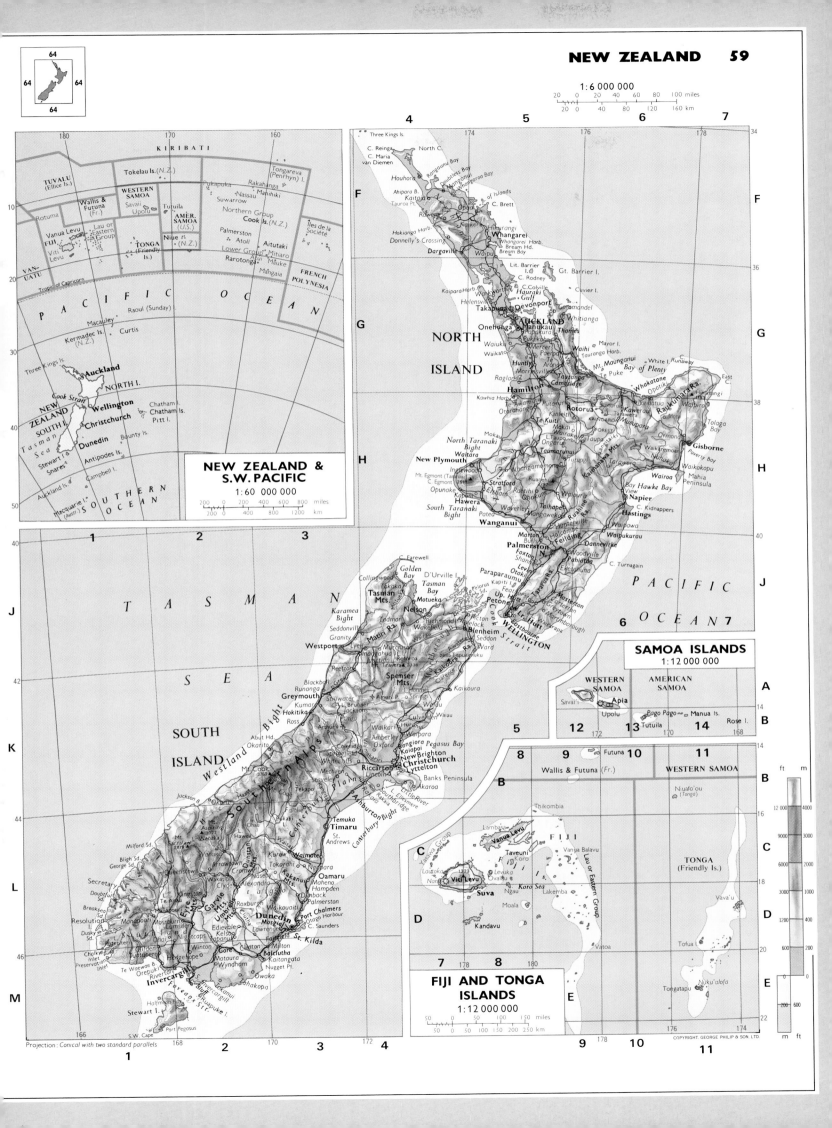

1:6 000 000

SAMOA ISLANDS
1:12 000 000

NEW ZEALAND &
S.W. PACIFIC
1:60 000 000

FIJI AND TONGA
ISLANDS
1:12 000 000

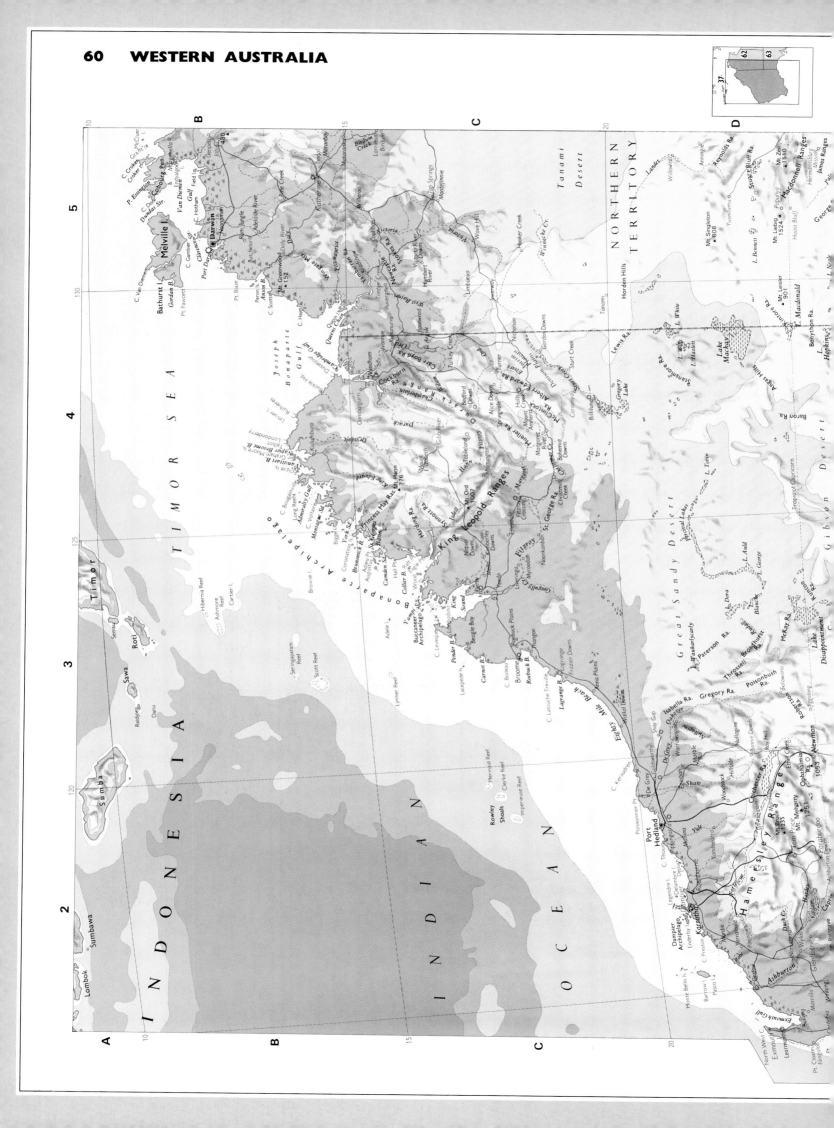

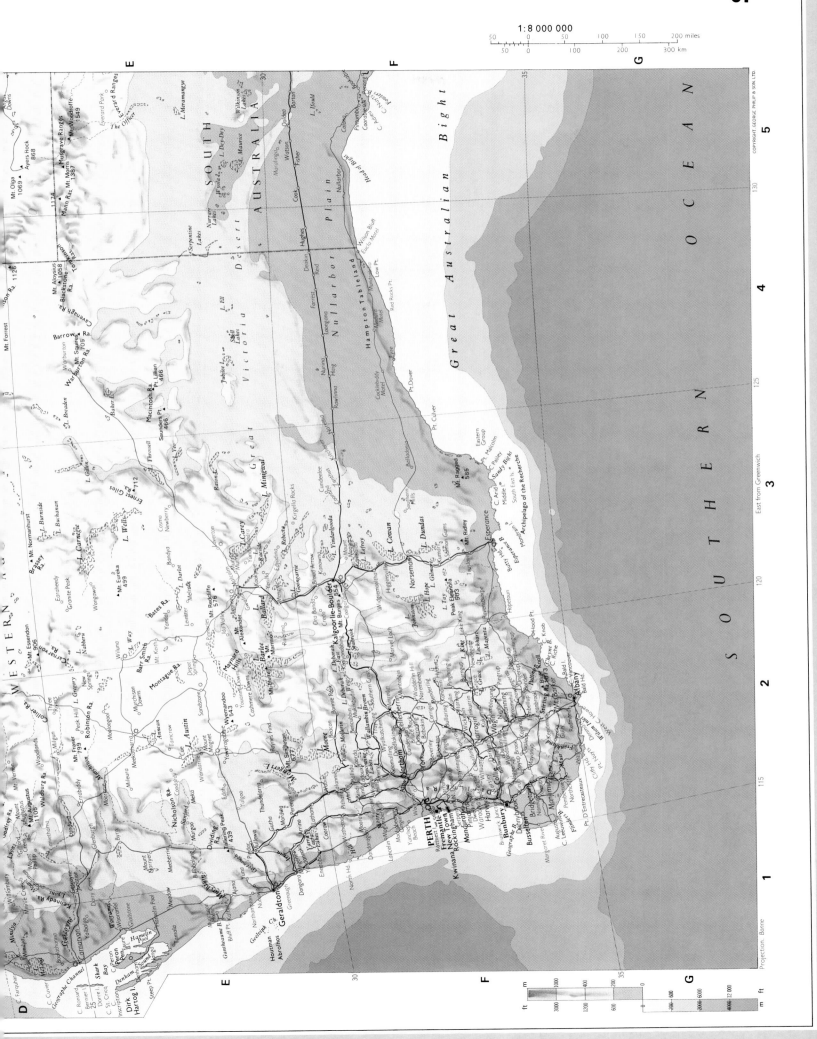

1 : 8 000 000

50   0   50   100   150   200 miles

50   0   100   200   300 km

Projection: Bonne

East from Greenwich

COPYRIGHT. GEORGE PHILIP & SON. LTD.

WESTERN AUSTRALIA

SOUTH AUSTRALIA

Great Victoria Desert

Nullarbor Plain

Hampton Tableland

Great Australian Bight

SOUTHERN OCEAN

PERTH
Fremantle
New Town
Kwinana
Rockingham
Bunbury
Busselton
Albany
Geraldton
Carnarvon

Kalgoorlie-Boulder
Esperance
Norseman

Ayers Rock 868
Mt. Olga 1069
Mann Ras. Mt. Morris 1387
Musgrave Ranges
Mt. Woodroffe 1549
Everard Ranges
The Officer

Mt. Forrest

Warburton Ra.
Mt. Squires 705
Macintosh Ra. Pt. Lillian 466
Saunders Pt. 466

ft   m
12 000   4000
6000   2000
4000   1200
2000   600
1000   400
600   200
200   0
0

m   ft
3000
1200
600
200
0

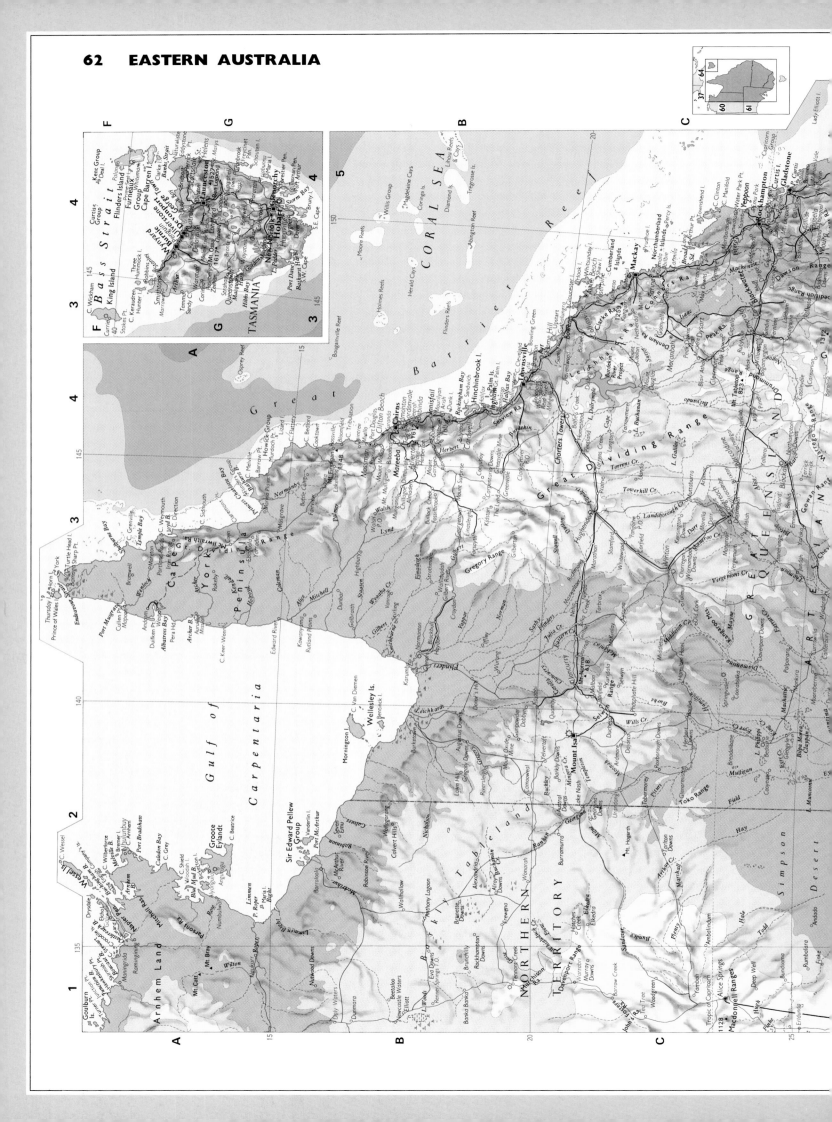

1:8 000 000

Projection: Bonne

COPYRIGHT GEORGE PHILIP & SON, LTD.

East from Greenwich

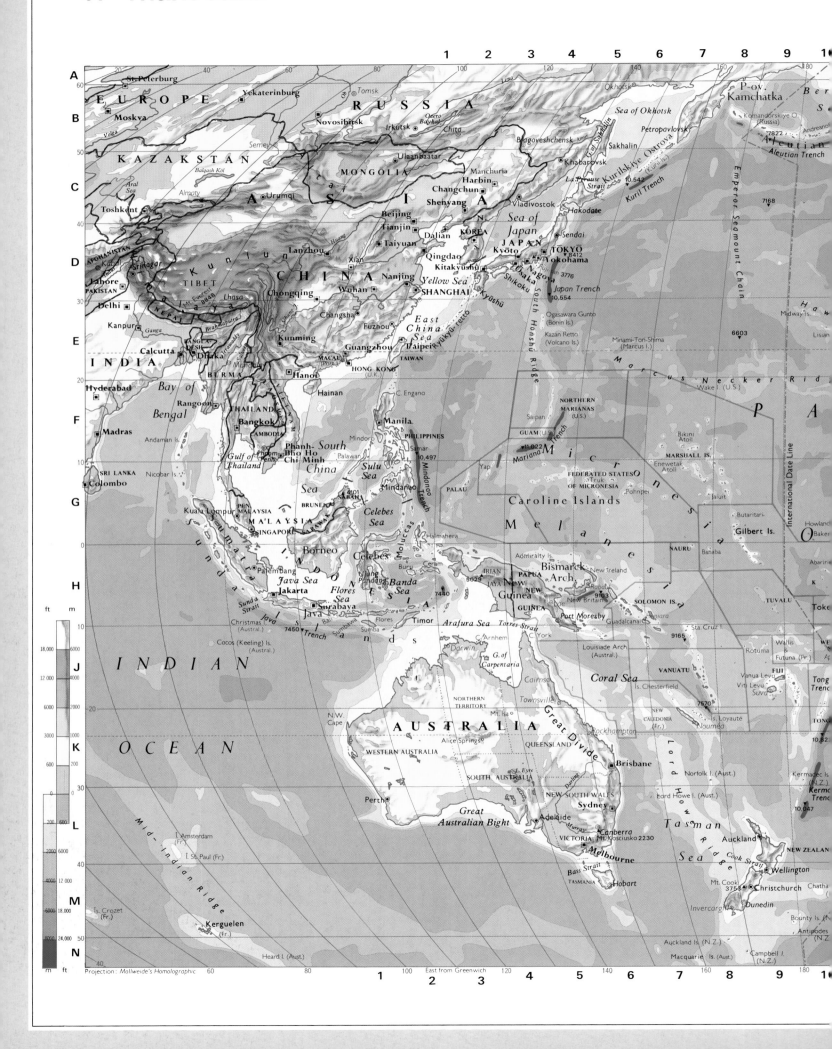

1:54 000 000

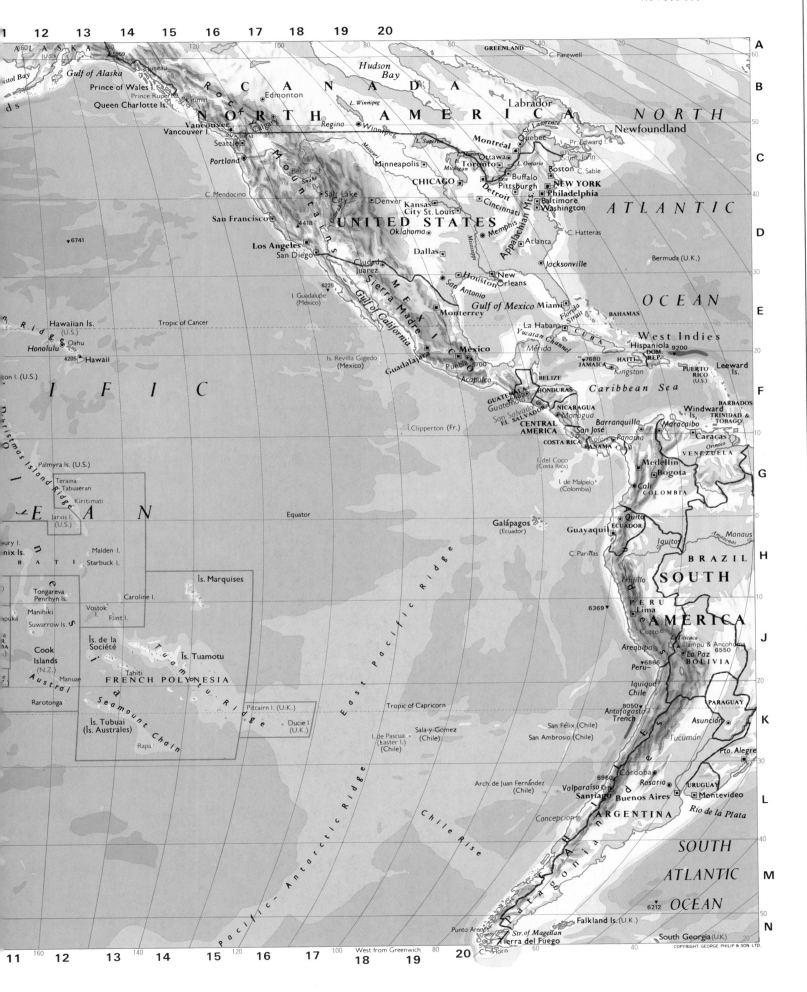

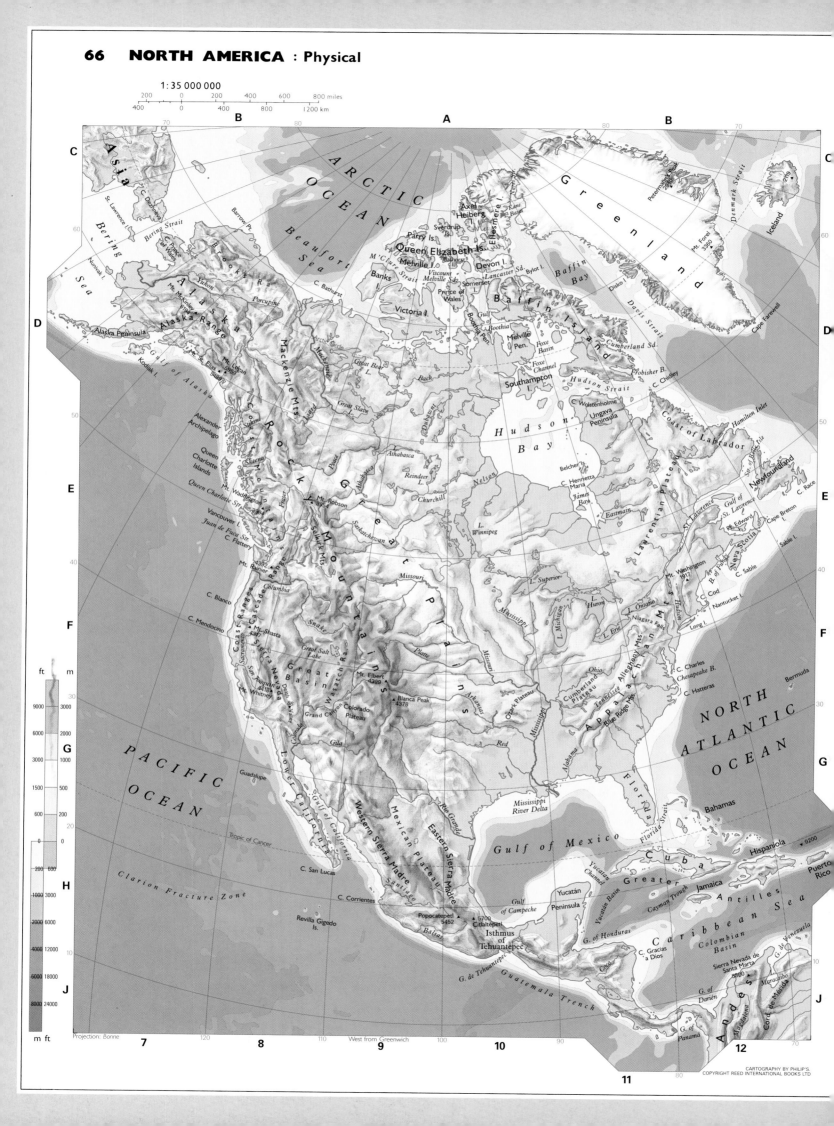

1 : 35 000 000

200   0   200   400   600   800 miles
400   0   400   800   1200 km

A

B   B

C   C
ARCTIC OCEAN

Asia
St. Lawrence I.
C. Dezhneva
Bering Strait
C. Prince of Wales
Barrow Pt.
Beaufort Sea

Greenland
Petermann Peak 2300
Mt. Forel 3380
Denmark Strait
Iceland

Numvak I.
Bering Sea
Brooks Ra.
Axel Heiberg I.
Sverdrup Is.
Parry Is.
Queen Elizabeth Is.
Melville I.
M'Clure Strait
Viscount Melville Sd.
Devon I.
Lancaster Sd.
Bylot I.
Baffin Bay
Kane Basin
Ellesmere I.
Bathurst
Somerset
Disko I.
Davis Strait

D   D
Alaska
Alaska Range
Mt. McKinley
Yukon
Porcupine
Banks I.
Victoria I.
Prince of Wales
Gulf of Boothia
Boothia Pen.
Melville Pen.
Foxe Basin
Foxe Channel
Cumberland Sd.
Baffin Island
Frobisher B.
C. Chidley
Cape Farewell

Alaska Peninsula
Kodiak I.
Gulf of Alaska
Mt. St. Elias 5950
Mackenzie Mts.
Liard
Mackenzie
Great Bear L.
Bach
Dubawnt
Southampton I.
Hudson Strait
C. Wolstenholme
Ungava Peninsula
Coast of Labrador
Hamilton Inlet

E   E
Alexander Archipelago
Skeena
Spatsie
Great Slave L.
Great Bear
Queen Charlotte Islands
Mt. Waddington 3994
Queen Charlotte Str.
Athabasca
Reindeer L.
Nelson
Belcher Is.
C. Henrietta Maria
James Bay
Eastmain
Laurentian Plateau
St. Lawrence
Gulf of St. Lawrence
Newfoundland
Str. of Belle Isle
C. Race

Vancouver I.
Juan de Fuca Str.
C. Flattery
Mt. Robson 3954
Selkirk Mts.
Fraser
Peace
Saskatchewan
Churchill
L. Winnipeg
L. Superior
St. Edward
Cape Breton
Nova Scotia
Sable I.

F   F
Mt. Rainier 4392
Cascade Range
Columbia
Snake
Missouri
Mississippi
L. Michigan
L. Huron
L. Ontario
L. Erie
Niagara Falls
Appalachian Mts.
Hudson
Long I.
Mt. Washington 1917
B. of Fundy
C. Cod
Nantucket I.

C. Blanco
C. Mendocino
Mt. Shasta 4317
Sacramento
Great Salt Lake
Wasatch Ra.
Platte
Missouri
Ohio
Cumberland Plateau
Tennessee
Allegheny Mts.
Blue Ridge Mts.
C. Charles
Chesapeake B.
C. Hatteras

G   G
Coast Ranges
Sierra Nevada
Mt. Whitney 4418
San Joaquin
Death Valley 86
Great Basin
Colorado Plateau
Grand Canyon
Colorado
Gila
Mt. Elbert 4399
Blanca Peak 4378
Arkansas
Red
Ozark Plateau
Mississippi
Alabama
Florida
Bermuda

NORTH ATLANTIC OCEAN

H   H
PACIFIC OCEAN
Guadalupe
Lower California
Gulf of California
Western Sierra Madre
Mexican Plateau
Eastern Sierra Madre
Rio Grande
Mississippi River Delta
Gulf of Mexico
Bahamas
Cuba
Florida Strait
Hispaniola 9200
Puerto Rico
Greater Antilles

Clarion Fracture Zone
Tropic of Cancer
C. San Lucas
C. Corrientes
Santiago
Balsas
Gulf of Campeche
Yucatán Peninsula
Yucatán Channel
Yucatán Basin
Cayman Trough
Jamaica
Antilles
Caribbean Sea

J   J
Revilla Gigedo Is.
Popocatepetl 5452
Citlaltepetl 5700
Isthmus of Tehuantepec
G. de Tehuantepec
Guatemala Trench
Coco
C. Gracias a Dios
G. of Honduras
Colombian Basin
Sierra Nevada de Santa Marta 5800
G. of Venezuela
G. of Darién
Maracaibo
Cord. de Mérida
Andes
G. of Panama

Projection: Bonne

7   120   8   110   West from Greenwich   100   10   90   70   12

11

CARTOGRAPHY BY PHILIP'S.
COPYRIGHT REED INTERNATIONAL BOOKS LTD

1 : 35 000 000

200   0   200   400   600   800 miles
400   0   400   800   1200 km

C   B   A   B   C

RUSSIA

Asia

ARCTIC

OCEAN

GREENLAND

(Denmark)

International Date Line

St. Lawrence

Bering Strait

Bering Sea

Beaufort Sea

Queen Elizabeth Is.

Ellesmere I.

ICELAND

Reykjavik

Denmark Strait

ALASKA (U.S.A.)

Yukon

Porcupine

Fairbanks

Anchorage

Kodiak I.

Gulf of Alaska

Victoria I.

Baffin Bay

Baffin Island

Godthaab

Cape Farewell

Davis Strait

D

YUKON TERRITORY

Whitehorse

Juneau

Arctic Circle

NORTHWEST TERRITORIES

Mackenzie

Great Bear L.

Back

Yellowknife

Great Slave L.

Hudson Strait

Hudson Bay

NEWFOUNDLAND

E

BRITISH COLUMBIA

Skeena

Fraser

Liard

Peace

ALBERTA

Edmonton

Calgary

Athabasca

SASKATCHEWAN

Saskatchewan

Churchill

Athabasca

CANADA

MANITOBA

L. Winnipeg

Nelson

Eastmain

ONTARIO

QUÉBEC

Labrador

St. Lawrence

St-Pierre Et Miquelon (Fr.)

St. John's

PRINCE EDWARD I.

Charlottetown

NEW BRUNSWICK

Fredericton

NOVA SCOTIA

Halifax

C. Sable

Victoria

Vancouver

Regina

Winnipeg

Montréal

Québec

Augusta

MAINE

Olympia

WASHINGTON

Seattle

Portland

Salem

Columbia

OREGON

MONTANA

Missouri

Helena

IDAHO

Boise

Snake

WYOMING

NORTH DAKOTA

Bismarck

SOUTH DAKOTA

MINNESOTA

Minneapolis

WISCONSIN

Madison

Milwaukee

L. Superior

L. Michigan

L. Huron

MICHIGAN

Lansing

Detroit

Toronto

Ottawa

Buffalo

NEW YORK

Concord

N.H.

Boston

MASS.

Providence

Hartford

NEW YORK CITY

PHILADELPHIA

VER.

F

Sacramento

San Francisco

San Jose

CALIFORNIA

Carson City

NEVADA

Salt Lake City

UTAH

Cheyenne

Denver

COLORADO

NEBRASKA

Lincoln

Topeka

KANSAS

IOWA

MISSOURI

St. Louis

ILLINOIS

CHICAGO

Springfield

INDIANA

Indianapolis

Cincinnati

OHIO

Columbus

Cleveland

Pittsburgh

Erie

PA.

Baltimore

Washington D.C.

Richmond

VIRGINIA

W.VA.

MD.

KENTUCKY

Nashville

TENNESSEE

Memphis

G

Los Angeles

San Diego

Las Vegas

ARIZONA

Phoenix

Tucson

NEW MEXICO

Albuquerque

Santa Fe

Colorado

El Paso

OKLAHOMA

Oklahoma City

ARKANSAS

Little Rock

MISSISSIPPI

Jackson

Birmingham

ALABAMA

Montgomery

Columbia

SOUTH CAROLINA

NORTH CAROLINA

Raleigh

Charlotte

Charleston

GEORGIA

Atlanta

Jacksonville

Bermuda (U.K.)

NORTH ATLANTIC OCEAN

PACIFIC OCEAN

Guadalupe (Mex.)

Hermosillo

Rio Grande

TEXAS

Dallas

Austin

Houston

LOUISIANA

Baton Rouge

New Orleans

Tallahassee

FLORIDA

Tampa

Miami

Florida Str.

Nassau

BAHAMAS

Turks & Caicos Is. (U.K.)

Tropic of Cancer

Culiacan

Monterrey

Gulf of Mexico

Havana

CUBA

Cayman Is. (U.K.)

HAITI

Port-au-Prince

DOMINICAN REP.

Santo Domingo

PUERTO RICO (U.S.A.)

San Juan

JAMAICA

Kingston

Caribbean Sea

MEXICO

Revilla Gigedo Is. (Mex.)

Guadalajara

MÉXICO

Puebla

Acapulco

Mérida

Belmopan

BELIZE

GUATEMALA

Guatemala

HONDURAS

Tegucigalpa

Maracaibo

San Salvador

EL SALVADOR

NICARAGUA

Managua

L. Nicaragua

Barranquilla

VENEZUELA

J

COSTA RICA

San José

PANAMA

Panama

COLOMBIA

Medellin

South America

Projection: Bonne

7   ■ MÉXICO Capital Cities   8

West from Greenwich

9   10   11   12

CARTOGRAPHY BY PHILIP'S
COPYRIGHT REED INTERNATIONAL BOOKS LTD

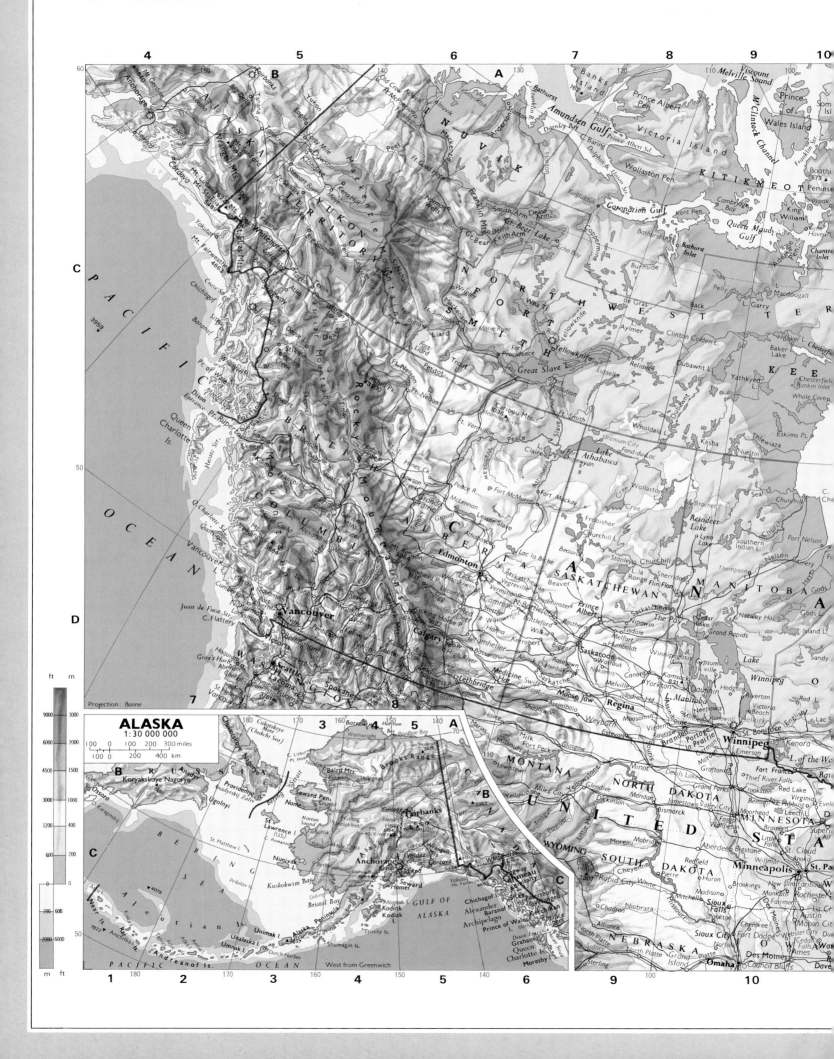

Projection: Bonne

ALASKA
1:30 000 000

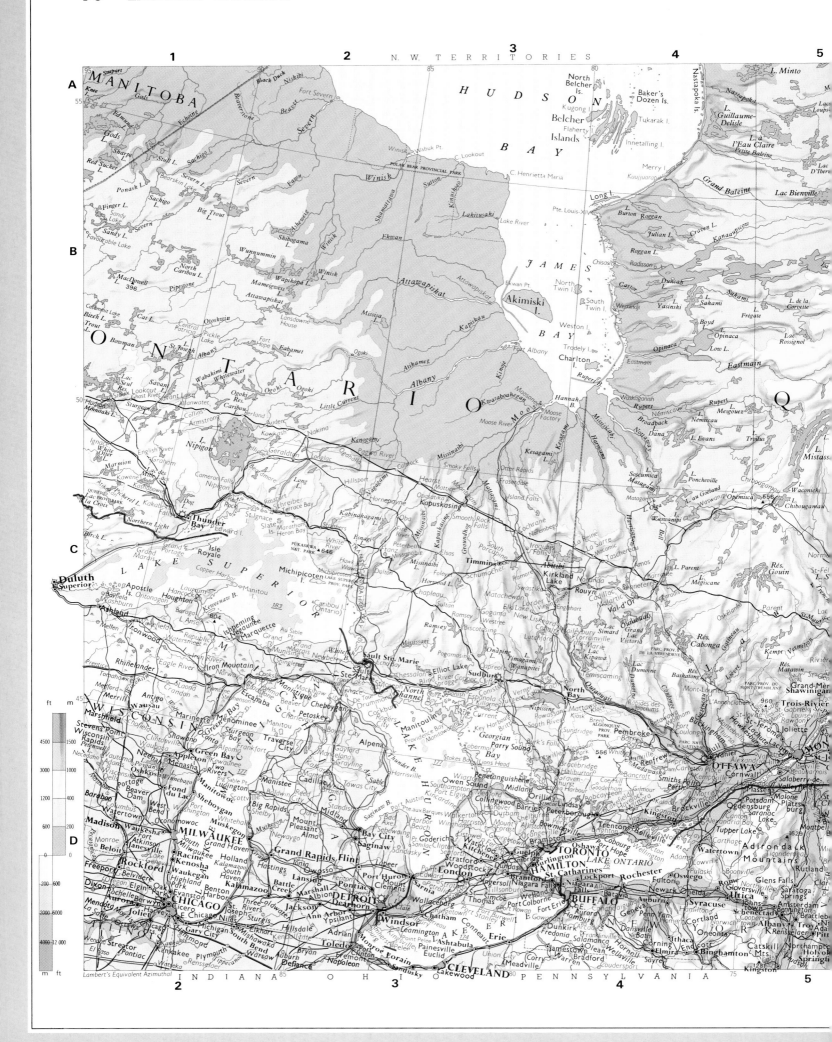

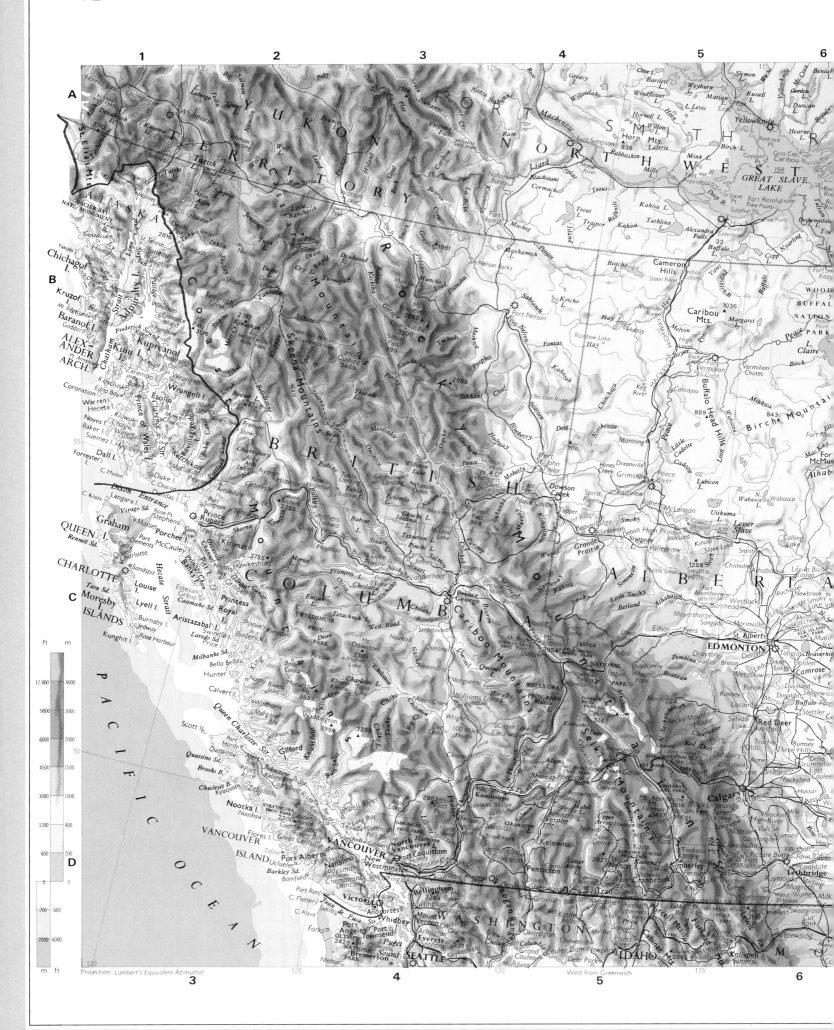

Projection: Lambert's Equivalent Azimuthal

West from Greenwich

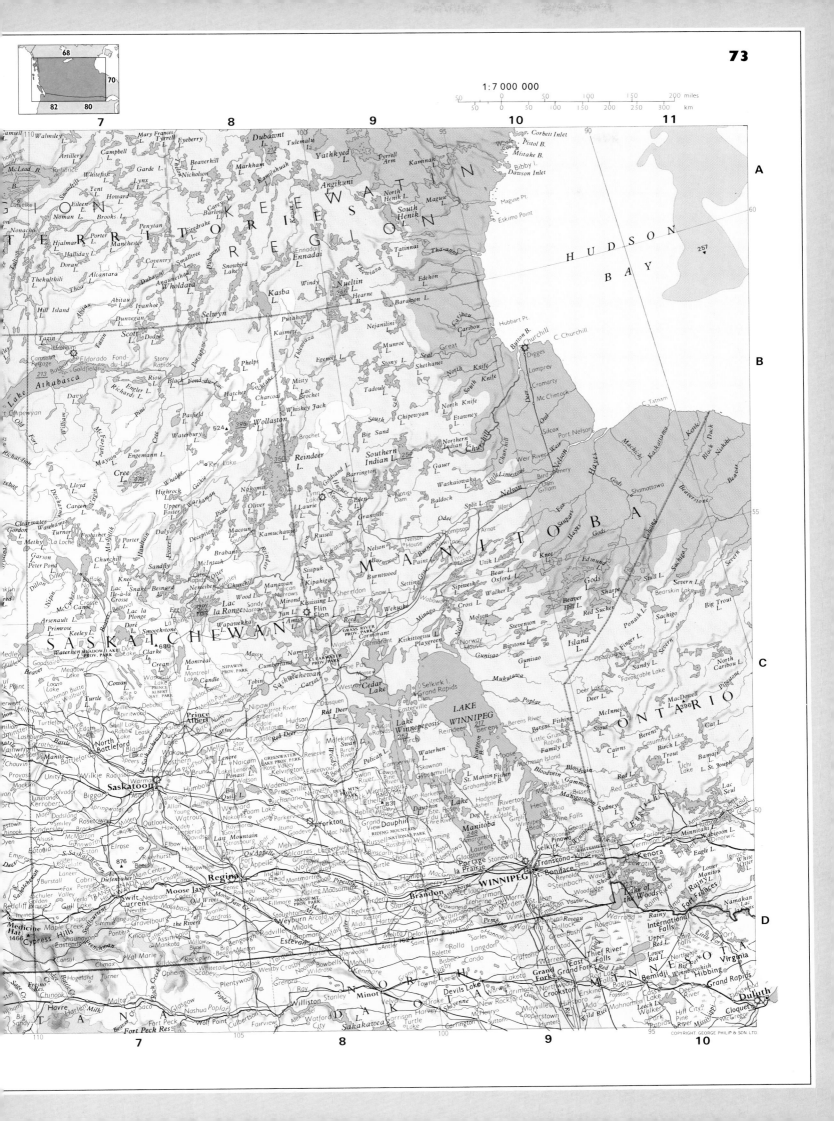

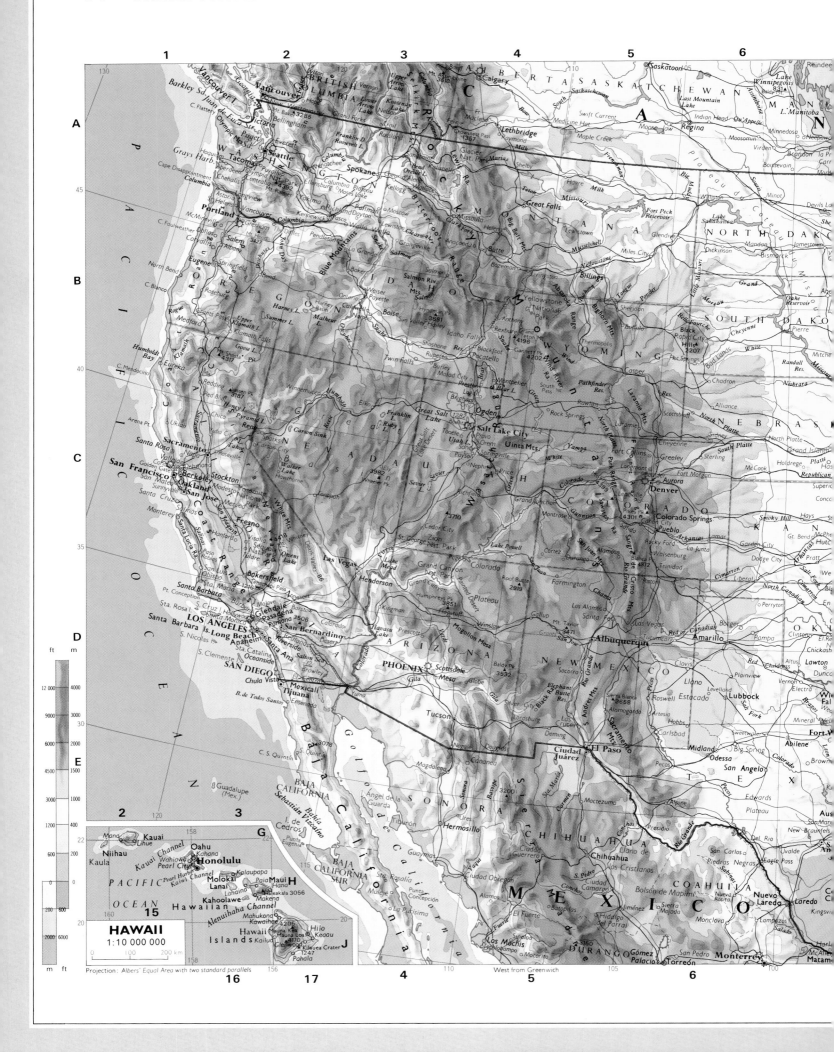

HAWAII
1:10 000 000

Projection: Albers' Equal Area with two standard parallels

West from Greenwich

68 69
86 87
8 9

1:12 000 000
50   100   150   200   250   300 miles
50 0 50 100 150 200 250 300 350 400 450 km

8   9   10   11   12   13

A

CANADA

Lake Winnipeg
Trout Lake   L. St. Joseph
English   L. Seul
Albany
Nakina   Longlac
Moosonee
Nottaway
L. au Goéland
L. Matagami
Chibougamau
Chicoutimi
Rimouski
St. Lawrence
Edmundston
NEW BRUNSWICK

Beren   Kenora
Winnipeg   Sioux Lookout
Lake of the Woods   Rainy   Ignace   Seine
Thunder Bay   St. Ignace
Hearst   Kapuskasing   Cochrane
Timmins   L. Abitibi
Rouyn   Rés. de Gouin
La Tuque   Rivière-du-Loup   Édmundston
Québec   Houlton

Thief River Falls
Grand Forks   Red Lake
Fort Frances
Royale
Michipicoten
Wawa   Sudbury   North Bay
Ottawa   Buckingham
Trois-Rivières
MONTREAL   Sherbrooke   MAINE   Bar Harbor
Presque Isle

45

MINNESOTA   Duluth
Lake Superior   Sault Ste. Marie
Manitoulin   Georgian Bay
Hull   Ottawa
VERMONT   N.H.   Bangor
Rockland   Penobscot Bay

Moorhead   Bemidji   Hibbing   Virginia
Ashland   Keweenaw Bay   Marquette   North Chan.
L. Nipissing
Pembroke   Peterborough   Kingston
Adirondack Mts.   Watertown   Rutland   Manchester
Portland

Fargo   Fergus Falls   St. Cloud   Merrill   Antigo   Escanaba
Parry Sound   Owen Sound   Orillia   Oshawa
TORONTO   Rochester   Syracuse   Schenectady
Concord   Lawrence   Boston
Fall River   New Bedford

B

Big Stone Lake
Willmar   Minneapolis   St. Paul   Stillwater   Green Bay
Lake Michigan   Lake Huron
Hamilton   Niagara Falls   Buffalo
Binghamton   Scranton   Springfield   Hartford   Providence
Waterbury   New Haven   Martha's Vineyard

WISCONSIN   Madison   Milwaukee   Racine   Kenosha
Grand Rapids   Lansing   Flint
DETROIT   Windsor   Erie
NEW YORK   Paterson   NEWARK   NEW YORK
Jersey City

40

IOWA   Waterloo   Cedar Rapids   Rockford
CHICAGO   Gary   Ft. Wayne
Cleveland   Akron   Youngstown
OHIO   Pittsburgh   PHILADELPHIA   Camden
Atlantic City

Des Moines   Davenport   Rock Island
Peoria   Bloomington   Lafayette   Marion   Lima
Mansfield   Canton   Wheeling
PENNSYLVANIA   Harrisburg   York   Wilmington   Baltimore   Delaware Bay

C

Council Bluffs   Omaha
ILLINOIS   Springfield   Decatur   Indianapolis   INDIANA
Dayton   Columbus   Ketterng
Cincinnati   WEST VIRGINIA   Washington D.C.
Richmond   Chesapeake Bay   Cape Charles

Kansas City   St. Louis
MISSOURI
Terre Haute   Louisville   Lexington
Huntington   Charleston   Roanoke
Lynchburg   Newport News   Norfolk   Virginia Beach
Portsmouth

Topeka   Lawrence
St. Joseph   Columbia   Jefferson City
Evansville   KENTUCKY   Frankfort
Beckley   Bristol   Winston   Greensboro   Durham
Raleigh

35

Wichita   El Dorado   Springfield   Rolla
OZARK Plateau
Bowling Green   Nashville
Knoxville   Asheville   NORTH CAROLINA
Winston-Salem   Raleigh
Cape Hatteras

Tulsa   Fayetteville   Boston Mts.
Memphis   Chattanooga   Greenville   Charlotte
SOUTH CAROLINA   Columbia   Wilmington
Onslow Bay

OKLAHOMA   Fort Smith   Little Rock   Hot Springs
ARKANSAS
TENNESSEE   Huntsville   Rome   Atlanta
Augusta   Charleston
Long Bay

D

DALLAS   Texarkana   Shreveport
MISSISSIPPI   ALABAMA   Birmingham   Montgomery
GEORGIA   Macon   Savannah

Tyler   Longview   Monroe   Jackson   Meridian
Columbus   Montgomery   Columbus   Dublin
Brunswick

HOUSTON   Beaumont   Port Arthur
LOUISIANA   Baton Rouge   New Orleans
Mobile   Pensacola   Tallahassee   Jacksonville
St. Augustine

30

Galveston   Lake Charles   Lafayette   New Iberia
Lake Pontchartrain   Biloxi   Gulfport
FLORIDA   Gainesville   Daytona Beach

Delta of the Mississippi   Apalachee B.
Panama City
Orlando   Melbourne   Palm Bay

E

GULF OF MEXICO
Tampa   Clearwater   St. Petersburg   Lakeland
West Palm Beach   Grand Bahama I.   Little Abaco
Gt. Abaco   BAHAMAS   Eleuthera I.

Sarasota   Arcadia   L. Okeechobee
Fort Lauderdale   N.W. Providence Chan.   N.E. Providence Channel

Charlotte Harb.   Cape Coral
Miami   Coral Gables   Nassau   New Providence   Cat I.
Exuma Sound

25

F

Florida Bay
Key West   Florida Keys   Andros I.

COPYRIGHT GEORGE PHILIP & SON LTD.

95   8   90   9   85   10   80   11   12

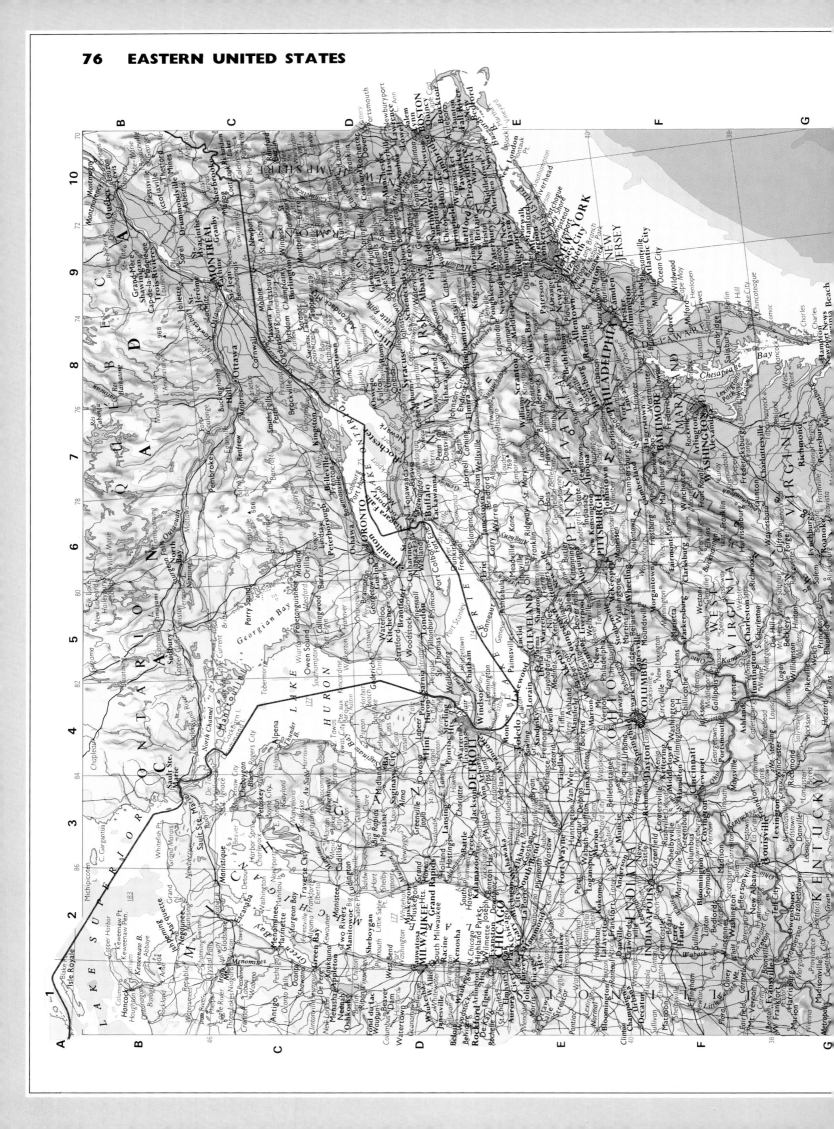

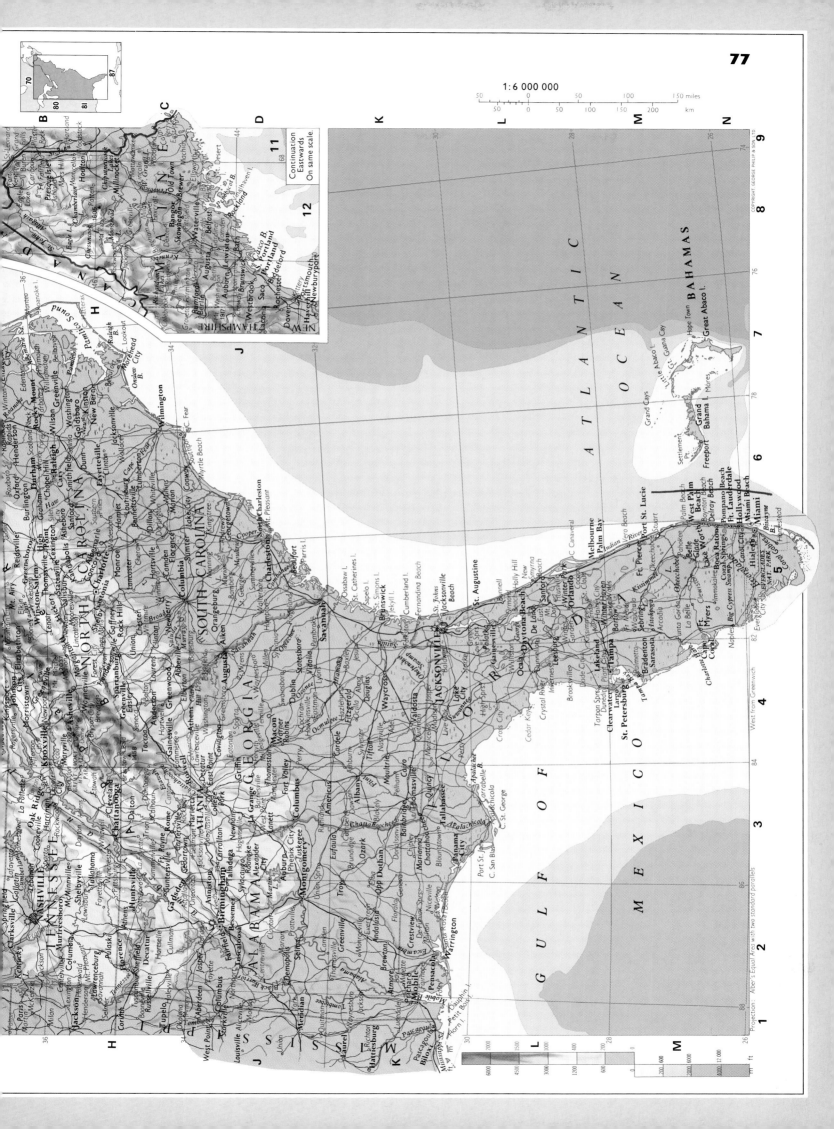

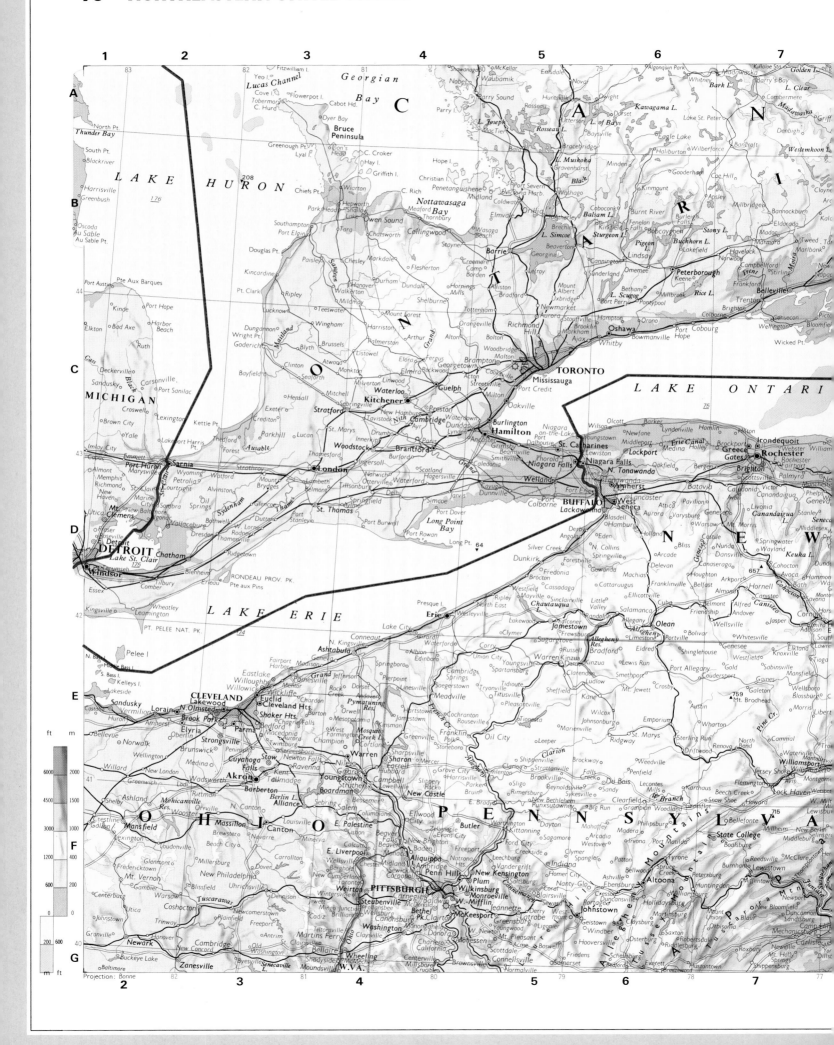

Projection: Bonne

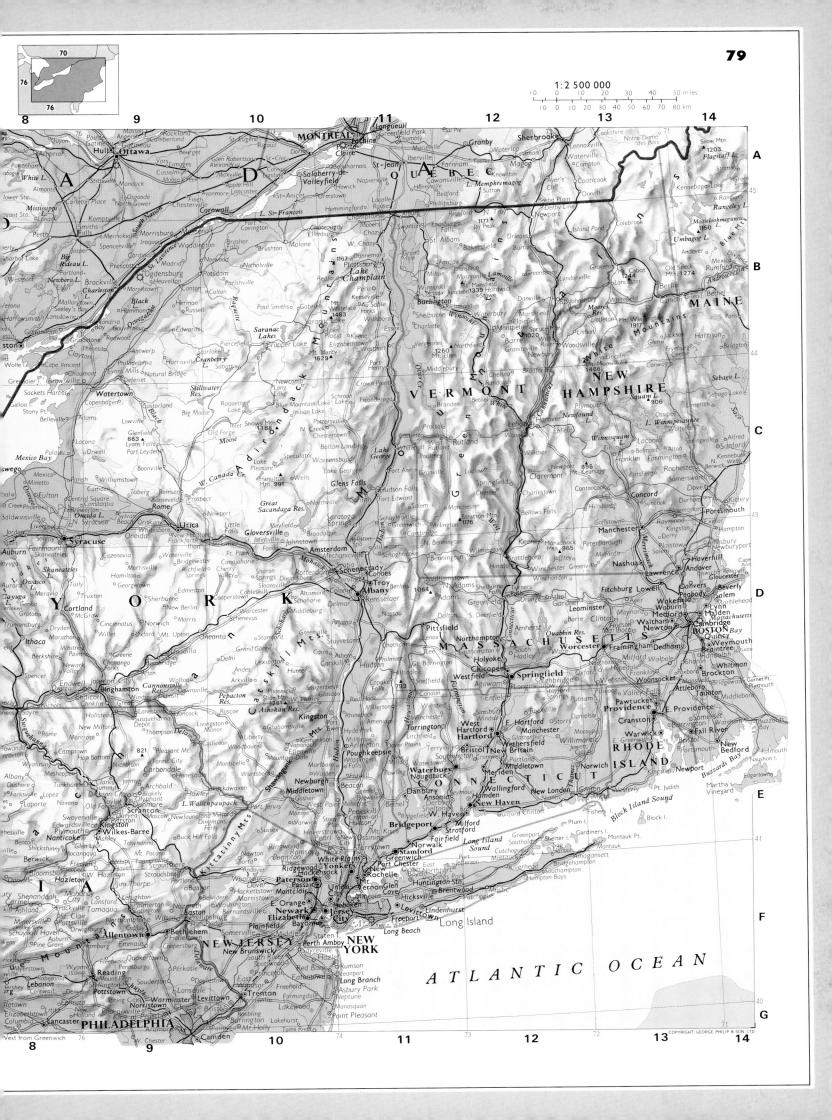

1:6 000 000

50   0   50   100   150 miles

50   0   50   100   150   200   km

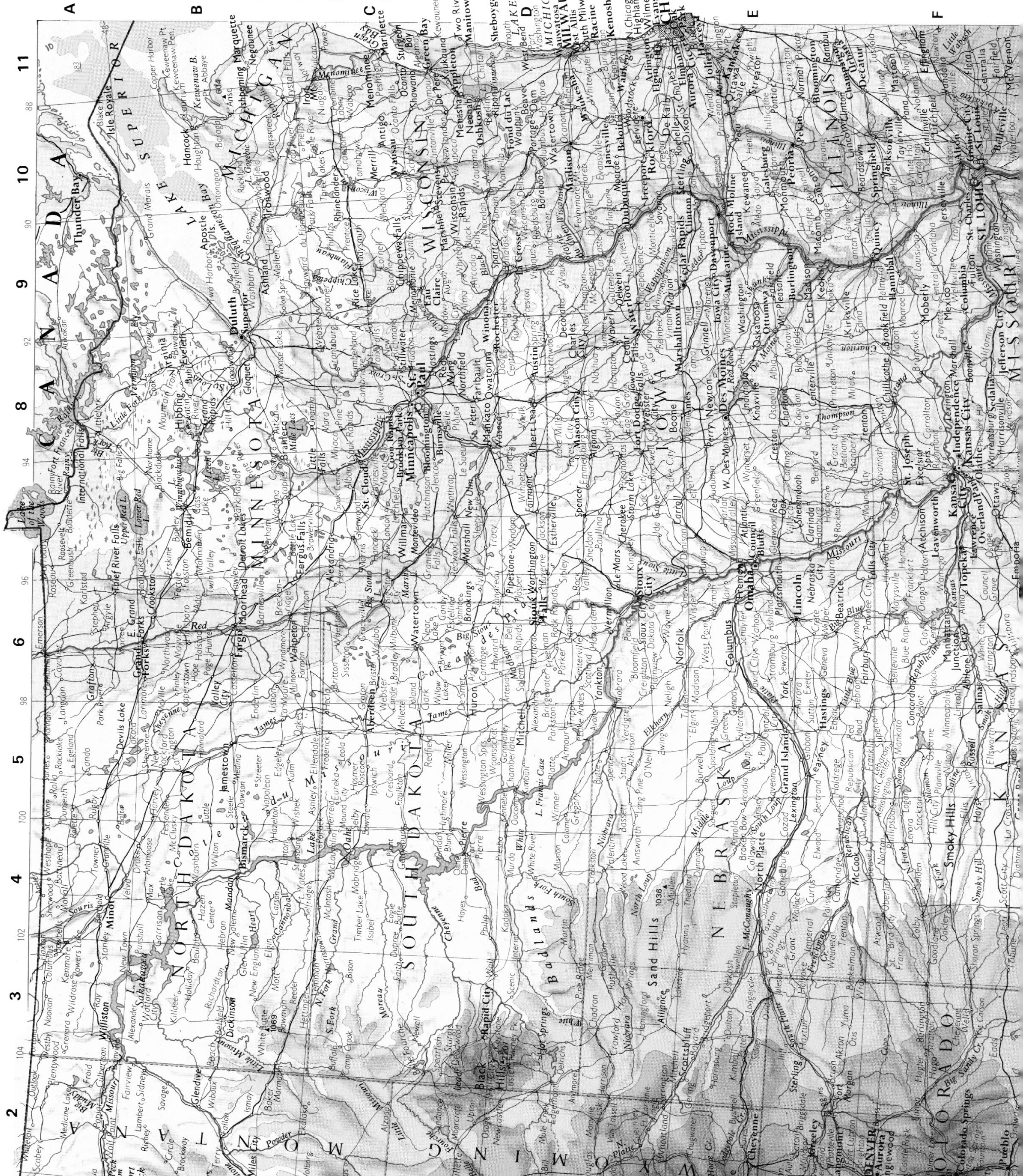

A   B   C   D   E   F

CANADA

LAKE SUPERIOR

MICHIGAN

WISCONSIN

MINNESOTA

NORTH DAKOTA

SOUTH DAKOTA

MONTANA

WYOMING

NEBRASKA

IOWA

ILLINOIS

MISSOURI

KANSAS

COLORADO

CHICAGO

MILWAUKEE

Duluth

Minneapolis
St. Paul

Omaha

Lincoln

Kansas City

Denver

St. Louis

Bismarck

Rapid City

Des Moines

Sioux Falls

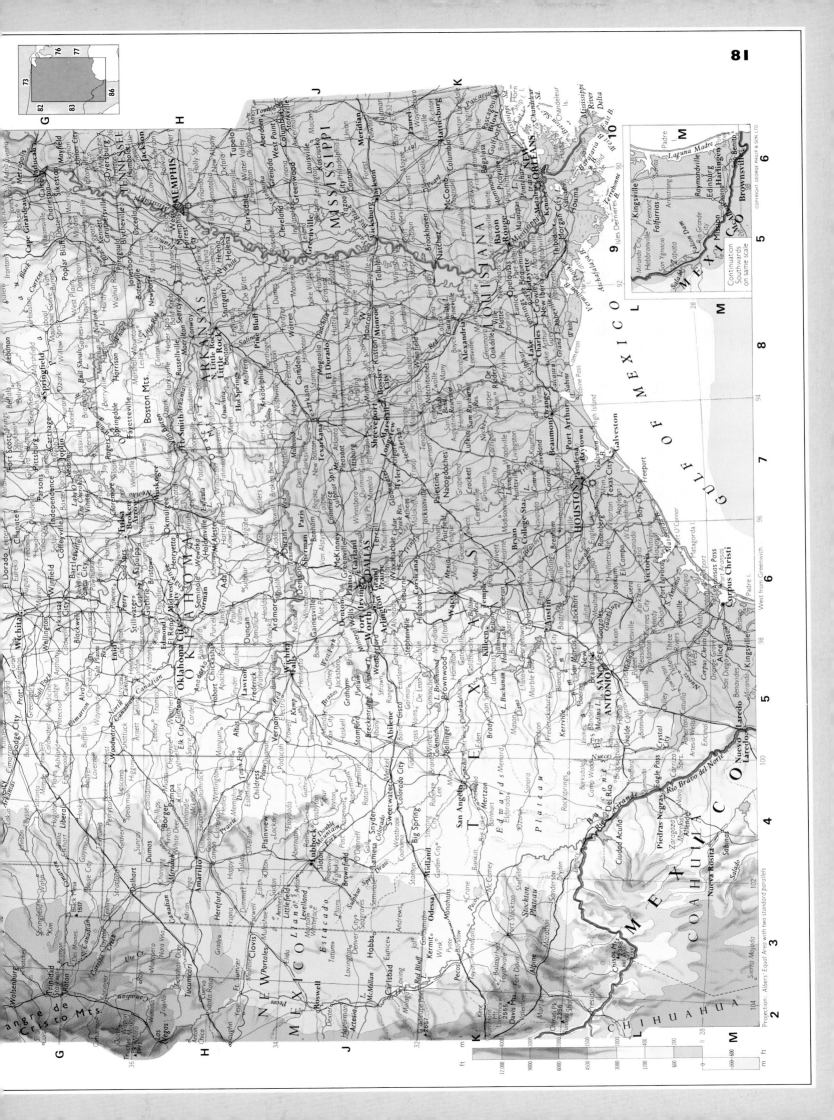

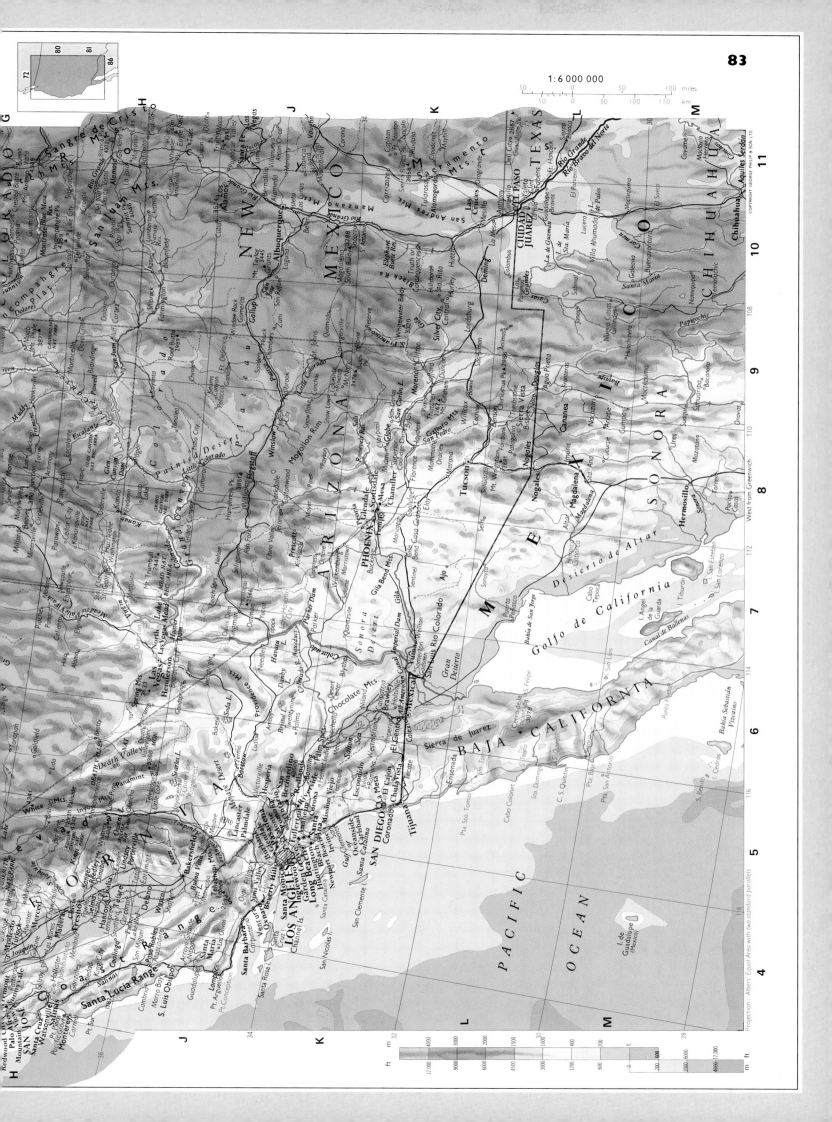

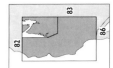

SEATTLE-PORTLAND
REGION
On same scale

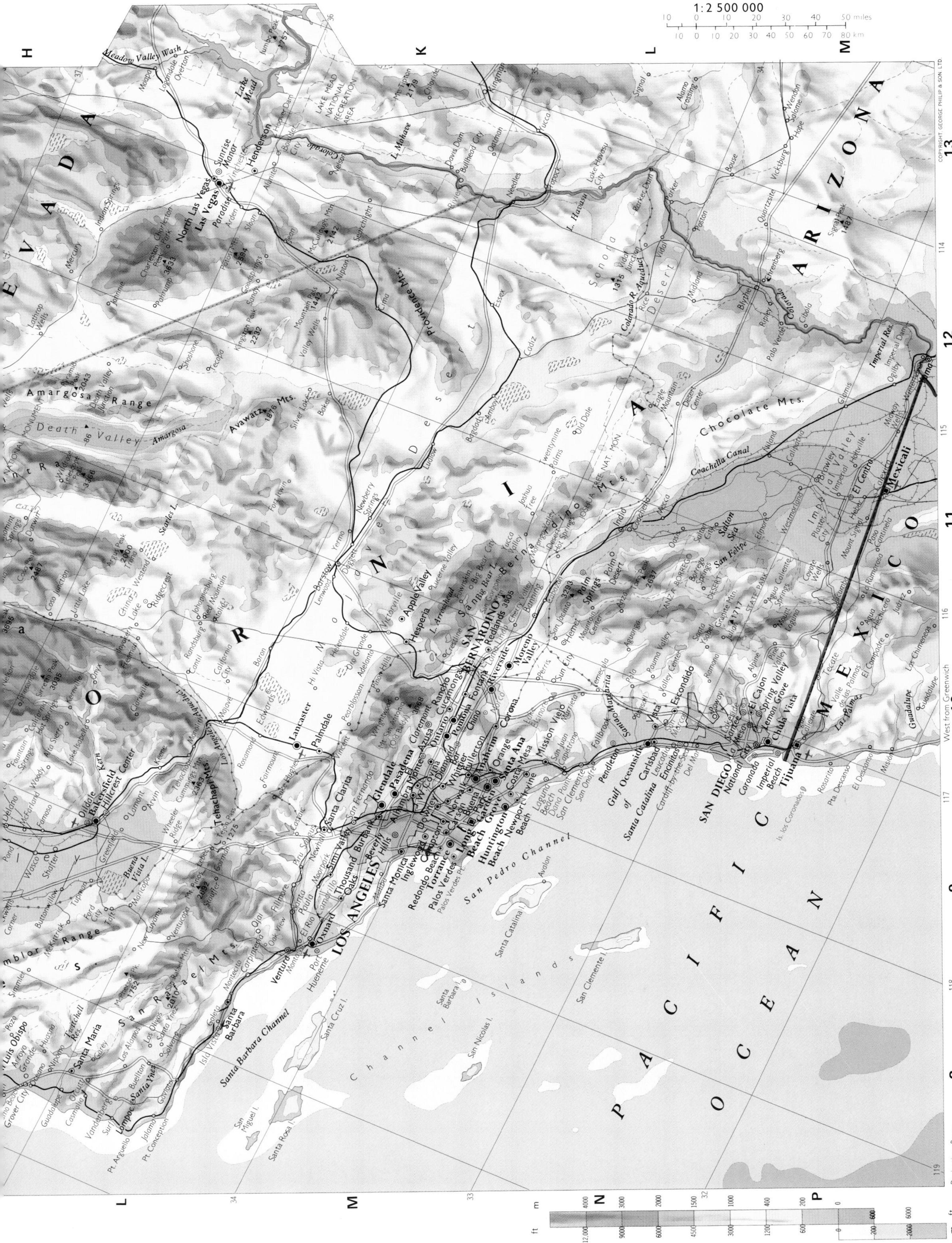

1:2 500 000

10   0   10   20   30   40   50 miles
10   0   10   20   30   40   50   60   70   80 km

H   J   K   L   M

NEVADA

ARIZONA

C   A   L   I   F   O   R   N   I   A

M   E   X   I   C   O

PACIFIC   OCEAN

Lake Mead
LAKE MEAD NATIONAL RECREATION AREA
Las Vegas
North Las Vegas
Henderson
Paradise
Sunrise Manor

Death Valley
Amargosa Range
DEATH VALLEY NATIONAL MONUMENT

Bakersfield
Oildale
Hillcrest Center

Mojave Desert

Lancaster
Palmdale
Victorville
Apple Valley
Hesperia
Barstow

SAN BERNARDINO
Redlands
Riverside
Moreno Valley
Corona
Ontario
Pomona
Pasadena
Glendale
Burbank
Santa Clarita
Thousand Oaks
Simi Valley

LOS ANGELES
Beverly Hills
Santa Monica
Inglewood
Torrance
Redondo Beach
Long Beach
Huntington Beach
Newport Beach
Anaheim
Fullerton
Garden Grove
Santa Ana
Orange
Costa Mesa
Mission Viejo

Ventura
Oxnard
Santa Barbara
Santa Maria
Lompoc
San Luis Obispo

Palos Verdes Pt.
San Pedro Channel
Santa Catalina I.
Avalon
San Clemente I.
San Nicolas I.
Santa Cruz I.
Santa Rosa I.
San Miguel I.
Santa Barbara I.
Channel Islands
Santa Barbara Channel

Oceanside
Carlsbad
Encinitas
Escondido
Vista
El Cajon
La Mesa
Chula Vista
SAN DIEGO
Coronado
Imperial Beach

Tijuana
Mexicali
El Centro
Brawley
Salton Sea
Coachella Canal
Imperial Valley
Imperial Dam
Yuma

Colorado R.
Needles
Blythe
Parker
Parker Dam
Davis Dam
Bullhead City
Kingman
Sonora Desert
Chocolate Mts.

West from Greenwich

Projection: Bonne

COPYRIGHT GEORGE PHILIP & SON, LTD.

m   ft
4000   12,000
3000   9000
2000   6000
1500   4500
1000   3000
600   1800
200   600
0   0
200   600
2000   6000

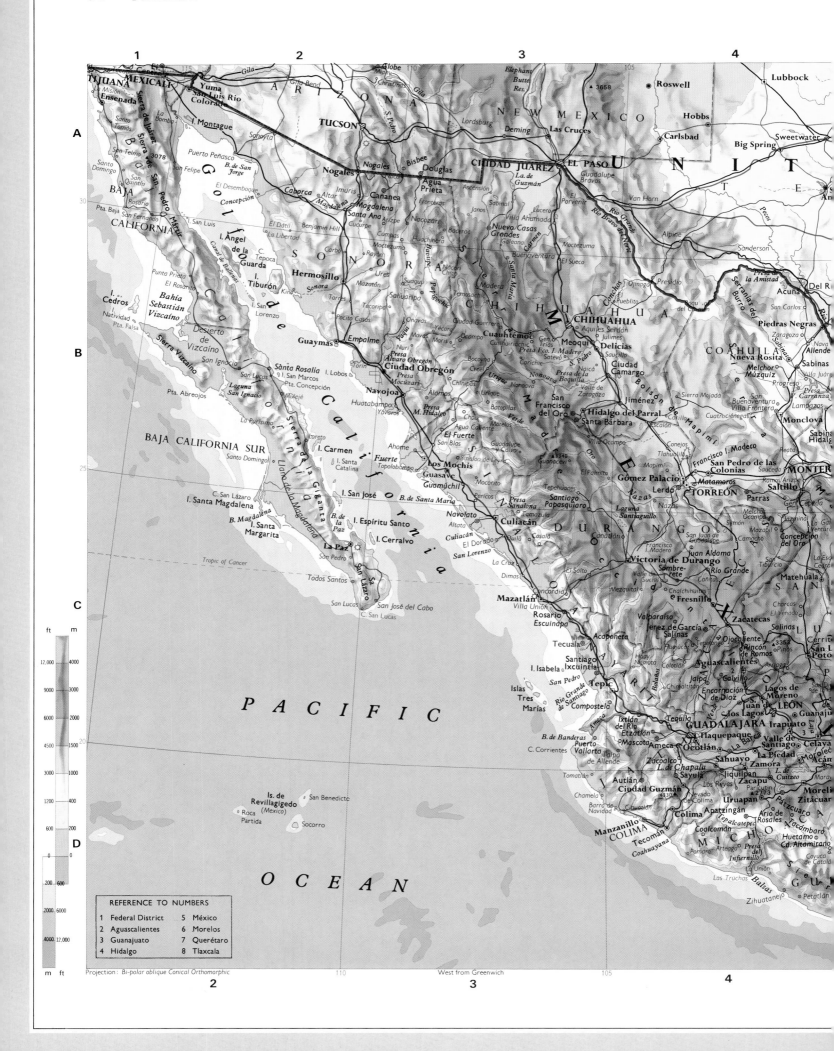

REFERENCE TO NUMBERS
1 Federal District   5 México
2 Aguascalientes   6 Morelos
3 Guanajuato   7 Querétaro
4 Hidalgo   8 Tlaxcala

Projection: *Bi-polar oblique Conical Orthomorphic*

West from Greenwich

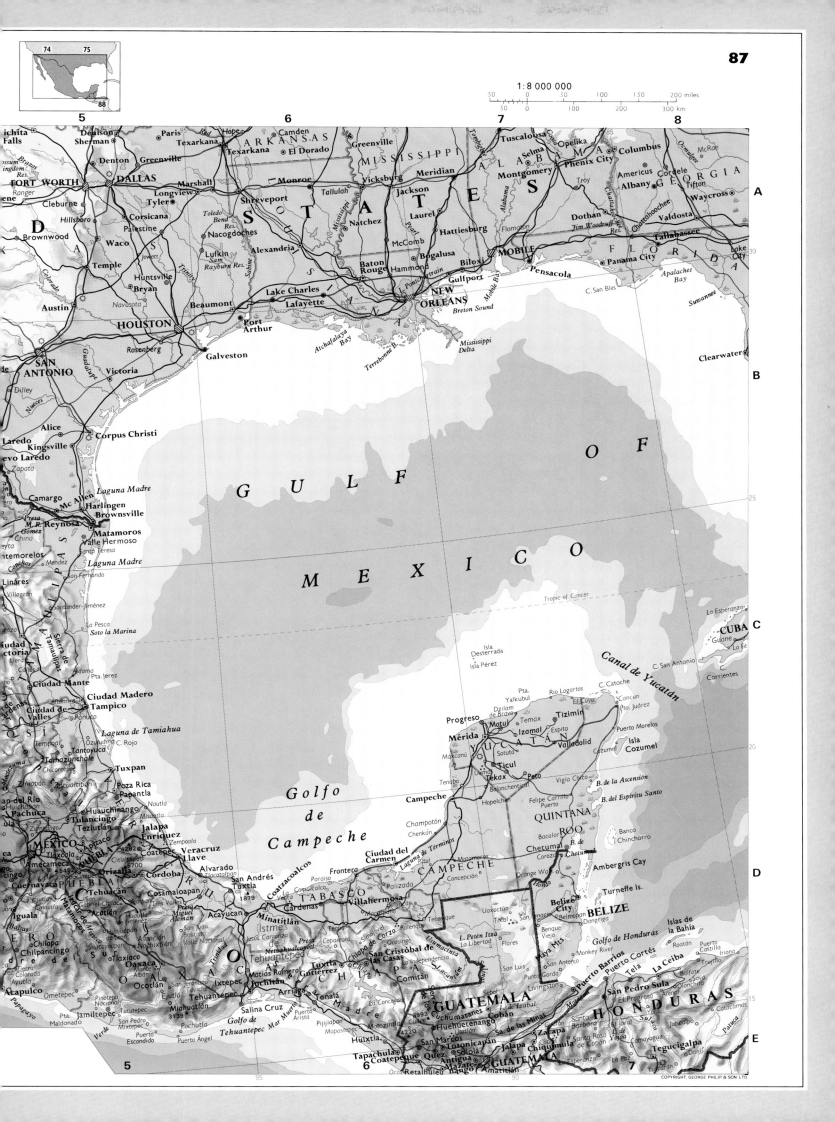

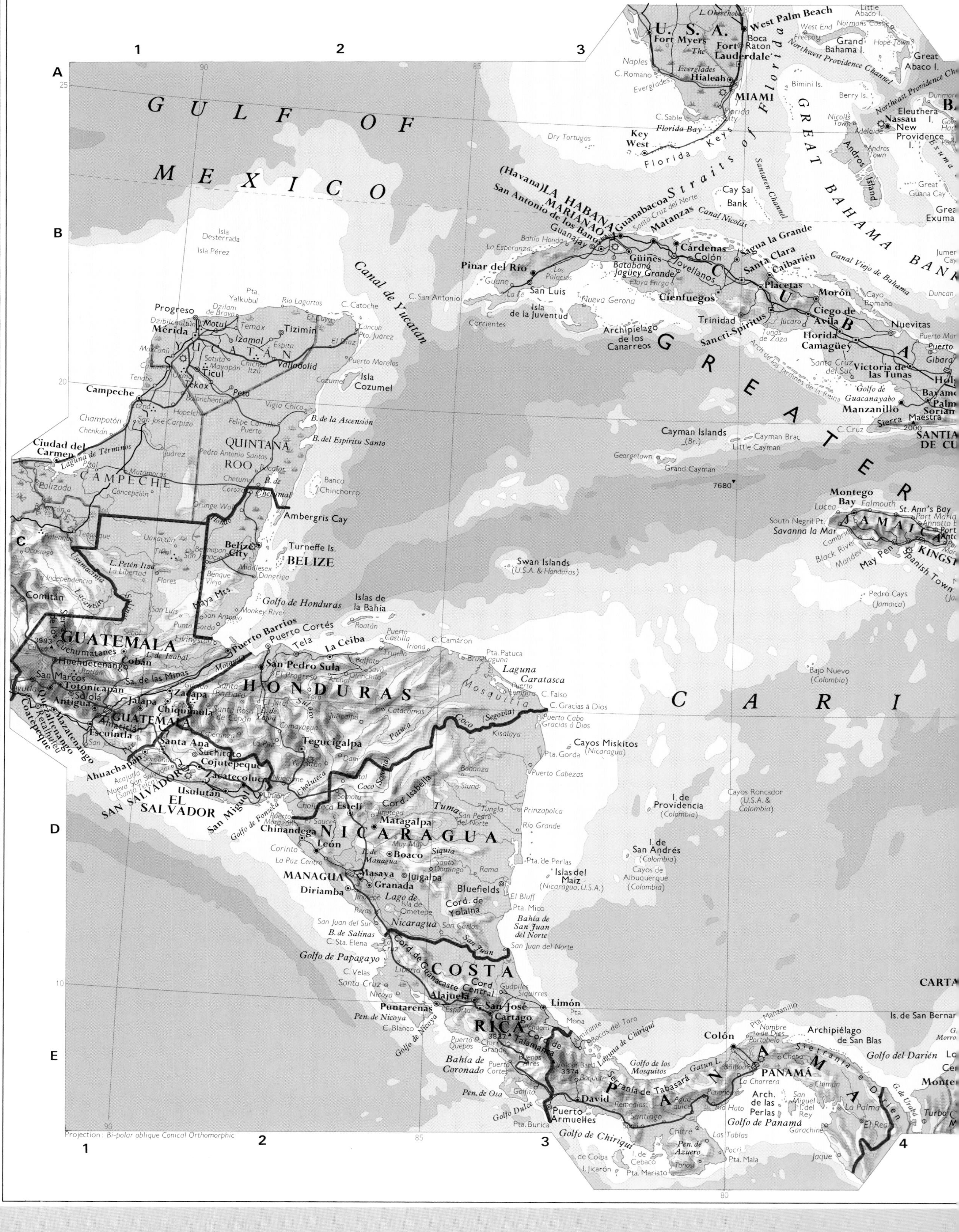

GULF OF MEXICO

U.S.A.

West Palm Beach
Fort Myers
Boca Raton
Fort Lauderdale
Naples
C. Romano
The Everglades
Everglades
Hialeah
MIAMI
C. Sable
Florida Bay
Key West
Dry Tortugas
Florida Keys
Straits of Florida

Little Abaco I.
Normans Cay
West End
Freeport
Hope Town
Grand Bahama I.
Great Abaco I.
Eleuthera I.
New Providence I.
Nassau
Adelaide
GREAT BAHAMA BANK
Great Guana Cay
Berry Is.
Bimini Is.
Nicoll's Town
Andros Town
Andros Island
Great Exuma

L. Okeechobee

(Havana) LA HABANA
MARIANAO
San Antonio de los Baños
Guanabacoa
Guanajay
Santa Cruz del Norte
Matanzas
Canal Nicolás
Bahía Honda
Lo Esperanza
Güines
Cárdenas
Colón
Sagua la Grande
Santa Clara
Caibarién
Canal Viejo de Bahama
Pinar del Río
Los Palacios
Batabanó
Jagüey Grande
Jovellanos
Placetas
Morón
Cayo Coco
Guane
San Luis
La Fé
Nueva Gerona
Isla de la Juventud
Cienfuegos
Sancti-Spíritus
Ciego de Ávila
Florida
Nuevitas
Puerto Padre
Gibara
Corrientes
Archipiélago de los Canarreos
Trinidad
Júcaro
Tunas de Zaza
Arch. de los Jardines de la Reina
Camagüey
Santa Cruz del Sur
Victoria de las Tunas
Holguín
Bayamo
Manzanillo
Palma Soriano
SANTIAGO DE CUBA
Golfo de Guacanayabo
Sierra Maestra

C U B A
G R E A T E R
CARIBBEAN

Cayman Islands (Br.)
Georgetown
Grand Cayman
Cayman Brac
Little Cayman
7680

Montego Bay
Lucea
Falmouth
St. Ann's Bay
Annotto Bay
South Negril Pt.
Savanna la Mar
JAMAICA
Black River
Mandeville
May Pen
Spanish Town
KINGSTON
Port Maria
Port Antonio
Morant Bay

Swan Islands (U.S.A. & Honduras)

Bajo Nuevo (Colombia)

Pedro Cays (Jamaica)

Progreso
Pta. Yalkubul
Dzilam de Bravo
Motul
Temax
Río Lagartos
C. Catoche
Tizimín
Mérida
Izamal
Espita
El Cuyo
Cancún
Pto. Juárez
YUCATÁN
Valladolid
Puerto Morelos
Ticul
Peto
Chichén Itzá
Isla Cozumel
Campeche
Champotón
Chenkan
Vigia Chico
B. de la Ascensión
QUINTANA ROO
B. del Espíritu Santo
Ciudad del Carmen
Laguna de Términos
Palizada
CAMPECHE
Pedro Antonio Santos
Isla Cozumel
Banco Chinchorro
Chetumal
Orange Walk
Corozal
Ambergris Cay
Turneffe Is.
Belize City
BELIZE
Uaxactún
Tikal
L. Petén Itzá
Flores
Benque Viejo
Middlesex
Dangriga
Monkey River
Comitán
La Independencia
La Libertad
Maya Mts.
San Luis
Punta Gorda
Golfo de Honduras
Islas de la Bahía

GUATEMALA
Huehuetenango
Cobán
3993
Totonicapán
Sololá
San Marcos
Quezaltenango
Antigua
GUATEMALA
Jalapa
Chiquimula
Zacapa
Esquintla
Mazatenango
Retalhuleu
Coatepeque
Ahuachapán
Santa Ana
Suchitoto
Cojutepeque
EL SALVADOR
SAN SALVADOR
Zacatecoluca
Usulután
San Miguel
Golfo de Fonseca

L. de Izabal
Puerto Barrios
Puerto Cortés
Tela
La Ceiba
Trujillo
Roatán
Puerto Castilla
C. Camarón
Pta. Patuca
San Pedro Sula
El Progreso
Santa Bárbara
HONDURAS
Comayagua
Tegucigalpa
Catacamas
Juticalpa
Laguna Caratasca
Mosquitia
C. Falso
C. Gracias á Dios
Puerto Cabo Gracias á Dios
Cayos Miskitos (Nicaragua)
Choluteca
Esteli
Matagalpa
NICARAGUA
Chinandega
León
Boaco
Prinzapolca
Puerto Cabezas
MANAGUA
Masaya
Granada
Juigalpa
Bluefields
Diriamba
L. de Managua
Lago de Nicaragua
Cord. de Yolaina
El Bluff
Pta. Mico
San Juan del Sur
Isla de Ometepe
Rivas
San Carlos
Bahía de San Juan del Norte
San Juan del Norte
B. de Salinas
C. Sta. Elena
Cord. de Guanacaste
Nicoya
Liberia
COSTA RICA
Santa Cruz
Cord. Central
Alajuela
SAN JOSÉ
Cartago
Limón
Puntarenas
Pen. de Nicoya
Golfo de Papagayo
Golfo de Nicoya
3827
Cord. de Talamanca
Pen. de Osa
Bahía de Coronado
Golfo Dulce
Puerto Armuelles
Pta. Burica
Golfo de Chiriqui
David
PANAMÁ
Colón
Portobelo
Archipiélago de San Blas
Golfo del Darién
Golfo de los Mosquitos
Laguna de Chiriqui
Bocas del Toro
Gatun L.
Serranía de Tabasará
La Chorrera
Arch. de las Perlas
Golfo de Panamá
Santiago
Chitré
Las Tablas
Pen. de Azuero
I. de Coiba
I. de Cebaco
Pta. Mariato
Pta. Mala

Islas del Maíz (Nicaragua, U.S.A.)
Cayos de Albuquerque (Colombia)
Cayos Roncador (U.S.A. & Colombia)
I. de Providencia (Colombia)
I. de San Andrés (Colombia)

Pedro Antonio Santos

C A R I B
C A R T A

Is. de San Bernardo

Sierra de San Blas

Serranía del Darién

Projection: Bi-polar oblique Conical Orthomorphic

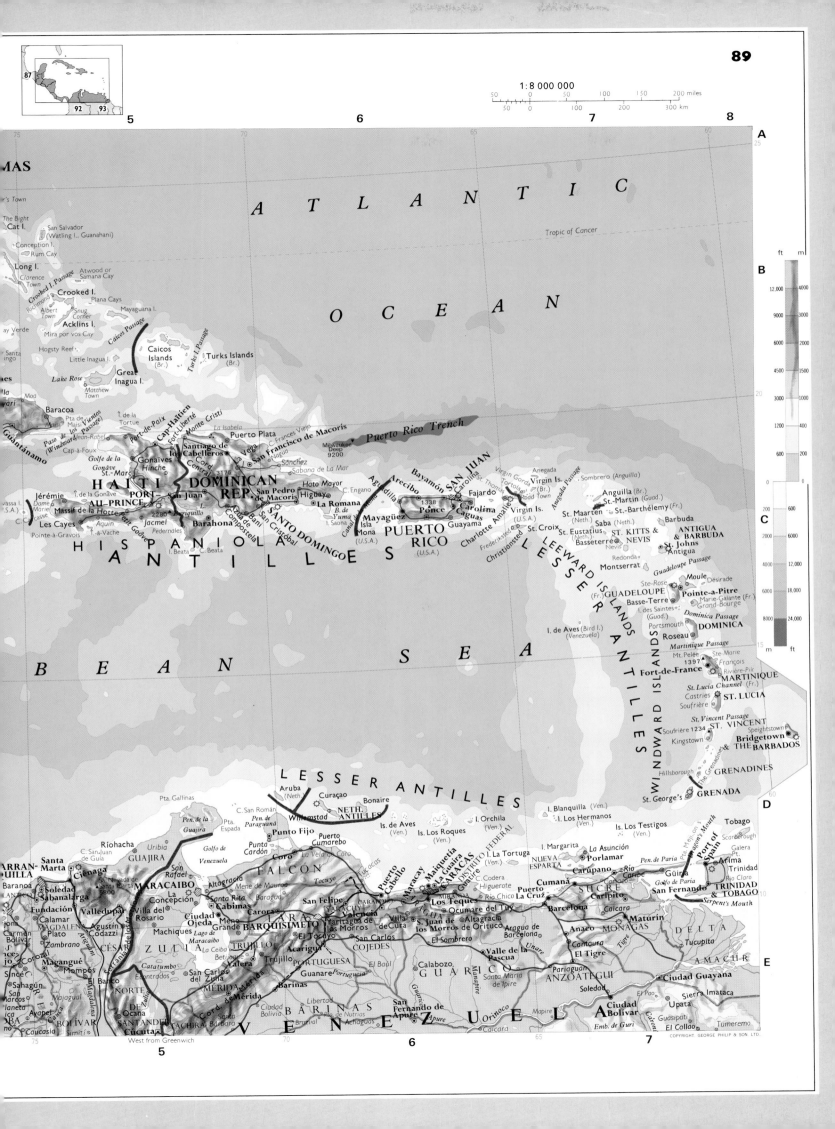

1:8 000 000

50   0   50   100   150   200 miles

50   0   100   200   300 km

A

ATLANTIC

OCEAN

Tropic of Cancer

B

ft   m

12,000   4000

9000   3000

6000   2000

4500   1500

3000   1000

1200   400

600   200

0   0

C

200   600

2000   6000

4000   12,000

6000   18,000

8000   24,000

m   ft

15

MAS

'r's Town

The Bight
Cat I.
Conception I.
Rum Cay
San Salvador
(Watling I., Guanahani)

Long I.

Clarence
Town
Crooked I. Passage
Crooked I.
Plana Cays
Richmond
Albert
Town
Snug
Corner
Atwood or
Samana Cay
Acklins I.
Mayaguana I.
Hogsty Reef
Little Inagua I.
Turks I. Passage
Mira por vos Cay
ay Verde
Caicos
Islands
(Br.)
Turks Islands
(Br.)
Lake Rose
Great
Inagua I.
Matthew
Town

Santa
ingo

Baracoa
Moa
yari

Guantánamo

Pta. de Maisí
Cap-à-Foux
(Windward)Jean-Rabel
Paso de
los Vientos
Passage
Port-de-Paix
Cap-Haïtien
Fort-Liberté
Monte Cristi
Î. de la
Tortue
La Isabela
Puerto Plata
C. Frances Viejo
Santiago de
los Caballeros
Cord.
Central
La Vega
Sánchez
Sabana de la Mar
San Francisco de Macorís
Nagua

Puerto Rico Trench

Milwaukee
Deep
9200

San Juan

Bayamón
Carolina
Virgin Is.
(Br.)
Anegada
Virgin Gorda
Tortola
Road Town
Sombrero (Anguilla)

Jérémie
Dame
I. de la Gonâve
HAITI
Massif de la Hotte
PORT-
AU-PRINCE
2280
Les Cayes
Aquin
Jacmel
DOMINICAN
REP.
San Juan
3175
Barahona
L.
Enriquillo
Pedernales
San Pedro
de Macorís
SANTO
DOMINGOE
San Cristóbal
Baní
Azua
Compostela
Higüey
C. Engaño
B. de
Yuma
I. Saona
La Romana
Mayagüez
Isla
Mona
(U.S.A.)
Arecibo
1338
Ponce
Caguas
Carolina
Guayama
PUERTO
RICO
(U.S.A.)
Fajardo
Charlotte Amalie
St. Thomas
Virgin Is.
(U.S.A.)
St. Croix
Christiansted
Frederiksted
St. Croix

Anguilla (Br.)
St.-Martin (Guad.)
St.-Barthélemy (Fr.)
St. Maarten
(Neth.)
Saba (Neth.)
St. Eustatius
(Neth.)
Basseterre
ST. KITTS &
NEVIS
Nevis
Redonda
Montserrat

Barbuda
ANTIGUA
& BARBUDA
St. Johns
Antigua

Jérémie

vassa I.
(U.S.A.)

Pointe-à-Gravois
Pointe-à-Gravois
Î.-à-Vache
I. Beata
C. Beata

HISPANIOLA

ANTILLES

Guadeloupe Passage
LEEWARD ISLANDS
GUADELOUPE
Basse-Terre
Ste-Rose
Marie-Galante
(Guad.)
Les Saintes
(Guad.)
Moule
Désirade
Pointe-à-Pitre (Fr.)
Grand-Bourg
Dominica Passage
Portsmouth
Roseau
DOMINICA

BEAN   SEA

I. de Aves (Bird I.)
(Venezuela)

LESSER
ANTILLES

Martinique Passage
Mt. Pelée
1397
Fort-de-France
Ste-Marie
François
Rivière-Pil
MARTINIQUE
(Fr.)

St. Lucia Channel
Castries
Soufrière
ST. LUCIA

St. Vincent Passage
Soufrière 1234
ST. VINCENT
Kingstown
Hillsborough
The Grenadines
GRENADINES
St. George's
GRENADA

Speightstown
Bridgetown
& THE BARBADOS

60

D

LESSER ANTILLES

Pta. Gallinas
Aruba
(Neth.)
Curaçao
NETH.
ANTILLES
Bonaire
Is. de Aves
(Ven.)
I. Orchila
(Ven.)
I. Blanquilla (Ven.)
I. Los Hermanos
(Ven.)
Tobago

Pen. de la
Guajira
Pta.
Espada
C. San Román
Pen. de
Paraguaná
Willemstad
I. Los Roques
(Ven.)
Is. Los Testigos
(Ven.)
Scarborough
Galera Pt.

Ríohacha
Uribia
San Juan
de Guía
GUAJIRA
Golfo de
Venezuela
Punta
Cardón
Punto Fijo
Puerto
Cumarebo
Coro
La Vela de Coro
Los Cocos
I. Margarita
La Asunción
NUEVA
ESPARTA
Porlamar
Pen. de Paria
I. La Tortuga
Carúpano
Río
Caribe
Güira
Port
of Spain
Arima
Trinidad

Santa
Marta
BARRAN-
QUILLA
C. San Juan
de Guía
Santa
Marta
Ciénaga
San
Rafael
Altagracia
FALCON
Puerto
Cabello
Maiquetía
La Guaira
CARACAS
DISTRITO
FEDERAL
Guatire
C. Codera
Higuerote
Río Chico
Puerto
La Cruz
Cumaná
SUCRE
Caripito
TRINIDAD
& TOBAGO
San Fernando
Serpent's Mouth

Baranoa
Soledad
Sabanalarga
Fundación
Calamar
MAGDALENA
Plato
Zambrano
Magangué
MARACAIBO
La
Concepción
Santa
Rita
Machiques
Mene de Mauroa
Barágua
Santa
Rita
San Felipe
YARACUY
Valencia
Villa
de Cura
S. Juan de
los Morros de Orituco
Ocumare del Tuy
Los Teques
Aragua de
Barcelona
Barcelona
Caicara
Anaco
Maturín
MONAGAS
DELTA
AMACUR
Tucupita

jons
San
Bolívar
Agustín
Codazzi
Valledupar
CÉSAR
Villa del
Rosario
Ciudad
Ojeda
5800
ZULIA
Lago de
Maracaibo
La Ceiba
TRUJILLO
Cabimas
LARA
BARQUISIMETO
Carora
El Tocuyo
Acarigua
COJEDES
San Carlos
Guanare
PORTUGUESA
Guanare
El Baúl
Calabozo
GUÁRICO
Santa María
de Ipire
El Sombrero
Valle de
la Pascua
Pariaguán
ANZOATEGUI
El Tigre
Contaura
El Tigre
Ciudad Guayana
Soledad
Ciudad Guayana
El Pao
Upata
Sierra Imataca

Sincé
Sahagún
San
Marcos
ica
BOLÍVAR
Simití
NORTE
DE
SANTANDER
Ocaña
Catatumbo
El Banco
Cúcuta
Cach ira
Santa
Bárbara
MÉRIDA
Mérida
Ciudad
Bolívia
Bruzual
Nula
BARINAS
San
Fernando de
Apure
Apure
Achaguas
Orinoco
San Fernando de
Apure
Ciudad
Bolívar
Emb. de Guri
El Callao
Guasipati
Tumeremo

Ayapel
Carmen
Majagual
de
Bolívar
Caucasia
NBA
Cauca
Magdalena
Barinas
VENEZUELA
Caicara

75   West from Greenwich   70   6   65   7

5   6   7

COPYRIGHT GEORGE PHILIP & SON LTD.

E

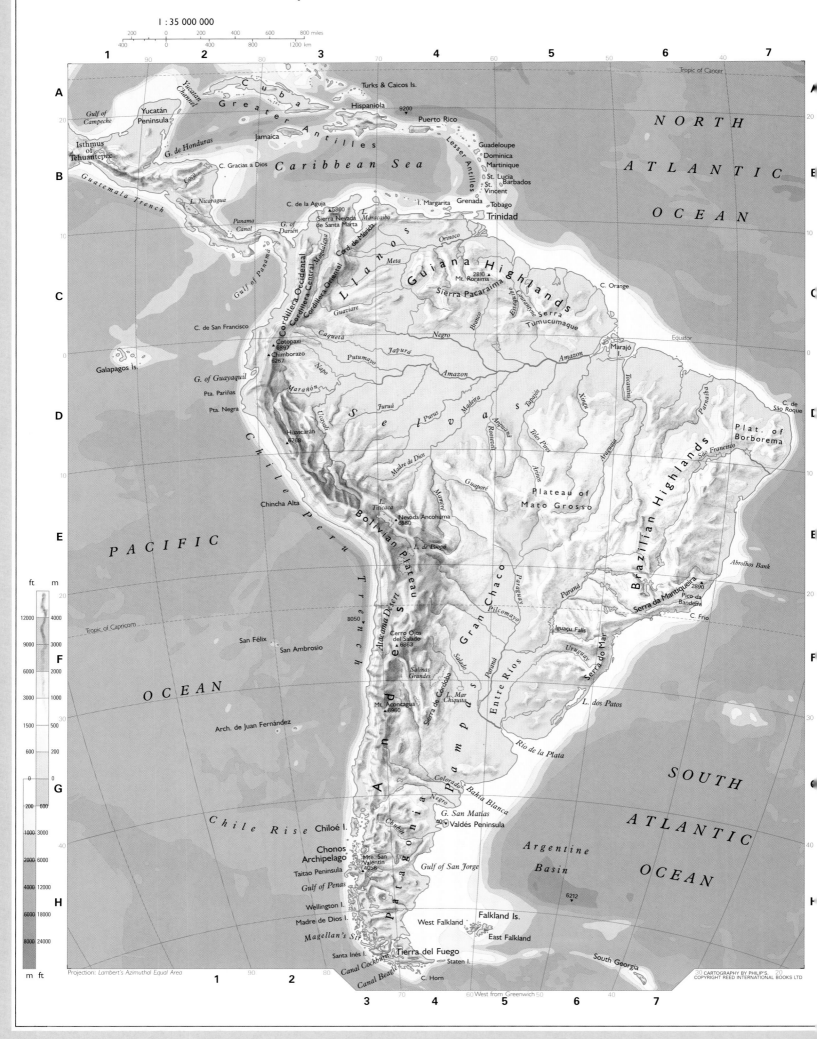

I : 35 000 000

Projection: *Lambert's Azimuthal Equal Area*

1 : 35 000 000

Tropic of Cancer

NORTH

ATLANTIC

OCEAN

Havana
BAHAMAS
CUBA
Turks & Caicos Is.
(U.K.)
HAITI
DOMINICAN
REP.
Port-au-Prince
San Juan
Virgin Is.
(U.K.)
PUERTO
RICO
(U.S.A.)
ST. KITTS-
NEVIS
ANTIGUA &
BARBUDA
Basse-Terre
GUADELOUPE
(Fr.)
DOMINICA
Fort-de-France
MARTINIQUE
(Fr.)
Castries
ST. LUCIA
ST. VINCENT
Kingstown
BARBADOS
Bridgetown
GRENADA
St. George's
TRINIDAD &
TOBAGO
JAMAICA
Kingston

MEXICO
BELIZE
GUATEMALA
HONDURAS
Tegucigalpa
Guatemala
San Salvador
EL SALVADOR
NICARAGUA
Managua
COSTA
RICA
San José
Panamá
PANAMA

Caribbean Sea

Barranquilla
C. de
la Aguja
Cartagena
Maracaibo
Aruba
Curaçao
Caracas
Port of
Spain
G. of
Darién
Barquisimeto
Valencia
Cúcuta
San Cristóbal
Orinoco
Ciudad Guayana
Medellín
Bucaramanga
Georgetown
Paramaribo
Cayenne
C. Orange
Bogotá
VENEZUELA
GUYANA
SURINAM
**FRENCH
GUIANA**
Cali
COLOMBIA
RORAIMA
Essequibo
Branco
AMAPÁ

Galapagos Is.
(Ecuador)
Quito
Equator
Japurá
Amazon
Marajó
I.
Belém
ECUADOR
Guayaquil
Putumayo
Napo
Manaus
Santarém
São Luís
Fortaleza
G. of Guayaquil
Marañón
Iquitos
Amazon
AMAZONAS
Madeira
PARÁ
Tocantins
MARANHÃO
Teresina
C. de
São Roque
CEARÁ
Furuá
Purus
Tapajós
Xingu
RIO G.
DO NORTE
Natal
Chiclayo
Trujillo
Ucayali
ACRE
Pôrto Velho
PARAÍBA
Campina Grande
Chimbote
RONDÔNIA
BRAZIL
TOCANTINS
PIAUÍ
PERNAMBUCO
Recife
PERU
Madre de Dios
Mamoré
ALAGOAS
Maceió
Callao
LIMA
Cuzco
MATO GROSSO
SERGIPE
Aracaju
L.
Titicaca
BOLIVIA
GOIÁS
São Francisco
BAHÍA
Salvador
La Paz
Cochabamba
Santa Cruz
Cuiabá
DIS. FED.
Brasília
Arequipa
Sucre
Goiânia
MINAS GERAIS
Iquique
Paraguay
MATO GROSSO
DO SUL
Belo
Horizonte
ESPÍRITO
SANTO
Ribeirão
Prêto
Vitória
Antofagasta
PARAGUAY
Pilcomayo
Paraná
SÃO PAULO
Juiz
de Fora
Campos
Salta
Asunción
PARANÁ
SÃO
PAULO
Campinas
RIO DE
JANEIRO
R. DE J.
Niterói
San Miguel
de Tucumán
Curitiba
SANTA CATARINA
Resistencia
Corrientes
Uruguay
RIO GRANDE
DO SUL
Porto Alegre
Córdoba
Santa Fe
Paraná
URUGUAY
Pelotas
San Juan
Mendoza
Rosario
Saladо
San Félix
(Chile)
San Ambrosio
(Chile)
ARGENTINA
Valparaíso
Viña del Mar
SANTIAGO
BUENOS AIRES
Montevideo
Arch. de Juan Fernández
(Chile)
Talca
La Plata
Río de la Plata
Concepción
Bahía
Blanca
Mar del Plata
CHILE
Colorado
Valdivia
Negro
Viedma

PACIFIC

OCEAN

Tropic of Capricorn

SOUTH

ATLANTIC

OCEAN

Puerto Montt
Comodoro Rivadavia
Gulf of San Jorge
Chubut
Gulf of Penas
Gulf of Penas
West Falkland
FALKLAND IS.
(U.K.)
Stanley
East Falkland
Magellan's Str.
Punta Arenas
Tierra del Fuego
South Georgia
(U.K.)
C. Horn

Projection: Lambert's Azimuthal Equal Area

West from Greenwich

LIMA   Capital Cities

CARTOGRAPHY BY PHILIP'S.
COPYRIGHT REED INTERNATIONAL BOOKS LTD

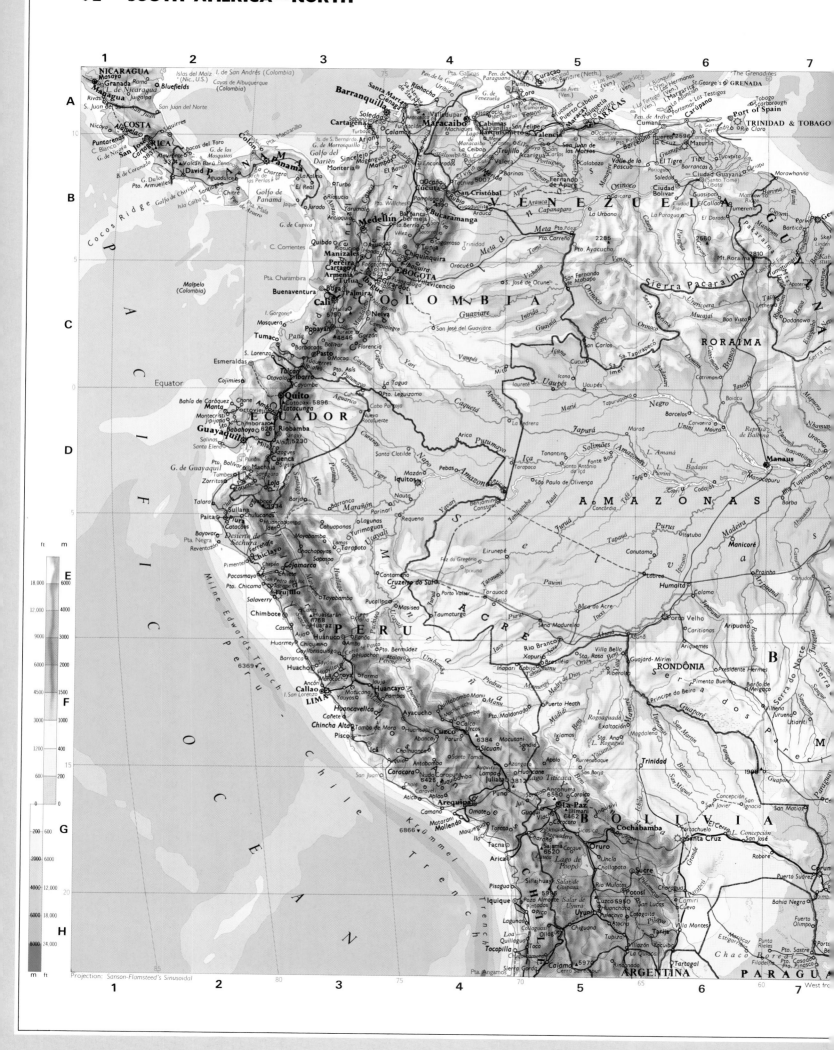

1:16 000 000

100 50 0   100   200   300 miles
100   0   100 200 300 400 km

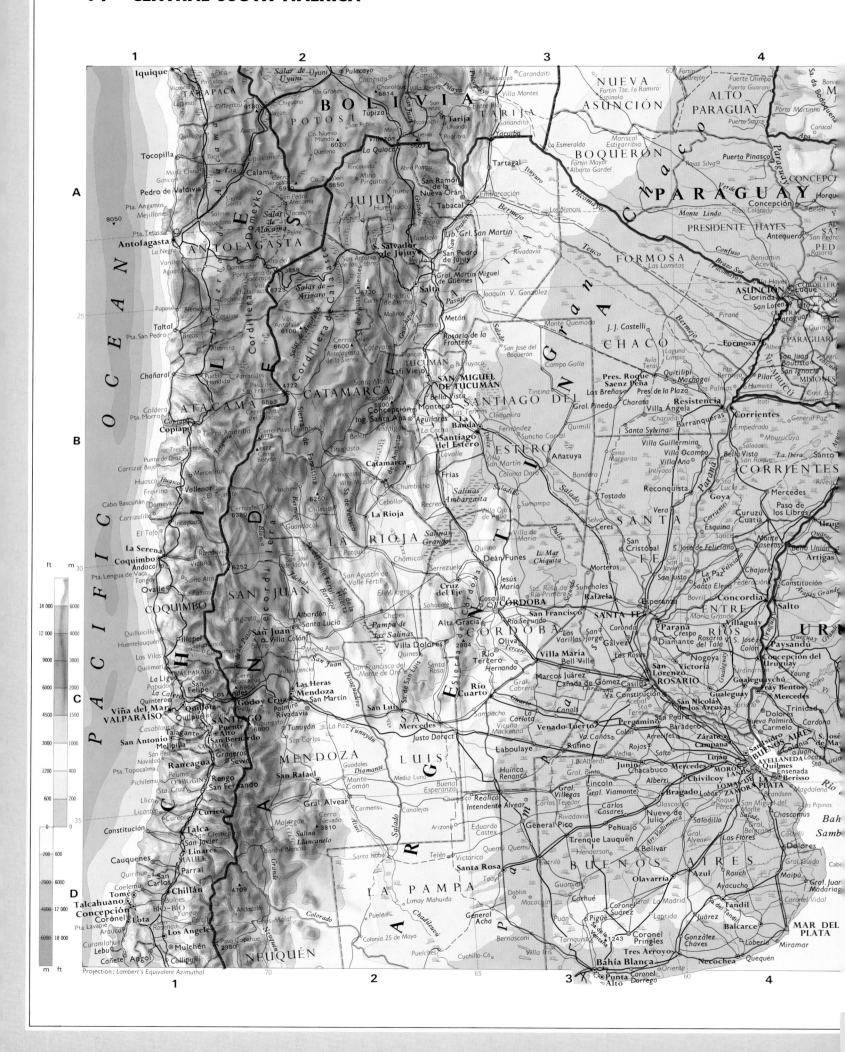

Projection: Lambert's Equivalent Azimuthal

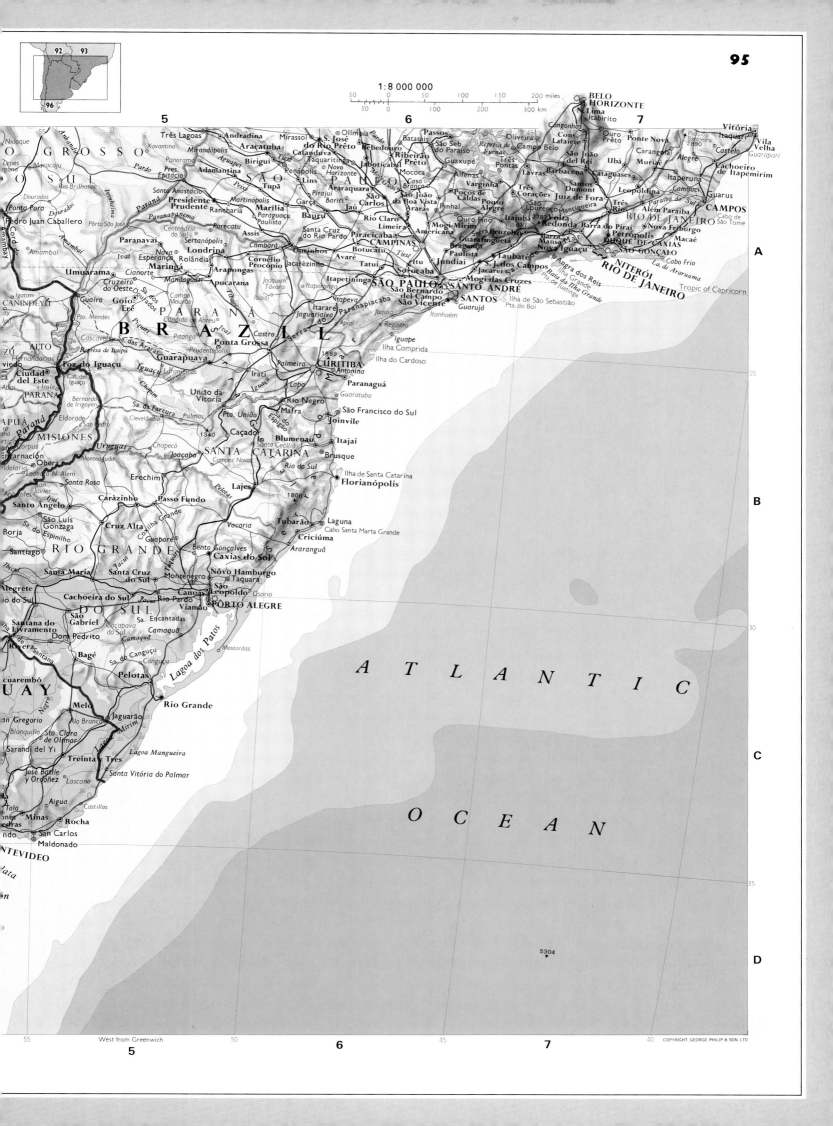

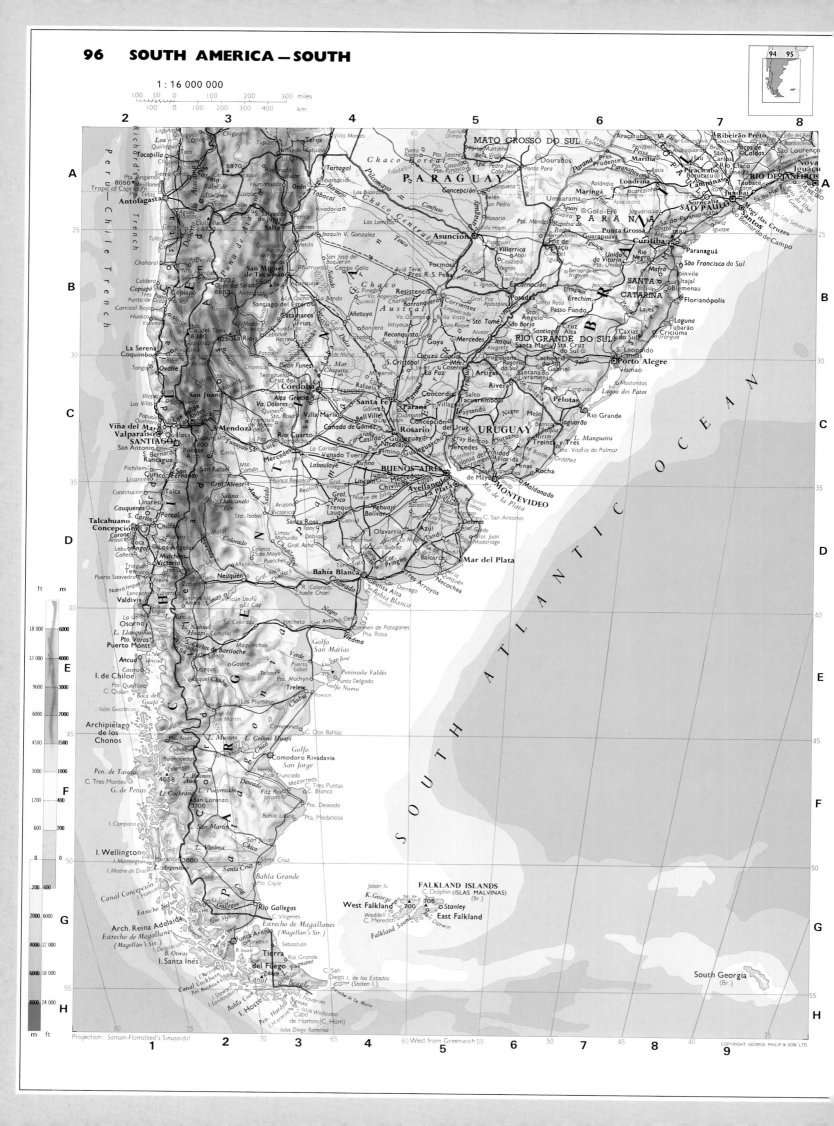

INDEX

The index contains the names of all the principal places and features shown on the World Maps. Each name is followed by an additional entry in italics giving the country or region within which it is located. The alphabetical order of names composed of two or more words is governed primarily by the first word and then by the second. This is an example of the rule:

Mīr Kūh, *Iran* . . . . **45 E8**   26 22 N   58 55 E
Mīr Shahdād, *Iran* . . . . **45 E8**   26 15 N   58 29 E
Miraj, *India* . . . . **40 L9**   16 50 N   74 45 E
Miram Shah, *Pakistan* . . . . . . **42 C4**   33 0 N   70 2 E
Miramar, *Mozam.* . . . . **57 C6**   23 50 S   35 35 E

Physical features composed of a proper name (Erie) and a description (Lake) are positioned alphabetically by the proper name. The description is positioned after the proper name and is usually abbreviated:

Erie, L., *N. Amer.* . . . . **78 D3**   42 15 N   81 0 W

Where a description forms part of a settlement or administrative name, however, it is always written in full and put in its true alphabetic position:

Mount Morris, *U.S.A.* . . . . **78 D7**   42 44 N   77 52 W

Names beginning with M' and Mc are indexed as if they were spelled Mac. Names beginning St. are alphabetized under Saint, but Sankt, Sint, Sant', Santa and San are all spelled in full and are alphabetized accordingly. If the same place name occurs two or more times in the index and all are in the same country, each is followed by the name of the administrative subdivision in which it is located. The names are placed in the alphabetical order of the subdivisions. For example:

Jackson, *Ky., U.S.A.* . . . . **76 G4**   37 33 N   83 23 W
Jackson, *Mich., U.S.A.* . . . . . . **76 D3**   42 15 N   84 24 W
Jackson, *Minn., U.S.A.* . . . . . . **80 D7**   43 37 N   95 1 W

The number in bold type which follows each name in the index refers to the number of the map page where that feature or place will be found. This is usually the largest scale at which the place or feature appears.

The letter and figure which are in bold type immediately after the page number give the grid square on the map page, within which the feature is situated. The letter represents the latitude and the figure the longitude.

In some cases the feature itself may fall within the specified square, while the name is outside. This is usually the case only with features which are larger than a grid square.

For a more precise location the geographical coordinates which follow the letter/figure references give the latitude and the longitude of each place. The first set of figures represent the latitude which is the distance north or south of the Equator measured as an angle at the centre of the Earth. The Equator is latitude 0°, the North Pole is 90°N, and the South Pole 90°S.

The second set of figures represent the longitude, which is the distance East or West of the prime meridian, which runs through Greenwich, England. Longitude is also measured as an angle at the centre of the earth and is given East or West of the prime meridian, from 0° to 180° in either direction.

The unit of measurement for latitude and longitude is the degree, which is subdivided into 60 minutes. Each index entry states the position of a place in degrees and minutes, a space being left between the degrees and the minutes.

The latitude is followed by N(orth) or S(outh) and the longitude by E(ast) or W(est).

Rivers are indexed to their mouths or confluences, and carry the symbol → after their names. A solid square ■ follows the name of a country while, an open square □ refers to a first order administrative area.

Abbreviations used in the index

A.C.T. — Australian Capital Territory
Afghan. — Afghanistan
Ala. — Alabama
Alta. — Alberta
Amer. — America(n)
Arch. — Archipelago
Ariz. — Arizona
Ark. — Arkansas
Atl. Oc. — Atlantic Ocean
B. — Baie, Bahía, Bay, Bucht, Bugt
B.C. — British Columbia
Bangla. — Bangladesh
Barr. — Barrage
Bos. & H. — Bosnia and Herzegovina
C. — Cabo, Cap, Cape, Coast
C.A.R. — Central African Republic
C. Prov. — Cape Province
Calif. — California
Cent. — Central
Chan. — Channel
Colo. — Colorado
Conn. — Connecticut
Cord. — Cordillera
Cr. — Creek
Czech. — Czech Republic
D.C. — District of Columbia
Del. — Delaware
Dep. — Dependency
Des. — Desert
Dist. — District
Dj. — Djebel
Domin. — Dominica
Dom. Rep. — Dominican Republic
E. — East

El Salv. — El Salvador
Eq. Guin. — Equatorial Guinea
Fla. — Florida
Falk. Is. — Falkland Is.
G. — Golfe, Golfo, Gulf, Guba, Gebel
Ga. — Georgia
Gt. — Great, Greater
Guinea-Biss. — Guinea-Bissau
H.K. — Hong Kong
H.P. — Himachal Pradesh
Hants. — Hampshire
Harb. — Harbor, Harbour
Hd. — Head
Hts. — Heights
I.(s). — Île, Ilha, Insel, Isla, Island, Isle
Ill. — Illinois
Ind. — Indiana
Ind. Oc. — Indian Ocean
Ivory C. — Ivory Coast
J. — Jabal, Jebel, Jazira
Junc. — Junction
K. — Kap, Kapp
Kans. — Kansas
Kep. — Kepulauan
Ky. — Kentucky
L. — Lac, Lacul, Lago, Lagoa, Lake, Limni, Loch, Lough
La. — Louisiana
Liech. — Liechtenstein
Lux. — Luxembourg
Mad. P. — Madhya Pradesh
Madag. — Madagascar
Man. — Manitoba
Mass. — Massachusetts

Md. — Maryland
Me. — Maine
Medit. S. — Mediterranean Sea
Mich. — Michigan
Minn. — Minnesota
Miss. — Mississippi
Mo. — Missouri
Mont. — Montana
Mozam. — Mozambique
Mt.(e). — Mont, Monte, Monti, Montaña, Mountain
N. — Nord, Norte, North, Northern, Nouveau
N.B. — New Brunswick
N.C. — North Carolina
N. Cal. — New Caledonia
N. Dak. — North Dakota
N.H. — New Hampshire
N.I. — North Island
N.J. — New Jersey
N. Mex. — New Mexico
N.S. — Nova Scotia
N.S.W. — New South Wales
N.W.T. — North West Territory
N.Y. — New York
N.Z. — New Zealand
Nebr. — Nebraska
Neths. — Netherlands
Nev. — Nevada
Nfld. — Newfoundland
Nic. — Nicaragua
O. — Oued, Ouadi
Occ. — Occidentale
Okla. — Oklahoma
Ont. — Ontario
Or. — Orientale

Oreg. — Oregon
Os. — Ostrov
Oz. — Ozero
P. — Pass, Passo, Pasul, Pulau
P.E.I. — Prince Edward Island
Pa. — Pennsylvania
Pac. Oc. — Pacific Ocean
Papua N.G. — Papua New Guinea
Pass. — Passage
Pen. — Peninsula, Péninsule
Phil. — Philippines
Pk. — Park, Peak
Plat. — Plateau
P-ov. — Poluostrov
Prov. — Province, Provincial
Pt. — Point
Pta. — Ponta, Punta
Pte. — Pointe
Qué. — Québec
Queens. — Queensland
R. — Rio, River
R.I. — Rhode Island
Ra.(s). — Range(s)
Raj. — Rajasthan
Reg. — Region
Rep. — Republic
Res. — Reserve, Reservoir
S. — San, South, Sea
Si. Arabia — Saudi Arabia
S.C. — South Carolina
S. Dak. — South Dakota
S.I. — South Island
S. Leone — Sierra Leone
Sa. — Serra, Sierra
Sask. — Saskatchewan
Scot. — Scotland

Sd. — Sound
Sev. — Severnaya
Sib. — Siberia
Sprs. — Springs
St. — Saint, Sankt, Sint
Sta. — Santa, Station
Ste. — Sainte
Sto. — Santo
Str. — Strait, Stretto
Switz. — Switzerland
Tas. — Tasmania
Tenn. — Tennessee
Tex. — Texas
Tg. — Tanjung
Trin. & Tob. — Trinidad & Tobago
U.A.E. — United Arab Emirates
U.K. — United Kingdom
U.S.A. — United States of America
Ut. P. — Uttar Pradesh
Va. — Virginia
Vdkhr. — Vodokhranilishche
Vf. — Vîrful
Vic. — Victoria
Vol. — Volcano
Vt. — Vermont
W. — Wadi, West
W. Va. — West Virginia
Wash. — Washington
Wis. — Wisconsin
Wlkp. — Wielkopolski
Wyo. — Wyoming
Yorks. — Yorkshire

A Coruña

A

A Coruña = La Coruña, Spain 19 A1 43 20N 8 25W
Aachen, Germany 16 C4 50 45N 6 6 E
Aalborg = Ålborg, Denmark 9 H13 57 2N 9 54 E
Aalen, Germany 16 D6 48 51N 10 6 E
Aalsmeer, Neths. 15 B4 52 17N 4 43 E
Aalst, Belgium 15 D4 50 56N 4 2 E
Aalten, Neths. 15 C6 51 56N 6 35 E
Äänekoski, Finland 9 E21 62 36N 25 44 E
Aarau, Switz. 16 E5 47 23N 8 4 E
Aare →, Switz. 16 E5 47 33N 8 14 E
Aarhus = Århus, Denmark 9 H14 56 8N 10 11 E
Aarschot, Belgium 15 D4 50 59N 4 49 E
Aba, Nigeria 50 G6 5 10N 7 19 E
Aba, Zaïre 54 B3 3 58N 30 17 E
Ābādān, Iran 45 D6 30 22N 48 20 E
Ābādeh, Iran 45 D7 31 8N 52 40 E
Abadla, Algeria 50 B4 31 2N 2 45W
Abaetetuba, Brazil 93 D9 1 40S 48 50W
Abagnar Qi, China 34 C9 43 52N 116 2 E
Abai, Paraguay 95 B4 25 58S 55 54W
Abakan, Russia 27 D10 53 40N 91 10 E
Abancay, Peru 92 F4 13 35S 72 55W
Abariringa, Kiribati 64 H10 2 50S 171 40W
Abarqū, Iran 45 D7 31 10N 53 20 E
Abashiri, Japan 30 B12 44 0N 144 15 E
Abashiri-Wan, Japan 30 B12 44 0N 144 30 E
Abay, Kazakstan 26 E8 49 38N 72 53 E
Abaya, L., Ethiopia 51 G12 6 30N 37 50 E
Abaza, Russia 26 D10 52 39N 90 6 E
'Abbāsābād, Iran 45 C8 33 34N 58 23 E
Abbay = Nîl el Azraq →, Sudan 51 E11 15 38N 32 31 E
Abbaye, Pt., U.S.A. 76 B1 46 58N 88 8W
Abbeville, France 18 A4 50 6N 1 49 E
Abbeville, La., U.S.A. 81 K8 29 58N 92 8W
Abbeville, S.C., U.S.A. 77 H4 34 11N 82 23W
Abbieglassie, Australia 63 D4 27 15S 147 28 E
Abbot Ice Shelf, Antarctica 5 D16 73 0S 92 0W
Abbotsford, Canada 72 D4 49 5N 122 20W
Abbotsford, U.S.A. 80 C9 44 57N 90 19W
Abbottabad, Pakistan 42 B5 34 10N 73 15 E
Abd al Kūrī, Ind. Oc. 46 E5 12 5N 52 20 E
Ābdar, Iran 45 D7 30 16N 55 19 E
'Abdolābād, Iran 45 C8 34 12N 56 30 E
Abéché, Chad 51 F9 13 50N 20 35 E
Åbenrå, Denmark 9 J13 55 3N 9 25 E
Abeokuta, Nigeria 50 G5 7 3N 3 19 E
Aber, Uganda 54 B3 2 12N 32 25 E
Aberaeron, U.K. 11 E3 52 15N 4 15W
Aberayron = Aberaeron, U.K. 11 E3 52 15N 4 15W
Aberconwy & Colwyn □, U.K. 10 D4 53 10N 3 44W
Abercorn = Mbala, Zambia 55 D3 8 46S 31 24 E
Abercorn, Australia 63 D5 25 12S 151 5 E
Aberdare, U.K. 11 F4 51 43N 3 27W
Aberdare Ra., Kenya 54 C4 0 15S 36 50 E
Aberdeen, Australia 63 E5 32 9S 150 56 E
Aberdeen, Canada 73 C7 52 20N 106 8W
Aberdeen, S. Africa 56 E3 32 28S 24 2 E
Aberdeen, U.K. 12 D6 57 9N 2 5W
Aberdeen, Ala., U.S.A. 77 J1 33 49N 88 33W
Aberdeen, Idaho, U.S.A. 82 E7 42 57N 112 50W
Aberdeen, S. Dak., U.S.A. 80 C5 45 28N 98 29W
Aberdeen, Wash., U.S.A. 84 D3 46 59N 123 50W
Aberdeenshire □, U.K. 12 D6 57 17N 2 36W
Aberdovey = Aberdyfi, U.K. 11 E3 52 33N 4 3W
Aberdyfi, U.K. 11 E3 52 33N 4 3W
Aberfeldy, U.K. 12 E5 56 37N 3 51W
Abergavenny, U.K. 11 F4 51 49N 3 1W
Abernathy, U.S.A. 81 J4 33 50N 101 51W
Abert, L., U.S.A. 82 E3 42 38N 120 14W
Aberystwyth, U.K. 11 E3 52 25N 4 5W
Abhar, Iran 45 B6 36 9N 49 13 E
Abhayapuri, India 43 F14 26 24N 90 38 E
Abidjan, Ivory C. 50 G4 5 26N 3 58W
Abilene, Kans., U.S.A. 80 F6 38 55N 97 13W
Abilene, Tex., U.S.A. 81 J5 32 28N 99 43W
Abingdon, U.K. 11 F6 51 40N 1 17W
Abingdon, Ill., U.S.A. 80 E9 40 48N 90 24W
Abingdon, Va., U.S.A. 77 G5 36 43N 81 59W
Abington Reef, Australia 62 B4 18 0S 149 35 E
Abitau →, Canada 73 B7 59 53N 109 3W
Abitau L., Canada 73 A7 60 27N 107 15W
Abitibi L., Canada 70 C4 48 40N 79 40W
Abkhaz Republic □ = Abkhazia □, Georgia 25 F7 43 12N 41 5 E
Abkhazia □, Georgia 25 F7 43 12N 41 5 E
Abkit, Russia 27 C16 64 10N 157 10 E
Abminga, Australia 63 D1 26 8S 134 51 E
Åbo = Turku, Finland 9 F20 60 30N 22 19 E
Abohar, India 42 D6 30 10N 74 10 E
Abomey, Benin 50 G5 7 10N 2 5 E
Abong-Mbang, Cameroon 52 D2 4 0N 13 8 E
Abou-Deïa, Chad 51 F8 11 20N 19 20 E
Aboyne, U.K. 12 D6 57 4N 2 47W
Abra Pampa, Argentina 94 A2 22 43S 65 42W
Abreojos, Pta., Mexico 86 B2 26 50N 113 40W
Abri, Sudan 51 D11 20 50N 30 27 E
Abrolhos, Banka, Brazil 93 G11 18 0S 38 0W
Abrud, Romania 17 E12 46 19N 23 5 E
Absaroka Range, U.S.A. 82 D9 44 45N 109 50W
Abū al Khaşīb, Iraq 45 D6 30 25N 48 0 E
Abū 'Alī, Si. Arabia 45 E6 27 20N 49 27 E
Abū 'Alī →, Lebanon 47 A4 34 25N 35 50 E
Abu 'Arīsh, Si. Arabia 46 D3 16 53N 42 48 E
Abu Dhabi = Abū Ẓāby, U.A.E. 45 E7 24 28N 54 22 E
Abû Dis, Sudan 51 E11 19 12N 33 38 E
Abū Du'ān, Syria 44 B3 36 25N 38 15 E
Abu el Gairi, W. →, Egypt 47 F2 29 35N 33 30 E
Abu Ga'da, W. →, Egypt 47 F1 29 15N 32 53 E
Abū Ḩadrīyah, Si. Arabia 45 E6 27 20N 48 58 E
Abu Hamed, Sudan 51 E11 19 32N 33 13 E
Abū Kamāl, Syria 44 C4 34 30N 41 0 E
Abū Madd, Ra's, Si. Arabia 44 E3 24 50N 37 7 E
Abu Matariq, Sudan 51 F10 10 59N 26 9 E
Abu Şafāt, W. →, Jordan 47 E5 30 24N 36 7 E
Abū Şukhayr, Iraq 44 D5 31 54N 44 30 E
Abu Tig, Egypt 51 C11 27 4N 31 15 E
Abû Zabad, Sudan 51 F10 12 25N 29 10 E
Abū Ẓāby, U.A.E. 45 E7 24 28N 54 22 E
Abū Zeydābād, Iran 45 C6 33 54N 51 45 E
Abuja, Nigeria 50 G6 9 16N 7 2 E
Abukuma-Gawa →, Japan 30 E10 38 6N 140 52 E
Abukuma-Sammyaku, Japan 30 F10 37 30N 140 45 E
Abunã, Brazil 92 E5 9 40S 65 20W
Abunã →, Brazil 92 E5 9 41S 65 20W
Aburo, Zaïre 54 B3 2 4N 30 53 E
Abut Hd., N.Z. 59 K3 43 7S 170 15 E
Abwong, Sudan 51 G11 9 2N 32 14 E
Acajutla, El Salv. 88 D2 13 36N 89 50W
Acámbaro, Mexico 86 C4 20 0N 100 40W
Acaponeta, Mexico 86 C3 22 30N 105 20W
Acapulco, Mexico 87 D5 16 51N 99 56W
Acarigua, Venezuela 92 B5 9 33N 69 12W
Acatlán, Mexico 87 D5 18 10N 98 3W
Acayucan, Mexico 87 D6 17 59N 94 58W
Accomac, U.S.A. 76 G8 37 43N 75 40W
Accra, Ghana 50 G4 5 35N 0 6W
Accrington, U.K. 10 D5 53 45N 2 22W
Acebal, Argentina 94 C3 33 20S 60 50W
Aceh □, Indonesia 36 D1 4 15N 97 30 E
Achalpur, India 40 J10 21 22N 77 32 E
Acheng, China 35 B14 45 30N 126 58 E
Acher, India 42 H5 23 10N 72 32 E
Achill, Ireland 13 C2 53 56N 9 55W
Achill Hd., Ireland 13 C1 53 58N 10 15W
Achill I., Ireland 13 C1 53 58N 10 1W
Achill Sd., Ireland 13 C2 53 54N 9 56W
Achinsk, Russia 27 D10 56 20N 90 20 E
Acireale, Italy 20 F6 37 37N 15 10 E
Ackerman, U.S.A. 81 J10 33 19N 89 11W
Acklins I., Bahamas 89 B5 22 30N 74 0W
Acme, Canada 72 C6 51 33N 113 30W
Aconcagua, Cerro, Argentina 94 C2 32 39S 70 0W
Aconquija, Mt., Argentina 94 B2 27 0S 66 0W
Açores, Is. dos = Azores, Atl. Oc. 48 C1 38 44N 29 0W
Acraman, L., Australia 63 E2 32 2S 135 23 E
Acre = 'Akko, Israel 47 C4 32 55N 35 4 E
Acre □, Brazil 92 E4 9 1S 71 0W
Acre →, Brazil 92 E5 8 45S 67 22W
Acton, Canada 78 C4 43 38N 80 3W
Ad Dammām, Si. Arabia 45 E6 26 20N 50 5 E
Ad Dawhah, Qatar 45 E6 25 15N 51 35 E
Ad Dawr, Iraq 44 C4 34 27N 43 47 E
Ad Dir'īyah, Si. Arabia 44 E5 24 44N 46 35 E
Ad Dīwānīyah, Iraq 44 D5 32 0N 45 0 E
Ad Dujayl, Iraq 44 C5 33 51N 44 14 E
Ad Durūz, J., Jordan 47 C5 32 35N 36 40 E
Ada, Minn., U.S.A. 80 B6 47 18N 96 31W
Ada, Okla., U.S.A. 81 H6 34 46N 96 41W
Adaja →, Spain 19 B3 41 32N 4 52W
Adamaoua, Massif de l', Cameroon 51 G7 7 20N 12 20 E
Adamawa Highlands = Adamaoua, Massif de l', Cameroon 51 G7 7 20N 12 20 E
Adamello, Mte., Italy 20 A4 46 9N 10 30 E
Adaminaby, Australia 63 F4 36 0S 148 45 E
Adams, Mass., U.S.A. 79 D11 42 38N 73 7W
Adams, N.Y., U.S.A. 79 C8 43 49N 76 1W
Adams, Wis., U.S.A. 80 D10 43 57N 89 49W
Adam's Bridge, Sri Lanka 40 Q11 9 15N 79 40 E
Adams L., Canada 72 C5 51 10N 119 40W
Adams Mt., U.S.A. 84 D5 46 12N 121 30W
Adam's Peak, Sri Lanka 40 R12 6 48N 80 30 E
Adana, Turkey 25 G6 37 0N 35 16 E
Adapazarı, Turkey 25 F5 40 48N 30 25 E
Adarama, Sudan 51 E11 17 10N 34 52 E
Adare, C., Antarctica 5 D11 71 0S 171 0 E
Adaut, Indonesia 37 F8 8 8S 131 7 E
Adavale, Australia 63 D3 25 52S 144 32 E
Adda →, Italy 20 B3 45 8N 9 53 E
Addis Ababa = Addis Abeba, Ethiopia 51 G12 9 2N 38 42 E
Addis Abeba, Ethiopia 51 G12 9 2N 38 42 E
Addis Alem, Ethiopia 51 G12 9 0N 38 17 E
Addison, U.S.A. 78 D7 42 1N 77 14W
Addo, S. Africa 56 E4 33 32S 25 45 E
Ādeh, Iran 44 B5 37 42N 45 11 E
Adel, U.S.A. 77 K4 31 8N 83 25W
Adelaide, Australia 63 E2 34 52S 138 30 E
Adelaide, Bahamas 88 A4 25 4N 77 31W
Adelaide, S. Africa 56 E4 32 42S 26 20 E
Adelaide I., Antarctica 5 C17 67 15S 68 30W
Adelaide Pen., Canada 68 B10 68 15N 97 30W
Adelaide River, Australia 60 B5 13 15S 131 7 E
Adelanto, U.S.A. 85 L9 34 35N 117 22W
Adele I., Australia 60 C3 15 32S 123 9 E
Adélie, Terre, Antarctica 5 C10 68 0S 140 0 E
Adélie Land = Adélie, Terre, Antarctica 5 C10 68 0S 140 0 E
Aden = Al 'Adan, Yemen 46 E4 12 45N 45 0 E
Aden, G. of, Asia 46 E4 12 30N 47 30 E
Adendorp, S. Africa 56 E3 32 15S 24 30 E
Adh Dhayd, U.A.E. 45 E7 25 17N 55 53 E
Adhoi, India 42 H4 23 26N 70 32 E
Adi, Indonesia 37 E8 4 15S 133 30 E
Adi Ugri, Eritrea 51 F12 14 58N 38 48 E
Adieu, C., Australia 61 F5 32 0S 132 10 E
Adieu Pt., Australia 60 C3 15 14S 124 35 E
Adige →, Italy 20 B5 45 9N 12 20 E
Adilabad, India 40 K11 19 33N 78 20 E
Adin, U.S.A. 82 F3 41 12N 120 57W
Adin Khel, Afghan. 40 C6 32 45N 68 5 E
Adirondack Mts., U.S.A. 79 C10 44 0N 74 0W
Adjumani, Uganda 54 B3 3 20N 31 50 E
Adlavik Is., Canada 71 B8 55 2N 57 45W
Admer, Algeria 50 D6 20 21N 5 27 E
Admiralty G., Australia 60 B4 14 20S 125 55 E
Admiralty I., U.S.A. 68 C6 57 30N 134 30W
Admiralty Inlet, U.S.A. 82 C2 48 8N 122 58W
Admiralty Is., Papua N. G. 64 H6 2 0S 147 0 E
Ado-Ekiti, Nigeria 50 G6 7 38N 5 12 E
Adonara, Indonesia 37 F6 8 15S 123 5 E
Adoni, India 40 M10 15 33N 77 18 E
Adour →, France 18 E3 43 32N 1 32W
Adra, India 43 H12 23 30N 86 42 E
Adra, Spain 19 D4 36 43N 3 3W
Adrano, Italy 20 F6 37 40N 14 50 E
Adrar, Algeria 50 C4 27 51N 0 11W
Adré, Chad 51 F9 13 40N 22 20 E
Adrī, Libya 51 C7 27 32N 13 2 E
Adrian, Mich., U.S.A. 76 E3 41 54N 84 2W
Adrian, Tex., U.S.A. 81 H3 35 16N 102 40W
Adriatic Sea, Medit. S. 20 C6 43 0N 16 0 E
Adua, Indonesia 37 E7 1 45S 129 50 E
Adwa, Ethiopia 51 F12 14 15N 38 52 E
Adzhar Republic □ = Ajaria □, Georgia 25 F7 41 30N 42 0 E
Ægean Sea, Medit. S. 21 E11 38 30N 25 0 E
Aerhtai Shan, Mongolia 32 B4 46 40N 92 45 E
'Afak, Iraq 44 C5 32 4N 45 15 E
Afándou, Greece 23 C10 36 18N 28 12 E
Afghanistan ■, Asia 40 C4 33 0N 65 0 E
Afgoi, Somali Rep. 46 G3 2 7N 44 59 E
Afognak I., U.S.A. 68 C4 58 15N 152 30W
'Afrīn, Syria 44 B3 36 32N 36 50 E
Afton, U.S.A. 79 D9 42 14N 75 32W
Afuá, Brazil 93 D8 0 15S 50 20W
Afula, Israel 47 C4 32 37N 35 17 E
Afyonkarahisar, Turkey 25 G5 38 45N 30 33 E
Agadès = Agadez, Niger 50 E6 16 58N 7 59 E
Agadez, Niger 50 E6 16 58N 7 59 E
Agadir, Morocco 50 B3 30 28N 9 55W
Agaete, Canary Is. 22 F4 28 6N 15 43W
Agapa, Russia 27 B9 71 27N 89 15 E
Agar, India 42 H7 23 40N 76 2 E
Agartala, India 41 H17 23 50N 91 23 E
Agassiz, Canada 72 D4 49 14N 121 46W
Agats, Indonesia 37 F9 5 33S 138 0 E
Agboville, Ivory C. 50 G4 5 55N 4 15W
Agde, France 18 E5 43 19N 3 28 E
Agen, France 18 D4 44 12N 0 38 E
Āgh Kand, Iran 45 B6 37 15N 48 4 E
Aginskoye, Russia 27 D12 51 6N 114 32 E
Agra, India 42 F7 27 17N 77 58 E
Agri →, Italy 20 D7 40 13N 16 44 E
Ağri Daği, Turkey 25 G7 39 50N 44 15 E
Ağri Karakose, Turkey 25 G7 39 44N 43 3 E
Agrigento, Italy 20 F5 37 19N 13 34 E
Agrinion, Greece 21 E9 38 37N 21 27 E
Agua Caliente, Baja Calif., Mexico 85 N10 32 29N 116 59W
Agua Caliente, Sinaloa, Mexico 86 B3 26 30N 108 20W
Agua Caliente Springs, U.S.A. 85 N10 32 56N 116 19W
Água Clara, Brazil 93 H8 20 25S 52 45W
Agua Hechicero, Mexico 85 N10 32 26N 116 14W
Agua Prieta, Mexico 86 A3 31 20N 109 32W
Aguadas, Colombia 92 B3 5 40N 75 38W
Aguadilla, Puerto Rico 89 C6 18 26N 67 10W
Aguadulce, Panama 88 E3 8 15N 80 32W
Aguanga, U.S.A. 85 M10 33 27N 116 51W
Aguanish, Canada 71 B7 50 14N 62 2W
Aguanus →, Canada 71 B7 50 13N 62 5W
Aguapey →, Argentina 94 B4 29 7S 56 36W
Aguaray Guazú →, Paraguay 94 A4 24 47S 57 19W
Aguarico →, Ecuador 92 D3 0 59S 75 11W
Aguas Blancas, Chile 94 A2 24 15S 69 55W
Aguas Calientes, Sierra de, Argentina 94 B2 25 26S 66 40W
Aguascalientes, Mexico 86 C4 21 53N 102 12W
Aguascalientes □, Mexico 86 C4 22 0N 102 20W
Aguilares, Argentina 94 B2 27 26S 65 35W
Aguilas, Spain 19 D5 37 23N 1 35W
Agüimes, Canary Is. 22 G4 27 58N 15 27W
Aguja, C. de la, Colombia 90 B3 11 18N 74 12W
Agulhas, C., S. Africa 56 E3 34 52S 20 0 E
Agulo, Canary Is. 22 F2 28 11N 17 12W
Agung, Indonesia 36 F5 8 20S 115 28 E
Agur, Uganda 54 B3 2 28N 32 55 E
Agusan →, Phil. 37 C7 9 0N 125 30 E
Aha Mts., Botswana 56 B3 19 45S 21 0 E
Ahaggar, Algeria 50 D6 23 0N 6 30 E
Ahar, Iran 44 B5 38 35N 47 0 E
Ahipara B., N.Z. 59 F4 35 5S 173 5 E
Ahiri, India 40 K12 19 30N 80 0 E
Ahmad Wal, Pakistan 42 E1 29 18N 65 58 E
Ahmadabad, India 42 H5 23 0N 72 40 E
Aḩmadābād, Khorāsān, Iran 45 C9 35 3N 60 50 E
Aḩmadābād, Khorāsān, Iran 45 C8 35 49N 59 42 E
Aḩmadī, Iran 45 E8 27 56N 56 42 E
Ahmadnagar, India 40 K9 19 7N 74 46 E
Ahmadpur, Pakistan 42 E4 29 12N 71 10 E
Ahmedabad = Ahmadabad, India 42 H5 23 0N 72 40 E
Ahmednagar = Ahmadnagar, India 40 K9 19 7N 74 46 E
Ahome, Mexico 86 B3 25 55N 109 11W
Ahram, Iran 45 D6 28 52N 51 16 E
Ahrax Pt., Malta 23 D1 35 59N 14 22 E
Āhū, Iran 45 C6 34 33N 50 2 E
Ahuachapán, El Salv. 88 D2 13 54N 89 52W
Ahvāz, Iran 45 D6 31 20N 48 40 E
Ahvenanmaa = Åland, Finland 9 F19 60 15N 20 0 E
Aḩwar, Yemen 46 E4 13 30N 46 40 E
Aichi □, Japan 31 G8 35 0N 137 15 E
Aigua, Uruguay 95 C5 34 13S 54 46W
Aigues-Mortes, France 18 E6 43 35N 4 12 E
Aihui, China 33 A7 50 10N 127 30 E
Aija, Peru 92 E3 9 50S 77 45W
Aikawa, Japan 30 E9 38 2N 138 15 E
Aiken, U.S.A. 77 J5 33 34N 81 43W
Aillik, Canada 71 A8 55 11N 59 18W
Ailsa Craig, U.K. 12 F3 55 15N 5 6W
'Ailūn, Jordan 47 C4 32 18N 35 47 E
Aim, Russia 27 D14 59 0N 133 55 E
Aimere, Indonesia 37 F6 8 45S 121 3 E
Aimogasta, Argentina 94 B2 28 33S 66 50W
Aimorés, Brazil 93 G10 19 30S 41 4W
Aïn Beïda, Algeria 50 A6 35 50N 7 29 E
Aïn Ben Tili, Mauritania 50 C3 25 59N 9 27W
Aïn-Sefra, Algeria 50 B4 32 47N 0 37W
'Ain Sudr, Egypt 47 F2 29 50N 33 6 E
Ainabo, Somali Rep. 46 F4 9 0N 46 25 E
Ainaži, Latvia 9 H21 57 50N 24 24 E
Ainsworth, U.S.A. 80 D5 42 33N 99 52W
Aïr, Niger 50 E6 18 30N 8 0 E
Air Hitam, Malaysia 39 M4 1 55N 103 11 E
Airdrie, U.K. 12 F5 55 52N 3 57W
Aire →, U.K. 10 D7 53 43N 0 55W
Aire, I. del, Spain 22 B11 39 48N 4 16 E
Airlie Beach, Australia 62 C4 20 16S 148 43 E
Aisne →, France 18 B5 49 26N 2 50 E
Aitkin, U.S.A. 80 B8 46 32N 93 42W
Aiud, Romania 17 E12 46 19N 23 44 E
Aix-en-Provence, France 18 E6 43 32N 5 27 E
Aix-la-Chapelle = Aachen, Germany 16 C4 50 45N 6 6 E
Aix-les-Bains, France 18 D6 45 41N 5 53 E
Aiyansh, Canada 72 B3 55 17N 129 2W
Aiyion, Greece 21 E10 38 15N 22 5 E
Aizawl, India 41 H18 23 40N 92 44 E
Aizkraukle, Latvia 9 H21 56 36N 25 11 E
Aizpute, Latvia 9 H19 56 43N 21 40 E
Aizuwakamatsu, Japan 30 F9 37 30N 139 56 E
Ajaccio, France 18 F8 41 55N 8 40 E
Ajalpan, Mexico 87 D5 18 22N 97 15W
Ajanta Ra., India 40 J9 20 28N 75 50 E
Ajari Rep. = Ajaria □, Georgia 25 F7 41 30N 42 0 E
Ajaria □, Georgia 25 F7 41 30N 42 0 E
Ajax, Canada 78 C5 43 50N 79 1W
Ajdâbiyah, Libya 51 B9 30 54N 20 4 E
Ajka, Hungary 17 E9 47 4N 17 31 E
'Ajmān, U.A.E. 45 E7 25 25N 55 30 E
Ajmer, India 42 F6 26 28N 74 37 E
Ajo, U.S.A. 83 K7 32 22N 112 52W
Ajo, C. de, Spain 19 A4 43 31N 3 35W
Akabira, Japan 30 C11 43 33N 142 5 E
Akamas □, Cyprus 23 D11 35 3N 32 18 E
Akanthou, Cyprus 23 D12 35 22N 33 45 E
Akaroa, N.Z. 59 K4 43 49S 172 59 E
Akashi, Japan 31 G7 34 45N 134 58 E
Akelamo, Indonesia 37 D7 1 35N 129 40 E
Aketi, Zaïre 52 D4 2 38N 23 47 E
Akharnaí, Greece 21 E10 38 5N 23 44 E
Akhelóös →, Greece 21 E9 38 19N 21 7 E
Akhisar, Turkey 21 E12 38 56N 27 48 E
Akhmîm, Egypt 51 C11 26 31N 31 47 E
Akhnur, India 43 C6 32 52N 74 45 E
Aki, Japan 31 H6 33 30N 133 54 E
Akimiski I., Canada 70 B3 52 50N 81 30W
Akita, Japan 30 E10 39 45N 140 7 E
Akita □, Japan 30 E10 39 40N 140 30 E
Akjoujt, Mauritania 50 E2 19 45N 14 15W
Akkeshi, Japan 30 C12 43 2N 144 51 E
'Akko, Israel 47 C4 32 55N 35 4 E
Akkol, Kazakstan 26 E8 45 0N 75 39 E
Aklavik, Canada 68 B6 68 12N 135 0W
Akmolinsk = Aqmola, Kazakstan 26 D8 51 10N 71 30 E
Akō, Japan 31 G7 34 45N 134 24 E
Akobo →, Ethiopia 51 G11 7 48N 33 3 E
Akola, India 40 J10 20 42N 77 2 E
Akordat, Eritrea 51 E12 15 30N 37 40 E
Akpatok I., Canada 69 B13 60 25N 68 8W
Åkrahamn, Norway 9 G11 59 15N 5 10 E
Akranes, Iceland 8 D2 64 19N 22 5W
Akreïjit, Mauritania 50 E3 18 19N 9 11W
Akron, Colo., U.S.A. 80 E3 40 10N 103 13W
Akron, Ohio, U.S.A. 78 E3 41 5N 81 31W
Akrotiri, Cyprus 23 E11 34 36N 32 57 E
Akrotiri Bay, Cyprus 23 E12 34 35N 33 10 E
Aksai Chin, India 43 B8 35 15N 79 55 E
Aksarka, Russia 26 C7 66 31N 67 50 E
Aksay, Kazakstan 24 D9 51 11N 53 0 E
Aksenovo Zilovskoye, Russia 27 D12 53 20N 117 40 E
Aksu, China 32 B3 41 5N 80 10 E
Aksum, Ethiopia 51 F12 14 5N 38 40 E
Aktogay, Kazakstan 26 E8 46 57N 79 40 E
Aktsyabrski, Belarus 17 B15 52 38N 28 53 E
Aktyubinsk = Aqtöbe, Kazakstan 25 D10 50 17N 57 10 E
Aku, Nigeria 50 G6 6 40N 7 18 E
Akure, Nigeria 50 G6 7 15N 5 5 E
Akureyri, Iceland 8 D4 65 40N 18 6W
Akuseki-Shima, Japan 31 K4 29 27N 129 37 E
Akyab = Sittwe, Burma 41 J18 20 18N 92 45 E
Al 'Adan, Yemen 46 E4 12 45N 45 0 E
Al Aḩsā, Si. Arabia 45 E6 25 50N 49 0 E
Al Ajfar, Si. Arabia 44 E4 27 26N 43 0 E
Al Amādīyah, Iraq 44 B4 37 5N 43 30 E
Al Amārah, Iraq 44 D5 31 55N 47 15 E
Al 'Aqabah, Jordan 47 F4 29 31N 35 0 E
Al Arak, Syria 44 C3 34 38N 38 35 E
Al 'Aramah, Si. Arabia 44 E5 25 30N 46 0 E
Al Arţāwīyah, Si. Arabia 44 E5 26 31N 45 20 E
Al 'Āşimah □, Jordan 47 D5 31 40N 36 30 E
Al' Assāfīyah, Si. Arabia 44 D3 28 17N 38 59 E
Al 'Ayn, Oman 45 E7 24 15N 55 45 E
Al 'Ayn, Si. Arabia 44 E3 25 4N 38 6 E
Al A'ẓamīyah, Iraq 44 C5 33 22N 44 22 E
Al 'Azīzīyah, Iraq 44 C5 32 54N 45 4 E
Al Bāb, Syria 44 B3 36 23N 37 29 E
Al Bad', Si. Arabia 44 D2 28 28N 35 1 E
Al Bādī, Iraq 44 C4 35 56N 41 32 E
Al Baḩrah, Kuwait 44 D5 29 40N 47 52 E
Al Balqā' □, Jordan 47 C4 32 5N 35 45 E
Al Bārūk, J., Lebanon 47 B4 33 39N 35 40 E
Al Başrah, Iraq 44 D5 30 30N 47 50 E
Al Baţḩā, Iraq 44 D5 31 6N 45 53 E
Al Batrūn, Lebanon 47 A4 34 15N 35 40 E
Al Bayḑā, Libya 51 B9 32 50N 21 44 E
Al Biqā □, Lebanon 47 A5 34 10N 36 10 E
Al Bi'r, Si. Arabia 44 D3 28 50N 36 16 E
Al Bu'ayrāt al Ḩasūn, Libya 51 B8 31 24N 15 44 E
Al Burayj, Syria 47 A5 34 15N 36 46 E
Al Fallūjah, Iraq 44 C4 33 20N 43 55 E
Al Fāw, Iraq 45 D6 30 0N 48 30 E
Al Fujayrah, U.A.E. 45 E8 25 7N 56 18 E
Al Ghadaf, W. →, Jordan 47 D5 31 26N 36 43 E
Al Ghammās, Iraq 44 D5 31 45N 44 37 E

Asike

Anzhero-Sudzhensk, Russia 26 D9 56 10N 86 0 E
Anzio, Italy 20 D5 41 27N 12 37 E
Aoga-Shima, Japan 31 H9 32 28N 139 46 E
Aomori, Japan 30 D10 40 45N 140 45 E
Aomori □, Japan 30 D10 40 45N 140 40 E
Aonla, India 43 E8 28 16N 79 11 E
Aosta, Italy 20 B2 45 45N 7 20 E
Aoudéras, Niger 50 E6 17 45N 8 20 E
Aoulef el Arab, Algeria 50 C5 26 55N 1 2 E
Apa ➝, S. Amer. 94 A4 22 6S 58 2W
Apache, U.S.A. 81 H5 34 54N 98 22W
Apalachee B., U.S.A. 77 L3 30 0N 84 0W
Apalachicola, U.S.A. 77 L3 29 43N 84 59W
Apalachicola ➝, U.S.A. 77 L3 29 43N 84 58W
Apaporis ➝, Colombia 92 D5 1 23S 69 25W
Aparri, Phil. 37 A6 18 22N 121 38 E
Apàtity, Russia 24 A5 67 34N 33 22 E
Apatzingán, Mexico 86 D4 19 0N 102 20W
Apeldoorn, Neths. 15 B5 52 13N 5 57 E
Apennines = Appennini, Italy 20 B4 44 0N 10 0 E
Apia, W. Samoa 59 A13 13 50S 171 50W
Apiacás, Serra dos, Brazil 92 E7 9 50S 57 0W
Apizaco, Mexico 87 D5 19 26N 98 9W
Aplao, Peru 92 G4 16 0S 72 40W
Apo, Mt., Phil. 37 C7 6 53N 125 14 E
Apolakkiá, Greece 23 C9 36 5N 27 48 E
Apolakkiá, Órmos, Greece 23 C9 36 5N 27 45 E
Apollonia = Marsá Susah, Libya 51 B9 32 52N 21 59 E
Apolo, Bolivia 92 F5 14 30S 68 30W
Apostle Is., U.S.A. 80 B9 47 0N 90 40W
Apóstoles, Argentina 95 B4 28 0S 56 0W
Apostolos Andreas, C., Cyprus 23 D13 35 42N 34 35 E
Apoteri, Guyana 92 C7 4 2N 58 32W
Appalachian Mts., U.S.A. 76 G6 38 0N 80 0W
Appennini, Italy 20 B4 44 0N 10 0 E
Apple Hill, Canada 79 A10 45 13N 74 46W
Apple Valley, U.S.A. 85 L9 34 32N 117 14W
Appleby-in-Westmorland, U.K. 10 C5 54 35N 2 29W
Appleton, U.S.A. 76 C1 44 16N 88 25W
Approuague, Fr. Guiana 93 C8 4 20N 52 0W
Aprília, Italy 20 D5 41 36N 12 39 E
Apucarana, Brazil 95 A5 23 55S 51 33W
Apure ➝, Venezuela 92 B5 7 37N 66 25W
Apurimac ➝, Peru 92 F4 12 17S 73 56W
Aqabah = Al 'Aqabah, Jordan 47 F4 29 31N 35 0 E
'Aqabah, Khalīj al, Red Sea 44 D2 28 15N 33 20 E
'Aqdā, Iran 45 C7 32 26N 53 37 E
Aqīq, Sudan 51 E12 18 14N 38 12 E
Aqmola, Kazakstan 26 D8 51 10N 71 30 E
Aqrah, Iraq 44 B4 36 46N 43 45 E
Aqtöbe, Kazakstan 25 D10 50 17N 57 10 E
Aquidauana, Brazil 93 H7 20 30S 55 50W
Aquiles Serdán, Mexico 86 B3 28 37N 105 54W
Aquin, Haiti 89 C5 18 16N 73 24W
Aquitain, Bassin, France 18 D3 44 0N 0 30W
Ar Rachidiya, Morocco 50 B4 31 58N 4 20W
Ar Rafid, Syria 47 C4 32 57N 35 52 E
Ar Raḩḩālīyah, Iraq 44 C4 32 44N 43 23 E
Ar Ramādī, Iraq 44 C4 33 25N 43 20 E
Ar Ramthā, Jordan 47 C5 32 34N 36 0 E
Ar Raqqah, Syria 44 C3 35 59N 39 8 E
Ar Rass, Si. Arabia 44 E4 25 50N 43 40 E
Ar Rifā'ī, Iraq 44 D5 31 50N 46 10 E
Ar Riyāḑ, Si. Arabia 46 C4 24 41N 46 42 E
Ar Ru'ays, Qatar 45 E6 26 8N 51 12 E
Ar Rukhaymīyah, Iraq 44 D5 29 22N 45 38 E
Ar Ruqayyidah, Si. Arabia 45 E6 25 21N 49 34 E
Ar Ruşāfah, Syria 44 C3 35 45N 38 49 E
Ar Ruṭbah, Iraq 44 C4 33 0N 40 15 E
Ara, India 43 G11 25 35N 84 32 E
'Arab, Bahr el ➝, Sudan 51 G10 9 0N 29 30 E
'Arabābād, Iran 45 C8 33 2N 57 41 E
Arabia, Asia 46 C4 25 0N 45 0 E
Arabian Desert = Es Sahrâ' Esh Sharqîya, Egypt 51 C11 27 30N 32 30 E
Arabian Gulf = Gulf, The, Asia 45 E6 27 0N 50 0 E
Arabian Sea, Ind. Oc. 29 H10 16 0N 65 0 E
Aracaju, Brazil 93 F11 10 55S 37 4W
Aracataca, Colombia 92 A4 10 38N 74 9W
Aracati, Brazil 93 D11 4 30S 37 44W
Araçatuba, Brazil 95 A5 21 10S 50 30W
Aracena, Spain 19 D2 37 53N 6 38W
Araçuaí, Brazil 93 G10 16 52S 42 4W
'Arad, Israel 47 D4 31 15N 35 12 E
Arad, Romania 17 E11 46 10N 21 20 E
Arada, Chad 51 F9 15 0N 20 20 E
Aradhippou, Cyprus 23 E12 34 57N 33 36 E
Arafura Sea, E. Indies 37 F8 9 0S 135 0 E
Aragón □, Spain 19 B5 41 25N 0 40W
Aragón ➝, Spain 19 A5 42 13N 1 44W
Araguacema, Brazil 93 E9 8 50S 49 20W
Araguaia ➝, Brazil 93 E9 5 21S 48 41W
Araguari, Brazil 93 G9 18 38S 48 11W
Araguari ➝, Brazil 93 C9 1 15N 49 55W
Arak, Algeria 50 C5 25 20N 3 45 E
Arāk, Iran 45 C6 34 0N 49 40 E
Arakan Coast, Burma 41 K19 19 0N 94 0 E
Arakan Yoma, Burma 41 K19 20 0N 94 40 E
Araks = Aras, Rūd-e ➝, Azerbaijan 44 B5 40 5N 48 29 E
Aral, Kazakstan 26 E7 46 41N 61 45 E
Aral Sea, Asia 26 E7 44 30N 60 0 E
Aral Tengizi = Aral Sea, Asia 26 E7 44 30N 60 0 E
Aralsk = Aral, Kazakstan 26 E7 46 41N 61 45 E
Aralskoye More = Aral Sea, Asia 26 E7 44 30N 60 0 E
Aramac, Australia 62 C4 22 58S 145 14 E
Arambag, India 43 H12 22 53N 87 48 E
Aran I., Ireland 13 B3 55 0N 8 30W
Aran Is., Ireland 13 C2 53 6N 9 38W
Aranda de Duero, Spain 19 B4 41 39N 3 42W
Arandān, Iran 44 C5 35 23N 46 55 E
Aranjuez, Spain 19 B4 40 1N 3 40W
Aranos, Namibia 56 C2 24 9S 19 7 E
Aransas Pass, U.S.A. 81 M6 27 55N 97 9W
Araouane, Mali 50 E4 18 55N 3 30W
Arapahoe, U.S.A. 80 E5 40 18N 99 54W
Arapey Grande ➝, Uruguay 94 C4 30 55S 57 49W
Arapiraca, Brazil 93 E11 9 45S 36 39W
Arapongas, Brazil 95 A5 23 29S 51 28W
Ar'ar, Si. Arabia 44 D4 30 59N 41 2 E
Araranguá, Brazil 95 B6 29 0S 49 30W
Araraquara, Brazil 93 H9 21 50S 48 0W
Ararás, Serra das, Brazil 95 B5 25 0S 53 10W
Ararat, Australia 63 F3 37 16S 143 0 E
Ararat, Mt. = Ağrı Dağı, Turkey 25 G7 39 50N 44 15 E
Araria, India 43 F12 26 9N 87 33 E
Araripe, Chapada do, Brazil 93 E11 7 20S 40 0W
Araruama, L. de, Brazil 95 A7 22 53S 42 12W
Aras, Rūd-e ➝, Azerbaijan 44 B5 40 5N 48 29 E
Arauca, Colombia 92 B4 7 0N 70 40W
Arauca ➝, Venezuela 92 B5 7 24N 66 35W
Arauco, Chile 94 D1 37 16S 73 25W
Arauco □, Chile 94 D1 37 40S 73 25W
Araxá, Brazil 93 G9 19 35S 46 55W
Araya, Pen. de, Venezuela 92 A6 10 40N 64 0W
Arbat, Iraq 44 C5 35 25N 45 35 E
Arbatax, Italy 20 E3 39 56N 9 42 E
Arbil, Iraq 44 B5 36 15N 44 5 E
Arborfield, Canada 73 C8 53 6N 103 39W
Arborg, Canada 73 C9 50 54N 97 13W
Arbroath, U.K. 12 E6 56 34N 2 35W
Arbuckle, U.S.A. 84 F4 39 1N 122 3W
Arcachon, France 18 D3 44 40N 1 10W
Arcade, U.S.A. 78 D6 42 32N 78 25W
Arcadia, Fla., U.S.A. 77 M5 27 13N 81 52W
Arcadia, La., U.S.A. 81 J8 32 33N 92 55W
Arcadia, Nebr., U.S.A. 80 E5 41 25N 99 8W
Arcadia, Pa., U.S.A. 78 F6 40 47N 78 51W
Arcadia, Wis., U.S.A. 80 C9 44 15N 91 30W
Arcata, U.S.A. 82 F1 40 52N 124 5W
Archangel = Arkhangelsk, Russia 24 B7 64 38N 40 36 E
Archbald, U.S.A. 79 E9 41 30N 75 32W
Archer ➝, Australia 62 A3 13 28S 141 41 E
Archer B., Australia 62 A3 13 20S 141 30 E
Archers Post, Kenya 54 B4 0 35N 37 35 E
Arcila = Asilah, Morocco 50 A3 35 29N 6 0W
Arckaringa, Australia 63 D1 27 56S 134 45 E
Arckaringa Cr. ➝, Australia 63 D2 28 10S 135 22 E
Arco, U.S.A. 82 E7 43 38N 113 18W
Arcola, Canada 73 D8 49 40N 102 30W
Arcos de la Frontera, Spain 19 D3 36 45N 5 49W
Arcot, India 40 N11 12 53N 79 20 E
Arcoverde, Brazil 93 E11 8 25S 37 4W
Arctic Bay, Canada 69 A11 73 1N 85 7W
Arctic Ocean, Arctic 4 B18 78 0N 160 0W
Arctic Red River, Canada 68 B6 67 15N 134 0W
Arda ➝, Bulgaria 21 D12 41 40N 26 29 E
Ardabīl, Iran 45 B6 38 15N 48 18 E
Ardakān = Sepīdān, Iran 45 D7 30 20N 52 5 E
Ardee, Ireland 13 C5 53 52N 6 33W
Arden, Canada 78 B8 44 43N 76 56W
Arden, Calif., U.S.A. 84 G5 38 36N 121 33W
Arden, Nev., U.S.A. 85 J11 36 1N 115 14W
Ardenne, Belgium 15 E5 49 50N 5 5 E
Ardennes = Ardenne, Belgium 15 E5 49 50N 5 5 E
Ardestān, Iran 45 C7 33 20N 52 25 E
Ardgour, U.K. 12 E3 56 45N 5 25W
Ardlethan, Australia 63 E4 34 22S 146 53 E
Ardmore, Australia 62 C2 21 39S 139 11 E
Ardmore, Okla., U.S.A. 81 H6 34 10N 97 8W
Ardmore, Pa., U.S.A. 79 G9 39 58N 75 18W
Ardmore, S. Dak., U.S.A. 80 D3 43 1N 103 40W
Ardnacrusha, Ireland 13 D3 52 43N 8 38W
Ardnamurchan, Pt. of, U.K. 12 E2 56 43N 6 14W
Ardrossan, Australia 63 E2 34 26S 137 53 E
Ardrossan, U.K. 12 F4 55 39N 4 49W
Ards □, U.K. 13 B6 54 35N 5 30W
Ards Pen., U.K. 13 B6 54 33N 5 34W
Arecibo, Puerto Rico 89 C6 18 29N 66 43W
Areia Branca, Brazil 93 D11 5 0S 37 0W
Arena, Pt., U.S.A. 84 G3 38 57N 123 44W
Arendal, Norway 9 G13 58 28N 8 46 E
Arequipa, Peru 92 G4 16 20S 71 30W
Arero, Ethiopia 51 H12 4 41N 38 50 E
Arévalo, Spain 19 B3 41 3N 4 43W
Arezzo, Italy 20 C4 43 25N 11 53 E
Argamakmur, Indonesia 36 E2 3 35S 102 0 E
Arganda, Spain 19 B4 40 19N 3 26W
Argentan, France 18 B3 48 45N 0 1W
Argentário, Mte., Italy 20 C4 42 24N 11 9 E
Argentia, Canada 71 C9 47 18N 53 58W
Argentina ■, S. Amer. 96 D3 35 0S 66 0W
Argentina Is., Antarctica 5 C17 66 0S 64 0W
Argentino, L., Argentina 96 G2 50 10S 73 0W
Argeş ➝, Romania 17 F14 44 11N 26 25 E
Arghandab ➝, Afghan. 42 D1 31 30N 64 15 E
Argo, Sudan 51 E11 19 28N 30 30 E
Argolikós Kólpos, Greece 21 F10 37 20N 22 52 E
Árgos, Greece 21 F10 37 40N 22 43 E
Argostólion, Greece 21 E9 38 12N 20 33 E
Arguello, Pt., U.S.A. 85 L6 34 35N 120 39W
Arguineguín, Canary Is. 22 G4 27 46N 15 41W
Argun ➝, Russia 27 D13 53 20N 121 28 E
Argungu, Nigeria 50 F5 12 40N 4 31 E
Argus Pk., U.S.A. 85 K9 35 52N 117 26W
Argyle, U.S.A. 80 A6 48 20N 96 49W
Argyle, L., Australia 60 C4 16 20S 128 40 E
Argyll & Bute □, U.K. 12 E3 56 13N 5 28W
Århus, Denmark 9 H14 56 8N 10 11 E
Ariadnoye, Russia 30 B7 45 8N 134 25 E
Ariamsvlei, Namibia 56 D2 28 9S 19 51 E
Arica, Chile 92 G4 18 32S 70 20W
Arica, Colombia 92 D4 2 0S 71 50W
Arico, Canary Is. 22 F3 28 9N 16 29W
Arid, C., Australia 61 F3 34 1S 123 10 E
Arida, Japan 31 G7 34 5N 135 8 E
Arīḩā, Syria 44 C3 35 49N 36 35 E
Arílla, Ákra, Greece 23 A3 39 43N 19 39 E
Arima, Trin. & Tob. 89 D7 10 38N 61 17W
Arinos ➝, Brazil 92 F7 10 25S 58 20W
Ario de Rosales, Mexico 86 D4 19 12N 102 0W
Aripuanã, Brazil 92 E6 9 25S 60 30W
Aripuanã ➝, Brazil 92 E6 5 7S 60 25W
Ariquemes, Brazil 92 E6 9 55S 63 6W
Arisaig, U.K. 12 E3 56 55N 5 51W
Aristazabal I., Canada 72 C3 52 40N 129 10W
Arivaca, U.S.A. 83 L8 31 37N 111 25W
Arivonimamo, Madag. 57 B8 19 1S 47 11 E
Arizaro, Salar de, Argentina 94 A2 24 40S 67 50W
Arizona, Argentina 94 D2 35 45S 65 25W
Arizona □, U.S.A. 83 J8 34 0N 112 0W
Arizpe, Mexico 86 A2 30 20N 110 11W
Arjeplog, Sweden 8 D18 66 3N 18 2 E
Arjona, Colombia 92 A3 10 14N 75 22W
Arjuno, Indonesia 37 G15 7 49S 112 34 E
Arka, Russia 27 C15 60 15N 142 0 E
Arkadelphia, U.S.A. 81 H8 34 7N 93 4W
Arkaig, L., U.K. 12 E3 56 59N 5 10W
Arkalyk = Arqalyk, Kazakstan 26 D7 50 13N 66 50 E
Arkansas □, U.S.A. 81 H8 35 0N 92 30W
Arkansas ➝, U.S.A. 81 J9 33 47N 91 4W
Arkansas City, U.S.A. 81 G6 37 4N 97 2W
Arkhángelos, Greece 23 C10 36 13N 28 7 E
Arkhangelsk, Russia 24 B7 64 38N 40 36 E
Arklow, Ireland 13 D5 52 48N 6 10W
Arkticheskiy, Mys, Russia 27 A10 81 10N 95 0 E
Arlanzón ➝, Spain 19 A3 42 3N 4 17W
Arlberg P., Austria 16 E6 47 9N 10 12 E
Arlee, U.S.A. 82 C6 47 10N 114 5W
Arles, France 18 E6 43 41N 4 40 E
Arlington, S. Africa 57 D4 28 1S 27 53 E
Arlington, Oreg., U.S.A. 82 D3 45 43N 120 12W
Arlington, S. Dak., U.S.A. 80 C6 44 22N 97 8W
Arlington, Va., U.S.A. 76 F7 38 53N 77 7W
Arlington, Wash., U.S.A. 84 B4 48 12N 122 8W
Arlington Heights, U.S.A. 76 D2 42 5N 87 59W
Arlon, Belgium 15 E5 49 42N 5 49 E
Armagh, U.K. 13 B5 54 21N 6 39W
Armagh □, U.K. 13 B5 54 18N 6 37W
Armavir, Russia 25 E7 45 2N 41 7 E
Armenia, Colombia 92 C3 4 35N 75 45W
Armenia ■, Asia 25 F7 40 20N 45 0 E
Armenistís, Ákra, Greece 23 C9 36 8N 27 42 E
Armidale, Australia 63 E5 30 30S 151 40 E
Armour, U.S.A. 80 D5 43 19N 98 21W
Armstrong, B.C., Canada 72 C5 50 25N 119 10W
Armstrong, Ont., Canada 70 B2 50 18N 89 4W
Armstrong, U.S.A. 81 M6 26 56N 97 47W
Armstrong ➝, Australia 60 C5 16 35S 131 40 E
Arnarfjörður, Iceland 8 D2 65 48N 23 40W
Arnaud ➝, Canada 69 B12 60 0N 70 0W
Arnauti, C., Cyprus 23 D11 35 6N 32 17 E
Arnett, U.S.A. 81 G5 36 8N 99 46W
Arnhem, Neths. 15 C5 51 58N 5 55 E
Arnhem, C., Australia 62 A2 12 20S 137 30 E
Arnhem B., Australia 62 A2 12 20S 136 10 E
Arnhem Land, Australia 62 A1 13 10S 134 30 E
Arno ➝, Italy 20 C4 43 41N 10 17 E
Arno Bay, Australia 63 E2 33 54S 136 34 E
Arnold, Calif., U.S.A. 84 G6 38 15N 120 20W
Arnold, Nebr., U.S.A. 80 E4 41 26N 100 12W
Arnot, Canada 73 B9 55 56N 96 41W
Arnøy, Norway 8 A19 70 9N 20 40 E
Arnprior, Canada 70 C4 45 26N 76 21W
Arnsberg, Germany 16 C5 51 24N 8 5 E
Aroab, Namibia 56 D2 26 41S 19 39 E
Arqalyk, Kazakstan 26 D7 50 13N 66 50 E
Arrabury, Australia 63 D3 26 45S 141 0 E
Arrah = Ara, India 43 G11 25 35N 84 32 E
Arran, U.K. 12 F3 55 34N 5 12W
Arrandale, Canada 72 C3 54 57N 130 0W
Arras, France 18 A5 50 17N 2 46 E
Arrecife, Canary Is. 22 F6 28 57N 13 37W
Arrecifes, Argentina 94 C3 34 6S 60 9W
Arrée, Mts. d', France 18 B2 48 26N 3 55W
Arriaga, Chiapas, Mexico 87 D6 16 15N 93 52W
Arriaga, San Luis Potosí, Mexico 86 C4 21 55N 101 23W
Arrilalah P.O., Australia 62 C3 23 43S 143 54 E
Arrino, Australia 61 E2 29 30S 115 40 E
Arrow, L., Ireland 13 B3 54 3N 8 19W
Arrow Rock Res., U.S.A. 82 E6 43 45N 115 50W
Arrowhead, Canada 72 C5 50 40N 117 55W
Arrowhead, L., U.S.A. 85 L9 34 16N 117 10W
Arrowtown, N.Z. 59 L2 44 57S 168 50 E
Arroyo Grande, U.S.A. 85 K6 35 7N 120 35W
Ars, Iran 44 B5 37 9N 47 46 E
Arsenault L., Canada 73 B7 55 6N 108 32W
Arsenev, Russia 30 B6 44 10N 133 15 E
Árta, Greece 21 E9 39 8N 21 2 E
Artá, Spain 22 B10 39 41N 3 21 E
Arteaga, Mexico 86 D4 18 50N 102 20W
Artem, Russia 30 C6 43 22N 132 13 E
Artemovsk, Russia 27 D10 54 45N 93 35 E
Artesia = Mosomane, Botswana 56 C4 24 2S 26 19 E
Artesia, U.S.A. 81 J2 32 51N 104 24W
Artesia Wells, U.S.A. 81 L5 28 17N 99 17W
Artesian, U.S.A. 80 C6 44 1N 97 55W
Arthur ➝, Australia 62 G3 41 2S 144 40 E
Arthur Cr. ➝, Australia 62 C2 22 30S 136 25 E
Arthur Pt., Australia 62 C5 22 7S 150 3 E
Arthur's Pass, N.Z. 59 K3 42 54S 171 35 E
Arthur's Town, Bahamas 89 B4 24 38N 75 42W
Artigas, Uruguay 94 C4 30 20S 56 30W
Artillery L., Canada 73 A7 63 9N 107 52W
Artois, France 18 A5 50 20N 2 30 E
Artsyz, Ukraine 17 E15 46 4N 29 26 E
Artvin, Turkey 25 F7 41 14N 41 44 E
Aru, Kepulauan, Indonesia 37 F8 6 0S 134 30 E
Aru Is. = Aru, Kepulauan, Indonesia 37 F8 6 0S 134 30 E
Aru Meru □, Tanzania 54 C4 3 20S 36 50 E
Arua, Uganda 54 B3 3 1N 30 58 E
Aruanã, Brazil 93 F8 14 54S 51 10W
Aruba ■, W. Indies 89 D6 12 30N 70 0W
Arucas, Canary Is. 22 F4 28 7N 15 32W
Arumpo, Australia 63 E3 33 48S 142 55 E
Arun ➝, Nepal 43 F12 26 55N 87 10 E
Arunachal Pradesh □, India 41 E19 28 0N 95 0 E
Arusha, Tanzania 54 C4 3 20S 36 40 E
Arusha □, Tanzania 54 C4 4 0S 36 30 E
Arusha Chini, Tanzania 54 C4 3 32S 37 20 E
Aruwimi ➝, Zaïre 54 B1 1 13N 23 36 E
Arvada, U.S.A. 82 D10 44 39N 106 8W
Árvi, Greece 23 E7 34 59N 25 28 E
Arvida, Canada 71 C5 48 25N 71 14W
Arvidsjaur, Sweden 8 D18 65 35N 19 10 E
Arvika, Sweden 9 G15 59 40N 12 36 E
Arvin, U.S.A. 85 K8 35 12N 118 50W
Arxan, China 33 B6 47 11N 119 57 E
Aryirádhes, Greece 23 B3 39 27N 19 58 E
Aryiroúpolis, Greece 23 D6 35 17N 24 20 E
Arys, Kazakstan 26 E7 42 26N 68 48 E
Arzamas, Russia 24 C7 55 27N 43 55 E
Arzew, Algeria 50 A4 35 50N 0 23W
Aş Şadr, U.A.E. 45 E7 24 40N 54 41 E
Aş Şafā, Syria 47 B6 33 10N 37 0 E
'As Saffānīyah, Si. Arabia 45 D6 28 5N 48 50 E
As Safīrah, Syria 44 B3 36 5N 37 21 E
Aş Şahm, Oman 45 E8 24 10N 56 53 E
As Sājir, Si. Arabia 44 E5 25 11N 44 36 E
As Salamīyah, Syria 44 C3 35 1N 37 2 E
As Salṭ, Jordan 47 C4 32 2N 35 43 E
As Sal'w'a, Qatar 45 E6 24 23N 50 50 E
As Samāwah, Iraq 44 D5 31 15N 45 15 E
As Sanamayn, Syria 47 B5 33 3N 36 10 E
As Sukhnah, Syria 44 C3 34 52N 38 52 E
As Sulaymānīyah, Iraq 44 C5 35 35N 45 29 E
As Sulaymī, Si. Arabia 44 E4 26 17N 41 21 E
As Summān, Si. Arabia 44 E5 25 0N 47 0 E
As Suwaydā', Syria 47 C5 32 40N 36 30 E
As Suwaydā' □, Syria 47 C5 32 45N 36 45 E
Aş Şuwayrah, Iraq 44 C5 32 55N 45 0 E
Asab, Namibia 56 D2 25 30S 18 0 E
Asahi-Gawa ➝, Japan 31 G6 34 36N 133 58 E
Asahigawa, Japan 30 C11 43 46N 142 22 E
Asansol, India 43 H12 23 40N 87 1 E
Asbesberge, S. Africa 56 D3 29 0S 23 0 E
Asbestos, Canada 71 C5 45 47N 71 58W
Asbury Park, U.S.A. 79 F10 40 13N 74 1W
Ascensión, Mexico 86 A3 31 6N 107 59W
Ascensión, B. de la, Mexico 87 D7 19 50N 87 20W
Ascension I., Atl. Oc. 49 G2 8 0S 14 15W
Aschaffenburg, Germany 16 D5 49 58N 9 6 E
Aschersleben, Germany 16 C6 51 45N 11 29 E
Áscoli Piceno, Italy 20 C5 42 51N 13 34 E
Ascope, Peru 92 E3 7 46S 79 8W
Ascotán, Chile 94 A2 21 45S 68 17W
Aseb, Eritrea 46 E3 13 0N 42 40 E
Asela, Ethiopia 51 G12 8 0N 39 0 E
Asenovgrad, Bulgaria 21 C11 42 1N 24 51 E
Asgata, Cyprus 23 E12 34 46N 33 15 E
Ash Fork, U.S.A. 83 J7 35 13N 112 29W
Ash Grove, U.S.A. 81 G8 37 19N 93 35W
Ash Shām, Bādiyat, Asia 28 F7 32 0N 40 0 E
Ash Shamāl □, Lebanon 47 A5 34 25N 36 0 E
Ash Shāmīyah, Iraq 44 D5 31 55N 44 35 E
Ash Shāriqah, U.A.E. 45 E7 25 23N 55 26 E
Ash Sharmah, Si. Arabia 44 D2 28 1N 35 16 E
Ash Sharqāt, Iraq 44 C4 35 27N 43 16 E
Ash Sharqi, Al Jabal, Lebanon 47 B5 33 40N 36 10 E
Ash Shaṭrah, Iraq 44 D5 31 30N 46 10 E
Ash Shawbak, Jordan 44 D2 30 32N 35 34 E
Ash Shawmari, J., Jordan 47 E5 30 35N 36 35 E
Ash Shaykh, J., Lebanon 47 B4 33 25N 35 50 E
Ash Shināfīyah, Iraq 44 D5 31 35N 44 39 E
Ash Shu'aybah, Si. Arabia 44 E5 27 53N 42 43 E
Ash Shumlūl, Si. Arabia 44 E5 26 31N 47 20 E
Ash Shūr'a, Iraq 44 C4 35 58N 43 13 E
Ash Shurayf, Si. Arabia 44 E3 25 43N 39 14 E
Ash Shuwayfāt, Lebanon 47 B4 33 45N 35 30 E
Asha, Russia 24 D10 55 0N 57 16 E
Ashau, Vietnam 38 D6 16 6N 107 22 E
Ashburn, U.S.A. 77 K4 31 43N 83 39W
Ashburton, N.Z. 59 K3 43 53S 171 48 E
Ashburton ➝, Australia 60 D1 21 40S 114 56 E
Ashburton Downs, Australia 60 D2 23 25S 117 4 E
Ashby de la Zouch, U.K. 10 E6 52 46N 1 29W
Ashcroft, Canada 72 C4 50 40N 121 20W
Ashdod, Israel 47 D3 31 49N 34 35 E
Asheboro, U.S.A. 77 H6 35 43N 79 49W
Asherton, U.S.A. 81 L5 28 27N 99 46W
Asheville, U.S.A. 77 H4 35 36N 82 33W
Asheweig ➝, Canada 70 B2 54 17N 87 12W
Ashford, Australia 63 D5 29 15S 151 3 E
Ashford, U.K. 11 F8 51 8N 0 53 E
Ashford, U.S.A. 82 C2 46 46N 122 2W
Ashgabat, Turkmenistan 26 F6 38 0N 57 50 E
Ashibetsu, Japan 30 C11 43 31N 142 11 E
Ashikaga, Japan 31 F9 36 28N 139 29 E
Ashizuri-Zaki, Japan 31 H6 32 44N 133 0 E
Ashkarkot, Afghan. 42 C2 33 3N 67 58 E
Ashkhabad = Ashgabat, Turkmenistan 26 F6 38 0N 57 50 E
Ashland, Kans., U.S.A. 81 G5 37 11N 99 46W
Ashland, Ky., U.S.A. 76 F4 38 28N 82 38W
Ashland, Maine, U.S.A. 71 C6 46 38N 68 24W
Ashland, Mont., U.S.A. 82 D10 45 36N 106 16W
Ashland, Nebr., U.S.A. 80 E6 41 3N 96 23W
Ashland, Ohio, U.S.A. 78 F2 40 52N 82 19W
Ashland, Oreg., U.S.A. 82 E2 42 12N 122 43W
Ashland, Pa., U.S.A. 79 F8 40 45N 76 22W
Ashland, Va., U.S.A. 76 G7 37 46N 77 29W
Ashland, Wis., U.S.A. 80 B9 46 35N 90 53W
Ashley, N. Dak., U.S.A. 80 B5 46 2N 99 22W
Ashley, Pa., U.S.A. 79 E9 41 12N 75 55W
Ashmont, Canada 72 C6 54 7N 111 35W
Ashmore Reef, Australia 60 B3 12 14S 123 5 E
Ashmyany, Belarus 9 J21 54 26N 25 52 E
Ashqelon, Israel 47 D3 31 42N 34 35 E
Ashtabula, U.S.A. 78 E4 41 52N 80 47W
Ashton, S. Africa 56 E3 33 50S 20 5 E
Ashton, U.S.A. 82 D8 44 4N 111 27W
Ashton under Lyne, U.K. 10 D5 53 29N 2 6W
Ashuanipi, L., Canada 71 B6 52 45N 66 15W
Asia, Kepulauan, Indonesia 37 D8 1 0N 131 13 E
Āsiā Bak, Iran 45 C6 35 19N 50 30 E
Asifabad, India 40 K11 19 20N 79 24 E
Asike, Indonesia 37 F10 6 39S 140 24 E

B

Barents Sea

Bihar

Belgorod, Russia 25 D6 50 35N 36 35 E
Belgorod-Dnestrovskiy = Bilhorod-Dnistrovskyy, Ukraine 25 E5 46 11N 30 23 E
Belgrade = Beograd, Serbia, Yug. 21 B9 44 50N 20 37 E
Belgrade, U.S.A. 82 D8 45 47N 111 11W
Belhaven, U.S.A. 77 H7 35 33N 76 37W
Beli Drim →, Europe 21 C9 42 6N 20 25 E
Belinga, Gabon 52 D2 1 10N 13 2 E
Belinyu, Indonesia 36 E3 1 35S 105 50 E
Beliton Is. = Belitung, Indonesia 36 E3 3 10S 107 50 E
Belitung, Indonesia 36 E3 3 10S 107 50 E
Belize ■, Cent. Amer. 87 D7 17 0N 88 30W
Belize City, Belize 87 D7 17 25N 88 0W
Belkovskiy, Ostrov, Russia 27 B14 75 32N 135 44 E
Bell →, Canada 70 C4 49 48N 77 38W
Bell Bay, Australia 62 G4 41 6S 146 53 E
Bell I., Canada 71 B8 50 46N 55 35W
Bell-Irving →, Canada 72 B3 56 12N 129 5W
Bell Peninsula, Canada 69 B11 63 50N 82 0W
Bell Ville, Argentina 94 C3 32 40S 62 40W
Bella Bella, Canada 72 C3 52 10N 128 10W
Bella Coola, Canada 72 C3 52 25N 126 40W
Bella Unión, Uruguay 94 C4 30 15S 57 40W
Bella Vista, Corrientes, Argentina 94 B4 28 33S 59 0W
Bella Vista, Tucuman, Argentina 94 B2 27 10S 65 25W
Bellaire, U.S.A. 78 F4 40 1N 80 45W
Bellary, India 40 M10 15 10N 76 56 E
Bellata, Australia 63 D4 29 53S 149 46 E
Belle Fourche, U.S.A. 80 C3 44 40N 103 51W
Belle Fourche →, U.S.A. 80 C3 44 26N 102 18W
Belle Glade, U.S.A. 77 M5 26 41N 80 40W
Belle-Ile, France 18 C2 47 20N 3 10W
Belle Isle, Canada 71 B8 51 57N 55 25W
Belle Isle, Str. of, Canada 71 B8 51 30N 56 30W
Belle Plaine, Iowa, U.S.A. 80 E8 41 54N 92 17W
Belle Plaine, Minn., U.S.A. 80 C8 44 37N 93 46W
Belledune, Canada 71 C6 47 55N 65 50W
Bellefontaine, U.S.A. 76 E4 40 22N 83 46W
Bellefonte, U.S.A. 78 F7 40 55N 77 47W
Belleoram, Canada 71 C8 47 31N 55 25W
Belleville, Canada 70 D4 44 10N 77 23W
Belleville, Ill., U.S.A. 80 F10 38 31N 89 59W
Belleville, Kans., U.S.A. 80 F6 39 50N 97 38W
Belleville, N.Y., U.S.A. 79 C8 43 46N 76 10W
Bellevue, Canada 72 D6 49 35N 114 22W
Bellevue, Idaho, U.S.A. 82 E6 43 28N 114 16W
Bellevue, Ohio, U.S.A. 78 E2 41 17N 82 51W
Bellevue, Wash., U.S.A. 84 C4 47 37N 122 12W
Bellin = Kangirsuk, Canada 69 B13 60 0N 70 0W
Bellingen, Australia 63 E5 30 25S 152 50 E
Bellingham, U.S.A. 84 B4 48 46N 122 29W
Bellingshausen Sea, Antarctica 5 C17 66 0S 80 0W
Bellinzona, Switz. 16 E5 46 11N 9 1 E
Bellows Falls, U.S.A. 79 C12 43 8N 72 27W
Bellpat, Pakistan 42 E3 29 0N 68 5 E
Belluno, Italy 20 A5 46 9N 12 13 E
Bellville, U.S.A. 81 L6 29 57N 96 15W
Bellwood, U.S.A. 78 F6 40 36N 78 20W
Belmont, Australia 63 E5 33 4S 151 42 E
Belmont, Canada 78 D3 42 53N 81 5W
Belmont, S. Africa 56 D3 29 28S 24 22 E
Belmont, U.S.A. 78 D6 42 14N 78 2W
Belmonte, Brazil 93 G11 16 0S 39 0W
Belmopan, Belize 87 D7 17 18N 88 30W
Belmullet, Ireland 13 B2 54 14N 9 58W
Belo Horizonte, Brazil 93 G10 19 55S 43 56W
Belo-sur-Mer, Madag. 57 C7 20 42S 44 0 E
Belo-Tsiribihina, Madag. 57 B7 19 40S 44 30 E
Belogorsk, Russia 27 D13 51 0N 128 20 E
Beloha, Madag. 57 D8 25 10S 45 3 E
Beloit, Kans., U.S.A. 80 F5 39 28N 98 6W
Beloit, Wis., U.S.A. 80 D10 42 31N 89 2W
Belokorovichi, Ukraine 17 C15 51 7N 28 2 E
Belomorsk, Russia 24 B5 64 35N 34 54 E
Belonia, India 41 H17 23 15N 91 30 E
Beloretsk, Russia 24 D10 53 58N 58 24 E
Belorussia ■ = Belarus ■, Europe 17 B14 53 30N 27 0 E
Belovo, Russia 26 D9 54 30N 86 0 E
Beloye, Ozero, Russia 24 B6 60 10N 37 35 E
Beloye More, Russia 24 A6 66 30N 38 0 E
Belozersk, Russia 24 B6 60 1N 37 45 E
Beltana, Australia 63 E2 30 48S 138 25 E
Belterra, Brazil 93 D8 2 45S 55 0W
Belton, S.C., U.S.A. 77 H4 34 31N 82 30W
Belton, Tex., U.S.A. 81 K6 31 3N 97 28W
Belton Res., U.S.A. 81 K6 31 8N 97 32W
Beltsy = Bălţi, Moldova 17 E14 47 48N 28 0 E
Belturbet, Ireland 13 B4 54 6N 7 26W
Belukha, Russia 26 E9 49 50N 86 50 E
Beluran, Malaysia 36 C5 5 48N 117 35 E
Belvidere, Ill., U.S.A. 80 D10 42 15N 88 50W
Belvidere, N.J., U.S.A. 79 F9 40 50N 75 5W
Belyando →, Australia 62 C4 21 38S 146 50 E
Belyy, Ostrov, Russia 26 B8 73 30N 71 0 E
Belyy Yar, Russia 26 D9 58 26N 84 39 E
Belzoni, U.S.A. 81 J9 33 11N 90 29W
Bemaraha, Lembalemban' i, Madag. 57 B7 18 40S 44 45 E
Bemarivo, Madag. 57 C7 21 45S 44 45 E
Bemarivo →, Madag. 57 B8 15 27S 47 40 E
Bemavo, Madag. 57 C8 21 33S 45 25 E
Bembéréke, Benin 50 F5 10 11N 2 43 E
Bembesi, Zimbabwe 55 F2 20 0S 28 58 E
Bembesi →, Zimbabwe 55 F2 18 57S 27 47 E
Bemidji, U.S.A. 80 B7 47 28N 94 53W
Ben, Iran 45 C6 32 32N 50 45 E
Ben Cruachan, U.K. 12 E3 56 26N 5 8W
Ben Dearg, U.K. 12 D4 57 47N 4 56W
Ben Gardane, Tunisia 51 B7 33 11N 11 11 E
Ben Hope, U.K. 12 C4 58 25N 4 36W
Ben Lawers, U.K. 12 E4 56 32N 4 14W
Ben Lomond, N.S.W., Australia 63 E5 30 1S 151 43 E
Ben Lomond, Tas., Australia 62 G4 41 38S 147 42 E
Ben Lomond, U.K. 12 E4 56 11N 4 38W
Ben Luc, Vietnam 39 G6 10 39N 106 29 E
Ben Macdhui, U.K. 12 D5 57 4N 3 40W
Ben Mhor, U.K. 12 D1 57 15N 7 18W
Ben More, Arg. & Bute, U.K. 12 E2 56 26N 6 1W
Ben More, Stirl., U.K. 12 E4 56 23N 4 32W
Ben More Assynt, U.K. 12 C4 58 8N 4 52W
Ben Nevis, U.K. 12 E4 56 48N 5 1W
Ben Quang, Vietnam 38 D6 17 3N 106 55 E
Ben Tre, Vietnam 39 G6 10 3N 106 36 E
Ben Vorlich, U.K. 12 E4 56 21N 4 14W
Ben Wyvis, U.K. 12 D4 57 40N 4 35W
Bena, Nigeria 50 F6 11 20N 5 50 E
Bena Dibele, Zaïre 52 E4 4 4S 22 50 E
Benagerie, Australia 63 E3 31 25S 140 22 E
Benalla, Australia 63 F4 36 30S 146 0 E
Benambra, Mt., Australia 63 F4 36 31S 147 34 E
Benares = Varanasi, India 43 G10 25 22N 83 0 E
Benavente, Spain 19 A3 42 2N 5 43W
Benavides, U.S.A. 81 M5 27 36N 98 25W
Benbecula, U.K. 12 D1 57 26N 7 21W
Benbonyathe, Australia 63 E2 30 25S 139 11 E
Bencubbin, Australia 61 F2 30 48S 117 52 E
Bend, U.S.A. 82 D3 44 4N 121 19W
Bender Beila, Somali Rep. 46 F5 9 30N 50 48 E
Bendering, Australia 61 F2 32 23S 118 18 E
Bendery = Tighina, Moldova 17 E15 46 50N 29 30 E
Bendigo, Australia 63 F3 36 40S 144 15 E
Benē Beraq, Israel 47 C3 32 6N 34 51 E
Benenitra, Madag. 57 C8 23 27S 45 5 E
Benevento, Italy 20 D6 41 8N 14 45 E
Benga, Mozam. 55 F3 16 11S 33 40 E
Bengal, Bay of, Ind. Oc. 41 K16 15 0N 90 0 E
Bengbu, China 35 H9 32 58N 117 20 E
Benghazi = Banghāzī, Libya 51 B9 32 11N 20 3 E
Bengkalis, Indonesia 36 D2 1 30N 102 10 E
Bengkulu, Indonesia 36 E2 3 50S 102 12 E
Bengkulu □, Indonesia 36 E2 3 48S 102 16 E
Bengough, Canada 73 D7 49 25N 105 10W
Benguela, Angola 53 G2 12 37S 13 25 E
Benguérua, I., Mozam. 57 C6 21 58S 35 28 E
Beni, Zaïre 54 B2 0 30N 29 27 E
Beni →, Bolivia 92 F5 10 23S 65 24W
Beni Abbès, Algeria 50 B4 30 5N 2 5W
Beni Mazâr, Egypt 51 C11 28 32N 30 44 E
Beni Mellal, Morocco 50 B3 32 21N 6 21W
Beni Ounif, Algeria 50 B4 32 0N 1 10W
Beni Suef, Egypt 51 C11 29 5N 31 6 E
Beniah L., Canada 72 A6 63 23N 112 17W
Benicia, U.S.A. 84 G4 38 3N 122 9W
Benidorm, Spain 19 C5 38 33N 0 9W
Benin ■, Africa 50 G5 10 0N 2 0 E
Benin, Bight of, W. Afr. 50 H5 5 0N 3 0 E
Benin City, Nigeria 50 G6 6 20N 5 31 E
Benitses, Greece 23 A3 39 32N 19 55 E
Benjamin Aceval, Paraguay 94 A4 24 58S 57 34W
Benjamin Constant, Brazil 92 D4 4 40S 70 15W
Benjamin Hill, Mexico 86 A2 30 10N 111 10W
Benkelman, U.S.A. 80 E4 40 3N 101 32W
Benlidi, Australia 62 C3 24 35S 144 50 E
Bennett, Canada 72 B2 59 56N 134 53W
Bennett, L., Australia 60 D5 22 50S 131 2 E
Bennett, Ostrov, Russia 27 B15 76 21N 148 56 E
Bennettsville, U.S.A. 77 H6 34 37N 79 41W
Bennington, U.S.A. 79 D11 43 0N 71 55W
Benoni, S. Africa 57 D4 26 11S 28 18 E
Benque Viejo, Belize 87 D7 17 5N 89 8W
Benson, U.S.A. 83 L8 31 58N 110 18W
Bent, Iran 45 E8 26 20N 59 31 E
Benteng, Indonesia 37 F6 6 10S 120 30 E
Bentinck I., Australia 62 B2 17 3S 139 35 E
Bento Gonçalves, Brazil 95 B5 29 10S 51 31W
Benton, Ark., U.S.A. 81 H8 34 34N 92 35W
Benton, Calif., U.S.A. 84 H8 37 48N 118 32W
Benton, Ill., U.S.A. 80 F10 38 0N 88 55W
Benton Harbor, U.S.A. 76 D2 42 6N 86 27W
Bentung, Malaysia 39 L3 3 31N 101 55 E
Benue →, Nigeria 50 G6 7 48N 6 46 E
Benxi, China 35 D12 41 20N 123 48 E
Beo, Indonesia 37 D7 4 25N 126 50 E
Beograd, Serbia, Yug. 21 B9 44 50N 20 37 E
Beowawe, U.S.A. 82 F5 40 35N 116 29W
Beppu, Japan 31 H5 33 15N 131 30 E
Beqaa Valley = Al Biqā □, Lebanon 47 A5 34 10N 36 10 E
Berati, Albania 21 D8 40 43N 19 59 E
Berau, Teluk, Indonesia 37 E8 2 30S 132 30 E
Berber, Sudan 51 E11 18 0N 34 0 E
Berbera, Somali Rep. 46 E4 10 30N 45 2 E
Berbérati, C.A.R. 52 D3 4 15N 15 40 E
Berberia, C. del, Spain 22 C7 38 39N 1 24 E
Berbice →, Guyana 92 B7 6 20N 57 32W
Berdichev = Berdychiv, Ukraine 17 D15 49 57N 28 30 E
Berdsk, Russia 26 D9 54 47N 83 2 E
Berdyansk, Ukraine 25 E6 46 45N 36 50 E
Berdychiv, Ukraine 17 D15 49 57N 28 30 E
Berea, U.S.A. 76 G3 37 34N 84 17W
Berebere, Indonesia 37 D7 2 25N 128 45 E
Bereda, Somali Rep. 46 E5 11 45N 51 0 E
Berehove, Ukraine 17 D12 48 15N 22 35 E
Berekum, Ghana 50 G4 7 29N 2 34W
Berens →, Canada 73 C9 52 25N 97 2W
Berens I., Canada 73 C9 52 18N 97 18W
Berens River, Canada 73 C9 52 25N 97 0W
Berestechko, Ukraine 17 C13 50 22N 25 5 E
Berevo, Mahajanga, Madag. 57 B7 17 14S 44 17 E
Berevo, Toliara, Madag. 57 B7 19 44S 44 58 E
Bereza, Belarus 17 B13 52 31N 24 51 E
Berezhany, Ukraine 17 D13 49 26N 24 58 E
Berezina = Byarezina →, Belarus 17 B16 52 33N 30 14 E
Berezniki, Russia 26 D6 59 24N 56 46 E
Berezovo, Russia 26 C7 64 0N 65 0 E
Berga, Spain 19 A6 42 6N 1 48 E
Bergama, Turkey 21 E12 39 8N 27 15 E
Bérgamo, Italy 20 B3 45 41N 9 43 E
Bergen, Neths. 15 B4 52 40N 4 43 E
Bergen, Norway 9 F11 60 20N 5 20 E
Bergen, U.S.A. 78 C7 43 5N 77 57W
Bergen-op-Zoom, Neths. 15 C4 51 28N 4 18 E
Bergerac, France 18 D4 44 51N 0 30 E
Bergum, Neths. 15 A5 53 13N 5 59 E
Bergville, S. Africa 57 D4 28 52S 29 18 E
Berhala, Selat, Indonesia 36 E2 1 0S 104 15 E
Berhampore = Baharampur, India 43 G13 24 2N 88 27 E
Berhampur, India 41 K14 19 15N 84 54 E
Bering Sea, Pac. Oc. 68 C1 58 0N 171 0 E
Bering Strait, U.S.A. 68 B3 65 30N 169 0W
Beringen, Belgium 15 C5 51 3N 5 14 E
Beringovskiy, Russia 27 C18 63 3N 179 19 E
Berisso, Argentina 94 C4 34 56S 57 50W
Berja, Spain 19 D4 36 50N 2 56W
Berkeley, U.K. 11 F5 51 41N 2 27W
Berkeley, U.S.A. 84 H4 37 52N 122 16W
Berkeley Springs, U.S.A. 76 F6 39 38N 78 14W
Berkner I., Antarctica 5 D18 79 30S 50 0W
Berkshire □, U.K. 11 F6 51 25N 1 17W
Berland →, Canada 72 C5 54 0N 116 50W
Berlin, Germany 16 B7 52 30N 13 25 E
Berlin, Md., U.S.A. 76 F8 38 20N 75 13W
Berlin, N.H., U.S.A. 79 B13 44 28N 71 11W
Berlin, Wis., U.S.A. 76 D1 43 58N 88 57W
Bermejo →, Formosa, Argentina 94 B4 26 51S 58 23W
Bermejo →, San Juan, Argentina 94 C2 32 30S 67 30W
Bermuda ■, Atl. Oc. 66 F13 32 45N 65 0W
Bern, Switz. 16 E4 46 57N 7 28 E
Bernado, U.S.A. 83 J10 34 30N 106 53W
Bernalillo, U.S.A. 83 J10 35 18N 106 33W
Bernardo de Irigoyen, Argentina 95 B5 26 15S 53 40W
Bernardo O'Higgins □, Chile 94 C1 34 15S 70 45W
Bernasconi, Argentina 94 D3 37 55S 63 44W
Bernburg, Germany 16 C6 51 47N 11 44 E
Berne = Bern, Switz. 16 E4 46 57N 7 28 E
Bernier I., Australia 61 D1 24 50S 113 12 E
Bernina, Piz, Switz. 16 E5 46 20N 9 54 E
Beroroha, Madag. 57 C8 21 40S 45 10 E
Beroun, Czech. 16 D8 49 57N 14 5 E
Berrechid, Morocco 50 B3 33 18N 7 36W
Berri, Australia 63 E3 34 14S 140 35 E
Berry, Australia 63 E5 34 46S 150 43 E
Berry, France 18 C5 46 50N 2 0 E
Berry Is., Bahamas 88 A4 25 40N 77 50W
Berryessa L., U.S.A. 84 G4 38 31N 122 6W
Berryville, U.S.A. 81 G8 36 22N 93 34W
Bershad, Ukraine 17 D15 48 22N 29 31 E
Berthold, U.S.A. 80 A4 48 19N 101 44W
Berthoud, U.S.A. 80 E2 40 19N 105 5W
Bertoua, Cameroon 52 D2 4 30N 13 45 E
Bertrand, U.S.A. 80 E5 40 32N 99 38W
Berwick, U.S.A. 79 E8 41 3N 76 14W
Berwick-upon-Tweed, U.K. 10 B5 55 46N 2 0W
Berwyn Mts., U.K. 10 E4 52 54N 3 26W
Besal, Pakistan 43 B5 35 4N 73 56 E
Besalampy, Madag. 57 B7 16 43S 44 29 E
Besançon, France 18 C7 47 15N 6 2 E
Besar, Indonesia 36 E5 2 40S 116 0 E
Besnard L., Canada 73 B7 55 25N 106 0W
Besor, N. →, Egypt 47 D3 31 28N 34 22 E
Bessarabiya, Moldova 17 E15 47 0N 28 10 E
Bessarabka = Basarabeasca, Moldova 17 E15 46 21N 28 58 E
Bessemer, Ala., U.S.A. 77 J2 33 24N 86 58W
Bessemer, Mich., U.S.A. 80 B9 46 29N 90 3W
Bet She'an, Israel 47 C4 32 30N 35 30 E
Bet Shemesh, Israel 47 D3 31 44N 35 0 E
Betafo, Madag. 57 B8 19 50S 46 51 E
Betancuria, Canary Is. 22 F5 28 25N 14 3W
Betanzos, Spain 19 A1 43 15N 8 12W
Bétaré Oya, Cameroon 52 C2 5 40N 14 5 E
Bethal, S. Africa 57 D4 26 27S 29 28 E
Bethanien, Namibia 56 D2 26 31S 17 8 E
Bethany, U.S.A. 80 E7 40 16N 94 2W
Bethel, Alaska, U.S.A. 68 B3 60 48N 161 45W
Bethel, Vt., U.S.A. 79 C12 43 50N 72 38W
Bethel Park, U.S.A. 78 F4 40 20N 80 1W
Bethlehem = Bayt Lahm, West Bank 47 D4 31 43N 35 12 E
Bethlehem, S. Africa 57 D4 28 14S 28 18 E
Bethlehem, U.S.A. 79 F9 40 37N 75 23W
Bethulie, S. Africa 56 E4 30 30S 25 59 E
Béthune, France 18 A5 50 30N 2 38 E
Bethungra, Australia 63 E4 34 45S 147 51 E
Betioky, Madag. 57 C7 23 48S 44 20 E
Betong, Thailand 39 K3 5 45N 101 5 E
Betoota, Australia 62 D3 25 45S 140 42 E
Betroka, Madag. 57 C8 23 16S 46 0 E
Betsiamites, Canada 71 C6 48 56N 68 40W
Betsiamites →, Canada 71 C6 48 56N 68 38W
Betsiboka →, Madag. 57 B8 16 3S 46 36 E
Bettiah, India 43 F11 26 48N 84 33 E
Betul, India 40 J10 21 58N 77 59 E
Beulah, U.S.A. 80 B4 47 16N 101 47W
Beverley, Australia 61 F2 32 9S 116 56 E
Beverley, U.K. 10 D7 53 51N 0 26W
Beverly, Mass., U.S.A. 79 D14 42 33N 70 53W
Beverly, Wash., U.S.A. 82 C4 46 50N 119 56W
Beverly Hills, U.S.A. 85 L8 34 4N 118 25W
Beverwijk, Neths. 15 B4 52 28N 4 38 E
Beya, Russia 27 D10 52 40N 92 30 E
Beyänlü, Iran 44 C5 36 0N 47 51 E
Beyla, Guinea 50 G3 8 30N 8 38W
Beyneu, Kazakstan 25 E10 45 18N 55 9 E
Beypazan, Turkey 25 F5 40 10N 31 56 E
Beyşehir Gölü, Turkey 25 G5 37 41N 31 33 E
Bezhitsa, Russia 24 D5 53 19N 34 17 E
Béziers, France 18 E5 43 20N 3 12 E
Bezwada = Vijayawada, India 41 L12 16 31N 80 39 E
Bhachau, India 40 H7 23 20N 70 16 E
Bhadarwah, India 43 C6 32 58N 75 46 E
Bhadrakh, India 41 J15 21 10N 86 30 E
Bhadravati, India 40 N9 13 49N 75 40 E
Bhagalpur, India 43 G12 25 10N 87 0 E
Bhakkar, Pakistan 42 D4 31 40N 71 5 E
Bhakra Dam, India 42 D7 31 30N 76 45 E
Bhamo, Burma 41 G20 24 15N 97 15 E
Bhandara, India 40 J11 21 5N 79 42 E
Bhanrer Ra., India 42 H8 23 40N 79 45 E
Bharat = India ■, Asia 40 K11 20 0N 78 0 E
Bharatpur, India 42 F7 27 15N 77 30 E
Bhatinda, India 42 D6 30 15N 74 57 E
Bhatpara, India 43 H13 22 50N 88 25 E
Bhaun, Pakistan 42 C5 32 55N 72 40 E
Bhaunagar = Bhavnagar, India 42 J5 21 45N 72 10 E
Bhavnagar, India 42 J5 21 45N 72 10 E
Bhawanipatna, India 41 K12 19 55N 80 10 E
Bhera, Pakistan 42 C5 32 29N 72 57 E
Bhilsa = Vidisha, India 42 H7 23 28N 77 53 E
Bhilwara, India 42 G6 25 25N 74 38 E
Bhima →, India 40 L10 16 25N 77 17 E
Bhimavaram, India 41 L12 16 30N 81 30 E
Bhimbar, Pakistan 43 C6 32 59N 74 3 E
Bhind, India 43 F8 26 30N 78 46 E
Bhiwandi, India 40 K8 19 20N 73 0 E
Bhiwani, India 42 E7 28 50N 76 9 E
Bhola, Bangla. 41 H17 22 45N 90 35 E
Bhopal, India 42 H7 23 20N 77 30 E
Bhubaneshwar, India 41 J14 20 15N 85 50 E
Bhuj, India 42 H3 23 15N 69 49 E
Bhumiphol Dam = Phumiphon, Khuan, Thailand 38 D2 17 15N 98 58 E
Bhusaval, India 40 J9 21 3N 75 46 E
Bhutan ■, Asia 41 F17 27 25N 90 30 E
Biafra, B. of = Bonny, Bight of, Africa 52 D1 3 30N 9 20 E
Biak, Indonesia 37 E9 1 10S 136 6 E
Biala Podlaska, Poland 17 B12 52 4N 23 6 E
Białogard, Poland 16 A8 54 2N 15 58 E
Białystok, Poland 17 B12 53 10N 23 10 E
Biārjmand, Iran 45 B7 36 6N 55 53 E
Biaro, Indonesia 37 D7 2 5N 125 26 E
Biarritz, France 18 E3 43 29N 1 33W
Bibai, Japan 30 C10 43 19N 141 52 E
Bibala, Angola 53 G2 14 44S 13 24 E
Bibby I., Canada 73 A10 61 55N 93 0W
Biberach, Germany 16 D5 48 5N 9 47 E
Bibiani, Ghana 50 G4 6 30N 2 8W
Biboohra, Australia 62 B4 16 56S 145 25 E
Bibungwa, Zaïre 54 C2 2 40S 28 15 E
Bic, Canada 71 C6 48 20N 68 41W
Bickerton I., Australia 62 A2 13 45S 136 10 E
Bicknell, Ind., U.S.A. 76 F2 38 47N 87 19W
Bicknell, Utah, U.S.A. 83 G8 38 20N 111 33W
Bida, Nigeria 50 G6 9 3N 5 58 E
Bidar, India 40 L10 17 55N 77 35 E
Biddeford, U.S.A. 71 D5 43 30N 70 28W
Bideford, U.K. 11 F3 51 1N 4 13W
Bidon 5 = Poste Maurice Cortier, Algeria 50 D5 22 14N 1 2 E
Bidor, Malaysia 39 K3 4 6N 101 15 E
Bié, Planalto de, Angola 53 G3 12 0S 16 0 E
Bieber, U.S.A. 82 F3 41 7N 121 8W
Biel, Switz. 16 E4 47 8N 7 14 E
Bielé Karpaty, Europe 17 D9 49 5N 18 0 E
Bielefeld, Germany 16 B5 52 1N 8 33 E
Biella, Italy 20 B3 45 34N 8 3 E
Bielsk Podlaski, Poland 17 B12 52 47N 23 12 E
Bielsko-Biała, Poland 17 D10 49 50N 19 2 E
Bien Hoa, Vietnam 39 G6 10 57N 106 49 E
Bienfait, Canada 73 D8 49 10N 102 50W
Bienne = Biel, Switz. 16 E4 47 8N 7 14 E
Bienville, L., Canada 70 A5 55 5N 72 40W
Biesiesfontein, S. Africa 56 E2 30 57S 17 58 E
Big →, Canada 71 B8 54 50N 58 55W
Big B., Canada 71 A7 55 43N 60 35W
Big Bear City, U.S.A. 85 L10 34 16N 116 51W
Big Bear Lake, U.S.A. 85 L10 34 15N 116 56W
Big Beaver, Canada 73 D7 49 10N 105 10W
Big Belt Mts., U.S.A. 82 C8 46 30N 111 25W
Big Bend, Swaziland 57 D5 26 50S 31 58 E
Big Bend National Park, U.S.A. 81 L3 29 20N 103 5W
Big Black →, U.S.A. 81 J9 32 3N 91 4W
Big Blue →, U.S.A. 80 F6 39 35N 96 34W
Big Cr. →, Canada 72 C4 51 42N 122 41W
Big Creek, U.S.A. 84 H7 37 11N 119 14W
Big Cypress Swamp, U.S.A. 77 M5 26 12N 81 10W
Big Falls, U.S.A. 80 A8 48 12N 93 48W
Big Fork →, U.S.A. 80 A8 48 31N 93 43W
Big Horn Mts. = Bighorn Mts., U.S.A. 82 D10 44 30N 107 30W
Big Lake, U.S.A. 81 K4 31 12N 101 28W
Big Moose, U.S.A. 79 C10 43 49N 74 58W
Big Muddy Cr. →, U.S.A. 80 A2 48 8N 104 36W
Big Pine, U.S.A. 83 H4 37 10N 118 17W
Big Piney, U.S.A. 82 E8 42 32N 110 7W
Big Quill L., Canada 73 C8 51 55N 104 50W
Big Rapids, U.S.A. 76 D3 43 42N 85 29W
Big River, Canada 73 C7 53 50N 107 0W
Big Run, U.S.A. 78 F6 40 57N 78 55W
Big Sable Pt., U.S.A. 76 C2 44 3N 86 1W
Big Sand L., Canada 73 B9 57 45N 99 45W
Big Sandy, U.S.A. 82 B8 48 11N 110 7W
Big Sandy Cr. →, U.S.A. 80 F3 38 7N 102 29W
Big Sioux →, U.S.A. 80 D6 42 29N 96 27W
Big Spring, U.S.A. 81 J4 32 15N 101 28W
Big Springs, U.S.A. 80 E3 41 4N 102 5W
Big Stone City, U.S.A. 80 C6 45 18N 96 28W
Big Stone Gap, U.S.A. 77 G4 36 52N 82 47W
Big Stone L., U.S.A. 80 C6 45 30N 96 35W
Big Sur, U.S.A. 84 J5 36 15N 121 48W
Big Timber, U.S.A. 82 D9 45 50N 109 57W
Big Trout L., Canada 70 B1 53 40N 90 0W
Biğa, Turkey 21 D12 40 13N 27 14 E
Bigadiç, Turkey 21 E13 39 22N 28 7 E
Bigfork, U.S.A. 82 B6 48 4N 114 4W
Biggar, Canada 73 C7 52 4N 108 0W
Biggar, U.K. 12 F5 55 38N 3 32W
Bigge I., Australia 60 B4 14 35S 125 10 E
Biggenden, Australia 63 D5 25 31S 152 4 E
Biggs, U.S.A. 84 F5 39 25N 121 43W
Bighorn, U.S.A. 82 C10 46 10N 107 27W
Bighorn →, U.S.A. 82 C10 46 10N 107 28W
Bighorn Mts., U.S.A. 82 D10 44 30N 107 30W
Bigstone L., Canada 73 C9 53 42N 95 44W
Bigwa, Tanzania 54 D4 7 10S 39 10 E
Bihać, Bos.-H. 16 F8 44 49N 15 57 E
Bihar, India 43 G11 25 5N 85 40 E

Bristol L.

Bolshoy Begichev, Ostrov, *Russia* **27 B12** 74 20N 112 30 E
Bolshoy Lyakhovskiy, Ostrov, *Russia* **27 B15** 73 35N 142 0 E
Bolshoy Tyuters, Ostrov, *Russia* **9 G22** 59 51N 27 13 E
Bolsward, *Neths.* **15 A5** 53 3N 5 32 E
Bolton, *Canada* **78 C5** 43 54N 79 45W
Bolton, *U.K.* **10 D5** 53 35N 2 26W
Bolu, *Turkey* **25 F5** 40 45N 31 35 E
Bolungavík, *Iceland* **8 C2** 66 9N 23 15W
Bolvadin, *Turkey* **25 G5** 38 45N 31 4 E
Bolzano, *Italy* **20 A4** 46 31N 11 22 E
Bom Despacho, *Brazil* **93 G9** 19 43S 45 15W
Bom Jesus da Lapa, *Brazil* **93 F10** 13 15S 43 25W
Boma, *Zaïre* **52 F2** 5 50S 13 4 E
Bomaderry, *Australia* **63 E5** 34 52S 150 37 E
Bombala, *Australia* **63 F4** 36 56S 149 15 E
Bombay, *India* **40 K8** 18 55N 72 50 E
Bomboma, *Zaïre* **52 D3** 2 25N 18 55 E
Bombombwa, *Zaïre* **54 B2** 1 40N 25 40 E
Bomili, *Zaïre* **54 B2** 1 45N 27 5 E
Bømlo, *Norway* **9 G11** 59 37N 5 13 E
Bomokandi →, *Zaïre* **54 B2** 3 39N 26 8 E
Bomongo, *Zaïre* **52 D3** 1 27N 18 21 E
Bomu →, *C.A.R.* **52 D4** 4 40N 22 30 E
Bon, C., *Tunisia* **51 A7** 37 1N 11 2 E
Bon Sar Pa, *Vietnam* **38 F6** 12 24N 107 35 E
Bonaire, *Neth. Ant.* **89 D6** 12 10N 68 15W
Bonang, *Australia* **63 F4** 37 11S 148 41 E
Bonanza, *Nic.* **88 D3** 13 54N 84 35W
Bonaparte Arch., *Australia* **60 B3** 14 0S 124 30 E
Bonaventure, *Canada* **71 C6** 48 5N 65 32W
Bonavista, *Canada* **71 C9** 48 40N 53 5W
Bonavista, C., *Canada* **71 C9** 48 42N 53 5W
Bondo, *Zaïre* **54 B1** 3 55N 23 53 E
Bondoukou, *Ivory C.* **50 G4** 8 2N 2 47W
Bondowoso, *Indonesia* **37 G15** 7 55S 113 49 E
Bone, Teluk, *Indonesia* **37 E6** 4 10S 120 50 E
Bonerate, *Indonesia* **37 F6** 7 25S 121 5 E
Bonerate, Kepulauan, *Indonesia* **37 F6** 6 30S 121 10 E
Bo'ness, *U.K.* **12 E5** 56 1N 3 37W
Bonete, Cerro, *Argentina* **94 B2** 27 55S 68 40W
Bong Son = Hoai Nhon, *Vietnam* **38 E7** 14 28N 109 1 E
Bongandanga, *Zaïre* **52 D4** 1 24N 21 3 E
Bongor, *Chad* **51 F8** 10 35N 15 20 E
Bonham, *U.S.A.* **81 J6** 33 35N 96 11W
Bonifacio, *France* **18 F8** 41 24N 9 10 E
Bonin Is. = Ogasawara Gunto, *Pac. Oc.* **28 G18** 27 0N 142 0 E
Bonn, *Germany* **16 C4** 50 46N 7 6 E
Bonne Terre, *U.S.A.* **81 G9** 37 55N 90 33W
Bonners Ferry, *U.S.A.* **82 B5** 48 42N 116 19W
Bonney, L., *Australia* **63 F3** 37 50S 140 20 E
Bonnie Downs, *Australia* **62 C3** 22 7S 143 50 E
Bonnie Rock, *Australia* **61 F2** 30 29S 118 22 E
Bonny, Bight of, *Africa* **52 D1** 3 30N 9 20 E
Bonnyville, *Canada* **73 C6** 54 20N 110 45W
Bonoi, *Indonesia* **37 E9** 1 45S 137 41 E
Bonsall, *U.S.A.* **85 M9** 33 16N 117 14W
Bontang, *Indonesia* **36 D5** 0 10N 117 30 E
Bonthain, *Indonesia* **37 F5** 5 34S 119 56 E
Bonthe, *S. Leone* **50 G2** 7 30N 12 33W
Bontoc, *Phil.* **37 A6** 17 7N 120 58 E
Bonython Ra., *Australia* **60 D4** 23 40S 128 45 E
Bookabie, *Australia* **61 F5** 31 50S 132 41 E
Booker, *U.S.A.* **81 G4** 36 27N 100 32W
Boolaboolka L., *Australia* **63 E3** 32 38S 143 10 E
Booligal, *Australia* **63 E3** 33 58S 144 53 E
Boom, *Belgium* **15 C4** 51 6N 4 20 E
Boonah, *Australia* **63 D5** 27 58S 152 41 E
Boone, *Iowa, U.S.A.* **80 D8** 42 4N 93 53W
Boone, *N.C., U.S.A.* **77 G5** 36 13N 81 41W
Booneville, *Ark., U.S.A.* **81 H8** 35 8N 93 55W
Booneville, *Miss., U.S.A.* **77 H1** 34 39N 88 34W
Boonville, *Calif., U.S.A.* **84 F3** 39 1N 123 22W
Boonville, *Ind., U.S.A.* **76 F2** 38 3N 87 16W
Boonville, *Mo., U.S.A.* **80 F8** 38 58N 92 44W
Boonville, *N.Y., U.S.A.* **79 C9** 43 29N 75 20W
Boorindal, *Australia* **63 E4** 30 22S 146 11 E
Boorowa, *Australia* **63 E4** 34 28S 148 44 E
Boothia, Gulf of, *Canada* **69 A11** 71 0N 90 0W
Boothia Pen., *Canada* **68 A10** 71 0N 94 0W
Bootle, *U.K.* **10 D4** 53 28N 3 1W
Booué, *Gabon* **52 E2** 0 5S 11 55 E
Boquete, *Panama* **88 E3** 8 46N 82 27W
Boquilla, Presa de la, *Mexico* **86 B3** 27 40N 105 30W
Boquillas del Carmen, *Mexico* **86 B4** 29 17N 102 53W
Bor, *Serbia, Yug.* **21 B10** 44 5N 22 7 E
Bôr, *Sudan* **51 G11** 6 10N 31 40 E
Bor Mashash, *Israel* **47 D3** 31 7N 34 50 E
Boradā →, *Syria* **47 B5** 33 33N 36 34 E
Borah Peak, *U.S.A.* **82 D7** 44 8N 113 47W
Borama, *Somali Rep.* **46 F3** 9 55N 43 7 E
Borås, *Sweden* **9 H15** 57 43N 12 56 E
Borāzjān, *Iran* **45 D6** 29 22N 51 10 E
Borba, *Brazil* **92 D7** 4 12S 59 34W
Borborema, Planalto da, *Brazil* **90 D7** 7 0S 37 0W
Bord Khūn-e Now, *Iran* **45 D6** 28 3N 51 28 E
Borda, C., *Australia* **63 F2** 35 45S 136 34 E
Bordeaux, *France* **18 D3** 44 50N 0 36W
Borden, *Australia* **61 F2** 34 3S 118 12 E
Borden, *Canada* **71 C7** 46 18N 63 47W
Borden I., *Canada* **4 B2** 78 30N 111 30W
Borders □, *U.K.* **12 F6** 55 35N 2 50W
Bordertown, *Australia* **63 F3** 36 19S 140 45 E
Borðeyri, *Iceland* **8 D3** 65 12N 21 6W
Bordj Fly Ste. Marie, *Algeria* **50 C4** 27 19N 2 32W
Bordj-in-Eker, *Algeria* **50 D6** 24 9N 5 3 E
Bordj Omar Driss, *Algeria* **50 C6** 28 10N 6 40 E
Bordj-Tarat, *Algeria* **50 C6** 25 55N 9 3 E
Borgå = Porvoo, *Finland* **9 F21** 60 24N 25 40 E
Borgarfjörður, *Iceland* **8 D7** 65 31N 13 49W
Borgarnes, *Iceland* **8 D3** 64 32N 21 55W
Børgefjellet, *Norway* **8 D15** 65 20N 13 45 E
Borger, *Neths.* **15 B6** 52 54N 6 44 E
Borger, *U.S.A.* **81 H4** 35 39N 101 24W
Borgholm, *Sweden* **9 H17** 56 52N 16 39 E
Borikhane, *Laos* **38 C4** 18 33N 103 43 E
Borisoglebsk, *Russia* **25 D7** 51 27N 42 5 E
Borisov = Barysaw, *Belarus* **17 A15** 54 17N 28 28 E
Borja, *Peru* **92 D3** 4 20S 77 40W
Borkou, *Chad* **51 E8** 18 15N 18 50 E
Borkum, *Germany* **16 B4** 53 34N 6 40 E
Borlänge, *Sweden* **9 F16** 60 29N 15 26 E
Borley, C., *Antarctica* **5 C5** 66 15S 52 30 E
Borneo, *E. Indies* **36 D5** 1 0N 115 0 E
Bornholm, *Denmark* **9 J16** 55 10N 15 0 E
Borobudur, *Indonesia* **37 G14** 7 36S 110 13 E
Borogontsy, *Russia* **27 C14** 62 42N 131 8 E
Boromo, *Burkina Faso* **50 F4** 11 45N 2 58W
Boron, *U.S.A.* **85 L9** 35 0N 117 39W
Borongan, *Phil.* **37 B7** 11 37N 125 26 E
Bororen, *Australia* **62 C5** 24 13S 151 33 E
Borovichi, *Russia* **24 C5** 58 25N 33 55 E
Borrego Springs, *U.S.A.* **85 M10** 33 15N 116 23W
Borroloola, *Australia* **62 B2** 16 4S 136 17 E
Borşa, *Romania* **17 E13** 47 41N 24 50 E
Borth, *U.K.* **11 E3** 52 29N 4 2W
Borūjerd, *Iran* **45 C6** 33 55N 48 50 E
Boryslav, *Ukraine* **17 D12** 49 18N 23 28 E
Borzya, *Russia* **27 D12** 50 24N 116 31 E
Bosa, *Italy* **20 D3** 40 18N 8 30 E
Bosanska Gradiška, *Bos.-H.* **20 B7** 45 10N 17 15 E
Bosaso, *Somali Rep.* **46 E4** 11 12N 49 18 E
Boscastle, *U.K.* **11 G3** 50 41N 4 42W
Boshan, *China* **35 F9** 36 28N 117 49 E
Boshof, *S. Africa* **56 D4** 28 31S 25 13 E
Boshrūyeh, *Iran* **45 C8** 33 50N 57 30 E
Bosna →, *Bos.-H.* **21 B8** 45 4N 18 29 E
Bosna i Hercegovina = Bosnia-Herzegovina ■, *Europe* **20 B7** 44 0N 17 0 E
Bosnia-Herzegovina ■, *Europe* **20 B7** 44 0N 17 0 E
Bosnik, *Indonesia* **37 E9** 1 5S 136 10 E
Bosobolo, *Zaïre* **52 D3** 4 15N 19 50 E
Bosporus = Karadeniz Boğazı, *Turkey* **21 D13** 41 10N 29 10 E
Bossangoa, *C.A.R.* **51 G8** 6 35N 17 30 E
Bossembélé, *C.A.R.* **51 G8** 5 25N 17 40 E
Bossier City, *U.S.A.* **81 J8** 32 31N 93 44W
Bosso, *Niger* **51 F7** 13 43N 13 19 E
Bostānābād, *Iran* **44 B5** 37 50N 46 50 E
Bosten Hu, *China* **32 B3** 41 55N 87 40 E
Boston, *U.K.* **10 E7** 52 59N 0 2W
Boston, *U.S.A.* **79 D13** 42 22N 71 4W
Boston Bar, *Canada* **72 D4** 49 52N 121 30W
Boswell, *Canada* **72 D5** 49 28N 116 45W
Boswell, *Okla., U.S.A.* **81 H7** 34 2N 95 52W
Boswell, *Pa., U.S.A.* **78 F5** 40 10N 79 2W
Botad, *India* **42 H4** 22 15N 71 40 E
Botany B., *Australia* **63 E5** 34 0S 151 14 E
Botene, *Laos* **38 D3** 17 35N 101 12 E
Bothaville, *S. Africa* **56 D4** 27 23S 26 34 E
Bothnia, G. of, *Europe* **8 E19** 63 0N 20 15 E
Bothwell, *Australia* **62 G4** 42 20S 147 1 E
Bothwell, *Canada* **78 D3** 42 38N 81 52W
Botletle →, *Botswana* **56 C3** 20 10S 23 15 E
Botoşani, *Romania* **17 E14** 47 42N 26 41 E
Botswana ■, *Africa* **56 C3** 22 0S 24 0 E
Bottineau, *U.S.A.* **80 A4** 48 50N 100 27W
Bottrop, *Germany* **15 C6** 51 31N 6 58 E
Botucatu, *Brazil* **95 A6** 22 55S 48 30W
Botwood, *Canada* **71 C8** 49 6N 55 23W
Bou Djébéha, *Mali* **50 E4** 18 25N 2 45W
Bou Izakarn, *Morocco* **50 C3** 29 12N 9 46W
Bouaké, *Ivory C.* **50 G3** 7 40N 5 2W
Bouar, *C.A.R.* **52 C3** 6 0N 15 40 E
Bouârfa, *Morocco* **50 B4** 32 32N 1 58W
Bouca, *C.A.R.* **51 G8** 6 45N 18 25 E
Boucaut B., *Australia* **62 A1** 12 0S 134 25 E
Bougainville, C., *Australia* **60 B4** 13 57S 126 4 E
Bougainville Reef, *Australia* **62 B4** 15 30S 147 5 E
Bougie = Bejaia, *Algeria* **50 A6** 36 42N 5 2 E
Bougouni, *Mali* **50 F3** 11 30N 7 20W
Bouillon, *Belgium* **15 E5** 49 44N 5 3 E
Boulder, *Colo., U.S.A.* **80 E2** 40 1N 105 17W
Boulder, *Mont., U.S.A.* **82 C7** 46 14N 112 7W
Boulder City, *U.S.A.* **85 K12** 35 59N 114 50W
Boulder Creek, *U.S.A.* **84 H4** 37 7N 122 7W
Boulder Dam = Hoover Dam, *U.S.A.* **85 K12** 36 1N 114 44W
Boulia, *Australia* **62 C2** 22 52S 139 51 E
Boulogne-sur-Mer, *France* **18 A4** 50 42N 1 36 E
Boultoum, *Niger* **50 F7** 14 45N 10 25 E
Boun Neua, *Laos* **38 B3** 21 38N 101 54 E
Boun Tai, *Laos* **38 B3** 21 23N 101 58 E
Bouna, *Ivory C.* **50 G4** 9 10N 3 0W
Boundary Peak, *U.S.A.* **84 H8** 37 51N 118 21W
Boundiali, *Ivory C.* **50 G3** 9 30N 6 20W
Bountiful, *U.S.A.* **82 F8** 40 53N 111 53W
Bounty Is., *Pac. Oc.* **64 M9** 48 0S 178 30 E
Bourbonnais, *France* **18 C5** 46 28N 3 0 E
Bourem, *Mali* **50 E4** 17 0N 0 24W
Bourg-en-Bresse, *France* **18 C6** 46 13N 5 12 E
Bourg-St.-Maurice, *France* **18 D7** 45 35N 6 46 E
Bourges, *France* **18 C5** 47 9N 2 25 E
Bourget, *Canada* **79 A9** 45 26N 75 9W
Bourgogne, *France* **18 C6** 47 0N 4 50 E
Bourke, *Australia* **63 E4** 30 8S 145 55 E
Bournemouth, *U.K.* **11 G6** 50 43N 1 52W
Bouse, *U.S.A.* **85 M13** 33 56N 114 0W
Bousso, *Chad* **51 F8** 10 34N 16 52 E
Boutilimit, *Mauritania* **50 E2** 17 45N 14 40W
Bouvet I. = Bouvetøya, *Antarctica* **3 G10** 54 26S 3 24 E
Bouvetøya, *Antarctica* **3 G10** 54 26S 3 24 E
Bovigny, *Belgium* **15 D5** 50 12N 5 55 E
Bovill, *U.S.A.* **82 C5** 46 51N 116 24W
Bow Island, *Canada* **72 D6** 49 50N 111 23W
Bowbells, *U.S.A.* **80 A3** 48 48N 102 15W
Bowdle, *U.S.A.* **80 C5** 45 27N 99 39W
Bowelling, *Australia* **61 F2** 33 25S 116 30 E
Bowen, *Australia* **62 C4** 20 0S 148 16 E
Bowen Mts., *Australia* **63 F4** 37 0S 147 50 E
Bowie, *Ariz., U.S.A.* **83 K9** 32 19N 109 29W
Bowie, *Tex., U.S.A.* **81 J6** 33 34N 97 51W
Bowkān, *Iran* **44 B5** 36 31N 46 12 E
Bowland, Forest of, *U.K.* **10 D5** 54 0N 2 30W
Bowling Green, *Ky., U.S.A.* **76 G2** 36 59N 86 27W
Bowling Green, *Ohio, U.S.A.* **76 E4** 41 23N 83 39W
Bowling Green, C., *Australia* **62 B4** 19 19S 147 25 E
Bowman, *U.S.A.* **80 B3** 46 11N 103 24W
Bowman I., *Antarctica* **5 C8** 65 0S 104 0 E
Bowmans, *Australia* **63 E2** 34 10S 138 17 E
Bowmanville, *Canada* **70 D4** 43 55N 78 41W
Bowmore, *U.K.* **12 F2** 55 45N 6 17W
Bowral, *Australia* **63 E5** 34 26S 150 27 E
Bowraville, *Australia* **63 E5** 30 37S 152 52 E
Bowron →, *Canada* **72 C4** 54 3N 121 50W
Bowser L., *Canada* **72 B3** 56 30N 129 30W
Bowsman, *Canada* **73 C8** 52 14N 101 12W
Bowwood, *Zambia* **55 F2** 17 5S 26 20 E
Boxtel, *Neths.* **15 C5** 51 36N 5 20 E
Boyce, *U.S.A.* **81 K8** 31 23N 92 40W
Boyer →, *Canada* **72 B5** 58 27N 115 57W
Boyle, *Ireland* **13 C3** 53 59N 8 18W
Boyne →, *Ireland* **13 C5** 53 43N 6 15W
Boyne City, *U.S.A.* **76 C3** 45 13N 85 1W
Boynton Beach, *U.S.A.* **77 M5** 26 32N 80 4W
Boyoma, Chutes, *Zaïre* **54 B2** 0 35N 25 23 E
Boyup Brook, *Australia* **61 F2** 33 50S 116 23 E
Boz Dağlan, *Turkey* **21 E13** 38 20N 28 0 E
Bozburun, *Turkey* **21 F13** 36 43N 28 8 E
Bozcaada, *Turkey* **21 E12** 39 49N 26 3 E
Bozdoğan, *Turkey* **21 F13** 37 40N 28 17 E
Bozeman, *U.S.A.* **82 D8** 45 41N 111 2W
Bozen = Bolzano, *Italy* **20 A4** 46 31N 11 22 E
Bozoum, *C.A.R.* **51 G8** 6 25N 16 35 E
Bra, *Italy* **20 B2** 44 42N 7 51 E
Brabant □, *Belgium* **15 D4** 50 46N 4 30 E
Brabant L., *Canada* **73 B8** 55 58N 103 43W
Brač, *Croatia* **20 C7** 43 20N 16 40 E
Bracadale, L., *U.K.* **12 D2** 57 20N 6 30W
Bracciano, L. di, *Italy* **20 C5** 42 7N 12 14 E
Bracebridge, *Canada* **70 C4** 45 2N 79 19W
Brach, *Libya* **51 C7** 27 31N 14 20 E
Bräcke, *Sweden* **9 E16** 62 45N 15 26 E
Brackettville, *U.S.A.* **81 L4** 29 19N 100 25W
Brad, *Romania* **17 E12** 46 10N 22 50 E
Bradenton, *U.S.A.* **77 M4** 27 30N 82 34W
Bradford, *Canada* **78 B5** 44 7N 79 34W
Bradford, *U.K.* **10 D6** 53 47N 1 45W
Bradford, *Pa., U.S.A.* **78 E6** 41 58N 78 38W
Bradford, *Vt., U.S.A.* **79 C12** 43 59N 72 9W
Bradley, *Ark., U.S.A.* **81 J8** 33 6N 93 39W
Bradley, *Calif., U.S.A.* **84 K6** 35 52N 120 48W
Bradley, *S. Dak., U.S.A.* **80 C6** 45 5N 97 39W
Bradley Institute, *Zimbabwe* **55 F3** 17 7S 31 25 E
Bradore Bay, *Canada* **71 B8** 51 27N 57 18W
Bradshaw, *Australia* **60 C5** 15 21S 130 16 E
Brady, *U.S.A.* **81 K5** 31 9N 99 20W
Braemar, *Australia* **63 E2** 33 12S 139 35 E
Braeside, *Canada* **79 A8** 45 28N 76 24W
Braga, *Portugal* **19 B1** 41 35N 8 25W
Bragado, *Argentina* **94 D3** 35 2S 60 27W
Bragança, *Brazil* **93 D9** 1 0S 47 2W
Bragança, *Portugal* **19 B2** 41 48N 6 50W
Bragança Paulista, *Brazil* **95 A6** 22 55S 46 32W
Brahmanbaria, *Bangla.* **41 H17** 23 58N 91 15 E
Brahmani →, *India* **41 J15** 20 39N 86 46 E
Brahmaputra →, *India* **43 G13** 23 58N 89 50 E
Braich-y-pwll, *U.K.* **10 E3** 52 47N 4 46W
Braidwood, *Australia* **63 F4** 35 27S 149 49 E
Brăila, *Romania* **17 F14** 45 19N 27 59 E
Brainerd, *U.S.A.* **80 B7** 46 22N 94 12W
Braintree, *U.K.* **11 F8** 51 53N 0 34 E
Braintree, *U.S.A.* **79 D14** 42 13N 71 0W
Brak →, *S. Africa* **56 D3** 29 35S 22 55 E
Brakwater, *Namibia* **56 C2** 22 28S 17 3 E
Bralorne, *Canada* **72 C4** 50 50N 122 50W
Brampton, *Canada* **70 D4** 43 45N 79 45W
Bramwell, *Australia* **62 A3** 12 8S 142 37 E
Branco →, *Brazil* **92 D6** 1 20S 61 50W
Brandenburg = Neubrandenburg, *Germany* **16 B7** 53 33N 13 15 E
Brandenburg, *Germany* **16 B7** 52 25N 12 33 E
Brandenburg □, *Germany* **16 B6** 52 50N 13 0 E
Brandfort, *S. Africa* **56 D4** 28 40S 26 30 E
Brandon, *Canada* **73 D9** 49 50N 99 57W
Brandon, *U.S.A.* **79 C11** 43 48N 73 4W
Brandon B., *Ireland* **13 D1** 52 17N 10 8W
Brandon Mt., *Ireland* **13 D1** 52 15N 10 15W
Brandsen, *Argentina* **94 D4** 35 10S 58 15W
Brandvlei, *S. Africa* **56 E3** 30 25S 20 30 E
Branford, *U.S.A.* **79 E12** 41 17N 72 49W
Braniewo, *Poland* **17 A10** 54 25N 19 50 E
Bransfield Str., *Antarctica* **5 C18** 63 0S 59 0W
Branson, *Colo., U.S.A.* **81 G3** 37 1N 103 53W
Branson, *Mo., U.S.A.* **81 G8** 36 39N 93 13W
Brantford, *Canada* **70 D3** 43 10N 80 15W
Branxholme, *Australia* **63 F3** 37 52S 141 49 E
Bras d'Or, L., *Canada* **71 C7** 45 50N 60 50W
Brasil, Planalto, *Brazil* **90 E6** 18 0S 46 30W
Brasiléia, *Brazil* **92 F5** 11 0S 68 45W
Brasília, *Brazil* **93 G9** 15 47S 47 55W
Braslaw, *Belarus* **9 J22** 55 38N 27 0 E
Braşov, *Romania* **17 F13** 45 38N 25 35 E
Brasschaat, *Belgium* **15 C4** 51 19N 4 27 E
Brassey, Banjaran, *Malaysia* **36 D5** 5 0N 117 15 E
Brassey Ra., *Australia* **61 E3** 25 8S 122 15 E
Brasstown Bald, *U.S.A.* **77 H4** 34 53N 83 49W
Brastad, *Sweden* **9 G14** 58 23N 11 30 E
Bratislava, *Slovak Rep.* **17 D9** 48 10N 17 7 E
Bratsk, *Russia* **27 D11** 56 10N 101 30 E
Brattleboro, *U.S.A.* **79 D12** 42 51N 72 34W
Braunau, *Austria* **16 D7** 48 15N 13 3 E
Braunschweig, *Germany* **16 B6** 52 15N 10 31 E
Braunton, *U.K.* **11 F3** 51 7N 4 10W
Brava, *Somali Rep.* **46 G3** 1 20N 44 8 E
Bravo del Norte →, *Mexico* **86 B5** 25 57N 97 9W
Bravo del Norte, R. → = Grande, Rio →, *U.S.A.* **81 N6** 25 58N 97 9W
Brawley, *U.S.A.* **85 N11** 32 59N 115 31W
Bray, *Ireland* **13 C5** 53 13N 6 7W
Bray, Mt., *Australia* **62 A1** 14 0S 134 30 E
Bray, Pays de, *France* **18 B4** 49 46N 1 26 E
Brazeau →, *Canada* **72 C5** 52 55N 115 14W
Brazil, *U.S.A.* **76 F2** 39 32N 87 8W
Brazil ■, *S. Amer.* **93 F9** 12 0S 50 0W
Brazilian Highlands = Brasil, Planalto, *Brazil* **90 E6** 18 0S 46 30W
Brazo Sur →, *S. Amer.* **94 B4** 25 21S 57 42W
Brazos →, *U.S.A.* **81 L7** 28 53N 95 23W
Brazzaville, *Congo* **52 E3** 4 9S 15 12 E
Brčko, *Bos.-H.* **21 B8** 44 54N 18 46 E
Breadalbane, *Australia* **62 C2** 23 50S 139 35 E
Breadalbane, *U.K.* **12 E4** 56 30N 4 15W
Breaden, L., *Australia* **61 E4** 25 51S 125 28 E
Breaksea Sd., *N.Z.* **59 L1** 45 35S 166 35 E
Bream B., *N.Z.* **59 F5** 35 56S 174 28 E
Bream Hd., *N.Z.* **59 F5** 35 51S 174 36 E
Breas, *Chile* **94 B1** 25 29S 70 24W
Brebes, *Indonesia* **37 G13** 6 52S 109 3 E
Brechin, *Canada* **78 B5** 44 32N 79 10W
Brechin, *U.K.* **12 E6** 56 44N 2 39W
Breckenridge, *Colo., U.S.A.* **82 G10** 39 29N 106 3W
Breckenridge, *Minn., U.S.A.* **80 B6** 46 16N 96 35W
Breckenridge, *Tex., U.S.A.* **81 J5** 32 45N 98 54W
Breckland, *U.K.* **11 E8** 52 30N 0 40 E
Brecon, *U.K.* **11 F4** 51 57N 3 23W
Brecon Beacons, *U.K.* **11 F4** 51 53N 3 26W
Breda, *Neths.* **15 C4** 51 35N 4 45 E
Bredasdorp, *S. Africa* **56 E3** 34 33S 20 2 E
Bredbo, *Australia* **63 F4** 35 58S 149 10 E
Bregenz, *Austria* **16 E5** 47 30N 9 45 E
Breiðafjörður, *Iceland* **8 D2** 65 15N 23 15W
Brejo, *Brazil* **93 D10** 3 41S 42 47W
Bremen, *Germany* **16 B5** 53 4N 8 47 E
Bremer I., *Australia* **62 A2** 12 5S 136 45 E
Bremerhaven, *Germany* **16 B5** 53 33N 8 36 E
Bremerton, *U.S.A.* **84 C4** 47 34N 122 38W
Brenham, *U.S.A.* **81 K6** 30 10N 96 24W
Brenner P., *Austria* **16 E6** 47 2N 11 30 E
Brent, *Canada* **70 C4** 46 2N 78 29W
Brent, *U.K.* **11 F7** 51 33N 0 16W
Brentwood, *U.K.* **11 F8** 51 37N 0 19 E
Brentwood, *U.S.A.* **79 F11** 40 47N 73 15W
Bréscia, *Italy* **20 B4** 45 33N 10 15 E
Breskens, *Neths.* **15 C3** 51 23N 3 33 E
Breslau = Wrocław, *Poland* **17 C9** 51 5N 17 5 E
Bressanone, *Italy* **20 A4** 46 43N 11 39 E
Bressay, *U.K.* **12 A7** 60 9N 1 6W
Brest, *Belarus* **17 B12** 52 10N 23 40 E
Brest, *France* **18 B1** 48 24N 4 31W
Brest-Litovsk = Brest, *Belarus* **17 B12** 52 10N 23 40 E
Bretagne, *France* **18 B2** 48 10N 3 0W
Breton, *Canada* **72 C6** 53 7N 114 28W
Breton Sd., *U.S.A.* **81 L10** 29 35N 89 15W
Brett, C., *N.Z.* **59 F5** 35 10S 174 20 E
Brevard, *U.S.A.* **77 H4** 35 14N 82 44W
Brewarrina, *Australia* **63 D4** 30 0S 146 51 E
Brewer, *U.S.A.* **71 D6** 44 48N 68 46W
Brewer, Mt., *U.S.A.* **84 J8** 36 44N 118 28W
Brewster, *N.Y., U.S.A.* **79 E11** 41 23N 73 37W
Brewster, *Wash., U.S.A.* **82 B4** 48 6N 119 47W
Brewster, Kap, *Greenland* **4 B6** 70 7N 22 0W
Brewton, *U.S.A.* **77 K2** 31 7N 87 4W
Breyten, *S. Africa* **57 D4** 26 16S 30 0 E
Brezhnev = Naberezhnyye Chelny, *Russia* **24 C9** 55 42N 52 19 E
Bria, *C.A.R.* **51 G9** 6 30N 21 58 E
Briançon, *France* **18 D7** 44 54N 6 39 E
Bribie I., *Australia* **63 D5** 27 0S 153 10 E
Bridgehampton, *U.S.A.* **79 F12** 40 56N 72 19W
Bridgend, *U.K.* **11 F4** 51 30N 3 34W
Bridgend □, *U.K.* **11 F4** 51 36N 3 36W
Bridgeport, *Calif., U.S.A.* **83 G4** 38 15N 119 14W
Bridgeport, *Conn., U.S.A.* **79 E11** 41 11N 73 12W
Bridgeport, *Nebr., U.S.A.* **80 E3** 41 40N 103 6W
Bridgeport, *Tex., U.S.A.* **81 J6** 33 13N 97 45W
Bridger, *U.S.A.* **82 D9** 45 18N 108 55W
Bridgeton, *U.S.A.* **76 F8** 39 26N 75 14W
Bridgetown, *Australia* **61 F2** 33 58S 116 7 E
Bridgetown, *Barbados* **89 D8** 13 5N 59 30W
Bridgetown, *Canada* **71 D6** 44 55N 65 18W
Bridgewater, *Canada* **71 D7** 44 25N 64 31W
Bridgewater, *Mass., U.S.A.* **79 E14** 41 59N 70 58W
Bridgewater, *S. Dak., U.S.A.* **80 D6** 43 33N 97 30W
Bridgewater, C., *Australia* **63 F3** 38 23S 141 23 E
Bridgnorth, *U.K.* **11 E5** 52 32N 2 25W
Bridgton, *U.S.A.* **79 B14** 44 3N 70 42W
Bridgwater, *U.K.* **11 F4** 51 8N 2 59W
Bridlington, *U.K.* **10 C7** 54 5N 0 12W
Bridport, *Australia* **62 G4** 40 59S 147 23 E
Bridport, *U.K.* **11 G5** 50 44N 2 45W
Brig, *Switz.* **16 E4** 46 18N 7 59 E
Brigg, *U.K.* **10 D7** 53 34N 0 28W
Briggsdale, *U.S.A.* **80 E2** 40 38N 104 20W
Brigham City, *U.S.A.* **82 F7** 41 31N 112 1W
Bright, *Australia* **63 F4** 36 42S 146 56 E
Brighton, *Australia* **63 F2** 35 5S 138 30 E
Brighton, *Canada* **70 D4** 44 2N 77 44W
Brighton, *U.K.* **11 G7** 50 49N 0 7W
Brighton, *U.S.A.* **80 F2** 39 59N 104 49W
Brilliant, *Canada* **72 D5** 49 19N 117 38W
Brilliant, *U.S.A.* **78 F4** 40 15N 80 39W
Bríndisi, *Italy* **21 D7** 40 39N 17 55 E
Brinkley, *U.S.A.* **81 H9** 34 53N 91 12W
Brinkworth, *Australia* **63 E2** 33 42S 138 26 E
Brinnon, *U.S.A.* **84 C4** 47 41N 122 54W
Brion, I., *Canada* **71 C7** 47 46N 61 26W
Brisbane, *Australia* **63 D5** 27 25S 153 2 E
Brisbane →, *Australia* **63 D5** 27 24S 153 9 E
Bristol, *U.K.* **11 F5** 51 26N 2 35W
Bristol, *Conn., U.S.A.* **79 E12** 41 40N 72 57W
Bristol, *Pa., U.S.A.* **79 F10** 40 6N 74 51W
Bristol, *R.I., U.S.A.* **79 E13** 41 40N 71 16W
Bristol, *S. Dak., U.S.A.* **80 C6** 45 21N 97 45W
Bristol, *Tenn., U.S.A.* **77 G4** 36 36N 82 11W
Bristol □, *U.K.* **11 F5** 51 27N 2 36W
Bristol B., *U.S.A.* **68 C4** 58 0N 160 0W
Bristol Channel, *U.K.* **11 F3** 51 18N 4 30W
Bristol I., *Antarctica* **5 B1** 58 45S 28 0W
Bristol L., *U.S.A.* **83 J5** 34 23N 116 50W

Bristow

Bristow, U.S.A. 81 H6 35 50N 96 23W
British Columbia □, Canada 72 C3 55 0N 125 15W
British Isles, Europe 6 E5 54 0N 4 0W
Brits, S. Africa 57 D4 25 37S 27 48 E
Britstown, S. Africa 56 E3 30 37S 23 30 E
Britt, Canada 70 C3 45 46N 80 34W
Brittany = Bretagne, France 18 B2 48 10N 3 0W
Britton, U.S.A. 80 C6 45 48N 97 45W
Brive-la-Gaillarde, France 18 D4 45 10N 1 32 E
Brixen = Bressanone, Italy 20 A4 46 43N 11 39 E
Brixton, Australia 62 C3 23 32S 144 57 E
Brlik, Kazakstan 26 E8 43 40N 73 49 E
Brno, Czech. 17 D9 49 10N 16 35 E
Broad →, U.S.A. 77 J5 34 1N 81 4W
Broad Arrow, Australia 61 F3 30 23S 121 15 E
Broad B., U.K. 12 C2 58 14N 6 18W
Broad Haven, Ireland 13 B2 54 20N 9 55W
Broad Law, U.K. 12 F5 55 30N 3 21W
Broad Sd., Australia 62 C4 22 0S 149 45 E
Broadhurst Ra., Australia 60 D3 22 30S 122 30 E
Broads, The, U.K. 10 E9 52 45N 1 30 E
Broadus, U.S.A. 80 C2 45 27N 105 25W
Broadview, Canada 73 C8 50 22N 102 35W
Brochet, Canada 73 B8 57 53N 101 40W
Brochet, L., Canada 73 B8 58 36N 101 35W
Brock, Canada 73 C7 51 26N 108 43W
Brocken, Germany 16 C6 51 47N 10 37 E
Brockport, U.S.A. 78 C7 43 13N 77 56W
Brockton, U.S.A. 79 D13 42 5N 71 1W
Brockville, Canada 70 D4 44 35N 75 41W
Brockway, Mont., U.S.A. 80 B2 47 18N 105 45W
Brockway, Pa., U.S.A. 78 E6 41 15N 78 47W
Brocton, U.S.A. 78 D5 42 23N 79 26W
Brodeur Pen., Canada 69 A11 72 30N 88 10W
Brodick, U.K. 12 F3 55 35N 5 9W
Brodnica, Poland 17 B10 53 15N 19 25 E
Brody, Ukraine 17 C13 50 5N 25 10 E
Brogan, U.S.A. 82 D5 44 15N 117 31W
Broken Arrow, U.S.A. 81 G7 36 3N 95 48W
Broken Bow, Nebr., U.S.A. 80 E5 41 24N 99 38W
Broken Bow, Okla., U.S.A. 81 H7 34 2N 94 44W
Broken Hill = Kabwe, Zambia 55 E2 14 30S 28 29 E
Broken Hill, Australia 63 E3 31 58S 141 29 E
Bromfield, U.K. 11 E5 52 24N 2 45W
Bromley, U.K. 11 F8 51 24N 0 2 E
Brønderslev, Denmark 9 H13 57 16N 9 57 E
Bronkhorstspruit, S. Africa 57 D4 25 46S 28 45 E
Brønnøysund, Norway 8 D15 65 28N 12 14 E
Bronte, U.S.A. 81 K4 31 53N 100 18W
Bronte Park, Australia 62 G4 42 8S 146 30 E
Brook Park, U.S.A. 78 E4 41 24N 80 51W
Brookfield, U.S.A. 80 F8 39 47N 93 4W
Brookhaven, U.S.A. 81 K9 31 35N 90 26W
Brookings, Oreg., U.S.A. 82 E1 42 3N 124 17W
Brookings, S. Dak., U.S.A. 80 C6 44 19N 96 48W
Brooklin, Canada 78 C6 43 55N 78 55W
Brooklyn Park, U.S.A. 80 C8 45 6N 93 23W
Brookmere, Canada 72 D4 49 52N 120 53W
Brooks, Canada 72 C6 50 35N 111 55W
Brooks B., Canada 72 C3 50 15N 127 55W
Brooks L., Canada 73 A7 61 55N 106 35W
Brooks Ra., U.S.A. 68 B5 68 40N 147 0W
Brooksville, U.S.A. 77 L4 28 33N 82 23W
Brookville, U.S.A. 76 F3 39 25N 85 1W
Brooloo, Australia 63 D5 26 30S 152 43 E
Broom, L., U.K. 12 D3 57 55N 5 15W
Broome, Australia 60 C3 18 0S 122 15 E
Broomehill, Australia 61 F2 33 51S 117 39 E
Brora, U.K. 12 C5 58 0N 3 52W
Brora →, U.K. 12 C5 58 0N 3 51W
Brosna →, Ireland 13 C4 53 14N 7 58W
Brothers, U.S.A. 82 E3 43 49N 120 36W
Brough, U.K. 10 C5 54 32N 2 18W
Broughton Island, Canada 69 B13 67 33N 63 0W
Broughty Ferry, U.K. 12 E6 56 29N 2 51W
Brouwershaven, Neths. 15 C3 51 45N 3 55 E
Browerville, U.S.A. 80 B7 46 5N 94 52W
Brown, Pt., Australia 63 E1 32 32S 133 50 E
Brown Willy, U.K. 11 G3 50 35N 4 37W
Brownfield, U.S.A. 81 J3 33 11N 102 17W
Browning, U.S.A. 82 B7 48 34N 113 1W
Brownlee, Canada 73 C7 50 43N 106 1W
Brownsville, Oreg., U.S.A. 82 D2 44 24N 122 59W
Brownsville, Tenn., U.S.A. 81 H10 35 36N 89 16W
Brownsville, Tex., U.S.A. 81 N6 25 54N 97 30W
Brownwood, U.S.A. 81 K5 31 43N 98 59W
Brownwood, L., U.S.A. 81 K5 31 51N 98 35W
Browse I., Australia 60 B3 14 7S 123 33 E
Bruas, Malaysia 39 K3 4 30N 100 47 E
Bruay-en-Artois, France 18 A5 50 29N 2 33 E
Bruce, Mt., Australia 60 D2 22 37S 118 8 E
Bruce Pen., Canada 78 A3 45 0N 81 30W
Bruce Rock, Australia 61 F2 31 52S 118 8 E
Bruck an der Leitha, Austria 17 D9 48 1N 16 47 E
Bruck an der Mur, Austria 16 E8 47 24N 15 16 E
Brue →, U.K. 11 F5 51 13N 2 59W
Bruges = Brugge, Belgium 15 C3 51 13N 3 13 E
Brugge, Belgium 15 C3 51 13N 3 13 E
Brûlé, Canada 72 C5 53 15N 117 58W
Brumado, Brazil 93 F10 14 14S 41 40W
Brumunddal, Norway 9 F14 60 53N 10 56 E
Brunchilly, Australia 62 B1 18 50S 134 30 E
Brundidge, U.S.A. 77 K3 31 43N 85 49W
Bruneau, U.S.A. 82 E6 42 53N 115 48W
Bruneau →, U.S.A. 82 E6 42 56N 115 57W
Brunei = Bandar Seri Begawan, Brunei 36 C4 4 52N 115 0 E
Brunei ■, Asia 36 D4 4 50N 115 0 E
Brunette Downs, Australia 62 B2 18 40S 135 55 E
Brunner, L., N.Z. 59 K3 42 37S 171 27 E
Bruno, Canada 73 C7 52 20N 105 30W
Brunswick = Braunschweig, Germany 16 B6 52 15N 10 31 E
Brunswick, Ga., U.S.A. 77 K5 31 10N 81 30W
Brunswick, Maine, U.S.A. 71 D6 43 55N 69 58W
Brunswick, Md., U.S.A. 76 F7 39 19N 77 38W
Brunswick, Mo., U.S.A. 80 F8 39 26N 93 8W
Brunswick, Ohio, U.S.A. 78 E3 41 14N 81 51W
Brunswick, Pen. de, Chile 96 G2 53 30S 71 30W
Brunswick B., Australia 60 C3 15 15S 124 50 E
Brunswick Junction, Australia 61 F2 33 15S 115 50 E
Bruny I., Australia 62 G4 43 20S 147 15 E
Brus Laguna, Honduras 88 C3 15 47N 84 35W
Brush, U.S.A. 80 E3 40 15N 103 37W
Brushton, U.S.A. 79 B10 44 50N 74 31W
Brusque, Brazil 95 B6 27 5S 49 0W
Brussel, Belgium 15 D4 50 51N 4 21 E
Brussels = Brussel, Belgium 15 D4 50 51N 4 21 E
Brussels, Canada 78 C3 43 44N 81 15W
Bruthen, Australia 63 F4 37 42S 147 50 E
Bruxelles = Brussel, Belgium 15 D4 50 51N 4 21 E
Bryan, Ohio, U.S.A. 76 E3 41 28N 84 33W
Bryan, Tex., U.S.A. 81 K6 30 40N 96 22W
Bryan, Mt., Australia 63 E2 33 30S 139 0 E
Bryansk, Russia 24 D5 53 13N 34 25 E
Bryant, U.S.A. 80 C6 44 35N 97 28W
Bryne, Norway 9 G11 58 44N 5 38 E
Bryson City, U.S.A. 77 H4 35 26N 83 27W
Bsharri, Lebanon 47 A5 34 15N 36 0 E
Bū Baqarah, U.A.E. 45 E8 25 35N 56 25 E
Bu Craa, W. Sahara 50 C2 26 45N 12 50W
Bū Ḥasā, U.A.E. 45 F7 23 30N 53 20 E
Bua Yai, Thailand 38 E4 15 33N 102 26 E
Buapinang, Indonesia 37 E6 4 40S 121 30 E
Buayan, Phil. 37 C7 6 3N 125 6 E
Bubanza, Burundi 54 C2 3 6S 29 23 E
Būbiyān, Kuwait 45 D6 29 45N 48 15 E
Bucaramanga, Colombia 92 B4 7 0N 73 0W
Buccaneer Arch., Australia 60 C3 16 7S 123 20 E
Buchach, Ukraine 17 D13 49 5N 25 25 E
Buchan, U.K. 12 D6 57 32N 2 21W
Buchan Ness, U.K. 12 D7 57 29N 1 46W
Buchanan, Canada 73 C8 51 40N 102 45W
Buchanan, Liberia 50 G2 5 57N 10 2W
Buchanan, L., Queens., Australia 62 C4 21 35S 145 52 E
Buchanan, L., W. Austral., Australia 61 E3 25 33S 123 2 E
Buchanan, L., U.S.A. 81 K5 30 45N 98 25W
Buchanan Cr. →, Australia 62 B2 19 13S 136 33 E
Buchans, Canada 71 C8 48 50N 56 52W
Bucharest = Bucureşti, Romania 17 F14 44 27N 26 10 E
Buchon, Pt., U.S.A. 84 K6 35 15N 120 54W
Buckeye, U.S.A. 83 K7 33 22N 112 35W
Buckhannon, U.S.A. 76 F5 39 0N 80 8W
Buckhaven, U.K. 12 E5 56 11N 3 3W
Buckie, U.K. 12 D6 57 41N 2 58W
Buckingham, Canada 70 C4 45 37N 75 24W
Buckingham, U.K. 11 F7 51 59N 0 57W
Buckingham B., Australia 62 A2 12 10S 135 40 E
Buckinghamshire □, U.K. 11 F7 51 53N 0 55W
Buckle Hd., Australia 60 B4 14 26S 127 52 E
Buckleboo, Australia 63 E2 32 54S 136 12 E
Buckley, U.S.A. 82 C2 47 10N 122 2W
Buckley →, Australia 62 C2 20 10S 138 49 E
Bucklin, U.S.A. 81 G5 37 33N 99 38W
Bucks L., U.S.A. 84 F5 39 54N 121 12W
Buctouche, Canada 71 C7 46 30N 64 45W
Bucureşti, Romania 17 F14 44 27N 26 10 E
Bucyrus, U.S.A. 76 E4 40 48N 82 59W
Budalin, Burma 41 H19 22 20N 95 10 E
Budapest, Hungary 17 E10 47 29N 19 5 E
Budaun, India 43 E8 28 5N 79 10 E
Budd Coast, Antarctica 5 C8 68 0S 112 0 E
Bude, U.K. 11 G3 50 49N 4 34W
Budennovsk, Russia 25 F7 44 50N 44 10 E
Budge Budge = Baj Baj, India 43 H13 22 30N 88 5 E
Budgewoi, Australia 63 E5 33 13S 151 34 E
Budjala, Zaïre 52 D3 2 50N 19 40 E
Buellton, U.S.A. 85 L6 34 37N 120 12W
Buena Park, U.S.A. 85 M9 33 52N 117 59W
Buena Vista, Colo., U.S.A. 83 G10 38 51N 106 8W
Buena Vista, Va., U.S.A. 76 G6 37 44N 79 21W
Buena Vista L., U.S.A. 85 K7 35 12N 119 18W
Buenaventura, Colombia 92 C3 3 53N 77 4W
Buenaventura, Mexico 86 B3 29 50N 107 30W
Buenos Aires, Argentina 94 C4 34 30S 58 20W
Buenos Aires, Costa Rica 88 E3 9 10N 83 20W
Buenos Aires □, Argentina 94 D4 36 30S 60 0W
Buenos Aires, L., Chile 96 F2 46 35S 72 30W
Buffalo, Mo., U.S.A. 81 G8 37 39N 93 6W
Buffalo, N.Y., U.S.A. 78 D6 42 53N 78 53W
Buffalo, Okla., U.S.A. 81 G5 36 50N 99 38W
Buffalo, S. Dak., U.S.A. 80 C3 45 35N 103 33W
Buffalo, Wyo., U.S.A. 82 D10 44 21N 106 42W
Buffalo →, Canada 72 A5 60 5N 115 5W
Buffalo Head Hills, Canada 72 B5 57 25N 115 55W
Buffalo L., Canada 72 C6 52 27N 112 54W
Buffalo Narrows, Canada 73 B7 55 51N 108 29W
Buffels →, S. Africa 56 D2 29 36S 17 3 E
Buford, U.S.A. 77 H4 34 10N 84 0W
Bug → = Buh →, Ukraine 25 E5 46 59N 31 58 E
Bug →, Poland 17 B11 52 31N 21 5 E
Buga, Colombia 92 C3 4 0N 76 15W
Buganda, Uganda 54 C3 0 0 31 30 E
Buganga, Uganda 54 C3 0 3S 32 0 E
Bugel, Tanjung, Indonesia 36 F4 6 26S 111 3 E
Bugibba, Malta 23 D1 35 57N 14 25 E
Bugsuk, Phil. 36 C5 8 15N 117 15 E
Bugulma, Russia 24 D9 54 33N 52 48 E
Bugun Shara, Mongolia 32 B5 49 0N 104 0 E
Buguruslan, Russia 24 D9 53 39N 52 26 E
Buh →, Ukraine 25 E5 46 59N 31 58 E
Buheirat-Murrat-el-Kubra, Egypt 51 B11 30 18N 32 26 E
Buhl, Idaho, U.S.A. 82 E6 42 36N 114 46W
Buhl, Minn., U.S.A. 80 B8 47 30N 92 46W
Buick, U.S.A. 81 G9 37 38N 91 2W
Builth Wells, U.K. 11 E4 52 9N 3 25W
Buir Nur, Mongolia 33 B6 47 50N 117 42 E
Bujumbura, Burundi 54 C2 3 16S 29 18 E
Bukachacha, Russia 27 D12 52 55N 116 50 E
Bukama, Zaïre 55 D2 9 10S 25 50 E
Bukavu, Zaïre 54 C2 2 20S 28 52 E
Bukene, Tanzania 54 C3 4 15S 32 48 E
Bukhara = Bukhoro, Uzbekistan 26 F7 39 48N 64 25 E
Bukhoro, Uzbekistan 26 F7 39 48N 64 25 E
Bukima, Tanzania 54 C3 1 50S 33 25 E
Bukit Mertajam, Malaysia 39 K3 5 22N 100 28 E
Bukittinggi, Indonesia 36 E2 0 20S 100 20 E
Bukoba, Tanzania 54 C3 1 20S 31 49 E
Bukoba □, Tanzania 54 C3 1 30S 32 0 E
Bukuya, Uganda 54 B3 0 40N 31 52 E
Bula, Indonesia 37 E8 3 6S 130 30 E
Bulahdelah, Australia 63 E5 32 23S 152 13 E
Bulan, Phil. 37 B6 12 40N 123 52 E
Bulandshahr, India 42 E7 28 28N 77 51 E
Bulawayo, Zimbabwe 55 G2 20 7S 28 32 E
Buldan, Turkey 21 E13 38 2N 28 50 E
Bulgaria ■, Europe 21 C11 42 35N 25 30 E
Bulgroo, Australia 63 D3 25 47S 143 58 E
Bulgunnia, Australia 63 E1 30 10S 134 53 E
Bulhar, Somali Rep. 46 E3 10 25N 44 30 E
Buli, Teluk, Indonesia 37 D7 1 5N 128 25 E
Buliluyan, C., Phil. 36 C5 8 20N 117 15 E
Bulkley →, Canada 72 B3 55 15N 127 40W
Bull Shoals L., U.S.A. 81 G8 36 22N 92 35W
Bullara, Australia 60 D1 22 40S 114 3 E
Bullaring, Australia 61 F2 32 30S 117 45 E
Bulli, Australia 63 E5 34 15S 150 57 E
Bullock Creek, Australia 62 B3 17 43S 144 31 E
Bulloo →, Australia 63 D3 28 43S 142 30 E
Bulloo Downs, Queens., Australia 63 D3 28 31S 142 57 E
Bulloo Downs, W. Austral., Australia 60 D2 24 0S 119 32 E
Bulloo L., Australia 63 D3 28 43S 142 25 E
Bulls, N.Z. 59 J5 40 10S 175 24 E
Bulnes, Chile 94 D1 36 42S 72 19W
Bulo Burti, Somali Rep. 46 G4 3 50N 45 33 E
Bulsar = Valsad, India 40 J8 20 40N 72 58 E
Bultfontein, S. Africa 56 D4 28 18S 26 10 E
Bulukumba, Indonesia 37 F6 5 33S 120 11 E
Bulun, Russia 27 B13 70 37N 127 30 E
Bulus, Russia 27 C13 63 10N 129 10 E
Bumba, Zaïre 52 D4 2 13N 22 30 E
Bumbiri I., Tanzania 54 C3 1 40S 31 55 E
Bumhpa Bum, Burma 41 F20 26 51N 97 14 E
Bumi →, Zimbabwe 55 F2 17 0S 28 20 E
Buna, Kenya 54 B4 2 58N 39 30 E
Bunazi, Tanzania 54 C3 1 3S 31 23 E
Bunbah, Khalīj, Libya 51 B9 32 20N 23 15 E
Bunbury, Australia 61 F2 33 20S 115 35 E
Buncrana, Ireland 13 A4 55 8N 7 27W
Bundaberg, Australia 63 C5 24 54S 152 22 E
Bundey →, Australia 62 C2 21 46S 135 37 E
Bundi, India 42 G6 25 30N 75 35 E
Bundooma, Australia 62 C1 24 54S 134 16 E
Bundoran, Ireland 13 B3 54 24N 8 16W
Bung Kan, Thailand 38 C4 18 23N 103 37 E
Bungatakada, Japan 31 H5 33 35N 131 25 E
Bungil Cr. →, Australia 62 D4 27 5S 149 5 E
Bungo-Suidō, Japan 31 H6 33 0N 132 15 E
Bungoma, Kenya 54 B3 0 34N 34 34 E
Bungu, Tanzania 54 D4 7 35S 39 0 E
Bunia, Zaïre 54 B3 1 35N 30 20 E
Bunji, Pakistan 43 B6 35 45N 74 40 E
Bunkie, U.S.A. 81 K8 30 57N 92 11W
Bunnell, U.S.A. 77 L5 29 28N 81 16W
Buntok, Indonesia 36 E4 1 40S 114 58 E
Bunyu, Indonesia 36 D5 3 35N 117 50 E
Buol, Indonesia 37 D6 1 15N 121 32 E
Buon Brieng, Vietnam 38 F7 13 9N 108 12 E
Buon Me Thuot, Vietnam 38 F7 12 40N 108 3 E
Buong Long, Cambodia 38 F6 13 44N 106 59 E
Buorkhaya, Mys, Russia 27 B14 71 50N 132 40 E
Buqayq, Si. Arabia 45 E6 26 0N 49 45 E
Bur Acaba, Somali Rep. 46 G3 3 12N 44 20 E
Bûr Safâga, Egypt 51 C11 26 43N 33 57 E
Bûr Sa'îd, Egypt 51 B11 31 16N 32 18 E
Bûr Sûdân, Sudan 51 E12 19 32N 37 9 E
Bura, Kenya 54 C4 1 4S 39 58 E
Burao, Somali Rep. 46 F4 9 32N 45 32 E
Burāq, Syria 47 B5 33 11N 36 29 E
Buras, U.S.A. 81 L10 29 22N 89 32W
Buraydah, Si. Arabia 44 E5 26 20N 44 8 E
Burbank, U.S.A. 85 L8 34 11N 118 19W
Burcher, Australia 63 E4 33 30S 147 16 E
Burdekin →, Australia 62 B4 19 38S 147 25 E
Burdett, Canada 72 D6 49 50N 111 32W
Burdur, Turkey 25 G5 37 45N 30 17 E
Burdwan = Barddhaman, India 43 H12 23 14N 87 39 E
Bure →, U.K. 10 E9 52 38N 1 43 E
Bureya →, Russia 27 E13 49 27N 129 30 E
Burford, Canada 78 C4 43 7N 80 27W
Burgas, Bulgaria 21 C12 42 33N 27 29 E
Burgeo, Canada 71 C8 47 37N 57 38W
Burgersdorp, S. Africa 56 E4 31 0S 26 20 E
Burges, Mt., Australia 61 F3 30 50S 121 5 E
Burgos, Spain 19 A4 42 21N 3 41W
Burgsvik, Sweden 9 H18 57 3N 18 19 E
Burgundy = Bourgogne, France 18 C6 47 0N 4 50 E
Burhaniye, Turkey 21 E12 39 30N 26 58 E
Burhanpur, India 40 J10 21 18N 76 14 E
Burias, Phil. 37 B6 12 55N 123 5 E
Burica, Pta., Costa Rica 88 E3 8 3N 82 51W
Burigi, L., Tanzania 54 C3 2 2S 31 22 E
Burin, Canada 71 C8 47 1N 55 14W
Buriram, Thailand 38 E4 15 0N 103 0 E
Burj Sāfitā, Syria 44 C3 34 48N 36 7 E
Burji, Ethiopia 51 G12 5 29N 37 51 E
Burkburnett, U.S.A. 81 H5 34 6N 98 34W
Burke, U.S.A. 82 C6 47 31N 115 49W
Burke →, Australia 62 C2 23 12S 139 33 E
Burketown, Australia 62 B2 17 45S 139 33 E
Burkina Faso ■, Africa 50 F4 12 0N 1 0W
Burk's Falls, Canada 70 C4 45 37N 79 24W
Burley, U.S.A. 82 E7 42 32N 113 48W
Burlingame, U.S.A. 84 H4 37 35N 122 21W
Burlington, Canada 78 C5 43 18N 79 45W
Burlington, Colo., U.S.A. 80 F3 39 18N 102 16W
Burlington, Iowa, U.S.A. 80 E9 40 49N 91 14W
Burlington, Kans., U.S.A. 80 F7 38 12N 95 45W
Burlington, N.C., U.S.A. 77 G6 36 6N 79 26W
Burlington, N.J., U.S.A. 79 F10 40 4N 74 51W
Burlington, Vt., U.S.A. 79 B11 44 29N 73 12W
Burlington, Wash., U.S.A. 84 B4 48 28N 122 20W
Burlington, Wis., U.S.A. 76 D1 42 41N 88 17W
Burlyu-Tyube, Kazakstan 26 E8 46 30N 79 10 E
Burma ■, Asia 41 J20 21 0N 96 30 E
Burnaby I., Canada 72 C2 52 25N 131 19W
Burnet, U.S.A. 81 K5 30 45N 98 14W
Burney, U.S.A. 82 F3 40 53N 121 40W
Burngup, Australia 61 F2 33 2S 118 42 E
Burnham, U.S.A. 78 F7 40 38N 77 34W
Burnie, Australia 62 G4 41 4S 145 56 E
Burnley, U.K. 10 D5 53 47N 2 14W
Burns, Oreg., U.S.A. 82 E4 43 35N 119 3W
Burns, Wyo., U.S.A. 80 E2 41 12N 104 21W
Burns Lake, Canada 72 C3 54 20N 125 45W
Burnside →, Canada 68 B9 66 51N 108 4W
Burnside, L., Australia 61 E3 25 22S 123 0 E
Burnsville, U.S.A. 80 C8 44 47N 93 17W
Burnt River, Canada 78 B6 44 41N 78 42W
Burntwood →, Canada 73 B9 56 8N 96 34W
Burntwood L., Canada 73 B8 55 22N 100 26W
Burqān, Kuwait 44 D5 29 0N 47 57 E
Burra, Australia 63 E2 33 40S 138 55 E
Burramurra, Australia 62 C2 20 25S 137 15 E
Burren Junction, Australia 63 E4 30 7S 148 59 E
Burrendong Dam, Australia 63 E4 32 39S 149 6 E
Burrinjuck Res., Australia 63 F4 35 0S 148 36 E
Burro, Serranías del, Mexico 86 B4 29 0N 102 0W
Burruyacú, Argentina 94 B3 26 30S 64 40W
Burry Port, U.K. 11 F3 51 41N 4 15W
Bursa, Turkey 21 D13 40 15N 29 5 E
Burstall, Canada 73 C7 50 39N 109 54W
Burton L., Canada 70 B4 54 45N 78 20W
Burton upon Trent, U.K. 10 E6 52 48N 1 38W
Burtundy, Australia 63 E3 33 45S 142 15 E
Buru, Indonesia 37 E7 3 30S 126 30 E
Burûn, Râs, Egypt 47 D2 31 14N 33 7 E
Burundi ■, Africa 54 C3 3 15S 30 0 E
Bururi, Burundi 54 C2 3 57S 29 37 E
Burutu, Nigeria 50 G6 5 20N 5 29 E
Burwell, U.S.A. 80 E5 41 47N 99 8W
Bury, U.K. 10 D5 53 35N 2 17W
Bury St. Edmunds, U.K. 11 E8 52 15N 0 43 E
Buryatia □, Russia 27 D11 53 0N 110 0 E
Busango Swamp, Zambia 55 E2 14 15S 25 45 E
Buşayrah, Syria 44 C4 35 9N 40 26 E
Buşayyah, Iraq 44 D5 30 0N 46 10 E
Būshehr, Iran 45 D6 28 55N 50 55 E
Būshehr □, Iran 45 D6 28 20N 51 45 E
Bushell, Canada 73 B7 59 31N 108 45W
Bushenyi, Uganda 54 C3 0 35S 30 10 E
Bushire = Būshehr, Iran 45 D6 28 55N 50 55 E
Bushnell, Ill., U.S.A. 80 E9 40 33N 90 31W
Bushnell, Nebr., U.S.A. 80 E3 41 14N 103 54W
Busia □, Kenya 54 B3 0 25N 34 6 E
Businga, Zaïre 52 D4 3 16N 20 59 E
Busra ash Shām, Syria 47 C5 32 30N 36 25 E
Busselton, Australia 61 F2 33 42S 115 15 E
Bussum, Neths. 15 B5 52 16N 5 10 E
Busto Arsizio, Italy 20 B3 45 37N 8 51 E
Busu-Djanoa, Zaïre 52 D4 1 43N 21 23 E
Busuanga, Phil. 37 B5 12 10N 120 0 E
Buta, Zaïre 54 B1 2 50N 24 53 E
Butare, Rwanda 54 C2 2 31S 29 52 E
Butaritari, Kiribati 64 G9 3 30N 174 0 E
Bute, U.K. 12 F3 55 48N 5 2W
Bute Inlet, Canada 72 C4 50 40N 124 53W
Butemba, Uganda 54 B3 1 9N 31 37 E
Butembo, Zaïre 54 B2 0 9N 29 18 E
Butha Qi, China 33 B7 48 0N 122 32 E
Butiaba, Uganda 54 B3 1 50N 31 20 E
Butler, Mo., U.S.A. 80 F7 38 16N 94 20W
Butler, Pa., U.S.A. 78 F5 40 52N 79 54W
Buton, Indonesia 37 E6 5 0S 122 45 E
Butte, Mont., U.S.A. 82 C7 46 0N 112 32W
Butte, Nebr., U.S.A. 80 D5 42 58N 98 51W
Butte Creek →, U.S.A. 84 F5 39 12N 121 56W
Butterworth = Gcuwa, S. Africa 57 E4 32 20S 28 11 E
Butterworth, Malaysia 39 K3 5 24N 100 23 E
Buttfield, Mt., Australia 61 D4 24 45S 128 9 E
Button B., Canada 73 B10 58 45N 94 23W
Buttonwillow, U.S.A. 85 K7 35 24N 119 28W
Butty Hd., Australia 61 F3 33 54S 121 39 E
Butuan, Phil. 37 C7 8 57N 125 33 E
Butung = Buton, Indonesia 37 E6 5 0S 122 45 E
Buturlinovka, Russia 25 D7 50 50N 40 35 E
Buxar, India 43 G10 25 34N 83 58 E
Buxtehude, Germany 16 B5 53 28N 9 39 E
Buxton, U.K. 10 D6 53 16N 1 54W
Buy, Russia 24 C7 58 28N 41 28 E
Büyük Menderes →, Turkey 21 F12 37 28N 27 11 E
Büyükçekmece, Turkey 21 D13 41 2N 28 35 E
Buzău, Romania 17 F14 45 10N 26 50 E
Buzău →, Romania 17 F14 45 26N 27 44 E
Buzen, Japan 31 H5 33 35N 131 5 E
Buzi →, Mozam. 55 F3 19 50S 34 43 E
Buzuluk, Russia 24 D9 52 48N 52 12 E
Buzzards Bay, U.S.A. 79 E14 41 45N 70 37W
Bwana Mkubwe, Zaïre 55 E2 13 8S 28 38 E
Byarezina →, Belarus 17 B16 52 33N 30 14 E
Bydgoszcz, Poland 17 B9 53 10N 18 0 E
Byelarus = Belarus ■, Europe 17 B14 53 30N 27 0 E
Byelorussia = Belarus ■, Europe 17 B14 53 30N 27 0 E
Byers, U.S.A. 80 F2 39 43N 104 14W
Byesville, U.S.A. 78 G3 39 58N 81 32W
Byhalia, U.S.A. 81 H10 34 52N 89 41W
Bykhaw, Belarus 17 B16 53 31N 30 14 E
Bykhov = Bykhaw, Belarus 17 B16 53 31N 30 14 E
Bylas, U.S.A. 83 K8 33 8N 110 7W
Bylot I., Canada 69 A12 73 13N 78 34W
Byrd, C., Antarctica 5 C17 69 38S 76 7W
Byro, Australia 61 E2 26 5S 116 11 E
Byrock, Australia 63 E4 30 40S 146 27 E
Byron Bay, Australia 63 D5 28 43S 153 37 E
Byrranga, Gory, Russia 27 B11 75 0N 100 0 E

Cape York Peninsula

Byrranga Mts. = Byrranga, Gory, *Russia* **27 B11** 75 0N 100 0 E
Byske, *Sweden* **8 D19** 64 57N 21 11 E
Byske älv →, *Sweden* **8 D19** 64 57N 21 13 E
Bytom, *Poland* **17 C10** 50 25N 18 54 E
Bytów, *Poland* **17 A9** 54 10N 17 30 E
Byumba, *Rwanda* **54 C3** 1 35S 30 4 E

C

Ca →, *Vietnam* **38 C5** 18 45N 105 45 E
Ca Mau = Quan Long, *Vietnam* **39 H5** 9 7N 105 8 E
Ca Mau, Mui = Bai Bung, Mui, *Vietnam* **39 H5** 8 38N 104 44 E
Ca Na, *Vietnam* **39 G7** 11 20N 108 54 E
Caacupé, *Paraguay* **94 B4** 25 23S 57 5W
Caála, *Angola* **53 G3** 12 46S 15 30 E
Caamano Sd., *Canada* **72 C3** 52 55N 129 25W
Caazapá, *Paraguay* **94 B4** 26 8S 56 19W
Caazapá □, *Paraguay* **95 B4** 26 10S 56 0W
Caballeria, C. de, *Spain* **22 A11** 40 5N 4 5 E
Cabanatuan, *Phil.* **37 A6** 15 30N 120 58 E
Cabano, *Canada* **71 C6** 47 40N 68 56W
Cabazon, *U.S.A.* **85 M10** 33 55N 116 47W
Cabedelo, *Brazil* **93 E12** 7 0S 34 50W
Cabildo, *Chile* **94 C1** 32 30S 71 5W
Cabimas, *Venezuela* **92 A4** 10 23N 71 25W
Cabinda, *Angola* **52 F2** 5 33S 12 11 E
Cabinda □, *Angola* **52 F2** 5 0S 12 30 E
Cabinet Mts., *U.S.A.* **82 C6** 48 0N 115 30W
Cabo Blanco, *Argentina* **96 F3** 47 15S 65 47W
Cabo Frio, *Brazil* **95 A7** 22 51S 42 3W
Cabo Pantoja, *Peru* **92 D3** 1 0S 75 10W
Cabonga, Réservoir, *Canada* **70 C4** 47 20N 76 40W
Cabool, *U.S.A.* **81 G8** 37 7N 92 6W
Caboolture, *Australia* **63 D5** 27 5S 152 58 E
Cabora Bassa Dam = Cahora Bassa Dam, *Mozam.* **55 F3** 15 20S 32 50 E
Caborca, *Mexico* **86 A2** 30 40N 112 10W
Cabot, Mt., *U.S.A.* **79 B13** 44 30N 71 25W
Cabot Str., *Canada* **71 C8** 47 15N 59 40W
Cabra, *Spain* **19 D3** 37 30N 4 28W
Cabrera, *Spain* **22 B9** 39 8N 2 57 E
Cabri, *Canada* **73 C7** 50 35N 108 25W
Cabriel →, *Spain* **19 C5** 39 14N 1 3W
Čačak, *Serbia, Yug.* **21 C9** 43 54N 20 20 E
Cáceres, *Brazil* **92 G7** 16 5S 57 40W
Cáceres, *Spain* **19 C2** 39 26N 6 23W
Cache Bay, *Canada* **70 C4** 46 22N 80 0W
Cache Cr. →, *U.S.A.* **84 G5** 38 42N 121 42W
Cachi, *Argentina* **94 B2** 25 5S 66 10W
Cachimbo, Serra do, *Brazil* **93 E7** 9 30S 55 30W
Cachoeira, *Brazil* **93 F11** 12 30S 39 0W
Cachoeira de Itapemirim, *Brazil* **95 A7** 20 51S 41 7W
Cachoeira do Sul, *Brazil* **95 C5** 30 3S 52 53W
Cacólo, *Angola* **52 G3** 10 9S 19 21 E
Caconda, *Angola* **53 G3** 13 48S 15 8 E
Cacongo, *Angola* **52 F2** 5 11S 12 5 E
Caddo, *U.S.A.* **81 H6** 34 7N 96 16W
Cadell Cr. →, *Australia* **62 C3** 22 35S 141 51 E
Cader Idris, *U.K.* **10 E4** 52 42N 3 53W
Cadibarrawirracanna, L., *Australia* **63 D2** 28 52S 135 27 E
Cadillac, *Canada* **70 C4** 48 14N 78 23W
Cadillac, *U.S.A.* **76 C3** 44 15N 85 24W
Cadiz, *Phil.* **37 B6** 10 57N 123 15 E
Cádiz, *Spain* **19 D2** 36 30N 6 20W
Cadiz, *U.S.A.* **78 F4** 40 22N 81 0W
Cádiz, G. de, *Spain* **19 D2** 36 40N 7 0W
Cadney Park, *Australia* **63 D1** 27 55S 134 3 E
Cadomin, *Canada* **72 C5** 53 2N 117 20W
Cadotte →, *Canada* **72 B5** 56 43N 117 10W
Cadoux, *Australia* **61 F2** 30 46S 117 7 E
Caen, *France* **18 B3** 49 10N 0 22W
Caernarfon, *U.K.* **10 D3** 53 8N 4 16W
Caernarfon B., *U.K.* **10 D3** 53 4N 4 40W
Caernarvon = Caernarfon, *U.K.* **10 D3** 53 8N 4 16W
Caerphilly, *U.K.* **11 F4** 51 35N 3 13W
Caerphilly □, *U.K.* **11 F4** 51 37N 3 12W
Caesarea, *Israel* **47 C3** 32 30N 34 53 E
Caeté, *Brazil* **93 G10** 19 55S 43 40W
Caetité, *Brazil* **93 F10** 13 50S 42 32W
Cafayate, *Argentina* **94 B2** 26 2S 66 0W
Cafu, *Angola* **56 B2** 16 30S 15 8 E
Cagayan →, *Phil.* **37 A6** 18 25N 121 42 E
Cagayan de Oro, *Phil.* **37 C6** 8 30N 124 40 E
Cágliari, *Italy* **20 E3** 39 13N 9 7 E
Cágliari, G. di, *Italy* **20 E3** 39 8N 9 11 E
Caguas, *Puerto Rico* **89 C6** 18 14N 66 2W
Caha Mts., *Ireland* **13 E2** 51 45N 9 40W
Cahama, *Angola* **56 B1** 16 17S 14 19 E
Caher, *Ireland* **13 D4** 52 22N 7 56W
Caherciveen, *Ireland* **13 E1** 51 56N 10 14W
Cahora Bassa Dam, *Mozam.* **55 F3** 15 20S 32 50 E
Cahore Pt., *Ireland* **13 D5** 52 33N 6 12W
Cahors, *France* **18 D4** 44 27N 1 27 E
Cahuapanas, *Peru* **92 E3** 5 15S 77 0W
Cahul, *Moldova* **17 F15** 45 50N 28 15 E
Cai Bau, Dao, *Vietnam* **38 B6** 21 10N 107 27 E
Cai Nuoc, *Vietnam* **39 H5** 8 56N 105 1 E
Caia, *Mozam.* **55 F4** 17 51S 35 24 E
Caianda, *Angola* **55 E1** 11 2S 23 31 E
Caibarién, *Cuba* **88 B4** 22 30N 79 30W
Caicara, *Venezuela* **92 B5** 7 38N 66 10W
Caicó, *Brazil* **93 E11** 6 20S 37 0W
Caicos Is., *W. Indies* **89 B5** 21 40N 71 40W
Caicos Passage, *W. Indies* **89 B5** 22 45N 72 45W
Caird Coast, *Antarctica* **5 D1** 75 0S 25 0W
Cairn Gorm, *U.K.* **12 D5** 57 7N 3 39W
Cairn Toul, *U.K.* **12 D5** 57 3N 3 44W
Cairngorm Mts., *U.K.* **12 D5** 57 6N 3 42W
Cairns, *Australia* **62 B4** 16 57S 145 45 E
Cairo = El Qâhira, *Egypt* **51 B11** 30 1N 31 14 E
Cairo, *Ga., U.S.A.* **77 K3** 30 52N 84 13W
Cairo, *Ill., U.S.A.* **81 G10** 37 0N 89 11W
Caithness, Ord of, *U.K.* **12 C5** 58 8N 3 36W
Caiundo, *Angola* **53 H3** 15 50S 17 28 E
Caiza, *Bolivia* **92 H5** 20 2S 65 40W
Cajamarca, *Peru* **92 E3** 7 5S 78 28W
Cajàzeiras, *Brazil* **93 E11** 6 52S 38 30W
Cala d'Or, *Spain* **22 B10** 39 23N 3 14 E
Cala Figuera, C., *Spain* **22 B9** 39 27N 2 31 E
Cala Forcat, *Spain* **22 A10** 40 0N 3 47 E
Cala Mayor, *Spain* **22 B9** 39 33N 2 37 E
Cala Mezquida, *Spain* **22 B11** 39 55N 4 16 E
Cala Millor, *Spain* **22 B10** 39 35N 3 22 E
Cala Ratjada, *Spain* **22 B10** 39 43N 3 27 E
Calabar, *Nigeria* **50 H6** 4 57N 8 20 E
Calábria □, *Italy* **20 E7** 39 0N 16 30 E
Calafate, *Argentina* **96 G2** 50 19S 72 15W
Calahorra, *Spain* **19 A5** 42 18N 1 59W
Calais, *France* **18 A4** 50 57N 1 56 E
Calais, *U.S.A.* **71 C6** 45 11N 67 17W
Calalaste, Cord. de, *Argentina* **94 B2** 25 0S 67 0W
Calama, *Brazil* **92 E6** 8 0S 62 50W
Calama, *Chile* **94 A2** 22 30S 68 55W
Calamar, Bolívar, *Colombia* **92 A4** 10 15N 74 55W
Calamar, Vaupés, *Colombia* **92 C4** 1 58N 72 32W
Calamian Group, *Phil.* **37 B5** 11 50N 119 55 E
Calamocha, *Spain* **19 B5** 40 50N 1 17W
Calán Porter, *Spain* **22 B11** 39 52N 4 8 E
Calang, *Indonesia* **36 D1** 4 37N 95 37 E
Calapan, *Phil.* **37 B6** 13 25N 121 7 E
Călăraşi, *Romania* **17 F14** 44 12N 27 20 E
Calatayud, *Spain* **19 B5** 41 20N 1 40W
Calauag, *Phil.* **37 B6** 13 55N 122 15 E
Calavite, C., *Phil.* **37 B6** 13 26N 120 20 E
Calbayog, *Phil.* **37 B6** 12 4N 124 38 E
Calca, *Peru* **92 F4** 13 22S 72 0W
Calcasieu L., *U.S.A.* **81 L8** 29 55N 93 18W
Calcutta, *India* **43 H13** 22 36N 88 24 E
Caldas da Rainha, *Portugal* **19 C1** 39 24N 9 8W
Calder →, *U.K.* **10 D6** 53 44N 1 22W
Caldera, *Chile* **94 B1** 27 5S 70 55W
Caldwell, *Idaho, U.S.A.* **82 E5** 43 40N 116 41W
Caldwell, *Kans., U.S.A.* **81 G6** 37 2N 97 37W
Caldwell, *Tex., U.S.A.* **81 K6** 30 32N 96 42W
Caledon, *S. Africa* **56 E2** 34 14S 19 26 E
Caledon →, *S. Africa* **56 E4** 30 31S 26 5 E
Caledon B., *Australia* **62 A2** 12 45S 137 0 E
Caledonia, *Canada* **78 C5** 43 7N 79 58W
Caledonia, *U.S.A.* **78 D7** 42 58N 77 51W
Calemba, *Angola* **56 B2** 16 0S 15 44 E
Calexico, *U.S.A.* **85 N11** 32 40N 115 30W
Calf of Man, *U.K.* **10 C3** 54 3N 4 48W
Calgary, *Canada* **72 C6** 51 0N 114 10W
Calheta, *Madeira* **22 D2** 32 44N 17 11W
Calhoun, *U.S.A.* **77 H3** 34 30N 84 57W
Cali, *Colombia* **92 C3** 3 25N 76 35W
Calicut, *India* **40 P9** 11 15N 75 43 E
Caliente, *U.S.A.* **83 H6** 37 37N 114 31W
California, *Mo., U.S.A.* **80 F8** 38 38N 92 34W
California, *Pa., U.S.A.* **78 F5** 40 4N 79 54W
California □, *U.S.A.* **83 H4** 37 30N 119 30W
California, Baja, *Mexico* **86 A1** 32 10N 115 12W
California, Baja, T.N. □ = Baja California □, *Mexico* **86 B2** 30 0N 115 0W
California, Baja, T.S. □ = Baja California Sur □, *Mexico* **86 B2** 25 50N 111 50W
California, G. de, *Mexico* **86 B2** 27 0N 111 0W
California City, *U.S.A.* **85 K9** 35 10N 117 55W
California Hot Springs, *U.S.A.* **85 K8** 35 51N 118 41W
Calingasta, *Argentina* **94 C2** 31 15S 69 30W
Calipatria, *U.S.A.* **85 M11** 33 8N 115 31W
Calistoga, *U.S.A.* **84 G4** 38 35N 122 35W
Calitzdorp, *S. Africa* **56 E3** 33 33S 21 42 E
Callabonna, L., *Australia* **63 D3** 29 40S 140 5 E
Callan, *Ireland* **13 D4** 52 32N 7 24W
Callander, *U.K.* **12 E4** 56 15N 4 13W
Callao, *Peru* **92 F3** 12 0S 77 0W
Callaway, *U.S.A.* **80 E5** 41 18N 99 56W
Calles, *Mexico* **87 C5** 23 2N 98 42W
Callide, *Australia* **62 C5** 24 18S 150 28 E
Calling Lake, *Canada* **72 B6** 55 15N 113 12W
Calliope, *Australia* **62 C5** 24 0S 151 16 E
Calola, *Angola* **56 B2** 16 25S 17 48 E
Caloundra, *Australia* **63 D5** 26 45S 153 10 E
Calpella, *U.S.A.* **84 F3** 39 14N 123 12W
Calpine, *U.S.A.* **84 F6** 39 40N 120 27W
Calstock, *Canada* **70 C3** 49 47N 84 9W
Caltagirone, *Italy* **20 F6** 37 14N 14 31 E
Caltanissetta, *Italy* **20 F6** 37 29N 14 4 E
Calulo, *Angola* **52 G2** 10 1S 14 56 E
Calumet, *U.S.A.* **76 B1** 47 14N 88 27W
Calunda, *Angola* **53 G4** 12 7S 23 36 E
Calvert, *U.S.A.* **81 K6** 30 59N 96 40W
Calvert →, *Australia* **62 B2** 16 17S 137 44 E
Calvert Hills, *Australia* **62 B2** 17 15S 137 20 E
Calvert I., *Canada* **72 C3** 51 30N 128 0W
Calvert Ra., *Australia* **60 D3** 24 0S 122 30 E
Calvi, *France* **18 E8** 42 34N 8 45 E
Calviá, *Spain* **19 C7** 39 34N 2 31 E
Calvillo, *Mexico* **86 C4** 21 51N 102 43W
Calvinia, *S. Africa* **56 E2** 31 28S 19 45 E
Calwa, *U.S.A.* **84 J7** 36 42N 119 46W
Cam →, *U.K.* **11 E8** 52 21N 0 16 E
Cam Lam, *Vietnam* **39 G7** 11 54N 109 10 E
Cam Pha, *Vietnam* **38 B6** 21 7N 107 18 E
Cam Ranh, *Vietnam* **39 G7** 11 54N 109 12 E
Cam Xuyen, *Vietnam* **38 C6** 18 15N 106 0 E
Camabatela, *Angola* **52 F3** 8 20S 15 26 E
Camacha, *Madeira* **22 D3** 32 41N 16 49W
Camacho, *Mexico* **86 C4** 24 25N 102 18W
Camacupa, *Angola* **53 G3** 11 58S 17 22 E
Camagüey, *Cuba* **88 B4** 21 20N 78 0W
Camaná, *Peru* **92 G4** 16 30S 72 50W
Camanche Reservoir, *U.S.A.* **84 G6** 38 14N 121 1W
Camaquã →, *Brazil* **95 C5** 31 17S 51 47W
Câmara de Lobos, *Madeira* **22 D3** 32 39N 16 59W
Camargo, *Bolivia* **92 H5** 20 38S 65 15W
Camargue, *France* **18 E6** 43 34N 4 34 E
Camarillo, *U.S.A.* **85 L7** 34 13N 119 2W
Camarón, C., *Honduras* **88 C2** 16 0N 85 5W
Camarones, *Argentina* **96 E3** 44 50S 65 40W
Camas, *U.S.A.* **84 E4** 45 35N 122 24W
Camas Valley, *U.S.A.* **82 E2** 43 2N 123 40W
Cambará, *Brazil* **95 A5** 23 2S 50 5W
Cambay = Khambhat, *India* **42 H5** 22 23N 72 33 E
Cambay, G. of = Khambat, G. of, *India* **42 J5** 20 45N 72 30 E
Cambodia ■, *Asia* **38 F5** 12 15N 105 0 E
Camborne, *U.K.* **11 G2** 50 12N 5 19W
Cambrai, *France* **18 A5** 50 11N 3 14 E
Cambria, *U.S.A.* **83 J3** 35 34N 121 5W
Cambrian Mts., *U.K.* **11 E4** 52 3N 3 57W
Cambridge, *Canada* **70 D3** 43 23N 80 15W
Cambridge, *Jamaica* **88 C4** 18 18N 77 54W
Cambridge, *N.Z.* **59 G5** 37 54S 175 29 E
Cambridge, *U.K.* **11 E8** 52 12N 0 8 E
Cambridge, *Idaho, U.S.A.* **82 D5** 44 34N 116 41W
Cambridge, *Mass., U.S.A.* **79 D13** 42 22N 71 6W
Cambridge, *Md., U.S.A.* **76 F7** 38 34N 76 5W
Cambridge, *Minn., U.S.A.* **80 C8** 45 34N 93 13W
Cambridge, *N.Y., U.S.A.* **79 C11** 43 2N 73 22W
Cambridge, *Nebr., U.S.A.* **80 E4** 40 17N 100 10W
Cambridge, *Ohio, U.S.A.* **78 F3** 40 2N 81 35W
Cambridge Bay, *Canada* **68 B9** 69 10N 105 0W
Cambridge G., *Australia* **60 B4** 14 55S 128 15 E
Cambridge Springs, *U.S.A.* **78 E4** 41 48N 80 4W
Cambridgeshire □, *U.K.* **11 E8** 52 25N 0 7W
Cambuci, *Brazil* **95 A7** 21 35S 41 55W
Cambundi-Catembo, *Angola* **52 G3** 10 10S 17 35 E
Camden, *Ala., U.S.A.* **77 K2** 31 59N 87 17W
Camden, *Ark., U.S.A.* **81 J8** 33 35N 92 50W
Camden, *Maine, U.S.A.* **71 D6** 44 13N 69 4W
Camden, *N.J., U.S.A.* **79 G9** 39 56N 75 7W
Camden, *S.C., U.S.A.* **77 H5** 34 16N 80 36W
Camden Sd., *Australia* **60 C3** 15 27S 124 25 E
Camdenton, *U.S.A.* **81 F8** 38 1N 92 45W
Cameron, *Ariz., U.S.A.* **83 J8** 35 53N 111 25W
Cameron, *La., U.S.A.* **81 L8** 29 48N 93 20W
Cameron, *Mo., U.S.A.* **80 F7** 39 44N 94 14W
Cameron, *Tex., U.S.A.* **81 K6** 30 51N 96 59W
Cameron Falls, *Canada* **70 C2** 49 8N 88 19W
Cameron Highlands, *Malaysia* **39 K3** 4 27N 101 22 E
Cameron Hills, *Canada* **72 B5** 59 48N 118 0W
Cameroon ■, *Africa* **51 G7** 6 0N 12 30 E
Cameroun, Mt., *Cameroon* **50 H6** 4 13N 9 10 E
Cametá, *Brazil* **93 D9** 2 12S 49 30W
Caminha, *Portugal* **19 B1** 41 50N 8 50W
Camino, *U.S.A.* **84 G6** 38 44N 120 41W
Camira Creek, *Australia* **63 D5** 29 15S 152 58 E
Camissombo, *Angola* **52 F4** 8 7S 20 38 E
Cammal, *U.S.A.* **78 E7** 41 24N 77 28W
Camocim, *Brazil* **93 D10** 2 55S 40 50W
Camooweal, *Australia* **62 B2** 19 56S 138 7 E
Camopi →, *Fr. Guiana* **93 C8** 3 10N 52 20W
Camp Crook, *U.S.A.* **80 C3** 45 33N 103 59W
Camp Nelson, *U.S.A.* **85 J8** 36 8N 118 39W
Camp Wood, *U.S.A.* **81 L4** 29 40N 100 1W
Campana, *Argentina* **94 C4** 34 10S 58 55W
Campana, I., *Chile* **96 F1** 48 20S 75 20W
Campanário, *Madeira* **22 D2** 32 39N 17 2W
Campánia □, *Italy* **20 D6** 41 0N 14 30 E
Campbell, *S. Africa* **56 D3** 28 48S 23 44 E
Campbell, *Calif., U.S.A.* **84 H5** 37 17N 121 57W
Campbell, *Ohio, U.S.A.* **78 E4** 41 5N 80 37W
Campbell I., *Pac. Oc.* **64 N8** 52 30S 169 0 E
Campbell L., *Canada* **73 A7** 63 14N 106 55W
Campbell River, *Canada* **72 C3** 50 5N 125 20W
Campbell Town, *Australia* **62 G4** 41 52S 147 30 E
Campbellford, *Canada* **78 B7** 44 18N 77 48W
Campbellpur, *Pakistan* **42 C5** 33 46N 72 26 E
Campbellsville, *U.S.A.* **76 G3** 37 21N 85 20W
Campbellton, *Canada* **71 C6** 47 57N 66 43W
Campbelltown, *Australia* **63 E5** 34 4S 150 49 E
Campbeltown, *U.K.* **12 F3** 55 26N 5 36W
Campeche, *Mexico* **87 D6** 19 50N 90 32W
Campeche □, *Mexico* **87 D6** 19 50N 90 32W
Campeche, B. de, *Mexico* **87 D6** 19 30N 93 0W
Camperdown, *Australia* **63 F3** 38 14S 143 9 E
Camperville, *Canada* **73 C8** 51 59N 100 9W
Campina Grande, *Brazil* **93 E11** 7 20S 35 47W
Campinas, *Brazil* **95 A6** 22 50S 47 0W
Campo, *Cameroon* **52 D1** 2 22N 9 50 E
Campo Belo, *Brazil* **93 H9** 20 52S 45 16W
Campo Formoso, *Brazil* **93 F10** 10 30S 40 20W
Campo Grande, *Brazil* **93 H8** 20 25S 54 40W
Campo Maior, *Brazil* **93 D10** 4 50S 42 12W
Campo Mourão, *Brazil* **95 A5** 24 3S 52 22W
Campoalegre, *Colombia* **92 C3** 2 41N 75 20W
Campobasso, *Italy* **20 D6** 41 34N 14 39 E
Campos, *Brazil* **95 A7** 21 50S 41 20W
Campos Belos, *Brazil* **93 F9** 13 10S 47 3W
Campos del Puerto, *Spain* **22 B10** 39 26N 3 1 E
Campos Novos, *Brazil* **95 B5** 27 21S 51 50W
Camptonville, *U.S.A.* **84 F5** 39 27N 121 3W
Campuya →, *Peru* **92 D4** 1 40S 73 30W
Camrose, *Canada* **72 C6** 53 0N 112 50W
Camsell Portage, *Canada* **73 B7** 59 37N 109 15W
Çan, *Turkey* **21 D12** 40 2N 27 3 E
Can Clavo, *Spain* **22 C7** 38 57N 1 27 E
Can Creu, *Spain* **22 C7** 38 58N 1 28 E
Can Gio, *Vietnam* **39 G6** 10 25N 106 58 E
Can Tho, *Vietnam* **39 G5** 10 2N 105 46 E
Canaan, *U.S.A.* **79 D11** 42 2N 73 20W
Canada ■, *N. Amer.* **68 C10** 60 0N 100 0W
Cañada de Gómez, *Argentina* **94 C3** 32 40S 61 30W
Canadian, *U.S.A.* **81 H4** 35 55N 100 23W
Canadian →, *U.S.A.* **81 H7** 35 28N 95 3W
Canadian Shield, *Canada* **69 C10** 53 0N 75 0W
Çanakkale, *Turkey* **21 D12** 40 8N 26 24 E
Çanakkale Boğazı, *Turkey* **21 D12** 40 17N 26 32 E
Canal Flats, *Canada* **72 C5** 50 10N 115 48W
Canalejas, *Argentina* **94 D2** 35 15S 66 34W
Canals, *Argentina* **94 C3** 33 35S 62 53W
Canandaigua, *U.S.A.* **78 D7** 42 54N 77 17W
Cananea, *Mexico* **86 A2** 31 0N 110 20W
Canarias, Is., *Atl. Oc.* **22 F4** 28 30N 16 0W
Canarreos, Arch. de los, *Cuba* **88 B3** 21 35N 81 40W
Canary Is. = Canarias, Is., *Atl. Oc.* **22 F4** 28 30N 16 0W
Canatlán, *Mexico* **86 C4** 24 31N 104 47W
Canaveral, C., *U.S.A.* **77 L5** 28 27N 80 32W
Canavieiras, *Brazil* **93 G11** 15 39S 39 0W
Canbelego, *Australia* **63 E4** 31 32S 146 18 E
Canberra, *Australia* **63 F4** 35 15S 149 8 E
Canby, *Calif., U.S.A.* **82 F3** 41 27N 120 52W
Canby, *Minn., U.S.A.* **80 C6** 44 43N 96 16W
Canby, *Oreg., U.S.A.* **84 E4** 45 16N 122 42W
Cancún, *Mexico* **87 C7** 21 8N 86 44W
Candala, *Somali Rep.* **46 E4** 11 30N 49 58 E
Candelaria, *Argentina* **95 B4** 27 29S 55 44W
Candelaria, *Canary Is.* **22 F3** 28 22N 16 22W
Candelo, *Australia* **63 F4** 36 47S 149 43 E
Candia = Iráklion, *Greece* **23 D7** 35 20N 25 12 E
Candle L., *Canada* **73 C7** 53 50N 105 18W
Candlemas I., *Antarctica* **5 B1** 57 3S 26 40W
Cando, *U.S.A.* **80 A5** 48 32N 99 12W
Canea = Khaniá, *Greece* **23 D6** 35 30N 24 4 E
Canelones, *Uruguay* **95 C4** 34 32S 56 17W
Cañete, *Chile* **94 D1** 37 50S 73 30W
Cañete, *Peru* **92 F3** 13 8S 76 30W
Cangas de Narcea, *Spain* **19 A2** 43 10N 6 32W
Canguaretama, *Brazil* **93 E11** 6 20S 35 5W
Canguçu, *Brazil* **95 C5** 31 22S 52 43W
Cangzhou, *China* **34 E9** 38 19N 116 52 E
Canicattì, *Italy* **20 F5** 37 21N 13 51 E
Canigou, Mt., *France* **18 E5** 42 31N 2 27 E
Canim Lake, *Canada* **72 C4** 51 47N 120 54W
Canindeyu □, *Paraguay* **95 A4** 24 10S 55 0W
Canipaan, *Phil.* **36 C5** 8 33N 117 15 E
Canisteo, *U.S.A.* **78 D7** 42 16N 77 36W
Canisteo →, *U.S.A.* **78 D7** 42 7N 77 8W
Cañitas, *Mexico* **86 C4** 23 36N 102 43W
Çankırı, *Turkey* **25 F5** 40 40N 33 37 E
Cankuzo, *Burundi* **54 C3** 3 10S 30 31 E
Canmore, *Canada* **72 C5** 51 7N 115 18W
Cann River, *Australia* **63 F4** 37 35S 149 7 E
Canna, *U.K.* **12 D2** 57 3N 6 33W
Cannanore, *India* **40 P9** 11 53N 75 27 E
Cannes, *France* **18 E7** 43 32N 7 1 E
Canning Town = Port Canning, *India* **43 H13** 22 23N 88 40 E
Cannington, *Canada* **78 B5** 44 20N 79 2W
Cannock, *U.K.* **10 E5** 52 41N 2 1W
Cannon Ball →, *U.S.A.* **80 B4** 46 20N 100 38W
Cannondale Mt., *Australia* **62 D4** 25 13S 148 57 E
Canoas, *Brazil* **95 B5** 29 56S 51 11W
Canoe L., *Canada* **73 B7** 55 10N 108 15W
Canon City, *U.S.A.* **80 F2** 38 27N 105 14W
Canora, *Canada* **73 C8** 51 40N 102 30W
Canowindra, *Australia* **63 E4** 33 35S 148 38 E
Canso, *Canada* **71 C7** 45 20N 61 0W
Cantabria □, *Spain* **19 A4** 43 10N 4 0W
Cantabrian Mts. = Cantábrica, Cordillera, *Spain* **19 A3** 43 0N 5 10W
Cantábrica, Cordillera, *Spain* **19 A3** 43 0N 5 10W
Cantal, Plomb du, *France* **18 D5** 45 3N 2 45 E
Canterbury, *Australia* **62 D3** 25 23S 141 53 E
Canterbury, *U.K.* **11 F9** 51 16N 1 6 E
Canterbury □, *N.Z.* **59 K3** 43 45S 171 19 E
Canterbury Bight, *N.Z.* **59 L3** 44 16S 171 55 E
Canterbury Plains, *N.Z.* **59 K3** 43 55S 171 22 E
Cantil, *U.S.A.* **85 K9** 35 18N 117 58W
Canton = Guangzhou, *China* **33 D6** 23 5N 113 10 E
Canton, *Ga., U.S.A.* **77 H3** 34 14N 84 29W
Canton, *Ill., U.S.A.* **80 E9** 40 33N 90 2W
Canton, *Miss., U.S.A.* **81 J9** 32 37N 90 2W
Canton, *Mo., U.S.A.* **80 E9** 40 8N 91 32W
Canton, *N.Y., U.S.A.* **79 B9** 44 36N 75 10W
Canton, *Ohio, U.S.A.* **78 F3** 40 48N 81 23W
Canton, *Okla., U.S.A.* **81 G5** 36 3N 98 35W
Canton, *S. Dak., U.S.A.* **80 D6** 43 18N 96 35W
Canton L., *U.S.A.* **81 G5** 36 6N 98 35W
Canudos, *Brazil* **92 E7** 7 13S 58 5W
Canutama, *Brazil* **92 E6** 6 30S 64 20W
Canutillo, *U.S.A.* **83 L10** 31 55N 106 36W
Canyon, *Tex., U.S.A.* **81 H4** 34 59N 101 55W
Canyon, *Wyo., U.S.A.* **82 D8** 44 43N 110 36W
Canyonlands National Park, *U.S.A.* **83 G9** 38 15N 110 0W
Canyonville, *U.S.A.* **82 E2** 42 56N 123 17W
Cao Bang, *Vietnam* **38 A6** 22 40N 106 15 E
Cao He →, *China* **35 D13** 40 10N 124 32 E
Cao Lanh, *Vietnam* **39 G5** 10 27N 105 38 E
Cao Xian, *China* **34 G8** 34 50N 115 35 E
Cap-aux-Meules, *Canada* **71 C7** 47 23N 61 52W
Cap-Chat, *Canada* **71 C6** 49 6N 66 40W
Cap-de-la-Madeleine, *Canada* **70 C5** 46 22N 72 31W
Cap-Haïtien, *Haiti* **89 C5** 19 40N 72 20W
Cap St.-Jacques = Vung Tau, *Vietnam* **39 G6** 10 21N 107 4 E
Capa, *Vietnam* **38 A4** 22 21N 103 50 E
Capaia, *Angola* **52 F4** 8 27S 20 13 E
Capanaparo →, *Venezuela* **92 B5** 7 1N 67 7W
Cape →, *Australia* **62 C4** 20 59S 146 51 E
Cape Barren I., *Australia* **62 G4** 40 25S 148 15 E
Cape Breton Highlands Nat. Park, *Canada* **71 C7** 46 50N 60 40W
Cape Breton I., *Canada* **71 C7** 46 0N 60 30W
Cape Charles, *U.S.A.* **76 G8** 37 16N 76 1W
Cape Coast, *Ghana* **50 G4** 5 5N 1 15W
Cape Coral, *U.S.A.* **77 M5** 26 33N 81 57W
Cape Dorset, *Canada* **69 B12** 64 14N 76 32W
Cape Dyer, *Canada* **69 B13** 66 30N 61 22W
Cape Fear →, *U.S.A.* **77 H6** 33 53N 78 1W
Cape Girardeau, *U.S.A.* **81 G10** 37 19N 89 32W
Cape Jervis, *Australia* **63 F2** 35 40S 138 5 E
Cape May, *U.S.A.* **76 F8** 38 56N 74 56W
Cape May Point, *U.S.A.* **75 C12** 38 56N 74 58W
Cape Tormentine, *Canada* **71 C7** 46 8N 63 47W
Cape Town, *S. Africa* **56 E2** 33 55S 18 22 E
Cape Verde Is. ■, *Atl. Oc.* **49 E1** 17 10N 25 20W
Cape Vincent, *U.S.A.* **79 B8** 44 8N 76 20W
Cape York Peninsula, *Australia* **62 A3** 12 0S 142 30 E

111

Dera Ghazi Khan

Dadri = Charkhi Dadri, India 42 E7 28 37N 76 17 E
Dadu, Pakistan 42 F2 26 45N 67 45 E
Daet, Phil. 37 B6 14 2N 122 55 E
Dagana, Senegal 50 E1 16 30N 15 35W
Dagestan □, Russia 25 F8 42 30N 47 0 E
Daggett, U.S.A. 85 L10 34 52N 116 52W
Daghestan Republic = Dagestan □, Russia 25 F8 42 30N 47 0 E
Dagö = Hiiumaa, Estonia 9 G20 58 50N 22 45 E
Dagu, China 35 E9 38 59N 117 40 E
Dagupan, Phil. 37 A6 16 3N 120 20 E
Dahlak Kebir, Eritrea 46 D3 15 50N 40 10 E
Dahlonega, U.S.A. 77 H4 34 32N 83 59W
Dahod, India 42 H6 22 50N 74 15 E
Dahomey = Benin ■, Africa 50 G5 10 0N 2 0 E
Dahra, Senegal 50 E1 15 22N 15 30W
Dai Hao, Vietnam 38 C6 18 1N 106 25 E
Dai-Sen, Japan 31 G6 35 22N 133 32 E
Dai Xian, China 34 E7 39 4N 112 58 E
Daicheng, China 34 E9 38 42N 116 38 E
Daingean, Ireland 13 C4 53 18N 7 17W
Daintree, Australia 62 B4 16 20S 145 20 E
Daiō-Misaki, Japan 31 G8 34 15N 136 45 E
Dairût, Egypt 51 C11 27 34N 30 43 E
Daisetsu-Zan, Japan 30 C11 43 30N 142 57 E
Dajarra, Australia 62 C2 21 42S 139 30 E
Dak Dam, Cambodia 38 F6 12 20N 107 21 E
Dak Nhe, Vietnam 38 E6 15 28N 107 48 E
Dak Pek, Vietnam 38 E6 15 4N 107 44 E
Dak Song, Vietnam 39 F6 12 19N 107 35 E
Dak Sui, Vietnam 38 E6 14 55N 107 43 E
Dakar, Senegal 50 F1 14 34N 17 29W
Dakhla, W. Sahara 50 D1 23 50N 15 53W
Dakhla, El Wâhât el-, Egypt 51 C10 25 30N 28 50 E
Dakhovskaya, Russia 25 F7 44 13N 40 13 E
Dakor, India 42 H5 22 45N 73 11 E
Dakota City, U.S.A. 80 D6 42 25N 96 25W
Đakovica, Serbia, Yug. 21 C9 42 22N 20 26 E
Dalachi, China 34 F3 36 48N 105 0 E
Dalai Nur, China 34 C9 43 20N 116 45 E
Dālakī, Iran 45 D6 29 26N 51 17 E
Dalälven, Sweden 9 F17 60 12N 16 43 E
Dalaman →, Turkey 21 F13 36 41N 28 43 E
Dalandzadgad, Mongolia 34 C3 43 27N 104 30 E
Dalarna, Sweden 9 F16 61 0N 14 0 E
Dālbandīn, Pakistan 40 E4 29 0N 64 23 E
Dalbeattie, U.K. 12 G5 54 56N 3 50W
Dalby, Australia 63 D5 27 10S 151 17 E
Dalgān, Iran 45 E8 27 31N 59 19 E
Dalhart, U.S.A. 81 G3 36 4N 102 31W
Dalhousie, Canada 71 C6 48 5N 66 26W
Dalhousie, India 42 C6 32 38N 75 58 E
Dali, Shaanxi, China 34 G5 34 48N 109 58 E
Dali, Yunnan, China 32 D5 25 40N 100 10 E
Dalian, China 35 E11 38 50N 121 40 E
Daliang Shan, China 32 D5 28 0N 102 45 E
Daling He →, China 35 D11 40 55N 121 40 E
Dāliyat el Karmel, Israel 47 C4 32 43N 35 2 E
Dalkeith, U.K. 12 F5 55 54N 3 4W
Dall I., U.S.A. 72 C2 54 59N 133 25W
Dallarnil, Australia 63 D5 25 19S 152 2 E
Dallas, Oreg., U.S.A. 82 D2 44 55N 123 19W
Dallas, Tex., U.S.A. 81 J6 32 47N 96 49W
Dalmacija, Croatia 20 C7 43 20N 17 0 E
Dalmatia = Dalmacija, Croatia 20 C7 43 20N 17 0 E
Dalmellington, U.K. 12 F4 55 19N 4 23W
Dalnegorsk, Russia 27 E14 44 32N 135 33 E
Dalnerechensk, Russia 27 E14 45 50N 133 40 E
Daloa, Ivory C. 50 G3 7 0N 6 30W
Dalsland, Sweden 9 G14 58 50N 12 15 E
Daltenganj, India 43 G11 24 0N 84 4 E
Dalton, Canada 70 C3 48 11N 84 1W
Dalton, Ga., U.S.A. 77 H3 34 46N 84 58W
Dalton, Mass., U.S.A. 79 D11 42 28N 73 11W
Dalton, Nebr., U.S.A. 80 E3 41 25N 102 58W
Dalton Iceberg Tongue, Antarctica 5 C9 66 15S 121 30 E
Dalvík, Iceland 8 D4 65 58N 18 32W
Daly →, Australia 60 B5 13 35S 130 19 E
Daly City, U.S.A. 84 H4 37 42N 122 28W
Daly L., Canada 73 B7 56 32N 105 39W
Daly Waters, Australia 62 B1 16 15S 133 24 E
Dam Doi, Vietnam 39 H5 8 50N 105 12 E
Dam Ha, Vietnam 38 B6 21 21N 107 36 E
Daman, India 40 J8 20 25N 72 57 E
Dāmaneh, Iran 45 C6 33 1N 50 29 E
Damanhûr, Egypt 51 B11 31 0N 30 30 E
Damanzhuang, China 34 E9 38 5N 116 35 E
Damar, Indonesia 37 F7 7 7S 128 40 E
Damaraland, Namibia 56 C2 21 0S 17 0 E
Damascus = Dimashq, Syria 47 B5 33 30N 36 18 E
Damāvand, Iran 45 C7 35 47N 52 0 E
Damāvand, Qolleh-ye, Iran 45 C7 35 56N 52 10 E
Damba, Angola 52 F3 6 44S 15 20 E
Dame Marie, Haiti 89 C5 18 36N 74 26W
Dāmghān, Iran 45 B7 36 10N 54 17 E
Damiel, Spain 19 C4 39 4N 3 37W
Damietta = Dumyât, Egypt 51 B11 31 24N 31 48 E
Daming, China 34 F8 36 15N 115 6 E
Damīr Qābū, Syria 44 B4 36 58N 41 51 E
Dammam = Ad Dammām, Si. Arabia 45 E6 26 20N 50 5 E
Damodar →, India 43 H12 23 17N 87 35 E
Damoh, India 43 H8 23 50N 79 28 E
Dampier, Australia 60 D2 20 41S 116 42 E
Dampier, Selat, Indonesia 37 E8 0 40S 131 0 E
Dampier Arch., Australia 60 D2 20 38S 116 32 E
Damrei, Chuor Phnum, Cambodia 39 G4 11 30N 103 0 E
Dana, Indonesia 37 F6 11 0S 122 52 E
Dana, L., Canada 70 B4 50 53N 77 20W
Dana, Mt., U.S.A. 84 H7 37 54N 119 12W
Danbury, U.S.A. 79 E11 41 24N 73 28W
Danby L., U.S.A. 83 J6 34 13N 115 5W
Dand, Afghan. 42 D1 31 28N 65 32 E
Dandaragan, Australia 61 F2 30 40S 115 40 E
Dandeldhura, Nepal 43 E9 29 20N 80 35 E
Dandeli, India 40 M9 15 5N 74 30 E
Dandenong, Australia 63 F4 38 0S 145 15 E
Dandong, China 35 D13 40 10N 124 20 E
Danfeng, China 34 H6 33 45N 110 25 E
Danforth, U.S.A. 71 C6 45 40N 67 52W
Danger Is. = Pukapuka, Cook Is. 65 J11 10 53S 165 49W
Danger Pt., S. Africa 56 E2 34 40S 19 17 E
Dangora, Nigeria 50 F6 11 30N 8 7 E
Dangrek, Phnom, Thailand 38 E5 14 15N 105 0 E
Dangriga, Belize 87 D7 17 0N 88 13W
Dangshan, China 34 G9 34 27N 116 22 E
Daniel, U.S.A. 82 E8 42 52N 110 4W
Daniel's Harbour, Canada 71 B8 50 13N 57 35W
Danielskuil, S. Africa 56 D3 28 11S 23 33 E
Danielson, U.S.A. 79 E13 41 48N 71 53W
Danilov, Russia 24 C7 58 16N 40 13 E
Daning, China 34 F6 36 28N 110 45 E
Danissa, Kenya 54 B5 3 15N 40 58 E
Dankhar Gompa, India 40 C11 32 10N 78 10 E
Danlí, Honduras 88 D2 14 4N 86 35W
Dannemora, U.S.A. 79 B11 44 43N 73 44W
Dannevirke, N.Z. 59 J6 40 12S 176 8 E
Dannhauser, S. Africa 57 D5 28 0S 30 3 E
Dansville, U.S.A. 78 D7 42 34N 77 42W
Dantan, India 43 J12 21 57N 87 20 E
Dante, Somali Rep. 46 E5 10 25N 51 16 E
Danube = Dunărea →, Europe 17 F15 45 20N 29 40 E
Danube →, Europe 6 F11 45 20N 29 40 E
Danvers, U.S.A. 79 D14 42 34N 70 56W
Danville, Ill., U.S.A. 76 E2 40 8N 87 37W
Danville, Ky., U.S.A. 76 G3 37 39N 84 46W
Danville, Va., U.S.A. 77 G6 36 36N 79 23W
Danzig = Gdańsk, Poland 17 A10 54 22N 18 40 E
Dao, Phil. 37 B6 10 30N 121 57 E
Daoud = Aïn Beïda, Algeria 50 A6 35 50N 7 29 E
Daqing Shan, China 34 D6 40 40N 111 0 E
Dar Banda, Africa 48 F6 8 0N 23 0 E
Dar el Beida = Casablanca, Morocco 50 B3 33 36N 7 36W
Dar es Salaam, Tanzania 54 D4 6 50S 39 12 E
Dar Mazār, Iran 45 D8 29 14N 57 20 E
Dar'ā, Syria 47 C5 32 36N 36 7 E
Dar'ā □, Syria 47 C5 32 55N 36 10 E
Dārāb, Iran 45 D7 28 50N 54 30 E
Daraj, Libya 50 B7 30 10N 10 28 E
Dārān, Iran 45 C6 32 59N 50 24 E
Dārayyā, Syria 47 B5 33 28N 36 15 E
Darband, Pakistan 42 B5 34 20N 72 50 E
Darband, Kūh-e, Iran 45 D8 31 34N 57 8 E
Darbhanga, India 43 F11 26 15N 85 55 E
Darby, U.S.A. 82 C6 46 1N 114 11W
Dardanelle, Ark., U.S.A. 81 H8 35 13N 93 9W
Dardanelle, Calif., U.S.A. 84 G7 38 20N 119 50W
Dardanelles = Çanakkale Boğazı, Turkey 21 D12 40 17N 26 32 E
Dārestān, Iran 45 D8 29 9N 58 42 E
Dârfûr, Sudan 51 F9 13 40N 24 0 E
Dargai, Pakistan 42 B4 34 25N 71 55 E
Dargan Ata, Uzbekistan 26 E7 40 29N 62 10 E
Dargaville, N.Z. 59 F4 35 57S 173 52 E
Darhan Muminggan Lianheqi, China 34 D6 41 40N 110 28 E
Danca, Turkey 21 D13 40 45N 29 23 E
Darién, G. del, Colombia 92 B3 9 0N 77 0W
Dariganga, Mongolia 34 B7 45 21N 113 45 E
Darjeeling = Darjiling, India 43 F13 27 3N 88 18 E
Darjiling, India 43 F13 27 3N 88 18 E
Dark Cove, Canada 71 C9 48 47N 54 13W
Darkan, Australia 61 F2 33 20S 116 43 E
Darkhazīneh, Iran 45 D6 31 54N 48 39 E
Darkot Pass, Pakistan 43 A5 36 45N 73 26 E
Darling →, Australia 63 E3 34 4S 141 54 E
Darling Downs, Australia 63 D5 27 30S 150 30 E
Darling Ra., Australia 61 F2 32 30S 116 0 E
Darlington, U.K. 10 C6 54 32N 1 33W
Darlington, S.C., U.S.A. 77 H6 34 18N 79 52W
Darlington, Wis., U.S.A. 80 D9 42 41N 90 7W
Darlington, L., S. Africa 56 E4 33 10S 25 9 E
Darlot, L., Australia 61 E3 27 48S 121 35 E
Darłowo, Poland 16 A9 54 25N 16 25 E
Darmstadt, Germany 16 D5 49 51N 8 39 E
Darnah, Libya 51 B9 32 45N 22 45 E
Darnall, S. Africa 57 D5 29 23S 31 18 E
Darnley, C., Antarctica 5 C6 68 0S 69 0 E
Darnley B., Canada 68 B7 69 30N 123 30W
Darr, Australia 62 C3 23 13S 144 7 E
Darr →, Australia 62 C3 23 39S 143 50 E
Darrington, U.S.A. 82 B3 48 15N 121 36W
Dart →, U.K. 11 G4 50 24N 3 39W
Dart, C., Antarctica 5 D14 73 6S 126 20W
Dartmoor, U.K. 11 G4 50 38N 3 57W
Dartmouth, Australia 62 C3 23 31S 144 44 E
Dartmouth, Canada 71 D7 44 40N 63 30W
Dartmouth, U.K. 11 G4 50 21N 3 36W
Dartmouth, L., Australia 63 D4 26 4S 145 18 E
Dartuch, C., Spain 22 B10 39 55N 3 49 E
Darvaza, Turkmenistan 26 E6 40 11N 58 24 E
Darvel, Teluk, Malaysia 37 D5 4 50N 118 20 E
Darwha, India 40 J10 20 15N 77 45 E
Darwin, Australia 60 B5 12 25S 130 51 E
Darwin, U.S.A. 85 J9 36 15N 117 35W
Darwin River, Australia 60 B5 12 50S 130 58 E
Daryoi Amu = Amudarya →, Uzbekistan 26 E6 43 58N 59 34 E
Dās, U.A.E. 45 E7 25 20N 53 30 E
Dashetai, China 34 D5 41 0N 109 5 E
Dashhowuz, Turkmenistan 26 E6 41 49N 59 58 E
Dasht, Iran 45 B8 37 17N 56 7 E
Dasht →, Pakistan 40 G2 25 10N 61 40 E
Dasht-e Mārgow, Afghan. 40 D3 30 40N 62 30 E
Dasht-i-Nawar, Afghan. 42 C3 33 52N 68 0 E
Daska, Pakistan 42 C6 32 20N 74 20 E
Datça, Turkey 21 F12 36 46N 27 40 E
Datia, India 43 G8 25 39N 78 27 E
Datong, China 34 D7 40 6N 113 18 E
Datu, Tanjung, Indonesia 36 D3 2 5N 109 39 E
Datu Piang, Phil. 37 C6 7 2N 124 30 E
Daugava →, Latvia 9 H21 57 4N 24 3 E
Daugavpils, Latvia 9 J22 55 53N 26 32 E
Daulpur, India 42 F7 26 45N 77 59 E
Dauphin, Canada 73 C8 51 9N 100 5W
Dauphin I., U.S.A. 77 K1 30 15N 88 11W
Dauphin L., Canada 73 C9 51 20N 99 45W
Dauphiné, France 18 D6 45 15N 5 25 E
Dausa, India 42 F7 26 52N 76 20 E
Davangere, India 40 M9 14 25N 75 55 E
Davao, Phil. 37 C7 7 0N 125 40 E
Davao, G. of, Phil. 37 C7 6 30N 125 48 E
Dāvar Panāh, Iran 45 E9 27 25N 62 15 E
Davenport, Calif., U.S.A. 84 H4 37 1N 122 12W
Davenport, Iowa, U.S.A. 80 E9 41 32N 90 35W
Davenport, Wash., U.S.A. 82 C4 47 39N 118 9W
Davenport Downs, Australia 62 C3 24 8S 141 7 E
Davenport Ra., Australia 62 C1 20 28S 134 0 E
David, Panama 88 E3 8 30N 82 30W
David City, U.S.A. 80 E6 41 15N 97 8W
David Gorodok = Davyd Haradok, Belarus 17 B14 52 4N 27 8 E
Davidson, Canada 73 C7 51 16N 105 59W
Davis, U.S.A. 84 G5 38 33N 121 44W
Davis Dam, U.S.A. 85 K12 35 11N 114 34W
Davis Inlet, Canada 71 A7 55 50N 60 59W
Davis Mts., U.S.A. 81 K2 30 50N 103 55W
Davis Sea, Antarctica 5 C7 66 0S 92 0 E
Davis Str., N. Amer. 69 B14 65 0N 58 0W
Davos, Switz. 16 E5 46 48N 9 49 E
Davy L., Canada 73 B7 58 53N 108 18W
Davyd Haradok, Belarus 17 B14 52 4N 27 8 E
Dawes Ra., Australia 62 C5 24 40S 150 40 E
Dawson, Canada 68 B6 64 10N 139 30W
Dawson, Ga., U.S.A. 77 K3 31 46N 84 27W
Dawson, N. Dak., U.S.A. 80 B5 46 52N 99 45W
Dawson, I., Chile 96 G2 53 50S 70 50W
Dawson Creek, Canada 72 B4 55 45N 120 15W
Dawson Inlet, Canada 73 A10 61 50N 93 25W
Dawson Ra., Australia 62 C4 24 30S 149 48 E
Dax, France 18 E3 43 44N 1 3W
Daxian, China 32 C5 31 15N 107 23 E
Daxindian, China 35 F11 37 30N 120 50 E
Daxinggou, China 35 C15 43 25N 129 40 E
Daxue Shan, China 32 C5 30 30N 101 30 E
Daylesford, Australia 63 F3 37 21S 144 9 E
Dayr az Zawr, Syria 44 C4 35 20N 40 5 E
Daysland, Canada 72 C6 52 50N 112 20W
Dayton, Nev., U.S.A. 84 F7 39 14N 119 36W
Dayton, Ohio, U.S.A. 76 F3 39 45N 84 12W
Dayton, Pa., U.S.A. 78 F5 40 53N 79 15W
Dayton, Tenn., U.S.A. 77 H3 35 30N 85 1W
Dayton, Wash., U.S.A. 82 C4 46 19N 117 59W
Daytona Beach, U.S.A. 77 L5 29 13N 81 1W
Dayville, U.S.A. 82 D4 44 28N 119 32W
De Aar, S. Africa 56 E3 30 39S 24 0 E
De Funiak Springs, U.S.A. 77 K2 30 43N 86 7W
De Grey, Australia 60 D2 20 12S 119 12 E
De Grey →, Australia 60 D2 20 12S 119 13 E
De Kalb, U.S.A. 80 E10 41 56N 88 46W
De Land, U.S.A. 77 L5 29 2N 81 18W
De Leon, U.S.A. 81 J5 32 7N 98 32W
De Pere, U.S.A. 76 C1 44 27N 88 4W
De Queen, U.S.A. 81 H7 34 2N 94 21W
De Quincy, U.S.A. 81 K8 30 27N 93 26W
De Ridder, U.S.A. 81 K8 30 51N 93 17W
De Smet, U.S.A. 80 C6 44 23N 97 33W
De Soto, U.S.A. 80 F9 38 8N 90 34W
De Tour Village, U.S.A. 76 C4 46 0N 83 56W
De Witt, U.S.A. 81 H9 34 18N 91 20W
Dead Sea, Asia 47 D4 31 30N 35 30 E
Deadwood, U.S.A. 80 C3 44 23N 103 44W
Deadwood L., Canada 72 B3 59 10N 128 30W
Deakin, Australia 61 F4 30 46S 128 58 E
Deal, U.K. 11 F9 51 13N 1 25 E
Deal I., Australia 62 F4 39 30S 147 20 E
Dealesville, S. Africa 56 D4 28 41S 25 44 E
Dean, Forest of, U.K. 11 F5 51 45N 2 33W
Deán Funes, Argentina 94 C3 30 20S 64 20W
Dearborn, U.S.A. 70 D3 42 19N 83 11W
Dease →, Canada 72 B3 59 56N 128 32W
Dease L., Canada 72 B2 58 40N 130 5W
Dease Lake, Canada 72 B2 58 25N 130 6W
Death Valley, U.S.A. 85 J10 36 15N 116 50W
Death Valley Junction, U.S.A. 85 J10 36 20N 116 25W
Death Valley National Monument, U.S.A. 85 J10 36 45N 117 15W
Deba Habe, Nigeria 50 F7 10 14N 11 20 E
Debar, Macedonia 21 D9 41 31N 20 30 E
Debden, Canada 73 C7 53 30N 106 50W
Dębica, Poland 17 C11 50 2N 21 25 E
Debolt, Canada 72 B5 55 12N 118 1W
Deborah East, L., Australia 61 F2 30 45S 119 0 E
Deborah West, L., Australia 61 F2 30 45S 118 50 E
Debre Markos, Ethiopia 51 F12 10 20N 37 40 E
Debre Tabor, Ethiopia 51 F12 11 50N 38 26 E
Debrecen, Hungary 17 E11 47 33N 21 42 E
Decatur, Ala., U.S.A. 77 H2 34 36N 86 59W
Decatur, Ga., U.S.A. 77 J3 33 47N 84 18W
Decatur, Ill., U.S.A. 80 F10 39 51N 88 57W
Decatur, Ind., U.S.A. 76 E3 40 50N 84 56W
Decatur, Tex., U.S.A. 81 J6 33 14N 97 35W
Deccan, India 40 M10 18 0N 79 0 E
Deception L., Canada 73 B8 56 33N 104 13W
Děčín, Czech. 16 C8 50 47N 14 12 E
Deckerville, U.S.A. 78 C2 43 32N 82 44W
Decorah, U.S.A. 80 D9 43 18N 91 48W
Dedéagach = Alexandroúpolis, Greece 21 D11 40 50N 25 54 E
Dedham, U.S.A. 79 D13 42 15N 71 10W
Dédougou, Burkina Faso 50 F4 12 30N 3 25W
Dedza, Malawi 55 E3 14 20S 34 20 E
Dee →, C. of Aberd., U.K. 12 D6 57 9N 2 5W
Dee →, Wales, U.K. 10 D4 53 22N 3 17W
Deep B., Canada 72 A5 61 15N 116 35W
Deep Well, Australia 62 C1 24 20S 134 0 E
Deepwater, Australia 63 D5 29 25S 151 51 E
Deer →, Canada 73 B10 58 23N 94 13W
Deer Lake, Nfld., Canada 71 C8 49 11N 57 27W
Deer Lake, Ont., Canada 73 C10 52 36N 94 20W
Deer Lodge, U.S.A. 82 C7 46 24N 112 44W
Deer Park, U.S.A. 82 C5 47 57N 117 28W
Deer River, U.S.A. 80 B8 47 20N 93 48W
Deeral, Australia 62 B4 17 14S 145 55 E
Deerdepoort, S. Africa 56 C4 24 37S 26 27 E
Deferiet, U.S.A. 79 B9 44 2N 75 41W
Defiance, U.S.A. 76 E3 41 17N 84 22W
Degeh Bur, Ethiopia 46 F3 8 11N 43 31 E
Deggendorf, Germany 16 D7 48 50N 12 57 E
Deh Bīd, Iran 45 D7 30 39N 53 11 E
Deh-e Shīr, Iran 45 D7 31 29N 53 45 E
Dehaj, Iran 45 D7 30 42N 54 53 E
Dehdez, Iran 45 D6 31 43N 50 17 E
Dehestān, Iran 45 D7 28 30N 55 35 E
Dehgolān, Iran 44 C5 35 17N 47 25 E
Dehi Titan, Afghan. 40 C3 33 45N 63 50 E
Dehibat, Tunisia 50 B7 32 0N 10 47 E
Dehlorān, Iran 44 C5 32 41N 47 16 E
Dehnow-e Kūhestān, Iran 45 E8 27 58N 58 32 E
Dehra Dun, India 42 D8 30 20N 78 4 E
Dehri, India 43 G11 24 50N 84 15 E
Dehui, China 35 B13 44 30N 125 40 E
Deinze, Belgium 15 D3 50 59N 3 32 E
Dej, Romania 17 E12 47 10N 23 52 E
Dekese, Zaïre 52 E4 3 24S 21 24 E
Del Mar, U.S.A. 85 N9 32 58N 117 16W
Del Norte, U.S.A. 83 H10 37 41N 106 21W
Del Rio, U.S.A. 81 L4 29 22N 100 54W
Delano, U.S.A. 85 K7 35 46N 119 15W
Delareyville, S. Africa 56 D4 26 41S 25 26 E
Delavan, U.S.A. 80 D10 42 38N 88 39W
Delaware, U.S.A. 76 E4 40 18N 83 4W
Delaware □, U.S.A. 76 F8 39 0N 75 20W
Delaware →, U.S.A. 76 F8 39 15N 75 20W
Delaware B., U.S.A. 75 C12 39 0N 75 10W
Delegate, Australia 63 F4 37 4S 148 56 E
Delft, Neths. 15 B4 52 1N 4 22 E
Delfzijl, Neths. 15 A6 53 20N 6 55 E
Delgado, C., Mozam. 55 E5 10 45S 40 40 E
Delgerhet, Mongolia 34 B6 45 50N 110 30 E
Delgo, Sudan 51 D11 20 6N 30 40 E
Delhi, Canada 78 D4 42 51N 80 30W
Delhi, India 42 E7 28 38N 77 17 E
Delhi, U.S.A. 79 D10 42 17N 74 55W
Delia, Canada 72 C6 51 38N 112 23W
Delice →, Turkey 25 G5 39 45N 34 15 E
Delicias, Mexico 86 B3 28 10N 105 30W
Delījān, Iran 45 C6 33 59N 50 40 E
Déline, Canada 68 B7 65 10N 123 30W
Dell City, U.S.A. 83 L11 31 56N 105 12W
Dell Rapids, U.S.A. 80 D6 43 50N 96 43W
Delmar, U.S.A. 79 D11 42 37N 73 47W
Delmenhorst, Germany 16 B5 53 3N 8 37 E
Delmiro Gouveia, Brazil 93 E11 9 24S 38 6W
Delong, Ostrova, Russia 27 B15 76 40N 149 20 E
Deloraine, Australia 62 G4 41 30S 146 40 E
Deloraine, Canada 73 D8 49 15N 100 29W
Delphi, U.S.A. 76 E2 40 36N 86 41W
Delphos, U.S.A. 76 E3 40 51N 84 21W
Delportshoop, S. Africa 56 D3 28 22S 24 20 E
Delray Beach, U.S.A. 77 M5 26 28N 80 4W
Delta, Colo., U.S.A. 83 G9 38 44N 108 4W
Delta, Utah, U.S.A. 82 G7 39 21N 112 35W
Delungra, Australia 63 D5 29 39S 150 51 E
Delvinë, Albania 21 E9 39 59N 20 4 E
Demanda, Sierra de la, Spain 19 A4 42 15N 3 0W
Demavand = Damāvand, Iran 45 C7 35 47N 52 0 E
Demba, Zaïre 52 F4 5 28S 22 15 E
Dembecha, Ethiopia 51 F12 10 32N 37 30 E
Dembia, Zaïre 54 B2 3 33N 25 48 E
Dembidolo, Ethiopia 51 G11 8 34N 34 50 E
Demer →, Belgium 15 D4 50 57N 4 42 E
Deming, N. Mex., U.S.A. 83 K10 32 16N 107 46W
Deming, Wash., U.S.A. 84 B4 48 50N 122 13W
Demini →, Brazil 92 D6 0 46S 62 56W
Demirci, Turkey 21 E13 39 2N 28 38 E
Demirköy, Turkey 21 D12 41 49N 27 45 E
Demopolis, U.S.A. 77 J2 32 31N 87 50W
Dempo, Indonesia 36 E2 4 2S 103 15 E
Den Burg, Neths. 15 A4 53 3N 4 47 E
Den Chai, Thailand 38 D3 17 59N 100 4 E
Den Haag = 's-Gravenhage, Neths. 15 B4 52 7N 4 17 E
Den Helder, Neths. 15 B4 52 57N 4 45 E
Den Oever, Neths. 15 B5 52 56N 5 2 E
Denain, France 15 D3 50 20N 3 22 E
Denair, U.S.A. 84 H6 37 32N 120 48W
Denau, Uzbekistan 26 F7 38 16N 67 54 E
Denbigh, U.K. 10 D4 53 12N 3 25W
Denbighshire □, U.K. 10 D4 53 8N 3 22W
Dendang, Indonesia 36 E3 3 7S 107 56 E
Dendermonde, Belgium 15 C4 51 2N 4 5 E
Dengfeng, China 34 G7 34 25N 113 2 E
Dengkou, China 34 D4 40 18N 106 55 E
Denham, Australia 61 E1 25 56S 113 31 E
Denham Ra., Australia 62 C4 21 55S 147 46 E
Denham Sd., Australia 61 E1 25 45S 113 15 E
Denia, Spain 19 C6 38 49N 0 8 E
Denial B., Australia 63 E1 32 14S 133 32 E
Deniliquin, Australia 63 F3 35 30S 144 58 E
Denison, Iowa, U.S.A. 80 D7 42 1N 95 21W
Denison, Tex., U.S.A. 81 J6 33 45N 96 33W
Denison Plains, Australia 60 C4 18 35S 128 0 E
Denizli, Turkey 25 G4 37 42N 29 2 E
Denman Glacier, Antarctica 5 C7 66 45S 99 25 E
Denmark, Australia 61 F2 34 59S 117 25 E
Denmark ■, Europe 9 J13 55 30N 9 0 E
Denmark Str., Atl. Oc. 4 C6 66 0N 30 0W
Dennison, U.S.A. 78 F3 40 24N 81 19W
Denpasar, Indonesia 36 F5 8 45S 115 14 E
Denton, Mont., U.S.A. 82 C9 47 19N 109 57W
Denton, Tex., U.S.A. 81 J6 33 13N 97 8W
D'Entrecasteaux, Pt., Australia 61 F2 34 50S 115 57 E
Denver, U.S.A. 80 F2 39 44N 104 59W
Denver City, U.S.A. 81 J3 32 58N 102 50W
Deoband, India 42 E7 29 42N 77 43 E
Deoghar, India 43 G12 24 30N 86 42 E
Deolali, India 40 K8 19 58N 73 50 E
Deoli = Devli, India 42 G6 25 50N 75 20 E
Deoria, India 43 F10 26 31N 83 48 E
Deosai Mts., Pakistan 43 B6 35 40N 75 0 E
Deping, China 35 F9 37 25N 116 58 E
Deposit, U.S.A. 79 D9 42 4N 75 25W
Depot Springs, Australia 61 E3 27 55S 120 3 E
Deputatskiy, Russia 27 C14 69 18N 139 54 E
Dera Ghazi Khan, Pakistan 42 D4 30 5N 70 43 E

Dera Ismail Khan

Dera Ismail Khan, Pakistan 42 D4 31 50N 70 50 E
Derbent, Russia 25 F8 42 5N 48 15 E
Derby, Australia 60 C3 17 18S 123 38 E
Derby, U.K. 10 E6 52 56N 1 28W
Derby, Conn., U.S.A. 79 E11 41 19N 73 5W
Derby, N.Y., U.S.A. 78 D6 42 41N 78 58W
Derbyshire □, U.K. 10 E6 53 11N 1 38W
Derg →, U.K. 13 B4 54 44N 7 26W
Derg, L., Ireland 13 D3 53 0N 8 20W
Dergaon, India 41 F19 26 45N 94 0 E
Dernieres, Isles, U.S.A. 81 L9 29 2N 90 50W
Derry = Londonderry, U.K. 13 B4 55 0N 7 20W
Derryveagh Mts., Ireland 13 B3 54 56N 8 11W
Derudub, Sudan 51 E12 17 31N 36 7 E
Derwent, Canada 73 C6 53 41N 110 58W
Derwent →, Derby, U.K. 10 E6 52 57N 1 28W
Derwent →, N. Yorks., U.K. 10 D7 53 45N 0 58W
Derwent Water, U.K. 10 C4 54 35N 3 9W
Des Moines, Iowa, U.S.A. 80 E8 41 35N 93 37W
Des Moines, N. Mex., U.S.A. 81 G3 36 46N 103 50W
Des Moines →, U.S.A. 80 E9 40 23N 91 25W
Desaguadero →, Argentina 94 C2 34 30S 66 46W
Desaguadero →, Bolivia 92 G5 16 35S 69 5W
Descanso, Pta., Mexico 85 N9 32 21N 117 3W
Deschaillons, Canada 71 C5 46 32N 72 7W
Descharme →, Canada 73 B7 56 51N 109 13W
Deschutes →, U.S.A. 82 D3 45 38N 120 55W
Dese, Ethiopia 46 E2 11 5N 39 40 E
Desert Center, U.S.A. 85 M11 33 43N 115 24W
Desert Hot Springs, U.S.A. 85 M10 33 58N 116 30W
Désirade, I., Guadeloupe 89 C7 16 18N 61 3W
Deskenatlata L., Canada 72 A6 60 55N 112 3W
Desna →, Ukraine 17 C16 50 33N 30 32 E
Desolación, I., Chile 96 G2 53 0S 74 0W
Despeñaperros, Paso, Spain 19 C4 38 24N 3 30W
Dessau, Germany 16 C7 51 51N 12 14 E
Dessye = Dese, Ethiopia 46 E2 11 5N 39 40 E
D'Estrees B., Australia 63 F2 35 55S 137 45 E
Desuri, India 42 G5 25 18N 73 35 E
Det Udom, Thailand 38 E5 14 54N 105 5 E
Dete, Zimbabwe 55 F2 18 38S 26 50 E
Detmold, Germany 16 C5 51 56N 8 52 E
Detour, Pt., U.S.A. 76 C2 45 40N 86 40W
Detroit, Mich., U.S.A. 75 B10 42 20N 83 3W
Detroit, Tex., U.S.A. 81 J7 33 40N 95 16W
Detroit Lakes, U.S.A. 80 B7 46 49N 95 51W
Deurne, Belgium 15 C4 51 12N 4 24 E
Deurne, Neths. 15 C5 51 27N 5 49 E
Deutsche Bucht, Germany 16 A5 54 15N 8 0 E
Deva, Romania 17 F12 45 53N 22 55 E
Devakottai, India 40 Q11 9 55N 78 45 E
Devaprayag, India 43 D8 30 13N 78 35 E
Deventer, Neths. 15 B6 52 15N 6 10 E
Deveron →, U.K. 12 D6 57 41N 2 32W
Devgadh Bariya, India 42 H5 22 40N 73 55 E
Devils Den, U.S.A. 84 K7 35 46N 119 58W
Devils Lake, U.S.A. 80 A5 48 7N 98 52W
Devils Paw, Canada 72 B2 58 47N 134 0W
Devizes, U.K. 11 F6 51 22N 1 58W
Devli, India 42 G6 25 50N 75 20 E
Devon, Canada 72 C6 53 24N 113 44W
Devon □, U.K. 11 G4 50 50N 3 40W
Devon I., Canada 4 B3 75 10N 85 0W
Devonport, Australia 62 G4 41 10S 146 22 E
Devonport, N.Z. 59 G5 36 49S 174 49 E
Devonport, U.K. 11 G3 50 22N 4 11W
Dewas, India 42 H7 22 59N 76 3 E
Dewetsdorp, S. Africa 56 D4 29 33S 26 39 E
Dewsbury, U.K. 10 D6 53 42N 1 37W
Dexter, Mo., U.S.A. 81 G9 36 48N 89 57W
Dexter, N. Mex., U.S.A. 81 J2 33 12N 104 22W
Dey-Dey, L., Australia 61 E5 29 12S 131 4 E
Deyhūk, Iran 45 C8 33 15N 57 30 E
Deyyer, Iran 45 E6 27 55N 51 55 E
Dezadeash L., Canada 72 A1 60 28N 136 58W
Dezfūl, Iran 45 C6 32 20N 48 30 E
Dezhneva, Mys, Russia 27 C19 66 5N 169 40W
Dezhou, China 34 F9 37 26N 116 18 E
Dháfni, Greece 23 D7 35 13N 25 3 E
Dhahiriya = Az Zāhirīyah, West Bank 47 D3 31 25N 34 58 E
Dhahran = Az Zahrān, Si. Arabia 45 E6 26 10N 50 7 E
Dhaka, Bangla. 43 H14 23 43N 90 26 E
Dhaka □, Bangla. 43 G14 24 25N 90 25 E
Dhali, Cyprus 23 D12 35 1N 33 25 E
Dhamar, Yemen 46 E3 14 30N 44 20 E
Dhampur, India 43 E8 29 19N 78 33 E
Dhamtari, India 41 J12 20 42N 81 35 E
Dhanbad, India 43 H12 23 50N 86 30 E
Dhangarhi, Nepal 41 E12 28 55N 80 40 E
Dhankuta, Nepal 43 F12 26 55N 87 40 E
Dhar, India 42 H6 22 35N 75 26 E
Dharampur, India 42 H6 22 13N 75 18 E
Dharamsala = Dharmsala, India 42 C7 32 16N 76 23 E
Dharmapuri, India 40 N11 12 10N 78 10 E
Dharmsala, India 42 C7 32 16N 76 23 E
Dharwad, India 40 M9 15 22N 75 15 E
Dhaulagiri, Nepal 43 E10 28 39N 83 28 E
Dhebar, L., India 42 G6 24 10N 74 0 E
Dheftera, Cyprus 23 D12 35 5N 33 16 E
Dhenkanal, India 41 J14 20 45N 85 35 E
Dherinia, Cyprus 23 D12 35 3N 33 57 E
Dhiarrizos →, Cyprus 23 E11 34 41N 32 34 E
Dhībān, Jordan 47 D4 31 30N 35 46 E
Dhíkti Óros, Greece 23 D7 35 8N 25 22 E
Dhírfis, Greece 21 E10 38 40N 23 54 E
Dhodhekánisos, Greece 21 F12 36 35N 27 0 E
Dholka, India 42 H5 22 44N 72 29 E
Dhoraji, India 42 J4 21 45N 70 37 E
Dhráhstis, Ákra, Greece 23 A3 39 48N 19 40 E
Dhrangadhra, India 42 H4 22 59N 71 31 E
Dhrápanon, Ákra, Greece 23 D6 35 28N 24 14 E
Dhrol, India 42 H4 22 33N 70 25 E
Dhuburi, India 41 F16 26 2N 89 59 E
Dhule, India 40 J9 20 58N 74 50 E
Dhut →, Somali Rep. 46 E5 10 30N 50 0 E
Di Linh, Vietnam 39 G7 11 35N 108 4 E
Di Linh, Cao Nguyen, Vietnam 39 G7 11 30N 108 0 E
Día, Greece 23 D7 35 28N 25 14 E
Diablo, Mt., U.S.A. 84 H5 37 53N 121 56W
Diablo Range, U.S.A. 84 J5 37 20N 121 25W
Diafarabé, Mali 50 F4 14 9N 4 57W
Diamante, Argentina 94 C3 32 5S 60 40W
Diamante →, Argentina 94 C2 34 30S 66 46W
Diamantina, Brazil 93 G10 18 17S 43 40W
Diamantina →, Australia 63 D2 26 45S 139 10 E
Diamantino, Brazil 93 F7 14 30S 56 30W
Diamond Bar, U.S.A. 85 L9 34 1N 117 48W
Diamond Harbour, India 43 H13 22 11N 88 14 E
Diamond Is., Australia 62 B5 17 25S 151 5 E
Diamond Mts., U.S.A. 82 G6 39 50N 115 30W
Diamond Springs, U.S.A. 84 G6 38 42N 120 49W
Diamondville, U.S.A. 82 F8 41 47N 110 32W
Diapaga, Burkina Faso 50 F5 12 5N 1 46 E
Dibā, Oman 45 E8 25 45N 56 16 E
Dibaya, Zaïre 52 F4 6 30S 22 57 E
Dibaya-Lubue, Zaïre 52 E3 4 12S 19 54 E
Dibbi, Ethiopia 46 G3 4 10N 41 52 E
Dibete, Botswana 56 C4 23 45S 26 32 E
Dibrugarh, India 41 F19 27 29N 94 55 E
Dickinson, U.S.A. 80 B3 46 53N 102 47W
Dickson, Russia 26 B9 73 40N 80 5 E
Dickson, U.S.A. 77 G2 36 5N 87 23W
Dickson City, U.S.A. 79 E9 41 29N 75 40W
Didiéni, Mali 50 F3 13 53N 8 6W
Didsbury, Canada 72 C6 51 35N 114 10W
Didwana, India 42 F6 27 23N 74 36 E
Diébougou, Burkina Faso 50 F4 11 0N 3 15W
Diefenbaker L., Canada 73 C7 51 0N 106 55W
Diego Garcia, Ind. Oc. 3 E13 7 50S 72 50 E
Diekirch, Lux. 15 E6 49 52N 6 10 E
Dien Ban, Vietnam 38 E7 15 53N 108 16 E
Dien Bien, Vietnam 38 B4 21 20N 103 0 E
Dien Khanh, Vietnam 39 F7 12 15N 109 6 E
Dieppe, France 18 B4 49 54N 1 4 E
Dieren, Neths. 15 B6 52 3N 6 6 E
Dierks, U.S.A. 81 H7 34 7N 94 1W
Diest, Belgium 15 D5 50 58N 5 4 E
Differdange, Lux. 15 E5 49 31N 5 54 E
Dig, India 42 F7 27 28N 77 20 E
Digba, Zaïre 54 B2 4 25N 25 48 E
Digby, Canada 71 D6 44 38N 65 50W
Digges, Canada 73 B10 58 40N 94 0W
Digges Is., Canada 69 B12 62 40N 77 50W
Dighinala, Bangla. 41 H18 23 15N 92 5 E
Dighton, U.S.A. 80 F4 38 29N 100 28W
Digne-les-Bains, France 18 D7 44 5N 6 12 E
Digos, Phil. 37 C7 6 45N 125 20 E
Digranes, Iceland 8 C6 66 4N 14 44W
Digul →, Indonesia 37 F9 7 7S 138 42 E
Dihang →, India 41 F19 27 48N 95 30 E
Dīhōk, Iraq 44 B3 36 50N 43 1 E
Dijlah, Nahr →, Asia 44 D5 31 0N 47 25 E
Dijon, France 18 C6 47 20N 5 3 E
Dikimdya, Russia 27 D13 59 1N 121 47 E
Dikomu di Kai, Botswana 56 C3 24 58S 24 36 E
Diksmuide, Belgium 15 C2 51 2N 2 52 E
Dikson = Dickson, Russia 26 B9 73 40N 80 5 E
Dikwa, Nigeria 51 F7 12 4N 13 30 E
Dili, Indonesia 37 F7 8 39S 125 34 E
Dilley, U.S.A. 81 L5 28 40N 99 10W
Dilling, Sudan 51 F10 12 3N 29 35 E
Dillingham, U.S.A. 68 C4 59 3N 158 28W
Dillon, Canada 73 B7 55 56N 108 35W
Dillon, Mont., U.S.A. 82 D7 45 13N 112 38W
Dillon, S.C., U.S.A. 77 H6 34 25N 79 22W
Dillon →, Canada 73 B7 55 56N 108 56W
Dilolo, Zaïre 52 G4 10 28S 22 18 E
Dilston, Australia 62 G4 41 22S 147 10 E
Dimas, Mexico 86 C3 23 43N 106 47W
Dimashq, Syria 47 B5 33 30N 36 18 E
Dimashq □, Syria 47 B5 33 30N 36 30 E
Dimbaza, S. Africa 57 E4 32 50S 27 14 E
Dimbokro, Ivory C. 50 G4 6 45N 4 46W
Dimboola, Australia 63 F3 36 28S 142 7 E
Dîmboviţa →, Romania 17 F14 44 5N 26 35 E
Dimbulah, Australia 62 B4 17 8S 145 4 E
Dimitrovgrad, Bulgaria 21 C11 42 5N 25 35 E
Dimitrovgrad, Russia 24 D8 54 14N 49 39 E
Dimitrovo = Pernik, Bulgaria 21 C10 42 35N 23 2 E
Dimmitt, U.S.A. 81 H3 34 33N 102 19W
Dimona, Israel 47 D4 31 2N 35 1 E
Dinagat, Phil. 37 B7 10 10N 125 40 E
Dinajpur, Bangla. 41 G16 25 33N 88 43 E
Dinan, France 18 B2 48 28N 2 2W
Dinān Āb, Iran 45 C8 32 4N 56 49 E
Dinant, Belgium 15 D4 50 16N 4 55 E
Dinapur, India 43 G11 25 38N 85 5 E
Dinār, Kūh-e, Iran 45 D6 30 42N 51 46 E
Dinara Planina, Croatia 20 C7 44 0N 16 30 E
Dinard, France 18 B2 48 38N 2 6W
Dinaric Alps = Dinara Planina, Croatia 20 C7 44 0N 16 30 E
Dindigul, India 40 P11 10 25N 78 0 E
Ding Xian, China 34 E8 38 30N 114 59 E
Dingbian, China 34 F4 37 35N 107 32 E
Dingle, Ireland 13 D1 52 9N 10 17W
Dingle B., Ireland 13 D1 52 3N 10 20W
Dingmans Ferry, U.S.A. 79 E10 41 13N 74 55W
Dingo, Australia 62 C4 23 38S 149 19 E
Dingtao, China 34 G8 35 5N 115 35 E
Dinguiraye, Guinea 50 F2 11 18N 10 49W
Dingwall, U.K. 12 D4 57 36N 4 26W
Dingxi, China 34 G3 35 30N 104 33 E
Dingxiang, China 34 E7 38 30N 112 58 E
Dinh, Mui, Vietnam 39 G7 11 22N 109 1 E
Dinh Lap, Vietnam 38 B6 21 33N 107 6 E
Dinokwe, Botswana 56 C4 23 29S 26 37 E
Dinosaur National Monument, U.S.A. 82 F9 40 30N 108 45W
Dinuba, U.S.A. 83 H4 36 32N 119 23W
Diourbel, Senegal 50 F1 14 39N 16 12W
Diplo, Pakistan 42 G3 24 35N 69 35 E
Dipolog, Phil. 37 C6 8 36N 123 20 E
Dir, Pakistan 40 B7 35 8N 71 59 E
Diré, Mali 50 E4 16 20N 3 25W
Dire Dawa, Ethiopia 46 F3 9 35N 41 45 E
Diriamba, Nic. 88 D2 11 51N 86 19W
Dirico, Angola 53 H4 17 50S 20 42 E
Dirk Hartog I., Australia 61 E1 25 50S 113 5 E
Dirranbandi, Australia 63 D4 28 33S 148 17 E
Disa, India 42 G5 24 18N 72 10 E
Disappointment, C., U.S.A. 82 C1 46 18N 124 5W
Disappointment, L., Australia 60 D3 23 20S 122 40 E
Disaster B., Australia 63 F4 37 15S 149 58 E
Discovery B., Australia 63 F3 38 10S 140 40 E
Disko, Greenland 4 C5 69 45N 53 30W
Disko Bugt, Greenland 4 C5 69 10N 52 0W
Disteghil Sar, Pakistan 43 A6 36 20N 75 12 E
Distrito Federal □, Brazil 93 G9 15 45S 47 45W
Diu, India 42 J4 20 45N 70 58 E
Dīvāndarreh, Iran 44 C5 35 55N 47 2 E
Divide, U.S.A. 82 D7 45 45N 112 45W
Dividing Ra., Australia 61 E2 27 45S 116 0 E
Divinópolis, Brazil 93 H10 20 10S 44 54W
Divnoye, Russia 25 E7 45 55N 43 21 E
Dīwāl Kol, Afghan. 42 B2 34 23N 67 52 E
Dixie Mt., U.S.A. 84 F6 39 55N 120 16W
Dixon, Calif., U.S.A. 84 G5 38 27N 121 49W
Dixon, Ill., U.S.A. 80 E10 41 50N 89 29W
Dixon, Mont., U.S.A. 82 C6 47 19N 114 19W
Dixon, N. Mex., U.S.A. 83 H11 36 12N 105 53W
Dixon Entrance, U.S.A. 72 C2 54 30N 132 0W
Dixonville, Canada 72 B5 56 32N 117 40W
Diyarbakır, Turkey 25 G7 37 55N 40 18 E
Djado, Niger 51 D7 21 4N 12 14 E
Djakarta = Jakarta, Indonesia 37 G12 6 9S 106 49 E
Djamba, Angola 56 B1 16 45S 13 58 E
Djambala, Congo 52 E2 2 32S 14 30 E
Djanet, Algeria 50 D6 24 35N 9 32 E
Djawa = Jawa, Indonesia 37 G14 7 0S 110 0 E
Djelfa, Algeria 50 B5 34 40N 3 15 E
Djema, C.A.R. 54 A2 6 3N 25 15 E
Djenné, Mali 50 F4 14 0N 4 30W
Djerba, I. de, Tunisia 51 B7 33 50N 10 48 E
Djerid, Chott, Tunisia 50 B6 33 42N 8 30 E
Djibo, Burkina Faso 50 F4 14 9N 1 35W
Djibouti, Djibouti 46 E3 11 30N 43 5 E
Djibouti ■, Africa 46 E3 12 0N 43 0 E
Djolu, Zaïre 52 D4 0 35N 22 5 E
Djougou, Benin 50 G5 9 40N 1 45 E
Djoum, Cameroon 52 D2 2 41N 12 35 E
Djourab, Chad 51 E8 16 40N 18 50 E
Djugu, Zaïre 54 B3 1 55N 30 35 E
Djúpivogur, Iceland 8 D6 64 39N 14 17W
Dmitriya Lapteva, Proliv, Russia 27 B15 73 0N 140 0 E
Dnepr → = Dnipro →, Ukraine 25 E5 46 30N 32 18 E
Dneprodzerzhinsk = Dniprodzerzhynsk, Ukraine 25 E5 48 32N 34 37 E
Dnepropetrovsk = Dnipropetrovsk, Ukraine 25 E5 48 30N 35 0 E
Dnestr → = Dnister →, Europe 17 E16 46 18N 30 17 E
Dnestrovski = Belgorod, Russia 25 D6 50 35N 36 35 E
Dnieper = Dnipro →, Ukraine 25 E5 46 30N 32 18 E
Dniester = Dnister →, Europe 17 E16 46 18N 30 17 E
Dnipro →, Ukraine 25 E5 46 30N 32 18 E
Dniprodzerzhynsk, Ukraine 25 E5 48 32N 34 37 E
Dnipropetrovsk, Ukraine 25 E5 48 30N 35 0 E
Dnister →, Europe 17 E16 46 18N 30 17 E
Dnistrovskyy Lyman, Ukraine 17 E16 46 15N 30 17 E
Dnyapro = Dnipro →, Ukraine 25 E5 46 30N 32 18 E
Doan Hung, Vietnam 38 B5 21 30N 105 10 E
Doba, Chad 51 G8 8 40N 16 50 E
Dobbyn, Australia 62 B3 19 44S 140 2 E
Dobele, Latvia 9 H20 56 37N 23 16 E
Doberai, Jazirah, Indonesia 37 E8 1 25S 133 0 E
Doblas, Argentina 94 D3 37 5S 64 0W
Dobo, Indonesia 37 F8 5 45S 134 15 E
Doboj, Bos.-H. 21 B8 44 46N 18 6 E
Dobreta-Turnu-Severin, Romania 17 F12 44 39N 22 41 E
Dobrich, Bulgaria 21 C12 43 37N 27 49 E
Dobruja, Romania 17 F15 44 30N 28 15 E
Dobrush, Belarus 17 B16 52 25N 31 22 E
Doc, Mui, Vietnam 38 D6 17 58N 106 30 E
Doda, India 43 C6 33 10N 75 34 E
Dodecanese = Dhodhekánisos, Greece 21 F12 36 35N 27 0 E
Dodge Center, U.S.A. 80 C8 44 2N 92 52W
Dodge City, U.S.A. 81 G5 37 45N 100 1W
Dodge L., Canada 73 B7 59 50N 105 36W
Dodgeville, U.S.A. 80 D9 42 58N 90 8W
Dodoma, Tanzania 54 D4 6 8S 35 45 E
Dodoma □, Tanzania 54 D4 6 0S 36 0 E
Dodsland, Canada 73 C7 51 50N 108 45W
Dodson, U.S.A. 82 B9 48 24N 108 15W
Doetinchem, Neths. 15 C6 51 59N 6 18 E
Dog Creek, Canada 72 C4 51 35N 122 14W
Dog L., Man., Canada 73 C9 51 2N 98 31W
Dog L., Ont., Canada 70 C2 48 48N 89 30W
Dogi, Afghan. 40 C3 32 20N 62 50 E
Dogran, Pakistan 42 D5 31 48N 73 35 E
Doha = Ad Dawhah, Qatar 45 E6 25 15N 51 35 E
Dohazari, Bangla. 41 H18 22 10N 92 5 E
Doi, Indonesia 37 D7 2 14N 127 49 E
Doi Luang, Thailand 38 C3 18 30N 101 0 E
Doi Saket, Thailand 38 C2 18 52N 99 9 E
Doig →, Canada 72 B4 56 25N 120 40W
Dois Irmãos, Sa., Brazil 93 E10 9 0S 42 30W
Dokkum, Neths. 15 A5 53 20N 5 59 E
Dokri, Pakistan 42 F3 27 25N 68 7 E
Doland, U.S.A. 80 C5 44 54N 98 6W
Dolbeau, Canada 71 C5 48 53N 72 18W
Dole, France 18 C6 47 7N 5 31 E
Dolgellau, U.K. 10 E4 52 45N 3 53W
Dolgelley = Dolgellau, U.K. 10 E4 52 45N 3 53W
Dollart, Neths. 15 A7 53 20N 7 10 E
Dolomites = Dolomiti, Italy 20 A4 46 23N 11 51 E
Dolomiti, Italy 20 A4 46 23N 11 51 E
Dolores, Argentina 94 D4 36 20S 57 40W
Dolores, Uruguay 94 C4 33 34S 58 15W
Dolores, U.S.A. 83 H9 37 28N 108 30W
Dolores →, U.S.A. 83 G9 38 49N 109 17W
Dolphin, C., Falk. Is. 96 G5 51 10S 59 0W
Dolphin and Union Str., Canada 68 B8 69 5N 114 45W
Dom Pedrito, Brazil 95 C5 31 0S 54 40W
Domasi, Malawi 55 F4 15 15S 35 22 E
Dombarovskiy, Russia 26 D6 50 46N 59 32 E
Dombås, Norway 9 E13 62 4N 9 8 E
Domburg, Neths. 15 C3 51 34N 3 30 E
Domeyko, Chile 94 B1 29 0S 71 0W
Domeyko, Cordillera, Chile 94 A2 24 30S 69 0W
Dominador, Chile 94 A2 24 21S 69 20W
Dominica ■, W. Indies 89 C7 15 20N 61 20W
Dominica Passage, W. Indies 89 C7 15 10N 61 20W
Dominican Rep. ■, W. Indies 89 C5 19 0N 70 30W
Domo, Ethiopia 46 F4 7 50N 47 10 E
Domodóssola, Italy 20 A3 46 7N 8 17 E
Domville, Mt., Australia 63 D5 28 1S 151 15 E
Don →, Russia 25 E6 47 4N 39 18 E
Don →, C. of Aberd., U.K. 12 D6 57 11N 2 5W
Don →, S. Yorks., U.K. 10 D7 53 41N 0 52W
Don, C., Australia 60 B5 11 18S 131 46 E
Don Benito, Spain 19 C3 38 53N 5 51W
Don Duong, Vietnam 39 G7 11 51N 108 35 E
Don Martín, Presa de, Mexico 86 B4 27 30N 100 50W
Dona Ana = Nhamaabué, Mozam. 55 F4 17 25S 35 5 E
Donaghadee, U.K. 13 B6 54 39N 5 33W
Donald, Australia 63 F3 36 23S 143 0 E
Donalda, Canada 72 C6 52 35N 112 34W
Donaldsonville, U.S.A. 81 K9 30 6N 90 59W
Donalsonville, U.S.A. 77 K3 31 3N 84 53W
Donau = Dunărea →, Europe 17 F15 45 20N 29 40 E
Donauwörth, Germany 16 D6 48 43N 10 47 E
Doncaster, U.K. 10 D6 53 32N 1 6W
Dondo, Angola 52 F2 9 45S 14 25 E
Dondo, Mozam. 55 F3 19 33S 34 46 E
Dondo, Teluk, Indonesia 37 D6 0 29N 120 30 E
Dondra Head, Sri Lanka 40 S12 5 55N 80 40 E
Donegal, Ireland 13 B3 54 39N 8 5W
Donegal □, Ireland 13 B4 54 53N 8 0W
Donegal B., Ireland 13 B3 54 31N 8 49W
Donets →, Russia 25 E7 47 33N 40 55 E
Donetsk, Ukraine 25 E6 48 0N 37 45 E
Dong Ba Thin, Vietnam 39 F7 12 8N 109 13 E
Dong Dang, Vietnam 38 B6 21 54N 106 42 E
Dong Giam, Vietnam 38 C5 19 25N 105 31 E
Dong Ha, Vietnam 38 D6 16 55N 107 8 E
Dong Hene, Laos 38 D5 16 40N 105 18 E
Dong Hoi, Vietnam 38 D6 17 29N 106 36 E
Dong Khe, Vietnam 38 A6 22 26N 106 27 E
Dong Ujimqin Qi, China 34 B9 45 32N 116 55 E
Dong Van, Vietnam 38 A5 23 16N 105 22 E
Dong Xoai, Vietnam 39 G6 11 32N 106 55 E
Dongara, Australia 61 E1 29 14S 114 57 E
Dongbei, China 35 D13 42 0N 125 0 E
Dongchuan, China 32 D5 26 8N 103 1 E
Dongfang, China 38 C7 18 50N 108 33 E
Dongfeng, China 35 C13 42 40N 125 34 E
Donggala, Indonesia 37 E5 0 30S 119 40 E
Donggou, China 35 E13 39 52N 124 10 E
Dongguang, China 34 F9 37 50N 116 30 E
Dongjingcheng, China 35 B15 44 5N 129 10 E
Dongning, China 35 B16 44 2N 131 5 E
Dongola, Sudan 51 E11 19 9N 30 22 E
Dongou, Congo 52 D3 2 0N 18 5 E
Dongping, China 34 G9 35 55N 116 20 E
Dongsheng, China 34 E6 39 50N 110 0 E
Dongtai, China 35 H11 32 51N 120 21 E
Dongting Hu, China 33 D6 29 18N 112 45 E
Donington, C., Australia 63 E2 34 45S 136 0 E
Doniphan, U.S.A. 81 G9 36 37N 90 50W
Dønna, Norway 8 C15 66 6N 12 30 E
Donna, U.S.A. 81 M5 26 9N 98 4W
Donnaconna, Canada 71 C5 46 41N 71 41W
Donnelly's Crossing, N.Z. 59 F4 35 42S 173 38 E
Donnybrook, Australia 61 F2 33 34S 115 48 E
Donnybrook, S. Africa 57 D4 29 59S 29 48 E
Donora, U.S.A. 78 F5 40 11N 79 52W
Donor's Hill, Australia 62 B3 18 42S 140 33 E
Donostia = San Sebastián, Spain 19 A5 43 17N 1 58W
Doon →, U.K. 12 F4 55 27N 4 39W
Dora, L., Australia 60 D3 22 0S 123 0 E
Dora Báltea →, Italy 20 B3 45 11N 8 3 E
Doran L., Canada 73 A7 61 13N 108 6W
Dorchester, U.K. 11 G5 50 42N 2 27W
Dorchester, C., Canada 69 B12 65 27N 77 27W
Dordogne →, France 18 D3 45 2N 0 36W
Dordrecht, Neths. 15 C4 51 48N 4 39 E
Dordrecht, S. Africa 56 E4 31 20S 27 3 E
Doré L., Canada 73 C7 54 46N 107 17W
Doré Lake, Canada 73 C7 54 38N 107 36W
Dori, Burkina Faso 50 F4 14 3N 0 2W
Doring →, S. Africa 56 E2 31 54S 18 39 E
Doringbos, S. Africa 56 E2 31 59S 19 16 E
Dorion, Canada 70 C5 45 23N 74 3W
Dornbirn, Austria 16 E5 47 25N 9 45 E
Dornoch, U.K. 12 D4 57 53N 4 2W
Dornoch Firth, U.K. 12 D4 57 51N 4 4W
Dornogovĭ □, Mongolia 34 B6 44 0N 110 0 E
Dorohoi, Romania 17 E14 47 56N 26 30 E
Döröö Nuur, Mongolia 32 B4 48 0N 93 0 E
Dorr, Iran 45 C6 33 17N 50 38 E
Dorre I., Australia 61 E1 25 13S 113 12 E
Dorrigo, Australia 63 E5 30 20S 152 44 E
Dorris, U.S.A. 82 F3 41 58N 121 55W
Dorset, Canada 78 A6 45 14N 78 54W
Dorset, U.S.A. 78 E4 41 4N 80 40W
Dorset □, U.K. 11 G5 50 45N 2 26W
Dortmund, Germany 16 C4 51 30N 7 28 E
Doruma, Zaïre 54 B2 4 42N 27 33 E
Dorūneh, Iran 45 C8 35 10N 57 18 E
Dos Bahías, C., Argentina 96 E3 44 58S 65 32W
Dos Hermanas, Spain 19 D3 37 16N 5 55W
Dos Palos, U.S.A. 84 J6 36 59N 120 37W

Eastport

Dosso, *Niger* **50 F5** 13 0N 3 13 E
Dothan, *U.S.A.* **77 K3** 31 13N 85 24W
Doty, *U.S.A.* **84 D3** 46 38N 123 17W
Douai, *France* **18 A5** 50 21N 3 4 E
Douala, *Cameroon* **50 H6** 4 0N 9 45 E
Douarnenez, *France* **18 B1** 48 6N 4 21W
Double Island Pt., *Australia* **63 D5** 25 56S 153 11 E
Doubs —►, *France* **18 C6** 46 53N 5 1 E
Doubtful Sd., *N.Z.* **59 L1** 45 20S 166 49 E
Doubtless B., *N.Z.* **59 F4** 34 55S 173 26 E
Douentza, *Mali* **50 F4** 14 58N 2 48W
Douglas, *S. Africa* **56 D3** 29 4S 23 46 E
Douglas, *U.K.* **10 C3** 54 10N 4 28W
Douglas, *Alaska, U.S.A.* **72 B2** 58 17N 134 24W
Douglas, *Ariz., U.S.A.* **83 L9** 31 21N 109 33W
Douglas, *Ga., U.S.A.* **77 K4** 31 31N 82 51W
Douglas, *Wyo., U.S.A.* **80 D2** 42 45N 105 24W
Douglastown, *Canada* **71 C7** 48 46N 64 24W
Douglasville, *U.S.A.* **77 J3** 33 45N 84 45W
Doumé, *Cameroon* **52 D2** 4 15N 13 25 E
Dounreay, *U.K.* **12 C5** 58 35N 3 44W
Dourados, *Brazil* **95 A5** 22 9S 54 50W
Dourados —►, *Brazil* **95 A5** 21 58S 54 18W
Douro —►, *Europe* **19 B1** 41 8N 8 40W
Dove —►, *U.K.* **10 E6** 52 51N 1 36W
Dove Creek, *U.S.A.* **83 H9** 37 46N 108 54W
Dover, *Australia* **62 G4** 43 18S 147 2 E
Dover, *U.K.* **11 F9** 51 7N 1 19 E
Dover, *Del., U.S.A.* **76 F8** 39 10N 75 32W
Dover, *N.H., U.S.A.* **79 C14** 43 12N 70 56W
Dover, *N.J., U.S.A.* **79 F10** 40 53N 74 34W
Dover, *Ohio, U.S.A.* **78 F3** 40 32N 81 29W
Dover, Pt., *Australia* **61 F4** 32 32S 125 32 E
Dover, Str. of, *Europe* **18 A4** 51 0N 1 30 E
Dover-Foxcroft, *U.S.A.* **71 C6** 45 11N 69 13W
Dover Plains, *U.S.A.* **79 E11** 41 43N 73 35W
Dovey = Dyfi —►, *U.K.* **11 E4** 52 32N 4 3W
Dovrefjell, *Norway* **9 E13** 62 15N 9 33 E
Dow Rūd, *Iran* **45 C6** 33 28N 49 4 E
Dowa, *Malawi* **55 E3** 13 38S 33 58 E
Dowagiac, *U.S.A.* **76 E2** 41 59N 86 6W
Dowgha'i, *Iran* **45 B8** 36 54N 58 32 E
Dowlatābād, *Iran* **45 D8** 28 20N 56 40 E
Down □, *U.K.* **13 B6** 54 23N 6 2W
Downey, *Calif., U.S.A.* **85 M8** 33 56N 118 7W
Downey, *Idaho, U.S.A.* **82 E7** 42 26N 112 7W
Downham Market, *U.K.* **11 E8** 52 37N 0 23 E
Downieville, *U.S.A.* **84 F6** 39 34N 120 50W
Downpatrick, *U.K.* **13 B6** 54 20N 5 43W
Downpatrick Hd., *Ireland* **13 B2** 54 20N 9 21W
Dowsārī, *Iran* **45 D8** 28 25N 57 59 E
Doyle, *U.S.A.* **84 E6** 40 2N 120 6W
Doylestown, *U.S.A.* **79 F9** 40 21N 75 10W
Draa, Oued —►, *Morocco* **50 C2** 28 40N 11 10W
Drachten, *Neths.* **15 A6** 53 7N 6 5 E
Drăgăşani, *Romania* **17 F13** 44 39N 24 17 E
Dragichyn, *Belarus* **17 B13** 52 15N 25 8 E
Dragoman, Prokhod, *Bulgaria* **21 C10** 42 58N 22 53 E
Dragonera, I., *Spain* **22 B9** 39 35N 2 19 E
Draguignan, *France* **18 E7** 43 32N 6 27 E
Drain, *U.S.A.* **82 E2** 43 40N 123 19W
Drake, *Australia* **63 D5** 28 55S 152 25 E
Drake, *U.S.A.* **80 B4** 47 55N 100 23W
Drake Passage, *S. Ocean* **5 B17** 58 0S 68 0W
Drakensberg, *S. Africa* **57 E4** 31 0S 28 0 E
Dráma, *Greece* **21 D11** 41 9N 24 10 E
Drammen, *Norway* **9 G14** 59 42N 10 12 E
Drangajökull, *Iceland* **8 C2** 66 9N 22 15W
Dras, *India* **43 B6** 34 25N 75 48 E
Drau = Drava —►, *Croatia* **21 B8** 45 33N 18 55 E
Drava —►, *Croatia* **21 B8** 45 33N 18 55 E
Drayton Valley, *Canada* **72 C6** 53 12N 114 58W
Drenthe □, *Neths.* **15 B6** 52 52N 6 40 E
Drepanum, C., *Cyprus* **23 E11** 34 54N 32 19 E
Dresden, *Canada* **78 D2** 42 35N 82 11W
Dresden, *Germany* **16 C7** 51 3N 13 44 E
Dreux, *France* **18 B4** 48 44N 1 23 E
Driffield, *U.K.* **10 C7** 54 0N 0 26W
Driftwood, *U.S.A.* **78 E6** 41 20N 78 8W
Driggs, *U.S.A.* **82 E8** 43 44N 111 6W
Drina —►, *Bos.-H.* **21 B8** 44 53N 19 21 E
Drini —►, *Albania* **21 C8** 42 1N 19 38 E
Drøbak, *Norway* **9 G14** 59 39N 10 39 E
Drochia, *Moldova* **17 D14** 48 2N 27 48 E
Drogheda, *Ireland* **13 C5** 53 43N 6 22W
Drogichin = Dragichyn, *Belarus* **17 B13** 52 15N 25 8 E
Drogobych = Drohobych, *Ukraine* **17 D12** 49 20N 23 30 E
Drohobych, *Ukraine* **17 D12** 49 20N 23 30 E
Droichead Atha = Drogheda, *Ireland* **13 C5** 53 43N 6 22W
Droichead Nua, *Ireland* **13 C5** 53 11N 6 48W
Droitwich, *U.K.* **11 E5** 52 16N 2 8W
Dromedary, C., *Australia* **63 F5** 36 17S 150 10 E
Dronfield, *Australia* **62 C3** 21 12S 140 3 E
Drumbo, *Canada* **78 C4** 43 16N 80 35W
Drumheller, *Canada* **72 C6** 51 25N 112 40W
Drummond, *U.S.A.* **82 C7** 46 40N 113 9W
Drummond I., *U.S.A.* **70 C3** 46 1N 83 39W
Drummond Pt., *Australia* **63 E2** 34 9S 135 16 E
Drummond Ra., *Australia* **62 C4** 23 45S 147 10 E
Drummondville, *Canada* **70 C5** 45 55N 72 25W
Drumright, *U.S.A.* **81 H6** 35 59N 96 36W
Druskininkai, *Lithuania* **9 J20** 54 3N 23 58 E
Drut —►, *Belarus* **17 B16** 53 8N 30 5 E
Druzhina, *Russia* **27 C15** 68 14N 145 18 E
Dry Tortugas, *U.S.A.* **88 B3** 24 38N 82 55W
Dryden, *Canada* **73 D10** 49 47N 92 50W
Dryden, *U.S.A.* **81 K3** 30 3N 102 7W
Drygalski I., *Antarctica* **5 C7** 66 0S 92 0 E
Drysdale —►, *Australia* **60 B4** 13 59S 126 51 E
Drysdale I., *Australia* **62 A2** 11 41S 136 0 E
Dschang, *Cameroon* **50 G7** 5 32N 10 3 E
Du Bois, *U.S.A.* **78 E6** 41 8N 78 46W
Du Quoin, *U.S.A.* **80 G10** 38 1N 89 14W
Duanesburg, *U.S.A.* **79 D10** 42 45N 74 11W
Duaringa, *Australia* **62 C4** 23 42S 149 42 E
Ḍubā, *Si. Arabia* **44 E2** 27 10N 35 40 E
Dubai = Dubayy, *U.A.E.* **45 E7** 25 18N 55 20 E
Dubăsari, *Moldova* **17 E15** 47 15N 29 10 E
Dubăsari Vdkhr., *Moldova* **17 E15** 47 30N 29 0 E
Dubawnt —►, *Canada* **73 A8** 64 33N 100 6W
Dubawnt, L., *Canada* **73 A8** 63 4N 101 42W
Dubayy, *U.A.E.* **45 E7** 25 18N 55 20 E
Dubbo, *Australia* **63 E4** 32 11S 148 35 E
Dubele, *Zaïre* **54 B2** 2 56N 29 35 E
Dublin, *Ireland* **13 C5** 53 21N 6 15W
Dublin, *Ga., U.S.A.* **77 J4** 32 32N 82 54W
Dublin, *Tex., U.S.A.* **81 J5** 32 5N 98 21W
Dublin □, *Ireland* **13 C5** 53 24N 6 20W
Dublin B., *Ireland* **13 C5** 53 18N 6 5W
Dubno, *Ukraine* **17 C13** 50 25N 25 45 E
Dubois, *U.S.A.* **82 D7** 44 10N 112 14W
Dubossary = Dubăsari, *Moldova* **17 E15** 47 15N 29 10 E
Dubossary Vdkhr. = Dubăsari Vdkhr., *Moldova* **17 E15** 47 30N 29 0 E
Dubovka, *Russia* **25 E7** 49 5N 44 50 E
Dubrajpur, *India* **43 H12** 23 48N 87 25 E
Dubréka, *Guinea* **50 G2** 9 46N 13 31W
Dubrovitsa = Dubrovytsya, *Ukraine* **17 C14** 51 31N 26 35 E
Dubrovnik, *Croatia* **21 C8** 42 39N 18 6 E
Dubrovskoye, *Russia* **27 D12** 58 55N 111 10 E
Dubrovytsya, *Ukraine* **17 C14** 51 31N 26 35 E
Dubuque, *U.S.A.* **80 D9** 42 30N 90 41W
Duchesne, *U.S.A.* **82 F8** 40 10N 110 24W
Duchess, *Australia* **62 C2** 21 20S 139 50 E
Ducie I., *Pac. Oc.* **65 K15** 24 40S 124 48W
Duck Cr. —►, *Australia* **60 D2** 22 37S 116 53 E
Duck Lake, *Canada* **73 C7** 52 50N 106 16W
Duck Mountain Prov. Park, *Canada* **73 C8** 51 45N 101 0W
Duckwall, Mt., *U.S.A.* **84 H6** 37 58N 120 7W
Dudhi, *India* **41 G13** 24 15N 83 10 E
Dudinka, *Russia* **27 C9** 69 30N 86 13 E
Dudley, *U.K.* **11 E5** 52 31N 2 5W
Duero = Douro —►, *Europe* **19 B1** 41 8N 8 40W
Dufftown, *U.K.* **12 D5** 57 27N 3 8W
Dugi Otok, *Croatia* **16 G8** 44 0N 15 3 E
Duifken Pt., *Australia* **62 A3** 12 33S 141 38 E
Duisburg, *Germany* **16 C4** 51 26N 6 45 E
Duiwelskloof, *S. Africa* **57 C5** 23 42S 30 10 E
Dūkdamīn, *Iran* **45 C8** 35 59N 57 43 E
Duke I., *U.S.A.* **72 C2** 54 50N 131 20W
Dukelský Průsmyk, *Slovak Rep.* **17 D11** 49 25N 21 42 E
Dukhān, *Qatar* **45 E6** 25 25N 50 50 E
Duki, *Pakistan* **40 D6** 30 14N 68 25 E
Duku, *Nigeria* **50 F7** 10 43N 10 43 E
Dulce —►, *Argentina* **94 C3** 30 32S 62 33W
Dulce, G., *Costa Rica* **88 E3** 8 40N 83 20W
Dulf, *Iraq* **44 C5** 35 7N 45 51 E
Dulit, Banjaran, *Malaysia* **36 D4** 3 15N 114 30 E
Duliu, *China* **34 E9** 39 2N 116 55 E
Dullewala, *Pakistan* **42 D4** 31 50N 71 25 E
Dulq Maghār, *Syria* **44 B3** 36 22N 38 39 E
Dululu, *Australia* **62 C5** 23 48S 150 15 E
Duluth, *U.S.A.* **80 B8** 46 47N 92 6W
Dum Dum, *India* **43 H13** 22 39N 88 33 E
Dum Duma, *India* **41 F19** 27 40N 95 40 E
Dum Hadjer, *Chad* **51 F8** 13 18N 19 41 E
Dūmā, *Lebanon* **47 A4** 34 12N 35 50 E
Dūmā, *Syria* **47 B5** 33 34N 36 24 E
Dumaguete, *Phil.* **37 C6** 9 17N 123 15 E
Dumai, *Indonesia* **36 D2** 1 35N 101 28 E
Dumaran, *Phil.* **37 B5** 10 33N 119 50 E
Dumas, *Ark., U.S.A.* **81 J9** 33 53N 91 29W
Dumas, *Tex., U.S.A.* **81 H4** 35 52N 101 58W
Dumbarton, *U.K.* **12 F4** 55 57N 4 33W
Dumbleyung, *Australia* **61 F2** 33 17S 117 42 E
Dumfries, *U.K.* **12 F5** 55 4N 3 37W
Dumfries & Galloway □, *U.K.* **12 F5** 55 9N 3 58W
Dumka, *India* **43 G12** 24 12N 87 15 E
Dumoine —►, *Canada* **70 C4** 46 13N 77 51W
Dumoine L., *Canada* **70 C4** 46 55N 77 55W
Dumraon, *India* **43 G11** 25 33N 84 8 E
Dumyât, *Egypt* **51 B11** 31 24N 31 48 E
Dún Dealgan = Dundalk, *Ireland* **13 B5** 54 1N 6 24W
Dun Laoghaire, *Ireland* **13 C5** 53 17N 6 8W
Duna = Dunărea —►, *Europe* **17 F15** 45 20N 29 40 E
Dunaj = Dunărea —►, *Europe* **17 F15** 45 20N 29 40 E
Dunakeszi, *Hungary* **17 E10** 47 37N 19 8 E
Dunărea —►, *Europe* **17 F15** 45 20N 29 40 E
Dunaújváros, *Hungary* **17 E10** 47 0N 18 57 E
Dunav = Dunărea —►, *Europe* **17 F15** 45 20N 29 40 E
Dunay, *Russia* **30 C6** 42 52N 132 22 E
Dunback, *N.Z.* **59 L3** 45 23S 170 36 E
Dunbar, *Australia* **62 B3** 16 0S 142 22 E
Dunbar, *U.K.* **12 E6** 56 0N 2 31W
Dunblane, *U.K.* **12 E5** 56 11N 3 58W
Duncan, *Canada* **72 D4** 48 45N 123 40W
Duncan, *Ariz., U.S.A.* **83 K9** 32 43N 109 6W
Duncan, *Okla., U.S.A.* **81 H6** 34 30N 97 57W
Duncan, L., *Canada* **70 B4** 53 29N 77 58W
Duncan L., *Canada* **72 A6** 62 51N 113 58W
Duncan Town, *Bahamas* **88 B4** 22 15N 75 45W
Duncannon, *U.S.A.* **78 F7** 40 23N 77 2W
Dundalk, *Canada* **78 B4** 44 10N 80 24W
Dundalk, *Ireland* **13 B5** 54 1N 6 24W
Dundalk Bay, *Ireland* **13 C5** 53 55N 6 15W
Dundas, *Canada* **70 D4** 43 17N 79 59W
Dundas, L., *Australia* **61 F3** 32 35S 121 50 E
Dundas I., *Canada* **72 C2** 54 30N 130 50W
Dundas Str., *Australia* **60 B5** 11 15S 131 35 E
Dundee, *S. Africa* **57 D5** 28 11S 30 15 E
Dundee, *U.K.* **12 E6** 56 28N 2 59W
Dundee City □, *U.K.* **12 E6** 56 30N 2 58W
Dundgovĭ □, *Mongolia* **34 B4** 45 10N 106 0 E
Dundoo, *Australia* **63 D3** 27 40S 144 37 E
Dundrum, *U.K.* **13 B6** 54 16N 5 52W
Dundrum B., *U.K.* **13 B6** 54 13N 5 47W
Dundwara, *India* **43 F8** 27 48N 79 9 E
Dunedin, *N.Z.* **59 L3** 45 50S 170 33 E
Dunedin, *U.S.A.* **77 L4** 28 1N 82 47W
Dunedin —►, *Canada* **72 B4** 59 30N 124 5W
Dunfermline, *U.K.* **12 E5** 56 5N 3 27W
Dungannon, *Canada* **78 C3** 43 51N 81 36W
Dungannon, *U.K.* **13 B5** 54 31N 6 46W
Dungannon □, *U.K.* **13 B5** 54 30N 6 55W
Dungarpur, *India* **42 H5** 23 52N 73 45 E
Dungarvan, *Ireland* **13 D4** 52 5N 7 37W
Dungarvan Harbour, *Ireland* **13 D4** 52 4N 7 35W
Dungeness, *U.K.* **11 G8** 50 54N 0 59 E
Dungo, L. do, *Angola* **56 B2** 17 15S 19 0 E
Dungog, *Australia* **63 E5** 32 22S 151 46 E
Dungu, *Zaïre* **54 B2** 3 40N 28 32 E
Dunhua, *China* **35 C15** 43 20N 128 14 E
Dunhuang, *China* **32 B4** 40 8N 94 36 E
Dunk I., *Australia* **62 B4** 17 59S 146 29 E
Dunkeld, *U.K.* **12 E5** 56 34N 3 35W
Dunkerque, *France* **18 A5** 51 2N 2 20 E
Dunkery Beacon, *U.K.* **11 F4** 51 9N 3 36W
Dunkirk = Dunkerque, *France* **18 A5** 51 2N 2 20 E
Dunkirk, *U.S.A.* **78 D5** 42 29N 79 20W
Dunkwa, *Ghana* **50 G4** 6 0N 1 47W
Dunlap, *U.S.A.* **80 E7** 41 51N 95 36W
Dúnleary = Dun Laoghaire, *Ireland* **13 C5** 53 17N 6 8W
Dunmanus B., *Ireland* **13 E2** 51 31N 9 50W
Dunmara, *Australia* **62 B1** 16 42S 133 25 E
Dunmore, *U.S.A.* **79 E9** 41 25N 75 38W
Dunmore Hd., *Ireland* **13 D1** 52 10N 10 35W
Dunmore Town, *Bahamas* **88 A4** 25 30N 76 39W
Dunn, *U.S.A.* **77 H6** 35 19N 78 37W
Dunnellon, *U.S.A.* **77 L4** 29 3N 82 28W
Dunnet Hd., *U.K.* **12 C5** 58 40N 3 21W
Dunning, *U.S.A.* **80 E4** 41 50N 100 6W
Dunnville, *Canada* **78 D5** 42 54N 79 36W
Dunolly, *Australia* **63 F3** 36 51S 143 44 E
Dunoon, *U.K.* **12 F4** 55 57N 4 56W
Dunqul, *Egypt* **51 D11** 23 26N 31 37 E
Duns, *U.K.* **12 F6** 55 47N 2 20W
Dunseith, *U.S.A.* **80 A4** 48 50N 100 3W
Dunsmuir, *U.S.A.* **82 F2** 41 13N 122 16W
Dunstable, *U.K.* **11 F7** 51 53N 0 32W
Dunstan Mts., *N.Z.* **59 L2** 44 53S 169 35 E
Dunster, *Canada* **72 C5** 53 8N 119 50W
Dunvegan L., *Canada* **73 A7** 60 8N 107 10W
Duolun, *China* **34 C9** 42 12N 116 28 E
Duong Dong, *Vietnam* **39 G4** 10 13N 103 58 E
Dupree, *U.S.A.* **80 C4** 45 4N 101 35W
Dupuyer, *U.S.A.* **82 B7** 48 13N 112 30W
Duque de Caxias, *Brazil* **95 A7** 22 45S 43 19W
Durack —►, *Australia* **60 C4** 15 33S 127 52 E
Durack Ra., *Australia* **60 C4** 16 50S 127 40 E
Durance —►, *France* **18 E6** 43 55N 4 45 E
Durand, *U.S.A.* **76 D4** 42 55N 83 59W
Durango = Victoria de Durango, *Mexico* **86 C4** 24 3N 104 39W
Durango, *Spain* **19 A4** 43 13N 2 40W
Durango, *U.S.A.* **83 H10** 37 16N 107 53W
Durango □, *Mexico* **86 C4** 25 0N 105 0W
Duranillin, *Australia* **61 F2** 33 30S 116 45 E
Durant, *U.S.A.* **81 J6** 33 59N 96 25W
Durazno, *Uruguay* **94 C4** 33 25S 56 31W
Durazzo = Durrësi, *Albania* **21 D8** 41 19N 19 28 E
Durban, *S. Africa* **57 D5** 29 49S 31 1 E
Düren, *Germany* **16 C4** 50 48N 6 29 E
Durg, *India* **41 J12** 21 15N 81 22 E
Durgapur, *India* **43 H12** 23 30N 87 20 E
Durham, *Canada* **78 B4** 44 10N 80 49W
Durham, *U.K.* **10 C6** 54 47N 1 34W
Durham, *Calif., U.S.A.* **84 F5** 39 39N 121 48W
Durham, *N.C., U.S.A.* **77 G6** 35 59N 78 54W
Durham □, *U.K.* **10 C6** 54 42N 1 45W
Durham Downs, *Australia* **63 D4** 26 6S 149 5 E
Durmitor, *Montenegro, Yug.* **21 C8** 43 10N 19 0 E
Durness, *U.K.* **12 C4** 58 34N 4 45W
Durrësi, *Albania* **21 D8** 41 19N 19 28 E
Durrie, *Australia* **62 D3** 25 40S 140 15 E
Dursunbey, *Turkey* **21 E13** 39 35N 28 37 E
Duru, *Zaïre* **54 B2** 4 14N 28 50 E
D'Urville, Tanjung, *Indonesia* **37 E9** 1 28S 137 54 E
D'Urville I., *N.Z.* **59 J4** 40 50S 173 55 E
Duryea, *U.S.A.* **79 E9** 41 20N 75 45W
Dusa Mareb, *Somali Rep.* **46 F4** 5 30N 46 15 E
Dushak, *Turkmenistan* **26 F7** 37 13N 60 1 E
Dushanbe, *Tajikistan* **26 F7** 38 33N 68 48 E
Dusky Sd., *N.Z.* **59 L1** 45 47S 166 30 E
Dussejour, C., *Australia* **60 B4** 14 45S 128 13 E
Düsseldorf, *Germany* **16 C4** 51 14N 6 47 E
Dutch Harbor, *U.S.A.* **68 C3** 53 53N 166 32W
Dutlwe, *Botswana* **56 C3** 23 58S 23 46 E
Dutton, *Canada* **78 D3** 42 39N 81 30W
Dutton —►, *Australia* **62 C3** 20 44S 143 10 E
Duyun, *China* **32 D5** 26 18N 107 29 E
Duzdab = Zāhedān, *Iran* **45 D9** 29 30N 60 50 E
Dvina, Severnaya —►, *Russia* **24 B7** 64 32N 40 30 E
Dvinsk = Daugavpils, *Latvia* **9 J22** 55 53N 26 32 E
Dvinskaya Guba, *Russia* **24 B6** 65 0N 39 0 E
Dwarka, *India* **42 H3** 22 18N 69 8 E
Dwellingup, *Australia* **61 F2** 32 43S 116 4 E
Dwight, *Canada* **78 A5** 45 20N 79 1W
Dwight, *U.S.A.* **76 E1** 41 5N 88 26W
Dyatlovo = Dzyatlava, *Belarus* **17 B13** 53 28N 25 28 E
Dyer, C., *Canada* **69 B13** 66 40N 61 0W
Dyer Plateau, *Antarctica* **5 D17** 70 45S 65 30W
Dyersburg, *U.S.A.* **81 G10** 36 3N 89 23W
Dyfi —►, *U.K.* **11 E4** 52 32N 4 3W
Dymer, *Ukraine* **17 C16** 50 47N 30 18 E
Dynevor Downs, *Australia* **63 D3** 28 10S 144 20 E
Dysart, *Canada* **73 C8** 50 57N 104 2W
Dzamin Üüd, *Mongolia* **34 C6** 43 50N 111 58 E
Dzerzhinsk, *Russia* **24 C7** 56 14N 43 30 E
Dzhalinda, *Russia* **27 D13** 53 26N 124 0 E
Dzhambul = Zhambyl, *Kazakstan* **26 E8** 42 54N 71 22 E
Dzhankoy, *Ukraine* **25 E5** 45 40N 34 20 E
Dzhardzhan, *Russia* **27 C13** 68 10N 124 10 E
Dzhetygara = Zhetiqara, *Kazakstan* **26 D7** 52 11N 61 12 E
Dzhezkazgan = Zhezqazghan, *Kazakstan* **26 E7** 47 44N 67 40 E
Dzhizak = Jizzakh, *Uzbekistan* **26 E7** 40 6N 67 50 E
Dzhugdzur, Khrebet, *Russia* **27 D14** 57 30N 138 0 E
Dzhungarskiye Vorota, *Kazakstan* **32 B3** 45 0N 82 0 E
Działdowa, *Poland* **17 B11** 53 15N 20 15 E
Dzierzoniów, *Poland* **17 C9** 50 45N 16 39 E
Dzilam de Bravo, *Mexico* **87 C7** 21 24N 88 53W
Dzungaria = Junggar Pendi, *China* **32 B3** 44 30N 86 0 E
Dzungarian Gates = Dzhungarskiye Vorota, *Kazakstan* **32 B3** 45 0N 82 0 E
Dzuumod, *Mongolia* **32 B5** 47 45N 106 58 E
Dzyarzhynsk, *Belarus* **17 B14** 53 40N 27 1 E
Dzyatlava, *Belarus* **17 B13** 53 28N 25 28 E

E

Eabamet, L., *Canada* **70 B2** 51 30N 87 46W
Eads, *U.S.A.* **80 F3** 38 29N 102 47W
Eagle, *U.S.A.* **82 G10** 39 39N 106 50W
Eagle —►, *Canada* **71 B8** 53 36N 57 26W
Eagle Butte, *U.S.A.* **80 C4** 45 0N 101 10W
Eagle Grove, *U.S.A.* **80 D8** 42 40N 93 54W
Eagle L., *Calif., U.S.A.* **82 F3** 40 39N 120 45W
Eagle L., *Maine, U.S.A.* **71 C6** 46 20N 69 22W
Eagle Lake, *U.S.A.* **81 L6** 29 35N 96 20W
Eagle Mountain, *U.S.A.* **85 M11** 33 49N 115 27W
Eagle Nest, *U.S.A.* **83 H11** 36 33N 105 16W
Eagle Pass, *U.S.A.* **81 L4** 28 43N 100 30W
Eagle Pk., *U.S.A.* **84 G7** 38 10N 119 25W
Eagle Pt., *Australia* **60 C3** 16 11S 124 23 E
Eagle River, *U.S.A.* **80 C10** 45 55N 89 15W
Ealing, *U.K.* **11 F7** 51 31N 0 20W
Earaheedy, *Australia* **61 E3** 25 34S 121 29 E
Earl Grey, *Canada* **73 C8** 50 57N 104 43W
Earle, *U.S.A.* **81 H9** 35 16N 90 28W
Earlimart, *U.S.A.* **85 K7** 35 53N 119 16W
Earn —►, *U.K.* **12 E5** 56 21N 3 18W
Earn, L., *U.K.* **12 E4** 56 23N 4 13W
Earnslaw, Mt., *N.Z.* **59 L2** 44 32S 168 27 E
Earth, *U.S.A.* **81 H3** 34 14N 102 24W
Easley, *U.S.A.* **77 H4** 34 50N 82 36W
East Angus, *Canada* **71 C5** 45 30N 71 40W
East Aurora, *U.S.A.* **78 D6** 42 46N 78 37W
East Ayrshire □, *U.K.* **12 F4** 55 26N 4 11W
East B., *U.S.A.* **81 L10** 29 0N 89 15W
East Bengal, *Bangla.* **41 G17** 24 0N 90 0 E
East Beskids = Vychodné Beskydy, *Europe* **17 D11** 49 20N 22 0 E
East Brady, *U.S.A.* **78 F5** 40 59N 79 36W
East C., *N.Z.* **59 G7** 37 42S 178 35 E
East Chicago, *U.S.A.* **76 E2** 41 38N 87 27W
East China Sea, *Asia* **33 C7** 30 5N 126 0 E
East Coulee, *Canada* **72 C6** 51 23N 112 27W
East Dunbartonshire □, *U.K.* **12 F4** 55 57N 4 13W
East Falkland, *Falk. Is.* **96 G5** 51 30S 58 30W
East Grand Forks, *U.S.A.* **80 B6** 47 56N 97 1W
East Greenwich, *U.S.A.* **79 E13** 41 40N 71 27W
East Hartford, *U.S.A.* **79 E12** 41 46N 72 39W
East Helena, *U.S.A.* **82 C8** 46 35N 111 56W
East Indies, *Asia* **37 E6** 0 0 120 0 E
East Jordan, *U.S.A.* **76 C3** 45 10N 85 7W
East Lansing, *U.S.A.* **76 D3** 42 44N 84 29W
East Liverpool, *U.S.A.* **78 F4** 40 37N 80 35W
East London, *S. Africa* **57 E4** 33 0S 27 55 E
East Lothian □, *U.K.* **12 F6** 55 58N 2 44W
East Main = Eastmain, *Canada* **70 B4** 52 10N 78 30W
East Orange, *U.S.A.* **79 F10** 40 46N 74 13W
East Pacific Ridge, *Pac. Oc.* **65 J17** 15 0S 110 0W
East Palestine, *U.S.A.* **78 F4** 40 50N 80 33W
East Pine, *Canada* **72 B4** 55 48N 120 12W
East Point, *U.S.A.* **77 J3** 33 41N 84 27W
East Providence, *U.S.A.* **79 E13** 41 49N 71 23W
East Pt., *Canada* **71 C7** 46 27N 61 58W
East Renfrewshire □, *U.K.* **12 F4** 55 46N 4 21W
East Retford = Retford, *U.K.* **10 D7** 53 19N 0 56W
East Riding □, *U.K.* **10 D7** 53 55N 0 30W
East St. Louis, *U.S.A.* **80 F9** 38 37N 90 9W
East Schelde —►= Oosterschelde, *Neths.* **15 C4** 51 33N 4 0 E
East Siberian Sea, *Russia* **27 B17** 73 0N 160 0 E
East Stroudsburg, *U.S.A.* **79 E9** 41 1N 75 11W
East Sussex □, *U.K.* **11 G8** 50 56N 0 19 E
East Tawas, *U.S.A.* **76 C4** 44 17N 83 29W
East Toorale, *Australia* **63 E4** 30 27S 145 28 E
East Walker —►, *U.S.A.* **84 G7** 38 52N 119 10W
Eastbourne, *N.Z.* **59 J5** 41 19S 174 55 E
Eastbourne, *U.K.* **11 G8** 50 46N 0 18 E
Eastend, *Canada* **73 D7** 49 32N 108 50W
Easter Islands = Pascua, I. de, *Pac. Oc.* **65 K17** 27 0S 109 0W
Eastern □, *Kenya* **54 B4** 0 0 38 30 E
Eastern □, *Uganda* **54 B3** 1 50N 33 45 E
Eastern Cape □, *S. Africa* **56 E4** 32 0S 26 0 E
Eastern Cr. —►, *Australia* **62 C3** 20 40S 141 35 E
Eastern Ghats, *India* **40 N11** 14 0N 78 50 E
Eastern Group = Lau Group, *Fiji* **59 C9** 17 0S 178 30W
Eastern Group, *Australia* **61 F3** 33 30S 124 30 E
Eastern Transvaal = Mpumalanga □, *S. Africa* **57 B5** 26 0S 30 0 E
Easterville, *Canada* **73 C9** 53 8N 99 49W
Easthampton, *U.S.A.* **79 D12** 42 16N 72 40W
Eastland, *U.S.A.* **81 J5** 32 24N 98 49W
Eastleigh, *U.K.* **11 G6** 50 58N 1 21W
Eastmain, *Canada* **70 B4** 52 10N 78 30W
Eastmain —►, *Canada* **70 B4** 52 27N 78 26W
Eastman, *Canada* **79 A12** 45 18N 72 19W
Eastman, *U.S.A.* **77 J4** 32 12N 83 11W
Easton, *Md., U.S.A.* **76 F7** 38 47N 76 5W
Easton, *Pa., U.S.A.* **79 F9** 40 41N 75 13W
Easton, *Wash., U.S.A.* **84 C5** 47 14N 121 11W
Eastport, *U.S.A.* **71 D6** 44 56N 67 0W

Fartak, Râs

Fartak, Râs, Si. Arabia 44 D2 28 5N 34 34 E
Fartura, Serra da, Brazil 95 B5 26 21S 52 52W
Fārūj, Iran 45 B8 37 14N 58 14 E
Farvel, Kap, Greenland 4 D5 59 48N 43 55W
Farwell, U.S.A. 81 H3 34 23N 103 2W
Fasā, Iran 45 D7 29 0N 53 39 E
Fasano, Italy 20 D7 40 50N 17 22 E
Fastiv, Ukraine 17 C15 50 7N 29 57 E
Fastnet Rock, Ireland 13 E2 51 22N 9 37W
Fastov = Fastiv, Ukraine 17 C15 50 7N 29 57 E
Fatagar, Tanjung, Indonesia 37 E8 2 46S 131 57 E
Fatehgarh, India 43 F8 27 25N 79 35 E
Fatehpur, Raj., India 42 F6 28 0N 74 40 E
Fatehpur, Ut. P., India 43 G9 25 56N 81 13 E
Fatima, Canada 71 C7 47 24N 61 53W
Faulkton, U.S.A. 80 C5 45 2N 99 8W
Faure I., Australia 61 E1 25 52S 113 50 E
Fauresmith, S. Africa 56 D4 29 44S 25 17 E
Fauske, Norway 8 C16 67 17N 15 25 E
Favara, Italy 20 F5 37 19N 13 39 E
Favaritx, C., Spain 22 A11 40 0N 4 15 E
Favignana, Italy 20 F5 37 56N 12 20 E
Favourable Lake, Canada 70 B1 52 50N 93 39W
Fawn →, Canada 70 A2 55 20N 87 35W
Fawnskin, U.S.A. 85 L10 34 16N 116 56W
Faxaflói, Iceland 8 D2 64 29N 23 0W
Faya-Largeau, Chad 51 E8 17 58N 19 6 E
Fayd, Si. Arabia 44 E4 27 1N 42 52 E
Fayette, Ala., U.S.A. 77 J2 33 41N 87 50W
Fayette, Mo., U.S.A. 80 F8 39 9N 92 41W
Fayetteville, Ark., U.S.A. 81 G7 36 4N 94 10W
Fayetteville, N.C., U.S.A. 77 H6 35 3N 78 53W
Fayetteville, Tenn., U.S.A. 77 H2 35 9N 86 34W
Fazilka, India 42 D6 30 27N 74 2 E
Fazilpur, Pakistan 42 E4 29 18N 70 29 E
Fdérik, Mauritania 50 D2 22 40N 12 45W
Feale →, Ireland 13 D2 52 27N 9 37W
Fear, C., U.S.A. 77 J7 33 50N 77 58W
Feather →, U.S.A. 82 G3 38 47N 121 36W
Feather Falls, U.S.A. 84 F5 39 36N 121 16W
Featherston, N.Z. 59 J5 41 6S 175 20 E
Featherstone, Zimbabwe 55 F3 18 42S 30 55 E
Fécamp, France 18 B4 49 45N 0 22 E
Federación, Argentina 94 C4 31 0S 57 55W
Fedeshkūh, Iran 45 D7 28 49N 53 50 E
Fehmarn, Germany 16 A6 54 27N 11 7 E
Fehmarn Bælt, Europe 9 J14 54 35N 11 20 E
Fei Xian, China 35 G9 35 18N 117 59 E
Feilding, N.Z. 59 J5 40 13S 175 35 E
Feira de Santana, Brazil 93 F11 12 15S 38 57W
Feixiang, China 34 F8 36 30N 114 45 E
Felanitx, Spain 22 B10 39 28N 3 9 E
Feldkirch, Austria 16 E5 47 15N 9 37 E
Felipe Carrillo Puerto, Mexico 87 D7 19 38N 88 3W
Felixstowe, U.K. 11 F9 51 58N 1 23 E
Felton, U.K. 10 B6 55 18N 1 42W
Felton, U.S.A. 84 H4 37 3N 122 4W
Femunden, Norway 9 E14 62 10N 11 53 E
Fen He →, China 34 G6 35 36N 110 42 E
Fenelon Falls, Canada 78 B6 44 32N 78 45W
Feng Xian, Jiangsu, China 34 G9 34 43N 116 35 E
Feng Xian, Shaanxi, China 34 H4 33 54N 106 40 E
Fengcheng, China 35 D13 40 28N 124 5 E
Fengfeng, China 34 F8 36 28N 114 8 E
Fengjie, China 33 C5 31 5N 109 36 E
Fengning, China 34 D9 41 10N 116 33 E
Fengqiu, China 34 G8 35 2N 114 25 E
Fengrun, China 35 E10 39 48N 118 8 E
Fengtai, China 34 E9 39 50N 116 18 E
Fengxiang, China 34 G4 34 29N 107 25 E
Fengyang, China 35 H9 32 51N 117 29 E
Fengzhen, China 34 D7 40 25N 113 2 E
Fenit, Ireland 13 D2 52 17N 9 51W
Fennimore, U.S.A. 80 D9 42 59N 90 39W
Fenoarivo Afovoany, Madag. 57 B8 18 26S 46 34 E
Fenoarivo Atsinanana, Madag. 57 B8 17 22S 49 25 E
Fens, The, U.K. 10 E8 52 38N 0 2W
Fenton, U.S.A. 76 D4 42 48N 83 42W
Fenxi, China 34 F6 36 40N 111 31 E
Fenyang, China 34 F6 37 18N 111 48 E
Feodosiya, Ukraine 25 E6 45 2N 35 16 E
Ferdows, Iran 45 C8 33 58N 58 2 E
Ferfer, Somali Rep. 46 F4 5 4N 45 9 E
Fergana = Farghona, Uzbekistan 26 E8 40 23N 71 19 E
Fergus, Canada 70 D3 43 43N 80 24W
Fergus Falls, U.S.A. 80 B6 46 17N 96 4W
Ferland, Canada 70 B2 50 19N 88 27W
Fermanagh □, U.K. 13 B4 54 21N 7 40W
Fermo, Italy 20 C5 43 9N 13 43 E
Fermoy, Ireland 13 D3 52 9N 8 16W
Fernández, Argentina 94 B3 27 55S 63 50W
Fernandina Beach, U.S.A. 77 K5 30 40N 81 27W
Fernando de Noronha, Brazil 93 D12 4 0S 33 10W
Fernando Póo = Bioko, Eq. Guin. 50 H6 3 30N 8 40 E
Ferndale, Calif., U.S.A. 82 F1 40 35N 124 16W
Ferndale, Wash., U.S.A. 84 B4 48 51N 122 36W
Fernie, Canada 72 D5 49 30N 115 5W
Fernlees, Australia 62 C4 23 51S 148 7 E
Fernley, U.S.A. 82 G4 39 36N 119 15W
Ferozepore = Firozpur, India 42 D6 30 55N 74 40 E
Ferrara, Italy 20 B4 44 50N 11 35 E
Ferreñafe, Peru 92 E3 6 42S 79 50W
Ferrerías, Spain 22 B11 39 59N 4 1 E
Ferret, C., France 18 D3 44 38N 1 15W
Ferriday, U.S.A. 81 K9 31 38N 91 33W
Ferrol = El Ferrol, Spain 19 A1 43 29N 8 15W
Ferron, U.S.A. 83 G8 39 5N 111 8W
Ferryland, Canada 71 C9 47 2N 52 53W
Fertile, U.S.A. 80 B6 47 32N 96 17W
Fès, Morocco 50 B4 34 0N 5 0W
Feshi, Zaïre 52 F3 6 8S 18 10 E
Fessenden, U.S.A. 80 B5 47 39N 99 38W
Feteşti, Romania 17 F14 44 22N 27 51 E
Fetlar, U.K. 12 A8 60 36N 0 52W
Feuilles →, Canada 69 C12 58 47N 70 4W
Fezzan, Libya 51 C8 27 0N 15 0 E
Ffestiniog, U.K. 10 E4 52 57N 3 55W
Fiambalá, Argentina 94 B2 27 45S 67 37W
Fianarantsoa, Madag. 57 C8 21 26S 47 5 E
Fianarantsoa □, Madag. 57 B8 19 30S 47 0 E
Fianga, Cameroon 51 G8 9 55N 15 9 E
Ficksburg, S. Africa 57 D4 28 51S 27 53 E
Field, Canada 70 C3 46 31N 80 1W
Field →, Australia 62 C2 23 48S 138 0 E
Field I., Australia 60 B5 12 5S 132 23 E
Fieri, Albania 21 D8 40 43N 19 33 E
Fife □, U.K. 12 E5 56 16N 3 1W
Fife Ness, U.K. 12 E6 56 17N 2 35W
Figeac, France 18 D5 44 37N 2 2 E
Figtree, Zimbabwe 55 G2 20 22S 28 20 E
Figueira da Foz, Portugal 19 B1 40 7N 8 54W
Figueras, Spain 19 A7 42 18N 2 58 E
Figuig, Morocco 50 B4 32 5N 1 11W
Fihaonana, Madag. 57 B8 18 36S 47 12 E
Fiherenana, Madag. 57 B8 18 29S 48 24 E
Fiherenana →, Madag. 57 C7 23 19S 43 37 E
Fiji ■, Pac. Oc. 59 C8 17 20S 179 0 E
Filer, U.S.A. 82 E6 42 34N 114 37W
Filey, U.K. 10 C7 54 12N 0 18W
Filfla, Malta 23 D1 35 47N 14 24 E
Filiatrá, Greece 21 F9 37 9N 21 35 E
Filipstad, Sweden 9 G16 59 43N 14 9 E
Fillmore, Canada 73 D8 49 50N 103 25W
Fillmore, Calif., U.S.A. 85 L8 34 24N 118 55W
Fillmore, Utah, U.S.A. 83 G7 38 58N 112 20W
Finch, Canada 79 A9 45 11N 75 7W
Findhorn →, U.K. 12 D5 57 38N 3 38W
Findlay, U.S.A. 76 E4 41 2N 83 39W
Finger L., Canada 73 C10 53 33N 93 30W
Fíngõe, Mozam. 55 E3 14 55S 31 50 E
Finisterre, C., Spain 19 A1 42 50N 9 19W
Finke, Australia 62 D1 25 34S 134 35 E
Finke →, Australia 63 D2 27 0S 136 10 E
Finland ■, Europe 8 E22 63 0N 27 0 E
Finland, G. of, Europe 9 G21 60 0N 26 0 E
Finlay →, Canada 72 B3 57 0N 125 10W
Finley, Australia 63 F4 35 38S 145 35 E
Finley, U.S.A. 80 B6 47 31N 97 50W
Finn →, Ireland 13 B4 54 51N 7 28W
Finnigan, Mt., Australia 62 B4 15 49S 145 17 E
Finniss, C., Australia 63 E1 33 8S 134 51 E
Finnmark, Norway 8 B20 69 37N 23 57 E
Finnsnes, Norway 8 B18 69 14N 18 0 E
Finspång, Sweden 9 G16 58 43N 15 47 E
Fiora →, Italy 20 C4 42 20N 11 34 E
Fiq, Syria 47 C4 32 46N 35 41 E
Firat = Furāt, Nahr al →, Asia 44 D5 31 0N 47 25 E
Fire River, Canada 70 C3 48 47N 83 21W
Firebag →, Canada 73 B6 57 45N 111 21W
Firebaugh, U.S.A. 84 J6 36 52N 120 27W
Firedrake L., Canada 73 A8 61 25N 104 30W
Firenze, Italy 20 C4 43 46N 11 15 E
Firk →, Iraq 44 D5 30 59N 44 34 E
Firozabad, India 43 F8 27 10N 78 25 E
Firozpur, India 42 D6 30 55N 74 40 E
Fīrūzābād, Iran 45 D7 28 52N 52 35 E
Fīrūzkūh, Iran 45 C7 35 50N 52 50 E
Firvale, Canada 72 C3 52 27N 126 13W
Fish →, Namibia 56 D2 28 7S 17 10 E
Fish →, S. Africa 56 E3 31 30S 20 16 E
Fisher, Australia 61 F5 30 30S 131 0 E
Fisher B., Canada 73 C9 51 35N 97 13W
Fishguard, U.K. 11 F3 52 0N 5 0W
Fishing L., Canada 73 C9 52 10N 95 24W
Fitchburg, U.S.A. 79 D13 42 35N 71 48W
Fitri, L., Chad 51 F8 12 50N 17 28 E
Fitz Roy, Argentina 96 F3 47 0S 67 0W
Fitzgerald, Canada 72 B6 59 51N 111 36W
Fitzgerald, U.S.A. 77 K4 31 43N 83 15W
Fitzmaurice →, Australia 60 B5 14 45S 130 5 E
Fitzroy →, Queens., Australia 62 C5 23 32S 150 52 E
Fitzroy →, W. Austral., Australia 60 C3 17 31S 123 35 E
Fitzroy Crossing, Australia 60 C4 18 9S 125 38 E
Fitzwilliam I., Canada 78 A3 45 30N 81 45W
Fiume = Rijeka, Croatia 16 F8 45 20N 14 21 E
Five Points, U.S.A. 84 J6 36 26N 120 6W
Fizi, Zaïre 54 C2 4 17S 28 55 E
Flagler, U.S.A. 80 F3 39 18N 103 4W
Flagstaff, U.S.A. 83 J8 35 12N 111 39W
Flaherty I., Canada 70 A4 56 15N 79 15W
Flåm, Norway 9 F12 60 50N 7 7 E
Flambeau →, U.S.A. 80 C9 45 18N 91 14W
Flamborough Hd., U.K. 10 C7 54 7N 0 5W
Flaming Gorge Dam, U.S.A. 82 F9 40 55N 109 25W
Flaming Gorge Reservoir, U.S.A. 82 F9 41 10N 109 25W
Flamingo, Teluk, Indonesia 37 F9 5 30S 138 0 E
Flanders = West-Vlaanderen □, Belgium 15 D3 51 0N 3 0 E
Flandre, Europe 16 C2 51 0N 3 0 E
Flandre Occidentale = West-Vlaanderen □, Belgium 15 D3 51 0N 3 0 E
Flandre Orientale = Oost-Vlaanderen □, Belgium 15 C3 51 5N 3 50 E
Flandreau, U.S.A. 80 C6 44 3N 96 36W
Flanigan, U.S.A. 84 E7 40 10N 119 53W
Flannan Is., U.K. 12 C1 58 9N 7 52W
Flåsjön, Sweden 8 D16 64 5N 15 40 E
Flat →, Canada 72 A3 61 33N 125 18W
Flat River, U.S.A. 81 G9 37 51N 90 31W
Flathead L., U.S.A. 82 C6 47 51N 114 8W
Flattery, C., Australia 62 A4 14 58S 145 21 E
Flattery, C., U.S.A. 84 B2 48 23N 124 29W
Flaxton, U.S.A. 80 A3 48 54N 102 24W
Fleetwood, U.K. 10 D4 53 55N 3 1W
Flekkefjord, Norway 9 G12 58 18N 6 39 E
Flemington, U.S.A. 78 E7 41 7N 77 28W
Flensburg, Germany 16 A5 54 47N 9 27 E
Flers, France 18 B3 48 47N 0 33W
Flesherton, Canada 78 B4 44 16N 80 33W
Flesko, Tanjung, Indonesia 37 D6 0 29N 124 30 E
Flevoland □, Neths. 15 B5 52 30N 5 30 E
Flin Flon, Canada 73 C8 54 46N 101 53W
Flinders →, Australia 62 B3 17 36S 140 36 E
Flinders B., Australia 61 F2 34 19S 115 19 E
Flinders Group, Australia 62 A3 14 11S 144 15 E
Flinders I., Australia 62 F4 40 0S 148 0 E
Flinders Ranges, Australia 63 E2 31 30S 138 30 E
Flinders Reefs, Australia 62 B4 17 37S 148 31 E
Flint, U.K. 10 D4 53 15N 3 8W
Flint, U.S.A. 76 D4 43 1N 83 41W
Flint →, U.S.A. 77 K3 30 57N 84 34W
Flint I., Kiribati 65 J12 11 26S 151 48W
Flinton, Australia 63 D4 27 55S 149 32 E
Flintshire □, U.K. 10 D4 53 17N 3 17W
Flodden, U.K. 10 B5 55 37N 2 8W
Floodwood, U.S.A. 80 B8 46 55N 92 55W
Flora, U.S.A. 76 F1 38 40N 88 29W
Florala, U.S.A. 77 K2 31 0N 86 20W
Florence = Firenze, Italy 20 C4 43 46N 11 15 E
Florence, Ala., U.S.A. 77 H2 34 48N 87 41W
Florence, Ariz., U.S.A. 83 K8 33 2N 111 23W
Florence, Colo., U.S.A. 80 F2 38 23N 105 8W
Florence, Oreg., U.S.A. 82 E1 43 58N 124 7W
Florence, S.C., U.S.A. 77 H6 34 12N 79 46W
Florence, L., Australia 63 D2 28 53S 138 9 E
Florennes, Belgium 15 D4 50 15N 4 35 E
Florenville, Belgium 15 E5 49 40N 5 19 E
Flores, Guatemala 88 C2 16 59N 89 50W
Flores, Indonesia 37 F6 8 35S 121 0 E
Flores I., Canada 72 D3 49 20N 126 10W
Flores Sea, Indonesia 37 F6 6 30S 120 0 E
Floreşti, Moldova 17 E15 47 53N 28 17 E
Floresville, U.S.A. 81 L5 29 8N 98 10W
Floriano, Brazil 93 E10 6 50S 43 0W
Florianópolis, Brazil 95 B6 27 30S 48 30W
Florida, Cuba 88 B4 21 32N 78 14W
Florida, Uruguay 95 C4 34 7S 56 10W
Florida □, U.S.A. 77 L5 28 0N 82 0W
Florida, Straits of, U.S.A. 88 B3 25 0N 80 0W
Florida B., U.S.A. 88 A3 25 0N 80 45W
Florida Keys, U.S.A. 75 F10 24 40N 81 0W
Flórina, Greece 21 D9 40 48N 21 26 E
Florø, Norway 9 F11 61 35N 5 1 E
Flower Station, Canada 79 A8 45 10N 76 41W
Flower's Cove, Canada 71 B8 51 14N 56 46W
Floydada, U.S.A. 81 J4 33 59N 101 20W
Fluk, Indonesia 37 E7 1 42S 127 44 E
Flushing = Vlissingen, Neths. 15 C3 51 26N 3 34 E
Flying Fish, C., Antarctica 5 D15 72 6S 102 29W
Foam Lake, Canada 73 C8 51 40N 103 32W
Foça, Turkey 21 E12 38 39N 26 46 E
Focşani, Romania 17 F14 45 41N 27 15 E
Fóggia, Italy 20 D6 41 27N 15 34 E
Fogo, Canada 71 C9 49 43N 54 17W
Fogo I., Canada 71 C9 49 40N 54 5W
Föhr, Germany 16 A5 54 43N 8 30 E
Foix, France 18 E4 42 58N 1 38 E
Folda, Nord-Trøndelag, Norway 8 D14 64 32N 10 30 E
Folda, Nordland, Norway 8 C16 67 38N 14 50 E
Foleyet, Canada 70 C3 48 15N 82 25W
Folgefonni, Norway 9 F12 60 3N 6 23 E
Foligno, Italy 20 C5 42 57N 12 42 E
Folkestone, U.K. 11 F9 51 5N 1 12 E
Folkston, U.S.A. 77 K5 30 50N 82 0W
Follett, U.S.A. 81 G4 36 26N 100 8W
Folsom Res., U.S.A. 84 G5 38 42N 121 9W
Fond-du-Lac, Canada 73 B7 59 19N 107 12W
Fond du Lac, U.S.A. 80 D10 43 47N 88 27W
Fond-du-Lac →, Canada 73 B7 59 17N 106 0W
Fonda, U.S.A. 79 D10 42 57N 74 22W
Fondi, Italy 20 D5 41 21N 13 25 E
Fonsagrada, Spain 19 A2 43 8N 7 4W
Fonseca, G. de, Cent. Amer. 88 D2 13 10N 87 40W
Fontainebleau, France 18 B5 48 24N 2 40 E
Fontana, U.S.A. 85 L9 34 6N 117 26W
Fontas →, Canada 72 B4 58 14N 121 48W
Fonte Boa, Brazil 92 D5 2 33S 66 0W
Fontenay-le-Comte, France 18 C3 46 28N 0 48W
Fontur, Iceland 8 C6 66 23N 14 32W
Foochow = Fuzhou, China 33 D6 26 5N 119 16 E
Foping, China 34 H4 33 41N 108 0 E
Forbes, Australia 63 E4 33 22S 148 0 E
Forbesganj, India 43 F12 26 17N 87 18 E
Ford City, Calif., U.S.A. 85 K7 35 9N 119 27W
Ford City, Pa., U.S.A. 78 F5 40 46N 79 32W
Førde, Norway 9 F11 61 27N 5 53 E
Ford's Bridge, Australia 63 D4 29 41S 145 29 E
Fordyce, U.S.A. 81 J8 33 49N 92 25W
Forécariah, Guinea 50 G2 9 28N 13 10W
Forel, Mt., Greenland 4 C6 66 52N 36 55W
Foremost, Canada 72 D6 49 26N 111 34W
Forest, Canada 78 C3 43 6N 82 0W
Forest, U.S.A. 81 J10 32 22N 89 29W
Forest City, Iowa, U.S.A. 80 D8 43 16N 93 39W
Forest City, N.C., U.S.A. 77 H5 35 20N 81 52W
Forest City, Pa., U.S.A. 79 E9 41 39N 75 28W
Forest Grove, U.S.A. 84 E3 45 31N 123 7W
Forestburg, Canada 72 C6 52 35N 112 1W
Foresthill, U.S.A. 84 F6 39 1N 120 49W
Forestier Pen., Australia 62 G4 43 0S 148 0 E
Forestville, Canada 71 C6 48 48N 69 2W
Forestville, Calif., U.S.A. 84 G4 38 28N 122 54W
Forestville, Wis., U.S.A. 76 C2 44 41N 87 29W
Forfar, U.K. 12 E6 56 39N 2 53W
Forks, U.S.A. 84 C2 47 57N 124 23W
Forlì, Italy 20 B5 44 13N 12 3 E
Forman, U.S.A. 80 B6 46 7N 97 38W
Formby Pt., U.K. 10 D4 53 33N 3 6W
Formentera, Spain 22 C7 38 43N 1 27 E
Formentor, C. de, Spain 22 B10 39 58N 3 13 E
Former Yugoslav Republic of Macedonia = Macedonia ■, Europe 21 D9 41 53N 21 40 E
Fórmia, Italy 20 D5 41 15N 13 37 E
Formosa = Taiwan ■, Asia 33 D7 23 30N 121 0 E
Formosa, Argentina 94 B4 26 15S 58 10W
Formosa □, Argentina 94 B3 25 0S 60 0W
Formosa, Serra, Brazil 93 F8 12 0S 55 0W
Formosa Bay, Kenya 54 C5 2 40S 40 20 E
Fornells, Spain 22 A11 40 3N 4 7 E
Føroyar, Atl. Oc. 8 F9 62 0N 7 0W
Forres, U.K. 12 D5 57 37N 3 37W
Forrest, Vic., Australia 63 F3 38 33S 143 47 E
Forrest, W. Austral., Australia 61 F4 30 51S 128 6 E
Forrest, Mt., Australia 61 D4 24 48S 127 45 E
Forrest City, U.S.A. 81 H9 35 1N 90 47W
Forsayth, Australia 62 B3 18 33S 143 34 E
Forssa, Finland 9 F20 60 49N 23 38 E
Forst, Germany 16 C8 51 45N 14 37 E
Forster, Australia 63 E5 32 12S 152 31 E
Forsyth, Ga., U.S.A. 77 J4 33 2N 83 56W
Forsyth, Mont., U.S.A. 82 C10 46 16N 106 41W
Fort Albany, Canada 70 B3 52 15N 81 35W
Fort Apache, U.S.A. 83 K9 33 50N 110 0W
Fort Assiniboine, Canada 72 C6 54 20N 114 45W
Fort Augustus, U.K. 12 D4 57 9N 4 42W
Fort Beaufort, S. Africa 56 E4 32 46S 26 40 E
Fort Benton, U.S.A. 82 C8 47 49N 110 40W
Fort Bragg, U.S.A. 82 G2 39 26N 123 48W
Fort Bridger, U.S.A. 82 F8 41 19N 110 23W
Fort Chipewyan, Canada 73 B6 58 42N 111 8W
Fort Collins, U.S.A. 80 E2 40 35N 105 5W
Fort-Coulonge, Canada 70 C4 45 50N 76 45W
Fort Davis, U.S.A. 81 K3 30 35N 103 54W
Fort-de-France, Martinique 89 D7 14 36N 61 2W
Fort de Possel = Possel, C.A.R. 52 C3 5 5N 19 10 E
Fort Defiance, U.S.A. 83 J9 35 45N 109 5W
Fort Dodge, U.S.A. 80 D7 42 30N 94 11W
Fort Edward, U.S.A. 79 C11 43 16N 73 35W
Fort Frances, Canada 73 D10 48 36N 93 24W
Fort Garland, U.S.A. 83 H11 37 26N 105 26W
Fort George = Chisasibi, Canada 70 B4 53 50N 79 0W
Fort Good-Hope, Canada 68 B7 66 14N 128 40W
Fort Hancock, U.S.A. 83 L11 31 18N 105 51W
Fort Hertz = Putao, Burma 41 F20 27 28N 97 30 E
Fort Hope, Canada 70 B2 51 30N 88 0W
Fort Irwin, U.S.A. 85 K10 35 16N 116 34W
Fort Jameson = Chipata, Zambia 55 E3 13 38S 32 28 E
Fort Kent, U.S.A. 71 C6 47 15N 68 36W
Fort Klamath, U.S.A. 82 E3 42 42N 122 0W
Fort-Lamy = Ndjamena, Chad 51 F7 12 10N 14 59 E
Fort Laramie, U.S.A. 80 D2 42 13N 104 31W
Fort Lauderdale, U.S.A. 77 M5 26 7N 80 8W
Fort Liard, Canada 72 A4 60 14N 123 30W
Fort Liberté, Haiti 89 C5 19 42N 71 51W
Fort Lupton, U.S.A. 80 E2 40 5N 104 49W
Fort Mackay, Canada 72 B6 57 12N 111 41W
Fort McKenzie, Canada 71 A6 57 20N 69 0W
Fort Macleod, Canada 72 D6 49 45N 113 30W
Fort MacMahon, Algeria 50 C5 29 43N 1 45 E
Fort McMurray, Canada 72 B6 56 44N 111 7W
Fort McPherson, Canada 68 B6 67 30N 134 55W
Fort Madison, U.S.A. 80 E9 40 38N 91 27W
Fort Meade, U.S.A. 77 M5 27 45N 81 48W
Fort Miribel, Algeria 50 C5 29 25N 2 55 E
Fort Morgan, U.S.A. 80 E3 40 15N 103 48W
Fort Myers, U.S.A. 77 M5 26 39N 81 52W
Fort Nelson, Canada 72 B4 58 50N 122 44W
Fort Nelson →, Canada 72 B4 59 32N 124 0W
Fort Norman = Tulita, Canada 68 B7 64 57N 125 30W
Fort Payne, U.S.A. 77 H3 34 26N 85 43W
Fort Peck, U.S.A. 82 B10 48 1N 106 27W
Fort Peck Dam, U.S.A. 82 C10 48 0N 106 26W
Fort Peck L., U.S.A. 82 C10 48 0N 106 26W
Fort Pierce, U.S.A. 77 M5 27 27N 80 20W
Fort Pierre, U.S.A. 80 C4 44 21N 100 22W
Fort Plain, U.S.A. 79 D10 42 56N 74 37W
Fort Portal, Uganda 54 B3 0 40N 30 20 E
Fort Providence, Canada 72 A5 61 3N 117 40W
Fort Qu'Appelle, Canada 73 C8 50 45N 103 50W
Fort Resolution, Canada 72 A6 61 10N 113 40W
Fort Rixon, Zimbabwe 55 G2 20 2S 29 17 E
Fort Rosebery = Mansa, Zambia 55 E2 11 13S 28 55 E
Fort Ross, U.S.A. 84 G3 38 32N 123 13W
Fort Rupert = Waskaganish, Canada 70 B4 51 30N 78 40W
Fort St. James, Canada 72 C4 54 30N 124 10W
Fort St. John, Canada 72 B4 56 15N 120 50W
Fort Sandeman, Pakistan 42 D3 31 20N 69 31 E
Fort Saskatchewan, Canada 72 C6 53 40N 113 15W
Fort Scott, U.S.A. 81 G7 37 50N 94 42W
Fort Severn, Canada 70 A2 56 0N 87 40W
Fort Shevchenko, Kazakstan 25 F9 44 35N 50 23 E
Fort Simpson, Canada 72 A4 61 45N 121 15W
Fort Smith, Canada 72 B6 60 0N 111 51W
Fort Smith, U.S.A. 81 H7 35 23N 94 25W
Fort Stanton, U.S.A. 83 K11 33 30N 105 31W
Fort Stockton, U.S.A. 81 K3 30 53N 102 53W
Fort Sumner, U.S.A. 81 H2 34 28N 104 15W
Fort Trinquet = Bir Mogrein, Mauritania 50 C2 25 10N 11 25W
Fort Valley, U.S.A. 77 J4 32 33N 83 53W
Fort Vermilion, Canada 72 B5 58 24N 116 0W
Fort Walton Beach, U.S.A. 77 K2 30 25N 86 36W
Fort Wayne, U.S.A. 76 E3 41 4N 85 9W
Fort William, U.K. 12 E3 56 49N 5 7W
Fort Worth, U.S.A. 81 J6 32 45N 97 18W
Fort Yates, U.S.A. 80 B4 46 5N 100 38W
Fort Yukon, U.S.A. 68 B5 66 34N 145 16W
Fortaleza, Brazil 93 D11 3 45S 38 35W
Forteau, Canada 71 B8 51 28N 56 58W
Forth →, U.K. 12 E5 56 9N 3 50W
Forth, Firth of, U.K. 12 E6 56 5N 2 55W
Fortrose, U.K. 12 D4 57 35N 4 9W
Fortuna, Calif., U.S.A. 82 F1 40 36N 124 9W
Fortuna, N. Dak., U.S.A. 80 A3 48 55N 103 47W
Fortune B., Canada 71 C8 47 30N 55 22W
Foshan, China 33 D6 23 4N 113 5 E
Fosna, Norway 8 E14 63 50N 10 20 E
Fosnavåg, Norway 9 E11 62 22N 5 38 E
Fossano, Italy 20 B2 44 33N 7 43 E
Fossil, U.S.A. 82 D3 45 0N 120 9W
Fossilbrook, Australia 62 B3 17 47S 144 29 E
Fosston, U.S.A. 80 B7 47 35N 95 45W
Foster, Canada 79 A12 45 17N 72 30W
Foster →, Canada 73 B7 55 47N 105 49W
Fosters Ra., Australia 62 C1 21 35S 133 48 E
Fostoria, U.S.A. 76 E4 41 10N 83 25W

Fougamou, *Gabon* **52 E2** 1 16S 10 30 E
Fougères, *France* **18 B3** 48 21N 1 14W
Foul Pt., *Sri Lanka* **40 Q12** 8 35N 81 18 E
Foula, *U.K.* **12 A6** 60 10N 2 5W
Foulness I., *U.K.* **11 F8** 51 36N 0 55 E
Foulpointe, *Madag.* **57 B8** 17 41S 49 31 E
Foumban, *Cameroon* **50 G7** 5 45N 10 50 E
Fountain, *Colo., U.S.A.* **80 F2** 38 41N 104 42W
Fountain, *Utah, U.S.A.* **82 G8** 39 41N 111 37W
Fountain Springs, *U.S.A.* **85 K8** 35 54N 118 51W
Fourchu, *Canada* **71 C7** 45 43N 60 17W
Fouriesburg, *S. Africa* **56 D4** 28 38S 28 14 E
Foúrnoi, *Greece* **21 F12** 37 36N 26 32 E
Fouta Djalon, *Guinea* **50 F2** 11 20N 12 10W
Foux, Cap-à-, *Haiti* **89 C5** 19 43N 73 27W
Foveaux Str., *N.Z.* **59 M2** 46 42S 168 10 E
Fowey, *U.K.* **11 G3** 50 20N 4 39W
Fowler, *Calif., U.S.A.* **83 H4** 36 38N 119 41W
Fowler, *Colo., U.S.A.* **80 F2** 38 8N 104 2W
Fowler, *Kans., U.S.A.* **81 G4** 37 23N 100 12W
Fowlers B., *Australia* **61 F5** 31 59S 132 34 E
Fowlerton, *U.S.A.* **81 L5** 28 28N 98 48W
Fox —►, *Canada* **73 B10** 56 3N 93 18W
Fox Valley, *Canada* **73 C7** 50 30N 109 25W
Foxe Basin, *Canada* **69 B12** 66 0N 77 0W
Foxe Chan., *Canada* **69 B11** 65 0N 80 0W
Foxe Pen., *Canada* **69 B12** 65 0N 76 0W
Foxpark, *U.S.A.* **82 F10** 41 5N 106 9W
Foxton, *N.Z.* **59 J5** 40 29S 175 18 E
Foyle, Lough, *U.K.* **13 A4** 55 7N 7 4W
Foynes, *Ireland* **13 D2** 52 37N 9 7W
Fóz do Cunene, *Angola* **56 B1** 17 15S 11 48 E
Foz do Gregório, *Brazil* **92 E4** 6 47S 70 44W
Foz do Iguaçu, *Brazil* **95 B5** 25 30S 54 30W
Frackville, *U.S.A.* **79 F8** 40 47N 76 14W
Framingham, *U.S.A.* **79 D13** 42 17N 71 25W
Franca, *Brazil* **93 H9** 20 33S 47 30W
Francavilla Fontana, *Italy* **21 D7** 40 32N 17 35 E
France ■, *Europe* **18 C5** 47 0N 3 0 E
Frances, *Australia* **63 F3** 36 41S 140 55 E
Frances —►, *Canada* **72 A3** 60 16N 129 10W
Frances L., *Canada* **72 A3** 61 23N 129 30W
Francés Viejo, C., *Dom. Rep.* **89 C6** 19 40N 69 55W
Franceville, *Gabon* **52 E2** 1 40S 13 32 E
Franche-Comté, *France* **18 C6** 46 50N 5 55 E
Francisco I. Madero, *Coahuila, Mexico* **86 B4** 25 48N 103 18W
Francisco I. Madero, *Durango, Mexico* **86 C4** 24 32N 104 22W
Francistown, *Botswana* **57 C4** 21 7S 27 33 E
François, *Canada* **71 C8** 47 35N 56 45W
François L., *Canada* **72 C3** 54 0N 125 30W
Franeker, *Neths.* **15 A5** 53 12N 5 33 E
Frankfort, *S. Africa* **57 D4** 27 17S 28 30 E
Frankfort, *Ind., U.S.A.* **76 E2** 40 17N 86 31W
Frankfort, *Kans., U.S.A.* **80 F6** 39 42N 96 25W
Frankfort, *Ky., U.S.A.* **76 F3** 38 12N 84 52W
Frankfort, *Mich., U.S.A.* **76 C2** 44 38N 86 14W
Frankfurt, *Brandenburg, Germany* **16 B8** 52 20N 14 32 E
Frankfurt, *Hessen, Germany* **16 C5** 50 7N 8 41 E
Fränkische Alb, *Germany* **16 D6** 49 10N 11 23 E
Frankland —►, *Australia* **61 G2** 35 0S 116 48 E
Franklin, *Ky., U.S.A.* **77 G2** 36 43N 86 35W
Franklin, *La., U.S.A.* **81 L9** 29 48N 91 30W
Franklin, *Mass., U.S.A.* **79 D13** 42 5N 71 24W
Franklin, *N.H., U.S.A.* **79 C13** 43 27N 71 39W
Franklin, *Nebr., U.S.A.* **80 E5** 40 6N 98 57W
Franklin, *Pa., U.S.A.* **78 E5** 41 24N 79 50W
Franklin, *Tenn., U.S.A.* **77 H2** 35 55N 86 52W
Franklin, *Va., U.S.A.* **77 G7** 36 41N 76 56W
Franklin, *W. Va., U.S.A.* **76 F6** 38 39N 79 20W
Franklin B., *Canada* **68 B7** 69 45N 126 0W
Franklin D. Roosevelt L., *U.S.A.* **82 B4** 48 18N 118 9W
Franklin I., *Antarctica* **5 D11** 76 10S 168 30 E
Franklin L., *U.S.A.* **82 F6** 40 25N 115 22W
Franklin Mts., *Canada* **68 B7** 65 0N 125 0W
Franklin Str., *Canada* **68 A10** 72 0N 96 0W
Franklinton, *U.S.A.* **81 K9** 30 51N 90 9W
Franklinville, *U.S.A.* **78 D6** 42 20N 78 27W
Franks Pk., *U.S.A.* **82 E9** 43 58N 109 18W
Frankston, *Australia* **63 F4** 38 8S 145 8 E
Frantsa Iosifa, Zemlya, *Russia* **26 A6** 82 0N 55 0 E
Franz, *Canada* **70 C3** 48 25N 84 30W
Franz Josef Land = Frantsa Iosifa, Zemlya, *Russia* **26 A6** 82 0N 55 0 E
Fraser —►, *B.C., Canada* **72 D4** 49 7N 123 11W
Fraser —►, *Nfld., Canada* **71 A7** 56 39N 62 10W
Fraser, Mt., *Australia* **61 E2** 25 35S 118 20 E
Fraser I., *Australia* **63 D5** 25 15S 153 10 E
Fraser Lake, *Canada* **72 C4** 54 0N 124 50W
Fraserburg, *S. Africa* **56 E3** 31 55S 21 30 E
Fraserburgh, *U.K.* **12 D6** 57 42N 2 1W
Fraserdale, *Canada* **70 C3** 49 55N 81 37W
Fray Bentos, *Uruguay* **94 C4** 33 10S 58 15W
Frazier Downs, *Australia* **60 C3** 18 48S 121 42 E
Fredericia, *Denmark* **9 J13** 55 34N 9 45 E
Frederick, *Md., U.S.A.* **76 F7** 39 25N 77 25W
Frederick, *Okla., U.S.A.* **81 H5** 34 23N 99 1W
Frederick, *S. Dak., U.S.A.* **80 C5** 45 50N 98 31W
Frederick Sd., *U.S.A.* **72 B2** 57 10N 134 0W
Fredericksburg, *Tex., U.S.A.* **81 K5** 30 16N 98 52W
Fredericksburg, *Va., U.S.A.* **76 F7** 38 18N 77 28W
Fredericktown, *U.S.A.* **81 G9** 37 34N 90 18W
Frederico I. Madero, Presa, *Mexico* **86 B3** 28 7N 105 40W
Fredericton, *Canada* **71 C6** 45 57N 66 40W
Fredericton Junc., *Canada* **71 C6** 45 41N 66 40W
Frederikshåb, *Greenland* **4 C5** 62 0N 49 43W
Frederikshavn, *Denmark* **9 H14** 57 28N 10 31 E
Frederiksted, *Virgin Is.* **89 C7** 17 43N 64 53W
Fredonia, *Ariz., U.S.A.* **83 H7** 36 57N 112 32W
Fredonia, *Kans., U.S.A.* **81 G7** 37 32N 95 49W
Fredonia, *N.Y., U.S.A.* **78 D5** 42 26N 79 20W
Fredrikstad, *Norway* **9 G14** 59 13N 10 57 E
Free State □, *S. Africa* **56 D4** 28 30S 27 0 E
Freehold, *U.S.A.* **79 F10** 40 16N 74 17W
Freel Peak, *U.S.A.* **84 G7** 38 52N 119 54W
Freeland, *U.S.A.* **79 E9** 41 1N 75 54W
Freels, C., *Canada* **71 C9** 49 15N 53 30W
Freeman, *Calif., U.S.A.* **85 K9** 35 35N 117 53W
Freeman, *S. Dak., U.S.A.* **80 D6** 43 21N 97 26W
Freeport, *Bahamas* **88 A4** 26 30N 78 47W
Freeport, *Canada* **71 D6** 44 15N 66 20W
Freeport, *Ill., U.S.A.* **80 D10** 42 17N 89 36W
Freeport, *N.Y., U.S.A.* **79 F11** 40 39N 73 35W
Freeport, *Tex., U.S.A.* **81 L7** 28 57N 95 21W
Freetown, *S. Leone* **50 G2** 8 30N 13 17W
Frégate, L., *Canada* **70 B5** 53 15N 74 45W
Fregenal de la Sierra, *Spain* **19 C2** 38 10N 6 39W
Freibourg = Fribourg, *Switz.* **16 E4** 46 49N 7 9 E
Freiburg, *Germany* **16 E4** 47 59N 7 51 E
Freire, *Chile* **96 D2** 38 54S 72 38W
Freirina, *Chile* **94 B1** 28 30S 71 10W
Freising, *Germany* **16 D6** 48 24N 11 45 E
Freistadt, *Austria* **16 D8** 48 30N 14 30 E
Fréjus, *France* **18 E7** 43 25N 6 44 E
Fremantle, *Australia* **61 F2** 32 7S 115 47 E
Fremont, *Calif., U.S.A.* **83 H2** 37 32N 121 57W
Fremont, *Mich., U.S.A.* **76 D3** 43 28N 85 57W
Fremont, *Nebr., U.S.A.* **80 E6** 41 26N 96 30W
Fremont, *Ohio, U.S.A.* **76 E4** 41 21N 83 7W
Fremont —►, *U.S.A.* **83 G8** 38 24N 110 42W
Fremont L., *U.S.A.* **82 E9** 42 57N 109 48W
French Camp, *U.S.A.* **84 H5** 37 53N 121 16W
French Creek —►, *U.S.A.* **78 E5** 41 24N 79 50W
French Guiana ■, *S. Amer.* **93 C8** 4 0N 53 0W
French Pass, *N.Z.* **59 J4** 40 55S 173 55 E
French Polynesia ■, *Pac. Oc.* **65 J13** 20 0S 145 0W
Frenchglen, *U.S.A.* **82 E4** 42 50N 118 55W
Frenchman Butte, *Canada* **73 C7** 53 35N 109 38W
Frenchman Cr. —►, *Mont., U.S.A.* **82 B10** 48 31N 107 10W
Frenchman Cr. —►, *Nebr., U.S.A.* **80 E4** 40 14N 100 50W
Fresco —►, *Brazil* **93 E8** 7 15S 51 30W
Freshfield, C., *Antarctica* **5 C10** 68 25S 151 10 E
Fresnillo, *Mexico* **86 C4** 23 10N 103 0W
Fresno, *U.S.A.* **83 H4** 36 44N 119 47W
Fresno Reservoir, *U.S.A.* **82 B9** 48 36N 109 57W
Frew —►, *Australia* **62 C2** 20 0S 135 38 E
Frewena, *Australia* **62 B2** 19 25S 135 25 E
Freycinet Pen., *Australia* **62 G4** 42 10S 148 25 E
Fria, C., *Namibia* **56 B1** 18 0S 12 0 E
Friant, *U.S.A.* **84 J7** 36 59N 119 43W
Frías, *Argentina* **94 B2** 28 40S 65 5W
Fribourg, *Switz.* **16 E4** 46 49N 7 9 E
Friday Harbor, *U.S.A.* **84 B3** 48 32N 123 1W
Friedrichshafen, *Germany* **16 E5** 47 39N 9 30 E
Friendly Is. = Tonga ■, *Pac. Oc.* **59 D11** 19 50S 174 30W
Friesland □, *Neths.* **15 A5** 53 5N 5 50 E
Frio —►, *U.S.A.* **81 L5** 28 26N 98 11W
Frio, C., *Brazil* **90 F6** 22 50S 41 50W
Friona, *U.S.A.* **81 H3** 34 38N 102 43W
Fritch, *U.S.A.* **81 H4** 35 38N 101 36W
Frobisher B., *Canada* **69 B13** 62 30N 66 0W
Frobisher Bay = Iqaluit, *Canada* **69 B13** 63 44N 68 31W
Frobisher L., *Canada* **73 B7** 56 20N 108 15W
Frohavet, *Norway* **8 E13** 64 0N 9 30 E
Froid, *U.S.A.* **80 A2** 48 20N 104 30W
Fromberg, *U.S.A.* **82 D9** 45 24N 108 54W
Frome, *U.K.* **11 F5** 51 14N 2 19W
Frome, L., *Australia* **63 E2** 30 45S 139 45 E
Frome Downs, *Australia* **63 E2** 31 13S 139 45 E
Front Range, *U.S.A.* **82 G11** 40 25N 105 45W
Front Royal, *U.S.A.* **76 F6** 38 55N 78 12W
Frontera, *Canary Is.* **22 G2** 27 47N 17 59W
Frontera, *Mexico* **87 D6** 18 30N 92 40W
Frosinone, *Italy* **20 D5** 41 38N 13 19 E
Frostburg, *U.S.A.* **76 F6** 39 39N 78 56W
Frostisen, *Norway* **8 B17** 68 14N 17 10 E
Frøya, *Norway* **8 E13** 63 43N 8 40 E
Frunze = Bishkek, *Kyrgyzstan* **26 E8** 42 54N 74 46 E
Frutal, *Brazil* **93 G9** 20 0S 49 0W
Frýdek-Místek, *Czech.* **17 D10** 49 40N 18 20 E
Fu Xian, *Liaoning, China* **35 E11** 39 38N 121 58 E
Fu Xian, *Shaanxi, China* **34 F5** 36 0N 109 20 E
Fucheng, *China* **34 F9** 37 50N 116 10 E
Fuchou = Fuzhou, *China* **33 D6** 26 5N 119 16 E
Fuchū, *Japan* **31 G6** 34 34N 133 14 E
Fuencaliente, *Canary Is.* **22 F2** 28 28N 17 50W
Fuencaliente, Pta., *Canary Is.* **22 F2** 28 27N 17 51W
Fuengirola, *Spain* **19 D3** 36 32N 4 41W
Fuentes de Oñoro, *Spain* **19 B2** 40 33N 6 52W
Fuerte —►, *Mexico* **86 B3** 25 50N 109 25W
Fuerte Olimpo, *Paraguay* **94 A4** 21 0S 57 51W
Fuerteventura, *Canary Is.* **22 F6** 28 30N 14 0W
Fufeng, *China* **34 G4** 34 22N 108 0 E
Fugou, *China* **34 G8** 34 3N 114 25 E
Fugu, *China* **34 E6** 39 2N 111 3 E
Fuhai, *China* **32 B3** 47 2N 87 25 E
Fuḩaymī, *Iraq* **44 C4** 34 16N 42 10 E
Fuji, *Japan* **31 G9** 35 9N 138 39 E
Fuji-San, *Japan* **31 G9** 35 22N 138 44 E
Fuji-yoshida, *Japan* **31 G9** 35 30N 138 46 E
Fujian □, *China* **33 D6** 26 0N 118 0 E
Fujinomiya, *Japan* **31 G9** 35 10N 138 40 E
Fujisawa, *Japan* **31 G9** 35 22N 139 29 E
Fukien = Fujian □, *China* **33 D6** 26 0N 118 0 E
Fukuchiyama, *Japan* **31 G7** 35 19N 135 9 E
Fukue-Shima, *Japan* **31 H4** 32 40N 128 45 E
Fukui, *Japan* **31 F8** 36 5N 136 10 E
Fukui □, *Japan* **31 G8** 36 0N 136 12 E
Fukuoka, *Japan* **31 H5** 33 39N 130 21 E
Fukuoka □, *Japan* **31 H5** 33 30N 131 0 E
Fukushima, *Japan* **30 F10** 37 44N 140 28 E
Fukushima □, *Japan* **30 F10** 37 30N 140 15 E
Fukuyama, *Japan* **31 G6** 34 35N 133 20 E
Fulda, *Germany* **16 C5** 50 32N 9 40 E
Fulda —►, *Germany* **16 C5** 51 25N 9 39 E
Fullerton, *Calif., U.S.A.* **85 M9** 33 53N 117 56W
Fullerton, *Nebr., U.S.A.* **80 E5** 41 22N 97 58W
Fulongquan, *China* **35 B13** 44 20N 124 42 E
Fulton, *Mo., U.S.A.* **80 F9** 38 52N 91 57W
Fulton, *N.Y., U.S.A.* **79 C8** 43 19N 76 25W
Fulton, *Tenn., U.S.A.* **77 G1** 36 31N 88 53W
Funabashi, *Japan* **31 G10** 35 45N 140 0 E
Funchal, *Madeira* **22 D3** 32 38N 16 54W
Fundación, *Colombia* **92 A4** 10 31N 74 11W
Fundão, *Portugal* **19 B2** 40 8N 7 30W
Fundy, B. of, *Canada* **71 D6** 45 0N 66 0W
Funing, *Hebei, China* **35 E10** 39 53N 119 12 E
Funing, *Jiangsu, China* **35 H10** 33 45N 119 50 E
Funiu Shan, *China* **34 H7** 33 30N 112 20 E
Funtua, *Nigeria* **50 F6** 11 30N 7 18 E
Fuping, *Hebei, China* **34 E8** 38 48N 114 12 E
Fuping, *Shaanxi, China* **34 G5** 34 42N 109 10 E
Furano, *Japan* **30 C11** 43 21N 142 23 E
Furāt, Nahr al —►, *Asia* **44 D5** 31 0N 47 25 E
Fūrg, *Iran* **45 D7** 28 18N 55 13 E
Furnás, *Spain* **22 B8** 39 3N 1 32 E
Furnas, Represa de, *Brazil* **95 A6** 20 50S 45 30W
Furneaux Group, *Australia* **62 G4** 40 10S 147 50 E
Furness, *U.K.* **10 C4** 54 14N 3 8W
Furqlus, *Syria* **47 A6** 34 36N 37 8 E
Fürstenwalde, *Germany* **16 B8** 52 22N 14 3 E
Fürth, *Germany* **16 D6** 49 28N 10 59 E
Furukawa, *Japan* **30 E10** 38 34N 140 58 E
Fury and Hecla Str., *Canada* **69 B11** 69 56N 84 0W
Fusagasuga, *Colombia* **92 C4** 4 21N 74 22W
Fushan, *Shandong, China* **35 F11** 37 30N 121 15 E
Fushan, *Shanxi, China* **34 G6** 35 58N 111 51 E
Fushun, *China* **35 D12** 41 50N 123 56 E
Fusong, *China* **35 C14** 42 20N 127 15 E
Futuna, *Wall. & F. Is.* **59 B8** 14 25S 178 20 E
Fuxin, *China* **35 C11** 42 5N 121 48 E
Fuyang, *China* **34 H8** 33 0N 115 48 E
Fuyang He —►, *China* **34 E9** 38 12N 117 0 E
Fuyu, *China* **35 B13** 45 12N 124 43 E
Fuzhou, *China* **33 D6** 26 5N 119 16 E
Fylde, *U.K.* **10 D5** 53 50N 2 58W
Fyn, *Denmark* **9 J14** 55 20N 10 30 E
Fyne, L., *U.K.* **12 F3** 55 59N 5 23W

G

Gabela, *Angola* **52 G2** 11 0S 14 24 E
Gabès, *Tunisia* **50 B7** 33 53N 10 2 E
Gabès, G. de, *Tunisia* **51 B7** 34 0N 10 30 E
Gabon ■, *Africa* **52 E2** 0 10S 10 0 E
Gaborone, *Botswana* **56 C4** 24 45S 25 57 E
Gabriels, *U.S.A.* **79 B10** 44 26N 74 12W
Gābrīk, *Iran* **45 E8** 25 44N 58 28 E
Gabrovo, *Bulgaria* **21 C11** 42 52N 25 19 E
Gāch Sār, *Iran* **45 B6** 36 7N 51 19 E
Gachsārān, *Iran* **45 D6** 30 15N 50 45 E
Gadag, *India* **40 M9** 15 30N 75 45 E
Gadap, *Pakistan* **42 G2** 25 5N 67 28 E
Gadarwara, *India* **43 H8** 22 50N 78 50 E
Gadhada, *India* **42 J4** 22 0N 71 35 E
Gadsden, *Ala., U.S.A.* **77 H2** 34 1N 86 1W
Gadsden, *Ariz., U.S.A.* **83 K6** 32 33N 114 47W
Gadwal, *India* **40 L10** 16 10N 77 50 E
Gaffney, *U.S.A.* **77 H5** 35 5N 81 39W
Gafsa, *Tunisia* **50 B6** 34 24N 8 43 E
Gagetown, *Canada* **71 C6** 45 46N 66 10W
Gagnoa, *Ivory C.* **50 G3** 6 56N 5 16W
Gagnon, *Canada* **71 B6** 51 50N 68 5W
Gagnon, L., *Canada* **73 A6** 62 3N 110 27W
Gahini, *Rwanda* **54 C3** 1 50S 30 30 E
Gahmar, *India* **43 G10** 25 27N 83 49 E
Gai Xian, *China* **35 D12** 40 22N 122 20 E
Gaïdhouronisi, *Greece* **23 E7** 34 53N 25 41 E
Gail, *U.S.A.* **81 J4** 32 46N 101 27W
Gaillimh = Galway, *Ireland* **13 C2** 53 17N 9 3W
Gaines, *U.S.A.* **78 E7** 41 46N 77 35W
Gainesville, *Fla., U.S.A.* **77 L4** 29 40N 82 20W
Gainesville, *Ga., U.S.A.* **77 H4** 34 18N 83 50W
Gainesville, *Mo., U.S.A.* **81 G8** 36 36N 92 26W
Gainesville, *Tex., U.S.A.* **81 J6** 33 38N 97 8W
Gainsborough, *U.K.* **10 D7** 53 24N 0 46W
Gairdner, L., *Australia* **63 E2** 31 30S 136 0 E
Gairloch, L., *U.K.* **12 D3** 57 43N 5 45W
Gakuch, *Pakistan* **43 A5** 36 7N 73 45 E
Galán, Cerro, *Argentina* **94 B2** 25 55S 66 52W
Galana —►, *Kenya* **54 C5** 3 9S 40 8 E
Galangue, *Angola* **53 G3** 13 42S 16 9 E
Galápagos, *Pac. Oc.* **90 D1** 0 0 91 0W
Galashiels, *U.K.* **12 F6** 55 37N 2 49W
Galaţi, *Romania* **17 F15** 45 27N 28 2 E
Galatina, *Italy* **21 D8** 40 10N 18 10 E
Galax, *U.S.A.* **77 G5** 36 40N 80 56W
Galbraith, *Australia* **62 B3** 16 25S 141 30 E
Galcaio, *Somali Rep.* **46 F4** 6 30N 47 30 E
Galdhøpiggen, *Norway* **9 F12** 61 38N 8 18 E
Galeana, *Mexico* **86 C4** 24 50N 100 4W
Galela, *Indonesia* **37 D7** 1 50N 127 49 E
Galera Point, *Trin. & Tob.* **89 D7** 10 8N 61 0W
Galesburg, *U.S.A.* **80 E9** 40 57N 90 22W
Galeton, *U.S.A.* **78 E7** 41 44N 77 39W
Galich, *Russia* **24 C7** 58 22N 42 24 E
Galicia □, *Spain* **19 A2** 42 43N 7 45W
Galilee = Hagalil, *Israel* **47 C4** 32 53N 35 18 E
Galilee, L., *Australia* **62 C4** 22 20S 145 50 E
Galilee, Sea of = Yam Kinneret, *Israel* **47 C4** 32 45N 35 35 E
Galinoporni, *Cyprus* **23 D13** 35 31N 34 18 E
Galion, *U.S.A.* **78 F2** 40 44N 82 47W
Galiuro Mts., *U.S.A.* **83 K8** 32 30N 110 20W
Gallabat, *Sudan* **51 F12** 12 58N 36 11 E
Gallatin, *U.S.A.* **77 G2** 36 24N 86 27W
Galle, *Sri Lanka* **40 R12** 6 5N 80 10 E
Gállego —►, *Spain* **19 B5** 41 39N 0 51W
Gallegos —►, *Argentina* **96 G3** 51 35S 69 0W
Galley Hd., *Ireland* **13 E3** 51 32N 8 55W
Gallinas, Pta., *Colombia* **92 A4** 12 28N 71 40W
Gallipoli = Gelibolu, *Turkey* **21 D12** 40 28N 26 43 E
Gallipoli, *Italy* **21 D8** 40 3N 17 58 E
Gallipolis, *U.S.A.* **76 F4** 38 49N 82 12W
Gällivare, *Sweden* **8 C19** 67 9N 20 40 E
Galloway, *U.K.* **12 G4** 55 1N 4 29W
Galloway, Mull of, *U.K.* **12 G4** 54 39N 4 52W
Gallup, *U.S.A.* **83 J9** 35 32N 108 45W
Galong, *Australia* **63 E4** 34 37S 148 34 E
Galoya, *Sri Lanka* **40 Q12** 8 10N 80 55 E
Galt, *U.S.A.* **84 G5** 38 15N 121 18W
Galty Mts., *Ireland* **13 D3** 52 22N 8 10W
Galtymore, *Ireland* **13 D3** 52 21N 8 11W
Galva, *U.S.A.* **80 E9** 41 10N 90 3W
Galveston, *U.S.A.* **81 L7** 29 18N 94 48W
Galveston B., *U.S.A.* **81 L7** 29 36N 94 50W
Gálvez, *Argentina* **94 C3** 32 0S 61 14W
Galway, *Ireland* **13 C2** 53 17N 9 3W
Galway □, *Ireland* **13 C2** 53 22N 9 1W
Galway B., *Ireland* **13 C2** 53 13N 9 10W
Gam —►, *Vietnam* **38 B5** 21 55N 105 12 E
Gamagori, *Japan* **31 G8** 34 50N 137 14 E
Gambaga, *Ghana* **50 F4** 10 30N 0 28W
Gambat, *Pakistan* **42 F3** 27 17N 68 26 E
Gambela, *Ethiopia* **51 G11** 8 14N 34 38 E
Gambia ■, *W. Afr.* **50 F1** 13 25N 16 0W
Gambia —►, *W. Afr.* **50 F1** 13 28N 16 34W
Gambier, C., *Australia* **60 B5** 11 56S 130 57 E
Gambier Is., *Australia* **63 F2** 35 3S 136 30 E
Gamboli, *Pakistan* **42 E3** 29 53N 68 24 E
Gamboma, *Congo* **52 E3** 1 55S 15 52 E
Gamerco, *U.S.A.* **83 J9** 35 34N 108 46W
Gamlakarleby = Kokkola, *Finland* **8 E20** 63 50N 23 8 E
Gammon —►, *Canada* **73 C9** 51 24N 95 44W
Gan Jiang —►, *China* **33 D6** 29 15N 116 0 E
Ganado, *Ariz., U.S.A.* **83 J9** 35 43N 109 33W
Ganado, *Tex., U.S.A.* **81 L6** 29 2N 96 31W
Gananoque, *Canada* **70 D4** 44 20N 76 10W
Ganāveh, *Iran* **45 D6** 29 35N 50 35 E
Gäncä, *Azerbaijan* **25 F8** 40 45N 46 20 E
Gand = Gent, *Belgium* **15 C3** 51 2N 3 42 E
Ganda, *Angola* **53 G2** 13 3S 14 35 E
Gandak —►, *India* **43 G11** 25 39N 85 13 E
Gandava, *Pakistan* **42 E2** 28 32N 67 32 E
Gander, *Canada* **71 C9** 48 58N 54 35W
Gander L., *Canada* **71 C9** 48 58N 54 35W
Ganderowe Falls, *Zimbabwe* **55 F2** 17 20S 29 10 E
Gandhi Sagar, *India* **42 G6** 24 40N 75 40 E
Gandi, *Nigeria* **50 F6** 12 55N 5 49 E
Gandia, *Spain* **19 C5** 38 58N 0 9W
Gando, Pta., *Canary Is.* **22 G4** 27 55N 15 22W
Ganedidalem = Gani, *Indonesia* **37 E7** 0 48S 128 14 E
Ganga —►, *India* **43 H14** 23 20N 90 30 E
Ganga, Mouths of the, *India* **43 J13** 21 30N 90 0 E
Ganganagar, *India* **42 E5** 29 56N 73 56 E
Gangapur, *India* **42 F7** 26 32N 76 49 E
Gangara, *Niger* **50 F6** 14 35N 8 29 E
Gangaw, *Burma* **41 H19** 22 5N 94 5 E
Gangdisê Shan, *China* **41 D12** 31 20N 81 0 E
Ganges = Ganga —►, *India* **43 H14** 23 20N 90 30 E
Gangoh, *India* **42 E7** 29 46N 77 18 E
Gangtok, *India* **41 F16** 27 20N 88 37 E
Gangu, *China* **34 G3** 34 40N 105 15 E
Gangyao, *China* **35 B14** 44 12N 126 37 E
Gani, *Indonesia* **37 E7** 0 48S 128 14 E
Ganj, *India* **43 F8** 27 45N 78 57 E
Gannett Peak, *U.S.A.* **82 E9** 43 11N 109 39W
Gannvalley, *U.S.A.* **80 C5** 44 2N 98 59W
Ganquan, *China* **34 F5** 36 20N 109 20 E
Gansu □, *China* **34 G3** 36 0N 104 0 E
Ganta, *Liberia* **50 G3** 7 15N 8 59W
Gantheaume, C., *Australia* **63 F2** 36 4S 137 32 E
Gantheaume B., *Australia* **61 E1** 27 40S 114 10 E
Gantsevichi = Hantsavichy, *Belarus* **17 B14** 52 49N 26 30 E
Ganyem, *Indonesia* **37 E10** 2 46S 140 12 E
Ganyu, *China* **35 G10** 34 50N 119 8 E
Ganzhou, *China* **33 D6** 25 51N 114 56 E
Gaomi, *China* **35 F10** 36 20N 119 42 E
Gaoping, *China* **34 G7** 35 45N 112 55 E
Gaotang, *China* **34 F9** 36 50N 116 15 E
Gaoua, *Burkina Faso* **50 F4** 10 20N 3 8W
Gaoual, *Guinea* **50 F2** 11 45N 13 25W
Gaoxiong = Kaohsiung, *Taiwan* **33 D7** 22 35N 120 16 E
Gaoyang, *China* **34 E8** 38 40N 115 45 E
Gaoyou Hu, *China* **35 H10** 32 45N 119 20 E
Gaoyuan, *China* **35 F9** 37 8N 117 58 E
Gap, *France* **18 D7** 44 33N 6 5 E
Gar, *China* **32 C2** 32 10N 79 58 E
Garabogazköl Aylagy, *Turkmenistan* **25 F9** 41 0N 53 30 E
Garachico, *Canary Is.* **22 F3** 28 22N 16 46W
Garachiné, *Panama* **88 E4** 8 0N 78 12W
Garafia, *Canary Is.* **22 F2** 28 48N 17 57W
Garajonay, *Canary Is.* **22 F2** 28 7N 17 14W
Garanhuns, *Brazil* **93 E11** 8 50S 36 30W
Garawe, *Liberia* **50 H3** 4 35N 8 0W
Garba Tula, *Kenya* **54 B4** 0 30N 38 32 E
Garber, *U.S.A.* **81 G6** 36 26N 97 35W
Garberville, *U.S.A.* **82 F2** 40 6N 123 48W
Gard, *Somali Rep.* **46 F4** 9 30N 49 6 E
Garda, L. di, *Italy* **20 B4** 45 40N 10 41 E
Garde L., *Canada* **73 A7** 62 50N 106 13W
Garden City, *Kans., U.S.A.* **81 G4** 37 58N 100 53W
Garden City, *Tex., U.S.A.* **81 K4** 31 52N 101 29W
Garden Grove, *U.S.A.* **85 M9** 33 47N 117 55W
Gardēz, *Afghan.* **42 C3** 33 37N 69 9 E
Gardiner, *U.S.A.* **82 D8** 45 2N 110 22W
Gardiners I., *U.S.A.* **79 E12** 41 6N 72 6W
Gardner, *U.S.A.* **79 D13** 42 34N 71 59W
Gardner Canal, *Canada* **72 C3** 53 27N 128 8W
Gardnerville, *U.S.A.* **84 G7** 38 56N 119 45W
Garey, *U.S.A.* **85 L6** 34 53N 120 19W
Garfield, *U.S.A.* **82 C5** 47 1N 117 9W
Gargano, Mte., *Italy* **20 D6** 41 43N 15 43 E
Garhshankar, *India* **42 D7** 31 13N 76 11 E
Garibaldi Prov. Park, *Canada* **72 D4** 49 50N 122 40W
Garies, *S. Africa* **56 E2** 30 32S 17 59 E
Garigliano —►, *Italy* **20 D5** 41 13N 13 45 E
Garissa, *Kenya* **54 C4** 0 25S 39 40 E
Garissa □, *Kenya* **54 C5** 0 20S 40 0 E
Garland, *Tex., U.S.A.* **81 J6** 32 55N 96 38W
Garland, *Utah, U.S.A.* **82 F7** 41 47N 112 10W
Garm, *Tajikistan* **26 F8** 39 0N 70 20 E

Greece

Gō-no-ura, *Japan* 31 H4 33 44N 129 40 E
Go Quao, *Vietnam* 39 H5 9 43N 105 17 E
Goa, *India* 40 M8 15 33N 73 59 E
Goa □, *India* 40 M8 15 33N 73 59 E
Goalen Hd., *Australia* 63 F5 36 33S 150 4 E
Goalpara, *India* 41 F17 26 10N 90 40 E
Goalundo Ghat, *Bangla.* 43 H13 23 50N 89 47 E
Goat Fell, *U.K.* 12 F3 55 38N 5 11W
Goba, *Ethiopia* 46 F2 7 1N 39 59 E
Goba, *Mozam.* 57 D5 26 15S 32 13 E
Gobabis, *Namibia* 56 C2 22 30S 19 0 E
Gobi, *Asia* 34 C5 44 0N 111 0 E
Gobō, *Japan* 31 H7 33 53N 135 10 E
Gochas, *Namibia* 56 C2 24 59S 18 55 E
Godavari →, *India* 41 L13 16 25N 82 18 E
Godavari Point, *India* 41 L13 17 0N 82 20 E
Godbout, *Canada* 71 C6 49 20N 67 38W
Godda, *India* 43 G12 24 50N 87 13 E
Goderich, *Canada* 70 D3 43 45N 81 41W
Godhavn, *Greenland* 4 C5 69 15N 53 38W
Godhra, *India* 42 H5 22 49N 73 40 E
Godoy Cruz, *Argentina* 94 C2 32 56S 68 52W
Gods →, *Canada* 73 B10 56 22N 92 51W
Gods L., *Canada* 73 C10 54 40N 94 15W
Godthåb, *Greenland* 69 B14 64 10N 51 35W
Godwin Austen = K2, *Pakistan* 43 B7 35 58N 76 32 E
Goeie Hoop, Kaap die = Good Hope, C. of, *S. Africa* 56 E2 34 24S 18 30 E
Goéland, L. au, *Canada* 70 C4 49 50N 76 48W
Goeree, *Neths.* 15 C3 51 50N 4 0 E
Goes, *Neths.* 15 C3 51 30N 3 55 E
Gogama, *Canada* 70 C3 47 35N 81 43W
Gogango, *Australia* 62 C5 23 40S 150 2 E
Gogebic, L., *U.S.A.* 80 B10 46 30N 89 35W
Gogra = Ghaghara →, *India* 43 G11 25 45N 84 40 E
Goiânia, *Brazil* 93 G9 16 43S 49 20W
Goiás, *Brazil* 93 G8 15 55S 50 10W
Goiás □, *Brazil* 93 F9 12 10S 48 0W
Goio-Ere, *Brazil* 95 A5 24 12S 53 1W
Gojō, *Japan* 31 G7 34 21N 135 42 E
Gojra, *Pakistan* 42 D5 31 10N 72 40 E
Gokarannath, *India* 43 F9 27 57N 80 39 E
Gökçeada, *Turkey* 21 D11 40 10N 25 50 E
Gokteik, *Burma* 41 H20 22 26N 97 0 E
Gokurt, *Pakistan* 42 E2 29 40N 67 26 E
Gola, *India* 43 E9 28 3N 80 32 E
Golakganj, *India* 43 F13 26 8N 89 52 E
Golan Heights = Hagolan, *Syria* 47 B4 33 0N 35 45 E
Golāshkerd, *Iran* 45 E8 27 59N 57 16 E
Golchikha, *Russia* 4 B12 71 45N 83 30 E
Golconda, *U.S.A.* 82 F5 40 58N 117 30W
Gold Beach, *U.S.A.* 82 E1 42 25N 124 25W
Gold Coast, *Australia* 63 D5 28 0S 153 25 E
Gold Coast, *W. Afr.* 48 F3 4 0N 1 40W
Gold Hill, *U.S.A.* 82 E2 42 26N 123 3W
Golden, *Canada* 72 C5 51 20N 116 59W
Golden, *U.S.A.* 80 F2 39 42N 105 15W
Golden B., *N.Z.* 59 J4 40 40S 172 50 E
Golden Gate, *U.S.A.* 82 H2 37 54N 122 30W
Golden Hinde, *Canada* 72 D3 49 40N 125 44W
Golden Lake, *Canada* 78 A7 45 34N 77 21W
Golden Prairie, *Canada* 73 C7 50 13N 109 37W
Golden Vale, *Ireland* 13 D3 52 33N 8 17W
Goldendale, *U.S.A.* 82 D3 45 49N 120 50W
Goldfield, *U.S.A.* 83 H5 37 42N 117 14W
Goldfields, *Canada* 73 B7 59 28N 108 29W
Goldsand L., *Canada* 73 B8 57 2N 101 8W
Goldsboro, *U.S.A.* 77 H7 35 23N 77 59W
Goldsmith, *U.S.A.* 81 K3 31 59N 102 37W
Goldsworthy, *Australia* 60 D2 20 21S 119 30 E
Goldthwaite, *U.S.A.* 81 K5 31 27N 98 34W
Goleniów, *Poland* 16 B8 53 35N 14 50 E
Golestānak, *Iran* 45 D7 30 36N 54 14 E
Goleta, *U.S.A.* 85 L7 34 27N 119 50W
Golfito, *Costa Rica* 88 E3 8 41N 83 5W
Golfo Aranci, *Italy* 20 D3 40 59N 9 38 E
Goliad, *U.S.A.* 81 L6 28 40N 97 23W
Golpāyegān, *Iran* 45 C6 33 27N 50 18 E
Golra, *Pakistan* 42 C5 33 37N 72 56 E
Golspie, *U.K.* 12 D5 57 58N 3 59W
Goma, *Rwanda* 54 C2 2 11S 29 18 E
Goma, *Zaïre* 54 C2 1 37S 29 10 E
Gomati →, *India* 43 G10 25 32N 83 11 E
Gombari, *Zaïre* 54 B2 2 45N 29 3 E
Gombe →, *Tanzania* 54 C3 4 38S 31 40 E
Gomel = Homyel, *Belarus* 17 B16 52 28N 31 0 E
Gomera, *Canary Is.* 22 F2 28 7N 17 14W
Gómez Palacio, *Mexico* 86 B4 25 40N 104 0W
Gomīshān, *Iran* 45 B7 37 4N 54 6 E
Gomogomo, *Indonesia* 37 F8 6 39S 134 43 E
Gomoh, *India* 41 H15 23 52N 86 10 E
Gompa = Ganta, *Liberia* 50 G3 7 15N 8 59W
Gonābād, *Iran* 45 C8 34 15N 58 45 E
Gonaïves, *Haiti* 89 C5 19 20N 72 42W
Gonâve, G. de la, *Haiti* 89 C5 19 29N 72 42W
Gonâve, I. de la, *Haiti* 89 C5 18 45N 73 0W
Gonbab-e Kāvūs, *Iran* 45 B7 37 20N 55 25 E
Gonda, *India* 43 F9 27 9N 81 58 E
Gondal, *India* 42 J4 21 58N 70 52 E
Gonder, *Ethiopia* 51 F12 12 39N 37 30 E
Gondia, *India* 40 J12 21 23N 80 10 E
Gondola, *Mozam.* 55 F3 19 10S 33 37 E
Gönen, *Turkey* 21 D12 40 6N 27 39 E
Gonghe, *China* 32 C5 36 18N 100 32 E
Gongolgon, *Australia* 63 E4 30 21S 146 54 E
Goniri, *Nigeria* 51 F7 11 30N 12 15 E
Gonzales, *Calif., U.S.A.* 83 H3 36 30N 121 26W
Gonzales, *Tex., U.S.A.* 81 L6 29 30N 97 27W
González Chaves, *Argentina* 94 D3 38 2S 60 5W
Good Hope, C. of, *S. Africa* 56 E2 34 24S 18 30 E
Gooderham, *Canada* 70 D4 44 54N 78 21W
Goodeve, *Canada* 73 C8 51 4N 103 10W
Gooding, *U.S.A.* 82 E6 42 56N 114 43W
Goodland, *U.S.A.* 80 F4 39 21N 101 43W
Goodnight, *U.S.A.* 81 H4 35 2N 101 11W
Goodooga, *Australia* 63 D4 29 3S 147 28 E
Goodsoil, *Canada* 73 C7 54 24N 109 13W
Goodsprings, *U.S.A.* 83 J6 35 50N 115 26W
Goole, *U.K.* 10 D7 53 42N 0 53W
Goolgowi, *Australia* 63 E4 33 58S 145 41 E
Goomalling, *Australia* 61 F2 31 15S 116 49 E
Goombalie, *Australia* 63 D4 29 59S 145 26 E
Goonda, *Mozam.* 55 F3 19 48S 33 57 E
Goondiwindi, *Australia* 63 D5 28 30S 150 21 E
Goongarrie, L., *Australia* 61 F3 30 3S 121 9 E
Goonyella, *Australia* 62 C4 21 47S 147 58 E
Goor, *Neths.* 15 B6 52 13N 6 33 E
Gooray, *Australia* 63 D5 28 25S 150 2 E
Goose →, *Canada* 71 B7 53 20N 60 35W
Goose L., *U.S.A.* 82 F3 41 56N 120 26W
Gop, *India* 40 H6 22 5N 69 50 E
Gopalganj, *India* 43 F11 26 28N 84 30 E
Göppingen, *Germany* 16 D5 48 42N 9 39 E
Gorakhpur, *India* 43 F10 26 47N 83 23 E
Goražde, *Bos.-H.* 21 C8 43 38N 18 58 E
Gorda, *U.S.A.* 84 K5 35 53N 121 26W
Gorda, Pta., *Canary Is.* 22 F2 28 45N 18 0W
Gorda, Pta., *Nic.* 88 D3 14 20N 83 10W
Gordan B., *Australia* 60 B5 11 35S 130 10 E
Gordon, *U.S.A.* 80 D3 42 48N 102 12W
Gordon →, *Australia* 62 G4 42 27S 145 30 E
Gordon Downs, *Australia* 60 C4 18 48S 128 33 E
Gordon L., *Alta., Canada* 73 B6 56 30N 110 25W
Gordon L., *N.W.T., Canada* 72 A6 63 5N 113 11W
Gordonvale, *Australia* 62 B4 17 5S 145 50 E
Gore, *Australia* 63 D5 28 17S 151 30 E
Goré, *Chad* 51 G8 7 59N 16 31 E
Gore, *Ethiopia* 51 G12 8 12N 35 32 E
Gore, *N.Z.* 59 M2 46 5S 168 58 E
Gore Bay, *Canada* 70 C3 45 57N 82 28W
Gorey, *Ireland* 13 D5 52 41N 6 18W
Gorg, *Iran* 45 D8 29 29N 59 43 E
Gorgān, *Iran* 45 B7 36 50N 54 29 E
Gorgona, I., *Colombia* 92 C3 3 0N 78 10W
Gorham, *U.S.A.* 79 B13 44 23N 71 10W
Gorinchem, *Neths.* 15 C4 51 50N 4 59 E
Gorízia, *Italy* 20 B5 45 56N 13 37 E
Gorki = Nizhniy Novgorod, *Russia* 24 C7 56 20N 44 0 E
Gorkiy = Nizhniy Novgorod, *Russia* 24 C7 56 20N 44 0 E
Gorkovskoye Vdkhr., *Russia* 24 C7 57 2N 43 4 E
Görlitz, *Germany* 16 C8 51 9N 14 58 E
Gorlovka = Horlivka, *Ukraine* 25 E6 48 19N 38 5 E
Gorman, *Calif., U.S.A.* 85 L8 34 47N 118 51W
Gorman, *Tex., U.S.A.* 81 J5 32 12N 98 41W
Gorna Dzhumayo = Blagoevgrad, *Bulgaria* 21 C10 42 2N 23 5 E
Gorna Oryakhovitsa, *Bulgaria* 21 C11 43 7N 25 40 E
Gorno-Altay □, *Russia* 26 D9 51 0N 86 0 E
Gorno-Altaysk, *Russia* 26 D9 51 50N 86 5 E
Gorno Slinkino = Gornopravdinsk, *Russia* 26 C8 60 5N 70 0 E
Gornopravdinsk, *Russia* 26 C8 60 5N 70 0 E
Gornyatski, *Russia* 24 A11 67 32N 64 3 E
Gornyi, *Russia* 30 B6 44 57N 133 59 E
Gorodenka = Horodenka, *Ukraine* 17 D13 48 41N 25 29 E
Gorodok = Horodok, *Ukraine* 17 D12 49 46N 23 32 E
Gorokhov = Horokhiv, *Ukraine* 17 C13 50 30N 24 45 E
Goromonzi, *Zimbabwe* 55 F3 17 52S 31 22 E
Gorongose →, *Mozam.* 57 C5 20 30S 34 40 E
Gorongoza, *Mozam.* 55 F3 18 44S 34 2 E
Gorongoza, Sa. da, *Mozam.* 55 F3 18 27S 34 2 E
Gorontalo, *Indonesia* 37 D6 0 35N 123 5 E
Gort, *Ireland* 13 C3 53 3N 8 49W
Gortis, *Greece* 23 D6 35 4N 24 58 E
Gorzów Wielkopolski, *Poland* 16 B8 52 43N 15 15 E
Gosford, *Australia* 63 E5 33 23S 151 18 E
Goshen, *Calif., U.S.A.* 84 J7 36 21N 119 25W
Goshen, *Ind., U.S.A.* 76 E3 41 35N 85 50W
Goshen, *N.Y., U.S.A.* 79 E10 41 24N 74 20W
Goshogawara, *Japan* 30 D10 40 48N 140 27 E
Goslar, *Germany* 16 C6 51 54N 10 25 E
Gospič, *Croatia* 16 F8 44 35N 15 23 E
Gosport, *U.K.* 11 G6 50 48N 1 9W
Gosse →, *Australia* 62 B1 19 32S 134 37 E
Göta älv →, *Sweden* 9 H14 57 42N 11 54 E
Göta kanal, *Sweden* 9 G16 58 30N 15 58 E
Götaland, *Sweden* 9 G15 57 30N 14 30 E
Göteborg, *Sweden* 9 H14 57 43N 11 59 E
Gotha, *Germany* 16 C6 50 56N 10 42 E
Gothenburg = Göteborg, *Sweden* 9 H14 57 43N 11 59 E
Gothenburg, *U.S.A.* 80 E4 40 56N 100 10W
Gotland, *Sweden* 9 H18 57 30N 18 33 E
Gotska Sandön, *Sweden* 9 G18 58 24N 19 15 E
Gōtsu, *Japan* 31 G6 35 0N 132 14 E
Göttingen, *Germany* 16 C5 51 31N 9 55 E
Gottwaldov = Zlin, *Czech.* 17 D9 49 14N 17 40 E
Goubangzi, *China* 35 D11 41 20N 121 52 E
Gouda, *Neths.* 15 B4 52 1N 4 42 E
Goúdhoura, Ákra, *Greece* 23 E8 34 59N 26 6 E
Gough I., *Atl. Oc.* 2 G9 40 10S 9 45W
Gouin, Rés., *Canada* 70 C5 48 35N 74 40W
Goulburn, *Australia* 63 E4 34 44S 149 44 E
Goulburn Is., *Australia* 62 A1 11 40S 133 20 E
Gounou-Gaya, *Chad* 51 G8 9 38N 15 31 E
Gouri, *Chad* 51 E8 19 36N 19 36 E
Gourits →, *S. Africa* 56 E3 34 21S 21 52 E
Gourma Rharous, *Mali* 50 E4 16 55N 1 50W
Goúrnais, *Greece* 23 D7 35 19N 25 16 E
Gourock Ra., *Australia* 63 F4 36 0S 149 25 E
Gouverneur, *U.S.A.* 79 B9 44 20N 75 28W
Gouviá, *Greece* 23 A3 39 39N 19 50 E
Govan, *Canada* 73 C8 51 20N 105 0W
Governador Valadares, *Brazil* 93 G10 18 15S 41 57W
Governor's Harbour, *Bahamas* 88 A4 25 10N 76 14W
Gowan Ra., *Australia* 62 C4 25 0S 145 0 E
Gowanda, *U.S.A.* 78 D6 42 28N 78 56W
Gowd-e Zirreh, *Afghan.* 40 E3 29 45N 62 0 E
Gower, *U.K.* 11 F3 51 35N 4 10W
Gowna, L., *Ireland* 13 C4 53 51N 7 34W
Goya, *Argentina* 94 B4 29 10S 59 10W
Goyder Lagoon, *Australia* 63 D2 27 3S 138 58 E
Goyllarisquisga, *Peru* 92 F3 10 31S 76 24W
Goz Beïda, *Chad* 51 F9 12 10N 21 20 E
Gozo, *Malta* 23 C1 36 3N 14 13 E
Graaff-Reinet, *S. Africa* 56 E3 32 13S 24 32 E
Gračac, *Croatia* 16 F8 44 18N 15 57 E
Grace, *U.S.A.* 82 E8 42 35N 111 44W
Graceville, *U.S.A.* 80 C6 45 34N 96 26W
Gracias a Dios, C., *Honduras* 88 C3 15 0N 83 10W
Graciosa, I., *Canary Is.* 22 E6 29 15N 13 32W
Grado, *Spain* 19 A2 43 23N 6 4W
Gradule, *Australia* 63 D4 28 32S 149 15 E
Grady, *U.S.A.* 81 H3 34 49N 103 19W
Grafton, *Australia* 63 D5 29 38S 152 58 E
Grafton, *U.S.A.* 80 A6 48 25N 97 25W
Graham, *Canada* 70 C1 49 20N 90 30W
Graham, *N.C., U.S.A.* 77 G6 36 5N 79 25W
Graham, *Tex., U.S.A.* 81 J5 33 6N 98 35W
Graham →, *Canada* 72 B4 56 31N 122 17W
Graham, Mt., *U.S.A.* 83 K9 32 42N 109 52W
Graham Bell, Os., *Russia* 26 A7 81 0N 62 0 E
Graham I., *Canada* 72 C2 53 40N 132 30W
Graham Land, *Antarctica* 5 C17 65 0S 64 0W
Grahamdale, *Canada* 73 C9 51 23N 98 30W
Grahamstown, *S. Africa* 56 E4 33 19S 26 31 E
Grain Coast, *W. Afr.* 48 F2 4 20N 10 0W
Grajaú, *Brazil* 93 E9 5 50S 46 4W
Grajaú →, *Brazil* 93 D10 3 41S 44 48W
Grampian Highlands = Grampian Mts., *U.K.* 12 E5 56 50N 4 0W
Grampian Mts., *U.K.* 12 E5 56 50N 4 0W
Gran Canaria, *Canary Is.* 22 F4 27 55N 15 35W
Gran Chaco, *S. Amer.* 94 B3 25 0S 61 0W
Gran Paradiso, *Italy* 20 B2 45 33N 7 17 E
Gran Sasso d'Italia, *Italy* 20 C5 42 27N 13 42 E
Granada, *Nic.* 88 D2 11 58N 86 0W
Granada, *Spain* 19 D4 37 10N 3 35W
Granada, *U.S.A.* 81 F3 38 4N 102 19W
Granadilla de Abona, *Canary Is.* 22 F3 28 7N 16 33W
Granard, *Ireland* 13 C4 53 47N 7 30W
Granbury, *U.S.A.* 81 J6 32 27N 97 47W
Granby, *Canada* 70 C5 45 25N 72 45W
Grand →, *Mo., U.S.A.* 80 F8 39 23N 93 7W
Grand →, *S. Dak., U.S.A.* 80 C4 45 40N 100 45W
Grand Bahama, *Bahamas* 88 A4 26 40N 78 30W
Grand Bank, *Canada* 71 C8 47 6N 55 48W
Grand Bassam, *Ivory C.* 50 G4 5 10N 3 49W
Grand-Bourg, *Guadeloupe* 89 C7 15 53N 61 19W
Grand Canal = Yun Ho →, *China* 35 E9 39 10N 117 10 E
Grand Canyon, *U.S.A.* 83 H7 36 3N 112 9W
Grand Canyon National Park, *U.S.A.* 83 H7 36 15N 112 30W
Grand Cayman, *Cayman Is.* 88 C3 19 20N 81 20W
Grand Coulee, *U.S.A.* 82 C4 47 57N 119 0W
Grand Coulee Dam, *U.S.A.* 82 C4 47 57N 118 59W
Grand Falls, *Canada* 71 C8 48 56N 55 40W
Grand Forks, *Canada* 72 D5 49 0N 118 30W
Grand Forks, *U.S.A.* 80 B6 47 55N 97 3W
Grand Haven, *U.S.A.* 76 D2 43 4N 86 13W
Grand I., *U.S.A.* 76 B2 46 31N 86 40W
Grand Island, *U.S.A.* 80 E5 40 55N 98 21W
Grand Isle, *U.S.A.* 81 L10 29 14N 90 0W
Grand Junction, *U.S.A.* 83 G9 39 4N 108 33W
Grand L., *N.B., Canada* 71 C6 45 57N 66 7W
Grand L., *Nfld., Canada* 71 C8 49 0N 57 30W
Grand L., *Nfld., Canada* 71 B7 53 40N 60 30W
Grand L., *U.S.A.* 81 L8 29 55N 92 47W
Grand Lac Victoria, *Canada* 70 C4 47 35N 77 35W
Grand Lahou, *Ivory C.* 50 G3 5 10N 5 5W
Grand Lake, *U.S.A.* 82 F11 40 15N 105 49W
Grand Manan I., *Canada* 71 D6 44 45N 66 52W
Grand Marais, *Canada* 80 B9 47 45N 90 25W
Grand Marais, *U.S.A.* 76 B3 46 40N 85 59W
Grand-Mère, *Canada* 70 C5 46 36N 72 40W
Grand Portage, *U.S.A.* 70 C2 47 58N 89 41W
Grand Prairie, *U.S.A.* 81 J6 32 47N 97 0W
Grand Rapids, *Canada* 73 C9 53 12N 99 19W
Grand Rapids, *Mich., U.S.A.* 76 D2 42 58N 85 40W
Grand Rapids, *Minn., U.S.A.* 80 B8 47 14N 93 31W
Grand St.-Bernard, Col du, *Europe* 16 F4 45 50N 7 10 E
Grand Teton, *U.S.A.* 82 E8 43 54N 111 50W
Grand Valley, *U.S.A.* 82 G9 39 27N 108 3W
Grand View, *Canada* 73 C8 51 10N 100 42W
Grande →, *Jujuy, Argentina* 94 A2 24 20S 65 2W
Grande →, *Mendoza, Argentina* 94 D2 36 52S 69 45W
Grande →, *Bolivia* 92 G6 15 51S 64 39W
Grande →, *Bahia, Brazil* 93 F10 11 30S 44 30W
Grande →, *Minas Gerais, Brazil* 93 H8 20 6S 51 4W
Grande, B., *Argentina* 96 G3 50 30S 68 20W
Grande, Rio →, *U.S.A.* 81 N6 25 58N 97 9W
Grande Baie, *Canada* 71 C5 48 19N 70 52W
Grande Baleine, R. de la →, *Canada* 70 A4 55 16N 77 47W
Grande Cache, *Canada* 72 C5 53 53N 119 8W
Grande de Santiago →, *Mexico* 86 C3 21 36N 105 26W
Grande-Entrée, *Canada* 71 C7 47 30N 61 40W
Grande Prairie, *Canada* 72 B5 55 10N 118 50W
Grande-Rivière, *Canada* 71 C7 48 26N 64 30W
Grande-Vallée, *Canada* 71 C6 49 14N 65 8W
Grandes-Bergeronnes, *Canada* 71 C6 48 16N 69 35W
Grandfalls, *U.S.A.* 81 K3 31 20N 102 51W
Grandoe Mines, *Canada* 72 B3 56 29N 129 54W
Grandview, *U.S.A.* 82 C4 46 15N 119 54W
Graneros, *Chile* 94 C1 34 5S 70 45W
Grangemouth, *U.K.* 12 E5 56 1N 3 42W
Granger, *Wash., U.S.A.* 82 C3 46 21N 120 11W
Granger, *Wyo., U.S.A.* 82 F9 41 35N 109 58W
Grangeville, *U.S.A.* 82 D5 45 56N 116 7W
Granite City, *U.S.A.* 80 F9 38 42N 90 9W
Granite Falls, *U.S.A.* 80 C7 44 49N 95 33W
Granite Mt., *U.S.A.* 85 M10 33 5N 116 28W
Granite Peak, *Australia* 61 E3 25 40S 121 20 E
Granite Peak, *U.S.A.* 82 D9 45 10N 109 48W
Granity, *N.Z.* 59 J3 41 39S 171 51 E
Granja, *Brazil* 93 D10 3 7S 40 50W
Granollers, *Spain* 19 B7 41 39N 2 18 E
Grant, *U.S.A.* 80 E4 40 53N 101 42W
Grant, Mt., *U.S.A.* 82 G4 38 34N 118 48W
Grant City, *U.S.A.* 80 E7 40 29N 94 25W
Grant I., *Australia* 60 B5 11 10S 132 52 E
Grant Range, *U.S.A.* 83 G6 38 30N 115 25W
Grantham, *U.K.* 10 E7 52 55N 0 38W
Grantown-on-Spey, *U.K.* 12 D5 57 20N 3 36W
Grants, *U.S.A.* 83 J10 35 9N 107 52W
Grants Pass, *U.S.A.* 82 E2 42 26N 123 19W
Grantsburg, *U.S.A.* 80 C8 45 47N 92 41W
Grantsville, *U.S.A.* 82 F7 40 36N 112 28W
Granville, *France* 18 B3 48 50N 1 35W
Granville, *N. Dak., U.S.A.* 80 A4 48 16N 100 47W
Granville, *N.Y., U.S.A.* 76 D9 43 24N 73 16W
Granville L., *Canada* 73 B8 56 18N 100 30W
Grapeland, *U.S.A.* 81 K7 31 30N 95 29W
Gras, L. de, *Canada* 68 B8 64 30N 110 30W
Graskop, *S. Africa* 57 C5 24 56S 30 49 E
Grass →, *Canada* 73 B9 56 3N 96 33W
Grass Range, *U.S.A.* 82 C9 47 0N 109 0W
Grass River Prov. Park, *Canada* 73 C8 54 40N 100 50W
Grass Valley, *Calif., U.S.A.* 84 F6 39 13N 121 4W
Grass Valley, *Oreg., U.S.A.* 82 D3 45 22N 120 47W
Grasse, *France* 18 E7 43 38N 6 56 E
Grassmere, *Australia* 63 E3 31 24S 142 38 E
Graulhet, *France* 18 E4 43 45N 1 59 E
Gravelbourg, *Canada* 73 D7 49 50N 106 35W
's-Gravenhage, *Neths.* 15 B4 52 7N 4 17 E
Gravenhurst, *Canada* 78 B5 44 52N 79 20W
Gravesend, *Australia* 63 D5 29 35S 150 20 E
Gravesend, *U.K.* 11 F8 51 26N 0 22 E
Gravois, Pointe-à-, *Haiti* 89 C5 18 15N 73 56W
Grayling, *U.S.A.* 76 C3 44 40N 84 43W
Grayling →, *Canada* 72 B3 59 21N 125 0W
Grays Harbor, *U.S.A.* 82 C1 46 59N 124 1W
Grays L., *U.S.A.* 82 E8 43 4N 111 26W
Grays River, *U.S.A.* 84 D3 46 21N 123 37W
Grayson, *Canada* 73 C8 50 45N 102 40W
Graz, *Austria* 16 E8 47 4N 15 27 E
Greasy L., *Canada* 72 A4 62 55N 122 12W
Great Abaco I., *Bahamas* 88 A4 26 25N 77 10W
Great Artesian Basin, *Australia* 62 C3 23 0S 144 0 E
Great Australian Bight, *Australia* 61 F5 33 30S 130 0 E
Great Bahama Bank, *Bahamas* 88 B4 23 15N 78 0W
Great Barrier I., *N.Z.* 59 G5 36 11S 175 25 E
Great Barrier Reef, *Australia* 62 B4 18 0S 146 50 E
Great Barrington, *U.S.A.* 79 D11 42 12N 73 22W
Great Basin, *U.S.A.* 82 G5 40 0N 117 0W
Great Bear →, *Canada* 68 B7 65 0N 124 0W
Great Bear L., *Canada* 68 B7 65 30N 120 0W
Great Belt = Store Bælt, *Denmark* 9 J14 55 20N 11 0 E
Great Bend, *Kans., U.S.A.* 80 F5 38 22N 98 46W
Great Bend, *Pa., U.S.A.* 79 E9 41 58N 75 45W
Great Blasket I., *Ireland* 13 D1 52 6N 10 32W
Great Britain, *Europe* 6 E5 54 0N 2 15W
Great Central, *Canada* 72 D3 49 20N 125 10W
Great Dividing Ra., *Australia* 62 C4 23 0S 146 0 E
Great Driffield = Driffield, *U.K.* 10 C7 54 0N 0 26W
Great Exuma I., *Bahamas* 88 B4 23 30N 75 50W
Great Falls, *Canada* 73 C9 50 27N 96 1W
Great Falls, *U.S.A.* 82 C8 47 30N 111 17W
Great Fish = Groot Vis →, *S. Africa* 56 E4 33 28S 27 5 E
Great Guana Cay, *Bahamas* 88 B4 24 0N 76 20W
Great Harbour Deep, *Canada* 71 B8 50 25N 56 32W
Great I., *Canada* 73 B9 58 53N 96 35W
Great Inagua I., *Bahamas* 89 B5 21 0N 73 20W
Great Indian Desert = Thar Desert, *India* 42 F4 28 0N 72 0 E
Great Karoo, *S. Africa* 56 E3 31 55S 21 0 E
Great Lake, *Australia* 62 G4 41 50S 146 40 E
Great Malvern, *U.K.* 11 E5 52 7N 2 18W
Great Ormes Head, *U.K.* 10 D4 53 20N 3 52W
Great Ouse →, *U.K.* 10 E8 52 48N 0 21 E
Great Palm I., *Australia* 62 B4 18 45S 146 40 E
Great Plains, *N. Amer.* 74 A6 47 0N 105 0W
Great Ruaha →, *Tanzania* 54 D4 7 56S 37 52 E
Great Saint Bernard P. = Grand St.-Bernard, Col du, *Europe* 16 F4 45 50N 7 10 E
Great Salt L., *U.S.A.* 82 F7 41 15N 112 40W
Great Salt Lake Desert, *U.S.A.* 82 F7 40 50N 113 30W
Great Salt Plains L., *U.S.A.* 81 G5 36 45N 98 8W
Great Sandy Desert, *Australia* 60 D3 21 0S 124 0 E
Great Sangi = Sangihe, P., *Indonesia* 37 D7 3 45N 125 30 E
Great Slave L., *Canada* 72 A5 61 23N 115 38W
Great Smoky Mts. Nat. Pk., *U.S.A.* 77 H4 35 40N 83 40W
Great Stour = Stour →, *U.K.* 11 F9 51 18N 1 22 E
Great Victoria Desert, *Australia* 61 E4 29 30S 126 30 E
Great Wall, *China* 34 E5 38 30N 109 30 E
Great Whernside, *U.K.* 10 C6 54 10N 1 58W
Great Yarmouth, *U.K.* 10 E9 52 37N 1 44 E
Greater Antilles, *W. Indies* 89 C5 17 40N 74 0W
Greater London □, *U.K.* 11 F7 51 31N 0 6W
Greater Manchester □, *U.K.* 10 D5 53 30N 2 15W
Greater Sunda Is., *Indonesia* 36 F4 7 0S 112 0 E
Greco, C., *Cyprus* 23 E13 34 57N 34 5 E
Gredos, Sierra de, *Spain* 19 B3 40 20N 5 0W
Greece, *U.S.A.* 78 C7 43 13N 77 41W
Greece ■, *Europe* 21 E9 40 0N 23 0 E

H

Heinze Is.

Hajipur, *India* **43 G11** 25 45N 85 13 E
Hājjī Muḩsin, *Iraq* **44 C5** 32 35N 45 29 E
Ḩājjīābād, *Eşfahan, Iran* **45 C7** 33 41N 54 50 E
Ḩājjīābād, *Hormozgān, Iran* **45 D7** 28 19N 55 55 E
Hajnówka, *Poland* **17 B12** 52 47N 23 35 E
Hakansson, Mts., *Zaïre* **55 D2** 8 40S 25 45 E
Hakken-Zan, *Japan* **31 G7** 34 10N 135 54 E
Hakodate, *Japan* **30 D10** 41 45N 140 44 E
Haku-San, *Japan* **31 F8** 36 9N 136 46 E
Hakui, *Japan* **31 F8** 36 53N 136 47 E
Hala, *Pakistan* **40 G6** 25 43N 68 20 E
Ḩalab, *Syria* **44 B3** 36 10N 37 15 E
Ḩalabjah, *Iraq* **44 C5** 35 10N 45 58 E
Halaib, *Sudan* **51 D12** 22 12N 36 30 E
Hālat 'Ammār, *Si. Arabia* **44 D3** 29 10N 36 4 E
Halbā, *Lebanon* **47 A5** 34 34N 36 6 E
Halberstadt, *Germany* **16 C6** 51 54N 11 3 E
Halcombe, *N.Z.* **59 J5** 40 8S 175 30 E
Halcon, Mt., *Phil.* **37 B6** 13 0N 121 30 E
Halden, *Norway* **9 G14** 59 9N 11 23 E
Haldia, *India* **41 H16** 22 5N 88 3 E
Haldwani, *India* **43 E8** 29 31N 79 30 E
Hale →, *Australia* **62 C2** 24 56S 135 53 E
Haleakala Crater, *U.S.A.* **74 H16** 20 43N 156 16W
Haleyville, *U.S.A.* **77 H2** 34 14N 87 37W
Halfway →, *Canada* **72 B4** 56 12N 121 32W
Haliburton, *Canada* **70 C4** 45 3N 78 30W
Halifax, *Australia* **62 B4** 18 32S 146 22 E
Halifax, *Canada* **71 D7** 44 38N 63 35W
Halifax, *U.K.* **10 D6** 53 43N 1 52W
Halifax B., *Australia* **62 B4** 18 50S 147 0 E
Halifax I., *Namibia* **56 D2** 26 38S 15 4 E
Halīl →, *Iran* **45 E8** 27 40N 58 30 E
Hall Beach, *Canada* **69 B11** 68 46N 81 12W
Hall Pt., *Australia* **60 C3** 15 40S 124 23 E
Halland, *Sweden* **9 H15** 57 8N 12 47 E
Halle, *Belgium* **15 D4** 50 44N 4 13 E
Halle, *Germany* **16 C6** 51 30N 11 56 E
Hällefors, *Sweden* **9 G16** 59 47N 14 31 E
Hallett, *Australia* **63 E2** 33 25S 138 55 E
Hallettsville, *U.S.A.* **81 L6** 29 27N 96 57W
Halliday, *U.S.A.* **80 B3** 47 21N 102 20W
Halliday L., *Canada* **73 A7** 61 21N 108 56W
Hallim, *S. Korea* **35 H14** 33 24N 126 15 E
Hallingdalselva →, *Norway* **9 F13** 60 40N 8 50 E
Hallock, *U.S.A.* **73 D9** 48 47N 96 57W
Halls Creek, *Australia* **60 C4** 18 16S 127 38 E
Hallsberg, *Sweden* **9 G16** 59 5N 15 7 E
Hallstead, *U.S.A.* **79 E9** 41 58N 75 45W
Halmahera, *Indonesia* **37 D7** 0 40N 128 0 E
Halmstad, *Sweden* **9 H15** 56 41N 12 52 E
Halq el Oued, *Tunisia* **51 A7** 36 53N 10 18 E
Hälsingborg = Helsingborg, *Sweden* **9 H15** 56 3N 12 42 E
Hälsingland, *Sweden* **9 F16** 61 40N 16 5 E
Halstad, *U.S.A.* **80 B6** 47 21N 96 50W
Halti, *Finland* **8 B19** 69 17N 21 18 E
Halul, *Qatar* **45 E7** 25 40N 52 40 E
Ḩalvān, *Iran* **45 C8** 33 57N 56 15 E
Ham Tan, *Vietnam* **39 G6** 10 40N 107 45 E
Ham Yen, *Vietnam* **38 A5** 22 4N 105 3 E
Hamab, *Namibia* **56 D2** 28 7S 19 16 E
Hamada, *Japan* **31 G6** 34 56N 132 4 E
Hamadān, *Iran* **45 C6** 34 52N 48 32 E
Hamadān □, *Iran* **45 C6** 35 0N 49 0 E
Hamāh, *Syria* **44 C3** 35 5N 36 40 E
Hamamatsu, *Japan* **31 G8** 34 45N 137 45 E
Hamar, *Norway* **9 F14** 60 48N 11 7 E
Hambantota, *Sri Lanka* **40 R12** 6 10N 81 10 E
Hamber Prov. Park, *Canada* **72 C5** 52 20N 118 0W
Hamburg, *Germany* **16 B5** 53 33N 9 59 E
Hamburg, *Ark., U.S.A.* **81 J9** 33 14N 91 48W
Hamburg, *Iowa, U.S.A.* **80 E7** 40 36N 95 39W
Hamburg, *N.Y., U.S.A.* **78 D6** 42 43N 78 50W
Hamburg, *Pa., U.S.A.* **79 F9** 40 33N 75 59W
Ḩamd, W. al →, *Si. Arabia* **44 E3** 24 55N 36 20 E
Hamden, *U.S.A.* **79 E12** 41 23N 72 54W
Häme, *Finland* **9 F20** 61 38N 25 10 E
Hämeenlinna, *Finland* **9 F21** 61 0N 24 28 E
Hamelin Pool, *Australia* **61 E1** 26 22S 114 20 E
Hameln, *Germany* **16 B5** 52 6N 9 21 E
Hamerkaz □, *Israel* **47 C3** 32 15N 34 55 E
Hamersley Ra., *Australia* **60 D2** 22 0S 117 45 E
Hamhung, *N. Korea* **35 E14** 39 54N 127 30 E
Hami, *China* **32 B4** 42 55N 93 25 E
Hamilton, *Australia* **63 F3** 37 45S 142 2 E
Hamilton, *Canada* **70 D4** 43 15N 79 50W
Hamilton, *N.Z.* **59 G5** 37 47S 175 19 E
Hamilton, *U.K.* **12 F4** 55 46N 4 2W
Hamilton, *Mo., U.S.A.* **80 F8** 39 45N 93 59W
Hamilton, *Mont., U.S.A.* **82 C6** 46 15N 114 10W
Hamilton, *N.Y., U.S.A.* **79 D9** 42 50N 75 33W
Hamilton, *Ohio, U.S.A.* **76 F3** 39 24N 84 34W
Hamilton, *Tex., U.S.A.* **81 K5** 31 42N 98 7W
Hamilton →, *Australia* **62 C2** 23 30S 139 47 E
Hamilton City, *U.S.A.* **84 F4** 39 45N 122 1W
Hamilton Hotel, *Australia* **62 C3** 22 45S 140 40 E
Hamilton Inlet, *Canada* **71 B8** 54 0N 57 30W
Hamina, *Finland* **9 F22** 60 34N 27 12 E
Hamiota, *Canada* **73 C8** 50 11N 100 38W
Hamlet, *U.S.A.* **77 H6** 34 53N 79 42W
Hamley Bridge, *Australia* **63 E2** 34 17S 138 35 E
Hamlin = Hameln, *Germany* **16 B5** 52 6N 9 21 E
Hamlin, *N.Y., U.S.A.* **78 C7** 43 17N 77 55W
Hamlin, *Tex., U.S.A.* **81 J4** 32 53N 100 8W
Hamm, *Germany* **16 C4** 51 40N 7 50 E
Hammerfest, *Norway* **8 A20** 70 39N 23 41 E
Hammond, *Ind., U.S.A.* **76 E2** 41 38N 87 30W
Hammond, *La., U.S.A.* **81 K9** 30 30N 90 28W
Hammonton, *U.S.A.* **76 F8** 39 39N 74 48W
Hampden, *N.Z.* **59 L3** 45 18S 170 50 E
Hampshire □, *U.K.* **11 F6** 51 7N 1 23W
Hampshire Downs, *U.K.* **11 F6** 51 15N 1 10W
Hampton, *Ark., U.S.A.* **81 J8** 33 32N 92 28W
Hampton, *Iowa, U.S.A.* **80 D8** 42 45N 93 13W
Hampton, *N.H., U.S.A.* **79 D14** 42 57N 70 50W
Hampton, *S.C., U.S.A.* **77 J5** 32 52N 81 7W
Hampton, *Va., U.S.A.* **76 G7** 37 2N 76 21W
Hampton Tableland, *Australia* **61 F4** 32 0S 127 0 E
Hamrat esh Sheykh, *Sudan* **51 F10** 14 38N 27 55 E
Hamyang, *S. Korea* **35 G14** 35 32N 127 42 E
Han Pijesak, *Bos.-H.* **21 B8** 44 5N 18 57 E
Hana, *U.S.A.* **74 H17** 20 45N 155 59W
Hanak, *Si. Arabia* **44 E3** 25 32N 37 0 E
Hanamaki, *Japan* **30 E10** 39 23N 141 7 E
Hanang, *Tanzania* **54 C4** 4 30S 35 25 E
Hanau, *Germany* **16 C5** 50 7N 8 56 E
Hanbogd, *Mongolia* **34 C4** 43 11N 107 10 E
Hancheng, *China* **34 G6** 35 31N 110 25 E
Hancock, *Mich., U.S.A.* **80 B10** 47 8N 88 35W
Hancock, *Minn., U.S.A.* **80 C7** 45 30N 95 48W
Hancock, *N.Y., U.S.A.* **79 E9** 41 57N 75 17W
Handa, *Japan* **31 G8** 34 53N 136 55 E
Handa, *Somali Rep.* **46 E5** 10 37N 51 2 E
Handan, *China* **34 F8** 36 35N 114 28 E
Handeni, *Tanzania* **54 D4** 5 25S 38 2 E
Handeni □, *Tanzania* **54 D4** 5 30S 38 0 E
Handwara, *India* **43 B6** 34 21N 74 20 E
Hanegev, *Israel* **47 E3** 30 50N 35 0 E
Haney, *Canada* **72 D4** 49 12N 122 40W
Hanford, *U.S.A.* **83 H4** 36 20N 119 39W
Hang Chat, *Thailand* **38 C2** 18 20N 99 21 E
Hang Dong, *Thailand* **38 C2** 18 41N 98 55 E
Hangang →, *S. Korea* **35 F14** 37 50N 126 30 E
Hangayn Nuruu, *Mongolia* **32 B4** 47 30N 99 0 E
Hangchou = Hangzhou, *China* **33 C7** 30 18N 120 11 E
Hanggin Houqi, *China* **34 D4** 40 58N 107 4 E
Hanggin Qi, *China* **34 E5** 39 52N 108 50 E
Hangu, *China* **35 E9** 39 18N 117 53 E
Hangzhou, *China* **33 C7** 30 18N 120 11 E
Hangzhou Wan, *China* **33 C7** 30 15N 120 45 E
Hanhongor, *Mongolia* **34 C3** 43 55N 104 28 E
Ḩanīdh, *Si. Arabia* **45 E6** 26 35N 48 38 E
Ḩanīsh, *Yemen* **46 E3** 13 45N 42 46 E
Hankinson, *U.S.A.* **80 B6** 46 4N 96 54W
Hanko, *Finland* **9 G20** 59 50N 22 57 E
Hanksville, *U.S.A.* **83 G8** 38 22N 110 43W
Hanle, *India* **43 C8** 32 42N 79 4 E
Hanmer Springs, *N.Z.* **59 K4** 42 32S 172 50 E
Hann →, *Australia* **60 C4** 17 26S 126 17 E
Hann, Mt., *Australia* **60 C4** 15 45S 126 0 E
Hanna, *Canada* **72 C6** 51 40N 111 54W
Hannaford, *U.S.A.* **80 B5** 47 19N 98 11W
Hannah, *U.S.A.* **80 A5** 48 58N 98 42W
Hannah B., *Canada* **70 B4** 51 40N 80 0W
Hannibal, *U.S.A.* **80 F9** 39 42N 91 22W
Hannover, *Germany* **16 B5** 52 22N 9 46 E
Hanoi, *Vietnam* **32 D5** 21 5N 105 55 E
Hanover = Hannover, *Germany* **16 B5** 52 22N 9 46 E
Hanover, *Canada* **78 B3** 44 9N 81 2W
Hanover, *S. Africa* **56 E3** 31 4S 24 29 E
Hanover, *N.H., U.S.A.* **79 C12** 43 42N 72 17W
Hanover, *Ohio, U.S.A.* **78 F2** 40 4N 82 16W
Hanover, *Pa., U.S.A.* **76 F7** 39 48N 76 59W
Hanover, I., *Chile* **96 G2** 51 0S 74 50W
Hansi, *India* **42 E6** 29 10N 75 57 E
Hanson, L., *Australia* **63 E2** 31 0S 136 15 E
Hantsavichy, *Belarus* **17 B14** 52 49N 26 30 E
Hanzhong, *China* **34 H4** 33 10N 107 1 E
Hanzhuang, *China* **35 G9** 34 33N 117 23 E
Haora, *India* **43 H13** 22 37N 88 20 E
Haparanda, *Sweden* **8 D21** 65 52N 24 8 E
Happy, *U.S.A.* **81 H4** 34 45N 101 52W
Happy Camp, *U.S.A.* **82 F2** 41 48N 123 23W
Happy Valley-Goose Bay, *Canada* **71 B7** 53 15N 60 20W
Hapsu, *N. Korea* **35 D15** 41 13N 128 51 E
Hapur, *India* **42 E7** 28 45N 77 45 E
Ḩaql, *Si. Arabia* **47 F3** 29 10N 34 58 E
Har, *Indonesia* **37 F8** 5 16S 133 14 E
Har-Ayrag, *Mongolia* **34 B5** 45 47N 109 16 E
Har Hu, *China* **32 C4** 38 20N 97 38 E
Har Us Nuur, *Mongolia* **32 B4** 48 0N 92 0 E
Har Yehuda, *Israel* **47 D3** 31 35N 34 57 E
Ḩaraḑ, *Si. Arabia* **46 C4** 24 22N 49 0 E
Haranomachi, *Japan* **30 F10** 37 38N 140 58 E
Harardera, *Somali Rep.* **46 G4** 4 33N 47 38 E
Harare, *Zimbabwe* **55 F3** 17 43S 31 2 E
Harazé, *Chad* **51 F8** 14 20N 19 12 E
Harbin, *China* **35 B14** 45 48N 126 40 E
Harbor Beach, *U.S.A.* **76 D4** 43 51N 82 39W
Harbor Springs, *U.S.A.* **76 C3** 45 26N 85 0W
Harbour Breton, *Canada* **71 C8** 47 29N 55 50W
Harbour Grace, *Canada* **71 C9** 47 40N 53 22W
Harda, *India* **42 H7** 22 27N 77 5 E
Hardangerfjorden, *Norway* **9 F12** 60 5N 6 0 E
Hardangervidda, *Norway* **9 F12** 60 7N 7 20 E
Hardap Dam, *Namibia* **56 C2** 24 32S 17 50 E
Hardenberg, *Neths.* **15 B6** 52 34N 6 37 E
Harderwijk, *Neths.* **15 B5** 52 21N 5 38 E
Hardey →, *Australia* **60 D2** 22 45S 116 8 E
Hardin, *U.S.A.* **82 D10** 45 44N 107 37W
Harding, *S. Africa* **57 E4** 30 35S 29 55 E
Harding Ra., *Australia* **60 C3** 16 17S 124 55 E
Hardisty, *Canada* **72 C6** 52 40N 111 18W
Hardman, *U.S.A.* **82 D4** 45 10N 119 41W
Hardoi, *India* **43 F9** 27 26N 80 6 E
Hardwar = Haridwar, *India* **42 E8** 29 58N 78 9 E
Hardwick, *U.S.A.* **79 B12** 44 30N 72 22W
Hardy, *U.S.A.* **81 G9** 36 19N 91 29W
Hardy, Pen., *Chile* **96 H3** 55 30S 68 20W
Hare B., *Canada* **71 B8** 51 15N 55 45W
Hareid, *Norway* **9 E12** 62 22N 6 1 E
Harer, *Ethiopia* **46 F3** 9 20N 42 8 E
Hargeisa, *Somali Rep.* **46 F3** 9 30N 44 2 E
Hari →, *Indonesia* **36 E2** 1 16S 104 5 E
Haria, *Canary Is.* **22 E6** 29 8N 13 32W
Haridwar, *India* **42 E8** 29 58N 78 9 E
Haringhata →, *Bangla.* **41 J16** 22 0N 89 58 E
Harīrūd →, *Asia* **40 A2** 37 24N 60 38 E
Härjedalen, *Sweden* **9 E15** 62 22N 13 5 E
Harlan, *Iowa, U.S.A.* **80 E7** 41 39N 95 19W
Harlan, *Ky., U.S.A.* **77 G4** 36 51N 83 19W
Harlech, *U.K.* **10 E3** 52 52N 4 6W
Harlem, *U.S.A.* **82 B9** 48 32N 108 47W
Harlingen, *Neths.* **15 A5** 53 11N 5 25 E
Harlingen, *U.S.A.* **81 M6** 26 12N 97 42W
Harlowton, *U.S.A.* **82 C9** 46 26N 109 50W
Harney Basin, *U.S.A.* **82 E4** 43 30N 119 0W
Harney L., *U.S.A.* **82 E4** 43 14N 119 8W
Harney Peak, *U.S.A.* **80 D3** 43 52N 103 32W
Härnösand, *Sweden* **9 E17** 62 38N 17 55 E
Harp L., *Canada* **71 A7** 55 5N 61 50W
Harrand, *Pakistan* **42 E4** 29 28N 70 3 E
Harriman, *U.S.A.* **77 H3** 35 56N 84 33W
Harrington Harbour, *Canada* **71 B8** 50 31N 59 30W
Harris, *U.K.* **12 D2** 57 50N 6 55W
Harris, Sd. of, *U.K.* **12 D1** 57 44N 7 6W
Harris L., *Australia* **63 E2** 31 10S 135 10 E
Harrisburg, *Ill., U.S.A.* **81 G10** 37 44N 88 32W
Harrisburg, *Nebr., U.S.A.* **80 E3** 41 33N 103 44W
Harrisburg, *Oreg., U.S.A.* **82 D2** 44 16N 123 10W
Harrisburg, *Pa., U.S.A.* **78 F8** 40 16N 76 53W
Harrismith, *S. Africa* **57 D4** 28 15S 29 8 E
Harrison, *Ark., U.S.A.* **81 G8** 36 14N 93 7W
Harrison, *Idaho, U.S.A.* **82 C5** 47 27N 116 47W
Harrison, *Nebr., U.S.A.* **80 D3** 42 41N 103 53W
Harrison, C., *Canada* **71 B8** 54 55N 57 55W
Harrison Bay, *U.S.A.* **68 A4** 70 40N 151 0W
Harrison L., *Canada* **72 D4** 49 33N 121 50W
Harrisonburg, *U.S.A.* **76 F6** 38 27N 78 52W
Harrisonville, *U.S.A.* **80 F7** 38 39N 94 21W
Harriston, *Canada* **70 D3** 43 57N 80 53W
Harrisville, *U.S.A.* **78 B1** 44 39N 83 17W
Harrogate, *U.K.* **10 D6** 54 0N 1 33W
Harrow, *U.K.* **11 F7** 51 35N 0 21W
Harsin, *Iran* **44 C5** 34 18N 47 33 E
Harstad, *Norway* **8 B17** 68 48N 16 30 E
Hart, *U.S.A.* **76 D2** 43 42N 86 22W
Hart, L., *Australia* **63 E2** 31 10S 136 25 E
Hartbees →, *S. Africa* **56 D3** 28 45S 20 32 E
Hartford, *Conn., U.S.A.* **79 E12** 41 46N 72 41W
Hartford, *Ky., U.S.A.* **76 G2** 37 27N 86 55W
Hartford, *S. Dak., U.S.A.* **80 D6** 43 38N 96 57W
Hartford, *Wis., U.S.A.* **80 D10** 43 19N 88 22W
Hartford City, *U.S.A.* **76 E3** 40 27N 85 22W
Hartland, *Canada* **71 C6** 46 20N 67 32W
Hartland Pt., *U.K.* **11 F3** 51 1N 4 32W
Hartlepool, *U.K.* **10 C6** 54 42N 1 13W
Hartlepool □, *U.K.* **10 C6** 54 42N 1 17W
Hartley Bay, *Canada* **72 C3** 53 25N 129 15W
Hartmannberge, *Namibia* **56 B1** 17 0S 13 0 E
Hartney, *Canada* **73 D8** 49 30N 100 35W
Harts →, *S. Africa* **56 D3** 28 24S 24 17 E
Hartselle, *U.S.A.* **77 H2** 34 27N 86 56W
Hartshorne, *U.S.A.* **81 H7** 34 51N 95 34W
Hartsville, *U.S.A.* **77 H5** 34 23N 80 4W
Hartwell, *U.S.A.* **77 H4** 34 21N 82 56W
Harunabad, *Pakistan* **42 E5** 29 35N 73 8 E
Harvand, *Iran* **45 D7** 28 25N 55 43 E
Harvey, *Australia* **61 F2** 33 5S 115 54 E
Harvey, *Ill., U.S.A.* **76 E2** 41 36N 87 50W
Harvey, *N. Dak., U.S.A.* **80 B5** 47 47N 99 56W
Harwich, *U.K.* **11 F9** 51 56N 1 17 E
Haryana □, *India* **42 E7** 29 0N 76 10 E
Haryn →, *Belarus* **17 B14** 52 7N 27 17 E
Harz, *Germany* **16 C6** 51 38N 10 44 E
Hasan Kīādeh, *Iran* **45 B6** 37 24N 49 58 E
Ḩasanābād, *Iran* **45 C7** 32 8N 52 44 E
Hasanpur, *India* **42 E8** 28 43N 78 17 E
Hashimoto, *Japan* **31 G7** 34 19N 135 37 E
Hashtjerd, *Iran* **45 C6** 35 52N 50 40 E
Haskell, *Okla., U.S.A.* **81 H7** 35 50N 95 40W
Haskell, *Tex., U.S.A.* **81 J5** 33 10N 99 44W
Hasselt, *Belgium* **15 D5** 50 56N 5 21 E
Hassi Inifel, *Algeria* **50 C5** 29 50N 3 41 E
Hassi Messaoud, *Algeria* **50 B6** 31 51N 6 1 E
Hässleholm, *Sweden* **9 H15** 56 10N 13 46 E
Hastings, *N.Z.* **59 H6** 39 39S 176 52 E
Hastings, *U.K.* **11 G8** 50 51N 0 35 E
Hastings, *Mich., U.S.A.* **76 D3** 42 39N 85 17W
Hastings, *Minn., U.S.A.* **80 C8** 44 44N 92 51W
Hastings, *Nebr., U.S.A.* **80 E5** 40 35N 98 23W
Hastings Ra., *Australia* **63 E5** 31 15S 152 14 E
Hat Yai, *Thailand* **39 J3** 7 1N 100 27 E
Hatanbulag, *Mongolia* **34 C5** 43 8N 109 5 E
Hatay = Antalya, *Turkey* **25 G5** 36 52N 30 45 E
Hatch, *U.S.A.* **83 K10** 32 40N 107 9W
Hatches Creek, *Australia* **62 C2** 20 56S 135 12 E
Hatchet L., *Canada* **73 B8** 58 36N 103 40W
Hateruma-Shima, *Japan* **31 M1** 24 3N 123 47 E
Hatfield P.O., *Australia* **63 E3** 33 54S 143 49 E
Hatgal, *Mongolia* **32 A5** 50 26N 100 9 E
Hathras, *India* **42 F8** 27 36N 78 6 E
Hatia, *Bangla.* **41 H17** 22 30N 91 5 E
Hato Mayor, *Dom. Rep.* **89 C6** 18 46N 69 15W
Hattah, *Australia* **63 E3** 34 48S 142 17 E
Hatteras, C., *U.S.A.* **77 H8** 35 14N 75 32W
Hattiesburg, *U.S.A.* **81 K10** 31 20N 89 17W
Hatvan, *Hungary* **17 E10** 47 40N 19 45 E
Hau Bon = Cheo Reo, *Vietnam* **38 F7** 13 25N 108 28 E
Hau Duc, *Vietnam* **38 E7** 15 20N 108 13 E
Haugesund, *Norway* **9 G11** 59 23N 5 13 E
Haukipudas, *Finland* **8 D21** 65 12N 25 20 E
Haultain →, *Canada* **73 B7** 55 51N 106 46W
Hauraki G., *N.Z.* **59 G5** 36 35S 175 5 E
Haut Atlas, *Morocco* **50 B3** 32 30N 5 0W
Haut Zaïre □, *Zaïre* **54 B2** 2 20N 26 0 E
Hauterive, *Canada* **71 C6** 49 10N 68 16W
Hautes Fagnes = Hohe Venn, *Belgium* **15 D6** 50 30N 6 5 E
Hauts Plateaux, *Algeria* **50 A5** 35 0N 1 0 E
Havana = La Habana, *Cuba* **88 B3** 23 8N 82 22W
Havana, *U.S.A.* **80 E9** 40 18N 90 4W
Havant, *U.K.* **11 G7** 50 51N 0 58W
Havasu, L., *U.S.A.* **85 L12** 34 18N 114 28W
Havel →, *Germany* **16 B7** 52 50N 12 3 E
Havelange, *Belgium* **15 D5** 50 23N 5 15 E
Havelian, *Pakistan* **42 B5** 34 2N 73 10 E
Havelock, *N.B., Canada* **71 C6** 46 2N 65 24W
Havelock, *Ont., Canada* **70 D4** 44 26N 77 53W
Havelock, *N.Z.* **59 J4** 41 17S 173 48 E
Haverfordwest, *U.K.* **11 F3** 51 48N 4 58W
Haverhill, *U.S.A.* **79 D13** 42 47N 71 5W
Havering, *U.K.* **11 F8** 51 34N 0 13 E
Haverstraw, *U.S.A.* **79 E11** 41 12N 73 58W
Havířov, *Czech Rep.* **17 D10** 49 46N 18 20 E
Havlíčkův Brod, *Czech.* **16 D8** 49 36N 15 33 E
Havre, *U.S.A.* **82 B9** 48 33N 109 41W
Havre-Aubert, *Canada* **71 C7** 47 12N 61 56W
Havre-St.-Pierre, *Canada* **71 B7** 50 18N 63 33W
Haw →, *U.S.A.* **77 H6** 35 36N 79 3W
Hawaii □, *U.S.A.* **74 H16** 19 30N 156 30W
Hawaii I., *Pac. Oc.* **74 J17** 20 0N 155 0W
Hawaiian Is., *Pac. Oc.* **74 H17** 20 30N 156 0W
Hawaiian Ridge, *Pac. Oc.* **65 E11** 24 0N 165 0W
Hawarden, *Canada* **73 C7** 51 25N 106 36W
Hawarden, *U.S.A.* **80 D6** 43 0N 96 29W
Hawea, L., *N.Z.* **59 L2** 44 28S 169 19 E
Hawera, *N.Z.* **59 H5** 39 35S 174 19 E
Hawick, *U.K.* **12 F6** 55 26N 2 47W
Hawk Junction, *Canada* **70 C3** 48 5N 84 38W
Hawke B., *N.Z.* **59 H6** 39 25S 177 20 E
Hawker, *Australia* **63 E2** 31 59S 138 22 E
Hawkesbury, *Canada* **70 C5** 45 37N 74 37W
Hawkesbury I., *Canada* **72 C3** 53 37N 129 3W
Hawkesbury Pt., *Australia* **62 A1** 11 55S 134 5 E
Hawkinsville, *U.S.A.* **77 J4** 32 17N 83 28W
Hawkwood, *Australia* **63 D5** 25 45S 150 50 E
Hawley, *U.S.A.* **80 B6** 46 53N 96 19W
Hawrān, *Syria* **47 C5** 32 45N 36 15 E
Hawsh Mūssá, *Lebanon* **47 B4** 33 45N 35 55 E
Hawthorne, *U.S.A.* **82 G4** 38 32N 118 38W
Haxtun, *U.S.A.* **80 E3** 40 39N 102 38W
Hay, *Australia* **63 E3** 34 30S 144 51 E
Hay →, *Australia* **62 C2** 24 50S 138 0 E
Hay →, *Canada* **72 A5** 60 50N 116 26W
Hay, C., *Australia* **60 B4** 14 5S 129 29 E
Hay L., *Canada* **72 B5** 58 50N 118 50W
Hay Lakes, *Canada* **72 C6** 53 12N 113 2W
Hay-on-Wye, *U.K.* **11 E4** 52 5N 3 8W
Hay River, *Canada* **72 A5** 60 51N 115 44W
Hay Springs, *U.S.A.* **80 D3** 42 41N 102 41W
Haya, *Indonesia* **37 E7** 3 19S 129 37 E
Hayachine-San, *Japan* **30 E10** 39 34N 141 29 E
Hayden, *Ariz., U.S.A.* **83 K8** 33 0N 110 47W
Hayden, *Colo., U.S.A.* **82 F10** 40 30N 107 16W
Haydon, *Australia* **62 B3** 18 0S 141 30 E
Hayes, *U.S.A.* **80 C4** 44 23N 101 1W
Hayes →, *Canada* **73 B10** 57 3N 92 12W
Haynesville, *U.S.A.* **81 J8** 32 58N 93 8W
Hayrabolu, *Turkey* **21 D12** 41 12N 27 5 E
Hays, *Canada* **72 C6** 50 6N 111 48W
Hays, *U.S.A.* **80 F5** 38 53N 99 20W
Haysyn, *Ukraine* **17 D15** 48 57N 29 25 E
Hayvoron, *Ukraine* **17 D15** 48 22N 29 52 E
Hayward, *Calif., U.S.A.* **84 H4** 37 40N 122 5W
Hayward, *Wis., U.S.A.* **80 B9** 46 1N 91 29W
Haywards Heath, *U.K.* **11 F7** 51 0N 0 5W
Hazafon □, *Israel* **47 C4** 32 40N 35 20 E
Hazarām, Kūh-e, *Iran* **45 D8** 29 30N 57 18 E
Hazard, *U.S.A.* **76 G4** 37 15N 83 12W
Hazaribag, *India* **43 H11** 23 58N 85 26 E
Hazaribag Road, *India* **43 G11** 24 12N 85 57 E
Hazelton, *Canada* **72 B3** 55 20N 127 42W
Hazelton, *U.S.A.* **80 B4** 46 29N 100 17W
Hazen, *N. Dak., U.S.A.* **80 B4** 47 18N 101 38W
Hazen, *Nev., U.S.A.* **82 G4** 39 34N 119 3W
Hazlehurst, *Ga., U.S.A.* **77 K4** 31 52N 82 36W
Hazlehurst, *Miss., U.S.A.* **81 K9** 31 52N 90 24W
Hazleton, *U.S.A.* **79 F9** 40 57N 75 59W
Hazlett, L., *Australia* **60 D4** 21 30S 128 48 E
Hazor, *Israel* **47 B4** 33 2N 35 32 E
Head of Bight, *Australia* **61 F5** 31 30S 131 25 E
Headlands, *Zimbabwe* **55 F3** 18 15S 32 2 E
Healdsburg, *U.S.A.* **84 G4** 38 37N 122 52W
Healdton, *U.S.A.* **81 H6** 34 14N 97 29W
Healesville, *Australia* **63 F4** 37 35S 145 30 E
Heanor, *U.K.* **10 D6** 53 1N 1 21W
Heard I., *Ind. Oc.* **3 G13** 53 0S 74 0 E
Hearne, *U.S.A.* **81 K6** 30 53N 96 36W
Hearne B., *Canada* **73 A9** 60 10N 99 10W
Hearne L., *Canada* **72 A6** 62 20N 113 10W
Hearst, *Canada* **70 C3** 49 40N 83 41W
Heart →, *U.S.A.* **80 B4** 46 46N 100 50W
Heart's Content, *Canada* **71 C9** 47 54N 53 27W
Heath Pt., *Canada* **71 C7** 49 8N 61 40W
Heath Steele, *Canada* **71 C6** 47 17N 66 5W
Heavener, *U.S.A.* **81 H7** 34 53N 94 36W
Hebbronville, *U.S.A.* **81 M5** 27 18N 98 41W
Hebei □, *China* **34 E9** 39 0N 116 0 E
Hebel, *Australia* **63 D4** 28 58S 147 47 E
Heber, *U.S.A.* **85 N11** 32 44N 115 32W
Heber Springs, *U.S.A.* **81 H9** 35 30N 92 2W
Hebert, *Canada* **73 C7** 50 30N 107 10W
Hebgen L., *U.S.A.* **82 D8** 44 52N 111 20W
Hebi, *China* **34 G8** 35 57N 114 7 E
Hebrides, *U.K.* **12 D1** 57 30N 7 0W
Hebron = Al Khalīl, *West Bank* **47 D4** 31 32N 35 6 E
Hebron, *Canada* **69 C13** 58 5N 62 30W
Hebron, *N. Dak., U.S.A.* **80 B3** 46 54N 102 3W
Hebron, *Nebr., U.S.A.* **80 E6** 40 10N 97 35W
Hecate Str., *Canada* **72 C2** 53 10N 130 30W
Hechi, *China* **32 D5** 24 40N 108 2 E
Hechuan, *China* **32 C5** 30 2N 106 12 E
Hecla, *U.S.A.* **80 C5** 45 53N 98 9W
Hecla I., *Canada* **73 C9** 51 10N 96 43W
Hede, *Sweden* **9 E15** 62 23N 13 30 E
Hedemora, *Sweden* **9 F16** 60 18N 15 58 E
Hedley, *U.S.A.* **81 H4** 34 52N 100 39W
Heemstede, *Neths.* **15 B4** 52 22N 4 37 E
Heerde, *Neths.* **15 B6** 52 24N 6 2 E
Heerenveen, *Neths.* **15 B5** 52 57N 5 55 E
Heerlen, *Neths.* **18 A6** 50 55N 5 58 E
Hefa, *Israel* **47 C3** 32 46N 35 0 E
Hefa □, *Israel* **47 C4** 32 40N 35 0 E
Hefei, *China* **33 C6** 31 52N 117 18 E
Hegang, *China* **33 B8** 47 20N 130 19 E
Heichengzhen, *China* **34 F4** 36 24N 106 3 E
Heidelberg, *Germany* **16 D5** 49 24N 8 42 E
Heidelberg, *S. Africa* **56 E3** 34 6S 20 59 E
Heilbron, *S. Africa* **57 D4** 27 16S 27 59 E
Heilbronn, *Germany* **16 D5** 49 9N 9 13 E
Heilongjiang □, *China* **35 B14** 48 0N 126 0 E
Heilunkiang = Heilongjiang □, *China* **35 B14** 48 0N 126 0 E
Heimaey, *Iceland* **8 E3** 63 26N 20 17W
Heinola, *Finland* **9 F22** 61 13N 26 2 E
Heinze Is., *Burma* **41 M20** 14 25N 97 45 E

Juan de Fuca Str.

J

Jabal Lubnān, Lebanon .. 47 B4 33 45N 35 40 E
Jabalpur, India .... 43 H8 23 9N 79 58 E
Jabbūl, Syria .... 44 B3 36 4N 37 30 E
Jablah, Syria .... 44 C3 35 20N 36 0 E
Jablanica, Macedonia ... 21 D9 41 15N 20 30 E
Jablonec, Czech. .... 16 C8 50 43N 15 10 E
Jaboatão, Brazil 93 E11 8 7S 35 1W
Jaboticabal, Brazil 95 A6 21 15S 48 17W
Jaburu, Brazil 92 E6 5 30S 64 0W
Jaca, Spain 19 A5 42 35N 0 33W
Jacarei, Brazil 95 A6 23 20S 46 0W
Jacarèzinho, Brazil 95 A6 23 5S 49 58W
Jackman, U.S.A. 71 C5 45 35N 70 17W
Jacksboro, U.S.A. 81 J5 33 14N 98 15W
Jackson, Australia ...... 63 D4 26 39S 149 39 E
Jackson, Ala., U.S.A. 77 K2 31 31N 87 53W
Jackson, Calif., U.S.A. ... 84 G6 38 21N 120 46W
Jackson, Ky., U.S.A. 76 G4 37 33N 83 23W
Jackson, Mich., U.S.A. .. 76 D3 42 15N 84 24W
Jackson, Minn., U.S.A. .. 80 D7 43 37N 95 1W
Jackson, Miss., U.S.A. ... 81 J9 32 18N 90 12W
Jackson, Mo., U.S.A. 81 G10 37 23N 89 40W
Jackson, Ohio, U.S.A. ... 76 F4 39 3N 82 39W
Jackson, Tenn., U.S.A. .. 77 H1 35 37N 88 49W
Jackson, Wyo., U.S.A. ... 82 E8 43 29N 110 46W
Jackson B., N.Z. .... 59 K2 43 58S 168 42 E
Jackson L., U.S.A. 82 E8 43 52N 110 36W
Jacksons, N.Z. .... 59 K3 42 46S 171 32 E
Jacksonville, Ala., U.S.A. 77 J3 33 49N 85 46W
Jacksonville, Calif., U.S.A. 84 H6 37 52N 120 24W
Jacksonville, Fla., U.S.A. . 77 K5 30 20N 81 39W
Jacksonville, Ill., U.S.A. .. 80 F9 39 44N 90 14W
Jacksonville, N.C., U.S.A. 77 H7 34 45N 77 26W
Jacksonville, Oreg., U.S.A. 82 E2 42 19N 122 57W
Jacksonville, Tex., U.S.A. 81 K7 31 58N 95 17W
Jacksonville Beach, U.S.A. 77 K5 30 17N 81 24W
Jacmel, Haiti 89 C5 18 14N 72 32W
Jacob Lake, U.S.A. 83 H7 36 43N 112 13W
Jacobabad, Pakistan .... 42 E3 28 20N 68 29 E
Jacobina, Brazil 93 F10 11 11S 40 30W
Jacques-Cartier, Mt., Canada 71 C6 48 57N 66 0W
Jacuí →, Brazil 95 C5 30 2S 51 15W
Jacumba, U.S.A. 85 N10 32 37N 116 11W
Jacundá →, Brazil 93 D8 1 57S 50 26W
Jadotville = Likasi, Zaïre 55 E2 10 55S 26 48 E
Jādū, Libya .... 51 B7 32 0N 12 0 E
Jaén, Peru 92 E3 5 25S 78 40W
Jaén, Spain 19 D4 37 44N 3 43W
Jaffa = Tel Aviv-Yafo, Israel .... 47 C3 32 4N 34 48 E
Jaffa, C., Australia ...... 63 F2 36 58S 139 40 E
Jaffna, Sri Lanka .... 40 Q12 9 45N 80 2 E
Jagadhri, India .... 42 D7 30 10N 77 20 E
Jagadishpur, India ...... 43 G11 25 30N 84 21 E
Jagdalpur, India .... 41 K12 19 3N 82 0 E
Jagersfontein, S. Africa .. 56 D4 29 44S 25 27 E
Jagraon, India .... 40 D9 30 50N 75 25 E
Jagtial, India .... 40 K11 18 50N 79 0 E
Jaguariaiva, Brazil 95 A6 24 10S 49 50W
Jaguaribe →, Brazil 93 D11 4 25S 37 45W
Jagüey Grande, Cuba ... 88 B3 22 35N 81 7W
Jahangirabad, India ..... 42 E8 28 19N 78 4 E
Jahrom, Iran .... 45 D7 28 30N 53 31 E
Jailolo, Indonesia .... 37 D7 1 5N 127 30 E
Jailolo, Selat, Indonesia . 37 D7 0 5N 129 5 E
Jaipur, India .... 42 F6 27 0N 75 50 E
Jājarm, Iran .... 45 B8 36 58N 56 27 E
Jakarta, Indonesia ...... 37 G12 6 9S 106 49 E
Jakobstad = Pietarsaari, Finland .... 8 E20 63 40N 22 43 E
Jal, U.S.A. 81 J3 32 7N 103 12W
Jalalabad, Afghan. ...... 42 B4 34 30N 70 29 E
Jalalabad, India .... 43 F8 27 41N 79 42 E
Jalalpur Jattan, Pakistan . 42 C6 32 38N 74 11 E
Jalama, U.S.A. 85 L6 34 29N 120 29W
Jalapa, Guatemala 88 D2 14 39N 89 59W
Jalapa Enríquez, Mexico . 87 D5 19 32N 96 55W
Jalasjärvi, Finland ...... 9 E20 62 29N 22 47 E
Jalaun, India .... 43 F8 26 8N 79 25 E
Jaleswar, Nepal .... 43 F11 26 38N 85 48 E
Jalgaon, Maharashtra, India .... 40 J10 21 2N 76 31 E
Jalgaon, Maharashtra, India .... 40 J9 21 0N 75 42 E
Jalībah, Iraq .... 44 D5 30 35N 46 32 E
Jalisco □, Mexico 86 C4 20 0N 104 0W
Jalkot, Pakistan .... 43 B5 35 14N 73 24 E
Jalna, India .... 40 K9 19 48N 75 38 E
Jalón →, Spain 19 B5 41 47N 1 4W
Jalpa, Mexico 86 C4 21 38N 102 58W
Jalpaiguri, India .... 41 F16 26 32N 88 46 E
Jaluit I., Pac. Oc. ...... 64 G8 6 0N 169 30 E
Jalūlā, Iraq .... 44 C5 34 16N 45 10 E
Jamaica ■, W. Indies 88 C4 18 10N 77 30W
Jamalpur, Bangla. ...... 41 G16 24 52N 89 56 E
Jamalpur, India .... 43 G12 25 18N 86 28 E
Jamalpurganj, India ..... 43 H13 23 2N 88 1 E
Jamanxim →, Brazil 93 D7 4 43S 56 18W
Jambe, Indonesia .... 37 E8 1 15S 132 10 E
Jambi, Indonesia .... 36 E2 1 38S 103 30 E
Jambi □, Indonesia ..... 36 E2 1 30S 102 30 E
Jambusar, India .... 42 H5 22 3N 72 51 E
James →, U.S.A. 80 D6 42 52N 97 18W
James B., Canada 69 C11 51 30N 80 0W
James Ras., Australia ... 60 D5 24 10S 132 30 E
James Ross I., Antarctica 5 C18 63 58S 57 50W
Jamestown, Australia ... 63 E2 33 10S 138 32 E
Jamestown, S. Africa ... 56 E4 31 6S 26 45 E
Jamestown, Ky., U.S.A. . 76 G3 36 59N 85 4W
Jamestown, N. Dak., U.S.A. 80 B5 46 54N 98 42W
Jamestown, N.Y., U.S.A. . 78 D5 42 6N 79 14W
Jamestown, Pa., U.S.A. .. 78 E4 41 29N 80 27W
Jamestown, Tenn., U.S.A. 77 G3 36 26N 84 56W
Jamīlābād, Iran .... 45 C6 34 24N 48 28 E
Jamiltepec, Mexico 87 D5 16 17N 97 49W
Jamkhandi, India .... 40 L9 16 30N 75 15 E
Jammu, India .... 42 C6 32 43N 74 54 E
Jammu & Kashmir □, India .... 43 B7 34 25N 77 0 E
Jamnagar, India .... 42 H4 22 30N 70 6 E
Jampur, Pakistan .... 42 E4 29 39N 70 40 E
Jamrud, Pakistan .... 42 C4 33 59N 71 24 E
Jämsä, Finland .... 9 F21 61 53N 25 10 E
Jamshedpur, India ..... 43 H12 22 44N 86 12 E
Jamtara, India .... 43 H12 23 59N 86 49 E
Jämtland, Sweden ...... 8 E15 63 31N 14 0 E
Jan L., Canada 73 C8 54 56N 102 55W
Jan Mayen, Arctic 4 B7 71 0N 9 0W
Janakkala, Finland ...... 9 F21 60 54N 24 36 E
Jand, Pakistan .... 42 C5 33 30N 72 6 E
Jandaq, Iran .... 45 C7 34 3N 54 22 E
Jandia, Canary Is. 22 F5 28 6N 14 21W
Jandia, Pta. de, Canary Is. 22 F5 28 3N 14 31W
Jandola, Pakistan .... 42 C4 32 20N 70 9 E
Jandowae, Australia .... 63 D5 26 45S 151 7 E
Janesville, U.S.A. 80 D10 42 41N 89 1W
Janīn, West Bank .... 47 C4 32 28N 35 18 E
Janos, Mexico 86 A3 30 45N 108 10W
Januária, Brazil 93 G10 15 25S 44 25W
Janubio, Canary Is. 22 F6 28 56N 13 50W
Jaora, India .... 42 H6 23 40N 75 10 E
Japan ■, Asia .... 31 G8 36 0N 136 0 E
Japan, Sea of, Asia ..... 30 E7 40 0N 135 0 E
Japan Trench, Pac. Oc. .. 28 F18 32 0N 142 0 E
Japen = Yapen, Indonesia 37 E9 1 50S 136 0 E
Japurá →, Brazil 92 D5 3 8S 65 46W
Jaque, Panama 92 B3 7 27N 78 8W
Jarābulus, Syria .... 44 B3 36 49N 38 1 E
Jarama →, Spain 19 B4 40 24N 3 32W
Jaranwala, Pakistan ..... 42 D5 31 15N 73 26 E
Jarash, Jordan .... 47 C4 32 17N 35 54 E
Jardim, Brazil 94 A4 21 28S 56 2W
Jardines de la Reina, Is., Cuba 88 B4 20 50N 78 50W
Jargalang, China .... 35 C12 43 5N 122 55 E
Jargalant = Hovd, Mongolia .... 32 B4 48 2N 91 37 E
Jarīr, W. al →, Si. Arabia 44 E4 25 38N 42 30 E
Jarosław, Poland .... 17 C12 50 2N 22 42 E
Jarrahdale, Australia .... 61 F2 32 24S 116 5 E
Jarres, Plaine des, Laos . 38 C4 19 27N 103 10 E
Jarso, Ethiopia .... 51 G12 5 15N 37 30 E
Jartai, China .... 34 E3 39 45N 105 48 E
Jarud Qi, China .... 35 B11 44 28N 120 50 E
Järvenpää, Finland ...... 9 F21 60 29N 25 5 E
Jarvis, Canada 78 D4 42 53N 80 6W
Jarvis I., Pac. Oc. 65 H12 0 15S 159 55W
Jarwa, India .... 43 F10 27 38N 82 30 E
Jāsimīyah, Iraq .... 44 C5 33 45N 44 41 E
Jasin, Malaysia .... 39 L4 2 20N 102 26 E
Jāsk, Iran .... 45 E8 25 38N 57 45 E
Jasło, Poland .... 17 D11 49 45N 21 30 E
Jasper, Alta., Canada ... 72 C5 52 55N 118 5W
Jasper, Ont., Canada ... 79 B9 44 52N 75 57W
Jasper, Ala., U.S.A. 77 J2 33 50N 87 17W
Jasper, Fla., U.S.A. 77 K4 30 31N 82 57W
Jasper, Minn., U.S.A. 80 D6 43 51N 96 24W
Jasper, Tex., U.S.A. 81 K8 30 56N 94 1W
Jasper Nat. Park, Canada 72 C5 52 50N 118 8W
Jászberény, Hungary .... 17 E10 47 30N 19 55 E
Jataí, Brazil 93 G8 17 58S 51 48W
Jati, Pakistan .... 42 G3 24 20N 68 19 E
Jatibarang, Indonesia ... 37 G13 6 28S 108 18 E
Jatinegara, Indonesia ... 37 G12 6 13S 106 52 E
Játiva, Spain 19 C5 39 0N 0 32W
Jaú, Brazil 95 A6 22 10S 48 30W
Jauja, Peru 92 F3 11 45S 75 15W
Jaunpur, India .... 43 G10 25 46N 82 44 E
Java = Jawa, Indonesia .. 37 G14 7 0S 110 0 E
Java Sea, Indonesia ..... 36 E3 4 35S 107 15 E
Java Trench, Ind. Oc. ... 64 H2 9 0S 105 0 E
Javhlant = Ulyasutay, Mongolia .... 32 B4 47 56N 97 28 E
Jawa, Indonesia .... 37 G14 7 0S 110 0 E
Jay, U.S.A. 81 G7 36 25N 94 48W
Jaya, Puncak, Indonesia . 37 E9 3 57S 137 17 E
Jayanti, India .... 41 F16 26 45N 89 40 E
Jayapura, Indonesia ..... 37 E10 2 28S 140 38 E
Jayawijaya, Pegunungan, Indonesia .... 37 E9 5 0S 139 0 E
Jaynagar, India .... 41 F15 26 43N 86 9 E
Jayrūd, Syria .... 44 C3 33 49N 36 44 E
Jayton, U.S.A. 81 J4 33 15N 100 34W
Jazīreh-ye Shīf, Iran .... 45 D6 29 4N 50 54 E
Jazminal, Mexico 86 C4 24 56N 101 25W
Jazzin, Lebanon .... 47 B4 33 31N 35 35 E
Jean, U.S.A. 85 K11 35 47N 115 20W
Jean Marie River, Canada 72 A4 61 32N 120 38W
Jean Rabel, Haiti 89 C5 19 50N 73 5W
Jeanerette, U.S.A. 81 L9 29 55N 91 40W
Jeanette, Ostrov, Russia . 27 B16 76 43N 158 0 E
Jeannette, U.S.A. 78 F5 40 20N 79 36W
Jebba, Nigeria .... 50 G5 9 9N 4 48 E
Jebel, Bahr el →, Sudan 51 G11 9 30N 30 25 E
Jedburgh, U.K. 12 F6 55 29N 2 33W
Jedda = Jiddah, Si. Arabia .... 46 C2 21 29N 39 10 E
Jędrzejów, Poland ...... 17 C11 50 35N 20 15 E
Jedway, Canada 72 C2 52 17N 131 14W
Jefferson, Iowa, U.S.A. .. 80 D7 42 1N 94 23W
Jefferson, Ohio, U.S.A. .. 78 E4 41 44N 80 46W
Jefferson, Tex., U.S.A. .. 81 J7 32 46N 94 21W
Jefferson, Wis., U.S.A. .. 80 D10 43 0N 88 48W
Jefferson, Mt., Nev., U.S.A. 82 G5 38 51N 117 0W
Jefferson, Mt., Oreg., U.S.A. 82 D3 44 41N 121 48W
Jefferson City, Mo., U.S.A. 80 F8 38 34N 92 10W
Jefferson City, Tenn., U.S.A. 77 G4 36 7N 83 30W
Jeffersonville, U.S.A. 76 F3 38 17N 85 44W
Jega, Nigeria .... 50 F5 12 15N 4 23 E
Jēkabpils, Latvia .... 9 H21 56 29N 25 57 E
Jelenia Góra, Poland .... 16 C8 50 50N 15 45 E
Jelgava, Latvia .... 9 H20 56 41N 23 49 E
Jellicoe, Canada 70 C2 49 40N 87 30W
Jemaja, Indonesia ...... 36 D3 3 5N 105 45 E
Jemaluang, Malaysia .... 39 L4 2 16N 103 52 E
Jember, Indonesia ...... 37 H15 8 11S 113 41 E
Jembongan, Malaysia ... 36 C5 6 45N 117 20 E
Jemeppe, Belgium ...... 15 D5 50 37N 5 30 E
Jena, Germany .... 16 C6 50 54N 11 35 E
Jena, U.S.A. 81 K8 31 41N 92 8W
Jenkins, U.S.A. 76 G4 37 10N 82 38W
Jenner, U.S.A. 84 G3 38 27N 123 7W
Jennings, U.S.A. 81 K8 30 13N 92 40W
Jennings →, Canada ... 72 B2 59 38N 132 5W
Jeparit, Australia .... 63 F3 36 8S 142 1 E
Jequié, Brazil 93 F10 13 51S 40 5W
Jequitinhonha, Brazil 93 G10 16 30S 41 0W
Jequitinhonha →, Brazil 93 G11 15 51S 38 53W
Jerada, Morocco 50 B4 34 17N 2 10W
Jerantut, Malaysia ...... 39 L4 3 56N 102 22 E
Jérémie, Haiti 89 C5 18 40N 74 10W
Jerez, Punta, Mexico ... 87 C5 22 58N 97 40W
Jerez de García Salinas, Mexico 86 C4 22 39N 103 0W
Jerez de la Frontera, Spain 19 D2 36 41N 6 7W
Jerez de los Caballeros, Spain 19 C2 38 20N 6 45W
Jericho = Arīḩā, Syria ... 44 C3 35 49N 36 35 E
Jericho = El Arīḩā, West Bank .... 47 D4 31 52N 35 27 E
Jericho, Australia ...... 62 C4 23 38S 146 6 E
Jerilderie, Australia .... 63 F4 35 20S 145 41 E
Jermyn, U.S.A. 79 E9 41 31N 75 31W
Jerome, U.S.A. 83 J8 34 45N 112 7W
Jersey, U.K. 11 H5 49 11N 2 7W
Jersey City, U.S.A. 79 F10 40 44N 74 4W
Jersey Shore, U.S.A. 78 E7 41 12N 77 15W
Jerseyville, U.S.A. 80 F9 39 7N 90 20W
Jerusalem, Israel .... 47 D4 31 47N 35 10 E
Jervis B., Australia ..... 63 F5 35 8S 150 46 E
Jesselton = Kota Kinabalu, Malaysia .... 36 C5 6 0N 116 4 E
Jessore, Bangla. .... 41 H16 23 10N 89 10 E
Jesup, U.S.A. 77 K5 31 36N 81 53W
Jesús Carranza, Mexico . 87 D5 17 28N 95 1W
Jesús María, Argentina .. 94 C3 30 59S 64 5W
Jetmore, U.S.A. 81 F5 38 4N 99 54W
Jetpur, India .... 42 J4 21 45N 70 10 E
Jevnaker, Norway ...... 9 F14 60 15N 10 26 E
Jewett, Ohio, U.S.A. 78 F3 40 22N 81 2W
Jewett, Tex., U.S.A. 81 K6 31 22N 96 9W
Jewett City, U.S.A. 79 E13 41 36N 72 0W
Jeyḩūnābād, Iran ...... 45 C6 34 58N 48 59 E
Jeypore, India .... 41 K13 18 50N 82 38 E
Jhajjar, India .... 42 E7 28 37N 76 42 E
Jhal Jhao, Pakistan .... 40 F4 26 20N 65 35 E
Jhalawar, India .... 42 G7 24 40N 76 10 E
Jhang Maghiana, Pakistan 42 D5 31 15N 72 22 E
Jhansi, India .... 43 G8 25 30N 78 36 E
Jharia, India .... 43 H12 23 45N 86 26 E
Jharsuguda, India ...... 41 J14 21 56N 84 5 E
Jhelum, Pakistan ...... 42 C5 33 0N 73 45 E
Jhelum →, Pakistan ... 42 D5 31 20N 72 10 E
Jhunjhunu, India ...... 42 E6 28 10N 75 30 E
Ji Xian, Hebei, China ... 34 F8 37 35N 115 30 E
Ji Xian, Henan, China ... 34 G8 35 22N 114 5 E
Ji Xian, Shanxi, China ... 34 F6 36 7N 110 40 E
Jia Xian, Henan, China .. 34 H7 33 59N 113 12 E
Jia Xian, Shaanxi, China . 34 E6 38 12N 110 28 E
Jiamusi, China .... 33 B8 46 40N 130 26 E
Ji'an, Jiangxi, China .... 33 D6 27 6N 114 59 E
Ji'an, Jilin, China ...... 35 D14 41 5N 126 10 E
Jianchang, China .... 35 D11 40 55N 120 35 E
Jianchangying, China ... 35 D10 40 10N 118 50 E
Jiangcheng, China ...... 32 D5 22 36N 101 52 E
Jiangmen, China .... 33 D6 22 32N 113 0 E
Jiangsu □, China ...... 35 H10 33 0N 120 0 E
Jiangxi □, China .... 33 D6 27 30N 116 0 E
Jiao Xian, China .... 35 F11 36 18N 120 1 E
Jiaohe, Hebei, China ... 34 E9 38 2N 116 20 E
Jiaohe, Jilin, China .... 35 C14 43 40N 127 22 E
Jiaozhou Wan, China ... 35 F11 36 5N 120 10 E
Jiaozuo, China .... 34 G7 35 16N 113 12 E
Jiawang, China .... 35 G9 34 28N 117 26 E
Jiaxiang, China .... 34 G9 35 25N 116 20 E
Jiaxing, China .... 33 C7 30 49N 120 45 E
Jiayi = Chiai, Taiwan ... 33 D7 23 29N 120 25 E
Jibuti = Djibouti ■, Africa 46 E3 12 0N 43 0 E
Jicarón, I., Panama 88 E3 7 10N 81 50W
Jiddah, Si. Arabia ...... 46 C2 21 29N 39 10 E
Jido, India .... 41 E19 29 2N 94 58 E
Jieshou, China .... 34 H8 33 18N 115 22 E
Jiexiu, China .... 34 F6 37 2N 111 55 E
Jiggalong, Australia .... 60 D3 23 21S 120 47 E
Jihlava, Czech. .... 16 D8 49 28N 15 35 E
Jihlava →, Czech. ..... 17 D9 48 55N 16 36 E
Jijel, Algeria .... 50 A6 36 52N 5 50 E
Jijiga, Ethiopia .... 46 F3 9 20N 42 50 E
Jilin, China .... 35 C14 43 44N 126 30 E
Jilin □, China .... 35 C13 44 0N 127 0 E
Jilong = Chilung, Taiwan 33 D7 25 3N 121 45 E
Jima, Ethiopia .... 51 G12 7 40N 36 47 E
Jiménez, Mexico 86 B4 27 10N 104 54W
Jimo, China .... 35 F11 36 23N 120 30 E
Jin Xian, Hebei, China .. 34 E8 38 2N 115 2 E
Jin Xian, Liaoning, China 35 E11 38 55N 121 42 E
Jinan, China .... 34 F9 36 38N 117 1 E
Jincheng, China .... 34 G7 35 29N 112 50 E
Jind, India .... 42 E7 29 19N 76 22 E
Jindabyne, Australia .... 63 F4 36 25S 148 35 E
Jindrichuv Hradeç, Czech. 16 D8 49 10N 15 2 E
Jing He →, China ..... 34 G5 34 27N 109 4 E
Jingbian, China .... 34 F5 37 20N 108 30 E
Jingchuan, China ...... 34 G4 35 20N 107 20 E
Jingdezhen, China ..... 33 D6 29 20N 117 11 E
Jinggu, China .... 32 D5 23 35N 100 41 E
Jinghai, China .... 34 E9 38 55N 116 55 E
Jingle, China .... 34 E6 38 20N 111 55 E
Jingning, China .... 34 G3 35 30N 105 43 E
Jingpo Hu, China ...... 35 C15 43 55N 128 55 E
Jingtai, China .... 34 F3 37 10N 104 6 E
Jingxing, China .... 34 E8 38 2N 114 8 E
Jingyang, China .... 34 G5 34 30N 108 50 E
Jingyu, China .... 35 C14 42 25N 126 45 E
Jingyuan, China .... 34 F3 36 30N 104 40 E
Jingziguan, China ..... 34 H6 33 15N 111 0 E
Jinhua, China .... 33 D6 29 8N 119 38 E
Jining, Nei Mongol Zizhiqu, China .... 34 D7 41 5N 113 0 E
Jining, Shandong, China 34 G9 35 22N 116 34 E
Jinja, Uganda .... 54 B3 0 25N 33 12 E
Jinjang, Malaysia ...... 39 L3 3 13N 101 39 E
Jinji, China .... 34 F4 37 58N 106 8 E
Jinnah Barrage, Pakistan 40 C7 32 58N 71 33 E
Jinotega, Nic. 88 D2 13 6N 85 59W
Jinotepe, Nic. 88 D2 11 50N 86 10W
Jinsha Jiang →, China . 32 D5 28 50N 104 36 E
Jinxi, China .... 35 D11 40 52N 120 50 E
Jinxiang, China .... 34 G9 35 5N 116 22 E
Jinzhou, China .... 35 D11 41 5N 121 3 E
Jiparaná →, Brazil 92 E6 8 3S 62 52W
Jipijapa, Ecuador 92 D2 1 0S 80 40W
Jiquilpan, Mexico 86 D4 19 57N 102 42W
Jishan, China .... 34 G6 35 34N 110 58 E
Jisr ash Shughūr, Syria . 44 C3 35 49N 36 18 E
Jitarning, Australia ..... 61 F2 32 48S 117 57 E
Jitra, Malaysia .... 39 J3 6 16N 100 25 E
Jiu →, Romania .... 17 F12 43 47N 23 48 E
Jiudengkou, China ..... 34 E4 39 56N 106 40 E
Jiujiang, China .... 33 D6 29 42N 115 58 E
Jiutai, China .... 35 B13 44 10N 125 50 E
Jiuxiangcheng, China ... 34 H8 33 12N 114 50 E
Jiuxincheng, China ..... 34 E8 39 17N 115 59 E
Jixi, China .... 35 B16 45 20N 130 50 E
Jiyang, China .... 35 F9 37 0N 117 12 E
Jīzān, Si. Arabia .... 46 D3 17 0N 42 20 E
Jize, China .... 34 F8 36 54N 114 56 E
Jizō-Zaki, Japan ...... 31 G6 35 34N 133 20 E
Jizzakh, Uzbekistan .... 26 E7 40 6N 67 50 E
Joaçaba, Brazil 95 B5 27 5S 51 31W
João Pessoa, Brazil 93 E12 7 10S 34 52W
Joaquín V. González, Argentina 94 B3 25 10S 64 0W
Jodhpur, India .... 42 F5 26 23N 73 8 E
Joensuu, Finland ...... 24 B4 62 37N 29 49 E
Jofane, Mozam. .... 57 C5 21 15S 34 18 E
Jõgeva, Estonia .... 9 G22 58 45N 26 24 E
Joggins, Canada 71 C7 45 42N 64 27W
Jogjakarta = Yogyakarta, Indonesia .... 37 G14 7 49S 110 22 E
Johannesburg, S. Africa . 57 D4 26 10S 28 2 E
Johannesburg, U.S.A. ... 85 K9 35 22N 117 38W
John Day, U.S.A. 82 D4 44 25N 118 57W
John Day →, U.S.A. ... 82 D3 45 44N 120 39W
John H. Kerr Reservoir, U.S.A. 77 G6 36 36N 78 18W
John o' Groats, U.K. 12 C5 58 38N 3 4W
Johnnie, U.S.A. 85 J10 36 25N 116 5W
John's Ra., Australia ... 62 C1 21 55S 133 23 E
Johnson, U.S.A. 81 G4 37 34N 101 45W
Johnson City, N.Y., U.S.A. 79 D9 42 7N 75 58W
Johnson City, Tenn., U.S.A. 77 G4 36 19N 82 21W
Johnson City, Tex., U.S.A. 81 K5 30 17N 98 25W
Johnsonburg, U.S.A. ... 78 E6 41 29N 78 41W
Johnsondale, U.S.A. ... 85 K8 35 58N 118 32W
Johnson's Crossing, Canada 72 A2 60 29N 133 18W
Johnston, L., Australia .. 61 F3 32 25S 120 30 E
Johnston Falls = Mambilima Falls, Zambia .... 55 E2 10 31S 28 45 E
Johnston I., Pac. Oc. ... 65 F11 17 10N 169 8W
Johnstone Str., Canada .. 72 C3 50 28N 126 0W
Johnstown, N.Y., U.S.A. . 79 C10 43 0N 74 22W
Johnstown, Pa., U.S.A. .. 78 F6 40 20N 78 55W
Johor Baharu, Malaysia . 39 M4 1 28N 103 46 E
Jõhvi, Estonia .... 9 G22 59 22N 27 27 E
Joinvile, Brazil 95 B6 26 15S 48 55W
Joinville I., Antarctica .. 5 C18 65 0S 55 30W
Jojutla, Mexico 87 D5 18 37N 99 11W
Jokkmokk, Sweden ..... 8 C18 66 35N 19 50 E
Jökulsá á Bru →, Iceland 8 D6 65 40N 14 16W
Jökulsá á Fjöllum →, Iceland 8 C5 66 10N 16 30W
Jolfā, Āzarbājān-e Sharqī, Iran .... 44 B5 38 57N 45 38 E
Jolfā, Eşfahan, Iran ..... 45 C6 32 58N 51 37 E
Joliet, U.S.A. 76 E1 41 32N 88 5W
Joliette, Canada 70 C5 46 3N 73 24W
Jolo, Phil. .... 37 C6 6 0N 121 0 E
Jolon, U.S.A. 84 K5 35 58N 121 9W
Jombang, Indonesia .... 37 G15 7 33S 112 14 E
Jome, Indonesia ...... 37 E7 1 16S 127 30 E
Jonava, Lithuania ..... 9 J21 55 8N 24 12 E
Jones Sound, Canada ... 4 B3 76 0N 85 0W
Jonesboro, Ark., U.S.A. .. 81 H9 35 50N 90 42W
Jonesboro, Ill., U.S.A. ... 81 G10 37 27N 89 16W
Jonesboro, La., U.S.A. .. 81 J8 32 15N 92 43W
Jonesport, U.S.A. 71 D6 44 32N 67 37W
Joniškis, Lithuania ..... 9 H20 56 13N 23 35 E
Jönköping, Sweden ..... 9 H16 57 45N 14 10 E
Jonquière, Canada 71 C5 48 27N 71 14W
Joplin, U.S.A. 81 G7 37 6N 94 31W
Jordan, U.S.A. 82 C10 47 19N 106 55W
Jordan ■, Asia .... 47 E5 31 0N 36 0 E
Jordan →, Asia .... 47 D4 31 48N 35 32 E
Jordan Valley, U.S.A. ... 82 E5 42 59N 117 3W
Jorhat, India .... 41 F19 26 45N 94 12 E
Jörn, Sweden .... 8 D19 65 4N 20 1 E
Jorong, Indonesia ..... 36 E4 3 58S 114 56 E
Jørpeland, Norway ..... 9 G11 59 3N 6 1 E
Jorquera →, Chile 94 B2 28 3S 69 58W
Jos, Nigeria .... 50 G6 9 53N 8 51 E
José Batlle y Ordóñez, Uruguay 95 C4 33 20S 55 10W
Joseph, U.S.A. 82 D5 45 21N 117 14W
Joseph, L., Nfld., Canada 71 B6 52 45N 65 18W
Joseph, L., Ont., Canada . 78 A5 45 10N 79 44W
Joseph Bonaparte G., Australia .... 60 B4 14 35S 128 50 E
Joseph City, U.S.A. 83 J8 34 57N 110 20W
Joshua Tree, U.S.A. 85 L10 34 8N 116 19W
Joshua Tree National Monument, U.S.A. 85 M10 33 55N 116 0W
Jostedalsbreen, Norway . 9 F12 61 40N 6 59 E
Jotunheimen, Norway ... 9 F13 61 35N 8 25 E
Jourdanton, U.S.A. 81 L5 28 55N 98 33W
Joussard, Canada 72 B5 55 22N 115 50W
Jovellanos, Cuba 88 B3 22 40N 81 10W
Ju Xian, China .... 35 F10 36 35N 118 20 E
Juan Aldama, Mexico ... 86 C4 24 20N 103 23W
Juan Bautista Alberdi, Argentina 94 C3 34 26S 61 48W
Juan de Fuca Str., Canada 84 B2 48 15N 124 0W

Juan de Nova

Juan de Nova, Ind. Oc. 57 B7 17 3S 43 45 E
Juan Fernández, Arch. de, Pac. Oc. 90 G2 33 50S 80 0W
Juan José Castelli, Argentina 94 B3 25 27S 60 57W
Juan L. Lacaze, Uruguay 94 C4 34 26S 57 25W
Juankoski, Finland 8 E23 63 3N 28 19 E
Juárez, Argentina 94 D4 37 40S 59 43W
Juárez, Mexico 85 N11 32 20N 115 57W
Juárez, Sierra de, Mexico 86 A1 32 0N 116 0W
Juàzeiro, Brazil 93 E10 9 30S 40 30W
Juàzeiro do Norte, Brazil 93 E11 7 10S 39 18W
Jubayl, Lebanon 47 A4 34 5N 35 39 E
Jubbah, Si. Arabia 44 D4 28 2N 40 56 E
Jubbulpore = Jabalpur, India 43 H8 23 9N 79 58 E
Jubilee L., Australia 61 E4 29 0S 126 50 E
Juby, C., Morocco 50 C2 28 0N 12 59W
Júcar →, Spain 19 C5 39 5N 0 10W
Júcaro, Cuba 88 B4 21 37N 78 51W
Juchitán, Mexico 87 D5 16 27N 95 5W
Judaea = Har Yehuda, Israel 47 D3 31 35N 34 57 E
Judith →, U.S.A. 82 C9 47 44N 109 39W
Judith, Pt., U.S.A. 79 E13 41 22N 71 29W
Judith Gap, U.S.A. 82 C9 46 41N 109 45W
Jugoslavia = Yugoslavia ■, Europe 21 B9 44 0N 20 0 E
Juigalpa, Nic. 88 D2 12 6N 85 26W
Juiz de Fora, Brazil 95 A7 21 43S 43 19W
Jujuy □, Argentina 94 A2 23 20S 65 40W
Julesburg, U.S.A. 80 E3 40 59N 102 16W
Juli, Peru 92 G5 16 10S 69 25W
Julia Cr. →, Australia 62 C3 20 0S 141 11 E
Julia Creek, Australia 62 C3 20 39S 141 44 E
Juliaca, Peru 92 G4 15 25S 70 10W
Julian, U.S.A. 85 M10 33 4N 116 38W
Julianehåb, Greenland 4 C5 60 43N 46 0W
Julimes, Mexico 86 B3 28 25N 105 27W
Jullundur, India 42 D6 31 20N 75 40 E
Julu, China 34 F8 37 15N 115 2 E
Jumbo, Zimbabwe 55 F3 17 30S 30 58 E
Jumbo Pk., U.S.A. 85 J12 36 12N 114 11W
Jumentos Cays, Bahamas 89 B4 23 0N 75 40W
Jumet, Belgium 15 D4 50 27N 4 25 E
Jumilla, Spain 19 C5 38 28N 1 19W
Jumla, Nepal 43 E10 29 15N 82 13 E
Jumna = Yamuna →, India 43 G9 25 30N 81 53 E
Junagadh, India 42 J4 21 30N 70 30 E
Junction, Tex., U.S.A. 81 K5 30 29N 99 46W
Junction, Utah, U.S.A. 83 G7 38 14N 112 13W
Junction B., Australia 62 A1 11 52S 133 55 E
Junction City, Kans., U.S.A. 80 F6 39 2N 96 50W
Junction City, Oreg., U.S.A. 82 D2 44 13N 123 12W
Junction Pt., Australia 62 A1 11 45S 133 50 E
Jundah, Australia 62 C3 24 46S 143 2 E
Jundiaí, Brazil 95 A6 23 10S 47 0W
Juneau, U.S.A. 68 C6 58 18N 134 25W
Junee, Australia 63 E4 34 53S 147 35 E
Jungfrau, Switz. 16 E4 46 32N 7 58 E
Junggar Pendi, China 32 B3 44 30N 86 0 E
Jungshahi, Pakistan 42 G2 24 52N 67 44 E
Juniata →, U.S.A. 78 F7 40 30N 77 40W
Junín, Argentina 94 C3 34 33S 60 57W
Junín de los Andes, Argentina 96 D2 39 45S 71 0W
Jūniyah, Lebanon 47 B4 33 59N 35 38 E
Juntura, U.S.A. 82 E4 43 45N 118 5W
Jupiter →, Canada 71 C7 49 29N 63 37W
Jur, Nahr el →, Sudan 51 G10 8 45N 29 15 E
Jura = Jura, Mts. du, Europe 18 C7 46 40N 6 5 E
Jura = Schwäbische Alb, Germany 16 D5 48 20N 9 30 E
Jura, U.K. 12 F3 56 0N 5 50W
Jura, Mts. du, Europe 18 C7 46 40N 6 5 E
Jura, Sd. of, U.K. 12 F3 55 57N 5 45W
Jurado, Colombia 92 B3 7 7N 77 46W
Jurbarkas, Lithuania 9 J20 55 6N 22 47 E
Jūrmala, Latvia 9 H20 56 58N 23 34 E
Juruá →, Brazil 92 D5 2 37S 65 44W
Juruena →, Brazil 92 E7 7 20S 58 3W
Juruti, Brazil 93 D7 2 9S 56 4W
Justo Daract, Argentina 94 C2 33 52S 65 12W
Juticalpa, Honduras 88 D2 14 40N 86 12W
Jutland = Jylland, Denmark 9 H13 56 25N 9 30 E
Juventud, I. de la, Cuba 88 B3 21 40N 82 40W
Juwain, Afghan. 40 D2 31 45N 61 30 E
Jūy Zar, Iran 44 C5 33 50N 46 18 E
Juye, China 34 G9 35 22N 116 5 E
Jylland, Denmark 9 H13 56 25N 9 30 E
Jyväskylä, Finland 9 E21 62 14N 25 50 E

K

K2, Pakistan 43 B7 35 58N 76 32 E
Kaap Plateau, S. Africa 56 D3 28 30S 24 0 E
Kaapkruis, Namibia 56 C1 21 55S 13 57 E
Kaapstad = Cape Town, S. Africa 56 E2 33 55S 18 22 E
Kabaena, Indonesia 37 F6 5 15S 122 0 E
Kabala, S. Leone 50 G2 9 38N 11 37W
Kabale, Uganda 54 C3 1 15S 30 0 E
Kabalo, Zaïre 54 D2 6 0S 27 0 E
Kabambare, Zaïre 54 C2 4 41S 27 39 E
Kabango, Zaïre 55 D2 8 35S 28 30 E
Kabanjahe, Indonesia 36 D1 3 6N 98 30 E
Kabara, Mali 50 E4 16 40N 2 50W
Kabardino-Balkar Republic = Kabardino Balkaria □, Russia 25 F7 43 30N 43 30 E
Kabardino Balkaria □, Russia 25 F7 43 30N 43 30 E
Kabare, Indonesia 37 E8 0 4S 130 58 E
Kabarega Falls, Uganda 54 B3 2 15N 31 30 E
Kabasalan, Phil. 37 C6 7 47N 122 44 E
Kabba, Nigeria 50 G6 7 50N 6 3 E
Kabin Buri, Thailand 38 F3 13 57N 101 43 E
Kabinakagami L., Canada 70 C3 48 54N 84 25W
Kabīr, Zab al →, Iraq 44 C4 36 1N 43 24 E
Kabkabīyah, Sudan 51 F9 13 50N 24 0 E
Kabompo, Zambia 55 E1 13 36S 24 14 E
Kabompo →, Zambia 53 G4 14 10S 23 11 E
Kabondo, Zaïre 55 D2 8 58S 25 40 E
Kabongo, Zaïre 54 D2 7 22S 25 33 E
Kabra, Australia 62 C5 23 25S 150 25 E
Kabūd Gonbad, Iran 45 B8 37 5N 59 45 E
Kābul, Afghan. 42 B3 34 28N 69 11 E
Kābul □, Afghan. 40 B6 34 30N 69 0 E
Kabul →, Pakistan 42 C5 33 55N 72 14 E
Kabunga, Zaïre 54 C2 1 38S 28 3 E
Kaburuang, Indonesia 37 D7 3 50N 126 30 E
Kabwe, Zambia 55 E2 14 30S 28 29 E
Kachchh, Gulf of, India 42 H3 22 50N 69 15 E
Kachchh, Rann of, India 42 G4 24 0N 70 0 E
Kachebera, Zambia 55 E3 13 50S 32 50 E
Kachin □, Burma 41 F20 26 0N 97 30 E
Kachira, L., Uganda 54 C3 0 40S 31 7 E
Kachiry, Kazakstan 26 D8 53 10N 75 50 E
Kachot, Cambodia 39 G4 11 30N 103 3 E
Kaçkar, Turkey 25 F7 40 45N 41 10 E
Kadan Kyun, Burma 36 B1 12 30N 98 20 E
Kadanai →, Afghan. 42 D1 31 22N 65 45 E
Kadi, India 42 H5 23 18N 72 23 E
Kadina, Australia 63 E2 33 55S 137 43 E
Kadiyevka = Stakhanov, Ukraine 25 E6 48 35N 38 40 E
Kadoka, U.S.A. 80 D4 43 50N 101 31W
Kadoma, Zimbabwe 55 F2 18 20S 29 52 E
Kâdugli, Sudan 51 F10 11 0N 29 45 E
Kaduna, Nigeria 50 F6 10 30N 7 21 E
Kaédi, Mauritania 50 E2 16 9N 13 28W
Kaelé, Cameroon 51 F7 10 7N 14 27 E
Kaeng Khoï, Thailand 38 E3 14 35N 101 0 E
Kaesŏng, N. Korea 35 F14 37 58N 126 35 E
Kāf, Si. Arabia 44 D3 31 25N 37 29 E
Kafakumba, Zaïre 52 F4 9 38S 23 46 E
Kafan = Kapan, Armenia 25 G8 39 18N 46 27 E
Kafanchan, Nigeria 50 G6 9 40N 8 20 E
Kaffrine, Senegal 50 F1 14 8N 15 36W
Kafia Kingi, Sudan 51 G9 9 20N 24 25 E
Kafinda, Zambia 55 E3 12 32S 30 20 E
Kafirévs, Ákra, Greece 21 E11 38 9N 24 38 E
Kafue, Zambia 55 F2 15 46S 28 9 E
Kafue →, Zambia 53 H5 15 30S 29 0 E
Kafue Flats, Zambia 55 F2 15 40S 27 25 E
Kafue Nat. Park, Zambia 55 F2 15 0S 25 30 E
Kafulwe, Zambia 55 D2 9 0S 29 1 E
Kaga, Afghan. 42 B4 34 14N 70 10 E
Kaga Bandoro, C.A.R. 51 G8 7 0N 19 10 E
Kagan, Uzbekistan 26 F7 39 43N 64 33 E
Kagawa □, Japan 31 G6 34 15N 134 0 E
Kagera □, Tanzania 54 C3 2 0S 31 30 E
Kagera →, Uganda 54 C3 0 57S 31 47 E
Kagoshima, Japan 31 J5 31 35N 130 33 E
Kagoshima □, Japan 31 J5 31 30N 130 30 E
Kagul = Cahul, Moldova 17 F15 45 50N 28 15 E
Kahak, Iran 45 B6 36 6N 49 46 E
Kahama, Tanzania 54 C3 4 8S 32 30 E
Kahama □, Tanzania 54 C3 3 50S 32 0 E
Kahang, Malaysia 39 L4 2 12N 103 32 E
Kahayan →, Indonesia 36 E4 3 40S 114 0 E
Kahe, Tanzania 54 C4 3 30S 37 25 E
Kahemba, Zaïre 52 F3 7 18S 18 55 E
Kahniah →, Canada 72 B4 58 15N 120 55W
Kahnūj, Iran 45 E8 27 55N 57 40 E
Kahoka, U.S.A. 80 E9 40 25N 91 44W
Kahoolawe, U.S.A. 74 H16 20 33N 156 37W
Kahramanmaraş, Turkey 25 G6 37 37N 36 53 E
Kahuta, Pakistan 42 C5 33 35N 73 24 E
Kai, Kepulauan, Indonesia 37 F8 5 55S 132 45 E
Kai Besar, Indonesia 37 F8 5 35S 133 0 E
Kai Is. = Kai, Kepulauan, Indonesia 37 F8 5 55S 132 45 E
Kai Kecil, Indonesia 37 F8 5 45S 132 40 E
Kaiama, Nigeria 50 G5 9 36N 4 1 E
Kaiapoi, N.Z. 59 K4 43 24S 172 40 E
Kaieteur Falls, Guyana 92 B7 5 1N 59 10W
Kaifeng, China 34 G8 34 48N 114 21 E
Kaikohe, N.Z. 59 F4 35 25S 173 49 E
Kaikoura, N.Z. 59 K4 42 25S 173 43 E
Kaikoura Ra., N.Z. 59 J4 41 59S 173 41 E
Kailu, China 35 C11 43 38N 121 18 E
Kailua Kona, U.S.A. 74 J17 19 39N 155 59W
Kaimana, Indonesia 37 E8 3 39S 133 45 E
Kaimanawa Mts., N.Z. 59 H5 39 15S 175 56 E
Kaimganj, India 43 F8 27 33N 79 24 E
Kaimur Hills, India 43 G9 24 30N 82 0 E
Kaingaroa Forest, N.Z. 59 H6 38 24S 176 30 E
Kainji Res., Nigeria 50 F5 10 1N 4 40 E
Kainuu, Finland 8 D23 64 30N 29 7 E
Kaipara Harbour, N.Z. 59 G5 36 25S 174 14 E
Kaipokok B., Canada 71 B8 54 54N 59 47W
Kairana, India 42 E7 29 24N 77 15 E
Kaironi, Indonesia 37 E8 0 47S 133 40 E
Kairouan, Tunisia 50 A7 35 45N 10 5 E
Kaiserslautern, Germany 16 D4 49 26N 7 45 E
Kaitaia, N.Z. 59 F4 35 8S 173 17 E
Kaitangata, N.Z. 59 M2 46 17S 169 51 E
Kaithal, India 42 E7 29 48N 76 26 E
Kaitu →, Pakistan 42 C4 33 10N 70 30 E
Kaiwi Channel, U.S.A. 74 H16 21 15N 157 30W
Kaiyuan, China 35 C13 42 28N 124 1 E
Kajaani, Finland 8 D22 64 17N 27 46 E
Kajabbi, Australia 62 B3 20 0S 140 1 E
Kajana = Kajaani, Finland 8 D22 64 17N 27 46 E
Kajang, Malaysia 39 L3 2 59N 101 48 E
Kajiado, Kenya 54 C4 1 53S 36 48 E
Kajiado □, Kenya 54 C4 2 0S 36 30 E
Kajo Kaji, Sudan 51 H11 3 58N 31 40 E
Kaka, Sudan 51 F11 10 38N 32 10 E
Kakabeka Falls, Canada 70 C2 48 24N 89 37W
Kakamas, S. Africa 56 D3 28 45S 20 33 E
Kakamega, Kenya 54 B3 0 20N 34 46 E
Kakamega □, Kenya 54 B3 0 20N 34 46 E
Kakanui Mts., N.Z. 59 L3 45 10S 170 30 E
Kake, Japan 31 G6 34 36N 132 19 E
Kakegawa, Japan 31 G9 34 45N 138 1 E
Kakeroma-Jima, Japan 31 K4 28 8N 129 14 E
Kakhovka, Ukraine 25 E5 46 45N 33 30 E
Kakhovske Vdskh., Ukraine 25 E5 47 5N 34 0 E
Kakinada, India 41 L13 16 57N 82 11 E
Kakisa →, Canada 72 A5 61 3N 118 10W
Kakisa L., Canada 72 A5 60 56N 117 43W
Kakogawa, Japan 31 G7 34 46N 134 51 E
Kakwa →, Canada 72 C5 54 37N 118 28W
Kāl Gūsheh, Iran 45 D8 30 59N 58 12 E
Kal Safīd, Iran 44 C5 34 52N 47 23 E
Kalabagh, Pakistan 42 C4 33 0N 71 28 E
Kalabahi, Indonesia 37 F6 8 13S 124 31 E
Kalabo, Zambia 53 G4 14 58S 22 40 E
Kalach, Russia 25 D7 50 22N 41 0 E
Kaladan →, Burma 41 J18 20 20N 93 5 E
Kaladar, Canada 78 B7 44 37N 77 5W
Kalahari, Africa 56 C3 24 0S 21 30 E
Kalahari Gemsbok Nat. Park, S. Africa 56 D3 25 30S 20 30 E
Kalajoki, Finland 8 D20 64 12N 24 10 E
Kālak, Iran 45 E8 25 29N 59 22 E
Kalakamati, Botswana 57 C4 20 40S 27 25 E
Kalakan, Russia 27 D12 55 15N 116 45 E
Kalakh, Syria 44 C3 34 55N 36 10 E
K'alak'unlun Shank'ou, Pakistan 43 B7 35 33N 77 46 E
Kalam, Pakistan 43 B5 35 34N 72 30 E
Kalama, U.S.A. 84 E4 46 1N 122 51W
Kalama, Zaïre 54 C2 2 52S 28 35 E
Kalámai, Greece 21 F10 37 3N 22 10 E
Kalamata = Kalámai, Greece 21 F10 37 3N 22 10 E
Kalamazoo, U.S.A. 76 D3 42 17N 85 35W
Kalamazoo →, U.S.A. 76 D2 42 40N 86 10W
Kalambo Falls, Tanzania 55 D3 8 37S 31 35 E
Kalannie, Australia 61 F2 30 22S 117 5 E
Kalāntarī, Iran 45 C7 32 10N 54 8 E
Kalao, Indonesia 37 F6 7 21S 121 0 E
Kalaotoa, Indonesia 37 F6 7 20S 121 50 E
Kalasin, Thailand 38 D4 16 26N 103 30 E
Kalat, Pakistan 40 E5 29 8N 66 31 E
Kalāteh, Iran 45 B7 36 33N 55 41 E
Kalāteh-ye-Ganj, Iran 45 E8 27 31N 57 55 E
Kalbarri, Australia 61 E1 27 40S 114 10 E
Kalce, Slovenia 16 F8 45 54N 14 13 E
Kale, Turkey 21 F13 37 27N 28 49 E
Kalegauk Kyun, Burma 41 M20 15 33N 97 35 E
Kalehe, Zaïre 54 C2 2 6S 28 50 E
Kalema, Tanzania 54 C3 1 12S 31 55 E
Kalemie, Zaïre 54 D2 5 55S 29 9 E
Kalewa, Burma 41 H19 23 10N 94 15 E
Kalgan = Zhangjiakou, China 34 D8 40 48N 114 55 E
Kalgoorlie-Boulder, Australia 61 F3 30 40S 121 22 E
Kaliakra, Nos, Bulgaria 21 C13 43 21N 28 30 E
Kalianda, Indonesia 36 F3 5 50S 105 45 E
Kalibo, Phil. 37 B6 11 43N 122 22 E
Kaliganj, Bangla. 43 H13 22 25N 89 8 E
Kalima, Zaïre 54 C2 2 33S 26 32 E
Kalimantan, Indonesia 36 E4 0 0 114 0 E
Kalimantan Barat □, Indonesia 36 E4 0 0 110 30 E
Kalimantan Selatan □, Indonesia 36 E5 2 30S 115 30 E
Kalimantan Tengah □, Indonesia 36 E4 2 0S 113 30 E
Kalimantan Timur □, Indonesia 36 D5 1 30N 116 30 E
Kálimnos, Greece 21 F12 37 0N 27 0 E
Kalimpong, India 43 F13 27 4N 88 35 E
Kalinin = Tver, Russia 24 C6 56 55N 35 55 E
Kaliningrad, Kaliningd., Russia 9 J19 54 42N 20 32 E
Kaliningrad, Moskva, Russia 24 C6 55 58N 37 54 E
Kalinkavichy, Belarus 17 B15 52 12N 29 20 E
Kalinkovichi = Kalinkavichy, Belarus 17 B15 52 12N 29 20 E
Kaliro, Uganda 54 B3 0 56N 33 30 E
Kalispell, U.S.A. 82 B6 48 12N 114 19W
Kalisz, Poland 17 C10 51 45N 18 8 E
Kaliua, Tanzania 54 D3 5 5S 31 48 E
Kalix, Sweden 8 D20 65 53N 23 12 E
Kalix →, Sweden 8 D20 65 50N 23 11 E
Kalka, India 42 D7 30 46N 76 57 E
Kalkaska, U.S.A. 76 C3 44 44N 85 11W
Kalkfeld, Namibia 56 C2 20 57S 16 14 E
Kalkfontein, Botswana 56 C3 22 4S 20 57 E
Kalkrand, Namibia 56 C2 24 1S 17 35 E
Kallavesi, Finland 8 E22 62 58N 27 30 E
Kallsjön, Sweden 8 E15 63 38N 13 0 E
Kalmar, Sweden 9 H17 56 40N 16 20 E
Kalmyk Republic = Kalmykia □, Russia 25 E8 46 5N 46 1 E
Kalmykia □, Russia 25 E8 46 5N 46 1 E
Kalmykovo, Kazakstan 25 E9 49 0N 51 47 E
Kalna, India 43 H13 23 13N 88 25 E
Kalocsa, Hungary 17 E10 46 32N 19 0 E
Kalokhorio, Cyprus 23 E12 34 51N 33 2 E
Kaloko, Zaïre 54 D2 6 47S 25 48 E
Kalol, Gujarat, India 42 H5 22 37N 73 31 E
Kalol, Gujarat, India 42 H5 23 15N 72 33 E
Kalomo, Zambia 55 F2 17 0S 26 30 E
Kalpi, India 43 F8 26 8N 79 47 E
Kalu, Pakistan 42 G2 25 5N 67 39 E
Kaluga, Russia 24 D6 54 35N 36 10 E
Kalulushi, Zambia 55 E2 12 50S 28 3 E
Kalundborg, Denmark 9 J14 55 41N 11 5 E
Kalush, Ukraine 17 D13 49 3N 24 23 E
Kalutara, Sri Lanka 40 R11 6 35N 80 0 E
Kalya, Russia 24 B10 60 15N 59 59 E
Kama, Zaïre 54 C2 3 30S 27 5 E
Kama →, Russia 24 C9 55 45N 52 0 E
Kamachumu, Tanzania 54 C3 1 37S 31 37 E
Kamaishi, Japan 30 E10 39 16N 141 53 E
Kamalia, Pakistan 42 D5 30 44N 72 42 E
Kamapanda, Zambia 55 E1 12 5S 24 0 E
Kamaran, Yemen 46 D3 15 21N 42 35 E
Kamativi, Zimbabwe 55 F2 18 15S 27 27 E
Kambalda, Australia 61 F3 31 10S 121 37 E
Kambar, Pakistan 42 F3 27 37N 68 1 E
Kambarka, Russia 24 C9 56 15N 54 11 E
Kambolé, Zambia 55 D3 8 47S 30 48 E
Kambos, Cyprus 23 D11 35 2N 32 44 E
Kambove, Zaïre 55 E2 10 51S 26 33 E
Kamchatka, P-ov., Russia 27 D16 57 0N 160 0 E
Kamchatka Pen. = Kamchatka, P-ov., Russia 27 D16 57 0N 160 0 E
Kamchiya →, Bulgaria 21 C12 43 4N 27 44 E
Kamen, Russia 26 D9 53 50N 81 30 E
Kamen-Rybolov, Russia 30 B6 44 46N 132 2 E
Kamenjak, Rt., Croatia 16 F7 44 47N 13 55 E
Kamenka, Russia 24 A7 65 58N 44 0 E
Kamenka Bugskaya = Kamyanka-Buzka, Ukraine 17 C13 50 8N 24 16 E
Kamensk Uralskiy, Russia 26 D7 56 25N 62 2 E
Kamenskoye, Russia 27 C17 62 45N 165 30 E
Kameoka, Japan 31 G7 35 0N 135 35 E
Kamiah, U.S.A. 82 C5 46 14N 116 2W
Kamieskroon, S. Africa 56 E2 30 9S 17 56 E
Kamilukuak, L., Canada 73 A8 62 22N 101 40W
Kamin-Kashyrskyy, Ukraine 17 C13 51 39N 24 56 E
Kamina, Zaïre 55 D1 8 45S 25 0 E
Kaminak L., Canada 73 A9 62 10N 95 0W
Kaminoyama, Japan 30 E10 38 9N 140 17 E
Kamiros, Greece 23 C9 36 20N 27 56 E
Kamituga, Zaïre 54 C2 3 2S 28 10 E
Kamloops, Canada 72 C4 50 40N 120 20W
Kamo, Japan 30 F9 37 39N 139 3 E
Kamoke, Pakistan 42 C6 32 4N 74 4 E
Kampala, Uganda 54 B3 0 20N 32 30 E
Kampar, Malaysia 39 K3 4 18N 101 9 E
Kampar →, Indonesia 36 D2 0 30N 103 8 E
Kampen, Neths. 15 B5 52 33N 5 53 E
Kamphaeng Phet, Thailand 38 D2 16 28N 99 30 E
Kampolombo, L., Zambia 55 E2 11 37S 29 42 E
Kampong To, Thailand 39 J3 6 3N 101 13 E
Kampot, Cambodia 39 G5 10 36N 104 10 E
Kampuchea = Cambodia ■, Asia 38 F5 12 15N 105 0 E
Kampung →, Indonesia 37 F9 5 44S 138 24 E
Kampung Air Putih, Malaysia 39 K4 4 15N 103 10 E
Kampung Jerangau, Malaysia 39 K4 4 50N 103 10 E
Kampung Raja, Malaysia 39 K4 5 45N 102 35 E
Kampungbaru = Tolitoli, Indonesia 37 D6 1 5N 120 50 E
Kamrau, Teluk, Indonesia 37 E8 3 30S 133 36 E
Kamsack, Canada 73 C8 51 34N 101 54W
Kamskoye Vdkhr., Russia 24 C10 58 41N 56 7 E
Kamuchawie L., Canada 73 B8 56 18N 101 59W
Kamui-Misaki, Japan 30 C10 43 20N 140 21 E
Kamyanets-Podilskyy, Ukraine 17 D14 48 45N 26 40 E
Kamyanka-Buzka, Ukraine 17 C13 50 8N 24 16 E
Kāmyārān, Iran 44 C5 34 47N 46 56 E
Kamyshin, Russia 25 D8 50 10N 45 24 E
Kanaaupscow, Canada 70 B4 54 2N 76 30W
Kanab, U.S.A. 83 H7 37 3N 112 32W
Kanab →, U.S.A. 83 H7 36 24N 112 38W
Kanagi, Japan 30 D10 40 54N 140 27 E
Kanairiktok →, Canada 71 A7 55 2N 60 18W
Kananga, Zaïre 52 F4 5 55S 22 18 E
Kanarraville, U.S.A. 83 H7 37 32N 113 11W
Kanash, Russia 24 C8 55 30N 47 32 E
Kanaskat, U.S.A. 84 C5 47 19N 121 54W
Kanastraion, Ákra = Palioúrion, Ákra, Greece 21 E10 39 57N 23 45 E
Kanawha →, U.S.A. 76 F4 38 50N 82 9W
Kanazawa, Japan 31 F8 36 30N 136 38 E
Kanchanaburi, Thailand 38 E2 14 2N 99 31 E
Kanchenjunga, Nepal 43 F13 27 50N 88 10 E
Kanchipuram, India 40 N11 12 52N 79 45 E
Kanda Kanda, Zaïre 52 F4 6 52S 23 48 E
Kandahar = Qandahār, Afghan. 40 D4 31 32N 65 30 E
Kandalaksha, Russia 24 A5 67 9N 32 30 E
Kandalakshkiy Zaliv, Russia 24 A5 66 0N 35 0 E
Kandalu, Afghan. 40 E3 29 55N 63 20 E
Kandangan, Indonesia 36 E5 2 50S 115 20 E
Kandanos, Greece 23 D5 35 19N 23 44 E
Kandhkot, Pakistan 42 E3 28 16N 69 8 E
Kandhla, India 42 E7 29 18N 77 19 E
Kandi, Benin 50 F5 11 7N 2 55 E
Kandi, India 43 H13 23 58N 88 5 E
Kandla, India 42 H4 23 0N 70 10 E
Kandos, Australia 63 E4 32 45S 149 58 E
Kandy, Sri Lanka 40 R12 7 18N 80 43 E
Kane, U.S.A. 78 E6 41 40N 78 49W
Kane Basin, Greenland 4 B4 79 1N 70 0W
Kangān, Fārs, Iran 45 E7 27 50N 52 3 E
Kangān, Hormozgān, Iran 45 E8 25 48N 57 28 E
Kangar, Malaysia 39 J3 6 27N 100 12 E
Kangaroo I., Australia 63 F2 35 45S 137 0 E
Kangasala, Finland 9 F21 61 28N 24 4 E
Kangāvar, Iran 45 C6 34 40N 48 0 E
Kangdong, N. Korea 35 E14 39 9N 126 5 E
Kangean, Kepulauan, Indonesia 36 F5 6 55S 115 23 E
Kangean Is. = Kangean, Kepulauan, Indonesia 36 F5 6 55S 115 23 E
Kanggye, N. Korea 35 D14 41 0N 126 35 E
Kanggyŏng, S. Korea 35 F14 36 10N 127 0 E
Kanghwa, S. Korea 35 F14 37 45N 126 30 E
Kangiqsualujjuaq, Canada 69 C13 58 30N 65 59W
Kangiqsujuaq, Canada 69 B12 61 30N 72 0W
Kangirsuk, Canada 69 B13 60 0N 70 0W
Kangnŭng, S. Korea 35 F15 37 45N 128 54 E
Kango, Gabon 52 D2 0 11N 10 14 E
Kangping, China 35 C12 42 43N 123 18 E
Kangto, India 41 F18 27 50N 92 35 E
Kaniama, Zaïre 54 D1 7 30S 24 12 E
Kaniapiskau →, Canada 71 A6 56 40N 69 30W
Kaniapiskau L., Canada 71 B6 54 10N 69 55W
Kanin, Poluostrov, Russia 24 A8 68 0N 45 0 E
Kanin Nos, Mys, Russia 24 A7 68 39N 43 32 E
Kanin Pen. = Kanin, Poluostrov, Russia 24 A8 68 0N 45 0 E
Kaniva, Australia 63 F3 36 22S 141 18 E
Kanjut Sar, Pakistan 43 A6 36 7N 75 25 E
Kankaanpää, Finland 9 F20 61 44N 22 50 E
Kankakee, U.S.A. 76 E2 41 7N 87 52W
Kankakee →, U.S.A. 76 E1 41 23N 88 15W
Kankan, Guinea 50 F3 10 23N 9 15W

Kenner

Kankendy = Xankändi, Azerbaijan 25 G8 39 52N 46 49 E
Kanker, India 41 J12 20 10N 81 40 E
Kankunskiy, Russia 27 D13 57 37N 126 8 E
Kannapolis, U.S.A. 77 H5 35 30N 80 37W
Kannauj, India 43 F8 27 3N 79 56 E
Kannod, India 40 H10 22 45N 76 40 E
Kano, Nigeria 50 F6 12 2N 8 30 E
Kan'onji, Japan 31 G6 34 7N 133 39 E
Kanowit, Malaysia 36 D4 2 14N 112 20 E
Kanowna, Australia 61 F3 30 32S 121 31 E
Kanoya, Japan 31 J5 31 25N 130 50 E
Kanpetlet, Burma 41 J18 21 10N 93 59 E
Kanpur, India 43 F9 26 28N 80 20 E
Kansas □, U.S.A. 80 F6 38 30N 99 0W
Kansas →, U.S.A. 80 F7 39 7N 94 37W
Kansas City, Kans., U.S.A. 80 F7 39 7N 94 38W
Kansas City, Mo., U.S.A. 80 F7 39 6N 94 35W
Kansenia, Zaïre 55 E2 10 20S 26 0 E
Kansk, Russia 27 D10 56 20N 95 37 E
Kansŏng, S. Korea 35 E15 38 24N 128 30 E
Kansu = Gansu □, China 34 G3 36 0N 104 0 E
Kantang, Thailand 39 J2 7 25N 99 31 E
Kantharalak, Thailand 38 E5 14 39N 104 39 E
Kantō □, Japan 31 F9 36 15N 139 30 E
Kantō-Sanchi, Japan 31 G9 35 59N 138 50 E
Kanturk, Ireland 13 D3 52 11N 8 54W
Kanuma, Japan 31 F9 36 34N 139 42 E
Kanus, Namibia 56 D2 27 50S 18 39 E
Kanye, Botswana 56 C4 24 55S 25 28 E
Kanzenze, Zaïre 55 E2 10 30S 25 12 E
Kanzi, Ras, Tanzania 54 D4 7 1S 39 33 E
Kaohsiung, Taiwan 33 D7 22 35N 120 16 E
Kaokoveld, Namibia 56 B1 19 15S 14 30 E
Kaolack, Senegal 50 F1 14 5N 16 8W
Kaoshan, China 35 B13 44 38N 124 50 E
Kapadvanj, India 42 H5 23 5N 73 0 E
Kapan, Armenia 25 G8 39 18N 46 27 E
Kapanga, Zaïre 52 F4 8 30S 22 40 E
Kapchagai = Qapshaghay, Kazakstan 26 E8 43 51N 77 14 E
Kapema, Zaïre 55 E2 10 45S 28 22 E
Kapfenberg, Austria 16 E8 47 26N 15 18 E
Kapiri Mposhi, Zambia 55 E2 13 59S 28 43 E
Kapiskau →, Canada 70 B3 52 47N 81 55W
Kapit, Malaysia 36 D4 2 0N 112 55 E
Kapiti I., N.Z. 59 J5 40 50S 174 56 E
Kapoe, Thailand 39 H2 9 34N 98 32 E
Kapoeta, Sudan 51 H11 4 50N 33 35 E
Kaposvár, Hungary 17 E9 46 25N 17 47 E
Kapowsin, U.S.A. 84 D4 46 59N 122 13W
Kapps, Namibia 56 C2 22 32S 17 18 E
Kapsan, N. Korea 35 D15 41 4N 128 19 E
Kapsukas = Marijampolė, Lithuania 9 J20 54 33N 23 19 E
Kapuas →, Indonesia 36 E3 0 25S 109 20 E
Kapuas Hulu, Pegunungan, Malaysia 36 D4 1 30N 113 30 E
Kapuas Hulu Ra. = Kapuas Hulu, Pegunungan, Malaysia 36 D4 1 30N 113 30 E
Kapulo, Zaïre 55 D2 8 18S 29 15 E
Kapunda, Australia 63 E2 34 20S 138 56 E
Kapuni, N.Z. 59 H5 39 29S 174 8 E
Kapurthala, India 42 D6 31 23N 75 25 E
Kapuskasing, Canada 70 C3 49 25N 82 30W
Kapuskasing →, Canada 70 C3 49 49N 82 0W
Kaputar, Australia 63 E5 30 15S 150 10 E
Kaputir, Kenya 54 B4 2 5N 35 28 E
Kara, Russia 26 C7 69 10N 65 0 E
Kara Bogaz Gol, Zaliv = Garabogazköl Aylagy, Turkmenistan 25 F9 41 0N 53 30 E
Kara Kalpak Republic □ = Karakalpakstan □, Uzbekistan 26 E6 43 0N 58 0 E
Kara Kum, Turkmenistan 26 F6 39 30N 60 0 E
Kara Sea, Russia 26 B7 75 0N 70 0 E
Karabiğa, Turkey 21 D12 40 24N 27 18 E
Karaburun, Turkey 21 E12 38 41N 26 28 E
Karabutak = Qarabutaq, Kazakstan 26 E7 49 59N 60 14 E
Karacabey, Turkey 21 D13 40 12N 28 21 E
Karacasu, Turkey 21 F13 37 43N 28 35 E
Karachi, Pakistan 42 G2 24 53N 67 0 E
Karad, India 40 L9 17 15N 74 10 E
Karadeniz Boğazı, Turkey 21 D13 41 10N 29 10 E
Karaganda = Qaraghandy, Kazakstan 26 E8 49 50N 73 10 E
Karagayly, Kazakstan 26 E8 49 26N 76 0 E
Karaginskiy, Ostrov, Russia 27 D17 58 45N 164 0 E
Karagiye, Vpadina, Kazakstan 25 F9 43 27N 51 45 E
Karagiye Depression = Karagiye, Vpadina, Kazakstan 25 F9 43 27N 51 45 E
Karagwe □, Tanzania 54 C3 2 0S 31 0 E
Karaikal, India 40 P11 10 59N 79 50 E
Karaikkudi, India 40 P11 10 5N 78 45 E
Karaj, Iran 45 C6 35 48N 51 0 E
Karak, Malaysia 39 L4 3 25N 102 2 E
Karakalpakstan □, Uzbekistan 26 E6 43 0N 58 0 E
Karakas, Kazakstan 26 E9 48 20N 83 30 E
Karakelong, Indonesia 37 D7 4 35N 126 50 E
Karakitang, Indonesia 37 D7 3 14N 125 28 E
Karaklis = Vanadzor, Armenia 25 F7 40 48N 44 30 E
Karakoram Pass, Pakistan 43 B7 35 33N 77 50 E
Karakoram Ra., Pakistan 43 B7 35 30N 77 0 E
Karalon, Russia 27 D12 57 5N 115 50 E
Karaman, Turkey 25 G5 37 14N 33 13 E
Karamay, China 32 B3 45 30N 84 58 E
Karambu, Indonesia 36 E5 3 53S 116 6 E
Karamea Bight, N.Z. 59 J3 41 22S 171 40 E
Karamsad, India 42 H5 22 35N 72 50 E
Karand, Iran 44 C5 34 16N 46 15 E
Karanganyar, Indonesia 37 G13 7 38S 109 37 E
Karasburg, Namibia 56 D2 28 0S 18 44 E
Karasino, Russia 26 C9 66 50N 86 50 E
Karasjok, Norway 8 B21 69 27N 25 30 E
Karasuk, Russia 26 D8 53 44N 78 2 E
Karasuyama, Japan 31 F10 36 39N 140 9 E
Karatau = Qarataū, Kazakstan 26 E8 43 10N 70 28 E
Karatau, Khrebet, Kazakstan 26 E7 43 30N 69 30 E
Karauli, India 42 F7 26 30N 77 4 E
Karavostasi, Cyprus 23 D11 35 8N 32 50 E
Karawang, Indonesia 37 G12 6 30S 107 15 E
Karawanken, Europe 16 E8 46 30N 14 40 E
Karazhal, Kazakstan 26 E8 48 2N 70 49 E
Karbalā, Iraq 44 C5 32 36N 44 3 E
Karcag, Hungary 17 E11 47 19N 20 57 E
Karcha →, Pakistan 43 B7 34 45N 76 10 E
Karda, Russia 27 D11 55 0N 103 16 E
Kardhítsa, Greece 21 E9 39 23N 21 54 E
Kärdla, Estonia 9 G20 58 50N 22 40 E
Kareeberge, S. Africa 56 E3 30 59S 21 50 E
Karelia □, Russia 24 A5 65 30N 32 30 E
Karelian Republic □ = Karelia □, Russia 24 A5 65 30N 32 30 E
Kārevāndar, Iran 45 E9 27 53N 60 44 E
Kargasok, Russia 26 D9 59 3N 80 53 E
Kargat, Russia 26 D9 55 10N 80 15 E
Kargil, India 43 B7 34 32N 76 12 E
Kargopol, Russia 24 B6 61 30N 38 58 E
Karīān, Iran 45 E8 26 57N 57 14 E
Kariba, Zimbabwe 55 F2 16 28S 28 50 E
Kariba, L., Zimbabwe 55 F2 16 40S 28 25 E
Kariba Dam, Zimbabwe 55 F2 16 30S 28 35 E
Kariba Gorge, Zambia 55 F2 16 30S 28 50 E
Karibib, Namibia 56 C2 22 0S 15 56 E
Karimata, Kepulauan, Indonesia 36 E3 1 25S 109 0 E
Karimata, Selat, Indonesia 36 E3 2 0S 108 40 E
Karimata Is. = Karimata, Kepulauan, Indonesia 36 E3 1 25S 109 0 E
Karimnagar, India 40 K11 18 26N 79 10 E
Karimunjawa, Kepulauan, Indonesia 36 F4 5 50S 110 30 E
Karin, Somali Rep. 46 E4 10 50N 45 52 E
Karīt, Iran 45 C8 33 29N 56 55 E
Kariya, Japan 31 G8 34 58N 137 1 E
Karkaralinsk = Qarqaraly, Kazakstan 26 E8 49 26N 75 30 E
Karkinitska Zatoka, Ukraine 25 E5 45 56N 33 0 E
Karkinitskiy Zaliv = Karkinitska Zatoka, Ukraine 25 E5 45 56N 33 0 E
Karl-Marx-Stadt = Chemnitz, Germany 16 C7 50 51N 12 54 E
Karlovac, Croatia 16 F8 45 31N 15 36 E
Karlovo, Bulgaria 21 C11 42 38N 24 47 E
Karlovy Vary, Czech. 16 C7 50 13N 12 51 E
Karlsbad = Karlovy Vary, Czech. 16 C7 50 13N 12 51 E
Karlsborg, Sweden 9 G16 58 33N 14 33 E
Karlshamn, Sweden 9 H16 56 10N 14 51 E
Karlskoga, Sweden 9 G16 59 22N 14 33 E
Karlskrona, Sweden 9 H16 56 10N 15 35 E
Karlsruhe, Germany 16 D5 49 0N 8 23 E
Karlstad, Sweden 9 G15 59 23N 13 30 E
Karlstad, U.S.A. 80 A6 48 35N 96 31W
Karnal, India 42 E7 29 42N 77 2 E
Karnali →, Nepal 43 E9 28 45N 81 16 E
Karnaphuli Res., Bangla. 41 H18 22 40N 92 20 E
Karnataka □, India 40 N10 13 15N 77 0 E
Karnes City, U.S.A. 81 L6 28 53N 97 54W
Karnische Alpen, Europe 16 E7 46 36N 13 0 E
Kärnten □, Austria 16 E8 46 52N 13 30 E
Karoi, Zimbabwe 55 F2 16 48S 29 45 E
Karonga, Malawi 55 D3 9 57S 33 55 E
Karoonda, Australia 63 F2 35 1S 139 59 E
Karora, Sudan 51 E12 17 44N 38 15 E
Karpasia □, Cyprus 23 D13 35 32N 34 15 E
Kárpathos, Greece 21 G12 35 37N 27 10 E
Karpinsk, Russia 24 C11 59 45N 60 1 E
Karpogory, Russia 24 B7 64 0N 44 27 E
Karpuz Burnu = Apostolos Andreas, C., Cyprus 23 D13 35 42N 34 35 E
Kars, Turkey 25 F7 40 40N 43 5 E
Karsakpay, Kazakstan 26 E7 47 55N 66 40 E
Karshi = Qarshi, Uzbekistan 26 F7 38 53N 65 48 E
Karsiyang, India 43 F13 26 56N 88 18 E
Karsun, Russia 24 D8 54 14N 46 57 E
Kartaly, Russia 26 D7 53 3N 60 40 E
Kartapur, India 42 D6 31 27N 75 32 E
Karthaus, U.S.A. 78 E6 41 8N 78 9W
Karufa, Indonesia 37 E8 3 50S 133 20 E
Karumba, Australia 62 B3 17 31S 140 50 E
Karumo, Tanzania 54 C3 2 25S 32 50 E
Karumwa, Tanzania 54 C3 3 12S 32 38 E
Karungu, Kenya 54 C3 0 50S 34 10 E
Karviná, Czech. 17 D10 49 53N 18 25 E
Karwar, India 40 M9 14 55N 74 13 E
Karwi, India 43 G9 25 12N 80 57 E
Kasache, Malawi 55 E3 13 25S 34 20 E
Kasai →, Zaïre 52 E3 3 30S 16 10 E
Kasai Oriental □, Zaïre 54 C1 5 0S 24 30 E
Kasaji, Zaïre 55 E1 10 25S 23 27 E
Kasama, Zambia 55 E3 10 16S 31 9 E
Kasan-dong, N. Korea 35 D14 41 18N 126 55 E
Kasane, Namibia 56 B3 17 34S 24 50 E
Kasanga, Tanzania 55 D3 8 30S 31 10 E
Kasangulu, Zaïre 52 E3 4 33S 15 15 E
Kasaragod, India 40 N9 12 30N 74 58 E
Kasba L., Canada 73 A8 60 20N 102 10W
Kāseh Garān, Iran 44 C5 34 5N 46 2 E
Kasempa, Zambia 55 E2 13 30S 25 44 E
Kasenga, Zaïre 55 E2 10 20S 28 45 E
Kasese, Uganda 54 B3 0 13N 30 3 E
Kasewa, Zambia 55 E2 14 28S 28 53 E
Kasganj, India 43 F8 27 48N 78 42 E
Kashabowie, Canada 70 C1 48 40N 90 26W
Kāshān, Iran 45 C6 34 5N 51 30 E
Kashi, China 32 C2 39 30N 76 2 E
Kashimbo, Zaïre 55 E2 11 12S 26 19 E
Kashipur, India 43 E8 29 15N 79 0 E
Kashiwazaki, Japan 31 F9 37 22N 138 33 E
Kashk-e Kohneh, Afghan. 40 B3 34 55N 62 30 E
Kāshmar, Iran 45 C8 35 16N 58 26 E
Kashmir, Asia 43 C7 34 0N 76 0 E
Kashmor, Pakistan 42 E3 28 28N 69 32 E
Kashun Noerh = Gaxun Nur, China 32 B5 42 22N 100 30 E
Kasimov, Russia 24 D7 54 55N 41 20 E
Kasinge, Zaïre 54 D2 6 15S 26 58 E
Kasiruta, Indonesia 37 E7 0 25S 127 12 E
Kaskaskia →, U.S.A. 80 G10 37 58N 89 57W
Kaskattama →, Canada 73 B10 57 3N 90 4W
Kaskinen, Finland 9 E19 62 22N 21 15 E
Kaslo, Canada 72 D5 49 55N 116 55W
Kasmere L., Canada 73 B8 59 34N 101 10W
Kasongo, Zaïre 54 C2 4 30S 26 33 E
Kasongo Lunda, Zaïre 52 F3 6 35S 16 49 E
Kásos, Greece 21 G12 35 20N 26 55 E
Kassalâ, Sudan 51 E12 15 30N 36 0 E
Kassel, Germany 16 C5 51 18N 9 26 E
Kassiópi, Greece 23 A3 39 48N 19 53 E
Kassue, Indonesia 37 F9 6 58S 139 21 E
Kastamonu, Turkey 25 F5 41 25N 33 43 E
Kastélli, Greece 23 D5 35 29N 23 38 E
Kastéllion, Greece 23 D7 35 12N 25 20 E
Kastoria, Greece 21 D9 40 30N 21 19 E
Kasulu, Tanzania 54 C3 4 37S 30 5 E
Kasulu □, Tanzania 54 C3 4 37S 30 5 E
Kasumi, Japan 31 G7 35 38N 134 38 E
Kasungu, Malawi 55 E3 13 0S 33 29 E
Kasur, Pakistan 42 D6 31 5N 74 25 E
Kata, Russia 27 D11 58 46N 102 40 E
Kataba, Zambia 55 F2 16 5S 25 10 E
Katako Kombe, Zaïre 54 C1 3 25S 24 20 E
Katale, Tanzania 54 C3 4 52S 31 7 E
Katamatite, Australia 63 F4 36 6S 145 41 E
Katanda, Kivu, Zaïre 54 C2 0 55S 29 21 E
Katanda, Shaba, Zaïre 54 D1 7 52S 24 13 E
Katanga = Shaba □, Zaïre 54 D2 8 0S 25 0 E
Katangi, India 40 J11 21 56N 79 50 E
Katangli, Russia 27 D15 51 42N 143 14 E
Katavi Swamp, Tanzania 54 D3 6 50S 31 10 E
Katerini, Greece 21 D10 40 18N 22 37 E
Katha, Burma 41 G20 24 10N 96 30 E
Katherine, Australia 60 B5 14 27S 132 20 E
Kathiawar, India 42 H4 22 20N 71 0 E
Kathikas, Cyprus 23 E11 34 55N 32 25 E
Katihar, India 43 G12 25 34N 87 36 E
Katima Mulilo, Zambia 56 B3 17 28S 24 13 E
Katimbira, Malawi 55 E3 12 40S 34 0 E
Katingan = Mendawai →, Indonesia 36 E4 3 30S 113 0 E
Katiola, Ivory C. 50 G3 8 10N 5 10W
Katmandu, Nepal 43 F11 27 45N 85 20 E
Káto Arkhánai, Greece 23 D7 35 15N 25 10 E
Káto Khorió, Greece 23 D7 35 3N 25 47 E
Kato Pyrgos, Cyprus 23 D11 35 11N 32 41 E
Katompe, Zaïre 54 D2 6 2S 26 23 E
Katonga →, Uganda 54 B3 0 34N 31 50 E
Katoomba, Australia 63 E5 33 41S 150 19 E
Katowice, Poland 17 C10 50 17N 19 5 E
Katrine, L., U.K. 12 E4 56 15N 4 30W
Katrineholm, Sweden 9 G17 59 9N 16 12 E
Katsepe, Madag. 57 B8 15 45S 46 15 E
Katsina, Nigeria 50 F6 13 0N 7 32 E
Katsumoto, Japan 31 H4 33 51N 129 42 E
Katsuura, Japan 31 G10 35 10N 140 20 E
Katsuyama, Japan 31 F8 36 3N 136 30 E
Kattaviá, Greece 23 D9 35 57N 27 46 E
Kattegat, Denmark 9 H14 57 0N 11 20 E
Katumba, Zaïre 54 D2 7 40S 25 17 E
Katungu, Kenya 54 C5 2 55S 40 3 E
Katwa, India 43 H13 23 30N 88 5 E
Katwijk-aan-Zee, Neths. 15 B4 52 12N 4 24 E
Kauai, U.S.A. 74 H15 22 3N 159 30W
Kauai Channel, U.S.A. 74 H15 21 45N 158 50W
Kaufman, U.S.A. 81 J6 32 35N 96 19W
Kauhajoki, Finland 9 E20 62 25N 22 10 E
Kaukauna, U.S.A. 76 C1 44 17N 88 17W
Kaukauveld, Namibia 56 C3 20 0S 20 15 E
Kaunas, Lithuania 9 J20 54 54N 23 54 E
Kaura Namoda, Nigeria 50 F6 12 37N 6 33 E
Kautokeino, Norway 8 B20 69 0N 23 4 E
Kavacha, Russia 27 C17 60 16N 169 51 E
Kavalerovo, Russia 30 B7 44 15N 135 4 E
Kavali, India 40 M12 14 55N 80 1 E
Kavála, Greece 21 D11 40 57N 24 28 E
Kavār, Iran 45 D7 29 11N 52 44 E
Kavos, Greece 23 B4 39 23N 20 3 E
Kaw, Fr. Guiana 93 C8 4 30N 52 15W
Kawagama L., Canada 78 A6 45 18N 78 45W
Kawagoe, Japan 31 G9 35 55N 139 29 E
Kawaguchi, Japan 31 G9 35 52N 139 45 E
Kawaihae, U.S.A. 74 H17 20 3N 155 50W
Kawambwa, Zambia 55 D2 9 48S 29 3 E
Kawanoe, Japan 31 G6 34 1N 133 34 E
Kawardha, India 43 J9 22 0N 81 17 E
Kawasaki, Japan 31 G9 35 35N 139 42 E
Kawene, Canada 70 C1 48 45N 91 15W
Kawerau, N.Z. 59 H6 38 7S 176 42 E
Kawhia Harbour, N.Z. 59 H5 38 5S 174 51 E
Kawio, Kepulauan, Indonesia 37 D7 4 30N 125 30 E
Kawnro, Burma 41 H21 22 48N 99 8 E
Kawthoolei = Kawthule □, Burma 41 L20 18 0N 97 30 E
Kawthule □, Burma 41 L20 18 0N 97 30 E
Kaya, Burkina Faso 50 F4 13 4N 1 10W
Kayah □, Burma 41 K20 19 15N 97 15 E
Kayan →, Indonesia 36 D5 2 55N 117 35 E
Kaycee, U.S.A. 82 E10 43 43N 106 38W
Kayeli, Indonesia 37 E7 3 20S 127 10 E
Kayenta, U.S.A. 83 H8 36 44N 110 15W
Kayes, Mali 50 F2 14 25N 11 30W
Kayoa, Indonesia 37 D7 0 1N 127 28 E
Kayomba, Zambia 55 E1 13 11S 24 2 E
Kayrunnera, Australia 63 E3 30 40S 142 30 E
Kayseri, Turkey 25 G6 38 45N 35 30 E
Kaysville, U.S.A. 82 F8 41 2N 111 56W
Kayuagung, Indonesia 36 E2 3 24S 104 50 E
Kazachye, Russia 27 B14 70 52N 135 58 E
Kazakstan ■, Asia 26 E7 50 0N 70 0 E
Kazan, Russia 24 C8 55 50N 49 10 E
Kazan-Rettō, Pac. Oc. 64 E6 25 0N 141 0 E
Kazanlŭk, Bulgaria 21 C11 42 38N 25 20 E
Kazatin = Kozyatyn, Ukraine 17 D15 49 45N 28 50 E
Kāzerūn, Iran 45 D6 29 38N 51 40 E
Kazumba, Zaïre 52 F4 6 25S 22 5 E
Kazuno, Japan 30 D10 40 10N 140 45 E
Kazym →, Russia 26 C7 63 54N 65 50 E
Ké-Macina, Mali 50 F3 14 5N 5 22W
Kéa, Greece 21 F11 37 35N 24 22 E
Keams Canyon, U.S.A. 83 J8 35 49N 110 12W
Kearney, U.S.A. 80 E5 40 42N 99 5W
Keban, Turkey 25 G6 38 50N 38 50 E
Kebnekaise, Sweden 8 C18 67 53N 18 33 E
Kebri Dehar, Ethiopia 46 F3 6 45N 44 17 E
Kebumen, Indonesia 37 G13 7 42S 109 40 E
Kechika →, Canada 72 B3 59 41N 127 12W
Kecskemét, Hungary 17 E10 46 57N 19 42 E
Kedgwick, Canada 71 C6 47 40N 67 20W
Kédhros Óros, Greece 23 D6 35 11N 24 37 E
Kedia Hill, Botswana 56 C3 21 28S 24 37 E
Kediniai, Lithuania 9 J21 55 15N 24 2 E
Kediri, Indonesia 37 G15 7 51S 112 1 E
Kédougou, Senegal 50 F2 12 35N 12 10W
Keeler, U.S.A. 84 J9 36 29N 117 52W
Keeley L., Canada 73 C7 54 54N 108 8W
Keeling Is. = Cocos Is., Ind. Oc. 64 J1 12 10S 96 55 E
Keene, Calif., U.S.A. 85 K8 35 13N 118 33W
Keene, N.H., U.S.A. 79 D12 42 56N 72 17W
Keeper Hill, Ireland 13 D3 52 45N 8 16W
Keer-Weer, C., Australia 62 A3 14 0S 141 32 E
Keeseville, U.S.A. 79 B11 44 29N 73 30W
Keetmanshoop, Namibia 56 D2 26 35S 18 8 E
Keewatin, U.S.A. 80 B8 47 24N 93 5W
Keewatin □, Canada 73 A9 63 20N 95 0W
Keewatin →, Canada 73 B8 56 29N 100 46W
Kefallinía, Greece 21 E9 38 20N 20 30 E
Kefamenanu, Indonesia 37 F6 9 28S 124 29 E
Keffi, Nigeria 50 G6 8 55N 7 43 E
Keflavík, Iceland 8 D2 64 2N 22 35W
Keg River, Canada 72 B5 57 54N 117 55W
Kegaska, Canada 71 B7 50 9N 61 18W
Keighley, U.K. 10 D6 53 52N 1 54W
Keila, Estonia 9 G21 59 18N 24 25 E
Keimoes, S. Africa 56 D3 28 41S 20 59 E
Keitele, Finland 8 E22 63 10N 26 20 E
Keith, Australia 63 F3 36 6S 140 20 E
Keith, U.K. 12 D6 57 32N 2 57W
Keith Arm, Canada 68 B7 64 20N 122 15W
Kejser Franz Joseph Fjord = Kong Franz Joseph Fd., Greenland 4 B6 73 30N 24 30W
Kekri, India 42 G6 26 0N 75 10 E
Kël, Russia 27 C13 69 30N 124 10 E
Kelan, China 34 E6 38 43N 111 31 E
Kelang, Malaysia 39 L3 3 2N 101 26 E
Kelantan →, Malaysia 39 J4 6 13N 102 14 E
Kelibia, Tunisia 51 A7 36 50N 11 3 E
Kellé, Congo 52 E2 0 8S 14 38 E
Keller, U.S.A. 82 B4 48 5N 118 41W
Kellerberrin, Australia 61 F2 31 36S 117 38 E
Kellett, C., Canada 4 B1 72 0N 126 0W
Kelleys I., U.S.A. 78 E2 41 36N 82 42W
Kellogg, U.S.A. 82 C5 47 32N 116 7W
Kells = Ceanannus Mor, Ireland 13 C5 53 44N 6 53W
Kélo, Chad 51 G8 9 10N 15 45 E
Kelokedhara, Cyprus 23 E11 34 48N 32 39 E
Kelowna, Canada 72 D5 49 50N 119 25W
Kelsey Bay, Canada 72 C3 50 25N 126 0W
Kelseyville, U.S.A. 84 G4 38 59N 122 50W
Kelso, N.Z. 59 L2 45 54S 169 15 E
Kelso, U.K. 12 F6 55 36N 2 26W
Kelso, U.S.A. 84 D4 46 9N 122 54W
Keluang, Malaysia 39 L4 2 3N 103 18 E
Kelvington, Canada 73 C8 52 10N 103 30W
Kem, Russia 24 B5 65 0N 34 38 E
Kem →, Russia 24 B5 64 57N 34 41 E
Kema, Indonesia 37 D7 1 22N 125 8 E
Kemano, Canada 72 C3 53 35N 128 0W
Kemasik, Malaysia 39 K4 4 25N 103 27 E
Kemerovo, Russia 26 D9 55 20N 86 5 E
Kemi, Finland 8 D21 65 44N 24 34 E
Kemi älv = Kemijoki →, Finland 8 D21 65 47N 24 32 E
Kemijärvi, Finland 8 C22 66 43N 27 22 E
Kemijoki →, Finland 8 D21 65 47N 24 32 E
Kemmerer, U.S.A. 82 F8 41 48N 110 32W
Kemmuna = Comino, Malta 23 C1 36 2N 14 20 E
Kemp, L., U.S.A. 81 J5 33 46N 99 9W
Kemp Land, Antarctica 5 C5 69 0S 55 0 E
Kempsey, Australia 63 E5 31 1S 152 50 E
Kempt, L., Canada 70 C5 47 25N 74 22W
Kempten, Germany 16 E6 47 45N 10 17 E
Kemptville, Canada 70 C4 45 0N 75 38W
Kendal, Indonesia 36 F4 6 56S 110 14 E
Kendal, U.K. 10 C5 54 20N 2 44W
Kendall, Australia 63 E5 31 35S 152 44 E
Kendall →, Australia 62 A3 14 4S 141 35 E
Kendallville, U.S.A. 76 E3 41 27N 85 16W
Kendari, Indonesia 37 E6 3 50S 122 30 E
Kendawangan, Indonesia 36 E4 2 32S 110 17 E
Kende, Nigeria 50 F5 11 30N 4 12 E
Kendenup, Australia 61 F2 34 30S 117 38 E
Kendrapara, India 41 J15 20 35N 86 30 E
Kendrew, S. Africa 56 E3 32 32S 24 30 E
Kendrick, U.S.A. 82 C5 46 37N 116 39W
Kene Thao, Laos 38 D3 17 44N 101 10 E
Kenedy, U.S.A. 81 L6 28 49N 97 51W
Kenema, S. Leone 50 G2 7 50N 11 14W
Keng Kok, Laos 38 D5 16 26N 105 12 E
Keng Tawng, Burma 41 J21 20 45N 98 18 E
Keng Tung, Burma 41 J21 21 0N 99 30 E
Kenge, Zaïre 52 E3 4 50S 17 4 E
Kengeja, Tanzania 54 D4 5 26S 39 45 E
Kenhardt, S. Africa 56 D3 29 19S 21 12 E
Kenitra, Morocco 50 B3 34 15N 6 40W
Kenli, China 35 F10 37 30N 118 20 E
Kenmare, Ireland 13 E2 51 53N 9 36W
Kenmare, U.S.A. 80 A3 48 41N 102 5W
Kenmare →, Ireland 13 E2 51 48N 9 51W
Kennebec, U.S.A. 80 D5 43 54N 99 52W
Kennedy, Zimbabwe 55 F2 18 52S 27 10 E
Kennedy Ra., Australia 61 D2 24 45S 115 10 E
Kennedy Taungdeik, Burma 41 H18 23 15N 93 45 E
Kenner, U.S.A. 81 L9 29 59N 90 15W

Korea, South

Kinston, *U.S.A.* **77 H7** 35 16N 77 35W
Kintampo, *Ghana* **50 G4** 8 5N 1 41W
Kintap, *Indonesia* **36 E5** 3 51S 115 13 E
Kintore Ra., *Australia* **60 D4** 23 15S 128 47 E
Kintyre, *U.K.* **12 F3** 55 30N 5 35W
Kintyre, Mull of, *U.K.* **12 F3** 55 17N 5 47W
Kinushseo →, *Canada* **70 A3** 55 15N 83 45W
Kinuso, *Canada* **72 B5** 55 20N 115 25W
Kinyangiri, *Tanzania* **54 C3** 4 25S 34 37 E
Kinzua, *U.S.A.* **78 E6** 41 52N 78 58W
Kinzua Dam, *U.S.A.* **78 E5** 41 53N 79 0W
Kiosk, *Canada* **70 C4** 46 6N 78 53W
Kiowa, *Kans., U.S.A.* **81 G5** 37 1N 98 29W
Kiowa, *Okla., U.S.A.* **81 H7** 34 43N 95 54W
Kipahigan L., *Canada* **73 B8** 55 20N 101 55W
Kipanga, *Tanzania* **54 D4** 6 15S 35 20 E
Kiparissía, *Greece* **21 F9** 37 15N 21 40 E
Kiparissiakós Kólpos, *Greece* **21 F9** 37 25N 21 25 E
Kipembawe, *Tanzania* **54 D3** 7 38S 33 27 E
Kipengere Ra., *Tanzania* **55 D3** 9 12S 34 15 E
Kipili, *Tanzania* **54 D3** 7 28S 30 32 E
Kipini, *Kenya* **54 C5** 2 30S 40 32 E
Kipling, *Canada* **73 C8** 50 6N 102 38W
Kippure, *Ireland* **13 C5** 53 11N 6 21W
Kipushi, *Zaïre* **55 E2** 11 48S 27 12 E
Kiratpur, *India* **42 E8** 29 32N 78 12 E
Kirensk, *Russia* **27 D11** 57 50N 107 55 E
Kirgella Rocks, *Australia* **61 F3** 30 5S 122 50 E
Kirghizia ■ = Kyrgyzstan ■, *Asia* **26 E8** 42 0N 75 0 E
Kirghizstan = Kyrgyzstan ■, *Asia* **26 E8** 42 0N 75 0 E
Kirgiziya Steppe, *Eurasia* **25 D10** 50 0N 55 0 E
Kiri, *Zaïre* **52 E3** 1 29S 19 0 E
Kiribati ■, *Pac. Oc.* **64 H10** 5 0S 180 0 E
Kırıkkale, *Turkey* **25 G5** 39 51N 33 32 E
Kirillov, *Russia* **24 C6** 59 49N 38 24 E
Kirin = Jilin, *China* **35 C14** 43 44N 126 30 E
Kirin = Jilin □, *China* **35 C13** 44 0N 127 0 E
Kiritimati, *Kiribati* **65 G12** 1 58N 157 27W
Kirkcaldy, *U.K.* **12 E5** 56 7N 3 9W
Kirkcudbright, *U.K.* **12 G4** 54 50N 4 2W
Kirkee, *India* **40 K8** 18 34N 73 56 E
Kirkenes, *Norway* **8 B23** 69 40N 30 5 E
Kirkintilloch, *U.K.* **12 F4** 55 56N 4 8W
Kirkjubæjarklaustur, *Iceland* **8 E4** 63 47N 18 4W
Kirkkonummi, *Finland* **9 F21** 60 8N 24 26 E
Kirkland, *U.S.A.* **83 J7** 34 25N 112 43W
Kirkland Lake, *Canada* **70 C3** 48 9N 80 2W
Kırklareli, *Turkey* **21 D12** 41 44N 27 15 E
Kirksville, *U.S.A.* **80 E8** 40 12N 92 35W
Kirkūk, *Iraq* **44 C5** 35 30N 44 21 E
Kirkwall, *U.K.* **12 C6** 58 59N 2 58W
Kirkwood, *S. Africa* **56 E4** 33 22S 25 15 E
Kirov, *Russia* **24 C8** 58 35N 49 40 E
Kirovabad = Gäncä, *Azerbaijan* **25 F8** 40 45N 46 20 E
Kirovakan = Vanadzor, *Armenia* **25 F7** 40 48N 44 30 E
Kirovograd = Kirovohrad, *Ukraine* **25 E5** 48 35N 32 20 E
Kirovohrad, *Ukraine* **25 E5** 48 35N 32 20 E
Kirovsk = Babadayhan, *Turkmenistan* **26 F7** 37 42N 60 23 E
Kirovsk, *Russia* **24 A5** 67 32N 33 41 E
Kirovskiy, *Kamchatka, Russia* **27 D16** 54 27N 155 42 E
Kirovskiy, *Primorsk, Russia* **30 B6** 45 7N 133 30 E
Kirriemuir, *U.K.* **12 E6** 56 41N 3 1W
Kirsanov, *Russia* **24 D7** 52 35N 42 40 E
Kırşehir, *Turkey* **25 G5** 39 14N 34 5 E
Kirthar Range, *Pakistan* **42 F2** 27 0N 67 0 E
Kiruna, *Sweden* **8 C19** 67 52N 20 15 E
Kirundu, *Zaïre* **54 C2** 0 50S 25 35 E
Kirup, *Australia* **61 F2** 33 40S 115 50 E
Kiryū, *Japan* **31 F9** 36 24N 139 20 E
Kisaga, *Tanzania* **54 C3** 4 30S 34 23 E
Kisalaya, *Nic.* **88 D3** 14 40N 84 3W
Kisámou, Kólpos, *Greece* **23 D5** 35 30N 23 38 E
Kisanga, *Zaïre* **54 B2** 2 30N 26 35 E
Kisangani, *Zaïre* **54 B2** 0 35N 25 15 E
Kisar, *Indonesia* **37 F7** 8 5S 127 10 E
Kisaran, *Indonesia* **36 D1** 3 0N 99 37 E
Kisarawe, *Tanzania* **54 D4** 6 53S 39 0 E
Kisarawe □, *Tanzania* **54 D4** 7 3S 39 0 E
Kisarazu, *Japan* **31 G9** 35 23N 139 55 E
Kiselevsk, *Russia* **26 D9** 54 5N 86 39 E
Kishanganga →, *Pakistan* **43 B5** 34 18N 73 28 E
Kishanganj, *India* **43 F13** 26 3N 88 14 E
Kishangarh, *India* **42 F4** 27 50N 70 30 E
Kishinev = Chişinău, *Moldova* **17 E15** 47 0N 28 50 E
Kishiwada, *Japan* **31 G7** 34 28N 135 22 E
Kishtwar, *India* **43 C6** 33 20N 75 48 E
Kisii, *Kenya* **54 C3** 0 40S 34 45 E
Kisii □, *Kenya* **54 C3** 0 40S 34 45 E
Kisiju, *Tanzania* **54 D4** 7 23S 39 19 E
Kisizi, *Uganda* **54 C2** 1 0S 29 58 E
Kiska I., *U.S.A.* **68 C1** 51 59N 177 30 E
Kiskittinaw →, *Canada* **72 B4** 56 8N 120 10W
Kiskittogisu L., *Canada* **73 C9** 54 13N 98 20W
Kiskörös, *Hungary* **17 E10** 46 37N 19 20 E
Kiskunfélegyháza, *Hungary* **17 E10** 46 42N 19 53 E
Kiskunhalas, *Hungary* **17 E10** 46 28N 19 37 E
Kislovodsk, *Russia* **25 F7** 43 50N 42 45 E
Kismayu = Chisimaio, *Somali Rep.* **49 G8** 0 22S 42 32 E
Kiso-Gawa →, *Japan* **31 G8** 35 20N 136 45 E
Kiso-Sammyaku, *Japan* **31 G8** 35 45N 137 45 E
Kisofukushima, *Japan* **31 G8** 35 52N 137 43 E
Kisoro, *Uganda* **54 C2** 1 17S 29 48 E
Kissidougou, *Guinea* **50 G2** 9 5N 10 5W
Kissimmee, *U.S.A.* **77 L5** 28 18N 81 24W
Kissimmee →, *U.S.A.* **77 M5** 27 9N 80 52W
Kississing L., *Canada* **73 B8** 55 10N 101 20W
Kissónerga, *Cyprus* **23 E11** 34 49N 32 24 E
Kisumu, *Kenya* **54 C3** 0 3S 34 45 E
Kiswani, *Tanzania* **54 C4** 4 5S 37 57 E
Kiswere, *Tanzania* **55 D4** 9 27S 39 30 E
Kit Carson, *U.S.A.* **80 F3** 38 46N 102 48W
Kita, *Mali* **50 F3** 13 5N 9 25W
Kitab, *Uzbekistan* **26 F7** 39 7N 66 52 E
Kitaibaraki, *Japan* **31 F10** 36 50N 140 45 E
Kitakami, *Japan* **30 E10** 39 20N 141 10 E
Kitakami-Gawa →, *Japan* **30 E10** 38 25N 141 19 E
Kitakami-Sammyaku, *Japan* **30 E10** 39 30N 141 30 E
Kitakata, *Japan* **30 F9** 37 39N 139 52 E
Kitakyūshū, *Japan* **31 H5** 33 50N 130 50 E
Kitale, *Kenya* **54 B4** 1 0N 35 0 E
Kitami, *Japan* **30 C11** 43 48N 143 54 E
Kitami-Sammyaku, *Japan* **30 B11** 44 22N 142 43 E
Kitangiri, L., *Tanzania* **54 C3** 4 5S 34 20 E
Kitaya, *Tanzania* **55 E5** 10 38S 40 8 E
Kitchener, *Australia* **61 F3** 30 55S 124 8 E
Kitchener, *Canada* **70 D3** 43 27N 80 29W
Kitega = Gitega, *Burundi* **54 C2** 3 26S 29 56 E
Kitengo, *Zaïre* **54 D1** 7 26S 24 8 E
Kiteto □, *Tanzania* **54 C4** 5 0S 37 0 E
Kitgum, *Uganda* **54 B3** 3 17N 32 52 E
Kíthira, *Greece* **21 F10** 36 8N 23 0 E
Kíthnos, *Greece* **21 F11** 37 26N 24 27 E
Kiti, *Cyprus* **23 E12** 34 50N 33 34 E
Kiti, C., *Cyprus* **23 E12** 34 48N 33 36 E
Kitikmeot □, *Canada* **68 A9** 70 0N 110 0W
Kitimat, *Canada* **72 C3** 54 3N 128 38W
Kitinen →, *Finland* **8 C22** 67 14N 27 27 E
Kitsuki, *Japan* **31 H5** 33 25N 131 37 E
Kittakittaooloo, L., *Australia* **63 D2** 28 3S 138 14 E
Kittanning, *U.S.A.* **78 F5** 40 49N 79 31W
Kittatinny Mts., *U.S.A.* **79 E10** 41 0N 75 0W
Kittery, *U.S.A.* **77 D10** 43 5N 70 45W
Kittilä, *Finland* **8 C21** 67 40N 24 51 E
Kitui, *Kenya* **54 C4** 1 17S 38 0 E
Kitui □, *Kenya* **54 C4** 1 30S 38 25 E
Kitwe, *Zambia* **55 E2** 12 54S 28 13 E
Kivarli, *India* **42 G5** 24 33N 72 46 E
Kivertsi, *Ukraine* **17 C13** 50 50N 25 28 E
Kividhes, *Cyprus* **23 E11** 34 46N 32 51 E
Kivu □, *Zaïre* **54 C2** 3 10S 27 0 E
Kivu, L., *Zaïre* **54 C2** 1 48S 29 0 E
Kiyev = Kyyiv, *Ukraine* **17 C16** 50 30N 30 28 E
Kiyevskoye Vdkhr. = Kyyivske Vdskh., *Ukraine* **17 C16** 51 0N 30 25 E
Kizel, *Russia* **24 C10** 59 3N 57 40 E
Kiziguru, *Rwanda* **54 C3** 1 46S 30 23 E
Kızıl Irmak →, *Turkey* **25 F6** 41 44N 35 58 E
Kizil Jilga, *India* **43 B8** 35 26N 78 50 E
Kizimkazi, *Tanzania* **54 D4** 6 28S 39 30 E
Kizlyar, *Russia* **25 F8** 43 51N 46 40 E
Kizyl-Arvat = Gyzylarbat, *Turkmenistan* **26 F6** 39 4N 56 23 E
Kjölur, *Iceland* **8 D4** 64 50N 19 25W
Kladno, *Czech.* **16 C8** 50 10N 14 7 E
Klaeng, *Thailand* **38 F3** 12 47N 101 39 E
Klagenfurt, *Austria* **16 E8** 46 38N 14 20 E
Klaipeda, *Lithuania* **9 J19** 55 43N 21 10 E
Klaksvík, *Færoe Is.* **8 E9** 62 14N 6 35W
Klamath →, *U.S.A.* **82 F1** 41 33N 124 5W
Klamath Falls, *U.S.A.* **82 E3** 42 13N 121 46W
Klamath Mts., *U.S.A.* **82 F2** 41 20N 123 0W
Klappan →, *Canada* **72 B3** 58 0N 129 43W
Klarälven →, *Sweden* **9 G15** 59 23N 13 32 E
Klaten, *Indonesia* **37 G14** 7 43S 110 36 E
Klatovy, *Czech.* **16 D7** 49 23N 13 18 E
Klawer, *S. Africa* **56 E2** 31 44S 18 36 E
Klawock, *U.S.A.* **72 B2** 55 33N 133 6W
Kleena Kleene, *Canada* **72 C4** 52 0N 124 59W
Klein, *U.S.A.* **82 C9** 46 24N 108 33W
Klein-Karas, *Namibia* **56 D2** 27 33S 18 7 E
Klerksdorp, *S. Africa* **56 D4** 26 53S 26 38 E
Kletsk = Klyetsk, *Belarus* **17 B14** 53 5N 26 45 E
Kletskiy, *Russia* **26 E5** 49 16N 43 11 E
Klickitat, *U.S.A.* **82 D3** 45 49N 121 9W
Klickitat →, *U.S.A.* **84 E5** 45 42N 121 17W
Klidhes, *Cyprus* **23 D13** 35 42N 34 36 E
Klin, *Russia* **26 D4** 56 20N 36 48 E
Klinaklini →, *Canada* **72 C3** 51 21N 125 40W
Klipdale, *S. Africa* **56 E2** 34 19S 19 57 E
Klipplaat, *S. Africa* **56 E3** 33 1S 24 22 E
Kłodzko, *Poland* **17 C9** 50 28N 16 38 E
Klondike, *Canada* **68 B6** 64 0N 139 26W
Klouto, *Togo* **50 G5** 6 57N 0 44 E
Kluane L., *Canada* **68 B6** 61 15N 138 40W
Kluczbork, *Poland* **17 C10** 50 58N 18 12 E
Klyetsk, *Belarus* **17 B14** 53 5N 26 45 E
Klyuchevskaya, Gora, *Russia* **27 D17** 55 50N 160 30 E
Knaresborough, *U.K.* **10 C6** 54 1N 1 28W
Knee L., *Man., Canada* **73 B10** 55 3N 94 45W
Knee L., *Sask., Canada* **73 B7** 55 51N 107 0W
Knight Inlet, *Canada* **72 C3** 50 45N 125 40W
Knighton, *U.K.* **11 E4** 52 21N 3 3W
Knights Ferry, *U.S.A.* **84 H6** 37 50N 120 40W
Knights Landing, *U.S.A.* **84 G5** 38 48N 121 43W
Knob, C., *Australia* **61 F2** 34 32S 119 16 E
Knockmealdown Mts., *Ireland* **13 D4** 52 14N 7 56W
Knokke, *Belgium* **15 C3** 51 20N 3 17 E
Knossós, *Greece* **23 D7** 35 16N 25 10 E
Knox, *U.S.A.* **76 E2** 41 18N 86 37W
Knox, C., *Canada* **72 C2** 54 11N 133 5W
Knox City, *U.S.A.* **81 J5** 33 25N 99 49W
Knox Coast, *Antarctica* **5 C8** 66 30S 108 0 E
Knoxville, *Iowa, U.S.A.* **80 E8** 41 19N 93 6W
Knoxville, *Tenn., U.S.A.* **77 H4** 35 58N 83 55W
Knysna, *S. Africa* **56 E3** 34 2S 23 2 E
Ko Kha, *Thailand* **38 C2** 18 11N 99 24 E
Ko Tao, *Thailand* **39 G2** 10 6N 99 48 E
Koartac = Quaqtaq, *Canada* **69 B13** 60 55N 69 40W
Koba, *Aru, Indonesia* **37 F8** 6 37S 134 37 E
Koba, *Bangka, Indonesia* **36 E3** 2 26S 106 14 E
Kobarid, *Slovenia* **16 E7** 46 15N 13 30 E
Kobayashi, *Japan* **31 J5** 31 56N 130 59 E
Kobdo = Hovd, *Mongolia* **32 B4** 48 2N 91 37 E
Kōbe, *Japan* **31 G7** 34 45N 135 10 E
København, *Denmark* **9 J15** 55 41N 12 34 E
Kōbi-Sho, *Japan* **31 M1** 25 56N 123 41 E
Koblenz, *Germany* **16 C4** 50 21N 7 36 E
Kobroor, Kepulauan, *Indonesia* **37 F8** 6 10S 134 30 E
Kobryn, *Belarus* **17 B13** 52 15N 24 22 E
Kocaeli = İzmit, *Turkey* **25 F4** 40 45N 29 50 E
Kočani, *Macedonia* **21 D10** 41 55N 22 25 E
Koch Bihar, *India* **41 F16** 26 22N 89 29 E
Kochang, *S. Korea* **35 G14** 35 41N 127 55 E
Kochas, *India* **43 G10** 25 15N 83 56 E
Kocheya, *Russia* **27 D13** 52 32N 120 42 E
Kōchi, *Japan* **31 H6** 33 30N 133 35 E
Kōchi □, *Japan* **31 H6** 33 40N 133 30 E
Kochiu = Gejiu, *China* **32 D5** 23 20N 103 10 E
Kodiak, *U.S.A.* **68 C4** 57 47N 152 24W
Kodiak I., *U.S.A.* **68 C4** 57 30N 152 45W
Kodinar, *India* **42 J4** 20 46N 70 46 E
Koes, *Namibia* **56 D2** 26 0S 19 15 E
Koffiefontein, *S. Africa* **56 D4** 29 30S 25 0 E
Kofiau, *Indonesia* **37 E7** 1 11S 129 50 E
Koforidua, *Ghana* **50 G4** 6 3N 0 17W
Kōfu, *Japan* **31 G9** 35 40N 138 30 E
Koga, *Japan* **31 F9** 36 11N 139 43 E
Kogaluk →, *Canada* **71 A7** 56 12N 61 44W
Kogan, *Australia* **63 D5** 27 2S 150 40 E
Køge, *Denmark* **9 J15** 55 27N 12 11 E
Koh-i-Bābā, *Afghan.* **40 B5** 34 30N 67 0 E
Koh-i-Khurd, *Afghan.* **42 C1** 33 30N 65 59 E
Kohat, *Pakistan* **42 C4** 33 40N 71 29 E
Kohima, *India* **41 G19** 25 35N 94 10 E
Kohkīlūyeh va Būyer Aḥmadi □, *Iran* **45 D6** 31 30N 50 30 E
Kohler Ra., *Antarctica* **5 D15** 77 0S 110 0W
Kohtla-Järve, *Estonia* **9 G22** 59 20N 27 20 E
Koillismaa, *Finland* **8 D23** 65 44N 28 36 E
Koin-dong, *N. Korea* **35 D14** 40 28N 126 18 E
Kojō, *N. Korea* **35 E14** 38 58N 127 58 E
Kojonup, *Australia* **61 F2** 33 48S 117 10 E
Kojūr, *Iran* **45 B6** 36 23N 51 43 E
Kokand = Qŭqon, *Uzbekistan* **26 E8** 40 30N 70 57 E
Kokanee Glacier Prov. Park, *Canada* **72 D5** 49 47N 117 10W
Kokas, *Indonesia* **37 E8** 2 42S 132 26 E
Kokchetav = Kökshetaū, *Kazakstan* **26 D7** 53 20N 69 25 E
Kokemäenjoki →, *Finland* **9 F19** 61 32N 21 44 E
Kokkola, *Finland* **8 E20** 63 50N 23 8 E
Koko Kyunzu, *Burma* **41 M18** 14 10N 93 25 E
Kokomo, *U.S.A.* **76 E2** 40 29N 86 8W
Kokonau, *Indonesia* **37 E9** 4 43S 136 26 E
Koksan, *N. Korea* **35 E14** 38 46N 126 40 E
Kökshetaū, *Kazakstan* **26 D7** 53 20N 69 25 E
Koksoak →, *Canada* **69 C13** 58 30N 68 10W
Kokstad, *S. Africa* **57 E4** 30 32S 29 29 E
Kokubu, *Japan* **31 J5** 31 44N 130 46 E
Kokuora, *Russia* **27 B15** 71 35N 144 50 E
Kola, *Indonesia* **37 F8** 5 35S 134 30 E
Kola, *Russia* **24 A5** 68 45N 33 8 E
Kola Pen. = Kolskiy Poluostrov, *Russia* **24 A6** 67 30N 38 0 E
Kolahoi, *India* **43 B6** 34 12N 75 22 E
Kolaka, *Indonesia* **37 E6** 4 3S 121 46 E
Kolar, *India* **40 N11** 13 12N 78 15 E
Kolar Gold Fields, *India* **40 N11** 12 58N 78 16 E
Kolari, *Finland* **8 C20** 67 20N 23 48 E
Kolayat, *India* **40 F8** 27 50N 72 50 E
Kolchugino = Leninsk-Kuznetskiy, *Russia* **26 D9** 54 44N 86 10 E
Kolda, *Senegal* **50 F2** 12 55N 14 57W
Kolding, *Denmark* **9 J13** 55 30N 9 29 E
Kole, *Zaïre* **52 E4** 3 16S 22 42 E
Kolepom = Yos Sudarso, Pulau, *Indonesia* **37 F9** 8 0S 138 30 E
Kolguyev, Ostrov, *Russia* **24 A8** 69 20N 48 30 E
Kolhapur, *India* **40 L9** 16 43N 74 15 E
Kolín, *Czech.* **16 C8** 50 2N 15 9 E
Kolkas Rags, *Latvia* **9 H20** 57 46N 22 37 E
Kolmanskop, *Namibia* **56 D2** 26 45S 15 14 E
Köln, *Germany* **16 C4** 50 56N 6 57 E
Koło, *Poland* **17 B10** 52 14N 18 40 E
Kołobrzeg, *Poland* **16 A8** 54 10N 15 35 E
Kolokani, *Mali* **50 F3** 13 35N 7 45W
Kolomna, *Russia* **24 C6** 55 8N 38 45 E
Kolomyya, *Ukraine* **17 D13** 48 31N 25 2 E
Kolonodale, *Indonesia* **37 E6** 2 3S 121 25 E
Kolosib, *India* **41 G18** 24 15N 92 45 E
Kolpashevo, *Russia* **26 D9** 58 20N 83 5 E
Kolpino, *Russia* **24 C5** 59 44N 30 39 E
Kolskiy Poluostrov, *Russia* **24 A6** 67 30N 38 0 E
Kolskiy Zaliv, *Russia* **24 A5** 69 23N 34 0 E
Kolwezi, *Zaïre* **55 E2** 10 40S 25 25 E
Kolyma →, *Russia* **27 C17** 69 30N 161 0 E
Kolymskoye Nagorye, *Russia* **27 C16** 63 0N 157 0 E
Komandorskiye Is. = Komandorskiye Ostrova, *Russia* **27 D17** 55 0N 167 0 E
Komandorskiye Ostrova, *Russia* **27 D17** 55 0N 167 0 E
Komárno, *Slovak Rep.* **17 E10** 47 49N 18 5 E
Komatipoort, *S. Africa* **57 D5** 25 25S 31 55 E
Komatou Yialou, *Cyprus* **23 D13** 35 25N 34 8 E
Komatsu, *Japan* **31 F8** 36 25N 136 30 E
Komatsujima, *Japan* **31 H7** 34 0N 134 35 E
Komi □, *Russia* **24 B10** 64 0N 55 0 E
Kommunarsk = Alchevsk, *Ukraine* **25 E6** 48 30N 38 45 E
Kommunizma, Pik, *Tajikistan* **26 F8** 39 0N 72 2 E
Komodo, *Indonesia* **37 F5** 8 37S 119 20 E
Komono, *Congo* **52 E2** 3 10S 13 20 E
Komoran, Pulau, *Indonesia* **37 F9** 8 18S 138 45 E
Komoro, *Japan* **31 F9** 36 19N 138 26 E
Komotini, *Greece* **21 D11** 41 9N 25 26 E
Kompasberg, *S. Africa* **56 E3** 31 45S 24 32 E
Kompong Bang, *Cambodia* **39 F5** 12 24N 104 40 E
Kompong Cham, *Cambodia* **39 F5** 12 0N 105 30 E
Kompong Chhnang, *Cambodia* **39 F5** 12 20N 104 35 E
Kompong Chikreng, *Cambodia* **38 F5** 13 5N 104 18 E
Kompong Kleang, *Cambodia* **38 F5** 13 6N 104 8 E
Kompong Luong, *Cambodia* **39 G5** 11 49N 104 48 E
Kompong Pranak, *Cambodia* **38 F5** 13 35N 104 55 E
Kompong Som, *Cambodia* **39 G4** 10 38N 103 30 E
Kompong Som, Chhung, *Cambodia* **39 G4** 10 50N 103 32 E
Kompong Speu, *Cambodia* **39 G5** 11 26N 104 32 E
Kompong Sralao, *Cambodia* **38 E5** 14 5N 105 46 E
Kompong Thom, *Cambodia* **38 F5** 12 35N 104 51 E
Kompong Trabeck, *Cambodia* **38 F5** 13 6N 105 14 E
Kompong Trabeck, *Cambodia* **39 G5** 11 9N 105 28 E
Kompong Trach, *Cambodia* **39 G5** 11 25N 105 48 E
Kompong Tralach, *Cambodia* **39 G5** 11 54N 104 47 E
Komrat = Comrat, *Moldova* **17 E15** 46 18N 28 40 E
Komsberg, *S. Africa* **56 E3** 32 40S 20 45 E
Komsomolets, Ostrov, *Russia* **27 A10** 80 30N 95 0 E
Komsomolsk, *Russia* **27 D14** 50 30N 137 0 E
Konarhá □, *Afghan.* **40 B7** 35 30N 71 3 E
Konārī, *Iran* **45 D6** 28 13N 51 36 E
Konawa, *U.S.A.* **81 H6** 34 58N 96 45W
Konch, *India* **43 G8** 26 0N 79 10 E
Kondakovo, *Russia* **27 C16** 69 36N 152 0 E
Konde, *Tanzania* **54 C4** 4 57S 39 45 E
Kondinin, *Australia* **61 F2** 32 34S 118 8 E
Kondoa, *Tanzania* **54 C4** 4 55S 35 50 E
Kondoa □, *Tanzania* **54 D4** 5 0S 36 0 E
Kondókali, *Greece* **23 A3** 39 38N 19 51 E
Kondopaga, *Russia* **24 B5** 62 12N 34 17 E
Kondratyevo, *Russia* **27 D10** 57 22N 98 15 E
Konduga, *Nigeria* **51 F7** 11 35N 13 26 E
Köneürgench, *Turkmenistan* **26 E6** 42 19N 59 10 E
Konevo, *Russia* **24 B6** 62 8N 39 20 E
Kong, *Ivory C.* **50 G4** 8 54N 4 36W
Kong →, *Cambodia* **38 F5** 13 32N 105 58 E
Kong, Koh, *Cambodia* **39 G4** 11 20N 103 0 E
Kong Christian IX.s Land, *Greenland* **4 C6** 68 0N 36 0W
Kong Christian X.s Land, *Greenland* **4 B6** 74 0N 29 0W
Kong Franz Joseph Fd., *Greenland* **4 B6** 73 30N 24 30W
Kong Frederik IX.s Land, *Greenland* **4 C5** 67 0N 52 0W
Kong Frederik VI.s Kyst, *Greenland* **4 C5** 63 0N 43 0W
Kong Frederik VIII.s Land, *Greenland* **4 B6** 78 30N 26 0W
Kong Oscar Fjord, *Greenland* **4 B6** 72 20N 24 0W
Kongju, *S. Korea* **35 F14** 36 30N 127 0 E
Konglu, *Burma* **41 F20** 27 13N 97 57 E
Kongolo, *Kasai Or., Zaïre* **54 D1** 5 26S 24 49 E
Kongolo, *Shaba, Zaïre* **54 D2** 5 22S 27 0 E
Kongor, *Sudan* **51 G11** 7 1N 31 27 E
Kongsberg, *Norway* **9 G13** 59 39N 9 39 E
Kongsvinger, *Norway* **9 F15** 60 12N 12 2 E
Kongwa, *Tanzania* **54 D4** 6 11S 36 26 E
Koni, *Zaïre* **55 E2** 10 40S 27 11 E
Koni, Mts., *Zaïre* **55 E2** 10 36S 27 10 E
Königsberg = Kaliningrad, *Russia* **9 J19** 54 42N 20 32 E
Konin, *Poland* **17 B10** 52 12N 18 15 E
Konjic, *Bos.-H.* **21 C7** 43 42N 17 58 E
Konkiep, *Namibia* **56 D2** 26 49S 17 15 E
Konosha, *Russia* **24 B7** 61 0N 40 5 E
Kōnosu, *Japan* **31 F9** 36 3N 139 31 E
Konotop, *Ukraine* **25 D5** 51 12N 33 7 E
Końskie, *Poland* **17 C11** 51 15N 20 23 E
Konstanz, *Germany* **16 E5** 47 40N 9 10 E
Kont, *Iran* **45 E9** 26 55N 61 50 E
Kontagora, *Nigeria* **50 F6** 10 23N 5 27 E
Kontum, *Vietnam* **38 E7** 14 24N 108 0 E
Kontum, Plateau du, *Vietnam* **38 E7** 14 30N 108 30 E
Konya, *Turkey* **25 G5** 37 52N 32 35 E
Konza, *Kenya* **54 C4** 1 45S 37 7 E
Kookynie, *Australia* **61 E3** 29 17S 121 22 E
Kooline, *Australia* **60 D2** 22 57S 116 20 E
Kooloonong, *Australia* **63 E3** 34 48S 143 10 E
Koolyanobbing, *Australia* **61 F2** 30 48S 119 36 E
Koondrook, *Australia* **63 F3** 35 33S 144 8 E
Koonibba, *Australia* **63 E1** 31 54S 133 25 E
Koorawatha, *Australia* **63 E4** 34 2S 148 33 E
Koorda, *Australia* **61 F2** 30 48S 117 35 E
Kooskia, *U.S.A.* **82 C6** 46 9N 115 59W
Kootenai →, *Canada* **82 B5** 49 15N 117 39W
Kootenay L., *Canada* **72 D5** 49 45N 116 50W
Kootenay Nat. Park, *Canada* **72 C5** 51 0N 116 0W
Kootjieskolk, *S. Africa* **56 E3** 31 15S 20 21 E
Kopaonik, *Serbia, Yug.* **21 C9** 43 10N 20 50 E
Kópavogur, *Iceland* **8 D3** 64 6N 21 55W
Koper, *Slovenia* **16 F7** 45 31N 13 44 E
Kopervik, *Norway* **9 G11** 59 17N 5 17 E
Kopeysk, *Russia* **26 D7** 55 7N 61 37 E
Kopi, *Australia* **63 E2** 33 24S 135 40 E
Köping, *Sweden* **9 G17** 59 31N 16 3 E
Koppies, *S. Africa* **57 D4** 27 20S 27 30 E
Koprivnica, *Croatia* **20 A7** 46 12N 16 45 E
Kopychyntsi, *Ukraine* **17 D13** 49 7N 25 58 E
Korab, *Macedonia* **21 D9** 41 44N 20 40 E
Korakiána, *Greece* **23 A3** 39 42N 19 45 E
Korba, *India* **43 H10** 22 20N 82 45 E
Korbu, G., *Malaysia* **39 K3** 4 41N 101 18 E
Korça, *Albania* **21 D9** 40 37N 20 50 E
Korce = Korça, *Albania* **21 D9** 40 37N 20 50 E
Korčula, *Croatia* **20 C7** 42 56N 16 57 E
Kord Kūy, *Iran* **45 B7** 36 48N 54 7 E
Kord Sheykh, *Iran* **45 D7** 28 31N 52 53 E
Kordestān □, *Iran* **44 C5** 36 0N 47 0 E
Kordofân, *Sudan* **51 F10** 13 0N 29 0 E
Korea, North ■, *Asia* **35 E14** 40 0N 127 0 E
Korea, South ■, *Asia* **35 F15** 36 0N 128 0 E

Korea Bay

Korea Bay, *Korea* **35 E13** 39 0N 124 0 E
Korea Strait, *Asia* **35 G15** 34 0N 129 30 E
Korets, *Ukraine* **17 C14** 50 40N 27 5 E
Korhogo, *Ivory C.* **50 G3** 9 29N 5 28W
Korim, *Indonesia* **37 E9** 0 58S 136 10 E
Korinthiakós Kólpos, *Greece* **21 E10** 38 16N 22 30 E
Kórinthos, *Greece* **21 F10** 37 56N 22 55 E
Koríssa, Límni, *Greece* **23 B3** 39 27N 19 53 E
Kōriyama, *Japan* **30 F10** 37 24N 140 23 E
Korla, *China* **32 B3** 41 45N 86 4 E
Kormakiti, C., *Cyprus* **23 D11** 35 23N 32 56 E
Korneshty = Corneşti, *Moldova* **17 E15** 47 21N 28 1 E
Koro, *Fiji* **59 C8** 17 19S 179 23 E
Koro, *Ivory C.* **50 G3** 8 32N 7 30W
Koro, *Mali* **50 F4** 14 1N 2 58W
Koro Sea, *Fiji* **59 C9** 17 30S 179 45W
Korogwe, *Tanzania* **54 D4** 5 5S 38 25 E
Korogwe □, *Tanzania* **54 D4** 5 0S 38 20 E
Koroit, *Australia* **63 F3** 38 18S 142 24 E
Koror, *Pac. Oc.* **37 C8** 7 20N 134 28 E
Körös →, *Hungary* **17 E11** 46 43N 20 12 E
Korosten, *Ukraine* **17 C15** 50 54N 28 36 E
Korostyshev, *Ukraine* **17 C15** 50 19N 29 4 E
Korraraika, Helodranon' i, *Madag.* **57 B7** 17 45S 43 57 E
Korsakov, *Russia* **27 E15** 46 36N 142 42 E
Korshunovo, *Russia* **27 D12** 58 37N 110 10 E
Korsør, *Denmark* **9 J14** 55 20N 11 9 E
Korti, *Sudan* **51 E11** 18 6N 31 33 E
Kortrijk, *Belgium* **15 D3** 50 50N 3 17 E
Korwai, *India* **42 G8** 24 7N 78 5 E
Koryakskoye Nagorye, *Russia* **27 C18** 61 0N 171 0 E
Koryŏng, *S. Korea* **35 G15** 35 44N 128 15 E
Kos, *Greece* **21 F12** 36 50N 27 15 E
Koschagyl, *Kazakstan* **25 E9** 46 40N 54 0 E
Kościan, *Poland* **17 B9** 52 5N 16 40 E
Kosciusko, *U.S.A.* **81 J10** 33 4N 89 35W
Kosciusko, Mt., *Australia* **63 F4** 36 27S 148 16 E
Kosciusko I., *U.S.A.* **72 B2** 56 0N 133 40W
Kosha, *Sudan* **51 D11** 20 50N 30 30 E
K'oshih = Kashi, *China* **32 C2** 39 30N 76 2 E
Koshiki-Rettō, *Japan* **31 J4** 31 45N 129 49 E
Kosi, *India* **42 F7** 27 48N 77 29 E
Košice, *Slovak Rep.* **17 D11** 48 42N 21 15 E
Koskhinoú, *Greece* **23 C10** 36 23N 28 13 E
Koslan, *Russia* **24 B8** 63 34N 49 14 E
Kosŏng, *N. Korea* **35 E15** 38 40N 128 22 E
Kosovo □, *Serbia, Yug.* **21 C9** 42 30N 21 0 E
Kosovska-Mitrovica = Titova-Mitrovica, *Serbia, Yug.* **21 C9** 42 54N 20 52 E
Kostamuksa, *Russia* **24 B5** 62 34N 32 44 E
Koster, *S. Africa* **56 D4** 25 52S 26 54 E
Kôstî, *Sudan* **51 F11** 13 8N 32 43 E
Kostopil, *Ukraine* **17 C14** 50 51N 26 22 E
Kostroma, *Russia* **24 C7** 57 50N 40 58 E
Kostrzyn, *Poland* **16 B8** 52 35N 14 39 E
Koszalin, *Poland* **16 A9** 54 11N 16 8 E
Kot Addu, *Pakistan* **42 D4** 30 30N 71 0 E
Kot Moman, *Pakistan* **42 C5** 32 13N 73 0 E
Kota, *India* **42 G6** 25 14N 75 49 E
Kota Baharu, *Malaysia* **39 J4** 6 7N 102 14 E
Kota Belud, *Malaysia* **36 C5** 6 21N 116 26 E
Kota Kinabalu, *Malaysia* **36 C5** 6 0N 116 4 E
Kota Tinggi, *Malaysia* **39 M4** 1 44N 103 53 E
Kotaagung, *Indonesia* **36 F2** 5 38S 104 29 E
Kotabaru, *Indonesia* **36 E5** 3 20S 116 20 E
Kotabumi, *Indonesia* **36 E2** 4 49S 104 54 E
Kotagede, *Indonesia* **37 G14** 7 54S 110 26 E
Kotamobagu, *Indonesia* **37 D6** 0 57N 124 31 E
Kotaneelee →, *Canada* **72 A4** 60 11N 123 42W
Kotawaringin, *Indonesia* **36 E4** 2 28S 111 27 E
Kotcho L., *Canada* **72 B4** 59 7N 121 12W
Kotelnich, *Russia* **24 C8** 58 22N 48 24 E
Kotelnikovo, *Russia* **26 E5** 47 38N 43 8 E
Kotelnyy, Ostrov, *Russia* **27 B14** 75 10N 139 0 E
Kothi, *India* **43 G9** 24 45N 80 40 E
Kotiro, *Pakistan* **42 F2** 26 17N 67 13 E
Kotka, *Finland* **9 F22** 60 28N 26 58 E
Kotlas, *Russia* **24 B8** 61 17N 46 43 E
Kotli, *Pakistan* **42 C5** 33 30N 73 55 E
Kotmul, *Pakistan* **43 B6** 35 32N 75 10 E
Kotor, *Montenegro, Yug.* **21 C8** 42 25N 18 47 E
Kotovsk, *Ukraine* **17 E15** 47 45N 29 35 E
Kotputli, *India* **42 F7** 27 43N 76 12 E
Kotri, *Pakistan* **42 G3** 25 22N 68 22 E
Kottayam, *India* **40 Q10** 9 35N 76 33 E
Kotturu, *India* **40 M10** 14 45N 76 10 E
Kotuy →, *Russia* **27 B11** 71 54N 102 6 E
Kotzebue, *U.S.A.* **68 B3** 66 53N 162 39W
Kouango, *C.A.R.* **52 C4** 5 0N 20 10 E
Koudougou, *Burkina Faso* **50 F4** 12 10N 2 20W
Koufonísi, *Greece* **23 E8** 34 56N 26 8 E
Kougaberge, *S. Africa* **56 E3** 33 48S 23 50 E
Kouilou →, *Congo* **52 E2** 4 10S 12 5 E
Kouki, *C.A.R.* **52 C3** 7 22N 17 3 E
Koula Moutou, *Gabon* **52 E2** 1 15S 12 25 E
Koulen, *Cambodia* **38 F5** 13 50N 104 40 E
Koulikoro, *Mali* **50 F3** 12 40N 7 50W
Kouloúra, *Greece* **23 A3** 39 42N 19 54 E
Koúm-bournoú, Ákra, *Greece* **23 C10** 36 15N 28 11 E
Koumala, *Australia* **62 C4** 21 38S 149 15 E
Koumra, *Chad* **51 G8** 8 50N 17 35 E
Kounradskiy, *Kazakstan* **26 E8** 46 59N 75 0 E
Kountze, *U.S.A.* **81 K7** 30 22N 94 19W
Kouris →, *Cyprus* **23 E11** 34 38N 32 54 E
Kouroussa, *Guinea* **50 F3** 10 45N 9 45W
Kousseri, *Cameroon* **51 F7** 12 0N 14 55 E
Koutiala, *Mali* **50 F3** 12 25N 5 23W
Kouvola, *Finland* **9 F22** 60 52N 26 43 E
Kovdor, *Russia* **24 A5** 67 34N 30 24 E
Kovel, *Ukraine* **17 C13** 51 11N 24 38 E
Kovrov, *Russia* **24 C7** 56 25N 41 25 E
Kowanyama, *Australia* **62 B3** 15 29S 141 44 E
Kowkash, *Canada* **70 B2** 50 20N 87 12W
Kowŏn, *N. Korea* **35 E14** 39 26N 127 14 E
Köyceğiz, *Turkey* **21 F13** 36 57N 28 40 E
Koyuk, *U.S.A.* **68 B3** 64 56N 161 9W
Koyukuk →, *U.S.A.* **68 B4** 64 55N 157 32W
Koza, *Japan* **31 L3** 26 19N 127 46 E
Kozáni, *Greece* **21 D9** 40 19N 21 47 E
Kozhikode = Calicut, *India* **40 P9** 11 15N 75 43 E
Kozhva, *Russia* **24 A10** 65 10N 57 0 E
Kozyatyn, *Ukraine* **17 D15** 49 45N 28 50 E
Kpalimé, *Togo* **50 G5** 6 57N 0 44 E
Kra, Isthmus of = Kra, Kho Khot, *Thailand* **39 G2** 10 15N 99 30 E
Kra, Kho Khot, *Thailand* **39 G2** 10 15N 99 30 E
Kra Buri, *Thailand* **39 G2** 10 22N 98 46 E
Krabi, *Thailand* **39 H2** 8 4N 98 55 E
Kragan, *Indonesia* **37 G14** 6 43S 111 38 E
Kragerø, *Norway* **9 G13** 58 52N 9 25 E
Kragujevac, *Serbia, Yug.* **21 B9** 44 2N 20 56 E
Krajina, *Bos.-H.* **20 B7** 44 45N 16 35 E
Krakatau = Rakata, Pulau, *Indonesia* **36 F3** 6 10S 105 20 E
Krakor, *Cambodia* **38 F5** 12 32N 104 12 E
Kraków, *Poland* **17 C10** 50 4N 19 57 E
Kraksaan, *Indonesia* **37 G15** 7 43S 113 23 E
Kralanh, *Cambodia* **38 F4** 13 35N 103 25 E
Kraljevo, *Serbia, Yug.* **21 C9** 43 44N 20 41 E
Kramatorsk, *Ukraine* **25 E6** 48 50N 37 30 E
Kramfors, *Sweden* **9 E17** 62 55N 17 48 E
Kranj, *Slovenia* **16 E8** 46 16N 14 22 E
Krankskop, *S. Africa* **57 D5** 28 0S 30 47 E
Krasavino, *Russia* **24 B8** 60 58N 46 29 E
Kraskino, *Russia* **27 E14** 42 44N 130 48 E
Kraśnik, *Poland* **17 C12** 50 55N 22 5 E
Krasnoarmeysk, *Russia* **26 D5** 51 0N 45 42 E
Krasnodar, *Russia* **25 E6** 45 5N 39 0 E
Krasnokamsk, *Russia* **24 C10** 58 4N 55 48 E
Krasnoperekopsk, *Ukraine* **25 E5** 46 0N 33 54 E
Krasnorechenskiy, *Russia* **30 B7** 44 41N 135 14 E
Krasnoselkupsk, *Russia* **26 C9** 65 20N 82 10 E
Krasnoturinsk, *Russia* **24 C11** 59 46N 60 12 E
Krasnoufimsk, *Russia* **24 C10** 56 36N 57 38 E
Krasnouralsk, *Russia* **24 C11** 58 21N 60 3 E
Krasnovishersk, *Russia* **24 B10** 60 23N 57 3 E
Krasnovodsk = Türkmenbashi, *Turkmenistan* **25 F9** 40 5N 53 5 E
Krasnoyarsk, *Russia* **27 D10** 56 8N 93 0 E
Krasnyy Luch, *Ukraine* **25 E6** 48 13N 39 0 E
Krasnyy Yar, *Russia* **25 E8** 46 43N 48 23 E
Kratie, *Cambodia* **38 F6** 12 32N 106 10 E
Krau, *Indonesia* **37 E10** 3 19S 140 5 E
Kravanh, Chuor Phnum, *Cambodia* **39 G4** 12 0N 103 32 E
Krefeld, *Germany* **16 C4** 51 20N 6 33 E
Kremen, *Croatia* **16 F8** 44 28N 15 53 E
Kremenchug = Kremenchuk, *Ukraine* **25 E5** 49 5N 33 25 E
Kremenchuk, *Ukraine* **25 E5** 49 5N 33 25 E
Kremenchuksk Vdskh., *Ukraine* **25 E5** 49 20N 32 30 E
Kremenets, *Ukraine* **17 C13** 50 8N 25 43 E
Kremmling, *U.S.A.* **82 F10** 40 4N 106 24W
Krems, *Austria* **16 D8** 48 25N 15 36 E
Kretinga, *Lithuania* **9 J19** 55 53N 21 15 E
Kribi, *Cameroon* **52 D1** 2 57N 9 56 E
Krichev = Krychaw, *Belarus* **17 B16** 53 40N 31 41 E
Kriós, Ákra, *Greece* **23 D5** 35 13N 23 34 E
Krishna →, *India* **41 M12** 15 57N 80 59 E
Krishnanagar, *India* **43 H13** 23 24N 88 33 E
Kristiansand, *Norway* **9 G13** 58 8N 8 1 E
Kristianstad, *Sweden* **9 H16** 56 2N 14 9 E
Kristiansund, *Norway* **8 E12** 63 7N 7 45 E
Kristiinankaupunki, *Finland* **9 E19** 62 16N 21 21 E
Kristinehamn, *Sweden* **9 G16** 59 18N 14 13 E
Kristinestad = Kristiinankaupunki, *Finland* **9 E19** 62 16N 21 21 E
Kríti, *Greece* **23 D7** 35 15N 25 0 E
Kritsá, *Greece* **23 D7** 35 10N 25 41 E
Krivoy Rog = Kryvyy Rih, *Ukraine* **25 E5** 47 51N 33 20 E
Krk, *Croatia* **16 F8** 45 8N 14 40 E
Krokodil →, *Mozam.* **57 D5** 25 14S 32 18 E
Kronprins Olav Kyst, *Antarctica* **5 C5** 69 0S 42 0 E
Kronshtadt, *Russia* **24 B4** 59 57N 29 51 E
Kroonstad, *S. Africa* **56 D4** 27 43S 27 19 E
Kropotkin, *Irkutsk, Russia* **27 D12** 59 0N 115 30 E
Kropotkin, *Krasnodar, Russia* **25 E7** 45 28N 40 28 E
Krosno, *Poland* **17 D11** 49 42N 21 46 E
Krotoszyn, *Poland* **17 C9** 51 42N 17 23 E
Kroussón, *Greece* **23 D6** 35 13N 24 59 E
Kruger Nat. Park, *S. Africa* **57 C5** 23 30S 31 40 E
Krugersdorp, *S. Africa* **57 D4** 26 5S 27 46 E
Kruisfontein, *S. Africa* **56 E3** 33 59S 24 43 E
Krung Thep = Bangkok, *Thailand* **38 F3** 13 45N 100 35 E
Krupki, *Belarus* **17 A15** 54 19N 29 8 E
Kruševac, *Serbia, Yug.* **21 C9** 43 35N 21 28 E
Kruzof I., *U.S.A.* **72 B1** 57 10N 135 40W
Krychaw, *Belarus* **17 B16** 53 40N 31 41 E
Krymskiy Poluostrov = Krymskyy Pivostriv, *Ukraine* **25 E5** 45 0N 34 0 E
Krymskyy Pivostriv, *Ukraine* **25 E5** 45 0N 34 0 E
Kryvyy Rih, *Ukraine* **25 E5** 47 51N 33 20 E
Ksar el Boukhari, *Algeria* **50 A5** 35 51N 2 52 E
Ksar el Kebir, *Morocco* **50 B3** 35 0N 6 0W
Ksar es Souk = Ar Rachidiya, *Morocco* **50 B4** 31 58N 4 20W
Kuala, *Indonesia* **36 D3** 2 55N 105 47 E
Kuala Berang, *Malaysia* **39 K4** 5 5N 103 1 E
Kuala Dungun, *Malaysia* **39 K4** 4 45N 103 25 E
Kuala Kangsar, *Malaysia* **39 K3** 4 46N 100 56 E
Kuala Kelawang, *Malaysia* **39 L4** 2 56N 102 5 E
Kuala Kerai, *Malaysia* **39 K4** 5 30N 102 12 E
Kuala Kubu Baharu, *Malaysia* **39 L3** 3 34N 101 39 E
Kuala Lipis, *Malaysia* **39 K4** 4 10N 102 3 E
Kuala Lumpur, *Malaysia* **39 L3** 3 9N 101 41 E
Kuala Nerang, *Malaysia* **39 J3** 6 16N 100 37 E
Kuala Pilah, *Malaysia* **39 L4** 2 45N 102 15 E
Kuala Rompin, *Malaysia* **39 L4** 2 49N 103 29 E
Kuala Selangor, *Malaysia* **39 L3** 3 20N 101 15 E
Kuala Terengganu, *Malaysia* **39 K4** 5 20N 103 8 E
Kualajelai, *Indonesia* **36 E4** 2 58S 110 46 E
Kualakapuas, *Indonesia* **36 E4** 2 55S 114 20 E
Kualakurun, *Indonesia* **36 E4** 1 10S 113 50 E
Kualapembuang, *Indonesia* **36 E4** 3 14S 112 38 E
Kualasimpang, *Indonesia* **36 D1** 4 17N 98 3 E
Kuancheng, *China* **35 D10** 40 37N 118 30 E
Kuandang, *Indonesia* **37 D6** 0 56N 123 1 E
Kuandian, *China* **35 D13** 40 45N 124 45 E
Kuangchou = Guangzhou, *China* **33 D6** 23 5N 113 10 E
Kuantan, *Malaysia* **39 L4** 3 49N 103 20 E
Kuba = Quba, *Azerbaijan* **25 F8** 41 21N 48 32 E
Kuban →, *Russia* **25 E6** 45 20N 37 30 E
Kubokawa, *Japan* **31 H6** 33 12N 133 8 E
Kucha Gompa, *India* **43 B7** 34 25N 76 56 E
Kuchaman, *India* **42 F6** 27 13N 74 47 E
Kuchino-eruba-Jima, *Japan* **31 J5** 30 28N 130 12 E
Kuchino-Shima, *Japan* **31 K4** 29 57N 129 55 E
Kuchinotsu, *Japan* **31 H5** 32 36N 130 11 E
Kucing, *Malaysia* **36 D4** 1 33N 110 25 E
Kud →, *Pakistan* **42 F2** 26 5N 66 20 E
Kuda, *India* **40 H7** 23 10N 71 15 E
Kudat, *Malaysia* **36 C5** 6 55N 116 55 E
Kudus, *Indonesia* **37 G14** 6 48S 110 51 E
Kudymkar, *Russia* **26 D6** 59 1N 54 39 E
Kueiyang = Guiyang, *China* **32 D5** 26 32N 106 40 E
Kufra Oasis = Al Kufrah, *Libya* **51 D9** 24 17N 23 15 E
Kufstein, *Austria* **16 E7** 47 35N 12 11 E
Kuglugtuk, *Canada* **68 B8** 67 50N 115 5W
Kugong I., *Canada* **70 A4** 56 18N 79 50W
Kūh-e-Hazārām, *Iran* **45 D8** 29 35N 57 20 E
Kūhak, *Iran* **40 F3** 27 12N 63 10 E
Kūhbonān, *Iran* **45 D8** 31 23N 56 19 E
Kūhestak, *Iran* **45 E8** 26 47N 57 2 E
Kūhīn, *Iran* **45 C6** 35 13N 48 25 E
Kūhīrī, *Iran* **45 E9** 26 55N 61 2 E
Kūhpāyeh, *Eşfahan, Iran* **45 C7** 32 44N 52 20 E
Kūhpāyeh, *Kermān, Iran* **45 D8** 30 35N 57 15 E
Kui Buri, *Thailand* **39 F2** 12 3N 99 52 E
Kuito, *Angola* **53 G3** 12 22S 16 55 E
Kujang, *N. Korea* **35 E14** 39 57N 126 1 E
Kuji, *Japan* **30 D10** 40 11N 141 46 E
Kujū-San, *Japan* **31 H5** 33 5N 131 15 E
Kukawa, *Nigeria* **51 F7** 12 58N 13 27 E
Kukerin, *Australia* **61 F2** 33 13S 118 0 E
Kukësi, *Albania* **21 C9** 42 5N 20 20 E
Kukup, *Malaysia* **39 M4** 1 20N 103 27 E
Kula, *Turkey* **21 E13** 38 32N 28 40 E
Kulai, *Malaysia* **39 M4** 1 44N 103 35 E
Kulal, Mt., *Kenya* **54 B4** 2 42N 36 57 E
Kulasekarappattinam, *India* **40 Q11** 8 20N 78 5 E
Kuldiga, *Latvia* **9 H19** 56 58N 21 59 E
Kuldja = Yining, *China* **26 E9** 43 58N 81 10 E
Kulgam, *India* **43 C6** 33 36N 75 2 E
Kulim, *Malaysia* **39 K3** 5 22N 100 34 E
Kulin, *Australia* **61 F2** 32 40S 118 2 E
Kulja, *Australia* **61 F2** 30 28S 117 18 E
Kulm, *U.S.A.* **80 B5** 46 18N 98 57W
Külob, *Tajikistan* **26 F7** 37 55N 69 50 E
Kulsary, *Kazakstan* **25 E9** 46 59N 54 1 E
Kulti, *India* **43 H12** 23 43N 86 50 E
Kulumbura, *Australia* **60 B4** 13 55S 126 35 E
Kulunda, *Russia* **26 D8** 52 35N 78 57 E
Kulungar, *Afghan.* **42 C3** 34 0N 69 2 E
Kūlvand, *Iran* **45 D7** 31 21N 54 35 E
Kulwin, *Australia* **63 F3** 35 0S 142 42 E
Kulyab = Külob, *Tajikistan* **26 F7** 37 55N 69 50 E
Kum Tekei, *Kazakstan* **26 E8** 43 10N 79 30 E
Kuma →, *Russia* **25 F8** 44 55N 47 0 E
Kumagaya, *Japan* **31 F9** 36 9N 139 22 E
Kumai, *Indonesia* **36 E4** 2 44S 111 43 E
Kumamba, Kepulauan, *Indonesia* **37 E9** 1 36S 138 45 E
Kumamoto, *Japan* **31 H5** 32 45N 130 45 E
Kumamoto □, *Japan* **31 H5** 32 55N 130 55 E
Kumanovo, *Macedonia* **21 C9** 42 9N 21 42 E
Kumara, *N.Z.* **59 K3** 42 37S 171 12 E
Kumarl, *Australia* **61 F3** 32 47S 121 33 E
Kumasi, *Ghana* **50 G4** 6 41N 1 38W
Kumayri = Gyumri, *Armenia* **25 F7** 40 47N 43 50 E
Kumba, *Cameroon* **50 H6** 4 36N 9 24 E
Kumbakonam, *India* **40 P11** 10 58N 79 25 E
Kumbarilla, *Australia* **63 D5** 27 15S 150 55 E
Kŭmchŏn, *N. Korea* **35 E14** 38 10N 126 29 E
Kumdok, *India* **43 C8** 33 32N 78 10 E
Kume-Shima, *Japan* **31 L3** 26 20N 126 47 E
Kumertau, *Russia* **24 D10** 52 45N 55 57 E
Kŭmhwa, *S. Korea* **35 E14** 38 17N 127 28 E
Kumi, *Uganda* **54 B3** 1 30N 33 58 E
Kumla, *Sweden* **9 G16** 59 8N 15 10 E
Kumo, *Nigeria* **50 F7** 10 1N 11 12 E
Kumon Bum, *Burma* **41 F20** 26 30N 97 15 E
Kunama, *Australia* **63 F4** 35 35S 148 4 E
Kunashir, Ostrov, *Russia* **27 E15** 44 0N 146 0 E
Kunda, *Estonia* **9 G22** 59 30N 26 34 E
Kundla, *India* **42 J4** 21 21N 71 25 E
Kungala, *Australia* **63 D5** 29 58S 153 7 E
Kunghit I., *Canada* **72 C2** 52 6N 131 3W
Kungrad = Qŭnghirot, *Uzbekistan* **26 E6** 43 6N 58 54 E
Kungsbacka, *Sweden* **9 H15** 57 30N 12 5 E
Kungur, *Russia* **24 C10** 57 25N 56 57 E
Kungurri, *Australia* **62 C4** 21 3S 148 46 E
Kunhar →, *Pakistan* **43 B5** 34 20N 73 30 E
Kuningan, *Indonesia* **37 G13** 6 59S 108 29 E
Kunlong, *Burma* **41 H21** 23 20N 98 50 E
Kunlun Shan, *Asia* **32 C3** 36 0N 86 30 E
Kunming, *China* **32 D5** 25 1N 102 41 E
Kunsan, *S. Korea* **35 G14** 35 59N 126 45 E
Kununurra, *Australia* **60 C4** 15 40S 128 50 E
Kunwarara, *Australia* **62 C5** 22 55S 150 9 E
Kunya-Urgench = Köneürgench, *Turkmenistan* **26 E6** 42 19N 59 10 E
Kuopio, *Finland* **8 E22** 62 53N 27 35 E
Kupa →, *Croatia* **16 F9** 45 28N 16 24 E
Kupang, *Indonesia* **37 F6** 10 19S 123 39 E
Kupyansk, *Ukraine* **26 E4** 49 52N 37 35 E
Kuqa, *China* **32 B3** 41 35N 82 30 E
Kür →, *Azerbaijan* **25 G8** 39 29N 49 15 E
Kura = Kür →, *Azerbaijan* **25 G8** 39 29N 49 15 E
Kuranda, *Australia* **62 B4** 16 48S 145 35 E
Kurashiki, *Japan* **31 G6** 34 40N 133 50 E
Kurayoshi, *Japan* **31 G6** 35 26N 133 50 E
Kŭrdzhali, *Bulgaria* **21 D11** 41 38N 25 21 E
Kure, *Japan* **31 G6** 34 14N 132 32 E
Kuressaare, *Estonia* **9 G20** 58 15N 22 30 E
Kurgaldzhinskiy, *Kazakstan* **26 D8** 50 35N 70 20 E
Kurgan, *Russia* **26 D7** 55 26N 65 18 E
Kuria Maria Is. = Khūriyā Mūriyā, Jazā 'ir, *Oman* **46 D6** 17 30N 55 58 E
Kuridala, *Australia* **62 C3** 21 16S 140 29 E
Kurigram, *Bangla.* **41 G16** 25 49N 89 39 E
Kurikka, *Finland* **9 E20** 62 36N 22 24 E
Kuril Is. = Kurilskiye Ostrova, *Russia* **27 E15** 45 0N 150 0 E
Kuril Trench, *Pac. Oc.* **28 E19** 44 0N 153 0 E
Kurilsk, *Russia* **27 E15** 45 14N 147 53 E
Kurilskiye Ostrova, *Russia* **27 E15** 45 0N 150 0 E
Kurino, *Japan* **31 J5** 31 57N 130 43 E
Kurmuk, *Sudan* **51 F11** 10 33N 34 21 E
Kurnool, *India* **40 M10** 15 45N 78 0 E
Kuro-Shima, *Kagoshima, Japan* **31 J4** 30 50N 129 57 E
Kuro-Shima, *Okinawa, Japan* **31 M2** 24 14N 124 1 E
Kurow, *N.Z.* **59 L3** 44 44S 170 29 E
Kurrajong, *Australia* **63 E5** 33 33S 150 42 E
Kurram →, *Pakistan* **42 C4** 32 36N 71 20 E
Kurri Kurri, *Australia* **63 E5** 32 50S 151 28 E
Kurshskiy Zaliv, *Russia* **9 J19** 55 9N 21 6 E
Kursk, *Russia* **24 D6** 51 42N 36 11 E
Kuruktag, *China* **32 B3** 41 0N 89 0 E
Kuruman, *S. Africa* **56 D3** 27 28S 23 28 E
Kuruman →, *S. Africa* **56 D3** 26 56S 20 39 E
Kurume, *Japan* **31 H5** 33 15N 130 30 E
Kurunegala, *Sri Lanka* **40 R12** 7 30N 80 23 E
Kurya, *Russia* **27 C11** 61 15N 108 10 E
Kus Gölü, *Turkey* **21 D12** 40 10N 27 55 E
Kuşadası, *Turkey* **21 F12** 37 52N 27 15 E
Kusatsu, *Japan* **31 F9** 36 37N 138 36 E
Kusawa L., *Canada* **72 A1** 60 20N 136 13W
Kushikino, *Japan* **31 J5** 31 44N 130 16 E
Kushima, *Japan* **31 J5** 31 29N 131 14 E
Kushimoto, *Japan* **31 H7** 33 28N 135 47 E
Kushiro, *Japan* **30 C12** 43 0N 144 25 E
Kushiro →, *Japan* **30 C12** 42 59N 144 23 E
Kūshk, *Iran* **45 D8** 28 46N 56 51 E
Kushka = Gushgy, *Turkmenistan* **26 F7** 35 20N 62 18 E
Kūshkī, *Īlām, Iran* **44 C5** 33 31N 47 13 E
Kūshkī, *Khorāsān, Iran* **45 B8** 37 2N 57 26 E
Kūshkū, *Iran* **45 E7** 27 19N 53 28 E
Kushol, *India* **43 C7** 33 40N 76 36 E
Kushtia, *Bangla.* **41 H16** 23 55N 89 5 E
Kushva, *Russia* **24 C10** 58 18N 59 45 E
Kuskokwim →, *U.S.A.* **68 B3** 60 5N 162 25W
Kuskokwim B., *U.S.A.* **68 C3** 59 45N 162 25W
Kussharo-Ko, *Japan* **30 C12** 43 38N 144 21 E
Kustanay = Qostanay, *Kazakstan* **26 D7** 53 10N 63 35 E
Kut, Ko, *Thailand* **39 G4** 11 40N 102 35 E
Kütahya, *Turkey* **25 G5** 39 30N 30 2 E
Kutaisi, *Georgia* **25 F7** 42 19N 42 40 E
Kutaraja = Banda Aceh, *Indonesia* **36 C1** 5 35N 95 20 E
Kutch, Gulf of = Kachchh, Gulf of, *India* **42 H3** 22 50N 69 15 E
Kutch, Rann of = Kachchh, Rann of, *India* **42 G4** 24 0N 70 0 E
Kutiyana, *India* **42 J4** 21 36N 70 2 E
Kutno, *Poland* **17 B10** 52 15N 19 23 E
Kuttabul, *Australia* **62 C4** 21 5S 148 48 E
Kutu, *Zaïre* **52 E3** 2 40S 18 11 E
Kutum, *Sudan* **51 F9** 14 10N 24 40 E
Kuujjuaq, *Canada* **69 C13** 58 6N 68 15W
Kuŭp-tong, *N. Korea* **35 D14** 40 45N 126 1 E
Kuusamo, *Finland* **8 D23** 65 57N 29 8 E
Kuusankoski, *Finland* **9 F22** 60 55N 26 38 E
Kuwait = Al Kuwayt, *Kuwait* **44 D5** 29 30N 48 0 E
Kuwait ■, *Asia* **44 D5** 29 30N 47 30 E
Kuwana, *Japan* **31 G8** 35 5N 136 43 E
Kuybyshev = Samara, *Russia* **24 D9** 53 8N 50 6 E
Kuybyshev, *Russia* **26 D8** 55 27N 78 19 E
Kuybyshevskoye Vdkhr., *Russia* **24 C8** 55 2N 49 30 E
Kuye He →, *China* **34 E6** 38 23N 110 46 E
Kūyeh, *Iran* **44 B5** 38 45N 47 57 E
Kūysanjaq, *Iraq* **44 B5** 36 5N 44 38 E
Kuyto, Ozero, *Russia* **24 B5** 65 6N 31 20 E
Kuyumba, *Russia* **27 C10** 60 58N 96 59 E
Kuzey Anadolu Dağları, *Turkey* **25 F6** 41 30N 35 0 E
Kuznetsk, *Russia* **24 D8** 53 12N 46 40 E
Kuzomen, *Russia* **24 A6** 66 22N 36 50 E
Kvænangen, *Norway* **8 A19** 70 5N 21 15 E
Kvaløy, *Norway* **8 B18** 69 40N 18 30 E
Kvarner, *Croatia* **16 F8** 44 50N 14 10 E
Kvarnerič, *Croatia* **16 F8** 44 43N 14 37 E
Kwabhaca, *S. Africa* **57 E4** 30 51S 29 0 E
Kwadacha →, *Canada* **72 B3** 57 28N 125 38W
Kwakhanai, *Botswana* **56 C3** 21 39S 21 16 E
Kwakoegron, *Surinam* **93 B7** 5 12N 55 25W
Kwale, *Kenya* **54 C4** 4 15S 39 31 E
Kwale □, *Kenya* **54 C4** 4 15S 39 10 E
KwaMashu, *S. Africa* **57 D5** 29 45S 30 58 E
Kwamouth, *Zaïre* **52 E3** 3 9S 16 12 E
Kwando →, *Africa* **56 B3** 18 27S 23 32 E
Kwangdaeri, *N. Korea* **35 D14** 40 31N 127 32 E
Kwangju, *S. Korea* **35 G14** 35 9N 126 54 E
Kwango →, *Zaïre* **49 G5** 3 14S 17 22 E
Kwangsi-Chuang = Guangxi Zhuangzu Zizhiqu □, *China* **33 D5** 24 0N 109 0 E
Kwangtung = Guangdong □, *China* **33 D6** 23 0N 113 0 E

Lansdowne

Kwataboahegan →, Canada 70 B3 51 9N 80 50W
Kwatisore, Indonesia 37 E8 3 18S 134 50 E
KwaZulu Natal □, S. Africa 57 D5 29 0S 30 0 E
Kweichow = Guizhou □, China 32 D5 27 0N 107 0 E
Kwekwe, Zimbabwe 55 F2 18 58S 29 48 E
Kwidzyn, Poland 17 B10 53 44N 18 55 E
Kwimba □, Tanzania 54 C3 3 0S 33 0 E
Kwinana New Town, Australia 61 F2 32 15S 115 47 E
Kwoka, Indonesia 37 E8 0 31S 132 27 E
Kyabé, Chad 51 G8 9 30N 19 0 E
Kyabra Cr. →, Australia 63 D3 25 36S 142 55 E
Kyabram, Australia 63 F4 36 19S 145 4 E
Kyaikto, Burma 38 D1 17 20N 97 3 E
Kyakhta, Russia 27 D11 50 30N 106 25 E
Kyancutta, Australia 63 E2 33 8S 135 33 E
Kyangin, Burma 41 K19 18 20N 95 20 E
Kyaukpadaung, Burma 41 J19 20 52N 95 8 E
Kyaukpyu, Burma 41 K18 19 28N 93 30 E
Kyaukse, Burma 41 J20 21 36N 96 10 E
Kyburz, U.S.A. 84 G6 38 47N 120 18W
Kyenjojo, Uganda 54 B3 0 40N 30 37 E
Kyle Dam, Zimbabwe 55 G3 20 15S 31 0 E
Kyle of Lochalsh, U.K. 12 D3 57 17N 5 44W
Kymijoki →, Finland 9 F22 60 30N 26 55 E
Kyneton, Australia 63 F3 37 10S 144 29 E
Kynuna, Australia 62 C3 21 37S 141 55 E
Kyō-ga-Saki, Japan 31 G7 35 45N 135 15 E
Kyoga, L., Uganda 54 B3 1 35N 33 0 E
Kyogle, Australia 63 D5 28 40S 153 0 E
Kyongju, S. Korea 35 G15 35 51N 129 14 E
Kyongpyaw, Burma 41 L19 17 12N 95 10 E
Kyŏngsŏng, N. Korea 35 D15 41 35N 129 36 E
Kyōto, Japan 31 G7 35 0N 135 45 E
Kyōto □, Japan 31 G7 35 15N 135 45 E
Kyparissovouno, Cyprus 23 D12 35 19N 33 10 E
Kyperounda, Cyprus 23 E11 34 56N 32 58 E
Kyren, Russia 27 D11 51 45N 101 45 E
Kyrenia, Cyprus 23 D12 35 20N 33 20 E
Kyrgyzstan ■, Asia 26 E8 42 0N 75 0 E
Kyrönjoki →, Finland 8 E19 63 14N 21 45 E
Kyrtylakh, Russia 27 C13 65 30N 123 40 E
Kystatyam, Russia 27 C13 67 20N 123 10 E
Kythréa, Cyprus 23 D12 35 15N 33 29 E
Kyulyunken, Russia 27 C14 64 10N 137 5 E
Kyunhla, Burma 41 H19 23 25N 95 15 E
Kyuquot, Canada 72 C3 50 3N 127 25W
Kyūshū, Japan 31 H5 33 0N 131 0 E
Kyūshū □, Japan 31 H5 33 0N 131 0 E
Kyūshū-Sanchi, Japan 31 H5 32 35N 131 17 E
Kyustendil, Bulgaria 21 C10 42 16N 22 41 E
Kyusyur, Russia 27 B13 70 19N 127 30 E
Kywong, Australia 63 E4 34 58S 146 44 E
Kyyiv, Ukraine 17 C16 50 30N 30 28 E
Kyyivske Vdskh., Ukraine 17 C16 51 0N 30 25 E
Kyzyl, Russia 27 D10 51 50N 94 30 E
Kyzyl Kum, Uzbekistan 26 E7 42 30N 65 0 E
Kyzyl-Kyya, Kyrgyzstan 26 E8 40 16N 72 8 E
Kzyl-Orda = Qyzylorda, Kazakstan 26 E7 44 48N 65 28 E

L

La Albufera, Spain 19 C5 39 20N 0 27W
La Alcarria, Spain 19 B4 40 31N 2 45W
La Asunción, Venezuela 92 A6 11 2N 63 53W
La Banda, Argentina 94 B3 27 45S 64 10W
La Barca, Mexico 86 C4 20 20N 102 40W
La Barge, U.S.A. 82 E8 42 16N 110 12W
La Belle, U.S.A. 77 M5 26 46N 81 26W
La Biche →, Canada 72 B4 59 57N 123 50W
La Bomba, Mexico 86 A1 31 53N 115 2W
La Calera, Chile 94 C1 32 50S 71 10W
La Canal, Spain 22 C7 38 51N 1 23 E
La Carlota, Argentina 94 C3 33 30S 63 20W
La Ceiba, Honduras 88 C2 15 40N 86 50W
La Chaux de Fonds, Switz. 16 E4 47 7N 6 50 E
La Cocha, Argentina 94 B2 27 50S 65 40W
La Concordia, Mexico 87 D6 16 8N 92 38W
La Conner, U.S.A. 82 B2 48 23N 122 30W
La Coruña, Spain 19 A1 43 20N 8 25W
La Crete, Canada 72 B5 58 11N 116 24W
La Crosse, Kans., U.S.A. 80 F5 38 32N 99 18W
La Crosse, Wis., U.S.A. 80 D9 43 48N 91 15W
La Cruz, Costa Rica 88 D2 11 4N 85 39W
La Cruz, Mexico 86 C3 23 55N 106 54W
La Dorada, Colombia 92 B4 5 30N 74 40W
La Escondida, Mexico 86 C5 24 6N 99 55W
La Esmeralda, Paraguay 94 A3 22 16S 62 33W
La Esperanza, Cuba 88 B3 22 46N 83 44W
La Esperanza, Honduras 88 D2 14 15N 88 10W
La Estrada, Spain 19 A1 42 43N 8 27W
La Fayette, U.S.A. 77 H3 34 42N 85 17W
La Fé, Cuba 88 B3 22 2N 84 15W
La Follette, U.S.A. 77 G3 36 23N 84 7W
La Grande, U.S.A. 82 D4 45 20N 118 5W
La Grange, Calif., U.S.A. 84 H6 37 42N 120 27W
La Grange, Ga., U.S.A. 77 J3 33 2N 85 2W
La Grange, Ky., U.S.A. 76 F3 38 25N 85 23W
La Grange, Tex., U.S.A. 81 L6 29 54N 96 52W
La Guaira, Venezuela 92 A5 10 36N 66 56W
La Güera, Mauritania 50 D1 20 51N 17 0W
La Habana, Cuba 88 B3 23 8N 82 22W
La Harpe, U.S.A. 80 E9 40 35N 90 58W
La Independencia, Mexico 87 D6 16 31N 91 47W
La Isabela, Dom. Rep. 89 C5 19 58N 71 2W
La Jara, U.S.A. 83 H11 37 16N 105 58W
La Junta, U.S.A. 81 F3 37 59N 103 33W
La Laguna, Canary Is. 22 F3 28 28N 16 18W
La Libertad, Guatemala 88 C1 16 47N 90 7W
La Libertad, Mexico 86 B2 29 55N 112 41W
La Ligua, Chile 94 C1 32 30S 71 16W
La Línea de la Concepción, Spain 19 D3 36 15N 5 23W
La Loche, Canada 73 B7 56 29N 109 26W
La Louvière, Belgium 15 D4 50 27N 4 10 E
La Malbaie, Canada 71 C5 47 40N 70 10W
La Mancha, Spain 19 C4 39 10N 2 54W
La Mesa, Calif., U.S.A. 85 N9 32 46N 117 3W
La Mesa, N. Mex., U.S.A. 83 K10 32 7N 106 42W
La Misión, Mexico 86 A1 32 5N 116 50W
La Moure, U.S.A. 80 B5 46 21N 98 18W
La Negra, Chile 94 A1 23 46S 70 18W
La Oliva, Canary Is. 22 F6 28 36N 13 57W
La Orotava, Canary Is. 22 F3 28 22N 16 31W
La Palma, Canary Is. 22 F2 28 40N 17 50W
La Palma, Panama 88 E4 8 15N 78 0W
La Palma del Condado, Spain 19 D2 37 21N 6 38W
La Paloma, Chile 94 C1 30 35S 71 0W
La Pampa □, Argentina 94 D2 36 50S 66 0W
La Paragua, Venezuela 92 B6 6 50N 63 20W
La Paz, Entre Ríos, Argentina 94 C4 30 50S 59 45W
La Paz, San Luis, Argentina 94 C2 33 30S 67 20W
La Paz, Bolivia 92 G5 16 20S 68 10W
La Paz, Honduras 88 D2 14 20N 87 47W
La Paz, Mexico 86 C2 24 10N 110 20W
La Paz Centro, Nic. 88 D2 12 20N 86 41W
La Pedrera, Colombia 92 D5 1 18S 69 43W
La Perouse Str., Asia 30 B11 45 40N 142 0 E
La Pesca, Mexico 87 C5 23 46N 97 47W
La Piedad, Mexico 86 C4 20 20N 102 1W
La Pine, U.S.A. 82 E3 43 40N 121 30W
La Plant, U.S.A. 80 C4 45 9N 100 39W
La Plata, Argentina 94 D4 35 0S 57 55W
La Porte, U.S.A. 76 E2 41 36N 86 43W
La Purísima, Mexico 86 B2 26 10N 112 4W
La Push, U.S.A. 84 C2 47 55N 124 38W
La Quiaca, Argentina 94 A2 22 5S 65 35W
La Reine, Canada 70 C4 48 50N 79 30W
La Restinga, Canary Is. 22 G2 27 38N 17 59W
La Rioja, Argentina 94 B2 29 20S 67 0W
La Rioja □, Argentina 94 B2 29 30S 67 0W
La Rioja □, Spain 19 A4 42 20N 2 20W
La Robla, Spain 19 A3 42 50N 5 41W
La Roche-sur-Yon, France 18 C3 46 40N 1 25W
La Rochelle, France 18 C3 46 10N 1 9W
La Roda, Spain 19 C4 39 13N 2 15W
La Romana, Dom. Rep. 89 C6 18 27N 68 57W
La Ronge, Canada 73 B7 55 5N 105 20W
La Rumorosa, Mexico 85 N10 32 33N 116 4W
La Sabina, Spain 22 C7 38 44N 1 25 E
La Salle, U.S.A. 80 E10 41 20N 89 6W
La Santa, Canary Is. 22 E6 29 5N 13 40W
La Sarre, Canada 70 C4 48 45N 79 15W
La Scie, Canada 71 C8 49 57N 55 36W
La Selva Beach, U.S.A. 84 J5 36 56N 121 51W
La Serena, Chile 94 B1 29 55S 71 10W
La Seyne-sur-Mer, France 18 E6 43 7N 5 52 E
La Spézia, Italy 20 B3 44 7N 9 50 E
La Tortuga, Venezuela 89 D6 11 0N 65 22W
La Tuque, Canada 70 C5 47 30N 72 50W
La Unión, Chile 96 E2 40 10S 73 0W
La Unión, El Salv. 88 D2 13 20N 87 50W
La Unión, Mexico 86 D4 17 58N 101 49W
La Urbana, Venezuela 92 B5 7 8N 66 56W
La Vega, Dom. Rep. 89 C5 19 20N 70 30W
La Venta, Mexico 87 D6 18 8N 94 3W
La Ventura, Mexico 86 C4 24 38N 100 54W
Labe = Elbe →, Europe 16 B5 53 50N 9 0 E
Labé, Guinea 50 F2 11 24N 12 16W
Laberge, L., Canada 72 A1 61 11N 135 12W
Labis, Malaysia 39 L4 2 22N 103 2 E
Laboulaye, Argentina 94 C3 34 10S 63 30W
Labrador, Coast of □, Canada 71 B7 53 20N 61 0W
Labrador City, Canada 71 B6 52 57N 66 55W
Lábrea, Brazil 92 E6 7 15S 64 51W
Labuan, Pulau, Malaysia 36 C5 5 21N 115 13 E
Labuha, Indonesia 37 E7 0 30S 127 30 E
Labuhan, Indonesia 37 G11 6 22S 105 50 E
Labuhanbajo, Indonesia 37 F6 8 28S 120 1 E
Labuk, Telok, Malaysia 36 C5 6 10N 117 50 E
Labyrinth, L., Australia 63 E2 30 40S 135 11 E
Labytnangi, Russia 24 A12 66 39N 66 21 E
Lac Allard, Canada 71 B7 50 33N 63 24W
Lac Bouchette, Canada 71 C5 48 16N 72 11W
Lac du Flambeau, U.S.A. 80 B10 45 58N 89 53W
Lac Édouard, Canada 70 C5 47 40N 72 16W
Lac La Biche, Canada 72 C6 54 45N 111 58W
Lac la Martre = Wha Ti, Canada 68 B8 63 8N 117 16W
Lac-Mégantic, Canada 71 C5 45 35N 70 53W
Lac Seul, Res., Canada 70 B1 50 25N 92 30W
Lac Thien, Vietnam 38 F7 12 25N 108 11 E
Lacanau, France 18 D3 44 58N 1 5W
Lacantúm →, Mexico 87 D6 16 36N 90 40W
Laccadive Is. = Lakshadweep Is., Ind. Oc. 28 H11 10 0N 72 30 E
Lacepede B., Australia 63 F2 36 40S 139 40 E
Lacepede Is., Australia 60 C3 16 55S 122 0 E
Lacerdónia, Mozam. 55 F4 18 3S 35 35 E
Lacey, U.S.A. 84 C4 47 7N 122 49W
Lachhmangarh, India 42 F6 27 50N 75 4 E
Lachi, Pakistan 42 C4 33 25N 71 20 E
Lachine, Canada 70 C5 45 30N 73 40W
Lachlan →, Australia 63 E3 34 22S 143 55 E
Lachute, Canada 70 C5 45 39N 74 21W
Lackawanna, U.S.A. 78 D6 42 50N 78 50W
Lacolle, Canada 79 A11 45 5N 73 22W
Lacombe, Canada 72 C6 52 30N 113 44W
Lacona, U.S.A. 79 C8 43 39N 76 10W
Laconia, U.S.A. 79 C13 43 32N 71 28W
Lacrosse, U.S.A. 82 C5 46 51N 117 58W
Ladakh Ra., India 43 B8 34 0N 78 0 E
Ladismith, S. Africa 56 E3 33 28S 21 15 E
Lādīz, Iran 45 D9 28 55N 61 15 E
Ladnun, India 42 F6 27 38N 74 25 E
Ladoga, L. = Ladozhskoye Ozero, Russia 24 B5 61 15N 30 30 E
Ladozhskoye Ozero, Russia 24 B5 61 15N 30 30 E
Lady Grey, S. Africa 56 E4 30 43S 27 13 E
Ladybrand, S. Africa 56 D4 29 9S 27 29 E
Ladysmith, Canada 72 D4 49 0N 123 49W
Ladysmith, S. Africa 57 D4 28 32S 29 46 E
Ladysmith, U.S.A. 80 C9 45 28N 91 12W
Lae, Papua N. G. 64 H6 6 40S 147 2 E
Laem Ngop, Thailand 39 F4 12 10N 102 26 E
Laem Pho, Thailand 39 J3 6 55N 101 19 E
Læsø, Denmark 9 H14 57 15N 10 53 E
Lafayette, Colo., U.S.A. 80 F2 39 58N 105 12W
Lafayette, Ind., U.S.A. 76 E2 40 25N 86 54W
Lafayette, La., U.S.A. 81 K9 30 14N 92 1W
Lafayette, Tenn., U.S.A. 77 G3 36 31N 86 2W
Laferte →, Canada 72 A5 61 53N 117 44W
Lafia, Nigeria 50 G6 8 30N 8 34 E
Lafleche, Canada 73 D7 49 45N 106 40W
Lagan →, U.K. 13 B6 54 36N 5 55W
Lagarfljót →, Iceland 8 D6 65 40N 14 18W
Lågen →, Oppland, Norway 9 F14 61 8N 10 25 E
Lågen →, Vestfold, Norway 9 G14 59 3N 10 3 E
Laghouat, Algeria 50 B5 33 50N 2 59 E
Lagonoy Gulf, Phil. 37 B6 13 50N 123 50 E
Lagos, Nigeria 50 G5 6 25N 3 27 E
Lagos, Portugal 19 D1 37 5N 8 41W
Lagos de Moreno, Mexico 86 C4 21 21N 101 55W
Lagrange, Australia 60 C3 18 45S 121 43 E
Lagrange B., Australia 60 C3 18 38S 121 42 E
Laguna, Brazil 95 B6 28 30S 48 50W
Laguna, U.S.A. 83 J10 35 2N 107 25W
Laguna Beach, U.S.A. 85 M9 33 33N 117 47W
Laguna Limpia, Argentina 94 B4 26 32S 59 45W
Laguna Madre, U.S.A. 87 B5 27 0N 97 20W
Lagunas, Chile 94 A2 21 0S 69 45W
Lagunas, Peru 92 E3 5 10S 75 35W
Lahad Datu, Malaysia 37 C5 5 0N 118 20 E
Lahan Sai, Thailand 38 E4 14 25N 102 52 E
Lahanam, Laos 38 D5 16 16N 105 16 E
Laharpur, India 43 F9 27 43N 80 56 E
Lahat, Indonesia 36 E2 3 45S 103 30 E
Lahewa, Indonesia 36 D1 1 22N 97 12 E
Lāhījān, Iran 45 B6 37 10N 50 6 E
Lahn →, Germany 16 C4 50 19N 7 37 E
Laholm, Sweden 9 H15 56 30N 13 2 E
Lahontan Reservoir, U.S.A. 82 G4 39 28N 119 4W
Lahore, Pakistan 42 D6 31 32N 74 22 E
Lahti, Finland 9 F21 60 58N 25 40 E
Lahtis = Lahti, Finland 9 F21 60 58N 25 40 E
Laï, Chad 51 G8 9 25N 16 18 E
Lai Chau, Vietnam 38 A4 22 5N 103 3 E
Laidley, Australia 63 D5 27 39S 152 20 E
Laikipia □, Kenya 54 B4 0 30N 36 30 E
Laingsburg, S. Africa 56 E3 33 9S 20 52 E
Lainio älv →, Sweden 8 C20 67 35N 22 40 E
Lairg, U.K. 12 C4 58 2N 4 24W
Laishui, China 34 E8 39 23N 115 45 E
Laiwu, China 35 F9 36 15N 117 40 E
Laixi, China 35 F11 36 50N 120 31 E
Laiyang, China 35 F11 36 59N 120 45 E
Laiyuan, China 34 E8 39 20N 114 40 E
Laizhou Wan, China 35 F10 37 30N 119 30 E
Laja →, Mexico 86 C4 20 55N 100 46W
Lajere, Nigeria 50 F7 12 10N 11 25 E
Lajes, Brazil 95 B5 27 48S 50 20W
Lak Sao, Laos 38 C5 18 11N 104 59 E
Lakaband, Pakistan 42 D3 31 2N 69 15 E
Lake Alpine, U.S.A. 84 G7 38 29N 120 0W
Lake Andes, U.S.A. 80 D5 43 9N 98 32W
Lake Anse, U.S.A. 76 B1 46 42N 88 25W
Lake Arthur, U.S.A. 81 K8 30 5N 92 41W
Lake Cargelligo, Australia 63 E4 33 15S 146 22 E
Lake Charles, U.S.A. 81 K8 30 14N 93 13W
Lake City, Colo., U.S.A. 83 G10 38 2N 107 19W
Lake City, Fla., U.S.A. 77 K4 30 11N 82 38W
Lake City, Iowa, U.S.A. 80 D7 42 16N 94 44W
Lake City, Mich., U.S.A. 76 C3 44 20N 85 13W
Lake City, Minn., U.S.A. 80 C8 44 27N 92 16W
Lake City, Pa., U.S.A. 78 D4 42 1N 80 21W
Lake City, S.C., U.S.A. 77 J6 33 52N 79 45W
Lake George, U.S.A. 79 C11 43 26N 73 43W
Lake Grace, Australia 61 F2 33 7S 118 28 E
Lake Harbour = Kimmirut, Canada 69 B13 62 50N 69 50W
Lake Havasu City, U.S.A. 85 L12 34 27N 114 22W
Lake Hughes, U.S.A. 85 L8 34 41N 118 26W
Lake Isabella, U.S.A. 85 K8 35 38N 118 28W
Lake King, Australia 61 F2 33 5S 119 45 E
Lake Lenore, Canada 73 C8 52 24N 104 59W
Lake Louise, Canada 72 C5 51 30N 116 10W
Lake Mead National Recreation Area, U.S.A. 85 K12 36 15N 114 30W
Lake Mills, U.S.A. 80 D8 43 25N 93 32W
Lake Nash, Australia 62 C2 20 57S 138 0 E
Lake Providence, U.S.A. 81 J9 32 48N 91 10W
Lake River, Canada 70 B3 54 30N 82 31W
Lake Superior Prov. Park, Canada 70 C3 47 45N 84 45W
Lake Village, U.S.A. 81 J9 33 20N 91 17W
Lake Wales, U.S.A. 77 M5 27 54N 81 35W
Lake Worth, U.S.A. 77 M5 26 37N 80 3W
Lakefield, Canada 70 D4 44 25N 78 16W
Lakeland, Australia 62 B3 15 49S 144 57 E
Lakeland, U.S.A. 77 L5 28 3N 81 57W
Lakemba, Fiji 59 D9 18 13S 178 47W
Lakeport, U.S.A. 84 F4 39 3N 122 55W
Lakes Entrance, Australia 63 F4 37 50S 148 0 E
Lakeside, Ariz., U.S.A. 83 J9 34 9N 109 58W
Lakeside, Calif., U.S.A. 85 N10 32 52N 116 55W
Lakeside, Nebr., U.S.A. 80 D3 42 3N 102 26W
Lakeview, U.S.A. 82 E3 42 11N 120 21W
Lakewood, Colo., U.S.A. 80 F2 39 44N 105 5W
Lakewood, N.J., U.S.A. 79 F10 40 6N 74 13W
Lakewood, Ohio, U.S.A. 78 E3 41 29N 81 48W
Lakewood Center, U.S.A. 84 C4 47 11N 122 32W
Lakhaniá, Greece 23 D9 35 58N 27 54 E
Lakhonpheng, Laos 38 E5 15 54N 105 34 E
Lakhpat, India 42 H3 23 48N 68 47 E
Lakin, U.S.A. 81 G4 37 57N 101 15W
Lakitusaki →, Canada 70 B3 54 21N 82 25W
Lákkoi, Greece 23 D5 35 24N 23 57 E
Lakonikós Kólpos, Greece 21 F10 36 40N 22 40 E
Lakor, Indonesia 37 F7 8 15S 128 17 E
Lakota, Ivory C. 50 G3 5 50N 5 30W
Lakota, U.S.A. 80 A5 48 2N 98 21W
Laksefjorden, Norway 8 A22 70 45N 26 50 E
Lakselv, Norway 8 A21 70 2N 25 0 E
Lakshadweep Is., Ind. Oc. 28 H11 10 0N 72 30 E
Lakshmikantapur, India 43 H13 22 5N 88 20 E
Lala Ghat, India 41 G18 24 30N 92 40 E
Lala Musa, Pakistan 42 C5 32 40N 73 57 E
Lalago, Tanzania 54 C3 3 28S 33 58 E
Lalapanzi, Zimbabwe 55 F3 19 20S 30 15 E
Lalganj, India 43 G11 25 52N 85 13 E
Lalibela, Ethiopia 51 F12 12 2N 39 2 E
Lalin, China 35 B14 45 12N 127 0 E
Lalín, Spain 19 A1 42 40N 8 5W
Lalin He →, China 35 B13 45 32N 125 40 E
Lalitapur = Patan, Nepal 41 F14 27 40N 85 20 E
Lalitpur, India 43 G8 24 42N 78 28 E
Lam, Vietnam 38 B6 21 21N 106 31 E
Lam Pao Res., Thailand 38 D4 16 50N 103 15 E
Lamaing, Burma 41 M20 15 25N 97 53 E
Lamar, Colo., U.S.A. 80 F3 38 5N 102 37W
Lamar, Mo., U.S.A. 81 G7 37 30N 94 16W
Lamas, Peru 92 E3 6 28S 76 31W
Lambaréné, Gabon 52 E2 0 41S 10 12 E
Lambasa, Fiji 59 C8 16 30S 179 10 E
Lambay I., Ireland 13 C5 53 29N 6 1W
Lambert, U.S.A. 80 B2 47 41N 104 37W
Lambert Glacier, Antarctica 5 D6 71 0S 70 0 E
Lamberts Bay, S. Africa 56 E2 32 5S 18 17 E
Lame, Nigeria 50 F6 10 30N 9 20 E
Lame Deer, U.S.A. 82 D10 45 37N 106 40W
Lamego, Portugal 19 B2 41 5N 7 52W
Lamèque, Canada 71 C7 47 45N 64 38W
Lameroo, Australia 63 F3 35 19S 140 33 E
Lamesa, U.S.A. 81 J4 32 44N 101 58W
Lamía, Greece 21 E10 38 55N 22 26 E
Lammermuir Hills, U.K. 12 F6 55 50N 2 40W
Lamon Bay, Phil. 37 B6 14 30N 122 20 E
Lamont, Canada 72 C6 53 46N 112 50W
Lamont, U.S.A. 85 K8 35 15N 118 55W
Lampa, Peru 92 G4 15 22S 70 22W
Lampang, Thailand 38 C2 18 16N 99 32 E
Lampasas, U.S.A. 81 K5 31 4N 98 11W
Lampazos de Naranjo, Mexico 86 B4 27 2N 100 32W
Lampedusa, Medit. S. 20 G5 35 36N 12 40 E
Lampeter, U.K. 11 E3 52 7N 4 4W
Lampione, Medit. S. 20 G5 35 33N 12 20 E
Lampman, Canada 73 D8 49 25N 102 50W
Lamprey, Canada 73 B10 58 33N 94 8W
Lampung □, Indonesia 36 F2 5 30S 104 30 E
Lamu, Kenya 54 C5 2 16S 40 55 E
Lamu □, Kenya 54 C5 2 0S 40 45 E
Lamy, U.S.A. 83 J11 35 29N 105 53W
Lan Xian, China 34 E6 38 15N 111 35 E
Lanai I., U.S.A. 74 H16 20 50N 156 55W
Lanak La, India 43 B8 34 27N 79 32 E
Lanak'o Shank'ou = Lanak La, India 43 B8 34 27N 79 32 E
Lanao, L., Phil. 37 C6 7 52N 124 15 E
Lanark, Canada 79 A8 45 1N 76 22W
Lanark, U.K. 12 F5 55 40N 3 47W
Lancang Jiang →, China 32 D5 21 40N 101 10 E
Lancashire □, U.K. 10 D5 53 50N 2 48W
Lancaster, Canada 79 A10 45 10N 74 30W
Lancaster, U.K. 10 C5 54 3N 2 48W
Lancaster, Calif., U.S.A. 85 L8 34 42N 118 8W
Lancaster, Ky., U.S.A. 76 G3 37 37N 84 35W
Lancaster, N.H., U.S.A. 79 B13 44 29N 71 34W
Lancaster, N.Y., U.S.A. 78 D6 42 54N 78 40W
Lancaster, Pa., U.S.A. 79 F8 40 2N 76 19W
Lancaster, S.C., U.S.A. 77 H5 34 43N 80 46W
Lancaster, Wis., U.S.A. 80 D9 42 51N 90 43W
Lancaster Sd., Canada 69 A11 74 13N 84 0W
Lancer, Canada 73 C7 50 48N 108 53W
Lanchow = Lanzhou, China 34 F2 36 1N 103 52 E
Lanciano, Italy 20 C6 42 14N 14 23 E
Lancun, China 35 F11 36 25N 120 10 E
Landeck, Austria 16 E6 47 9N 10 34 E
Landen, Belgium 15 D5 50 45N 5 3 E
Lander, U.S.A. 82 E9 42 50N 108 44W
Lander →, Australia 60 D5 22 0S 132 0 E
Landes, France 18 D3 44 0N 1 0W
Landi Kotal, Pakistan 42 B4 34 7N 71 6 E
Landor, Australia 61 E2 25 10S 116 54 E
Land's End, U.K. 11 G2 50 4N 5 44W
Landsborough Cr. →, Australia 62 C3 22 28S 144 35 E
Landshut, Germany 16 D7 48 34N 12 8 E
Landskrona, Sweden 9 J15 55 53N 12 50 E
Lanesboro, U.S.A. 79 E9 41 57N 75 34W
Lanett, U.S.A. 77 J3 32 52N 85 12W
Lang Bay, Canada 72 D4 49 45N 124 21W
Lang Qua, Vietnam 38 A5 22 16N 104 27 E
Lang Shan, China 34 D4 41 0N 106 30 E
Lang Son, Vietnam 38 B6 21 52N 106 42 E
Lang Suan, Thailand 39 H2 9 57N 99 4 E
La'nga Co, China 41 D12 30 45N 81 15 E
Langar, Iran 45 C9 35 23N 60 25 E
Langara I., Canada 72 C2 54 14N 133 1W
Langdon, U.S.A. 80 A5 48 45N 98 22W
Langeberg, S. Africa 56 E3 33 55S 21 0 E
Langeberge, S. Africa 56 D3 28 15S 22 33 E
Langeland, Denmark 9 J14 54 56N 10 48 E
Langenburg, Canada 73 C8 50 51N 101 43W
Langholm, U.K. 12 F6 55 9N 3 0W
Langjökull, Iceland 8 D3 64 39N 20 12W
Langkawi, P., Malaysia 39 J2 6 25N 99 45 E
Langklip, S. Africa 56 D3 28 12S 20 20 E
Langkon, Malaysia 36 C5 6 30N 116 40 E
Langlade, St- P. & M. 71 C8 46 50N 56 20W
Langlois, U.S.A. 82 E1 42 56N 124 27W
Langøya, Norway 8 B16 68 45N 14 50 E
Langres, France 18 C6 47 52N 5 20 E
Langres, Plateau de, France 18 C6 47 45N 5 3 E
Langsa, Indonesia 36 D1 4 30N 97 57 E
Langtry, U.S.A. 81 L4 29 49N 101 34W
Langu, Thailand 39 J2 6 53N 99 47 E
Languedoc, France 18 E5 43 58N 3 55 E
Langxiangzhen, China 34 E9 39 43N 116 8 E
Lanigan, Canada 73 C7 51 51N 105 2W
Lankao, China 34 G8 34 48N 114 50 E
Länkäran, Azerbaijan 25 G8 38 48N 48 52 E
Lannion, France 18 B2 48 46N 3 29W
L'Annonciation, Canada 70 C5 46 25N 74 55W
Lansdale, U.S.A. 79 F9 40 14N 75 17W
Lansdowne, Australia 63 E5 31 48S 152 30 E
Lansdowne, Canada 79 B8 44 24N 76 1W

Lansdowne House

Lansdowne House, *Canada* **70 B2** 52 14N 87 53W
L'Anse, *U.S.A.* **70 C2** 46 45N 88 27W
L'Anse au Loup, *Canada* **71 B8** 51 32N 56 50W
Lansford, *U.S.A.* **79 F9** 40 50N 75 53W
Lansing, *U.S.A.* **76 D3** 42 44N 84 33W
Lanta Yai, Ko, *Thailand* **39 J2** 7 35N 99 3 E
Lantian, *China* **34 G5** 34 11N 109 20 E
Lanus, *Argentina* **94 C4** 34 44S 58 27W
Lanusei, *Italy* **20 E3** 39 52N 9 34 E
Lanzarote, *Canary Is.* **22 E6** 29 0N 13 40W
Lanzhou, *China* **34 F2** 36 1N 103 52 E
Lao Bao, *Laos* **38 D6** 16 35N 106 30 E
Lao Cai, *Vietnam* **38 A4** 22 30N 103 57 E
Laoag, *Phil.* **37 A6** 18 7N 120 34 E
Laoang, *Phil.* **37 B7** 12 32N 125 8 E
Laoha He →, *China* **35 C11** 43 25N 120 35 E
Laois □, *Ireland* **13 D4** 52 57N 7 36W
Laon, *France* **18 B5** 49 33N 3 35 E
Laona, *U.S.A.* **76 C1** 45 34N 88 40W
Laos ■, *Asia* **38 D5** 17 45N 105 0 E
Lapa, *Brazil* **95 B6** 25 46S 49 44W
Laparan, *Phil.* **37 C6** 6 0N 120 0 E
Lapeer, *U.S.A.* **76 D4** 43 3N 83 19W
Lapithos, *Cyprus* **23 D12** 35 21N 33 11 E
Lapland = Lappland, *Europe* **8 B21** 68 7N 24 0 E
Laporte, *U.S.A.* **79 E8** 41 25N 76 30W
Lappeenranta, *Finland* **9 F23** 61 3N 28 12 E
Lappland, *Europe* **8 B21** 68 7N 24 0 E
Laprida, *Argentina* **94 D3** 37 34S 60 45W
Lapseki, *Turkey* **21 D12** 40 20N 26 41 E
Laptev Sea, *Russia* **27 B13** 76 0N 125 0 E
Lapua, *Finland* **8 E20** 62 58N 23 0 E
L'Áquila, *Italy* **20 C5** 42 22N 13 22 E
Lār, *Āzarbājān-e Sharqī, Iran* **44 B5** 38 30N 47 52 E
Lār, *Fārs, Iran* **45 E7** 27 40N 54 14 E
Larache, *Morocco* **50 A3** 35 10N 6 5W
Laramie, *U.S.A.* **80 E2** 41 19N 105 35W
Laramie Mts., *U.S.A.* **80 E2** 42 0N 105 30W
Laranjeiras do Sul, *Brazil* **95 B5** 25 23S 52 23W
Larantuka, *Indonesia* **37 F6** 8 21S 122 55 E
Larap, *Phil.* **37 B6** 14 18N 122 39 E
Larat, *Indonesia* **37 F8** 7 0S 132 0 E
Larde, *Mozam.* **55 F4** 16 28S 39 43 E
Larder Lake, *Canada* **70 C4** 48 5N 79 40W
Lardhos, Ákra, *Greece* **23 C10** 36 4N 28 10 E
Lardhos, Órmos, *Greece* **23 C10** 36 4N 28 2 E
Laredo, *U.S.A.* **81 M5** 27 30N 99 30W
Laredo Sd., *Canada* **72 C3** 52 30N 128 53W
Largo, *U.S.A.* **77 M4** 27 55N 82 47W
Largs, *U.K.* **12 F4** 55 47N 4 52W
Lariang, *Indonesia* **37 E5** 1 26S 119 17 E
Larimore, *U.S.A.* **80 B6** 47 54N 97 38W
Lārīn, *Iran* **45 C7** 35 55N 52 19 E
Lárisa, *Greece* **21 E10** 39 36N 22 27 E
Larkana, *Pakistan* **42 F3** 27 32N 68 18 E
Larnaca, *Cyprus* **23 E12** 34 55N 33 38 E
Larnaca Bay, *Cyprus* **23 E12** 34 53N 33 45 E
Larne, *U.K.* **13 B6** 54 51N 5 51W
Larned, *U.S.A.* **80 F5** 38 11N 99 6W
Larrimah, *Australia* **60 C5** 15 35S 133 12 E
Larsen Ice Shelf, *Antarctica* **5 C17** 67 0S 62 0W
Larvik, *Norway* **9 G14** 59 4N 10 0 E
Laryak, *Russia* **26 C8** 61 15N 80 0 E
Las Animas, *U.S.A.* **80 F3** 38 4N 103 13W
Las Anod, *Somali Rep.* **46 F4** 8 26N 47 19 E
Las Brenãs, *Argentina* **94 B3** 27 5S 61 7W
Las Chimeneas, *Mexico* **85 N10** 32 8N 116 5W
Las Cruces, *U.S.A.* **83 K10** 32 19N 106 47W
Las Flores, *Argentina* **94 D4** 36 10S 59 7W
Las Heras, *Argentina* **94 C2** 32 51S 68 49W
Las Khoreh, *Somali Rep.* **46 E4** 11 10N 48 20 E
Las Lajas, *Argentina* **96 D2** 38 30S 70 25W
Las Lomitas, *Argentina* **94 A3** 24 43S 60 35W
Las Palmas, *Argentina* **94 B4** 27 8S 58 45W
Las Palmas, *Canary Is.* **22 F4** 28 7N 15 26W
Las Palmas →, *Mexico* **85 N10** 32 26N 116 54W
Las Piedras, *Uruguay* **95 C4** 34 44S 56 14W
Las Pipinas, *Argentina* **94 D4** 35 30S 57 19W
Las Plumas, *Argentina* **96 E3** 43 40S 67 15W
Las Rosas, *Argentina* **94 C3** 32 30S 61 35W
Las Tablas, *Panama* **88 E3** 7 49N 80 14W
Las Termas, *Argentina* **94 B3** 27 29S 64 52W
Las Truchas, *Mexico* **86 D4** 17 57N 102 13W
Las Varillas, *Argentina* **94 C3** 31 50S 62 50W
Las Vegas, *N. Mex., U.S.A.* **83 J11** 35 36N 105 13W
Las Vegas, *Nev., U.S.A.* **85 J11** 36 10N 115 9W
Lascano, *Uruguay* **95 C5** 33 35S 54 12W
Lashburn, *Canada* **73 C7** 53 10N 109 40W
Lashio, *Burma* **41 H20** 22 56N 97 45 E
Lashkar, *India* **42 F8** 26 10N 78 10 E
Lasíthi, *Greece* **23 D7** 35 11N 25 31 E
Lasíthi □, *Greece* **23 D7** 35 5N 25 50 E
Lassen Pk., *U.S.A.* **82 F3** 40 29N 121 31W
Last Mountain L., *Canada* **73 C7** 51 5N 105 14W
Lastchance Cr. →, *U.S.A.* **84 E5** 40 2N 121 15W
Lastoursville, *Gabon* **52 E2** 0 55S 12 38 E
Lastovo, *Croatia* **20 C7** 42 46N 16 55 E
Lat Yao, *Thailand* **38 E2** 15 45N 99 48 E
Latacunga, *Ecuador* **92 D3** 0 50S 78 35W
Latakia = Al Lādhiqīyah, *Syria* **44 C2** 35 30N 35 45 E
Latchford, *Canada* **70 C4** 47 20N 79 50W
Latham, *Australia* **61 E2** 29 44S 116 20 E
Lathrop Wells, *U.S.A.* **85 J10** 36 39N 116 24W
Latina, *Italy* **20 D5** 41 28N 12 52 E
Latium = Lazio □, *Italy* **20 C5** 42 10N 12 30 E
Laton, *U.S.A.* **84 J7** 36 26N 119 41W
Latouche Treville, C., *Australia* **60 C3** 18 27S 121 49 E
Latrobe, *Australia* **62 G4** 41 14S 146 30 E
Latrobe, *U.S.A.* **78 F5** 40 19N 79 23W
Latvia ■, *Europe* **9 H20** 56 50N 24 0 E
Lau Group, *Fiji* **59 C9** 17 0S 178 30W
Lauchhammer, *Germany* **16 C7** 51 29N 13 47 E
Laukaa, *Finland* **9 E21** 62 24N 25 56 E
Launceston, *Australia* **62 G4** 41 24S 147 8 E
Launceston, *U.K.* **11 G3** 50 38N 4 22W
Laune →, *Ireland* **13 D2** 52 7N 9 47W
Laura, *Australia* **62 B3** 15 32S 144 32 E
Laurel, *Miss., U.S.A.* **81 K10** 31 41N 89 8W
Laurel, *Mont., U.S.A.* **82 D9** 45 40N 108 46W
Laurencekirk, *U.K.* **12 E6** 56 50N 2 28W
Laurens, *U.S.A.* **77 H4** 34 30N 82 1W
Laurentian Plateau, *Canada* **71 B6** 52 0N 70 0W
Laurentides, Parc Prov. des, *Canada* **71 C5** 47 45N 71 15W
Lauria, *Italy* **20 E6** 40 2N 15 50 E
Laurie L., *Canada* **73 B8** 56 35N 101 57W
Laurinburg, *U.S.A.* **77 H6** 34 47N 79 28W
Laurium, *U.S.A.* **76 B1** 47 14N 88 27W
Lausanne, *Switz.* **16 E4** 46 32N 6 38 E
Laut, *Indonesia* **36 D3** 4 45N 108 0 E
Laut Kecil, Kepulauan, *Indonesia* **36 E5** 4 45S 115 40 E
Lautoka, *Fiji* **59 C7** 17 37S 177 27 E
Lauzon, *Canada* **71 C5** 46 48N 71 10W
Lava Hot Springs, *U.S.A.* **82 E7** 42 37N 112 1W
Laval, *France* **18 B3** 48 4N 0 48W
Lavalle, *Argentina* **94 B2** 28 15S 65 15W
Laverne, *U.S.A.* **81 G5** 36 43N 99 54W
Laverton, *Australia* **61 E3** 28 44S 122 29 E
Lavras, *Brazil* **95 A7** 21 20S 45 0W
Lavrentiya, *Russia* **27 C19** 65 35N 171 0W
Lávrion, *Greece* **21 F11** 37 40N 24 4 E
Lávris, *Greece* **23 D6** 35 25N 24 40 E
Lavumisa, *Swaziland* **57 D5** 27 20S 31 55 E
Lawas, *Malaysia* **36 D5** 4 55N 115 25 E
Lawele, *Indonesia* **37 F6** 5 16S 123 3 E
Lawn Hill, *Australia* **62 B2** 18 36S 138 33 E
Lawng Pit, *Burma* **41 G20** 25 30N 97 25 E
Lawqah, *Si. Arabia* **44 D4** 29 49N 42 45 E
Lawrence, *N.Z.* **59 L2** 45 55S 169 41 E
Lawrence, *Kans., U.S.A.* **80 F7** 38 58N 95 14W
Lawrence, *Mass., U.S.A.* **79 D13** 42 43N 71 10W
Lawrenceburg, *Ind., U.S.A.* **76 F3** 39 6N 84 52W
Lawrenceburg, *Tenn., U.S.A.* **77 H2** 35 14N 87 20W
Lawrenceville, *U.S.A.* **77 J4** 33 57N 83 59W
Laws, *U.S.A.* **84 H8** 37 24N 118 20W
Lawton, *U.S.A.* **81 H5** 34 37N 98 25W
Lawu, *Indonesia* **37 G14** 7 40S 111 13 E
Laxford, L., *U.K.* **12 C3** 58 24N 5 6W
Laylān, *Iraq* **44 C5** 35 18N 44 31 E
Laysan I., *Pac. Oc.* **65 E11** 25 30N 167 0W
Laytonville, *U.S.A.* **82 G2** 39 41N 123 29W
Lazio □, *Italy* **20 C5** 42 10N 12 30 E
Lazo, *Russia* **30 C6** 43 25N 133 55 E
Le Creusot, *France* **18 C6** 46 48N 4 24 E
Le François, *Martinique* **89 D7** 14 38N 60 57W
Le Havre, *France* **18 B4** 49 30N 0 5 E
Le Mans, *France* **18 C4** 48 0N 0 10 E
Le Mars, *U.S.A.* **80 D6** 42 47N 96 10W
Le Mont-St.-Michel, *France* **18 B3** 48 40N 1 30W
Le Moule, *Guadeloupe* **89 C7** 16 20N 61 22W
Le Puy-en-Velay, *France* **18 D5** 45 3N 3 52 E
Le Roy, *U.S.A.* **81 F7** 38 5N 95 38W
Le Sueur, *U.S.A.* **80 C8** 44 28N 93 55W
Le Thuy, *Vietnam* **38 D6** 17 14N 106 49 E
Le Touquet-Paris-Plage, *France* **18 A4** 50 30N 1 36 E
Le Tréport, *France* **18 A4** 50 3N 1 20 E
Le Verdon-sur-Mer, *France* **18 D3** 45 33N 1 4W
Lea →, *U.K.* **11 F7** 51 31N 0 1 E
Leach, *Cambodia* **39 F4** 12 21N 103 46 E
Lead, *U.S.A.* **80 C3** 44 21N 103 46W
Leader, *Canada* **73 C7** 50 50N 109 30W
Leadhills, *U.K.* **12 F5** 55 25N 3 45W
Leadville, *U.S.A.* **83 G10** 39 15N 106 18W
Leaf →, *U.S.A.* **81 K10** 30 59N 88 44W
Leakey, *U.S.A.* **81 L5** 29 44N 99 46W
Leamington, *Canada* **70 D3** 42 3N 82 36W
Leamington, *U.S.A.* **82 G7** 39 32N 112 17W
Leamington Spa = Royal Leamington Spa, *U.K.* **11 E6** 52 18N 1 31W
Leandro Norte Alem, *Argentina* **95 B4** 27 34S 55 15W
Learmonth, *Australia* **60 D1** 22 13S 114 10 E
Leask, *Canada* **73 C7** 53 5N 106 45W
Leavenworth, *Kans., U.S.A.* **80 F7** 39 19N 94 55W
Leavenworth, *Wash., U.S.A.* **82 C3** 47 36N 120 40W
Lebak, *Phil.* **37 C6** 6 32N 124 5 E
Lebam, *U.S.A.* **84 D3** 46 34N 123 33W
Lebanon, *Ind., U.S.A.* **76 E2** 40 3N 86 28W
Lebanon, *Kans., U.S.A.* **80 F5** 39 49N 98 33W
Lebanon, *Ky., U.S.A.* **76 G3** 37 34N 85 15W
Lebanon, *Mo., U.S.A.* **81 G8** 37 41N 92 40W
Lebanon, *Oreg., U.S.A.* **82 D2** 44 32N 122 55W
Lebanon, *Pa., U.S.A.* **79 F8** 40 20N 76 26W
Lebanon, *Tenn., U.S.A.* **77 G2** 36 12N 86 18W
Lebanon ■, *Asia* **47 B4** 34 0N 36 0 E
Lebec, *U.S.A.* **85 L8** 34 50N 118 52W
Lebomboberge, *S. Africa* **57 C5** 24 30S 32 0 E
Lębork, *Poland* **17 A9** 54 33N 17 46 E
Lebrija, *Spain* **19 D2** 36 53N 6 5W
Lebu, *Chile* **94 D1** 37 40S 73 47W
Lecce, *Italy* **21 D8** 40 23N 18 11 E
Lecco, *Italy* **20 B3** 45 51N 9 23 E
Lech →, *Germany* **16 D6** 48 43N 10 56 E
Łęczyca, *Poland* **17 B10** 52 5N 19 15 E
Ledbury, *U.K.* **11 E5** 52 2N 2 25W
Ledong, *China* **38 C7** 18 41N 109 5 E
Leduc, *Canada* **72 C6** 53 15N 113 30W
Lee, *U.S.A.* **79 D11** 42 19N 73 15W
Lee →, *Ireland* **13 E3** 51 53N 8 56W
Lee Vining, *U.S.A.* **84 H7** 37 58N 119 7W
Leech L., *U.S.A.* **80 B7** 47 10N 94 24W
Leedey, *U.S.A.* **81 H5** 35 52N 99 21W
Leeds, *U.K.* **10 D6** 53 48N 1 33W
Leeds, *U.S.A.* **77 J2** 33 33N 86 33W
Leek, *U.K.* **10 D5** 53 7N 2 1W
Leer, *Germany* **16 B4** 53 13N 7 26 E
Leesburg, *U.S.A.* **77 L5** 28 49N 81 53W
Leesville, *U.S.A.* **81 K8** 31 9N 93 16W
Leeton, *Australia* **63 E4** 34 33S 146 23 E
Leetonia, *U.S.A.* **78 F4** 40 53N 80 45W
Leeu Gamka, *S. Africa* **56 E3** 32 47S 21 59 E
Leeuwarden, *Neths.* **15 A5** 53 15N 5 48 E
Leeuwin, C., *Australia* **61 F2** 34 20S 115 9 E
Leeward Is., *Atl. Oc.* **89 C7** 16 30N 63 30W
Lefka, *Cyprus* **23 D11** 35 6N 32 51 E
Lefkoniko, *Cyprus* **23 D12** 35 18N 33 44 E
Lefors, *U.S.A.* **81 H4** 35 26N 100 48W
Lefroy, L., *Australia* **61 F3** 31 21S 121 40 E
Legal, *Canada* **72 C6** 53 55N 113 35W
Leganés, *Spain* **19 B4** 40 19N 3 45W
Legazpi, *Phil.* **37 B6** 13 10N 123 45 E
Legendre I., *Australia* **60 D2** 20 22S 116 55 E
Leghorn = Livorno, *Italy* **20 C4** 43 33N 10 19 E
Legionowo, *Poland* **17 B11** 52 25N 20 50 E
Legnago, *Italy* **20 B4** 45 11N 11 18 E
Legnica, *Poland* **16 C9** 51 12N 16 10 E
Legume, *Australia* **63 D5** 28 20S 152 19 E
Leh, *India* **43 B7** 34 9N 77 35 E
Lehi, *U.S.A.* **82 F8** 40 24N 111 51W
Lehighton, *U.S.A.* **79 F9** 40 50N 75 43W
Lehututu, *Botswana* **56 C3** 23 54S 21 55 E
Leiah, *Pakistan* **42 D4** 30 58N 70 58 E
Leicester, *U.K.* **11 E6** 52 38N 1 8W
Leicestershire □, *U.K.* **11 E6** 52 41N 1 17W
Leichhardt →, *Australia* **62 B2** 17 35S 139 48 E
Leichhardt Ra., *Australia* **62 C4** 20 46S 147 40 E
Leiden, *Neths.* **15 B4** 52 9N 4 30 E
Leie →, *Belgium* **15 C3** 51 2N 3 45 E
Leine →, *Germany* **16 B5** 52 43N 9 36 E
Leinster, *Australia* **61 E3** 27 51S 120 36 E
Leinster □, *Ireland* **13 C4** 53 3N 7 8W
Leinster, Mt., *Ireland* **13 D5** 52 37N 6 46W
Leipzig, *Germany* **16 C7** 51 18N 12 22 E
Leiria, *Portugal* **19 C1** 39 46N 8 53W
Leirvik, *Norway* **9 G11** 59 47N 5 28 E
Leisler, Mt., *Australia* **60 D4** 23 23S 129 20 E
Leith, *U.K.* **12 F5** 55 59N 3 11W
Leith Hill, *U.K.* **11 F7** 51 11N 0 22W
Leitrim, *Ireland* **13 B3** 54 0N 8 5W
Leitrim □, *Ireland* **13 B3** 54 8N 8 0W
Leizhou Bandao, *China* **33 D6** 21 0N 110 0 E
Lek →, *Neths.* **15 C4** 51 54N 4 35 E
Leka, *Norway* **8 D14** 65 5N 11 35 E
Leksula, *Indonesia* **37 E7** 3 46S 126 31 E
Lékva Ori, *Greece* **23 D6** 35 18N 24 3 E
Leland, *U.S.A.* **81 J9** 33 24N 90 54W
Leland Lakes, *Canada* **73 A6** 60 0N 110 59W
Leleque, *Argentina* **96 E2** 42 28S 71 0W
Lelystad, *Neths.* **15 B5** 52 30N 5 25 E
Léman, L., *Europe* **16 E4** 46 26N 6 30 E
Lemera, *Zaïre* **54 C2** 3 0S 28 55 E
Lemhi Ra., *U.S.A.* **82 D7** 44 30N 113 30W
Lemmer, *Neths.* **15 B5** 52 51N 5 43 E
Lemmon, *U.S.A.* **80 C3** 45 57N 102 10W
Lemon Grove, *U.S.A.* **85 N9** 32 45N 117 2W
Lemoore, *U.S.A.* **83 H4** 36 18N 119 46W
Lemvig, *Denmark* **9 H13** 56 33N 8 20 E
Lena →, *Russia* **27 B13** 72 52N 126 40 E
Léndas, *Greece* **23 E6** 34 56N 24 56 E
Lendeh, *Iran* **45 D6** 30 58N 50 25 E
Lenggong, *Malaysia* **39 K3** 5 6N 100 58 E
Lengua de Vaca, Pta., *Chile* **94 C1** 30 14S 71 38W
Leninabad = Khudzhand, *Tajikistan* **26 E7** 40 17N 69 37 E
Leninakan = Gyumri, *Armenia* **25 F7** 40 47N 43 50 E
Leningrad = Sankt-Peterburg, *Russia* **24 C5** 59 55N 30 20 E
Leninogorsk, *Kazakstan* **26 D9** 50 20N 83 30 E
Leninsk, *Russia* **25 E8** 48 40N 45 15 E
Leninsk-Kuznetskiy, *Russia* **26 D9** 54 44N 86 10 E
Leninskoye, *Russia* **27 E14** 47 56N 132 38 E
Lenkoran = Länkäran, *Azerbaijan* **25 G8** 38 48N 48 52 E
Lenmalu, *Indonesia* **37 E8** 1 45S 130 15 E
Lennoxville, *Canada* **79 A13** 45 22N 71 51W
Lenoir, *U.S.A.* **77 H5** 35 55N 81 32W
Lenoir City, *U.S.A.* **77 H3** 35 48N 84 16W
Lenora, *U.S.A.* **80 F4** 39 37N 100 0W
Lenore L., *Canada* **73 C8** 52 30N 104 59W
Lenox, *U.S.A.* **79 D11** 42 22N 73 17W
Lens, *France* **18 A5** 50 26N 2 50 E
Lensk, *Russia* **27 C12** 60 48N 114 55 E
Lentini, *Italy* **20 F6** 37 17N 15 0 E
Lenwood, *U.S.A.* **85 L9** 34 53N 117 7W
Leoben, *Austria* **16 E8** 47 22N 15 5 E
Leodhas = Lewis, *U.K.* **12 C2** 58 9N 6 40W
Leola, *U.S.A.* **80 C5** 45 43N 98 56W
Leominster, *U.K.* **11 E5** 52 14N 2 43W
Leominster, *U.S.A.* **79 D13** 42 32N 71 46W
León, *Mexico* **86 C4** 21 7N 101 40W
León, *Nic.* **88 D2** 12 20N 86 51W
León, *Spain* **19 A3** 42 38N 5 34W
Leon, *U.S.A.* **80 E8** 40 44N 93 45W
León, Montañas de, *Spain* **19 A2** 42 30N 6 18W
Leonardtown, *U.S.A.* **76 F7** 38 17N 76 38W
Leongatha, *Australia* **63 F4** 38 30S 145 58 E
Leonora, *Australia* **61 E3** 28 49S 121 19 E
Léopold II, Lac = Mai-Ndombe, L., *Zaïre* **52 E3** 2 0S 18 20 E
Leopoldina, *Brazil* **95 A7** 21 28S 42 40W
Leopoldsburg, *Belgium* **15 C5** 51 7N 5 13 E
Léopoldville = Kinshasa, *Zaïre* **52 E3** 4 20S 15 15 E
Leoti, *U.S.A.* **80 F4** 38 29N 101 21W
Leova, *Moldova* **17 E15** 46 28N 28 15 E
Leoville, *Canada* **73 C7** 53 39N 107 33W
Lépa, L. do, *Angola* **56 B2** 17 0S 19 0 E
Lepel = Lyepyel, *Belarus* **24 D4** 54 50N 28 40 E
Lepikha, *Russia* **27 C13** 64 45N 125 55 E
Leppävirta, *Finland* **9 E22** 62 29N 27 46 E
Lerdo, *Mexico* **86 B4** 25 32N 103 32W
Léré, *Chad* **51 G7** 9 39N 14 13 E
Leribe, *Lesotho* **57 D4** 28 51S 28 3 E
Lérida, *Spain* **19 B6** 41 37N 0 39 E
Lerwick, *U.K.* **12 A7** 60 9N 1 9W
Les Cayes, *Haiti* **89 C5** 18 15N 73 46W
Les Étroits, *Canada* **71 C6** 47 24N 68 54W
Les Sables-d'Olonne, *France* **18 C3** 46 30N 1 45W
Lesbos = Lésvos, *Greece* **21 E12** 39 10N 26 20 E
Leshan, *China* **32 D5** 29 33N 103 41 E
Leshukonskoye, *Russia* **24 B8** 64 54N 45 46 E
Leskov I., *Antarctica* **5 B1** 56 0S 28 0W
Leskovac, *Serbia, Yug.* **21 C9** 43 0N 21 58 E
Leslie, *U.S.A.* **81 H8** 35 50N 92 34W
Lesopilnoye, *Russia* **30 A7** 46 44N 134 20 E
Lesotho ■, *Africa* **57 D4** 29 40S 28 0 E
Lesozavodsk, *Russia* **27 E14** 45 30N 133 29 E
Lesse →, *Belgium* **15 D4** 50 15N 4 54 E
Lesser Antilles, *W. Indies* **89 C7** 15 0N 61 0W
Lesser Slave L., *Canada* **72 B5** 55 30N 115 25W
Lesser Sunda Is., *Indonesia* **37 F6** 7 0S 120 0 E
Lessines, *Belgium* **15 D3** 50 42N 3 50 E
Lester, *U.S.A.* **84 C5** 47 12N 121 29W
Lestock, *Canada* **73 C8** 51 19N 103 59W
Lesuer I., *Australia* **60 B4** 13 50S 127 17 E
Lésvos, *Greece* **21 E12** 39 10N 26 20 E
Leszno, *Poland* **17 C9** 51 50N 16 30 E
Letchworth, *U.K.* **11 F7** 51 59N 0 13W
Lethbridge, *Canada* **72 D6** 49 45N 112 45W
Leti, Kepulauan, *Indonesia* **37 F7** 8 10S 128 0 E
Leti Is. = Leti, Kepulauan, *Indonesia* **37 F7** 8 10S 128 0 E
Letiahau →, *Botswana* **56 C3** 21 16S 24 0 E
Leticia, *Colombia* **92 D4** 4 9S 70 0W
Leting, *China* **35 E10** 39 23N 118 55 E
Letjiesbos, *S. Africa* **56 E3** 32 34S 22 16 E
Letlhakeng, *Botswana* **56 C3** 24 0S 24 59 E
Letpadan, *Burma* **41 L19** 17 45N 95 45 E
Letpan, *Burma* **41 K19** 19 28N 94 10 E
Letterkenny, *Ireland* **13 B4** 54 57N 7 45W
Leucadia, *U.S.A.* **85 M9** 33 4N 117 18W
Leuser, G., *Indonesia* **36 D1** 3 46N 97 12 E
Leuven, *Belgium* **15 D4** 50 52N 4 42 E
Leuze, *Hainaut, Belgium* **15 D3** 50 36N 3 37 E
Leuze, *Namur, Belgium* **15 D4** 50 33N 4 54 E
Levádhia, *Greece* **21 E10** 38 27N 22 54 E
Levan, *U.S.A.* **82 G8** 39 33N 111 52W
Levanger, *Norway* **8 E14** 63 45N 11 19 E
Levelland, *U.S.A.* **81 J3** 33 35N 102 23W
Leven, *U.K.* **12 E6** 56 12N 3 0W
Leven, L., *U.K.* **12 E5** 56 12N 3 22W
Leven, Toraka, *Madag.* **57 A8** 12 30S 47 45 E
Leveque C., *Australia* **60 C3** 16 20S 123 0 E
Levice, *Slovak Rep.* **17 D10** 48 13N 18 35 E
Levin, *N.Z.* **59 J5** 40 37S 175 18 E
Lévis, *Canada* **71 C5** 46 48N 71 9W
Levis, L., *Canada* **72 A5** 62 37N 117 58W
Levittown, *N.Y., U.S.A.* **79 F11** 40 44N 73 31W
Levittown, *Pa., U.S.A.* **79 F10** 40 9N 74 51W
Levkás, *Greece* **21 E9** 38 40N 20 43 E
Levkímmi, *Greece* **23 B4** 39 25N 20 3 E
Levkímmi, Ákra, *Greece* **23 B4** 39 29N 20 4 E
Levkôsia = Nicosia, *Cyprus* **23 D12** 35 10N 33 25 E
Levskigrad = Karlovo, *Bulgaria* **21 C11** 42 38N 24 47 E
Lewellen, *U.S.A.* **80 E3** 41 20N 102 9W
Lewes, *U.K.* **11 G8** 50 52N 0 1 E
Lewes, *U.S.A.* **76 F8** 38 46N 75 9W
Lewis, *U.K.* **12 C2** 58 9N 6 40W
Lewis →, *U.S.A.* **84 E4** 45 51N 122 48W
Lewis, Butt of, *U.K.* **12 C2** 58 31N 6 16W
Lewis Ra., *Australia* **60 D4** 20 3S 128 50 E
Lewis Range, *U.S.A.* **82 C7** 48 5N 113 5W
Lewisburg, *Pa., U.S.A.* **78 F8** 40 58N 76 54W
Lewisburg, *Tenn., U.S.A.* **77 H2** 35 27N 86 48W
Lewisporte, *Canada* **71 C8** 49 15N 55 3W
Lewiston, *Idaho, U.S.A.* **82 C5** 46 25N 117 1W
Lewiston, *Maine, U.S.A.* **77 C11** 44 6N 70 13W
Lewistown, *Mont., U.S.A.* **82 C9** 47 4N 109 26W
Lewistown, *Pa., U.S.A.* **78 F7** 40 36N 77 34W
Lexington, *Ill., U.S.A.* **80 E10** 40 39N 88 47W
Lexington, *Ky., U.S.A.* **76 F3** 38 3N 84 30W
Lexington, *Miss., U.S.A.* **81 J9** 33 7N 90 3W
Lexington, *Mo., U.S.A.* **80 F8** 39 11N 93 52W
Lexington, *N.C., U.S.A.* **77 H5** 35 49N 80 15W
Lexington, *Nebr., U.S.A.* **80 E5** 40 47N 99 45W
Lexington, *Ohio, U.S.A.* **78 F2** 40 41N 82 35W
Lexington, *Oreg., U.S.A.* **82 D4** 45 27N 119 42W
Lexington, *Tenn., U.S.A.* **77 H1** 35 39N 88 24W
Lexington Park, *U.S.A.* **76 F7** 38 16N 76 27W
Leyte, *Phil.* **37 B6** 11 0N 125 0 E
Lezha, *Albania* **21 D8** 41 47N 19 42 E
Lhasa, *China* **32 D4** 29 25N 90 58 E
Lhazê, *China* **32 D3** 29 5N 87 38 E
Lhokkruet, *Indonesia* **36 D1** 4 55N 95 24 E
Lhokseumawe, *Indonesia* **36 C1** 5 10N 97 10 E
Lhuntsi Dzong, *India* **41 F17** 27 39N 91 10 E
Li, *Thailand* **38 D2** 17 48N 98 57 E
Li Xian, *Gansu, China* **34 G3** 34 10N 105 5 E
Li Xian, *Hebei, China* **34 E8** 38 30N 115 35 E
Lianga, *Phil.* **37 C7** 8 38N 126 6 E
Liangcheng, *Nei Mongol Zizhiqu, China* **34 D7** 40 28N 112 25 E
Liangcheng, *Shandong, China* **35 G10** 35 32N 119 37 E
Liangdang, *China* **34 H4** 33 56N 106 18 E
Lianshanguan, *China* **35 D12** 40 53N 123 43 E
Lianshui, *China* **35 H10** 33 42N 119 20 E
Lianyungang, *China* **35 G10** 34 40N 119 11 E
Liao He →, *China* **35 D11** 41 0N 121 50 E
Liaocheng, *China* **34 F8** 36 28N 115 58 E
Liaodong Bandao, *China* **35 E12** 40 0N 122 30 E
Liaodong Wan, *China* **35 D11** 40 20N 121 10 E
Liaoning □, *China* **35 D12** 41 40N 122 30 E
Liaoyang, *China* **35 D12** 41 15N 122 58 E
Liaoyuan, *China* **35 C13** 42 58N 125 2 E
Liaozhong, *China* **35 D12** 41 23N 122 50 E
Liard →, *Canada* **72 A4** 61 51N 121 18W
Liari, *Pakistan* **42 G2** 25 37N 66 30 E
Libau = Liepāja, *Latvia* **9 H19** 56 30N 21 0 E
Libby, *U.S.A.* **82 B6** 48 23N 115 33W
Libenge, *Zaïre* **52 D3** 3 40N 18 55 E
Liberal, *Kans., U.S.A.* **81 G4** 37 3N 100 55W
Liberal, *Mo., U.S.A.* **81 G7** 37 34N 94 31W
Liberec, *Czech.* **16 C8** 50 47N 15 7 E
Liberia, *Costa Rica* **88 D2** 10 40N 85 30W
Liberia ■, *W. Afr.* **50 G3** 6 30N 9 30W
Liberty, *Mo., U.S.A.* **80 F7** 39 15N 94 25W
Liberty, *Tex., U.S.A.* **81 K7** 30 3N 94 48W
Lībīya, Sahrâ', *Africa* **51 C9** 25 0N 25 0 E
Libobo, Tanjung, *Indonesia* **37 E7** 0 54S 128 28 E
Libode, *S. Africa* **57 E4** 31 33S 29 2 E
Libonda, *Zambia* **53 G4** 14 28S 23 12 E
Libourne, *France* **18 D3** 44 55N 0 14W
Libramont, *Belgium* **15 E5** 49 55N 5 23 E
Libreville, *Gabon* **52 D1** 0 25N 9 26 E
Libya ■, *N. Afr.* **51 C8** 27 0N 17 0 E

Maluku

McGehee, U.S.A. 81 J9 33 38N 91 24W
McGill, U.S.A. 82 G6 39 23N 114 47W
Macgillycuddy's Reeks, Ireland 13 D2 51 58N 9 45W
MacGregor, Canada 73 D9 49 57N 98 48W
McGregor, U.S.A. 80 D9 43 1N 91 11W
McGregor —►, Canada 72 B4 55 10N 122 0W
McGregor Ra., Australia 63 D3 27 0S 142 45 E
Mach, Pakistan 40 E5 29 50N 67 20 E
Māch Kowr, Iran 45 E9 25 48N 61 28 E
Machado = Jiparaná —►, Brazil 92 E6 8 3S 62 52W
Machagai, Argentina 94 B3 26 56S 60 2W
Machakos, Kenya 54 C4 1 30S 37 15 E
Machakos □, Kenya 54 C4 1 30S 37 15 E
Machala, Ecuador 92 D3 3 20S 79 57W
Machanga, Mozam. 57 C6 20 59S 35 0 E
Machattie, L., Australia 62 C2 24 50S 139 48 E
Machava, Mozam. 57 D5 25 54S 32 28 E
Machece, Mozam. 55 F4 19 15S 35 32 E
Machevna, Russia 27 C18 61 20N 172 20 E
Machias, U.S.A. 71 D6 44 43N 67 28W
Machichi —►, Canada 73 B10 57 3N 92 6W
Machico, Madeira 22 D3 32 43N 16 44W
Machilipatnam, India 41 L12 16 12N 81 8 E
Machiques, Venezuela 92 A4 10 4N 72 34W
Machupicchu, Peru 92 F4 13 8S 72 30W
Machynlleth, U.K. 11 E4 52 35N 3 50W
McIlwraith Ra., Australia 62 A3 13 50S 143 20 E
McIntosh, U.S.A. 80 C4 45 55N 101 21W
McIntosh L., Canada 73 B8 55 45N 105 0W
Macintosh Ra., Australia 61 E4 27 39S 125 32 E
Macintyre —►, Australia 63 D5 28 37S 150 47 E
Mackay, Australia 62 C4 21 8S 149 11 E
Mackay, U.S.A. 82 E7 43 55N 113 37W
MacKay —►, Canada 72 B6 57 10N 111 38W
Mackay, L., Australia 60 D4 22 30S 129 0 E
McKay Ra., Australia 60 D3 23 0S 122 30 E
McKeesport, U.S.A. 78 F5 40 21N 79 52W
McKenna, U.S.A. 84 D4 46 56N 122 33W
Mackenzie, Canada 72 B4 55 20N 123 5W
McKenzie, U.S.A. 77 G1 36 8N 88 31W
Mackenzie —►, Australia 62 C4 23 38S 149 46 E
Mackenzie —►, Canada 68 B6 69 10N 134 20W
McKenzie —►, U.S.A. 82 D2 44 7N 123 6W
Mackenzie Bay, Canada 4 B1 69 0N 137 30W
Mackenzie City = Linden, Guyana 92 B7 6 0N 58 10W
Mackenzie Highway, Canada 72 B5 58 0N 117 15W
Mackenzie Mts., Canada 68 B6 64 0N 130 0W
Mackinaw City, U.S.A. 76 C3 45 47N 84 44W
McKinlay, Australia 62 C3 21 16S 141 18 E
McKinlay —►, Australia 62 C3 20 50S 141 28 E
McKinley, Mt., U.S.A. 68 B4 63 4N 151 0W
McKinley Sea, Arctic 4 A7 82 0N 0 0 E
McKinney, U.S.A. 81 J6 33 12N 96 37W
Mackinnon Road, Kenya 54 C4 3 40S 39 1 E
Macksville, Australia 63 E5 30 40S 152 56 E
McLaughlin, U.S.A. 80 C4 45 49N 100 49W
Maclean, Australia 63 D5 29 26S 153 16 E
McLean, U.S.A. 81 H4 35 14N 100 36W
McLeansboro, U.S.A. 80 F10 38 6N 88 32W
Maclear, S. Africa 57 E4 31 2S 28 23 E
Macleay —►, Australia 63 E5 30 56S 153 0 E
McLennan, Canada 72 B5 55 42N 116 50W
MacLeod, B., Canada 73 A7 62 53N 110 0W
McLeod, L., Australia 61 D1 24 9S 113 47 E
MacLeod Lake, Canada 72 C4 54 58N 123 0W
McLoughlin, Mt., U.S.A. 82 E2 42 27N 122 19W
McLure, Canada 72 C4 51 2N 120 13W
McMechen, U.S.A. 78 G4 39 57N 80 44W
McMillan, L., U.S.A. 81 J2 32 36N 104 21W
McMinnville, Oreg., U.S.A. 82 D2 45 13N 123 12W
McMinnville, Tenn., U.S.A. 77 H3 35 41N 85 46W
McMorran, Canada 73 C7 51 19N 108 42W
McMurdo Sd., Antarctica 5 D11 77 0S 170 0 E
McMurray = Fort McMurray, Canada 72 B6 56 44N 111 7W
McMurray, U.S.A. 84 B4 48 19N 122 14W
McNary, U.S.A. 83 J9 34 4N 109 51W
MacNutt, Canada 73 C8 51 5N 101 36W
Macodoene, Mozam. 57 C6 23 32S 35 5 E
Macomb, U.S.A. 80 E9 40 27N 90 40W
Mâcon, France 18 C6 46 19N 4 50 E
Macon, Ga., U.S.A. 77 J4 32 51N 83 38W
Macon, Miss., U.S.A. 77 J1 33 7N 88 34W
Macon, Mo., U.S.A. 80 F8 39 44N 92 28W
Macondo, Angola 53 G4 12 37S 23 46 E
Macossa, Mozam. 55 F3 17 55S 33 56 E
Macoun L., Canada 73 B8 56 32N 103 40W
Macovane, Mozam. 57 C6 21 30S 35 2 E
McPherson, U.S.A. 80 F6 38 22N 97 40W
McPherson Pk., U.S.A. 85 L7 34 53N 119 53W
McPherson Ra., Australia 63 D5 28 15S 153 15 E
Macquarie Harbour, Australia 62 G4 42 15S 145 23 E
Macquarie Is., Pac. Oc. 64 N7 54 36S 158 55 E
MacRobertson Land, Antarctica 5 D6 71 0S 64 0 E
Macroom, Ireland 13 E3 51 54N 8 57W
Macroy, Australia 60 D2 20 53S 118 2 E
MacTier, Canada 78 A5 45 9N 79 46W
Macubela, Mozam. 55 F4 16 53S 37 49 E
Macuiza, Mozam. 55 F3 18 7S 34 29 E
Macuse, Mozam. 55 F4 17 45S 37 10 E
Macuspana, Mexico 87 D6 17 46N 92 36W
Macusse, Angola 56 B3 17 48S 20 23 E
McVille, U.S.A. 80 B5 47 46N 98 11W
Madadeni, S. Africa 57 D5 27 43S 30 3 E
Madagali, Nigeria 51 F7 10 56N 13 33 E
Madagascar ■, Africa 57 C8 20 0S 47 0 E
Madā'in Sālih, Si. Arabia 44 E3 26 46N 37 57 E
Madama, Niger 51 D7 22 0N 13 40 E
Madame I., Canada 71 C7 45 30N 60 58W
Madaoua, Niger 50 F6 14 5N 6 27 E
Madaripur, Bangla. 41 H17 23 19N 90 15 E
Madauk, Burma 41 L20 17 56N 96 52 E
Madawaska, Canada 78 A7 45 30N 78 0W
Madawaska —►, Canada 78 A8 45 27N 76 21W
Madaya, Burma 41 H20 22 12N 96 10 E
Maddalena, Italy 20 D3 41 16N 9 23 E
Madeira, Atl. Oc. 22 D3 32 50N 17 0W
Madeira —►, Brazil 92 D7 3 22S 58 45W
Madeleine, Is. de la, Canada 71 C7 47 30N 61 40W
Madera, U.S.A. 83 H3 36 57N 120 3W
Madha, India 40 L9 18 0N 75 30 E
Madhubani, India 43 F12 26 21N 86 7 E
Madhya Pradesh □, India 42 J7 22 50N 78 0 E
Madikeri, India 40 N9 12 30N 75 45 E
Madill, U.S.A. 81 H6 34 6N 96 46W
Madimba, Zaïre 52 E3 4 58S 15 5 E
Ma'din, Syria 44 C3 35 45N 39 36 E
Madīnat ash Sha'b, Yemen 46 E3 12 50N 45 0 E
Madingou, Congo 52 E2 4 10S 13 33 E
Madirovalo, Madag. 57 B8 16 26S 46 32 E
Madison, Calif., U.S.A. 84 G5 38 41N 121 59W
Madison, Fla., U.S.A. 77 K4 30 28N 83 25W
Madison, Ind., U.S.A. 76 F3 38 44N 85 23W
Madison, Nebr., U.S.A. 80 E6 41 50N 97 27W
Madison, Ohio, U.S.A. 78 E3 41 46N 81 3W
Madison, S. Dak., U.S.A. 80 D6 44 0N 97 7W
Madison, Wis., U.S.A. 80 D10 43 4N 89 24W
Madison —►, U.S.A. 82 D8 45 56N 111 31W
Madisonville, Ky., U.S.A. 76 G2 37 20N 87 30W
Madisonville, Tex., U.S.A. 81 K7 30 57N 95 55W
Madista, Botswana 56 C4 21 15S 25 6 E
Madiun, Indonesia 37 G14 7 38S 111 32 E
Madley, U.K. 11 E5 52 2N 2 51W
Madona, Latvia 9 H22 56 53N 26 5 E
Madras = Tamil Nadu □, India 40 P10 11 0N 77 0 E
Madras, India 40 N12 13 8N 80 19 E
Madras, U.S.A. 82 D3 44 38N 121 8W
Madre, L., Mexico 87 B5 25 0N 97 30W
Madre, Laguna, U.S.A. 81 M6 27 0N 97 30W
Madre, Sierra, Phil. 37 A6 17 0N 122 0 E
Madre de Dios —►, Bolivia 92 F5 10 59S 66 8W
Madre de Dios, I., Chile 96 G1 50 20S 75 10W
Madre del Sur, Sierra, Mexico 87 D5 17 30N 100 0W
Madre Occidental, Sierra, Mexico 86 B3 27 0N 107 0W
Madre Oriental, Sierra, Mexico 86 C4 25 0N 100 0W
Madri, India 42 G5 24 16N 73 32 E
Madrid, Spain 19 B4 40 25N 3 45W
Madura, Selat, Indonesia 37 G15 7 30S 113 20 E
Madura Motel, Australia 61 F4 31 55S 127 0 E
Madurai, India 40 Q11 9 55N 78 10 E
Madurantakam, India 40 N11 12 30N 79 50 E
Mae Chan, Thailand 38 B2 20 9N 99 52 E
Mae Hong Son, Thailand 38 C2 19 16N 98 1 E
Mae Khlong —►, Thailand 38 F3 13 24N 100 0 E
Mae Phrik, Thailand 38 D2 17 27N 99 7 E
Mae Ramat, Thailand 38 D2 16 58N 98 31 E
Mae Rim, Thailand 38 C2 18 54N 98 57 E
Mae Sot, Thailand 38 D2 16 43N 98 34 E
Mae Suai, Thailand 38 C2 19 39N 99 33 E
Mae Tha, Thailand 38 C2 18 28N 99 8 E
Maebashi, Japan 31 F9 36 24N 139 4 E
Maesteg, U.K. 11 F4 51 36N 3 40W
Maestra, Sierra, Cuba 88 B4 20 15N 77 0W
Maestrazgo, Mts. del, Spain 19 B5 40 30N 0 25W
Maevatanana, Madag. 57 B8 16 56S 46 49 E
Mafeking = Mafikeng, S. Africa 56 D4 25 50S 25 38 E
Mafeking, Canada 73 C8 52 40N 101 10W
Mafeteng, Lesotho 56 D4 29 51S 27 15 E
Maffra, Australia 63 F4 37 53S 146 58 E
Mafia I., Tanzania 54 D4 7 45S 39 50 E
Mafikeng, S. Africa 56 D4 25 50S 25 38 E
Mafra, Brazil 95 B6 26 10S 49 55W
Mafra, Portugal 19 C1 38 55N 9 20W
Mafungabusi Plateau, Zimbabwe 55 F2 18 30S 29 8 E
Magadan, Russia 27 D16 59 38N 150 50 E
Magadi, Kenya 54 C4 1 54S 36 19 E
Magadi, L., Kenya 54 C4 1 54S 36 19 E
Magaliesburg, S. Africa 57 D4 26 0S 27 32 E
Magallanes, Estrecho de, Chile 96 G2 52 30S 75 0W
Magangué, Colombia 92 B4 9 14N 74 45W
Magburaka, S. Leone 50 G2 8 47N 12 0W
Magdalen Is. = Madeleine, Is. de la, Canada 71 C7 47 30N 61 40W
Magdalena, Argentina 94 D4 35 5S 57 30W
Magdalena, Bolivia 92 F6 13 13S 63 57W
Magdalena, Malaysia 36 D5 4 25N 117 55 E
Magdalena, Mexico 86 A2 30 50N 112 0W
Magdalena, U.S.A. 83 J10 34 7N 107 15W
Magdalena —►, Colombia 92 A4 11 6N 74 51W
Magdalena —►, Mexico 86 A2 30 40N 112 25W
Magdalena, B., Mexico 86 C2 24 30N 112 10W
Magdalena, Llano de la, Mexico 86 C2 25 0N 111 30W
Magdeburg, Germany 16 B6 52 7N 11 38 E
Magdelaine Cays, Australia 62 B5 16 33S 150 18 E
Magee, U.S.A. 81 K10 31 52N 89 44W
Magee, I., U.K. 13 B6 54 48N 5 43W
Magelang, Indonesia 37 G14 7 29S 110 13 E
Magellan's Str. = Magallanes, Estrecho de, Chile 96 G2 52 30S 75 0W
Magenta, L., Australia 61 F2 33 30S 119 2 E
Magerøya, Norway 8 A21 71 3N 25 40 E
Maggiore, L., Italy 20 B3 45 57N 8 39 E
Magherafelt, U.K. 13 B5 54 45N 6 37W
Magistralnyy, Russia 27 D11 56 16N 107 36 E
Magnetic Pole (North) = North Magnetic Pole, Canada 4 B2 77 58N 102 8W
Magnetic Pole (South) = South Magnetic Pole, Antarctica 5 C9 64 8S 138 8 E
Magnitogorsk, Russia 24 D10 53 27N 59 4 E
Magnolia, Ark., U.S.A. 81 J8 33 16N 93 14W
Magnolia, Miss., U.S.A. 81 K9 31 9N 90 28W
Magog, Canada 71 C5 45 18N 72 9W
Magoro, Uganda 54 B3 1 45N 34 12 E
Magosa = Famagusta, Cyprus 23 D12 35 8N 33 55 E
Magouládhes, Greece 23 A3 39 45N 19 42 E
Magoye, Zambia 55 F2 16 1S 27 30 E
Magpie L., Canada 71 B7 51 0N 64 41W
Magrath, Canada 72 D6 49 25N 112 50W
Magu □, Tanzania 54 C3 2 31S 33 28 E
Maguarinho, C., Brazil 93 D9 0 15S 48 30W
Mağusa = Famagusta, Cyprus 23 D12 35 8N 33 55 E
Maguse L., Canada 73 A9 61 40N 95 10W
Maguse Pt., Canada 73 A10 61 20N 93 50W
Magwe, Burma 41 J19 20 10N 95 0 E
Maha Sarakham, Thailand 38 D4 16 12N 103 16 E
Mahābād, Iran 44 B5 36 50N 45 45 E
Mahabharat Lekh, Nepal 43 E9 28 30N 82 0 E
Mahabo, Madag. 57 C7 20 23S 44 40 E
Mahadeo Hills, India 42 H8 22 20N 78 30 E
Mahagi, Zaïre 54 B3 2 20N 31 0 E
Mahajamba —►, Madag. 57 B8 15 33S 47 8 E
Mahajamba, Helodranon' i, Madag. 57 B8 15 24S 47 5 E
Mahajan, India 42 E5 28 48N 73 56 E
Mahajanga, Madag. 57 B8 15 40S 46 25 E
Mahajanga □, Madag. 57 B8 17 0S 47 0 E
Mahajilo —►, Madag. 57 B8 19 42S 45 22 E
Mahakam —►, Indonesia 36 E5 0 35S 117 17 E
Mahalapye, Botswana 56 C4 23 1S 26 51 E
Maḩallāt, Iran 45 C6 33 55N 50 30 E
Māhān, Iran 45 D8 30 5N 57 18 E
Mahanadi —►, India 41 J15 20 20N 86 25 E
Mahanoro, Madag. 57 B8 19 54S 48 48 E
Mahanoy City, U.S.A. 79 F8 40 49N 76 9W
Maharashtra □, India 40 J9 20 30N 75 30 E
Mahari Mts., Tanzania 54 D2 6 20S 30 0 E
Mahasham, W. —►, Egypt 47 E3 30 15N 34 10 E
Mahasolo, Madag. 57 B8 19 7S 46 22 E
Mahattat ash Shīdīyah, Jordan 47 F4 29 55N 35 55 E
Mahattat 'Unayzah, Jordan 47 E4 30 30N 35 47 E
Mahaxay, Laos 38 D5 17 22N 105 12 E
Mahbubnagar, India 40 L10 16 45N 77 59 E
Maḩḑah, Oman 45 E7 24 24N 55 59 E
Mahdia, Tunisia 51 A7 35 28N 11 0 E
Mahe, India 43 C8 33 10N 78 32 E
Mahenge, Tanzania 55 D4 8 45S 36 41 E
Maheno, N.Z. 59 L3 45 10S 170 50 E
Mahesana, India 42 H5 23 39N 72 26 E
Mahia Pen., N.Z. 59 H6 39 9S 177 55 E
Mahilyow, Belarus 17 B16 53 55N 30 18 E
Mahmud Kot, Pakistan 42 D4 30 16N 71 0 E
Mahnomen, U.S.A. 80 B7 47 19N 95 58W
Mahoba, India 43 G8 25 15N 79 55 E
Mahón, Spain 22 B11 39 53N 4 16 E
Mahone Bay, Canada 71 D7 44 30N 64 20W
Mai-Ndombe, L., Zaïre 52 E3 2 0S 18 20 E
Mai-Sai, Thailand 38 B2 20 20N 99 55 E
Maicurú —►, Brazil 93 D8 2 14S 54 17W
Maidan Khula, Afghan. 42 C3 33 36N 69 50 E
Maidenhead, U.K. 11 F7 51 31N 0 42W
Maidstone, Canada 73 C7 53 5N 109 20W
Maidstone, U.K. 11 F8 51 16N 0 32 E
Maiduguri, Nigeria 51 F7 12 0N 13 20 E
Maijdi, Bangla. 41 H17 22 48N 91 10 E
Maikala Ra., India 41 J12 22 0N 81 0 E
Mailsi, Pakistan 42 E5 29 48N 72 15 E
Main —►, Germany 16 C5 50 0N 8 18 E
Main —►, U.K. 13 B5 54 48N 6 18W
Main Centre, Canada 73 C7 50 35N 107 21W
Maine, France 18 C3 47 55N 0 25W
Maine □, U.S.A. 71 C6 45 20N 69 0W
Maine —►, Ireland 13 D2 52 9N 9 45W
Maingkwan, Burma 41 F20 26 15N 96 37 E
Mainit, L., Phil. 37 C7 9 31N 125 30 E
Mainland, Orkney, U.K. 12 C5 58 59N 3 8W
Mainland, Shet., U.K. 12 A7 60 15N 1 22W
Mainpuri, India 43 F8 27 18N 79 4 E
Maintirano, Madag. 57 B7 18 3S 44 1 E
Mainz, Germany 16 C5 50 1N 8 14 E
Maipú, Argentina 94 D4 36 52S 57 50W
Maiquetía, Venezuela 92 A5 10 36N 66 57W
Mairabari, India 41 F18 26 30N 92 22 E
Maisi, Cuba 89 B5 20 17N 74 9W
Maisi, Pta. de, Cuba 89 B5 20 10N 74 10W
Maitland, N.S.W., Australia 63 E5 32 33S 151 36 E
Maitland, S. Austral., Australia 63 E2 34 23S 137 40 E
Maitland —►, Canada 78 C3 43 45N 81 43W
Maiz, Is. del, Nic. 88 D3 12 15N 83 4W
Maizuru, Japan 31 G7 35 25N 135 22 E
Majalengka, Indonesia 37 G13 6 50S 108 13 E
Majene, Indonesia 37 E5 3 38S 118 57 E
Maji, Ethiopia 51 G12 6 12N 35 30 E
Major, Canada 73 C7 51 52N 109 37W
Majorca = Mallorca, Spain 22 B10 39 30N 3 0 E
Maka, Senegal 50 F2 13 40N 14 10W
Makale, Indonesia 37 E5 3 6S 119 51 E
Makamba, Burundi 54 C2 4 8S 29 49 E
Makari, Cameroon 52 B2 12 35N 14 28 E
Makarikari = Makgadikgadi Salt Pans, Botswana 56 C4 20 40S 25 45 E
Makarovo, Russia 27 D11 57 40N 107 45 E
Makasar = Ujung Pandang, Indonesia 37 F5 5 10S 119 20 E
Makasar, Selat, Indonesia 37 E5 1 0S 118 20 E
Makasar, Str. of = Makasar, Selat, Indonesia 37 E5 1 0S 118 20 E
Makat, Kazakstan 25 E9 47 39N 53 19 E
Makedhonía □, Greece 21 D10 40 39N 22 0 E
Makedonija = Macedonia ■, Europe 21 D9 41 53N 21 40 E
Makena, U.S.A. 74 H16 20 39N 156 27W
Makeni, S. Leone 50 G2 8 55N 12 5W
Makeyevka = Makiyivka, Ukraine 25 E6 48 0N 38 0 E
Makgadikgadi Salt Pans, Botswana 56 C4 20 40S 25 45 E
Makhachkala, Russia 25 F8 43 0N 47 30 E
Makhmūr, Iraq 44 C4 35 46N 43 35 E
Makian, Indonesia 37 D7 0 20N 127 20 E
Makindu, Kenya 54 C4 2 18S 37 50 E
Makinsk, Kazakstan 26 D8 52 37N 70 26 E
Makiyivka, Ukraine 25 E6 48 0N 38 0 E
Makkah, Si. Arabia 46 C2 21 30N 39 54 E
Makkovik, Canada 71 A8 55 10N 59 10W
Makó, Hungary 17 E11 46 14N 20 33 E
Makokou, Gabon 52 D2 0 40N 12 50 E
Makongo, Zaïre 54 B2 3 25N 26 17 E
Makoro, Zaïre 54 B2 3 10N 29 59 E
Makoua, Congo 52 E3 0 5S 15 50 E
Makrai, India 40 H10 22 2N 77 0 E
Makran Coast Range, Pakistan 40 G4 25 40N 64 0 E
Makrana, India 42 F6 27 2N 74 46 E
Makriyialos, Greece 23 D7 35 2N 25 59 E
Maksimkin Yar, Russia 26 D9 58 42N 86 50 E
Mākū, Iran 44 B5 39 15N 44 31 E
Makumbi, Zaïre 52 F4 5 50S 20 43 E
Makunda, Botswana 56 C3 22 30S 20 7 E
Makurazaki, Japan 31 J5 31 15N 130 20 E
Makurdi, Nigeria 50 G6 7 43N 8 35 E
Makūyeh, Iran 45 D7 28 7N 53 9 E
Makwassie, S. Africa 56 D4 27 17S 26 0 E
Mal B., Ireland 13 D2 52 50N 9 30W
Mala, Pta., Panama 88 E3 7 28N 80 2W
Malabang, Phil. 37 C6 7 36N 124 3 E
Malabar Coast, India 40 P9 11 0N 75 0 E
Malabo = Rey Malabo, Eq. Guin. 50 H6 3 45N 8 50 E
Malacca, Str. of, Indonesia 39 L3 3 0N 101 0 E
Malad City, U.S.A. 82 E7 42 12N 112 15W
Maladzyechna, Belarus 17 A14 54 20N 26 50 E
Málaga, Spain 19 D3 36 43N 4 23W
Malaga, U.S.A. 81 J2 32 14N 104 4W
Malagarasi, Tanzania 54 D3 5 5S 30 50 E
Malagarasi —►, Tanzania 54 D2 5 12S 29 47 E
Malaimbandy, Madag. 57 C8 20 20S 45 36 E
Malakâl, Sudan 51 G11 9 33N 31 40 E
Malakand, Pakistan 42 B4 34 40N 71 55 E
Malakoff, U.S.A. 81 J7 32 10N 96 1W
Malamyzh, Russia 27 E14 49 50N 136 50 E
Malang, Indonesia 37 G15 7 59S 112 45 E
Malangen, Norway 8 B18 69 24N 18 37 E
Malanje, Angola 52 F3 9 36S 16 17 E
Mälaren, Sweden 9 G17 59 30N 17 10 E
Malargüe, Argentina 94 D2 35 32S 69 30W
Malartic, Canada 70 C4 48 9N 78 9W
Malaryta, Belarus 17 C13 51 50N 24 3 E
Malatya, Turkey 25 G6 38 25N 38 20 E
Malawi ■, Africa 55 E3 11 55S 34 0 E
Malawi, L., Africa 55 E3 12 30S 34 30 E
Malay Pen., Asia 39 J3 7 25N 100 0 E
Malaybalay, Phil. 37 C7 8 5N 125 7 E
Malāyer, Iran 45 C6 34 19N 48 51 E
Malaysia ■, Asia 36 D4 5 0N 110 0 E
Malazgirt, Turkey 25 G7 39 10N 42 33 E
Malbon, Australia 62 C3 21 5S 140 17 E
Malbooma, Australia 63 E1 30 41S 134 11 E
Malbork, Poland 17 B10 54 3N 19 1 E
Malcolm, Australia 61 E3 28 51S 121 25 E
Malcolm, Pt., Australia 61 F3 33 48S 123 45 E
Maldegem, Belgium 15 C3 51 14N 3 26 E
Malden, Mass., U.S.A. 79 D13 42 26N 71 4W
Malden, Mo., U.S.A. 81 G10 36 34N 89 57W
Malden I., Kiribati 65 H12 4 3S 155 1W
Maldives ■, Ind. Oc. 29 J11 5 0N 73 0 E
Maldonado, Uruguay 95 C5 34 59S 55 0W
Maldonado, Punta, Mexico 87 D5 16 19N 98 35W
Malé Karpaty, Slovak Rep. 17 D9 48 30N 17 20 E
Maléa, Ákra, Greece 21 F10 36 28N 23 7 E
Malegaon, India 40 J9 20 30N 74 38 E
Malei, Mozam. 55 F4 17 12S 36 58 E
Malek Kandī, Iran 44 B5 37 9N 46 6 E
Malela, Zaïre 54 C2 4 22S 26 8 E
Malema, Mozam. 55 E4 14 57S 37 20 E
Máleme, Greece 23 D5 35 31N 23 49 E
Malerkotla, India 42 D6 30 32N 75 58 E
Máles, Greece 23 D7 35 6N 25 35 E
Malgomaj, Sweden 8 D17 64 40N 16 30 E
Malha, Sudan 51 E10 15 8N 25 10 E
Malheur —►, U.S.A. 82 D5 44 4N 116 59W
Malheur L., U.S.A. 82 E4 43 20N 118 48W
Mali ■, Africa 50 E4 17 0N 3 0W
Mali —►, Burma 41 G20 25 40N 97 40 E
Malibu, U.S.A. 85 L8 34 2N 118 41W
Malik, Indonesia 37 E6 0 39S 123 16 E
Malili, Indonesia 37 E6 2 42S 121 6 E
Malimba, Mts., Zaïre 54 D2 7 30S 29 30 E
Malin Hd., Ireland 13 A4 55 23N 7 23W
Malindi, Kenya 54 C5 3 12S 40 5 E
Malines = Mechelen, Belgium 15 C4 51 2N 4 29 E
Malino, Indonesia 37 D6 1 0N 121 0 E
Malinyi, Tanzania 55 D4 8 56S 36 0 E
Malita, Phil. 37 C7 6 19N 125 39 E
Malkara, Turkey 21 D12 40 53N 26 53 E
Mallacoota, Australia 63 F4 37 40S 149 40 E
Mallacoota Inlet, Australia 63 F4 37 34S 149 40 E
Mallaig, U.K. 12 E3 57 0N 5 50W
Mallawan, India 43 F9 27 4N 80 12 E
Mallawi, Egypt 51 C11 27 44N 30 44 E
Mállia, Greece 23 D7 35 17N 25 27 E
Mallión, Kólpos, Greece 23 D7 35 19N 25 27 E
Mallorca, Spain 22 B10 39 30N 3 0 E
Mallorytown, Canada 79 B9 44 29N 75 53W
Mallow, Ireland 13 D3 52 8N 8 39W
Malmberget, Sweden 8 C19 67 11N 20 40 E
Malmédy, Belgium 15 D6 50 25N 6 2 E
Malmesbury, S. Africa 56 E2 33 28S 18 41 E
Malmö, Sweden 9 J15 55 36N 12 59 E
Malolos, Phil. 37 B6 14 50N 120 49 E
Malombe L., Malawi 55 E4 14 40S 35 15 E
Malone, U.S.A. 79 B10 44 51N 74 18W
Måløy, Norway 9 F11 61 57N 5 6 E
Malozemelskaya Tundra, Russia 24 A9 67 0N 50 0 E
Malpaso, Canary Is. 22 G1 27 43N 18 3W
Malpelo, Colombia 92 C2 4 3N 81 35W
Malta, Idaho, U.S.A. 82 E7 42 18N 113 22W
Malta, Mont., U.S.A. 82 B10 48 21N 107 52W
Malta ■, Europe 23 D1 35 50N 14 30 E
Maltahöhe, Namibia 56 C2 24 55S 17 0 E
Malton, Canada 78 C5 43 42N 79 38W
Malton, U.K. 10 C7 54 8N 0 49W
Maluku, Indonesia 37 E7 1 0S 127 0 E
Maluku □, Indonesia 37 E7 3 0S 128 0 E

Maluku Sea

Maluku Sea = Molucca Sea, Indonesia 37 E6 2 0S 124 0 E
Malvan, India 40 L8 16 2N 73 30 E
Malvern, U.S.A. 81 H8 34 22N 92 49W
Malvern Hills, U.K. 11 E5 52 0N 2 19W
Malvinas, Is. = Falkland Is. □, Atl. Oc. 96 G5 51 30S 59 0W
Malya, Tanzania 54 C3 3 5S 33 38 E
Malyn, Ukraine 17 C15 50 46N 29 3 E
Malyy Lyakhovskiy, Ostrov, Russia 27 B15 74 7N 140 36 E
Malyy Nimnyr, Russia 27 D13 57 50N 125 10 E
Mama, Russia 27 D12 58 18N 112 54 E
Mamanguape, Brazil 93 E11 6 50S 35 4W
Mamasa, Indonesia 37 E5 2 55S 119 20 E
Mambasa, Zaïre 54 B2 1 22N 29 3 E
Mamberamo →, Indonesia 37 E9 2 0S 137 50 E
Mambilima Falls, Zambia 55 E2 10 31S 28 45 E
Mambirima, Zaïre 55 E2 11 25S 27 33 E
Mambo, Tanzania 54 C4 4 52S 38 22 E
Mambrui, Kenya 54 C5 3 5S 40 5 E
Mamburao, Phil. 37 B6 13 13N 120 39 E
Mameigwess L., Canada 70 B2 52 35N 87 50W
Mamfe, Cameroon 50 G6 5 50N 9 15 E
Mammoth, U.S.A. 83 K8 32 43N 110 39W
Mamoré →, Bolivia 92 F5 10 23S 65 53W
Mamou, Guinea 50 F2 10 15N 12 0W
Mamuju, Indonesia 37 E5 2 41S 118 50 E
Man, Ivory C. 50 G3 7 30N 7 40W
Man, I. of, U.K. 10 C3 54 15N 4 30W
Man Na, Burma 41 H20 23 27N 97 19 E
Mana, Fr. Guiana 93 B8 5 45N 53 55W
Manaar, G. of = Mannar, G. of, Asia 40 Q11 8 30N 79 0 E
Manacapuru, Brazil 92 D6 3 16S 60 37W
Manacor, Spain 22 B10 39 34N 3 13 E
Manado, Indonesia 37 D6 1 29N 124 51 E
Managua, Nic. 88 D2 12 6N 86 20W
Managua, L., Nic. 88 D2 12 20N 86 30W
Manakara, Madag. 57 C8 22 8S 48 1 E
Manama = Al Manāmah, Bahrain 45 E6 26 10N 50 30 E
Manambao →, Madag. 57 B7 17 35S 44 0 E
Manambato, Madag. 57 A8 13 43S 49 7 E
Manambolo →, Madag. 57 B7 19 18S 44 22 E
Manambolosy, Madag. 57 B8 16 2S 49 40 E
Mananara, Madag. 57 B8 16 10S 49 46 E
Mananara →, Madag. 57 C8 23 21S 47 42 E
Mananjary, Madag. 57 C8 21 13S 48 20 E
Manantenina, Madag. 57 C8 24 17S 47 19 E
Manaos = Manaus, Brazil 92 D7 3 0S 60 0W
Manapouri, N.Z. 59 L1 45 34S 167 39 E
Manapouri, L., N.Z. 59 L1 45 32S 167 32 E
Manas, China 32 B3 44 17N 85 56 E
Manas →, India 41 F17 26 12N 90 40 E
Manaslu, Nepal 43 E11 28 33N 84 33 E
Manasquan, U.S.A. 79 F10 40 8N 74 3W
Manassa, U.S.A. 83 H11 37 11N 105 56W
Manaung, Burma 41 K18 18 45N 93 40 E
Manaus, Brazil 92 D7 3 0S 60 0W
Manawan L., Canada 73 B8 55 24N 103 14W
Manay, Phil. 37 C7 7 17N 126 33 E
Manbij, Syria 44 B3 36 31N 37 57 E
Mancelona, U.S.A. 76 C3 44 54N 85 4W
Manchester, U.K. 10 D5 53 29N 2 12W
Manchester, Calif., U.S.A. 84 G3 38 58N 123 41W
Manchester, Conn., U.S.A. 79 E12 41 47N 72 31W
Manchester, Ga., U.S.A. 77 J3 32 51N 84 37W
Manchester, Iowa, U.S.A. 80 D9 42 29N 91 27W
Manchester, Ky., U.S.A. 76 G4 37 9N 83 46W
Manchester, N.H., U.S.A. 79 D13 42 59N 71 28W
Manchester, N.Y., U.S.A. 78 D7 42 56N 77 16W
Manchester, Vt., U.S.A. 79 C11 43 10N 73 5W
Manchester L., Canada 73 A7 61 28N 107 29W
Manchuria = Dongbei, China 35 D13 42 0N 125 0 E
Manchurian Plain, China 28 E16 47 0N 124 0 E
Mand →, Iran 45 D7 28 20N 52 30 E
Manda, Chunya, Tanzania 54 D3 6 51S 32 29 E
Manda, Ludewe, Tanzania 55 E3 10 30S 34 40 E
Mandabé, Madag. 57 C7 21 0S 44 55 E
Mandaguari, Brazil 95 A5 23 32S 51 42W
Mandah, Mongolia 34 B5 44 27N 108 2 E
Mandal, Norway 9 G12 58 2N 7 25 E
Mandalay, Burma 41 J20 22 0N 96 4 E
Mandale = Mandalay, Burma 41 J20 22 0N 96 4 E
Mandalgovi, Mongolia 34 B4 45 45N 106 10 E
Mandalī, Iraq 44 C5 33 43N 45 28 E
Mandan, U.S.A. 80 B4 46 50N 100 54W
Mandar, Teluk, Indonesia 37 E5 3 35S 119 15 E
Mandaue, Phil. 37 B6 10 20N 123 56 E
Mandera, Kenya 54 B5 3 55N 41 53 E
Mandera □, Kenya 54 B5 3 30N 41 0 E
Mandi, India 42 D7 31 39N 76 58 E
Mandimba, Mozam. 55 E4 14 20S 35 40 E
Mandioli, Indonesia 37 E7 0 40S 127 20 E
Mandla, India 43 H9 22 39N 80 30 E
Mandoto, Madag. 57 B8 19 34S 46 17 E
Mandra, Pakistan 42 C5 33 23N 73 12 E
Mandrare →, Madag. 57 D8 25 10S 46 30 E
Mandritsara, Madag. 57 B8 15 50S 48 49 E
Mandsaur, India 42 G6 24 3N 75 8 E
Mandurah, Australia 61 F2 32 36S 115 48 E
Mandvi, India 42 H3 22 51N 69 22 E
Mandya, India 40 N10 12 30N 77 0 E
Mandzai, Pakistan 42 D2 30 55N 67 6 E
Maneh, Iran 45 B8 37 39N 57 7 E
Maneroo, Australia 62 C3 23 22S 143 53 E
Maneroo Cr. →, Australia 62 C3 23 21S 143 53 E
Manfalût, Egypt 51 C11 27 20N 30 52 E
Manfred, Australia 63 E3 33 19S 143 45 E
Manfredónia, Italy 20 D6 41 38N 15 55 E
Mangalia, Romania 17 G15 43 50N 28 35 E
Mangalore, India 40 N9 12 55N 74 47 E
Mangaweka, N.Z. 59 H5 39 48S 175 47 E
Manggar, Indonesia 36 E3 2 50S 108 10 E
Manggawitu, Indonesia 37 E8 4 8S 133 32 E
Mangkalihat, Tanjung, Indonesia 37 D5 1 2N 118 59 E
Mangla Dam, Pakistan 43 C5 33 9N 73 44 E
Manglaur, India 42 E7 29 44N 77 49 E
Mangnai, China 32 C4 37 52N 91 43 E
Mango, Togo 50 F5 10 20N 0 30 E
Mangoche, Malawi 55 E4 14 25S 35 16 E
Mangoky →, Madag. 57 C7 21 29S 43 41 E
Mangole, Indonesia 37 E7 1 50S 125 55 E
Mangombe, Zaïre 54 C2 1 20S 26 48 E
Mangonui, N.Z. 59 F4 35 1S 173 32 E
Mangueigne, Chad 51 F9 10 30N 21 15 E
Mangueira, L. da, Brazil 95 C5 33 0S 52 50W
Mangum, U.S.A. 81 H5 34 53N 99 30W
Mangyshlak Poluostrov, Kazakstan 26 E6 44 30N 52 30 E
Manhattan, U.S.A. 80 F6 39 11N 96 35W
Manhiça, Mozam. 57 D5 25 23S 32 49 E
Manhuaçu, Brazil 93 H10 20 15S 42 2W
Mania →, Madag. 57 B8 19 42S 45 22 E
Manica, Mozam. 57 B5 18 58S 32 59 E
Manica e Sofala □, Mozam. 57 B5 19 10S 33 45 E
Manicaland □, Zimbabwe 55 F3 19 0S 32 30 E
Manicoré, Brazil 92 E6 5 48S 61 16W
Manicouagan →, Canada 71 C6 49 30N 68 30W
Manīfah, Si. Arabia 45 E6 27 44N 49 0 E
Manifold, Australia 62 C5 22 41S 150 40 E
Manifold, C., Australia 62 C5 22 41S 150 50 E
Manigotagan, Canada 73 C9 51 6N 96 18W
Manihiki, Cook Is. 65 J11 10 24S 161 1W
Manika, Plateau de la, Zaïre 55 E2 10 0S 25 5 E
Manila, Phil. 37 B6 14 40N 121 3 E
Manila, U.S.A. 82 F9 40 59N 109 43W
Manila B., Phil. 37 B6 14 40N 120 35 E
Manilla, Australia 63 E5 30 45S 150 43 E
Maningrida, Australia 62 A1 12 3S 134 13 E
Manipur □, India 41 G18 25 0N 94 0 E
Manipur →, Burma 41 H19 23 45N 94 20 E
Manisa, Turkey 21 E12 38 38N 27 30 E
Manistee, U.S.A. 76 C2 44 15N 86 19W
Manistee →, U.S.A. 76 C2 44 15N 86 21W
Manistique, U.S.A. 76 C2 45 57N 86 15W
Manito L., Canada 73 C7 52 43N 109 43W
Manitoba □, Canada 73 B9 55 30N 97 0W
Manitoba, L., Canada 73 C9 51 0N 98 45W
Manitou, Canada 73 D9 49 15N 98 32W
Manitou I., U.S.A. 70 C2 47 25N 87 37W
Manitou Is., U.S.A. 76 C2 45 8N 86 0W
Manitou L., Canada 71 B6 50 55N 65 17W
Manitou Springs, U.S.A. 80 F2 38 52N 104 55W
Manitoulin I., Canada 70 C3 45 40N 82 30W
Manitowaning, Canada 70 C3 45 46N 81 49W
Manitowoc, U.S.A. 76 C2 44 5N 87 40W
Manizales, Colombia 92 B3 5 5N 75 32W
Manja, Madag. 57 C7 21 26S 44 20 E
Manjacaze, Mozam. 57 C5 24 45S 34 0 E
Manjakandriana, Madag. 57 B8 18 55S 47 47 E
Manjhand, Pakistan 42 G3 25 50N 68 10 E
Manjil, Iran 45 B6 36 46N 49 30 E
Manjimup, Australia 61 F2 34 15S 116 6 E
Manjra →, India 40 K10 18 49N 77 52 E
Mankato, Kans., U.S.A. 80 F5 39 47N 98 13W
Mankato, Minn., U.S.A. 80 C8 44 10N 94 0W
Mankayane, Swaziland 57 D5 26 40S 31 4 E
Mankono, Ivory C. 50 G3 8 1N 6 10W
Mankota, Canada 73 D7 49 25N 107 5W
Manlay, Mongolia 34 B4 44 9N 107 0 E
Manly, Australia 63 E5 33 48S 151 17 E
Manmad, India 40 J9 20 18N 74 28 E
Mann Ras., Australia 61 E5 26 6S 130 5 E
Manna, Indonesia 36 E2 4 25S 102 55 E
Mannahill, Australia 63 E3 32 25S 140 0 E
Mannar, Sri Lanka 40 Q11 9 1N 79 54 E
Mannar, G. of, Asia 40 Q11 8 30N 79 0 E
Mannar I., Sri Lanka 40 Q11 9 5N 79 45 E
Mannheim, Germany 16 D5 49 29N 8 29 E
Manning, Canada 72 B5 56 53N 117 39W
Manning, Oreg., U.S.A. 84 E3 45 45N 123 13W
Manning, S.C., U.S.A. 77 J5 33 42N 80 13W
Manning Prov. Park, Canada 72 D4 49 5N 120 45W
Mannington, U.S.A. 76 F5 39 32N 80 21W
Mannum, Australia 63 E2 34 50S 139 20 E
Mano, S. Leone 50 G2 8 3N 12 2W
Manokwari, Indonesia 37 E8 0 54S 134 0 E
Manombo, Madag. 57 C7 22 57S 43 28 E
Manono, Zaïre 54 D2 7 15S 27 25 E
Manosque, France 18 E6 43 49N 5 47 E
Manouane, L., Canada 71 B5 50 45N 70 45W
Manpojin, N. Korea 35 D14 41 6N 126 24 E
Manresa, Spain 19 B6 41 48N 1 50 E
Mansa, Gujarat, India 42 H5 23 27N 72 45 E
Mansa, Punjab, India 42 E6 30 0N 75 27 E
Mansa, Zambia 55 E2 11 13S 28 55 E
Mansehra, Pakistan 42 B5 34 20N 73 15 E
Mansel I., Canada 69 B11 62 0N 80 0W
Mansfield, Australia 63 F4 37 4S 146 6 E
Mansfield, U.K. 10 D6 53 9N 1 11W
Mansfield, La., U.S.A. 81 J8 32 2N 93 43W
Mansfield, Mass., U.S.A. 79 D13 42 2N 71 13W
Mansfield, Ohio, U.S.A. 78 F2 40 45N 82 31W
Mansfield, Pa., U.S.A. 78 E7 41 48N 77 5W
Mansfield, Wash., U.S.A. 82 C4 47 49N 119 38W
Manson Creek, Canada 72 B4 55 37N 124 32W
Manta, Ecuador 92 D2 1 0S 80 40W
Mantalingajan, Mt., Phil. 36 C5 8 55N 117 45 E
Mantare, Tanzania 54 C3 2 42S 33 13 E
Manteca, U.S.A. 83 H3 37 48N 121 13W
Manteo, U.S.A. 77 H8 35 55N 75 40W
Mantes-la-Jolie, France 18 B4 48 58N 1 41 E
Manthani, India 40 K11 18 40N 79 35 E
Manti, U.S.A. 82 G8 39 16N 111 38W
Mantiqueira, Serra da, Brazil 95 A7 22 0S 44 0W
Manton, U.S.A. 76 C3 44 25N 85 24W
Mántova, Italy 20 B4 45 9N 10 48 E
Mänttä, Finland 9 E21 62 0N 24 40 E
Mantua = Mántova, Italy 20 B4 45 9N 10 48 E
Manu, Peru 92 F4 12 10S 70 51W
Manua Is., Amer. Samoa 59 B14 14 13S 169 35W
Manuae, Cook Is. 65 J12 19 30S 159 0W
Manuel Alves →, Brazil 93 F9 11 19S 48 28W
Manui, Indonesia 37 E6 3 35S 123 5 E
Manville, U.S.A. 80 D2 42 47N 104 37W
Many, U.S.A. 81 K8 31 34N 93 29W
Manyara, L., Tanzania 54 C4 3 40S 35 50 E
Manych-Gudilo, Ozero, Russia 25 E7 46 24N 42 38 E
Manyonga →, Tanzania 54 C3 4 10S 34 15 E
Manyoni, Tanzania 54 D3 5 45S 34 55 E
Manyoni □, Tanzania 54 D3 6 30S 34 30 E
Manzai, Pakistan 42 C4 32 12N 70 15 E
Manzanares, Spain 19 C4 39 2N 3 22W
Manzanillo, Cuba 88 B4 20 20N 77 31W
Manzanillo, Mexico 86 D4 19 0N 104 20W
Manzanillo, Pta., Panama 88 E4 9 30N 79 40W
Manzano Mts., U.S.A. 83 J10 34 40N 106 20W
Manzarīyeh, Iran 45 C6 34 53N 50 50 E
Manzhouli, China 33 B6 49 35N 117 25 E
Manzini, Swaziland 57 D5 26 30S 31 25 E
Mao, Chad 51 F8 14 4N 15 19 E
Maoke, Pegunungan, Indonesia 37 E9 3 40S 137 30 E
Maolin, China 35 C12 43 58N 123 30 E
Maoming, China 33 D6 21 50N 110 54 E
Maoxing, China 35 B13 45 28N 124 40 E
Mapam Yumco, China 32 C3 30 45N 81 28 E
Mapastepec, Mexico 87 D6 15 26N 92 54W
Mapia, Kepulauan, Indonesia 37 D8 0 50N 134 20 E
Mapimí, Mexico 86 B4 25 50N 103 50W
Mapimí, Bolsón de, Mexico 86 B4 27 30N 104 15W
Mapinga, Tanzania 54 D4 6 40S 39 12 E
Mapinhane, Mozam. 57 C6 22 20S 35 0 E
Maple Creek, Canada 73 D7 49 55N 109 29W
Maple Valley, U.S.A. 84 C4 47 25N 122 3W
Mapleton, U.S.A. 82 D2 44 2N 123 52W
Mapuera →, Brazil 92 D7 1 5S 57 2W
Maputo, Mozam. 57 D5 25 58S 32 32 E
Maputo, B. de, Mozam. 57 D5 25 50S 32 45 E
Maqiaohe, China 35 B16 44 40N 130 30 E
Maqnā, Si. Arabia 44 D2 28 25N 34 50 E
Maquela do Zombo, Angola 52 F3 6 0S 15 15 E
Maquinchao, Argentina 96 E3 41 15S 68 50W
Maquoketa, U.S.A. 80 D9 42 4N 90 40W
Mar, Serra do, Brazil 95 B6 25 30S 49 0W
Mar Chiquita, L., Argentina 94 C3 30 40S 62 50W
Mar del Plata, Argentina 94 D4 38 0S 57 30W
Mar Menor, Spain 19 D5 37 40N 0 45W
Mara, Tanzania 54 C3 1 30S 34 32 E
Mara □, Tanzania 54 C3 1 45S 34 20 E
Maraã, Brazil 92 D5 1 52S 65 25W
Marabá, Brazil 93 E9 5 20S 49 5W
Maracá, I. de, Brazil 93 C8 2 10N 50 30W
Maracaibo, Venezuela 92 A4 10 40N 71 37W
Maracaibo, L. de, Venezuela 92 B4 9 40N 71 30W
Maracaju, Brazil 95 A4 21 38S 55 9W
Maracay, Venezuela 92 A5 10 15N 67 28W
Marādah, Libya 51 C8 29 15N 19 15 E
Maradi, Niger 50 F6 13 29N 7 20 E
Marāgheh, Iran 44 B5 37 30N 46 12 E
Marāh, Si. Arabia 44 E5 25 0N 45 35 E
Marajó, I. de, Brazil 93 D9 1 0S 49 30W
Marākand, Iran 44 B5 38 51N 45 16 E
Maralal, Kenya 54 B4 1 0N 36 38 E
Maralinga, Australia 61 F5 30 13S 131 32 E
Marama, Australia 63 F3 35 10S 140 10 E
Marampa, S. Leone 50 G2 8 45N 12 28W
Maran, Malaysia 39 L4 3 35N 102 45 E
Marana, U.S.A. 83 K8 32 27N 111 13W
Maranboy, Australia 60 B5 14 40S 132 39 E
Marand, Iran 44 B5 38 30N 45 45 E
Marang, Malaysia 39 K4 5 12N 103 13 E
Maranguape, Brazil 93 D11 3 55S 38 50W
Maranhão = São Luís, Brazil 93 D10 2 39S 44 15W
Maranhão □, Brazil 93 E9 5 0S 46 0W
Maranoa →, Australia 63 D4 27 50S 148 37 E
Marañón →, Peru 92 D4 4 30S 73 35W
Marão, Mozam. 57 C5 24 18S 34 2 E
Maraş = Kahramanmaraş, Turkey 25 G6 37 37N 36 53 E
Marathasa □, Cyprus 23 E11 34 59N 32 51 E
Marathon, Australia 62 C3 20 51S 143 32 E
Marathon, Canada 70 C2 48 44N 86 23W
Marathon, N.Y., U.S.A. 79 D8 42 27N 76 2W
Marathon, Tex., U.S.A. 81 K3 30 12N 103 15W
Marathóvouno, Cyprus 23 D12 35 13N 33 37 E
Maratua, Indonesia 37 D5 2 10N 118 35 E
Maravatío, Mexico 86 D4 19 51N 100 25W
Marāwih, U.A.E. 45 E7 24 18N 53 18 E
Marbella, Spain 19 D3 36 30N 4 57W
Marble Bar, Australia 60 D2 21 9S 119 44 E
Marble Falls, U.S.A. 81 K5 30 35N 98 16W
Marblehead, U.S.A. 79 D14 42 30N 70 51W
Marburg, Germany 16 C5 50 47N 8 46 E
March, U.K. 11 E8 52 33N 0 5 E
Marche, France 18 C4 46 5N 1 20 E
Marche-en-Famenne, Belgium 15 D5 50 14N 5 19 E
Marchena, Spain 19 D3 37 18N 5 23W
Marcos Juárez, Argentina 94 C3 32 42S 62 5W
Marcus I. = Minami-Tori-Shima, Pac. Oc. 64 E7 24 0N 153 45 E
Marcus Necker Ridge, Pac. Oc. 64 F9 20 0N 175 0 E
Marcy, Mt., U.S.A. 79 B11 44 7N 73 56W
Mardan, Pakistan 42 B5 34 20N 72 0 E
Mardie, Australia 60 D2 21 12S 115 59 E
Mardin, Turkey 25 G7 37 20N 40 43 E
Maree, L., U.K. 12 D3 57 40N 5 26W
Mareeba, Australia 62 B4 16 59S 145 28 E
Marek = Stanke Dimitrov, Bulgaria 21 C10 42 17N 23 9 E
Marek, Indonesia 37 E6 4 41S 120 24 E
Marengo, U.S.A. 80 E8 41 48N 92 4W
Marenyi, Kenya 54 C4 4 22S 39 8 E
Marerano, Madag. 57 C7 21 23S 44 52 E
Marfa, U.S.A. 81 K2 30 19N 104 1W
Marfa Pt., Malta 23 D1 35 59N 14 19 E
Margaret →, Australia 60 C4 18 9S 125 41 E
Margaret Bay, Canada 72 C3 51 20N 127 35W
Margaret L., Canada 72 B5 58 56N 115 25W
Margaret River, Australia 60 C4 18 38S 126 52 E
Margarita, I. de, Venezuela 92 A6 11 0N 64 0W
Margaritovo, Russia 30 C7 43 25N 134 45 E
Margate, S. Africa 57 E5 30 50S 30 20 E
Margate, U.K. 11 F9 51 23N 1 23 E
Margelan = Marghilon, Uzbekistan 26 E8 40 27N 71 42 E
Marghilon, Uzbekistan 26 E8 40 27N 71 42 E
Marguerite, Canada 72 C4 52 30N 122 25W
Mari El □, Russia 24 C8 56 30N 48 0 E
Mari Republic □ = Mari El □, Russia 24 C8 56 30N 48 0 E
María Elena, Chile 94 A2 22 18S 69 40W
María Grande, Argentina 94 C4 31 45S 59 55W
Maria I., N. Terr., Australia 62 A2 14 52S 135 45 E
Maria I., Tas., Australia 62 G4 42 35S 148 0 E
Maria van Diemen, C., N.Z. 59 F4 34 29S 172 40 E
Mariakani, Kenya 54 C4 3 50S 39 27 E
Marian L., Canada 72 A5 63 0N 116 15W
Mariana Trench, Pac. Oc. 28 H18 13 0N 145 0 E
Marianao, Cuba 88 B3 23 8N 82 24W
Marianna, Ark., U.S.A. 81 H9 34 46N 90 46W
Marianna, Fla., U.S.A. 77 K3 30 46N 85 14W
Marias →, U.S.A. 82 C8 47 56N 110 30W
Mariato, Punta, Panama 88 E3 7 12N 80 52W
Ma'rib, Yemen 46 D4 15 25N 45 21 E
Maribor, Slovenia 16 E8 46 36N 15 40 E
Marico →, Africa 56 C4 23 35S 26 57 E
Maricopa, Ariz., U.S.A. 83 K7 33 4N 112 3W
Maricopa, Calif., U.S.A. 85 K7 35 4N 119 24W
Maricourt, Canada 69 C12 56 34N 70 49W
Marîdî, Sudan 51 H10 4 55N 29 25 E
Marie Byrd Land, Antarctica 5 D14 79 30S 125 0W
Marie-Galante, Guadeloupe 89 C7 15 56N 61 16W
Mariecourt = Kangiqsujuaq, Canada 69 B12 61 30N 72 0W
Marienberg, Neths. 15 B6 52 2N 6 35 E
Marienbourg, Belgium 15 D4 50 6N 4 31 E
Mariental, Namibia 56 C2 24 36S 18 0 E
Marienville, U.S.A. 78 E5 41 28N 79 8W
Mariestad, Sweden 9 G15 58 43N 13 50 E
Marietta, Ga., U.S.A. 77 J3 33 57N 84 33W
Marietta, Ohio, U.S.A. 76 F5 39 25N 81 27W
Marieville, Canada 79 A11 45 26N 73 10W
Mariinsk, Russia 26 D9 56 10N 87 20 E
Marijampolė, Lithuania 9 J20 54 33N 23 19 E
Marília, Brazil 95 A5 22 13S 50 0W
Marillana, Australia 60 D2 22 37S 119 16 E
Marín, Spain 19 A1 42 23N 8 42W
Marina, U.S.A. 84 J5 36 41N 121 48W
Marina Plains, Australia 62 A3 14 37S 143 57 E
Marinduque, Phil. 37 B6 13 25N 122 0 E
Marine City, U.S.A. 76 D4 42 43N 82 30W
Marinette, U.S.A. 76 C2 45 6N 87 38W
Maringá, Brazil 95 A5 23 26S 52 2W
Marion, Ala., U.S.A. 77 J2 32 38N 87 19W
Marion, Ill., U.S.A. 81 G10 37 44N 88 56W
Marion, Ind., U.S.A. 76 E3 40 32N 85 40W
Marion, Iowa, U.S.A. 80 D9 42 2N 91 36W
Marion, Kans., U.S.A. 80 F6 38 21N 97 1W
Marion, Mich., U.S.A. 76 C3 44 6N 85 9W
Marion, N.C., U.S.A. 77 H4 35 41N 82 1W
Marion, Ohio, U.S.A. 76 E4 40 35N 83 8W
Marion, S.C., U.S.A. 77 H6 34 11N 79 24W
Marion, Va., U.S.A. 77 G5 36 50N 81 31W
Marion, L., U.S.A. 77 J5 33 28N 80 10W
Mariposa, U.S.A. 83 H4 37 29N 119 58W
Mariscal Estigarribia, Paraguay 94 A3 22 3S 60 40W
Maritime Alps = Maritimes, Alpes, Europe 16 F4 44 10N 7 10 E
Maritimes, Alpes, Europe 16 F4 44 10N 7 10 E
Maritsa = Évros →, Bulgaria 21 D12 41 40N 26 34 E
Maritsa, Greece 23 C10 36 22N 28 10 E
Mariupol, Ukraine 25 E6 47 5N 37 31 E
Marīvān, Iran 44 C5 35 30N 46 25 E
Markazī □, Iran 45 C6 35 0N 49 30 E
Markdale, Canada 78 B4 44 19N 80 39W
Marked Tree, U.S.A. 81 H9 35 32N 90 25W
Marken, Neths. 15 B5 52 26N 5 12 E
Market Drayton, U.K. 10 E5 52 54N 2 29W
Market Harborough, U.K. 11 E7 52 29N 0 55W
Markham, Canada 78 C5 43 52N 79 16W
Markham, Mt., Antarctica 5 E11 83 0S 164 0 E
Markham L., Canada 73 A8 62 30N 102 35W
Markleeville, U.S.A. 84 G7 38 42N 119 47W
Markovo, Russia 27 C17 64 40N 169 40 E
Marks, Russia 24 D8 51 45N 46 50 E
Marksville, U.S.A. 81 K8 31 8N 92 4W
Marla, Australia 63 D1 27 19S 133 33 E
Marlboro, U.S.A. 79 D13 42 19N 71 33W
Marlborough, Australia 62 C4 22 46S 149 52 E
Marlborough Downs, U.K. 11 F6 51 27N 1 53W
Marlin, U.S.A. 81 K6 31 18N 96 54W
Marlow, U.S.A. 81 H6 34 39N 97 58W
Marmagao, India 40 M8 15 25N 73 56 E
Marmara, Turkey 21 D12 40 35N 27 38 E
Marmara, Sea of = Marmara Denizi, Turkey 21 D13 40 45N 28 15 E
Marmara Denizi, Turkey 21 D13 40 45N 28 15 E
Marmaris, Turkey 21 F13 36 50N 28 14 E
Marmarth, U.S.A. 80 B3 46 18N 103 54W
Marmion, Mt., Australia 61 E2 29 16S 119 50 E
Marmion L., Canada 70 C1 48 55N 91 20W
Marmolada, Mte., Italy 20 A4 46 26N 11 51 E
Marmora, Canada 70 D4 44 28N 77 41W
Marne →, France 18 B5 48 48N 2 24 E
Maroala, Madag. 57 B8 15 23S 47 59 E
Maroantsetra, Madag. 57 B8 15 26S 49 44 E
Maromandia, Madag. 57 A8 14 13S 48 5 E
Marondera, Zimbabwe 55 F3 18 5S 31 42 E
Maroni →, Fr. Guiana 93 B8 5 30N 54 0W
Maroochydore, Australia 63 D5 26 29S 153 5 E
Maroona, Australia 63 F3 37 27S 142 54 E
Marosakoa, Madag. 57 B8 15 26S 46 38 E
Maroua, Cameroon 51 F7 10 40N 14 20 E
Marovoay, Madag. 57 B8 16 6S 46 39 E
Marquard, S. Africa 56 D4 28 40S 27 28 E
Marquesas Is. = Marquises, Is., Pac. Oc. 65 H14 9 30S 140 0W
Marquette, U.S.A. 76 B2 46 33N 87 24W
Marquises, Is., Pac. Oc. 65 H14 9 30S 140 0W

Mekhtar

Marracuene, Mozam. 57 D5 25 45S 32 35 E
Marrakech, Morocco 50 B3 31 9N 8 0W
Marrawah, Australia 62 G3 40 55S 144 42 E
Marree, Australia 63 D2 29 39S 138 1 E
Marrilla, Australia 60 D1 22 31S 114 25 E
Marrimane, Mozam. 57 C5 22 58S 33 34 E
Marromeu, Mozam. 57 B6 18 15S 36 25 E
Marrowie Cr. →, Australia 63 E4 33 23S 145 40 E
Marrubane, Mozam. 55 F4 18 0S 37 0 E
Marrupa, Mozam. 55 E4 13 8S 37 30 E
Marsá Matrûh, Egypt 51 B10 31 19N 27 9 E
Marsá Susah, Libya 51 B9 32 52N 21 59 E
Marsabit, Kenya 54 B4 2 18N 38 0 E
Marsabit □, Kenya 54 B4 2 45N 37 45 E
Marsala, Italy 20 F5 37 48N 12 26 E
Marsalforn, Malta 23 C1 36 4N 14 15 E
Marsden, Australia 63 E4 33 47S 147 32 E
Marseille, France 18 E6 43 18N 5 23 E
Marseilles = Marseille, France 18 E6 43 18N 5 23 E
Marsh I., U.S.A. 81 L9 29 34N 91 53W
Marsh L., U.S.A. 80 C6 45 5N 96 0W
Marshall, Liberia 50 G2 6 8N 10 22W
Marshall, Ark., U.S.A. 81 H8 35 55N 92 38W
Marshall, Mich., U.S.A. 76 D3 42 16N 84 58W
Marshall, Minn., U.S.A. 80 C7 44 25N 95 45W
Marshall, Mo., U.S.A. 80 F8 39 7N 93 12W
Marshall, Tex., U.S.A. 81 J7 32 33N 94 23W
Marshall →, Australia 62 C2 22 59S 136 59 E
Marshall Is. ■, Pac. Oc. 64 G9 9 0N 171 0 E
Marshalltown, U.S.A. 80 D8 42 3N 92 55W
Marshfield, Mo., U.S.A. 81 G8 37 15N 92 54W
Marshfield, Wis., U.S.A. 80 C9 44 40N 90 10W
Marshūn, Iran 45 B6 36 19N 49 23 E
Märsta, Sweden 9 G17 59 37N 17 52 E
Mart, U.S.A. 81 K6 31 33N 96 50W
Martaban, Burma 41 L20 16 30N 97 35 E
Martaban, G. of, Burma 41 L20 16 5N 96 30 E
Martapura, Kalimantan, Indonesia 36 E4 3 22S 114 47 E
Martapura, Sumatera, Indonesia 36 E2 4 19S 104 22 E
Marte, Nigeria 51 F7 12 23N 13 46 E
Martelange, Belgium 15 E5 49 49N 5 43 E
Martha's Vineyard, U.S.A. 79 E14 41 25N 70 38W
Martigny, Switz. 16 E4 46 6N 7 3 E
Martigues, France 18 E6 43 24N 5 4 E
Martin, Slovak Rep. 17 D10 49 6N 18 48 E
Martin, S. Dak., U.S.A. 80 D4 43 11N 101 44W
Martin, Tenn., U.S.A. 81 G10 36 21N 88 51W
Martin L., U.S.A. 77 J3 32 41N 85 55W
Martina Franca, Italy 20 D7 40 42N 17 20 E
Martinborough, N.Z. 59 J5 41 14S 175 29 E
Martinez, U.S.A. 84 G4 38 1N 122 8W
Martinique ■, W. Indies 89 D7 14 40N 61 0W
Martinique Passage, W. Indies 89 C7 15 15N 61 0W
Martinópolis, Brazil 95 A5 22 11S 51 12W
Martins Ferry, U.S.A. 78 F4 40 6N 80 44W
Martinsburg, Pa., U.S.A. 78 F6 40 19N 78 20W
Martinsburg, W. Va., U.S.A. 76 F7 39 27N 77 58W
Martinsville, Ind., U.S.A. 76 F2 39 26N 86 25W
Martinsville, Va., U.S.A. 77 G6 36 41N 79 52W
Marton, N.Z. 59 J5 40 4S 175 23 E
Martos, Spain 19 D4 37 44N 3 58W
Marudi, Malaysia 36 D4 4 11N 114 19 E
Ma'ruf, Afghan. 40 D5 31 30N 67 6 E
Marugame, Japan 31 G6 34 15N 133 40 E
Marulan, Australia 63 E5 34 43S 150 3 E
Marunga, Angola 56 B3 17 28S 20 2 E
Marungu, Mts., Zaïre 54 D2 7 30S 30 0 E
Marvast, Iran 45 D7 30 30N 54 15 E
Marwar, India 42 G5 25 43N 73 45 E
Mary, Turkmenistan 26 F7 37 40N 61 50 E
Mary Frances L., Canada 73 A7 63 19N 106 13W
Mary Kathleen, Australia 62 C2 20 44S 139 48 E
Maryborough = Port Laoise, Ireland 13 C4 53 2N 7 18W
Maryborough, Queens., Australia 63 D5 25 31S 152 37 E
Maryborough, Vic., Australia 63 F3 37 0S 143 44 E
Maryfield, Canada 73 D8 49 50N 101 35W
Maryland □, U.S.A. 76 F7 39 0N 76 30W
Maryland Junction, Zimbabwe 55 F3 17 45S 30 31 E
Maryport, U.K. 10 C4 54 44N 3 28W
Mary's Harbour, Canada 71 B8 52 18N 55 51W
Marystown, Canada 71 C8 47 10N 55 10W
Marysvale, U.S.A. 83 G7 38 27N 112 14W
Marysville, Canada 72 D5 49 35N 116 0W
Marysville, Calif., U.S.A. 84 F5 39 9N 121 35W
Marysville, Kans., U.S.A. 80 F6 39 51N 96 39W
Marysville, Mich., U.S.A. 78 D2 42 54N 82 29W
Marysville, Ohio, U.S.A. 76 E4 40 14N 83 22W
Marysville, Wash., U.S.A. 84 B4 48 3N 122 11W
Maryvale, Australia 63 D5 28 4S 152 12 E
Maryville, U.S.A. 77 H4 35 46N 83 58W
Marzūq, Libya 51 C7 25 53N 13 57 E
Masahunga, Tanzania 54 C3 2 6S 33 18 E
Masai, Malaysia 39 M4 1 29N 103 55 E
Masai Steppe, Tanzania 54 C4 4 30S 36 30 E
Masaka, Uganda 54 C3 0 21S 31 45 E
Masalembo, Kepulauan, Indonesia 36 F4 5 35S 114 30 E
Masalima, Kepulauan, Indonesia 36 F5 5 4S 117 5 E
Masamba, Indonesia 37 E6 2 30S 120 15 E
Masan, S. Korea 35 G15 35 11N 128 32 E
Masasi, Tanzania 55 E4 10 45S 38 52 E
Masasi □, Tanzania 55 E4 10 45S 38 50 E
Masaya, Nic. 88 D2 12 0N 86 7W
Masbate, Phil. 37 B6 12 21N 123 36 E
Mascara, Algeria 50 A5 35 26N 0 6 E
Mascota, Mexico 86 C4 20 30N 104 50W
Masela, Indonesia 37 F7 8 9S 129 51 E
Maseru, Lesotho 56 D4 29 18S 27 30 E
Mashaba, Zimbabwe 55 G3 20 2S 30 29 E
Mashābih, Si. Arabia 44 E3 25 35N 36 30 E
Masherbrum, Pakistan 43 B7 35 38N 76 18 E
Mashhad, Iran 45 B8 36 20N 59 35 E
Mashīz, Iran 45 D8 29 56N 56 37 E
Mashkel, Hamun-i-, Pakistan 40 E3 28 30N 63 0 E
Mashki Chāh, Pakistan 40 E3 29 5N 62 30 E
Mashonaland Central □, Zimbabwe 57 B5 17 30S 31 0 E
Mashonaland East □, Zimbabwe 57 B5 18 0S 32 0 E
Mashonaland West □, Zimbabwe 57 B4 17 30S 29 30 E
Masi Manimba, Zaïre 52 E3 4 40S 17 54 E
Masindi, Uganda 54 B3 1 40N 31 43 E
Masindi Port, Uganda 54 B3 1 43N 32 2 E
Masisea, Peru 92 E4 8 35S 74 22W
Masisi, Zaïre 54 C2 1 23S 28 49 E
Masjed Soleyman, Iran 45 D6 31 55N 49 18 E
Mask, L., Ireland 13 C2 53 36N 9 22W
Masoala, Tanjon' i, Madag. 57 B9 15 59S 50 13 E
Masoarivo, Madag. 57 B7 19 3S 44 19 E
Masohi, Indonesia 37 E7 3 20S 128 55 E
Masomeloka, Madag. 57 C8 20 17S 48 37 E
Mason, Nev., U.S.A. 84 G7 38 56N 119 8W
Mason, Tex., U.S.A. 81 K5 30 45N 99 14W
Mason City, U.S.A. 80 D8 43 9N 93 12W
Maspalomas, Canary Is. 22 G4 27 46N 15 35W
Maspalomas, Pta., Canary Is. 22 G4 27 43N 15 36W
Masqat, Oman 46 C6 23 37N 58 36 E
Massa, Italy 20 B4 44 1N 10 9 E
Massachusetts □, U.S.A. 79 D12 42 30N 72 0W
Massachusetts B., U.S.A. 79 D14 42 20N 70 50W
Massaguet, Chad 51 F8 12 28N 15 26 E
Massakory, Chad 51 F8 13 0N 15 49 E
Massanella, Spain 22 B9 39 48N 2 51 E
Massangena, Mozam. 57 C5 21 34S 33 0 E
Massawa = Mitsiwa, Eritrea 51 E12 15 35N 39 25 E
Massena, U.S.A. 79 B10 44 56N 74 54W
Massénya, Chad 51 F8 11 21N 16 9 E
Masset, Canada 72 C2 54 2N 132 10W
Massif Central, France 18 D5 44 55N 3 0 E
Massillon, U.S.A. 78 F3 40 48N 81 32W
Massinga, Mozam. 57 C6 23 15S 35 22 E
Masson, Canada 79 A9 45 32N 75 25W
Masson I., Antarctica 5 C7 66 10S 93 20 E
Mastanli = Momchilgrad, Bulgaria 21 D11 41 33N 25 23 E
Masterton, N.Z. 59 J5 40 56S 175 39 E
Mastuj, Pakistan 43 A5 36 20N 72 36 E
Mastung, Pakistan 40 E5 29 50N 66 56 E
Masty, Belarus 17 B13 53 27N 24 38 E
Masuda, Japan 31 G5 34 40N 131 51 E
Masvingo, Zimbabwe 55 G3 20 8S 30 49 E
Masvingo □, Zimbabwe 55 G3 21 0S 31 30 E
Maswa □, Tanzania 54 C3 3 30S 34 0 E
Maşyāf, Syria 44 C3 35 4N 36 20 E
Matabeleland North □, Zimbabwe 55 F2 19 0S 28 0 E
Matabeleland South □, Zimbabwe 55 G2 21 0S 29 0 E
Mataboor, Indonesia 37 E9 1 41S 138 3 E
Matachewan, Canada 70 C3 47 56N 80 39W
Matadi, Zaïre 52 F2 5 52S 13 31 E
Matagalpa, Nic. 88 D2 13 0N 85 58W
Matagami, Canada 70 C4 49 45N 77 34W
Matagami, L., Canada 70 C4 49 50N 77 40W
Matagorda, U.S.A. 81 L7 28 42N 95 58W
Matagorda B., U.S.A. 81 L6 28 40N 96 0W
Matagorda I., U.S.A. 81 L6 28 15N 96 30W
Matak, P., Indonesia 39 L6 3 18N 106 16 E
Matakana, Australia 63 E4 32 59S 145 54 E
Mátala, Greece 23 E6 34 59N 24 45 E
Matam, Senegal 50 E2 15 34N 13 17W
Matamoros, Campeche, Mexico 87 D6 18 50N 90 50W
Matamoros, Coahuila, Mexico 86 B4 25 33N 103 15W
Matamoros, Puebla, Mexico 87 D5 18 2N 98 17W
Matamoros, Tamaulipas, Mexico 87 B5 25 50N 97 30W
Ma'ţan as Sarra, Libya 51 D9 21 45N 22 0 E
Matandu →, Tanzania 55 D3 8 45S 34 19 E
Matane, Canada 71 C6 48 50N 67 33W
Matanzas, Cuba 88 B3 23 0N 81 40W
Matapan, C. = Taínaron, Ákra, Greece 21 F10 36 22N 22 27 E
Matapédia, Canada 71 C6 48 0N 66 59W
Matara, Sri Lanka 40 S12 5 58N 80 30 E
Mataram, Indonesia 36 F5 8 41S 116 10 E
Matarani, Peru 92 G4 17 0S 72 10W
Mataranka, Australia 60 B5 14 55S 133 4 E
Matarma, Râs, Egypt 47 E1 30 27N 32 44 E
Mataró, Spain 19 B7 41 32N 2 29 E
Matatiele, S. Africa 57 E4 30 20S 28 49 E
Mataura, N.Z. 59 M2 46 11S 168 51 E
Matehuala, Mexico 86 C4 23 40N 100 40W
Mateke Hills, Zimbabwe 55 G3 21 48S 31 0 E
Matera, Italy 20 D7 40 40N 16 36 E
Matetsi, Zimbabwe 55 F2 18 12S 26 0 E
Matheson Island, Canada 73 C9 51 45N 96 56W
Mathis, U.S.A. 81 L6 28 6N 97 50W
Mathura, India 42 F7 27 30N 77 40 E
Mati, Phil. 37 C7 6 55N 126 15 E
Matías Romero, Mexico 87 D5 16 53N 95 2W
Matibane, Mozam. 55 E5 14 49S 40 45 E
Matima, Botswana 56 C3 20 15S 24 26 E
Matiri Ra., N.Z. 59 J4 41 38S 172 20 E
Matlock, U.K. 10 D6 53 9N 1 33W
Matmata, Tunisia 50 B6 33 37N 9 59 E
Mato Grosso □, Brazil 93 F8 14 0S 55 0W
Mato Grosso, Planalto do, Brazil 93 G8 15 0S 55 0W
Mato Grosso, Plateau of, Brazil 90 E5 15 0S 54 0W
Mato Grosso do Sul □, Brazil 93 G8 18 0S 55 0W
Matochkin Shar, Russia 26 B6 73 10N 56 40 E
Matopo Hills, Zimbabwe 55 G2 20 36S 28 20 E
Matopos, Zimbabwe 55 G2 20 20S 28 29 E
Matosinhos, Portugal 19 B1 41 11N 8 42W
Matsue, Japan 31 G6 35 25N 133 10 E
Matsumae, Japan 30 D10 41 26N 140 7 E
Matsumoto, Japan 31 F9 36 15N 138 0 E
Matsusaka, Japan 31 G8 34 34N 136 32 E
Matsuura, Japan 31 H4 33 20N 129 49 E
Matsuyama, Japan 31 H6 33 45N 132 45 E
Mattagami →, Canada 70 B3 50 43N 81 29W
Mattancheri, India 40 Q10 9 50N 76 15 E
Mattawa, Canada 70 C4 46 20N 78 45W
Mattawamkeag, U.S.A. 71 C6 45 32N 68 21W
Matterhorn, Switz. 16 F4 45 58N 7 39 E
Matthew Town, Bahamas 89 B5 20 57N 73 40W
Matthew's Ridge, Guyana 92 B6 7 37N 60 10W
Mattice, Canada 70 C3 49 40N 83 20W
Mattituck, U.S.A. 79 F12 40 59N 72 32W
Matuba, Mozam. 57 C5 24 28S 32 49 E
Matucana, Peru 92 F3 11 55S 76 25W
Matun, Afghan. 42 C3 33 22N 69 58 E
Maturín, Venezuela 92 B6 9 45N 63 11W
Mau, India 43 G10 25 56N 83 33 E
Mau Escarpment, Kenya 54 C4 0 40S 36 0 E
Mau Ranipur, India 43 G8 25 16N 79 8 E
Maubeuge, France 18 A6 50 17N 3 57 E
Maud, Pt., Australia 60 D1 23 6S 113 45 E
Maude, Australia 63 E3 34 29S 144 18 E
Maudin Sun, Burma 41 M19 16 0N 94 30 E
Maués, Brazil 92 D7 3 20S 57 45W
Mauganj, India 41 G12 24 50N 81 55 E
Maui, U.S.A. 74 H16 20 48N 156 20W
Maulamyaing = Moulmein, Burma 41 L20 16 30N 97 40 E
Maule □, Chile 94 D1 36 5S 72 30W
Maumee, U.S.A. 76 E4 41 34N 83 39W
Maumee →, U.S.A. 76 E4 41 42N 83 28W
Maumere, Indonesia 37 F6 8 38S 122 13 E
Maun, Botswana 56 B3 20 0S 23 26 E
Mauna Kea, U.S.A. 74 J17 19 50N 155 28W
Mauna Loa, U.S.A. 74 J17 19 30N 155 35W
Maungmagan Kyunzu, Burma 41 M20 14 0N 97 48 E
Maupin, U.S.A. 82 D3 45 11N 121 5W
Maurepas, L., U.S.A. 81 K9 30 15N 90 30W
Maurice, L., Australia 61 E5 29 30S 131 0 E
Mauritania ■, Africa 50 D3 20 50N 10 0W
Mauritius ■, Ind. Oc. 49 J9 20 0S 57 0 E
Mauston, U.S.A. 80 D9 43 48N 90 5W
Mavinga, Angola 53 H4 15 50S 20 21 E
Mavli, India 42 G5 24 45N 73 55 E
Mavuradonha Mts., Zimbabwe 55 F3 16 30S 31 30 E
Mawa, Zaïre 54 B2 2 45N 26 40 E
Mawana, India 42 E7 29 6N 77 58 E
Mawand, Pakistan 42 E3 29 33N 68 38 E
Mawk Mai, Burma 41 J20 20 14N 97 37 E
Mawlaik, Burma 41 H19 23 40N 94 26 E
Mawquq, Si. Arabia 44 E4 27 25N 41 8 E
Mawson Coast, Antarctica 5 C6 68 30S 63 0 E
Max, U.S.A. 80 B4 47 49N 101 18W
Maxcanú, Mexico 87 C6 20 40N 92 0W
Maxesibeni, S. Africa 57 E4 30 49S 29 23 E
Maxhamish L., Canada 72 B4 59 50N 123 17W
Maxixe, Mozam. 57 C6 23 54S 35 17 E
Maxville, Canada 79 A10 45 17N 74 51W
Maxwell, U.S.A. 84 F4 39 17N 122 11W
Maxwelton, Australia 62 C3 20 43S 142 41 E
May Downs, Australia 62 C4 22 38S 148 55 E
May Pen, Jamaica 88 C4 17 58N 77 15W
Maya →, Russia 27 D14 60 28N 134 28 E
Maya Mts., Belize 87 D7 16 30N 89 0W
Mayaguana, Bahamas 89 B5 22 30N 72 44W
Mayagüez, Puerto Rico 89 C6 18 12N 67 9W
Mayāmey, Iran 45 B7 36 24N 55 42 E
Mayarí, Cuba 89 B4 20 40N 75 41W
Maybell, U.S.A. 82 F9 40 31N 108 5W
Maydān, Iraq 44 C5 34 55N 45 37 E
Maydena, Australia 62 G4 42 45S 146 30 E
Mayenne →, France 18 C3 47 30N 0 32W
Mayer, U.S.A. 83 J7 34 24N 112 14W
Mayerthorpe, Canada 72 C5 53 57N 115 8W
Mayfield, U.S.A. 77 G1 36 44N 88 38W
Mayhill, U.S.A. 83 K11 32 53N 105 29W
Maykop, Russia 25 F7 44 35N 40 10 E
Maymyo, Burma 38 A1 22 2N 96 28 E
Maynard, U.S.A. 84 C4 47 59N 122 55W
Maynard Hills, Australia 61 E2 28 28S 119 49 E
Mayne →, Australia 62 C3 23 40S 141 55 E
Maynooth, Ireland 13 C5 53 23N 6 34W
Mayo, Canada 68 B6 63 38N 135 57W
Mayo □, Ireland 13 C2 53 53N 9 3W
Mayo L., Canada 68 B6 63 45N 135 0W
Mayon Volcano, Phil. 37 B6 13 15N 123 41 E
Mayor I., N.Z. 59 G6 37 16S 176 17 E
Mayotte, I., Mayotte 49 H8 12 50S 45 10 E
Mayson L., Canada 73 B7 57 55N 107 10W
Maysville, U.S.A. 76 F4 38 39N 83 46W
Mayu, Indonesia 37 D7 1 30N 126 30 E
Mayville, N. Dak., U.S.A. 80 B6 47 30N 97 20W
Mayville, N.Y., U.S.A. 78 D5 42 15N 79 30W
Mayya, Russia 27 C14 61 44N 130 18 E
Mazabuka, Zambia 55 F2 15 52S 27 44 E
Mazagán = El Jadida, Morocco 50 B3 33 11N 8 17W
Mazagão, Brazil 93 D8 0 7S 51 16W
Mazán, Peru 92 D4 3 30S 73 0W
Māzandarān □, Iran 45 B7 36 30N 52 0 E
Mazapil, Mexico 86 C4 24 38N 101 34W
Mazara del Vallo, Italy 20 F5 37 39N 12 35 E
Mazarredo, Argentina 96 F3 47 10S 66 50W
Mazarrón, Spain 19 D5 37 38N 1 19W
Mazaruni →, Guyana 92 B7 6 25N 58 35W
Mazatán, Mexico 86 B2 29 0N 110 8W
Mazatenango, Guatemala 88 D1 14 35N 91 30W
Mazatlán, Mexico 86 C3 23 13N 106 25W
Mažeikiai, Lithuania 9 H20 56 20N 22 20 E
Māzhān, Iran 45 C8 32 30N 59 0 E
Mazīnān, Iran 45 B8 36 19N 56 56 E
Mazoe, Mozam. 55 F3 16 42S 33 7 E
Mazoe →, Mozam. 55 F3 16 20S 33 30 E
Mazowe, Zimbabwe 55 F3 17 28S 30 58 E
Mazurian Lakes = Mazurski, Pojezierze, Poland 17 B11 53 50N 21 0 E
Mazurski, Pojezierze, Poland 17 B11 53 50N 21 0 E
Mazyr, Belarus 17 B15 51 59N 29 15 E
Mbabane, Swaziland 57 D5 26 18S 31 6 E
Mbaïki, C.A.R. 52 D3 3 53N 18 1 E
Mbala, Zambia 55 D3 8 46S 31 24 E
Mbale, Uganda 54 B3 1 8N 34 12 E
Mbalmayo, Cameroon 52 D2 3 33N 11 33 E
Mbamba Bay, Tanzania 55 E3 11 13S 34 49 E
Mbandaka, Zaïre 52 D3 0 1N 18 18 E
Mbanza Congo, Angola 52 F2 6 18S 14 16 E
Mbanza Ngungu, Zaïre 52 F2 5 12S 14 53 E
Mbarara, Uganda 54 C3 0 35S 30 40 E
Mbashe →, S. Africa 57 E4 32 15S 28 54 E
Mbenkuru →, Tanzania 55 D4 9 25S 39 50 E
Mberengwa, Zimbabwe 55 G2 20 29S 29 57 E
Mberengwa, Mt., Zimbabwe 55 G2 20 37S 29 55 E
Mbesuma, Zambia 55 D3 10 0S 32 2 E
Mbeya, Tanzania 55 D3 8 54S 33 29 E
Mbeya □, Tanzania 54 D3 8 15S 33 30 E
Mbinga, Tanzania 55 E4 10 50S 35 0 E
Mbinga □, Tanzania 55 E3 10 50S 35 0 E
Mbini □, Eq. Guin. 52 D2 1 30N 10 0 E
Mbour, Senegal 50 F1 14 22N 16 54W
Mbout, Mauritania 50 E2 16 1N 12 38W
Mbozi □, Tanzania 55 D3 9 0S 32 50 E
Mbuji-Mayi, Zaïre 54 D1 6 9S 23 40 E
Mbulu, Tanzania 54 C4 3 45S 35 30 E
Mbulu □, Tanzania 54 C4 3 52S 35 33 E
Mburucuyá, Argentina 94 B4 28 1S 58 14W
Mchinja, Tanzania 55 D4 9 44S 39 45 E
Mchinji, Malawi 55 E3 13 47S 32 58 E
Mead, L., U.S.A. 85 J12 36 1N 114 44W
Meade, U.S.A. 81 G4 37 17N 100 20W
Meadow, Australia 61 E1 26 35S 114 40 E
Meadow Lake, Canada 73 C7 54 10N 108 26W
Meadow Lake Prov. Park, Canada 73 C7 54 27N 109 0W
Meadow Valley Wash →, U.S.A. 85 J12 36 40N 114 34W
Meadville, U.S.A. 78 E4 41 39N 80 9W
Meaford, Canada 70 D3 44 36N 80 35W
Mealy Mts., Canada 71 B8 53 10N 58 0W
Meander River, Canada 72 B5 59 2N 117 42W
Meares, C., U.S.A. 82 D2 45 37N 124 0W
Mearim →, Brazil 93 D10 3 4S 44 35W
Meath □, Ireland 13 C5 53 40N 6 57W
Meath Park, Canada 73 C7 53 27N 105 22W
Meaux, France 18 B5 48 58N 2 50 E
Mebechi-Gawa →, Japan 30 D10 40 31N 141 31 E
Mecanhelas, Mozam. 55 F4 15 12S 35 54 E
Mecca = Makkah, Si. Arabia 46 C2 21 30N 39 54 E
Mecca, U.S.A. 85 M10 33 34N 116 5W
Mechanicsburg, U.S.A. 78 F8 40 13N 77 1W
Mechanicville, U.S.A. 79 D11 42 54N 73 41W
Mechelen, Belgium 15 C4 51 2N 4 29 E
Mecheria, Algeria 50 B4 33 35N 0 18W
Mecklenburg, Germany 16 B6 53 33N 11 40 E
Mecklenburger Bucht, Germany 16 A6 54 20N 11 40 E
Meconta, Mozam. 55 E4 14 59S 39 50 E
Meda, Australia 60 C3 17 22S 123 59 E
Medan, Indonesia 36 D1 3 40N 98 38 E
Medanosa, Pta., Argentina 96 F3 48 8S 66 0W
Medéa, Algeria 50 A5 36 12N 2 50 E
Medellín, Colombia 92 B3 6 15N 75 35W
Medelpad, Sweden 9 E17 62 33N 16 30 E
Medemblik, Neths. 15 B5 52 46N 5 8 E
Mederdra, Mauritania 50 E1 17 0N 15 38W
Medford, Mass., U.S.A. 79 D13 42 25N 71 7W
Medford, Oreg., U.S.A. 82 E2 42 19N 122 52W
Medford, Wis., U.S.A. 80 C9 45 9N 90 20W
Medgidia, Romania 17 F15 44 15N 28 19 E
Media Agua, Argentina 94 C2 31 58S 68 25W
Media Luna, Argentina 94 C2 34 45S 66 44W
Mediaş, Romania 17 E13 46 9N 24 22 E
Medical Lake, U.S.A. 82 C5 47 34N 117 41W
Medicine Bow, U.S.A. 82 F10 41 54N 106 12W
Medicine Bow Pk., U.S.A. 82 F10 41 21N 106 19W
Medicine Bow Ra., U.S.A. 82 F10 41 10N 106 25W
Medicine Hat, Canada 73 D6 50 0N 110 45W
Medicine Lake, U.S.A. 80 A2 48 30N 104 30W
Medicine Lodge, U.S.A. 81 G5 37 17N 98 35W
Medina = Al Madīnah, Si. Arabia 46 C2 24 35N 39 52 E
Medina, N. Dak., U.S.A. 80 B5 46 54N 99 18W
Medina, N.Y., U.S.A. 78 C6 43 13N 78 23W
Medina, Ohio, U.S.A. 78 E3 41 8N 81 52W
Medina →, U.S.A. 81 L5 29 16N 98 29W
Medina del Campo, Spain 19 B3 41 18N 4 55W
Medina L., U.S.A. 81 L5 29 32N 98 56W
Medina-Sidonia, Spain 19 D3 36 28N 5 57W
Medinipur, India 43 H12 22 25N 87 21 E
Mediterranean Sea, Europe 6 H7 35 0N 15 0 E
Medley, Canada 73 C6 54 25N 110 16W
Médoc, France 18 D3 45 10N 0 50W
Medstead, Canada 73 C7 53 19N 108 5W
Medveditsa →, Russia 25 E7 49 35N 42 41 E
Medvezhi, Ostrava, Russia 27 B17 71 0N 161 0 E
Medvezhyegorsk, Russia 24 B5 63 0N 34 25 E
Medway →, U.K. 11 F8 51 27N 0 46 E
Meeberrie, Australia 61 E2 26 57S 115 51 E
Meekatharra, Australia 61 E2 26 32S 118 29 E
Meeker, U.S.A. 82 F10 40 2N 107 55W
Meerut, India 42 E7 29 1N 77 42 E
Meeteetse, U.S.A. 82 D9 44 9N 108 52W
Mega, Ethiopia 51 H12 3 57N 38 19 E
Mégara, Greece 21 F10 37 58N 23 22 E
Meghalaya □, India 41 G17 25 50N 91 0 E
Mégiscane, L., Canada 70 C4 48 35N 75 55W
Mehndawal, India 43 F10 26 58N 83 5 E
Mehr Jān, Iran 45 C7 33 50N 55 6 E
Mehrābād, Iran 44 B5 36 53N 47 55 E
Mehrān, Iran 44 C5 33 7N 46 10 E
Mehrīz, Iran 45 D7 31 35N 54 28 E
Mei Xian, Guangdong, China 33 D6 24 16N 116 6 E
Mei Xian, Shaanxi, China 34 G4 34 18N 107 55 E
Meiganga, Cameroon 52 C2 6 30N 14 25 E
Meiktila, Burma 41 J19 20 53N 95 54 E
Meissen, Germany 16 C7 51 9N 13 29 E
Mejillones, Chile 94 A1 23 10S 70 30W
Meka, Australia 61 E2 27 25S 116 48 E
Mékambo, Gabon 52 D2 1 2N 13 50 E
Mekdela, Ethiopia 51 F12 11 24N 39 10 E
Mekhtar, Pakistan 40 D6 30 30N 69 15 E

Meknès

Meknès, Morocco 50 B3 33 57N 5 33W
Mekong →, Asia 39 H6 9 30N 106 15 E
Mekongga, Indonesia 37 E6 3 39S 121 15 E
Mekvari = Kür →, Azerbaijan 25 G8 39 29N 49 15 E
Melagiri Hills, India 40 N10 12 20N 77 30 E
Melaka, Malaysia 39 L4 2 15N 102 15 E
Melalap, Malaysia 36 C5 5 10N 116 5 E
Mélambes, Greece 23 D6 35 8N 24 40 E
Melanesia, Pac. Oc. 64 H7 4 0S 155 0 E
Melbourne, Australia 63 F3 37 50S 145 0 E
Melbourne, U.S.A. 77 L5 28 5N 80 37W
Melchor Múzquiz, Mexico 86 B4 27 50N 101 30W
Melchor Ocampo, Mexico 86 C4 24 52N 101 40W
Mélèzes →, Canada 69 C12 57 30N 71 0W
Melfi, Chad 51 F8 11 0N 17 59 E
Melfort, Canada 73 C8 52 50N 104 37W
Melfort, Zimbabwe 55 F3 18 0S 31 25 E
Melhus, Norway 8 E14 63 17N 10 18 E
Melilla, N. Afr. 19 E4 35 21N 2 57W
Melipilla, Chile 94 C1 33 42S 71 15W
Mélissa, Ákra, Greece 23 D6 35 6N 24 33 E
Melita, Canada 73 D8 49 15N 101 0W
Melitopol, Ukraine 25 E6 46 50N 35 22 E
Melk, Austria 16 D8 48 13N 15 20 E
Mellansel, Sweden 8 E18 63 25N 18 17 E
Mellen, U.S.A. 80 B9 46 20N 90 40W
Mellerud, Sweden 9 G15 58 41N 12 28 E
Mellette, U.S.A. 80 C5 45 9N 98 30W
Mellieha, Malta 23 D1 35 57N 14 21 E
Melo, Uruguay 95 C5 32 20S 54 10W
Melolo, Indonesia 37 F6 9 53S 120 40 E
Melouprey, Cambodia 38 F5 13 48N 105 16 E
Melrose, N.S.W., Australia 63 E4 32 42S 146 57 E
Melrose, W. Austral., Australia 61 E3 27 50S 121 15 E
Melrose, U.K. 12 F6 55 36N 2 43W
Melrose, U.S.A. 81 H3 34 26N 103 38W
Melstone, U.S.A. 82 C10 46 36N 107 52W
Melton Mowbray, U.K. 11 E7 52 47N 0 54W
Melun, France 18 B5 48 32N 2 39 E
Melut, Sudan 51 F11 10 30N 32 13 E
Melville, Canada 73 C8 50 55N 102 50W
Melville, C., Australia 62 A3 14 11S 144 30 E
Melville, L., Canada 71 B8 53 30N 60 0W
Melville B., Australia 62 A2 12 0S 136 45 E
Melville I., Australia 60 B5 11 30S 131 0 E
Melville I., Canada 4 B2 75 30N 112 0W
Melville Pen., Canada 69 B11 68 0N 84 0W
Melvin →, Canada 72 B5 59 11N 117 31W
Memba, Mozam. 55 E5 14 11S 40 30 E
Memboro, Indonesia 37 F5 9 30S 119 30 E
Memel = Klaipėda, Lithuania 9 J19 55 43N 21 10 E
Memel, S. Africa 57 D4 27 38S 29 36 E
Memmingen, Germany 16 E6 47 58N 10 10 E
Mempawah, Indonesia 36 D3 0 30N 109 5 E
Memphis, Tenn., U.S.A. 81 H10 35 8N 90 3W
Memphis, Tex., U.S.A. 81 H4 34 44N 100 33W
Mena, U.S.A. 81 H7 34 35N 94 15W
Menai Strait, U.K. 10 D3 53 11N 4 13W
Ménaka, Mali 50 E5 15 59N 2 18 E
Menan = Chao Phraya →, Thailand 38 F3 13 32N 100 36 E
Menarandra →, Madag. 57 D7 25 17S 44 30 E
Menard, U.S.A. 81 K5 30 55N 99 47W
Menasha, U.S.A. 76 C1 44 13N 88 26W
Menate, Indonesia 36 E4 0 12S 113 3 E
Mendawai →, Indonesia 36 E4 3 30S 113 0 E
Mende, France 18 D5 44 31N 3 30 E
Mendez, Mexico 87 B5 25 7N 98 34W
Mendhar, India 43 C6 33 35N 74 10 E
Mendip Hills, U.K. 11 F5 51 17N 2 40W
Mendocino, U.S.A. 82 G2 39 19N 123 48W
Mendocino, C., U.S.A. 82 F1 40 26N 124 25W
Mendota, Calif., U.S.A. 83 H3 36 45N 120 23W
Mendota, Ill., U.S.A. 80 E10 41 33N 89 7W
Mendoza, Argentina 94 C2 32 50S 68 52W
Mendoza □, Argentina 94 C2 33 0S 69 0W
Mene Grande, Venezuela 92 B4 9 49N 70 56W
Menemen, Turkey 21 E12 38 34N 27 3 E
Menen, Belgium 15 D3 50 47N 3 7 E
Menggala, Indonesia 36 E3 4 30S 105 15 E
Mengjin, China 34 G7 34 55N 112 45 E
Mengyin, China 35 G9 35 40N 117 58 E
Mengzi, China 32 D5 23 20N 103 22 E
Menihek L., Canada 71 B6 54 0N 67 0W
Menin = Menen, Belgium 15 D3 50 47N 3 7 E
Menindee, Australia 63 E3 32 20S 142 25 E
Menindee L., Australia 63 E3 32 20S 142 25 E
Meningie, Australia 63 F2 35 50S 139 18 E
Menlo Park, U.S.A. 84 H4 37 27N 122 12W
Menominee, U.S.A. 76 C2 45 6N 87 37W
Menominee →, U.S.A. 76 C2 45 6N 87 36W
Menomonie, U.S.A. 80 C9 44 53N 91 55W
Menongue, Angola 53 G3 14 48S 17 52 E
Menorca, Spain 22 B11 40 0N 4 0 E
Mentakab, Malaysia 39 L4 3 29N 102 21 E
Mentawai, Kepulauan, Indonesia 36 E1 2 0S 99 0 E
Menton, France 18 E7 43 50N 7 29 E
Mentor, U.S.A. 78 E3 41 40N 81 21W
Menzelinsk, Russia 24 C9 55 47N 53 11 E
Menzies, Australia 61 E3 29 40S 121 2 E
Me'ona, Israel 47 B4 33 1N 35 15 E
Meoqui, Mexico 86 B3 28 17N 105 29W
Mepaco, Mozam. 55 F3 15 57S 30 48 E
Meppel, Neths. 15 B6 52 42N 6 12 E
Mer Rouge, U.S.A. 81 J9 32 47N 91 48W
Merabéllou, Kólpos, Greece 23 D7 35 10N 25 50 E
Meramangye, L., Australia 61 E5 28 25S 132 13 E
Meran = Merano, Italy 20 A4 46 40N 11 9 E
Merano, Italy 20 A4 46 40N 11 9 E
Merauke, Indonesia 37 F10 8 29S 140 24 E
Merbabu, Indonesia 37 G14 7 30S 110 40 E
Merbein, Australia 63 E3 34 10S 142 2 E
Merca, Somali Rep. 46 G3 1 48N 44 50 E
Mercadal, Spain 22 B11 39 59N 4 5 E
Merced, U.S.A. 83 H3 37 18N 120 29W
Merced Pk., U.S.A. 84 H7 37 36N 119 24W
Mercedes, Buenos Aires, Argentina 94 C4 34 40S 59 30W
Mercedes, Corrientes, Argentina 94 B4 29 10S 58 5W
Mercedes, San Luis, Argentina 94 C2 33 40S 65 21W
Mercedes, Uruguay 94 C4 33 12S 58 0W
Merceditas, Chile 94 B1 28 20S 70 35W
Mercer, N.Z. 59 G5 37 16S 175 5 E
Mercer, U.S.A. 78 E4 41 14N 80 15W
Mercury, U.S.A. 85 J11 36 40N 115 58W
Mercy C., Canada 69 B13 65 0N 63 30W
Meredith, C., Falk. Is. 96 G4 52 15S 60 40W
Meredith, L., U.S.A. 81 H4 35 43N 101 33W
Merga = Nukheila, Sudan 51 E10 19 1N 26 21 E
Mergui Arch. = Myeik Kyunzu, Burma 39 G1 11 30N 97 30 E
Mérida, Mexico 87 C7 20 58N 89 37W
Mérida, Spain 19 C2 38 55N 6 25W
Mérida, Venezuela 92 B4 8 24N 71 8W
Mérida, Cord. de, Venezuela 90 C3 9 0N 71 0W
Meriden, U.S.A. 79 E12 41 32N 72 48W
Meridian, Calif., U.S.A. 84 F5 39 9N 121 55W
Meridian, Idaho, U.S.A. 82 E5 43 37N 116 24W
Meridian, Miss., U.S.A. 77 J1 32 22N 88 42W
Meridian, Tex., U.S.A. 81 K6 31 56N 97 39W
Meriruma, Brazil 93 C8 1 15N 54 50W
Merkel, U.S.A. 81 J4 32 28N 100 1W
Merksem, Belgium 15 C4 51 16N 4 25 E
Mermaid Reef, Australia 60 C2 17 6S 119 36 E
Merowe, Sudan 51 E11 18 29N 31 46 E
Merredin, Australia 61 F2 31 28S 118 18 E
Merrick, U.K. 12 F4 55 8N 4 28W
Merrickville, Canada 79 B9 44 55N 75 50W
Merrill, Oreg., U.S.A. 82 E3 42 1N 121 36W
Merrill, Wis., U.S.A. 80 C10 45 11N 89 41W
Merriman, U.S.A. 80 D4 42 55N 101 42W
Merritt, Canada 72 C4 50 10N 120 45W
Merriwa, Australia 63 E5 32 6S 150 22 E
Merriwagga, Australia 63 E4 33 47S 145 43 E
Merry I., Canada 70 A4 55 29N 77 31W
Merrygoen, Australia 63 E4 31 51S 149 12 E
Merryville, U.S.A. 81 K8 30 45N 93 33W
Mersa Fatma, Eritrea 46 E3 14 57N 40 17 E
Mersch, Lux. 15 E6 49 44N 6 7 E
Merseburg, Germany 16 C6 51 22N 11 59 E
Mersey →, U.K. 10 D5 53 25N 3 1W
Merseyside □, U.K. 10 D5 53 31N 3 2W
Mersin, Turkey 25 G5 36 51N 34 36 E
Mersing, Malaysia 39 L4 2 25N 103 50 E
Merta, India 42 F6 26 39N 74 4 E
Merthyr Tydfil, U.K. 11 F4 51 45N 3 22W
Merthyr Tydfil □, U.K. 11 F4 51 46N 3 21W
Mértola, Portugal 19 D2 37 40N 7 40W
Mertzon, U.S.A. 81 K4 31 16N 100 49W
Meru, Kenya 54 B4 0 3N 37 40 E
Meru, Tanzania 54 C4 3 15S 36 46 E
Meru □, Kenya 54 B4 0 3N 37 46 E
Mesa, U.S.A. 83 K8 33 25N 111 50W
Mesanagrós, Greece 23 C9 36 1N 27 49 E
Mesaoría □, Cyprus 23 D12 35 12N 33 14 E
Mesarás, Kólpos, Greece 23 D6 35 6N 24 47 E
Mesgouez, L., Canada 70 B4 51 20N 75 0W
Meshed = Mashhad, Iran 45 B8 36 20N 59 35 E
Meshoppen, U.S.A. 79 E8 41 36N 76 3W
Meshra er Req, Sudan 51 G10 8 25N 29 18 E
Mesick, U.S.A. 76 C3 44 24N 85 43W
Mesilinka →, Canada 72 B4 56 6N 124 30W
Mesilla, U.S.A. 83 K10 32 16N 106 48W
Mesolóngion, Greece 21 E9 38 21N 21 28 E
Mesopotamia = Al Jazirah, Iraq 44 C5 33 30N 44 0 E
Mesquite, U.S.A. 83 H6 36 47N 114 6W
Mess Cr. →, Canada 72 B2 57 55N 131 14W
Messalo →, Mozam. 55 E4 12 25S 39 15 E
Messina, Italy 20 E6 38 11N 15 34 E
Messina, S. Africa 57 C5 22 20S 30 5 E
Messina, Str. di, Italy 20 F6 38 15N 15 35 E
Messini, Greece 21 F10 37 4N 22 1 E
Messiniakós Kólpos, Greece 21 F10 36 45N 22 5 E
Messonghi, Greece 23 B3 39 29N 19 56 E
Mesta →, Bulgaria 21 D11 40 54N 24 49 E
Meta →, S. Amer. 92 B5 6 12N 67 28W
Metairie, U.S.A. 81 L9 29 58N 90 10W
Metaline Falls, U.S.A. 82 B5 48 52N 117 22W
Metán, Argentina 94 B3 25 30S 65 0W
Metangula, Mozam. 55 E3 12 40S 34 50 E
Metema, Ethiopia 51 F12 12 56N 36 13 E
Metengobalame, Mozam. 55 E3 14 49S 34 30 E
Methven, N.Z. 59 K3 43 38S 171 40 E
Methy L., Canada 73 B7 56 28N 109 30W
Metil, Mozam. 55 F4 16 24S 39 0 E
Metlakatla, U.S.A. 72 B2 55 8N 131 35W
Metropolis, U.S.A. 81 G10 37 9N 88 44W
Mettur Dam, India 40 P10 11 45N 77 45 E
Metz, France 18 B7 49 8N 6 10 E
Meulaboh, Indonesia 36 D1 4 11N 96 3 E
Meureudu, Indonesia 36 C1 5 19N 96 10 E
Meuse →, Europe 18 A6 50 45N 5 41 E
Mexborough, U.K. 10 D6 53 30N 1 15W
Mexia, U.S.A. 81 K6 31 41N 96 29W
Mexiana, I., Brazil 93 C9 0 0 49 30W
Mexicali, Mexico 86 A1 32 40N 115 30W
Mexican Plateau, Mexico 66 G9 25 0N 104 0W
México, Mexico 87 D5 19 20N 99 10W
Mexico, Maine, U.S.A. 79 B14 44 34N 70 33W
Mexico, Mo., U.S.A. 80 F9 39 10N 91 53W
México □, Mexico 86 D5 19 20N 99 10W
Mexico ■, Cent. Amer. 86 C4 25 0N 105 0W
Mexico, G. of, Cent. Amer. 87 C7 25 0N 90 0W
Meymaneh, Afghan. 40 B4 35 53N 64 38 E
Mezen, Russia 24 A7 65 50N 44 20 E
Mezen →, Russia 24 A7 65 44N 44 22 E
Mézene, France 18 D6 44 54N 4 11 E
Mezökövesd, Hungary 17 E11 47 49N 20 35 E
Mezötúr, Hungary 17 E11 46 58N 20 41 E
Mezquital, Mexico 86 C4 23 29N 104 23W
Mgeta, Tanzania 55 D4 8 22S 36 6 E
Mhlaba Hills, Zimbabwe 55 F3 18 30S 30 30 E
Mhow, India 42 H6 22 33N 75 50 E
Miahuatlán, Mexico 87 D5 16 21N 96 36W
Miallo, Australia 62 B4 16 28S 145 22 E
Miami, Ariz., U.S.A. 83 K8 33 24N 110 52W
Miami, Fla., U.S.A. 77 N5 25 47N 80 11W
Miami, Tex., U.S.A. 81 H4 35 42N 100 38W
Miami →, U.S.A. 76 F3 39 20N 84 40W
Miami Beach, U.S.A. 77 N5 25 47N 80 8W
Mian Xian, China 34 H4 33 10N 106 32 E
Mianchi, China 34 G6 34 48N 111 48 E
Mīāndowāb, Iran 44 B5 37 0N 46 5 E
Miandrivazo, Madag. 57 B8 19 31S 45 29 E
Mīāneh, Iran 44 B5 37 30N 47 40 E
Mianwali, Pakistan 42 C4 32 38N 71 28 E
Miarinarivo, Madag. 57 B8 18 57S 46 55 E
Miass, Russia 24 D11 54 59N 60 6 E
Michalovce, Slovak Rep. 17 D11 48 47N 21 58 E
Michigan □, U.S.A. 76 C3 44 0N 85 0W
Michigan, L., U.S.A. 76 C2 44 0N 87 0W
Michigan City, U.S.A. 76 E2 41 43N 86 54W
Michikamau L., Canada 71 B7 54 20N 63 10W
Michipicoten, Canada 70 C3 47 55N 84 55W
Michipicoten I., Canada 70 C2 47 40N 85 40W
Michoacan □, Mexico 86 D4 19 0N 102 0W
Michurin, Bulgaria 21 C12 42 9N 27 51 E
Michurinsk, Russia 24 D7 52 58N 40 27 E
Miclere, Australia 62 C4 22 34S 147 32 E
Mico, Pta., Nic. 88 D3 12 0N 83 30W
Micronesia, Federated States of ■, Pac. Oc. 64 G7 9 0N 150 0 E
Midai, P., Indonesia 39 L6 3 0N 107 47 E
Midale, Canada 73 D8 49 25N 103 20W
Middelburg, Neths. 15 C3 51 30N 3 36 E
Middelburg, Eastern Cape, S. Africa 56 E3 31 30S 25 0 E
Middelburg, Mpumalanga, S. Africa 57 D4 25 49S 29 28 E
Middelwit, S. Africa 56 C4 24 51S 27 3 E
Middle Alkali L., U.S.A. 82 F3 41 27N 120 5W
Middle Fork Feather →, U.S.A. 84 F5 38 33N 121 30W
Middle I., Australia 61 F3 34 6S 123 11 E
Middle Loup →, U.S.A. 80 E5 41 17N 98 24W
Middleboro, U.S.A. 79 E14 41 54N 70 55W
Middleburg, N.Y., U.S.A. 79 D10 42 36N 74 20W
Middleburg, Pa., U.S.A. 78 F7 40 47N 77 3W
Middlebury, U.S.A. 79 B11 44 1N 73 10W
Middleport, U.S.A. 76 F4 39 0N 82 3W
Middlesboro, U.S.A. 77 G4 36 36N 83 43W
Middlesbrough, U.K. 10 C6 54 35N 1 13W
Middlesbrough □, U.K. 10 C6 54 28N 1 13W
Middlesex, Belize 88 C2 17 2N 88 31W
Middlesex, U.S.A. 79 F10 40 36N 74 30W
Middleton, Australia 62 C3 22 22S 141 32 E
Middleton, Canada 71 D6 44 57N 65 4W
Middletown, Calif., U.S.A. 84 G4 38 45N 122 37W
Middletown, Conn., U.S.A. 79 E12 41 34N 72 39W
Middletown, N.Y., U.S.A. 79 E10 41 27N 74 25W
Middletown, Ohio, U.S.A. 76 F3 39 31N 84 24W
Middletown, Pa., U.S.A. 79 F8 40 12N 76 44W
Midi, Canal du →, France 18 E4 43 45N 1 21 E
Midland, Canada 70 D4 44 45N 79 50W
Midland, Calif., U.S.A. 85 M12 33 52N 114 48W
Midland, Mich., U.S.A. 76 D3 43 37N 84 14W
Midland, Pa., U.S.A. 78 F4 40 39N 80 27W
Midland, Tex., U.S.A. 81 K3 32 0N 102 3W
Midlands □, Zimbabwe 55 F2 19 40S 29 0 E
Midleton, Ireland 13 E3 51 55N 8 10W
Midlothian, U.S.A. 81 J6 32 30N 97 0W
Midlothian □, U.K. 12 F5 55 51N 3 5W
Midongy, Tangorombohitr' i, Madag. 57 C8 23 30S 47 0 E
Midongy Atsimo, Madag. 57 C8 23 35S 47 1 E
Midway Is., Pac. Oc. 64 E10 28 13N 177 22W
Midway Wells, U.S.A. 85 N11 32 41N 115 7W
Midwest, U.S.A. 75 B9 42 0N 90 0W
Midwest, Wyo., U.S.A. 82 E10 43 25N 106 16W
Midwest City, U.S.A. 81 H6 35 27N 97 24W
Midzŏr, Bulgaria 21 C10 43 24N 22 40 E
Mie □, Japan 31 G8 34 30N 136 10 E
Międzychód, Poland 16 B8 52 35N 15 53 E
Międzyrzec Podlaski, Poland 17 C12 51 58N 22 45 E
Mielec, Poland 17 C11 50 15N 21 25 E
Mienga, Angola 56 B2 17 12S 19 48 E
Miercurea Ciuc, Romania 17 E13 46 21N 25 48 E
Mieres, Spain 19 A3 43 18N 5 48W
Mifflintown, U.S.A. 78 F7 40 34N 77 24W
Mifraz Hefa, Israel 47 C4 32 52N 35 0 E
Migdāl, Israel 47 C4 32 51N 35 30 E
Miguel Alemán, Presa, Mexico 87 D5 18 15N 96 40W
Miguel Alves, Brazil 93 D10 4 11S 42 55W
Mihara, Japan 31 G6 34 24N 133 5 E
Mikese, Tanzania 54 D4 6 48S 37 55 E
Mikhaylovgrad, Bulgaria 21 C10 43 27N 23 16 E
Mikkeli, Finland 9 F22 61 43N 27 15 E
Mikkwa →, Canada 72 B6 58 25N 114 46W
Mikonos, Greece 21 F11 37 30N 25 25 E
Mikumi, Tanzania 54 D4 7 26S 37 0 E
Mikun, Russia 24 B9 62 20N 50 0 E
Milaca, U.S.A. 80 C8 45 45N 93 39W
Milagro, Ecuador 92 D3 2 11S 79 36W
Milan = Milano, Italy 20 B3 45 28N 9 12 E
Milan, Mo., U.S.A. 80 E8 40 12N 93 7W
Milan, Tenn., U.S.A. 77 H1 35 55N 88 46W
Milang, Australia 63 E2 32 2S 139 10 E
Milange, Mozam. 55 F4 16 3S 35 45 E
Milano, Italy 20 B3 45 28N 9 12 E
Milâs, Turkey 21 F12 37 20N 27 50 E
Milatos, Greece 23 D7 35 18N 25 34 E
Milazzo, Italy 20 E6 38 13N 15 15 E
Milbank, U.S.A. 80 C6 45 13N 96 38W
Milden, Canada 73 C7 51 29N 107 32W
Mildmay, Canada 78 B3 44 3N 81 7W
Mildura, Australia 63 E3 34 13S 142 9 E
Miles, Australia 63 D5 26 40S 150 9 E
Miles, U.S.A. 81 K4 31 36N 100 11W
Miles City, U.S.A. 80 B2 46 25N 105 51W
Milestone, Canada 73 D8 49 59N 104 31W
Miletus, Turkey 21 F12 37 30N 27 18 E
Mileura, Australia 61 E2 26 22S 117 20 E
Milford, Calif., U.S.A. 84 E6 40 10N 120 22W
Milford, Conn., U.S.A. 79 E11 41 14N 73 3W
Milford, Del., U.S.A. 76 F8 38 55N 75 26W
Milford, Mass., U.S.A. 79 D13 42 8N 71 31W
Milford, Pa., U.S.A. 79 E10 41 19N 74 48W
Milford, Utah, U.S.A. 83 G7 38 24N 113 1W
Milford Haven, U.K. 11 F2 51 42N 5 7W
Milford Sd., N.Z. 59 L1 44 41S 167 47 E
Milgun, Australia 61 D2 24 56S 118 18 E
Milḥ, Baḥr al, Iraq 44 C4 32 40N 43 35 E
Miliana, Algeria 50 C5 27 20N 2 32 E
Miling, Australia 61 F2 30 30S 116 17 E
Milk →, U.S.A. 82 B10 48 4N 106 19W
Milk River, Canada 72 D6 49 10N 112 5W
Mill City, U.S.A. 82 D2 44 45N 122 29W
Mill I., Antarctica 5 C8 66 0S 101 30 E
Mill Valley, U.S.A. 84 H4 37 54N 122 32W
Millau, France 18 D5 44 8N 3 4 E
Millbridge, Canada 78 B7 44 41N 77 36W
Millbrook, Canada 78 B6 44 10N 78 29W
Mille Lacs, L. des, Canada 70 C1 48 45N 90 35W
Mille Lacs L., U.S.A. 80 B8 46 15N 93 39W
Milledgeville, U.S.A. 77 J4 33 5N 83 14W
Millen, U.S.A. 77 J5 32 48N 81 57W
Miller, U.S.A. 80 C5 44 31N 98 59W
Millersburg, Ohio, U.S.A. 78 F3 40 33N 81 55W
Millersburg, Pa., U.S.A. 78 F8 40 32N 76 58W
Millerton, U.S.A. 79 E11 41 57N 73 31W
Millerton L., U.S.A. 84 J7 37 1N 119 41W
Millicent, Australia 63 F3 37 34S 140 21 E
Millinocket, U.S.A. 71 C6 45 39N 68 43W
Millmerran, Australia 63 D5 27 53S 151 16 E
Mills L., Canada 72 A5 61 30N 118 20W
Millsboro, U.S.A. 78 G4 40 0N 80 0W
Milltown Malbay, Ireland 13 D2 52 52N 9 24W
Millville, U.S.A. 76 F8 39 24N 75 2W
Millwood L., U.S.A. 81 J8 33 42N 93 58W
Milne →, Australia 62 C2 21 10S 137 33 E
Milne Inlet, Canada 69 A11 72 30N 80 0W
Milnor, U.S.A. 80 B6 46 16N 97 27W
Milo, Canada 72 C6 50 34N 112 53W
Milos, Greece 21 F11 36 44N 24 25 E
Milparinka P.O., Australia 63 D3 29 46S 141 57 E
Milton, Canada 78 C5 43 31N 79 53W
Milton, N.Z. 59 M2 46 7S 169 59 E
Milton, U.K. 12 D4 57 18N 4 32W
Milton, Calif., U.S.A. 84 G6 38 3N 120 51W
Milton, Fla., U.S.A. 77 K2 30 38N 87 3W
Milton, Pa., U.S.A. 78 F8 41 1N 76 51W
Milton-Freewater, U.S.A. 82 D4 45 56N 118 23W
Milton Keynes, U.K. 11 E7 52 1N 0 44W
Miltou, Chad 51 F8 10 14N 17 26 E
Milverton, Canada 78 C4 43 34N 80 55W
Milwaukee, U.S.A. 76 D2 43 2N 87 55W
Milwaukee Deep, Atl. Oc. 89 C6 19 50N 68 0W
Milwaukie, U.S.A. 84 E4 45 27N 122 38W
Min Chiang →, China 33 D6 26 0N 119 35 E
Min Jiang →, China 32 D5 28 45N 104 48 E
Min Xian, China 34 G3 34 25N 104 5 E
Mina, U.S.A. 83 G4 38 24N 118 7W
Mina Pirquitas, Argentina 94 A2 22 40S 66 30W
Mīnā Su'ud, Si. Arabia 45 D6 28 45N 48 28 E
Mīnā'al Aḥmadī, Kuwait 45 D6 29 5N 48 10 E
Mīnāb, Iran 45 E8 27 10N 57 1 E
Minago →, Canada 73 C9 54 33N 98 59W
Minaki, Canada 73 D10 49 59N 94 40W
Minamata, Japan 31 H5 32 10N 130 30 E
Minami-Tori-Shima, Pac. Oc. 64 E7 24 0N 153 45 E
Minas, Uruguay 95 C4 34 20S 55 10W
Minas, Sierra de las, Guatemala 88 C2 15 9N 89 31W
Minas Basin, Canada 71 C7 45 20N 64 12W
Minas Gerais □, Brazil 93 G9 18 50S 46 0W
Minatitlán, Mexico 87 D6 17 59N 94 31W
Minbu, Burma 41 J19 20 10N 94 52 E
Mindanao, Phil. 37 C6 8 0N 125 0 E
Mindanao Sea = Bohol Sea, Phil. 37 C6 9 0N 124 0 E
Mindanao Trench, Pac. Oc. 37 B7 12 0N 126 6 E
Minden, Canada 78 B6 44 55N 78 43W
Minden, Germany 16 B5 52 17N 8 55 E
Minden, La., U.S.A. 81 J8 32 37N 93 17W
Minden, Nev., U.S.A. 84 G7 38 57N 119 46W
Mindiptana, Indonesia 37 F10 5 55S 140 22 E
Mindoro, Phil. 37 B6 13 0N 121 0 E
Mindoro Str., Phil. 37 B6 12 30N 120 30 E
Mindouli, Congo 52 E2 4 12S 14 28 E
Mine, Japan 31 G5 34 12N 131 7 E
Minehead, U.K. 11 F4 51 12N 3 29W
Mineola, U.S.A. 81 J7 32 40N 95 29W
Mineral King, U.S.A. 84 J8 36 27N 118 36W
Mineral Wells, U.S.A. 81 J5 32 48N 98 7W
Minersville, Pa., U.S.A. 79 F8 40 41N 76 16W
Minersville, Utah, U.S.A. 83 G7 38 13N 112 56W
Minerva, U.S.A. 78 F3 40 44N 81 6W
Minetto, U.S.A. 79 C8 43 24N 76 28W
Mingäçevir Su Anbarı, Azerbaijan 25 F8 40 57N 46 50 E
Mingan, Canada 71 B7 50 20N 64 0W
Mingechaurskoye Vdkhr. = Mingäçevir Su Anbarı, Azerbaijan 25 F8 40 57N 46 50 E
Mingela, Australia 62 B4 19 52S 146 38 E
Mingenew, Australia 61 E2 29 12S 115 21 E
Mingera Cr. →, Australia 62 C2 20 38S 137 45 E
Mingin, Burma 41 H19 22 50N 94 30 E
Mingt'iehkaitafan = Mintaka Pass, Pakistan 43 A6 37 0N 74 58 E
Mingyuegue, China 35 C15 43 2N 128 50 E
Minho = Miño →, Spain 19 A2 41 52N 8 40W
Minho, Portugal 19 B1 41 25N 8 20W
Minidoka, U.S.A. 82 E7 42 45N 113 29W
Minigwal, L., Australia 61 E3 29 31S 123 14 E
Minilya, Australia 61 D1 23 55S 114 0 E
Minilya →, Australia 61 D1 23 45S 114 0 E
Minipi, L., Canada 71 B7 52 25N 60 45W
Mink L., Canada 72 A5 61 54N 117 40W
Minna, Nigeria 50 G6 9 37N 6 30 E
Minneapolis, Kans., U.S.A. 80 F6 39 8N 97 42W
Minneapolis, Minn., U.S.A. 80 C8 44 59N 93 16W
Minnedosa, Canada 73 C9 50 14N 99 50W
Minnesota □, U.S.A. 80 B7 46 0N 94 15W
Minnie Creek, Australia 61 D2 24 3S 115 42 E
Minnipa, Australia 63 E2 32 51S 135 9 E
Minnitaki L., Canada 70 C1 49 57N 92 10W
Mino, Japan 31 G8 35 32N 136 55 E
Miño →, Spain 19 A2 41 52N 8 40W
Minorca = Menorca, Spain 22 B11 40 0N 4 0 E

Moonie

Minore, *Australia* **63 E4** 32 14S 148 27 E
Minot, *U.S.A.* **80 A4** 48 14N 101 18W
Minqin, *China* **34 E2** 38 38N 103 20 E
Minsk, *Belarus* **17 B14** 53 52N 27 30 E
Mińsk Mazowiecki, *Poland* **17 B11** 52 10N 21 33 E
Mintaka Pass, *Pakistan* **43 A6** 37 0N 74 58 E
Minto, *U.S.A.* **68 B5** 64 53N 149 11W
Minton, *Canada* **73 D8** 49 10N 104 35W
Minturn, *U.S.A.* **82 G10** 39 35N 106 26W
Minusinsk, *Russia* **27 D10** 53 50N 91 20 E
Minutang, *India* **41 E20** 28 15N 96 30 E
Minvoul, *Gabon* **52 D2** 2 9N 12 8 E
Mir, *Niger* **51 F7** 14 5N 11 59 E
Mīr Kūh, *Iran* **45 E8** 26 22N 58 55 E
Mīr Shahdād, *Iran* **45 E8** 26 15N 58 29 E
Mira, *Italy* **20 B5** 45 26N 12 8 E
Mira por vos Cay, *Bahamas* **89 B5** 22 9N 74 30W
Miraj, *India* **40 L9** 16 50N 74 45 E
Miram Shah, *Pakistan* **42 C4** 33 0N 70 2 E
Miramar, *Argentina* **94 D4** 38 15S 57 50W
Miramar, *Mozam.* **57 C6** 23 50S 35 35 E
Miramichi B., *Canada* **71 C7** 47 15N 65 0W
Miranda, *Brazil* **93 H7** 20 10S 56 15W
Miranda de Ebro, *Spain* **19 A4** 42 41N 2 57W
Miranda do Douro, *Portugal* **19 B2** 41 30N 6 16W
Mirando City, *U.S.A.* **81 M5** 27 26N 99 0W
Mirandópolis, *Brazil* **95 A5** 21 9S 51 6W
Mirango, *Malawi* **55 E3** 13 32S 34 58 E
Mirani, *Australia* **62 C4** 21 9S 148 53 E
Mirassol, *Brazil* **95 A6** 20 46S 49 28W
Mirbāţ, *Oman* **46 D5** 17 0N 54 45 E
Miri, *Malaysia* **36 D4** 4 23N 113 59 E
Miriam Vale, *Australia* **62 C5** 24 20S 151 33 E
Mirim, L., *S. Amer.* **95 C5** 32 45S 52 50W
Mirnyy, *Russia* **27 C12** 62 33N 113 53 E
Mirond L., *Canada* **73 B8** 55 6N 102 47W
Mirpur, *Pakistan* **43 C5** 33 32N 73 56 E
Mirpur Bibiwari, *Pakistan* **42 E2** 28 33N 67 44 E
Mirpur Khas, *Pakistan* **42 G3** 25 30N 69 0 E
Mirpur Sakro, *Pakistan* **42 G2** 24 33N 67 41 E
Mirror, *Canada* **72 C6** 52 30N 113 7W
Miryang, *S. Korea* **35 G15** 35 31N 128 44 E
Mirzapur, *India* **43 G10** 25 10N 82 34 E
Mirzapur-cum-Vindhyachal = Mirzapur, *India* **43 G10** 25 10N 82 34 E
Misantla, *Mexico* **87 D5** 19 56N 96 50W
Misawa, *Japan* **30 D10** 40 41N 141 24 E
Miscou I., *Canada* **71 C7** 47 57N 64 31W
Mish'āb, Ra'as al, *Si. Arabia* **45 D6** 28 15N 48 43 E
Mishan, *China* **33 B8** 45 37N 131 48 E
Mishawaka, *U.S.A.* **76 E2** 41 40N 86 11W
Mishima, *Japan* **31 G9** 35 10N 138 52 E
Misión, *Mexico* **85 N10** 32 6N 116 53W
Misiones □, *Argentina* **95 B5** 27 0S 55 0W
Misiones □, *Paraguay* **94 B4** 27 0S 56 0W
Miskah, *Si. Arabia* **44 E4** 24 49N 42 56 E
Miskitos, Cayos, *Nic.* **88 D3** 14 26N 82 50W
Miskolc, *Hungary* **17 D11** 48 7N 20 50 E
Misoke, *Zaïre* **54 C2** 0 42S 28 2 E
Misool, *Indonesia* **37 E8** 1 52S 130 10 E
Misrātah, *Libya* **51 B8** 32 24N 15 3 E
Missanabie, *Canada* **70 C3** 48 20N 84 6W
Missinaibi →, *Canada* **70 B3** 50 43N 81 29W
Missinaibi L., *Canada* **70 C3** 48 23N 83 40W
Mission, *S. Dak., U.S.A.* **80 D4** 43 18N 100 39W
Mission, *Tex., U.S.A.* **81 M5** 26 13N 98 20W
Mission City, *Canada* **72 D4** 49 10N 122 15W
Mission Viejo, *U.S.A.* **85 M9** 33 36N 117 40W
Missisa L., *Canada* **70 B2** 52 20N 85 7W
Missisagi →, *Canada* **70 C3** 46 15N 83 9W
Mississippi □, *U.S.A.* **81 J10** 33 0N 90 0W
Mississippi →, *U.S.A.* **81 L10** 29 9N 89 15W
Mississippi L., *Canada* **79 A8** 45 5N 76 10W
Mississippi River Delta, *U.S.A.* **81 L9** 29 10N 89 15W
Mississippi Sd., *U.S.A.* **81 K10** 30 20N 89 0W
Missoula, *U.S.A.* **82 C6** 46 52N 114 1W
Missouri □, *U.S.A.* **80 F8** 38 25N 92 30W
Missouri →, *U.S.A.* **80 F9** 38 49N 90 7W
Missouri Valley, *U.S.A.* **80 E7** 41 34N 95 53W
Mist, *U.S.A.* **84 E3** 45 59N 123 15W
Mistake B., *Canada* **73 A10** 62 8N 93 0W
Mistassini →, *Canada* **71 C5** 48 42N 72 20W
Mistassini L., *Canada* **70 B5** 51 0N 73 30W
Mistastin L., *Canada* **71 A7** 55 57N 63 20W
Mistatim, *Canada* **73 C8** 52 52N 103 22W
Misty L., *Canada* **73 B8** 58 53N 101 40W
Misurata = Misrātah, *Libya* **51 B8** 32 24N 15 3 E
Mitchell, *Australia* **63 D4** 26 29S 147 58 E
Mitchell, *Canada* **78 C3** 43 28N 81 12W
Mitchell, *Ind., U.S.A.* **76 F2** 38 44N 86 28W
Mitchell, *Nebr., U.S.A.* **80 E3** 41 57N 103 49W
Mitchell, *Oreg., U.S.A.* **82 D3** 44 34N 120 9W
Mitchell, *S. Dak., U.S.A.* **80 D5** 43 43N 98 2W
Mitchell →, *Australia* **62 B3** 15 12S 141 35 E
Mitchell, Mt., *U.S.A.* **77 H4** 35 46N 82 16W
Mitchell Ras., *Australia* **62 A2** 12 49S 135 36 E
Mitchelstown, *Ireland* **13 D3** 52 15N 8 16W
Mitha Tiwana, *Pakistan* **42 C5** 32 13N 72 6 E
Mitilíni, *Greece* **21 E12** 39 6N 26 35 E
Mito, *Japan* **31 F10** 36 20N 140 30 E
Mitrovica = Titova-Mitrovica, *Serbia, Yug.* **21 C9** 42 54N 20 52 E
Mitsinjo, *Madag.* **57 B8** 16 1S 45 52 E
Mitsiwa, *Eritrea* **51 E12** 15 35N 39 25 E
Mitsukaidō, *Japan* **31 F9** 36 1N 139 59 E
Mittagong, *Australia* **63 E5** 34 28S 150 29 E
Mitú, *Colombia* **92 C4** 1 8N 70 3W
Mitumba, *Tanzania* **54 D3** 7 8S 31 2 E
Mitumba, Chaîne des, *Zaïre* **54 D2** 7 0S 27 30 E
Mitumba Mts. = Mitumba, Chaîne des, *Zaïre* **54 D2** 7 0S 27 30 E
Mitwaba, *Zaïre* **55 D2** 8 2S 27 17 E
Mityana, *Uganda* **54 B3** 0 23N 32 2 E
Mitzic, *Gabon* **52 D2** 0 45N 11 40 E
Mixteco →, *Mexico* **87 D5** 18 11N 98 30W
Miyagi □, *Japan* **30 E10** 38 15N 140 45 E
Miyāh, W. el →, *Syria* **44 C3** 34 44N 39 57 E
Miyake-Jima, *Japan* **31 G9** 34 5N 139 30 E
Miyako, *Japan* **30 E10** 39 40N 141 59 E
Miyako-Jima, *Japan* **31 M2** 24 45N 125 20 E
Miyako-Rettō, *Japan* **31 M2** 24 24N 125 0 E
Miyakonojō, *Japan* **31 J5** 31 40N 131 5 E
Miyanoura-Dake, *Japan* **31 J5** 30 20N 130 31 E
Miyazaki, *Japan* **31 J5** 31 56N 131 30 E
Miyazaki □, *Japan* **31 H5** 32 30N 131 30 E
Miyazu, *Japan* **31 G7** 35 35N 135 10 E
Miyet, Bahr el = Dead Sea, *Asia* **47 D4** 31 30N 35 30 E
Miyoshi, *Japan* **31 G6** 34 48N 132 51 E
Miyun, *China* **34 D9** 40 28N 116 50 E
Miyun Shuiku, *China* **35 D9** 40 30N 117 0 E
Mizdah, *Libya* **51 B7** 31 30N 13 0 E
Mizen Hd., *Cork, Ireland* **13 E2** 51 27N 9 50W
Mizen Hd., *Wick., Ireland* **13 D5** 52 51N 6 4W
Mizhi, *China* **34 F6** 37 47N 110 12 E
Mizoram □, *India* **41 H18** 23 30N 92 40 E
Mizpe Ramon, *Israel* **47 E3** 30 34N 34 49 E
Mizusawa, *Japan* **30 E10** 39 8N 141 8 E
Mjölby, *Sweden* **9 G16** 58 20N 15 10 E
Mjøsa, *Norway* **9 F14** 60 40N 11 0 E
Mkata, *Tanzania* **54 D4** 5 45S 38 20 E
Mkokotoni, *Tanzania* **54 D4** 5 55S 39 15 E
Mkomazi, *Tanzania* **54 C4** 4 40S 38 7 E
Mkomazi →, *S. Africa* **57 E5** 30 12S 30 50 E
Mkulwe, *Tanzania* **55 D3** 8 37S 32 20 E
Mkumbi, Ras, *Tanzania* **54 D4** 7 38S 39 55 E
Mkushi, *Zambia* **55 E2** 14 25S 29 15 E
Mkushi River, *Zambia* **55 E2** 13 32S 29 45 E
Mkuze, *S. Africa* **57 D5** 27 10S 32 0 E
Mladá Boleslav, *Czech.* **16 C8** 50 27N 14 53 E
Mlala Hills, *Tanzania* **54 D3** 6 50S 31 40 E
Mlange, *Malawi* **55 F4** 16 2S 35 33 E
Mława, *Poland* **17 B11** 53 9N 20 25 E
Mljet, *Croatia* **20 C7** 42 43N 17 30 E
Mmabatho, *S. Africa* **56 D4** 25 49S 25 30 E
Mo i Rana, *Norway* **8 C16** 66 20N 14 7 E
Moa, *Indonesia* **37 F7** 8 0S 128 0 E
Moab, *U.S.A.* **83 G9** 38 35N 109 33W
Moabi, *Gabon* **52 E2** 2 24S 10 59 E
Moala, *Fiji* **59 D8** 18 36S 179 53 E
Moalie Park, *Australia* **63 D3** 29 42S 143 3 E
Moba, *Zaïre* **54 D2** 7 0S 29 48 E
Mobārakābād, *Iran* **45 D7** 28 24N 53 20 E
Mobārakīyeh, *Iran* **45 C6** 32 23N 51 37 E
Mobaye, *C.A.R.* **52 D4** 4 25N 21 5 E
Mobayi, *Zaïre* **52 D4** 4 15N 21 8 E
Moberly, *U.S.A.* **80 F8** 39 25N 92 26W
Moberly →, *Canada* **72 B4** 56 12N 120 55W
Mobile, *U.S.A.* **77 K1** 30 41N 88 3W
Mobile B., *U.S.A.* **77 K2** 30 30N 88 0W
Mobridge, *U.S.A.* **80 C4** 45 32N 100 26W
Mobutu Sese Seko, L. = Albert L., *Africa* **54 B3** 1 30N 31 0 E
Moc Chau, *Vietnam* **38 B5** 20 50N 104 38 E
Moc Hoa, *Vietnam* **39 G5** 10 46N 105 56 E
Mocabe Kasari, *Zaïre* **55 D2** 9 58S 26 12 E
Moçambique, *Mozam.* **55 F5** 15 3S 40 42 E
Moçâmedes = Namibe, *Angola* **53 H2** 15 7S 12 11 E
Mochudi, *Botswana* **56 C4** 24 27S 26 7 E
Mocimboa da Praia, *Mozam.* **55 E5** 11 25S 40 20 E
Moclips, *U.S.A.* **84 C2** 47 14N 124 13W
Mocoa, *Colombia* **92 C3** 1 7N 76 35W
Mococa, *Brazil* **95 A6** 21 28S 47 0W
Mocorito, *Mexico* **86 B3** 25 30N 107 53W
Moctezuma, *Mexico* **86 B3** 29 50N 109 0W
Moctezuma →, *Mexico* **87 C5** 21 59N 98 34W
Mocuba, *Mozam.* **55 F4** 16 54S 36 57 E
Mocúzari, Presa, *Mexico* **86 B3** 27 10N 109 10W
Modane, *France* **18 D7** 45 12N 6 40 E
Modasa, *India* **42 H5** 23 30N 73 21 E
Modder →, *S. Africa* **56 D3** 29 2S 24 37 E
Modderrivier, *S. Africa* **56 D3** 29 2S 24 38 E
Módena, *Italy* **20 B4** 44 40N 10 55 E
Modena, *U.S.A.* **83 H7** 37 48N 113 56W
Modesto, *U.S.A.* **83 H3** 37 39N 121 0W
Módica, *Italy* **20 F6** 36 52N 14 46 E
Moe, *Australia* **63 F4** 38 12S 146 19 E
Moebase, *Mozam.* **55 F4** 17 3S 38 41 E
Moengo, *Surinam* **93 B8** 5 45N 54 20W
Moffat, *U.K.* **12 F5** 55 21N 3 27W
Moga, *India* **42 D6** 30 48N 75 8 E
Mogadishu = Muqdisho, *Somali Rep.* **46 G4** 2 2N 45 25 E
Mogador = Essaouira, *Morocco* **50 B3** 31 32N 9 42W
Mogalakwena →, *S. Africa* **57 C4** 22 38S 28 40 E
Mogami →, *Japan* **30 E10** 38 45N 140 0 E
Mogán, *Canary Is.* **22 G4** 27 53N 15 43W
Mogaung, *Burma* **41 G20** 25 20N 97 0 E
Mogi das Cruzes, *Brazil* **95 A6** 23 31S 46 11W
Mogi-Guaçu →, *Brazil* **95 A6** 20 53S 48 10W
Mogi-Mirim, *Brazil* **95 A6** 22 29S 47 0W
Mogilev = Mahilyow, *Belarus* **17 B16** 53 55N 30 18 E
Mogilev-Podolskiy = Mohyliv-Podilskyy, *Ukraine* **17 D14** 48 26N 27 48 E
Mogincual, *Mozam.* **55 F5** 15 35S 40 25 E
Mogocha, *Russia* **27 D12** 53 40N 119 50 E
Mogoi, *Indonesia* **37 E8** 1 55S 133 10 E
Mogok, *Burma* **41 H20** 23 0N 96 40 E
Mogumber, *Australia* **61 F2** 31 2S 116 3 E
Mohács, *Hungary* **17 F10** 45 58N 18 41 E
Mohales Hoek, *Lesotho* **56 E4** 30 7S 27 26 E
Mohall, *U.S.A.* **80 A4** 48 46N 101 31W
Moḩammadābād, *Iran* **45 B8** 37 52N 59 5 E
Mohave, L., *U.S.A.* **85 K12** 35 12N 114 34W
Mohawk →, *U.S.A.* **79 D11** 42 47N 73 41W
Mohoro, *Tanzania* **54 D4** 8 6S 39 8 E
Mohyliv-Podilskyy, *Ukraine* **17 D14** 48 26N 27 48 E
Moidart, L., *U.K.* **12 E3** 56 47N 5 52W
Moires, *Greece* **23 D6** 35 4N 24 56 E
Moisaküla, *Estonia* **9 G21** 58 3N 25 12 E
Moisie, *Canada* **71 B6** 50 12N 66 1W
Moisie →, *Canada* **71 B6** 50 14N 66 5W
Moïssala, *Chad* **51 G8** 8 21N 17 46 E
Mojave, *U.S.A.* **85 K8** 35 3N 118 10W
Mojave Desert, *U.S.A.* **85 L10** 35 0N 116 30W
Mojo, *Bolivia* **94 A2** 21 48S 65 33W
Mojokerto, *Indonesia* **37 G15** 7 28S 112 26 E
Mokai, *N.Z.* **59 H5** 38 32S 175 56 E
Mokambo, *Zaïre* **55 E2** 12 25S 28 20 E
Mokameh, *India* **43 G11** 25 24N 85 55 E
Mokelumne →, *U.S.A.* **84 G5** 38 13N 121 28W
Mokelumne Hill, *U.S.A.* **84 G6** 38 18N 120 43W
Mokhós, *Greece* **23 D7** 35 16N 25 27 E
Mokhotlong, *Lesotho* **57 D4** 29 22S 29 2 E
Mokokchung, *India* **41 F19** 26 15N 94 30 E
Mokra Gora, *Serbia, Yug.* **21 C9** 42 50N 20 30 E
Mol, *Belgium* **15 C5** 51 11N 5 5 E
Molchanovo, *Russia* **26 D9** 57 40N 83 50 E
Mold, *U.K.* **10 D4** 53 9N 3 8W
Moldavia ■ = Moldova ■, *Europe* **17 E15** 47 0N 28 0 E
Molde, *Norway* **8 E12** 62 45N 7 9 E
Moldova ■, *Europe* **17 E15** 47 0N 28 0 E
Moldoveana, *Romania* **17 F13** 45 36N 24 45 E
Molepolole, *Botswana* **56 C4** 24 28S 25 28 E
Molfetta, *Italy* **20 D7** 41 12N 16 36 E
Moline, *U.S.A.* **80 E9** 41 30N 90 31W
Molinos, *Argentina* **94 B2** 25 28S 66 15W
Moliro, *Zaïre* **54 D3** 8 12S 30 30 E
Mollahat, *Bangla.* **43 H13** 22 56N 89 48 E
Mollendo, *Peru* **92 G4** 17 0S 72 0W
Mollerin, L., *Australia* **61 F2** 30 30S 117 35 E
Mölndal, *Sweden* **9 H15** 57 40N 12 3 E
Molodechno = Maladzyechna, *Belarus* **17 A14** 54 20N 26 50 E
Molokai, *U.S.A.* **74 H16** 21 8N 157 0W
Molong, *Australia* **63 E4** 33 5S 148 54 E
Molopo →, *Africa* **56 D3** 27 30S 20 13 E
Molotov = Perm, *Russia* **24 C10** 58 0N 56 10 E
Moloundou, *Cameroon* **52 D3** 2 8N 15 15 E
Molson L., *Canada* **73 C9** 54 22N 96 40W
Molteno, *S. Africa* **56 E4** 31 22S 26 22 E
Molu, *Indonesia* **37 F8** 6 45S 131 40 E
Molucca Sea, *Indonesia* **37 E6** 2 0S 124 0 E
Moluccas = Maluku, *Indonesia* **37 E7** 1 0S 127 0 E
Moma, *Mozam.* **55 F4** 16 47S 39 4 E
Moma, *Zaïre* **54 C1** 1 35S 23 52 E
Mombasa, *Kenya* **54 C4** 4 2S 39 43 E
Mombetsu, *Japan* **30 B11** 44 21N 143 22 E
Momchilgrad, *Bulgaria* **21 D11** 41 33N 25 23 E
Momi, *Zaïre* **54 C2** 1 42S 27 0 E
Mompós, *Colombia* **92 B4** 9 14N 74 26W
Møn, *Denmark* **9 J15** 54 57N 12 15 E
Mon →, *Burma* **41 J19** 20 25N 94 30 E
Mona, Canal de la, *W. Indies* **89 C6** 18 30N 67 45W
Mona, Isla, *Puerto Rico* **89 C6** 18 5N 67 54W
Mona, Pta., *Costa Rica* **88 E3** 9 37N 82 36W
Monach Is., *U.K.* **12 D1** 57 32N 7 40W
Monaco ■, *Europe* **18 E7** 43 46N 7 23 E
Monadhliath Mts., *U.K.* **12 D4** 57 10N 4 4W
Monaghan, *Ireland* **13 B5** 54 15N 6 57W
Monaghan □, *Ireland* **13 B5** 54 11N 6 56W
Monahans, *U.S.A.* **81 K3** 31 36N 102 54W
Monapo, *Mozam.* **55 E5** 14 56S 40 19 E
Monarch Mt., *Canada* **72 C3** 51 55N 125 57W
Monastir = Bitola, *Macedonia* **21 D9** 41 5N 21 10 E
Monastir, *Tunisia* **51 A7** 35 50N 10 49 E
Moncayo, Sierra del, *Spain* **19 B5** 41 48N 1 50W
Monchegorsk, *Russia* **24 A5** 67 54N 32 58 E
Mönchengladbach, *Germany* **16 C4** 51 11N 6 27 E
Monchique, *Portugal* **19 D1** 37 19N 8 38W
Monclova, *Mexico* **86 B4** 26 50N 101 30W
Moncton, *Canada* **71 C7** 46 7N 64 51W
Mondego →, *Portugal* **19 B1** 40 9N 8 52W
Mondeodo, *Indonesia* **37 E6** 3 34S 122 9 E
Mondovì, *Italy* **20 B2** 44 23N 7 49 E
Mondovi, *U.S.A.* **80 C9** 44 34N 91 40W
Mondrain I., *Australia* **61 F3** 34 9S 122 14 E
Monduli □, *Tanzania* **54 C4** 3 0S 36 0 E
Monessen, *U.S.A.* **78 F5** 40 9N 79 54W
Monett, *U.S.A.* **81 G8** 36 55N 93 55W
Monforte de Lemos, *Spain* **19 A2** 42 31N 7 33W
Mong Hsu, *Burma* **41 J21** 21 54N 98 30 E
Mong Kung, *Burma* **41 J20** 21 35N 97 35 E
Mong Nai, *Burma* **41 J20** 20 32N 97 46 E
Mong Pawk, *Burma* **41 H21** 22 4N 99 16 E
Mong Ton, *Burma* **41 J21** 20 17N 98 45 E
Mong Wa, *Burma* **41 J22** 21 26N 100 27 E
Mong Yai, *Burma* **41 H21** 22 21N 98 3 E
Mongalla, *Sudan* **51 G11** 5 8N 31 42 E
Mongers, L., *Australia* **61 E2** 29 25S 117 5 E
Monghyr = Munger, *India* **43 G12** 25 23N 86 30 E
Mongibello = Etna, *Italy* **20 F6** 37 50N 14 55 E
Mongo, *Chad* **51 F8** 12 14N 18 43 E
Mongolia ■, *Asia* **27 E10** 47 0N 103 0 E
Mongororo, *Chad* **51 F9** 12 3N 22 26 E
Mongu, *Zambia* **53 H4** 15 16S 23 12 E
Mônguo, *Angola* **56 B2** 16 43S 15 20 E
Monkey Bay, *Malawi* **55 E4** 14 7S 35 1 E
Monkey River, *Belize* **87 D7** 16 22N 88 29W
Monkira, *Australia* **62 C3** 24 46S 140 30 E
Monkoto, *Zaïre* **52 E4** 1 38S 20 35 E
Monmouth, *U.K.* **11 F5** 51 48N 2 42W
Monmouth, *U.S.A.* **80 E9** 40 55N 90 39W
Monmouthshire □, *U.K.* **11 F5** 51 48N 2 54W
Mono L., *U.S.A.* **83 H4** 38 1N 119 1W
Monolith, *U.S.A.* **85 K8** 35 7N 118 22W
Monólithos, *Greece* **23 C9** 36 7N 27 45 E
Monongahela, *U.S.A.* **78 F5** 40 12N 79 56W
Monópoli, *Italy* **20 D7** 40 57N 17 18 E
Monqoumba, *C.A.R.* **52 D3** 3 33N 18 40 E
Monroe, *Ga., U.S.A.* **77 J4** 33 47N 83 43W
Monroe, *La., U.S.A.* **81 J8** 32 30N 92 7W
Monroe, *Mich., U.S.A.* **76 E4** 41 55N 83 24W
Monroe, *N.C., U.S.A.* **77 H5** 34 59N 80 33W
Monroe, *N.Y., U.S.A.* **79 E10** 41 20N 74 11W
Monroe, *Utah, U.S.A.* **83 G7** 38 38N 112 7W
Monroe, *Wash., U.S.A.* **84 C5** 47 51N 121 58W
Monroe, *Wis., U.S.A.* **80 D10** 42 36N 89 38W
Monroe City, *U.S.A.* **80 F9** 39 39N 91 44W
Monroeville, *Ala., U.S.A.* **77 K2** 31 31N 87 20W
Monroeville, *Pa., U.S.A.* **78 F5** 40 26N 79 45W
Monrovia, *Liberia* **50 G2** 6 18N 10 47W
Mons, *Belgium* **15 D3** 50 27N 3 58 E
Monse, *Indonesia* **37 E6** 4 0S 123 10 E
Mont-de-Marsan, *France* **18 E3** 43 54N 0 31W
Mont-Joli, *Canada* **71 C6** 48 37N 68 10W
Mont-Laurier, *Canada* **70 C4** 46 35N 75 30W
Mont-St.-Michel, Le = Le Mont-St.-Michel, *France* **18 B3** 48 40N 1 30W
Mont Tremblant Prov. Park, *Canada* **70 C5** 46 30N 74 30W
Montagu, *S. Africa* **56 E3** 33 45S 20 8 E
Montagu I., *Antarctica* **5 B1** 58 25S 26 20W
Montague, *Canada* **71 C7** 46 10N 62 39W
Montague, *U.S.A.* **82 F2** 41 44N 122 32W
Montague, I., *Mexico* **86 A2** 31 40N 114 56W
Montague Ra., *Australia* **61 E2** 27 15S 119 30 E
Montague Sd., *Australia* **60 B4** 14 28S 125 20 E
Montalbán, *Spain* **19 B5** 40 50N 0 45W
Montalvo, *U.S.A.* **85 L7** 34 15N 119 12W
Montaña, *Peru* **92 E4** 6 0S 73 0W
Montana □, *U.S.A.* **82 C9** 47 0N 110 0W
Montaña Clara, I., *Canary Is.* **22 E6** 29 17N 13 33W
Montargis, *France* **18 C5** 47 59N 2 43 E
Montauban, *France* **18 D4** 44 2N 1 21 E
Montauk, *U.S.A.* **79 E13** 41 3N 71 57W
Montauk Pt., *U.S.A.* **79 E13** 41 4N 71 52W
Montbéliard, *France* **18 C7** 47 31N 6 48 E
Montceau-les-Mines, *France* **18 C6** 46 40N 4 23 E
Montclair, *U.S.A.* **79 F10** 40 49N 74 13W
Monte Albán, *Mexico* **87 D5** 17 2N 96 45W
Monte Alegre, *Brazil* **93 D8** 2 0S 54 0W
Monte Azul, *Brazil* **93 G10** 15 9S 42 53W
Monte Bello Is., *Australia* **60 D2** 20 30S 115 45 E
Monte-Carlo, *Monaco* **16 G4** 43 46N 7 23 E
Monte Caseros, *Argentina* **94 C4** 30 10S 57 50W
Monte Comán, *Argentina* **94 C2** 34 40S 67 53W
Monte Cristi, *Dom. Rep.* **89 C5** 19 52N 71 39W
Monte Lindo →, *Paraguay* **94 A4** 23 56S 57 12W
Monte Quemado, *Argentina* **94 B3** 25 53S 62 41W
Monte Rio, *U.S.A.* **84 G4** 38 28N 123 0W
Monte Santu, C. di, *Italy* **20 D3** 40 5N 9 44 E
Monte Vista, *U.S.A.* **83 H10** 37 35N 106 9W
Monteagudo, *Argentina* **95 B5** 27 14S 54 8W
Montebello, *Canada* **70 C5** 45 40N 74 55W
Montecito, *U.S.A.* **85 L7** 34 26N 119 40W
Montecristi, *Ecuador* **92 D2** 1 0S 80 40W
Montecristo, *Italy* **20 C4** 42 20N 10 19 E
Montego Bay, *Jamaica* **88 C4** 18 30N 78 0W
Montejinnie, *Australia* **60 C5** 16 40S 131 38 E
Montélimar, *France* **18 D6** 44 33N 4 45 E
Montello, *U.S.A.* **80 D10** 43 48N 89 20W
Montemorelos, *Mexico* **87 B5** 25 11N 99 42W
Montenegro, *Brazil* **95 B5** 29 39S 51 29W
Montenegro □, *Yugoslavia* **21 C8** 42 40N 19 20 E
Montepuez, *Mozam.* **55 E4** 13 8S 38 59 E
Montepuez →, *Mozam.* **55 E5** 12 32S 40 27 E
Monterey, *U.S.A.* **83 H3** 36 37N 121 55W
Monterey B., *U.S.A.* **84 J5** 36 45N 122 0W
Montería, *Colombia* **92 B3** 8 46N 75 53W
Monteros, *Argentina* **94 B2** 27 11S 65 30W
Monterrey, *Mexico* **86 B4** 25 40N 100 30W
Montes Claros, *Brazil* **93 G10** 16 30S 43 50W
Montesano, *U.S.A.* **84 D3** 46 59N 123 36W
Montesilvano Marina, *Italy* **20 C6** 42 29N 14 8 E
Montevideo, *Uruguay* **95 C4** 34 50S 56 11W
Montevideo, *U.S.A.* **80 C7** 44 57N 95 43W
Montezuma, *U.S.A.* **80 E8** 41 35N 92 32W
Montgomery = Sahiwal, *Pakistan* **42 D5** 30 45N 73 8 E
Montgomery, *U.K.* **11 E4** 52 34N 3 8W
Montgomery, *Ala., U.S.A.* **77 J2** 32 23N 86 19W
Montgomery, *W. Va., U.S.A.* **76 F5** 38 11N 81 19W
Monticello, *Ark., U.S.A.* **81 J9** 33 38N 91 47W
Monticello, *Fla., U.S.A.* **77 K4** 30 33N 83 52W
Monticello, *Ind., U.S.A.* **76 E2** 40 45N 86 46W
Monticello, *Iowa, U.S.A.* **80 D9** 42 15N 91 12W
Monticello, *Ky., U.S.A.* **77 G3** 36 50N 84 51W
Monticello, *Minn., U.S.A.* **80 C8** 45 18N 93 48W
Monticello, *Miss., U.S.A.* **81 K9** 31 33N 90 7W
Monticello, *N.Y., U.S.A.* **79 E10** 41 39N 74 42W
Monticello, *Utah, U.S.A.* **83 H9** 37 52N 109 21W
Montijo, *Portugal* **19 C1** 38 41N 8 54W
Montilla, *Spain* **19 D3** 37 36N 4 40W
Montluçon, *France* **18 C5** 46 22N 2 36 E
Montmagny, *Canada* **71 C5** 46 58N 70 34W
Montmartre, *Canada* **73 C8** 50 14N 103 27W
Montmorency, *Canada* **71 C5** 46 53N 71 11W
Montmorillon, *France* **18 C4** 46 26N 0 50 E
Monto, *Australia* **62 C5** 24 52S 151 6 E
Montoro, *Spain* **19 C3** 38 1N 4 27W
Montour Falls, *U.S.A.* **78 D8** 42 21N 76 51W
Montpelier, *Idaho, U.S.A.* **82 E8** 42 19N 111 18W
Montpelier, *Ohio, U.S.A.* **76 E3** 41 35N 84 37W
Montpelier, *Vt., U.S.A.* **79 B12** 44 16N 72 35W
Montpellier, *France* **18 E5** 43 37N 3 52 E
Montréal, *Canada* **70 C5** 45 31N 73 34W
Montreal L., *Canada* **73 C7** 54 20N 105 45W
Montreal Lake, *Canada* **73 C7** 54 3N 105 46W
Montreux, *Switz.* **16 E4** 46 26N 6 55 E
Montrose, *U.K.* **12 E6** 56 44N 2 27W
Montrose, *Colo., U.S.A.* **83 G10** 38 29N 107 53W
Montrose, *Pa., U.S.A.* **79 E9** 41 50N 75 53W
Monts, Pte. des, *Canada* **71 C6** 49 20N 67 12W
Montserrat ■, *W. Indies* **89 C7** 16 40N 62 10W
Montuiri, *Spain* **22 B9** 39 34N 2 59 E
Monveda, *Zaïre* **52 D4** 2 52N 21 30 E
Monywa, *Burma* **41 H19** 22 7N 95 11 E
Monza, *Italy* **20 B3** 45 35N 9 16 E
Monze, *Zambia* **55 F2** 16 17S 27 29 E
Monze, C., *Pakistan* **42 G2** 24 47N 66 37 E
Monzón, *Spain* **19 B6** 41 52N 0 10 E
Mooi River, *S. Africa* **57 D4** 29 13S 29 50 E
Moolawatana, *Australia* **63 D2** 29 55S 139 45 E
Mooliabeenee, *Australia* **61 F2** 31 20S 116 2 E
Mooloogool, *Australia* **61 E2** 26 2S 119 5 E
Moomin Cr. →, *Australia* **63 D4** 29 44S 149 20 E
Moonah →, *Australia* **62 C2** 22 3S 138 33 E
Moonbeam, *Canada* **70 C3** 49 20N 82 10W
Moonda, L., *Australia* **62 D3** 25 52S 140 25 E
Moonie, *Australia* **63 D5** 27 46S 150 20 E
Moonie →, *Australia* **63 D4** 29 19S 148 43 E

Namwala

Mull, *U.K.* **12 E3** 56 25N 5 56W
Mullaittvu, *Sri Lanka* **40 Q12** 9 15N 80 49 E
Mullen, *U.S.A.* **80 D4** 42 3N 101 1W
Mullengudgery, *Australia* **63 E4** 31 43S 147 23 E
Mullens, *U.S.A.* **76 G5** 37 35N 81 23W
Muller, Pegunungan, *Indonesia* **36 D4** 0 30N 113 30 E
Mullet Pen., *Ireland* **13 B1** 54 13N 10 2W
Mullewa, *Australia* **61 E2** 28 29S 115 30 E
Mulligan →, *Australia* **62 C2** 25 0S 139 0 E
Mullin, *U.S.A.* **81 K5** 31 33N 98 40W
Mullingar, *Ireland* **13 C4** 53 31N 7 21W
Mullins, *U.S.A.* **77 H6** 34 12N 79 15W
Mullumbimby, *Australia* **63 D5** 28 30S 153 30 E
Mulobezi, *Zambia* **55 F2** 16 45S 25 7 E
Multan, *Pakistan* **42 D4** 30 15N 71 36 E
Mulumbe, Mts., *Zaïre* **55 D2** 8 40S 27 30 E
Mulungushi Dam, *Zambia* **55 E2** 14 48S 28 48 E
Mulvane, *U.S.A.* **81 G6** 37 29N 97 15W
Mulwala, *Australia* **63 F4** 35 59S 146 0 E
Mumbaï = Bombay, *India* **40 K8** 18 55N 72 50 E
Mumbwa, *Zambia* **55 E2** 15 0S 27 0 E
Mun →, *Thailand* **38 E5** 15 19N 105 30 E
Muna, *Indonesia* **37 F6** 5 0S 122 30 E
Munamagi, *Estonia* **9 H22** 57 43N 27 4 E
München, *Germany* **16 D6** 48 8N 11 34 E
Munchen-Gladbach = Mönchengladbach, *Germany* **16 C4** 51 11N 6 27 E
Muncho Lake, *Canada* **72 B3** 59 0N 125 50W
Munchŏn, *N. Korea* **35 E14** 39 14N 127 19 E
Muncie, *U.S.A.* **76 E3** 40 12N 85 23W
Muncoonie, L., *Australia* **62 D2** 25 12S 138 40 E
Mundala, *Indonesia* **37 E10** 4 30S 141 0 E
Mundare, *Canada* **72 C6** 53 35N 112 20W
Munday, *U.S.A.* **81 J5** 33 27N 99 38W
Münden, *Germany* **16 C5** 51 25N 9 38 E
Mundiwindi, *Australia* **60 D3** 23 47S 120 9 E
Mundo Novo, *Brazil* **93 F10** 11 50S 40 29W
Mundra, *India* **42 H3** 22 54N 69 48 E
Mundrabilla, *Australia* **61 F4** 31 52S 127 51 E
Mungallala, *Australia* **63 D4** 26 28S 147 34 E
Mungallala Cr. →, *Australia* **63 D4** 28 53S 147 5 E
Mungana, *Australia* **62 B3** 17 8S 144 27 E
Mungaoli, *India* **42 G8** 24 24N 78 7 E
Mungari, *Mozam.* **55 F3** 17 12S 33 30 E
Mungbere, *Zaïre* **54 B2** 2 36N 28 28 E
Munger, *India* **43 G12** 25 23N 86 30 E
Mungindi, *Australia* **63 D4** 28 58S 149 1 E
Munhango, *Angola* **53 G3** 12 10S 18 38 E
Munich = München, *Germany* **16 D6** 48 8N 11 34 E
Munising, *U.S.A.* **76 B2** 46 25N 86 40W
Munku-Sardyk, *Russia* **27 D11** 51 45N 100 20 E
Muñoz Gamero, Pen., *Chile* **96 G2** 52 30S 73 5W
Munroe L., *Canada* **73 B9** 59 13N 98 35W
Munsan, *S. Korea* **35 F14** 37 51N 126 48 E
Münster, *Germany* **16 C4** 51 58N 7 37 E
Munster □, *Ireland* **13 D3** 52 18N 8 44W
Muntadgin, *Australia* **61 F2** 31 45S 118 33 E
Muntok, *Indonesia* **36 E3** 2 5S 105 10 E
Munyama, *Zambia* **55 F2** 16 5S 28 31 E
Muong Beng, *Laos* **38 B3** 20 23N 101 46 E
Muong Boum, *Vietnam* **38 A4** 22 24N 102 49 E
Muong Et, *Laos* **38 B5** 20 49N 104 1 E
Muong Hai, *Laos* **38 B3** 21 3N 101 49 E
Muong Hiem, *Laos* **38 B4** 20 5N 103 22 E
Muong Houn, *Laos* **38 B3** 20 8N 101 23 E
Muong Hung, *Vietnam* **38 B4** 20 56N 103 53 E
Muong Kau, *Laos* **38 E5** 15 6N 105 47 E
Muong Khao, *Laos* **38 C4** 19 38N 103 32 E
Muong Khoua, *Laos* **38 B4** 21 5N 102 31 E
Muong Liep, *Laos* **38 C3** 18 29N 101 40 E
Muong May, *Laos* **38 E6** 14 49N 106 56 E
Muong Ngeun, *Laos* **38 B3** 20 36N 101 3 E
Muong Ngoi, *Laos* **38 B4** 20 43N 102 41 E
Muong Nhie, *Vietnam* **38 A4** 22 12N 102 28 E
Muong Nong, *Laos* **38 D6** 16 22N 106 30 E
Muong Ou Tay, *Laos* **38 A3** 22 7N 101 48 E
Muong Oua, *Laos* **38 C3** 18 18N 101 20 E
Muong Peun, *Laos* **38 B4** 20 13N 103 52 E
Muong Phalane, *Laos* **38 D5** 16 39N 105 34 E
Muong Phieng, *Laos* **38 C3** 19 6N 101 32 E
Muong Phine, *Laos* **38 D6** 16 32N 106 2 E
Muong Sai, *Laos* **38 B3** 20 42N 101 59 E
Muong Saiapoun, *Laos* **38 C3** 18 24N 101 31 E
Muong Sen, *Vietnam* **38 C5** 19 24N 104 8 E
Muong Sing, *Laos* **38 B3** 21 11N 101 9 E
Muong Son, *Laos* **38 B4** 20 27N 103 19 E
Muong Soui, *Laos* **38 C4** 19 33N 102 52 E
Muong Va, *Laos* **38 B4** 21 53N 102 19 E
Muong Xia, *Vietnam* **38 B5** 20 19N 104 50 E
Muonio, *Finland* **8 C20** 67 57N 23 40 E
Muonionjoki →, *Finland* **8 C20** 67 11N 23 34 E
Mupa, *Angola* **53 H3** 16 5S 15 50 E
Muping, *China* **35 F11** 37 22N 121 36 E
Muqdisho, *Somali Rep.* **46 G4** 2 2N 45 25 E
Mur →, *Austria* **17 E9** 46 18N 16 52 E
Murakami, *Japan* **30 E9** 38 14N 139 29 E
Murallón, Cuerro, *Chile* **96 F2** 49 48S 73 30W
Muranda, *Rwanda* **54 C2** 1 52S 29 20 E
Murang'a, *Kenya* **54 C4** 0 45S 37 9 E
Murashi, *Russia* **24 C8** 59 30N 49 0 E
Muratlı, *Turkey* **21 D12** 41 10N 27 29 E
Murayama, *Japan* **30 E10** 38 30N 140 25 E
Murban, *U.A.E.* **45 F7** 23 50N 53 45 E
Murchison →, *Australia* **61 E1** 27 45S 114 0 E
Murchison, Mt., *Antarctica* **5 D11** 73 0S 168 0 E
Murchison Falls = Kabarega Falls, *Uganda* **54 B3** 2 15N 31 30 E
Murchison House, *Australia* **61 E1** 27 39S 114 14 E
Murchison Ra., *Australia* **62 C1** 20 0S 134 10 E
Murchison Rapids, *Malawi* **55 F3** 15 55S 34 35 E
Murcia, *Spain* **19 D5** 38 5N 1 10W
Murcia □, *Spain* **19 D5** 37 50N 1 30W
Murdo, *U.S.A.* **80 D4** 43 53N 100 43W
Murdoch Pt., *Australia* **62 A3** 14 37S 144 55 E
Mureş →, *Romania* **17 E11** 46 15N 20 13 E
Mureşul = Mureş →, *Romania* **17 E11** 46 15N 20 13 E
Murfreesboro, *U.S.A.* **77 H2** 35 51N 86 24W
Murgab = Murghob, *Tajikistan* **26 F8** 38 10N 74 2 E
Murghob, *Tajikistan* **26 F8** 38 10N 74 2 E
Murgon, *Australia* **63 D5** 26 15S 151 54 E
Murgoo, *Australia* **61 E2** 27 24S 116 28 E
Muria, *Indonesia* **37 G14** 6 36S 110 53 E
Muriaé, *Brazil* **95 A7** 21 8S 42 23W
Muriel Mine, *Zimbabwe* **55 F3** 17 14S 30 40 E
Müritz-see, *Germany* **16 B7** 53 25N 12 42 E
Murka, *Kenya* **54 C4** 3 27S 38 0 E
Murmansk, *Russia* **24 A5** 68 57N 33 10 E
Muro, *Spain* **22 B10** 39 44N 3 3 E
Murom, *Russia* **24 C7** 55 35N 42 3 E
Muroran, *Japan* **30 C10** 42 25N 141 0 E
Muroto, *Japan* **31 H7** 33 18N 134 9 E
Muroto-Misaki, *Japan* **31 H7** 33 15N 134 10 E
Murphy, *U.S.A.* **82 E5** 43 13N 116 33W
Murphys, *U.S.A.* **84 G6** 38 8N 120 28W
Murphysboro, *U.S.A.* **81 G10** 37 46N 89 20W
Murray, *Ky., U.S.A.* **77 G1** 36 37N 88 19W
Murray, *Utah, U.S.A.* **82 F8** 40 40N 111 53W
Murray →, *Australia* **63 F2** 35 20S 139 22 E
Murray →, *Canada* **72 B4** 56 11N 120 45W
Murray, L., *U.S.A.* **77 H5** 34 3N 81 13W
Murray Bridge, *Australia* **63 F2** 35 6S 139 14 E
Murray Downs, *Australia* **62 C1** 21 4S 134 40 E
Murray Harbour, *Canada* **71 C7** 46 0N 62 28W
Murraysburg, *S. Africa* **56 E3** 31 58S 23 47 E
Murree, *Pakistan* **42 C5** 33 56N 73 28 E
Murrieta, *U.S.A.* **85 M9** 33 33N 117 13W
Murrin Murrin, *Australia* **61 E3** 28 58S 121 33 E
Murrumbidgee →, *Australia* **63 E3** 34 43S 143 12 E
Murrumburrah, *Australia* **63 E4** 34 32S 148 22 E
Murrurundi, *Australia* **63 E5** 31 42S 150 51 E
Murshidabad, *India* **43 G13** 24 11N 88 19 E
Murtle L., *Canada* **72 C5** 52 8N 119 38W
Murtoa, *Australia* **63 F3** 36 35S 142 28 E
Murungu, *Tanzania* **54 C3** 4 12S 31 10 E
Murwara, *India* **43 H9** 23 46N 80 28 E
Murwillumbah, *Australia* **63 D5** 28 18S 153 27 E
Mürzzuschlag, *Austria* **16 E8** 47 36N 15 41 E
Muş, *Turkey* **25 G7** 38 45N 41 30 E
Mûsa, G., *Egypt* **51 C11** 28 33N 33 59 E
Musa Khel, *Pakistan* **42 D3** 30 59N 69 52 E
Mūsá Qal'eh, *Afghan.* **40 C4** 32 20N 64 50 E
Musaffargarh, *Pakistan* **40 D7** 30 10N 71 10 E
Musala, *Bulgaria* **21 C10** 42 13N 23 37 E
Musala, *Indonesia* **36 D1** 1 41N 98 28 E
Musan, *N. Korea* **35 C15** 42 12N 129 12 E
Musangu, *Zaïre* **55 E1** 10 28S 23 55 E
Musasa, *Tanzania* **54 C3** 3 25S 31 30 E
Musay'īd, *Qatar* **45 E6** 25 0N 51 33 E
Muscat = Masqat, *Oman* **46 C6** 23 37N 58 36 E
Muscat & Oman = Oman ■, *Asia* **46 C6** 23 0N 58 0 E
Muscatine, *U.S.A.* **80 E9** 41 25N 91 3W
Musgrave, *Australia* **62 A3** 14 47S 143 30 E
Musgrave Ras., *Australia* **61 E5** 26 0S 132 0 E
Mushie, *Zaïre* **52 E3** 2 56S 16 55 E
Musi →, *Indonesia* **36 E2** 2 20S 104 56 E
Muskeg →, *Canada* **72 A4** 60 20N 123 20W
Muskegon, *U.S.A.* **76 D2** 43 14N 86 16W
Muskegon →, *U.S.A.* **76 D2** 43 14N 86 21W
Muskegon Heights, *U.S.A.* **76 D2** 43 12N 86 16W
Muskogee, *U.S.A.* **81 H7** 35 45N 95 22W
Muskwa →, *Canada* **72 B4** 58 47N 122 48W
Muslīmiyah, *Syria* **44 B3** 36 19N 37 12 E
Musmar, *Sudan* **51 E12** 18 13N 35 40 E
Musofu, *Zambia* **55 E2** 13 30S 29 0 E
Musoma, *Tanzania* **54 C3** 1 30S 33 48 E
Musoma □, *Tanzania* **54 C3** 1 50S 34 30 E
Musquaro, L., *Canada* **71 B7** 50 38N 61 5W
Musquodoboit Harbour, *Canada* **71 D7** 44 50N 63 9W
Musselburgh, *U.K.* **12 F5** 55 57N 3 2W
Musselshell →, *U.S.A.* **82 C10** 47 21N 107 57W
Mussoorie, *India* **42 D8** 30 27N 78 6 E
Mussuco, *Angola* **56 B2** 17 2S 19 3 E
Mustafakemalpaşa, *Turkey* **21 D13** 40 2N 28 24 E
Mustang, *Nepal* **43 E10** 29 10N 83 55 E
Musters, L., *Argentina* **96 F3** 45 20S 69 25W
Musudan, *N. Korea* **35 D15** 40 50N 129 43 E
Muswellbrook, *Australia* **63 E5** 32 16S 150 56 E
Mût, *Egypt* **51 C10** 25 28N 28 58 E
Mutanda, *Mozam.* **57 C5** 21 0S 33 34 E
Mutanda, *Zambia* **55 E2** 12 24S 26 13 E
Mutare, *Zimbabwe* **55 F3** 18 58S 32 38 E
Muting, *Indonesia* **37 F10** 7 23S 140 20 E
Mutoray, *Russia* **27 C11** 60 56N 101 0 E
Mutshatsha, *Zaïre* **55 E1** 10 35S 24 20 E
Mutsu, *Japan* **30 D10** 41 5N 140 55 E
Mutsu-Wan, *Japan* **30 D10** 41 5N 140 55 E
Muttaburra, *Australia* **62 C3** 22 38S 144 29 E
Mutuáli, *Mozam.* **55 E4** 14 55S 37 0 E
Muweilih, *Egypt* **47 E3** 30 42N 34 19 E
Muxima, *Angola* **52 F2** 9 33S 13 58 E
Muy Muy, *Nic.* **88 D2** 12 39N 85 36W
Muyinga, *Burundi* **54 C3** 3 14S 30 33 E
Muynak, *Uzbekistan* **26 E6** 43 44N 59 10 E
Muzaffarabad, *Pakistan* **43 B5** 34 25N 73 30 E
Muzaffargarh, *Pakistan* **42 D4** 30 5N 71 14 E
Muzaffarnagar, *India* **42 E7** 29 26N 77 40 E
Muzaffarpur, *India* **43 F11** 26 7N 85 23 E
Muzhi, *Russia* **26 C7** 65 25N 64 40 E
Muzon, C., *U.S.A.* **72 C2** 54 40N 132 42W
Mvuma, *Zimbabwe* **55 F3** 19 16S 30 30 E
Mvurwi, *Zimbabwe* **55 F3** 17 0S 30 57 E
Mwadui, *Tanzania* **54 C3** 3 26S 33 32 E
Mwambo, *Tanzania* **55 E5** 10 30S 40 22 E
Mwandi, *Zambia* **55 F1** 17 30S 24 51 E
Mwanza, *Tanzania* **54 C3** 2 30S 32 58 E
Mwanza, *Zaïre* **54 D2** 7 55S 26 43 E
Mwanza, *Zambia* **55 F1** 16 58S 24 28 E
Mwanza □, *Tanzania* **54 C3** 2 0S 33 0 E
Mwaya, *Tanzania* **55 D3** 9 32S 33 55 E
Mweelrea, *Ireland* **13 C2** 53 39N 9 49W
Mweka, *Zaïre* **52 E4** 4 50S 21 34 E
Mwenezi, *Zimbabwe* **55 G3** 21 15S 30 48 E
Mwenezi →, *Mozam.* **55 G3** 22 40S 31 50 E
Mwenga, *Zaïre* **54 C2** 3 1S 28 28 E
Mweru, L., *Zambia* **55 D2** 9 0S 28 40 E
Mweza Range, *Zimbabwe* **55 G3** 21 0S 30 0 E
Mwilambwe, *Zaïre* **54 D5** 8 7S 25 5 E
Mwimbi, *Tanzania* **55 D3** 8 38S 31 39 E
Mwinilunga, *Zambia* **55 E1** 11 43S 24 25 E
My Tho, *Vietnam* **39 G6** 10 29N 106 23 E
Myajlar, *India* **42 F4** 26 15N 70 20 E
Myanaung, *Burma* **41 K19** 18 18N 95 22 E
Myanmar = Burma ■, *Asia* **41 J20** 21 0N 96 30 E
Myaungmya, *Burma* **41 L19** 16 30N 94 40 E
Mycenæ, *Greece* **21 F10** 37 39N 22 52 E
Myeik Kyunzu, *Burma* **39 G1** 11 30N 97 30 E
Myerstown, *U.S.A.* **79 F8** 40 22N 76 19W
Myingyan, *Burma* **41 J19** 21 30N 95 20 E
Myitkyina, *Burma* **41 G20** 25 24N 97 26 E
Mykines, *Fære Is.* **8 E9** 62 7N 7 35W
Mykolayiv, *Ukraine* **25 E5** 46 58N 32 0 E
Mymensingh, *Bangla.* **41 G17** 24 45N 90 24 E
Mynydd Du, *U.K.* **11 F4** 51 52N 3 50W
Mýrdalsjökull, *Iceland* **8 E4** 63 40N 19 6W
Myroodah, *Australia* **60 C3** 18 7S 124 16 E
Myrtle Beach, *U.S.A.* **77 J6** 33 42N 78 53W
Myrtle Creek, *U.S.A.* **82 E2** 43 1N 123 17W
Myrtle Point, *U.S.A.* **82 E1** 43 4N 124 8W
Myrtou, *Cyprus* **23 D12** 35 18N 33 4 E
Mysia, *Turkey* **21 E12** 39 50N 27 0 E
Mysore = Karnataka □, *India* **40 N10** 13 15N 77 0 E
Mysore, *India* **40 N10** 12 17N 76 41 E
Mystic, *U.S.A.* **79 E13** 41 21N 71 58W
Myszków, *Poland* **17 C10** 50 45N 19 22 E
Mytishchi, *Russia* **24 C6** 55 50N 37 50 E
Myton, *U.S.A.* **82 F8** 40 12N 110 4W
Mývatn, *Iceland* **8 D5** 65 36N 17 0W
Mzimba, *Malawi* **55 E3** 11 55S 33 39 E
Mzimkulu →, *S. Africa* **57 E5** 30 44S 30 28 E
Mzimvubu →, *S. Africa* **57 E4** 31 38S 29 33 E
Mzuzu, *Malawi* **55 E3** 11 30S 33 55 E

N

Na Hearadh = Harris, *U.K.* **12 D2** 57 50N 6 55W
Na Noi, *Thailand* **38 C3** 18 19N 100 43 E
Na Phao, *Laos* **38 D5** 17 35N 105 44 E
Na Sam, *Vietnam* **38 A6** 22 3N 106 37 E
Na San, *Vietnam* **38 B5** 21 12N 104 2 E
Naab →, *Germany* **16 D6** 49 1N 12 2 E
Naantali, *Finland* **9 F19** 60 29N 22 2 E
Naas, *Ireland* **13 C5** 53 12N 6 40W
Nababiep, *S. Africa* **56 D2** 29 36S 17 46 E
Nabadwip = Navadwip, *India* **43 H13** 23 34N 88 20 E
Nabari, *Japan* **31 G8** 34 37N 136 5 E
Nabawa, *Australia* **61 E1** 28 30S 114 48 E
Nabberu, L., *Australia* **61 E3** 25 50S 120 30 E
Naberezhnyye Chelny, *Russia* **24 C9** 55 42N 52 19 E
Nabeul, *Tunisia* **51 A7** 36 30N 10 44 E
Nabha, *India* **42 D7** 30 26N 76 14 E
Nabīd, *Iran* **45 D8** 29 40N 57 38 E
Nabire, *Indonesia* **37 E9** 3 15S 135 26 E
Nabisar, *Pakistan* **42 G3** 25 8N 69 40 E
Nabisipi →, *Canada* **71 B7** 50 14N 62 13W
Nabiswera, *Uganda* **54 B3** 1 27N 32 15 E
Nablus = Nābulus, *West Bank* **47 C4** 32 14N 35 15 E
Naboomspruit, *S. Africa* **57 C4** 24 32S 28 40 E
Nābulus, *West Bank* **47 C4** 32 14N 35 15 E
Nacala, *Mozam.* **55 E5** 14 31S 40 34 E
Nacala-Velha, *Mozam.* **55 E5** 14 32S 40 34 E
Nacaome, *Honduras* **88 D2** 13 31N 87 30W
Nacaroa, *Mozam.* **55 E4** 14 22S 39 56 E
Naches, *U.S.A.* **82 C3** 46 44N 120 42W
Naches →, *U.S.A.* **84 D6** 46 38N 120 31W
Nachingwea, *Tanzania* **55 E4** 10 23S 38 49 E
Nachingwea □, *Tanzania* **55 E4** 10 30S 38 30 E
Nachna, *India* **42 F4** 27 34N 71 41 E
Nacimiento Reservoir, *U.S.A.* **84 K6** 35 46N 120 53W
Nackara, *Australia* **63 E2** 32 48S 139 12 E
Naco, *Mexico* **86 A3** 31 20N 109 56W
Naco, *U.S.A.* **83 L9** 31 20N 109 57W
Nacogdoches, *U.S.A.* **81 K7** 31 36N 94 39W
Nácori Chico, *Mexico* **86 B3** 29 39N 109 1W
Nacozari, *Mexico* **86 A3** 30 24N 109 39W
Nadiad, *India* **42 H5** 22 41N 72 56 E
Nadur, *Malta* **23 C1** 36 2N 14 17 E
Nadūshan, *Iran* **45 C7** 32 2N 53 35 E
Nadvirna, *Ukraine* **17 D13** 48 37N 24 30 E
Nadvoitsy, *Russia* **24 B5** 63 52N 34 14 E
Nadvornaya = Nadvirna, *Ukraine* **17 D13** 48 37N 24 30 E
Nadym, *Russia* **26 C8** 65 35N 72 42 E
Nadym →, *Russia* **26 C8** 66 12N 72 0 E
Nærbø, *Norway* **9 G11** 58 40N 5 39 E
Næstved, *Denmark* **9 J14** 55 13N 11 44 E
Nafada, *Nigeria* **50 F7** 11 8N 11 20 E
Naftshahr, *Iran* **44 C5** 34 0N 45 30 E
Nafud Desert = An Nafūd, *Si. Arabia* **44 D4** 28 15N 41 0 E
Naga, *Phil.* **37 B6** 13 38N 123 15 E
Nagagami →, *Canada* **70 C3** 49 40N 84 40W
Nagahama, *Japan* **31 G8** 35 23N 136 16 E
Nagai, *Japan* **30 E10** 38 6N 140 2 E
Nagaland □, *India* **41 F19** 26 0N 94 30 E
Nagano, *Japan* **31 F9** 36 40N 138 10 E
Nagano □, *Japan* **31 F9** 36 15N 138 0 E
Nagaoka, *Japan* **31 F9** 37 27N 138 51 E
Nagappattinam, *India* **40 P11** 10 46N 79 51 E
Nagar Parkar, *Pakistan* **42 G4** 24 28N 70 46 E
Nagasaki, *Japan* **31 H4** 32 47N 129 50 E
Nagasaki □, *Japan* **31 H4** 32 50N 129 40 E
Nagato, *Japan* **31 G5** 34 19N 131 5 E
Nagaur, *India* **42 F5** 27 15N 73 45 E
Nagercoil, *India* **40 Q10** 8 12N 77 26 E
Nagina, *India* **43 E8** 29 30N 78 30 E
Nagineh, *Iran* **45 C8** 34 20N 57 15 E
Nagir, *Pakistan* **43 A6** 36 12N 74 42 E
Nagoorin, *Australia* **62 C5** 24 17S 151 15 E
Nagornyy, *Russia* **27 D13** 55 58N 124 57 E
Nagoya, *Japan* **31 G8** 35 10N 136 50 E
Nagpur, *India* **40 J11** 21 8N 79 10 E
Nagua, *Dom. Rep.* **89 C6** 19 23N 69 50W
Nagykanizsa, *Hungary* **17 E9** 46 28N 17 0 E
Nagykőrös, *Hungary* **17 E10** 47 5N 19 48 E
Naha, *Japan* **31 L3** 26 13N 127 42 E
Nahanni Butte, *Canada* **72 A4** 61 2N 123 31W
Nahanni Nat. Park, *Canada* **72 A3** 61 15N 125 0W
Nahariyya, *Israel* **44 C2** 33 1N 35 5 E
Nahāvand, *Iran* **45 C6** 34 10N 48 22 E
Nahlin, *Canada* **72 B2** 58 55N 131 38W
Naicá, *Mexico* **86 B3** 27 53N 105 31W
Naicam, *Canada* **73 C8** 52 30N 104 30W
Nā'ifah, *Si. Arabia* **46 D5** 19 59N 50 46 E
Nain, *Canada* **71 A7** 56 34N 61 40W
Nā'īn, *Iran* **45 C7** 32 54N 53 0 E
Naini Tal, *India* **43 E8** 29 30N 79 30 E
Nainpur, *India* **40 H12** 22 30N 80 10 E
Naira, *Indonesia* **37 E7** 4 28S 130 0 E
Nairn, *U.K.* **12 D5** 57 35N 3 53W
Nairobi, *Kenya* **54 C4** 1 17S 36 48 E
Naissaar, *Estonia* **9 G21** 59 34N 24 29 E
Naivasha, *Kenya* **54 C4** 0 40S 36 30 E
Naivasha, L., *Kenya* **54 C4** 0 48S 36 20 E
Najafābād, *Iran* **45 C6** 32 40N 51 15 E
Najibabad, *India* **42 E8** 29 40N 78 20 E
Najin, *N. Korea* **35 C16** 42 12N 130 15 E
Najmah, *Si. Arabia* **45 E6** 26 42N 50 6 E
Naju, *S. Korea* **35 G14** 35 3N 126 43 E
Nakadōri-Shima, *Japan* **31 H4** 32 57N 129 4 E
Nakalagba, *Zaïre* **54 B2** 2 50N 27 58 E
Nakaminato, *Japan* **31 F10** 36 21N 140 36 E
Nakamura, *Japan* **31 H6** 33 0N 133 0 E
Nakano, *Japan* **31 F9** 36 45N 138 22 E
Nakano-Shima, *Japan* **31 K4** 29 51N 129 52 E
Nakashibetsu, *Japan* **30 C12** 43 33N 144 59 E
Nakfa, *Eritrea* **51 E12** 16 40N 38 32 E
Nakhichevan = Naxçıvan, *Azerbaijan* **25 G8** 39 12N 45 15 E
Nakhichevan Republic □ = Naxçıvan □, *Azerbaijan* **25 G8** 39 25N 45 26 E
Nakhl, *Egypt* **47 F2** 29 55N 33 43 E
Nakhl-e Taqī, *Iran* **45 E7** 27 28N 52 36 E
Nakhodka, *Russia* **27 E14** 42 53N 132 54 E
Nakhon Nayok, *Thailand* **38 E3** 14 12N 101 13 E
Nakhon Pathom, *Thailand* **38 F3** 13 49N 100 3 E
Nakhon Phanom, *Thailand* **38 D5** 17 23N 104 43 E
Nakhon Ratchasima, *Thailand* **38 E4** 14 59N 102 12 E
Nakhon Sawan, *Thailand* **38 E3** 15 35N 100 10 E
Nakhon Si Thammarat, *Thailand* **39 H3** 8 29N 100 0 E
Nakhon Thai, *Thailand* **38 D3** 17 5N 100 44 E
Nakina, *B.C., Canada* **72 B2** 59 12N 132 52W
Nakina, *Ont., Canada* **70 B2** 50 10N 86 40W
Nakodar, *India* **42 D6** 31 8N 75 31 E
Nakskov, *Denmark* **9 J14** 54 50N 11 8 E
Naktong →, *S. Korea* **35 G15** 35 7N 128 57 E
Nakuru, *Kenya* **54 C4** 0 15S 36 4 E
Nakuru □, *Kenya* **54 C4** 0 15S 35 5 E
Nakuru, L., *Kenya* **54 C4** 0 23S 36 5 E
Nakusp, *Canada* **72 C5** 50 20N 117 45W
Nal →, *Pakistan* **42 G1** 25 20N 65 30 E
Nalchik, *Russia* **25 F7** 43 30N 43 33 E
Nalgonda, *India* **40 L11** 17 6N 79 15 E
Nalhati, *India* **43 G12** 24 17N 87 52 E
Nallamalai Hills, *India* **40 M11** 15 30N 78 50 E
Nālūt, *Libya* **51 B7** 31 54N 11 0 E
Nam Can, *Vietnam* **39 H5** 8 46N 104 59 E
Nam Co, *China* **32 C4** 30 30N 90 45 E
Nam Dinh, *Vietnam* **38 B6** 20 25N 106 5 E
Nam Du, Hon, *Vietnam* **39 H5** 9 41N 104 21 E
Nam Ngum Dam, *Laos* **38 C4** 18 35N 102 34 E
Nam-Phan, *Vietnam* **39 G6** 10 30N 106 0 E
Nam Phong, *Thailand* **38 D4** 16 42N 102 52 E
Nam Tha, *Laos* **38 B3** 20 58N 101 30 E
Nam Tok, *Thailand* **38 E2** 14 21N 99 4 E
Namacunde, *Angola* **56 B2** 17 18S 15 50 E
Namacurra, *Mozam.* **57 B6** 17 30S 36 50 E
Namak, Daryācheh-ye, *Iran* **45 C7** 34 30N 52 0 E
Namak, Kavir-e, *Iran* **45 C8** 34 30N 57 30 E
Namaland, *Namibia* **56 C2** 24 30S 17 0 E
Namangan, *Uzbekistan* **26 E8** 41 0N 71 40 E
Namapa, *Mozam.* **55 E4** 13 43S 39 50 E
Namaqualand, *S. Africa* **56 D2** 30 0S 17 25 E
Namasagali, *Uganda* **54 B3** 1 2N 33 0 E
Namber, *Indonesia* **37 E8** 1 2S 134 49 E
Nambour, *Australia* **63 D5** 26 32S 152 58 E
Nambucca Heads, *Australia* **63 E5** 30 37S 153 0 E
Namcha Barwa, *China* **32 D4** 29 40N 95 10 E
Namche Bazar, *Nepal* **43 F12** 27 51N 86 47 E
Namchonjŏm, *N. Korea* **35 E14** 38 15N 126 26 E
Namecunda, *Mozam.* **55 E4** 14 54S 37 37 E
Nameh, *Indonesia* **36 D5** 2 34N 116 21 E
Nameponda, *Mozam.* **55 F4** 15 50S 39 50 E
Nametil, *Mozam.* **55 F4** 15 40S 39 21 E
Namew L., *Canada* **73 C8** 54 14N 101 56W
Namib Desert = Namibwoestyn, *Namibia* **56 C2** 22 30S 15 0 E
Namibe, *Angola* **53 H2** 15 7S 12 11 E
Namibe □, *Angola* **56 B1** 16 35S 12 30 E
Namibia ■, *Africa* **56 C2** 22 0S 18 9 E
Namibwoestyn, *Namibia* **56 C2** 22 30S 15 0 E
Namlea, *Indonesia* **37 E7** 3 18S 127 5 E
Namoi →, *Australia* **63 E4** 30 12S 149 30 E
Nampa, *U.S.A.* **82 E5** 43 34N 116 34W
Nampō-Shotō, *Japan* **31 J10** 32 0N 140 0 E
Nampula, *Mozam.* **55 F4** 15 6S 39 15 E
Namrole, *Indonesia* **37 E7** 3 46S 126 46 E
Namse Shankou, *China* **41 E13** 30 0N 82 25 E
Namsen →, *Norway* **8 D14** 64 28N 11 37 E
Namsos, *Norway* **8 D14** 64 29N 11 30 E
Namtsy, *Russia* **27 C13** 62 43N 129 37 E
Namtu, *Burma* **41 H20** 23 5N 97 28 E
Namtumbo, *Tanzania* **55 E4** 10 30S 36 4 E
Namu, *Canada* **72 C3** 51 52N 127 50W
Namur, *Belgium* **15 D4** 50 27N 4 52 E
Namur □, *Belgium* **15 D4** 50 17N 5 0 E
Namutoni, *Namibia* **56 B2** 18 49S 16 55 E
Namwala, *Zambia* **55 F2** 15 44S 26 30 E

Namwŏn

Namwŏn, S. Korea **35 G14** 35 23N 127 23 E
Nan, Thailand **38 C3** 18 48N 100 46 E
Nan →, Thailand **38 E3** 15 42N 100 9 E
Nanaimo, Canada **72 D4** 49 10N 124 0W
Nanam, N. Korea **35 D15** 41 44N 129 40 E
Nanango, Australia **63 D5** 26 40S 152 0 E
Nanao, Japan **31 F8** 37 0N 137 0 E
Nanchang, China **33 D6** 28 42N 115 55 E
Nanching = Nanjing, China **33 C6** 32 2N 118 47 E
Nanchong, China **32 C5** 30 43N 106 2 E
Nancy, France **18 B7** 48 42N 6 12 E
Nanda Devi, India **43 D8** 30 23N 79 59 E
Nandan, Japan **31 G7** 34 10N 134 42 E
Nanded, India **40 K10** 19 10N 77 20 E
Nandewar Ra., Australia **63 E5** 30 15S 150 35 E
Nandi, Fiji **59 C7** 17 42S 177 20 E
Nandi □, Kenya **54 B4** 0 15N 35 0 E
Nandurbar, India **40 J9** 21 20N 74 15 E
Nandyal, India **40 M11** 15 30N 78 30 E
Nanga, Australia **61 E1** 26 7S 113 45 E
Nanga-Eboko, Cameroon **52 D2** 4 41N 12 22 E
Nanga Parbat, Pakistan **43 B6** 35 10N 74 35 E
Nangade, Mozam. **55 E4** 11 5S 39 36 E
Nangapinoh, Indonesia **36 E4** 0 20S 111 44 E
Nangarhár □, Afghan. **40 B7** 34 20N 70 0 E
Nangatayap, Indonesia **36 E4** 1 32S 110 34 E
Nangeya Mts., Uganda **54 B3** 3 30N 33 30 E
Nangong, China **34 F8** 37 23N 115 22 E
Nanhuang, China **35 F11** 36 58N 121 48 E
Nanjeko, Zambia **55 F1** 15 31S 23 30 E
Nanjing, China **33 C6** 32 2N 118 47 E
Nanjirinji, Tanzania **55 D4** 9 41S 39 5 E
Nankana Sahib, Pakistan **42 D5** 31 27N 73 38 E
Nanking = Nanjing, China **33 C6** 32 2N 118 47 E
Nankoku, Japan **31 H6** 33 39N 133 44 E
Nanning, China **32 D5** 22 48N 108 20 E
Nannup, Australia **61 F2** 33 59S 115 48 E
Nanpara, India **43 F9** 27 52N 81 33 E
Nanpi, China **34 E9** 38 2N 116 45 E
Nanping, China **33 D6** 26 38N 118 10 E
Nanripe, Mozam. **55 E4** 13 52S 38 52 E
Nansei-Shotō = Ryūkyū-rettō, Japan **31 M2** 26 0N 126 0 E
Nansen Sd., Canada **4 A3** 81 0N 91 0W
Nansio, Tanzania **54 C3** 2 3S 33 4 E
Nantes, France **18 C3** 47 12N 1 33W
Nanticoke, U.S.A. **79 E8** 41 12N 76 0W
Nanton, Canada **72 C6** 50 21N 113 46W
Nantong, China **33 C7** 32 1N 120 52 E
Nantucket I., U.S.A. **66 E12** 41 16N 70 5W
Nanuque, Brazil **93 G10** 17 50S 40 21W
Nanusa, Kepulauan, Indonesia **37 D7** 4 45N 127 1 E
Nanutarra, Australia **60 D2** 22 32S 115 30 E
Nanyang, China **34 H7** 33 11N 112 30 E
Nanyuan, China **34 E9** 39 44N 116 22 E
Nanyuki, Kenya **54 B4** 0 2N 37 4 E
Nao, C. de la, Spain **19 C6** 38 44N 0 14 E
Naococane L., Canada **71 B5** 52 50N 70 45W
Naoetsu, Japan **31 F9** 37 12N 138 10 E
Napa, U.S.A. **84 G4** 38 18N 122 17W
Napa →, U.S.A. **84 G4** 38 10N 122 19W
Napanee, Canada **70 D4** 44 15N 77 0W
Napanoch, U.S.A. **79 E10** 41 44N 74 22W
Nape, Laos **38 C5** 18 18N 105 6 E
Nape Pass = Keo Neua, Deo, Vietnam **38 C5** 18 23N 105 10 E
Napier, N.Z. **59 H6** 39 30S 176 56 E
Napier Broome B., Australia **60 B4** 14 2S 126 37 E
Napier Downs, Australia **60 C3** 17 11S 124 36 E
Napier Pen., Australia **62 A2** 12 4S 135 43 E
Naples = Nápoli, Italy **20 D6** 40 50N 14 15 E
Naples, U.S.A. **77 M5** 26 8N 81 48W
Napo →, Peru **92 D4** 3 20S 72 40W
Napoleon, N. Dak., U.S.A. **80 B5** 46 30N 99 46W
Napoleon, Ohio, U.S.A. **76 E3** 41 23N 84 8W
Nápoli, Italy **20 D6** 40 50N 14 15 E
Napopo, Zaïre **54 B2** 4 15N 28 0 E
Nappa Merrie, Australia **63 D3** 27 36S 141 7 E
Naqqāsh, Iran **45 C6** 35 40N 49 6 E
Nara, Japan **31 G7** 34 40N 135 49 E
Nara, Mali **50 E3** 15 10N 7 20W
Nara □, Japan **31 G8** 34 30N 136 0 E
Nara Canal, Pakistan **42 G3** 24 30N 69 20 E
Nara Visa, U.S.A. **81 H3** 35 37N 103 6W
Naracoorte, Australia **63 F3** 36 58S 140 45 E
Naradhan, Australia **63 E4** 33 34S 146 17 E
Narasapur, India **41 L12** 16 26N 81 40 E
Narathiwat, Thailand **39 J3** 6 30N 101 48 E
Narayanganj, Bangla. **41 H17** 23 40N 90 33 E
Narayanpet, India **40 L10** 16 45N 77 30 E
Narbonne, France **18 E5** 43 11N 3 0 E
Nardīn, Iran **45 B7** 37 3N 55 59 E
Nardò, Italy **21 D8** 40 11N 18 2 E
Narembeen, Australia **61 F2** 32 7S 118 24 E
Nares Str., Arctic **66 A13** 80 0N 70 0W
Naretha, Australia **61 F3** 31 0S 124 45 E
Narew →, Poland **17 B11** 52 26N 20 41 E
Nari →, Pakistan **42 E2** 28 0N 67 40 E
Narin, Afghan. **40 A6** 36 5N 69 0 E
Narindra, Helodranon' i, Madag. **57 A8** 14 55S 47 30 E
Narita, Japan **31 G10** 35 47N 140 19 E
Narmada →, India **42 J5** 21 38N 72 36 E
Narmland, Sweden **9 F15** 60 0N 13 30 E
Narnaul, India **42 E7** 28 5N 76 11 E
Narodnaya, Russia **24 A10** 65 5N 59 58 E
Narok, Kenya **54 C4** 1 55S 35 52 E
Narok □, Kenya **54 C4** 1 20S 36 30 E
Narooma, Australia **63 F5** 36 14S 150 4 E
Narowal, Pakistan **42 C6** 32 6N 74 52 E
Narrabri, Australia **63 E4** 30 19S 149 46 E
Narran →, Australia **63 D4** 28 37S 148 12 E
Narrandera, Australia **63 E4** 34 42S 146 31 E
Narraway →, Canada **72 B5** 55 44N 119 55W
Narrogin, Australia **61 F2** 32 58S 117 14 E
Narromine, Australia **63 E4** 32 12S 148 12 E
Narsimhapur, India **43 H8** 22 54N 79 14 E
Naruto, Japan **31 G7** 34 11N 134 37 E
Narva, Estonia **24 C4** 59 23N 28 12 E
Narva →, Russia **9 G22** 59 27N 28 2 E
Narvik, Norway **8 B17** 68 28N 17 26 E
Narwana, India **42 E7** 29 39N 76 6 E
Naryan-Mar, Russia **24 A9** 67 42N 53 12 E
Naryilco, Australia **63 D3** 28 37S 141 53 E
Narym, Russia **26 D9** 59 0N 81 30 E
Narymskoye, Kazakstan **26 E9** 49 10N 84 15 E
Naryn, Kyrgyzstan **26 E8** 41 26N 75 58 E
Nasa, Norway **8 C16** 66 29N 15 23 E
Nasarawa, Nigeria **50 G6** 8 32N 7 41 E
Naseby, N.Z. **59 L3** 45 1S 170 10 E
Naselle, U.S.A. **84 D3** 46 22N 123 49W
Naser, Buheirat en, Egypt **51 D11** 23 0N 32 30 E
Nashua, Iowa, U.S.A. **80 D8** 42 57N 92 32W
Nashua, Mont., U.S.A. **82 B10** 48 8N 106 22W
Nashua, N.H., U.S.A. **79 D13** 42 45N 71 28W
Nashville, Ark., U.S.A. **81 J8** 33 57N 93 51W
Nashville, Ga., U.S.A. **77 K4** 31 12N 83 15W
Nashville, Tenn., U.S.A. **77 G2** 36 10N 86 47W
Nasik, India **40 K8** 19 58N 73 50 E
Nasirabad, India **42 F6** 26 15N 74 45 E
Naskaupi →, Canada **71 B7** 53 47N 60 51W
Naṣriān-e Pā'īn, Iran **44 C5** 32 52N 46 52 E
Nass →, Canada **72 B3** 55 0N 129 40W
Nassau, Bahamas **88 A4** 25 5N 77 20W
Nassau, U.S.A. **79 D11** 42 31N 73 37W
Nassau, B., Chile **96 H3** 55 20S 68 0W
Nasser, L. = Naser, Buheirat en, Egypt **51 D11** 23 0N 32 30 E
Nässjö, Sweden **9 H16** 57 39N 14 42 E
Nat Kyizin, Burma **41 M20** 14 57N 97 59 E
Nata, Botswana **56 C4** 20 12S 26 12 E
Natagaima, Colombia **92 C3** 3 37N 75 6W
Natal, Brazil **93 E11** 5 47S 35 13W
Natal, Canada **72 D6** 49 43N 114 51W
Natal, Indonesia **36 D1** 0 35N 99 7 E
Naṭanz, Iran **45 C6** 33 30N 51 55 E
Natashquan, Canada **71 B7** 50 14N 61 46W
Natashquan →, Canada **71 B7** 50 7N 61 50W
Natchez, U.S.A. **81 K9** 31 34N 91 24W
Natchitoches, U.S.A. **81 K8** 31 46N 93 5W
Nathalia, Australia **63 F4** 36 1S 145 13 E
Nathdwara, India **42 G5** 24 55N 73 50 E
Nati, Pta., Spain **22 A10** 40 3N 3 50 E
Natimuk, Australia **63 F3** 36 42S 142 0 E
Nation →, Canada **72 B4** 55 30N 123 32W
National City, U.S.A. **85 N9** 32 41N 117 6W
Natitingou, Benin **50 F5** 10 20N 1 26 E
Natividad, I., Mexico **86 B1** 27 50N 115 10W
Natoma, U.S.A. **80 F5** 39 11N 99 2W
Natron, L., Tanzania **54 C4** 2 20S 36 0 E
Natrona Heights, U.S.A. **78 F5** 40 37N 79 44W
Natuna Besar, Kepulauan, Indonesia **39 L7** 4 0N 108 15 E
Natuna Is. = Natuna Besar, Kepulauan, Indonesia **39 L7** 4 0N 108 15 E
Natuna Selatan, Kepulauan, Indonesia **39 L7** 2 45N 109 0 E
Natural Bridge, U.S.A. **79 B9** 44 5N 75 30W
Naturaliste, C., Australia **62 G4** 40 50S 148 15 E
Nau Qala, Afghan. **42 B3** 34 5N 68 5 E
Naubinway, U.S.A. **70 C2** 46 6N 85 27W
Naugatuck, U.S.A. **79 E11** 41 30N 73 3W
Naumburg, Germany **16 C6** 51 9N 11 47 E
Nā'ūr at Tunayb, Jordan **47 D4** 31 48N 35 57 E
Nauru ■, Pac. Oc. **64 H8** 1 0S 166 0 E
Naushahra = Nowshera, Pakistan **40 B8** 34 0N 72 0 E
Nauta, Peru **92 D4** 4 31S 73 35W
Nautanwa, India **41 F13** 27 20N 83 25 E
Nautla, Mexico **87 C5** 20 20N 96 50W
Nava, Mexico **86 B4** 28 25N 100 46W
Navadwip, India **43 H13** 23 34N 88 20 E
Navahrudak, Belarus **17 B13** 53 40N 25 50 E
Navajo Reservoir, U.S.A. **83 H10** 36 48N 107 36W
Navalmoral de la Mata, Spain **19 C3** 39 52N 5 33W
Navan = An Uaimh, Ireland **13 C5** 53 39N 6 41W
Navarino, I., Chile **96 H3** 55 0S 67 40W
Navarra □, Spain **19 A5** 42 40N 1 40W
Navarre, U.S.A. **78 F3** 40 43N 81 31W
Navarro →, U.S.A. **84 F3** 39 11N 123 45W
Navasota, U.S.A. **81 K6** 30 23N 96 5W
Navassa, W. Indies **89 C4** 18 30N 75 0W
Naver →, U.K. **12 C4** 58 32N 4 14W
Navidad, Chile **94 C1** 33 57S 71 50W
Năvodari, Romania **17 F15** 44 19N 28 36 E
Navoi = Nawoiy, Uzbekistan **26 E7** 40 9N 65 22 E
Navojoa, Mexico **86 B3** 27 0N 109 30W
Navolato, Mexico **86 C3** 24 47N 107 42W
Návpaktos, Greece **21 E9** 38 23N 21 50 E
Návplion, Greece **21 F10** 37 33N 22 50 E
Navsari, India **40 J8** 20 57N 72 59 E
Nawa Kot, Pakistan **42 E4** 28 21N 71 24 E
Nawabganj, Ut. P., India **43 F9** 26 56N 81 14 E
Nawabganj, Ut. P., India **43 E8** 28 32N 79 40 E
Nawabshah, Pakistan **42 F3** 26 15N 68 25 E
Nawada, India **43 G11** 24 50N 85 33 E
Nawakot, Nepal **43 F11** 27 55N 85 10 E
Nawalgarh, India **42 F6** 27 50N 75 15 E
Nawanshahr, India **43 C6** 32 33N 74 48 E
Nawoiy, Uzbekistan **26 E7** 40 9N 65 22 E
Naxçıvan, Azerbaijan **25 G8** 39 12N 45 15 E
Naxçıvan □, Azerbaijan **25 G8** 39 25N 45 26 E
Náxos, Greece **21 F11** 37 8N 25 25 E
Nāy Band, Iran **45 E7** 27 20N 52 40 E
Nayakhan, Russia **27 C16** 61 56N 159 0 E
Nayarit □, Mexico **86 C4** 22 0N 105 0W
Nayoro, Japan **30 B11** 44 21N 142 28 E
Nayyāl, W. →, Si. Arabia **44 D3** 28 35N 39 4 E
Nazareth = Naẓerat, Israel **47 C4** 32 42N 35 17 E
Nazas, Mexico **86 B4** 25 10N 104 6W
Nazas →, Mexico **86 B4** 25 35N 103 25W
Naze, The, U.K. **11 F9** 51 53N 1 18 E
Naẓerat, Israel **47 C4** 32 42N 35 17 E
Nāzik, Iran **44 B5** 39 1N 45 4 E
Nazilli, Turkey **21 F13** 37 55N 28 15 E
Nazir Hat, Bangla. **41 H17** 22 35N 91 49 E
Nazko, Canada **72 C4** 53 1N 123 37W
Nazko →, Canada **72 C4** 53 7N 123 34W
Nchanga, Zambia **55 E2** 12 30S 27 49 E
Ncheu, Malawi **55 E3** 14 50S 34 47 E
Ndala, Tanzania **54 C3** 4 45S 33 15 E
Ndalatando, Angola **52 F2** 9 12S 14 48 E
Ndareda, Tanzania **54 C4** 4 12S 35 30 E
Ndélé, C.A.R. **51 G9** 8 25N 20 36 E
Ndendé, Gabon **52 E2** 2 22S 11 23 E
Ndjamena, Chad **51 F7** 12 10N 14 59 E
Ndjolé, Gabon **52 E2** 0 10S 10 45 E
Ndola, Zambia **55 E2** 13 0S 28 34 E
Ndoto Mts., Kenya **54 B4** 2 0N 37 0 E
Nduguti, Tanzania **54 C3** 4 18S 34 41 E
Neagh, Lough, U.K. **13 B5** 54 37N 6 25W
Neah Bay, U.S.A. **84 B2** 48 22N 124 37W
Neale, L., Australia **60 D5** 24 15S 130 0 E
Neápolis, Greece **23 D7** 35 15N 25 37 E
Near Is., U.S.A. **68 C1** 53 0N 172 0 E
Neath, U.K. **11 F4** 51 39N 3 48W
Neath Port Talbot □, U.K. **11 F4** 51 42N 3 45W
Nebine Cr. →, Australia **63 D4** 29 27S 146 56 E
Nebitdag, Turkmenistan **25 G9** 39 30N 54 22 E
Nebraska □, U.S.A. **80 E5** 41 30N 99 30W
Nebraska City, U.S.A. **80 E7** 40 41N 95 52W
Nébrodi, Monti, Italy **20 F6** 37 54N 14 35 E
Necedah, U.S.A. **80 C9** 44 2N 90 4W
Nechako →, Canada **72 C4** 53 30N 122 44W
Neches →, U.S.A. **81 L8** 29 58N 93 51W
Neckar →, Germany **16 D5** 49 27N 8 29 E
Necochea, Argentina **94 D4** 38 30S 58 50W
Needles, U.S.A. **85 L12** 34 51N 114 37W
Needles, The, U.K. **11 G6** 50 39N 1 35W
Ñeembucú □, Paraguay **94 B4** 27 0S 58 0W
Neemuch = Nimach, India **42 G6** 24 30N 74 56 E
Neenah, U.S.A. **76 C1** 44 11N 88 28W
Neepawa, Canada **73 C9** 50 15N 99 30W
Nefta, Tunisia **50 B6** 33 53N 7 50 E
Neftçala, Azerbaijan **25 G8** 39 19N 49 12 E
Neftyannyye Kamni, Azerbaijan **25 F9** 40 20N 50 55 E
Negapatam = Nagappattinam, India **40 P11** 10 46N 79 51 E
Negaunee, U.S.A. **76 B2** 46 30N 87 36W
Negele, Ethiopia **46 F2** 5 20N 39 36 E
Negev Desert = Hanegev, Israel **47 E3** 30 50N 35 0 E
Negombo, Sri Lanka **40 R11** 7 12N 79 50 E
Negotin, Serbia, Yug. **21 B10** 44 16N 22 37 E
Negra, Pta., Peru **90 D2** 6 6S 81 10W
Negra Pt., Phil. **37 A6** 18 40N 120 50 E
Negrais, C. = Maudin Sun, Burma **41 M19** 16 0N 94 30 E
Negro →, Argentina **96 E4** 41 2S 62 47W
Negro →, Brazil **92 D6** 3 0S 60 0W
Negro →, Uruguay **95 C4** 33 24S 58 22W
Negros, Phil. **37 C6** 9 30N 122 40 E
Nehalem →, U.S.A. **84 E3** 45 40N 123 56W
Nehāvand, Iran **45 C6** 35 56N 49 31 E
Nehbandān, Iran **45 D9** 31 35N 60 5 E
Nei Monggol Zizhiqu □, China **34 C6** 42 0N 112 0 E
Neidpath, Canada **73 C7** 50 12N 107 20W
Neihart, U.S.A. **82 C8** 47 0N 110 44W
Neijiang, China **32 D5** 29 35N 104 55 E
Neilton, U.S.A. **82 C2** 47 25N 123 53W
Neiqiu, China **34 F8** 37 15N 114 30 E
Neiva, Colombia **92 C3** 2 56N 75 18W
Neixiang, China **34 H6** 33 10N 111 52 E
Nejanilini L., Canada **73 B9** 59 33N 97 48W
Nekā, Iran **45 B7** 36 39N 53 19 E
Nekemte, Ethiopia **51 G12** 9 4N 36 30 E
Neksø, Denmark **9 J16** 55 4N 15 8 E
Nelia, Australia **62 C3** 20 39S 142 12 E
Neligh, U.S.A. **80 D5** 42 8N 98 2W
Nelkan, Russia **27 D14** 57 40N 136 4 E
Nellore, India **40 M11** 14 27N 79 59 E
Nelma, Russia **27 E14** 47 39N 139 0 E
Nelson, Canada **72 D5** 49 30N 117 20W
Nelson, N.Z. **59 J4** 41 18S 173 16 E
Nelson, U.K. **10 D5** 53 50N 2 13W
Nelson, U.S.A. **83 J7** 35 31N 113 19W
Nelson →, Canada **73 C9** 54 33N 98 2W
Nelson, C., Australia **63 F3** 38 26S 141 32 E
Nelson, Estrecho, Chile **96 G2** 51 30S 75 0W
Nelson Forks, Canada **72 B4** 59 30N 124 0W
Nelson House, Canada **73 B9** 55 47N 98 51W
Nelson L., Canada **73 B8** 55 48N 100 7W
Nelspoort, S. Africa **56 E3** 32 7S 23 0 E
Nelspruit, S. Africa **57 D5** 25 29S 30 59 E
Néma, Mauritania **50 E3** 16 40N 7 15W
Neman, Russia **9 J20** 55 2N 22 2 E
Neman →, Lithuania **9 J19** 55 25N 21 10 E
Nemeiben L., Canada **73 B7** 55 20N 105 20W
Nemunas = Neman →, Lithuania **9 J19** 55 25N 21 10 E
Nemuro, Japan **30 C12** 43 20N 145 35 E
Nemuro-Kaikyō, Japan **30 C12** 43 30N 145 30 E
Nemuy, Russia **27 D14** 55 40N 136 9 E
Nen Jiang →, China **35 B13** 45 28N 124 30 E
Nenagh, Ireland **13 D3** 52 52N 8 11W
Nenana, U.S.A. **68 B5** 64 34N 149 5W
Nenasi, Malaysia **39 L4** 3 9N 103 23 E
Nene →, U.K. **10 E8** 52 49N 0 11 E
Nenjiang, China **33 B7** 49 10N 125 10 E
Neno, Malawi **55 F3** 15 25S 34 40 E
Neodesha, U.S.A. **81 G7** 37 25N 95 41W
Neosho, U.S.A. **81 G7** 36 52N 94 22W
Neosho →, U.S.A. **81 H7** 36 48N 95 18W
Nepal ■, Asia **43 F11** 28 0N 84 30 E
Nepalganj, Nepal **43 E9** 28 5N 81 40 E
Nephi, U.S.A. **82 G8** 39 43N 111 50W
Nephin, Ireland **13 B2** 54 1N 9 22W
Neptune, U.S.A. **79 F10** 40 13N 74 2W
Nerchinsk, Russia **27 D12** 52 0N 116 39 E
Nerchinskiy Zavod, Russia **27 D12** 51 20N 119 40 E
Néret L., Canada **71 B5** 54 45N 70 44W
Neretva →, Croatia **21 C7** 43 1N 17 27 E
Neringa, Lithuania **9 J19** 55 30N 21 5 E
Ness, L., U.K. **12 D4** 57 15N 4 32W
Nesterov, Ukraine **17 C12** 50 4N 23 58 E
Nesvizh = Nyasvizh, Belarus **17 B14** 53 14N 26 38 E
Netanya, Israel **47 C3** 32 20N 34 51 E
Nète →, Belgium **15 C4** 51 7N 4 14 E
Netherdale, Australia **62 C4** 21 10S 148 33 E
Netherlands ■, Europe **15 C5** 52 0N 5 30 E
Netherlands Antilles ■, W. Indies **92 A5** 12 15N 69 0W
Nettilling L., Canada **69 B12** 66 30N 71 0W
Netzahualcoyotl, Presa, Mexico **87 D6** 17 10N 93 30W
Neubrandenburg, Germany **16 B7** 53 33N 13 15 E
Neuchâtel, Switz. **16 E4** 47 0N 6 55 E
Neuchâtel, Lac de, Switz. **16 E4** 46 53N 6 50 E
Neufchâteau, Belgium **15 E5** 49 50N 5 25 E
Neumünster, Germany **16 A5** 54 4N 9 58 E
Neunkirchen, Germany **16 D4** 49 20N 7 9 E
Neuquén, Argentina **96 D3** 38 55S 68 0W
Neuquén □, Argentina **94 D2** 38 0S 69 50W
Neuruppin, Germany **16 B7** 52 55N 12 48 E
Neuse →, U.S.A. **77 H7** 35 6N 76 29W
Neusiedler See, Austria **17 E9** 47 50N 16 47 E
Neuss, Germany **15 C6** 51 11N 6 42 E
Neustrelitz, Germany **16 B7** 53 21N 13 4 E
Neva →, Russia **24 C5** 59 50N 30 30 E
Nevada, U.S.A. **81 G7** 37 51N 94 22W
Nevada □, U.S.A. **82 G5** 39 0N 117 0W
Nevada, Sierra, Spain **19 D4** 37 3N 3 15W
Nevada, Sierra, U.S.A. **82 G3** 39 0N 120 30W
Nevada City, U.S.A. **84 F6** 39 16N 121 1W
Nevado, Cerro, Argentina **94 D2** 35 30S 68 32W
Nevanka, Russia **27 D10** 56 31N 98 55 E
Nevers, France **18 C5** 47 0N 3 9 E
Nevertire, Australia **63 E4** 31 50S 147 44 E
Neville, Canada **73 D7** 49 58N 107 39W
Nevinnomyssk, Russia **25 F7** 44 40N 42 0 E
Nevis, W. Indies **89 C7** 17 0N 62 30W
Nevyansk, Russia **24 C11** 57 30N 60 13 E
New Albany, Ind., U.S.A. **76 F3** 38 18N 85 49W
New Albany, Miss., U.S.A. **81 H10** 34 29N 89 0W
New Albany, Pa., U.S.A. **79 E8** 41 36N 76 27W
New Amsterdam, Guyana **92 B7** 6 15N 57 36W
New Angledool, Australia **63 D4** 29 5S 147 55 E
New Bedford, U.S.A. **79 E14** 41 38N 70 56W
New Bern, U.S.A. **77 H7** 35 7N 77 3W
New Bethlehem, U.S.A. **78 E5** 41 0N 79 20W
New Bloomfield, U.S.A. **78 F7** 40 25N 77 11W
New Boston, U.S.A. **81 J7** 33 28N 94 25W
New Braunfels, U.S.A. **81 L5** 29 42N 98 8W
New Brighton, N.Z. **59 K4** 43 29S 172 43 E
New Brighton, U.S.A. **78 F4** 40 42N 80 19W
New Britain, Papua N. G. **64 H7** 5 50S 150 20 E
New Britain, U.S.A. **79 E12** 41 40N 72 47W
New Brunswick, U.S.A. **79 F10** 40 30N 74 27W
New Brunswick □, Canada **71 C6** 46 50N 66 30W
New Caledonia ■, Pac. Oc. **64 K8** 21 0S 165 0 E
New Castle, Ind., U.S.A. **76 F3** 39 55N 85 22W
New Castle, Pa., U.S.A. **78 E4** 41 0N 80 21W
New City, U.S.A. **79 E11** 41 9N 73 59W
New Cumberland, U.S.A. **78 F4** 40 30N 80 36W
New Cuyama, U.S.A. **85 L7** 34 57N 119 38W
New Delhi, India **42 E7** 28 37N 77 13 E
New Denver, Canada **72 D5** 50 0N 117 25W
New Don Pedro Reservoir, U.S.A. **84 H6** 37 43N 120 24W
New England, U.S.A. **80 B3** 46 32N 102 52W
New England Ra., Australia **63 E5** 30 20S 151 45 E
New Forest, U.K. **11 G6** 50 53N 1 34W
New Glasgow, Canada **71 C7** 45 35N 62 36W
New Guinea, Oceania **28 K17** 4 0S 136 0 E
New Hamburg, Canada **78 C4** 43 23N 80 42W
New Hampshire □, U.S.A. **79 C13** 44 0N 71 30W
New Hampton, U.S.A. **80 D8** 43 3N 92 19W
New Hanover, S. Africa **57 D5** 29 22S 30 31 E
New Haven, Conn., U.S.A. **79 E12** 41 18N 72 55W
New Haven, Mich., U.S.A. **78 D2** 42 44N 82 48W
New Hazelton, Canada **72 B3** 55 20N 127 30W
New Hebrides = Vanuatu ■, Pac. Oc. **64 J8** 15 0S 168 0 E
New Iberia, U.S.A. **81 K9** 30 1N 91 49W
New Ireland, Papua N. G. **64 H7** 3 20S 151 50 E
New Jersey □, U.S.A. **79 F10** 40 0N 74 30W
New Kensington, U.S.A. **78 F5** 40 34N 79 46W
New Lexington, U.S.A. **76 F4** 39 43N 82 13W
New Liskeard, Canada **70 C4** 47 31N 79 41W
New London, Conn., U.S.A. **79 E12** 41 22N 72 6W
New London, Minn., U.S.A. **80 C7** 45 18N 94 56W
New London, Ohio, U.S.A. **78 E2** 41 5N 82 24W
New London, Wis., U.S.A. **80 C10** 44 23N 88 45W
New Madrid, U.S.A. **81 G10** 36 36N 89 32W
New Meadows, U.S.A. **82 D5** 44 58N 116 18W
New Melones L., U.S.A. **84 H6** 37 57N 120 31W
New Mexico □, U.S.A. **83 J10** 34 30N 106 0W
New Milford, Conn., U.S.A. **79 E11** 41 35N 73 25W
New Milford, Pa., U.S.A. **79 E9** 41 52N 75 44W
New Norcia, Australia **61 F2** 30 57S 116 13 E
New Norfolk, Australia **62 G4** 42 46S 147 2 E
New Orleans, U.S.A. **81 K9** 29 58N 90 4W
New Philadelphia, U.S.A. **78 F3** 40 30N 81 27W
New Plymouth, N.Z. **59 H5** 39 4S 174 5 E
New Plymouth, U.S.A. **82 E5** 43 58N 116 49W
New Providence, Bahamas **88 A4** 25 25N 78 35W
New Radnor, U.K. **11 E4** 52 15N 3 9W
New Richmond, U.S.A. **80 C8** 45 7N 92 32W
New Roads, U.S.A. **81 K9** 30 42N 91 26W
New Rochelle, U.S.A. **79 F11** 40 55N 73 47W
New Rockford, U.S.A. **80 B5** 47 41N 99 8W
New Ross, Ireland **13 D5** 52 23N 6 57W
New Salem, U.S.A. **80 B4** 46 51N 101 25W
New Scone, U.K. **12 E5** 56 25N 3 24W
New Siberian Is. = Novaya Sibir, Ostrov, Russia **27 B16** 75 10N 150 0 E
New Siberian Is. = Novosibirskiye Ostrova, Russia **27 B15** 75 0N 142 0 E
New Smyrna Beach, U.S.A. **77 L5** 29 1N 80 56W
New South Wales □, Australia **63 E4** 33 0S 146 0 E
New Springs, Australia **61 E3** 25 49S 120 1 E
New Town, U.S.A. **80 A3** 47 59N 102 30W
New Ulm, U.S.A. **80 C7** 44 19N 94 28W

147

North Las Vegas

North Las Vegas, *U.S.A.* . **85 J11** 36 12N 115 7W
North Lincolnshire □, *U.K.* **10 D7** 53 36N 0 30W
North Little Rock, *U.S.A.* . **81 H8** 34 45N 92 16W
North Loup →, *U.S.A.* . . **80 E5** 41 17N 98 24W
North Magnetic Pole,
Canada **4 B2** 77 58N 102 8W
North Minch, *U.K.* **12 C3** 58 5N 5 55W
North Nahanni →,
Canada **72 A4** 62 15N 123 20W
North Olmsted, *U.S.A.* . . **78 E3** 41 25N 81 56W
North Ossetia □, *Russia* . **25 F7** 43 30N 44 30 E
North Pagai, I. = Pagai
Utara, *Indonesia* . . . . . . **36 E2** 2 35S 100 0 E
North Palisade, *U.S.A.* . . . **83 H4** 37 6N 118 31W
North Platte, *U.S.A.* **80 E4** 41 8N 100 46W
North Platte →, *U.S.A.* . **80 E4** 41 7N 100 42W
North Pole, *Arctic* . . . . . . **4 A** 90 0N 0 0 E
North Portal, *Canada* **73 D8** 49 0N 102 33W
North Powder, *U.S.A.* . . . **82 D5** 45 2N 117 55W
North Pt., *Canada* **71 C7** 47 5N 64 0W
North Rhine Westphalia □
= Nordrhein-
Westfalen □, *Germany* **16 C4** 51 45N 7 30 E
North Ronaldsay, *U.K.* . . . **12 B6** 59 22N 2 26W
North Saskatchewan →,
Canada **73 C7** 53 15N 105 5W
North Sea, *Europe* . . . . . . **6 D6** 56 0N 4 0 E
North Somerset □, *U.K.* . . **11 F5** 51 24N 2 45W
North Sporades = Voríai
Sporádhes, *Greece* . . . . **21 E10** 39 15N 23 30 E
North Sydney, *Canada* . . **71 C7** 46 12N 60 15W
North Taranaki Bight, *N.Z.* **59 H5** 38 50S 174 15 E
North Thompson →,
Canada **72 C4** 50 40N 120 20W
North Tonawanda, *U.S.A.* **78 C6** 43 2N 78 53W
North Troy, *U.S.A.* **79 B12** 45 0N 72 24W
North Truchas Pk., *U.S.A.* **83 J11** 36 0N 105 30W
North Twin I., *Canada* . . . **70 B3** 53 20N 80 0W
North Tyne →, *U.K.* **10 C5** 55 0N 2 8W
North Uist, *U.K.* **12 D1** 57 40N 7 15W
North Vancouver, *Canada* **72 D4** 49 25N 123 3W
North Vernon, *U.S.A.* . . . **76 F3** 39 0N 85 38W
North Wabasca L., *Canada* **72 B6** 56 0N 113 55W
North Walsham, *U.K.* . . . **10 E9** 52 50N 1 22 E
North-West □, *S. Africa* . **56 D4** 27 0S 25 0 E
North West C., *Australia* . **60 D1** 21 45S 114 9 E
North West Christmas I.
Ridge, *Pac. Oc.* **65 G11** 6 30N 165 0W
North West Frontier □,
Pakistan . . . . **42 C4** 34 0N 72 0 E
North West Highlands,
U.K. **12 D3** 57 33N 4 58W
North West Providence
Channel, *W. Indies* **88 A4** 26 0N 78 0W
North West River, *Canada* **71 B7** 53 30N 60 10W
North West Territories □,
Canada **68 B9** 67 0N 110 0W
North Western □, *Zambia* **55 E2** 13 30S 25 30 E
North York Moors, *U.K.* . **10 C7** 54 23N 0 53W
North Yorkshire □, *U.K.* . **10 C6** 54 15N 1 25W
Northallerton, *U.K.* **10 C6** 54 20N 1 26W
Northam, *S. Africa* . . . . . . **56 C4** 24 56S 27 18 E
Northampton, *Australia* . . **61 E1** 28 27S 114 33 E
Northampton, *U.K.* **11 E7** 52 15N 0 53W
Northampton, *Mass.,*
U.S.A. **79 D12** 42 19N 72 38W
Northampton, *Pa., U.S.A.* **79 F9** 40 41N 75 30W
Northampton Downs,
Australia . . . . **62 C4** 24 35S 145 48 E
Northamptonshire □, *U.K.* **11 E7** 52 16N 0 55W
Northbridge, *U.S.A.* **79 D13** 42 9N 71 39W
Northcliffe, *Australia* . . . . **61 F2** 34 39S 116 7 E
Northern □, *Malawi* . . . . **55 E3** 11 0S 34 0 E
Northern □, *Uganda* . . . . **54 B3** 3 5N 32 30 E
Northern □, *Zambia* . . . . **55 E3** 10 30S 31 0 E
Northern Cape □, *S. Africa* **56 D3** 30 0S 20 0 E
Northern Circars, *India* . . **41 L13** 17 30N 82 30 E
Northern Indian L.,
Canada **73 B9** 57 20N 97 20W
Northern Ireland □, *U.K.* . **13 B5** 54 45N 7 0W
Northern Light, L., *Canada* **70 C1** 48 15N 90 39W
Northern Marianas ■,
Pac. Oc. . . . . **64 F6** 17 0N 145 0 E
Northern Territory □,
Australia . . . . **60 D5** 20 0S 133 0 E
Northern Transvaal □,
S. Africa . . . . **57 C4** 24 0S 29 0 E
Northfield, *U.S.A.* **80 C8** 44 27N 93 9W
Northland □, *N.Z.* . . . . . . **59 F4** 35 30S 173 30 E
Northome, *U.S.A.* **80 B7** 47 52N 94 17W
Northport, *Ala., U.S.A.* . . . **77 J2** 33 14N 87 35W
Northport, *Mich., U.S.A.* . **76 C3** 45 8N 85 37W
Northport, *Wash., U.S.A.* **82 B5** 48 55N 117 48W
Northumberland □, *U.K.* . **10 B5** 55 12N 2 0W
Northumberland, C.,
Australia . . . . **63 F3** 38 5S 140 40 E
Northumberland Is.,
Australia . . . . **62 C4** 21 30S 149 50 E
Northumberland Str.,
Canada **71 C7** 46 20N 64 0W
Northwich, *U.K.* **10 D5** 53 15N 2 31W
Northwood, *Iowa, U.S.A.* **80 D8** 43 27N 93 13W
Northwood, *N. Dak.,*
U.S.A. **80 B6** 47 44N 97 34W
Norton, *U.S.A.* **80 F5** 39 50N 99 53W
Norton, *Zimbabwe* . . . . . . **55 F3** 17 52S 30 40 E
Norton Sd., *U.S.A.* **68 B3** 63 50N 164 0W
Norwalk, *Calif., U.S.A.* . . . **85 M8** 33 54N 118 5W
Norwalk, *Conn., U.S.A.* . . **79 E11** 41 7N 73 22W
Norwalk, *Ohio, U.S.A.* . . . **78 E2** 41 15N 82 37W
Norway, *U.S.A.* **76 C2** 45 47N 87 55W
Norway ■, *Europe* . . . . . . **8 E14** 63 0N 11 0 E
Norway House, *Canada* . **73 C9** 53 59N 97 50W
Norwegian Sea, *Atl. Oc.* . . **4 C8** 66 0N 1 0 E
Norwich, *Canada* **78 D4** 42 59N 80 36W
Norwich, *U.K.* . . . . **10 E9** 52 38N 1 18 E
Norwich, *Conn., U.S.A.* . . . **79 E12** 41 31N 72 5W
Norwich, *N.Y., U.S.A.* . . . **79 D9** 42 32N 75 32W
Norwood, *Canada* **78 B7** 44 23N 77 59W
Noshiro, *Japan* . . . . **30 D10** 40 12N 140 0 E
Nosok, *Russia* . . . . **26 B9** 70 10N 82 20 E
Noss Hd., *U.K.* **12 C5** 58 28N 3 3W
Nossob →, *S. Africa* . . . **56 D3** 26 55S 20 45 E
Nosy Bé, *Madag.* . . . . **53 G9** 13 25S 48 15 E
Nosy Boraha, *Madag.* . . . **57 B8** 16 50S 49 55 E
Nosy Mitsio, *Madag.* . . . . **53 G9** 12 54S 48 36 E
Nosy Varika, *Madag.* . . . . **57 C8** 20 35S 48 32 E
Noteć →, *Poland* . . . . . . **16 B8** 52 44N 15 26 E
Notigi Dam, *Canada* **73 B9** 56 40N 99 10W
Notikewin →, *Canada* . . **72 B5** 57 2N 117 38W
Notodden, *Norway* . . . . . **9 G13** 59 35N 9 17 E
Notre-Dame, *Canada* **71 C7** 46 18N 64 46W
Notre Dame B., *Canada* . **71 C8** 49 45N 55 30W
Notre Dame de Koartac =
Quaqtaq, *Canada* **69 B13** 60 55N 69 40W
Notre Dame d'Ivugivic =
Ivujivik, *Canada* **69 B12** 62 24N 77 55W
Nottaway →, *Canada* . . . **70 B4** 51 22N 78 55W
Nottingham, *U.K.* **10 E6** 52 58N 1 10W
Nottinghamshire □, *U.K.* **10 D7** 53 10N 1 3W
Nottoway →, *U.S.A.* **76 G7** 36 33N 76 55W
Notwane →, *Botswana* . . **56 C4** 23 35S 26 58 E
Nouâdhibou, *Mauritania* . **50 D1** 20 54N 17 0W
Nouâdhibou, Ras,
Mauritania **50 D1** 20 50N 17 0W
Nouakchott, *Mauritania* . . **50 E1** 18 9N 15 58W
Nouméa, *N. Cal.* . . . . **64 K8** 22 17S 166 30 E
Noupoort, *S. Africa* . . . . . **56 E3** 31 10S 24 57 E
Nouveau Comptoir =
Wemindji, *Canada* **70 B4** 53 0N 78 49W
Nouvelle-Calédonie =
New Caledonia ■,
Pac. Oc. . . . . **64 K8** 21 0S 165 0 E
Nova Casa Nova, *Brazil* . . **93 E10** 9 25S 41 5W
Nova Cruz, *Brazil* **93 E11** 6 28S 35 25W
Nova Esperança, *Brazil* . . **95 A5** 23 8S 52 24W
Nova Friburgo, *Brazil* . . . **95 A7** 22 16S 42 30W
Nova Gaia = Cambundi-
Catembo, *Angola* . . . . . **52 G3** 10 10S 17 35 E
Nova Iguaçu, *Brazil* **95 A7** 22 45S 43 28W
Nova Iorque, *Brazil* **93 E10** 7 0S 44 5W
Nova Lima, *Brazil* **95 A7** 19 59S 43 51W
Nova Lisboa = Huambo,
Angola . . . . **53 G3** 12 42S 15 54 E
Nova Lusitânia, *Mozam.* . **55 F3** 19 50S 34 34 E
Nova Mambone, *Mozam.* . **57 C6** 21 0S 35 3 E
Nova Scotia □, *Canada* . . **71 C7** 45 10N 63 0W
Nova Sofala, *Mozam.* . . . **57 C5** 20 7S 34 42 E
Nova Venécia, *Brazil* **93 G10** 18 45S 40 24W
Nova Zagora, *Bulgaria* . . **21 C11** 42 32N 25 59 E
Novara, *Italy* . . . . **20 B3** 45 28N 8 38 E
Novato, *U.S.A.* **84 G4** 38 6N 122 35W
Novaya Ladoga, *Russia* . . **24 B5** 60 7N 32 16 E
Novaya Lyalya, *Russia* . . **26 D7** 59 4N 60 45 E
Novaya Sibir, Ostrov,
Russia . . . . **27 B16** 75 10N 150 0 E
Novaya Zemlya, *Russia* . . **26 B6** 75 0N 56 0 E
Nové Zámky, *Slovak Rep.* . **17 D10** 48 2N 18 8 E
Novgorod, *Russia* . . . . . . **24 C5** 58 30N 31 25 E
Novgorod-Severskiy =
Novhorod-Siverskyy,
Ukraine . . . . **24 D5** 52 2N 33 10 E
Novhorod-Siverskyy,
Ukraine . . . . **24 D5** 52 2N 33 10 E
Novi Ligure, *Italy* . . . . **20 B3** 44 46N 8 47 E
Novi Pazar, *Serbia, Yug.* . . **21 C9** 43 12N 20 28 E
Novi Sad, *Serbia, Yug.* . . . **21 B8** 45 18N 19 52 E
Nôvo Hamburgo, *Brazil* . . **95 B5** 29 37S 51 7W
Novo Mesto, *Slovenia* . . . . **16 F8** 45 48N 15 10 E
Novo Remanso, *Brazil* . . . **93 E10** 9 41S 42 4W
Novoataysk, *Russia* . . . . . **26 D9** 53 30N 84 0 E
Novocherkassk, *Russia* . . . **25 E7** 47 27N 40 15 E
Novogrudok =
Navahrudak, *Belarus* . . **17 B13** 53 40N 25 50 E
Novohrad-Volynskyy,
Ukraine . . . . **17 C14** 50 34N 27 35 E
Novokachalinsk, *Russia* . **30 B6** 45 5N 132 0 E
Novokazalinsk =
Zhangaqazaly,
Kazakstan . . . . **26 E7** 45 48N 62 6 E
Novokuybyshevsk, *Russia* **24 D8** 53 7N 49 58 E
Novokuznetsk, *Russia* . . . **26 D9** 53 45N 87 10 E
Novomoskovsk, *Russia* . . **24 D6** 54 5N 38 15 E
Novorossiysk, *Russia* . . . . **25 F6** 44 43N 37 46 E
Novorybnoye, *Russia* . . . . **27 B11** 72 50N 105 50 E
Novoselytsya, *Ukraine* . . . **17 D14** 48 14N 26 15 E
Novoshakhtinsk, *Russia* . . **25 E6** 47 46N 39 58 E
Novosibirsk, *Russia* . . . . . **26 D9** 55 0N 83 5 E
Novosibirskiye Ostrova,
Russia . . . . **27 B15** 75 0N 142 0 E
Novotroitsk, *Russia* . . . . . **26 D6** 51 10N 58 15 E
Novouzensk, *Russia* . . . . . **25 D8** 50 32N 48 17 E
Novovolynsk, *Ukraine* . . . **17 C13** 50 45N 24 4 E
Novska, *Croatia* . . . . **20 B7** 45 19N 17 0 E
Novvy Port, *Russia* . . . . . . **26 C8** 67 40N 72 30 E
Now Shahr, *Iran* . . . . **45 B6** 36 40N 51 30 E
Nowa Sól, *Poland* . . . . **16 C8** 51 48N 15 44 E
Nowbarān, *Iran* . . . . **45 C6** 35 8N 49 42 E
Nowghāb, *Iran* . . . . **45 C8** 33 53N 59 4 E
Nowgong, *India* . . . . **41 F18** 26 20N 92 50 E
Nowra, *Australia* . . . . **63 E5** 34 53S 150 35 E
Nowshera, *Pakistan* . . . . . **40 B8** 34 0N 72 0 E
Nowy Sącz, *Poland* . . . . . **17 D11** 49 40N 20 41 E
Nowy Targ, *Poland* . . . . . **17 D11** 49 29N 20 2 E
Nowy Tomyśl, *Poland* . . . **16 B9** 52 19N 16 10 E
Noxen, *U.S.A.* **79 E8** 41 25N 76 4W
Noxon, *U.S.A.* **82 C6** 48 0N 115 43W
Noyes I., *U.S.A.* **72 B2** 55 30N 133 40W
Noyon, *France* . . . . **18 B5** 49 34N 2 59 E
Noyon, *Mongolia* . . . . **34 C2** 43 2N 102 4 E
Nsanje, *Malawi* . . . . **55 F4** 16 55S 35 12 E
Nsawam, *Ghana* **50 G4** 5 50N 0 24W
Nsomba, *Zambia* . . . . **55 E2** 10 45S 29 51 E
Nsukka, *Nigeria* . . . . **50 G6** 6 51N 7 29 E
Nu Jiang →, *China* . . . . . **32 D4** 29 58N 97 25 E
Nu Shan, *China* . . . . **32 D4** 26 0N 99 20 E
Nubia, *Africa* . . . . **48 D7** 21 0N 32 0 E
Nubian Desert = Nûbîya,
Es Sahrâ En, *Sudan* . . . **51 D11** 21 30N 33 30 E
Nûbîya, Es Sahrâ En,
Sudan . . . . **51 D11** 21 30N 33 30 E
Ñuble □, *Chile* **94 D1** 37 0S 72 0W
Nuboai, *Indonesia* . . . . . . **37 E9** 2 10S 136 30 E
Nubra →, *India* . . . . **43 B7** 34 35N 77 35 E
Nueces →, *U.S.A.* **81 M6** 27 51N 97 30W
Nueltin L., *Canada* **73 A9** 60 30N 99 30W
Nueva Asunción □,
Paraguay **94 A3** 21 0S 61 0W
Nueva Gerona, *Cuba* **88 B3** 21 53N 82 49W
Nueva Imperial, *Chile* . . . **96 D2** 38 45S 72 58W
Nueva Palmira, *Uruguay* . . **94 C4** 33 52S 58 20W
Nueva Rosita, *Mexico* . . . **86 B4** 28 0N 101 11W
Nueva San Salvador,
El Salv. **88 D2** 13 40N 89 18W
Nuéve de Julio, *Argentina* **94 D3** 35 30S 61 0W
Nuevitas, *Cuba* **88 B4** 21 30N 77 20W
Nuevo, G., *Argentina* **96 E4** 43 0S 64 30W
Nuevo Guerrero, *Mexico* . **87 B5** 26 34N 99 15W
Nuevo Laredo, *Mexico* . . . **87 B5** 27 30N 99 30W
Nuevo León □, *Mexico* . . **86 C4** 25 0N 100 0W
Nugget Pt., *N.Z.* . . . . **59 M2** 46 27S 169 50 E
Nuhaka, *N.Z.* . . . . **59 H6** 39 3S 177 45 E
Nukey Bluff, *Australia* . . . **63 E2** 32 26S 135 29 E
Nukheila, *Sudan* . . . . **51 E10** 19 1N 26 21 E
Nuku'alofa, *Tonga* **59 E11** 21 10S 174 0W
Nukus, *Uzbekistan* . . . . . . **26 E6** 42 27N 59 41 E
Nulato, *U.S.A.* **68 B4** 64 43N 158 6W
Nullagine →, *Australia* . . **60 D3** 21 20S 120 20 E
Nullarbor, *Australia* . . . . . **61 F5** 31 28S 130 55 E
Nullarbor Plain, *Australia* **61 F4** 31 10S 129 0 E
Numalla, L., *Australia* . . . **63 D3** 28 43S 144 20 E
Numan, *Nigeria* . . . . **51 G7** 9 29N 12 3 E
Numata, *Japan* . . . . **31 F9** 36 45N 139 4 E
Numazu, *Japan* . . . . **31 G9** 35 7N 138 51 E
Numbulwar, *Australia* . . . **62 A2** 14 15S 135 45 E
Numfoor, *Indonesia* . . . . . **37 E8** 1 0S 134 50 E
Numurkah, *Australia* . . . . **63 F4** 36 5S 145 26 E
Nunaksaluk I., *Canada* . . . **71 A7** 55 49N 60 20W
Nuneaton, *U.K.* **11 E6** 52 32N 1 27W
Nungo, *Mozam.* . . . . **55 E4** 13 23S 37 43 E
Nungwe, *Tanzania* . . . . . . **54 C3** 2 48S 32 2 E
Nunivak I., *U.S.A.* **68 B3** 60 10N 166 30W
Nunkun, *India* . . . . **43 C7** 33 57N 76 2 E
Nunspeet, *Neths.* . . . . **15 B5** 52 21N 5 45 E
Núoro, *Italy* . . . . **20 D3** 40 20N 9 20 E
Nūrābād, *Iran* . . . . **45 E8** 27 47N 57 12 E
Nuremberg = Nürnberg,
Germany . . . . **16 D6** 49 27N 11 3 E
Nuri, *Mexico* **86 B3** 28 2N 109 22W
Nurina, *Australia* . . . . **61 F4** 30 56S 126 33 E
Nuriootpa, *Australia* . . . . . **63 E2** 34 27S 139 0 E
Nurmes, *Finland* . . . . **8 E23** 63 33N 29 10 E
Nürnberg, *Germany* . . . . . **16 D6** 49 27N 11 3 E
Nurran, L. = Terewah, L.,
Australia . . . . **63 D4** 29 52S 147 35 E
Nurrari Lakes, *Australia* . **61 E5** 29 1S 130 5 E
Nusa Barung, *Indonesia* . **37 H15** 8 10S 113 30 E
Nusa Kambangan,
Indonesia . . . . **37 G13** 7 40S 108 10 E
Nusa Tenggara Barat □,
Indonesia . . . . **36 F5** 8 50S 117 30 E
Nusa Tenggara Timur □,
Indonesia . . . . **37 F6** 9 30S 122 0 E
Nusaybin, *Turkey* . . . . **25 G7** 37 3N 41 10 E
Nushki, *Pakistan* . . . . **42 E2** 29 35N 66 0 E
Nutak, *Canada* **69 C13** 57 28N 61 59W
Nutwood Downs, *Australia* **62 B1** 15 49S 134 10 E
Nuuk = Godthåb,
Greenland **69 B14** 64 10N 51 35W
Nuwakot, *Nepal* . . . . **43 E10** 28 10N 83 55 E
Nuweveldberge, *S. Africa* **56 E3** 32 10S 21 45 E
Nuyts, C., *Australia* . . . . . **61 F5** 32 2S 132 21 E
Nuyts Arch., *Australia* . . . **63 E1** 32 35S 133 20 E
Nxau-Nxau, *Botswana* . . . **56 B3** 18 57S 21 4 E
Nyack, *U.S.A.* **79 E11** 41 5N 73 55W
Nyah West, *Australia* . . . . **63 F3** 35 16S 143 21 E
Nyahanga, *Tanzania* . . . . . **54 C3** 2 20S 33 37 E
Nyahua, *Tanzania* . . . . **54 D3** 5 25S 33 23 E
Nyahururu, *Kenya* . . . . **54 B4** 0 2N 36 27 E
Nyainqentanglha Shan,
China . . . . **32 D3** 30 0N 90 0 E
Nyakanazi, *Tanzania* . . . . **54 C3** 3 2S 31 10 E
Nyâlâ, *Sudan* . . . . **51 F9** 12 2N 24 58 E
Nyamandhlovu,
Zimbabwe . . . . **55 F2** 19 55S 28 16 E
Nyambiti, *Tanzania* . . . . . **54 C3** 2 48S 33 27 E
Nyamwaga, *Tanzania* . . . . **54 C3** 1 27S 34 33 E
Nyandekwa, *Tanzania* . . . **54 C3** 3 57S 32 32 E
Nyandoma, *Russia* . . . . . . **24 B7** 61 40N 40 12 E
Nyangana, *Namibia* . . . . . **56 B3** 18 0S 20 40 E
Nyanguge, *Tanzania* . . . . . **54 C3** 2 30S 33 12 E
Nyanza, *Burundi* . . . . **54 C2** 4 21S 29 36 E
Nyanza, *Rwanda* . . . . **54 C2** 2 20S 29 42 E
Nyanza □, *Kenya* . . . . **54 C3** 0 10S 34 15 E
Nyarling →, *Canada* **72 A6** 60 41N 113 23W
Nyasa, L. = Malawi, L.,
Africa . . . . **55 E3** 12 30S 34 30 E
Nyasvizh, *Belarus* . . . . **17 B14** 53 14N 26 38 E
Nyazepetrovsk, *Russia* . . **24 C10** 56 3N 59 36 E
Nyazura, *Zimbabwe* . . . . . **55 F3** 18 40S 32 16 E
Nyazwidzi →, *Zimbabwe* **55 F3** 20 0S 31 17 E
Nybro, *Sweden* . . . . **9 H16** 56 44N 15 55 E
Nyda, *Russia* . . . . **26 C8** 66 40N 72 58 E
Nyeri, *Kenya* . . . . **54 C4** 0 23S 36 56 E
Nyíregyháza, *Hungary* . . . **17 E11** 47 58N 21 47 E
Nykøbing, *Storstrøm,*
Denmark . . . . **9 J14** 54 56N 11 52 E
Nykøbing, *Vestsjælland,*
Denmark . . . . **9 J14** 55 55N 11 40 E
Nykøbing, *Viborg,*
Denmark . . . . **9 H13** 56 48N 8 51 E
Nyköping, *Sweden* . . . . . . **9 G17** 58 45N 17 0 E
Nylstroom, *S. Africa* . . . . **57 C4** 24 42S 28 22 E
Nymagee, *Australia* . . . . . **63 E4** 32 7S 146 20 E
Nynäshamn, *Sweden* . . . . **9 G17** 58 54N 17 57 E
Nyngan, *Australia* . . . . **63 E4** 31 30S 147 8 E
Nyoman = Neman →,
Lithuania . . . . **9 J19** 55 25N 21 10 E
Nysa, *Poland* . . . . **17 C9** 50 30N 17 22 E
Nysa →, *Europe* . . . . **16 B8** 52 4N 14 46 E
Nyssa, *U.S.A.* **82 E5** 43 53N 117 0W
Nyunzu, *Zaïre* . . . . **54 D2** 5 57S 27 58 E
Nyurbe, *Russia* . . . . **27 C12** 63 17N 118 28 E
Nzega, *Tanzania* . . . . **54 C3** 4 10S 33 12 E
Nzega □, *Tanzania* . . . . . **54 C3** 4 10S 33 10 E
N'Zérékoré, *Guinea* **50 G3** 7 49N 8 48W
Nzeto, *Angola* . . . . **52 F2** 7 10S 12 52 E
Nzilo, Chutes de, *Zaïre* . . **55 E2** 10 18S 25 27 E
Nzubuka, *Tanzania* . . . . . . **54 C3** 4 45S 32 50 E

O

Ō-Shima, *Nagasaki, Japan* **31 G4** 34 29N 129 33 E
Ō-Shima, *Shizuoka, Japan* **31 G9** 34 44N 139 24 E
Oacoma, *U.S.A.* **80 D5** 43 48N 99 24W
Oahe, L., *U.S.A.* **80 C4** 44 27N 100 24W
Oahe Dam, *U.S.A.* **80 C4** 44 27N 100 24W
Oahu, *U.S.A.* **74 H16** 21 28N 157 58W
Oak Creek, *U.S.A.* **82 F10** 40 16N 106 57W
Oak Harbor, *U.S.A.* **84 B4** 48 18N 122 39W
Oak Hill, *U.S.A.* **76 G5** 37 59N 81 9W
Oak Park, *U.S.A.* **76 E2** 41 53N 87 47W
Oak Ridge, *U.S.A.* **77 G3** 36 1N 84 16W
Oak View, *U.S.A.* **85 L7** 34 24N 119 18W
Oakan-Dake, *Japan* . . . . . **30 C12** 43 27N 144 10 E
Oakbank, *Australia* . . . . . . **63 E3** 33 4S 140 33 E
Oakdale, *Calif., U.S.A.* . . . **83 H3** 37 46N 120 51W
Oakdale, *La., U.S.A.* **81 K8** 30 49N 92 40W
Oakengates, *U.K.* **10 E5** 52 41N 2 26W
Oakes, *U.S.A.* **80 B5** 46 8N 98 6W
Oakesdale, *U.S.A.* **82 C5** 47 8N 117 15W
Oakey, *Australia* . . . . **63 D5** 27 25S 151 43 E
Oakham, *U.K.* **10 E7** 52 40N 0 43W
Oakhurst, *U.S.A.* **84 H7** 37 19N 119 40W
Oakland, *Calif., U.S.A.* . . . **83 H2** 37 49N 122 16W
Oakland, *Oreg., U.S.A.* . . . **82 E2** 43 25N 123 18W
Oakland City, *U.S.A.* **76 F2** 38 20N 87 21W
Oakley, *Idaho, U.S.A.* **82 E7** 42 15N 113 53W
Oakley, *Kans., U.S.A.* **80 F4** 39 8N 100 51W
Oakover →, *Australia* . . **60 D3** 21 0S 120 40 E
Oakridge, *U.S.A.* **82 E2** 43 45N 122 28W
Oakville, *U.S.A.* **84 D3** 46 51N 123 14W
Oamaru, *N.Z.* . . . . **59 L3** 45 5S 170 59 E
Oasis, *Calif., U.S.A.* **85 M10** 33 28N 116 6W
Oasis, *Nev., U.S.A.* **84 H9** 37 29N 117 55W
Oates Land, *Antarctica* . . **5 C11** 69 0S 160 0 E
Oatman, *U.S.A.* **85 K12** 35 1N 114 19W
Oaxaca, *Mexico* **87 D5** 17 2N 96 40W
Oaxaca □, *Mexico* **87 D5** 17 0N 97 0W
Ob →, *Russia* . . . . **26 C7** 66 45N 69 30 E
Oba, *Canada* **70 C3** 49 4N 84 7W
Obama, *Japan* . . . . **31 G7** 35 30N 135 45 E
Oban, *U.K.* **12 E3** 56 25N 5 29W
Obbia, *Somali Rep.* . . . . . . **46 F4** 5 25N 48 30 E
Obed, *Canada* **72 C5** 53 30N 117 10W
Obera, *Argentina* **95 B4** 27 21S 55 2W
Oberhausen, *Germany* . . . **16 C4** 51 28N 6 51 E
Oberlin, *Kans., U.S.A.* . . . **80 F4** 39 49N 100 32W
Oberlin, *La., U.S.A.* **81 K8** 30 37N 92 46W
Oberlin, *Ohio, U.S.A.* **78 E2** 41 18N 82 13W
Oberon, *Australia* . . . . **63 E4** 33 45S 149 52 E
Obi, Kepulauan, *Indonesia* **37 E7** 1 23S 127 45 E
Obi Is. = Obi, Kepulauan,
Indonesia . . . . **37 E7** 1 23S 127 45 E
Óbidos, *Brazil* **93 D7** 1 50S 55 30W
Obihiro, *Japan* . . . . **30 C11** 42 56N 143 12 E
Obilatu, *Indonesia* . . . . . . **37 E7** 1 25S 127 20 E
Obluchye, *Russia* . . . . **27 E14** 49 1N 131 4 E
Obo, *C.A.R.* . . . . **54 A2** 5 20N 26 32 E
Oboa, Mt., *Uganda* . . . . . . **54 B3** 1 45N 34 45 E
Oboyan, *Russia* . . . . **26 D4** 51 15N 36 21 E
Obozerskaya =
Obozerskiy, *Russia* . . . . **26 C5** 63 34N 40 21 E
Obozerskiy, *Russia* . . . . . **26 C5** 63 34N 40 21 E
Observatory Inlet, *Canada* **72 B3** 55 10N 129 54W
Obshchi Syrt, *Russia* . . . . **6 E16** 52 0N 53 0 E
Obskaya Guba, *Russia* . . . **26 C8** 69 0N 73 0 E
Obuasi, *Ghana* **50 G4** 6 17N 1 40W
Ocala, *U.S.A.* **77 L4** 29 11N 82 8W
Ocampo, *Mexico* **86 B3** 28 9N 108 24W
Ocaña, *Spain* **19 C4** 39 55N 3 30W
Ocanomowoc, *U.S.A.* . . . **80 D10** 43 7N 88 30W
Ocate, *U.S.A.* **81 G2** 36 11N 105 3W
Occidental, Cordillera,
Colombia **92 C3** 5 0N 76 0W
Ocean City, *N.J., U.S.A.* . . **76 F8** 39 17N 74 35W
Ocean City, *Wash., U.S.A.* **84 C2** 47 4N 124 10W
Ocean I. = Banaba,
Kiribati . . . . **64 H8** 0 45S 169 50 E
Ocean Park, *U.S.A.* **84 D2** 46 30N 124 3W
Oceano, *U.S.A.* **85 K6** 35 6N 120 37W
Oceanport, *U.S.A.* **79 F10** 40 19N 74 3W
Oceanside, *U.S.A.* **85 M9** 33 12N 117 23W
Ochil Hills, *U.K.* **12 E5** 56 14N 3 40W
Ochre River, *Canada* **73 C9** 51 4N 99 47W
Ocilla, *U.S.A.* **77 K4** 31 36N 83 15W
Ocmulgee →, *U.S.A.* **77 K4** 31 58N 82 33W
Ocnița, *Moldova* . . . . **17 D14** 48 25N 27 30 E
Oconee →, *U.S.A.* **77 K4** 31 58N 82 33W
Oconto, *U.S.A.* **76 C2** 44 53N 87 52W
Oconto Falls, *U.S.A.* **76 C1** 44 52N 88 9W
Ocosingo, *Mexico* **87 D6** 17 10N 92 15W
Ocotal, *Nic.* **88 D2** 13 41N 86 31W
Ocotlán, *Mexico* **86 C4** 20 21N 102 42W
Octave, *U.S.A.* **83 J7** 34 10N 112 43W
Ocumare del Tuy,
Venezuela **92 A5** 10 7N 66 46W
Ōda, *Japan* . . . . **31 G6** 35 11N 132 30 E
Ódáðahraun, *Iceland* **8 D5** 65 5N 17 0W
Odate, *Japan* . . . . **30 D10** 40 16N 140 34 E
Odawara, *Japan* . . . . **31 G9** 35 20N 139 6 E
Odda, *Norway* . . . . **9 F12** 60 3N 6 35 E
Oddur, *Somali Rep.* . . . . . . **46 G3** 4 11N 43 52 E
Odei →, *Canada* **73 B9** 56 6N 96 54W
Ödemiș, *Turkey* . . . . **21 E13** 38 15N 28 0 E
Odendaalsrus, *S. Africa* . . **56 D4** 27 48S 26 45 E
Odense, *Denmark* . . . . **9 J14** 55 22N 10 23 E
Oder →, *Germany* . . . . . . **16 B8** 53 33N 14 38 E
Odesa, *Ukraine* . . . . **25 E5** 46 30N 30 45 E
Odessa = Odesa, *Ukraine* **25 E5** 46 30N 30 45 E
Odessa, *Canada* **79 B8** 44 17N 76 43W
Odessa, *Tex., U.S.A.* **81 K3** 31 52N 102 23W
Odessa, *Wash., U.S.A.* . . . **82 C4** 47 20N 118 41W
Odiakwe, *Botswana* . . . . . **56 C4** 20 12S 25 17 E
Odienné, *Ivory C.* **50 G3** 9 30N 7 34W
Odintsovo, *Russia* . . . . **24 C6** 55 39N 37 15 E
O'Donnell, *U.S.A.* **81 J4** 32 58N 101 50W
Odorheiu Secuiesc,
Romania . . . . **17 E13** 46 21N 25 21 E
Odra = Oder →,
Germany . . . . **16 B8** 53 33N 14 38 E

Oshnovīyeh

Oshnovīyeh, *Iran* **44 B5** 37 2N 45 6 E
Oshogbo, *Nigeria* **50 G5** 7 48N 4 37 E
Oshtorīnān, *Iran* **45 C6** 34 1N 48 38 E
Oshwe, *Zaïre* **52 E3** 3 25 S 19 28 E
Osijek, *Croatia* **21 B8** 45 34N 18 41 E
Osipenko = Berdyansk, *Ukraine* **25 E6** 46 45N 36 50 E
Osipovichi = Asipovichy, *Belarus* **17 B15** 53 19N 28 33 E
Osizweni, *S. Africa* **57 D5** 27 49 S 30 7 E
Oskaloosa, *U.S.A.* **80 E8** 41 18N 92 39W
Oskarshamn, *Sweden* **9 H17** 57 15N 16 27 E
Oskélanéo, *Canada* **70 C4** 48 5N 75 15W
Öskemen, *Kazakstan* **26 E9** 50 0N 82 36 E
Oslo, *Norway* **9 G14** 59 55N 10 45 E
Oslob, *Phil.* **37 C6** 9 31N 123 26 E
Oslofjorden, *Norway* **9 G14** 59 20N 10 35 E
Osmanabad, *India* **40 K10** 18 5N 76 10 E
Osmaniye, *Turkey* **25 G6** 37 5N 36 10 E
Osnabrück, *Germany* **16 B5** 52 17N 8 3 E
Osorio, *Brazil* **95 B5** 29 53 S 50 17W
Osorno, *Chile* **96 E2** 40 25 S 73 0W
Osoyoos, *Canada* **72 D5** 49 0N 119 30W
Osøyri, *Norway* **9 F11** 60 9N 5 30 E
Ospika →, *Canada* **72 B4** 56 20N 124 0W
Osprey Reef, *Australia* **62 A4** 13 52 S 146 36 E
Oss, *Neths.* **15 C5** 51 46N 5 32 E
Ossa, Mt., *Australia* **62 G4** 41 52 S 146 3 E
Óssa, Oros, *Greece* **21 E10** 39 47N 22 42 E
Ossabaw I., *U.S.A.* **77 K5** 31 50N 81 5W
Ossining, *U.S.A.* **79 E11** 41 10N 73 55W
Ossipee, *U.S.A.* **79 C13** 43 41N 71 7W
Ossokmanuan L., *Canada* **71 B7** 53 25N 65 0W
Ossora, *Russia* **27 D17** 59 20N 163 13 E
Ostend = Oostende, *Belgium* **15 C2** 51 15N 2 54 E
Oster, *Ukraine* **17 C16** 50 57N 30 53 E
Österdalälven, *Sweden* **9 F16** 61 30N 13 45 E
Østerdalen, *Norway* **9 F14** 61 40N 10 50 E
Östersund, *Sweden* **8 E16** 63 10N 14 38 E
Ostfriesische Inseln, *Germany* **16 B4** 53 42N 7 0 E
Ostrava, *Czech.* **17 D10** 49 51N 18 18 E
Ostróda, *Poland* **17 B10** 53 42N 19 58 E
Ostroh, *Ukraine* **17 C14** 50 20N 26 30 E
Ostrołęka, *Poland* **17 B11** 53 4N 21 32 E
Ostrów Mazowiecka, *Poland* **17 B11** 52 50N 21 51 E
Ostrów Wielkopolski, *Poland* **17 C9** 51 36N 17 44 E
Ostrowiec-Świętokrzyski, *Poland* **17 C11** 50 55N 21 22 E
Ostuni, *Italy* **21 D7** 40 44N 17 35 E
Ōsumi-Kaikyō, *Japan* **31 J5** 30 55N 131 0 E
Ōsumi-Shotō, *Japan* **31 J5** 30 30N 130 0 E
Osuna, *Spain* **19 D3** 37 14N 5 8W
Oswego, *U.S.A.* **79 C8** 43 27N 76 31W
Oswestry, *U.K.* **10 E4** 52 52N 3 3W
Oświęcim, *Poland* **17 C10** 50 2N 19 11 E
Otago □, *N.Z.* **59 L2** 45 15 S 170 0 E
Otago Harbour, *N.Z.* **59 L3** 45 47 S 170 42 E
Ōtake, *Japan* **31 G6** 34 12N 132 13 E
Otaki, *N.Z.* **59 J5** 40 45 S 175 10 E
Otaru, *Japan* **30 C10** 43 10N 141 0 E
Otaru-Wan = Ishikari-Wan, *Japan* **30 C10** 43 25N 141 1 E
Otavalo, *Ecuador* **92 C3** 0 13N 78 20W
Otavi, *Namibia* **56 B2** 19 40 S 17 24 E
Otchinjau, *Angola* **56 B1** 16 30 S 13 56 E
Othello, *U.S.A.* **82 C4** 46 50N 119 10W
Otira Gorge, *N.Z.* **59 K3** 42 53 S 171 33 E
Otis, *U.S.A.* **80 E3** 40 9N 102 58W
Otjiwarongo, *Namibia* **56 C2** 20 30 S 16 33 E
Otoineppu, *Japan* **30 B11** 44 44N 142 16 E
Otorohanga, *N.Z.* **59 H5** 38 12 S 175 14 E
Otoskwin →, *Canada* **70 B2** 52 13N 88 6W
Otosquen, *Canada* **73 C8** 53 17N 102 1W
Otra →, *Norway* **9 G13** 58 9N 8 1 E
Otranto, *Italy* **21 D8** 40 9N 18 28 E
Otranto, C. d', *Italy* **21 D8** 40 7N 18 30 E
Otranto, Str. of, *Italy* **21 D8** 40 15N 18 40 E
Otse, *S. Africa* **56 D4** 25 2 S 25 45 E
Ōtsu, *Japan* **31 G7** 35 0N 135 50 E
Ōtsuki, *Japan* **31 G9** 35 36N 138 57 E
Ottawa = Outaouais →, *Canada* **70 C5** 45 27N 74 8W
Ottawa, *Canada* **70 C4** 45 27N 75 42W
Ottawa, *Ill., U.S.A.* **80 E10** 41 21N 88 51W
Ottawa, *Kans., U.S.A.* **80 F7** 38 37N 95 16W
Ottawa Is., *Canada* **69 C11** 59 35N 80 10W
Otter L., *Canada* **73 B8** 55 35N 104 39W
Otter Rapids, *Ont., Canada* **70 B3** 50 11N 81 39W
Otter Rapids, *Sask., Canada* **73 B8** 55 38N 104 44W
Otterville, *Canada* **78 D4** 42 55N 80 36W
Otto Beit Bridge, *Zimbabwe* **55 F2** 15 59 S 28 56 E
Ottosdal, *S. Africa* **56 D4** 26 46 S 25 59 E
Ottumwa, *U.S.A.* **80 E8** 41 1N 92 25W
Oturkpo, *Nigeria* **50 G6** 7 16N 8 8 E
Otway, B., *Chile* **96 G2** 53 30 S 74 0W
Otway, C., *Australia* **63 F3** 38 52 S 143 30 E
Otwock, *Poland* **17 B11** 52 5N 21 20 E
Ou →, *Laos* **38 B4** 20 4N 102 13 E
Ou Neua, *Laos* **38 A3** 22 18N 101 48 E
Ou-Sammyaku, *Japan* **30 E10** 39 20N 140 35 E
Ouachita →, *U.S.A.* **81 K9** 31 38N 91 49W
Ouachita, L., *U.S.A.* **81 H8** 34 34N 93 12W
Ouachita Mts., *U.S.A.* **81 H7** 34 40N 94 25W
Ouadâne, *Mauritania* **50 D2** 20 50N 11 40W
Ouadda, *C.A.R.* **51 G9** 8 15N 22 20 E
Ouagadougou, *Burkina Faso* **50 F4** 12 25N 1 30W
Ouahran = Oran, *Algeria* **50 A4** 35 45N 0 39W
Ouallene, *Algeria* **50 D5** 24 41N 1 11 E
Ouanda Djallé, *C.A.R.* **51 G9** 8 55N 22 53 E
Ouango, *C.A.R.* **52 D4** 4 19N 22 30 E
Ouargla, *Algeria* **50 B6** 31 59N 5 16 E
Ouarzazate, *Morocco* **50 B3** 30 55N 6 50W
Oubangi →, *Zaïre* **52 E3** 0 30 S 17 50 E
Ouddorp, *Neths.* **15 C3** 51 50N 3 57 E
Oude Rijn →, *Neths.* **15 B4** 52 12N 4 24 E
Oudenaarde, *Belgium* **15 D3** 50 50N 3 37 E
Oudtshoorn, *S. Africa* **56 E3** 33 35 S 22 14 E
Ouessant, I. d', *France* **18 B1** 48 28N 5 6W
Ouesso, *Congo* **52 D3** 1 37N 16 5 E
Ouest, Pte., *Canada* **71 C7** 49 52N 64 40W
Ouezzane, *Morocco* **50 B3** 34 51N 5 35W
Ouidah, *Benin* **50 G5** 6 25N 2 0 E
Oujda, *Morocco* **50 B4** 34 41N 1 55W
Oujeft, *Mauritania* **50 D2** 20 2N 13 0W
Oulainen, *Finland* **8 D21** 64 17N 24 47 E
Ouled Djellal, *Algeria* **50 B6** 34 28N 5 2 E
Oulu, *Finland* **8 D21** 65 1N 25 29 E
Oulujärvi, *Finland* **8 D22** 64 25N 27 15 E
Oulujoki →, *Finland* **8 D21** 65 1N 25 30 E
Oum Chalouba, *Chad* **51 E9** 15 48N 20 46 E
Ounasjoki →, *Finland* **8 C21** 66 31N 25 40 E
Ounguati, *Namibia* **56 C2** 22 0S 15 46 E
Ounianga-Kébir, *Chad* **51 E9** 19 4N 20 29 E
Ounianga Sérir, *Chad* **51 E9** 18 54N 20 51 E
Our →, *Lux.* **15 E6** 49 55N 6 5 E
Ouray, *U.S.A.* **83 G10** 38 1N 107 40W
Ourense = Orense, *Spain* **19 A2** 42 19N 7 55W
Ouricuri, *Brazil* **93 E10** 7 53 S 40 5W
Ourinhos, *Brazil* **95 A6** 23 0S 49 54W
Ouro Fino, *Brazil* **95 A6** 22 16 S 46 25W
Ouro Prêto, *Brazil* **95 A7** 20 20 S 43 30W
Ourthe →, *Belgium* **15 D5** 50 29N 5 35 E
Ouse, *Australia* **62 G4** 42 38 S 146 42 E
Ouse →, *E. Susx., U.K.* **11 G8** 50 47N 0 4 E
Ouse →, *N. Yorks., U.K.* **10 C8** 53 44N 0 55W
Outaouais →, *Canada* **70 C5** 45 27N 74 8W
Outardes →, *Canada* **71 C6** 49 24N 69 30W
Outer Hebrides, *U.K.* **12 D1** 57 30N 7 40W
Outer I., *Canada* **71 B8** 51 10N 58 35W
Outjo, *Namibia* **56 C2** 20 5S 16 7 E
Outlook, *Canada* **73 C7** 51 30N 107 0W
Outlook, *U.S.A.* **80 A2** 48 53N 104 47W
Outokumpu, *Finland* **8 E23** 62 43N 29 1 E
Ouyen, *Australia* **63 F3** 35 1S 142 22 E
Ovalau, *Fiji* **59 C8** 17 40 S 178 48 E
Ovalle, *Chile* **94 C1** 30 33 S 71 18W
Ovamboland, *Namibia* **56 B2** 18 30 S 16 0 E
Overflakkee, *Neths.* **15 C4** 51 44N 4 10 E
Overijssel □, *Neths.* **15 B6** 52 25N 6 35 E
Overland Park, *U.S.A.* **80 F7** 38 55N 94 50W
Overpelt, *Belgium* **15 C5** 51 12N 5 20 E
Overton, *U.S.A.* **85 J12** 36 33N 114 27W
Övertorneå, *Sweden* **8 C20** 66 23N 23 38 E
Ovid, *U.S.A.* **80 E3** 40 58N 102 23W
Oviedo, *Spain* **19 A3** 43 25N 5 50W
Oviši, *Latvia* **9 H19** 57 33N 21 44 E
Övör Hangay □, *Mongolia* **34 B2** 45 0N 102 30 E
Øvre Årdal, *Norway* **9 F12** 61 19N 7 48 E
Ovruch, *Ukraine* **17 C15** 51 25N 28 45 E
Owaka, *N.Z.* **59 M2** 46 27 S 169 40 E
Owambo = Ovamboland, *Namibia* **56 B2** 18 30 S 16 0 E
Owase, *Japan* **31 G8** 34 7N 136 12 E
Owatonna, *U.S.A.* **80 C8** 44 5N 93 14W
Owbeh, *Afghan.* **40 B3** 34 28N 63 10 E
Owego, *U.S.A.* **79 D8** 42 6N 76 16W
Owen Falls Dam, *Uganda* **54 B3** 0 30N 33 5 E
Owen Sound, *Canada* **70 D3** 44 35N 80 55W
Owendo, *Gabon* **52 D1** 0 17N 9 30 E
Owens →, *U.S.A.* **84 J9** 36 32N 117 59W
Owens L., *U.S.A.* **85 J9** 36 26N 117 57W
Owensboro, *U.S.A.* **76 G2** 37 46N 87 7W
Owensville, *U.S.A.* **80 F9** 38 21N 91 30W
Owl →, *Canada* **73 B10** 57 51N 92 44W
Owo, *Nigeria* **50 G6** 7 10N 5 39 E
Owosso, *U.S.A.* **76 D3** 43 0N 84 10W
Owyhee, *U.S.A.* **82 F5** 41 57N 116 6W
Owyhee →, *U.S.A.* **82 E5** 43 49N 117 2W
Owyhee, L., *U.S.A.* **82 E5** 43 38N 117 14W
Öxarfjörður, *Iceland* **8 C5** 66 15N 16 45W
Oxelösund, *Sweden* **9 G17** 58 43N 17 15 E
Oxford, *N.Z.* **59 K4** 43 18 S 172 11 E
Oxford, *U.K.* **11 F6** 51 46N 1 15W
Oxford, *Miss., U.S.A.* **81 H10** 34 22N 89 31W
Oxford, *N.C., U.S.A.* **77 G6** 36 19N 78 35W
Oxford, *Ohio, U.S.A.* **76 F3** 39 31N 84 45W
Oxford L., *Canada* **73 C9** 54 51N 95 37W
Oxfordshire □, *U.K.* **11 F6** 51 48N 1 16W
Oxley, *Australia* **63 E3** 34 11 S 144 6 E
Oxnard, *U.S.A.* **85 L7** 34 12N 119 11W
Oxus = Amudarya →, *Uzbekistan* **26 E6** 43 58N 59 34 E
Oya, *Malaysia* **36 D4** 2 55N 111 55 E
Oyama, *Japan* **31 F9** 36 18N 139 48 E
Oyem, *Gabon* **52 D2** 1 34N 11 31 E
Oyen, *Canada* **73 C6** 51 22N 110 28W
Oykel →, *U.K.* **12 D4** 57 56N 4 26W
Oymyakon, *Russia* **27 C15** 63 25N 142 44 E
Oyo, *Nigeria* **50 G5** 7 46N 3 56 E
Oyster Bay, *U.S.A.* **79 F11** 40 52N 73 32W
Ōyūbari, *Japan* **30 C11** 43 1N 142 5 E
Ozamiz, *Phil.* **37 C6** 8 15N 123 50 E
Ozark, *Ala., U.S.A.* **77 K3** 31 28N 85 39W
Ozark, *Ark., U.S.A.* **81 H8** 35 29N 93 50W
Ozark, *Mo., U.S.A.* **81 G8** 37 1N 93 12W
Ozark Plateau, *U.S.A.* **81 G9** 37 20N 91 40W
Ozarks, L. of the, *U.S.A.* **80 F8** 38 12N 92 38W
Ózd, *Hungary* **17 D11** 48 14N 20 15 E
Ozette L., *U.S.A.* **84 B2** 48 6N 124 38W
Ozona, *U.S.A.* **81 K4** 30 43N 101 12W
Ozuluama, *Mexico* **87 C5** 21 40N 97 50W

P

Pa-an, *Burma* **41 L20** 16 51N 97 40 E
Pa Mong Dam, *Thailand* **38 D4** 18 0N 102 22 E
Paamiut = Frederikshåb, *Greenland* **4 C5** 62 0N 49 43W
Paarl, *S. Africa* **56 E2** 33 45 S 18 56 E
Paauilo, *U.S.A.* **74 H17** 20 2N 155 22W
Pab Hills, *Pakistan* **42 F2** 26 30N 66 45 E
Pabianice, *Poland* **17 C10** 51 40N 19 20 E
Pabna, *Bangla.* **41 G16** 24 1N 89 18 E
Pabo, *Uganda* **54 B3** 3 1N 32 10 E
Pacaja →, *Brazil* **93 D8** 1 56 S 50 50W
Pacaraima, Sierra, *Venezuela* **92 C6** 4 0N 62 30W
Pacasmayo, *Peru* **92 E3** 7 20 S 79 35W
Pachhar, *India* **42 G7** 24 40N 77 42 E
Pachpadra, *India* **40 G8** 25 58N 72 10 E
Pachuca, *Mexico* **87 C5** 20 10N 98 40W
Pacific, *Canada* **72 C3** 54 48N 128 28W
Pacific-Antarctic Ridge, *Pac. Oc.* **65 M16** 43 0S 115 0W
Pacific Grove, *U.S.A.* **83 H3** 36 38N 121 56W
Pacific Ocean, *Pac. Oc.* **65 G14** 10 0N 140 0W
Pacifica, *U.S.A.* **84 H4** 37 36N 122 30W
Pacitan, *Indonesia* **37 H14** 8 12 S 111 7 E
Packwood, *U.S.A.* **84 D5** 46 36N 121 40W
Padaido, Kepulauan, *Indonesia* **37 E9** 1 5S 138 0 E
Padang, *Indonesia* **36 E2** 1 0S 100 20 E
Padangpanjang, *Indonesia* **36 E2** 0 40S 100 20 E
Padangsidempuan, *Indonesia* **36 D1** 1 30N 99 15 E
Paddockwood, *Canada* **73 C7** 53 30N 105 30W
Paderborn, *Germany* **16 C5** 51 42N 8 45 E
Padloping Island, *Canada* **69 B13** 67 0N 62 50W
Pádova, *Italy* **20 B4** 45 25N 11 53 E
Padra, *India* **42 H5** 22 15N 73 7 E
Padrauna, *India* **43 F10** 26 54N 83 59 E
Padre I., *U.S.A.* **81 M6** 27 10N 97 25W
Padstow, *U.K.* **11 G3** 50 33N 4 58W
Padua = Pádova, *Italy* **20 B4** 45 25N 11 53 E
Paducah, *Ky., U.S.A.* **76 G1** 37 5N 88 37W
Paducah, *Tex., U.S.A.* **81 H4** 34 1N 100 18W
Paengnyong-do, *S. Korea* **35 F13** 37 57N 124 40 E
Paeroa, *N.Z.* **59 G5** 37 23 S 175 41 E
Pafúri, *Mozam.* **57 C5** 22 28 S 31 17 E
Pag, *Croatia* **16 F8** 44 25N 15 3 E
Pagadian, *Phil.* **37 C6** 7 55N 123 30 E
Pagai Selatan, P., *Indonesia* **36 E2** 3 0S 100 15 E
Pagai Utara, *Indonesia* **36 E2** 2 35 S 100 0 E
Pagalu = Annobón, *Atl. Oc.* **49 G4** 1 25 S 5 36 E
Pagastikós Kólpos, *Greece* **21 E10** 39 15N 23 0 E
Pagatan, *Indonesia* **36 E5** 3 33 S 115 59 E
Page, *Ariz., U.S.A.* **83 H8** 36 57N 111 27W
Page, *N. Dak., U.S.A.* **80 B6** 47 10N 97 34W
Pago Pago, *Amer. Samoa* **59 B13** 14 16 S 170 43W
Pagosa Springs, *U.S.A.* **83 H10** 37 16N 107 1W
Pagwa River, *Canada* **70 B2** 50 2N 85 14W
Pahala, *U.S.A.* **74 J17** 19 12N 155 29W
Pahang →, *Malaysia* **39 L4** 3 30N 103 9 E
Pahiatua, *N.Z.* **59 J5** 40 27 S 175 50 E
Pahokee, *U.S.A.* **77 M5** 26 50N 80 40W
Pahrump, *U.S.A.* **85 J11** 36 12N 115 59W
Pahute Mesa, *U.S.A.* **84 H10** 37 20N 116 45W
Pai, *Thailand* **38 C2** 19 19N 98 27 E
Paia, *U.S.A.* **74 H16** 20 54N 156 22W
Paicines, *U.S.A.* **84 J5** 36 44N 121 17W
Paide, *Estonia* **9 G21** 58 57N 25 31 E
Paignton, *U.K.* **11 G4** 50 26N 3 35W
Päijänne, *Finland* **9 F21** 61 30N 25 30 E
Painan, *Indonesia* **36 E2** 1 21 S 100 34 E
Painesville, *U.S.A.* **78 E3** 41 43N 81 15W
Paint Hills = Wemindji, *Canada* **70 B4** 53 0N 78 49W
Paint L., *Canada* **73 B9** 55 28N 97 57W
Paint Rock, *U.S.A.* **81 K5** 31 31N 99 55W
Painted Desert, *U.S.A.* **83 J8** 36 0N 111 0W
Paintsville, *U.S.A.* **76 G4** 37 49N 82 48W
País Vasco □, *Spain* **19 A4** 42 50N 2 45W
Paisley, *Canada* **78 B3** 44 18N 81 16W
Paisley, *U.K.* **12 F4** 55 50N 4 25W
Paisley, *U.S.A.* **82 E3** 42 42N 120 32W
Paita, *Peru* **92 E2** 5 11 S 81 9W
Pajares, Puerto de, *Spain* **19 A3** 42 58N 5 46W
Pak Lay, *Laos* **38 C3** 18 15N 101 27 E
Pak Phanang, *Thailand* **39 H3** 8 21N 100 12 E
Pak Sane, *Laos* **38 C4** 18 22N 103 39 E
Pak Song, *Laos* **38 E6** 15 11N 106 14 E
Pak Suong, *Laos* **38 C4** 19 58N 102 15 E
Pakaraima Mts., *Guyana* **92 B6** 6 0N 60 0W
Pákhnes, *Greece* **23 D6** 35 16N 24 4 E
Pakistan ■, *Asia* **42 E3** 30 0N 70 0 E
Pakkading, *Laos* **38 C4** 18 19N 103 59 E
Pakokku, *Burma* **41 J19** 21 20N 95 0 E
Pakpattan, *Pakistan* **42 D5** 30 25N 73 27 E
Pakse, *Laos* **38 E5** 15 5N 105 52 E
Paktīā □, *Afghan.* **40 C6** 33 0N 69 15 E
Pakwach, *Uganda* **54 B3** 2 28N 31 27 E
Pala, *Chad* **51 G8** 9 25N 15 5 E
Pala, *U.S.A.* **85 M9** 33 22N 117 5W
Pala, *Zaïre* **54 D2** 6 45 S 29 30 E
Palabek, *Uganda* **54 B3** 3 22N 32 33 E
Palacios, *U.S.A.* **81 L6** 28 42N 96 13W
Palagruža, *Croatia* **20 C7** 42 24N 16 15 E
Palaiókastron, *Greece* **23 D8** 35 12N 26 15 E
Palaiokhóra, *Greece* **23 D5** 35 16N 23 39 E
Palam, *India* **40 K10** 19 0N 77 0 E
Palampur, *India* **42 C7** 32 10N 76 30 E
Palana, *Australia* **62 F4** 39 45 S 147 55 E
Palana, *Russia* **27 D16** 59 10N 159 59 E
Palanan, *Phil.* **37 A6** 17 8N 122 29 E
Palanan Pt., *Phil.* **37 A6** 17 17N 122 30 E
Palandri, *Pakistan* **43 C5** 33 42N 73 40 E
Palanga, *Lithuania* **9 J19** 55 58N 21 3 E
Palangkaraya, *Indonesia* **36 E4** 2 16 S 113 56 E
Palani Hills, *India* **40 P10** 10 14N 77 33 E
Palanpur, *India* **42 G5** 24 10N 72 25 E
Palanro, *Indonesia* **37 E5** 3 21 S 119 23 E
Palapye, *Botswana* **56 C4** 22 30 S 27 7 E
Palas, *Pakistan* **43 B5** 35 4N 73 14 E
Palatka, *Russia* **27 C16** 60 6N 150 54 E
Palatka, *U.S.A.* **77 L5** 29 39N 81 38W
Palau ■, *Pac. Oc.* **28 J17** 7 30N 134 30 E
Palawan, *Phil.* **36 C5** 9 30N 118 30 E
Palayankottai, *India* **40 Q10** 8 45N 77 45 E
Paldiski, *Estonia* **9 G21** 59 23N 24 9 E
Paleleh, *Indonesia* **37 D6** 1 10N 121 50 E
Palembang, *Indonesia* **36 E2** 3 0S 104 50 E
Palencia, *Spain* **19 A3** 42 1N 4 34W
Paleokastrítsa, *Greece* **23 A3** 39 40N 19 41 E
Paleometokho, *Cyprus* **23 D12** 35 7N 33 11 E
Palermo, *Italy* **20 E5** 38 7N 13 22 E
Palermo, *U.S.A.* **82 G3** 39 26N 121 33W
Palestine, *Asia* **47 D4** 32 0N 35 0 E
Palestine, *U.S.A.* **81 K7** 31 46N 95 38W
Paletwa, *Burma* **41 J18** 21 10N 92 50 E
Palghat, *India* **40 P10** 10 46N 76 42 E
Palgrave, Mt., *Australia* **60 D2** 23 22 S 115 58 E
Pali, *India* **42 G5** 25 50N 73 20 E
Paliouríon, Ákra, *Greece* **21 E10** 39 57N 23 45 E
Palisade, *U.S.A.* **80 E4** 40 21N 101 7W
Palitana, *India* **42 J4** 21 32N 71 49 E
Palizada, *Mexico* **87 D6** 18 18N 92 8W
Palk Bay, *Asia* **40 Q11** 9 30N 79 15 E
Palk Strait, *Asia* **40 Q11** 10 0N 79 45 E
Palkānah, *Iraq* **44 C5** 35 49N 44 26 E
Palla Road = Dinokwe, *Botswana* **56 C4** 23 29 S 26 37 E
Pallanza = Verbánia, *Italy* **20 B3** 45 56N 8 33 E
Pallisa, *Uganda* **54 B3** 1 12N 33 43 E
Pallu, *India* **42 E6** 28 59N 74 14 E
Palm Bay, *U.S.A.* **77 L5** 28 2N 80 35W
Palm Beach, *U.S.A.* **77 M6** 26 43N 80 2W
Palm Desert, *U.S.A.* **85 M10** 33 43N 116 22W
Palm Is., *Australia* **62 B4** 18 40 S 146 35 E
Palm Springs, *U.S.A.* **85 M10** 33 50N 116 33W
Palma, *Mozam.* **55 E5** 10 46 S 40 29 E
Palma →, *Brazil* **93 F9** 12 33 S 47 52W
Palma, B. de, *Spain* **22 B9** 39 30N 2 39 E
Palma de Mallorca, *Spain* **22 B9** 39 35N 2 39 E
Palma Soriano, *Cuba* **88 B4** 20 15N 76 0W
Palmares, *Brazil* **93 E11** 8 41 S 35 28W
Palmas, *Brazil* **95 B5** 26 29 S 52 0W
Palmas, C., *Liberia* **50 H3** 4 27N 7 46W
Pálmas, G. di, *Italy* **20 E3** 39 0N 8 30 E
Palmdale, *U.S.A.* **85 L8** 34 35N 118 7W
Palmeira dos Índios, *Brazil* **93 E11** 9 25 S 36 37W
Palmeirinhas, Pta. das, *Angola* **52 F2** 9 2 S 12 57 E
Palmer, *U.S.A.* **68 B5** 61 36N 149 7W
Palmer →, *Australia* **62 B3** 16 0S 142 26 E
Palmer Arch., *Antarctica* **5 C17** 64 15 S 65 0W
Palmer Lake, *U.S.A.* **80 F2** 39 7N 104 55W
Palmer Land, *Antarctica* **5 D18** 73 0S 63 0W
Palmerston, *Canada* **78 C4** 43 50N 80 51W
Palmerston, *N.Z.* **59 L3** 45 29 S 170 43 E
Palmerston North, *N.Z.* **59 J5** 40 21 S 175 39 E
Palmerton, *U.S.A.* **79 F9** 40 48N 75 37W
Palmetto, *U.S.A.* **77 M4** 27 31N 82 34W
Palmi, *Italy* **20 E6** 38 21N 15 51 E
Palmira, *Argentina* **94 C2** 32 59 S 68 34W
Palmira, *Colombia* **92 C3** 3 32N 76 16W
Palmyra = Tudmur, *Syria* **44 C3** 34 36N 38 15 E
Palmyra, *Mo., U.S.A.* **80 F9** 39 48N 91 32W
Palmyra, *N.Y., U.S.A.* **78 C7** 43 5N 77 18W
Palmyra Is., *Pac. Oc.* **65 G11** 5 52N 162 5W
Palo Alto, *U.S.A.* **83 H2** 37 27N 122 10W
Palo Verde, *U.S.A.* **85 M12** 33 26N 114 44W
Palopo, *Indonesia* **37 E6** 3 0S 120 16 E
Palos, C. de, *Spain* **19 D5** 37 38N 0 40W
Palos Verdes, *U.S.A.* **85 M8** 33 48N 118 23W
Palos Verdes, Pt., *U.S.A.* **85 M8** 33 43N 118 26W
Palouse, *U.S.A.* **82 C5** 46 55N 117 4W
Palparara, *Australia* **62 C3** 24 47 S 141 28 E
Palu, *Indonesia* **37 E5** 1 0S 119 52 E
Palu, *Turkey* **25 G7** 38 45N 40 0 E
Paluan, *Phil.* **37 B6** 13 26N 120 29 E
Palwal, *India* **42 E7** 28 8N 77 19 E
Pama, *Burkina Faso* **50 F5** 11 19N 0 44 E
Pamanukan, *Indonesia* **37 G12** 6 16 S 107 49 E
Pamekasan, *Indonesia* **37 G15** 7 10 S 113 28 E
Pamiers, *France* **18 E4** 43 7N 1 39 E
Pamirs, *Tajikistan* **26 F8** 37 40N 73 0 E
Pamlico →, *U.S.A.* **77 H7** 35 20N 76 28W
Pamlico Sd., *U.S.A.* **77 H8** 35 20N 76 0W
Pampa, *U.S.A.* **81 H4** 35 32N 100 58W
Pampa de las Salinas, *Argentina* **94 C2** 32 1S 66 58W
Pampanua, *Indonesia* **37 E6** 4 16 S 120 8 E
Pampas, *Argentina* **94 D3** 35 0S 63 0W
Pampas, *Peru* **92 F4** 12 20 S 74 50W
Pamplona, *Colombia* **92 B4** 7 23N 72 39W
Pamplona, *Spain* **19 A5** 42 48N 1 38W
Pampoenpoort, *S. Africa* **56 E3** 31 3S 22 40 E
Pana, *U.S.A.* **80 F10** 39 23N 89 5W
Panaca, *U.S.A.* **83 H6** 37 47N 114 23W
Panaitan, *Indonesia* **37 G11** 6 36 S 105 12 E
Panaji, *India* **40 M8** 15 25N 73 50 E
Panamá, *Panama* **88 E4** 9 0N 79 25W
Panama ■, *Cent. Amer.* **88 E4** 8 48N 79 55W
Panamá, G. de, *Panama* **88 E4** 8 4N 79 20W
Panama Canal, *Panama* **88 E4** 9 10N 79 37W
Panama City, *U.S.A.* **77 K3** 30 10N 85 40W
Panamint Range, *U.S.A.* **85 J9** 36 20N 117 20W
Panamint Springs, *U.S.A.* **85 J9** 36 20N 117 28W
Panão, *Peru* **92 E3** 9 55 S 75 55W
Panare, *Thailand* **39 J3** 6 51N 101 30 E
Panarukan, *Indonesia* **37 G15** 7 42 S 113 56 E
Panay, *Phil.* **37 B6** 11 10N 122 30 E
Panay, G., *Phil.* **37 B6** 11 0N 122 30 E
Pancake Range, *U.S.A.* **83 G6** 38 30N 115 50W
Pančevo, *Serbia, Yug.* **21 B9** 44 52N 20 41 E
Pandan, *Phil.* **37 B6** 11 45N 122 10 E
Pandegelang, *Indonesia* **37 G12** 6 25 S 106 5 E
Pandharpur, *India* **40 L9** 17 41N 75 20 E
Pando, *Uruguay* **95 C4** 34 44 S 56 0W
Pando, L. = Hope, L., *Australia* **63 D2** 28 24 S 139 18 E
Pandokrátor, *Greece* **23 A3** 39 45N 19 50 E
Pandora, *Costa Rica* **88 E3** 9 43N 83 3W
Panevėžys, *Lithuania* **9 J21** 55 42N 24 25 E
Panfilov, *Kazakstan* **26 E8** 44 10N 80 0 E
Pang-Long, *Burma* **41 H21** 23 11N 98 45 E
Pang-Yang, *Burma* **41 H21** 22 7N 98 48 E
Panga, *Zaïre* **54 B2** 1 52N 26 18 E
Pangalanes, Canal des, *Madag.* **57 C8** 22 48 S 47 50 E
Pangani, *Tanzania* **54 D4** 5 25 S 38 58 E
Pangani □, *Tanzania* **54 D4** 5 25 S 39 0 E
Pangani →, *Tanzania* **54 D4** 5 26 S 38 58 E
Pangfou = Bengbu, *China* **35 H9** 32 58N 117 20 E
Pangil, *Zaïre* **54 C2** 3 10 S 26 35 E
Pangkah, Tanjung, *Indonesia* **37 G15** 6 51 S 112 33 E
Pangkajene, *Indonesia* **37 E5** 4 46 S 119 34 E
Pangkalanbrandan, *Indonesia* **36 D1** 4 1N 98 20 E
Pangkalanbuun, *Indonesia* **36 E4** 2 41 S 111 37 E

Penny

Pangkalansusu, Indonesia 36 D1 4 2N 98 13 E
Pangkalpinang, Indonesia 36 E3 2 0S 106 0 E
Pangkoh, Indonesia 36 E4 3 5S 114 8 E
Pangnirtung, Canada 69 B13 66 8N 65 54W
Pangrango, Indonesia 37 G12 6 46S 107 1 E
Panguitch, U.S.A. 83 H7 37 50N 112 26W
Pangutaran Group, Phil. 37 C6 6 18N 120 34 E
Panhandle, U.S.A. 81 H4 35 21N 101 23W
Pani Mines, India 42 H5 22 29N 73 50 E
Pania-Mutombo, Zaïre 54 D1 5 11S 23 51 E
Panipat, India 42 E7 29 25N 77 2 E
Panjal Range, India 42 C7 32 30N 76 50 E
Panjgur, Pakistan 40 F4 27 0N 64 5 E
Panjim = Panaji, India 40 M8 15 25N 73 50 E
Panjinad Barrage, Pakistan 40 E7 29 22N 71 15 E
Panjwai, Afghan. 42 D1 31 26N 65 27 E
Panmunjŏm, N. Korea 35 F14 37 59N 126 38 E
Panna, India 43 G9 24 40N 80 15 E
Panna Hills, India 43 G9 24 40N 81 15 E
Pano Lefkara, Cyprus 23 E12 34 53N 33 20 E
Pano Panayia, Cyprus 23 E11 34 55N 32 38 E
Panorama, Brazil 95 A5 21 21S 51 51W
Pánormon, Greece 23 D6 35 25N 24 41 E
Panshan, China 35 D12 41 3N 122 2 E
Panshi, China 35 C14 42 58N 126 5 E
Pantar, Indonesia 37 F6 8 28S 124 10 E
Pante Macassar, Indonesia 37 F6 9 30S 123 58 E
Pantelleria, Italy 20 F4 36 50N 11 57 E
Pánuco, Mexico 87 C5 22 0N 98 15W
Panyam, Nigeria 50 G6 9 27N 9 8 E
Paola, Malta 23 D2 35 52N 14 30 E
Paola, U.S.A. 80 F7 38 35N 94 53W
Paonia, U.S.A. 83 G10 38 52N 107 36W
Paoting = Baoding, China 34 E8 38 50N 115 28 E
Paot'ou = Baotou, China 34 D6 40 32N 110 2 E
Paoua, C.A.R. 51 G8 7 9N 16 20 E
Pápa, Hungary 17 E9 47 22N 17 30 E
Papagayo →, Mexico 87 D5 16 36N 99 43W
Papagayo, G. de, Costa Rica 88 D2 10 30N 85 50W
Papakura, N.Z. 59 G5 37 4S 174 59 E
Papantla, Mexico 87 C5 20 30N 97 30W
Papar, Malaysia 36 C5 5 45N 116 0 E
Paphos, Cyprus 23 E11 34 46N 32 25 E
Papien Chiang = Da →, Vietnam 38 B5 21 15N 105 20 E
Papigochic →, Mexico 86 B3 29 9N 109 40W
Paposo, Chile 94 B1 25 0S 70 30W
Papoutsa, Cyprus 23 E12 34 54N 33 4 E
Papua New Guinea ■, Oceania 64 H6 8 0S 145 0 E
Papudo, Chile 94 C1 32 29S 71 27W
Papun, Burma 41 K20 18 2N 97 30 E
Papunya, Australia 60 D5 23 15S 131 54 E
Pará = Belém, Brazil 93 D9 1 20S 48 30W
Pará □, Brazil 93 D8 3 20S 52 0W
Paraburdoo, Australia 60 D2 23 14S 117 32 E
Paracatu, Brazil 93 G9 17 10S 46 50W
Paracel Is., S. China Sea 36 A4 15 50N 112 0 E
Parachilna, Australia 63 E2 31 10S 138 21 E
Parachinar, Pakistan 42 C4 33 55N 70 5 E
Paradhísi, Greece 23 C10 36 18N 28 7 E
Paradip, India 41 J15 20 15N 86 35 E
Paradise, Calif., U.S.A. 84 F5 39 46N 121 37W
Paradise, Mont., U.S.A. 82 C6 47 23N 114 48W
Paradise, Nev., U.S.A. 85 J11 36 9N 115 10W
Paradise →, Canada 71 B8 53 27N 57 19W
Paradise Valley, U.S.A. 82 F5 41 30N 117 32W
Parado, Indonesia 37 F5 8 42S 118 30 E
Paragould, U.S.A. 81 G9 36 3N 90 29W
Paragua →, Venezuela 92 B6 6 55N 62 55W
Paraguaçu →, Brazil 93 F11 12 45S 38 54W
Paraguaçu Paulista, Brazil 95 A5 22 22S 50 35W
Paraguaná, Pen. de, Venezuela 92 A4 12 0N 70 0W
Paraguarí, Paraguay 94 B4 25 36S 57 0W
Paraguarí □, Paraguay 94 B4 26 0S 57 10W
Paraguay ■, S. Amer. 94 A4 23 0S 57 0W
Paraguay →, Paraguay 94 B4 27 18S 58 38W
Paraíba = João Pessoa, Brazil 93 E12 7 10S 34 52W
Paraíba □, Brazil 93 E11 7 0S 36 0W
Paraíba do Sul →, Brazil 95 A7 21 37S 41 3W
Parainen, Finland 9 F20 60 18N 22 18 E
Paraiso, Mexico 87 D6 18 24N 93 14W
Parak, Iran 45 E7 27 38N 52 25 E
Parakou, Benin 50 G5 9 25N 2 40 E
Paralimni, Cyprus 23 D12 35 2N 33 58 E
Paramaribo, Surinam 93 B7 5 50N 55 10W
Paramushir, Ostrov, Russia 27 D16 50 24N 156 0 E
Paran →, Israel 47 E4 30 20N 35 10 E
Paraná, Argentina 94 C3 31 45S 60 30W
Paranã, Brazil 93 F9 12 30S 47 48W
Paraná □, Brazil 95 A5 24 30S 51 0W
Paraná →, Argentina 94 C4 33 43S 59 15W
Paranaguá, Brazil 95 B6 25 30S 48 30W
Paranaíba →, Brazil 93 H8 20 6S 51 4W
Paranapanema →, Brazil 95 A5 22 40S 53 9W
Paranapiacaba, Serra do, Brazil 95 A6 24 31S 48 35W
Paranavaí, Brazil 95 A5 23 4S 52 56W
Parang, Jolo, Phil. 37 C6 5 55N 120 54 E
Parang, Mindanao, Phil. 37 C6 7 23N 124 16 E
Paratinga, Brazil 93 F10 12 40S 43 10W
Paratoo, Australia 63 E2 32 42S 139 20 E
Parattah, Australia 62 G4 42 22S 147 23 E
Parbati →, India 42 G7 25 50N 76 30 E
Parbhani, India 40 K10 19 8N 76 52 E
Parchim, Germany 16 B6 53 26N 11 52 E
Pardes Hanna, Israel 47 C3 32 28N 34 57 E
Pardo →, Bahia, Brazil 93 G11 15 40S 39 0W
Pardo →, Mato Grosso, Brazil 95 A5 21 46S 52 9W
Pardo →, São Paulo, Brazil 93 H9 20 10S 48 38W
Pardubice, Czech. 16 C8 50 3N 15 45 E
Pare, Indonesia 37 G15 7 43S 112 12 E
Pare □, Tanzania 54 C4 4 10S 38 0 E
Pare Mts., Tanzania 54 C4 4 0S 37 45 E
Parecis, Serra dos, Brazil 92 F7 13 0S 60 0W
Pareh, Iran 44 B5 38 52N 45 42 E
Paren, Russia 27 C17 62 30N 163 15 E
Parent, Canada 70 C5 47 55N 74 35W
Parent, L., Canada 70 C4 48 31N 77 1W
Parepare, Indonesia 37 E5 4 0S 119 40 E
Párga, Greece 21 E9 39 15N 20 29 E
Pargo, Pta. do, Madeira 22 D2 32 49N 17 17W
Parguba, Russia 24 B5 62 20N 34 27 E
Pariaguán, Venezuela 92 B6 8 51N 64 34W
Pariaman, Indonesia 36 E2 0 47S 100 11 E
Paricutín, Cerro, Mexico 86 D4 19 28N 102 15W
Parigi, Java, Indonesia 37 G13 7 42S 108 29 E
Parigi, Sulawesi, Indonesia 37 E6 0 50S 120 5 E
Parika, Guyana 92 B7 6 50N 58 20W
Parima, Serra, Brazil 92 C6 2 30N 64 0W
Parinari, Peru 92 D4 4 35S 74 25W
Pariñas, Pta., S. Amer. 90 D2 4 30S 82 0W
Parîngul Mare, Romania 17 F12 45 20N 23 37 E
Parintins, Brazil 93 D7 2 40S 56 50W
Pariparit Kyun, Burma 41 M18 14 55N 93 45 E
Paris, Canada 70 D3 43 12N 80 25W
Paris, France 18 B5 48 50N 2 20 E
Paris, Idaho, U.S.A. 82 E8 42 14N 111 24W
Paris, Ky., U.S.A. 76 F3 38 13N 84 15W
Paris, Tenn., U.S.A. 77 G1 36 18N 88 19W
Paris, Tex., U.S.A. 81 J7 33 40N 95 33W
Parish, U.S.A. 79 C8 43 25N 76 8W
Pariti, Indonesia 37 F6 10 15S 123 45 E
Park, U.S.A. 84 B4 48 45N 122 18W
Park City, U.S.A. 82 F8 40 39N 111 30W
Park Falls, U.S.A. 80 C9 45 56N 90 27W
Park Range, U.S.A. 82 G10 40 0N 106 30W
Park Rapids, U.S.A. 80 B7 46 55N 95 4W
Park River, U.S.A. 80 A6 48 24N 97 45W
Park Rynie, S. Africa 57 E5 30 25S 30 45 E
Parkā Bandar, Iran 45 E8 25 55N 59 35 E
Parkano, Finland 9 E20 62 1N 23 0 E
Parker, Ariz., U.S.A. 85 L12 34 9N 114 17W
Parker, S. Dak., U.S.A. 80 D6 43 24N 97 8W
Parker Dam, U.S.A. 85 L12 34 18N 114 8W
Parkersburg, U.S.A. 76 F5 39 16N 81 34W
Parkerview, Canada 73 C8 51 21N 103 18W
Parkes, Australia 63 E4 33 9S 148 11 E
Parkfield, U.S.A. 84 K6 35 54N 120 26W
Parkland, U.S.A. 84 C4 47 9N 122 26W
Parkside, Canada 73 C7 53 10N 106 33W
Parkston, U.S.A. 80 D5 43 24N 97 59W
Parksville, Canada 72 D4 49 20N 124 21W
Parla, Spain 19 B4 40 14N 3 46W
Parma, Italy 20 B4 44 48N 10 20 E
Parma, Idaho, U.S.A. 82 E5 43 47N 116 57W
Parma, Ohio, U.S.A. 78 E3 41 23N 81 43W
Parnaguá, Brazil 93 F10 10 10S 44 38W
Parnaíba, Piauí, Brazil 93 D10 2 54S 41 47W
Parnaíba, São Paulo, Brazil 93 G8 19 34S 51 14W
Parnaíba →, Brazil 93 D10 3 0S 41 50W
Parnassós, Greece 21 E10 38 35N 22 30 E
Pärnu, Estonia 9 G21 58 28N 24 33 E
Paroo →, Australia 63 E3 31 28S 143 32 E
Páros, Greece 21 F11 37 5N 25 12 E
Parowan, U.S.A. 83 H7 37 51N 112 50W
Parral, Chile 94 D1 36 10S 71 52W
Parramatta, Australia 63 E5 33 48S 151 1 E
Parras, Mexico 86 B4 25 30N 102 20W
Parrett →, U.K. 11 F5 51 12N 3 1W
Parris I., U.S.A. 77 J5 32 20N 80 41W
Parrsboro, Canada 71 C7 45 30N 64 25W
Parry Is., Canada 4 B2 77 0N 110 0W
Parry Sound, Canada 70 C3 45 20N 80 0W
Parshall, U.S.A. 80 B3 47 57N 102 8W
Parsnip →, Canada 72 B4 55 10N 123 2W
Parsons, U.S.A. 81 G7 37 20N 95 16W
Parsons Ra., Australia 62 A2 13 30S 135 15 E
Partinico, Italy 20 E5 38 3N 13 7 E
Paru →, Brazil 93 D8 1 33S 52 38W
Paruro, Peru 92 F4 13 45S 71 50W
Parvān □, Afghan. 40 B6 35 0N 69 0 E
Parvatipuram, India 41 K13 18 50N 83 25 E
Parys, S. Africa 56 D4 26 52S 27 29 E
Pasadena, Calif., U.S.A. 85 L8 34 9N 118 9W
Pasadena, Tex., U.S.A. 81 L7 29 43N 95 13W
Pasaje, Ecuador 92 D3 3 23S 79 50W
Pasaje →, Argentina 94 B3 25 39S 63 56W
Pascagoula, U.S.A. 81 K10 30 21N 88 33W
Pascagoula →, U.S.A. 81 K10 30 23N 88 37W
Paşcani, Romania 17 E14 47 14N 26 45 E
Pasco, U.S.A. 82 C4 46 14N 119 6W
Pasco, Cerro de, Peru 92 F3 10 45S 76 10W
Pascua, I. de, Pac. Oc. 65 K17 27 0S 109 0W
Pasfield L., Canada 73 B7 58 24N 105 20W
Pashiwari, Pakistan 43 B6 34 40N 75 10 E
Pashmakli = Smolyan, Bulgaria 21 D11 41 36N 24 38 E
Pasirian, Indonesia 37 H15 8 13S 113 8 E
Paskūh, Iran 45 E9 27 34N 61 39 E
Pasley, C., Australia 61 F3 33 52S 123 35 E
Pašman, Croatia 16 G8 43 58N 15 20 E
Pasni, Pakistan 40 G3 25 15N 63 27 E
Paso Cantinela, Mexico 85 N11 32 33N 115 47W
Paso de Indios, Argentina 96 E3 43 55S 69 0W
Paso de los Libres, Argentina 94 B4 29 44S 57 10W
Paso de los Toros, Uruguay 94 C4 32 45S 56 30W
Paso Robles, U.S.A. 83 J3 35 38N 120 41W
Paspébiac, Canada 71 C6 48 3N 65 17W
Pasrur, Pakistan 42 C6 32 16N 74 43 E
Passage West, Ireland 13 E3 51 52N 8 21W
Passaic, U.S.A. 79 F10 40 51N 74 7W
Passau, Germany 16 D7 48 34N 13 28 E
Passero, C., Italy 20 F6 36 41N 15 10 E
Passo Fundo, Brazil 95 B5 28 10S 52 20W
Passos, Brazil 93 H9 20 45S 46 37W
Pastavy, Belarus 9 J22 55 4N 26 50 E
Pastaza →, Peru 92 D3 4 50S 76 52W
Pasto, Colombia 92 C3 1 13N 77 17W
Pasuruan, Indonesia 37 G15 7 40S 112 44 E
Patagonia, Argentina 96 F3 45 0S 69 0W
Patagonia, U.S.A. 83 L8 31 33N 110 45W
Patambar, Iran 45 D9 29 45N 60 17 E
Patan, India 40 H8 23 54N 72 14 E
Patan, Maharashtra, India 42 H5 23 54N 72 14 E
Patan, Nepal 41 F14 27 40N 85 20 E
Patani, Indonesia 37 D7 0 20N 128 50 E
Pataudi, India 42 E7 28 18N 76 48 E
Patchewollock, Australia 63 F3 35 22S 142 12 E
Patchogue, U.S.A. 79 F11 40 46N 73 1W
Patea, N.Z. 59 H5 39 45S 174 30 E
Pategi, Nigeria 50 G6 8 50N 5 45 E
Patensie, S. Africa 56 E3 33 46S 24 49 E
Paternò, Italy 20 F6 37 34N 14 54 E
Pateros, U.S.A. 82 B4 48 3N 119 54W
Paterson, U.S.A. 79 F10 40 55N 74 11W
Paterson Ra., Australia 60 D3 21 45S 122 10 E
Pathankot, India 42 C6 32 18N 75 45 E
Pathfinder Reservoir, U.S.A. 82 E10 42 28N 106 51W
Pathiu, Thailand 39 G2 10 42N 99 19 E
Pathum Thani, Thailand 38 E3 14 1N 100 32 E
Pati, Indonesia 37 G14 6 45S 111 1 E
Patiala, India 42 D7 30 23N 76 26 E
Patkai Bum, India 41 F19 27 0N 95 30 E
Pátmos, Greece 21 F12 37 21N 26 36 E
Patna, India 43 G11 25 35N 85 12 E
Patonga, Uganda 54 B3 2 45N 33 15 E
Patos, L. dos, Brazil 95 C5 31 20S 51 0W
Patos de Minas, Brazil 93 G9 18 35S 46 32W
Patquía, Argentina 94 C2 30 2S 66 55W
Pátrai, Greece 21 E9 38 14N 21 47 E
Pátraikós Kólpos, Greece 21 E9 38 17N 21 30 E
Patras = Pátrai, Greece 21 E9 38 14N 21 47 E
Patrocínio, Brazil 93 G9 18 57S 47 0W
Patta, Kenya 54 C5 2 10S 41 0 E
Pattani, Thailand 39 J3 6 48N 101 15 E
Patten, U.S.A. 71 C6 46 0N 68 38W
Patterson, Calif., U.S.A. 83 H3 37 28N 121 8W
Patterson, La., U.S.A. 81 L9 29 42N 91 18W
Patterson, Mt., U.S.A. 84 G7 38 29N 119 20W
Patti, India 42 D6 31 17N 74 54 E
Pattoki, Pakistan 42 D5 31 5N 73 52 E
Patton, U.S.A. 78 F6 40 38N 78 39W
Patuakhali, Bangla. 41 H17 22 20N 90 25 E
Patuca →, Honduras 88 C3 15 50N 84 18W
Patuca, Punta, Honduras 88 C3 15 49N 84 14W
Pátzcuaro, Mexico 86 D4 19 30N 101 40W
Pau, France 18 E3 43 19N 0 25W
Pauini →, Brazil 92 D6 1 42S 62 50W
Pauk, Burma 41 J19 21 27N 94 30 E
Paul I., Canada 71 A7 56 30N 61 20W
Paulis = Isiro, Zaïre 54 B2 2 53N 27 40 E
Paulistana, Brazil 93 E10 8 9S 41 9W
Paullina, U.S.A. 80 D7 42 59N 95 41W
Paulo Afonso, Brazil 93 E11 9 21S 38 15W
Paulpietersburg, S. Africa 57 D5 27 23S 30 50 E
Pauls Valley, U.S.A. 81 H6 34 44N 97 13W
Pauma Valley, U.S.A. 85 M10 33 16N 116 58W
Pāveh, Iran 44 C5 35 3N 46 22 E
Pavia, Italy 20 B3 45 7N 9 8 E
Pāvilosta, Latvia 9 H19 56 53N 21 14 E
Pavlodar, Kazakstan 26 D8 52 33N 77 0 E
Pavlograd = Pavlohrad, Ukraine 25 E6 48 30N 35 52 E
Pavlohrad, Ukraine 25 E6 48 30N 35 52 E
Pavlovo, Oka, Russia 24 C7 55 58N 43 5 E
Pavlovo, Sakha, Russia 27 C12 63 5N 115 25 E
Pavlovsk, Russia 25 D7 50 26N 40 5 E
Pawhuska, U.S.A. 81 G6 36 40N 96 20W
Pawling, U.S.A. 79 E11 41 34N 73 36W
Pawnee, U.S.A. 81 G6 36 20N 96 48W
Pawnee City, U.S.A. 80 E6 40 7N 96 9W
Pawtucket, U.S.A. 79 E13 41 53N 71 23W
Paximádhia, Greece 23 D6 35 0N 24 35 E
Paxoí, Greece 21 E9 39 14N 20 12 E
Paxton, Ill., U.S.A. 76 E1 40 27N 88 6W
Paxton, Nebr., U.S.A. 80 E4 41 7N 101 21W
Payakumbuh, Indonesia 36 E2 0 20S 100 35 E
Payette, U.S.A. 82 D5 44 5N 116 56W
Payne Bay = Kangirsuk, Canada 69 B13 60 0N 70 0W
Paynes Find, Australia 61 E2 29 15S 117 42 E
Paynesville, U.S.A. 80 C7 45 23N 94 43W
Paysandú, Uruguay 94 C4 32 19S 58 8W
Payson, Ariz., U.S.A. 83 J8 34 14N 111 20W
Payson, Utah, U.S.A. 82 F8 40 3N 111 44W
Paz →, Guatemala 88 D1 13 44N 90 10W
Paz, B. la, Mexico 86 C2 24 15N 110 25W
Pāzanān, Iran 45 D6 30 35N 49 59 E
Pazardzhik, Bulgaria 21 C11 42 12N 24 20 E
Pe Ell, U.S.A. 84 D3 46 34N 123 18W
Peabody, U.S.A. 79 D14 42 31N 70 56W
Peace →, Canada 72 B6 59 0N 111 25W
Peace Point, Canada 72 B6 59 7N 112 27W
Peace River, Canada 72 B5 56 15N 117 18W
Peach Springs, U.S.A. 83 J7 35 32N 113 25W
Peak, The = Kinder Scout, U.K. 10 D6 53 24N 1 52W
Peak Downs, Australia 62 C4 22 55S 148 5 E
Peak Downs Mine, Australia 62 C4 22 17S 148 11 E
Peak Hill, N.S.W., Australia 63 E4 32 47S 148 11 E
Peak Hill, W. Austral., Australia 61 E2 25 35S 118 43 E
Peak Ra., Australia 62 C4 22 50S 148 20 E
Peake, Australia 63 F2 35 25S 139 55 E
Peake Cr. →, Australia 63 D2 28 2S 136 7 E
Peale, Mt., U.S.A. 83 G9 38 26N 109 14W
Pearblossom, U.S.A. 85 L9 34 30N 117 55W
Pearl →, U.S.A. 81 K10 30 11N 89 32W
Pearl City, U.S.A. 74 H16 21 24N 157 59W
Pearsall, U.S.A. 81 L5 28 54N 99 6W
Pearse I., Canada 72 C2 54 52N 130 14W
Peary Land, Greenland 4 A6 82 40N 33 0W
Pease →, U.S.A. 81 H5 34 12N 99 2W
Pebane, Mozam. 55 F4 17 10S 38 8 E
Pebas, Peru 92 D4 3 10S 71 46W
Pebble Beach, U.S.A. 84 J5 36 34N 121 57W
Peć, Serbia, Yug. 21 C9 42 40N 20 17 E
Pechenga, Russia 24 A5 69 29N 31 4 E
Pechenizhyn, Ukraine 17 D13 48 30N 24 48 E
Pechiguera, Pta., Canary Is. 22 F6 28 51N 13 53W
Pechora →, Russia 24 A9 68 13N 54 15 E
Pechorskaya Guba, Russia 24 A9 68 40N 54 0 E
Pečory, Russia 9 H22 57 48N 27 40 E
Pecos, U.S.A. 81 K3 31 26N 103 30W
Pecos →, U.S.A. 81 L3 29 42N 101 22W
Pécs, Hungary 17 E10 46 5N 18 15 E
Pedder, L., Australia 62 G4 42 55S 146 10 E
Peddie, S. Africa 57 E4 33 14S 27 7 E
Pedernales, Dom. Rep. 89 C5 18 2N 71 44W
Pedieos →, Cyprus 23 D12 35 10N 33 54 E
Pedirka, Australia 63 D2 26 40S 135 14 E
Pedra Azul, Brazil 93 G10 16 2S 41 17W
Pedreiras, Brazil 93 D10 4 32S 44 40W
Pedro Afonso, Brazil 93 E9 9 0S 48 10W
Pedro Cays, Jamaica 88 C4 17 5N 77 48W
Pedro de Valdivia, Chile 94 A2 22 55S 69 38W
Pedro Juan Caballero, Paraguay 95 A4 22 30S 55 40W
Peebinga, Australia 63 E3 34 52S 140 57 E
Peebles, U.K. 12 F5 55 40N 3 11W
Peekskill, U.S.A. 79 E11 41 17N 73 55W
Peel, U.K. 10 C3 54 13N 4 40W
Peel →, Australia 63 E5 30 50S 150 29 E
Peel →, Canada 68 B6 67 0N 135 0W
Peera Peera Poolanna L., Australia 63 D2 26 30S 138 0 E
Peers, Canada 72 C5 53 40N 116 0W
Pegasus Bay, N.Z. 59 K4 43 20S 173 10 E
Pegu, Burma 41 L20 17 20N 96 29 E
Pegu Yoma, Burma 41 K19 19 0N 96 0 E
Pehuajó, Argentina 94 D3 35 45S 62 0W
Pei Xian, China 34 G9 34 44N 116 55 E
Peine, Chile 94 A2 23 45S 68 8W
Peine, Germany 16 B6 52 19N 10 14 E
Peip'ing = Beijing, China 34 E9 39 55N 116 20 E
Peipus, L. = Chudskoye, Oz., Russia 9 G22 58 13N 27 30 E
Peixe, Brazil 93 F9 12 0S 48 40W
Pekalongan, Indonesia 37 G13 6 53S 109 40 E
Pekan, Malaysia 39 L4 3 30N 103 25 E
Pekanbaru, Indonesia 36 D2 0 30N 101 15 E
Pekin, U.S.A. 80 E10 40 35N 89 40W
Peking = Beijing, China 34 E9 39 55N 116 20 E
Pelabuhan Kelang, Malaysia 39 L3 3 0N 101 23 E
Pelabuhan Ratu, Teluk, Indonesia 37 G12 7 5S 106 30 E
Pelabuhanratu, Indonesia 37 G12 7 0S 106 32 E
Pelagie, Is., Italy 20 G5 35 39N 12 33 E
Pelaihari, Indonesia 36 E4 3 55S 114 45 E
Peleaga, Vf., Romania 17 F12 45 22N 22 55 E
Pelée, Mt., Martinique 89 D7 14 48N 61 10W
Pelee, Pt., Canada 70 D3 41 54N 82 31W
Pelee I., Canada 70 D3 41 47N 82 40W
Pelekech, Kenya 54 B4 3 52N 35 8 E
Peleng, Indonesia 37 E6 1 20S 123 30 E
Pelham, U.S.A. 77 K3 31 8N 84 9W
Pelican L., Canada 73 C8 52 28N 100 20W
Pelican Narrows, Canada 73 B8 55 10N 102 56W
Pelican Rapids, Canada 73 C8 52 45N 100 42W
Pelješac, Croatia 20 C7 42 55N 17 25 E
Pelkosenniemi, Finland 8 C22 67 6N 27 28 E
Pella, S. Africa 56 D2 29 1S 19 6 E
Pella, U.S.A. 80 E8 41 25N 92 55W
Pello, Finland 8 C21 66 47N 23 59 E
Pelly →, Canada 68 B6 62 47N 137 19W
Pelly Bay, Canada 69 B11 68 38N 89 50W
Pelly L., Canada 68 B9 66 0N 102 0W
Peloponnese = Pelopónnisos □, Greece 21 F10 37 10N 22 0 E
Pelopónnisos □, Greece 21 F10 37 10N 22 0 E
Peloro, C., Italy 20 E6 38 16N 15 39 E
Pelorus Sd., N.Z. 59 J4 40 59S 173 59 E
Pelotas, Brazil 95 C5 31 42S 52 23W
Pelvoux, Massif du, France 18 D7 44 52N 6 20 E
Pemalang, Indonesia 37 G13 6 53S 109 23 E
Pematangsiantar, Indonesia 36 D1 2 57N 99 5 E
Pemba, Mozam. 55 E5 12 58S 40 30 E
Pemba, Zambia 55 F2 16 30S 27 28 E
Pemba Channel, Tanzania 54 D4 5 0S 39 37 E
Pemba I., Tanzania 54 D4 5 0S 39 45 E
Pemberton, Australia 61 F2 34 30S 116 0 E
Pemberton, Canada 72 C4 50 25N 122 50W
Pembina, U.S.A. 80 A6 48 58N 97 15W
Pembina →, U.S.A. 73 D9 48 58N 97 14W
Pembine, U.S.A. 76 C2 45 38N 87 59W
Pembroke, Canada 70 C4 45 50N 77 7W
Pembroke, U.K. 11 F3 51 41N 4 55W
Pembroke, U.S.A. 77 J5 32 8N 81 37W
Pembrokeshire □, U.K. 11 F3 51 52N 4 56W
Pen-y-Ghent, U.K. 10 C5 54 10N 2 14W
Penang = Pinang, Malaysia 39 K3 5 25N 100 15 E
Penápolis, Brazil 95 A6 21 30S 50 0W
Peñarroya-Pueblonuevo, Spain 19 C3 38 19N 5 16W
Peñas, C. de, Spain 19 A3 43 42N 5 52W
Penas, G. de, Chile 96 F2 47 0S 75 0W
Peñas del Chache, Canary Is. 22 E6 29 6N 13 33W
Pench'i = Benxi, China 35 D12 41 20N 123 48 E
Pend Oreille →, U.S.A. 82 B5 49 4N 117 37W
Pend Oreille L., U.S.A. 82 C5 48 10N 116 21W
Pendembu, S. Leone 50 G2 9 7N 12 14W
Pender B., Australia 60 C3 16 45S 122 42 E
Pendleton, Calif., U.S.A. 85 M9 33 16N 117 23W
Pendleton, Oreg., U.S.A. 82 D4 45 40N 118 47W
Penedo, Brazil 93 F11 10 15S 36 36W
Penetanguishene, Canada 70 D4 44 50N 79 55W
Pengalengan, Indonesia 37 G12 7 9S 107 30 E
Penge, Kasai Or., Zaïre 54 D1 5 30S 24 33 E
Penge, Kivu, Zaïre 54 C2 4 27S 28 25 E
Penglai, China 35 F11 37 48N 120 42 E
Penguin, Australia 62 G4 41 8S 146 6 E
Penhalonga, Zimbabwe 55 F3 18 52S 32 40 E
Peniche, Portugal 19 C1 39 19N 9 22W
Penicuik, U.K. 12 F5 55 50N 3 13W
Penida, Indonesia 36 F5 8 45S 115 30 E
Peninsular Malaysia □, Malaysia 39 L4 4 0N 102 0 E
Penmarch, Pte. de, France 18 C1 47 48N 4 22W
Penn Hills, U.S.A. 78 F5 40 28N 79 52W
Penn Yan, U.S.A. 78 D7 42 40N 77 3W
Pennant, Canada 73 C7 50 32N 108 14W
Penner →, India 40 M12 14 35N 80 10 E
Pennines, U.K. 10 C5 54 45N 2 27W
Pennington, U.S.A. 84 F5 39 15N 121 47W
Pennsylvania □, U.S.A. 76 E6 40 45N 77 30W
Penny, Canada 72 C4 53 51N 121 20W

153

Potrerillos

154

Ravena

Qasr 'Amra, *Jordan* **44 D3** 31 48N 36 35 E
Qaşr-e Qand, *Iran* **45 E9** 26 15N 60 45 E
Qasr Farâfra, *Egypt* **51 C10** 27 0N 28 1 E
Qatanâ, *Syria* **47 B5** 33 26N 36 4 E
Qatar ■, *Asia* **45 E6** 25 30N 51 15 E
Qatlīsh, *Iran* **45 B8** 37 50N 57 19 E
Qattâra, Munkhafed el, *Egypt* **51 C10** 29 30N 27 30 E
Qattâra Depression = Qattâra, Munkhafed el, *Egypt* **51 C10** 29 30N 27 30 E
Qawām al Ḥamzah, *Iraq* **44 D5** 31 43N 44 58 E
Qāyen, *Iran* **45 C8** 33 40N 59 10 E
Qazaqstan = Kazakstan ■, *Asia* **26 E7** 50 0N 70 0 E
Qazvin, *Iran* **45 B6** 36 15N 50 0 E
Qena, *Egypt* **51 C11** 26 10N 32 43 E
Qeqertarsuaq = Disko, *Greenland* **4 C5** 69 45N 53 30W
Qeqertarsuaq = Godhavn, *Greenland* **4 C5** 69 15N 53 38W
Qeshlāq, *Iran* **44 C5** 34 55N 46 28 E
Qeshm, *Iran* **45 E8** 26 55N 56 10 E
Qezi'ot, *Israel* **47 E3** 30 52N 34 26 E
Qi Xian, *China* **34 G8** 34 40N 114 48 E
Qian Gorlos, *China* **35 B13** 45 5N 124 42 E
Qian Xian, *China* **34 G5** 34 31N 108 15 E
Qianyang, *China* **34 G4** 34 40N 107 8 E
Qibā', *Si. Arabia* **44 E5** 27 24N 44 20 E
Qila Safed, *Pakistan* **40 E2** 29 0N 61 30 E
Qila Saifullāh, *Pakistan* **42 D3** 30 45N 68 17 E
Qilian Shan, *China* **32 C4** 38 30N 96 0 E
Qin He →, *China* **34 G7** 35 1N 113 22 E
Qin Ling = Qinling Shandi, *China* **34 H5** 33 50N 108 10 E
Qin'an, *China* **34 G3** 34 48N 105 40 E
Qing Xian, *China* **34 E9** 38 35N 116 45 E
Qingcheng, *China* **35 F9** 37 15N 117 40 E
Qingdao, *China* **35 F11** 36 5N 120 20 E
Qingfeng, *China* **34 G8** 35 52N 115 8 E
Qinghai □, *China* **32 C4** 36 0N 98 0 E
Qinghai Hu, *China* **32 C5** 36 40N 100 10 E
Qinghecheng, *China* **35 D13** 41 15N 124 30 E
Qinghemen, *China* **35 D11** 41 48N 121 25 E
Qingjian, *China* **34 F6** 37 8N 110 8 E
Qingjiang, *China* **35 H10** 33 30N 119 2 E
Qingshui, *China* **34 G4** 34 48N 106 8 E
Qingshuihe, *China* **34 E6** 39 55N 111 35 E
Qingtongxia Shuiku, *China* **34 F3** 37 50N 105 58 E
Qingxu, *China* **34 F7** 37 34N 112 22 E
Qingyang, *China* **34 F4** 36 2N 107 55 E
Qingyuan, *China* **35 C13** 42 10N 124 55 E
Qingyun, *China* **35 F9** 37 45N 117 20 E
Qinhuangdao, *China* **35 E10** 39 56N 119 30 E
Qinling Shandi, *China* **34 H5** 33 50N 108 10 E
Qinshui, *China* **34 G7** 35 40N 112 8 E
Qinyang, *China* **34 G7** 35 7N 112 57 E
Qinyuan, *China* **34 F7** 36 29N 112 20 E
Qinzhou, *China* **32 D5** 21 58N 108 38 E
Qionghai, *China* **38 C8** 19 15N 110 26 E
Qiongshan, *China* **38 C8** 19 51N 110 26 E
Qiongzhou Haixia, *China* **38 B8** 20 10N 110 15 E
Qiqihar, *China* **27 E13** 47 26N 124 0 E
Qiraîya, W. →, *Egypt* **47 E3** 30 27N 34 0 E
Qiryat Ata, *Israel* **47 C4** 32 47N 35 6 E
Qiryat Gat, *Israel* **47 D3** 31 32N 34 46 E
Qiryat Mal'akhi, *Israel* **47 D3** 31 44N 34 44 E
Qiryat Shemona, *Israel* **47 B4** 33 13N 35 35 E
Qiryat Yam, *Israel* **47 C4** 32 51N 35 4 E
Qishan, *China* **34 G4** 34 25N 107 38 E
Qitai, *China* **32 B3** 44 2N 89 35 E
Qixia, *China* **35 F11** 37 17N 120 52 E
Qojūr, *Iran* **44 B5** 36 12N 47 55 E
Qom, *Iran* **45 C6** 34 40N 51 0 E
Qomsheh, *Iran* **45 D6** 32 0N 51 55 E
Qostanay, *Kazakstan* **26 D7** 53 10N 63 35 E
Qu Xian, *China* **33 D6** 28 57N 118 54 E
Quairading, *Australia* **61 F2** 32 0S 117 21 E
Quakertown, *U.S.A.* **79 F9** 40 26N 75 21W
Qualeup, *Australia* **61 F2** 33 48S 116 48 E
Quambatook, *Australia* **63 F3** 35 49S 143 34 E
Quambone, *Australia* **63 E4** 30 57S 147 53 E
Quamby, *Australia* **62 C3** 20 22S 140 17 E
Quan Long, *Vietnam* **39 H5** 9 7N 105 8 E
Quanah, *U.S.A.* **81 H5** 34 18N 99 44W
Quandialla, *Australia* **63 E4** 34 1S 147 47 E
Quang Ngai, *Vietnam* **38 E7** 15 13N 108 58 E
Quang Yen, *Vietnam* **38 B6** 20 56N 106 52 E
Quantock Hills, *U.K.* **11 F4** 51 8N 3 10W
Quanzhou, *China* **33 D6** 24 55N 118 34 E
Quaqtaq, *Canada* **69 B13** 60 55N 69 40W
Quaraí, *Brazil* **94 C4** 30 15S 56 20W
Quartu Sant'Elena, *Italy* **20 E3** 39 15N 9 10 E
Quartzsite, *U.S.A.* **85 M12** 33 40N 114 13W
Quatsino, *Canada* **72 C3** 50 30N 127 40W
Quatsino Sd., *Canada* **72 C3** 50 25N 127 58W
Quba, *Azerbaijan* **25 F8** 41 21N 48 32 E
Qūchān, *Iran* **45 B8** 37 10N 58 27 E
Queanbeyan, *Australia* **63 F4** 35 17S 149 14 E
Québec, *Canada* **71 C5** 46 52N 71 13W
Québec □, *Canada* **71 B6** 48 0N 74 0W
Queen Alexandra Ra., *Antarctica* **5 E11** 85 0S 170 0 E
Queen Charlotte, *Canada* **72 C2** 53 15N 132 2W
Queen Charlotte Is., *Canada* **72 C2** 53 20N 132 10W
Queen Charlotte Str., *Canada* **72 C3** 51 0N 128 0W
Queen Elizabeth Is., *Canada* **66 B10** 76 0N 95 0W
Queen Elizabeth Nat. Park, *Uganda* **54 C3** 0 0 30 0 E
Queen Mary Land, *Antarctica* **5 D7** 70 0S 95 0 E
Queen Maud G., *Canada* **68 B9** 68 15N 102 30W
Queen Maud Land, *Antarctica* **5 D3** 72 30S 12 0 E
Queen Maud Mts., *Antarctica* **5 E13** 86 0S 160 0W
Queens Chan., *Australia* **60 C4** 15 0S 129 30 E
Queenscliff, *Australia* **63 F3** 38 16S 144 39 E
Queensland □, *Australia* **62 C3** 22 0S 142 0 E
Queenstown, *Australia* **62 G4** 42 4S 145 35 E
Queenstown, *N.Z.* **59 L2** 45 1S 168 40 E
Queenstown, *S. Africa* **56 E4** 31 52S 26 52 E
Queets, *U.S.A.* **84 C2** 47 32N 124 20W
Queguay Grande →, *Uruguay* **94 C4** 32 9S 58 9W
Queimadas, *Brazil* **93 F11** 11 0S 39 38W
Quela, *Angola* **52 F3** 9 10S 16 56 E
Quelimane, *Mozam.* **55 F4** 17 53S 36 58 E
Quelpart = Cheju Do, *S. Korea* **35 H14** 33 29N 126 34 E
Quemado, *N. Mex., U.S.A.* **83 J9** 34 20N 108 30W
Quemado, *Tex., U.S.A.* **81 L4** 28 58N 100 35W
Quemú-Quemú, *Argentina* **94 D3** 36 3S 63 36W
Quequén, *Argentina* **94 D4** 38 30S 58 30W
Querétaro, *Mexico* **86 C4** 20 36N 100 23W
Querétaro □, *Mexico* **86 C5** 20 30N 100 0W
Queshan, *China* **34 H8** 32 55N 114 2 E
Quesnel, *Canada* **72 C4** 53 0N 122 30W
Quesnel →, *Canada* **72 C4** 52 58N 122 29W
Quesnel L., *Canada* **72 C4** 52 30N 121 20W
Questa, *U.S.A.* **83 H11** 36 42N 105 36W
Quetico Prov. Park, *Canada* **70 C1** 48 30N 91 45W
Quetta, *Pakistan* **42 D2** 30 15N 66 55 E
Quezaltenango, *Guatemala* **88 D1** 14 50N 91 30W
Quezon City, *Phil.* **37 B6** 14 38N 121 0 E
Qufār, *Si. Arabia* **44 E4** 27 26N 41 37 E
Qui Nhon, *Vietnam* **38 F7** 13 40N 109 13 E
Quibaxe, *Angola* **52 F2** 8 24S 14 27 E
Quibdo, *Colombia* **92 B3** 5 42N 76 40W
Quiberon, *France* **18 C2** 47 29N 3 9W
Quick, *Canada* **72 C3** 54 36N 126 54W
Quiet L., *Canada* **72 A2** 61 5N 133 5W
Quiindy, *Paraguay* **94 B4** 25 58S 57 14W
Quila, *Mexico* **86 C3** 24 23N 107 13W
Quilán, C., *Chile* **96 E2** 43 15S 74 30W
Quilcene, *U.S.A.* **84 C4** 47 49N 122 53W
Quilengues, *Angola* **53 G2** 14 12S 14 12 E
Quilimarí, *Chile* **94 C1** 32 5S 71 30W
Quilino, *Argentina* **94 C3** 30 14S 64 29W
Quillabamba, *Peru* **92 F4** 12 50S 72 50W
Quillagua, *Chile* **94 A2** 21 40S 69 40W
Quillaicillo, *Chile* **94 C1** 31 17S 71 40W
Quillota, *Chile* **94 C1** 32 54S 71 16W
Quilmes, *Argentina* **94 C4** 34 43S 58 15W
Quilon, *India* **40 Q10** 8 50N 76 38 E
Quilpie, *Australia* **63 D3** 26 35S 144 11 E
Quilpué, *Chile* **94 C1** 33 5S 71 33W
Quilua, *Mozam.* **55 F4** 16 17S 39 54 E
Quimilí, *Argentina* **94 B3** 27 40S 62 30W
Quimper, *France* **18 B1** 48 0N 4 9W
Quimperlé, *France* **18 C2** 47 53N 3 33W
Quinault →, *U.S.A.* **84 C2** 47 21N 124 18W
Quincy, *Calif., U.S.A.* **84 F6** 39 56N 120 57W
Quincy, *Fla., U.S.A.* **77 K3** 30 35N 84 34W
Quincy, *Ill., U.S.A.* **80 F9** 39 56N 91 23W
Quincy, *Mass., U.S.A.* **79 D14** 42 15N 71 0W
Quincy, *Wash., U.S.A.* **82 C4** 47 22N 119 56W
Quines, *Argentina* **94 C2** 32 13S 65 48W
Quinga, *Mozam.* **55 F5** 15 49S 40 15 E
Quintana Roo □, *Mexico* **87 D7** 19 0N 88 0W
Quintanar de la Orden, *Spain* **19 C4** 39 36N 3 5W
Quintero, *Chile* **94 C1** 32 45S 71 30W
Quinyambie, *Australia* **63 E3** 30 15S 141 0 E
Quipungo, *Angola* **53 G2** 14 37S 14 40 E
Quirihue, *Chile* **94 D1** 36 15S 72 35W
Quirindi, *Australia* **63 E5** 31 28S 150 40 E
Quissanga, *Mozam.* **55 E5** 12 24S 40 28 E
Quitilipi, *Argentina* **94 B3** 26 50S 60 13W
Quitman, *Ga., U.S.A.* **77 K4** 30 47N 83 34W
Quitman, *Miss., U.S.A.* **77 J1** 32 2N 88 44W
Quitman, *Tex., U.S.A.* **81 J7** 32 48N 95 27W
Quito, *Ecuador* **92 D3** 0 15S 78 35W
Quixadá, *Brazil* **93 D11** 4 55S 39 0W
Quixaxe, *Mozam.* **55 F5** 15 17S 40 4 E
Qumbu, *S. Africa* **57 E4** 31 10S 28 48 E
Quneitra, *Syria* **47 B4** 33 7N 35 48 E
Qŭnghirot, *Uzbekistan* **26 E6** 43 6N 58 54 E
Quoin I., *Australia* **60 B4** 14 54S 129 32 E
Quoin Pt., *S. Africa* **56 E2** 34 46S 19 37 E
Quondong, *Australia* **63 E3** 33 6S 140 18 E
Quorn, *Australia* **63 E2** 32 25S 138 5 E
Qŭqon, *Uzbekistan* **26 E8** 40 30N 70 57 E
Qurnat as Sawdā', *Lebanon* **47 A5** 34 18N 36 6 E
Qûs, *Egypt* **51 C11** 25 55N 32 50 E
Qusaybah, *Iraq* **44 C4** 34 24N 40 59 E
Quseir, *Egypt* **51 C11** 26 7N 34 16 E
Qūshchī, *Iran* **44 B5** 37 59N 45 3 E
Quthing, *Lesotho* **57 E4** 30 25S 27 36 E
Qūţīābād, *Iran* **45 C6** 35 47N 48 30 E
Quwo, *China* **34 G6** 35 38N 111 25 E
Quyang, *China* **34 E8** 38 35N 114 40 E
Quynh Nhai, *Vietnam* **38 B4** 21 49N 103 33 E
Quzi, *China* **34 F4** 36 20N 107 20 E
Qyzylorda, *Kazakstan* **26 E7** 44 48N 65 28 E

R

Ra, Ko, *Thailand* **39 H2** 9 13N 98 16 E
Raahe, *Finland* **8 D21** 64 40N 24 28 E
Raasay, *U.K.* **12 D2** 57 25N 6 4W
Raasay, Sd. of, *U.K.* **12 D2** 57 30N 6 8W
Raba, *Indonesia* **37 F5** 8 36S 118 55 E
Rába →, *Hungary* **17 E9** 47 38N 17 38 E
Rabai, *Kenya* **54 C4** 3 50S 39 31 E
Rabat, *Malta* **23 D1** 35 53N 14 25 E
Rabat, *Morocco* **50 B3** 34 2N 6 48W
Rabaul, *Papua N. G.* **64 H7** 4 24S 152 18 E
Rabbit →, *Canada* **72 B3** 59 41N 127 12W
Rabbit Lake, *Canada* **73 C7** 53 8N 107 46W
Rabbitskin →, *Canada* **72 A4** 61 47N 120 42W
Rābor, *Iran* **45 D8** 29 17N 56 55 E
Race, C., *Canada* **71 C9** 46 40N 53 5W
Rach Gia, *Vietnam* **39 G5** 10 5N 105 5 E
Racibórz, *Poland* **17 C10** 50 7N 18 18 E
Racine, *U.S.A.* **76 D2** 42 41N 87 51W
Rackerby, *U.S.A.* **84 F5** 39 26N 121 22W
Radama, Nosy, *Madag.* **57 A8** 14 0S 47 47 E
Radama, Saikanosy, *Madag.* **57 A8** 14 16S 47 53 E
Rădăuţi, *Romania* **17 E13** 47 50N 25 59 E
Radekhiv, *Ukraine* **17 C13** 50 25N 24 32 E
Radekhov = Radekhiv, *Ukraine* **17 C13** 50 25N 24 32 E
Radford, *U.S.A.* **76 G5** 37 8N 80 34W
Radhanpur, *India* **42 H4** 23 50N 71 38 E
Radisson, *Canada* **73 C7** 52 30N 107 20W
Radium Hot Springs, *Canada* **72 C5** 50 35N 116 2W
Radnor Forest, *U.K.* **11 E4** 52 17N 3 10W
Radom, *Poland* **17 C11** 51 23N 21 12 E
Radomsko, *Poland* **17 C10** 51 5N 19 28 E
Radomyshl, *Ukraine* **17 C15** 50 30N 29 12 E
Radstock, *U.K.* **11 F5** 51 17N 2 26W
Radstock, C., *Australia* **63 E1** 33 12S 134 20 E
Radviliškis, *Lithuania* **9 J20** 55 49N 23 33 E
Radville, *Canada* **73 D8** 49 30N 104 15W
Rae, *Canada* **72 A5** 62 50N 116 3W
Rae Bareli, *India* **43 F9** 26 18N 81 20 E
Rae Isthmus, *Canada* **69 B11** 66 40N 87 30W
Raeren, *Belgium* **15 D6** 50 41N 6 7 E
Raeside, L., *Australia* **61 E3** 29 20S 122 0 E
Raetihi, *N.Z.* **59 H5** 39 25S 175 17 E
Rafaela, *Argentina* **94 C3** 31 10S 61 30W
Rafah, *Gaza Strip* **47 D3** 31 18N 34 14 E
Rafai, *C.A.R.* **54 B1** 4 59N 23 58 E
Rafḥā, *Si. Arabia* **44 D4** 29 35N 43 35 E
Rafsanjān, *Iran* **45 D8** 30 30N 56 5 E
Raft Pt., *Australia* **60 C3** 16 4S 124 26 E
Ragachow, *Belarus* **17 B16** 53 8N 30 5 E
Ragama, *Sri Lanka* **40 R11** 7 0N 79 50 E
Ragged, Mt., *Australia* **61 F3** 33 27S 123 25 E
Raglan, *Australia* **62 C5** 23 42S 150 49 E
Raglan, *N.Z.* **59 G5** 37 55S 174 55 E
Ragusa, *Italy* **20 F6** 36 55N 14 44 E
Raha, *Indonesia* **37 E6** 4 55S 123 0 E
Rahad al Bardī, *Sudan* **51 F9** 11 20N 23 40 E
Rahaeng = Tak, *Thailand* **38 D2** 16 52N 99 8 E
Raḥīmah, *Si. Arabia* **45 E6** 26 42N 50 4 E
Rahimyar Khan, *Pakistan* **42 E4** 28 30N 70 25 E
Rāhjerd, *Iran* **45 C6** 34 22N 50 22 E
Raichur, *India* **40 L10** 16 10N 77 20 E
Raiganj, *India* **43 G13** 25 37N 88 10 E
Raigarh, *India* **41 J13** 21 56N 83 25 E
Raijua, *Indonesia* **37 F6** 10 37S 121 36 E
Railton, *Australia* **62 G4** 41 25S 146 28 E
Rainbow Lake, *Canada* **72 B5** 58 30N 119 23W
Rainier, *U.S.A.* **84 D4** 46 53N 122 41W
Rainier, Mt., *U.S.A.* **84 D5** 46 52N 121 46W
Rainy L., *Canada* **73 D10** 48 42N 93 10W
Rainy River, *Canada* **73 D10** 48 43N 94 29W
Raippaluoto, *Finland* **8 E19** 63 13N 21 14 E
Raipur, *India* **41 J12** 21 17N 81 45 E
Raisio, *Finland* **9 F20** 60 28N 22 11 E
Raj Nandgaon, *India* **41 J12** 21 5N 81 5 E
Raja, Ujung, *Indonesia* **36 D1** 3 40N 96 25 E
Raja Ampat, Kepulauan, *Indonesia* **37 E7** 0 30S 130 0 E
Rajahmundry, *India* **41 L12** 17 1N 81 48 E
Rajang →, *Malaysia* **36 D4** 2 30N 112 0 E
Rajapalaiyam, *India* **40 Q10** 9 25N 77 35 E
Rajasthan □, *India* **42 F5** 26 45N 73 30 E
Rajasthan Canal, *India* **42 E5** 28 0N 72 0 E
Rajauri, *India* **43 C6** 33 25N 74 21 E
Rajgarh, *Mad. P., India* **42 G7** 24 2N 76 45 E
Rajgarh, *Raj., India* **42 E6** 28 40N 75 25 E
Rajkot, *India* **42 H4** 22 15N 70 56 E
Rajmahal Hills, *India* **43 G12** 24 30N 87 30 E
Rajpipla, *India* **40 J8** 21 50N 73 30 E
Rajpura, *India* **42 D7** 30 25N 76 32 E
Rajshahi, *Bangla.* **41 G16** 24 22N 88 39 E
Rajshahi □, *Bangla.* **43 G13** 25 0N 89 0 E
Rakaia, *N.Z.* **59 K4** 43 45S 172 1 E
Rakaia →, *N.Z.* **59 K4** 43 36S 172 15 E
Rakan, Ra's, *Qatar* **45 E6** 26 10N 51 20 E
Rakaposhi, *Pakistan* **43 A6** 36 10N 74 25 E
Rakata, Pulau, *Indonesia* **36 F3** 6 10S 105 20 E
Rakhiv, *Ukraine* **17 D13** 48 3N 24 12 E
Rakhni, *Pakistan* **42 D3** 30 4N 69 56 E
Rakitnoye, *Russia* **30 B7** 45 36N 134 17 E
Rakops, *Botswana* **56 C3** 21 1S 24 28 E
Rakvere, *Estonia* **9 G22** 59 20N 26 25 E
Raleigh, *U.S.A.* **77 H6** 35 47N 78 39W
Raleigh B., *U.S.A.* **77 H7** 34 50N 76 15W
Ralls, *U.S.A.* **81 J4** 33 41N 101 24W
Ram →, *Canada* **72 A4** 62 1N 123 41W
Rām Allāh, *West Bank* **47 D4** 31 55N 35 10 E
Ram Hd., *Australia* **63 F4** 37 47S 149 30 E
Rama, *Nic.* **88 D3** 12 9N 84 15W
Raman, *Thailand* **39 J3** 6 29N 101 18 E
Ramanathapuram, *India* **40 Q11** 9 25N 78 55 E
Ramanetaka, B. de, *Madag.* **57 A8** 14 13S 47 52 E
Ramat Gan, *Israel* **47 C3** 32 4N 34 48 E
Ramatlhabama, *S. Africa* **56 D4** 25 37S 25 33 E
Ramban, *India* **43 C6** 33 14N 75 12 E
Rambipuji, *Indonesia* **37 H15** 8 12S 113 37 E
Ramea, *Canada* **71 C8** 47 31N 57 23W
Ramechhap, *Nepal* **43 F12** 27 25N 86 10 E
Ramelau, *Indonesia* **37 F7** 8 55S 126 22 E
Ramgarh, *Bihar, India* **43 H11** 23 40N 85 35 E
Ramgarh, *Raj., India* **42 F6** 27 16N 75 14 E
Ramgarh, *Raj., India* **42 F4** 27 30N 70 36 E
Rāmhormoz, *Iran* **45 D6** 31 15N 49 35 E
Ramīān, *Iran* **45 B7** 37 3N 55 16 E
Ramingining, *Australia* **62 A2** 12 19S 135 3 E
Ramla, *Israel* **47 D3** 31 55N 34 52 E
Ramnad = Ramanathapuram, *India* **40 Q11** 9 25N 78 55 E
Ramnagar, *India* **43 C6** 32 47N 75 18 E
Ramona, *U.S.A.* **85 M10** 33 2N 116 52W
Ramore, *Canada* **70 C3** 48 30N 80 25W
Ramotswa, *Botswana* **56 C4** 24 50S 25 52 E
Rampur, *H.P., India* **42 D7** 31 26N 77 43 E
Rampur, *Mad. P., India* **42 H5** 23 25N 73 53 E
Rampur, *Ut. P., India* **43 E8** 28 50N 79 5 E
Rampur Hat, *India* **43 G12** 24 10N 87 50 E
Rampura, *India* **42 G6** 24 30N 75 27 E
Ramree I. = Ramree Kyun, *Burma* **41 K18** 19 0N 94 0 E
Ramree Kyun, *Burma* **41 K18** 19 0N 94 0 E
Rāmsar, *Iran* **45 B6** 36 53N 50 41 E
Ramsey, *Canada* **70 C3** 47 25N 82 20W
Ramsey, *U.K.* **10 C3** 54 20N 4 22W
Ramsgate, *U.K.* **11 F9** 51 20N 1 25 E
Ramtek, *India* **40 J11** 21 20N 79 15 E
Ranaghat, *India* **43 H13** 23 15N 88 35 E
Ranahu, *Pakistan* **42 G3** 25 55N 69 45 E
Ranau, *Malaysia* **36 C5** 6 2N 116 40 E
Rancagua, *Chile* **94 C1** 34 10S 70 50W
Rancheria →, *Canada* **72 A3** 60 13N 129 7W
Ranchester, *U.S.A.* **82 D10** 44 54N 107 10W
Ranchi, *India* **43 H11** 23 19N 85 27 E
Rancho Cucamonga, *U.S.A.* **85 L9** 34 10N 117 30W
Randers, *Denmark* **9 H14** 56 29N 10 1 E
Randfontein, *S. Africa* **57 D4** 26 8S 27 45 E
Randle, *U.S.A.* **84 D5** 46 32N 121 57W
Randolph, *Mass., U.S.A.* **79 D13** 42 10N 71 2W
Randolph, *N.Y., U.S.A.* **78 D6** 42 10N 78 59W
Randolph, *Utah, U.S.A.* **82 F8** 41 40N 111 11W
Randolph, *Vt., U.S.A.* **79 C12** 43 55N 72 40W
Råne älv →, *Sweden* **8 D20** 65 50N 22 20 E
Rangae, *Thailand* **39 J3** 6 19N 101 44 E
Rangaunu B., *N.Z.* **59 F4** 34 51S 173 15 E
Rangeley, *U.S.A.* **79 B14** 44 58N 70 39W
Rangely, *U.S.A.* **82 F9** 40 5N 108 48W
Ranger, *U.S.A.* **81 J5** 32 28N 98 41W
Rangia, *India* **41 F17** 26 28N 91 38 E
Rangiora, *N.Z.* **59 K4** 43 19S 172 36 E
Rangitaiki →, *N.Z.* **59 G6** 37 54S 176 49 E
Rangitata →, *N.Z.* **59 K3** 43 45S 171 15 E
Rangkasbitung, *Indonesia* **37 G12** 6 21S 106 15 E
Rangon →, *Burma* **41 L20** 16 28N 96 40 E
Rangoon, *Burma* **41 L20** 16 45N 96 20 E
Rangpur, *Bangla.* **41 G16** 25 42N 89 22 E
Rangsit, *Thailand* **38 F3** 13 59N 100 37 E
Ranibennur, *India* **40 M9** 14 35N 75 30 E
Raniganj, *India* **43 H12** 23 40N 87 5 E
Raniwara, *India* **40 G8** 24 50N 72 10 E
Rāniyah, *Iraq* **44 B5** 36 15N 44 53 E
Ranken →, *Australia* **62 C2** 20 31S 137 36 E
Rankin, *U.S.A.* **81 K4** 31 13N 101 56W
Rankin Inlet, *Canada* **68 B10** 62 30N 93 0W
Rankins Springs, *Australia* **63 E4** 33 49S 146 14 E
Rannoch, L., *U.K.* **12 E4** 56 41N 4 20W
Rannoch Moor, *U.K.* **12 E4** 56 38N 4 48W
Ranobe, Helodranon' i, *Madag.* **57 C7** 23 3S 43 33 E
Ranohira, *Madag.* **57 C8** 22 29S 45 24 E
Ranomafana, Toamasina, *Madag.* **57 B8** 18 57S 48 50 E
Ranomafana, Toliara, *Madag.* **57 C8** 24 34S 47 0 E
Ranong, *Thailand* **39 H2** 9 56N 98 40 E
Rānsa, *Iran* **45 C6** 33 39N 48 18 E
Ransiki, *Indonesia* **37 E8** 1 30S 134 10 E
Rantau, *Indonesia* **36 E5** 2 56S 115 9 E
Rantauprapat, *Indonesia* **36 D1** 2 15N 99 50 E
Rantemario, *Indonesia* **37 E5** 3 15S 119 57 E
Rantoul, *U.S.A.* **76 E1** 40 19N 88 9W
Raoyang, *China* **34 E8** 38 15N 115 45 E
Rapa, *Pac. Oc.* **65 K13** 27 35S 144 20W
Rapallo, *Italy* **20 B3** 44 21N 9 14 E
Rāpch, *Iran* **45 E8** 25 40N 59 15 E
Rapid →, *Canada* **72 B3** 59 15N 129 5W
Rapid City, *U.S.A.* **80 D3** 44 5N 103 14W
Rapid River, *U.S.A.* **76 C2** 45 55N 86 58W
Rapides des Joachims, *Canada* **70 C4** 46 13N 77 43W
Rapla, *Estonia* **9 G21** 59 1N 24 52 E
Rarotonga, *Cook Is.* **65 K12** 21 30S 160 0W
Ra's al 'Ayn, *Syria* **44 B4** 36 45N 40 12 E
Ra's al Khaymah, *U.A.E.* **45 E8** 25 50N 56 5 E
Ra's al-Unuf, *Libya* **51 B8** 30 46N 18 11 E
Ra's an Naqb, *Jordan* **47 F4** 30 0N 35 29 E
Ras Bânâs, *Egypt* **51 D12** 23 57N 35 59 E
Ras Dashen, *Ethiopia* **51 F12** 13 8N 38 26 E
Râs Timirist, *Mauritania* **50 E1** 19 21N 16 30W
Rasa, Punta, *Argentina* **96 E4** 40 50S 62 15W
Rasca, Pta. de la, *Canary Is.* **22 G3** 27 59N 16 41W
Raseiniai, *Lithuania* **9 J20** 55 25N 23 5 E
Rashad, *Sudan* **51 F11** 11 55N 31 0 E
Rashîd, *Egypt* **51 B11** 31 21N 30 22 E
Rasht, *Iran* **45 B6** 37 20N 49 40 E
Rasi Salai, *Thailand* **38 E5** 15 20N 104 9 E
Rason L., *Australia* **61 E3** 28 45S 124 25 E
Rasra, *India* **43 G10** 25 50N 83 50 E
Rat Buri, *Thailand* **38 F2** 13 30N 99 54 E
Rat Islands, *U.S.A.* **68 C1** 52 0N 178 0 E
Rat River, *Canada* **72 A6** 61 7N 112 36W
Ratangarh, *India* **42 E6** 28 5N 74 35 E
Raţāwī, *Iraq* **44 D5** 30 38N 47 13 E
Rath, *India* **43 G8** 25 36N 79 37 E
Rath Luirc, *Ireland* **13 D3** 52 21N 8 40W
Rathdrum, *Ireland* **13 D5** 52 56N 6 14W
Rathenow, *Germany* **16 B7** 52 37N 12 19 E
Rathkeale, *Ireland* **13 D3** 52 32N 8 56W
Rathlin I., *U.K.* **13 A5** 55 18N 6 14W
Rathlin O'Birne I., *Ireland* **13 B3** 54 40N 8 49W
Ratibor = Racibórz, *Poland* **17 C10** 50 7N 18 18 E
Ratlam, *India* **42 H6** 23 20N 75 0 E
Ratnagiri, *India* **40 L8** 16 57N 73 18 E
Raton, *U.S.A.* **81 G2** 36 54N 104 24W
Rattaphum, *Thailand* **39 J3** 7 8N 100 16 E
Rattray Hd., *U.K.* **12 D7** 57 38N 1 50W
Ratz, Mt., *Canada* **72 B2** 57 23N 132 12W
Raub, *Malaysia* **39 L3** 3 47N 101 52 E
Rauch, *Argentina* **94 D4** 36 45S 59 5W
Raufarhöfn, *Iceland* **8 C6** 66 27N 15 57W
Raufoss, *Norway* **9 F14** 60 44N 10 37 E
Raukumara Ra., *N.Z.* **59 H6** 38 5S 177 55 E
Rauma, *Finland* **9 F19** 61 10N 21 30 E
Raurkela, *India* **43 H11** 22 14N 84 50 E
Rausu-Dake, *Japan* **30 B12** 44 4N 145 7 E
Rava-Ruska, *Ukraine* **17 C12** 50 15N 23 42 E
Rava Russkaya = Rava-Ruska, *Ukraine* **17 C12** 50 15N 23 42 E
Rāvansar, *Iran* **44 C5** 34 43N 46 40 E
Rāvar, *Iran* **45 D8** 31 20N 56 51 E
Ravena, *U.S.A.* **79 D11** 42 28N 73 49W

Robertson Ra., Australia 60 D3 23 15S 121 0 E
Robertsport, Liberia 50 G2 6 45N 11 26W
Robertstown, Australia 63 E2 33 58S 139 5 E
Roberval, Canada 71 C5 48 32N 72 15W
Robeson Chan., Greenland 4 A4 82 0N 61 30W
Robinson →, Australia 62 B2 16 3S 137 16 E
Robinson Ra., Australia 61 E2 25 40S 119 0 E
Robinson River, Australia 62 B2 16 45S 136 58 E
Robinvale, Australia 63 E3 34 40S 142 45 E
Roblin, Canada 73 C8 51 14N 101 21W
Roboré, Bolivia 92 G7 18 10S 59 45W
Robson, Mt., Canada 72 C5 53 10N 119 10W
Robstown, U.S.A. 81 M6 27 47N 97 40W
Roca, C. da, Portugal 19 C1 38 40N 9 31W
Roca Partida, I., Mexico 86 D2 19 1N 112 2W
Rocas, I., Brazil 93 D12 4 0S 34 1W
Rocha, Uruguay 95 C5 34 30S 54 25W
Rochdale, U.K. 10 D5 53 38N 2 9W
Rochefort, Belgium 15 D5 50 9N 5 12 E
Rochefort, France 18 D3 45 56N 0 57W
Rochelle, U.S.A. 80 E10 41 56N 89 4W
Rocher River, Canada 72 A6 61 23N 112 44W
Rochester, Canada 72 C6 54 22N 113 27W
Rochester, U.K. 11 F8 51 23N 0 31 E
Rochester, Ind., U.S.A. 76 E2 41 4N 86 13W
Rochester, Minn., U.S.A. 80 C8 44 1N 92 28W
Rochester, N.H., U.S.A. 79 C14 43 18N 70 59W
Rochester, N.Y., U.S.A. 78 C7 43 10N 77 37W
Rock →, Canada 72 A3 60 7N 127 7W
Rock Hill, U.S.A. 77 H5 34 56N 81 1W
Rock Island, U.S.A. 80 E9 41 30N 90 34W
Rock Rapids, U.S.A. 80 D6 43 26N 96 10W
Rock River, U.S.A. 82 F11 41 44N 105 58W
Rock Sound, Bahamas 88 B4 24 54N 76 12W
Rock Springs, Mont., U.S.A. 82 C10 46 49N 106 15W
Rock Springs, Wyo., U.S.A. 82 F9 41 35N 109 14W
Rock Valley, U.S.A. 80 D6 43 12N 96 18W
Rockall, Atl. Oc. 6 D3 57 37N 13 42W
Rockdale, Tex., U.S.A. 81 K6 30 39N 97 0W
Rockdale, Wash., U.S.A. 84 C5 47 22N 121 28W
Rockefeller Plateau, Antarctica 5 E14 80 0S 140 0W
Rockford, U.S.A. 80 D10 42 16N 89 6W
Rockglen, Canada 73 D7 49 11N 105 57W
Rockhampton, Australia 62 C5 23 22S 150 32 E
Rockhampton Downs, Australia 62 B2 18 57S 135 10 E
Rockingham, Australia 61 F2 32 15S 115 38 E
Rockingham B., Australia 62 B4 18 5S 146 10 E
Rockingham Forest, U.K. 11 E7 52 29N 0 42W
Rocklake, U.S.A. 80 A5 48 47N 99 15W
Rockland, Canada 79 A9 45 33N 75 17W
Rockland, Idaho, U.S.A. 82 E7 42 34N 112 53W
Rockland, Maine, U.S.A. 71 D6 44 6N 69 7W
Rockland, Mich., U.S.A. 80 B10 46 44N 89 11W
Rocklin, U.S.A. 84 G5 38 48N 121 14W
Rockmart, U.S.A. 77 H3 34 0N 85 3W
Rockport, Mo., U.S.A. 80 E7 40 25N 95 31W
Rockport, Tex., U.S.A. 81 L6 28 2N 97 3W
Rocksprings, U.S.A. 81 K4 30 1N 100 13W
Rockville, Conn., U.S.A. 79 E12 41 52N 72 28W
Rockville, Md., U.S.A. 76 F7 39 5N 77 9W
Rockwall, U.S.A. 81 J6 32 56N 96 28W
Rockwell City, U.S.A. 80 D7 42 24N 94 38W
Rockwood, U.S.A. 77 H3 35 52N 84 41W
Rocky Ford, U.S.A. 80 F3 38 3N 103 43W
Rocky Gully, Australia 61 F2 34 30S 116 57 E
Rocky Lane, Canada 72 B5 58 31N 116 22W
Rocky Mount, U.S.A. 77 H7 35 57N 77 48W
Rocky Mountain House, Canada 72 C6 52 22N 114 55W
Rocky Mts., N. Amer. 72 C4 55 0N 121 0W
Rockyford, Canada 72 C6 51 14N 113 10W
Rod, Pakistan 40 E3 28 10N 63 5 E
Rødbyhavn, Denmark 9 J14 54 39N 11 22 E
Roddickton, Canada 71 B8 50 51N 56 8W
Roderick I., Canada 72 C3 52 38N 128 22W
Rodez, France 18 D5 44 21N 2 33 E
Rodhopoú, Greece 23 D5 35 34N 23 45 E
Ródhos, Greece 23 C10 36 15N 28 10 E
Rodney, Canada 78 D3 42 34N 81 41W
Rodney, C., N.Z. 59 G5 36 17S 174 50 E
Rodriguez, Ind. Oc. 3 E13 19 45S 63 20 E
Roe →, U.K. 13 A5 55 6N 6 59W
Roebling, U.S.A. 79 F10 40 7N 74 47W
Roebourne, Australia 60 D2 20 44S 117 9 E
Roebuck B., Australia 60 C3 18 5S 122 20 E
Roebuck Plains, Australia 60 C3 17 56S 122 28 E
Roermond, Neths. 15 C5 51 12N 6 0 E
Roes Welcome Sd., Canada 69 B11 65 0N 87 0W
Roeselare, Belgium 15 D3 50 57N 3 7 E
Rogachev = Ragachow, Belarus 17 B16 53 8N 30 5 E
Rogagua, L., Bolivia 92 F5 13 43S 66 50W
Rogatyn, Ukraine 17 D13 49 24N 24 36 E
Rogdhia, Greece 23 D7 35 22N 25 1 E
Rogers, U.S.A. 81 G7 36 20N 94 7W
Rogers City, U.S.A. 76 C4 45 25N 83 49W
Rogerson, U.S.A. 82 E6 42 13N 114 36W
Rogersville, U.S.A. 77 G4 36 24N 83 1W
Roggan River, Canada 70 B4 54 25N 79 32W
Roggeveldberge, S. Africa 56 E3 32 10S 20 10 E
Rogoaguado, L., Bolivia 92 F5 13 0S 65 30W
Rogue →, U.S.A. 82 E1 42 26N 124 26W
Róhda, Greece 23 A3 39 48N 19 46 E
Rohnert Park, U.S.A. 84 G4 38 16N 122 40W
Rohri, Pakistan 42 F3 27 45N 68 51 E
Rohri Canal, Pakistan 42 F3 26 15N 68 27 E
Rohtak, India 42 E7 28 55N 76 43 E
Roi Et, Thailand 38 D4 16 4N 103 40 E
Roja, Latvia 9 H20 57 29N 22 43 E
Rojas, Argentina 94 C3 34 10S 60 45W
Rojo, C., Mexico 87 C5 21 33N 97 20W
Rokan →, Indonesia 36 D2 2 0N 100 50 E
Rokeby, Australia 62 A3 13 39S 142 40 E
Rokiškis, Lithuania 9 J21 55 55N 25 35 E
Rolândia, Brazil 95 A5 23 18S 51 23W
Rolette, U.S.A. 80 A5 48 40N 99 51W
Rolla, Kans., U.S.A. 81 G4 37 7N 101 38W
Rolla, Mo., U.S.A. 81 G9 37 57N 91 46W
Rolla, N. Dak., U.S.A. 80 A5 48 52N 99 37W
Rolleston, Australia 62 C4 24 28S 148 35 E
Rollingstone, Australia 62 B4 19 2S 146 24 E
Roma, Australia 63 D4 26 32S 148 49 E
Roma, Italy 20 D5 41 54N 12 29 E
Roma, Sweden 9 H18 57 32N 18 26 E
Roman, Romania 17 E14 46 57N 26 55 E
Roman, Russia 27 C12 60 4N 112 14 E
Romang, Indonesia 37 F7 7 30S 127 20 E
Români, Egypt 47 E1 30 59N 32 38 E
Romania ■, Europe 17 F12 46 0N 25 0 E
Romano, Cayo, Cuba 88 B4 22 0N 77 30W
Romanovka = Basarabeasca, Moldova 17 E15 46 21N 28 58 E
Romans-sur-Isère, France 18 D6 45 3N 5 3 E
Romblon, Phil. 37 B6 12 33N 122 17 E
Rombo □, Tanzania 54 C4 3 10S 37 30 E
Rome = Roma, Italy 20 D5 41 54N 12 29 E
Rome, Ga., U.S.A. 77 H3 34 15N 85 10W
Rome, N.Y., U.S.A. 79 C9 43 13N 75 27W
Romney, U.S.A. 76 F6 39 21N 78 45W
Romney Marsh, U.K. 11 F8 51 2N 0 54 E
Rømø, Denmark 9 J13 55 10N 8 30 E
Romorantin-Lanthenay, France 18 C4 47 21N 1 45 E
Romsdalen, Norway 9 E12 62 25N 7 52 E
Ron, Vietnam 38 D6 17 53N 106 27 E
Rona, U.K. 12 D3 57 34N 5 59W
Ronan, U.S.A. 82 C6 47 32N 114 6W
Roncador, Cayos, Caribbean 88 D3 13 32N 80 4W
Roncador, Serra do, Brazil 93 F8 12 30S 52 30W
Ronceverte, U.S.A. 76 G5 37 45N 80 28W
Ronda, Spain 19 D3 36 46N 5 12W
Rondane, Norway 9 F13 61 57N 9 50 E
Rondônia □, Brazil 92 F6 11 0S 63 0W
Rondonópolis, Brazil 93 G8 16 28S 54 38W
Ronge, L. la, Canada 73 B7 55 6N 105 17W
Rønne, Denmark 9 J16 55 6N 14 43 E
Ronne Ice Shelf, Antarctica 5 D18 78 0S 60 0W
Ronsard, C., Australia 61 D1 24 46S 113 10 E
Ronse, Belgium 15 D3 50 45N 3 35 E
Roodepoort, S. Africa 57 D4 26 11S 27 54 E
Roof Butte, U.S.A. 83 H9 36 28N 109 5W
Roorkee, India 42 E7 29 52N 77 59 E
Roosendaal, Neths. 15 C4 51 32N 4 29 E
Roosevelt, Minn., U.S.A. 80 A7 48 48N 95 6W
Roosevelt, Utah, U.S.A. 82 F8 40 18N 109 59W
Roosevelt →, Brazil 92 E6 7 35S 60 20W
Roosevelt, Mt., Canada 72 B3 58 26N 125 20W
Roosevelt I., Antarctica 5 D12 79 30S 162 0W
Roosevelt Res., U.S.A. 83 K8 33 46N 111 0W
Roper →, Australia 62 A2 14 43S 135 27 E
Ropesville, U.S.A. 81 J3 33 26N 102 9W
Roque Pérez, Argentina 94 D4 35 25S 59 24W
Roquetas de Mar, Spain 19 D4 36 46N 2 36W
Roraima □, Brazil 92 C6 2 0N 61 30W
Roraima, Mt., Venezuela 92 B6 5 10N 60 40W
Rorketon, Canada 73 C9 51 24N 99 35W
Røros, Norway 9 E14 62 35N 11 23 E
Rosa, Zambia 55 D3 9 33S 31 15 E
Rosa, Monte, Europe 16 F4 45 57N 7 53 E
Rosalia, U.S.A. 82 C5 47 14N 117 22W
Rosamond, U.S.A. 85 L8 34 52N 118 10W
Rosario, Argentina 94 C3 33 0S 60 40W
Rosário, Brazil 93 D10 3 0S 44 15W
Rosario, Baja Calif., Mexico 86 A1 30 0N 115 50W
Rosario, Sinaloa, Mexico 86 C3 23 0N 105 52W
Rosario, Paraguay 94 A4 24 30S 57 35W
Rosario de la Frontera, Argentina 94 B3 25 50S 65 0W
Rosario de Lerma, Argentina 94 A2 24 59S 65 35W
Rosario del Tala, Argentina 94 C4 32 20S 59 10W
Rosário do Sul, Brazil 95 C5 30 15S 54 55W
Rosarito, Mexico 85 N9 32 18N 117 4W
Rosas, G. de, Spain 19 A7 42 10N 3 15 E
Roscoe, U.S.A. 80 C5 45 27N 99 20W
Roscommon, Ireland 13 C3 53 38N 8 11W
Roscommon, U.S.A. 76 C3 44 30N 84 35W
Roscommon □, Ireland 13 C3 53 49N 8 23W
Roscrea, Ireland 13 D4 52 57N 7 49W
Rose →, Australia 62 A2 14 16S 135 45 E
Rose Blanche, Canada 71 C8 47 38N 58 45W
Rose Harbour, Canada 72 C2 52 15N 131 10W
Rose Pt., Canada 72 C2 54 11N 131 39W
Rose Valley, Canada 73 C8 52 19N 103 49W
Roseau, Domin. 89 C7 15 20N 61 24W
Roseau, U.S.A. 80 A7 48 51N 95 46W
Rosebery, Australia 62 G4 41 46S 145 33 E
Rosebud, U.S.A. 81 K6 31 4N 96 59W
Roseburg, U.S.A. 82 E2 43 13N 123 20W
Rosedale, Australia 62 C5 24 38S 151 53 E
Rosedale, U.S.A. 81 J9 33 51N 91 2W
Roseland, U.S.A. 84 G4 38 25N 122 43W
Rosemary, Canada 72 C6 50 46N 112 5W
Rosenberg, U.S.A. 81 L7 29 34N 95 49W
Rosenheim, Germany 16 E7 47 51N 12 7 E
Rosetown, Canada 73 C7 51 35N 107 59W
Rosetta = Rashîd, Egypt 51 B11 31 21N 30 22 E
Roseville, U.S.A. 84 G5 38 45N 121 17W
Rosewood, N. Terr., Australia 60 C4 16 28S 128 58 E
Rosewood, Queens., Australia 63 D5 27 38S 152 36 E
Roshkhvār, Iran 45 C8 34 58N 59 37 E
Rosignano Marittimo, Italy 20 C4 43 24N 10 28 E
Rosignol, Guyana 92 B7 6 15N 57 30W
Roşiori-de-Vede, Romania 17 F13 44 7N 24 59 E
Roskilde, Denmark 9 J15 55 38N 12 3 E
Roslavl, Russia 24 D5 53 57N 32 55 E
Roslyn, Australia 63 E4 34 29S 149 37 E
Rosmead, S. Africa 56 E4 31 29S 25 8 E
Ross, Australia 62 G4 42 2S 147 30 E
Ross, N.Z. 59 K3 42 53S 170 49 E
Ross I., Antarctica 5 D11 77 30S 168 0 E
Ross Ice Shelf, Antarctica 5 E12 80 0S 180 0 E
Ross L., U.S.A. 82 B3 48 44N 121 4W
Ross-on-Wye, U.K. 11 F5 51 54N 2 34W
Ross Sea, Antarctica 5 D11 74 0S 178 0 E
Rossan Pt., Ireland 13 B3 54 42N 8 47W
Rossano Cálabro, Italy 20 E7 39 36N 16 39 E
Rossburn, Canada 73 C8 50 40N 100 49W
Rosseau, Canada 78 A5 45 16N 79 39W
Rossignol, L., Canada 70 B5 52 43N 73 40W
Rossignol Res., Canada 71 D6 44 12N 65 10W
Rossland, Canada 72 D5 49 6N 117 50W
Rosslare, Ireland 13 D5 52 17N 6 24W
Rosso, Mauritania 50 E1 16 40N 15 45W
Rossosh, Russia 25 D6 50 15N 39 28 E
Rossport, Canada 70 C2 48 50N 87 30W
Røssvatnet, Norway 8 D16 65 45N 14 5 E
Rossville, Australia 62 B4 15 48S 145 15 E
Røst, Norway 8 C15 67 32N 12 0 E
Rosthern, Canada 73 C7 52 40N 106 20W
Rostock, Germany 16 A7 54 5N 12 8 E
Rostov, Don, Russia 25 E6 47 15N 39 45 E
Rostov, Yarosl., Russia 24 C6 57 14N 39 25 E
Roswell, Ga., U.S.A. 77 H3 34 2N 84 22W
Roswell, N. Mex., U.S.A. 81 J2 33 24N 104 32W
Rosyth, U.K. 12 E5 56 2N 3 25W
Rotan, U.S.A. 81 J4 32 51N 100 28W
Rother →, U.K. 11 G8 50 59N 0 45 E
Rotherham, U.K. 10 D6 53 26N 1 20W
Rothes, U.K. 12 D5 57 32N 3 13W
Rothesay, Canada 71 C6 45 23N 66 0W
Rothesay, U.K. 12 F3 55 50N 5 3W
Roti, Indonesia 37 F6 10 50S 123 0 E
Roto, Australia 63 E4 33 0S 145 30 E
Rotondo Mte., France 18 E8 42 14N 9 8 E
Rotoroa, L., N.Z. 59 J4 41 55S 172 39 E
Rotorua, N.Z. 59 H6 38 9S 176 16 E
Rotorua, L., N.Z. 59 H6 38 5S 176 18 E
Rotterdam, Neths. 15 C4 51 55N 4 30 E
Rottnest I., Australia 61 F2 32 0S 115 27 E
Rottumeroog, Neths. 15 A6 53 33N 6 34 E
Rottweil, Germany 16 D5 48 9N 8 37 E
Rotuma, Fiji 64 J9 12 25S 177 5 E
Roubaix, France 18 A5 50 40N 3 10 E
Rouen, France 18 B4 49 27N 1 4 E
Rouleau, Canada 73 C8 50 10N 104 56W
Round Mountain, U.S.A. 82 G5 38 43N 117 4W
Round Mt., Australia 63 E5 30 26S 152 16 E
Roundup, U.S.A. 82 C9 46 27N 108 33W
Rousay, U.K. 12 B5 59 10N 3 2W
Rouses Point, U.S.A. 79 B11 44 59N 73 22W
Roussillon, France 18 E5 42 30N 2 35 E
Rouxville, S. Africa 56 E4 30 25S 26 50 E
Rouyn, Canada 70 C4 48 20N 79 0W
Rovaniemi, Finland 8 C21 66 29N 25 41 E
Rovereto, Italy 20 B4 45 53N 11 3 E
Rovigo, Italy 20 B4 45 4N 11 47 E
Rovinj, Croatia 16 F7 45 5N 13 40 E
Rovno = Rivne, Ukraine 17 C14 50 40N 26 10 E
Rovuma →, Tanzania 55 E5 10 29S 40 28 E
Row'ān, Iran 45 C6 35 8N 48 51 E
Rowena, Australia 63 D4 29 48S 148 55 E
Rowley Shoals, Australia 60 C2 17 30S 119 0 E
Roxas, Phil. 37 B6 11 36N 122 49 E
Roxboro, U.S.A. 77 G6 36 24N 78 59W
Roxborough Downs, Australia 62 C2 22 30S 138 45 E
Roxburgh, N.Z. 59 L2 45 33S 169 19 E
Roy, Mont., U.S.A. 82 C9 47 20N 108 58W
Roy, N. Mex., U.S.A. 81 H2 35 57N 104 12W
Roy Hill, Australia 60 D2 22 37S 119 58 E
Royal Leamington Spa, U.K. 11 E6 52 18N 1 31W
Royal Tunbridge Wells, U.K. 11 F8 51 7N 0 16 E
Royan, France 18 D3 45 37N 1 2W
Rozdilna, Ukraine 17 E16 46 50N 30 2 E
Rozhyshche, Ukraine 17 C13 50 54N 25 15 E
Rtishchevo, Russia 24 C7 52 18N 43 46 E
Ruacaná, Angola 56 B1 17 20S 14 12 E
Ruahine Ra., N.Z. 59 H6 39 55S 176 2 E
Ruapehu, N.Z. 59 H5 39 17S 175 35 E
Ruapuke I., N.Z. 59 M2 46 46S 168 31 E
Ruâq, W. →, Egypt 47 F2 30 0N 33 49 E
Rub' al Khali, Si. Arabia 46 D4 18 0N 48 0 E
Rubeho Mts., Tanzania 54 D4 6 50S 36 25 E
Rubh a' Mhail, U.K. 12 F2 55 56N 6 8W
Rubha Hunish, U.K. 12 D2 57 42N 6 20W
Rubha Robhanais = Lewis, Butt of, U.K. 12 C2 58 31N 6 16W
Rubicon →, U.S.A. 84 G5 38 53N 121 4W
Rubio, Venezuela 92 B4 7 43N 72 22W
Rubtsovsk, Russia 26 D9 51 30N 81 10 E
Ruby L., U.S.A. 82 F6 40 10N 115 28W
Ruby Mts., U.S.A. 82 F6 40 30N 115 20W
Rūd Sar, Iran 45 B6 37 8N 50 18 E
Rudall, Australia 63 E2 33 43S 136 17 E
Rudall →, Australia 60 D3 22 34S 122 13 E
Rudewa, Tanzania 55 E3 10 7S 34 40 E
Rudnichnyy, Russia 24 C9 59 38N 52 26 E
Rudnogorsk, Russia 27 D11 57 15N 103 42 E
Rudnyy, Kazakstan 26 D7 52 57N 63 7 E
Rudolf, Ostrov, Russia 26 A6 81 45N 58 30 E
Rudyard, U.S.A. 76 B3 46 14N 84 36W
Rufa'a, Sudan 51 F11 14 44N 33 22 E
Rufiji □, Tanzania 54 D4 8 0S 38 30 E
Rufiji →, Tanzania 54 D4 7 50S 39 15 E
Rufino, Argentina 94 C3 34 20S 62 50W
Rufisque, Senegal 50 F1 14 40N 17 15W
Rufunsa, Zambia 55 F2 15 4S 29 34 E
Rugby, U.K. 11 E6 52 23N 1 16W
Rugby, U.S.A. 80 A5 48 22N 100 0W
Rügen, Germany 16 A7 54 22N 13 24 E
Ruhengeri, Rwanda 54 C2 1 30S 29 36 E
Ruhnu saar, Estonia 9 H20 57 48N 23 15 E
Ruhr →, Germany 16 C4 51 27N 6 43 E
Ruhuhu →, Tanzania 55 E3 10 31S 34 34 E
Ruidosa, U.S.A. 81 L2 29 59N 104 41W
Ruidoso, U.S.A. 83 K11 33 20N 105 41W
Ruivo, Pico, Madeira 22 D3 32 45N 16 56W
Rujm Tal'at al Jamā'ah, Jordan 47 E4 30 24N 35 30 E
Ruk, Pakistan 42 F3 27 50N 68 42 E
Rukwa □, Tanzania 54 D3 7 0S 31 30 E
Rukwa L., Tanzania 54 D3 8 0S 32 20 E
Rulhieres, C., Australia 60 B4 13 56S 127 22 E
Rum = Rhum, U.K. 12 E2 57 0N 6 20W
Rum Cay, Bahamas 89 B5 23 40N 74 58W
Rum Jungle, Australia 60 B5 13 0S 130 59 E
Rumāḩ, Si. Arabia 44 E5 25 29N 47 10 E
Rumania = Romania ■, Europe 17 F12 46 0N 25 0 E
Rumaylah, Iraq 44 D5 30 47N 47 37 E
Rumbalara, Australia 62 D1 25 20S 134 29 E
Rumbêk, Sudan 51 G10 6 54N 29 37 E
Rumford, U.S.A. 79 B14 44 33N 70 33W
Rumia, Poland 17 A10 54 37N 18 25 E
Rumoi, Japan 30 C10 43 56N 141 39 E
Rumonge, Burundi 54 C2 3 59S 29 26 E
Rumsey, Canada 72 C6 51 51N 112 48W
Rumula, Australia 62 B4 16 35S 145 20 E
Rumuruti, Kenya 54 B4 0 17N 36 32 E
Runan, China 34 H8 33 0N 114 30 E
Runanga, N.Z. 59 K3 42 25S 171 15 E
Runaway, C., N.Z. 59 G6 37 32S 177 59 E
Runcorn, U.K. 10 D5 53 21N 2 44W
Rungwa, Tanzania 54 D3 6 55S 33 32 E
Rungwa →, Tanzania 54 D3 7 36S 31 50 E
Rungwe, Tanzania 55 D3 9 11S 33 32 E
Rungwe □, Tanzania 55 D3 9 25S 33 32 E
Runton Ra., Australia 60 D3 23 31S 123 6 E
Ruoqiang, China 32 C3 38 55N 88 10 E
Rupa, India 41 F18 27 15N 92 21 E
Rupar, India 42 D7 31 2N 76 38 E
Rupat, Indonesia 36 D2 1 45N 101 40 E
Rupert →, Canada 70 B4 51 29N 78 45W
Rupert House = Waskaganish, Canada 70 B4 51 30N 78 40W
Rurrenabaque, Bolivia 92 F5 14 30S 67 32W
Rusambo, Zimbabwe 55 F3 16 30S 32 4 E
Rusape, Zimbabwe 55 F3 18 35S 32 8 E
Ruschuk = Ruse, Bulgaria 21 C12 43 48N 25 59 E
Ruse, Bulgaria 21 C12 43 48N 25 59 E
Rushan, China 35 F11 36 56N 121 30 E
Rushden, U.K. 11 E7 52 18N 0 35W
Rushford, U.S.A. 80 D9 43 49N 91 46W
Rushville, Ill., U.S.A. 80 E9 40 7N 90 34W
Rushville, Ind., U.S.A. 76 F3 39 37N 85 27W
Rushville, Nebr., U.S.A. 80 D3 42 43N 102 28W
Rushworth, Australia 63 F4 36 32S 145 1 E
Russas, Brazil 93 D11 4 55S 37 50W
Russell, Canada 73 C8 50 50N 101 20W
Russell, U.S.A. 80 F5 38 54N 98 52W
Russell L., Man., Canada 73 B8 56 15N 101 30W
Russell L., N.W.T., Canada 72 A5 63 5N 115 44W
Russellkonda, India 41 K14 19 57N 84 42 E
Russellville, Ala., U.S.A. 77 H2 34 30N 87 44W
Russellville, Ark., U.S.A. 81 H8 35 17N 93 8W
Russellville, Ky., U.S.A. 77 G2 36 51N 86 53W
Russia ■, Eurasia 27 C11 62 0N 105 0 E
Russian →, U.S.A. 84 G3 38 27N 123 8W
Russkaya Polyana, Kazakstan 26 D8 53 47N 73 53 E
Russkoye Ustie, Russia 4 B15 71 0N 149 0 E
Rustam, Pakistan 42 B5 34 25N 72 13 E
Rustam Shahr, Pakistan 42 F2 26 58N 66 6 E
Rustavi, Georgia 25 F8 41 30N 45 0 E
Rustenburg, S. Africa 56 D4 25 41S 27 14 E
Ruston, U.S.A. 81 J8 32 32N 92 38W
Rutana, Burundi 54 C2 3 55S 30 0 E
Ruteng, Indonesia 37 F6 8 35S 120 30 E
Ruth, Mich., U.S.A. 78 C2 43 42N 82 45W
Ruth, Nev., U.S.A. 82 G6 39 17N 114 59W
Rutherford, U.S.A. 84 G4 38 26N 122 24W
Rutherglen, U.K. 12 F4 55 49N 4 13W
Rutland Plains, Australia 62 B3 15 38S 141 43 E
Rutledge →, Canada 73 A6 61 4N 112 0W
Rutledge L., Canada 73 A6 61 33N 110 47W
Rutshuru, Zaïre 54 C2 1 13S 29 25 E
Ruurlo, Neths. 15 B6 52 5N 6 24 E
Ruvu, Tanzania 54 D4 6 49S 38 43 E
Ruvu →, Tanzania 54 D4 6 23S 38 52 E
Ruvuma □, Tanzania 55 E4 10 20S 36 0 E
Ruwais, U.A.E. 45 E7 24 5N 52 50 E
Ruwenzori, Africa 54 B2 0 30N 29 55 E
Ruyigi, Burundi 54 C3 3 29S 30 15 E
Ružomberok, Slovak Rep. 17 D10 49 3N 19 17 E
Rwanda ■, Africa 54 C3 2 0S 30 0 E
Ryan, L., U.K. 12 G3 55 0N 5 2W
Ryazan, Russia 24 D6 54 40N 39 40 E
Ryazhsk, Russia 24 D7 53 45N 40 3 E
Rybache = Rybachye, Kazakstan 26 E9 46 40N 81 20 E
Rybachiy Poluostrov, Russia 24 A5 69 43N 32 0 E
Rybachye = Ysyk-Köl, Kyrgyzstan 28 E11 42 26N 76 12 E
Rybachye, Kazakstan 26 E9 46 40N 81 20 E
Rybinsk, Russia 24 C6 58 5N 38 50 E
Rybinskoye Vdkhr., Russia 24 C6 58 30N 38 25 E
Rybnitsa = Rîbniţa, Moldova 17 E15 47 45N 29 0 E
Ryde, U.K. 11 G6 50 43N 1 9W
Ryderwood, U.S.A. 84 D3 46 23N 123 3W
Rye, U.K. 11 G8 50 57N 0 45 E
Rye →, U.K. 10 C7 54 11N 0 44W
Rye Patch Reservoir, U.S.A. 82 F4 40 28N 118 19W
Ryegate, U.S.A. 82 C9 46 18N 109 15W
Rylstone, Australia 63 E4 32 46S 149 58 E
Ryōthu, Japan 30 E9 38 5N 138 26 E
Rypin, Poland 17 B10 53 3N 19 25 E
Ryūgasaki, Japan 31 G10 35 54N 140 11 E
Ryūkyū Is. = Ryūkyū-rettō, Japan 31 M2 26 0N 126 0 E
Ryūkyū-rettō, Japan 31 M2 26 0N 126 0 E
Rzeszów, Poland 17 C11 50 5N 21 58 E
Rzhev, Russia 24 C5 56 20N 34 20 E

S

Sa, Thailand 38 C3 18 34N 100 45 E
Sa Dec, Vietnam 39 G5 10 20N 105 46 E
Sa'ādatābād, Fārs, Iran 45 D7 30 10N 53 5 E
Sa'ādatābād, Kermān, Iran 45 D7 28 3N 55 53 E
Saale →, Germany 16 C6 51 56N 11 54 E
Saalfeld, Germany 16 C6 50 38N 11 21 E
Saar →, Europe 16 D4 49 41N 6 32 E

Saarbrücken

Saarbrücken, Germany 16 D4 49 14N 6 59 E
Saaremaa, Estonia 9 G20 58 30N 22 30 E
Saarijärvi, Finland 9 E21 62 43N 25 16 E
Saariselkä, Finland 8 B23 68 16N 28 15 E
Saarland □, Germany 15 E7 49 20N 7 0 E
Sab 'Ābar, Syria 44 C3 33 46N 37 41 E
Saba, W. Indies 89 C7 17 42N 63 26W
Šabac, Serbia, Yug. 21 B8 44 48N 19 42 E
Sabadell, Spain 19 B7 41 28N 2 7 E
Sabah □, Malaysia 36 C5 6 0N 117 0 E
Sabak Bernam, Malaysia 39 L3 3 46N 100 58 E
Sábana de la Mar, Dom. Rep. 89 C6 19 7N 69 24W
Sábanalarga, Colombia 92 A4 10 38N 74 55W
Sabang, Indonesia 36 C1 5 50N 95 15 E
Sabará, Brazil 93 G10 19 55S 43 46W
Sabattis, U.S.A. 79 B10 44 6N 74 40W
Saberania, Indonesia 37 E9 2 5S 138 18 E
Sabhah, Libya 51 C7 27 9N 14 29 E
Sabie, S. Africa 57 D5 25 10S 30 48 E
Sabinal, Mexico 86 A3 30 58N 107 25W
Sabinal, U.S.A. 81 L5 29 19N 99 28W
Sabinas, Mexico 86 B4 27 50N 101 10W
Sabinas →, Mexico 86 B4 27 37N 100 42W
Sabinas Hidalgo, Mexico 86 B4 26 33N 100 10W
Sabine →, U.S.A. 81 L8 29 59N 93 47W
Sabine L., U.S.A. 81 L8 29 53N 93 51W
Sabine Pass, U.S.A. 81 L8 29 44N 93 54W
Sabkhet el Bardawîl, Egypt 47 D2 31 10N 33 15 E
Sablayan, Phil. 37 B6 12 50N 120 50 E
Sable, C., Canada 71 D6 43 29N 65 38W
Sable, C., U.S.A. 75 E10 25 9N 81 8W
Sable I., Canada 71 D8 44 0N 60 0W
Sabrina Coast, Antarctica 5 C9 68 0S 120 0 E
Sabulubek, Indonesia 36 E1 1 36S 98 40 E
Sabzevār, Iran 45 B8 36 15N 57 40 E
Sabzvārān, Iran 45 D8 28 45N 57 50 E
Sac City, U.S.A. 80 D7 42 25N 95 0W
Săcele, Romania 17 F13 45 37N 25 41 E
Sachigo →, Canada 70 A2 55 6N 88 58W
Sachigo, L., Canada 70 B1 53 50N 92 12W
Sachsen □, Germany 16 C7 50 55N 13 10 E
Sachsen-Anhalt □, Germany 16 C7 52 0N 12 0 E
Sackets Harbor, U.S.A. 79 C8 43 57N 76 7W
Saco, Maine, U.S.A. 77 D10 43 30N 70 27W
Saco, Mont., U.S.A. 82 B10 48 28N 107 21W
Sacramento, U.S.A. 84 G5 38 35N 121 29W
Sacramento →, U.S.A. 84 G5 38 3N 121 56W
Sacramento Mts., U.S.A. 83 K11 32 30N 105 30W
Sacramento Valley, U.S.A. 84 G5 39 30N 122 0W
Sadani, Tanzania 54 D4 5 58S 38 35 E
Sadao, Thailand 39 J3 6 38N 100 26 E
Sadd el Aali, Egypt 51 D11 23 54N 32 54 E
Saddle Mt., U.S.A. 84 E3 45 58N 123 41W
Sadimi, Zaïre 55 D1 9 25S 23 32 E
Sado, Japan 30 E9 38 0N 138 25 E
Sadon, Burma 41 G20 25 28N 97 55 E
Sæby, Denmark 9 H14 57 21N 10 30 E
Saegerstown, U.S.A. 78 E4 41 43N 80 9W
Şafājah, Si. Arabia 44 E3 26 25N 39 0 E
Säffle, Sweden 9 G15 59 8N 12 55 E
Safford, U.S.A. 83 K9 32 50N 109 43W
Saffron Walden, U.K. 11 E8 52 1N 0 16 E
Safi, Morocco 50 B3 32 18N 9 20W
Şafīābād, Iran 45 B8 36 45N 57 58 E
Safīd Dasht, Iran 45 C6 33 27N 48 11 E
Safīd Kūh, Afghan. 40 B3 34 45N 63 0 E
Safwān, Iraq 44 D5 30 7N 47 43 E
Sag Harbor, U.S.A. 79 F12 41 0N 72 18W
Saga, Indonesia 37 E8 2 40S 132 55 E
Saga, Japan 31 H5 33 15N 130 16 E
Saga □, Japan 31 H5 33 15N 130 20 E
Sagae, Japan 30 E10 38 22N 140 17 E
Sagala, Mali 50 F3 14 9N 6 38W
Sagar, India 40 M9 14 14N 75 6 E
Sagara, L., Tanzania 54 D3 5 20S 31 0 E
Saginaw, U.S.A. 76 D4 43 26N 83 56W
Saginaw B., U.S.A. 76 D4 43 50N 83 40W
Sağir, Zāb aş →, Iraq 44 C4 35 17N 43 29 E
Saglouc = Salluit, Canada 69 B12 62 14N 75 38W
Sagŏ-ri, S. Korea 35 G14 35 25N 126 49 E
Sagua la Grande, Cuba 88 B3 22 50N 80 10W
Saguache, U.S.A. 83 G10 38 5N 106 8W
Saguenay →, Canada 71 C5 48 22N 71 0W
Sagunto, Spain 19 C5 39 42N 0 18W
Sahagún, Spain 19 A3 42 18N 5 2W
Saḩam al Jawlān, Syria 47 C4 32 45N 35 55 E
Sahand, Kūh-e, Iran 44 B5 37 44N 46 27 E
Sahara, Africa 50 D5 23 0N 5 0 E
Saharan Atlas = Saharien, Atlas, Algeria 50 B5 33 30N 1 0 E
Saharanpur, India 42 E7 29 58N 77 33 E
Saharien, Atlas, Algeria 50 B5 33 30N 1 0 E
Sahasinaka, Madag. 57 C8 21 49S 47 49 E
Sahaswan, India 43 E8 28 5N 78 45 E
Sahibganj, India 43 G12 25 12N 87 40 E
Sāḩilīyah, Iraq 44 C4 33 43N 42 42 E
Sahiwal, Pakistan 42 D5 30 45N 73 8 E
Şahneh, Iran 44 C5 34 29N 47 41 E
Sahtaneh →, Canada 72 B4 59 2N 122 28W
Sahuaripa, Mexico 86 B3 29 0N 109 13W
Sahuarita, U.S.A. 83 L8 31 57N 110 58W
Sahuayo, Mexico 86 C4 20 4N 102 43W
Sai Buri, Thailand 39 J3 6 43N 101 45 E
Sa'id Bundas, Sudan 51 G9 8 24N 24 48 E
Saïda, Algeria 50 B5 34 50N 0 11 E
Sa'īdābād, Kermān, Iran 45 D7 29 30N 55 45 E
Sa'īdābād, Semnān, Iran 45 B7 36 8N 54 11 E
Sa'īdīyeh, Iran 45 B6 36 20N 48 55 E
Saidpur, Bangla. 41 G16 25 48N 89 0 E
Saidu, Pakistan 43 B5 34 43N 72 24 E
Saigon = Phanh Bho Ho Chi Minh, Vietnam 39 G6 10 58N 106 40 E
Saijō, Japan 31 H6 33 55N 133 11 E
Saikhoa Ghat, India 41 F19 27 50N 95 40 E
Saiki, Japan 31 H5 32 58N 131 51 E
Sailolof, Indonesia 37 E8 1 7S 130 46 E
Saimaa, Finland 9 F23 61 15N 28 15 E
Şa'in Dezh, Iran 44 B5 36 40N 46 25 E
St. Abb's Head, U.K. 12 F6 55 55N 2 8W
St. Alban's, Canada 71 C8 47 51N 55 50W
St. Albans, U.K. 11 F7 51 45N 0 19W
St. Albans, Vt., U.S.A. 79 B11 44 49N 73 5W
St. Albans, W. Va., U.S.A. 76 F5 38 23N 81 50W
St. Alban's Head, U.K. 11 G5 50 34N 2 4W
St. Albert, Canada 72 C6 53 37N 113 32W
St. Andrew's, Canada 71 C8 47 45N 59 15W
St. Andrews, U.K. 12 E6 56 20N 2 47W
St-Anicet, Canada 79 A10 45 8N 74 22W
St. Ann B., Canada 71 C7 46 22N 60 25W
St. Ann's Bay, Jamaica 88 C4 18 26N 77 15W
St. Anthony, Canada 71 B8 51 22N 55 35W
St. Anthony, U.S.A. 82 E8 43 58N 111 41W
St. Arnaud, Australia 63 F3 36 40S 143 16 E
St. Arthur, Canada 71 C6 47 33N 67 46W
St. Asaph, U.K. 10 D4 53 15N 3 27W
St-Augustin-Saguenay, Canada 71 B8 51 13N 58 38W
St. Augustine, U.S.A. 77 L5 29 54N 81 19W
St. Austell, U.K. 11 G3 50 20N 4 47W
St.-Barthélemy, I., W. Indies 89 C7 17 50N 62 50W
St. Bees Hd., U.K. 10 C4 54 31N 3 38W
St. Boniface, Canada 73 D9 49 53N 97 5W
St. Bride's, Canada 71 C9 46 56N 54 10W
St. Brides B., U.K. 11 F2 51 49N 5 9W
St.-Brieuc, France 18 B2 48 30N 2 46W
St. Catharines, Canada 70 D4 43 10N 79 15W
St. Catherines I., U.S.A. 77 K5 31 40N 81 10W
St. Catherine's Pt., U.K. 11 G6 50 34N 1 18W
St.-Chamond, France 18 D6 45 28N 4 31 E
St. Charles, Ill., U.S.A. 76 E1 41 54N 88 19W
St. Charles, Mo., U.S.A. 80 F9 38 47N 90 29W
St. Christopher = St. Kitts, W. Indies 89 C7 17 20N 62 40W
St. Christopher-Nevis ■ = St. Kitts & Nevis ■, W. Indies 89 C7 17 20N 62 40W
St. Clair, Mich., U.S.A. 78 D2 42 50N 82 30W
St. Clair, Pa., U.S.A. 79 F8 40 43N 76 12W
St. Clair, L., Canada 70 D3 42 30N 82 45W
St. Clairsville, U.S.A. 78 F4 40 5N 80 54W
St. Claude, Canada 73 D9 49 40N 98 20W
St. Cloud, Fla., U.S.A. 77 L5 28 15N 81 17W
St. Cloud, Minn., U.S.A. 80 C7 45 34N 94 10W
St-Coeur de Marie, Canada 71 C5 48 39N 71 43W
St. Cricq, C., Australia 61 E1 25 17S 113 6 E
St. Croix, Virgin Is. 89 C7 17 45N 64 45W
St. Croix →, U.S.A. 80 C8 44 45N 92 48W
St. Croix Falls, U.S.A. 80 C8 45 24N 92 38W
St. David's, Canada 71 C8 48 12N 58 52W
St. David's, U.K. 11 F2 51 53N 5 16W
St. David's Head, U.K. 11 F2 51 54N 5 19W
St.-Denis, France 18 B5 48 56N 2 22 E
St.-Dizier, France 18 B6 48 38N 4 56 E
St. Elias, Mt., U.S.A. 68 B5 60 18N 140 56W
St. Elias Mts., Canada 72 A1 60 33N 139 28W
St.-Étienne, France 18 D6 45 27N 4 22 E
St. Eugène, Canada 79 A10 45 30N 74 28W
St. Eustatius, W. Indies 89 C7 17 20N 63 0W
St-Félicien, Canada 70 C5 48 40N 72 25W
St.-Flour, France 18 D5 45 2N 3 6 E
St. Francis, U.S.A. 80 F4 39 47N 101 48W
St. Francis →, U.S.A. 81 H9 34 38N 90 36W
St. Francis, C., S. Africa 56 E3 34 14S 24 49 E
St. Francisville, U.S.A. 81 K9 30 47N 91 23W
St-François, L., Canada 79 A10 45 10N 74 22W
St-Gabriel-de-Brandon, Canada 70 C5 46 17N 73 24W
St. Gallen = Sankt Gallen, Switz. 16 E5 47 26N 9 22 E
St.-Gaudens, France 18 E4 43 6N 0 44 E
St. George, Australia 63 D4 28 1S 148 30 E
St. George, Canada 71 C6 45 11N 66 50W
St. George, S.C., U.S.A. 77 J5 33 11N 80 35W
St. George, Utah, U.S.A. 83 H7 37 6N 113 35W
St. George, C., Canada 71 C8 48 30N 59 16W
St. George, C., U.S.A. 77 L3 29 40N 85 5W
St. George Ra., Australia 60 C4 18 40S 125 0 E
St-Georges, Belgium 15 D5 50 37N 5 20 E
St. George's, Canada 71 C8 48 26N 58 31W
St-Georges, Canada 71 C5 46 8N 70 40W
St.-Georges, Fr. Guiana 93 C8 4 0N 52 0W
St. George's, Grenada 89 D7 12 5N 61 43W
St. George's B., Canada 71 C8 48 24N 58 53W
St. Georges Basin, Australia 60 C4 15 23S 125 2 E
St. George's Channel, Europe 13 E6 52 0N 6 0W
St. Georges Hd., Australia 63 F5 35 12S 150 42 E
St. Gotthard P. = San Gottardo, P. del, Switz. 16 E5 46 33N 8 33 E
St. Helena, U.S.A. 82 G2 38 30N 122 28W
St. Helena ■, Atl. Oc. 49 H3 15 55S 5 44W
St. Helena, Mt., U.S.A. 84 G4 38 40N 122 36W
St. Helena B., S. Africa 56 E2 32 40S 18 10 E
St. Helens, Australia 62 G4 41 20S 148 15 E
St. Helens, U.K. 10 D5 53 27N 2 44W
St. Helens, U.S.A. 84 E4 45 52N 122 48W
St. Helens, Mt., U.S.A. 84 D4 46 12N 122 12W
St. Helier, U.K. 11 H5 49 10N 2 7W
St-Hubert, Belgium 15 D5 50 2N 5 23 E
St-Hyacinthe, Canada 70 C5 45 40N 72 58W
St. Ignace, U.S.A. 76 C3 45 52N 84 44W
St. Ignace I., Canada 70 C2 48 45N 88 0W
St. Ignatius, U.S.A. 82 C6 47 19N 114 6W
St. Ives, Cambs., U.K. 11 E7 52 20N 0 4W
St. Ives, Corn., U.K. 11 G2 50 12N 5 30W
St. James, U.S.A. 80 D7 43 59N 94 38W
St-Jean, Canada 70 C5 45 20N 73 20W
St-Jean →, Canada 71 B7 50 17N 64 20W
St-Jean, L., Canada 71 C5 48 40N 72 0W
St. Jean Baptiste, Canada 73 D9 49 15N 97 20W
St-Jean-Port-Joli, Canada 71 C5 47 15N 70 13W
St-Jérôme, Qué., Canada 70 C5 45 47N 74 0W
St-Jérôme, Qué., Canada 71 C5 48 26N 71 53W
St. John, Canada 71 C6 45 20N 66 8W
St. John, Kans., U.S.A. 81 G5 38 0N 98 46W
St. John, N. Dak., U.S.A. 80 A5 48 57N 99 43W
St. John →, U.S.A. 71 C6 45 12N 66 5W
St. John, C., Canada 71 B8 50 0N 55 32W
St. John's, Antigua 89 C7 17 6N 61 51W
St. John's, Canada 71 C9 47 35N 52 40W
St. Johns, Ariz., U.S.A. 83 J9 34 30N 109 22W
St. Johns, Mich., U.S.A. 76 D3 43 0N 84 33W
St. Johns →, U.S.A. 77 K5 30 24N 81 24W
St. Johnsbury, U.S.A. 79 B12 44 25N 72 1W
St. Johnsville, U.S.A. 79 C10 43 0N 74 43W
St. Joseph, La., U.S.A. 81 K9 31 55N 91 14W
St. Joseph, Mich., U.S.A. 76 D2 42 6N 86 29W
St. Joseph, Mo., U.S.A. 80 F7 39 46N 94 50W
St. Joseph →, U.S.A. 76 D2 42 7N 86 29W
St. Joseph, I., Canada 70 C3 46 12N 83 58W
St. Joseph, L., Canada 70 B1 51 10N 90 35W
St-Jovite, Canada 70 C5 46 8N 74 38W
St. Kilda, N.Z. 59 L3 45 53S 170 31 E
St. Kitts, W. Indies 89 C7 17 20N 62 40W
St. Kitts & Nevis ■, W. Indies 89 C7 17 20N 62 40W
St. Laurent, Canada 73 C9 50 25N 97 58W
St.-Laurent, Fr. Guiana 93 B8 5 29N 54 3W
St. Lawrence, Australia 62 C4 22 16S 149 31 E
St. Lawrence, Canada 71 C8 46 54N 55 23W
St. Lawrence →, Canada 71 C6 49 30N 66 0W
St. Lawrence, Gulf of, Canada 71 C7 48 25N 62 0W
St. Lawrence I., U.S.A. 68 B3 63 30N 170 30W
St. Leonard, Canada 71 C6 47 12N 67 58W
St. Lewis →, Canada 71 B8 52 26N 56 11W
St.-Lô, France 18 B3 49 7N 1 5W
St-Louis, Senegal 50 E1 16 8N 16 27W
St. Louis, Mich., U.S.A. 76 D3 43 25N 84 36W
St. Louis, Mo., U.S.A. 80 F9 38 37N 90 12W
St. Louis →, U.S.A. 80 B8 47 15N 92 45W
St. Lucia ■, W. Indies 89 D7 14 0N 60 50W
St. Lucia, L., S. Africa 57 D5 28 5S 32 30 E
St. Lucia Channel, W. Indies 89 D7 14 15N 61 0W
St. Lunaire-Griquet, Canada 71 B8 51 31N 55 28W
St. Maarten, W. Indies 89 C7 18 0N 63 5W
St.-Malo, France 18 B2 48 39N 2 1W
St-Marc, Haiti 89 C5 19 10N 72 41W
St. Maries, U.S.A. 82 C5 47 19N 116 35W
St-Martin, W. Indies 89 C7 18 0N 63 0W
St. Martin, L., Canada 73 C9 51 40N 98 30W
St. Martins, Canada 71 C6 45 22N 65 34W
St. Martinville, U.S.A. 81 K9 30 7N 91 50W
St. Mary Pk., Australia 63 E2 31 32S 138 34 E
St. Marys, Australia 62 G4 41 35S 148 11 E
St. Marys, Canada 78 C3 43 20N 81 10W
St. Mary's, U.K. 11 H1 49 55N 6 18W
St. Marys, U.S.A. 78 E6 41 26N 78 34W
St. Mary's, C., Canada 71 C9 46 50N 54 12W
St. Mary's B., Canada 71 C9 46 50N 53 50W
St. Marys Bay, Canada 71 D6 44 25N 66 10W
St.-Mathieu, Pte., France 18 B1 48 20N 4 45W
St. Matthews, I. = Zadetkyi Kyun, Burma 39 H2 10 0N 98 25 E
St-Maurice →, Canada 70 C5 46 21N 72 31W
St. Michael's Mount, U.K. 11 G2 50 7N 5 29W
St.-Nazaire, France 18 C2 47 17N 2 12W
St. Neots, U.K. 11 E7 52 14N 0 15W
St. Niklass = Sint Niklaas, Belgium 15 C4 51 10N 4 9 E
St.-Omer, France 18 A5 50 45N 2 15 E
St-Pacome, Canada 71 C6 47 24N 69 58W
St-Pamphile, Canada 71 C6 46 58N 69 48W
St. Pascal, Canada 71 C6 47 32N 69 48W
St. Paul, Canada 72 C6 54 0N 111 17W
St. Paul, Minn., U.S.A. 80 C8 44 57N 93 6W
St. Paul, Nebr., U.S.A. 80 E5 41 13N 98 27W
St. Paul, I., Ind. Oc. 3 F13 38 55S 77 34 E
St. Paul I., Canada 71 C7 47 12N 60 9W
St. Peter, U.S.A. 80 C8 44 20N 93 57W
St. Peter Port, U.K. 11 H5 49 26N 2 33W
St. Peters, N.S., Canada 71 C7 45 40N 60 53W
St. Peters, P.E.I., Canada 71 C7 46 25N 62 35W
St. Petersburg = Sankt-Peterburg, Russia 24 C5 59 55N 30 20 E
St. Petersburg, U.S.A. 77 M4 27 46N 82 39W
St.-Pierre, St- P. & M. 71 C8 46 46N 56 12W
St.-Pierre, L., Canada 70 C5 46 12N 72 52W
St.-Pierre et Miquelon □, St- P. & M. 71 C8 46 55N 56 10W
St.-Quentin, France 18 B5 49 50N 3 16 E
St. Regis, U.S.A. 82 C6 47 18N 115 6W
St. Sebastien, Tanjon' i, Madag. 57 A8 12 26S 48 44 E
St-Siméon, Canada 71 C6 47 51N 69 54W
St. Stephen, Canada 71 C6 45 16N 67 17W
St. Thomas, Canada 70 D3 42 45N 81 10W
St. Thomas I., Virgin Is. 89 C7 18 20N 64 55W
St-Tite, Canada 70 C5 46 45N 72 34W
St.-Tropez, France 18 E7 43 17N 6 38 E
St. Troud = Sint Truiden, Belgium 15 D5 50 48N 5 10 E
St. Vincent, W. Indies 89 D7 13 10N 61 10W
St. Vincent, G., Australia 63 F2 35 0S 138 0 E
St. Vincent & the Grenadines ■, W. Indies 89 D7 13 0N 61 10W
St. Vincent Passage, W. Indies 89 D7 13 30N 61 0W
St-Vith, Belgium 15 D6 50 17N 6 9 E
Ste-Agathe-des-Monts, Canada 70 C5 46 3N 74 17W
Ste-Anne de Beaupré, Canada 71 C5 47 2N 70 58W
Ste-Anne-des-Monts, Canada 71 C6 49 8N 66 30W
Ste. Genevieve, U.S.A. 80 G9 37 59N 90 2W
Ste-Marguerite →, Canada 71 B6 50 9N 66 36W
Ste.-Marie, Martinique 89 D7 14 48N 61 1W
Ste-Marie de la Madeleine, Canada 71 C5 46 26N 71 0W
Ste.-Rose, Guadeloupe 89 C7 16 20N 61 45W
Ste. Rose du Lac, Canada 73 C9 51 4N 99 30W
Saintes, France 18 D3 45 45N 0 37W
Saintes, I. des, Guadeloupe 89 C7 15 50N 61 35W
Saintonge, France 18 D3 45 40N 0 50W
Saipan, Pac. Oc. 64 F6 15 12N 145 45 E
Sairang, India 41 H18 23 50N 92 45 E
Sairecábur, Cerro, Bolivia 94 A2 22 43S 67 54W
Saitama □, Japan 31 F9 36 25N 139 30 E
Sajama, Bolivia 92 G5 18 7S 69 0W
Sajó, Hungary 17 D11 48 12N 20 44 E
Sajum, India 43 C8 33 20N 79 0 E
Sak →, S. Africa 56 E3 30 52S 20 25 E
Sakai, Japan 31 G7 34 30N 135 30 E
Sakaide, Japan 31 G6 34 15N 133 50 E
Sakaiminato, Japan 31 G6 35 38N 133 11 E
Sakākah, Si. Arabia 44 D4 30 0N 40 8 E
Sakakawea, L., U.S.A. 80 B3 47 30N 101 25W
Sakami, L., Canada 70 B4 53 15N 77 0W
Sakania, Zaïre 55 E2 12 43S 28 30 E
Sakarya = Adapazarı, Turkey 25 F5 40 48N 30 25 E
Sakarya →, Turkey 25 F5 41 7N 30 39 E
Sakashima-Guntō, Japan 31 M2 24 46N 124 0 E
Sakata, Japan 30 E9 38 55N 139 50 E
Sakchu, N. Korea 35 D13 40 23N 125 2 E
Sakeny →, Madag. 57 C8 20 0S 45 25 E
Sakha □, Russia 27 C13 62 0N 130 0 E
Sakhalin, Russia 27 D15 51 0N 143 0 E
Sakhalinskiy Zaliv, Russia 27 D15 54 0N 141 0 E
Šakiai, Lithuania 9 J20 54 59N 23 0 E
Sakon Nakhon, Thailand 38 D5 17 10N 104 9 E
Sakrand, Pakistan 42 F3 26 10N 68 15 E
Sakrivier, S. Africa 56 E3 30 54S 20 28 E
Sakuma, Japan 31 G8 35 3N 137 49 E
Sakurai, Japan 31 G7 34 30N 135 51 E
Sala, Sweden 9 G17 59 58N 16 35 E
Sala Consilina, Italy 20 D6 40 23N 15 36 E
Sala-y-Gómez, Pac. Oc. 65 K17 26 28S 105 28W
Salaberry-de-Valleyfield, Canada 70 C5 45 15N 74 8W
Saladas, Argentina 94 B4 28 15S 58 40W
Saladillo, Argentina 94 D4 35 40S 59 55W
Salado →, Buenos Aires, Argentina 94 D4 35 44S 57 22W
Salado →, La Pampa, Argentina 96 D3 37 30S 67 0W
Salado →, Santa Fe, Argentina 94 C3 31 40S 60 41W
Salado →, Mexico 86 B5 26 52N 99 19W
Salaga, Ghana 50 G4 8 31N 0 31W
Şalāḩ, Syria 47 C5 32 40N 36 45 E
Sálakhos, Greece 23 C9 36 17N 27 57 E
Şalālah, Oman 46 D5 16 56N 53 59 E
Salamanca, Chile 94 C1 31 46S 70 59W
Salamanca, Spain 19 B3 40 58N 5 39W
Salamanca, U.S.A. 78 D6 42 10N 78 43W
Salāmatābād, Iran 44 C5 35 39N 47 50 E
Salamis, Cyprus 23 D12 35 11N 33 54 E
Salamís, Greece 21 F10 37 56N 23 30 E
Salar de Atacama, Chile 94 A2 23 30S 68 25W
Salar de Uyuni, Bolivia 92 H5 20 30S 67 45W
Salatiga, Indonesia 37 G14 7 19S 110 30 E
Salavat, Russia 24 D10 53 21N 55 55 E
Salaverry, Peru 92 E3 8 15S 79 0W
Salawati, Indonesia 37 E8 1 7S 130 52 E
Salayar, Indonesia 37 F6 6 7S 120 30 E
Salcombe, U.K. 11 G4 50 14N 3 47W
Saldanha, S. Africa 56 E2 33 0S 17 58 E
Saldanha B., S. Africa 56 E2 33 6S 18 0 E
Saldus, Latvia 9 H20 56 38N 22 30 E
Sale, Australia 63 F4 38 6S 147 6 E
Salé, Morocco 50 B3 34 3N 6 48W
Sale, U.K. 10 D5 53 26N 2 19W
Salekhard, Russia 24 A12 66 30N 66 35 E
Salem, India 40 P11 11 40N 78 11 E
Salem, Ind., U.S.A. 76 F2 38 36N 86 6W
Salem, Mass., U.S.A. 79 D14 42 31N 70 53W
Salem, Mo., U.S.A. 81 G9 37 39N 91 32W
Salem, N.J., U.S.A. 76 F8 39 34N 75 28W
Salem, Ohio, U.S.A. 78 F4 40 54N 80 52W
Salem, Oreg., U.S.A. 82 D2 44 56N 123 2W
Salem, S. Dak., U.S.A. 80 D6 43 44N 97 23W
Salem, Va., U.S.A. 76 G5 37 18N 80 3W
Salerno, Italy 20 D6 40 41N 14 47 E
Salford, U.K. 10 D5 53 30N 2 18W
Salgótarján, Hungary 17 D10 48 5N 19 47 E
Salida, U.S.A. 74 C5 38 32N 106 0W
Salihli, Turkey 21 E13 38 28N 28 8 E
Salihorsk, Belarus 17 B14 52 51N 27 27 E
Salima, Malawi 53 G6 13 47S 34 28 E
Salina, Italy 20 E6 38 34N 14 50 E
Salina, U.S.A. 80 F6 38 50N 97 37W
Salina Cruz, Mexico 87 D5 16 10N 95 10W
Salinas, Brazil 93 G10 16 10S 42 10W
Salinas, Chile 94 A2 23 31S 69 29W
Salinas, Ecuador 92 D2 2 10S 80 58W
Salinas, U.S.A. 83 H3 36 40N 121 39W
Salinas →, Guatemala 87 D6 16 28N 90 31W
Salinas →, U.S.A. 83 H3 36 45N 121 48W
Salinas, B. de, Nic. 88 D2 11 4N 85 45W
Salinas, C. de, Spain 22 B10 39 16N 3 4 E
Salinas, Pampa de las, Argentina 94 C2 31 58S 66 42W
Salinas Ambargasta, Argentina 94 B3 29 0S 65 0W
Salinas de Hidalgo, Mexico 86 C4 22 30N 101 40W
Salinas Grandes, Argentina 94 B2 30 0S 65 0W
Saline →, Ark., U.S.A. 81 J8 33 10N 92 8W
Saline →, Kans., U.S.A. 80 F6 38 52N 97 30W
Salines, Spain 22 B10 39 21N 3 3 E
Salinópolis, Brazil 93 D9 0 40S 47 20W
Salisbury = Harare, Zimbabwe 55 F3 17 43S 31 2 E
Salisbury, Australia 63 E2 34 46S 138 40 E
Salisbury, U.K. 11 F6 51 4N 1 47W
Salisbury, Md., U.S.A. 76 F8 38 22N 75 36W
Salisbury, N.C., U.S.A. 77 H5 35 40N 80 29W
Salisbury Plain, U.K. 11 F6 51 14N 1 55W
Şalkhad, Syria 47 C5 32 29N 36 43 E
Salla, Finland 8 C23 66 50N 28 49 E
Sallisaw, U.S.A. 81 H7 35 28N 94 47W
Salluit, Canada 69 B12 62 14N 75 38W
Salmās, Iran 44 B5 38 11N 44 47 E
Salmo, Canada 72 D5 49 10N 117 20W
Salmon, U.S.A. 82 D7 45 11N 113 54W
Salmon →, Canada 72 C4 54 3N 122 40W
Salmon →, U.S.A. 82 D5 45 51N 116 47W
Salmon Arm, Canada 72 C5 50 40N 119 15W
Salmon Falls, U.S.A. 82 E6 42 48N 114 59W
Salmon Gums, Australia 61 F3 32 59S 121 38 E

Sanders

Salmon Res., Canada . . . 71 C8 48 5N 56 0W
Salmon River Mts., U.S.A. 82 D6 45 0N 114 30W
Salo, Finland . . . . 9 F20 60 22N 23 10 E
Salome, U.S.A. 85 M13 33 47N 113 37W
Salon-de-Provence, France 18 E6 43 39N 5 6 E
Salonica = Thessaloníki, Greece . . . . 21 D10 40 38N 22 58 E
Salonta, Romania . . . . . . 17 E11 46 49N 21 42 E
Salpausselkä, Finland . . . 9 F22 61 0N 27 0 E
Salsacate, Argentina 94 C2 31 20S 65 5W
Salsk, Russia . . . . 25 E7 46 28N 41 30 E
Salso →, Italy . . . . 20 F5 37 6N 13 57 E
Salt →, Canada 72 B6 60 0N 112 25W
Salt →, U.S.A. 83 K7 33 23N 112 19W
Salt Creek, Australia . . . . 63 F2 36 8S 139 38 E
Salt Fork Arkansas →, U.S.A. 81 G6 36 36N 97 3W
Salt Lake City, U.S.A. . . . 82 F8 40 45N 111 53W
Salt Range, Pakistan . . . . 42 C5 32 30N 72 25 E
Salta, Argentina 94 A2 24 57S 65 25W
Salta □, Argentina 94 A2 24 48S 65 30W
Saltcoats, U.K. 12 F4 55 38N 4 47W
Saltee Is., Ireland 13 D5 52 7N 6 37W
Saltfjellet, Norway . . . . . . 8 C16 66 40N 15 15 E
Saltfjorden, Norway . . . . 8 C16 67 15N 14 10 E
Saltillo, Mexico 86 B4 25 25N 101 0W
Salto, Argentina 94 C3 34 20S 60 15W
Salto, Uruguay 94 C4 31 27S 57 50W
Salto →, Italy . . . . 20 C5 42 26N 12 25 E
Salton City, U.S.A. 85 M11 33 29N 115 51W
Salton Sea, U.S.A. 85 M11 33 15N 115 45W
Saltpond, Ghana 50 G4 5 15N 1 3W
Saltville, U.S.A. 76 G5 36 53N 81 46W
Saluda →, U.S.A. 77 H5 34 1N 81 4W
Salûm, Egypt . . . . 51 B10 31 31N 25 7 E
Salûm, Khâlig el, Egypt . . 51 B10 31 35N 25 24 E
Salur, India . . . . 41 K13 18 27N 83 18 E
Salvador, Brazil 93 F11 13 0S 38 30W
Salvador, Canada 73 C7 52 10N 109 32W
Salvador, L., U.S.A. 81 L9 29 43N 90 15W
Salween →, Burma . . . . . 41 L20 16 31N 97 37 E
Salyan, Azerbaijan . . . . . . 25 G8 39 33N 48 59 E
Salyersville, U.S.A. 76 G4 37 45N 83 4W
Salzach →, Austria . . . . . 16 D7 48 12N 12 56 E
Salzburg, Austria . . . . . . 16 E7 47 48N 13 2 E
Salzgitter, Germany . . . . . 16 B6 52 9N 10 19 E
Salzwedel, Germany . . . . . 16 B6 52 52N 11 10 E
Sam Neua, Laos . . . . 38 B5 20 29N 104 5 E
Sam Ngao, Thailand . . . . 38 D2 17 18N 99 0 E
Sam Rayburn Reservoir, U.S.A. 81 K7 31 4N 94 5W
Sam Son, Vietnam . . . . . . 38 C5 19 44N 105 54 E
Sam Teu, Laos . . . . 38 C5 19 59N 104 38 E
Sama, Russia . . . . 26 C7 60 12N 60 22 E
Sama de Langreo, Spain . . 19 A3 43 18N 5 40W
Samagaltay, Russia . . . . . 27 D10 50 36N 95 3 E
Samales Group, Phil. . . . . 37 C6 6 0N 122 0 E
Samana, India . . . . 42 D7 30 10N 76 13 E
Samana Cay, Bahamas . . . 89 B5 23 3N 73 45W
Samanga, Tanzania . . . . . 55 D4 8 20S 39 13 E
Samangwa, Zaïre . . . . 54 C1 4 23S 24 10 E
Samani, Japan . . . . 30 C11 42 7N 142 56 E
Samar, Phil. . . . . 37 B7 12 0N 125 0 E
Samara, Russia . . . . 24 D9 53 8N 50 6 E
Samaria = Shōmrōn, West Bank . . . . 47 C4 32 15N 35 13 E
Samariá, Greece . . . . 23 D5 35 17N 23 58 E
Samarinda, Indonesia . . . . 36 E5 0 30S 117 9 E
Samarkand = Samarqand, Uzbekistan . . . . 26 F7 39 40N 66 55 E
Samarqand, Uzbekistan . . . 26 F7 39 40N 66 55 E
Sāmarrā, Iraq . . . . 44 C4 34 12N 43 52 E
Samastipur, India . . . . . . 43 G11 25 50N 85 50 E
Samba, India . . . . 43 C6 32 32N 75 10 E
Samba, Zaïre . . . . 54 C2 4 38S 26 22 E
Sambalpur, India . . . . 41 J14 21 28N 84 4 E
Sambar, Tanjung, Indonesia . . . . 36 E4 2 59S 110 19 E
Sambas, Indonesia . . . . . . 36 D3 1 20N 109 20 E
Sambava, Madag. . . . . . . 57 A9 14 16S 50 10 E
Sambawizi, Zimbabwe . . . . 55 F2 18 24S 26 13 E
Sambhal, India . . . . 43 E8 28 35N 78 37 E
Sambhar, India . . . . 42 F6 26 52N 75 6 E
Sambiase, Italy . . . . 20 E7 38 58N 16 17 E
Sambir, Ukraine . . . . 17 D12 49 30N 23 10 E
Sambor, Cambodia . . . . . . 38 F6 12 46N 106 0 E
Sambre →, Europe . . . . . 15 D4 50 27N 4 52 E
Samburu □, Kenya . . . . . . 54 B4 1 10N 37 0 E
Samchŏk, S. Korea . . . . . 35 F15 37 30N 129 10 E
Samchonpo, S. Korea . . . . 35 G15 35 0N 128 6 E
Same, Tanzania . . . . 54 C4 4 2S 37 38 E
Samfya, Zambia . . . . 55 E2 11 22S 29 31 E
Samnah, Si. Arabia . . . . . 44 E3 25 10N 37 15 E
Samo Alto, Chile 94 C1 30 22S 71 0W
Samokov, Bulgaria . . . . . . 21 C10 42 18N 23 35 E
Samoorombón, B., Argentina 94 D4 36 5S 57 20W
Sámos, Greece . . . . 21 F12 37 45N 26 50 E
Samothráki, Évros, Greece 21 D11 40 28N 25 28 E
Samothráki, Kérkira, Greece . . . . 23 A3 39 48N 19 31 E
Sampacho, Argentina 94 C3 33 20S 64 50W
Sampang, Indonesia . . . . . 37 G15 7 11S 113 13 E
Sampit, Indonesia . . . . . . 36 E4 2 34S 113 0 E
Sampit, Teluk, Indonesia . . 36 E4 3 5S 113 3 E
Samrong, Cambodia . . . . . 38 E4 14 15N 103 30 E
Samrong, Thailand . . . . . . 38 E3 15 10N 100 40 E
Samsø, Denmark . . . . 9 J14 55 50N 10 35 E
Samsun, Turkey . . . . 25 F6 41 15N 36 22 E
Samui, Ko, Thailand . . . . . 39 H3 9 30N 100 0 E
Samusole, Zaïre . . . . 55 E1 10 2S 24 0 E
Samut Prakan, Thailand . . 38 F3 13 32N 100 40 E
Samut Sakhon, Thailand . . 38 F3 13 31N 100 13 E
Samut Songkhram →, Thailand . . . . 38 F3 13 24N 100 1 E
Samwari, Pakistan . . . . . . 42 E2 28 30N 66 46 E
San, Mali 50 F4 13 15N 4 57W
San →, Cambodia . . . . . . 38 F5 13 32N 105 57 E
San →, Poland . . . . 17 C11 50 45N 21 51 E
San Agustin, C., Phil. . . . . 37 C7 6 20N 126 13 E
San Agustín de Valle Fértil, Argentina 94 C2 30 35S 67 30W
San Ambrosio, Pac. Oc. . . 90 F3 26 28S 79 53W
San Andreas, U.S.A. 84 G6 38 12N 120 41W
San Andrés, I. de, Caribbean 88 D3 12 42N 81 46W
San Andres Mts., U.S.A. . 83 K10 33 0N 106 30W
San Andrés Tuxtla, Mexico 87 D5 18 30N 95 20W
San Angelo, U.S.A. 81 K4 31 28N 100 26W
San Anselmo, U.S.A. 84 H4 37 59N 122 34W
San Antonio, Belize 87 D7 16 15N 89 2W
San Antonio, Chile 94 C1 33 40S 71 40W
San Antonio, Spain . . . . . 22 C7 38 59N 1 19 E
San Antonio, N. Mex., U.S.A. 83 K10 33 55N 106 52W
San Antonio, Tex., U.S.A. 81 L5 29 25N 98 30W
San Antonio →, U.S.A. . 81 L6 28 30N 96 54W
San Antonio, C., Argentina 94 D4 36 15S 56 40W
San Antonio, C., Cuba . . . 88 B3 21 50N 84 57W
San Antonio, Mt., U.S.A. . 85 L9 34 17N 117 38W
San Antonio de los Baños, Cuba 88 B3 22 54N 82 31W
San Antonio de los Cobres, Argentina 94 A2 24 10S 66 17W
San Antonio Oeste, Argentina 96 E4 40 40S 65 0W
San Ardo, U.S.A. 84 J6 36 1N 120 54W
San Augustín, Canary Is. . . 22 G4 27 47N 15 32W
San Augustine, U.S.A. . . . 81 K7 31 30N 94 7W
San Bartolomé, Canary Is. 22 F6 28 59N 13 37W
San Bartolomé de Tirajana, Canary Is. . . . 22 G4 27 54N 15 34W
San Benedetto del Tronto, Italy . . . . 20 C5 42 57N 13 53 E
San Benedicto, I., Mexico 86 D2 19 18N 110 49W
San Benito, U.S.A. 81 M6 26 8N 97 38W
San Benito →, U.S.A. . . 84 J5 36 53N 121 34W
San Benito Mt., U.S.A. . . 84 J6 36 22N 120 37W
San Bernardino, U.S.A. . . 85 L9 34 7N 117 19W
San Bernardino Mts., U.S.A. 85 L10 34 10N 116 45W
San Bernardino Str., Phil. 37 B6 13 0N 125 0 E
San Bernardo, Chile 94 C1 33 40S 70 50W
San Bernardo, I. de, Colombia 92 B3 9 45N 75 50W
San Blas, Mexico 86 B3 26 4N 108 46W
San Blas, Arch. de, Panama 88 E4 9 50N 78 31W
San Blas, C., U.S.A. 77 L3 29 40N 85 21W
San Borja, Bolivia 92 F5 14 50S 66 52W
San Buenaventura, Mexico 86 B4 27 5N 101 32W
San Carlos, Argentina . . . 94 C2 33 50S 69 0W
San Carlos, Chile 94 D1 36 10S 72 0W
San Carlos, Mexico 86 B4 29 0N 100 54W
San Carlos, Nic. 88 D3 11 12N 84 50W
San Carlos, Phil. . . . . 37 B6 10 29N 123 25 E
San Carlos, Spain . . . . . . 22 B8 39 3N 1 34 E
San Carlos, Uruguay 95 C5 34 46S 54 58W
San Carlos, U.S.A. 83 K8 33 21N 110 27W
San Carlos, Amazonas, Venezuela 92 C5 1 55N 67 4W
San Carlos, Cojedes, Venezuela 92 B5 9 40N 68 36W
San Carlos de Bariloche, Argentina 96 E2 41 10S 71 25W
San Carlos del Zulia, Venezuela 92 B4 9 1N 71 55W
San Carlos L., U.S.A. . . . 83 K8 33 11N 110 32W
San Clemente, Chile 94 D1 35 30S 71 29W
San Clemente, U.S.A. . . . 85 M9 33 26N 117 37W
San Clemente I., U.S.A. . . 85 N8 32 53N 118 29W
San Cristóbal, Argentina . . 94 C3 30 20S 61 10W
San Cristóbal, Dom. Rep. . 89 C5 18 25N 70 6W
San Cristóbal, Mexico . . . 87 D6 16 50N 92 33W
San Cristóbal, Spain . . . . 22 B11 39 57N 4 3 E
San Cristóbal, Venezuela . 92 B4 7 46N 72 14W
San Diego, Calif., U.S.A. . 85 N9 32 43N 117 9W
San Diego, Tex., U.S.A. . . 81 M5 27 46N 98 14W
San Diego, C., Argentina . 96 G3 54 40S 65 10W
San Diego de la Unión, Mexico 86 C4 21 28N 100 52W
San Dimitri, Ras, Malta . . 23 C1 36 4N 14 11 E
San Estanislao, Paraguay . 94 A4 24 39S 56 26W
San Felipe, Chile 94 C1 32 43S 70 42W
San Felipe, Mexico 86 A2 31 0N 114 52W
San Felipe, Venezuela . . . 92 A5 10 20N 68 44W
San Felipe →, U.S.A. . . 85 M11 33 12N 115 49W
San Feliu de Guíxols, Spain . . . . 19 B7 41 45N 3 1 E
San Félix, Pac. Oc. 90 F2 26 23S 80 0W
San Fernando, Chile 94 C1 34 30S 71 0W
San Fernando, Mexico . . . 86 B1 29 55N 115 10W
San Fernando, La Union, Phil. . . . . 37 A6 16 40N 120 23 E
San Fernando, Pampanga, Phil. . . . . 37 A6 15 5N 120 37 E
San Fernando, Baleares, Spain . . . . 22 C7 38 42N 1 28 E
San Fernando, Cádiz, Spain 19 D2 36 28N 6 17W
San Fernando, Trin. & Tob. 89 D7 10 20N 61 30W
San Fernando, U.S.A. . . . 85 L8 34 17N 118 26W
San Fernando →, Mexico 86 C5 24 55N 98 10W
San Fernando de Apure, Venezuela 92 B5 7 54N 67 15W
San Fernando de Atabapo, Venezuela 92 C5 4 3N 67 42W
San Francisco, Argentina 94 C3 31 30S 62 5W
San Francisco, U.S.A. . . . 83 H2 37 47N 122 25W
San Francisco →, U.S.A. 83 K9 32 59N 109 22W
San Francisco, Paso de, S. Amer. 94 B2 27 0S 68 0W
San Francisco de Macorîs, Dom. Rep. 89 C5 19 19N 70 15W
San Francisco del Monte de Oro, Argentina 94 C2 32 36S 66 8W
San Francisco del Oro, Mexico 86 B3 26 52N 105 50W
San Francisco Javier, Spain . . . . 22 C7 38 42N 1 26 E
San Francisco Solano, Pta., Colombia 90 C3 6 18N 77 29W
San Gil, Colombia 92 B4 6 33N 73 8W
San Gorgonio Mt., U.S.A. 85 L10 34 7N 116 51W
San Gottardo, P. del, Switz. . . . . 16 E5 46 33N 8 33 E
San Gregorio, Uruguay . . 95 C4 32 37S 55 40W
San Gregorio, U.S.A. 84 H4 37 20N 122 23W
San Ignacio, Belize 87 D7 17 10N 89 0W
San Ignacio, Bolivia 92 G6 16 20S 60 55W
San Ignacio, Mexico 86 B2 27 27N 113 0W
San Ignacio, Paraguay . . . 94 B4 26 52S 57 3W
San Ignacio, L., Mexico . . 86 B2 26 50N 113 11W
San Ildefonso, C., Phil. . . 37 A6 16 0N 122 1 E
San Isidro, Argentina 94 C4 34 29S 58 31W
San Jacinto, U.S.A. 85 M10 33 47N 116 57W
San Jaime, Spain . . . . . . 22 B11 39 54N 4 4 E
San Javier, Misiones, Argentina 95 B4 27 55S 55 5W
San Javier, Santa Fe, Argentina 94 C4 30 40S 59 55W
San Javier, Bolivia 92 G6 16 18S 62 30W
San Javier, Chile 94 D1 35 40S 71 45W
San Jeronimo Taviche, Mexico 87 D5 16 38N 96 32W
San Joaquin, U.S.A. 84 J6 36 36N 120 11W
San Joaquin →, U.S.A. . . 83 G3 38 4N 121 51W
San Joaquin Valley, U.S.A. 84 J6 37 20N 121 0W
San Jordi, Spain . . . . 22 B9 39 33N 2 46 E
San Jorge, Argentina 94 C3 31 54S 61 50W
San Jorge, Spain . . . . 22 C7 38 54N 1 24 E
San Jorge, B. de, Mexico . 86 A2 31 20N 113 20W
San Jorge, G., Argentina . . 96 F3 46 0S 66 0W
San Jorge, G. de, Spain . . 19 B6 40 53N 1 2 E
San Jorge, G. of, Argentina 90 H4 46 0S 66 0W
San José, Bolivia 92 G6 17 53S 60 50W
San José, Costa Rica 88 E3 9 55N 84 2W
San José, Guatemala 88 D1 14 0N 90 50W
San José, Mexico 86 C2 25 0N 110 50W
San Jose, Phil. . . . . 37 A6 15 45N 120 55 E
San José, Spain . . . . 22 C7 38 55N 1 18 E
San Jose, U.S.A. 83 H3 37 20N 121 53W
San Jose →, U.S.A. . . . 83 J10 34 25N 106 45W
San Jose de Buenovista, Phil. . . . . 37 B6 12 27N 121 4 E
San José de Feliciano, Argentina 94 C4 30 26S 58 46W
San José de Jáchal, Argentina 94 C2 30 15S 68 46W
San José de Mayo, Uruguay 94 C4 34 27S 56 40W
San José de Ocune, Colombia 92 C4 4 15N 70 20W
San José del Cabo, Mexico 86 C3 23 0N 109 40W
San José del Guaviare, Colombia 92 C4 2 35N 72 38W
San Juan, Argentina 94 C2 31 30S 68 30W
San Juan, Mexico 86 C4 21 20N 102 50W
San Juan, Phil. . . . . 37 C7 8 25N 126 20 E
San Juan, Puerto Rico . . . 89 C6 18 28N 66 7W
San Juan □, Argentina . . . 94 C2 31 9S 69 0W
San Juan →, Argentina . . 94 C2 32 20S 67 25W
San Juan →, Nic. 88 D3 10 56N 83 42W
San Juan →, U.S.A. 83 H8 37 16N 110 26W
San Juan, C., Eq. Guin. . . 52 D1 1 5N 9 20 E
San Juan Bautista, Paraguay 94 B4 26 37S 57 6W
San Juan Bautista, Spain . 22 B8 39 5N 1 31 E
San Juan Bautista, U.S.A. 83 H3 36 51N 121 32W
San Juan Bautista Valle Nacional, Mexico 87 D5 17 47N 96 19W
San Juan Capistrano, U.S.A. 85 M9 33 30N 117 40W
San Juan Cr. →, U.S.A. 84 J5 35 40N 120 22W
San Juan de Guadalupe, Mexico 86 C4 24 38N 102 44W
San Juan de los Morros, Venezuela 92 B5 9 55N 67 21W
San Juan del Norte, Nic. . . 88 D3 10 58N 83 40W
San Juan del Norte, B. de, Nic. 88 D3 11 0N 83 40W
San Juan del Río, Mexico 87 C5 20 25N 100 0W
San Juan del Sur, Nic. . . . 88 D2 11 20N 85 51W
San Juan I., U.S.A. 84 B3 48 32N 123 5W
San Juan Mts., U.S.A. . . . 83 H10 37 30N 107 0W
San Julián, Argentina 96 F3 49 15S 67 45W
San Justo, Argentina 94 C3 30 47S 60 30W
San Kamphaeng, Thailand 38 C2 18 45N 99 8 E
San Lázaro, C., Mexico . . . 86 C2 24 50N 112 18W
San Lázaro, Sa., Mexico . . 86 C3 23 25N 110 0W
San Leandro, U.S.A. 83 H2 37 44N 122 9W
San Lorenzo, Argentina . . . 94 C3 32 45S 60 45W
San Lorenzo, Ecuador 92 C3 1 15N 78 50W
San Lorenzo, Paraguay . . . 94 B4 25 20S 57 32W
San Lorenzo, Spain . . . . . 22 B10 39 37N 3 17 E
San Lorenzo →, Mexico . . 86 C3 24 15N 107 24W
San Lorenzo, I., Mexico . . 86 B2 28 35N 112 50W
San Lorenzo, I., Peru 92 F3 12 7S 77 15W
San Lorenzo, Mt., Argentina 96 F2 47 40S 72 20W
San Lucas, Bolivia 92 H5 20 5S 65 7W
San Lucas, Baja Calif. S., Mexico 86 C3 22 53N 109 54W
San Lucas, Baja Calif. S., Mexico 86 B2 27 10N 112 14W
San Lucas, U.S.A. 84 J5 36 8N 121 1W
San Lucas, C., Mexico . . . 86 C3 22 50N 110 0W
San Luis, Argentina 94 C2 33 20S 66 20W
San Luis, Cuba 88 B3 22 17N 83 46W
San Luis, Guatemala 88 C2 16 14N 89 27W
San Luis, U.S.A. 83 H11 37 12N 105 25W
San Luis □, Argentina . . . 94 C2 34 0S 66 0W
San Luis, I., Mexico 86 B2 29 58N 114 26W
San Luis, Sierra de, Argentina 94 C2 32 30S 66 10W
San Luis de la Paz, Mexico 86 C4 21 19N 100 32W
San Luis Obispo, U.S.A. . . 85 K6 35 17N 120 40W
San Luis Potosí, Mexico . . 86 C4 22 9N 100 59W
San Luis Potosí □, Mexico 86 C4 22 10N 101 0W
San Luis Reservoir, U.S.A. 84 H5 37 4N 121 5W
San Luis Río Colorado, Mexico 86 A2 32 29N 114 58W
San Marcos, Guatemala . . 88 D1 14 59N 91 52W
San Marcos, Mexico 86 B2 27 13N 112 6W
San Marcos, U.S.A. 81 L6 29 53N 97 56W
San Marino, San Marino . 16 G7 43 55N 12 30 E
San Marino ■, Europe . . 20 C5 43 56N 12 25 E
San Martín, Argentina . . . 94 C2 33 5S 68 28W
San Martín, L., Argentina . 96 F2 48 50S 72 50W
San Mateo, Spain . . . . . . 22 B7 39 3N 1 23 E
San Mateo, U.S.A. 83 H2 37 34N 122 19W
San Matías, Bolivia 92 G7 16 25S 58 20W
San Matías, G., Argentina 96 E4 41 30S 64 0W
San Miguel, El Salv. 88 D2 13 30N 88 12W
San Miguel, Panama 88 E4 8 27N 78 55W
San Miguel, Spain . . . . . . 22 B7 39 3N 1 26 E
San Miguel, U.S.A. 83 J3 35 45N 120 42W
San Miguel →, Bolivia . . 92 F6 13 52S 63 56W
San Miguel de Tucumán, Argentina 94 B2 26 50S 65 20W
San Miguel del Monte, Argentina 94 D4 35 23S 58 50W
San Miguel I., U.S.A. 85 L6 34 2N 120 23W
San Narciso, Phil. . . . . . . 37 A6 15 2N 120 3 E
San Nicolás, Canary Is. . . 22 G4 27 58N 15 47W
San Nicolás de los Arroyas, Argentina 94 C3 33 25S 60 10W
San Nicolas I., U.S.A. . . . 85 M7 33 15N 119 30W
San Onofre, U.S.A. 85 M9 33 22N 117 34W
San Pablo, Bolivia 94 A2 21 43S 66 38W
San Pedro, Buenos Aires, Argentina 95 B5 26 30S 54 10W
San Pedro, Jujuy, Argentina 94 A3 24 12S 64 55W
San-Pédro, Ivory C. 50 H3 4 50N 6 33W
San Pedro, Mexico 86 C2 23 55N 110 17W
San Pedro □, Paraguay . . 94 A4 24 0S 57 0W
San Pedro →, Chihuahua, Mexico . . . 86 B3 28 20N 106 10W
San Pedro →, Michoacan, Mexico . . . 86 D4 19 23N 103 51W
San Pedro →, Nayarit, Mexico 86 C3 21 45N 105 30W
San Pedro →, U.S.A. . . . 83 K8 32 59N 110 47W
San Pedro, Pta., Chile . . . 94 B1 25 30S 70 38W
San Pedro Channel, U.S.A. 85 M8 33 30N 118 25W
San Pedro de Atacama, Chile 94 A2 22 55S 68 15W
San Pedro de Jujuy, Argentina 94 A3 24 12S 64 55W
San Pedro de las Colonias, Mexico 86 B4 25 50N 102 59W
San Pedro de Lloc, Peru . 92 E3 7 15S 79 28W
San Pedro de Macorís, Dom. Rep. 89 C6 18 30N 69 18W
San Pedro del Norte, Nic. 88 D3 13 4N 84 33W
San Pedro del Paraná, Paraguay 94 B4 26 43S 56 13W
San Pedro Mártir, Sierra, Mexico 86 A1 31 0N 115 30W
San Pedro Mixtepec, Mexico 87 D5 16 2N 97 7W
San Pedro Ocampo = Melchor Ocampo, Mexico 86 C4 24 52N 101 40W
San Pedro Sula, Honduras 88 C2 15 30N 88 0W
San Pieto, Italy . . . . 20 E3 39 8N 8 17 E
San Quintín, Mexico 86 A1 30 29N 115 57W
San Rafael, Argentina . . . 94 C2 34 40S 68 21W
San Rafael, Calif., U.S.A. . 84 H4 37 58N 122 32W
San Rafael, N. Mex., U.S.A. 83 J10 35 7N 107 53W
San Rafael Mt., U.S.A. . . . 85 L7 34 41N 119 52W
San Rafael Mts., U.S.A. . . 85 L7 34 40N 119 50W
San Ramón de la Nueva Orán, Argentina 94 A3 23 10S 64 20W
San Remo, Italy . . . . 20 C2 43 49N 7 46 E
San Roque, Argentina . . . 94 B4 28 25S 58 45W
San Roque, Spain 19 D3 36 17N 5 21W
San Rosendo, Chile 94 D1 37 16S 72 43W
San Saba, U.S.A. 81 K5 31 12N 98 43W
San Salvador, Bahamas . . 89 B5 24 0N 74 40W
San Salvador, El Salv. . . . 88 D2 13 40N 89 10W
San Salvador, Spain . . . . 22 B10 39 27N 3 11 E
San Salvador de Jujuy, Argentina 94 A3 24 10S 64 48W
San Salvador I., Bahamas 89 B5 24 0N 74 32W
San Sebastián, Argentina . 96 G3 53 10S 68 30W
San Sebastián, Spain . . . 19 A5 43 17N 1 58W
San Sebastian de la Gomera, Canary Is. . . . 22 F2 28 5N 17 7W
San Serra, Spain . . . . 22 B10 39 43N 3 13 E
San Severo, Italy . . . . 20 D6 41 41N 15 23 E
San Simeon, U.S.A. 84 K5 35 39N 121 11W
San Simon, U.S.A. 83 K9 32 16N 109 14W
San Telmo, Mexico 86 A1 30 58N 116 6W
San Telmo, Spain . . . . . . 22 B9 39 35N 2 21 E
San Tiburcio, Mexico 86 C4 24 8N 101 32W
San Valentin, Mte., Chile 96 F2 46 30S 73 30W
San Vicente de la Barquera, Spain 19 A3 43 23N 4 29W
San Ygnacio, U.S.A. 81 M5 27 3N 99 26W
Sana', Yemen . . . . 46 D3 15 27N 44 12 E
Sana →, Bos.-H. . . . . . . 16 F9 45 3N 16 23 E
Sanaga →, Cameroon . . 50 H6 3 35N 9 38 E
Sanaloa, Presa, Mexico . . 86 C3 24 50N 107 20W
Sanana, Indonesia . . . . . . 37 E7 2 4S 125 58 E
Sanand, India . . . . 42 H5 22 59N 72 25 E
Sanandaj, Iran . . . . 44 C5 35 18N 47 1 E
Sanandita, Bolivia 94 A3 21 40S 63 45W
Sanawad, India . . . . 42 H7 22 11N 76 5 E
Sancellas, Spain . . . . 22 B9 39 39N 2 54 E
Sanchahe, China . . . . 35 B14 44 50N 126 2 E
Sánchez, Dom. Rep. 89 C6 19 15N 69 36W
Sanchor, India . . . . 42 G4 24 45N 71 55 E
Sanco Pt., Phil. . . . . 37 C7 8 15N 126 27 E
Sancti-Spíritus, Cuba . . . 88 B4 21 52N 79 33W
Sancy, Puy de, France . . . 18 D5 45 32N 2 50 E
Sand →, S. Africa . . . . . 57 C5 22 25S 30 5 E
Sand Springs, U.S.A. 81 G6 36 9N 96 7W
Sanda, Japan . . . . 31 G7 34 53N 135 14 E
Sandakan, Malaysia . . . . . 36 C5 5 53N 118 4 E
Sandan = Sambor, Cambodia . . . . 38 F6 12 46N 106 0 E
Sandanski, Bulgaria . . . . . 21 D10 41 35N 23 16 E
Sanday, U.K. 12 B6 59 16N 2 31W
Sandefjord, Norway . . . . . 9 G14 59 10N 10 15 E
Sanders, U.S.A. 83 J9 35 13N 109 20W

Sanderson

160

Shāndak

Shāndak, Iran **45 D9** 28 28N 60 27 E
Shandon, U.S.A. **84 K6** 35 39N 120 23W
Shandong □, China **35 F10** 36 0N 118 0 E
Shandong Bandao, China **35 F11** 37 0N 121 0 E
Shang Xian, China **34 H5** 33 50N 109 58 E
Shangalowe, Zaïre **55 E2** 10 50S 26 30 E
Shangani →, Zimbabwe **55 F2** 18 41S 27 10 E
Shangbancheng, China **35 D10** 40 50N 118 1 E
Shangdu, China **34 D7** 41 30N 113 30 E
Shanghai, China **33 C7** 31 15N 121 26 E
Shanghe, China **35 F9** 37 20N 117 10 E
Shangnan, China **34 H6** 33 32N 110 50 E
Shangqiu, China **34 G8** 34 26N 115 36 E
Shangrao, China **33 D6** 28 25N 117 59 E
Shangshui, China **34 H8** 33 42N 114 35 E
Shangzhi, China **35 B14** 45 22N 127 56 E
Shanhetun, China **35 B14** 44 33N 127 15 E
Shaniko, U.S.A. **82 D3** 45 0N 120 45W
Shannon, N.Z. **59 J5** 40 33S 175 25 E
Shannon →, Ireland **13 D2** 52 35N 9 30W
Shansi = Shanxi □, China **34 F7** 37 0N 112 0 E
Shantar, Ostrov Bolshoy, Russia **27 D14** 55 9N 137 40 E
Shantipur, India **43 H13** 23 17N 88 25 E
Shantou, China **33 D6** 23 18N 116 40 E
Shantung = Shandong □, China **35 F10** 36 0N 118 0 E
Shanxi □, China **34 F7** 37 0N 112 0 E
Shanyang, China **34 H5** 33 31N 109 55 E
Shanyin, China **34 E7** 39 25N 112 56 E
Shaoguan, China **33 D6** 24 48N 113 35 E
Shaoxing, China **33 C7** 30 0N 120 35 E
Shaoyang, China **33 D6** 27 14N 111 25 E
Shapinsay, U.K. **12 B6** 59 3N 2 51W
Shaqra', Si. Arabia **44 E5** 25 15N 45 16 E
Shaqrā', Yemen **46 E4** 13 22N 45 44 E
Sharbot Lake, Canada **79 B8** 44 46N 76 41W
Shari, Japan **30 C12** 43 55N 144 40 E
Sharjah = Ash Shāriqah, U.A.E. **45 E7** 25 23N 55 26 E
Shark B., Australia **61 E1** 25 30S 113 32 E
Sharon, Mass., U.S.A. **79 D13** 42 7N 71 11W
Sharon, Pa., U.S.A. **78 E4** 41 14N 80 31W
Sharon Springs, U.S.A. **80 F4** 38 54N 101 45W
Sharp Pt., Australia **62 A3** 10 58S 142 43 E
Sharpe L., Canada **73 C10** 54 24N 93 40W
Sharpsville, U.S.A. **78 E4** 41 15N 80 29W
Sharya, Russia **24 C8** 58 22N 45 20 E
Shashi, Botswana **57 C4** 21 15S 27 27 E
Shashi, China **33 C6** 30 25N 112 14 E
Shashi →, Africa **55 G2** 21 14S 29 20 E
Shasta, Mt., U.S.A. **82 F2** 41 25N 122 12W
Shasta L., U.S.A. **82 F2** 40 43N 122 25W
Shatt al'Arab →, Iraq **45 D6** 29 57N 48 34 E
Shattuck, U.S.A. **81 G5** 36 16N 99 53W
Shaunavon, Canada **73 D7** 49 35N 108 25W
Shaver L., U.S.A. **84 H7** 37 9N 119 18W
Shaw →, Australia **60 D2** 20 21S 119 17 E
Shaw I., Australia **62 C4** 20 30S 149 2 E
Shawanaga, Canada **78 A4** 45 31N 80 17W
Shawano, U.S.A. **76 C1** 44 47N 88 36W
Shawinigan, Canada **70 C5** 46 35N 72 50W
Shawnee, U.S.A. **81 H6** 35 20N 96 55W
Shaybārā, Si. Arabia **44 E3** 25 26N 36 47 E
Shaykh Sa'īd, Iraq **44 C5** 32 34N 46 17 E
Shcherbakov = Rybinsk, Russia **24 C6** 58 5N 38 50 E
Shchuchinsk, Kazakstan **26 D8** 52 56N 70 12 E
She Xian, China **34 F7** 36 30N 113 40 E
Shebele = Scebeli, Wabi →, Somali Rep. **46 G3** 2 0N 44 0 E
Sheboygan, U.S.A. **76 D2** 43 46N 87 45W
Shediac, Canada **71 C7** 46 14N 64 32W
Sheelin, L., Ireland **13 C4** 53 48N 7 20W
Sheep Haven, Ireland **13 A4** 55 11N 7 52W
Sheerness, U.K. **11 F8** 51 26N 0 47 E
Sheet Harbour, Canada **71 D7** 44 56N 62 31W
Sheffield, U.K. **10 D6** 53 23N 1 28W
Sheffield, Ala., U.S.A. **77 H2** 34 46N 87 41W
Sheffield, Mass., U.S.A. **79 D11** 42 5N 73 21W
Sheffield, Pa., U.S.A. **78 E5** 41 42N 79 3W
Sheffield, Tex., U.S.A. **81 K4** 30 41N 101 49W
Sheho, Canada **73 C8** 51 35N 103 13W
Sheikhpura, India **43 G11** 25 9N 85 53 E
Shekhupura, Pakistan **42 D5** 31 42N 73 58 E
Shelburne, N.S., Canada **71 D6** 43 47N 65 20W
Shelburne, Ont., Canada **70 D3** 44 4N 80 15W
Shelburne, U.S.A. **79 B11** 44 23N 73 14W
Shelburne B., Australia **62 A3** 11 50S 142 50 E
Shelburne Falls, U.S.A. **79 D12** 42 36N 72 45W
Shelby, Mich., U.S.A. **76 D2** 43 37N 86 22W
Shelby, Mont., U.S.A. **82 B8** 48 30N 111 51W
Shelby, N.C., U.S.A. **77 H5** 35 17N 81 32W
Shelby, Ohio, U.S.A. **78 F2** 40 53N 82 40W
Shelbyville, Ill., U.S.A. **80 F10** 39 24N 88 48W
Shelbyville, Ind., U.S.A. **76 F3** 39 31N 85 47W
Shelbyville, Tenn., U.S.A. **77 H2** 35 29N 86 28W
Sheldon, U.S.A. **80 D7** 43 11N 95 51W
Sheldrake, Canada **71 B7** 50 20N 64 51W
Shelikhova, Zaliv, Russia **27 D16** 59 30N 157 0 E
Shell Lake, Canada **73 C7** 53 19N 107 2W
Shell Lakes, Australia **61 E4** 29 20S 127 30 E
Shellbrook, Canada **73 C7** 53 13N 106 24W
Shellharbour, Australia **63 E5** 34 31S 150 51 E
Shelling Rocks, Ireland **13 E1** 51 45N 10 35W
Shelton, Conn., U.S.A. **79 E11** 41 19N 73 5W
Shelton, Wash., U.S.A. **84 C3** 47 13N 123 6W
Shen Xian, China **34 F8** 36 15N 115 40 E
Shenandoah, Iowa, U.S.A. **80 E7** 40 46N 95 22W
Shenandoah, Pa., U.S.A. **79 F8** 40 49N 76 12W
Shenandoah, Va., U.S.A. **76 F6** 38 29N 78 37W
Shenandoah →, U.S.A. **76 F7** 39 19N 77 44W
Shenchi, China **34 E7** 39 8N 112 10 E
Shendam, Nigeria **50 G6** 8 49N 9 30 E
Shendî, Sudan **51 E11** 16 46N 33 22 E
Shengfang, China **34 E9** 39 3N 116 42 E
Shenjingzi, China **35 B13** 44 40N 124 30 E
Shenmu, China **34 E6** 38 50N 110 29 E
Shenqiu, China **34 H8** 33 25N 115 5 E
Shenqiucheng, China **34 H8** 33 24N 115 2 E
Shensi = Shaanxi □, China **34 G5** 35 0N 109 0 E
Shenyang, China **35 D12** 41 48N 123 27 E
Sheopur Kalan, India **40 G10** 25 40N 76 40 E
Shepetivka, Ukraine **17 C14** 50 10N 27 10 E
Shepetovka = Shepetivka, Ukraine **17 C14** 50 10N 27 10 E
Shepparton, Australia **63 F4** 36 23S 145 26 E
Sheqi, China **34 H7** 33 12N 112 57 E
Sher Qila, Pakistan **43 A6** 36 7N 74 2 E
Sherborne, U.K. **11 G5** 50 57N 2 31W
Sherbro I., S. Leone **50 G2** 7 30N 12 40W
Sherbrooke, Canada **71 C5** 45 28N 71 57W
Sheridan, Ark., U.S.A. **81 H8** 34 19N 92 24W
Sheridan, Wyo., U.S.A. **82 D10** 44 48N 106 58W
Sherkot, India **43 E8** 29 22N 78 35 E
Sherman, U.S.A. **81 J6** 33 40N 96 35W
Sherridon, Canada **73 B8** 55 8N 101 5W
Sherwood, N. Dak., U.S.A. **80 A4** 48 57N 101 38W
Sherwood, Tex., U.S.A. **81 K4** 31 18N 100 45W
Sherwood Forest, U.K. **10 D6** 53 6N 1 7W
Sheslay, Canada **72 B2** 58 17N 131 52W
Sheslay →, Canada **72 B2** 58 48N 132 5W
Shethanei L., Canada **73 B9** 58 48N 97 50W
Shetland □, U.K. **12 A7** 60 30N 1 30W
Shetland Is., U.K. **12 A7** 60 30N 1 30W
Sheyenne, U.S.A. **80 B5** 47 50N 99 7W
Sheyenne →, U.S.A. **80 B6** 47 2N 96 50W
Shibām, Yemen **46 D4** 16 0N 48 36 E
Shibata, Japan **30 F9** 37 57N 139 20 E
Shibecha, Japan **30 C12** 43 17N 144 36 E
Shibetsu, Japan **30 B11** 44 10N 142 23 E
Shibogama L., Canada **70 B2** 53 35N 88 15W
Shibushi, Japan **31 J5** 31 25N 131 8 E
Shickshock Mts. = Chic-Chocs, Mts., Canada **71 C6** 48 55N 66 0W
Shidao, China **35 F12** 36 50N 122 25 E
Shido, Japan **31 G7** 34 19N 134 10 E
Shiel, L., U.K. **12 E3** 56 48N 5 34W
Shield, C., Australia **62 A2** 13 20S 136 20 E
Shiga □, Japan **31 G8** 35 20N 136 0 E
Shigaib, Sudan **51 E9** 15 5N 23 35 E
Shiguaigou, China **34 D6** 40 52N 110 15 E
Shihchiachuangi = Shijiazhuang, China **34 E8** 38 2N 114 28 E
Shijiazhuang, China **34 E8** 38 2N 114 28 E
Shikarpur, India **42 E8** 28 17N 78 7 E
Shikarpur, Pakistan **42 F3** 27 57N 68 39 E
Shikoku □, Japan **31 H6** 33 30N 133 30 E
Shikoku-Sanchi, Japan **31 H6** 33 30N 133 30 E
Shilabo, Ethiopia **46 F3** 6 22N 44 32 E
Shiliguri, India **41 F16** 26 45N 88 25 E
Shilka, Russia **27 D12** 52 0N 115 55 E
Shilka →, Russia **27 D13** 53 20N 121 26 E
Shillelagh, Ireland **13 D5** 52 45N 6 32W
Shillong, India **41 G17** 25 35N 91 53 E
Shilo, West Bank **47 C4** 32 4N 35 18 E
Shilou, China **34 F6** 37 0N 110 48 E
Shimabara, Japan **31 H5** 32 48N 130 20 E
Shimada, Japan **31 G9** 34 49N 138 10 E
Shimane □, Japan **31 G6** 35 0N 132 30 E
Shimanovsk, Russia **27 D13** 52 15N 127 30 E
Shimizu, Japan **31 G9** 35 0N 138 30 E
Shimodate, Japan **31 F9** 36 20N 139 55 E
Shimoga, India **40 N9** 13 57N 75 32 E
Shimoni, Kenya **54 C4** 4 38S 39 20 E
Shimonoseki, Japan **31 H5** 33 58N 130 55 E
Shimpuru Rapids, Angola **56 B2** 17 45S 19 55 E
Shin, L., U.K. **12 C4** 58 5N 4 30W
Shin-Tone →, Japan **31 G10** 35 44N 140 51 E
Shinano →, Japan **31 F9** 36 50N 138 30 E
Shīndand, Afghan. **40 C3** 33 12N 62 8 E
Shingleton, U.S.A. **70 C2** 46 21N 86 28W
Shingū, Japan **31 H7** 33 40N 135 55 E
Shinjō, Japan **30 E10** 38 46N 140 18 E
Shinshār, Syria **47 A5** 34 36N 36 43 E
Shinyanga, Tanzania **54 C3** 3 45S 33 27 E
Shinyanga □, Tanzania **54 C3** 3 50S 34 0 E
Shiogama, Japan **30 E10** 38 19N 141 1 E
Shiojiri, Japan **31 F8** 36 6N 137 58 E
Ship I., U.S.A. **81 K10** 30 13N 88 55W
Shipehenski Prokhod, Bulgaria **21 C11** 42 45N 25 15 E
Shiping, China **32 D5** 23 45N 102 23 E
Shipki La, India **40 D11** 31 45N 78 40 E
Shippegan, Canada **71 C7** 47 45N 64 45W
Shippensburg, U.S.A. **78 F7** 40 3N 77 31W
Shiprock, U.S.A. **83 H9** 36 47N 108 41W
Shiqma, N. →, Israel **47 D3** 31 37N 34 30 E
Shiquan, China **34 H5** 33 5N 108 15 E
Shīr Kūh, Iran **45 D7** 31 39N 54 3 E
Shiragami-Misaki, Japan **30 D10** 41 24N 140 12 E
Shirakawa, Fukushima, Japan **31 F10** 37 7N 140 13 E
Shirakawa, Gifu, Japan **31 F8** 36 17N 136 56 E
Shirane-San, Gumma, Japan **31 F9** 36 48N 139 22 E
Shirane-San, Yamanashi, Japan **31 G9** 35 42N 138 9 E
Shiraoi, Japan **30 C10** 42 33N 141 21 E
Shīrāz, Iran **45 D7** 29 42N 52 30 E
Shire →, Africa **55 F4** 17 42S 35 19 E
Shiretoko-Misaki, Japan **30 B12** 44 21N 145 20 E
Shirinab →, Pakistan **42 D2** 30 15N 66 28 E
Shiriya-Zaki, Japan **30 D10** 41 25N 141 30 E
Shiroishi, Japan **30 E10** 38 0N 140 37 E
Shīrvān, Iran **45 B8** 37 30N 57 50 E
Shirwa, L. = Chilwa, L., Malawi **55 F4** 15 15S 35 40 E
Shivpuri, India **42 G7** 25 26N 77 42 E
Shixian, China **35 C15** 43 5N 129 50 E
Shizuishan, China **34 E4** 39 15N 106 50 E
Shizuoka, Japan **31 G9** 34 57N 138 24 E
Shizuoka □, Japan **31 G9** 35 15N 138 40 E
Shklov = Shklow, Belarus **17 A16** 54 16N 30 15 E
Shklow, Belarus **17 A16** 54 16N 30 15 E
Shkoder = Shkodra, Albania **21 C8** 42 4N 19 32 E
Shkodra, Albania **21 C8** 42 4N 19 32 E
Shkumbini →, Albania **21 D8** 41 2N 19 31 E
Shmidta, O., Russia **27 A10** 81 0N 91 0 E
Shō-Gawa →, Japan **31 F8** 36 47N 137 4 E
Shoal Lake, Canada **73 C8** 50 30N 100 35W
Shōdo-Shima, Japan **31 G7** 34 30N 134 15 E
Shoeburyness, U.K. **11 F8** 51 32N 0 49 E
Sholapur = Solapur, India **40 L9** 17 43N 75 56 E
Shologontsy, Russia **27 C12** 66 13N 114 0 E
Shōmrōn, West Bank **47 C4** 32 15N 35 13 E
Shoshone, Calif., U.S.A. **85 K10** 35 58N 116 16W
Shoshone, Idaho, U.S.A. **82 E6** 42 56N 114 25W
Shoshone L., U.S.A. **82 D8** 44 22N 110 43W
Shoshone Mts., U.S.A. **82 G5** 39 20N 117 25W
Shoshong, Botswana **56 C4** 22 56S 26 31 E
Shoshoni, U.S.A. **82 E9** 43 14N 108 7W
Shouguang, China **35 F10** 37 52N 118 45 E
Shouyang, China **34 F7** 37 54N 113 8 E
Show Low, U.S.A. **83 J9** 34 15N 110 2W
Shreveport, U.S.A. **81 J8** 32 31N 93 45W
Shrewsbury, U.K. **10 E5** 52 43N 2 45W
Shrirampur, India **43 H13** 22 44N 88 21 E
Shropshire □, U.K. **11 E5** 52 36N 2 45W
Shu, Kazakstan **26 E8** 43 36N 73 42 E
Shu →, Kazakstan **28 E10** 45 0N 67 44 E
Shuangcheng, China **35 B14** 45 20N 126 15 E
Shuanggou, China **35 G9** 34 2N 117 30 E
Shuangliao, China **35 C12** 43 29N 123 30 E
Shuangshanzi, China **35 D10** 40 20N 119 8 E
Shuangyang, China **35 C13** 43 28N 125 40 E
Shuangyashan, China **33 B8** 46 28N 131 5 E
Shuguri Falls, Tanzania **55 D4** 8 33S 37 22 E
Shuiye, China **34 F8** 36 7N 114 8 E
Shujalpur, India **42 H7** 23 18N 76 46 E
Shukpa Kunzang, India **43 B8** 34 22N 78 22 E
Shulan, China **35 B14** 44 28N 127 0 E
Shule, China **32 C2** 39 25N 76 3 E
Shumagin Is., U.S.A. **68 C4** 55 7N 159 45W
Shumikha, Russia **26 D7** 55 10N 63 15 E
Shungnak, U.S.A. **68 B4** 66 52N 157 9W
Shuo Xian, China **34 E7** 39 20N 112 33 E
Shūr →, Iran **45 D7** 28 30N 55 0 E
Shūr Āb, Iran **45 C6** 34 23N 51 11 E
Shūr Gaz, Iran **45 D8** 29 10N 59 20 E
Shūrāb, Iran **45 C8** 33 43N 56 29 E
Shūrjestān, Iran **45 D7** 31 24N 52 25 E
Shurugwi, Zimbabwe **55 F3** 19 40S 30 0 E
Shūsf, Iran **45 D9** 31 50N 60 5 E
Shūshtar, Iran **45 D6** 32 0N 48 50 E
Shuswap L., Canada **72 C5** 50 55N 119 3W
Shuyang, China **35 G10** 34 10N 118 42 E
Shūzū, Iran **45 D7** 29 52N 54 30 E
Shwebo, Burma **41 H19** 22 30N 95 45 E
Shwegu, Burma **41 G20** 24 15N 96 26 E
Shweli →, Burma **41 H20** 23 45N 96 45 E
Shymkent, Kazakstan **26 E7** 42 18N 69 36 E
Shyok, India **43 B8** 34 15N 78 12 E
Shyok →, Pakistan **43 B6** 35 13N 75 53 E
Si Chon, Thailand **39 H2** 9 0N 99 54 E
Si Kiang = Xi Jiang →, China **33 D6** 22 5N 113 20 E
Si-ngan = Xi'an, China **34 G5** 34 15N 109 0 E
Si Prachan, Thailand **38 E3** 14 37N 100 9 E
Si Racha, Thailand **38 F3** 13 10N 100 48 E
Si Xian, China **35 H9** 33 30N 117 50 E
Siahan Range, Pakistan **40 F4** 27 30N 64 40 E
Siaksriindrapura, Indonesia **36 D2** 0 51N 102 0 E
Sialkot, Pakistan **42 C6** 32 32N 74 30 E
Siam = Thailand ■, Asia **38 E4** 16 0N 102 0 E
Siantan, P., Indonesia **39 L6** 3 10N 106 15 E
Siāreh, Iran **45 D9** 28 5N 60 14 E
Siargao, Phil. **37 C7** 9 52N 126 3 E
Siari, Pakistan **43 B7** 34 55N 76 40 E
Siasi, Phil. **37 C6** 5 34N 120 50 E
Siau, Indonesia **37 D7** 2 50N 125 25 E
Šiauliai, Lithuania **9 J20** 55 56N 23 15 E
Siaya □, Kenya **54 B3** 0 0 34 20 E
Sibay, Russia **24 D10** 52 42N 58 39 E
Sibayi, L., S. Africa **57 D5** 27 20S 32 45 E
Šibenik, Croatia **20 C6** 43 48N 15 54 E
Siberia, Russia **4 D13** 60 0N 100 0 E
Siberut, Indonesia **36 E1** 1 30S 99 0 E
Sibi, Pakistan **42 E2** 29 30N 67 54 E
Sibil, Indonesia **37 E10** 4 59S 140 35 E
Sibiti, Congo **52 E2** 3 38S 13 19 E
Sibiu, Romania **17 F13** 45 45N 24 9 E
Sibley, Iowa, U.S.A. **80 D7** 43 24N 95 45W
Sibley, La., U.S.A. **81 J8** 32 33N 93 18W
Sibolga, Indonesia **36 D1** 1 42N 98 45 E
Sibsagar, India **41 F19** 27 0N 94 36 E
Sibu, Malaysia **36 D4** 2 18N 111 49 E
Sibuco, Phil. **37 C6** 7 20N 122 10 E
Sibuguey B., Phil. **37 C6** 7 50N 122 45 E
Sibut, C.A.R. **51 G8** 5 46N 19 10 E
Sibutu, Phil. **37 D5** 4 45N 119 30 E
Sibutu Passage, E. Indies **37 D5** 4 50N 120 0 E
Sibuyan, Phil. **37 B6** 12 25N 122 40 E
Sibuyan Sea, Phil. **37 B6** 12 30N 122 20 E
Sicamous, Canada **72 C5** 50 49N 119 0W
Sichuan □, China **32 C5** 31 0N 104 0 E
Sicilia, Italy **20 F6** 37 30N 14 30 E
Sicily = Sicilia, Italy **20 F6** 37 30N 14 30 E
Sicuani, Peru **92 F4** 14 21S 71 10W
Sidári, Greece **23 A3** 39 47N 19 41 E
Siddhapur, India **42 H5** 23 56N 72 25 E
Siddipet, India **40 K11** 18 5N 78 51 E
Sidéradougou, Burkina Faso **50 F4** 10 42N 4 12W
Sídheros, Ákra, Greece **23 D8** 35 19N 26 19 E
Sîdi Barrâni, Egypt **51 B10** 31 38N 25 58 E
Sidi-bel-Abbès, Algeria **50 A4** 35 13N 0 39W
Sidlaw Hills, U.K. **12 E5** 56 32N 3 2W
Sidley, Mt., Antarctica **5 D14** 77 2S 126 2W
Sidmouth, U.K. **11 G4** 50 40N 3 15W
Sidmouth, C., Australia **62 A3** 13 25S 143 36 E
Sidney, Canada **72 D4** 48 39N 123 24W
Sidney, Mont., U.S.A. **80 B2** 47 43N 104 9W
Sidney, N.Y., U.S.A. **79 D9** 42 19N 75 24W
Sidney, Nebr., U.S.A. **80 E3** 41 8N 102 59W
Sidney, Ohio, U.S.A. **76 E3** 40 17N 84 9W
Sidoarjo, Indonesia **37 G15** 7 27S 112 43 E
Sidon = Saydā, Lebanon **47 B4** 33 35N 35 25 E
Sidra, G. of = Surt, Khalīj, Libya **51 B8** 31 40N 18 30 E
Sidra, G. of, Libya **48 C5** 31 40N 18 30 E
Siedlce, Poland **17 B12** 52 10N 22 20 E
Sieg →, Germany **16 C4** 50 46N 7 6 E
Siegen, Germany **16 C5** 50 51N 8 0 E
Siem Pang, Cambodia **38 E6** 14 7N 106 23 E
Siem Reap, Cambodia **38 F4** 13 20N 103 52 E
Siena, Italy **20 C4** 43 19N 11 21 E
Sieradz, Poland **17 C10** 51 37N 18 41 E
Sierra Blanca, U.S.A. **83 L11** 31 11N 105 22W
Sierra Blanca Peak, U.S.A. **83 K11** 33 23N 105 49W
Sierra City, U.S.A. **84 F6** 39 34N 120 38W
Sierra Colorada, Argentina **96 E3** 40 35S 67 50W
Sierra Gorda, Chile **94 A2** 22 50S 69 15W
Sierra Leone ■, W. Afr. **50 G2** 9 0N 12 0W
Sierra Madre, Mexico **87 D6** 16 0N 93 0W
Sierra Mojada, Mexico **86 B4** 27 19N 103 42W
Sierraville, U.S.A. **84 F6** 39 36N 120 22W
Sífnos, Greece **21 F11** 37 0N 24 45 E
Sifton, Canada **73 C8** 51 21N 100 8W
Sifton Pass, Canada **72 B3** 57 52N 126 15W
Sighetu-Marmatiei, Romania **17 E12** 47 57N 23 52 E
Sighişoara, Romania **17 E13** 46 12N 24 50 E
Sigli, Indonesia **36 C1** 5 25N 96 0 E
Siglufjörður, Iceland **8 C4** 66 12N 18 55W
Signal, U.S.A. **85 L13** 34 30N 113 38W
Signal Pk., U.S.A. **85 M12** 33 20N 114 2W
Sigsig, Ecuador **92 D3** 3 0S 78 50W
Sigtuna, Sweden **9 G17** 59 36N 17 44 E
Sigüenza, Spain **19 B4** 41 3N 2 40W
Siguiri, Guinea **50 F3** 11 31N 9 10W
Sigulda, Latvia **9 H21** 57 10N 24 55 E
Sigurd, U.S.A. **83 G8** 38 50N 111 58W
Sihanoukville = Kompong Som, Cambodia **39 G4** 10 38N 103 30 E
Siikajoki →, Finland **8 D21** 64 50N 24 43 E
Siilinjärvi, Finland **8 E22** 63 4N 27 39 E
Sijarira Ra., Zimbabwe **55 F2** 17 36S 27 45 E
Sikao, Thailand **39 J2** 7 34N 99 21 E
Sikar, India **42 F6** 27 33N 75 10 E
Sikasso, Mali **50 F3** 11 18N 5 35W
Sikeston, U.S.A. **81 G10** 36 53N 89 35W
Sikhote Alin, Khrebet, Russia **27 E14** 45 0N 136 0 E
Sikhote Alin Ra. = Sikhote Alin, Khrebet, Russia **27 E14** 45 0N 136 0 E
Síkinos, Greece **21 F11** 36 40N 25 8 E
Sikkani Chief →, Canada **72 B4** 57 47N 122 15W
Sikkim □, India **41 F16** 27 50N 88 30 E
Sikotu-Ko, Japan **30 C10** 42 45N 141 25 E
Sil →, Spain **19 A2** 42 27N 7 43W
Silacayoapan, Mexico **87 D5** 17 30N 98 9W
Silchar, India **41 G18** 24 49N 92 48 E
Silcox, Canada **73 B10** 57 12N 94 10W
Siler City, U.S.A. **77 H6** 35 44N 79 28W
Silesia = Śląsk, Poland **16 C9** 51 0N 16 30 E
Silgarhi Doti, Nepal **43 E9** 29 15N 81 0 E
Silghat, India **41 F18** 26 35N 93 0 E
Silifke, Turkey **25 G5** 36 22N 33 58 E
Siliguri = Shiliguri, India **41 F16** 26 45N 88 25 E
Siling Co, China **32 C3** 31 50N 89 20 E
Silistra, Bulgaria **21 B12** 44 6N 27 19 E
Silivri, Turkey **21 D13** 41 4N 28 14 E
Siljan, Sweden **9 F16** 60 55N 14 45 E
Silkeborg, Denmark **9 H13** 56 10N 9 32 E
Sillajhuay, Cordillera, Chile **92 G5** 19 46S 68 40W
Sillamäe, Estonia **9 G22** 59 24N 27 45 E
Siloam Springs, U.S.A. **81 G7** 36 11N 94 32W
Silsbee, U.S.A. **81 K7** 30 21N 94 11W
Šilute, Lithuania **9 J19** 55 21N 21 33 E
Silva Porto = Kuito, Angola **53 G3** 12 22S 16 55 E
Silver City, N. Mex., U.S.A. **83 K9** 32 46N 108 17W
Silver City, Nev., U.S.A. **82 G4** 39 15N 119 48W
Silver Cr. →, U.S.A. **82 E4** 43 16N 119 13W
Silver Creek, U.S.A. **78 D5** 42 33N 79 10W
Silver L., Calif., U.S.A. **84 G6** 38 39N 120 6W
Silver L., Calif., U.S.A. **85 K10** 35 21N 116 7W
Silver Lake, U.S.A. **82 E3** 43 8N 121 3W
Silver Streams, S. Africa **56 D3** 28 20S 23 33 E
Silverton, Colo., U.S.A. **83 H10** 37 49N 107 40W
Silverton, Tex., U.S.A. **81 H4** 34 28N 101 19W
Silvies →, U.S.A. **82 E4** 43 34N 119 2W
Simanggang, Malaysia **36 D4** 1 15N 111 32 E
Simard, L., Canada **70 C4** 47 40N 78 40W
Simav, Turkey **21 E13** 39 4N 28 58 E
Simba, Tanzania **54 C4** 2 10S 37 36 E
Simbirsk, Russia **24 D8** 54 20N 48 25 E
Simbo, Tanzania **54 C2** 4 51S 29 41 E
Simcoe, Canada **70 D3** 42 50N 80 20W
Simcoe, L., Canada **70 D4** 44 25N 79 20W
Simenga, Russia **27 C11** 62 42N 108 25 E
Simeria, Romania **17 F12** 45 51N 23 1 E
Simeulue, Indonesia **36 D1** 2 45N 95 45 E
Simferopol, Ukraine **25 F5** 44 55N 34 3 E
Sími, Greece **21 F12** 36 35N 27 50 E
Simi Valley, U.S.A. **85 L8** 34 16N 118 47W
Simikot, Nepal **43 E9** 30 0N 81 50 E
Simla, India **42 D7** 31 2N 77 9 E
Simmie, Canada **73 D7** 49 56N 108 6W
Simmler, U.S.A. **85 K7** 35 21N 119 59W
Simojoki →, Finland **8 D21** 65 35N 25 1 E
Simojovel, Mexico **87 D6** 17 12N 92 38W
Simonette →, Canada **72 B5** 55 9N 118 15W
Simonstown, S. Africa **56 E2** 34 14S 18 26 E
Simplon P., Switz. **16 E5** 46 15N 8 3 E
Simpson Desert, Australia **62 D2** 25 0S 137 0 E
Simpungdong, N. Korea **35 D15** 40 56N 129 29 E
Simrishamn, Sweden **9 J16** 55 33N 14 22 E
Simunjan, Malaysia **36 D4** 1 25N 110 45 E
Simushir, Ostrov, Russia **27 E16** 46 50N 152 30 E
Sinabang, Indonesia **36 D1** 2 30N 96 24 E
Sinadogo, Somali Rep. **46 F4** 5 50N 47 0 E
Sinai = Es Sînâ', Egypt **51 C11** 29 0N 34 0 E
Sinai, Mt. = Mûsa, G., Egypt **51 C11** 28 33N 33 59 E
Sinai Peninsula, Egypt **47 F2** 29 30N 34 0 E
Sinaloa □, Mexico **86 C3** 25 0N 107 30W
Sinaloa de Levya, Mexico **86 B3** 25 50N 108 20W
Sinarádhes, Greece **23 A3** 39 34N 19 51 E
Sīnāwan, Libya **50 B7** 31 0N 10 37 E
Sincelejo, Colombia **92 B3** 9 18N 75 24W
Sinchang, N. Korea **35 D15** 40 7N 128 28 E
Sinchang-ni, N. Korea **35 E14** 39 24N 126 8 E
Sinclair, U.S.A. **82 F10** 41 47N 107 7W
Sinclair Mills, Canada **72 C4** 54 5N 121 40W
Sincorá, Serra do, Brazil **93 F10** 13 30S 41 0W
Sind, Pakistan **42 G3** 26 0N 68 30 E

Sweetwater

Stillwater, *Okla., U.S.A.* **81 G6** 36 7N 97 4W
Stillwater Range, *U.S.A.* **82 G4** 39 50N 118 5W
Stilwell, *U.S.A.* **81 H7** 35 49N 94 38W
Štip, *Macedonia* **21 D10** 41 42N 22 10 E
Stirling, *Australia* **62 B3** 17 12S 141 35 E
Stirling, *Canada* **72 D6** 49 30N 112 30W
Stirling, *U.K.* **12 E5** 56 8N 3 57W
Stirling □, *U.K.* **12 E4** 56 12N 4 18W
Stirling Ra., *Australia* **61 F2** 34 23S 118 0 E
Stittsville, *Canada* **79 A9** 45 15N 75 55W
Stjernøya, *Norway* **8 A20** 70 20N 22 40 E
Stjørdalshalsen, *Norway* **8 E14** 63 29N 10 51 E
Stockerau, *Austria* **16 D9** 48 24N 16 12 E
Stockett, *U.S.A.* **82 C8** 47 21N 111 10W
Stockholm, *Sweden* **9 G18** 59 20N 18 3 E
Stockport, *U.K.* **10 D5** 53 25N 2 9W
Stockton, *Calif., U.S.A.* **83 H3** 37 58N 121 17W
Stockton, *Kans., U.S.A.* **80 F5** 39 26N 99 16W
Stockton, *Mo., U.S.A.* **81 G8** 37 42N 93 48W
Stockton-on-Tees, *U.K.* **10 C6** 54 35N 1 19W
Stockton-on-Tees □, *U.K.* **10 C6** 54 35N 1 19W
Stoke on Trent, *U.K.* **10 D5** 53 1N 2 11W
Stokes Bay, *Canada* **70 C3** 45 0N 81 28W
Stokes Pt., *Australia* **62 G3** 40 10S 143 56 E
Stokes Ra., *Australia* **60 C5** 15 50S 130 50 E
Stokksnes, *Iceland* **8 D6** 64 14N 14 58W
Stokmarknes, *Norway* **8 B16** 68 34N 14 54 E
Stolac, *Bos.-H.* **21 C7** 43 8N 17 59 E
Stolbovaya, *Russia* **27 C16** 64 50N 153 50 E
Stolbovoy, Ostrov, *Russia* **27 D17** 74 44N 135 14 E
Stolbtsy = Stowbtsy, *Belarus* **17 B14** 53 30N 26 43 E
Stolin, *Belarus* **17 C14** 51 53N 26 50 E
Stomion, *Greece* **23 D5** 35 21N 23 32 E
Stonehaven, *U.K.* **12 E6** 56 59N 2 12W
Stonehenge, *Australia* **62 C3** 24 22S 143 17 E
Stonewall, *Canada* **73 C9** 50 10N 97 19W
Stony L., *Man., Canada* **73 B9** 58 51N 98 40W
Stony L., *Ont., Canada* **78 B6** 44 30N 78 5W
Stony Rapids, *Canada* **73 B7** 59 16N 105 50W
Stony Tunguska = Podkamennaya Tunguska →, *Russia* **27 C10** 61 50N 90 13 E
Stonyford, *U.S.A.* **84 F4** 39 23N 122 33W
Stora Lulevatten, *Sweden* **8 C18** 67 10N 19 30 E
Storavan, *Sweden* **8 D18** 65 45N 18 10 E
Stord, *Norway* **9 G11** 59 52N 5 23 E
Store Bælt, *Denmark* **9 J14** 55 20N 11 0 E
Store Creek, *Australia* **63 E4** 32 54S 149 6 E
Storm B., *Australia* **62 G4** 43 10S 147 30 E
Storm Lake, *U.S.A.* **80 D7** 42 39N 95 13W
Stormberge, *S. Africa* **56 E4** 31 16S 26 17 E
Stormsrivier, *S. Africa* **56 E3** 33 59S 23 52 E
Stornoway, *U.K.* **12 C2** 58 13N 6 23W
Storozhinets = Storozhynets, *Ukraine* **17 D13** 48 14N 25 45 E
Storozhynets, *Ukraine* **17 D13** 48 14N 25 45 E
Storsjön, *Sweden* **8 E16** 63 9N 14 30 E
Storuman, *Sweden* **8 D17** 65 5N 17 10 E
Storuman, sjö, *Sweden* **8 D17** 65 13N 16 50 E
Stoughton, *Canada* **73 D8** 49 40N 103 0W
Stour →, *Dorset, U.K.* **11 G5** 50 43N 1 47W
Stour →, *Here. & Worcs., U.K.* **11 E5** 52 21N 2 17W
Stour →, *Kent, U.K.* **11 F9** 51 18N 1 22 E
Stour →, *Suffolk, U.K.* **11 F9** 51 57N 1 4 E
Stourbridge, *U.K.* **11 E5** 52 28N 2 8W
Stout, L., *Canada* **73 C10** 52 0N 94 40W
Stove Pipe Wells Village, *U.S.A.* **85 J9** 36 35N 117 11W
Stowbtsy, *Belarus* **17 B14** 53 30N 26 43 E
Stowmarket, *U.K.* **11 E9** 52 12N 1 0 E
Strabane, *U.K.* **13 B4** 54 50N 7 27W
Strabane □, *U.K.* **13 B4** 54 45N 7 25W
Strahan, *Australia* **62 G4** 42 9S 145 20 E
Stralsund, *Germany* **16 A7** 54 18N 13 4 E
Strand, *S. Africa* **56 E2** 34 9S 18 48 E
Stranda, *Møre og Romsdal, Norway* **9 E12** 62 19N 6 58 E
Stranda, *Nord-Trøndelag, Norway* **8 E14** 63 33N 10 14 E
Strangford L., *U.K.* **13 B6** 54 30N 5 37W
Strangsville, *U.S.A.* **78 E3** 41 19N 81 50W
Stranraer, *U.K.* **12 G3** 54 54N 5 1W
Strasbourg, *Canada* **73 C8** 51 4N 104 55W
Strasbourg, *France* **18 B7** 48 35N 7 42 E
Strasburg, *U.S.A.* **80 B4** 46 8N 100 10W
Stratford, *Canada* **70 D3** 43 23N 81 0W
Stratford, *N.Z.* **59 H5** 39 20S 174 19 E
Stratford, *Calif., U.S.A.* **83 H4** 36 11N 119 49W
Stratford, *Conn., U.S.A.* **79 E11** 41 12N 73 8W
Stratford, *Tex., U.S.A.* **81 G3** 36 20N 102 4W
Stratford-upon-Avon, *U.K.* **11 E6** 52 12N 1 42W
Strath Spey, *U.K.* **12 D5** 57 9N 3 49W
Strathalbyn, *Australia* **63 F2** 35 13S 138 53 E
Strathcona Prov. Park, *Canada* **72 D3** 49 38N 125 40W
Strathmore, *Australia* **62 B3** 17 50S 142 35 E
Strathmore, *Canada* **72 C6** 51 5N 113 18W
Strathmore, *U.K.* **12 E5** 56 37N 3 7W
Strathmore, *U.S.A.* **84 J7** 36 9N 119 4W
Strathnaver, *Canada* **72 C4** 53 20N 122 33W
Strathpeffer, *U.K.* **12 D4** 57 35N 4 32W
Strathroy, *Canada* **70 D3** 42 58N 81 38W
Strathy Pt., *U.K.* **12 C4** 58 36N 4 1W
Stratton, *U.S.A.* **80 F3** 39 19N 102 36W
Straubing, *Germany* **16 D7** 48 52N 12 34 E
Straumnes, *Iceland* **8 C2** 66 26N 23 8W
Strawberry Reservoir, *U.S.A.* **82 F8** 40 8N 111 9W
Strawn, *U.S.A.* **81 J5** 32 33N 98 30W
Streaky B., *Australia* **63 E1** 32 48S 134 13 E
Streaky Bay, *Australia* **63 E1** 32 51S 134 18 E
Streator, *U.S.A.* **80 E10** 41 8N 88 50W
Streeter, *U.S.A.* **80 B5** 46 39N 99 21W
Streetsville, *Canada* **78 C5** 43 35N 79 42W
Strelka, *Russia* **27 D10** 58 5N 93 3 E
Streng →, *Cambodia* **38 F4** 13 12N 103 37 E
Streymoy, *Færoe Is.* **8 E9** 62 8N 7 5W
Strezhevoy, *Russia* **26 C8** 60 42N 77 34 E
Strimón →, *Greece* **21 D10** 40 46N 23 51 E
Strimonikós Kólpos, *Greece* **21 D11** 40 33N 24 0 E
Strómboli, *Italy* **20 E6** 38 47N 15 13 E
Stromeferry, *U.K.* **12 D3** 57 21N 5 33W
Stromness, *U.K.* **12 C5** 58 58N 3 17W
Stromsburg, *U.S.A.* **80 E6** 41 7N 97 36W
Strömstad, *Sweden* **9 G14** 58 56N 11 10 E
Strömsund, *Sweden* **8 E16** 63 51N 15 33 E
Stronsay, *U.K.* **12 B6** 59 7N 2 35W
Stroud, *U.K.* **11 F5** 51 45N 2 13W
Stroud Road, *Australia* **63 E5** 32 18S 151 57 E
Stroudsburg, *U.S.A.* **79 F9** 40 59N 75 12W
Stroumbi, *Cyprus* **23 E11** 34 53N 32 29 E
Struer, *Denmark* **9 H13** 56 30N 8 35 E
Strumica, *Macedonia* **21 D10** 41 28N 22 41 E
Struthers, *Canada* **70 C2** 48 41N 85 51W
Struthers, *U.S.A.* **78 E4** 41 4N 80 39W
Stryker, *U.S.A.* **82 B6** 48 41N 114 46W
Stryy, *Ukraine* **17 D12** 49 16N 23 48 E
Strzelecki Cr. →, *Australia* **63 D2** 29 37S 139 59 E
Stuart, *Fla., U.S.A.* **77 M5** 27 12N 80 15W
Stuart, *Nebr., U.S.A.* **80 D5** 42 36N 99 8W
Stuart →, *Canada* **72 C4** 54 0N 123 35W
Stuart Bluff Ra., *Australia* **60 D5** 22 50S 131 52 E
Stuart L., *Canada* **72 C4** 54 30N 124 30W
Stuart Ra., *Australia* **63 D1** 29 10S 134 56 E
Stull, L., *Canada* **70 B1** 54 24N 92 34W
Stung Treng, *Cambodia* **38 F5** 13 31N 105 58 E
Stupart →, *Canada* **73 B10** 56 0N 93 25W
Sturgeon B., *Canada* **73 C9** 52 0N 97 50W
Sturgeon Bay, *U.S.A.* **76 C2** 44 50N 87 23W
Sturgeon Falls, *Canada* **70 C4** 46 25N 79 57W
Sturgeon L., *Alta., Canada* **72 B5** 55 6N 117 32W
Sturgeon L., *Ont., Canada* **70 B1** 50 0N 90 45W
Sturgeon L., *Ont., Canada* **78 B6** 44 28N 78 43W
Sturgis, *Mich., U.S.A.* **76 E3** 41 48N 85 25W
Sturgis, *S. Dak., U.S.A.* **80 C3** 44 25N 103 31W
Sturt Cr. →, *Australia* **60 C4** 19 8S 127 50 E
Sturt Creek, *Australia* **60 C4** 19 12S 128 8 E
Stutterheim, *S. Africa* **56 E4** 32 33S 27 28 E
Stuttgart, *Germany* **16 D5** 48 48N 9 11 E
Stuttgart, *U.S.A.* **81 H9** 34 30N 91 33W
Stuyvesant, *U.S.A.* **79 D11** 42 23N 73 45W
Stykkishólmur, *Iceland* **8 D2** 65 2N 22 40W
Styria = Steiermark □, *Austria* **16 E8** 47 26N 15 0 E
Su Xian, *China* **34 H9** 33 41N 116 59 E
Suakin, *Sudan* **51 E12** 19 8N 37 20 E
Suan, *N. Korea* **35 E14** 38 42N 126 22 E
Suaqui, *Mexico* **86 B3** 29 12N 109 41W
Subang, *Indonesia* **37 G12** 6 34S 107 45 E
Subansiri →, *India* **41 F18** 26 48N 93 50 E
Subayhah, *Si. Arabia* **44 D3** 30 2N 38 50 E
Subi, *Indonesia* **39 L7** 2 58N 108 50 E
Subotica, *Serbia, Yug.* **21 A8** 46 6N 19 39 E
Success, *Canada* **73 C7** 50 28N 108 6W
Suceava, *Romania* **17 E14** 47 38N 26 16 E
Suchan, *Russia* **30 C6** 43 8N 133 9 E
Suchitoto, *El Salv.* **88 D2** 13 56N 89 0W
Suchou = Suzhou, *China* **33 C7** 31 19N 120 38 E
Süchow = Xuzhou, *China* **35 G9** 34 18N 117 10 E
Suck →, *Ireland* **13 C3** 53 17N 8 3W
Sucre, *Bolivia* **92 G5** 19 0S 65 15W
Sud, Pte., *Canada* **71 C7** 49 3N 62 14W
Sud-Ouest, Pte. du, *Canada* **71 C7** 49 23N 63 36W
Sudan, *U.S.A.* **81 H3** 34 4N 102 32W
Sudan ■, *Africa* **51 E11** 15 0N 30 0 E
Sudbury, *Canada* **70 C3** 46 30N 81 0W
Sudbury, *U.K.* **11 E8** 52 2N 0 45 E
Sûdd, *Sudan* **51 G11** 8 20N 30 0 E
Sudeten Mts. = Sudety, *Europe* **17 C9** 50 20N 16 45 E
Sudety, *Europe* **17 C9** 50 20N 16 45 E
Suðuroy, *Færoe Is.* **8 F9** 61 32N 6 50W
Sudi, *Tanzania* **55 E4** 10 11S 39 57 E
Sudirman, Pegunungan, *Indonesia* **37 E9** 4 30S 137 0 E
Sueca, *Spain* **19 C5** 39 12N 0 21W
Suez = El Suweis, *Egypt* **51 C11** 29 58N 32 31 E
Suez, G. of = Suweis, Khalîg el, *Egypt* **51 C11** 28 40N 33 0 E
Suffield, *Canada* **73 C6** 50 12N 111 10W
Suffolk, *U.S.A.* **76 G7** 36 44N 76 35W
Suffolk □, *U.K.* **11 E9** 52 16N 1 0 E
Sugar City, *U.S.A.* **80 F3** 38 14N 103 40W
Sugluk = Salluit, *Canada* **69 B12** 62 14N 75 38W
Suhār, *Oman* **45 E8** 24 20N 56 40 E
Sühbaatar □, *Mongolia* **34 B8** 45 30N 114 0 E
Suhl, *Germany* **16 C6** 50 36N 10 42 E
Sui Xian, *China* **34 G8** 34 25N 115 2 E
Suide, *China* **34 F6** 37 30N 110 12 E
Suifenhe, *China* **35 B16** 44 25N 131 10 E
Suihua, *China* **33 B7** 46 32N 126 55 E
Suining, *China* **35 H9** 33 56N 117 58 E
Suiping, *China* **34 H7** 33 10N 113 59 E
Suir →, *Ireland* **13 D4** 52 16N 7 9W
Suiyang, *China* **35 B16** 44 30N 130 56 E
Suizhong, *China* **35 D11** 40 21N 120 20 E
Sujangarh, *India* **42 F6** 27 42N 74 31 E
Sukabumi, *Indonesia* **37 G12** 6 56S 106 50 E
Sukadana, *Kalimantan, Indonesia* **36 E3** 1 10S 110 0 E
Sukadana, *Sumatera, Indonesia* **36 F3** 5 5S 105 33 E
Sukagawa, *Japan* **31 F10** 37 17N 140 23 E
Sukaraja, *Indonesia* **36 E4** 2 28S 110 25 E
Sukarnapura = Jayapura, *Indonesia* **37 E10** 2 28S 140 38 E
Sukchŏn, *N. Korea* **35 E13** 39 22N 125 35 E
Sukhona →, *Russia* **24 C6** 61 15N 46 39 E
Sukhothai, *Thailand* **38 D2** 17 1N 99 49 E
Sukhumi = Sokhumi, *Georgia* **25 F7** 43 0N 41 0 E
Sukkur, *Pakistan* **42 F3** 27 42N 68 54 E
Sukkur Barrage, *Pakistan* **42 F3** 27 40N 68 50 E
Sukumo, *Japan* **31 H6** 32 56N 132 44 E
Sukunka →, *Canada* **72 B4** 55 45N 121 15W
Sula, Kepulauan, *Indonesia* **37 E7** 1 45S 125 0 E
Sulaco →, *Honduras* **88 C2** 15 2N 87 44W
Sulaiman Range, *Pakistan* **42 D3** 30 30N 69 50 E
Sūlār, *Iran* **45 D6** 31 53N 51 54 E
Sulawesi □, *Indonesia* **37 E6** 2 0S 120 0 E
Sulawesi Sea = Celebes Sea, *Indonesia* **37 D6** 3 0N 123 0 E
Sulima, *S. Leone* **50 G2** 6 58N 11 32W
Sulina, *Romania* **17 F15** 45 10N 29 40 E
Sulitjelma, *Norway* **8 C17** 67 9N 16 3 E
Sullana, *Peru* **92 D2** 4 52S 80 39W
Sullivan, *Ill., U.S.A.* **80 F10** 39 36N 88 37W
Sullivan, *Ind., U.S.A.* **76 F2** 39 6N 87 24W
Sullivan, *Mo., U.S.A.* **80 F9** 38 13N 91 10W
Sullivan Bay, *Canada* **72 C3** 50 55N 126 50W
Sulphur, *La., U.S.A.* **81 K8** 30 14N 93 23W
Sulphur, *Okla., U.S.A.* **81 H6** 34 31N 96 58W
Sulphur Pt., *Canada* **72 A6** 60 56N 114 48W
Sulphur Springs, *U.S.A.* **81 J7** 33 8N 95 36W
Sulphur Springs Draw →, *U.S.A.* **81 J4** 32 12N 101 36W
Sultan, *Canada* **70 C3** 47 36N 82 47W
Sultan, *U.S.A.* **84 C5** 47 52N 121 49W
Sultanpur, *India* **43 F10** 26 18N 82 4 E
Sultsa, *Russia* **24 B8** 63 27N 46 2 E
Sulu Arch., *Phil.* **37 C6** 6 0N 121 0 E
Sulu Sea, *E. Indies* **37 C6** 8 0N 120 0 E
Suluq, *Libya* **51 B9** 31 44N 20 14 E
Sulzberger Ice Shelf, *Antarctica* **5 D10** 78 0S 150 0 E
Sumalata, *Indonesia* **37 D6** 1 0N 122 31 E
Sumampa, *Argentina* **94 B3** 29 25S 63 29W
Sumatera □, *Indonesia* **36 D2** 0 40N 100 20 E
Sumatra = Sumatera □, *Indonesia* **36 D2** 0 40N 100 20 E
Sumatra, *U.S.A.* **82 C10** 46 37N 107 33W
Sumba, *Indonesia* **37 F5** 9 45S 119 35 E
Sumba, Selat, *Indonesia* **37 F5** 9 0S 118 40 E
Sumbawa, *Indonesia* **36 F5** 8 26S 117 30 E
Sumbawa Besar, *Indonesia* **36 F5** 8 30S 117 26 E
Sumbawanga □, *Tanzania* **54 D3** 8 0S 31 30 E
Sumbe, *Angola* **52 G2** 11 10S 13 48 E
Sumburgh Hd., *U.K.* **12 B7** 59 52N 1 17W
Sumdo, *India* **43 B8** 35 6N 78 41 E
Sumedang, *Indonesia* **37 G12** 6 52S 107 55 E
Šumen, *Bulgaria* **21 C12** 43 18N 26 55 E
Sumenep, *Indonesia* **37 G15** 7 1S 113 52 E
Sumgait = Sumqayıt, *Azerbaijan* **25 F8** 40 34N 49 38 E
Summer L., *U.S.A.* **82 E3** 42 50N 120 45W
Summerland, *Canada* **72 D5** 49 32N 119 41W
Summerside, *Canada* **71 C7** 46 24N 63 47W
Summerville, *Ga., U.S.A.* **77 H3** 34 29N 85 21W
Summerville, *S.C., U.S.A.* **77 J5** 33 1N 80 11W
Summit Lake, *Canada* **72 C4** 54 20N 122 40W
Summit Peak, *U.S.A.* **83 H10** 37 21N 106 42W
Sumner, *Iowa, U.S.A.* **80 D8** 42 51N 92 6W
Sumner, *Wash., U.S.A.* **84 C4** 47 12N 122 14W
Sumoto, *Japan* **31 G7** 34 21N 134 54 E
Šumperk, *Czech.* **17 D9** 49 59N 17 0 E
Sumqayıt, *Azerbaijan* **25 F8** 40 34N 49 38 E
Sumter, *U.S.A.* **77 J5** 33 55N 80 21W
Sumy, *Ukraine* **25 D5** 50 57N 34 50 E
Sun City, *Ariz., U.S.A.* **83 K7** 33 36N 112 17W
Sun City, *Calif., U.S.A.* **85 M9** 33 42N 117 11W
Sunagawa, *Japan* **30 C10** 43 29N 141 55 E
Sunan, *N. Korea* **35 E13** 39 15N 125 40 E
Sunart, L., *U.K.* **12 E3** 56 42N 5 43W
Sunburst, *U.S.A.* **82 B8** 48 53N 111 55W
Sunbury, *Australia* **63 F3** 37 35S 144 44 E
Sunbury, *U.S.A.* **79 F8** 40 52N 76 48W
Sunchales, *Argentina* **94 C3** 30 58S 61 35W
Suncho Corral, *Argentina* **94 B3** 27 55S 63 27W
Sunchon, *S. Korea* **35 G14** 34 52N 127 31 E
Suncook, *U.S.A.* **79 C13** 43 8N 71 27W
Sunda, Selat, *Indonesia* **36 F3** 6 20S 105 30 E
Sunda Is., *Indonesia* **28 K14** 5 0S 105 0 E
Sunda Str. = Sunda, Selat, *Indonesia* **36 F3** 6 20S 105 30 E
Sundance, *U.S.A.* **80 C2** 44 24N 104 23W
Sundarbans, The, *Asia* **41 J16** 22 0N 89 0 E
Sundargarh, *India* **41 H14** 22 4N 84 5 E
Sundays = Sondags →, *S. Africa* **56 E4** 33 44S 25 51 E
Sunderland, *Canada* **78 B5** 44 16N 79 4W
Sunderland, *U.K.* **10 C6** 54 55N 1 23W
Sundre, *Canada* **72 C6** 51 49N 114 38W
Sundridge, *Canada* **70 C4** 45 45N 79 25W
Sundsvall, *Sweden* **9 E17** 62 23N 17 17 E
Sung Hei, *Vietnam* **39 G6** 10 20N 106 2 E
Sungai Kolok, *Thailand* **39 J3** 6 2N 101 58 E
Sungai Lembing, *Malaysia* **39 L4** 3 55N 103 3 E
Sungai Patani, *Malaysia* **39 K3** 5 37N 100 30 E
Sungaigerong, *Indonesia* **36 E2** 2 59S 104 52 E
Sungailiat, *Indonesia* **36 E3** 1 51S 106 8 E
Sungaipakning, *Indonesia* **36 D2** 1 19N 102 0 E
Sungaipenuh, *Indonesia* **36 E2** 2 1S 101 20 E
Sungaitiram, *Indonesia* **36 E5** 0 45S 117 8 E
Sungari = Songhua Jiang →, *China* **33 B8** 47 45N 132 30 E
Sungguminasa, *Indonesia* **37 F5** 5 17S 119 30 E
Sunghua Chiang = Songhua Jiang →, *China* **33 B8** 47 45N 132 30 E
Sunndalsøra, *Norway* **9 E13** 62 40N 8 33 E
Sunnyside, *Utah, U.S.A.* **82 G8** 39 34N 110 23W
Sunnyside, *Wash., U.S.A.* **82 C3** 46 20N 120 0W
Sunnyvale, *U.S.A.* **83 H2** 37 23N 122 2W
Sunray, *U.S.A.* **81 G4** 36 1N 101 49W
Suntar, *Russia* **27 C12** 62 15N 117 30 E
Suomenselkä, *Finland* **8 E21** 62 52N 24 0 E
Suomussalmi, *Finland* **8 D23** 64 54N 29 10 E
Suoyarvi, *Russia* **24 B5** 62 3N 32 20 E
Supai, *U.S.A.* **83 H7** 36 15N 112 41W
Supaul, *India* **43 F12** 26 10N 86 40 E
Superior, *Ariz., U.S.A.* **83 K8** 33 18N 111 6W
Superior, *Mont., U.S.A.* **82 C6** 47 12N 114 53W
Superior, *Nebr., U.S.A.* **80 E5** 40 1N 98 4W
Superior, *Wis., U.S.A.* **80 B8** 46 44N 92 6W
Superior, L., *U.S.A.* **70 C2** 47 0N 87 0W
Suphan Buri, *Thailand* **38 E3** 14 14N 100 10 E
Supiori, *Indonesia* **37 E9** 1 0S 136 0 E
Supung Sk., *China* **35 D13** 40 35N 124 50 E
Sūq Suwayq, *Si. Arabia* **44 E3** 24 23N 38 27 E
Suqian, *China* **35 H10** 33 54N 118 8 E
Sūr, *Lebanon* **47 B4** 33 19N 35 16 E
Sur, Pt., *U.S.A.* **83 H3** 36 18N 121 54W
Sura →, *Russia* **24 C8** 56 6N 46 0 E
Surab, *Pakistan* **42 E2** 28 25N 66 15 E
Surabaja = Surabaya, *Indonesia* **37 G15** 7 17S 112 45 E
Surabaya, *Indonesia* **37 G15** 7 17S 112 45 E
Surakarta, *Indonesia* **37 G14** 7 35S 110 48 E
Surat, *Australia* **63 D4** 27 10S 149 6 E
Surat, *India* **40 J8** 21 12N 72 55 E
Surat Thani, *Thailand* **39 H2** 9 6N 99 20 E
Suratgarh, *India* **42 E5** 29 18N 73 55 E
Sûre = Sauer →, *Germany* **15 E6** 49 44N 6 31 E
Surendranagar, *India* **42 H4** 22 45N 71 40 E
Surf, *U.S.A.* **85 L6** 34 41N 120 36W
Surgut, *Russia* **26 C8** 61 14N 73 20 E
Suriapet, *India* **40 L11** 17 10N 79 40 E
Surigao, *Phil.* **37 C7** 9 47N 125 29 E
Surin, *Thailand* **38 E4** 14 50N 103 34 E
Surin Nua, Ko, *Thailand* **39 H1** 9 30N 97 55 E
Surinam ■, *S. Amer.* **93 C7** 4 0N 56 0W
Suriname ■ = Surinam ■, *S. Amer.* **93 C7** 4 0N 56 0W
Suriname →, *Surinam* **93 B7** 5 50N 55 15W
Sūrmaq, *Iran* **45 D7** 31 3N 52 48 E
Surprise L., *Canada* **72 B2** 59 40N 133 15W
Surrey □, *U.K.* **11 F7** 51 15N 0 31W
Surt, *Libya* **51 B8** 31 11N 16 39 E
Surt, Khalīj, *Libya* **51 B8** 31 40N 18 30 E
Surtsey, *Iceland* **8 E3** 63 20N 20 30W
Suruga-Wan, *Japan* **31 G9** 34 45N 138 30 E
Susaki, *Japan* **31 H6** 33 22N 133 17 E
Süsangerd, *Iran* **45 D6** 31 35N 48 6 E
Susanino, *Russia* **27 D15** 52 50N 140 14 E
Susanville, *U.S.A.* **82 F3** 40 25N 120 39W
Susquehanna →, *U.S.A.* **79 G8** 39 33N 76 5W
Susquehanna Depot, *U.S.A.* **79 E9** 41 57N 75 36W
Susques, *Argentina* **94 A2** 23 35S 66 25W
Sussex, *Canada* **71 C6** 45 45N 65 37W
Sussex, *U.S.A.* **79 E10** 41 13N 74 37W
Sussex, E. □, *U.K.* **11 G8** 51 0N 0 20 E
Sussex, W. □, *U.K.* **11 G7** 51 0N 0 30W
Sustut →, *Canada* **72 B3** 56 20N 127 30W
Susuman, *Russia* **27 C15** 62 47N 148 10 E
Susunu, *Indonesia* **37 E8** 3 20S 133 25 E
Susurluk, *Turkey* **21 E13** 39 54N 28 8 E
Sutherland, *S. Africa* **56 E3** 32 24S 20 40 E
Sutherland, *U.S.A.* **80 E4** 41 10N 101 8W
Sutherland Falls, *N.Z.* **59 L1** 44 48S 167 46 E
Sutherlin, *U.S.A.* **82 E2** 43 23N 123 19W
Sutlej →, *Pakistan* **42 E4** 29 23N 71 3 E
Sutter, *U.S.A.* **84 F5** 39 10N 121 45W
Sutter Creek, *U.S.A.* **84 G6** 38 24N 120 48W
Sutton, *Canada* **79 A12** 45 6N 72 37W
Sutton, *U.S.A.* **80 E6** 40 36N 97 52W
Sutton →, *Canada* **70 A3** 55 15N 83 45W
Sutton in Ashfield, *U.K.* **10 D6** 53 8N 1 16W
Suttor →, *Australia* **62 C4** 21 36S 147 2 E
Suttsu, *Japan* **30 C10** 42 48N 140 14 E
Suva, *Fiji* **59 D8** 18 6S 178 30 E
Suva Planina, *Serbia, Yug.* **21 C10** 43 10N 22 5 E
Suvorov Is. = Suwarrow Is., *Cook Is.* **65 J11** 15 0S 163 0W
Suwałki, *Poland* **17 A12** 54 8N 22 59 E
Suwannaphum, *Thailand* **38 E4** 15 33N 103 47 E
Suwannee →, *U.S.A.* **77 L4** 29 17N 83 10W
Suwanose-Jima, *Japan* **31 K4** 29 38N 129 43 E
Suwarrow Is., *Cook Is.* **65 J11** 15 0S 163 0W
Suwayq aş Şuqban, *Iraq* **44 D5** 31 32N 46 7 E
Suweis, Khalîg el, *Egypt* **51 C11** 28 40N 33 0 E
Suwŏn, *S. Korea* **35 F14** 37 17N 127 1 E
Suzdal, *Russia* **24 C7** 56 29N 40 26 E
Suzhou, *China* **33 C7** 31 19N 120 38 E
Suzu, *Japan* **31 F8** 37 25N 137 17 E
Suzu-Misaki, *Japan* **31 F8** 37 31N 137 21 E
Suzuka, *Japan* **31 G8** 34 55N 136 36 E
Svalbard, *Arctic* **4 B8** 78 0N 17 0 E
Svappavaara, *Sweden* **8 C19** 67 40N 21 3 E
Svartisen, *Norway* **8 C15** 66 40N 13 50 E
Svay Chek, *Cambodia* **38 F4** 13 48N 102 58 E
Svay Rieng, *Cambodia* **39 G5** 11 5N 105 48 E
Svealand □, *Sweden* **9 G16** 59 55N 15 0 E
Sveg, *Sweden* **9 E16** 62 2N 14 21 E
Svendborg, *Denmark* **9 J14** 55 4N 10 35 E
Sverdlovsk = Yekaterinburg, *Russia* **24 C11** 56 50N 60 30 E
Sverdrup Is., *Canada* **4 B3** 79 0N 97 0W
Svetlaya, *Russia* **30 A9** 46 33N 138 18 E
Svetlogorsk = Svyetlahorsk, *Belarus* **17 B15** 52 38N 29 46 E
Svetozarevo, *Serbia, Yug.* **21 C9** 44 5N 21 15 E
Svir →, *Russia* **24 B5** 60 30N 32 48 E
Svishtov, *Bulgaria* **21 C11** 43 36N 25 23 E
Svislach, *Belarus* **17 B13** 53 3N 24 2 E
Svobodnyy, *Russia* **27 D13** 51 20N 128 0 E
Svolvær, *Norway* **8 B16** 68 15N 14 34 E
Svyetlahorsk, *Belarus* **17 B15** 52 38N 29 46 E
Swabian Alps = Schwäbische Alb, *Germany* **16 D5** 48 20N 9 30 E
Swainsboro, *U.S.A.* **77 J4** 32 36N 82 20W
Swakopmund, *Namibia* **56 C1** 22 37S 14 30 E
Swale →, *U.K.* **10 C6** 54 5N 1 20W
Swan Hill, *Australia* **63 F3** 35 20S 143 33 E
Swan Hills, *Canada* **72 C5** 54 42N 115 24W
Swan Is., *W. Indies* **88 C3** 17 22N 83 57W
Swan L., *Canada* **73 C8** 52 30N 100 40W
Swan River, *Canada* **73 C8** 52 10N 101 16W
Swanage, *U.K.* **11 G6** 50 36N 1 58W
Swansea, *Australia* **63 E5** 33 3S 151 35 E
Swansea, *U.K.* **11 F4** 51 37N 3 57W
Swansea □, *U.K.* **11 F3** 51 38N 4 3W
Swar →, *Pakistan* **43 B5** 34 40N 72 5 E
Swartberge, *S. Africa* **56 E3** 33 20S 22 0 E
Swartmodder, *S. Africa* **56 D3** 28 1S 20 32 E
Swartruggens, *S. Africa* **56 D4** 25 39S 26 42 E
Swastika, *Canada* **70 C3** 48 7N 80 6W
Swatow = Shantou, *China* **33 D6** 23 18N 116 40 E
Swaziland ■, *Africa* **57 D5** 26 30S 31 30 E
Sweden ■, *Europe* **9 G16** 57 0N 15 0 E
Sweet Home, *U.S.A.* **82 D2** 44 24N 122 44W
Sweetwater, *Nev., U.S.A.* **84 G7** 38 27N 119 9W
Sweetwater, *Tex., U.S.A.* **81 J4** 32 28N 100 25W

Sweetwater

167

Toronto, *Australia* 63 E5 33 0S 151 30 E
Toronto, *Canada* 70 D4 43 39N 79 20W
Toronto, *U.S.A.* 78 F4 40 28N 80 36W
Toropets, *Russia* 24 C5 56 30N 31 40 E
Tororo, *Uganda* 54 B3 0 45N 34 12 E
Toros Dağlan, *Turkey* 25 G5 37 0N 32 30 E
Torquay, *Canada* 73 D8 49 9N 103 30W
Torquay, *U.K.* 11 G4 50 27N 3 32W
Torrance, *U.S.A.* 85 M8 33 50N 118 19W
Tôrre de Moncorvo, *Portugal* 19 B2 41 12N 7 8W
Torre del Greco, *Italy* 20 D6 40 47N 14 22 E
Torrejón de Ardoz, *Spain* 19 B4 40 27N 3 29W
Torrelavega, *Spain* 19 A3 43 20N 4 5W
Torremolinos, *Spain* 19 D3 36 38N 4 30W
Torrens, L., *Australia* 63 E2 31 0S 137 50 E
Torrens Cr. →, *Australia* 62 C4 22 23S 145 9 E
Torrens Creek, *Australia* 62 C4 20 48S 145 3 E
Torrente, *Spain* 19 C5 39 27N 0 28W
Torreón, *Mexico* 86 B4 25 33N 103 26W
Torres, *Mexico* 86 B2 28 46N 110 47W
Torres Strait, *Australia* 64 H6 9 50S 142 20 E
Torres Vedras, *Portugal* 19 C1 39 5N 9 15W
Torrevieja, *Spain* 19 D5 37 59N 0 42W
Torrey, *U.S.A.* 83 G8 38 18N 111 25W
Torridge →, *U.K.* 11 G3 51 0N 4 13W
Torridon, L., *U.K.* 12 D3 57 35N 5 50W
Torrington, *Conn., U.S.A.* 79 E11 41 48N 73 7W
Torrington, *Wyo., U.S.A.* 80 D2 42 4N 104 11W
Tórshavn, *Færoe Is.* 8 E9 62 5N 6 56W
Tortola, *Virgin Is.* 89 C7 18 19N 64 45W
Tortosa, *Spain* 19 B6 40 49N 0 31 E
Tortosa, C. de, *Spain* 19 B6 40 41N 0 52 E
Tortue, I. de la, *Haiti* 89 B5 20 5N 72 57W
Ţorūd, *Iran* 45 C7 35 25N 55 5 E
Toruń, *Poland* 17 B10 53 2N 18 39 E
Tory I., *Ireland* 13 A3 55 16N 8 14W
Tosa, *Japan* 31 H6 33 24N 133 23 E
Tosa-Shimizu, *Japan* 31 H6 32 52N 132 58 E
Tosa-Wan, *Japan* 31 H6 33 15N 133 30 E
Toscana □, *Italy* 20 C4 43 25N 11 0 E
Toshkent, *Uzbekistan* 26 E7 41 20N 69 10 E
Tostado, *Argentina* 94 B3 29 15S 61 50W
Tostón, Pta. de, *Canary Is.* 22 F5 28 42N 14 2W
Tosu, *Japan* 31 H5 33 22N 130 31 E
Toteng, *Botswana* 56 C3 20 22S 22 58 E
Totma, *Russia* 24 C7 60 0N 42 40 E
Totnes, *U.K.* 11 G4 50 26N 3 42W
Totonicapán, *Guatemala* 88 D1 14 58N 91 12W
Totten Glacier, *Antarctica* 5 C8 66 45S 116 10 E
Tottenham, *Australia* 63 E4 32 14S 147 21 E
Tottenham, *Canada* 78 B5 44 1N 79 49W
Tottori, *Japan* 31 G7 35 30N 134 15 E
Tottori □, *Japan* 31 G7 35 30N 134 12 E
Touba, *Ivory C.* 50 G3 8 22N 7 40W
Toubkal, Djebel, *Morocco* 50 B3 31 0N 8 0W
Tougan, *Burkina Faso* 50 F4 13 11N 2 58W
Touggourt, *Algeria* 50 B6 33 6N 6 4 E
Tougué, *Guinea* 50 F2 11 25N 11 50W
Toul, *France* 18 B6 48 40N 5 53 E
Toulepleu, *Ivory C.* 50 G3 6 32N 8 24W
Toulon, *France* 18 E6 43 10N 5 55 E
Toulouse, *France* 18 E4 43 37N 1 27 E
Toummo, *Niger* 51 D7 22 45N 14 8 E
Toungoo, *Burma* 41 K20 19 0N 96 30 E
Touraine, *France* 18 C4 47 20N 0 30 E
Tourane = Da Nang, *Vietnam* 38 D7 16 4N 108 13 E
Tourcoing, *France* 18 A5 50 42N 3 10 E
Touriñán, C., *Spain* 19 A1 43 3N 9 18W
Tournai, *Belgium* 15 D3 50 35N 3 25 E
Tournon, *France* 18 D6 45 4N 4 50 E
Tours, *France* 18 C4 47 22N 0 40 E
Touwsrivier, *S. Africa* 56 E3 33 20S 20 2 E
Towada, *Japan* 30 D10 40 37N 141 13 E
Towada-Ko, *Japan* 30 D10 40 28N 140 55 E
Towamba, *Australia* 63 F4 37 6S 149 43 E
Towanda, *U.S.A.* 79 E8 41 46N 76 27W
Towang, *India* 41 F17 27 37N 91 50 E
Tower, *U.S.A.* 80 B8 47 48N 92 17W
Towerhill Cr. →, *Australia* 62 C3 22 28S 144 35 E
Towner, *U.S.A.* 80 A4 48 21N 100 25W
Townsend, *U.S.A.* 82 C8 46 19N 111 31W
Townshend I., *Australia* 62 C5 22 10S 150 31 E
Townsville, *Australia* 62 B4 19 15S 146 45 E
Towson, *U.S.A.* 76 F7 39 24N 76 36W
Toya-Ko, *Japan* 30 C10 42 35N 140 51 E
Toyah, *U.S.A.* 81 K3 31 19N 103 48W
Toyahvale, *U.S.A.* 81 K3 30 57N 103 47W
Toyama, *Japan* 31 F8 36 40N 137 15 E
Toyama □, *Japan* 31 F8 36 45N 137 30 E
Toyama-Wan, *Japan* 31 F8 37 0N 137 30 E
Toyohashi, *Japan* 31 G8 34 45N 137 25 E
Toyokawa, *Japan* 31 G8 34 48N 137 27 E
Toyonaka, *Japan* 31 G7 34 50N 135 28 E
Toyooka, *Japan* 31 G7 35 35N 134 48 E
Toyota, *Japan* 31 G8 35 3N 137 7 E
Tozeur, *Tunisia* 50 B6 33 56N 8 8 E
Trá Li = Tralee, *Ireland* 13 D2 52 16N 9 42W
Tra On, *Vietnam* 39 H5 9 58N 105 55 E
Trabzon, *Turkey* 25 F6 41 0N 39 45 E
Tracadie, *Canada* 71 C7 47 30N 64 55W
Tracy, *Calif., U.S.A.* 83 H3 37 44N 121 26W
Tracy, *Minn., U.S.A.* 80 C7 44 14N 95 37W
Trafalgar, C., *Spain* 19 D2 36 10N 6 2W
Trail, *Canada* 72 D5 49 5N 117 40W
Trainor L., *Canada* 72 A4 60 24N 120 17W
Trákhonas, *Cyprus* 23 D12 35 12N 33 21 E
Tralee, *Ireland* 13 D2 52 16N 9 42W
Tralee B., *Ireland* 13 D2 52 17N 9 55W
Tramore, *Ireland* 13 D4 52 10N 7 10W
Tran Ninh, Cao Nguyen, *Laos* 38 C4 19 30N 103 10 E
Tranås, *Sweden* 9 G16 58 3N 14 59 E
Trancas, *Argentina* 94 B2 26 11S 65 20W
Trang, *Thailand* 39 J2 7 33N 99 38 E
Trangahy, *Madag.* 57 B7 19 7S 44 31 E
Trangan, *Indonesia* 37 F8 6 40S 134 20 E
Trangie, *Australia* 63 E4 32 4S 148 0 E
Trani, *Italy* 20 D7 41 17N 16 25 E
Tranoroa, *Madag.* 57 C8 24 42S 45 4 E
Tranqueras, *Uruguay* 95 C4 31 13S 55 45W
Trans Nzoia □, *Kenya* 54 B3 1 0N 35 0 E
Transantarctic Mts., *Antarctica* 5 E12 85 0S 170 0W
Transcaucasia = Zakavkazye, *Asia* 25 F7 42 0N 44 0 E
Transcona, *Canada* 73 D9 49 55N 97 0W
Transilvania, *Romania* 17 E12 45 19N 25 0 E
Transilvanian Alps = Carpaţii Meridionali, *Romania* 17 F13 45 30N 25 0 E
Transylvania = Transilvania, *Romania* 17 E12 45 19N 25 0 E
Trápani, *Italy* 20 E5 38 1N 12 29 E
Trapper Pk., *U.S.A.* 82 D6 45 54N 114 18W
Traralgon, *Australia* 63 F4 38 12S 146 34 E
Trasimeno, L., *Italy* 20 C5 43 8N 12 6 E
Trat, *Thailand* 39 F4 12 14N 102 33 E
Traun, *Austria* 16 D8 48 14N 14 15 E
Traveller's L., *Australia* 63 E3 33 20S 142 0 E
Travemünde, *Germany* 16 B6 53 57N 10 52 E
Travers, Mt., *N.Z.* 59 K4 42 1S 172 45 E
Traverse City, *U.S.A.* 76 C3 44 46N 85 38W
Travnik, *Bos.-H.* 21 B7 44 17N 17 39 E
Trayning, *Australia* 61 F2 31 7S 117 40 E
Trébbia →, *Italy* 20 B3 45 4N 9 41 E
Třebíč, *Czech.* 16 D8 49 14N 15 55 E
Trebinje, *Bos.-H.* 21 C8 42 44N 18 22 E
Tredegar, *U.K.* 11 F4 51 47N 3 14W
Tregaron, *U.K.* 11 E4 52 14N 3 56W
Tregrosse Is., *Australia* 62 B5 17 41S 150 43 E
Treherne, *Canada* 73 D9 49 38N 98 42W
Treinta y Tres, *Uruguay* 95 C5 33 16S 54 17W
Trelew, *Argentina* 96 E3 43 10S 65 20W
Trelleborg, *Sweden* 9 J15 55 20N 13 10 E
Tremonton, *U.S.A.* 82 F7 41 43N 112 10W
Tremp, *Spain* 19 A6 42 10N 0 52 E
Trenche →, *Canada* 70 C5 47 46N 72 53W
Trenčín, *Slovak Rep.* 17 D10 48 52N 18 4 E
Trenggalek, *Indonesia* 37 H14 8 3S 111 43 E
Trenque Lauquen, *Argentina* 94 D3 36 5S 62 45W
Trent →, *U.K.* 10 D7 53 41N 0 42W
Trento, *Italy* 20 A4 46 4N 11 8 E
Trenton, *Canada* 70 D4 44 10N 77 34W
Trenton, *Mo., U.S.A.* 80 E8 40 5N 93 37W
Trenton, *N.J., U.S.A.* 79 F10 40 14N 74 46W
Trenton, *Nebr., U.S.A.* 80 E4 40 11N 101 1W
Trenton, *Tenn., U.S.A.* 81 H10 35 59N 88 56W
Trepassey, *Canada* 71 C9 46 43N 53 25W
Tres Arroyos, *Argentina* 94 D3 38 26S 60 20W
Três Corações, *Brazil* 95 A6 21 44S 45 15W
Três Lagoas, *Brazil* 93 H8 20 50S 51 43W
Tres Marías, *Mexico* 86 C3 21 25N 106 28W
Tres Montes, C., *Chile* 96 F1 46 50S 75 30W
Tres Pinos, *U.S.A.* 84 J5 36 48N 121 19W
Três Pontas, *Brazil* 95 A6 21 23S 45 29W
Tres Puentes, *Chile* 94 B1 27 50S 70 15W
Tres Puntas, C., *Argentina* 96 F3 47 0S 66 0W
Três Rios, *Brazil* 95 A7 22 6S 43 15W
Tres Valles, *Mexico* 87 D5 18 15N 96 8W
Treviso, *Italy* 20 B5 45 40N 12 15 E
Triabunna, *Australia* 62 G4 42 30S 147 55 E
Triánda, *Greece* 23 C10 36 25N 28 10 E
Triang, *Malaysia* 39 L4 3 15N 102 26 E
Tribulation, C., *Australia* 62 B4 16 5S 145 29 E
Tribune, *U.S.A.* 80 F4 38 28N 101 45W
Trichinopoly = Tiruchchirappalli, *India* 40 P11 10 45N 78 45 E
Trichur, *India* 40 P10 10 30N 76 18 E
Trida, *Australia* 63 E4 33 1S 145 1 E
Trier, *Germany* 16 D4 49 45N 6 38 E
Trieste, *Italy* 20 B5 45 40N 13 46 E
Triglav, *Slovenia* 16 E7 46 21N 13 50 E
Tríkkala, *Greece* 21 E9 39 34N 21 47 E
Trikomo, *Cyprus* 23 D12 35 17N 33 52 E
Trikora, Puncak, *Indonesia* 37 E9 4 15S 138 45 E
Trim, *Ireland* 13 C5 53 33N 6 48W
Trincomalee, *Sri Lanka* 40 Q12 8 38N 81 15 E
Trindade, I., *Atl. Oc.* 2 F8 20 20S 29 50W
Trinidad, *Bolivia* 92 F6 14 46S 64 50W
Trinidad, *Colombia* 92 B4 5 25N 71 40W
Trinidad, *Cuba* 88 B3 21 48N 80 0W
Trinidad, *Uruguay* 94 C4 33 30S 56 50W
Trinidad, *U.S.A.* 81 G2 37 10N 104 31W
Trinidad, *W. Indies* 89 D7 10 30N 61 15W
Trinidad →, *Mexico* 87 D5 17 49N 95 9W
Trinidad, I., *Argentina* 96 D4 39 10S 62 0W
Trinidad & Tobago ■, *W. Indies* 89 D7 10 30N 61 20W
Trinity, *Canada* 71 C9 48 59N 53 55W
Trinity, *U.S.A.* 81 K7 30 57N 95 22W
Trinity →, *Calif., U.S.A.* 82 F2 41 11N 123 42W
Trinity →, *Tex., U.S.A.* 81 L7 29 45N 94 43W
Trinity B., *Canada* 71 C9 48 20N 53 10W
Trinity Range, *U.S.A.* 82 F4 40 15N 118 45W
Trinkitat, *Sudan* 51 E12 18 45N 37 51 E
Trion, *U.S.A.* 77 H3 34 33N 85 19W
Tripoli = Tarābulus, *Lebanon* 47 A4 34 31N 35 50 E
Tripoli = Tarābulus, *Libya* 51 B7 32 49N 13 7 E
Trípolis, *Greece* 21 F10 37 31N 22 25 E
Tripolitania, *N. Afr.* 48 C5 31 0N 13 0 E
Tripp, *U.S.A.* 80 D6 43 13N 97 58W
Tripura □, *India* 41 H17 24 0N 92 0 E
Trípylos, *Cyprus* 23 E11 34 59N 32 41 E
Tristan da Cunha, *Atl. Oc.* 49 K2 37 6S 12 20W
Trivandrum, *India* 40 Q10 8 41N 77 0 E
Trnava, *Slovak Rep.* 17 D9 48 23N 17 35 E
Trochu, *Canada* 72 C6 51 50N 113 13W
Trodely I., *Canada* 70 B4 52 15N 79 26W
Troglav, *Croatia* 20 C7 43 56N 16 36 E
Troilus, L., *Canada* 70 B5 50 50N 74 35W
Trois-Pistoles, *Canada* 71 C6 48 5N 69 10W
Trois-Rivières, *Canada* 70 C5 46 25N 72 34W
Troitsk, *Russia* 26 D7 54 10N 61 35 E
Troitsko Pechorsk, *Russia* 24 B10 62 40N 56 10 E
Trölladyngja, *Iceland* 8 D5 64 54N 17 16W
Trollhättan, *Sweden* 9 G15 58 17N 12 20 E
Trollheimen, *Norway* 8 E13 62 46N 9 1 E
Tromsø, *Norway* 8 B18 69 40N 18 56 E
Trona, *U.S.A.* 85 K9 35 46N 117 23W
Tronador, *Argentina* 96 E2 41 10S 71 50W
Trøndelag, *Norway* 8 D14 64 17N 11 50 E
Trondheim, *Norway* 8 E14 63 36N 10 25 E
Trondheimsfjorden, *Norway* 8 E14 63 35N 10 30 E
Troodos, *Cyprus* 23 E11 34 55N 32 52 E
Troon, *U.K.* 12 F4 55 33N 4 39W
Tropic, *U.S.A.* 83 H7 37 37N 112 5W
Trossachs, The, *U.K.* 12 E4 56 14N 4 24W
Trostan, *U.K.* 13 A5 55 3N 6 10W
Trotternish, *U.K.* 12 D2 57 32N 6 15W
Troup, *U.S.A.* 81 J7 32 9N 95 7W
Trout →, *Canada* 72 A5 61 19N 119 51W
Trout L., *N.W.T., Canada* 72 A4 60 40N 121 14W
Trout L., *Ont., Canada* 73 C10 51 20N 93 15W
Trout Lake, *Mich., U.S.A.* 70 C2 46 12N 85 1W
Trout Lake, *Wash., U.S.A.* 84 E5 46 0N 121 32W
Trout River, *Canada* 71 C8 49 29N 58 8W
Trouville-sur-Mer, *France* 18 B4 49 21N 0 5 E
Trowbridge, *U.K.* 11 F5 51 18N 2 12W
Troy, *Turkey* 21 E12 39 57N 26 12 E
Troy, *Ala., U.S.A.* 77 K3 31 48N 85 58W
Troy, *Idaho, U.S.A.* 82 C5 46 44N 116 46W
Troy, *Kans., U.S.A.* 80 F7 39 47N 95 5W
Troy, *Mo., U.S.A.* 80 F9 38 59N 90 59W
Troy, *Mont., U.S.A.* 82 B6 48 28N 115 53W
Troy, *N.Y., U.S.A.* 79 D11 42 44N 73 41W
Troy, *Ohio, U.S.A.* 76 E3 40 2N 84 12W
Troyes, *France* 18 B6 48 19N 4 3 E
Trucial States = United Arab Emirates ■, *Asia* 45 F7 23 50N 54 0 E
Truckee, *U.S.A.* 84 F6 39 20N 120 11W
Trudovoye, *Russia* 30 C6 43 17N 132 5 E
Trujillo, *Honduras* 88 C2 16 0N 86 0W
Trujillo, *Peru* 92 E3 8 6S 79 0W
Trujillo, *Spain* 19 C3 39 28N 5 55W
Trujillo, *U.S.A.* 81 H2 35 32N 104 42W
Trujillo, *Venezuela* 92 B4 9 22N 70 38W
Truk, *Pac. Oc.* 64 G7 7 25N 151 46 E
Trumann, *U.S.A.* 81 H9 35 41N 90 31W
Trumbull, Mt., *U.S.A.* 83 H7 36 25N 113 8W
Trundle, *Australia* 63 E4 32 53S 147 35 E
Trung-Phan, *Vietnam* 38 E7 16 0N 108 0 E
Truro, *Canada* 71 C7 45 21N 63 14W
Truro, *U.K.* 11 G2 50 16N 5 4W
Truskavets, *Ukraine* 17 D12 49 17N 23 30 E
Truslove, *Australia* 61 F3 33 20S 121 45 E
Truth or Consequences, *U.S.A.* 83 K10 33 8N 107 15W
Trutnov, *Czech.* 16 C8 50 37N 15 54 E
Tryon, *U.S.A.* 77 H4 35 13N 82 14W
Tryonville, *U.S.A.* 78 E5 41 42N 79 48W
Tsaratanana, *Madag.* 57 B8 16 47S 47 39 E
Tsaratanana, Mt. de, *Madag.* 57 A8 14 0S 49 0 E
Tsarevo = Michurin, *Bulgaria* 21 C12 42 9N 27 51 E
Tsau, *Botswana* 56 C3 20 8S 22 22 E
Tselinograd = Aqmola, *Kazakstan* 26 D8 51 10N 71 30 E
Tsetserleg, *Mongolia* 32 B5 47 36N 101 32 E
Tshabong, *Botswana* 56 D3 26 2S 22 29 E
Tshane, *Botswana* 56 C3 24 5S 21 54 E
Tshela, *Zaïre* 52 E2 4 57S 13 4 E
Tshesebe, *Botswana* 57 C4 21 51S 27 32 E
Tshibeke, *Zaïre* 54 C2 2 40S 28 35 E
Tshibinda, *Zaïre* 54 C2 2 23S 28 43 E
Tshikapa, *Zaïre* 52 F4 6 28S 20 48 E
Tshilenge, *Zaïre* 54 D1 6 17S 23 48 E
Tshinsenda, *Zaïre* 55 E2 12 20S 28 0 E
Tshofa, *Zaïre* 54 D2 5 13S 25 16 E
Tshwane, *Botswana* 56 C3 22 24S 22 1 E
Tsigara, *Botswana* 56 C4 20 22S 25 54 E
Tsihombe, *Madag.* 57 D8 25 10S 45 41 E
Tsimlyansk Res. = Tsimlyanskoye Vdkhr., *Russia* 25 E7 48 0N 43 0 E
Tsimlyanskoye Vdkhr., *Russia* 25 E7 48 0N 43 0 E
Tsinan = Jinan, *China* 34 F9 36 38N 117 1 E
Tsineng, *S. Africa* 56 D3 27 5S 23 5 E
Tsinghai = Qinghai □, *China* 32 C4 36 0N 98 0 E
Tsingtao = Qingdao, *China* 35 F11 36 5N 120 20 E
Tsinjomitondraka, *Madag.* 57 B8 15 40S 47 8 E
Tsiroanomandidy, *Madag.* 57 B8 18 46S 46 2 E
Tsivory, *Madag.* 57 C8 24 4S 46 5 E
Tskhinvali, *Georgia* 25 F7 42 14N 44 1 E
Tsna →, *Russia* 24 D7 54 55N 41 58 E
Tso Moriri, L., *India* 43 C8 32 50N 78 20 E
Tsodilo Hill, *Botswana* 56 B3 18 49S 21 43 E
Tsogttsetsiy, *Mongolia* 34 C3 43 43N 105 35 E
Tsolo, *S. Africa* 57 E4 31 18S 28 37 E
Tsomo, *S. Africa* 57 E4 32 0S 27 42 E
Tsu, *Japan* 31 G8 34 45N 136 25 E
Tsu L., *Canada* 72 A6 60 40N 111 52W
Tsuchiura, *Japan* 31 F10 36 5N 140 15 E
Tsugaru-Kaikyō, *Japan* 30 D10 41 35N 141 0 E
Tsumeb, *Namibia* 56 B2 19 9S 17 44 E
Tsumis, *Namibia* 56 C2 23 39S 17 29 E
Tsuruga, *Japan* 31 G8 35 45N 136 2 E
Tsurugi-San, *Japan* 31 H7 33 51N 134 6 E
Tsuruoka, *Japan* 30 E9 38 44N 139 50 E
Tsushima, *Gifu, Japan* 31 G8 35 10N 136 43 E
Tsushima, *Nagasaki, Japan* 31 G4 34 20N 129 20 E
Tsyelyakhany, *Belarus* 17 B13 52 30N 25 46 E
Tual, *Indonesia* 37 F8 5 38S 132 44 E
Tuam, *Ireland* 13 C3 53 31N 8 51W
Tuamotu Arch. = Tuamotu Is., *Pac. Oc.* 65 J13 17 0S 144 0W
Tuamotu Is., *Pac. Oc.* 65 J13 17 0S 144 0W
Tuamotu Ridge, *Pac. Oc.* 65 K14 20 0S 138 0W
Tuao, *Phil.* 37 A6 17 55N 121 22 E
Tuapse, *Russia* 25 F6 44 5N 39 10 E
Tuatapere, *N.Z.* 59 M1 46 8S 167 41 E
Tuba City, *U.S.A.* 83 H8 36 8N 111 14W
Tuban, *Indonesia* 37 G15 6 54S 112 3 E
Tubarão, *Brazil* 95 B6 28 30S 49 0W
Ţūbās, *West Bank* 47 C4 32 20N 35 22 E
Tubau, *Malaysia* 36 D4 3 10N 113 40 E
Tübingen, *Germany* 16 D5 48 31N 9 4 E
Tubruq, *Libya* 51 B9 32 7N 23 55 E
Tubuai Is., *Pac. Oc.* 65 K12 25 0S 150 0W
Tuc Trung, *Vietnam* 39 G6 11 1N 107 12 E
Tucacas, *Venezuela* 92 A5 10 48N 68 19W
Tuchodi →, *Canada* 72 B4 58 17N 123 42W
Tucson, *U.S.A.* 83 K8 32 13N 110 58W
Tucumán □, *Argentina* 94 B2 26 48S 66 2W
Tucumcari, *U.S.A.* 81 H3 35 10N 103 44W
Tucupita, *Venezuela* 92 B6 9 2N 62 3W
Tucuruí, *Brazil* 93 D9 3 42S 49 44W
Tucuruí, Reprêsa de, *Brazil* 93 D9 4 0S 49 30W
Tudela, *Spain* 19 A5 42 4N 1 39W
Tudmur, *Syria* 44 C3 34 36N 38 15 E
Tudor, L., *Canada* 71 A6 55 50N 65 25W
Tuen, *Australia* 63 D4 28 33S 145 37 E
Tugela →, *S. Africa* 57 D5 29 14S 31 30 E
Tuguegarao, *Phil.* 37 A6 17 35N 121 42 E
Tugur, *Russia* 27 D14 53 44N 136 45 E
Tuineje, *Canary Is.* 22 F5 28 19N 14 3W
Tukangbesi, Kepulauan, *Indonesia* 37 F6 6 0S 124 0 E
Tukarak I., *Canada* 70 A4 56 15N 78 45W
Tukayyid, *Iraq* 44 D5 29 47N 45 36 E
Tūkrah, *Libya* 51 B9 32 30N 20 37 E
Tuktoyaktuk, *Canada* 68 B6 69 27N 133 2W
Tukums, *Latvia* 9 H20 57 2N 23 10 E
Tukuyu, *Tanzania* 55 D3 9 17S 33 35 E
Tula, *Hidalgo, Mexico* 87 C5 20 5N 99 20W
Tula, *Tamaulipas, Mexico* 87 C5 23 0N 99 40W
Tula, *Russia* 24 D6 54 13N 37 38 E
Tulancingo, *Mexico* 87 C5 20 5N 99 22W
Tulare, *U.S.A.* 83 H4 36 13N 119 21W
Tulare Lake Bed, *U.S.A.* 83 J4 36 0N 119 48W
Tularosa, *U.S.A.* 83 K10 33 5N 106 1W
Tulbagh, *S. Africa* 56 E2 33 16S 19 6 E
Tulcán, *Ecuador* 92 C3 0 48N 77 43W
Tulcea, *Romania* 17 F15 45 13N 28 46 E
Tulchyn, *Ukraine* 17 D15 48 41N 28 49 E
Tūleh, *Iran* 45 C7 34 35N 52 33 E
Tulemalu L., *Canada* 73 A9 62 58N 99 25W
Tuli, *Indonesia* 37 E6 1 24S 122 26 E
Tuli, *Zimbabwe* 55 G2 21 58S 29 13 E
Tulia, *U.S.A.* 81 H4 34 32N 101 46W
Tulita, *Canada* 68 B7 64 57N 125 30W
Ţūlkarm, *West Bank* 47 C4 32 19N 35 2 E
Tullahoma, *U.S.A.* 77 H2 35 22N 86 13W
Tullamore, *Australia* 63 E4 32 39S 147 36 E
Tullamore, *Ireland* 13 C4 53 16N 7 31W
Tulle, *France* 18 D4 45 16N 1 46 E
Tullibigeal, *Australia* 63 E4 33 25S 146 44 E
Tullow, *Ireland* 13 D4 52 49N 6 45W
Tully, *Australia* 62 B4 17 56S 145 55 E
Ţulmaythah, *Libya* 51 B9 32 40N 20 55 E
Tulmur, *Australia* 62 C3 22 40S 142 20 E
Tulsa, *U.S.A.* 81 G7 36 10N 95 55W
Tulsequah, *Canada* 72 B2 58 39N 133 35W
Tulua, *Colombia* 92 C3 4 6N 76 11W
Tulun, *Russia* 27 D11 54 32N 100 35 E
Tulungagung, *Indonesia* 36 F4 8 5S 111 54 E
Tum, *Indonesia* 37 E8 3 36S 130 21 E
Tuma →, *Nic.* 88 D3 13 6N 84 35W
Tumaco, *Colombia* 92 C3 1 50N 78 45W
Tumatumari, *Guyana* 92 B7 5 20N 58 55W
Tumba, *Sweden* 9 G17 59 12N 17 48 E
Tumba, L., *Zaïre* 52 E3 0 50S 18 0 E
Tumbarumba, *Australia* 63 F4 35 44S 148 0 E
Tumbaya, *Argentina* 94 A2 23 50S 65 26W
Túmbes, *Peru* 92 D2 3 37S 80 27W
Tumbwe, *Zaïre* 55 E2 11 25S 27 15 E
Tumby Bay, *Australia* 63 E2 34 21S 136 8 E
Tumd Youqi, *China* 34 D6 40 30N 110 30 E
Tumen, *China* 35 C15 43 0N 129 50 E
Tumen Jiang →, *China* 35 C16 42 20N 130 35 E
Tumeremo, *Venezuela* 92 B6 7 18N 61 30W
Tumkur, *India* 40 N10 13 18N 77 6 E
Tummel, L., *U.K.* 12 E5 56 43N 3 55W
Tump, *Pakistan* 40 F3 26 7N 62 16 E
Tumpat, *Malaysia* 39 J4 6 11N 102 10 E
Tumu, *Ghana* 50 F4 10 56N 1 56W
Tumucumaque, Serra, *Brazil* 93 C8 2 0N 55 0W
Tumut, *Australia* 63 F4 35 16S 148 13 E
Tumwater, *U.S.A.* 82 C2 47 1N 122 54W
Tunas de Zaza, *Cuba* 88 B4 21 39N 79 34W
Tunbridge Wells = Royal Tunbridge Wells, *U.K.* 11 F8 51 7N 0 16 E
Tuncurry, *Australia* 63 E5 32 17S 152 29 E
Tunduru, *Tanzania* 55 E4 11 8S 37 25 E
Tunduru □, *Tanzania* 55 E4 11 5S 37 22 E
Tundzha →, *Bulgaria* 21 C11 41 40N 26 35 E
Tunga Pass, *India* 41 E19 29 0N 94 14 E
Tungabhadra →, *India* 40 M11 15 57N 78 15 E
Tungaru, *Sudan* 51 F11 10 9N 30 52 E
Tungla, *Nic.* 88 D3 13 24N 84 21W
Tungsten, *Canada* 72 A3 61 57N 128 16W
Tunguska, Nizhnyaya →, *Russia* 27 C9 65 48N 88 4 E
Tunica, *U.S.A.* 81 H9 34 41N 90 23W
Tunis, *Tunisia* 50 A7 36 50N 10 11 E
Tunisia ■, *Africa* 50 B6 33 30N 9 10 E
Tunja, *Colombia* 92 B4 5 33N 73 25W
Tunkhannock, *U.S.A.* 79 E9 41 32N 75 57W
Tunliu, *China* 34 F7 36 13N 112 52 E
Tunnsjøen, *Norway* 8 D15 64 45N 13 25 E
Tunungayualok I., *Canada* 71 A7 56 0N 61 0W
Tunuyán, *Argentina* 94 C2 33 35S 69 0W
Tunuyán →, *Argentina* 94 C2 33 33S 67 30W
Tunxi, *China* 33 D6 29 42N 118 25 E
Tuolumne, *U.S.A.* 83 H3 37 58N 120 15W
Tuolumne →, *U.S.A.* 84 H5 37 36N 121 13W
Tuoy-Khaya, *Russia* 27 C12 62 32N 111 25 E
Tūp Āghāj, *Iran* 44 B5 36 3N 47 50 E
Tupã, *Brazil* 95 A5 21 57S 50 28W
Tupelo, *U.S.A.* 77 H1 34 16N 88 43W
Tupik, *Russia* 27 D12 54 26N 119 57 E
Tupinambaranas, *Brazil* 92 D7 3 0S 58 0W
Tupiza, *Bolivia* 94 A2 21 30S 65 40W
Tupman, *U.S.A.* 85 K7 35 18N 119 21W
Tupper, *Canada* 72 B4 55 32N 120 1W
Tupper Lake, *U.S.A.* 79 B10 44 14N 74 28W
Tupungato, Cerro, *S. Amer.* 94 C2 33 15S 69 50W
Tuquan, *China* 35 B11 45 18N 121 38 E
Túquerres, *Colombia* 92 C3 1 5N 77 37W
Tura, *Russia* 27 C11 64 20N 100 17 E

Vienna

Usure, *Tanzania* **54 C3** 4 40S 34 22 E
Uta, *Indonesia* **37 E9** 4 33S 136 0 E
Utah □, *U.S.A.* **82 G8** 39 20N 111 30W
Utah, L., *U.S.A.* **82 F8** 40 10N 111 58W
Ute Creek →, *U.S.A.* **81 H3** 35 21N 103 50W
Utena, *Lithuania* **9 J21** 55 27N 25 40 E
Utete, *Tanzania* **54 D4** 8 0S 38 45 E
Uthai Thani, *Thailand* **38 E3** 15 22N 100 3 E
Uthal, *Pakistan* **42 G2** 25 44N 66 40 E
Utiariti, *Brazil* **92 F7** 13 0S 58 10W
Utica, *N.Y., U.S.A.* **79 C9** 43 6N 75 14W
Utica, *Ohio, U.S.A.* **78 F2** 40 14N 82 27W
Utik L., *Canada* **73 B9** 55 15N 96 0W
Utikuma L., *Canada* **72 B5** 55 50N 115 30W
Utrecht, *Neths.* **15 B5** 52 5N 5 8 E
Utrecht, *S. Africa* **57 D5** 27 38S 30 20 E
Utrecht □, *Neths.* **15 B5** 52 6N 5 7 E
Utrera, *Spain* **19 D3** 37 12N 5 48W
Utsjoki, *Finland* **8 B22** 69 51N 26 59 E
Utsunomiya, *Japan* **31 F9** 36 30N 139 50 E
Uttar Pradesh □, *India* **43 F9** 27 0N 80 0 E
Uttaradit, *Thailand* **38 D3** 17 36N 100 5 E
Uttoxeter, *U.K.* **10 E6** 52 54N 1 52W
Uummannarsuaq = Farvel, Kap, *Greenland* **4 D5** 59 48N 43 55W
Uusikaarlepyy, *Finland* **8 E20** 63 32N 22 31 E
Uusikaupunki, *Finland* **9 F19** 60 47N 21 25 E
Uva, *Russia* **24 C9** 56 59N 52 13 E
Uvalde, *U.S.A.* **81 L5** 29 13N 99 47W
Uvat, *Russia* **26 D7** 59 5N 68 50 E
Uvinza, *Tanzania* **54 D3** 5 5S 30 24 E
Uvira, *Zaïre* **54 C2** 3 22S 29 3 E
Uvs Nuur, *Mongolia* **32 A4** 50 20N 92 30 E
Uwajima, *Japan* **31 H6** 33 10N 132 35 E
Uxbridge, *Canada* **78 B5** 44 6N 79 7W
Uxin Qi, *China* **34 E5** 38 50N 109 5 E
Uxmal, *Mexico* **87 C7** 20 22N 89 46W
Uyandi, *Russia* **27 C15** 69 19N 141 0 E
Uyuni, *Bolivia* **92 H5** 20 28S 66 47W
Uzbekistan ■, *Asia* **26 E7** 41 30N 65 0 E
Uzen, *Kazakstan* **25 F9** 43 29N 52 54 E
Uzerche, *France* **18 D4** 45 25N 1 34 E
Uzh →, *Ukraine* **17 C16** 51 15N 30 12 E
Uzhgorod = Uzhhorod, *Ukraine* **17 D12** 48 36N 22 18 E
Uzhhorod, *Ukraine* **17 D12** 48 36N 22 18 E
Uzunköprü, *Turkey* **21 D12** 41 16N 26 43 E

V

Vaal →, *S. Africa* **56 D3** 29 4S 23 38 E
Vaal Dam, *S. Africa* **57 D4** 27 0S 28 14 E
Vaalwater, *S. Africa* **57 C4** 24 15S 28 8 E
Vaasa, *Finland* **8 E19** 63 6N 21 38 E
Vác, *Hungary* **17 E10** 47 49N 19 10 E
Vacaria, *Brazil* **95 B5** 28 31S 50 52W
Vacaville, *U.S.A.* **84 G5** 38 21N 121 59W
Vach → = Vakh →, *Russia* **26 C8** 60 45N 76 45 E
Vache, Î.-à-, *Haiti* **89 C5** 18 2N 73 35W
Vadnagar, *India* **42 H5** 23 47N 72 40 E
Vadodara, *India* **42 H5** 22 20N 73 10 E
Vadsø, *Norway* **8 A23** 70 3N 29 50 E
Vaduz, *Liech.* **16 E5** 47 8N 9 31 E
Værøy, *Norway* **8 C15** 67 40N 12 40 E
Vágar, *Færoe Is.* **8 E9** 62 5N 7 15W
Vågsfjorden, *Norway* **8 B17** 68 50N 16 50 E
Váh →, *Slovak Rep.* **17 D9** 47 43N 18 7 E
Vahsel B., *Antarctica* **5 D1** 75 0S 35 0W
Vaï, *Greece* **23 D8** 35 15N 26 18 E
Vaigach, *Russia* **26 B6** 70 10N 59 0 E
Vakh →, *Russia* **26 C8** 60 45N 76 45 E
Val d'Or, *Canada* **70 C4** 48 7N 77 47W
Val Marie, *Canada* **73 D7** 49 15N 107 45W
Valahia, *Romania* **17 F13** 44 35N 25 0 E
Valandovo, *Macedonia* **21 D10** 41 19N 22 34 E
Valcheta, *Argentina* **96 E3** 40 40S 66 8W
Valdayskaya Vozvyshennost, *Russia* **24 C5** 57 0N 33 30 E
Valdepeñas, *Spain* **19 C4** 38 43N 3 25W
Valdés, Pen., *Argentina* **96 E4** 42 30S 63 45W
Valdez, *U.S.A.* **68 B5** 61 7N 146 16W
Valdivia, *Chile* **96 D2** 39 50S 73 14W
Valdosta, *U.S.A.* **77 K4** 30 50N 83 17W
Valdres, *Norway* **9 F13** 61 5N 9 5 E
Vale, *U.S.A.* **82 E5** 43 59N 117 15W
Vale of Glamorgan □, *U.K.* **11 F4** 51 28N 3 25W
Valença, *Brazil* **93 F11** 13 20S 39 5W
Valença do Piaui, *Brazil* **93 E10** 6 20S 41 45W
Valence, *France* **18 D6** 44 57N 4 54 E
Valencia, *Spain* **19 C5** 39 27N 0 23W
Valencia, *Venezuela* **92 A5** 10 11N 68 0W
Valencia □, *Spain* **19 C5** 39 20N 0 40W
Valencia, G. de, *Spain* **19 C6** 39 30N 0 20 E
Valencia de Alcántara, *Spain* **19 C2** 39 25N 7 14W
Valencia Harbour, *Ireland* **13 E1** 51 56N 10 19W
Valencia I., *Ireland* **13 E1** 51 54N 10 22W
Valenciennes, *France* **18 A5** 50 20N 3 34 E
Valentim, Sa. do, *Brazil* **93 E10** 6 0S 43 30W
Valentin, *Russia* **30 C7** 43 8N 134 17 E
Valentine, *Nebr., U.S.A.* **80 D4** 42 52N 100 33W
Valentine, *Tex., U.S.A.* **81 K2** 30 35N 104 30W
Valera, *Venezuela* **92 B4** 9 19N 70 37W
Valga, *Estonia* **9 H22** 57 47N 26 2 E
Valier, *U.S.A.* **82 B7** 48 18N 112 16W
Valjevo, *Serbia, Yug.* **21 B8** 44 18N 19 53 E
Valka, *Latvia* **9 H21** 57 42N 25 57 E
Valkeakoski, *Finland* **9 F20** 61 16N 24 2 E
Valkenswaard, *Neths.* **15 C5** 51 21N 5 29 E
Vall de Uxó, *Spain* **19 C5** 39 49N 0 15W
Valladolid, *Mexico* **87 C7** 20 40N 88 11W
Valladolid, *Spain* **19 B3** 41 38N 4 43W
Valldemosa, *Spain* **22 B9** 39 43N 2 37 E
Valle de la Pascua, *Venezuela* **92 B5** 9 13N 66 0W
Valle de las Palmas, *Mexico* **85 N10** 32 20N 116 43W
Valle de Santiago, *Mexico* **86 C4** 20 25N 101 15W
Valle de Suchil, *Mexico* **86 C4** 23 38N 103 55W
Valle de Zaragoza, *Mexico* **86 B3** 27 28N 105 49W
Valle Fértil, Sierra del, *Argentina* **94 C2** 30 20S 68 0W
Valle Hermoso, *Mexico* **87 B5** 25 35N 97 40W
Valledupar, *Colombia* **92 A4** 10 29N 73 15W
Vallehermoso, *Canary Is.* **22 F2** 28 10N 17 15W
Vallejo, *U.S.A.* **84 G4** 38 7N 122 14W
Vallenar, *Chile* **94 B1** 28 30S 70 50W
Valletta, *Malta* **23 D2** 35 54N 14 31 E
Valley Center, *U.S.A.* **85 M9** 33 13N 117 2W
Valley City, *U.S.A.* **80 B6** 46 55N 98 0W
Valley Falls, *U.S.A.* **82 E3** 42 29N 120 17W
Valley Springs, *U.S.A.* **84 G6** 38 12N 120 50W
Valley Wells, *U.S.A.* **85 K11** 35 27N 115 46W
Valleyview, *Canada* **72 B5** 55 5N 117 17W
Vallimanca, Arroyo, *Argentina* **94 D4** 35 40S 59 10W
Valls, *Spain* **19 B6** 41 18N 1 15 E
Valmiera, *Latvia* **9 H21** 57 37N 25 29 E
Valognes, *France* **18 B3** 49 30N 1 28W
Valona = Vlóra, *Albania* **21 D8** 40 32N 19 28 E
Valozhyn, *Belarus* **17 A14** 54 3N 26 30 E
Valparaíso, *Chile* **94 C1** 33 2S 71 40W
Valparaíso, *Mexico* **86 C4** 22 50N 103 32W
Valparaiso, *U.S.A.* **76 E2** 41 28N 87 4W
Valparaíso □, *Chile* **94 C1** 33 2S 71 40W
Vals →, *S. Africa* **56 D4** 27 23S 26 30 E
Vals, Tanjung, *Indonesia* **37 F9** 8 26S 137 25 E
Valsad, *India* **40 J8** 20 40N 72 58 E
Valverde, *Canary Is.* **22 G2** 27 48N 17 55W
Valverde del Camino, *Spain* **19 D2** 37 35N 6 47W
Vammala, *Finland* **9 F20** 61 20N 22 54 E
Vámos, *Greece* **23 D6** 35 24N 24 13 E
Van, *Turkey* **25 G7** 38 30N 43 20 E
Van, L. = Van Gölü, *Turkey* **25 G7** 38 30N 43 0 E
Van Alstyne, *U.S.A.* **81 J6** 33 25N 96 35W
Van Bruyssel, *Canada* **71 C5** 47 56N 72 9W
Van Buren, *Canada* **71 C6** 47 10N 67 55W
Van Buren, *Ark., U.S.A.* **81 H7** 35 26N 94 21W
Van Buren, *Maine, U.S.A.* **77 B11** 47 10N 67 58W
Van Buren, *Mo., U.S.A.* **81 G9** 37 0N 91 1W
Van Canh, *Vietnam* **38 F7** 13 37N 109 0 E
Van Diemen, C., *N. Terr., Australia* **60 B5** 11 9S 130 24 E
Van Diemen, C., *Queens., Australia* **62 B2** 16 30S 139 46 E
Van Diemen G., *Australia* **60 B5** 11 45S 132 0 E
Van Gölü, *Turkey* **25 G7** 38 30N 43 0 E
Van Horn, *U.S.A.* **81 K2** 31 3N 104 50W
Van Ninh, *Vietnam* **38 F7** 12 42N 109 14 E
Van Rees, Pegunungan, *Indonesia* **37 E9** 2 35S 138 15 E
Van Tassell, *U.S.A.* **80 D2** 42 40N 104 5W
Van Wert, *U.S.A.* **76 E3** 40 52N 84 35W
Van Yen, *Vietnam* **38 B5** 21 4N 104 42 E
Vanadzor, *Armenia* **25 F7** 40 48N 44 30 E
Vanavara, *Russia* **27 C11** 60 22N 102 16 E
Vancouver, *Canada* **72 D4** 49 15N 123 10W
Vancouver, *U.S.A.* **84 E4** 45 38N 122 40W
Vancouver, C., *Australia* **61 G2** 35 2S 118 11 E
Vancouver I., *Canada* **72 D3** 49 50N 126 0W
Vandalia, *Ill., U.S.A.* **80 F10** 38 58N 89 6W
Vandalia, *Mo., U.S.A.* **80 F9** 39 19N 91 29W
Vandenburg, *U.S.A.* **85 L6** 34 35N 120 33W
Vanderbijlpark, *S. Africa* **57 D4** 26 42S 27 54 E
Vandergrift, *U.S.A.* **78 F5** 40 36N 79 34W
Vanderhoof, *Canada* **72 C4** 54 0N 124 0W
Vanderkloof Dam, *S. Africa* **56 E3** 30 4S 24 40 E
Vanderlin I., *Australia* **62 B2** 15 44S 137 2 E
Vandyke, *Australia* **62 C4** 24 10S 147 51 E
Vänern, *Sweden* **9 G15** 58 47N 13 30 E
Vänersborg, *Sweden* **9 G15** 58 26N 12 19 E
Vang Vieng, *Laos* **38 C4** 18 58N 102 32 E
Vanga, *Kenya* **54 C4** 4 35S 39 12 E
Vangaindrano, *Madag.* **57 C8** 23 21S 47 36 E
Vanguard, *Canada* **73 D7** 49 55N 107 20W
Vanier, *Canada* **70 C4** 45 27N 75 40W
Vankleek Hill, *Canada* **70 C5** 45 32N 74 40W
Vanna, *Norway* **8 A18** 70 6N 19 50 E
Vännäs, *Sweden* **8 E18** 63 58N 19 48 E
Vannes, *France* **18 C2** 47 40N 2 47W
Vanrhynsdorp, *S. Africa* **56 E2** 31 36S 18 44 E
Vanrook, *Australia* **62 B3** 16 57S 141 57 E
Vansbro, *Sweden* **9 F16** 60 32N 14 15 E
Vansittart B., *Australia* **60 B4** 14 3S 126 17 E
Vantaa, *Finland* **9 F21** 60 18N 24 58 E
Vanthli, *India* **42 J4** 21 28N 70 25 E
Vanua Levu, *Fiji* **59 C8** 16 33S 179 15 E
Vanua Mbalavu, *Fiji* **59 C9** 17 40S 178 57W
Vanuatu ■, *Pac. Oc.* **64 J8** 15 0S 168 0 E
Vanwyksvlei, *S. Africa* **56 E3** 30 18S 21 49 E
Vanzylsrus, *S. Africa* **56 D3** 26 52S 22 4 E
Vapnyarka, *Ukraine* **17 D15** 48 32N 28 45 E
Varanasi, *India* **43 G10** 25 22N 83 0 E
Varanger-halvøya, *Norway* **8 A23** 70 25N 29 30 E
Varangerfjorden, *Norway* **8 A23** 70 3N 29 25 E
Varaždin, *Croatia* **16 E9** 46 20N 16 20 E
Varberg, *Sweden* **9 H15** 57 6N 12 20 E
Vardar = Axiós →, *Greece* **21 D10** 40 57N 22 35 E
Varde, *Denmark* **9 J13** 55 38N 8 29 E
Vardø, *Norway* **8 A24** 70 23N 31 5 E
Varella, Mui, *Vietnam* **38 F7** 12 54N 109 26 E
Varena, *Lithuania* **9 J21** 54 12N 24 30 E
Varese, *Italy* **20 B3** 45 48N 8 50 E
Varginha, *Brazil* **95 A6** 21 33S 45 25W
Variadero, *U.S.A.* **81 H2** 35 43N 104 17W
Varillas, *Chile* **94 A1** 24 0S 70 10W
Varkaus, *Finland* **9 E22** 62 19N 27 50 E
Varna, *Bulgaria* **21 C12** 43 13N 27 56 E
Värnamo, *Sweden* **9 H16** 57 10N 14 3 E
Vars, *Canada* **79 A9** 45 21N 75 21W
Varzaneh, *Iran* **45 C7** 32 25N 52 40 E
Vasa Barris →, *Brazil* **93 F11** 11 10S 37 10W
Vascongadas = País Vasco □, *Spain* **19 A4** 42 50N 2 45W
Vasht = Khāsh, *Iran* **40 E2** 28 15N 61 15 E
Vasilevichi, *Belarus* **17 B15** 52 15N 29 50 E
Vasilkov = Vasylkiv, *Ukraine* **17 C16** 50 7N 30 15 E
Vaslui, *Romania* **17 E14** 46 38N 27 42 E
Vassar, *Canada* **73 D9** 49 10N 95 55W
Vassar, *U.S.A.* **76 D4** 43 22N 83 35W
Västerås, *Sweden* **9 G17** 59 37N 16 38 E
Västerbotten, *Sweden* **8 D18** 64 36N 20 4 E
Västerdalälven →, *Sweden* **9 F16** 60 30N 14 7 E
Västervik, *Sweden* **9 H17** 57 43N 16 33 E
Västmanland, *Sweden* **9 G16** 59 45N 16 20 E
Vasto, *Italy* **20 C6** 42 8N 14 40 E
Vasylkiv, *Ukraine* **17 C16** 50 7N 30 15 E
Vatican City ■, *Europe* **20 D5** 41 54N 12 27 E
Vatili, *Cyprus* **23 D12** 35 6N 33 40 E
Vatnajökull, *Iceland* **8 D5** 64 30N 16 48W
Vatoa, *Fiji* **59 D9** 19 50S 178 13W
Vatólakkos, *Greece* **23 D5** 35 27N 23 53 E
Vatoloha, *Madag.* **57 B8** 17 52S 47 48 E
Vatomandry, *Madag.* **57 B8** 19 20S 48 59 E
Vatra-Dornei, *Romania* **17 E13** 47 22N 25 22 E
Vättern, *Sweden* **9 G16** 58 25N 14 30 E
Vaughn, *Mont., U.S.A.* **82 C8** 47 33N 111 33W
Vaughn, *N. Mex., U.S.A.* **83 J11** 34 36N 105 13W
Vaupés = Uaupés →, *Brazil* **92 C5** 0 2N 67 16W
Vauxhall, *Canada* **72 C6** 50 5N 112 9W
Vava'u, *Tonga* **59 D11** 18 36S 174 0W
Vawkavysk, *Belarus* **17 B13** 53 9N 24 30 E
Växjö, *Sweden* **9 H16** 56 52N 14 50 E
Vaygach, Ostrov, *Russia* **26 C6** 70 0N 60 0 E
Váyia, Ákra, *Greece* **23 C10** 36 15N 28 11 E
Vechte →, *Neths.* **15 B6** 52 34N 6 6 E
Vedea →, *Romania* **17 G13** 43 53N 25 59 E
Vedia, *Argentina* **94 C3** 34 30S 61 31W
Vedra, I. del, *Spain* **22 C7** 38 52N 1 12 E
Veendam, *Neths.* **15 A6** 53 5N 6 52 E
Veenendaal, *Neths.* **15 B5** 52 2N 5 34 E
Vefsna →, *Norway* **8 D15** 65 48N 13 10 E
Vega, *Norway* **8 D14** 65 40N 11 55 E
Vega, *U.S.A.* **81 H3** 35 15N 102 26W
Veghel, *Neths.* **15 C5** 51 37N 5 32 E
Vegreville, *Canada* **72 C6** 53 30N 112 5W
Vejer de la Frontera, *Spain* **19 D3** 36 15N 5 59W
Vejle, *Denmark* **9 J13** 55 43N 9 30 E
Velas, C., *Costa Rica* **88 D2** 10 21N 85 52W
Velasco, Sierra de, *Argentina* **94 B2** 29 20S 67 10W
Velddrif, *S. Africa* **56 E2** 32 42S 18 11 E
Velebit Planina, *Croatia* **16 F8** 44 50N 15 20 E
Vélez, *Colombia* **92 B4** 6 1N 73 41W
Vélez Málaga, *Spain* **19 D3** 36 48N 4 5W
Vélez Rubio, *Spain* **19 D4** 37 41N 2 5W
Velhas →, *Brazil* **93 G10** 17 13S 44 49W
Velika Kapela, *Croatia* **16 F8** 45 10N 15 5 E
Velikaya →, *Russia* **24 C4** 57 48N 28 10 E
Velikaya Kema, *Russia* **30 B8** 45 30N 137 12 E
Veliki Ustyug, *Russia* **24 B8** 60 47N 46 20 E
Velikiye Luki, *Russia* **24 C5** 56 25N 30 32 E
Veliko Tŭrnovo, *Bulgaria* **21 C11** 43 5N 25 41 E
Velikonda Range, *India* **40 M11** 14 45N 79 10 E
Velletri, *Italy* **20 D5** 41 41N 12 47 E
Vellore, *India* **40 N11** 12 57N 79 10 E
Velsen-Noord, *Neths.* **15 B4** 52 27N 4 40 E
Velsk, *Russia* **24 B7** 61 10N 42 5 E
Velva, *U.S.A.* **80 A4** 48 4N 100 56W
Venado Tuerto, *Argentina* **94 C3** 33 50S 62 0W
Vendée □, *France* **18 C3** 46 50N 1 35W
Vendôme, *France* **18 C4** 47 47N 1 3 E
Venézia, *Italy* **20 B5** 45 27N 12 21 E
Venézia, G. di, *Italy* **20 B5** 45 15N 13 0 E
Venezuela ■, *S. Amer.* **92 B5** 8 0N 66 0W
Venezuela, G. de, *Venezuela* **92 A4** 11 30N 71 0W
Vengurla, *India* **40 M8** 15 53N 73 45 E
Venice = Venézia, *Italy* **20 B5** 45 27N 12 21 E
Venkatapuram, *India* **41 K12** 18 20N 80 30 E
Venlo, *Neths.* **15 C6** 51 22N 6 11 E
Vennesla, *Norway* **9 G12** 58 15N 8 0 E
Venraij, *Neths.* **15 C5** 51 31N 6 0 E
Ventana, Punta de la, *Mexico* **86 C3** 24 4N 109 48W
Ventana, Sa. de la, *Argentina* **94 D3** 38 0S 62 30W
Ventersburg, *S. Africa* **56 D4** 28 7S 27 9 E
Venterstad, *S. Africa* **56 E4** 30 47S 25 48 E
Ventnor, *U.K.* **11 G6** 50 36N 1 12W
Ventotene, *Italy* **20 D5** 40 47N 13 25 E
Ventoux, Mt., *France* **18 D6** 44 10N 5 17 E
Ventspils, *Latvia* **9 H19** 57 25N 21 32 E
Ventuarí →, *Venezuela* **92 C5** 3 58N 67 2W
Ventucopa, *U.S.A.* **85 L7** 34 50N 119 29W
Ventura, *U.S.A.* **85 L7** 34 17N 119 18W
Venus B., *Australia* **63 F4** 38 40S 145 42 E
Vera, *Argentina* **94 B3** 29 30S 60 20W
Vera, *Spain* **19 D5** 37 15N 1 51W
Veracruz, *Mexico* **87 D5** 19 10N 96 10W
Veracruz □, *Mexico* **87 D5** 19 0N 96 15W
Veraval, *India* **42 J4** 20 53N 70 27 E
Verbánia, *Italy* **20 B3** 45 56N 8 33 E
Vercelli, *Italy* **20 B3** 45 19N 8 25 E
Verdalsøra, *Norway* **8 E14** 63 48N 11 30 E
Verde →, *Argentina* **96 E3** 41 56S 65 5W
Verde →, *Chihuahua, Mexico* **86 B3** 26 29N 107 58W
Verde →, *Oaxaca, Mexico* **87 D5** 15 59N 97 50W
Verde →, *Veracruz, Mexico* **86 C4** 21 10N 102 50W
Verde →, *Paraguay* **94 A4** 23 9S 57 37W
Verde, Cay, *Bahamas* **88 B4** 23 0N 75 5W
Verden, *Germany* **16 B5** 52 55N 9 14 E
Verdi, *U.S.A.* **84 F7** 39 31N 119 59W
Verdigre, *U.S.A.* **80 D5** 42 36N 98 2W
Verdun, *France* **18 B6** 49 9N 5 24 E
Vereeniging, *S. Africa* **57 D4** 26 38S 27 57 E
Vérendrye, Parc Prov. de la, *Canada* **70 C4** 47 20N 76 40W
Verga, C., *Guinea* **50 F2** 10 30N 14 10W
Vergemont, *Australia* **62 C3** 23 33S 143 1 E
Vergemont Cr. →, *Australia* **62 C3** 24 16S 143 16 E
Vergennes, *U.S.A.* **79 B11** 44 10N 73 15W
Verín, *Spain* **19 B2** 41 57N 7 27W
Verkhnevilyuysk, *Russia* **27 C13** 63 27N 120 18 E
Verkhneye Kalinino, *Russia* **27 D11** 59 54N 108 8 E
Verkhniy Baskunchak, *Russia* **25 E8** 48 14N 46 44 E
Verkhnyaya Amga, *Russia* **27 D13** 59 50N 127 0 E
Verkhoyansk, *Russia* **27 C14** 67 35N 133 25 E
Verkhoyansk Ra. = Verkhoyanskiy Khrebet, *Russia* **27 C13** 66 0N 129 0 E
Verkhoyanskiy Khrebet, *Russia* **27 C13** 66 0N 129 0 E
Verlo, *Canada* **73 C7** 50 19N 108 35W
Vermilion, *Canada* **73 C6** 53 20N 110 50W
Vermilion →, *Alta., Canada* **73 C6** 53 22N 110 51W
Vermilion →, *Qué., Canada* **70 C5** 47 38N 72 56W
Vermilion, B., *U.S.A.* **81 L9** 29 45N 91 55W
Vermilion Bay, *Canada* **73 D10** 49 51N 93 34W
Vermilion Chutes, *Canada* **72 B6** 58 22N 114 51W
Vermilion L., *U.S.A.* **80 B8** 47 53N 92 26W
Vermillion, *U.S.A.* **80 D6** 42 47N 96 56W
Vermont □, *U.S.A.* **79 C12** 44 0N 73 0W
Vernal, *U.S.A.* **82 F9** 40 27N 109 32W
Vernalis, *U.S.A.* **84 H5** 37 36N 121 17W
Verner, *Canada* **70 C3** 46 25N 80 8W
Verneukpan, *S. Africa* **56 D3** 30 0S 21 0 E
Vernon, *Canada* **72 C5** 50 20N 119 15W
Vernon, *U.S.A.* **81 H5** 34 9N 99 17W
Vernonia, *U.S.A.* **84 E3** 45 52N 123 11W
Vero Beach, *U.S.A.* **77 M5** 27 38N 80 24W
Véroia, *Greece* **21 D10** 40 34N 22 12 E
Verona, *Italy* **20 B4** 45 27N 11 0 E
Versailles, *France* **18 B5** 48 48N 2 8 E
Vert, C., *Senegal* **50 F1** 14 45N 17 30W
Verulam, *S. Africa* **57 D5** 29 38S 31 2 E
Verviers, *Belgium* **15 D5** 50 37N 5 52 E
Veselovskoye Vdkhr., *Russia* **25 E7** 46 58N 41 25 E
Vesoul, *France* **18 C7** 47 40N 6 11 E
Vesterålen, *Norway* **8 B16** 68 45N 15 0 E
Vestfjorden, *Norway* **8 C15** 67 55N 14 0 E
Vestmannaeyjar, *Iceland* **8 E3** 63 27N 20 15W
Vestspitsbergen, *Svalbard* **4 B8** 78 40N 17 0 E
Vestvågøy, *Norway* **8 B15** 68 18N 13 50 E
Vesuvio, *Italy* **20 D6** 40 49N 14 26 E
Vesuvius, Mt. = Vesuvio, *Italy* **20 D6** 40 49N 14 26 E
Veszprém, *Hungary* **17 E9** 47 8N 17 57 E
Vetlanda, *Sweden* **9 H16** 57 24N 15 3 E
Vetlugu →, *Russia* **26 D5** 56 36N 46 4 E
Vettore, Mte., *Italy* **20 C5** 42 49N 13 16 E
Veurne, *Belgium* **15 C2** 51 5N 2 40 E
Veys, *Iran* **45 D6** 31 30N 49 0 E
Vezhen, *Bulgaria* **21 C11** 42 50N 24 20 E
Vi Thanh, *Vietnam* **39 H5** 9 42N 105 26 E
Viacha, *Bolivia* **92 G5** 16 39S 68 18W
Viamão, *Brazil* **95 C5** 30 5S 51 0W
Viana, *Brazil* **93 D10** 3 13S 44 55W
Viana do Alentejo, *Portugal* **19 C2** 38 17N 7 59W
Viana do Castelo, *Portugal* **19 B1** 41 42N 8 50W
Vianópolis, *Brazil* **93 G9** 16 40S 48 35W
Viaréggio, *Italy* **20 C4** 43 52N 10 14 E
Vibank, *Canada* **73 C8** 50 20N 103 56W
Vibo Valéntia, *Italy* **20 E7** 38 40N 16 6 E
Viborg, *Denmark* **9 H13** 56 27N 9 23 E
Vicenza, *Italy* **20 B4** 45 33N 11 33 E
Vich, *Spain* **19 B7** 41 58N 2 19 E
Vichy, *France* **18 C5** 46 9N 3 26 E
Vicksburg, *Ariz., U.S.A.* **85 M13** 33 45N 113 45W
Vicksburg, *Mich., U.S.A.* **76 D3** 42 7N 85 32W
Vicksburg, *Miss., U.S.A.* **81 J9** 32 21N 90 53W
Viçosa, *Brazil* **93 E11** 9 28S 36 14W
Victor, *India* **42 J4** 21 0N 71 30 E
Victor, *Colo., U.S.A.* **80 F2** 38 43N 105 9W
Victor, *N.Y., U.S.A.* **78 D7** 42 58N 77 24W
Victor Harbor, *Australia* **63 F2** 35 30S 138 37 E
Victoria, *Argentina* **94 C3** 32 40S 60 10W
Victoria, *Canada* **72 D4** 48 30N 123 25W
Victoria, *Chile* **96 D2** 38 13S 72 20W
Victoria, *Guinea* **50 F2** 10 50N 14 32W
Victoria, *Malaysia* **36 C5** 5 20N 115 14 E
Victoria, *Malta* **23 C1** 36 2N 14 14 E
Victoria, *Kans., U.S.A.* **80 F5** 38 52N 99 9W
Victoria, *Tex., U.S.A.* **81 L6** 28 48N 97 0W
Victoria □, *Australia* **63 F3** 37 0S 144 0 E
Victoria →, *Australia* **60 C4** 15 10S 129 40 E
Victoria, Grand L., *Canada* **70 C4** 47 31N 77 30W
Victoria, L., *Africa* **54 C3** 1 0S 33 0 E
Victoria, L., *Australia* **63 E3** 33 57S 141 15 E
Victoria Beach, *Canada* **73 C9** 50 40N 96 35W
Victoria de Durango, *Mexico* **86 C4** 24 3N 104 39W
Victoria de las Tunas, *Cuba* **88 B4** 20 58N 76 59W
Victoria Falls, *Zimbabwe* **55 F2** 17 58S 25 52 E
Victoria Harbour, *Canada* **70 D4** 44 45N 79 45W
Victoria I., *Canada* **68 A8** 71 0N 111 0W
Victoria Ld., *Antarctica* **5 D11** 75 0S 160 0 E
Victoria Nile →, *Uganda* **54 B3** 2 14N 31 26 E
Victoria Res., *Canada* **71 C8** 48 20N 57 27W
Victoria River Downs, *Australia* **60 C5** 16 25S 131 0 E
Victoria Taungdeik, *Burma* **41 J18** 21 15N 93 55 E
Victoria West, *S. Africa* **56 E3** 31 25S 23 4 E
Victoriaville, *Canada* **71 C5** 46 4N 71 56W
Victorica, *Argentina* **94 D2** 36 20S 65 30W
Victorville, *U.S.A.* **85 L9** 34 32N 117 18W
Vicuña, *Chile* **94 C1** 30 0S 70 50W
Vicuña Mackenna, *Argentina* **94 C3** 33 53S 64 25W
Vidal, *U.S.A.* **85 L12** 34 7N 114 31W
Vidal Junction, *U.S.A.* **85 L12** 34 11N 114 34W
Vidalia, *U.S.A.* **77 J4** 32 13N 82 25W
Vídho, *Greece* **23 A3** 39 38N 19 55 E
Vidin, *Bulgaria* **21 C10** 43 59N 22 50 E
Vidisha, *India* **42 H7** 23 28N 77 53 E
Vidzy, *Belarus* **9 J22** 55 23N 26 37 E
Viedma, *Argentina* **96 E4** 40 50S 63 0W
Viedma, L., *Argentina* **96 F2** 49 30S 72 30W
Vieng Pou Kha, *Laos* **38 B3** 20 41N 101 4 E
Vienna = Wien, *Austria* **16 D9** 48 12N 16 22 E

Westby

Wallingford, *U.S.A.* **79 E12** 41 27N 72 50W
Wallis & Futuna, Is., *Pac. Oc.* **64 J10** 13 18S 176 10W
Wallowa, *U.S.A.* **82 D5** 45 34N 117 32W
Wallowa Mts., *U.S.A.* **82 D5** 45 20N 117 30W
Wallsend, *Australia* **63 E5** 32 55S 151 40 E
Wallsend, *U.K.* **10 C6** 54 59N 1 31W
Wallula, *U.S.A.* **82 C4** 46 5N 118 54W
Wallumbilla, *Australia* **63 D4** 26 33S 149 9 E
Walmsley, L., *Canada* **73 A7** 63 25N 108 36W
Walney, I. of, *U.K.* **10 C4** 54 6N 3 15W
Walnut Creek, *U.S.A.* **84 H4** 37 54N 122 4W
Walnut Ridge, *U.S.A.* **81 G9** 36 4N 90 57W
Walsall, *U.K.* **11 E6** 52 35N 1 58W
Walsenburg, *U.S.A.* **81 G2** 37 38N 104 47W
Walsh, *U.S.A.* **81 G3** 37 23N 102 17W
Walsh →, *Australia* **62 B3** 16 31S 143 42 E
Walsh P.O., *Australia* **62 B3** 16 40S 144 0 E
Walterboro, *U.S.A.* **77 J5** 32 55N 80 40W
Walters, *U.S.A.* **81 H5** 34 22N 98 19W
Waltham, *U.S.A.* **79 D13** 42 23N 71 14W
Waltham Station, *Canada* **70 C4** 45 57N 76 57W
Waltman, *U.S.A.* **82 E10** 43 4N 107 12W
Walton, *U.S.A.* **79 D9** 42 10N 75 8W
Walvisbaai, *Namibia* **56 C1** 23 0S 14 28 E
Wamba, *Kenya* **54 B4** 0 58N 37 19 E
Wamba, *Zaïre* **54 B2** 2 10N 27 57 E
Wamego, *U.S.A.* **80 F6** 39 12N 96 18W
Wamena, *Indonesia* **37 E9** 4 4S 138 57 E
Wamulan, *Indonesia* **37 E7** 3 27S 126 7 E
Wan Xian, *China* **34 E8** 38 47N 115 7 E
Wana, *Pakistan* **42 C3** 32 20N 69 32 E
Wanaaring, *Australia* **63 D3** 29 38S 144 9 E
Wanaka, *N.Z.* **59 L2** 44 42S 169 9 E
Wanaka L., *N.Z.* **59 L2** 44 33S 169 7 E
Wanapiri, *Indonesia* **37 E9** 4 30S 135 59 E
Wanapitei L., *Canada* **70 C3** 46 45N 80 40W
Wanbi, *Australia* **63 E3** 34 46S 140 17 E
Wandarrie, *Australia* **61 E2** 27 50S 117 52 E
Wandel Sea = McKinley Sea, *Arctic* **4 A7** 82 0N 0 0 E
Wanderer, *Zimbabwe* **55 F3** 19 36S 30 1 E
Wandoan, *Australia* **63 D4** 26 5S 149 55 E
Wanfu, *China* **35 D12** 40 8N 122 38 E
Wang →, *Thailand* **38 D2** 17 8N 99 2 E
Wang Noi, *Thailand* **38 E3** 14 13N 100 44 E
Wang Saphung, *Thailand* **38 D3** 17 18N 101 46 E
Wang Thong, *Thailand* **38 D3** 16 50N 100 26 E
Wanga, *Zaïre* **54 B2** 2 58N 29 12 E
Wangal, *Indonesia* **37 F8** 6 8S 134 9 E
Wanganella, *Australia* **63 F3** 35 6S 144 49 E
Wanganui, *N.Z.* **59 H5** 39 56S 175 3 E
Wangaratta, *Australia* **63 F4** 36 21S 146 19 E
Wangary, *Australia* **63 E2** 34 35S 135 29 E
Wangdu, *China* **34 E8** 38 40N 115 7 E
Wangerooge, *Germany* **16 B4** 53 47N 7 54 E
Wangi, *Kenya* **54 C5** 1 58S 40 58 E
Wangiwangi, *Indonesia* **37 F6** 5 22S 123 37 E
Wangqing, *China* **35 C15** 43 12N 129 42 E
Wankaner, *India* **42 H4** 22 35N 71 0 E
Wanless, *Canada* **73 C8** 54 11N 101 21W
Wanon Niwat, *Thailand* **38 D4** 17 38N 103 46 E
Wanquan, *China* **34 D8** 40 50N 114 40 E
Wanrong, *China* **34 G6** 35 25N 110 50 E
Wanxian, *China* **33 C5** 30 42N 108 20 E
Wapakoneta, *U.S.A.* **76 E3** 40 34N 84 12W
Wapato, *U.S.A.* **82 C3** 46 27N 120 25W
Wapawekka L., *Canada* **73 C8** 54 55N 104 40W
Wapikopa L., *Canada* **70 B2** 52 56N 87 53W
Wappingers Falls, *U.S.A.* **79 E11** 41 36N 73 55W
Wapsipinicon →, *U.S.A.* **80 E9** 41 44N 90 19W
Warangal, *India* **40 L11** 17 58N 79 35 E
Waratah, *Australia* **62 G4** 41 30S 145 30 E
Waratah B., *Australia* **63 F4** 38 54S 146 5 E
Warburton, *Vic., Australia* **63 F4** 37 47S 145 42 E
Warburton, *W. Austral., Australia* **61 E4** 26 8S 126 35 E
Warburton Ra., *Australia* **61 E4** 25 55S 126 28 E
Ward, *N.Z.* **59 J5** 41 49S 174 11 E
Ward →, *Australia* **63 D4** 26 28S 146 6 E
Ward Cove, *U.S.A.* **72 B2** 55 25N 132 43W
Ward Mt., *U.S.A.* **84 H8** 37 12N 118 54W
Warden, *S. Africa* **57 D4** 27 50S 29 0 E
Wardha, *India* **40 J11** 20 45N 78 39 E
Wardha →, *India* **40 K11** 19 57N 79 11 E
Wardlow, *Canada* **72 C6** 50 56N 111 31W
Ware, *Canada* **72 B3** 57 26N 125 41W
Ware, *U.S.A.* **79 D12** 42 16N 72 14W
Wareham, *U.S.A.* **79 E14** 41 46N 70 43W
Warialda, *Australia* **63 D5** 29 29S 150 33 E
Wariap, *Indonesia* **37 E8** 1 30S 134 5 E
Warin Chamrap, *Thailand* **38 E5** 15 12N 104 53 E
Warkopi, *Indonesia* **37 E8** 1 12S 134 9 E
Warley, *U.K.* **11 E6** 52 30N 1 59W
Warm Springs, *U.S.A.* **83 G5** 38 10N 116 20W
Warman, *Canada* **73 C7** 52 19N 106 30W
Warmbad, *Namibia* **56 D2** 28 25S 18 42 E
Warmbad, *S. Africa* **57 C4** 24 51S 28 19 E
Warnambool Downs, *Australia* **62 C3** 22 48S 142 52 E
Warner, *Canada* **72 D6** 49 17N 112 12W
Warner Mts., *U.S.A.* **82 F3** 41 40N 120 15W
Warner Robins, *U.S.A.* **77 J4** 32 37N 83 36W
Waroona, *Australia* **61 F2** 32 50S 115 58 E
Warracknabeal, *Australia* **63 F3** 36 9S 142 26 E
Warragul, *Australia* **63 F4** 38 10S 145 58 E
Warrawagine, *Australia* **60 D3** 20 51S 120 42 E
Warrego →, *Australia* **63 E4** 30 24S 145 21 E
Warrego Ra., *Australia* **62 C4** 24 58S 146 0 E
Warren, *Australia* **63 E4** 31 42S 147 51 E
Warren, *Ark., U.S.A.* **81 J8** 33 37N 92 4W
Warren, *Mich., U.S.A.* **76 D4** 42 30N 83 0W
Warren, *Minn., U.S.A.* **80 A6** 48 12N 96 46W
Warren, *Ohio, U.S.A.* **78 E4** 41 14N 80 49W
Warren, *Pa., U.S.A.* **78 E5** 41 51N 79 9W
Warrenpoint, *U.K.* **13 B5** 54 6N 6 15W
Warrensburg, *U.S.A.* **80 F8** 38 46N 93 44W
Warrenton, *S. Africa* **56 D3** 28 9S 24 47 E
Warrenton, *U.S.A.* **84 D3** 46 10N 123 56W
Warrenville, *Australia* **63 D4** 25 48S 147 22 E
Warri, *Nigeria* **50 G6** 5 30N 5 41 E
Warrina, *Australia* **63 D2** 28 12S 135 50 E
Warrington, *U.K.* **10 D5** 53 24N 2 35W
Warrington, *U.S.A.* **77 K2** 30 23N 87 17W
Warrnambool, *Australia* **63 F3** 38 25S 142 30 E
Warroad, *U.S.A.* **80 A7** 48 54N 95 19W
Warsa, *Indonesia* **37 E9** 0 47S 135 55 E
Warsaw = Warszawa, *Poland* **17 B11** 52 13N 21 0 E
Warsaw, *Ind., U.S.A.* **76 E3** 41 14N 85 51W
Warsaw, *N.Y., U.S.A.* **78 D6** 42 45N 78 8W
Warsaw, *Ohio, U.S.A.* **78 F2** 40 20N 82 0W
Warszawa, *Poland* **17 B11** 52 13N 21 0 E
Warta →, *Poland* **16 B8** 52 35N 14 39 E
Warthe = Warta →, *Poland* **16 B8** 52 35N 14 39 E
Waru, *Indonesia* **37 E8** 3 30S 130 36 E
Warwick, *Australia* **63 D5** 28 10S 152 1 E
Warwick, *U.K.* **11 E6** 52 18N 1 35W
Warwick, *U.S.A.* **79 E13** 41 42N 71 28W
Warwickshire □, *U.K.* **11 E6** 52 14N 1 38W
Wasaga Beach, *Canada* **78 B4** 44 31N 80 1W
Wasatch Ra., *U.S.A.* **82 F8** 40 30N 111 15W
Wasbank, *S. Africa* **57 D5** 28 15S 30 9 E
Wasco, *Calif., U.S.A.* **85 K7** 35 36N 119 20W
Wasco, *Oreg., U.S.A.* **82 D3** 45 36N 120 42W
Waseca, *U.S.A.* **80 C8** 44 5N 93 30W
Wasekamio L., *Canada* **73 B7** 56 45N 108 45W
Wash, The, *U.K.* **10 E8** 52 58N 0 20 E
Washago, *Canada* **78 B5** 44 45N 79 20W
Washburn, *N. Dak., U.S.A.* **80 B4** 47 17N 101 2W
Washburn, *Wis., U.S.A.* **80 B9** 46 40N 90 54W
Washim, *India* **40 J10** 20 3N 77 0 E
Washington, *D.C., U.S.A.* **76 F7** 38 54N 77 2W
Washington, *Ga., U.S.A.* **77 J4** 33 44N 82 44W
Washington, *Ind., U.S.A.* **76 F2** 38 40N 87 10W
Washington, *Iowa, U.S.A.* **80 E9** 41 18N 91 42W
Washington, *Mo., U.S.A.* **80 F9** 38 33N 91 1W
Washington, *N.C., U.S.A.* **77 H7** 35 33N 77 3W
Washington, *N.J., U.S.A.* **79 F10** 40 46N 74 59W
Washington, *Pa., U.S.A.* **78 F4** 40 10N 80 15W
Washington, *Utah, U.S.A.* **83 H7** 37 8N 113 31W
Washington □, *U.S.A.* **82 C3** 47 30N 120 30W
Washington, Mt., *U.S.A.* **79 B13** 44 16N 71 18W
Washington I., *U.S.A.* **76 C2** 45 23N 86 54W
Washougal, *U.S.A.* **84 E4** 45 35N 122 21W
Wasian, *Indonesia* **37 E8** 1 47S 133 19 E
Wasior, *Indonesia* **37 E8** 2 43S 134 30 E
Waskaganish, *Canada* **70 B4** 51 30N 78 40W
Waskaiowaka, L., *Canada* **73 B9** 56 33N 96 23W
Waskesiu Lake, *Canada* **73 C7** 53 55N 106 5W
Wassenaar, *Neths.* **15 B4** 52 8N 4 24 E
Wasserkuppe, *Germany* **16 C5** 50 29N 9 55 E
Waswanipi, *Canada* **70 C4** 49 40N 76 29W
Waswanipi, L., *Canada* **70 C4** 49 35N 76 40W
Watangpone, *Indonesia* **37 E6** 4 29S 120 25 E
Water Park Pt., *Australia* **62 C5** 22 56S 150 47 E
Water Valley, *U.S.A.* **81 H10** 34 10N 89 38W
Waterberge, *S. Africa* **57 C4** 24 10S 28 0 E
Waterbury, *Conn., U.S.A.* **79 E11** 41 33N 73 3W
Waterbury, *Vt., U.S.A.* **79 B12** 44 20N 72 46W
Waterbury L., *Canada* **73 B8** 58 10N 104 22W
Waterdown, *Canada* **78 C5** 43 20N 79 53W
Waterford, *Canada* **78 D4** 42 56N 80 17W
Waterford, *Ireland* **13 D4** 52 15N 7 8W
Waterford, *U.S.A.* **84 H6** 37 38N 120 46W
Waterford □, *Ireland* **13 D4** 52 10N 7 40W
Waterford Harbour, *Ireland* **13 D5** 52 8N 6 58W
Waterhen L., *Man., Canada* **73 C9** 52 10N 99 40W
Waterhen L., *Sask., Canada* **73 C7** 54 28N 108 25W
Waterloo, *Belgium* **15 D4** 50 43N 4 25 E
Waterloo, *Ont., Canada* **70 D3** 43 30N 80 32W
Waterloo, *Qué., Canada* **79 A12** 45 22N 72 32W
Waterloo, *S. Leone* **50 G2** 8 26N 13 8W
Waterloo, *Ill., U.S.A.* **80 F9** 38 20N 90 9W
Waterloo, *Iowa, U.S.A.* **80 D8** 42 30N 92 21W
Waterloo, *N.Y., U.S.A.* **78 D8** 42 54N 76 52W
Watersmeet, *U.S.A.* **80 B10** 46 16N 89 11W
Waterton-Glacier International Peace Park, *U.S.A.* **82 B7** 48 45N 115 0W
Watertown, *Conn., U.S.A.* **79 E11** 41 36N 73 7W
Watertown, *N.Y., U.S.A.* **79 C9** 43 59N 75 55W
Watertown, *S. Dak., U.S.A.* **80 C6** 44 54N 97 7W
Watertown, *Wis., U.S.A.* **80 D10** 43 12N 88 43W
Waterval-Boven, *S. Africa* **57 D5** 25 40S 30 18 E
Waterville, *Canada* **79 A13** 45 16N 71 54W
Waterville, *Maine, U.S.A.* **71 D6** 44 33N 69 38W
Waterville, *N.Y., U.S.A.* **79 D9** 42 56N 75 23W
Waterville, *Pa., U.S.A.* **78 E7** 41 19N 77 21W
Waterville, *Wash., U.S.A.* **82 C3** 47 39N 120 4W
Watervliet, *U.S.A.* **79 D11** 42 44N 73 42W
Wates, *Indonesia* **37 G14** 7 51S 110 10 E
Watford, *Canada* **78 D3** 42 57N 81 53W
Watford, *U.K.* **11 F7** 51 40N 0 24W
Watford City, *U.S.A.* **80 B3** 47 48N 103 17W
Wathaman →, *Canada* **73 B8** 57 16N 102 59W
Watheroo, *Australia* **61 F2** 30 15S 116 0 E
Wating, *China* **34 G4** 35 40N 106 38 E
Watkins Glen, *U.S.A.* **78 D8** 42 23N 76 52W
Watling I. = San Salvador, *Bahamas* **89 B5** 24 0N 74 40W
Watonga, *U.S.A.* **81 H5** 35 51N 98 25W
Watrous, *Canada* **73 C7** 51 40N 105 25W
Watrous, *U.S.A.* **81 H2** 35 48N 104 59W
Watsa, *Zaïre* **54 B2** 3 4N 29 30 E
Watseka, *U.S.A.* **76 E2** 40 47N 87 44W
Watson, *Australia* **61 F5** 30 29S 131 31 E
Watson, *Canada* **73 C8** 52 10N 104 30W
Watson Lake, *Canada* **72 A3** 60 6N 128 49W
Watsonville, *U.S.A.* **83 H3** 36 55N 121 45W
Wattiwarriganna Cr. →, *Australia* **63 D2** 28 57S 136 10 E
Watuata = Batuata, *Indonesia* **37 F6** 6 12S 122 42 E
Watubela, Kepulauan, *Indonesia* **37 E8** 4 28S 131 35 E
Watubela Is. = Watubela, Kepulauan, *Indonesia* **37 E8** 4 28S 131 35 E
Wau, *Sudan* **49 F6** 7 45N 28 1 E
Waubamik, *Canada* **78 A4** 45 27N 80 1W
Waubay, *U.S.A.* **80 C6** 45 20N 97 18W
Waubra, *Australia* **63 F3** 37 21S 143 39 E
Wauchope, *Australia* **63 E5** 31 28S 152 45 E
Wauchula, *U.S.A.* **77 M5** 27 33N 81 49W
Waugh, *Canada* **73 D9** 49 40N 95 11W
Waukarlycarly, L., *Australia* **60 D3** 21 18S 121 56 E
Waukegan, *U.S.A.* **76 D2** 42 22N 87 50W
Waukesha, *U.S.A.* **76 D1** 43 1N 88 14W
Waukon, *U.S.A.* **80 D9** 43 16N 91 29W
Wauneta, *U.S.A.* **80 E4** 40 25N 101 23W
Waupaca, *U.S.A.* **80 C10** 44 21N 89 5W
Waupun, *U.S.A.* **80 D10** 43 38N 88 44W
Waurika, *U.S.A.* **81 H6** 34 10N 98 0W
Wausau, *U.S.A.* **80 C10** 44 58N 89 38W
Wautoma, *U.S.A.* **80 C10** 44 4N 89 18W
Wauwatosa, *U.S.A.* **76 D2** 43 3N 88 0W
Wave Hill, *Australia* **60 C5** 17 32S 131 0 E
Waveney →, *U.K.* **11 E9** 52 35N 1 39 E
Waverley, *N.Z.* **59 H5** 39 46S 174 37 E
Waverly, *Iowa, U.S.A.* **80 D8** 42 44N 92 29W
Waverly, *N.Y., U.S.A.* **79 D8** 42 1N 76 32W
Wavre, *Belgium* **15 D4** 50 43N 4 38 E
Wâw, *Sudan* **51 G10** 7 45N 28 1 E
Wāw al Kabīr, *Libya* **51 C8** 25 20N 16 43 E
Wawa, *Canada* **70 C3** 47 59N 84 47W
Wawanesa, *Canada* **73 D9** 49 36N 99 40W
Wawona, *U.S.A.* **84 H7** 37 32N 119 39W
Waxahachie, *U.S.A.* **81 J6** 32 24N 96 51W
Way, L., *Australia* **61 E3** 26 45S 120 16 E
Wayabula Rau, *Indonesia* **37 D7** 2 29N 128 17 E
Wayatinah, *Australia* **62 G4** 42 19S 146 27 E
Waycross, *U.S.A.* **77 K4** 31 13N 82 21W
Wayne, *Nebr., U.S.A.* **80 D6** 42 14N 97 1W
Wayne, *W. Va., U.S.A.* **76 F4** 38 13N 82 27W
Waynesboro, *Ga., U.S.A.* **77 J4** 33 6N 82 1W
Waynesboro, *Miss., U.S.A.* **77 K1** 31 40N 88 39W
Waynesboro, *Pa., U.S.A.* **76 F7** 39 45N 77 35W
Waynesboro, *Va., U.S.A.* **76 F6** 38 4N 78 53W
Waynesburg, *U.S.A.* **76 F5** 39 54N 80 11W
Waynesville, *U.S.A.* **77 H4** 35 28N 82 58W
Waynoka, *U.S.A.* **81 G5** 36 35N 98 53W
Wazirabad, *Pakistan* **42 C6** 32 30N 74 8 E
We, *Indonesia* **36 C1** 5 51N 95 18 E
Weald, The, *U.K.* **11 F8** 51 4N 0 20 E
Wear →, *U.K.* **10 C6** 54 55N 1 23W
Weatherford, *Okla., U.S.A.* **81 H5** 35 32N 98 43W
Weatherford, *Tex., U.S.A.* **81 J6** 32 46N 97 48W
Weaverville, *U.S.A.* **82 F2** 40 44N 122 56W
Webb City, *U.S.A.* **81 G7** 37 9N 94 28W
Webster, *Mass., U.S.A.* **79 D13** 42 3N 71 53W
Webster, *N.Y., U.S.A.* **78 C7** 43 13N 77 26W
Webster, *S. Dak., U.S.A.* **80 C6** 45 20N 97 31W
Webster, *Wis., U.S.A.* **80 C8** 45 53N 92 22W
Webster City, *U.S.A.* **80 D8** 42 28N 93 49W
Webster Green, *U.S.A.* **80 F9** 38 38N 90 20W
Webster Springs, *U.S.A.* **76 F5** 38 29N 80 25W
Weda, *Indonesia* **37 D7** 0 21N 127 50 E
Weda, Teluk, *Indonesia* **37 D7** 0 30N 127 50 E
Weddell I., *Falk. Is.* **96 G4** 51 50S 61 0W
Weddell Sea, *Antarctica* **5 D1** 72 30S 40 0W
Wedderburn, *Australia* **63 F3** 36 26S 143 33 E
Wedgeport, *Canada* **71 D6** 43 44N 65 59W
Wedza, *Zimbabwe* **55 F3** 18 40S 31 33 E
Wee Waa, *Australia* **63 E4** 30 11S 149 26 E
Weed, *U.S.A.* **82 F2** 41 25N 122 23W
Weed Heights, *U.S.A.* **84 G7** 38 59N 119 13W
Weedsport, *U.S.A.* **79 C8** 43 3N 76 35W
Weedville, *U.S.A.* **78 E6** 41 17N 78 30W
Weemelah, *Australia* **63 D4** 29 2S 149 15 E
Weenen, *S. Africa* **57 D5** 28 48S 30 7 E
Weert, *Neths.* **15 C5** 51 15N 5 43 E
Wei He →, *Hebei, China* **34 F8** 36 10N 115 45 E
Wei He →, *Shaanxi, China* **34 G6** 34 38N 110 15 E
Weichang, *China* **35 D9** 41 58N 117 49 E
Weichuan, *China* **34 G7** 34 20N 113 59 E
Weiden, *Germany* **16 D7** 49 41N 12 10 E
Weifang, *China* **35 F10** 36 44N 119 7 E
Weihai, *China* **35 F12** 37 30N 122 6 E
Weimar, *Germany* **16 C6** 50 58N 11 19 E
Weinan, *China* **34 G5** 34 31N 109 29 E
Weipa, *Australia* **62 A3** 12 40S 141 50 E
Weir →, *Australia* **63 D4** 28 20S 149 50 E
Weir →, *Canada* **73 B10** 56 54N 93 21W
Weir River, *Canada* **73 B10** 56 49N 94 6W
Weirton, *U.S.A.* **78 F4** 40 24N 80 35W
Weiser, *U.S.A.* **82 D5** 44 10N 117 0W
Weishan, *China* **35 G9** 34 47N 117 5 E
Weiyuan, *China* **34 G3** 35 7N 104 10 E
Wejherowo, *Poland* **17 A10** 54 35N 18 12 E
Wekusko L., *Canada* **73 C9** 54 40N 99 50W
Welbourn Hill, *Australia* **63 D1** 27 21S 134 6 E
Welch, *U.S.A.* **76 G5** 37 26N 81 35W
Welkom, *S. Africa* **56 D4** 28 0S 26 46 E
Welland, *Canada* **70 D4** 43 0N 79 15W
Welland →, *U.K.* **10 E7** 52 51N 0 5W
Wellesley Is., *Australia* **62 B2** 16 42S 139 30 E
Wellin, *Belgium* **15 D5** 50 5N 5 6 E
Wellingborough, *U.K.* **11 E7** 52 19N 0 41W
Wellington, *Australia* **63 E4** 32 35S 148 59 E
Wellington, *Canada* **70 D4** 43 57N 77 20W
Wellington, *N.Z.* **59 J5** 41 19S 174 46 E
Wellington, *S. Africa* **56 E2** 33 38S 19 1 E
Wellington, *Shrops., U.K.* **10 E5** 52 42N 2 30W
Wellington, *Somst., U.K.* **11 G4** 50 58N 3 13W
Wellington, *Colo., U.S.A.* **80 E2** 40 42N 105 0W
Wellington, *Kans., U.S.A.* **81 G6** 37 16N 97 24W
Wellington, *Nev., U.S.A.* **84 G7** 38 45N 119 23W
Wellington, *Ohio, U.S.A.* **78 E2** 41 10N 82 13W
Wellington, *Tex., U.S.A.* **81 H4** 34 51N 100 13W
Wellington, I., *Chile* **96 F1** 49 30S 75 0W
Wellington, L., *Australia* **63 F4** 38 6S 147 20 E
Wells, *U.K.* **11 F5** 51 13N 2 39W
Wells, *Maine, U.S.A.* **79 C14** 43 20N 70 35W
Wells, *Minn., U.S.A.* **80 D8** 43 45N 93 44W
Wells, *Nev., U.S.A.* **82 F6** 41 7N 114 58W
Wells, L., *Australia* **61 E3** 26 44S 123 15 E
Wells Gray Prov. Park, *Canada* **72 C4** 52 30N 120 15W
Wells-next-the-Sea, *U.K.* **10 E8** 52 57N 0 51 E
Wells River, *U.S.A.* **79 B12** 44 9N 72 4W
Wellsboro, *U.S.A.* **78 E7** 41 45N 77 18W
Wellsburg, *U.S.A.* **78 F4** 40 16N 80 37W
Wellsville, *Mo., U.S.A.* **80 F9** 39 4N 91 34W
Wellsville, *N.Y., U.S.A.* **78 D7** 42 7N 77 57W
Wellsville, *Ohio, U.S.A.* **78 F4** 40 36N 80 39W
Wellsville, *Utah, U.S.A.* **82 F8** 41 38N 111 56W
Wellton, *U.S.A.* **83 K6** 32 40N 114 8W
Wels, *Austria* **16 D8** 48 9N 14 1 E
Welshpool, *U.K.* **11 E4** 52 39N 3 8W
Wem, *U.K.* **10 E5** 52 52N 2 44W
Wembere →, *Tanzania* **54 C3** 4 10S 34 15 E
Wemindji, *Canada* **70 B4** 53 0N 78 49W
Wen Xian, *Gansu, China* **34 H3** 32 43N 104 36 E
Wen Xian, *Henan, China* **34 G7** 34 55N 113 5 E
Wenatchee, *U.S.A.* **82 C3** 47 25N 120 19W
Wenchang, *China* **38 C8** 19 38N 110 42 E
Wenchi, *Ghana* **50 G4** 7 46N 2 8W
Wenchow = Wenzhou, *China* **33 D7** 28 0N 120 38 E
Wendell, *U.S.A.* **82 E6** 42 47N 114 42W
Wenden, *U.S.A.* **85 M13** 33 49N 113 33W
Wendeng, *China* **35 F12** 37 15N 122 5 E
Wendesi, *Indonesia* **37 E8** 2 30S 134 17 E
Wendover, *U.S.A.* **82 F6** 40 44N 114 2W
Wenlock →, *Australia* **62 A3** 12 2S 141 55 E
Wenshan, *China* **32 D5** 23 20N 104 18 E
Wenshang, *China* **34 G9** 35 45N 116 30 E
Wenshui, *China* **34 F7** 37 26N 112 1 E
Wensu, *China* **32 B3** 41 15N 80 10 E
Wentworth, *Australia* **63 E3** 34 2S 141 54 E
Wenut, *Indonesia* **37 E8** 3 11S 133 19 E
Wenxi, *China* **34 G6** 35 20N 111 10 E
Wenzhou, *China* **33 D7** 28 0N 120 38 E
Weott, *U.S.A.* **82 F2** 40 20N 123 55W
Wepener, *S. Africa* **56 D4** 29 42S 27 3 E
Werda, *Botswana* **56 D3** 25 24S 23 15 E
Werder, *Ethiopia* **46 F4** 6 58N 45 1 E
Weri, *Indonesia* **37 E8** 3 10S 132 38 E
Werra →, *Germany* **16 C5** 51 26N 9 39 E
Werribee, *Australia* **63 F3** 37 54S 144 40 E
Werrimull, *Australia* **63 E3** 34 25S 141 38 E
Werris Creek, *Australia* **63 E5** 31 18S 150 38 E
Wersar, *Indonesia* **37 E8** 1 30S 131 55 E
Weser →, *Germany* **16 B5** 53 36N 8 28 E
Wesiri, *Indonesia* **37 F7** 7 30S 126 30 E
Wesley Vale, *U.S.A.* **83 J10** 35 3N 106 2W
Wesleyville, *Canada* **71 C9** 49 8N 53 36W
Wesleyville, *U.S.A.* **78 D4** 42 9N 80 0W
Wessel, C., *Australia* **62 A2** 10 59S 136 46 E
Wessel Is., *Australia* **62 A2** 11 10S 136 45 E
Wessington, *U.S.A.* **80 C5** 44 27N 98 42W
Wessington Springs, *U.S.A.* **80 C5** 44 5N 98 34W
West, *U.S.A.* **81 K6** 31 48N 97 6W
West Allis, *U.S.A.* **76 D1** 43 1N 88 0W
West B., *U.S.A.* **81 L10** 29 3N 89 22W
West Baines →, *Australia* **60 C4** 15 38S 129 59 E
West Bank □, *Asia* **47 C4** 32 6N 35 13 E
West Bend, *U.S.A.* **76 D1** 43 25N 88 11W
West Bengal □, *India* **43 H12** 23 0N 88 0 E
West Beskids = Západné Beskydy, *Europe* **17 D10** 49 30N 19 0 E
West Branch, *U.S.A.* **76 C3** 44 17N 84 14W
West Bromwich, *U.K.* **11 E5** 52 32N 1 59W
West Cape Howe, *Australia* **61 G2** 35 8S 117 36 E
West Chazy, *U.S.A.* **79 B11** 44 49N 73 28W
West Chester, *U.S.A.* **76 F8** 39 58N 75 36W
West Columbia, *U.S.A.* **81 L7** 29 9N 95 39W
West Covina, *U.S.A.* **85 L9** 34 4N 117 54W
West Des Moines, *U.S.A.* **80 E8** 41 35N 93 43W
West Dunbartonshire □, *U.K.* **12 F4** 55 59N 4 30W
West End, *Bahamas* **88 A4** 26 41N 78 58W
West Falkland, *Falk. Is.* **96 G4** 51 40S 60 0W
West Fjord = Vestfjorden, *Norway* **8 C15** 67 55N 14 0 E
West Frankfort, *U.S.A.* **80 G10** 37 54N 88 55W
West Hartford, *U.S.A.* **79 E12** 41 45N 72 44W
West Haven, *U.S.A.* **79 E12** 41 17N 72 57W
West Helena, *U.S.A.* **81 H9** 34 33N 90 38W
West Ice Shelf, *Antarctica* **5 C7** 67 0S 85 0 E
West Indies, *Cent. Amer.* **89 C7** 15 0N 65 0W
West Lorne, *Canada* **78 D3** 42 36N 81 36W
West Lothian □, *U.K.* **12 F5** 55 54N 3 36W
West Lunga →, *Zambia* **55 E1** 13 6S 24 39 E
West Memphis, *U.S.A.* **81 H9** 35 9N 90 11W
West Midlands □, *U.K.* **11 E6** 52 26N 2 0W
West Mifflin, *U.S.A.* **78 F5** 40 22N 79 52W
West Monroe, *U.S.A.* **81 J8** 32 31N 92 9W
West Newton, *U.S.A.* **78 F5** 40 14N 79 46W
West Nicholson, *Zimbabwe* **55 G2** 21 2S 29 20 E
West Palm Beach, *U.S.A.* **77 M5** 26 43N 80 3W
West Plains, *U.S.A.* **81 G9** 36 44N 91 51W
West Point, *Ga., U.S.A.* **77 J3** 32 53N 85 11W
West Point, *Miss., U.S.A.* **77 J1** 33 36N 88 39W
West Point, *Nebr., U.S.A.* **80 E6** 41 51N 96 43W
West Point, *Va., U.S.A.* **76 G7** 37 32N 76 48W
West Pokot □, *Kenya* **54 B4** 1 30N 35 15 E
West Pt. = Ouest, Pte., *Canada* **71 C7** 49 52N 64 40W
West Pt., *Australia* **63 F2** 35 1S 135 56 E
West Road →, *Canada* **72 C4** 53 18N 122 53W
West Rutland, *U.S.A.* **79 C11** 43 38N 73 5W
West Schelde = Westerschelde →, *Neths.* **15 C3** 51 25N 3 25 E
West Seneca, *U.S.A.* **78 D6** 42 51N 78 48W
West Siberian Plain, *Russia* **28 C11** 62 0N 75 0 E
West Sussex □, *U.K.* **11 G7** 50 55N 0 30W
West-Terschelling, *Neths.* **15 A5** 53 22N 5 13 E
West Valley City, *U.S.A.* **82 F8** 40 42N 111 57W
West Virginia □, *U.S.A.* **76 F5** 38 45N 80 30W
West-Vlaanderen □, *Belgium* **15 D3** 51 0N 3 0 E
West Walker →, *U.S.A.* **84 G7** 38 54N 119 9W
West Wyalong, *Australia* **63 E4** 33 56S 147 10 E
West Yellowstone, *U.S.A.* **82 D8** 44 40N 111 6W
West Yorkshire □, *U.K.* **10 D6** 53 45N 1 40W
Westall Pt., *Australia* **63 E1** 32 55S 134 4 E
Westbrook, *Maine, U.S.A.* **77 D10** 43 41N 70 22W
Westbrook, *Tex., U.S.A.* **81 J4** 32 21N 101 1W
Westbury, *Australia* **62 G4** 41 30S 146 51 E
Westby, *U.S.A.* **80 A2** 48 52N 104 3W

Westend

Westend, U.S.A. 85 K9 35 42N 117 24W
Westerland, Germany ... 9 J13 54 54N 8 17 E
Western □, Kenya ...... 54 B3 0 30N 34 30 E
Western □, Uganda .... 54 B3 1 45N 31 30 E
Western □, Zambia .... 55 F1 15 15S 24 30 E
Western Australia □,
  Australia .... 61 E2 25 0S 118 0 E
Western Cape □, S. Africa 56 E3 34 0S 20 0 E
Western Dvina =
  Daugava →, Latvia . 9 H21 57 4N 24 3 E
Western Ghats, India .... 40 N9 14 0N 75 0 E
Western Isles □, U.K. .. 12 D1 57 30N 7 10W
Western Sahara ■, Africa 50 D2 25 0N 13 0W
Western Samoa ■,
  Pac. Oc. 59 A13 14 0S 172 0W
Westernport, U.S.A. 76 F6 39 29N 79 3W
Westerschelde →, Neths. 15 C3 51 25N 3 25 E
Westerwald, Germany ... 16 C4 50 38N 7 56 E
Westfield, Mass., U.S.A. . 79 D12 42 7N 72 45W
Westfield, N.Y., U.S.A. .. 78 D5 42 20N 79 35W
Westfield, Pa., U.S.A. ... 78 E7 41 55N 77 32W
Westhope, U.S.A. 80 A4 48 55N 101 1W
Westland Bight, N.Z. ... 59 K3 42 55S 170 5 E
Westlock, Canada 72 C6 54 9N 113 55W
Westmeath □, Ireland .. 13 C4 53 33N 7 34W
Westminster, U.S.A. 76 F7 39 34N 76 59W
Westmorland, U.S.A. ... 83 K6 33 2N 115 37W
Weston, Malaysia ...... 36 C5 5 10N 115 35 E
Weston, Oreg., U.S.A. .. 82 D4 45 49N 118 26W
Weston, W. Va., U.S.A. .. 76 F5 39 2N 80 28W
Weston I., Canada 70 B4 52 33N 79 36W
Weston-super-Mare, U.K. 11 F5 51 21N 2 58W
Westport, Canada 79 B8 44 40N 76 25W
Westport, Ireland 13 C2 53 48N 9 31W
Westport, N.Z. .... 59 J3 41 46S 171 37 E
Westport, Oreg., U.S.A. . 84 D3 46 8N 123 23W
Westport, Wash., U.S.A. . 82 C1 46 53N 124 6W
Westray, Canada 73 C8 53 36N 101 24W
Westray, U.K. 12 B6 59 18N 3 0W
Westree, Canada 70 C3 47 26N 81 34W
Westville, Calif., U.S.A. . 84 F6 39 8N 120 42W
Westville, Ill., U.S.A. ... 76 E2 40 2N 87 38W
Westville, Okla., U.S.A. . 81 G7 35 58N 94 40W
Westwood, U.S.A. 82 F3 40 18N 121 0W
Wetar, Indonesia ...... 37 F7 7 30S 126 30 E
Wetaskiwin, Canada 72 C6 52 55N 113 24W
Wethersfield, U.S.A. 79 E12 41 42N 72 40W
Wetteren, Belgium ..... 15 D3 51 0N 3 52 E
Wetzlar, Germany ...... 16 C5 50 32N 8 31 E
Wewoka, U.S.A. 81 H6 35 9N 96 30W
Wexford, Ireland 13 D5 52 20N 6 28W
Wexford □, Ireland 13 D5 52 20N 6 25W
Wexford Harbour, Ireland 13 D5 52 20N 6 25W
Weyburn, Canada 73 D8 49 40N 103 50W
Weyburn L., Canada 72 A5 63 0N 117 59W
Weymouth, Canada 71 D6 44 30N 66 1W
Weymouth, U.K. 11 G5 50 37N 2 28W
Weymouth, U.S.A. 79 D14 42 13N 70 58W
Weymouth, C., Australia . 62 A3 12 37S 143 27 E
Wha Ti, Canada 68 B8 63 8N 117 16W
Whakatane, N.Z. ...... 59 G6 37 57S 177 1 E
Whale →, Canada 71 A6 58 15N 67 40W
Whale Cove, Canada ... 73 A10 62 11N 92 36W
Whales, B. of, Antarctica . 5 D12 78 0S 165 0W
Whalsay, U.K. 12 A7 60 22N 0 59W
Whangamomona, N.Z. .. 59 H5 39 8S 174 44 E
Whangarei, N.Z. .... 59 F5 35 43S 174 21 E
Whangarei Harb., N.Z. .. 59 F5 35 45S 174 28 E
Wharfe →, U.K. 10 D6 53 51N 1 9W
Wharfedale, U.K. 10 C5 54 6N 2 1W
Wharton, N.J., U.S.A. ... 79 F10 40 54N 74 35W
Wharton, Pa., U.S.A. ... 78 E6 41 31N 78 1W
Wharton, Tex., U.S.A. ... 81 L6 29 19N 96 6W
Wheatland, Calif., U.S.A. 84 F5 39 1N 121 25W
Wheatland, Wyo., U.S.A. 80 D2 42 3N 104 58W
Wheatley, Canada 78 D2 42 6N 82 27W
Wheaton, U.S.A. 80 C6 45 48N 96 30W
Wheelbarrow Pk., U.S.A. 84 H10 37 26N 116 5W
Wheeler, Oreg., U.S.A. . 82 D2 45 41N 123 53W
Wheeler, Tex., U.S.A. ... 81 H4 35 27N 100 16W
Wheeler →, Canada ... 73 B7 57 25N 105 30W
Wheeler Pk., N. Mex.,
  U.S.A. 83 H11 36 34N 105 25W
Wheeler Pk., Nev., U.S.A. 83 G6 38 57N 114 15W
Wheeler Ridge, U.S.A. .. 85 L8 35 0N 118 57W
Wheeling, U.S.A. 78 F4 40 4N 80 43W
Whernside, U.K. 10 C5 54 14N 2 24W
Whidbey I., U.S.A. 72 D4 48 12N 122 17W
Whiskey Gap, Canada ... 72 D6 49 0N 113 3W
Whiskey Jack L., Canada 73 B8 58 23N 101 55W
Whistleduck Cr. →,
  Australia .... 62 C2 20 15S 135 18 E
Whitby, Canada 78 C6 43 52N 78 56W
Whitby, U.K. 10 C7 54 29N 0 37W
White →, Ark., U.S.A. .. 81 J9 33 57N 91 5W
White →, Ind., U.S.A. .. 76 F2 38 25N 87 45W
White →, S. Dak., U.S.A. 80 D5 43 42N 99 27W
White →, Utah, U.S.A. . 82 F9 40 4N 109 41W
White →, Wash., U.S.A. 84 C4 47 12N 122 15W
White, L., Australia .... 60 D4 21 9S 128 56 E
White B., Canada 71 B8 50 0N 56 35W
White Bear Res., Canada 71 C8 48 10N 57 5W
White Bird, U.S.A. 82 D5 45 46N 116 18W
White Butte, U.S.A. 80 B3 46 23N 103 18W
White City, U.S.A. 80 F6 38 48N 96 44W
White Cliffs, Australia .. 63 E3 30 50S 143 10 E
White Deer, U.S.A. 81 H4 35 26N 101 10W
White Hall, U.S.A. 80 F9 39 26N 90 24W
White Haven, U.S.A. 79 E9 41 4N 75 47W
White Horse, Vale of, U.K. 11 F6 51 37N 1 30W
White I., N.Z. .... 59 G6 37 30S 177 13 E
White L., Australia 79 A8 61 18N 76 31W
White L., U.S.A. 81 L8 29 44N 92 30W
White Mts., Calif., U.S.A. 83 H4 37 30N 118 15W
White Mts., N.H., U.S.A. 79 B12 44 15N 71 15W
White Nile = Nîl el
  Abyad →, Sudan ... 51 E11 15 38N 32 31 E
White Otter L., Canada . 70 C1 49 5N 91 55W
White Pass, Canada 72 B1 59 40N 135 3W
White Pass, U.S.A. 84 D5 46 38N 121 24W
White Plains, U.S.A. ... 79 E11 41 2N 73 46W
White River, Canada ... 70 C2 48 35N 85 20W
White River, S. Africa .. 57 D5 25 20S 31 0 E

White River, U.S.A. 80 D4 43 34N 100 45W
White Russia = Belarus ■,
  Europe .... 17 B14 53 30N 27 0 E
White Sea = Beloye More,
  Russia .... 24 A6 66 30N 38 0 E
White Sulphur Springs,
  Mont., U.S.A. 82 C8 46 33N 110 54W
White Sulphur Springs,
  W. Va., U.S.A. 76 G5 37 48N 80 18W
White Swan, U.S.A. 84 D6 46 23N 120 44W
Whitecliffs, N.Z. ...... 59 K3 43 26S 171 55 E
Whitecourt, Canada ... 72 C5 54 10N 115 45W
Whiteface, U.S.A. 81 J3 33 36N 102 37W
Whitefield, U.S.A. 79 B13 44 23N 71 37W
Whitefish, Canada 13 A7 62 41N 106 48W
Whitefish, U.S.A. 82 B6 48 25N 114 20W
Whitefish Point, U.S.A. . 76 B3 46 45N 84 59W
Whitegull, L., Canada .. 71 A7 55 27N 64 17W
Whitehall, Mich., U.S.A. 76 D2 43 24N 86 21W
Whitehall, Mont., U.S.A. 82 D7 45 52N 112 6W
Whitehall, N.Y., U.S.A. . 79 C11 43 33N 73 24W
Whitehall, Wis., U.S.A. . 80 C9 44 22N 91 19W
Whitehaven, U.K. 10 C4 54 33N 3 35W
Whitehorse, Canada ... 72 A1 60 43N 135 3W
Whitemark, Australia .. 62 G4 40 7S 148 3 E
Whitemouth, Canada ... 73 D9 49 57N 95 58W
Whitesboro, N.Y., U.S.A. 79 C9 43 7N 75 18W
Whitesboro, Tex., U.S.A. 81 J6 33 39N 96 54W
Whiteshell Prov. Park,
  Canada 73 C9 50 0N 95 40W
Whitetail, U.S.A. 80 A2 48 54N 105 10W
Whiteville, U.S.A. 77 H6 34 20N 78 42W
Whitewater, U.S.A. 76 D1 42 50N 88 44W
Whitewater Baldy, U.S.A. 83 K9 33 20N 108 39W
Whitewater L., Canada . 70 B2 50 50N 89 10W
Whitewood, Australia .. 62 C3 21 28S 143 30 E
Whitewood, Canada 73 C8 50 20N 102 20W
Whitfield, Australia .... 63 F4 36 42S 146 24 E
Whithorn, U.K. 12 G4 54 44N 4 26W
Whitianga, N.Z. .... 59 G5 36 47S 175 41 E
Whitman, U.S.A. 79 D14 42 5N 70 56W
Whitmire, U.S.A. 77 H5 34 30N 81 37W
Whitney, Canada 78 A6 45 31N 78 14W
Whitney, Mt., U.S.A. ... 83 H4 36 35N 118 18W
Whitney Point, U.S.A. .. 79 D9 42 20N 75 58W
Whitstable, U.K. .... 11 F9 51 21N 1 3 E
Whitsunday I., Australia . 62 C4 20 15S 149 4 E
Whittier, U.S.A. 85 M8 33 58N 118 3W
Whittlesea, Australia .. 63 F4 37 27S 145 9 E
Whitwell, U.S.A. 77 H3 35 12N 85 31W
Wholdaia L., Canada ... 73 A8 60 43N 104 20W
Whyalla, Australia ..... 63 E2 33 2S 137 30 E
Whyjonta, Australia ... 63 D3 29 41S 142 28 E
Wiarton, Canada 78 B3 44 40N 81 10W
Wibaux, U.S.A. 80 B2 46 59N 104 11W
Wichian Buri, Thailand . 38 E3 15 39N 101 7 E
Wichita, U.S.A. 81 G6 37 42N 97 20W
Wichita Falls, U.S.A. ... 81 J5 33 54N 98 30W
Wick, U.K. 12 C5 58 26N 3 5W
Wickenburg, U.S.A. 83 K7 33 58N 112 44W
Wickepin, Australia .... 61 F2 32 50S 117 30 E
Wickham, C., Australia . 62 F3 39 35S 143 57 E
Wickliffe, U.S.A. 78 E3 41 36N 81 28W
Wicklow, Ireland 13 D5 52 59N 6 3W
Wicklow □, Ireland 13 D5 52 57N 6 25W
Wicklow Hd., Ireland .. 13 D5 52 58N 6 0W
Widgiemooltha, Australia 61 F3 31 30S 121 34 E
Widnes, U.K. 10 D5 53 23N 2 45W
Wieluń, Poland .... 17 C10 51 15N 18 34 E
Wien, Austria .... 16 D9 48 12N 16 22 E
Wiener Neustadt, Austria 16 E9 47 49N 16 16 E
Wierden, Neths. .... 15 B6 52 22N 6 35 E
Wiesbaden, Germany .. 16 C5 50 4N 8 14 E
Wigan, U.K. 10 D5 53 33N 2 38W
Wiggins, Colo., U.S.A. .. 80 E2 40 14N 104 4W
Wiggins, Miss., U.S.A. . 81 K10 30 51N 89 8W
Wight, I. of □, U.K. 11 G6 50 40N 1 20W
Wigtown, U.K. 12 G4 54 53N 4 27W
Wigtown B., U.K. 12 G4 54 46N 4 15W
Wilber, U.S.A. 80 E6 40 29N 96 58W
Wilberforce, Canada ... 78 A6 45 2N 78 13W
Wilberforce, C., Australia 62 A2 11 54S 136 35 E
Wilburton, U.S.A. 81 H7 34 55N 95 19W
Wilcannia, Australia ... 63 E3 31 30S 143 26 E
Wilcox, U.S.A. 78 E6 41 35N 78 41W
Wildrose, Calif., U.S.A. . 85 J9 36 14N 117 11W
Wildrose, N. Dak., U.S.A. 80 A3 48 38N 103 11W
Wildspitze, Austria .... 16 E6 46 53N 10 53 E
Wildwood, U.S.A. 76 F8 38 59N 74 50W
Wilge →, S. Africa .... 57 D4 27 3S 28 20 E
Wilhelm II Coast,
  Antarctica .... 5 C7 68 0S 90 0 E
Wilhelmshaven, Germany 16 B5 53 31N 8 7 E
Wilhelmstal, Namibia .. 56 C2 21 58S 16 21 E
Wilkes-Barre, U.S.A. ... 79 E9 41 15N 75 53W
Wilkesboro, U.S.A. 77 G5 36 9N 81 10W
Wilkie, Canada 73 C7 52 27N 108 42W
Wilkinsburg, U.S.A. 78 F5 40 26N 79 53W
Wilkinson Lakes, Australia 61 E5 29 40S 132 39 E
Willamina, U.S.A. 82 D2 45 5N 123 29W
Willandra Billabong
  Creek →, Australia . 63 E4 33 22S 145 52 E
Willapa B., U.S.A. 82 C2 46 40N 124 0W
Willapa Hills, U.S.A. ... 84 D3 46 35N 123 25W
Willard, N. Mex., U.S.A. 83 J10 34 36N 106 2W
Willard, Utah, U.S.A. ... 82 F7 41 25N 112 2W
Willcox, U.S.A. 83 K9 32 15N 109 50W
Willemstad, Neth. Ant. . 89 D6 12 5N 69 0W
Willeroo, Australia .... 60 C5 15 14S 131 37 E
William →, Canada ... 73 B7 59 8N 109 19W
William Creek, Australia 63 D2 28 58S 136 22 E
Williambury, Australia . 61 D2 23 45S 115 12 E
Williams, Australia ... 61 F2 33 2S 116 52 E
Williams, Ariz., U.S.A. . 83 J7 35 15N 112 11W
Williams, Calif., U.S.A. . 84 F4 39 9N 122 9W
Williams Lake, Canada . 72 C4 52 10N 122 10W
Williamsburg, Ky., U.S.A. 77 G3 36 44N 84 10W
Williamsburg, Pa., U.S.A. 78 F6 40 28N 78 12W
Williamsburg, Va., U.S.A. 76 G7 37 17N 76 44W
Williamson, N.Y., U.S.A. 78 C7 43 14N 77 11W
Williamson, W. Va., U.S.A. 76 G4 37 41N 82 17W
Williamsport, U.S.A. ... 78 E7 41 15N 77 0W
Williamston, U.S.A. 77 H7 35 51N 77 4W

Williamstown, Australia . 63 F3 37 51S 144 52 E
Williamstown, Mass.,
  U.S.A. 79 D11 42 41N 73 12W
Williamstown, N.Y., U.S.A. 79 C9 43 26N 75 53W
Williamsville, U.S.A. ... 81 G9 36 58N 90 33W
Willimantic, U.S.A. 79 E12 41 43N 72 13W
Willis Group, Australia . 62 B5 16 18S 150 0 E
Williston, S. Africa .... 56 E3 31 20S 20 53 E
Williston, Fla., U.S.A. .. 77 L4 29 23N 82 27W
Williston, N. Dak., U.S.A. 80 A3 48 9N 103 37W
Williston L., Canada ... 72 B4 56 0N 124 0W
Willits, U.S.A. 82 G2 39 25N 123 21W
Willmar, U.S.A. 80 C7 45 7N 95 3W
Willoughby, U.S.A. 78 E3 41 39N 81 24W
Willow Bunch, Canada . 73 D7 49 20N 105 35W
Willow L., Canada 72 A5 62 10N 119 8W
Willow Lake, Canada ... 80 C6 44 38N 97 38W
Willow Springs, U.S.A. . 81 G8 37 0N 91 58W
Willow Wall, The, China 35 C12 42 10N 122 0 E
Willowlake →, Canada . 72 A4 62 42N 123 8W
Willowmore, S. Africa .. 56 E3 33 15S 23 30 E
Willows, Australia ..... 62 C4 23 39S 147 25 E
Willows, U.S.A. 84 F4 39 31N 122 12W
Willowvale = Gatyana,
  S. Africa .... 57 E4 32 16S 28 31 E
Wills, L., Australia .... 60 D4 21 25S 128 51 E
Wills Cr. →, Australia . 62 C3 22 43S 140 2 E
Wills Point, U.S.A. 81 J7 32 43N 96 1W
Willunga, Australia .... 63 F2 35 15S 138 30 E
Wilmette, U.S.A. 76 D2 42 5N 87 42W
Wilmington, Australia .. 63 E2 32 39S 138 7 E
Wilmington, Del., U.S.A. 76 F8 39 45N 75 33W
Wilmington, Ill., U.S.A. . 76 E1 41 18N 88 9W
Wilmington, N.C., U.S.A. 77 H7 34 14N 77 55W
Wilmington, Ohio, U.S.A. 76 F4 39 27N 83 50W
Wilpena Cr. →, Australia 63 E2 31 25S 139 29 E
Wilsall, U.S.A. 82 D8 45 59N 110 38W
Wilson, U.S.A. 77 H7 35 44N 77 55W
Wilson →, Queens.,
  Australia .... 63 D3 27 38S 141 24 E
Wilson →, W. Austral.,
  Australia .... 60 C4 16 48S 128 16 E
Wilson Bluff, Australia . 61 F4 31 41S 129 0 E
Wilsons Promontory,
  Australia .... 63 F4 38 55S 146 25 E
Wilton, U.K. 11 F6 51 5N 1 51W
Wilton, U.S.A. 80 B4 47 10N 100 47W
Wilton →, Australia ... 62 A1 14 45S 134 33 E
Wiltshire □, U.K. 11 F6 51 18N 1 53W
Wiltz, Lux. .... 15 E5 49 57N 5 55 E
Wiluna, Australia ...... 61 E3 26 36S 120 14 E
Wimmera →, Australia 63 F3 36 8S 141 56 E
Winam G., Kenya ..... 54 C3 0 20S 34 15 E
Winburg, S. Africa .... 56 D4 28 30S 27 2 E
Winchendon, U.S.A. ... 79 D12 42 41N 72 3W
Winchester, U.K. 11 F6 51 4N 1 18W
Winchester, Conn., U.S.A. 79 E11 41 53N 73 9W
Winchester, Idaho, U.S.A. 82 C5 46 14N 116 38W
Winchester, Ind., U.S.A. 76 E3 40 10N 84 59W
Winchester, Ky., U.S.A. 76 G3 38 0N 84 11W
Winchester, N.H., U.S.A. 79 D12 42 46N 72 23W
Winchester, Nev., U.S.A. 85 J11 36 6N 115 10W
Winchester, Tenn., U.S.A. 77 H2 35 11N 86 7W
Winchester, Va., U.S.A. 76 F6 39 11N 78 10W
Wind →, U.S.A. 82 E9 43 12N 108 12W
Wind River Range, U.S.A. 82 E9 43 0N 109 30W
Windau = Ventspils,
  Latvia .... 9 H19 57 25N 21 32 E
Windber, U.S.A. 78 F6 40 14N 78 50W
Windermere, L., U.K. ... 10 C5 54 22N 2 56W
Windfall, Canada 72 C5 54 12N 116 13W
Windflower L., Canada . 72 A5 62 52N 118 30W
Windhoek, Namibia ... 56 C2 22 35S 17 4 E
Windom, U.S.A. 80 D7 43 52N 95 7W
Windorah, Australia ... 62 D3 25 24S 142 36 E
Window Rock, U.S.A. .. 83 J9 35 41N 109 3W
Windrush →, U.K. 11 F6 51 43N 1 24W
Windsor, Australia .... 63 E5 33 37S 150 50 E
Windsor, N.S., Canada . 71 D7 44 59N 64 5W
Windsor, Nfld., Canada 71 C8 48 57N 55 40W
Windsor, Ont., Canada . 70 D3 42 18N 83 0W
Windsor, U.K. 11 F7 51 29N 0 36W
Windsor, Colo., U.S.A. . 80 E2 40 29N 104 54W
Windsor, Conn., U.S.A. . 79 E12 41 50N 72 39W
Windsor, Mo., U.S.A. .. 80 F8 38 32N 93 31W
Windsor, N.Y., U.S.A. .. 79 D9 42 5N 75 37W
Windsor, Vt., U.S.A. ... 79 C12 43 29N 72 24W
Windsorton, S. Africa .. 56 D3 28 16S 24 44 E
Windward Is., W. Indies . 89 D7 13 0N 61 0W
Windward Passage =
  Vientos, Paso de los,
  Caribbean 89 C5 20 0N 74 0W
Windy L., Canada 73 A8 60 20N 100 2W
Winefred L., Canada ... 73 B6 55 30N 110 30W
Winfield, U.S.A. 81 G6 37 15N 96 59W
Wingate Mts., Australia 60 B5 14 25S 130 40 E
Wingen, Australia ..... 63 E5 31 54S 150 54 E
Wingham, Australia ... 63 E5 31 48S 152 22 E
Wingham, Canada 70 D3 43 55N 81 20W
Winifred, U.S.A. 82 C9 47 34N 109 23W
Winisk, Canada 70 A2 55 20N 85 15W
Winisk →, Canada ... 70 A2 55 17N 85 5W
Winisk L., Canada 70 B2 52 55N 87 22W
Wink, U.S.A. 81 K3 31 45N 103 9W
Winkler, Canada 73 D9 49 10N 97 56W
Winlock, U.S.A. 84 D4 46 30N 122 56W
Winneba, Ghana 50 G4 5 25N 0 36W
Winnebago, U.S.A. 80 D7 43 46N 94 10W
Winnebago, L., U.S.A. . 76 D1 44 0N 88 26W
Winnecke Cr. →,
  Australia .... 60 C5 18 35S 131 34 E
Winnemucca, U.S.A. .. 82 F5 40 58N 117 44W
Winnemucca, L., U.S.A. 82 F4 40 7N 119 21W
Winner, U.S.A. 80 D5 43 22N 99 52W
Winnett, U.S.A. 82 C9 47 0N 108 21W
Winnfield, U.S.A. 81 K8 31 56N 92 38W
Winnibigoshish, L., U.S.A. 80 B7 47 27N 94 13W
Winning, Australia .... 60 D1 23 9S 114 30 E
Winnipeg, Canada 73 D9 49 54N 97 9W
Winnipeg →, Canada . 73 C9 50 38N 96 19W
Winnipeg, L., Canada .. 73 C9 52 0N 97 0W
Winnipeg Beach, Canada 73 C9 50 30N 96 58W
Winnipegosis, Canada . 73 C9 51 39N 99 55W
Winnipegosis L., Canada 73 C9 52 30N 100 0W

Winnipesaukee, L., U.S.A. 79 C13 43 38N 71 21W
Winnsboro, La., U.S.A. . 81 J9 32 10N 91 43W
Winnsboro, S.C., U.S.A. 77 H5 34 23N 81 5W
Winnsboro, Tex., U.S.A. 81 J7 32 58N 95 17W
Winokapau, L., Canada . 71 B7 53 15N 62 50W
Winona, Minn., U.S.A. . 80 C9 44 3N 91 39W
Winona, Miss., U.S.A. . 81 J10 33 29N 89 44W
Winooski, U.S.A. 79 B11 44 29N 73 11W
Winschoten, Neths. ... 15 A7 53 9N 7 3 E
Winslow, Ariz., U.S.A. . 83 J8 35 2N 110 42W
Winslow, Wash., U.S.A. 84 C4 47 38N 122 31W
Winsted, U.S.A. 79 E11 41 55N 73 4W
Winston-Salem, U.S.A. . 77 G5 36 6N 80 15W
Winter Garden, U.S.A. . 77 L5 28 34N 81 35W
Winter Haven, U.S.A. .. 77 M5 28 1N 81 44W
Winter Park, U.S.A. ... 77 L5 28 36N 81 20W
Winterhaven, U.S.A. ... 85 N12 32 47N 114 39W
Winters, Calif., U.S.A. . 84 G5 38 32N 121 58W
Winters, Tex., U.S.A. .. 81 K5 31 58N 99 58W
Winterset, U.S.A. 80 E7 41 20N 94 1W
Wintersville, U.S.A. ... 78 F4 40 23N 80 42W
Winterswijk, Neths. ... 15 C6 51 58N 6 43 E
Winterthur, Switz. ..... 16 E5 47 30N 8 44 E
Winthrop, Minn., U.S.A. 80 C7 44 32N 94 22W
Winthrop, Wash., U.S.A. 82 B3 48 28N 120 10W
Winton, Australia ..... 62 C3 22 24S 143 3 E
Winton, N.Z. .... 59 M2 46 8S 168 20 E
Winton, U.S.A. 77 G7 36 24N 76 56W
Wirral, U.K. 10 D4 53 25N 3 0W
Wirrulla, Australia .... 63 E1 32 24S 134 31 E
Wisbech, U.K. .... 10 E8 52 41N 0 9 E
Wisconsin □, U.S.A. .. 80 C10 44 45N 89 30W
Wisconsin →, U.S.A. . 80 D9 43 0N 91 15W
Wisconsin Dells, U.S.A. 80 D10 43 38N 89 46W
Wisconsin Rapids, U.S.A. 80 C10 44 23N 89 49W
Wisdom, U.S.A. 82 D7 45 37N 113 27W
Wishaw, U.K. 12 F5 55 46N 3 54W
Wishek, U.S.A. 80 B5 46 16N 99 33W
Wisła →, Poland ..... 17 A10 54 22N 18 55 E
Wismar, Germany ..... 16 B6 53 54N 11 29 E
Wisner, U.S.A. 80 E6 41 59N 96 55W
Witbank, S. Africa ..... 57 D4 25 51S 29 14 E
Witdraai, S. Africa .... 56 D3 26 58S 20 48 E
Witham →, U.K. 10 D7 52 59N 0 2W
Withernsea, U.K. ...... 10 D8 53 44N 0 1 E
Witney, U.K. 11 F6 51 48N 1 28W
Witnossob →, Namibia 56 D3 26 55S 20 37 E
Witten, Germany ...... 15 C7 51 26N 7 20 E
Wittenberg, Germany . 16 C7 51 53N 12 39 E
Wittenberge, Germany . 16 B6 53 0N 11 45 E
Wittenoom, Australia .. 60 D2 22 15S 118 20 E
Wkra →, Poland ...... 17 B11 52 27N 20 44 E
Wlingi, Indonesia ..... 37 H15 8 5S 112 25 E
Włocławek, Poland .... 17 B10 52 40N 19 3 E
Włodawa, Poland ..... 17 C12 51 33N 23 31 E
Woburn, U.S.A. 79 D13 42 29N 71 9W
Wodian, China .... 34 H7 32 50N 112 35 E
Wodonga, Australia ... 63 F4 36 5S 146 50 E
Wokam, Indonesia .... 37 F8 5 45S 134 28 E
Wolf →, Canada 72 A2 60 17N 132 33W
Wolf Creek, U.S.A. 82 C7 47 0N 112 4W
Wolf L., Canada 72 A2 60 24N 131 40W
Wolf Point, U.S.A. 80 A2 48 5N 105 39W
Wolfe I., Canada 70 D4 44 7N 76 20W
Wolfsberg, Austria .... 16 E8 46 50N 14 52 E
Wolfsburg, Germany .. 16 B6 52 25N 10 48 E
Wolin, Poland .... 16 B8 53 50N 14 37 E
Wollaston, Is., Chile ... 96 H3 55 40S 67 30W
Wollaston L., Canada .. 73 B8 58 7N 103 10W
Wollaston Pen., Canada 68 B8 69 30N 115 0W
Wollogorang, Australia . 62 B2 17 13S 137 57 E
Wollongong, Australia . 63 E5 34 25S 150 54 E
Wolmaransstad, S. Africa 56 D4 27 12S 25 59 E
Wolseley, Australia .... 63 F3 36 23S 140 54 E
Wolseley, Canada 73 C8 50 25N 103 15W
Wolseley, S. Africa .... 56 E2 33 26S 19 7 E
Wolstenholme, C., Canada 66 C12 62 35N 77 30W
Wolvega, Neths. ...... 15 B6 52 52N 6 0 E
Wolverhampton, U.K. .. 11 E5 52 35N 2 7W
Wonarah, Australia .... 62 B2 19 55S 136 20 E
Wondai, Australia ..... 63 D5 26 20S 151 49 E
Wongalarroo L., Australia 63 E3 31 32S 144 0 E
Wongan Hills, Australia 61 F2 30 51S 116 37 E
Wongawol, Australia .. 61 E3 26 5S 121 55 E
Wŏnju, S. Korea ...... 35 F14 37 22N 127 58 E
Wonosari, Indonesia .. 37 G14 7 58S 110 36 E
Wŏnsan, N. Korea .... 35 E14 39 11N 127 27 E
Wonthaggi, Australia .. 63 F4 38 37S 145 37 E
Woocalla, Australia ... 63 E2 31 42S 137 12 E
Wood Buffalo Nat. Park,
  Canada 72 B6 59 0N 113 41W
Wood Is., Australia .... 60 C3 16 24S 123 19 E
Wood L., Canada 73 B8 55 17N 103 17W
Wood Lake, U.S.A. 80 D4 42 38N 100 14W
Woodah I., Australia .. 62 A2 13 27S 136 10 E
Woodanilling, Australia 61 F2 33 31S 117 24 E
Woodbridge, Canada .. 78 C5 43 47N 79 36W
Woodburn, Australia .. 63 D5 29 6S 153 23 E
Woodenbong, Australia 63 D5 28 24S 152 39 E
Woodend, Australia ... 63 F3 37 20S 144 33 E
Woodfords, U.S.A. 84 G7 38 47N 119 50W
Woodgreen, Australia . 62 C1 22 26S 134 12 E
Woodlake, U.S.A. 84 J7 36 25N 119 6W
Woodland, U.S.A. 84 G5 38 41N 121 46W
Woodlands, Australia . 60 D2 24 46S 118 8 E
Woodpecker, Canada .. 72 C4 53 30N 122 40W
Woodridge, Canada ... 73 D9 49 20N 96 9W
Woodroffe, Mt., Australia 61 E5 26 20S 131 45 E
Woodruff, Ariz., U.S.A. 83 J8 34 51N 110 1W
Woodruff, Utah, U.S.A. 82 F8 41 31N 111 10W
Woods, L., Australia ... 62 B1 17 50S 133 30 E
Woods, L., Canada 71 B6 54 30N 65 13W
Woods, L. of the, Canada 73 D10 49 15N 94 45W
Woodstock, Queens.,
  Australia .... 62 B4 19 35S 146 50 E
Woodstock, W. Austral.,
  Australia .... 60 D2 21 41S 118 57 E
Woodstock, N.B., Canada 71 C6 46 11N 67 37W
Woodstock, Ont., Canada 70 D3 43 10N 80 45W
Woodstock, U.K. 11 F6 51 51N 1 20W
Woodstock, Ill., U.S.A. 80 D10 42 19N 88 27W
Woodstock, Vt., U.S.A. 79 C12 43 37N 72 31W
Woodsville, U.S.A. 79 B13 44 9N 72 2W
Woodville, N.Z. .... 59 J5 40 20S 175 53 E